From the Wadsworth Series in Theatre

Anderson/Anderson, *Costume Design,* Second Edition

Barranger, *Theatre: A Way of Seeing,* Fifth Edition

Barton, *Acting: On Stage and Off,* Third Edition

Brockett/Ball, *The Essential Theatre,* Seventh Edition

Brockett/Ball, *Plays for the Theatre,* Seventh Edition

Brockett/Pape, *World Drama*

Dean/Carra, *Fundamentals of Play Directing,* Fifth Edition

Downs/Wright, *Playwriting: From Formula to Form*

Essig, *Lighting and the Design Idea*

Huberman/Pope/Ludwig, *The Theatrical Imagination,* Second Edition

Hudson, *How to Write About Theatre*

Jonas/Proehl/Lupo, *Dramaturgy in American Theatre: A Source Book*

Madden, *A Pocketful of Plays: Vintage Drama*

McGraw/Clark, *Acting Is Believing: A Basic Method,* Seventh Edition

Olivieri, *Shakespeare Without Fear: A User-Friendly Guide to Acting Shakespeare*

O'Neill, *The Actor's Checklist,* Second Edition

Parker/Wolf/Block, *Scene Design and Stage Lighting,* Eighth Edition

Schneider, *The Art and Craft of Stage Management*

Shapiro, *An Actor Performs*

Shapiro, *The Director's Companion*

Watt/Richardson, *American Drama: Colonial to Contemporary*

Worthen, *The Harcourt Anthology of Drama,* Brief Edition

Worthen, *The Harcourt Brace Anthology of Drama,* Third Edition

Scene Design and Stage Lighting

Eighth Edition

W. OREN PARKER

Carnegie Mellon University

R. CRAIG WOLF

San Diego State University

DICK BLOCK

Carnegie Mellon University

THOMSON ™ WADSWORTH

Australia ■ Canada ■ Mexico ■ Singapore ■ Spain
United Kingdom ■ United States

THOMSON
WADSWORTH

Publisher: Holly J. Allen
Development Editor: Eric Carlson
Editorial Assistant: Mele Alusa
Marketing Manager: Kimberly Russell
Project Manager, Editorial Production: Cathy Linberg
Print/Media Buyer: Barbara Britton
Permissions Editor: Joohee Lee
Production Service: Ideas to Images
Text Designer: Gary Palmatier, Ideas to Images
Art Editor: Gary Palmatier, Ideas to Images
Photo Researcher: Judy K. Brody, Elsa Peterson, Ltd.
Copy Editor: Molly Roth
Cover Designer: Preston Thomas
Cover Image: Ming Cho Lee
Compositor: Robaire Ream, Ideas to Images
Printer: Phoenix Color Corp

Printed in the United States of America

1 2 3 4 5 6 7 06 05 04 03 02

For more information about our products, contact us at:
Thomson Learning Academic Resource Center
1-800-423-0563

For permission to use material from this text, contact us by:
Phone: 1-800-730-2214
Fax: 1-800-730-2215
Web: http://www.thomsonrights.com

Library of Congress Control Number: 2002103124

Student Edition with InfoTrac College Edition: ISBN 0-15-506114-3

Student Edition without InfoTrac College Edition: ISBN 0-534-25985-5

About the cover:

The word *collaboration* is often used when discussing theatre. The more closely a production team works together, the more gratifying the project is likely to be. The design on the cover is a production of *Traveler in the Dark.* Ming Cho Lee, the set designer for this production, eloquently expresses this experience:

"The process of arriving at the design was a particularly satisfying one. During our first short meeting, the director, Gordon Davidson, and I asked Marsha Norman (the playwright) some key questions—the specific location of the play, the season ('sweater season,' with fallen leaves on the ground)—and I thought that it should have the look of a Wyeth landscape.

"During the second meeting, it was Gordon who suggested that perhaps the house should not be placed at the center of the stage, but rather in a less dominant position somewhere upstage on the side, to give greater importance to the landscape. I did an 1/8" sketch and showed it to Marsha, who said, 'I've been there!' The lighting designer was Marilyn Rennagel, and with her lighting the production had moments of breathtaking beauty."

Wadsworth/Thomson Learning
10 Davis Drive
Belmont, CA 94002-3098
USA

Asia
Thomson Learning
5 Shenton Way #01-01
UIC Building
Singapore 068808

Australia
Nelson Thomson Learning
102 Dodds Street
South Melbourne, Victoria 3205
Australia

Canada
Nelson Thomson Learning
1120 Birchmount Road
Toronto, Ontario M1K 5G4
Canada

Europe/Middle East/Africa
Thomson Learning
High Holborn House
50/51 Bedford Row
London WC1R 4LR
United Kingdom

Contents

Preface

This eighth edition of *Scene Design and Stage Lighting* reflects our most extensive revision in many years—every topic has been carefully examined with attention to relevance and technical detail. Although the thrust of the material remains centered on theatrical design and the collaborative process, focus on design and technical production as applied to fields other than theatre has been increased. Marginal glossary terms have been added to assist the reader in comprehension of key terms and concepts, and Web page URLs are included to aid students with further research into a topic or manufacturer. Illustrations and photographs have been updated to reflect current technology and practices.

The most significant change has been the addition of our third author, Dick Block. Dick served as an assistant author for the scene design and technology sections of the seventh edition. For this edition he assumes full responsibilities from Oren Parker, who has retired from the pressures of writing, happy to pass on the stress of deadlines to someone else. Dick and I take great pleasure in dedicating this edition to Oren, without whom *Scene Design and Stage Lighting* would have never provided such a significant resource to our students and faculty—and the theatre industry as a whole.

As specialization and technological changes grow exponentially, our reliance on the assistance of experts in the field also increases. We wish to acknowledge and thank the following individuals, who have contributed so greatly to this edition.

We are delighted that designer Ming Cho Lee agreed to supply the cover art. Thank you Ming, Betsy, and the Mark Taper Forum.

To provide a broader spectrum of approaches to scenery, the majority of the scenic designs represented in this edition are new. The color plates have been updated and expanded to provide a better sense of how color itself is used by designers, and a clearer and more in-depth discussion of the design and collaboration process is included. New drawings have been added, to better illustrate more-contemporary graphic styles of communication. We heartily thank all of the scenic designers who so graciously allowed us to use their work, especially Tim Saternow, Anne Mundell, Timothy Averill, Frank Ludwig, and Steven L. Gilliam, who provided numerous drawings and designs.

The chapters on tools, scenery construction, and handling have been updated to include modern techniques with an eye to current methods used by regional and commercial theatres. This would not have been possible without the expert help of David Randolph, Ben Carter, Norman Beck, and Kevin Hines. We are also grateful to Stephen Found of Found Design, who painstakingly reworked a majority of the tool drawings.

As has been the case for the past two editions, sound designer/engineer Peter Nordyke was instrumental in rewriting the sound chapters. Our chapter on sound design has been extensively revised, reflecting modern techniques made possible by advanced computer software. As one might expect, the subsequent chapter on sound systems and equipment is entirely updated, with emphasis on how to use the new equipment and software now available to theatrical sound designers and engineers.

The lighting design and technology section has many new photographs of both designs and equipment. We are indebted to Ralph Funicello, Chris Parry, Beeb Salzer, Cindy Limauro, Peter Maradudin, Don Hill, and Scott O'Donnell for their design contributions. For the first time, we have included exclusive interviews with several distinguished lighting designers from a variety of theatre-related fields: Broadway and regional theatre designer Donald Holder, regional theatre designer Chris Parry, architectural lighting designer Robert Shook, television designer Dennis Size, industrial lighting designer Ann Archbold, and themed-entertainment designer Tom Ruzika. We thank each of these talented people for their contributions of time and design work. The lighting section of this edition also contains all-new black-and-white and more color photographs. We appreciate the assistance of the many manufacturers who supplied information and product photos, especially Joe Tawil and Tamara Guion of GAMProducts. Finally, we want to thank Travis Richardson, who took the time to read through the draft of the lighting and sound sections from a student's perspective.

We also want to thank the many fine and thoughtful reviewers who helped shape this edition. They include: Ron Steger, professor, Department of Theatre and Dance, University of Wyoming; William Peeler, Department of Theatre, Southwest Texas State University; Ken Golden, associate professor of theatre, Hartwick College; Daniel Ionazzi, Department of Theatre, University of California, Los Angeles; Charles Williams, professor of design, University of Toledo; and the many other faculty members and students who have provided valuable feedback throughout the life of this text.

Many wonderful people have worked on the production of this edition, but special thanks go to the talented book production team at Ideas to Images, in particular the patient and understanding Gary Palmatier, and our copy editor, Molly Roth.

Finally, we would like to acknowledge the patience and infinite support of our partners, Barbara and Jane, as well as Zach and Daisy, who have helped make this edition a reality.

Craig Wolf
San Diego, California

Dick Block
Pittsburgh, Pennsylvania

PART I

Creating a Design

"I have often found that the set is the geometry of the eventual play, so that a wrong set makes many scenes impossible to play, and even destroys many possibilities for the actors. The best designer evolves step by step with the director, going back, changing, scrapping, as a conception of the whole gradually takes form....

"This is the essence of theatrical thinking: a true designer will think of his designs as being all the time in motion, in action, in relation to what the actor brings to a scene as it unfolds."

PETER BROOK

THE EMPTY SPACE

1

Introduction

Although design in the theatre may branch off into various areas of specialization, it is primarily seen in terms of four basic forms: first, as an environmental background, or scenery*; then as* costumes *for the actor within that setting; third, as* stage lighting *visually enhancing and unifying the first two forms; and, finally, as* sound.

The paths leading to a career of designing in the theatre are numerous and varied. They may come from within the theatre itself or elsewhere. Many a would-be actor has discovered more excitement in design; directors with a strong visual sense have sometimes become designers. There are trained visual artists who, equipped with the practical ability to draw and paint, possess a strong desire to be in the theatre and have forged careers as designers.

A student standing at the threshold of training for a career in design for the theatre may wonder what the future holds. Never before has theatre training made more sense, for today people with a solid grasp of theatrical design are being hired and are working in myriad related industries. The sudden but transitory flush of excitement involving one's first experiences in the theatre should not obscure the need for a long-range artistic commitment to hard work. Anyone interested in achieving creative and personal fulfillment as a scene, costume, lighting, or sound designer must first thoroughly understand the complexity of theatre as an art form.

Theatre is ever evolving. Over the past century, it has faced significant changes in its literary, physical, and theatrical form; these reflect the views of society as well as advances in technology. A wide range of influences have affected theatre, the most obvious perhaps being television and film—more and more scripts are written as series of short scenes in numerous locales. Multiculturalism has enabled us to understand and appreciate the lives of those with different backgrounds. Theatre's attempt to be more inclusive and allow the audience to be more directly involved physically and emotionally has increased the popularity of thrust stages and allowed us to consider wholly new forms of "theatre" such as conceptual and performance art. Possibly the most significant influence has been digital technology and the computer. New technology has allowed for more control of complex physical movement of scenery and light, it has revolutionized the way we manipulate and re-create sound in the theatre, and in many cases it has changed the way that designers think as well as how they develop and present their work. Audience expectations are now different as well. All of these changes greatly affect designers and their function in the theatre.

THEATRICAL FORM

Theatrical form in its simplest description is the communication of ideas between two groups: performers and audience. The assembly of audience and performer, or *performance,* is the presentation of ideas by the performers to the audience. These ideas may range from the ancient to the most topical, from the profound to the absurd, and at the same time be either sentimentally obvious or intellectually obscure. Performance and physical form have a major effect on style.

Other factors that influence style include the quality and personality of the actors, and the audience itself. Whatever the form, good theatre is still about telling a story. The challenge is to do so in an exciting, intriguing, and provocative way.

Most types of theatrical forms involve the designer. The most obvious are the literary form, or drama, emphasizing the spoken word; the musical form, including opera, book musicals, and revues, in which music tells part of the story; and ballet and modern dance, in which sight and sound rather than the spoken word matter most (see Figure 1-1). There are many other possible outlets for design that should not be overlooked, including film and television, trade shows or "industrials" (promoting a product or company), themed entertainment (rock concerts, videos, and theme parks), museum and display design, and performance art.

Of these forms, the literary form has so dominated theatre historically that the word *drama* has nearly become synonymous with *theatre.* The significance of drama to the designer is evidenced by the fact that a major portion of a designer's training for the theatre is spent in learning to interpret the ideas of the playwright and find a method to express that interpretation visually or aurally. This is the basis for all design in the theatre—finding a way to tell the playwright's story.

The literary form has met many challenges in recent decades in terms of both music and the spoken word. We tend to categorize things because doing so makes understanding them easier. But theatre often refuses to let us do that. Many musicals, for example, could be considered opera (*Sweeney Todd* is a good example). Any number of plays have much music that is sung. Are they no longer to be considered "straight" drama? Does a play by an Asian playwright necessarily mean it is an "Asian" play? For example, *M Butterfly* deals with attitudes of both Eastern and Western society.

As audiences have gotten more sophisticated, artists in theatre have pushed forward. The search for "meaning" in a play, or musical or opera, is all-important. We expect the design to reflect that search in a way that enhances the experience for the audience. At the same time, many people today want to see "spectacle," theatre that "wows" them by the use of sophisticated

a

b

c

a & b PHOTOS COURTESY RALPH FUNICELLO
c PHOTO COURTESY CINDY LIMAURO

1-1

Theatrical Forms

a Dance. Movement and music are the means of communicating in this modern dance performance of *Window Dressers* presented by Malashock Dance & Company at the Old Globe Theatre. Choreography, John Malashock; lighting, Ashley York Kennedy; costumes, Deborah Dryden; set design, Ralph Funicello.

b Drama. Theatrics at their most dramatic in *Hamlet* at the Old Globe Theatre, San Diego, 1990. Director, Jack O'Brien; set design, Ralph Funicello; lighting, Peter Maradudin; costumes, Lewis Brown.

c Opera. *Lucia di Lammermoor.* Lighting design by Cindy Limauro for the Opera Theatre of Pittsburgh.

technology. Computer technology has made this even easier in recent years, allowing for more-complex images, rapid changes of scenery and lighting, and far more control of stage movement than ever before. Virtual reality is an extreme version of this—but is it not really a form of theatre in which the audience member is directly involved in the story? It is easy to be dazzled by pyrotechnics and special effects and it is great fun. The downside of "spectacle" is that it often negates any intellectual challenge. There is nothing wrong with theatre being no more than sheer entertainment, but the result is often less than artistically fulfilling.

PHYSICAL FORM

The various types of theatrical form often determine in a general way their physical form. For example, the size of a theatre for most musical productions tends to be rather large, in part to accommodate a larger cast, an orchestra, and often more scenery. A two-hander (a play with only two characters) would get lost in a large space, denying the audience any connection to the characters; a smaller, more intimate venue providing closer proximity would make more sense. Many plays benefit from the traditional **proscenium** arrangement, in which the actors and audience essentially face one another (see Figure 1-2).

proscenium The architectural frame that separates the audience from the performers.

1-2

Proscenium Theatre

This proscenium house was originally built for vaudeville performances and, like many theatres of its day, was eventually used as a movie house. It has since been fully renovated and returned to its old glory and is now a small touring house.

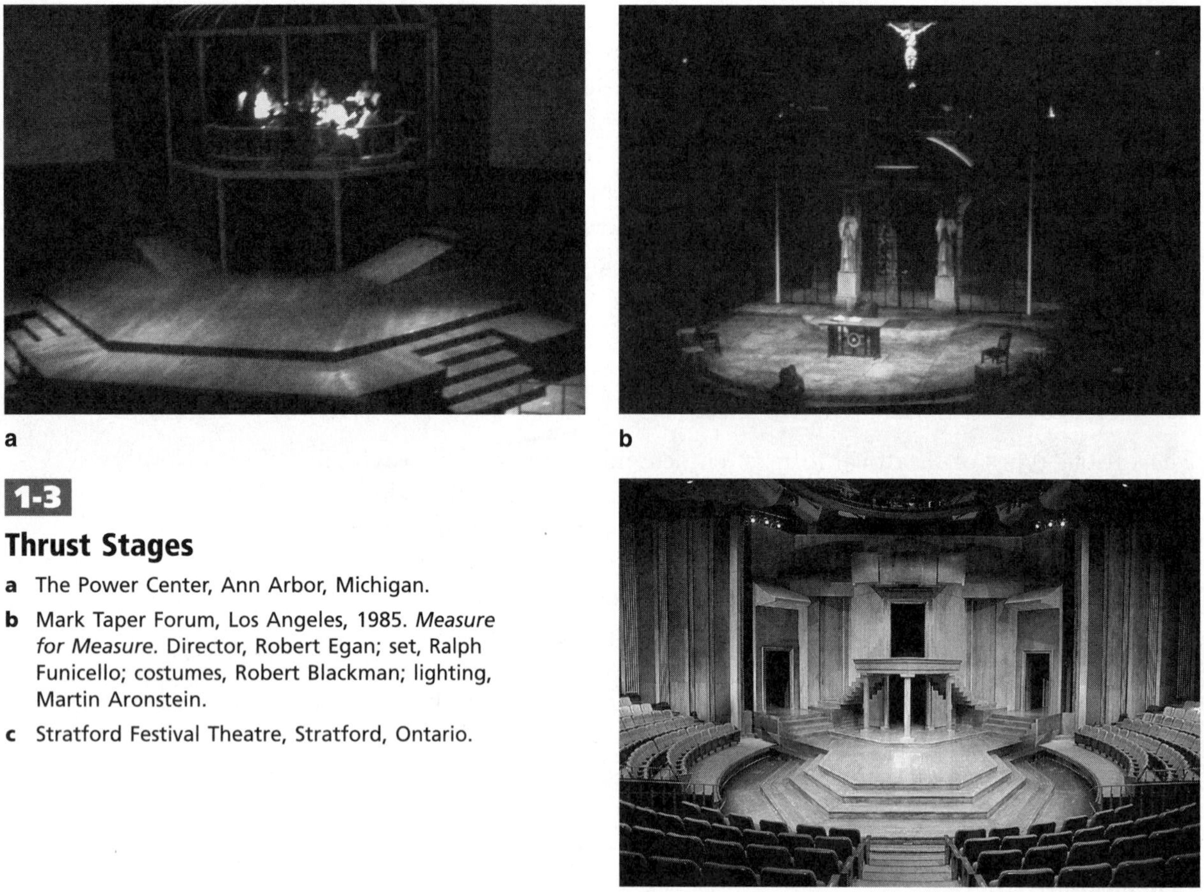

a b c

1-3

Thrust Stages

a The Power Center, Ann Arbor, Michigan.

b Mark Taper Forum, Los Angeles, 1985. *Measure for Measure.* Director, Robert Egan; set, Ralph Funicello; costumes, Robert Blackman; lighting, Martin Aronstein.

c Stratford Festival Theatre, Stratford, Ontario.

a & b PHOTOS COURTESY RALPH FUNICELLO
c PHOTO COURTESY THE STRATFORD FESTIVAL OF CANADA

This allows for a more formal "presentation" of a play and, for the designers, a bit more control over what the audience can and cannot see. The last several decades have seen a growth in the variety of physical arrangements in theatres, either variations of the proscenium or forms that are completely unique. Some try to combine both by converting from a conventional form to an unconventional one.

thrust stage A stage in which the audience sits around three sides of the acting space.

arena stage Theatre in which the audience sits on all sides of the acting space. Sometimes referred to as *theatre-in-the-round.*

Many recent theatres have taken on the new–old forms of the **thrust** and **arena stages** (see Figures 1-3 and 1-4). Prompted by the desire to bring the audience closer to the actor, these variations either partially or completely surround the acting area with seats (see Chapter 2). Although initially created primarily for drama and possibly intimate musicals, innovative staging and contemporary interpretations have broadened our idea of what can be played in these spaces. These shapes give the theatre back to the actor and the playwright. The use of the thrust and arena staging suggests a more sculptural rather than pictorial type of design, presenting many different challenges to the designer. A different sort of space should automatically suggest a different approach to a design.

In an effort to find a physical arrangement midway between thrust and proscenium staging, different configurations of the proscenium form have evolved. In one such case, the strict picture-frame feeling is reduced by extending the apron of the stage (see Figure 1-5). The result gives the illusion of a thrust into the audience and at the same time provides a stage that can function scenically like the proscenium.

a

a SCOTT SUCHMAN, ARENA STAGE, WASHINGTON, D.C.

1-4

Arena Theatres

a The Arena Stage in Washington, D.C., is a classic example of theatre-in-the-round.

b Not really a thrust and not really an arena, this stage is three-quarter round. The design on stage is *Macbeth* designed by David Centers for The Human Race, Dayton, Ohio, 2002.

b

b PHOTO COURTESY SCOTT KIMMINS

PHOTO COURTESY STEVEN L. GILLIAM

1-5

Extended Apron

All's Well That Ends Well was designed by Steven L. Gilliam for the Colorado Shakespeare Festival open stage production.

The "black box" (Figure 1-6) is a name given to a flexible space within which a variety of audience–performer arrangements can be created. This flexibility allows for the creation of the most appropriate type of physical space for the production being done. Various configurations of the black box create different challenges. At all times, however, the production should be both functionally simple and theatrically expressive.

It is no longer rare for a theatre to be created in a wide range of nontheatre structures (Figure 1-7). The audience–performer arrangement has been altered to fit into an old garage, a deserted warehouse, a gymnasium, a ballroom, an out-of-use church, and many other unexpected locations. The often unusual relationship between the seating arrangement and performance area is part of the theatrical experience and can function as an element of the production. Unconventional arrangements free the audience and the performer from any preconceived notions of what will be seen or heard or accomplished.

PHOTOGRAPHY BY STEVEN A. GUNTHER AND PHOTO COURTESY CALARTS

1-6

Black Box Theatre

A unique example of a black box. The Walt Disney Modular Theatre at the California Institute of the Arts has moveable floor units and wall panels that allow for multiple set configurations. The theatre was designed by Jules Fisher in collaboration with Herb Blau.

a

b

1-7

Nontheatre Forms

a Outdoor production of *The Music Man* at St. Louis MUNY Opera. Set design by Steven L. Gilliam.

b The Hip Pocket Theatre in Fort Worth, Texas, an outdoor theatre built around a tree.

c The outside of City Theatre in Pittsburgh, Pennsylvania. This old church was renovated and turned into a theatre that can be converted into proscenium or thrust configuration.

c

a PHOTO COURTESY DAVID BURNSIDE
b PHOTO BY MICHAEL BODYCOMB COURTESY HIP POCKET THEATRE, FORT WORTH, TX

SCENE DESIGN

The creation of an environment in which the action of the play might happen can be very exciting. The written words of the playwright are transformed for the audience by the director in collaboration with the artistic team, who provide a physical and visual world for the play. Theatrical production requires the integration of many related arts, and scene design is one of several vital parts.

The Total Dramatic Effect

Design in the modern theatre is concerned with the total visual and aural effect of a dramatic production. In any production, this overall effect is the sum of all the elements that provide the audience with clues about the world of the play. Scene design, the physical and visual environment, is often the strongest visual element that supports the spoken word of the dramatic form. The design of a setting, however, is not confined to creating the color and shape of scenery pieces alone. It also includes the selection and style of the furniture and set-dressing, all of which must relate to the nature of the production. Careful consideration of the costumes and the quality of the lighting and the sound is critical as well. This is true whether the visual requirements of a script are as simple as those of Thornton Wilder's play *Our Town,* which all but eliminates physical elements of scenery, or as complicated as those of Jerome Kern's *Showboat,* which requires vast quantities of spectacular background.

Qualities of Designers

Beginning designers are expected to know so many things at once that they may wonder where to begin. They soon find that anyone who aspires to be a designer will need the vision and imagination of the creative artist, the ingenuity and skills of the stage artisan, and above all the knowledge and sense of theatre of the actor, director, and playwright.

To function as creative artists in the theatre, designers must show talent in their use of line, color, and form. They must be able to bring meaning and visual significance to a stage picture through imaginative and creative qualities developed by training in the nonverbal techniques of design, drawing, and painting (both hand- and computer-generated). They must be collaborative in nature, for their individual design is only part of a complex whole.

As stage artisans, designers must be able, through the use of unique materials and theatrical techniques, to bring substance to their ideas with skill and dispatch and within the structural limitations of their medium. To create a design that can be wholly realized, they must know the structure of scenery, the limitations of materials, and the methods of movement. Likewise, the lighting designer must have a working knowledge of available equipment and the latest technologies. The same is true for costume and sound designers. In all cases, designers must have a general understanding and appreciation of the other areas of design.

As collaborating artists, the scenic, costume, and lighting designers make an important visual contribution to the dramatic form. The study of dramatic structure and perception of the playwright's intent helps the designer bring an appropriate visual interpretation onto the stage. The ability to understand the ideas of the playwright, remaining true to the intent of the play while allowing an artistic vision to develop, is a difficult but vital part of the designer's job. The better a designer can juggle those tasks, the easier it will be to provide a theatrical flair while keeping the designs in proportion to the dramatic import of the play. A successful visual interpretation requires an understanding of not only all of the physical and textual elements but also the actor's needs, a sense of space and movement, and a strong vision.

Design Collaboration

Productions are rarely designed by fewer than four designers. As noted, the design of a production is usually divided among a scene designer, a costume designer, a lighting designer, and a sound designer. These four work together in collaboration with the director, forming an artistic team. Each area of design is directly influenced by the others and creates the total atmosphere of any theatrical production. For this reason, involvement of all designers in the initial stages of conceptualization is highly desirable. The visual and aural effect is created by a response to the script and the overall approach to the production as determined by the artistic team. Each of the designers cannot with integrity design without concern for his or her colleagues. Do the clothes suggest the same kind of world as the set? If the costumes will be big due to padding or some other understructure, as is typical of several periods, is the set large enough to accommodate them? Is it possible for the lighting designer to light an actor in any area of the set? Does the set provide ample positions for sound speaker placement? Does the setting allow for lighting that can achieve the mood of the play? Is there a consistent sense of color throughout the various designs? Constant communication among the designers and with the director is critical throughout the production process.

The design team must also consider how the director will use the space for the production—physically and visually. Although the final action and staging of the actors is the prerogative of the director, the arrangement of the scenic pieces has a direct bearing on everything that happens in that space. Part of the scene designer's job is to allow the director to create theatrical stage pictures by arranging the actors within the setting in a manner appropriate to the script. The floor plan of a setting influences the ease and effectiveness of the actors' movements. A successful floor plan will make the physical arrangement of actors onstage obvious.

Light brings atmosphere and focus to a production as well as a flexible means of modifying color and modeling scenic forms. The lighting reveals or hides what is necessary—sometimes subtly, sometimes blatantly. It is innately theatrical. A good lighting designer will illuminate the actors and the set in such a way that members of the audience sense the mood and the tone of the moment, often without being aware of how they are being manipulated. The scene designer must be aware of the design potential of light in the theatre and provide the lighting designer ample opportunity to achieve that potential.

Costume design is an essential part of the total visual effect, and although it most directly concerns the actor, it affects the scene and lighting design also. The color, line, and period style of the costumes must complement the other design work. Costumes help define the individual character while placing him or her in proper relationship to the world of the play.

Sound in theatrical production is a powerful means of establishing locale and reinforcing the action of a play. Like lighting, it can establish mood in a way unnoticed by the audience. The style of sound in a production must compliment that of the scenery, lighting, and costumes.

Each of the designers must work to bring all of their contributions together to form one whole. If the design team has helped to create the world of the play in a given production, they have done their job well. Although an audience may leave the theatre with a lasting impression of the scenery, the lighting, the costumes, or the sound they come to the theatre to see a world in which the play can take place. This can happen only through a series of discussions in which each member of the artistic team brings ideas to the table. It is the melding of those ideas and the development of them that allows theatre to happen. One of the most exciting times for the designer is that point in which the director or fellow designer has taken an idea and developed it in a different direction than was initially conceived. This exploration of the ideas of the play through visual means is what makes theatre exciting and alive for the designers as well as for the audience. The more fully developed the ideas of the artistic team, the more fulfilling the production will be for the audience.

2

Scene Design and the Theatre

Many things influence the form of a final design for the theatre. The text itself (the raw material) and the conceptual work done by the artistic team (the interpretation of the text) are equally necessary and form the basis for the design. As part of the overall dramatic form of theatre, however, design does not stand alone. It is part of an event that includes and involves the actor and the audience as well. A scene designer, for example, may draw sketches or make models, but designs do not reach a full state of expression until they are onstage and inhabited by actors in front of an audience. As a result, the scene designer is concerned with not only the manner in which the design is presented to the artistic team, but also how it will be used in production and in what physical form.

THE THEATRICAL MEDIUM

Because audiences respond to their physical surroundings, including the space in which a design is used, an intelligent designer will regard the theatre itself as a medium of expression. Theatre varies in terms of the physical space available and the manner in which design work is done. Further, theatre functions in several ways simultaneously—as a complex organized business, a form of entertainment, and a technological machine. Each of these functions presents opportunities as well as limitations to designers.

Theatre as an Organization

The preparation of any production requires the close cooperation of many specialists. The theatrical medium brings together the writer, actors, director, designers, and audience. Regardless of the level of theatre, certain elements are critical to ensure the success of a play. The producing organization must always be efficient in (1) selecting a play; (2) casting and rehearsing the actors; (3) designing the scenery, lighting, costumes, and sound; (4) producing the physical production (i.e., building and painting the sets and costumes, lighting the production, and creating the sound); and (5) promoting the play to an audience. Professional theatre, as well as some college, university, and

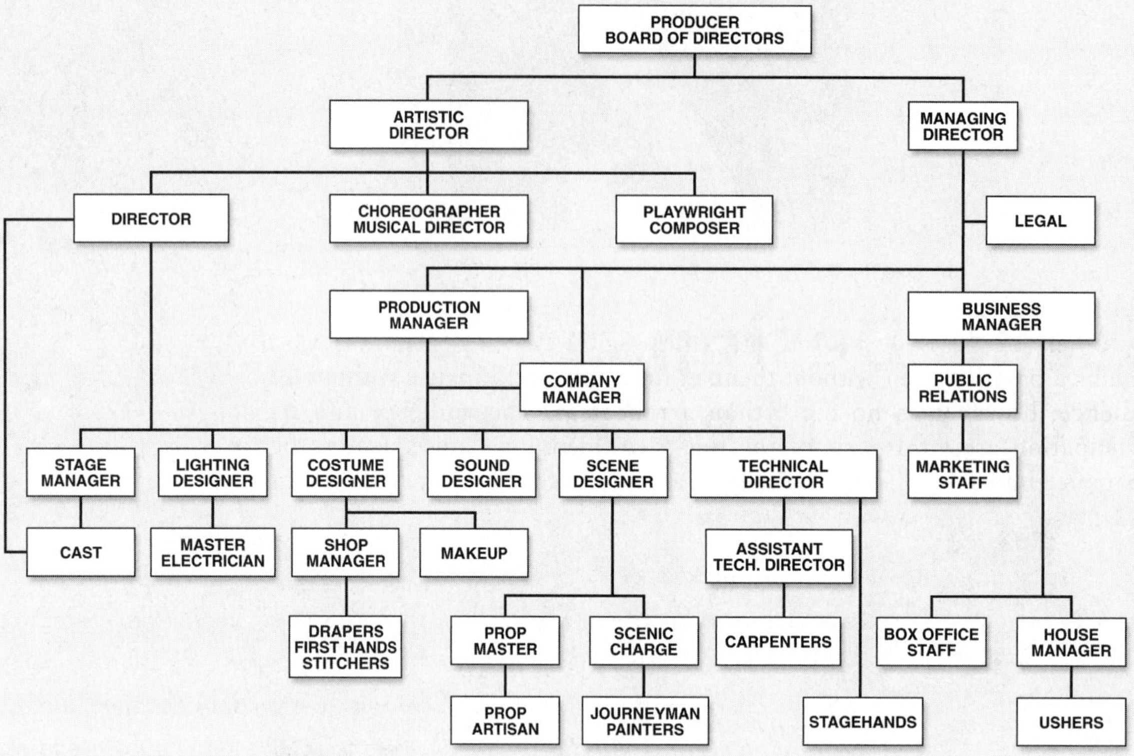

2-1

A Producing Theatre's Organizational Chart

This is typical; specifics concerning personnel and hierarchy will vary by the particular needs and types of productions of individual theatres.

URL http://www.livebroadway.com/community.html

URL http://www.tcg.org

community theatres, must also consider procuring financial backing and establishing the budget and selecting a theatre. Lack of cooperation or understanding, complicated by faulty planning in any phase of the production, can weaken it as a whole (see Figure 2-1).

To function well, any organization must have a guiding force or chief interpretive artist. This could be the director, producer, department chair, or another leader, depending on the given situation. It is the director's overall approach, however, that brings a unifying control to the production, including the visual elements, acting style, and literary interpretation. The designers' contribution to the production is, of course, a vital part of the visual statement. As a part of the organization and its collaborative effort, this may mean subordinating personal triumph to the good of the whole. Great moments of unified achievement in the theatre are usually experienced when the goal of the production is placed above individual gain.

In addition to being aware of their general relationship to the overall production plans, designers need to know the specifics of their own area of theatre, such as how the physical space backstage is set up, the standard theatre equipment that is available, and any limitations in terms of time and use of the space. A thorough knowledge of backstage and scene shop organization leads to a more efficient production as well as a more faithful reproduction of design ideas. The designer collaborates largely with the artisans in the various shops, in particular the technical director and props person. Just as important, the designers must be able to work with all of the other areas of the theatre organization, including the production manager, the actors, public relations, and the box office. Because of its specialized nature, the personnel and organization of design and technical production is discussed in Chapter 10.

Theatre as a Show

The designer's awareness of theatre as a show emphasizes the temporal quality of scenery, the dramatic qualities of the visual elements, and above all the sense of joining with an audience to give a performance. As a performing art, the theatre has an immediacy and a unique relationship with the audience that other art forms do not provide. Although a painting has viewers, it remains a painting even without them. A theatrical performance without an audience, however, is no more than a rehearsal. The audience and its participation are vital parts of the theatrical medium. Consequently, the theatre's almost total dependence on an audience gives it a quality of immediacy that becomes an intrinsic part of the medium.

This quality brings about a specific attitude toward scene design and the structure of scenery, for although scenery may look solid for the most part, it must be lightweight and portable to move easily from scene to scene or from audience to audience. The specifics will of course vary depending on the length of the production's run. Scenery built for a touring production must clearly last much longer than for a production that will have only ten performances. Finally, when the production reaches its last curtain, the usefulness of the scenery ends. It is doomed to storage, rebuilding, or destruction.

The performance aspect of the theatre has a direct bearing on the attitude of designers. People tend to think that the actors are the only performers, which is not the case. If a performance is truly a collaborative effort, then *all* the artists and workers in the theatre can be considered performers. Theatrical success depends on teamwork. Any sense of achievement lies in the reaction of the audience to a good performance, and most audiences respond to their overall experience rather than to an individual performance. Again, collaboration is essential to this success.

The designer achieves the dramatic qualities of scenery mainly through the creative manipulation of the visual art form. More specifically, this involves the use of proportion or scale. The theatre, more than other art forms, is an overstatement of life. Even a realistic play is drawn to be a little sharper and greater than real life. Even a relatively small idea, stated theatrically, can affect an audience. Much of this depends on the size and distance of the audience in relation to the performers, which in turn influences the scale of any scenery. If, for example, the theatre is large and the audience is at a great distance from the performers, the scenery has to take on an increased scale just to be in proportion to the size of the auditorium and stage. But whether it be a massive spectacle at an outdoor arena or a drama of intimate proportions in a vest-pocket theatre, the theatrical medium can touch the emotions of the audience in electrifying ways.

Theatre as a Machine

Although other people control the technological aspects of the theatre, the designer should be aware of the backstage operations. Most scenery-moving techniques occur on the stage of the proscenium theatre, where the specific concern is guaranteeing the smooth run of the production. The effortless movement of scenery, either in view of the audience or hidden by a curtain, is part of its theatrical magic.

Scenery and properties are, of course, moved in the thrust and arena stages, as well as in the black box theatres. The movement can be mechanized, but more often it is either a part of the action of the performance or is moved in view of the audience as an accepted feature of theatrical form.

Typical scenery-moving machines include the following. A rigging system, which allows scenery to fly, is particular to the proscenium theatre, although modified versions can be used in a thrust or arena theatre. Tracked wagons for lateral or diagonal movement and a turntable or revolving stage are also commonly used. Elevators and sliding pallets can be part of a design. Some stages are equipped with a built-in revolving stage or elevator system. All of these systems might have an influence on the production scheme.

The computer has added efficiency to the control of backstage movement as well as greater safety, and it is rapidly becoming a common tool for designers. Most lighting systems are now run by computer, and although still prohibitively expensive for some theatres, the computer is more and more frequently a built-in feature of stage equipment. It is already commonly used as a design tool. For a more thorough discussion of scenery-moving techniques, please see Chapter 10.

THE PHYSICAL STAGE AND ITS AUDITORIUM

URL http://www.theatres.uwa.edu.au

The most important step for beginning designers in learning their new medium is to become acquainted with the physical stage. Knowledge of the actual shape and physical makeup of the performance area is a must, for they define the space in which a designer must work.

Proscenium Theatre

In the contemporary theatre, the stage takes on various forms based on the relationship of the audience to the stage. The most common form is the proscenium type of theatre, where the audience is arranged on one side of a raised stage area. The enclosed stage is open to the audience through the proscenium opening. Early proscenium openings were surrounded by a decorative frame to separate the audience from the play in an artificial and often unrelated manner. The proscenium wall of the modern stage is often much simpler, functioning as architectural masking to hide stage machinery, lights, and stored scenery.

The Proscenium Opening The modern proscenium theatre attempts to minimize the frame of the opening separating the audience from the stage. It is less of a demarcation than the old picture-frame prosceniums. The relationship of the design space to the proscenium opening is an early and critical decision for the designer, because it is the first statement of scale. Does the setting relate or attach to the frame of the opening, hold free in an open staging manner, or pierce the opening to extend onto the apron? Figure 2-2 provides some examples. Each has different visual and staging capabilities. Closing in the opening reduces the scale of the production but may provide more backstage space for the storage of scenery. Little or no framing expands the design space into open staging. And piercing the opening reaches toward the audience as if to break through the plane of the opening.

a

b

c

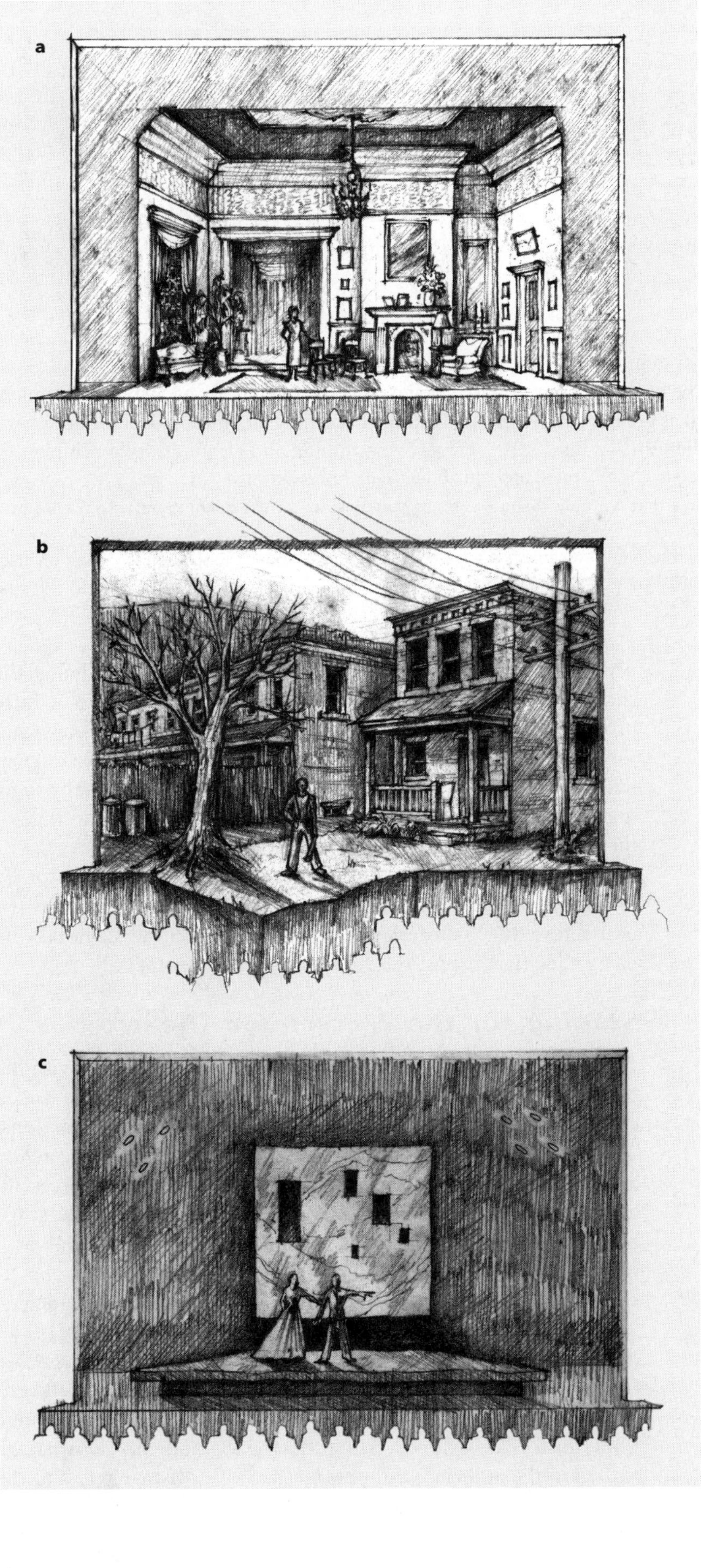

a–c COURTESY ANNE MUNDELL

2-2

The Proscenium Opening

These drawings show three variations in the use of the proscenium opening.

a One can alter the proportions and shape of the proscenium to fit the scale and the style of design. Here, the designer has lowered the horizontal frame and narrowed the right and left frames. The corners are shaped to conform to the cornice in the design of the room.

b Having a portion of the set push through the proscenium arch achieves a different sense of the environment.

c The complete lack of the proscenium arch establishes a surrounding environment that may be harmonious or in contrast to the scenic elements.

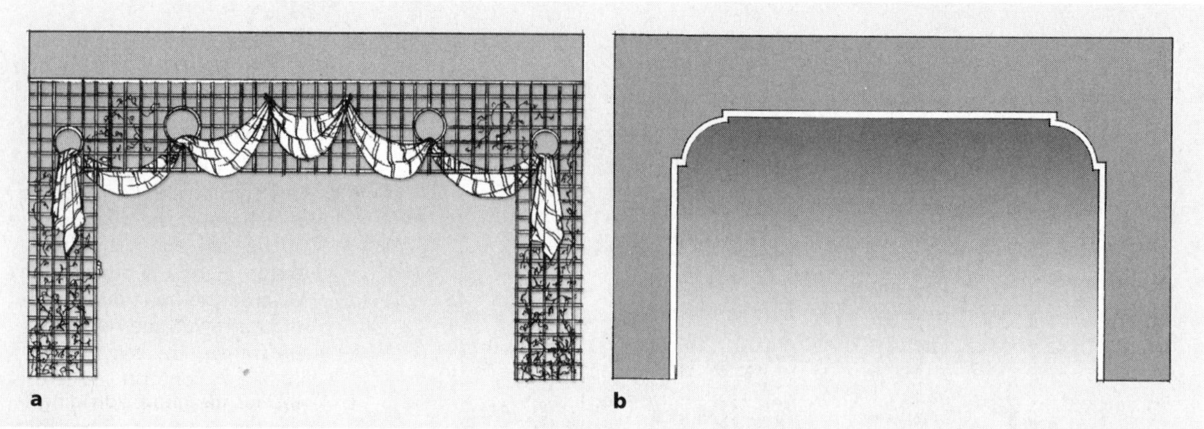

2-3

The Show Portal/False Proscenium

Both the show portal and the false proscenium are located upstage of the fixed proscenium arch.

a The *show portal* is a decorative frame that not only changes the size and/or shape of the opening but also frames the production in the style of the design.

b Most often neutral or black in color, the *false proscenium* is a frame that simply changes the size and/or shape of the opening. It can be used to bring unity to a variety of scenes.

Show Portal Sometimes it is desirable to close in or change the shape of the proscenium opening. This is done with a **false proscenium,** which is almost always neutral in design, or with a **show portal.** The show portal is designed to make a visual statement that sets the tone of the show and is sometimes used visually to tie together multiple sets. Either one is usually hung just upstage of the proscenium arch (see Figure 2-3).

The proscenium opening can also be reduced in proportion by lowering an inner overhead masking known as a **border** (in the past referred to as a **teaser**), and by closing in the side masking using a **leg** (in the past referred to as the **tormentor**).

false proscenium A neutral frame, most often black, that either reduces the opening of the proscenium arch or alters its shape.

show portal A decorative frame that is designed for a particular production and is used either to pull together multiple sets visually or to help establish the character of the production.

border Overhead masking, usually in reference to opaque black fabric, hanging from a batten and running laterally across the stage.

teaser A rarely used term referring to the first border upstage of the proscenium arch.

leg Side masking, usually in reference to opaque black fabric, hanging from a batten and running vertically to the floor.

tormentor A rarely used term referring to the first leg upstage of the proscenium arch.

Staging for the Proscenium Theatre

When planning the staging, the designer in collaboration with the director maps out the arrangement of properties, levels, and a general floor plan to facilitate the easy flow of the play's actions. The staging is much more than just a traffic pattern for the actors and requires the designer to think like a director. A successful ground plan allows the director to create appropriate stage pictures, bringing into focus each scene or moment in the play with the proper degree of importance relative to the other moments. It can also help the director establish relationships among characters.

Because actors and audience essentially face each other, directions can become confusing. On the stage, all directions relate to the actors' right or left as they face the audience. **Stage left** is to the actors' left, and the reverse holds for **stage right.** Because stage floors historically sloped down toward the audience, **downstage** is toward the audience and **upstage** is away. **Offstage** refers to the

stage left Direction to the actor's left as he or she faces the audience.

stage right Direction to the actor's right as he or she faces the audience.

downstage Direction toward the audience.

upstage Direction away from the audience.

offstage (1) Direction away from the center of the stage. (2) The stage areas to the right and left of the set.

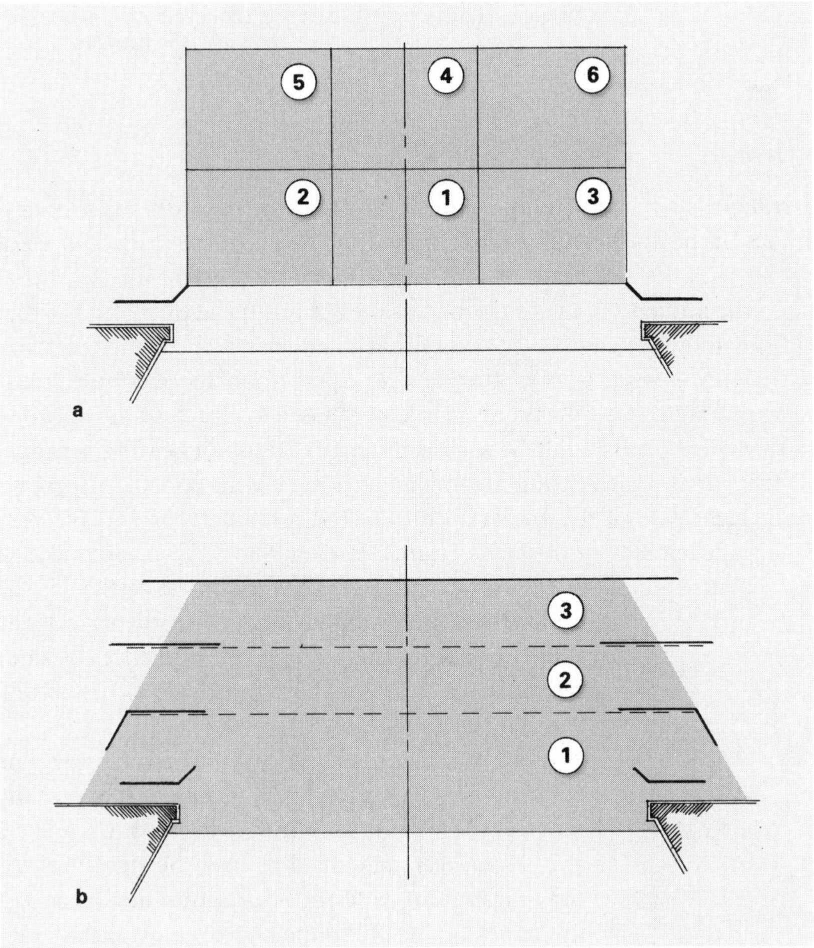

2-4

Stage Areas

a For easy identification, the stage area is divided into basic areas that are numbered here in order of relative importance:

1 Downstage center.
2 Downstage right.
3 Downstage left.
4 Upstage center.
5 Upstage right.
6 Upstage left.

b A second method of dividing the stage is a series of horizontal planes determined by the location of portals or wings and numbered from downstage to upstage. They are often referred to as "in-one," "in-two," "in-three," and so on.

right and left areas out of view, while **backstage** is the entire area behind the proscenium. (The same directions apply to the thrust stage. In an arena space, however, this system does not work. Rather, the stage directions are commonly given in terms of the hands of a clock, the position of "12" being an arbitrary choice.)

backstage All of the area upstage of the proscenium arch. Often used synonymously with *offstage*.

The designer, through composition of the visual elements, can alter the basic value of any stage area. Because of their relative position on the bare stage, certain areas are stronger than others. The nature of the proscenium theatre makes an actor standing downstage nearer the audience more important than an actor in an upstage position. The relative importance of the various positions on a bare stage is shown in Figure 2-4a by first dividing the stage into six equal parts and then numbering the areas in the order of their importance.

A set designer might employ certain devices to increase the importance of a stage area that is normally weak. For example, raking or angling the side walls of a set forces the upstage action toward the center; careful placement of furniture can bring important scenes downstage or more toward the center; using levels in the upstage areas can increase their importance.

When the stage is divided, left to right, by a series of portals or large arches, the staging becomes more two-dimensional. It falls into a series of horizontal planes related to the portals, each traditionally referred to by number. Beginning at the **apron,** the downstage strip is number one, the next one is

apron The area of the stage just in front of the proscenium arch. Synonymous with *forestage*.

number two, and so on upstage. The staging can be directed by indicating whether an actor or piece of scenery is to be in "one," "two," or "three," as desired (Figure 2-4b).

Sightlines

sightline Line of sight from an audience seat to a point onstage.

After learning the size and shape of the stage area, the designer must review the **sightlines** of the auditorium to determine how much of the stage is in view. The designer uses the sightlines of a theatre to guarantee two things: (1) that everyone in the audience can see the necessary action of the play and (2) that no one in the audience can see anything that is not pertinent to the environment as designed—what is seen through an open door, for example, must relate to the design. The proscenium theatre has a characteristic sightline problem that varies only slightly with different patterns of seating arrangements. If the flare of the seating arrangement is very wide, people sitting on the extreme right side of the auditorium (referred to as house right) see very little of the stage left side of the stage, and vice versa. Similarly, persons sitting in a steep second balcony see very little of the back wall of the setting. If the auditorium floor is flat without a gradient, or if the stage floor is unusually high, the audience does not see the stage floor and even sees little of the actors' legs as they walk upstage.

The designer must know these extreme sightline conditions in order to plan a setting that brings the most important areas into the view of all the audience. Designers need to find the sightlines for only the extreme or critical locations, not every seat in the house. The extreme horizontal sightlines are drawn from the seats farthest to the right and left in the audience. The horizontal sightlines are located on the plan of the stage and auditorium. The extreme vertical sightlines are drawn from the front row upward and from the last row in the balcony downward. These are located on the section view (see Chapter 5). On occasion, when a large balcony overhangs a considerable portion of the orchestra, it is necessary to consider a vertical sightline from the last row of orchestra seats.

From the pattern of extreme sightlines, the designer can see how much of the stage is in view to each member of the audience. In Figure 2-5, for example, the horizontal sightline shows the designer how far onstage a person sitting in this seat can see and how much of the stage-right wall cannot be seen. Figure 2-6 shows that portion of the stage that everyone in the house can see—a considerably smaller area. In this manner, the designer consults the sightlines of an auditorium in relation to the design (Figure 2-7), making the most efficient use of stage areas for staging the action of the play.

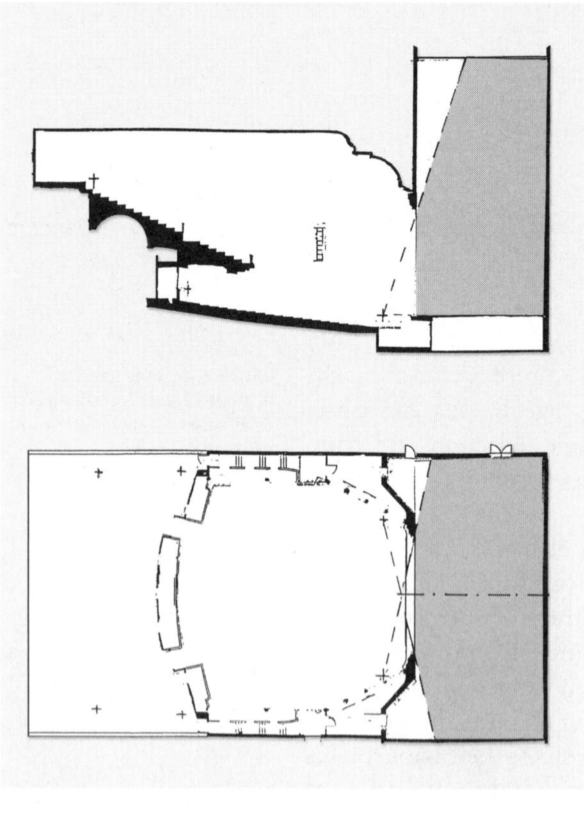

2-5

Sightlines—Area Visible to Someone

These drawings (cross sectional view and plan of auditorium and stage) show the largest amount of stage area that is visible from the extreme house right and left seats in the front row of the audience. The shaded portion is the visible stage area.

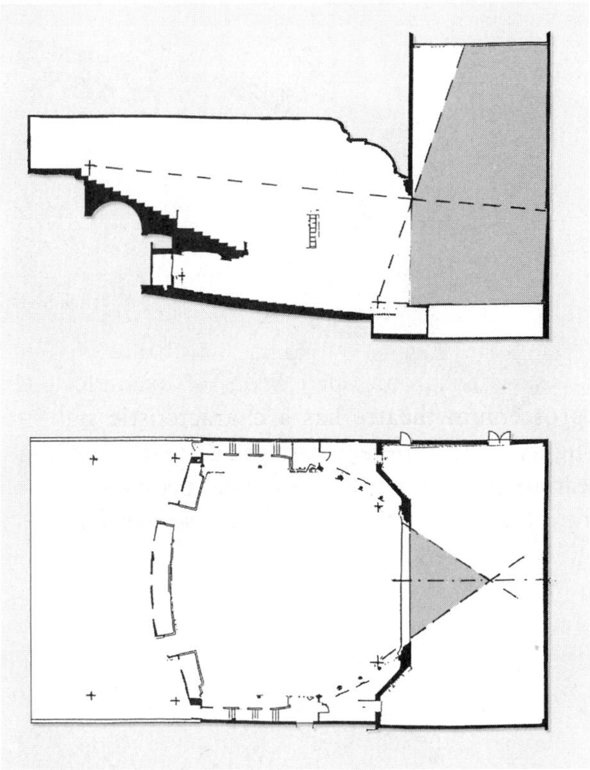

2-6

Sightlines—Area Visible to All

These drawings (cross sectional view and plan of auditorium and stage) show the amount of stage area (shaded) that is visible to everyone in the audience. The sightlines are from the closest and lowest seats and from the farthest back and highest seats (in the balcony).

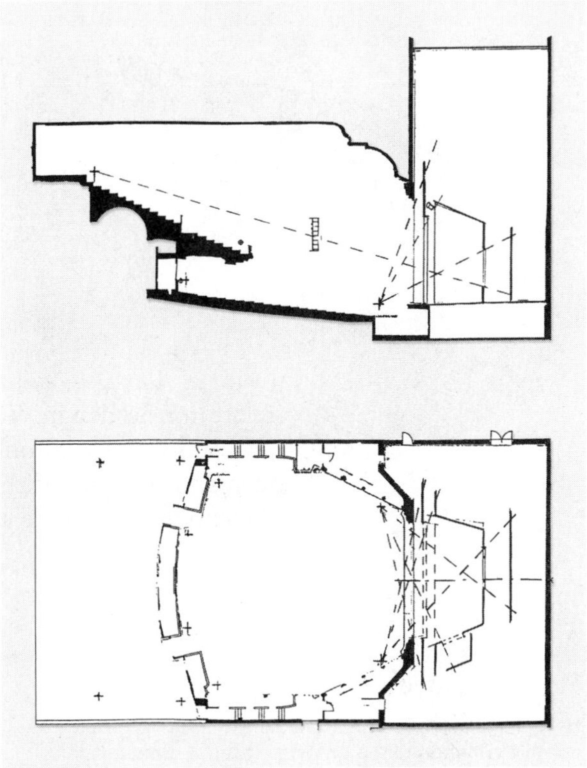

2-7

Sightline with a Set

These drawings (cross sectional view and plan of auditorium and stage) show how the sightlines of a specific set are checked from the extreme seats in the house.

Staging in Front of the Proscenium

Two variations of the proscenium theatre are the **extended apron** and the thrust stage. Both are outgrowths of the desire to reduce the distance between the audience and the actor. Each is a part of the movement away from the romantic theatricality of the past, which depended on a certain aesthetic distance to complete its illusion. Although the extended apron and thrust stage are not new forms in the theatre, they are very much a part of present day staging and represent spaces in which today's stage designer must be prepared to work.

extended apron An apron that projects out into the house.

Extended Apron The extended apron breaks the proscenium line, bringing the action farther downstage without losing the sense of the picture frame of the opening. It plays to a seating arrangement similar to that of the proscenium theatre with only slight differences in sightlines. The extended apron is often equipped with access openings or doors within each flanking wall downstage of the proscenium opening. The forestage area may be used in conjunction

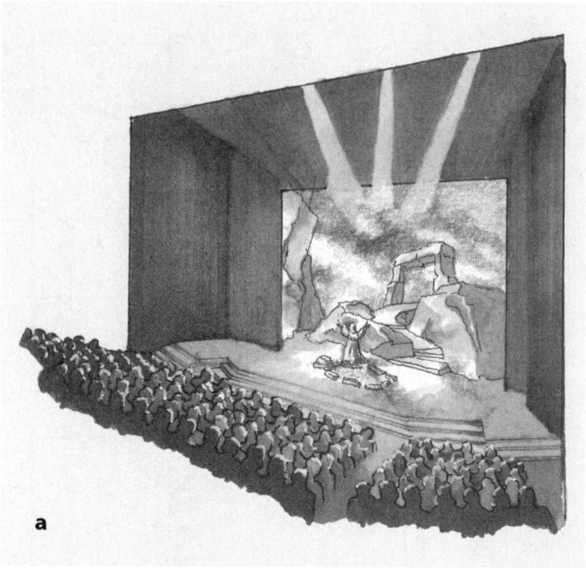

a

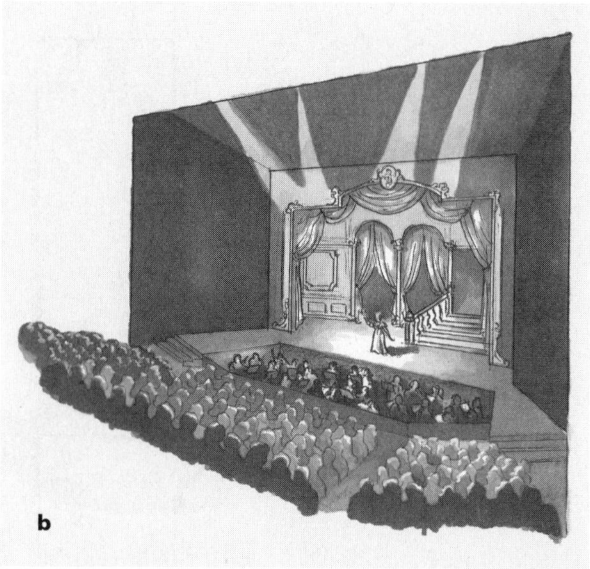

b

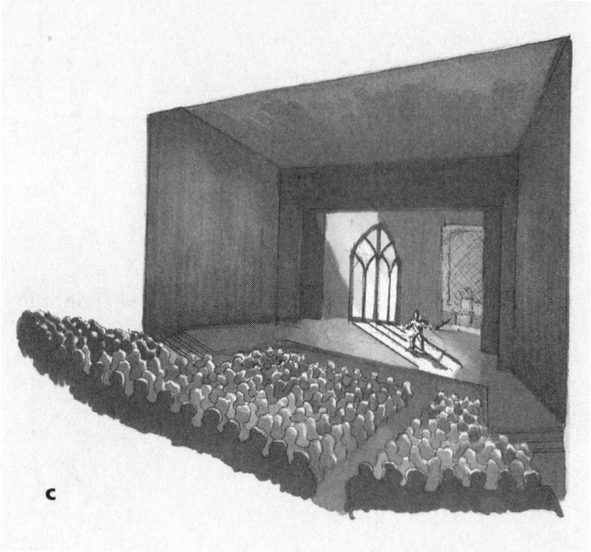

c

2-8

Flexible Aprons

Here is a proscenium theatre equipped with a flexible apron that when raised or lowered can assume several different shapes.

a With the apron raised to stage level, the apron extends well beyond the proscenium arch, allowing for entrances from the front and side.

b The apron has been lowered to orchestra pit level for a musical.

c The apron at house level allows for extra seats and for the audience to be closer to the action of the play.

side stage The area right and left and in front of the proscenium arch. Sometimes used as acting area.

with proscenium staging, allowing elements of the scene to spill out onto the **side stages**, or in a more formalized manner, with all action originating on the apron.

The most flexible form of apron stage is illustrated in Figure 2-8, which shows how the area ahead of the proscenium opening can be modified by the use of elevators or removable platforms and seats to one of three variations: (a) full extended apron, (b) side stages with orchestra pit, or (c) regular proscenium staging with additional seats.

Thrust Stage The thrust stage is, as the name suggests, a stage thrust out into the audience area. With seats arranged on three sides of a peninsula-shaped acting space, the bulk of the audience is closer to the actors than it would be in proscenium seating. The necessity to keep an actor in full view and in a position well ahead of the proscenium results in a house with a steeper rise in each successive row of seats, changing the vertical sightlines.

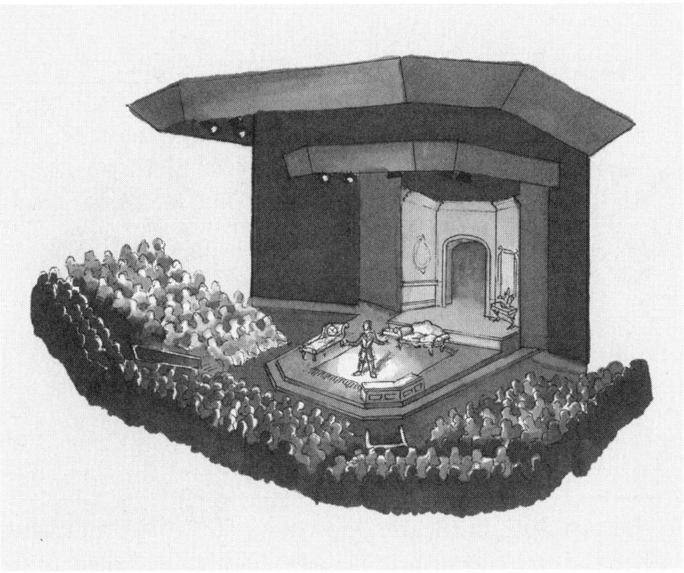

2-9

Thrust Stage

With seats on three sides of the stage area, the thrust stage and its background can assume a great variety of forms other than the conventional living room interior shown here. Entrances can be made from the audience (usually below the audience from tunnels called voms, or vomitories), from the sides, from the back, or through traps in the stage floor.

Semipermanent elements of scenery or an architectural background make up the fourth side of the theatre, as in Figure 2-9.

Though the thrust stage appears structurally similar to the proscenium theatre, its chronological development stems from the arena theatre. The long-felt need in theatre-in-the-round for greater variety of staging and a stronger axis of visual composition led to a semicircular grouping of seats around the thrust stage. At the same time, the widely diversified sightlines are an obvious improvement over the limited viewing angle of the proscenium theatre. Because the upstage portion of the stage is anchored to the structural part of the theatre, a rather important axis is established in the opposite direction.

The strong visual axis, however, has its shortcomings. The people sitting in the end seats of the right and left sides have a radically different compositional view. This effect increases if the seating arc is greater than a semicircle, in which case the audience in the extreme side seats may find themselves enjoying a vista that approaches a rear view. The ideal configuration seems to be slightly less than semicircular, thereby providing a more equitable distribution of seats without losing the sense of close contact with the actors, which is so much a part of both the thrust stage and arena theatre concepts.

The features of an ideal thrust stage that influence design are the extreme conditions of both the horizontal and vertical sightlines. The abnormally wide horizontal sightlines force the location of large scenic pieces to the back wall and support the use of furniture and properties to establish the locale. The sharp vertical sightlines, owing to the steeper rake of the audience (sometimes referred to as **arena seating**), make the floor treatment a more important part of the design.

arena seating Also referred to as *stadium seating* in which the slope of the audience seating is quite steep. Most often found in arena and thrust theatres (as well as in sports stadiums).

Because of their exposed positions, both the apron and thrust stages work most easily with one fixed setting or relatively simple modifications during act changes. Because the audience will see it, any speedy change of locale requires highly specialized technology or clever staging by the director.

Apron and thrust stages potentially provide more flexibility of staging. The three-quarters facing of the thrust stage plus the proximity of actors to the audience continuously encourage a greater use of style and design detail

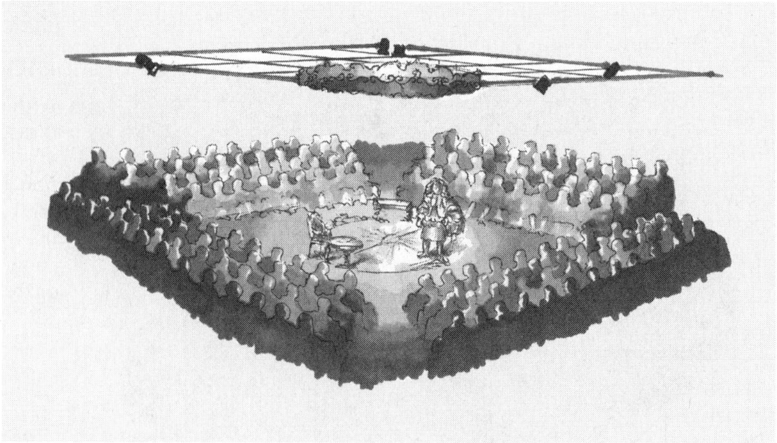

2-10

Arena Stage

The audience surrounds the stage area in an arena stage. The acting area may or may not be raised. Any use of scenic elements is limited because of obvious sightline issues.

than is called for in the proscenium theatre. Costumes and properties often become the center of the visual composition, while lighting is called on to isolate one area of the stage or another.

Arena Theatre

URL http://www.arenastage.org

Another familiar stage form is the arena, where the audience encircles the acting area (see Figure 2-10). The scale of an arena stage can vary from an intimate theatre-in-the-round to an arena the size of Madison Square Garden, with many sizes and variations in between.

The sightlines of arena staging differ drastically from the proscenium type of theatre and present a unique set of challenges and opportunities to the designer. For example, hiding actors, props, or machinery is much more difficult in arena than in proscenium staging. The visual elements normally have to be confined to small, low units or open pieces that can be seen through. As with the thrust stage, there is more of an emphasis on the design of the floor. The area above the acting area is also often used for scenic elements.

Design detail becomes more important because of the intimacy of the theatre and the lack of larger elements of scenery in the composition. This type of staging is intentionally simple, often depending on a suggestion of scenery to set the scene and stimulate the audience's imagination to fill in the rest.

Flexible Staging

Clearly, arena, thrust, and proscenium theatres all have advantages and disadvantages. Some plays lend themselves to one particular type of acting space while others allow for broader approaches. Flexibility of the physical space allows the director and designer a wide range of conceptual possibilities in creating a production.

black box theatre A theater that is usually small and that allows flexibility in the arrangement of audience to acting space. It is so named because the walls are usually painted black.

Flexible staging, as a technique, is associated with the **black box theatre** form, which provides an area for easy changing of the stage-audience arrangement (Figure 2-11). Within this flexible space, the staging can be altered from arena staging to three-quarters round or to proscenium-type staging. A further variation called *aisle staging* has the audience on two sides and a small stage or bit of scenery at one end, or both. Sightlines vary, of course, depending on the type of staging. When the seats are arranged for proscenium-type staging (as in Figure 2-12), sightlines are decidedly better than those in a

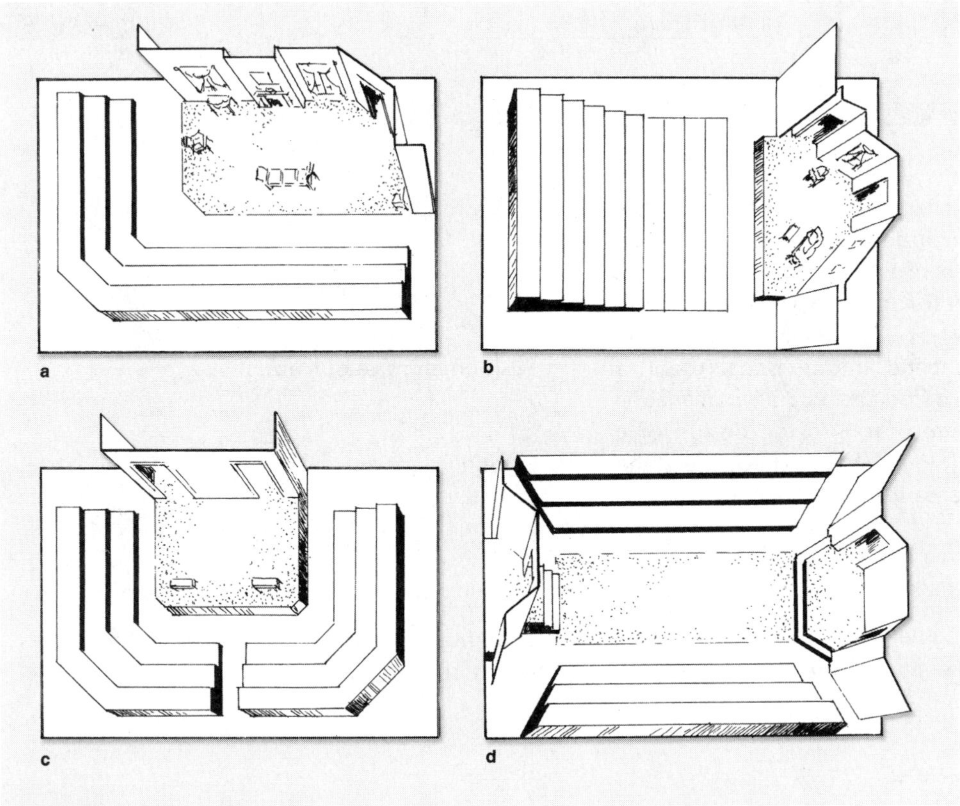

2-11

Flexible Staging

The moveable seat platforms and stage can facilitate a variety of audience–actor configurations. Depending on the arrangement, the audience may partially surround the stage area, limiting the potential for scenery.

- **a** L-shaped arrangement.
- **b** Proscenium arrangement.
- **c** U-shaped, with the audience on three sides of the stage.
- **d** The audience split on either side of the acting area.

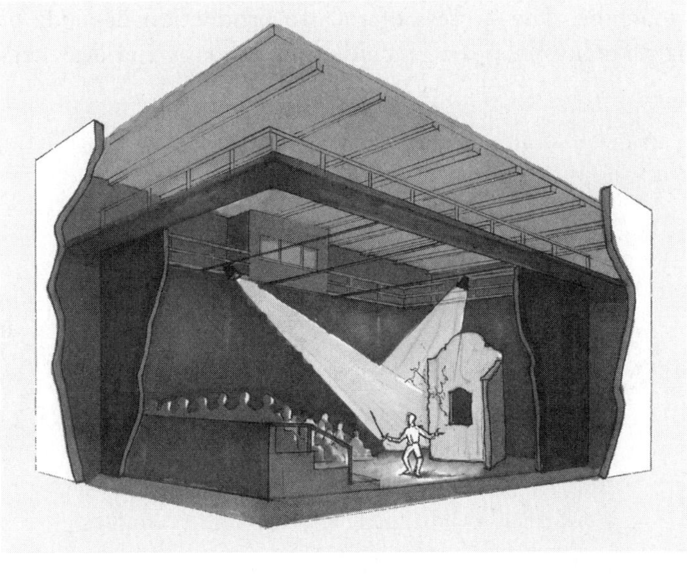

2-12

The Black Box Theatre

This cutaway section reveals the basic areas of the flexible theatre. The corridor or passageway surrounding the audience-performance space has adjustable openings to provide entrances and exits to accommodate a specific arrangement. The encircling catwalk provides easy access to the tension-wire grid covering the entire theatre space. Flexible lighting positions are available as well as limited flying or hanging of scenic elements.

Designing for the Real World

Working with the Physical Space

URL http://www.oecenter.com

Because every production is unique, the designer must receive basic information about the theatre in which he or she will be working. Any well-run theatre will provide drawings of the physical space as well as a "spec sheet" of equipment and limitations to its use. This most often will come from the production manager. Before venturing too far into the design of a production, the designer should check the stage and performance area for the following:

- Floor plan drawn to scale showing onstage and offstage space
- Section showing heights and flying system (number of lines and spacing; see Chapter 5)
- Indication of any line sets that are movable or not
- Indication of any line sets that are not available
- Position and size of traps, if any
- Sightline positions
- Lighting positions
- Overhead or offstage obstructions (ducts, vents, storage areas, etc.)
- Load-in door—size and access to stage
- Local fire-code restrictions (for example, is it allowable to break fire curtain line?)

conventional proscenium theatre. The seating is usually arranged with a negligible flare, thereby creating good sightlines for the entire house.

Flexible staging offers many exciting design and directing possibilities. Its main drawback is the relatively small audience capacity, which limits its commercial use. A more serious handicap is the loss of time and energy that occurs during the changing of the theatre from one arrangement to another. It is, however, an excellent staging medium for experimenting with new dramatic forms and for establishing greater intimacy between the actors and the audience.

Clearly, designers need to be aware of the physical aspects of each theatre they work in, from sightlines to fire codes. They also need to have a thorough understanding of the three functions of theatre—as organization, as entertainment, and as machine. The success of theatre production depends on cooperation among its many "players," including technicians and designers.

3

Scene Design as a Visual Art

The exciting interplay of line, color, and form in a vibrant stage setting or the subtle refinements of an inconspicuous scenic background do not happen by chance. To create a setting, the scene designer uses, either consciously or intuitively, well-established rules and the fundamentals of design common to all the visual arts. The beginning designer should have a knowledge of these fundamentals to aid in the development of final design forms.

DESIGN AND THE DESIGNER

We think of design as an orderly creation produced by an artist. Artists bring two things to their work: emotion and intellect. Both are expressed in the feeling and rationale of a work of art. The emotional aspect of creating is individual and introspective. It is hard to quantify and impossible to teach this relatively intangible quality, often referred to as "talent." The intellectual side of design, however, can be measured and defined in terms of **composition.** Within emotion or feeling lie desire, imagination, and a sense of theatre, all of which are necessary to creativity. On the other hand, the mind or intellect cultivates the practical skills as well as the conceptual and interpretive powers of design. The merging of emotion and intellect is the beginning of the creative process that spawns the design form.

composition The organization of design elements into a unified form. Light reveals composition.

Beginning designers may wonder how this abstract definition of design applies to their special interest in the theatre. It means that during the process of designing, two forces are at work—a personal vision or feeling for the final design form and the practical realities that are tempered by thoughtful judgment and taste. Both are regulated by the needs of the play and the production. In other words, emotion and feeling become the *ideal,* thought and intellect the *reality;* the first being the *goal* and the second the *realization.* The greater the skill and ability to realize the ideal, the more successful the designer.

COMPOSITION AND THE ELEMENTS OF DESIGN

URL http://www.metmuseum.org

URL http://www.louvre.fr/louvrea.htm

URL http://www.moma.org

Composition, in general terms, is the organizing of the elements of design in space into a unified *form*. The result may be a single form or the interaction of several forms acting as a whole. The elements of design are the basic factors that make up the visual form, whether it be a two-dimensional shape or a three-dimensional object. Museums provide an excellent place to examine the use of composition. Careful analysis of how an artist guides the spectator's eye through a painting or sculpture can inspire ideas for new designs and for controlling the elements of design.

The elements of design can also be thought of as forces that, by manipulation, can singly dominate a composition and help give the form meaning. The reason for, or meaning of, any visual form provides the composition with a unity of purpose that is particularly important in the theatre. After all, plays are about ideas. The meaning attached to the design of a visual form may be dictated from the outside, or it may come from within the artist, often formulated by the simple desire for personal expression.

Here are the elements of design that make up a visual form:

- Line
- Scale
- Movement
- Light
- Color
- Texture

Of these elements, line and color are often the most forceful, but any one of the six may be emphasized. All the elements interact, one influencing the other as the composition takes shape. Although none stands alone, each has unique features that contribute to the overall effect sought by the designer.

Line

line (1) A form that has length and width, although the width is often so narrow it is usually not recognized. (2) In geometric terms, a series of points.

Line, as an element of design, defines form. Its importance in composition stems from its versatility. Line can enclose space as *outline* and create shape (two-dimensional form), or it can suggest three-dimensional form. Line in a composition can appear as *real line* in many different modes (straight, curved, spiral, and so on), as *linear shapes* that take on a linelike quality, or as *suggested line* simulated by the eye as it follows a sequence of related shapes (see Figure 3-1). Line also has different qualities such as direction, length, and thickness.

Line is a path of action and therefore cannot help but take on a sense of *direction* and sometimes *movement.* Horizontal and vertical lines follow the direction of the frame and therefore suggest no movement. Diagonal lines, in contrast, suggest action. In an arrangement of several linear shapes, the lines not only assume a direction but also take on an *attitude* toward each other, be it one of harmony or opposition. Because of this, the use of line, suggested line, and shape with linear characteristics becomes a vital force in any

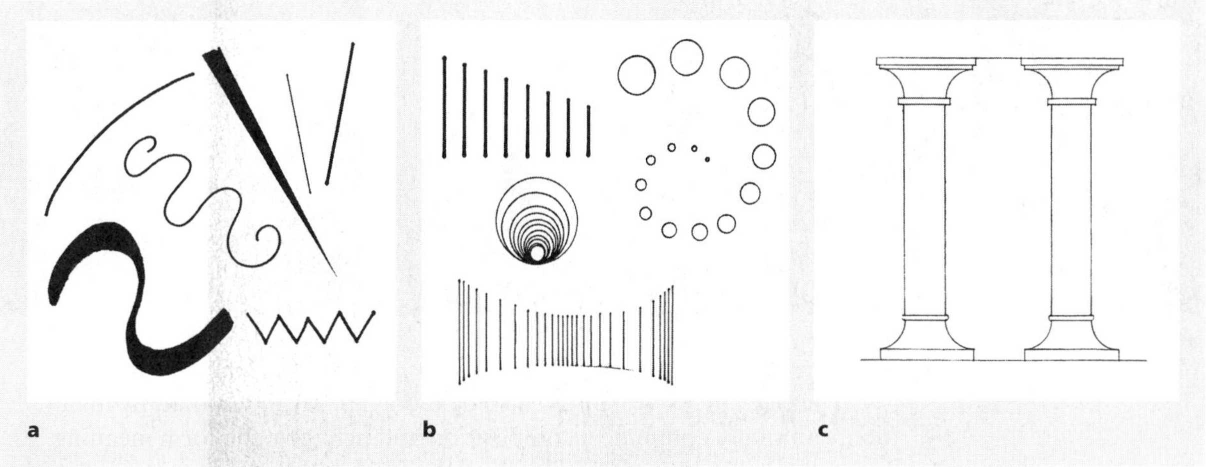

3-1

Line Types and Linear Shapes

a Examples of different kinds of line: straight, curved, thin, thick, subtle, strong, jagged, curvilinear.

b Line can enclose shape or suggest shape. The eye will follow a line suggested by repetition or shape, parallel lines, concentric circles, gradation of size or color, or a shape that points.

c Negative space. The space between two or more shapes can create a focal point of negative space.

arrangement of forms. A composition may use line as a dynamic force with a sense of violent action or as a static force with a feeling of strength and stability (see Figure 3-2).

PHOTO COURTESY RALPH FUNICELLO

3-2

Linear Form in Composition

The production of *Twelfth Night* presented in San Diego's Old Globe Theatre in 1994 exhibits clear use of linear form in its composition. Director, Laird Williamson; lighting, Chris Parry; costumes, Andrew Yelusich; scenery, Ralph Funicello.

a

b

a PHOTO COURTESY DAN NEMTEANU
b COURTESY BRUCE GOODRICH

3-3

Actor in Frame—Scale

Actors shown in two greatly differing scales of production. The amount of air and space surrounding a single actor changes the way in which an audience will respond.

a *Red Noses,* set design by Dan Nemteanu.

b *Mrs. Cage,* set design by Bruce Goodrich.

Scale

scale The size or mass of a form.

proportion The size of a form relative to another form.

Scale is the *size* or *mass* of form. As an element of design, scale is also concerned with the relationship of one shape to another—large to small, large to larger, and so forth—properly called **proportion.** Real dimension is always present in a two-dimensional shape, but, of course, it becomes suggested dimension when a three-dimensional form is represented on a two-dimensional surface.

One of the first decisions a designer makes is the scale of a production, based always on the relationship of the stage to the actor (see Figure 3-3). Recall that although the proscenium arch establishes an architectural limit, it can be adjusted with the use of a false proscenium, the designer's initial statement of scale. Some plays require a larger space, while others may need a smaller one to capture an intimate feeling for the production.

Scale can be used to create theatricality. We expect objects to be a familiar size. Increasing the scale of a common object can help establish an atmosphere that is overwhelming, or perhaps oppressive, in part by making the actor seem small and insignificant onstage (see Figure 3-4). Conversely, decreasing the scale of an object will make the surroundings seem larger than normal.

negative space The space between two or more forms.

In addition, scale includes the amount of space between forms in a composition, referred to as **negative space.** The size of the negative space has a definite effect on the apparent size or mass of the forms and their proportional relationship. A form's prominence or recession as well as its size and mass is of course influenced further by the use of color, light, and texture. The proportional relationship between negative space and mass also begins to establish a rhythm or sense of movement (see Figure 3-1).

Movement

movement The action of form.

Movement is the *action* of form—the kinetic energy of composition. Every design, even a static composition, presents or suggests motion. What we call the *real movement* of form within a composition, or actual physical movement, is very much a part of stage design. This includes the movement of light, of

3-4

Dimensional Relationship

The scale of form and proportional relationship to other forms in a composition is important: large to small, small to small, and so on. Scene from Eugene O'Neill's *Emperor Jones.*

the actors, and of animated elements of scenery. In particular, actors onstage move almost constantly throughout a performance, although sometimes this motion is quite subtle.

Simulated movement, as the term indicates, is the implied movement in a static medium such as a drawing, color sketch, or sculpture. The designer or artist may suggest motion in a sketch, for instance, by the blurring of a shape or the indication of fabric flowing in the air. For example, the costume sketch in Figure 3-5a illustrates simulated movement in the flow of the skirt.

Any fixed arrangement of forms engages the movement of the eye, or *optical motion.* For instance, the use of suggested line stimulates optical motion as the eye is led from one shape to the next. Optical motion basically "fools" viewers by drawing on their intuitive sense of orientation. This allows them to experience a feeling of movement frequently so subtle that they do not recognize the effect as a product of optical motion. The tendency of the viewer, for example, to interpret a diagonal line extending from the lower left to the upper right of a composition as an upward motion is a product of the left-to-right orientation common to all of us. It also involves the human association of a top and bottom to all composition. See Figure 3-5a for another example of real movement suggested by optical motion.

a

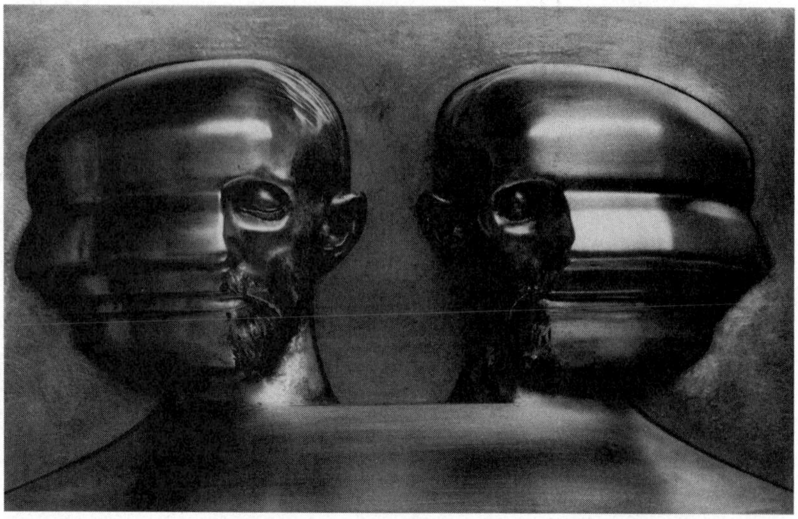

b

a COURTESY JAMES HAYCOCK
b PHOTO COURTESY HAROLD TOVICH

3-5

Simulated Movement

Movement in the costume sketch is suggested in the action of the skirt and the eccentric balance of the figure.

a Costume designed by James Haycock.

b Detail of a bronze relief sculpture, *Passage,* suggesting the fluidity of movement. Sculpture by New England artist Harold Tovich.

Optical motion also involves the fourth dimension—time. The characteristics and placement of forms cause a specific kind of eye movement or rhythm. This rhythm may be staccato, pulsating, or ponderous. The timing of the rhythm, or *tempo,* can vary as well, from quick to slow. The vibration of repeated shapes, complementary colors, rapid changes of direction, and high-contrast areas are all examples of techniques that cause optical motion.

Although orientation brings an instinctive sense of movement to a composition, the designer has many means of controlling optical motion. Strong direction can be countered, reversed, or subtly changed by altering the position or attitude of the forms in relation to each other. The outline of the form itself can establish a direction as can the other elements of design, such as color and light.

Both real motion and optical motion can be transferred to a static object; this technique is referred to as *transferability.* A simple figure or shape placed against a busy or pulsating background will appear to vibrate. This unwanted optical motion can happen to pictures, for example, when hung against vibrant wallpaper. Real motion can also be transferred from a moving background to a fixed object in the foreground. Most everyone has experienced a sense of motion while sitting in a stationary train car or bus when the adjacent vehicle begins to move. The technique of moving the background behind the actor or fixed scene to create the illusion of movement in the scene is frequently used onstage.

Movement on the stage must be carefully controlled and coordinated. Because movement catches the eye—an audience will automatically look toward a moving versus a static object—it can detract from the focus of a scene as easily as it can enhance it. Ask any actor who has been "upstaged" by the innocent waving of a handkerchief by another actor.

3-6

Light in Composition

The use of distribution, color, and movement of light in this production of *Prometheus Bound,* designed by Donald Oenslager, was unique for its time. Produced at Yale in 1939 and conceived much earlier, it represents the kind of innovative use of light we accept as modern practice. Technicians could penetrate the "gray gauze box" with light, wash it with color, project forms onto its surfaces, or make it disappear before our eyes. Within this simple box, the audience watched the anguishes of Prometheus unfold. Lighting, Stanley McCandless; costume, Frank Bevan.

A stage composition is in a constant state of flux. Actors change position and grouping; elements of scenery change location; a static arrangement changes by the movement of light. Figure 3-6 illustrates with four drawings how composition can be changed by the movement of light and the positioning of actors.

Light

Light *reveals* form. Although it has only recently been viewed as an element of design, light is a most dominant presence in all areas of stage design. As such, it must be considered a basic influence at the beginning of the creative process and not something to be added later.

Light can be thought of in three different ways: first, as *real light* capable of revealing form; second, as real light having its *own design form;* and last, as *simulated light* as it might appear in a two-dimensional representation of a three-dimensional form.

Physical Characteristics of Light The design potential of light stems from its physical characteristics: intensity, color, distribution, and movement. The control of these characteristics is essential to creating design. *Intensity* is the actual or comparative brightness of light. As with movement, our eye tends toward the brightest object onstage. The ability of light to transmit and reveal *color* is one of its most dramatic qualities. Color modification and the mixing of colored light are two basic concepts that all designers must understand (see Chapter 16 for more).

Distribution refers to both the direction and quality of light. The control of the distribution of light gives it both direction and texture as design features. The *direction* of light can cause a scenic element to be seen or not. It can create great shadow or its complete absence; it can emphasize texture or deny it. The sharp versus soft-edged quality of a light beam, coupled with its degree of brightness, gives an innate *texture* to light. In addition, light can be further textured by applying diffusion media to the beam or actually creating a pattern in the beam through the use of gobos (see Chapter 14).

It is easy to see how the knowledge of the distribution of light can affect the design form by the introduction of highlight, shade, shadow, and texture into composition. Besides the atmospheric quality that light can add to a composition, an exposed light source such as candelabra, chandeliers, or other visible lighting instruments can add much to the design of a set.

The fourth variant of light is movement. Stage lighting involves a nearly constant state of motion. The *movement* of light can be defined as the visible change of any or all of the other three qualities of light. A subtle change of intensity, the use of a follow spot, or the change of color in a sky or background can alter the focus or modify the atmosphere or mood of a scene. It can also have a dramatic or emotional impact on the audience, such as that experienced during the vibrant movement of light in a rock concert.

As mentioned before, real light can also take on its own design form. Patterns of light can be projected over a form as a part of the composition, or the projected image can be the entire composition. The use of light as projected scenery is a medium in itself. It draws on the same fundamentals of design for its realization but requires specialized knowledge and skill. (See Chapter 19 for more on projection.)

The use of light should be present in the designer's sketch showing its effects in the composition. Although *line* is used first to represent three dimensions, the added use of light and its shades and shadows is the designer's most effective way of representing three-dimensional form in a sketch or backdrop. However, the most successful use of light in a sketch or painting is based on a firsthand knowledge of what real light can and does do.

Light and the Scene Designer Of all techniques within the theatrical medium affecting scene design, lighting is the most influential, providing designers a greater flexibility in composition than any other visual art form. Because lighting technique will be covered in great detail later, here we shall simply point out its general influence on the materials and structure of scenery.

The two most active and vital components that make up a stage composition are the actor and light. The power of light to animate form makes it a forceful design element in a stage composition. The energy of light reveals, brightens, and adds color to an inert object, thereby increasing its vitality. For a dynamic example of designing with light, refer to Chapter 14, Figure 14-1.

The scene designer must consider in advance relative changes in the intensity of light and the position of the light source. Aside from its design possibilities, light on the stage has an unavoidable effect on the structure and materials of scenery, which, if controlled, can be extremely useful. Light can be used to create opaque, translucent, or transparent scenery. In the construction of transparent or translucent scenery, the pattern of the framing and the location of seams have to be carefully considered in collaboration with the lighting designer. Frequently such designs need to be altered slightly to conceal or modify a seam or structural element. Conversely, opaque areas should not be neglected, for a strong backing light may reveal an interesting but unwanted pattern of framing.

If the design of the lighting comes late in the planning of a setting, almost as an afterthought, the entire visual picture suffers. This sometimes reflects an indifference or unawareness of the power and compositional value of light itself. Lighting is too important not to be considered at the beginning of the theatrical design process.

Color

Although color is a critical aspect of light, it can be discussed as another and equally important element of design. Color is a powerful stimulus that can change the dimension of form, reverse the direction of line, alter the interval between forms, and generate optical motion. Color in the theatre comes from two basic sources: pigment or dye present on the surface of the form or color transmitted by light.

Color in either light or pigment has three variants: **hue, value,** and **chroma.** A specific color can be thought of in terms of its *hue,* which is the color's wavelength or position in the spectrum (or, most simply put, the name of the color); its *value,* signifying the color's black-to-white relationship; and its *chroma,* indicating the color's degree of purity (saturation) or freedom from neutrality.

hue The name of a color; the color's wavelength or position in the spectrum.

value The presence of white or black in a color; the lightness or darkness of a color.

chroma The purity of a color or the amount of adulteration (neutrality); often referred to as *intensity* or *saturation.*

Because of our emotional associations, color most often generates the strongest response of all artistic elements. Warm colors such as yellows, reds, and oranges generally evoke happiness, while cool colors such as blues and greens suggest sadder emotions. These generalizations might be useful but run the risk of becoming trite. For more on color, see Chapter 8.

Although value has been defined as a variant of color, it is an important medium of expression on its own. Suggested form can be modeled on paper without color in shades and highlights using various black-to-white tones, as illustrated in Figure 3-7. Value is experienced early in the process of designing scenery. Many designers will do preliminary work in the form of value sketches.

COURTESY FRANK LUDWIG

3-7

Value Sketch

Value sketch for *Antigone.* Set designer, Frank Ludwig.

Texture

Texture is the *tactile* aspect of form. As a design feature, it adds interest by embellishing the surface and thereby giving character to the finished form. The composition takes on a temperament partially inspired by the makeup of its texture. Surfaces may vary from the extremes of highly polished to rough/natural in quality (Figure 3-8). A rough-hewn surface or decorative bas-relief, for example, each stimulates different emotional responses.

The reason for using texture in a scenic design is to catch, interrupt, and reflect light. The irregular shadows and highlights of a textured surface enrich a design form; thus, the dependency of texture on light is a crucial component of design.

Texture, whether real or simulated, adds interest and character to a design. *Real* texture is three-dimensional, as in the use of fabricated brick, stucco, or plastic leaves (Figure 3-9a). *Simulated* texture is two-dimensional but suggests a third dimension most commonly achieved by painting (Figure 3-9b). Wallpaper, parquetry, and other patterns can be used as well to suggest texture.

Light and Texture Real texture is best revealed by directional side-lighting, while painted texture appears more real under a wash of light without a strong sense of direction. A wash of light is shadowless and therefore does not expose the simulated texture as a painted surface. Conversely, a wash of light on a textured detail such as a cornice or molding will deny its three-dimensionality

a

b

a PHOTO COURTESY NADINE CHARLSEN
b PHOTO COURTESY MIHAI CIUPE

c

c PHOTO COURTESY SCOTT BRADLEY

3-8

Texture and Light

a Texture use for *As You Like It.* Designer, Nadine Charlsen.

b Texture use in *Macbeth.* Designer, Mihai Ciupe.

c Set for *Seven Guitars.* Designer, Scott Bradley.

a PHOTO COURTESY DANIEL GUYETTE
b PHOTO COURTESY TIM SATERNOW

a

b

3-9

Texture

a Real texture used in a model piece. Designer, Dan Guyette.

b Painted texture for Charles Busch's *The Mystery of Irma Vep.* Designer, Tim Saternow.

a PHOTO COURTESY DOUGLAS MCCULLOUGH
b PHOTO COURTESY MICHAEL J. DEMPSEY

and sometimes require the addition of painted shadows and highlights to create the appearance of reality.

Using Texture to Design for Light The function of real texture is to divide light into interesting shadows and highlights as a design feature. The large scale of scenery can heighten that function (see Figure 3-10). Most

a

b

3-10

Designing for Light

a Dramatic use of lighting for *'Tis Pity She's a Whore.* Set design, Douglas McCullough.

b Lighting clearly establishes both mood and atmosphere in this moment from *To Gillian on Her 37th Birthday.* Set design, Michael J. Dempsey.

importantly, the successful unity of light and scenic form results most often from the close creative collaboration of the lighting and scene designers.

The theatrical value of light to scenic forms, first envisioned by Adolphe Appia and Edward Gordon Craig at the beginning of the twentieth century and more fully realized later by the inventiveness of Josef Svoboda, is very much a part of present-day scenography. Moveable lights and computer-generated and other types of projected images have greatly broadened the possibilities for creating texture. The use of abrupt surface changes, reflective coverings, and density variations from opaque to transparent, as well as the addition of highly textured areas, all contribute to the unity of lighting and scenic forms.

PRINCIPLES OF COMPOSITION

harmony A pleasing or congruent arrangement of scenic forms, creating an aesthetic unity, often achieved through repetition.

contrast In scenery, dissimilarity of forms used to create interest. In lighting, a difference in color, intensity, or distribution.

The *elements* of design are the raw materials ready to be brought together into some order or purpose, creating a *composition.* The *principles* of composition are the various ways the designer can control and use the design elements to bring interest and meaning to the stage. A good composition brings into play two controls, **harmony** and **contrast.** The manipulation of these controls through variation, emphasis, gradation, and so forth is how the designer creates interest in a stage setting.

Harmony

The simplest act of bringing order to disorder is to sort unrelated objects into groups that have some sequential relationship or continuity. The objects may have similar shapes, colors, or textures. Control is often achieved through repetition. The repeated use of linear forms, for example, can dominate a composition even though other elements, such as contrast, are present. (As with the elements of design, the principles of composition are not mutually exclusive.)

Although repetition is one of the easiest and quickest ways to bring harmonious control to a composition, it suffers the danger of becoming monotonous. This can be relieved with contrast or variation.

Contrast

The designer depends on contrast to create form and interest; form cannot be revealed without contrast. For example, in nature the protective coloration of an animal or bird reduces contrast to the point of making it invisible against its habitat. But in the theatre, such lack of contrast—an actress in a red gown sitting on a matching sofa—would be disastrous. Between the two extremes lie infinite variations.

The most visible example of harmony and contrast are found in the use of color and value. A design with a single color scheme would be harmonious. The farther apart colors are in the spectrum, the greater the contrast. The same thing occurs with value coupling. Black and white, for example, are extreme value contrasts. Again, refer to Chapter 8 for further discussion on color.

Variation

When the repetition of one element produces monotony, a **variation** of one or more of the other elements can add interest to the composition. In Donald Oenslager's designs for Aeschylus's *Prometheus Bound* (Figure 3-6), the use of light dominates the design. However, manipulation of the direction, distribution, and intensity of light varies greatly, bringing interest to a rather simple form. The color of the scenic form in this production was held under strict control. The overall tonality was gray or neutral, with moments of color achieved through the use of colored light.

variation Slight or major changes in the elements or principles of a form that prevent monotony.

Emphasis

Part of the function of the designer is to guide the audience's view of the stage, providing a **focal point** or **emphasis.** This is a point in the composition (not necessarily the center) to which the eye of the viewer is led by either obvious or subtle means. In addition to the focal point, secondary areas of interest as well as intriguing bits of detail within the composition may hold the audience's attention without detracting from the main focus. Although a stage setting is usually designed around a strong focal point with important secondary areas, the true center of interest in the total picture must be the actor.

focal point Center of interest.

emphasis Visual prominence using the elements and principles of design to guide the viewer to a specific area of the design.

To create emphasis, designers use both the elements and the principles of design. Contrast provides perhaps the easiest means of doing this. If all but one of the scenic pieces are small, our eye will logically go to the large piece, creating emphasis by use of contrast in scale. One single light object in a picture of dark objects creates emphasis by contrast in value.

Isolation or placement can also create emphasis. Within a frame such as a proscenium, the center of the space is the strongest point. Careful framing can guide our eye right to the point of interest. Placing one object away from everything else will also achieve this.

Fortunately, stage lighting, costume colors, and the movement of actors all help to make any change of emphasis rather simple. By dimming most of the lights and brightening one area, stage lighting can easily bring focus to a specific point on the stage, as can the color of a costume in relation to the setting and to other costumes in the scene. The movement of the actor can also change the center of focus, as in a ballet or other dance composition. The mobility of the actor allows the director to use groups of actors as a compositional tool for focusing the interest of the audience on any portion of the stage setting.

Gradation

Designers often want to establish a feeling of movement or change in a stage setting through relatively subtle means. Sharp contrasts can be reduced by the use of **gradation**, which by transitional steps softens contrasting elements yet brings a feeling of movement into the stage picture. The graded wash of a sky drop, with the dark blue at the top gradually becoming lighter near the bottom, is an example of gradation of value (see Figure 3-11). The use of gradation may occur in line, shape, or any other element of design.

gradation Transitional steps in a sequence used to create emphasis and a feeling of movement in a design.

a

b

a COURTESY JOHN BINKLEY
b COURTESY STEVEN L. GILLIAM

3-11

Gradation

The use of gradation can help focus the audience.

a In this idea sketch for *Faust,* designer John Binkley uses increasingly smaller circles, leading the eye to the smallest.

b This sketch, by Steven L. Gilliam for *The Sound of Music,* is subtler. Note the strong verticals that move from very narrow on the outside to quite broad in the center.

COMPOSITION, SPACE, AND DEPTH

Space is to the scene designer what a block of wood or stone is to the sculptor. The spaces in and around the stage become an area to enclose or leave open, to light or leave dark, to flatten out or deepen.

Space has meaning only if it has been in some way defined. An actor standing alone without any limiting device stands in a vacuum. The proscenium arch (or the stage deck in the case of arena and thrust theatre) begins to establish limits to a space. And, indeed, it is the province of the designer to define the space that the actors will ultimately be using.

One of the first devices that the designer uses to define the relationship of actor to stage is frame. The proscenium arch is just that—a large frame. Within that particular architectural limit, the designer will find other ways to frame the actor. A series of portals is the most obvious choice, but there are an infinite number of others. A set of columns, arches, and doors; a trellis; lines of trees—whatever draws our focus to an actor in a particular place on the stage—can be effective (Figure 3-12). The type and size of the frames will start to define the nature of the space that is appropriate for the production.

Depth defines three-dimensional space. As figures or large shapes are overlapped, the illusion of depth can be achieved. A wing-and-drop set in which subsequent portals get slightly smaller is a good example. The flat plane of each wing when contrasted against the adjacent wing gives an illusion of space that belies their two-dimensionality, especially when other signs of space use used.

To heighten the three-dimensional quality of the form, designers create the illusion of a sharp light coming from a specific direction. The direction of the light and the cast shadows help to describe the form and place it in space, as seen in Figure 3-13.

The final tool that designers use to show depth when planning forms is perspective drawing, which creates the illusion of literally breaking through the plane of the paper. Perspective and the shadows of directional lighting are combined to achieve a total effect, a feeling of space in a two-dimensional form.

PHOTO COURTESY FRANK LUDWIG

3-12

Frame

The squares in this photo of Anouilh's *Antigone,* designed by Frank Ludwig, not only separate the areas of the set visually, but they can also be used to frame the actors, thus providing them with focus.

a

b

b PHOTO COURTESY SCOTT BRADLEY

3-13

Sets Under Light

In both of these designs, the light is being used to establish the mood of the moment as well as to focus the audience on the immediate action.

a *Cat on a Hot Tin Roof.* Set and costume design, Michael Olich at the Institute of Dramatic Arts, Tokyo.

b The opera *Akhanaten* for Boston Lyric Opera. Design, Scott Bradley.

COMPOSITION AND UNITY

The composition of a stage setting is expected to bring a unity to the overall arrangements of the visual forms. The strength of unity depends on more than harmony, however. The compositional unity of scene design depends first on *balance and movement* and then on *proportion and rhythm.* At first glance, balance and movement may seem identical to proportion and rhythm;

however, a closer analysis will show that they are related but not the same. Balance and movement are the outward, more obvious expressions of the subtler, more sensitive effects of proportion and rhythm.

Unity suggests a *balance* of the forces within the composition. These are the forces of tension, attraction, and attention that exist among the forms of a stage design. This balance involves *movement,* or how forces and forms change over time. Further, all scenery forms have mass and size (scale), which means that their *proportion* must be considered. And lastly, the proportional relationship between forms cannot help but bring *rhythm* into the composition, whether it is static or dynamic in feeling.

Balance and Movement

balance Equalization of visual weight or opposing forces within a composition.

Balance is described as the relationship of forces within a composition. One of those forces, tension, is found in the spacing of scenery masses, the grouping of furniture, or the relationship of the actor to the scenery and furniture. The degree of tension depends on the interval or space among forms and creates a feeling of balance or imbalance. For example, the space between the finger of God and Adam gives life to man in Michelangelo's fresco in the Sistine Chapel. If the fingers were touching, or moved farther apart, there would be no tension.

Gravity is the other force in composition, made important by the viewer's unconscious reaction to it. Gravity has probably the greatest effect on balance. A viewer reacts to visual signs with an organic sense of balance schooled by a lifetime of living with the pull of gravity. Because of this, an unsupported heavy object may seem to be falling, as does a leaning object, unless its center of gravity holds it in balance. Also, a recognizable shape in an unnatural position may cause a feeling of imbalance. Such imbalance makes us feel like there is something wrong, a problem that can be useful in a design.

Movement can change the balance over a period of time. In the theatre, as has been noted, the time–movement relationship is quite apparent. The actors move from area to area; the lights dim and brighten; scenery on occasion moves in view of the audience. All these are part of the composition of the dramatic form and involve the element of time.

Time, however, exists in a fixed composition. There is an interval of time as the eye follows the pattern of movement through a composition. The interval is minute, of course, when compared with the broader movements on stage. Visual changes can lead the eye, abruptly or gradually, over the movement of a composition.

Proportion and Rhythm

The second means of obtaining unity in a composition is through the use of proportion and rhythm. A certain amount can be acquired by training and be sharpened by analysis, but a sense of proportion is largely intuitive.

Proportion can be linked to the reason or function of a visual form. The proportion of a chair as a visual form depends on how the chair is to be used. A simple dining room side chair is small when compared with the scale and grandeur of a canopied throne. That same chair next to a small stool will seem much larger and probably more important.

Although the primary concern regarding proportion onstage is how it relates to the human figure, a proportional relationship exists between one form and another and among the spaces between forms (negative space). Perhaps more important is the proportional relationship of forms to their surrounding space. The rhythm and proportions of a sculptural arrangement of forms set in an unbound space may seem different from a similar arrangement of shapes framed or confined within a rectangular shape like the proscenium opening.

Scene design is concerned with this rectangular frame as well as with the freer compositions of the nonproscenium stage. Designing for nonproscenium theatre requires more sculptural techniques to create a desirable proportional relationship among forms. Whereas the composition within a proscenium frame is viewed pictorially, nonproscenium scenic forms have to be composed satisfactorily for viewers from all directions.

As balance is linked to movement, so proportion relates to **rhythm.** Rhythm is a type of movement that recurs at intervals or creates a cycle. The space among forms and the attitude of one shape to another create a rhythm in the composition. The subdivision of a single form does the same. Rhythm may appear in the quiet dignity of a formal arrangement or in the vigorous movement of a dynamic composition. It may be expressed in the rhythmic flow of harmonious forms or in the nervous staccato organization of shapes.

rhythm Patterns of repeated visual movement.

Rhythm as a unifying factor is usually expressed in the lines or linear qualities of a stage composition. The use of actual lines or the feeling of a line caused by the position and direction of one shape in relation to another results in a rhythmic movement that may be as strong or as subdued as the designer desires. Diagonal lines give a greater sense of movement than the use of strong horizontal and vertical lines, which tend to stop movement.

Although the rhythm of straight lines is bolder than that of curved lines, the latter provide infinitely greater variety. The rhythm of a curved line may have the grace of flowing lines, the turbulence of reverse curves, the whirl of a spiral, as well as the repetition and order of interlaced geometric curves such as circles and ellipses.

Whether dominated by straight or curved lines, the rhythm of a stage composition eventually becomes a part of the basic movement plan. Likewise, the proportional relationship of forms, which determines the rhythm, forms a balance, resulting in a greater feeling of unity, especially when the rhythm is obviously repetitious.

COMPOSITION AND INTEREST

In addition to maintaining unity in a stage composition, the designer tries to bring interest and meaning to the setting. Any meaning attached to the scenic form of the composition is, of course, part of the designer's interpretation of the scenic requirements of the play or an attempt to bring visual substance to the playwright's ideas.

A stage setting, like a piece of fine art, can do all of this and still not be very interesting. What makes one setting for a play more interesting than another? A unique and daring visual interpretation of an idea is what stimulates an intellectual and emotional response on the part of the audience. This is frequently possible when the play is a classic or one familiar to the audience. European scene designers have long been credited with consistently producing exciting and innovative designs, because they approach plays differently than do many designers in the United States. Changes in the training of designers in this country is beginning to reflect more conceptual thinking. It is the novel thinking that is appealing, to say nothing of the skills demonstrated in the designs.

The manner in which a designer achieves balance in composition also accounts for one design being more appealing than another. A mechanical balance of the design forms may bring unity to a composition but still be monotonous. A better composition varies or stretches the balance into a more exciting arrangement of forms without losing unity.

Creating an exciting setting is desirable but it is more important to be true to the text of the play. There is always a danger that the conceptual work will overwhelm the play in order to create visual stimuli. The storytelling aspects of the play must take precedence over any design.

4

The Design Process

A design is concerned first with the function it will perform. A scenic idea may warrant pure decoration, as for an awards program, the mood-inducing staging of a ballet, or a realistic environment for a detergent commercial. A costume may be contemporary, everyday clothing, an otherworldly fantastic garment, or a leotard and tights allowing for complete freedom of movement. Lighting may realistically establish time of day and season or suggest a surreal world. Sound can amplify an announcer's voice or evoke atmosphere or mood. Whatever the form of design, its most important function is to serve the unfolding story line.

FUNCTION OF SCENE DESIGN FOR DRAMA

The creation of an environment to fulfill a purpose or function in scene design is obviously linked to the dramatic form it serves. The basic concept of present-day theatre as a union of playwriting and production has brought scenery out of the "pretty background" class into full partnership with the production of a play. The scene designer brings to the production a visual interpretation and expression of the author's aim. Thus, scene design becomes a fusing of a visual statement and the basic intent of the play into a single dramatic impression. This alone does not separate it from the other forms of theatre design, however; what makes scene design unique is the way in which it achieves this. (The same can be said for costume, lighting, and sound design.)

Creating this single dramatic impression is difficult and requires great skill, thought, and vision. Alone it would be a daunting task, but it is made considerably more difficult by the need to meld with the other designs as well as consider the director and the actors. This collaboration is what makes success in the theatre both extremely difficult and extremely exciting.

We can best see the function of scene design by looking at the dramatic form of the play itself. The form of the play should enable the designers to understand the relationship of scenery to the action and the actors, the dominant mood, the theme, and the story in general.

Placing the Action

If scene design is supposed to bring to the play a visual expression of the author's intent, the designer must first examine the *action* of the play and the kind of people involved in the action. Unless completely abstract, every play (or any other storytelling theatrical form, such as ballet or pantomime) presents a conflict. Out of the conflict, whether heroic or domestic, comes the action of the play, the force that moves it forward and makes it a living, breathing form. Dramatic action is a combination of physical or bodily action, visual movement, dialogue, and characterization. Characterization creates sympathy or repulsion in the audience for the figures involved in the action. The characters either create the conflict or are shaped by the conflict in the ensuing action. Careful analysis of the action and characters can help lead the designer to understand the playwright's intent.

The Scene of Action Scene design produces more than just a place where the scene of action occurs. It generates an environment in which the action can happen and that helps the audience understand the purpose of the story being told. Sometimes the scene or elements of the scene become a part of the action, such as in the frankly theatrical use of scenery in a musical comedy. The use of the falling chandelier in *Phantom of the Opera* immediately establishes an environment of danger. The treadmills that were heavily used in the original production of *Annie* provided a specific lateral movement for the scenery as well as a pattern for choreography. Alternatively, the scene may recede into the background and be more felt than seen—a witness to the action. A good design is never neutral; it always comments on the people or action of the play.

Characterization Character development or *characterization* bears an important relationship to the environment of the scene. The people in the action react in accordance with, or in opposition to, their surroundings as well as one another. The influence of the characters on scene design can be sometimes subtle, sometimes obvious, and on occasion symbolic. When, for example, the setting is an interior, a study of the people living in the house gives the designer many important clues for detail work. The family of Grandpa Vanderhof and his bizarre friends in Kaufman and Hart's *You Can't Take It with You* certainly contribute a wealth of detail about the kind of house and collection of curios that make up the environment of the play. In *Richard III*, the actions of the characters suggest in a much more abstract way the nature of the environment.

Time and Place The action of the play must occur in a specific *time* and *place,* which are usually calculated by the author to establish the proper atmospheric surroundings for the action. Place, even though it may be limbo, makes a visual impression on the audience. A specific time in the historical past can prepare a state of mind in the audience as much as the absence of a specific time or place can.

Although time and place are linked with the overall atmospherics, the connection is sometimes rather loose and may merely suggest a place that connotes the atmosphere inherent in the play. The design for *Red Noses* (Figure 4-1) suggests a world that is not normal, although we recognize elements of the "real" world. Architectural elements such as the gothic arches suggest a

PHOTO COURTESY MARY SCHRADER

4-1

Atmosphere Inherent in a Play

This set for *Red Noses,* designed by Mary Schrader, clearly indicates a world in which not all is right.

time period, but by skewing the perspective, the designer informs us that the environment of this play is very much out of balance. Specific time is of very little importance, which the language of the play makes more obvious.

Establishing Mood

The second function of scene design is to establish in the visual elements of the surroundings an expression of the dominant atmosphere, or *mood.* In this first impression on the audience, scene design tries to create an expression of the mood and its relationship to the action and characters. *Mood* can be described as the quality of a play that, when properly transmitted, creates a state of mind and emotional response in the audience. It can be expressed in such words as *sparkling, warm, gloomy, violent, earthy, mystic,* and so forth. The terms *tragedy, comedy,* and *farce* refer to **genre** but suggest as well a broader idea of atmosphere. It would be unusual to use the same words to describe the mood in a farce like *A Flea in Her Ear* as in a tragedy like *Oedipus.* Figure 4-2 provides two illustrations of how creative set design can establish different moods.

genre A general category, such as farce, mystery, and tragedy, distinguished by form, style, content, and other characteristics.

Arguably, a play is the dramatization of a mood, a theme, and a story. All three elements are always present in a play, but one may be emphasized over the other two. Hence, plays may primarily dramatize mood, with theme and story in a secondary position; such plays seem to be at the extreme ends of the emotional scale. A tragedy is usually a mood-dominated play, as is a low comedy or farce.

a

b

4-2

Mood

a Dramatic use of light is seen in this photograph of *Man of La Mancha,* designed by Tim Saternow.

b A different mood is seen in the architectural detail in the setting of Shaw's *Misalliance,* designed by Michael J. Dempsey.

a PHOTO COURTESY TIM SATERNOW
b PHOTO COURTESY MICHAEL J. DEMPSEY

The relationship of mood to action matters in any play. Occasionally, the atmosphere established visually contrasts with the apparent mood of a play. For example, comedy scenes are sometimes played against a haunted house, or tragedy against a raucous street carnival. The contrasting moods combine into a single dramatic impression. Hence, fun in the haunted house might turn into farce, and murder at the Mardi Gras may become irony. Tragedy, of course, frequently begins in a lighter mood that may or may not be expressed in the surroundings. A festive scene may have an air of foreboding that anticipates the approaching tragedy.

Reinforcing the Theme

Theme is, of course, closely linked with mood as well as with the storytelling part of the dramatic form. *Theme* is defined as the main idea of a play, or the main point that the author wants the audience to realize. The theme of some plays is clear, especially if the author is using the dramatic form as a soapbox to lampoon society or government. Comedy often carries a serious message to an unsuspecting audience as effectively as other forms of drama do. Because one can convey a thematic statement in so many ways, the collaborative efforts of the artistic team determine the specifics for each production (see Figure 4-3).

The expression of theme in scenery is not always easily achieved. More often the theme is treated with subtlety, achieved through elements known only to the designer and his or her muse. The most obvious example of a theme-oriented play is found in political theatre. Removed from the fictional format of literary theatre, political theatre is free to move to its objective with dramatic and theatrical directness. The most familiar political theatre, stemming from Germany in the 1930s, is that of Bertolt Brecht.

a PHOTO COURTESY BRUCE GOODRICH

a

b

4-3

Theme

Any artistic team brings its own sensibility to a production, so two versions of the same play might differ greatly while expressing the same theme. This is particularly true of a play like Dickens's *A Christmas Carol,* in which the theme is so universal.

a This photograph shows a production that is fairly traditional in that it evokes the world of nineteenth-century London as Dickens lived it. Set design, Bruce Goodrich.

b This approach to the same story is quite different, relying on a cacophony of theatrical props that allow the actors to create the scene from pieces that are sitting around. Set design, Dick Block.

To determine the theme of the play, designers find it helpful to understand the background of the playwright as well as the time period in which (and sometimes about which) the play was written. Plays comment on the human condition, which changes over time and in relation to varying social and political ideas. Knowledge of social norms is therefore important.

Determining the theme also involves looking beyond the words of the play and examining the overall structure, language, and ideas that are being expressed through the characters and the action. In some plays this does not require much thought; in others, several readings of the play and background reading may be necessary.

Staging the Story

Story is the thread that holds together the elements in a complete dramatic form. It is the series of related incidents bringing continuity to the many events in a play. Story is probably more important to the theatre than to other art forms. The expression of an idea in the theatre depends on having and holding the audience's attention every moment. If confused, the theatre audience cannot go back and reread a passage for clarification, the way a novel reader can. A clear and exciting story, however, can hold an audience spellbound. A good storyteller, of course, uses mood to create the atmosphere for a story. The storyteller can also use the story to make a point, as in plays with strong themes. Any good play usually has a good story, but a play that is dominated by the dramatization of story is primarily dedicated to telling an interesting tale, whether it be of love, adventure, intrigue—the list is long and varied.

When the environment of a story-dominated play is real, the design problem becomes one of selection of realistic details and forms that place the action and establish the mood. This, more often than not, has already been accomplished by the author through the choice of a realistic location for the action. More important than realistic detail is the manner in which the director fits the action of the play to the stage space, for which the designer provides logical choices. Called **staging,** this involves the placement and movement of actors within and around the physical environment of the set. Successful staging helps ensure the continuous flow of action necessary to telling a good story. The importance of this cannot be overemphasized.

staging The arrangement of actors in the environment, creating stage pictures that help to tell the story of the play.

The many English and French bedroom farces are story-dominated plays that depend heavily on staging. The skillful juxtaposition of hallways, doors, closets, and the ever-present bedroom—all visible to the audience—facilitates the fast pace and split-second timing of the nonsensical action of the story. An unusual example of imaginative farce staging is Alan Ayckburn's *Taking Steps.* The three floors of a house are staged on one level. Light helps to define the change of floor levels, as do the actors when they pantomime going up and down nonexistent stairs. Once the audience catches on to the convention, they easily imagine the different levels of the house. The cleverness of the staging adds humor to the performance and develops an interesting production style.

Every choice that the designer makes in the ground plan of the physical space both limits and provides opportunities for the director in terms of movement patterns and stage pictures. The decision to use an overstuffed armchair instead of a simpler tall-backed wooden chair, for example, means that the director will not be able to move the chair easily during the course of a scene. However, it might instead allow the director to perch an actor on the arm or even the back of the chair.

Sometimes a director will ask the designer for a "bare stage." Because this can mean many things, the designer and director must define it clearly. If, for example, one chair is needed on the bare stage, the exact placement of the chair becomes critical. The direction that the chair faces also becomes significant. If two chairs are used, their relative position is just as important. An intimate love scene staged with two chairs in proximity differs greatly from a love scene that has chairs on opposite sides of the stage or that face away from each other.

The responsibility the scene designer has in establishing the physical space makes the importance of collaboration with the director obvious when working out the ground plan. Although at times they may seem minor, all of these decisions will have a direct effect on the staging.

DESIGN AND OTHER THEATRICAL FORMS

Theme and mood are present in any theatrical form—ballet, mime, and multimedia performances as well as dramatic work. The high-tech lighting of a rock show imparts an atmospheric theme as it supports and enhances the music. Although classical ballet usually has a story line, modern dance frequently does not. Ballet's decorative background, which sets the locale and mood of the dance, has given way to limited use of scenery in the form of stylized properties, more expressive of theme than anything else. Mime, both group and solo, is highly theatrical. Imagination supplies the scenic background and hand props. The skill of the performer, rather than the designer, creates the mood of the locale in the minds of the audience.

The Challenge

Design Questions

Whatever type of theatrical event a designer may be asked to do, essentially the same questions are appropriate:

1. What is the reason for the event? (commercial, charity function, historical celebration, etc.)
2. What is the atmosphere or mood? (happy, serious, etc.)
3. What is the playwright's intent in writing this play? What is the theme? (How will scenery, costumes, lighting, and sound help you convey it?)
4. How and in what type of venue will it be staged? (theatre, stadium, on the street, etc.)
5. What is the style? (entertainment, documentary, pageant, etc.)

HOW TO BEGIN

At this point as a beginning designer you should be conscious of the importance of scene design in relation to the play. You should be aware of the influences of the theatrical medium and be familiar with the intricacies of the creative process. But, you may ask, how does one get an idea for a design?

Like any other art form, scene design is a personal method of expression. Because every designer approaches the process subjectively and intuitively, setting down universal rules for developing a design idea is impossible. Each designer must develop his or her own method of reaching the inner reservoir of creative ideas. Although we can make recommendations and point to examples of good design, the evolution of an idea is the designer's individual struggle.

Of course, the design does not find its complete expression until the play becomes a production and the written word becomes dialogue and visible action. Design is the individual expression of artistic imagination, theatrical sense, and technical ingenuity through the visual control of line, color, and form. The design concept is often evident as a visual theme with variations that weave through a complicated setting or series of settings, bringing unity of thought to the whole. Many times the theme is so subtle that only the trained eye of another designer can see it. Although the designer must be able to articulate the approach that is taken with a production, the audience does not necessarily need to be able to do so. Whatever the designer's approach, it must be consistent with that of the director and the rest of the design team. If it is, the ideas will be inherent in the production and will help guide the audience to a better understanding of the play.

The design idea is aimed at stimulating an intellectual or emotional response in the audience. The design elements may be broad and sensational to arouse basic emotions, or they may be subtle and refined to stimulate an intellectual response. Good design is the result of logical and imaginative thinking and intuition expressed through an idea or central theme.

A remarkable event or an appealing image may inspire the ideas for a setting—or inspiration may seem to appear out of thin air. A good designer is always open to moments of inspiration. Some designers carry a notebook; some keep sketch books to capture ideas on paper. Others simply keep new ideas on file in their minds. The trick is to recognize an exciting idea and be open to surprises and varied ways of thinking.

Analysis of the Script, Libretto, or Scenario

The Script Because all parts of a production are based on the written words of the play, the designer logically begins his or her conceptual work with the study of the play's text. Ideally, the play is analyzed from several separate readings. Each subsequent reading of the script will likely lead to a better understanding of the play.

The designer's first reading of the play is for its *content.* The designer should react as a member of the audience, avoiding any preconceived image of the scenery other than the author's description. (Some designers ignore even that on first reading.) In this way a first impression can serve as an overall response that will help answer these questions: What kind of a play is it? What is the action and where is it taking place? What is the dominant mood? Is the play a comedy or a tongue-in-cheek satire with political overtones? Is it a tragedy of classical proportions or a domestic misunderstanding? Writing down one's first impressions of a script is a good idea. Over the course of developing a design, one can easily forget this initial response, and it is impossible to re-create it. Having a record of it can remind designers of their original intent.

The atmosphere and mood of the play can usually be determined from the first reading. The scene of the action often suggests or sets the *atmosphere* of a play. A deserted house on a stormy night for a mystery or candlelight for a love scene are typical examples. As we have seen, however, the action may be in opposition or in contrast to its environment. The mood of a play or scene often suggests *color* to the designer. Out of the mood of the environment comes the overall tonality of the play, which often can be expressed most forcefully with color or even the absence of color.

The second, more careful, reading is for the play's *intent.* Designers must read "between the lines" to answer questions like these: What is the author saying? What is the theme? What is the style? Has the author expressed a point of view through allegory or in daily-life realism? Designers must also pay close attention to how the playwright has used language. Has the playwright soared into the realm of epic poetry or dropped into the lusty prose of street talk? The imagery that the playwright uses also serves as a guide to the designer. Design ideas often develop directly from specific images in the text. It is frequently helpful to use a metaphor for the play as an approach. In the style of the play, the designer finds clues to the degree of reality or unreality of the scenic environment.

A certain amount of organization is usually necessary in order to understand a play for design purposes. It might be as simple as a list of the various locales in the play; it could be a graphic of the relationships among the characters in a complex story. Determining the structure of the play also helps. As the play tells a story, so does each act and even each scene. Articulating the purpose and idea of each scene can tell the designer a great deal about the structure of the play. This effort inevitably leads to ideas about the theme.

Understanding the theme of the play allows the designer to find visual images and metaphors that help lead to an overall approach to the design. The style of the play usually suggests the form of the design. A realistic style implies realistic forms; a fantasy or dream points to unreal forms.

All of the elements just discussed help designers use their medium to create the world of the play. Designers typically continue rereading the play throughout the production process.

The Opera Libretto The **libretto** is the text or dialogue of an opera, sung rather than spoken. Like plays, operas vary widely. Some opera librettos are stilted and void of drama, while others are full of action and are highly dramatic. Because the music contains most of the excitement and atmosphere, the only way to comprehend the full dramatic intensity of an opera is to listen to it.

libretto The text or dialogue of an opera.

Opera is a "larger than life" performance style; therefore, the designer looks for more than a functional background. He or she searches for a visual image or metaphor in the music to support the theme of the text.

The Ballet Scenario Because ballet is a stylized performance technique relying on pantomime to tell the story, the scenery is often highly decorative and atmospheric. The *scenario* of a ballet is an outline of the story with an occasional description of the action, all of which provides minimal information for the designer. However, many classical ballets are based on familiar stories that can be researched for additional background.

As with opera, the ballet designer should listen to the music and learn from the choreographer the movement patterns that will be used. Because ballet is dance, the music will convey the mood and tempo of the movement. The choreographer who plans the movement, however, may interpret a familiar story and musical composition in an individualistic style. There are, for example, many versions of the *Nutcracker* ballet. Hence the designer must not only be familiar with the scenario and the music but also rely heavily on the choreographer for information and inspiration. Although these obstacles may seem restrictive, ballet provides an opportunity for imaginative and creative design that does not exist in other theatrical forms.

Determining the Visual Style

Style can be defined as the degree of reality expressed in the writing or literary form of the play, which in turn influences the mode of the performance and the form of the scenery and costumes. Because style in the theatre is felt, heard, and seen in so many different ways, it is difficult to define in specific terms. Literary, acting, directing, and visual styles, as well as period styles, unite to form a single production style. Style is sometimes visually obvious, but more often the audience will not notice it unless some element of it is jarring or inconsistent in terms of the whole.

Production Style and Reality The overall style of a production is expressed in the degree of reality of the performance. There are many kinds of reality in the theatre: the lifelike copy of nature *(naturalism),* the *fantasy* of dreams, the *make-believe* quality of storytelling, the immediacy of *documentary* or of *improvisational* style, and the performance reality of the *theatrical* style.

The interpretation of a play and the kind of response that is desired by the artistic team will determine the specific style of a production. For example, a play like *A Christmas Carol* can be the telling of a very dark and sad story or it can be lighter fare and filled with laughs. If Hamlet is justified in killing Claudius, that suggests a different style of production than if he is seen as a petulant, selfish young man or simply as crazy. Whatever the style, its consistency and integrity allow an audience to accept what it sees as the world of the play. This consistency is directly attributable to the collaborative work of the artistic team.

Occasionally production styles are combined. The docudrama style (documentary and literary styles) is used (more often in film than in theatre) to capture the emotion of an actual occurrence or event. It has the factual reality of a documentary but is actually a fictional style. The documentary format heightens the sense of reality and holds the audience while the story unfolds.

As human beings we often feel the need to categorize, but this can be limiting. Some contemporary plays do not clearly belong in a single category of style. By labeling a play, a designer runs the risk of limiting an approach to its production. It is best to use any perception of a play's style as a guide, not an absolute. To be innovative artists, designers must remain open to working outside the "norm" of these categories and allow themselves to look at plays with a fresh eye.

Visual Style and Form The effect of style on form is more easily seen in the physical production than in the performance styles just discussed, although the two are related. Visual styles can be defined similarly, in terms of degrees of reality.

The **representational** style, for example, is lifelike. The design form is represented in a painting or sculpture rendered as near to its natural form and color as the technical skill of the artist allows. The opposite of this, the **nonrepresentational** style, is ornamental. Because its goal is sensation, the interplay of abstract form and color becomes important. The designer does not attempt to create a form that bears any resemblance to actual objects. Between these two extremes lie as many degrees of realism, symbolism, abstraction, or complete subjectivity as designers care to define.

representational A form of art that directly relates to real or lifelike objects.

nonrepresentational A form of art that is abstract and ornamental, not based on real-life objects and shapes.

In nonrepresentationl style, the effect of form is more apparent. The form is distorted into an abstract but recognizable shape. For example, in Figure 4-4, there are certainly elements of trees and tree branches, but each design treats the representation of trees a bit differently. The realistic tree in *A Girl's Life* contrasts with the abstract texture of trees in the forest scene of *Macbeth*.

As a visual art, scenery styles conform to the same degrees of reality that production styles do. Scenery style, in fact, is the most important visual element supporting the overall production style. Several examples of various styles are shown in Figure 4-5.

URL http://www.brookes.ac.uk/VL/theatre/images.htm

URL http://www.siue.edu/PROJECT2000

URL http://vl-theatre.com

a PHOTO COURTESY MIHAI CIUPE
b PHOTO COURTESY KATHLEEN WIDOMSKI

a

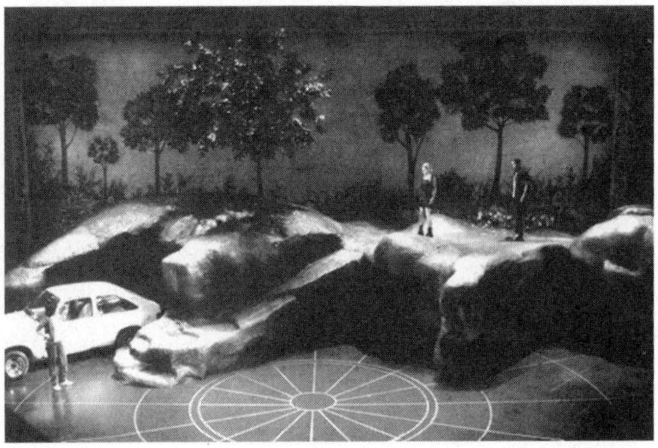

b

4-4

Style and Form

Designers are always exploring ways of suggesting foliage artistically. This is often a difficult task, but the following examples work successfully.

a *Macbeth,* designed by Mihai Ciupe, treats the foliage as an overall texture.

b A realistic tree is backed by painted foliage for *A Girl's Life,* designed by Kathleen Widomski for GEVA.

a

b

c

d

4-5

Styles of Scenery

The designs shown here are various approaches to creating an environment that is appropriate for a specific production of a play. Because classifying each as a certain "style" is problematic and limiting, the thought process and main idea behind the design are presented instead, mostly in the designers' own words.

a *Rumors,* designed by Michael J. Riha, is very much a realistic setting. Novice designers tend to assume that "realistic" box sets are easy to do. Actually, they are the hardest to do precisely because they must appear to be real.

b Designer Peter Beudert: "*The Firebugs* design is skeletal but suggests a menacing volume and variety of spaces around the central playing area. Light permeates through the framework of the structure as a psychological score to the action."

c Designer Mihai Ciupe: "My goal [for *Hedda Gabler*] was to create an elegant prison-like environment. Instead of using the cliché metal bars I decided to create this fragile web between the audience and the actors. The director and I were looking for a metaphoric space that would be a deadly trap for Hedda's spirit."

d Designer Dick Block: "One of the elements of *Oklahoma* that is important is the vast amount of air and space that surrounds these people. In trying to create a landscape that went far into the distance, we used a series of progressively smaller portals, much like an old-fashioned wing-and-drop set. These were painted as an abstraction of the sky to establish a feeling of openness and air."

e Designer Timothy Averill: "*The Kafka Project* was a very presentational design, all about where the characters

a PHOTO COURTESY MICHAEL J. RIHA
b PHOTO COURTESY PETER BEUDERT
c PHOTO COURTESY MIHAI CIUPE
d PHOTO COURTESY LISA LAKE
e PHOTO COURTESY TIMOTHY AVERILL

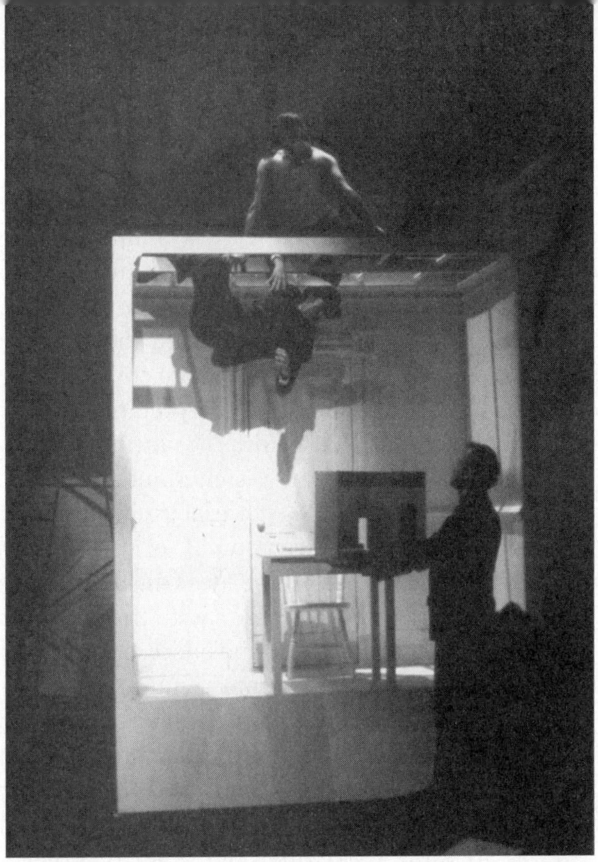

e

f PHOTO COURTESY DUNSI DAI
g PHOTO COURTESY JOHN BINKLEY

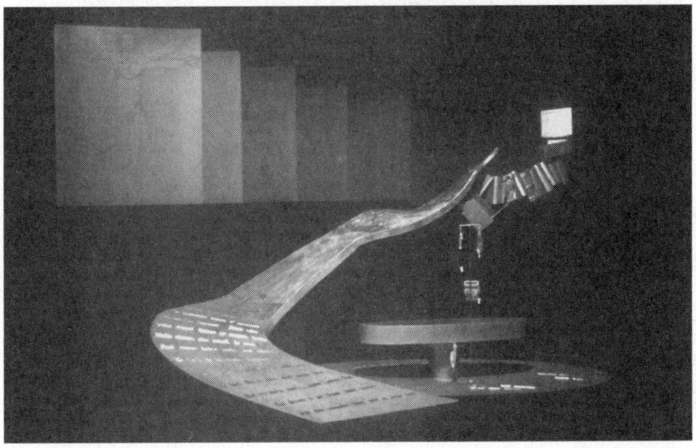

f

g

were in space on the stage and how that placement and containment affected them emotionally. The white box allowed the Kafka character to be outside the stories but the audience could watch him respond to the action, parallel with our experience of it. The white box spun in the transformation sequence, using a sleight-of-hand trick that squished the Kafka character into a tight cell of disappointment and loss."

f Designer Dunsi Dai for the Repertory Theatre of St. Louis: "*Wit* is a highly intellectual piece. The set tries to go with the spirit of the main character, avoiding the commitment to any specific location. It is featured with elements of the intellectual and the academic with a high spirit leading to an unknown world."

g Designer John Binkley: "The one thing that impressed me about the images [of the Dust Bowl] was the way that the wind literally reshaped the terrain. So much of the story [of *The Grapes of Wrath*] is about the earth and man's struggle for survival, I wanted there to be terrain the actors had to physically encounter. I designed an environment that evoked the wind reshaping the landscape."

Style and Costumes The influence of style on form in costume is not the same as in scenery. Unlike scenery, a costume design is always linked to the character and lifestyle envisioned by the playwright, as well as the human form of the actor. The author has created the character in the same style, be it realistic, allegorical, or symbolic, as the rest of the play. The actor and the costume interpret the character within the parameters of the director's concept. The costume designer may also strongly influence character interpretation. Often the costumes (as well as the scenery) are designed before the casting is done. When that is the case, the body type indicated by the designer in the costume sketch (i.e., large-boned and tall, excessively thin, etc.) may determine the body type of the actor that is to be cast in that part. This assumes, of course, that the costume designer and the director have agreed on the ideas manifest in the costume design. Any style choice in costumes usually starts with the director's concept of the play, which might be a spoof of a period piece or a radical departure in form, such as the changing of a drama into a musical.

The costume designer can use various types of *stylization* to help express the overall style of a play. In general, the more stylized a costume, the less realistic it is, engaging a more imaginative response from the audience. For example, a realistic bear costume meant to represent a bear is not a stylized costume; however, the design for Lyle the Crocodile (Figure 4-6a) shows a lot of stylization. If the bear is suggested by only a headpiece or mask, then this reflects a greater degree of stylization than the full suit does. The degrees of stylization vary. For instance, a designer may stylize a realistic costume slightly to achieve a particular effect. In Figure 4-6b, each costume is varied to reflect subtle character differences. Consider also the style statement created by the clothing of any female lead in a television sitcom—realistic, yet with some stylization.

The British musical *Cats* offers a wonderful example of costume stylization. The actors and dancers suggest that they are cats with stylized makeup, painted body tights, and movement. Their performance, however, is not to imply that they are humans impersonating cats, but that cats are like humans.

The focus of a theatrical performance is on the actors (characters) and their costumes. Of all the elements of a stage composition, costume style affects viewers the most. Its brilliance, cleverness, or dullness can stimulate or confuse an audience.

Style and Light Lighting and scene designers must visually support (and occasionally contrast) the acting, literary, and directing styles to help create a unified production. A lighting style can be developed by the manipulation of the *qualities of light.* The varying proportions of *intensity* (brightness), *color, distribution,* and *movement* of light contribute to the production style and the degree of reality in the stage picture, as shown in the examples in Figure 4-7.

How realistic light is on the stage depends on its degree of conformity (or lack of comformity) to light in nature. We are so used to seeing each other under the sun's light—its angles, distribution, and colors—that when these angles deviate from the norm, or when colors change too much, we consider

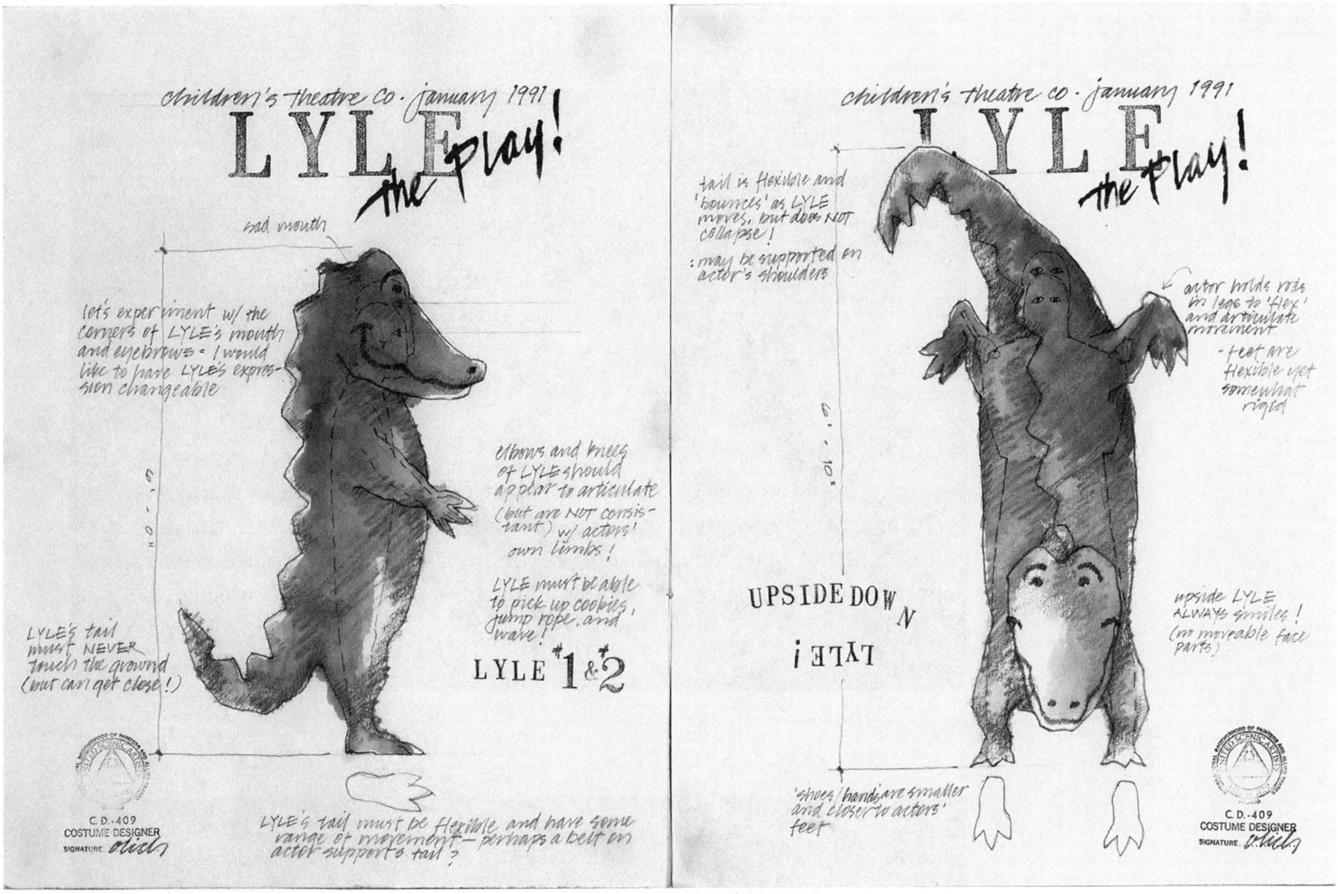

a COURTESY MICHAEL OLICH

a

b COURTESY SUSAN TSU

b

4-6

Costume Style

Categorizing the "style" of costumes creates the same problem as that of scenery. Here are two quite different approaches to designing costumes for the stage:

a This design for *Lyle the Crocodile* by Michael Olich shows a clever and fun solution to putting an actor onstage in an animal suit—upside down as well as right-side up! Note that within the sketch the designer has shown the actor.

b Period style with subtle character differences are clearly shown in this design by Susan Tsu for the Cut Purses in *Cyrano de Bergerac.*

a

b

b PHOTO COURTESY RALPH FUNICELLO

4-7

Style and Light

a The abstract use of light, form, and costumes in a production of Harold Pinter's *Old Times.* Lighting designer, R. Craig Wolf.

b A light-conscious design allowing the atmospheric, motivated, and decorative use of light in *She Stoops to Folly.* Designer, Ralph Funicello.

the light "unreal" or "theatrical." Ironically, the low angle and rich colors of a sunset are frequently so dramatic that they seem to belong on the stage. For the same reason, light on an actor from a low angle seems unnatural or stylized.

Although much of stage lighting may seem naturalistic, some types of theatrical productions and performances depend more on a style of color, distribution, and movement of light than on general illumination or visibility. Ballet, for example, is a theatrical extension of life into a highly stylized performance technique. Realistic illumination is less important than the theatrical atmosphere, exotic colors, and arbitrary angles of light that make up this style of production. In addition, many plays call for lighting to be more theatrical, using unusual angles and colors. As has been stated before, such choices depend on the unique interpretation of each production.

At times, lighting instruments are exposed to the view of the audience. This reinforces the feeling that what we are seeing is happening now, on the stage, in the reality of the performance. It may also increase the inherent theatricality of a production. In a proscenium house, this is a design decision. In a thrust or arena space, this is an accepted convention because there is no way to mask the lights.

It is of course vital that the scene and lighting designers discuss not only their individual ideas but the ways in which they will be able to work together. This might mean negotiation of fly space (space above the scenery; see Chapter 10) if, for instance, both designers want to use the downstage line sets; it may even mean working out the placement of lighting positions in the scenery itself. At the very least it implies that they will be using the same images as a starting point. Collaboration at work means that all members of the artistic team are striving for the same idea and are taking advantage of the elements provided by one another. In terms of scenery and lighting, this might be as simple as using a stained-glass window through which light can stream in on the actor, providing an excuse for the lighting designer to use a wider variety of colors for that one scene. Perhaps it means adding a practical lamp on a set, allowing the lighting designer to add light in a particular area of the set, thereby creating more focus on the actor.

Developing the Design Approach

A design approach is the *idea* or *visual theme* of design. It is the product of creative thinking, visual imagination, and collaboration with the director. The approach provides *control* and *direction* toward a final design. The clearer and stronger the design idea, the easier every subsequent design decision will be.

The approach to the production can begin with ideas from any or all members of the artistic team. Most often the director makes the initial statement. If the director is firm in his or her thinking, the parameters of the approach are established immediately. There are times, however, when the director does not know the specifics and wants to discuss the play with the artistic team. In any event, the designer should approach the first discussion with ideas about the production. If they lie outside the parameters of the director's ideas, they need not be brought into the discussion. Part of the initial task is to find a common vocabulary, a method of functioning as a team. Like each designer, every director is different, and it is important for the designers to learn how to work with individual directors.

The time spent discussing the production can and should be a very exciting and stimulating period in the development of a design. Every decision that a designer makes will have ramifications for every other member of the artistic team. If this process works, the result will be an amalgam of many ideas, not attributable to any one person—this is the true meaning of collaboration.

In this collaboration, many concerns arise. The first is often whether a historical style is needed and how to achieve it. How the physical form of the stage limits or creates alternatives and what the written play suggests are also initial collaborative concerns. Once such basic ideas are addressed, the designer can begin to form the design concept, meeting often with the director and others as the concept develops.

Historical Style and Concept Both historical and cultural periods are significant in their own right. The effect of each period on form is quite clear. The geometric and flamboyant tracery of Gothic, for example, is distinct from the reverse curve of the baroque and the whiplash of art nouveau. The same is true of national styles. There is a difference, for example, in the forms of the rococo in France, Germany, and Austria.

When a historical style is used on the stage, however, it becomes part of the design approach, for it is not the period that is being demonstrated but a conceptualization of the historical style. The historical scenes in Miller's *The Crucible,* for example, are conceptual versions of seventeenth-century America. It is not too difficult to see that period style can take on many degrees of reality. A historical period can be authentically reproduced, suggested, or even spoofed.

Historical moments in theatre frequently serve as a framework for a contemporary idea. The Shevelove/Gilbart/Sondheim musical *A Funny Thing Happened on the Way to the Forum,* for example, is a burlesque of Roman comedy with a present-day message. *The Boy Friend* is a nostalgic spoof of life in the 1920s. The melodramatic revival of such plays as *Under the Gaslight* is an exaggeration of period mannerism.

Style and Theatre Forms The proscenium theatre depends on aesthetic distance and an objective relationship with its audience. An interesting contrast of styles has developed in the production concepts of the two nonproscenium theatre forms, the thrust and the arena stages (Figure 4-8). The use of scenery on the proscenium stage is more obvious than on thrust and arena stages. The thrust and arena stages call on the imagination of the audience to complete the scene. Invisible walls and doors, different locales indicated by levels on the floor, hanging fragments overhead, and the color of light are common theatrical conventions on thrust and arena stages. They establish an abstract degree of reality the audience is asked to accept. Because the audience is physically closer to the action, furniture and hand properties are often painstakingly real, and the actors' costumes are fully detailed in a contrast of styles. The audience can therefore feel they are in the scene and a part of the action. There is a more subjective or intimate alliance of audience and performer when the proscenium wall is removed, although the reality remains theatrical.

Acting and Literary Styles Dramatic form combines the literary and acting styles with those of the scenery, costumes, lighting, and sound. Each style affects the others, and all must together provide some degree of unity in order to create a strong dramatic form.

a PHOTO COURTESY RIC EVANS

a

b COURTESY KATHLEEN WIDOMSKI

b

4-8

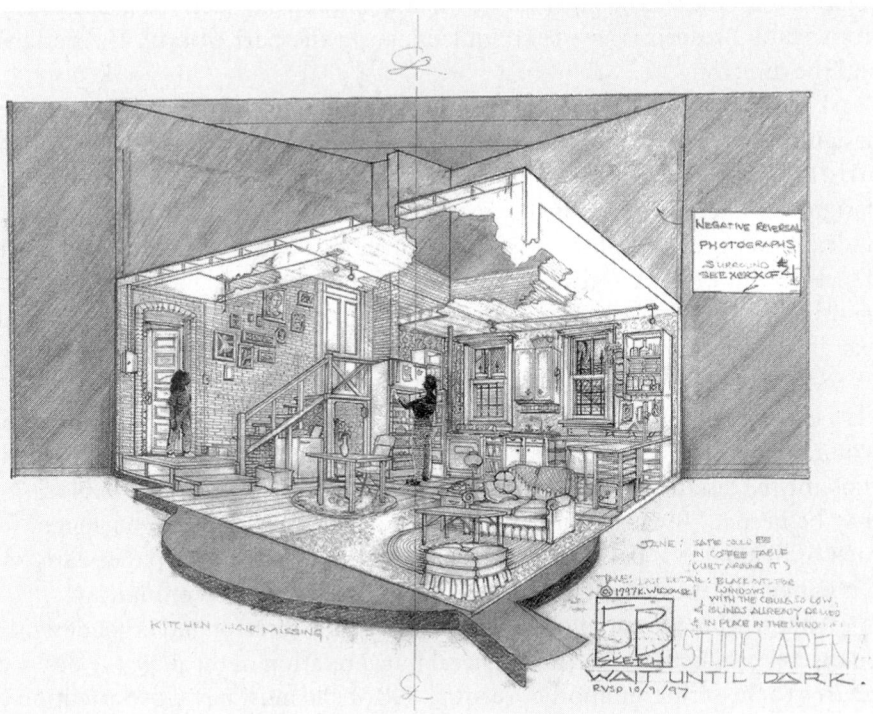

Style and Theatre Form

The thrust and arena stages often force the designer into the theatrical conventions or stylization inherent in the scale and sightlines of the stages' physical forms.

a O'Neill's *A Moon for the Misbegotten,* designed by Anne Mundell for the Pittsburgh Public Theatre.

b A sketch for *Wait Until Dark,* designed by Kathleen Widomski for Buffalo Studio Arena.

The acting style of today, for the most part, is believably real when compared with the highly mannered period examples of the seventeenth, eighteenth, and nineteenth centuries. Acting style, however, may vary from naturalism to conform with the style of a specific drama. It takes its cue, as do the designs, from the literary style of the play.

Scene design, as a visual art, can reinforce and heighten literary and acting styles. Strangely enough, it can on occasion contrast the acting style without breaking the unity of the production. Stylized scenery does not necessarily call for stylized acting, as was demonstrated so expertly in Jo Mielziner's setting for Miller's *Death of a Salesman.* The reverse, however, is not true. If the acting is stylized, the scenery must be, too. The important thing is that the audience will accept any degree of departure from the real in scenery as long as it is consistent, has integrity, and is in good taste. After all, the purpose of scenery is not necessarily to create a "real" world but to create one in which the action of the play can occur.

Working with the Director/Design Meetings As stated earlier, designers need to communicate closely with the director. Directorial influence on design can vary from a complete hands-off "solve-it-yourself" attitude to a "this-is-exactly-what-I-want" directive. A more equally balanced collaboration is, naturally, ideal. One-sided domination can lead to frustration and lack of creative fulfillment. The most successful and unified productions usually result from mutual respect and open-mindedness on the part of both the designer and the director.

The collaboration, of course, begins with talking; this is done at a series of design meetings. Preliminary discussions should include all members of the artistic team (the director and the scenic, costume, lighting, and sound designers). Each member of this team is expected to have at least a general understanding of the play for the first meeting. Most designers and many directors will bring initial pieces of research to the table. This might include paintings to suggest a design style or color, images that the designer finds exciting in relation to the play, or anything else that will lead the team toward a production idea. It is not unusual for a designer to ask for clarification if the play is complex. Images, the nature of the play, and the general atmosphere (colors, style, staging, and directorial concept) desired for this production will probably be discussed. Some agreement may be reached or further exploration may be needed. Because words have a way of triggering different images for each individual, the designer must put visual impressions on paper early on. Only then can the designers and director really begin to communicate.

After reaching a mutual understanding with the director and other designers on theme, production style, and general interpretation of the play, the designer returns to the script for another reading. He or she must pay close attention to the physical requirements of the plot structure and any changes of locale. Then he or she needs to examine the action and staging requirements. The designer must determine the number of people in a scene, the types of entrances and exits, specific references in the dialogue to the scene, action hidden from one actor but visible to the audience, and so on—all leading to the development of the basic idea and scheme of production.

At the second meeting, preliminary designs will be shown and discussed. Certainly more research based on the initial discussion will have been done. Depending on what was decided at the previous meeting, the scenic designer might show a rough sketch and ground plan, a rough model, or perhaps even a collage that addresses the tone of the play. This all depends on the working style of the artistic team and the individual designer. If this is the first time the designer and director have worked together, a certain amount of time discovering a "common language" or way to communicate with each other may be necessary. The director, for example, may ask for three different versions of a design or may want a particular kind of research. In any case, the designer should oblige. Subsequent meetings will narrow the discussion.

An understanding and agreement about the production style is probably the most important part of the designer–director collaboration, and certainly the most difficult. Only by the exploration of ideas through the use of drawings and/or models among the artistic team can the final determination of "production style" be found. This may happen over a short period or over several months. The number of meetings needed and the number of versions of a design will vary with every production.

During production, the director is the only one with an overall view and therefore must be responsible for coordinating the various styles as the show is being put together. The lack of immediate communication to the designer or designers of directorial changes or style adjustments in other areas of design can lead to conflicts at a time in the production schedule when it is too late to make changes. A good stage manager can be of great assistance in this regard. The best-laid plans can go astray without constant communication on the part of all members of the artistic team. An experienced designer soon learns to not take anything for granted and makes frequent checks with the director and other designers.

Rereading the Play

It is a good idea to reread the play after initial designs are prepared. This is a chance to rethink the play with design in mind. Often this rereading will point out specific problems with the design and perhaps suggest better answers to questions about staging or the "look" of the design. Further readings might prove necessary during the course of production.

Planning the Scheme of Production

The design solution of a multiscene play, or a *scheme of production,* brings scenery-handling techniques into the design concept. The design idea is developed around a method of handling the numerous changes of scene. The kinds of changes and the methods of handling scenery, such as wagons and turntables, are discussed fully in Chapter 10 and indicate the necessity of designing a large production around at least a basic scheme for moving the scenery.

Although discussed separately, a scheme of production is, of course, closely related to style. Many times the designer, through a scheme of production, establishes certain conventions that the audience is expected to accept and that, consequently, create a scenery style. Conversely, a scenery style may dictate how the scenery is to be handled, thereby becoming part of a scheme of production.

Unit Setting The movement of scenery may be reduced by the various uses of a **unit setting** (Color Plate 4-1). This form of setting is based on the retention or reuse of certain elements of scenery for more than one scene. The design shapes and colors, for example, may be varied in each setting although

unit setting A setting based on the retention or reuse of certain elements of scenery for more than one scene.

4-9

The Unit Setting

A production of *To Kill a Mockingbird*. Minor changes in the set—including the use of an added panel, louvres, and most especially lighting—established different locales. Designer, Dick Block.

they are placed in identical floor plans, or the same shape can be moved to a variety of positions.

A unit setting can be used in two different ways, either as a cleverly camouflaged method of reusing scenery or as an obvious device that becomes a unifying force for the production, as well as a means of simplifying scene changes (Figure 4-9).

Projected Scenery Light projections as scenery are included with many production schemes for handling multiscene shows. The rear projection of a design onto a translucent screen makes the shifting of a scene as simple as the changing of a slide.

Because projected scenery is light and not paint, it has a strong dramatic quality that tends to dominate the scene. It becomes in a sense an actor rather than scenery. When used correctly as an integral part of the play, projected scenery functions best in a nonrealistic or abstract production where the scenery is part of the action and not just background (see Color Plate 4-2).

Brecht, for example, used the screen as an actor. He frequently projected instructive messages or illustrative images on the screen, more as an instrument of propaganda or idea than as a visual background to set the scene. This classroom or documentary technique, used in dramatic surroundings, served to heighten his epic theatre.

In spite of its limitations and dominating characteristics, projected scenery can be used as a highly dramatic and exciting production scheme. Joseph Svoboda was a master at this. Many production designs have been based on projected scenery with successful results (Figures 4-10 and 4-11).

a & b PHOTOS COURTESY JOSHUA KRALL

a

b

c

4-10

Projected Scenery

a Projections for *Lost in a Mirror.* The different positions of the panels and the striking projected images established both mood and locale. Design and projections, Joshua Krall.

b Another variation of the projections for *Lost in a Mirror.*

c Sometimes the screen is as interesting as the projection. This intricate screen is a part of the design for *Faith, Hope, Charity* by Ödön von Horvath. Designer, William Mathews.

PHOTO COURTESY JOSHUA KRALL

4-11

Projections on Scenery

The use of isolated light and projections for *Lost in a Mirror* creates a stark atmosphere with incredible depth. Design, Joshua Krall.

VISUAL PRESENTATION OF THE DESIGN IDEA

The designer communicates his or her ideas to the other members of the design and production team not only verbally but also through visual means. The designer might, at varying points in the production process, present color sketches, ground plans, and/or models. The importance placed on each form of presentation can vary with the director (some will only be able to understand models, some like to see sketches, etc.), the particular skills of the designer, and perhaps the type of theatre company or the scale of production. The sketch, for example, might be a collage expressing the atmosphere and visual impact of the setting, while placing more emphasis on a larger scaled model with more detail. On the other hand, a single setting with many changes of scenic elements and lighting might be best presented with a series of photographs. Every production is different. Designers should play to their strengths but be prepared to present their work in any way or ways that best communicate the design ideas.

Preliminary Studies

The designer's first impressions of a design may be substantially revised or rejected after a closer study of the script in the second and third readings. A first impression is often correct, but when it does not work, the designer may find it difficult to change. For this reason the beginning designer may be wise during the first reading of a new play to keep an open mind, free of preconceptions, and not become too attached to one idea. This is the time to graphically explore many ideas in order to discover what will best suit the production.

Preliminary studies usually consist of small, freehand, thumbnail sketches and rough ground plans (Figure 4-12). After consultation with the director, the tentative ideas of the designer are ready to be expanded into a more complete form of presentation. These first sketches are visual ideas that will be developed in detail later. It is wise to keep all of these sketches for later reference. It is not uncommon to explore a series of designs only to return to initial ideas.

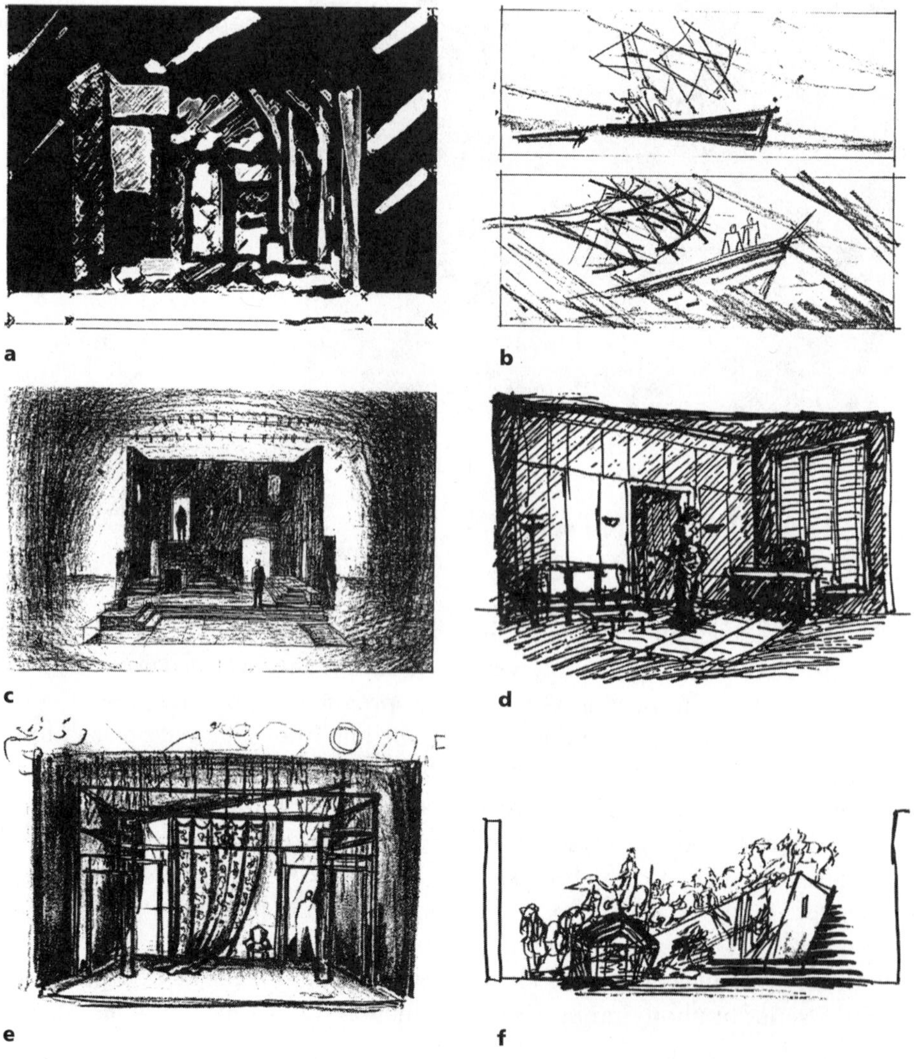

4-12

Rough Sketches

Every designer does rough sketches differently and often with different goals. Some are meant to explore an idea, others to look at quality of light and space. Proportion, scale, and mood can be determined in part by rough sketches. Not all rough sketches are meant for the director's eyes—some are only for the designer's use. Shown here are a variety of styles and uses for rough sketches.

- **a** *Benefactor,* Frank Ludwig.
- **b** *Moby Dick,* Anne Mundell and Dick Block.
- **c** *Hamlet,* Timothy Averill.
- **d** *Lady in the Dark,* Kathleen Widomski.
- **e** *The Three Sisters,* Timothy Averill.
- **f** *Henry IV, Part I,* Kathleen Widomski.

a COURTESY FRANK LUDWIG
b COURTESY ANNE MUNDELL
c COURTESY TIMOTHY AVERILL
d COURTESY KATHLEEN WIDOMSKI
e COURTESY TIMOTHY AVERILL
f COURTESY KATHLEEN WIDOMSKI

Some designers use a "mood sketch" to study the atmosphere of a scene. By working off a dark or black background, such as gray or black velour paper, the scenic forms are easily revealed in an atmospheric light.

The Sketch

Although scene design is essentially a three-dimensional art form, the two-dimensional sketch is one way to present the design idea, especially initially. This perspective sketch, most often rendered in black and white, reveals an atmosphere that would be difficult to accomplish in a model (although, if time permits, a rough model can be extremely useful). A series of sketches can be made to show changes in lighting, scenery, and composition of the actors. More importantly, the sketch can be done relatively quickly, so less time and energy (and soul) are invested in a single drawing. It is easier to accept the rejection of a sketched design if the designer remembers that it represents no more than an idea still to be developed.

Individual designers will make different kinds of sketches for a variety of purposes. Some are for the eyes of the designer only, perhaps to establish composition or to explore scale. The particular use of the sketch will suggest how "finished" or polished it needs to be (Figure 4-13). Regardless of its purpose and style, every sketch and model should have a scale figure.

a

a COURTESY BRUCE GOODRICH

b

b COURTESY TIM SATERNOW

c

c COURTESY TIMOTHY AVERILL

4-13

Preliminary Sketches

More finished than a rough sketch, a preliminary sketch serves as an important way for the designer to explore ideas and communicate them to the director and the rest of the artistic team, who can then contribute more ideas. This stage of the production is often the point where decisions about scale, proportion, and style are made.

a *Greetings,* Bruce Goodrich.

b *The Mystery of Edwin Drood,* Tim Saternow.

c *The Three Sisters,* Timothy Averill.

What is represented on the sketch depends somewhat on the working relationship between the designer and the director (or producer). If everyone on the artistic team has knowledge of one another's working habits, it is easier to determine the kinds of presentations that will prove successful. The design is accepted on the strength of the sketch and the accompanying explanation. How the ideas are verbalized will tell the director how to look at the design. This is one reason why the designer needs to know and understand the play thoroughly. The director may feel free to ask about the staging for any given moment—"How do you envision this scene happening?"

The sketch should catch a significant moment in the play. The designer usually picks a moment that will best show the setting and still express the dominant mood of the play. The *sketch* is an idealized drawing of the total visual picture, meaning the inclusion of costumed characters under lights; this can serve as a suggestion for the lighting designer. Color, if used in the sketch, should work toward the same purpose. Supplementary sketches are sometimes needed to show what would happen at other dramatic moments, with different lighting and actor groupings.

In the purest sense, the sketch is only a means of presenting an idea. It is not the final design and therefore should not be displayed or judged as a complete art form. A stage setting is not complete until it is on the stage, lighted, and viewed in the context of the action of the play and the actors' movements. The judgment of the success or failure of a design in the final analysis is based on how it functions under finished performance conditions rather than as a beautiful sketch.

ground plan A view of a set from above, as if cut across horizontally (usually at 3 feet above the stage deck).

The sketch is always accompanied by a **ground plan,** so that the director can examine the amount of floor space that the actors can use. With a scale drawing and ground plan, the director and others concerned with the production can form an accurate opinion as to how the actual setting will look as well as how it can be used. See Figure 4-14 for examples of sketches.

4-14

Designer's Sketches

a An atmospheric sketch for *Benedictions,* designed by Frank Ludwig.

a

a COURTESY FRANK LUDWIG

b

c COURTESY DEX EDWARDS

c

b Lighting plays an important role in this sketch for the barn scene of Dürenmatt's *The Visit.*

c *Gypsy,* designed by Dex Edwards.

The Model

Although the sketch has been presented as being one of the prime means of presenting an idea, it is often superseded by a model (Figure 4-15). Most directors today expect a model, but the need for one depends on the individuals involved. Because of the three-dimensionality of scenery, some designers prefer to work through models rather than sketches. The model gives a true indication of the spatial relationships of scenery and actors and is, therefore, helpful to the director when planning the staging.

Within the model, each piece of scenery is constructed to an accurate scale, thus giving the designer a miniature version of how the setting is going to look. Because the model is three-dimensional, composition and sightlines can be checked from all angles of view. In addition to being a means of presentation, the model can also be used to check the appropriateness of scale, proportion,

4-15

Sketch, Model, and Set

Scene for *The King and I*, designed by Anne Mundell.

a Designer's sketch.

b Designer's model.

c The completed set.

a

b

c

a–c COURTESY ANNE MUNDELL

or shape. If the model is for the designer's use only, a rough version can be built, saving time and energy.

The scale of the model varies with the designer. Some like to work at the scale of ½ inch equal to 1 foot, while others prefer a smaller scale. Models at ½-inch scale can be accurate, detailed, and extremely informative, but they are expensive and time-consuming. In addition, they are awkward to transport. The ¼-inch scale model is a more convenient size for faster execution, which sometimes is important. This smaller scale allows for easier changes and experimentation with the design than does a larger scale while still providing enough detail without the model becoming cumbersome (Figure 4-16). Some designers will work in scale as small as ⅛ inch to 1 foot. The advantage of this scale is that the overall sense of the design can be determined quickly and little time is spent on details—the scale itself makes that impossible. It is also much easier to carry a very small model to a design meeting if it can impart the needed information. It is also cheaper—less material is needed—and easier to store. What this ultimately means is that the designer can explore the ideas of the design without investing huge amounts of time or money.

Sometimes called a working model, the *sketch model* is made of paper (two-ply Bristol board) and is used by the designer to check the three-

a

b

4-16

Model and Production Shot

Design for the musical *Moby Dick.* Designers, Anne Mundell and Dick Block.

a Photo of the model.

b Production shot.

4-17

Model

Model for *Look Homeward Angel* on a thrust stage. Views from the front and from above show a clever asymmetrical arrangement of levels, allowing the audience to see several rooms of the house at once. Designer, Tim Saternow.

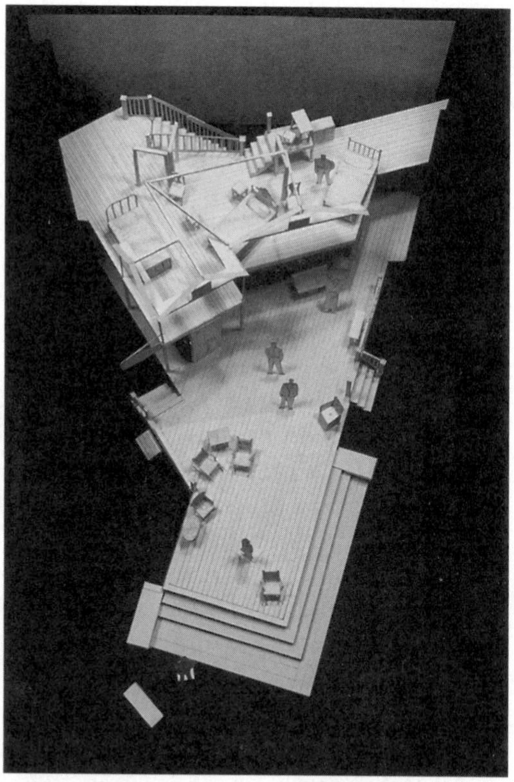

PHOTOS COURTESY TIM SATERNOW

dimensional qualities of a setting or portions of a set (Figure 4-17). The model is usually uncolored, but if three-ply Bristol board is used and the paint is applied before cutting and shaping, the model can be made in full color (see Color Plates 4-4, 4-5, and 4-6).

A carefully detailed scale model is of great value to those who will be constructing the scenery (Figure 4-18). It does not, however, provide enough information for the shop to develop construction drawings. A full set a draftings (see Chapter 5) will still need to be done.

The Computer Model

The term *model* has also come to refer to three-dimensional computer drawings. Technology now allows us to create a view of a set that can be rotated, allowing the designer to check for the same sightlines as with a physical model. Applications such as Studio 3-D Max are ideal for this.

In simple terms, designers develop a computer model by following these four steps:

1. The basic sketch outline, or *wire frame* of the design form, is modeled into a three-dimensional drawing. To give definition and dimension to the model, its surfaces may be textured.
2. A *texture mapping* program allows the designer to choose, from a library of textures, the most suitable texture and color or tone for the individual areas throughout the composition. The texture adds shape, direction, and a sense of detail to the design as well as providing each surface a degree of absorption and reflection of light.

COURTESY ANNE MUNDELL

4-18

Model

Setting for *Man of La Mancha*. Designer, Anne Mundell.

3. From an object library, the designer chooses furniture or properties to be placed in the setting, along with figures and their dress.

4. The final step, the lighting of the composition, is the most exciting and time-consuming. Through a lighting editor program, the designer can select offstage positions for motivating light sources, front lighting positions for the actors, as well as atmospheric background illumination. Light sources on the stage—such as lamps, torches, or candelabras—are also established. The computer analyzes the distribution of each light source, calculates the amount of reflection off the various textures, and plots the direction of the many overlapping shadows cast by the numerous light sources. The photographic realism of the printout is an excellent presentation of a design idea (Figure 4-19).

a

b

4-19

Computer-Generated Design

Here are two approaches to using the computer as a design tool:

a One of many computer-generated drawings for *Lost in a Mirror.* Design, Joshua Krall.

b One of a series of costume sketches for a dance project designed and drawn on the computer by Jessica Noble.

a COURTESY JOSHUA KRALL
b COURTESY JESSICA NOBLE

Computer-Generated Design

The entire design process, not simply the design model, can now be generated on the computer. Applications such as Adobe Illustrator, Corel Draw, AutoCAD, VectorWorks, and Adobe Photoshop can be used to create anything from rough sketches to fully developed color models (see Color Plate 4-7).

Scanners and digital cameras allow the designer to transfer images directly into the computer. Because these images can be manipulated in many ways to create a design, the computer makes it easy to explore a variety of ideas. Some designers use images together in a collagelike form to express a design. Others scan in a pencil drawing and adjust it in the computer. The possibilities are endless. The ability to change images rapidly is starting to alter how designers think about design. Thanks to the computer, new styles of design are also being explored.

The advantage of working on the computer is that changes can be made quickly. The downside of this is that the learning curve for these applications is still quite steep. The designer must spend serious time to become facile with these programs. As well, both the hardware and the software are still quite expensive.

Although extremely useful as a tool, the computer cannot serve as a panacea for solving problems. A pencil sketch and a computer sketch still require a vision and an artistic hand. The computer allows the designer to change, adapt, or rethink work quickly and easily but only if there is an idea to explore in the first place.

PHOTOS COURTESY TIM SATERNOW

CP4-1

Unit Setting

Unit setting in *Arden of Faversham;* setting and lighting designed by Tim Saternow for *The Empty Space* in Seattle, Washington, 1991.

PHOTO © DAVID COOPER, COURTESY SHAW FESTIVAL COLLECTION, ARCHIVAL AND SPECIAL COLLECTIONS, UNIVERSITY OF GUELPH LIBRARY

CP4-2

Projections on Scenery

Bringing the outside into the interior in an interesting setting for *Berkeley Square.* Designer, Cameron Porteous.

PHOTO COURTESY RALPH FUNICELLO

PHOTO COURTESY RALPH FUNICELLO

CP4-3

Light and Realism

Interesting use of light and realism in *Romeo and Juliet.* Designer, Ralph Funicello.

CP4-4

Production Model

A ¼-inch model for a production of *Hamlet* directed by Jack O'Brien. Scenery, Ralph Funicello; lighting, Peter Maradudin; costumes, Lewis Brown. Produced by The Old Globe Theatre, San Diego, California, 1990.

CP4-5

Model

Model of Beaumarchais's *The Marriage of Figaro.* Designer, Karl Brake.

PHOTO COURTESY ANNE MUNDELL

a

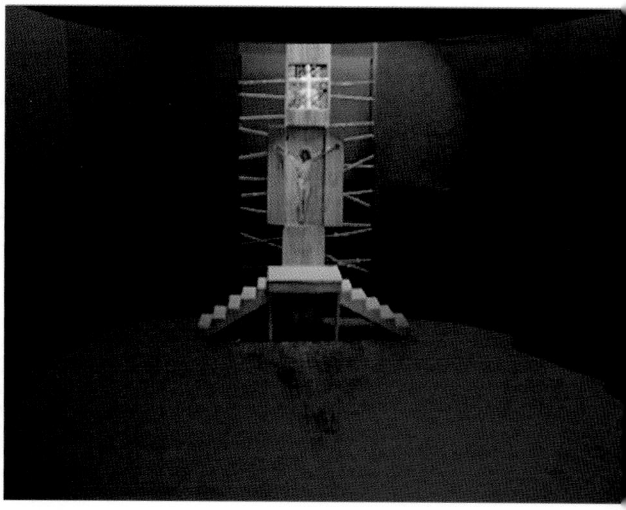

b

a PHOTO COURTESY TIM SATERNOW
b PHOTO COURTESY MIHAI CIUPE

CP4-6

Models

a Full color model for *The House of Blue Leaves.* Designer, Tim Saternow.

b Full color model for *Edith Stein.* Designer, Mihai Ciupe.

a

b

a COURTESY SAMUEL BALL
b COURTESY JEFF HINCHEE

CP4-7

Computer-Generated Art

a Design created on Photoshop program to serve as one of many projected backgrounds for *Much Ado About Nothing,* Orlando Shakespeare Festival. Designer, Samuel Ball.

b Computer-generated design using several programs, including sketch, perspective, color, texture, and light, *Volpone.* Designer, Jeff Hinchee.

CP4-8

Painter's Elevations

- **a** Backdrop for *Countess Maritza,* designed by Steven L. Gilliam.
- **b** Mirkwood drop for *The Hobbit,* designed by Kevin L. Raper.
- **c** Paint elevation for *The Secret Garden,* designed by Karl Brake.
- **d** Nighttime cityscape drop designed by Anne Mundell.

a

a COURTESY STEVEN L. GILLIAM

b

b COURTESY KEVIN L. RAPER

c

c COURTESY KARL BRAKE

d

d COURTESY ANNE MUNDELL

Designer's Preparations for the Shops

Once a design idea has been fully developed and is ready to be translated into full-scale reality, the designer has to prepare a series of detailed drawings for the artisans who will be building and painting the setting.

Designer's Elevations These are scaled and dimensioned drawings that provide information as to the profile, size, and location of openings and decorative detail of every unit of scenery. The designer and the design staff prepare these drawings in the form of designer's elevations, from which the technical director develops construction drawings. All are discussed in detail in Chapter 5. Design elevations are usually presented at a scale of ½ inch to 1 foot. These elevations can also be extremely helpful as a guide to the scenic artist in laying out work for decorative painting.

Painter's Elevations For the artists who will be painting the scenery, the designer prepares scaled elevations that indicate the colors and painting technique of each unit of scenery. Figure 4-20 shows the presentation of a large drop representing a garden. The first drawing (Figure 4-20a) is the

4-20

Painter's Elevation and Line Drawing

Elevations for the scenic artist are logically developed in two major steps: first the line drawing, then the paint elevation. Between the two, any and all information that is pertinent to the painting of the scenic unit will be indicated: color, techniques, opaque and translucent areas. This drop was designed by Anne Mundell.

a The line drawing supplies the scenic artists with the layout of the design. Any gridding will most often be done in the shop by the scenic artist, although some designers prefer to prepare this on their own.

b The paint elevation provides the scenic artist with color and painting techniques.

a & b COURTESY ANNE MUNDELL

cartoon, or line drawing indicating the basic layout of the composition. The cartoon is important to the painter, for as can be seen in Figure 4-20b, some of the outline is lost in the fully painted scene.

The two drawings (cartoon and painter's elevation) provide the scenic artist with information for the layout, open spaces, translucent and opaque areas, colors, and painting techniques. For a more detailed explanation of methods of layout, proportional enlargement, and scenery-painting techniques, please refer to Chapter 9. See also Color Plate 4-8.

The Costume Sketch

Just like the scenic designer, the costume designer's ideas are presented in sketch form (Figure 4-21) in full color and most often with fabric swatches. The costume sketch differs from the set design sketch in that it must serve several purposes. Besides presenting a design to be viewed in correlation with the overall tonality and style of the production, it is first and foremost the designer's interpretation of an individual character. For this reason, the actor is also interested in the costume sketch to gather visual reinforcement of and insight into his or her character and lifestyle. In addition, the costume sketch will be a working drawing the shops will use for construction information.

a

b

b COURTESY MICHAEL OLICH

4-21

Costume Design Presentation

a Unusual presentation of group costumes by Susan Tsu for *Plough and the Stars.*

b Costume design by Michael Olich for *La Dame aux Camelias.* Note the sketch to the side showing the back view of the dress as well as the numerous written construction notes for the costume shop.

When necessary, further drawings will be provided. Additional views or penciled details are common additions. The costume sketch also indicates the true colors of the costume, not the colors that may appear under stage lighting.

Lighting Design Presentation

As a member of the artistic team, the lighting designer should be present at discussions of the play. His or her unique point of view will provide insights to the production that differ from the other designers' contributions. His or her ideas can be instrumental in developing the production style as well as influencing the floor plan and setting. The set and lighting designers need to work hand in hand during the initial stages of the design process.

The lighting designer has been influenced by the script and has formed some general ideas of atmosphere and color. Images of light and shadow as well as those suggesting the right "feel" for the production may be displayed and discussed. An early discussion of color in light is important, especially to the costume designer. Swatch books of gel colors are convenient, if imperfect, aids for indicating light colors to others.

At later production meetings, the lighting designer will be able to present visual indications of color, distribution, and atmosphere through the use of **value sketches** or a **storyboard.** With simple tones, a storyboard illustrates the basic forms of the setting, the changes or movement of intensity, and the direction of light within a scene or from scene to scene (Figure 4-22). The use of computer applications like Photoshop have proven invaluable for creating storyboards.

value sketch A sketch that emphasizes the light and shadow of a set.

storyboard A series of sketches that provide a moment by moment view of a scene, act, and so forth.

4-22

Lighting Design Presentation

The lighting storyboard, an early presentation before the light plot, is a variation of the mood sketch showing atmospheric and distribution changes scene by scene. Shown here are two of many changes. This is one way for lighting designers to communicate their ideas to the director and the rest of the artistic team.

light plot A plan that indicates the exact placement, type, size, color, and number of each lighting instrument being used for a production.

lighting section A cross section of a set drawn as if cut vertically at the center line and showing the position (height) of each electric being used in a production.

As the lighting concept is developed, the lighting designer turns to his or her final presentation: the light plot and section. The **light plot** is a top view of the layout of all lighting instruments in the production, and a **lighting section** shows the height and position of the lights, scenery location and height, and vertical sightlines. Next to each fixture is a brief notation of the instrument's number, type, color, circuit, and channel. For more on the light plot as well as the lighting designer's presentation techniques, see Chapter 20.

THEATRICAL DESIGN OUTSIDE THE THEATRE

Many theatrically trained designers design for related commercially oriented venues, using theatrical techniques. Figure 4-23a shows one example. Such spheres as trade shows (e.g., auto or fashion shows), television and film, pageants, and themed entertainment call on the talents of the theatrical designer.

Trade Shows

The design approach and presentation for trade shows is basically the same as for theatre, although the goal is different. Instead of visually reinforcing a playwright's idea, the designer is called on to provide theatrical flair to the selling of a product or the promotion of a marketing technique to a captive audience of company personnel. The use of dramatic form and theatrical staging adds interest and excitement to what could be a dull subject.

Television and Film

Television is another outlet for theatre techniques. Both local and national broadcasting companies create original work, ranging from full-scale television movies and prime-time productions to simpler talk shows or news programs (Figure 4-23b). Although the scale is often smaller and the work is sometimes closer to architecture and interior design, television is a perfectly valid outlet for a designer. With the popularity of music videos and the heavy use of computer-generated artwork, the need for designers is likely to grow, especially for those with both computer and theatrical skills.

Historical Pageants

Usually performed outdoors in an amphitheatre or stadium, the pageant is a large-scale event. Often having a historical or documentary style, a pageant uses a narrator to advance the story line.

The scene of action may be a fixed group of exteriors or interiors or a natural setting, with the action moving from one area to the next. On the other hand, elaborate means can be employed, such as a water canal for ships or barges, tracked wagons or a treadmill for scenery or actors, and on occasion, horses. The climax of the evening may be a chase, a race, or a full-scale battle scene with pyrotechnics. The opportunities for scenery, costume, and lighting designers are obvious.

The pageant wagon is part of theatre history. A present-day example can be seen in the famous Mardi Gras floats in New Orleans. Traditionally part of

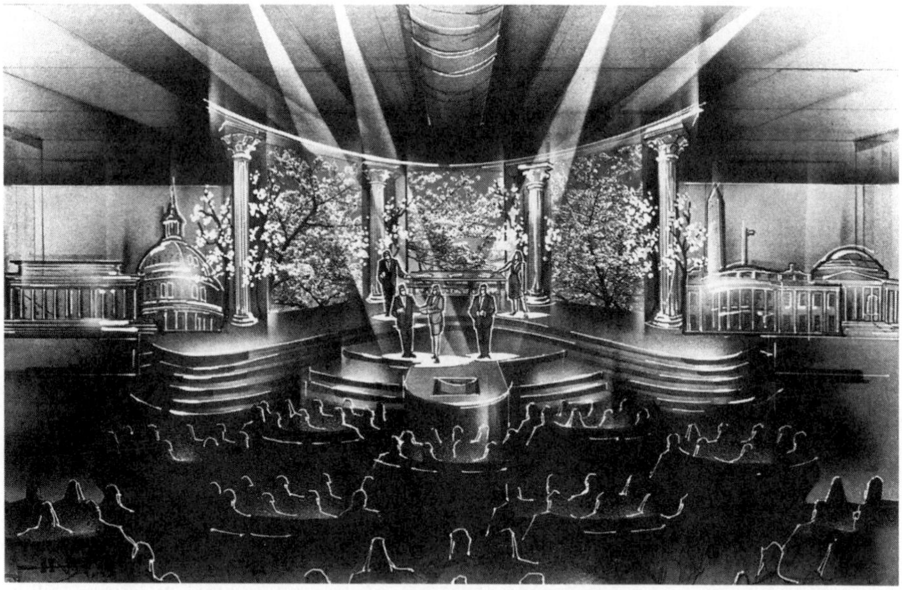

a

b

a COURTESY HOTOPP ASSOCIATES, LTD.

b COURTESY JOHN SHAFFNER AND JOE STEWART

4-23

Design Outside the Theatre

a Industrial show design by HOTOPP Associates, Ltd.

b Television—*Daytime Emmy Awards 2001.* Designers, Joe Stewart and John Shaffner.

the celebration of the beginning of Lent, the floats are a creative outlet for both costume and scene design.

Theme Parks

Theme parks have boomed over the past decade and need good designers. Working for a theme park can include a wide range of possibilities, from designing the scenery for musical entertainment to designing the rides to creating some of the buildings the vendors use. In all of these venues, the designer must call into play all of his or her theatrical training.

5

Drafting the Design

Although scene design is three-dimensional in final form, most of the presentation of the design idea in preparation for construction is two-dimensional in character. The graphics of presentation are the visual language or fundamental means of communication among the designer, stage technicians, and director. The planning of a production throughout all its phases relies on a common knowledge of simple drafting conventions that communicate technical and artistic information. The designer must provide simple, clear, and accurate information so that all ideas can be carried out efficiently and accurately.

DRAFTING EQUIPMENT

The student designer needs to become acquainted with certain tools and materials. Drafting for the theatre is similar to architectural drafting and engineering drawing but is not as elaborate. (Although more designers are using the computer to draft for the theatre, we discuss only the equipment needed for hand drafting.)

A good *drawing board* is made of clear white pine and cleated to prevent warping. When placed on a stand, it is referred to as a *drafting table*. As most typical drafting is 24 by 36 inches, common sizes for both drafting tables and boards are about 32 by 41 or 36 by 42 inches, although a variety of sizes is available.

Drawing boards need to be padded to prevent the pencil from following the grain of the wood. The best surface is a vinyl plastic cover that is tinted pale green on one side and off-white on the other, such as VYCO or BORCO. Although expensive, this material provides an excellent drafting surface and will last a lifetime.

The *T-square* serves as a guide for drawing lines. The head rests along the right or left edge, with the long center arm extending across the board as the drawing guide. Its accuracy depends on the straightness of the working edge and the squareness of the head and blade. A T-square made of hardwood with a transparent-edge blade and fixed head is best for most purposes. It must reach all the way across the drafting board. A traveling parallel straightedge, called a *parallel rule,* serves the same function as a T-square but is easier to use although more expensive. As wide as the board, it is guided by cables attached permanently to the top and bottom of a drafting table, and it is as wide as the board.

Two transparent plastic *triangles* provide the customary set of angles as well as perpendicular lines when used with the T-square or parallel rule. An 8- or 10-inch 45-degree and an 8- or 10-inch 30-60-90-degree triangle are the smallest useful sizes; some designers prefer to use larger triangles.

An instrument that lends itself to drawing the many odd angles so frequently found in a stage setting is the *adjustable triangle.* This combination of triangle and protractor has an adjustable edge that allows the selection of any angle between 45 and 90 degrees.

Figure 5-1 illustrates the equipment just described. The designer needs other instruments as well, most of which are shown in Figure 5-2.

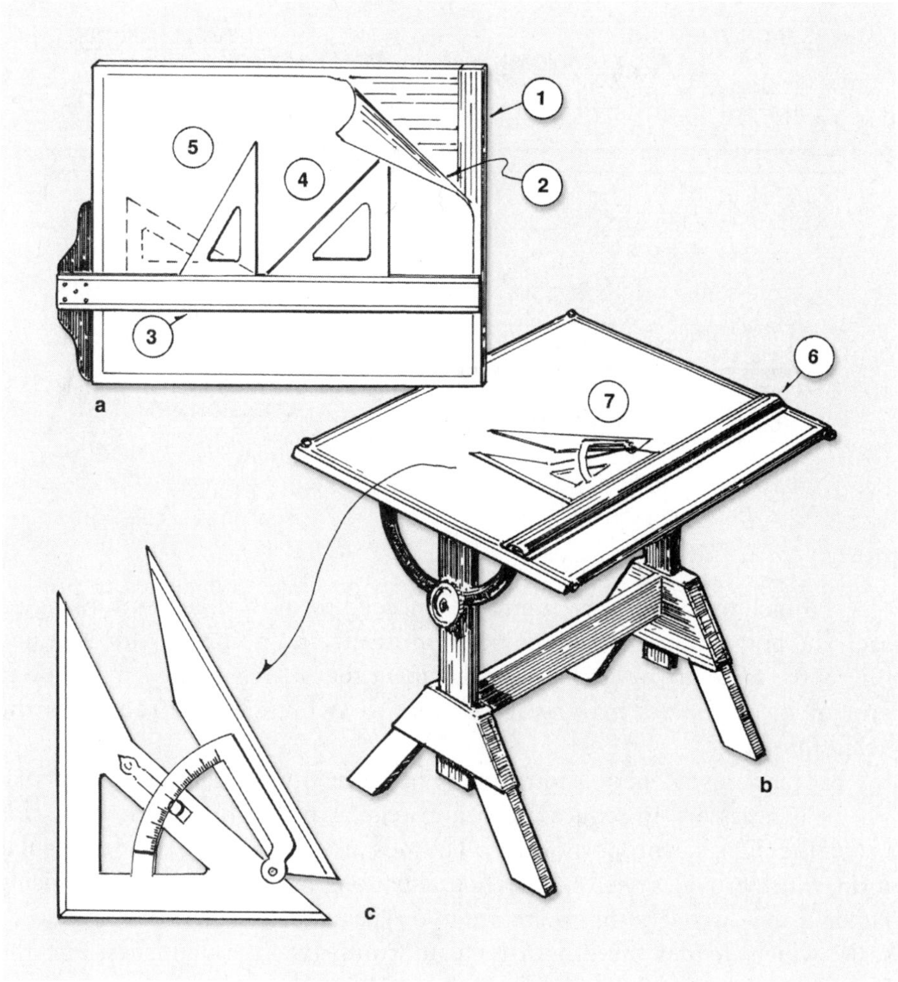

5-1

Drafting Equipment

- **a** Drawing board and tools.
  - **1** Cleated white-pine drawing board.
  - **2** Tinted vinyl padding for drawing board surface.
  - **3** T-square.
  - **4** 45-degree triangle.
  - **5** 30-60-90-degree triangle.
- **b** Drafting table with adjustable tilt and height.
  - **6** Parallel rule (straightedge) attached to the top of the drawing table by a cable system that allows it to travel from top to bottom and remain parallel.
  - **7** Adjustable triangle.
- **c** Detail of adjustable triangle.

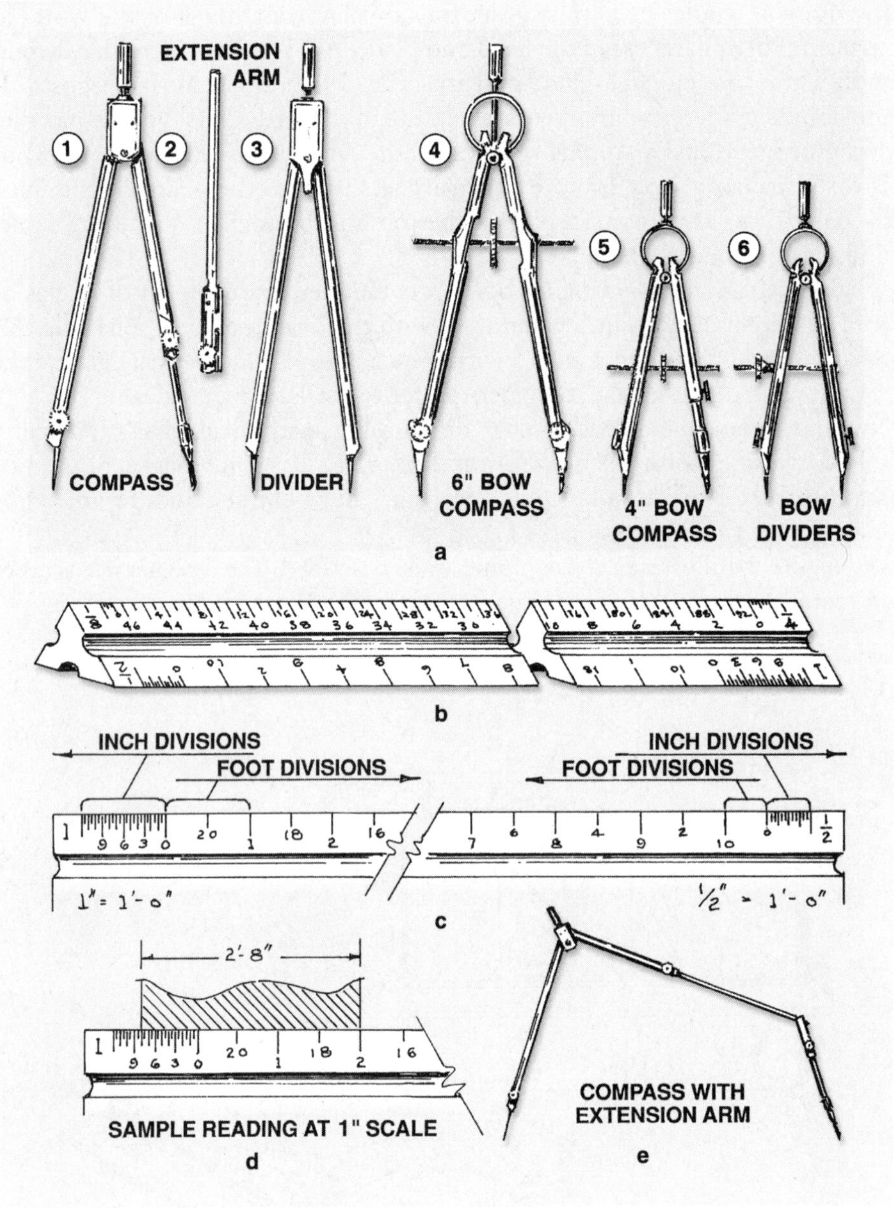

5-2

Drafting Instruments

a The minimum set of drafting instruments.
- **1** Compass.
- **2** Extension arm.
- **3** Dividers.
- **4** 6-inch bow compass.
- **5** 4-inch bow compass.
- **6** Bow dividers.

b Architect's scale rule, triangular form: three edges, six faces, and twelve scales.

c Drawing of one face to demonstrate the method of reading scale rule. The face shown contains two scales: 1" = 1'-0" to the left and ½" = 1'-0" to the right. To read the one-inch scale, for example, inches are read to the left of zero while foot divisions are read to the right.

d Drawing showing a sample reading of a surface 2'-8" in dimension at scale 1" = 1'-0".

e Compass with extension arm attached to increase radius.

A 6-inch or larger bow compass is needed to draw a circle or swing an arc. The bow compass holds its position firmly and accurately for repeated use on the same arc or circle. An attachment that increases the length of one arm of the compass, making it possible to swing a larger radius, is the *extension bar.*

Because most scenery is too large to be represented in a drawing at actual size, it is necessary to reduce the size in regular proportions. The *scale rule* makes the change in proportion easy. The most useful scale rule is the triangular form, which provides twelve different graduations. To the beginner, a confusing factor is the discovery that there are two types of scale rules: the Architect's scale, which divides the proportional foot into twelfths or inches, and the Engineer's scale, which divides the inch into decimals or tenths, with divisions from ten to sixty. The names are trade names, not an indication of the profession

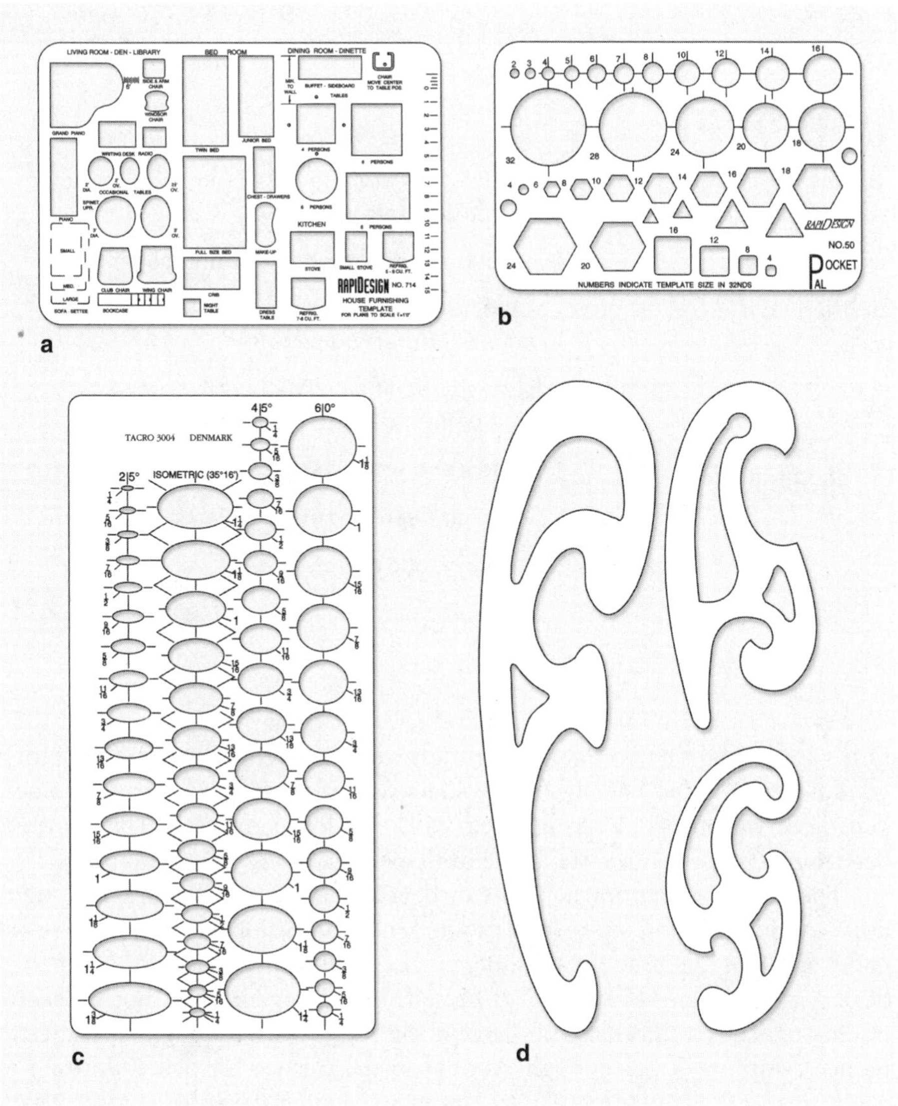

5-3

Drafting Templates and French Curves

- **a** Furniture template, scaled: ¼" = 1'-0".
- **b** Circles, squares, triangles, and hexagons.
- **c** Ellipse template.
- **d** French curves.

using them—engineers have as much use for the Architect's scale as do architects. Because stage sets, like houses, are built in feet and inches, designers use the Architect's scale rule.

To save time and increase accuracy, the designer often uses various *templates* to trace geometric shapes, eccentric curves, or furniture outlines onto a floor plan. Figure 5-3 shows templates for house furnishings; circles, squares, and other geometric shapes; ellipses; and French curves that can all provide edges for clear drafting. In addition, a spline (flexible piece of metal or hard rubber) can be used to create accurate curved lines that are not geometrical.

Drawing pencils and *leads* for lead holders have varying degrees of hardness and softness. Soft lead produces a blacker line than does hard lead, as under pressure it releases more graphite. The leads are graded by letter—from 6B, which is very soft, through HB and H, which are medium soft to firm, to 6H, the hardest lead. Designers usually find the combination of H, 2H, and 4H leads the most useful. It should be noted, however, that, of course, every designer drafts a bit differently, some with a light hand and some with a heavier hand.

Tools of the Trade

Drafting Equipment

In summary, basic drafting equipment includes the following:

1. A drawing board or drafting table
2. Drawing board cover
3. T-square or parallel rule
4. Two triangles: 30-60-90 degree and 45 degree
5. 6-inch bow compass
6. Architect's scale rule
7. Tracing paper and good drafting paper
8. Lead holder, mechanical pencil (and lead for either), or drafting pencils
9. Lead-sharpening device: pencil sharpener or lead pointer (for use with lead holder)
10. Erasers and erasing shield
11. Drawing cleaning powder or art gum eraser
12. Drafting tape or dots

Other leads might be needed to give the variety in line quality necessary for a good print. Drafting pencils, lead holders with separate leads, or mechanical pencils of various sizes can be used with equal effectiveness. The choice is determined by personal taste of the draftsperson.

The choice of *drafting paper* can depend on the type of drafting being done. Almost all drafting requires some kind of translucent paper. There are many different kinds, so the beginner is wise to seek the advice of a competent dealer or test various kinds him- or herself. Vellum, an excellent but expensive tracing paper, is a durable, 100 percent rag stock, with a nonglare surface to reduce eyestrain. It has enough "tooth" in the surface for pencil drafting to produce an excellent print. To save money, inexpensive rolls of thin canary yellow or white tracing paper can be used for preliminary drawings, with the good drafting paper saved for the finished drafting.

In addition, the draftsperson should have the following: something to sharpen the leads, such as a *lead pointer* for use with a lead holder or an electric or battery-powered pencil sharpener for use with drafting pencils; an *eraser* and *erasing shield* for erasing pencil-line mistakes; an *art gum eraser* or *drawing cleaning powder* to help keep the drawing paper clean; and *drafting tape* or dots, which are used to fasten the tracing paper to the drawing board.

THE GRAPHICS OF DESIGN

Drafting practices in the theatre are so numerous and loosely defined that they cannot easily be categorized. There are as many ways to draft a production as there are designers. A close inspection, however, reveals that each designer differs only in the amount of information given and in the way the material is organized. All have in common a background of engineering drawing and its basic principle, orthographic projection.

In spite of its academic sound, the orthographic projection is a simple drawing. Orthographic means "straight line." A straight-line projection is a method of representing the exact shape of an object in a two-dimensional drawing (Figure 5-4). This straight-line projection is the basis of most drafting.

For example, it is easy to recognize a three-step unit from a perspective drawing (Figure 5-4a). The carpenter, however, who needs more information than a pretty sketch, wants to know height, width, and depth. An **orthographic projection** is a way of drawing the unit to give this information: it reveals the object one view at a time and from as many angles as needed. The observer is free to "move" around the object to view it from front to rear and from top to bottom, with the drawing usually showing the top, front, and side. Each view is seen in true dimension by straight-line projection so it can be measured.

orthographic projection A straight-line projection drawing of an object showing three views, typically the top, the front, and the side.

A series of views of an object must relate to one another in order for them to have any value to the designer. One of the basic drafting conventions is the arrangement of these views.

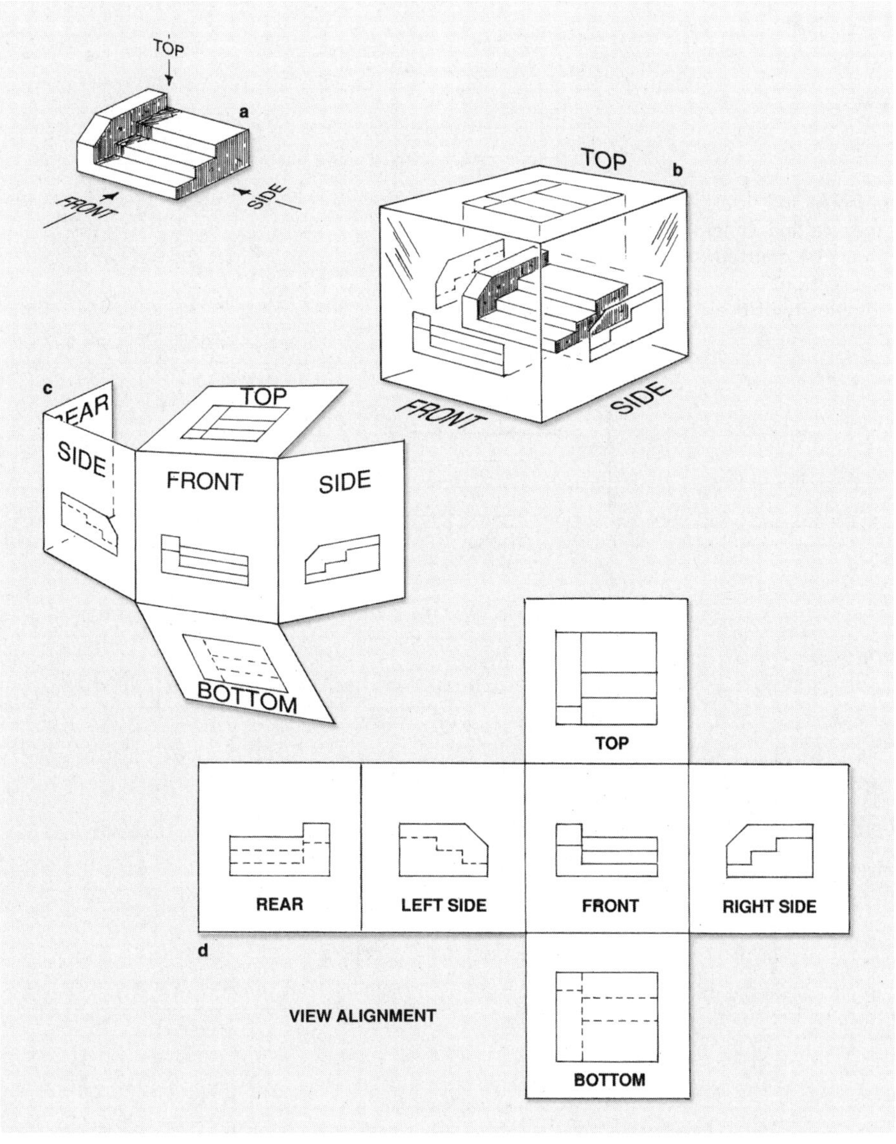

5-4

The Orthographic Projection

- **a** Pictorial view of a three-step unit.
- **b** Three-step unit surrounded by transparent cube with projection of each side.
- **c** Transparent cube unfolded.
- **d** View alignment.

To understand the method of transposing the views of the object in space onto the drawing board requires some visual imagination. Imagine for example that the three-step unit is in the center of a transparent cube (Figure 5-4b). Projected on each side of the cube is a line drawing of the object as it appears in each view. With the side containing the front view as the center, the other faces of the cube are unfolded to either side, to the top, and to the bottom (Figures 5-4c and d).

The front view is always the most recognizable one, showing the main characteristics of the object. It is the key view, giving the carpenter a bearing on visualizing the three-step unit in three dimensions. The top and side views are shown above and to the sides of the front view. These are the three principal views of the object. In architecture, horizontal views, in which the viewer's line of sight is perpendicular to the object, are called **elevations.** These include the front elevation, side elevations, and rear elevation. With the addition of dimensions to the three principal views, as well as some material specifications, the carpenter is ready to start building (Figure 5-5).

elevation A view of an object in which the line of sight of the viewer is perpendicular to the object, sometimes referred to as a *projection.*

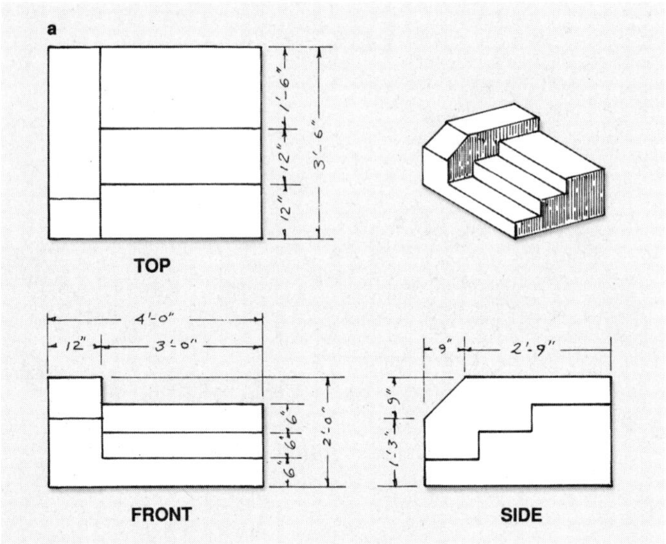

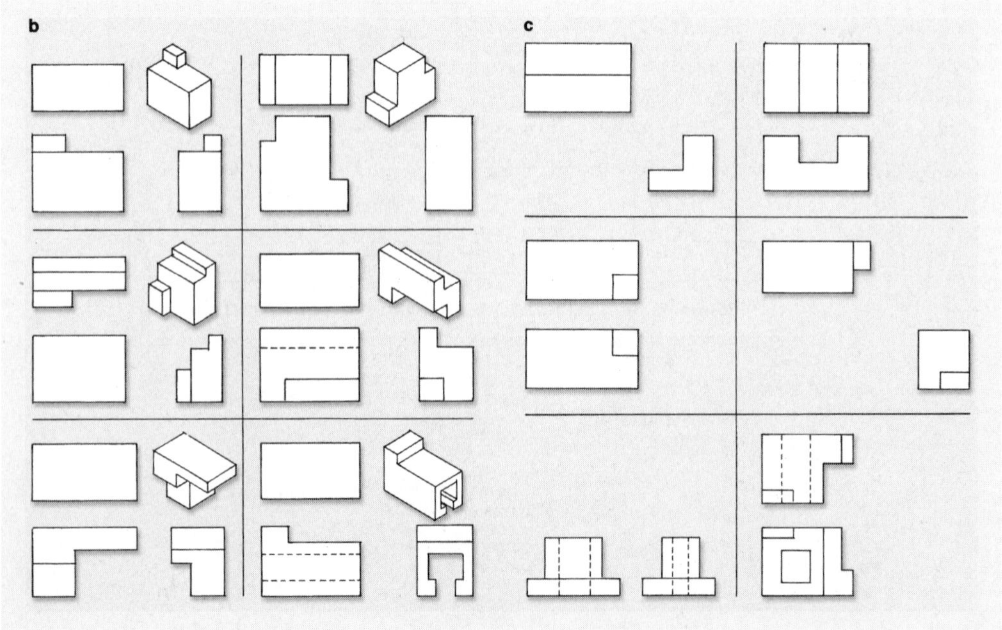

5-5

Scaled and Dimensioned Drawings, Problems

Designer's drawings:

a Three views of an object (top, front, and side) are generally shown. Drawn to scale and dimensioned. Occasionally one view may be omitted or an additional view (such as a section) included, depending on the complexity of the subject.

Orthographic problems:

b Supply the missing lines.

c Construct the missing views.

DRAFTING CONVENTIONS

As the designer begins to make working drawings, which are flat and less descriptive than the original sketch, he or she soon discovers that drafting has a way of making the lines speak for themselves, with symbols and conventions providing the words. The basic "vocabulary" of drafting includes lines of all types. There are thick lines, thin lines, dotted lines, dashed lines, straight lines, and curved lines, each with a different meaning and function. To correctly read a set of working drawings, one needs a thorough knowledge of the symbols used, just as one needs to know the conventions of English in order to read this textbook.

Line Symbols

The first and simplest convention is the drawing of lines in different weights or thickness. Most scene designers draft with three weights of line. For speed or for a simple drawing, sometimes only two weights of line are used. The goal is clarity of presentation and accuracy of representation. The United States Institute for Theatre Technology (USITT) Graphic Standard Board recommends for drafting in pencil the following guide to line weight: 0.3mm (3⁄10 of a millimeter) for a lightweight line, 0.5mm for a medium-weight line, and 0.9mm for a heavy-weight line. In practice, the different weights are consistent within a drawing but not necessarily between drawings. That is, a heavy line in one may be 0.9mm but a bit heavier or lighter in another. Because the scene designer drafts in so many scales and each designer is unique, standardization of thickness or number of weights is impossible. However, consistency within drawings ensures clarity.

A line is made heavy or light depending on its importance. Obviously, heavyweight lines are going to catch the eye first, medium-weight lines second, and lightweight lines last. The use of these different lines gives the print a feeling of depth. This slight third dimension makes the print easier to read. The weight of a line also determines its function, as shown in Figure 5-6. That is, different types of lines are used for different and quite specific purposes.

5-6

Line Symbols

a Lightweight lines.
b Medium-weight lines.
c Heavy-weight lines.
d Types of dimensions.

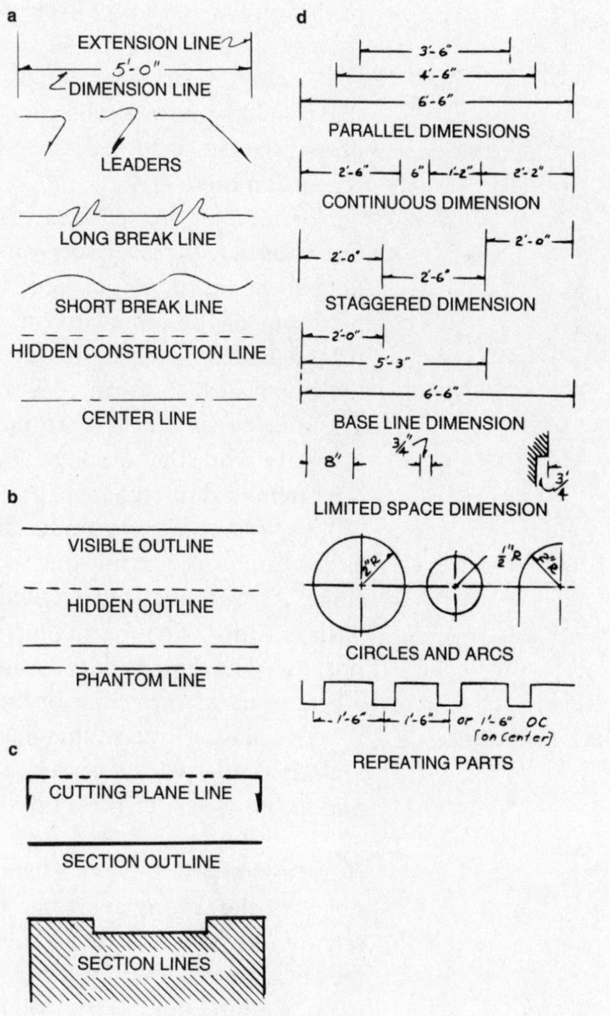

Medium-Weight Lines Medium-weight lines are used most frequently and have already been seen in the orthographic projection of the three-step unit (Figure 5-4). They are the *outline* or *object lines* that represent the shape of the object, showing visible edges of all surfaces as they appear at the angle of view. The visible outline is a solid, medium-weight line.

Occasionally a view will cover or hide a surface outline (see Figure 5-4d). It then becomes a **hidden outline** and is drawn as a dotted line or series of small dashes.

hidden outline The outline of an object that is hidden from view, drawn in dotted line.

Lightweight Lines Lightweight lines are used for reference or imaginary lines. Their function is to give additional information about the object without detracting from the overall picture created by the outlines.

Dimension lines, with arrowheads at the ends, mark the extent of the surface that is being dimensioned. The dimension itself, set into the line, shows the exact distance or length and is medium weight. If dimension lines are set too close to the drawing, or within the drawing, they may become confused with outlines. To keep the dimension line away from the object, *extension lines* are used. These solid lines are drawn perpendicular to the surface of the object. As the name implies, they extend the surface to the dimension line. Although the arrowheads of the dimension line touch the extension line, the extension line itself is held clear of the object, about 1⁄16 inch. (See Figure 5-13 for an example.)

Leaders, relatives of dimension lines, are made with one-sided arrowheads that touch the surface where a note or dimension applies. If the leader is always drawn slanted or curved, there is less chance for anyone to confuse it with the dimension line.

Break lines are space savers that denote a shortening of length or height. Occasionally, the draftsperson wants to draw a unit of scenery that is too long to fit on the paper. A reduction of length is accomplished by taking a piece out of the center and using a break line to show that the piece is not represented in full length. The break line can also be used to indicate that the outer surface of an object has been cut away to show inner structure. The *long break line* is a straight line with spasmodic eruptions occurring at intervals, while the *short break line* is a subtle curve with less regularity. These are often used interchangeably.

The *center line* is unique. Although it is a reference line, it is often drafted as a medium-weight line due to its great importance in locating scenery on the stage. As well, it is represented by a special dotted line: an alternating long dash and dot. This particular dotted line should not be used for any other purpose. The center line is a familiar symbol in the floor plan of a stage setting, where it marks the center of the stage or proscenium opening.

The **plaster line,** an imaginary line on the upstage edge of the proscenium arch, is similar to the center line. In spite of its being an imaginary line, the plaster line is of such great importance that it is drafted in medium-weight line.

plaster line Imaginary line on the upstage edge of the proscenium arch.

Heavy-Weight Lines Heavy-weight lines indicate the cross section of an object or the cutting away and removing of a portion to reveal the inside. The *section line,* which is drawn over an adjoining view to locate the position of the cut, consists of a repeating long line and a double short line. Arrowheads point the direction seen in the section view. The outline of an object at this point is drawn in solid, heavy-weight line, referred to as the *section outline.*

Scaled Drawings

The most important part of a set of working drawings is the dimension. A carpenter cannot begin to build without some indication of size. Scaled or dimensioned drawings are crucial for such information. Most misunderstandings that occur between the drawing board and the finished setting are over dimensions, such as the wall that is too small for the sideboard or the door that is too large for the door opening.

A carefully drawn object gives the carpenter a way to figure sizes. It also gives the designer a fairly accurate basis for studying the proportional relationship of various elements of the set.

The usual scale of a working drawing is ½ inch equals one foot (½" = 1'-0"), which means that every half inch on the drawing is equal to one foot at full-scale or actual size. Decorative details that might not be clear at the small scale are frequently increased to the scale of 1 inch or more to 1 foot. Any important bits of detail that the designer wants accurately reproduced—such as wallpaper patterns, scrolls, brackets, railings, and the like—are presented at full scale.

THE GROUND PLAN

It is impossible to overstate the importance of the *ground plan.* Because the staging of the production depends on the use of the floor space, the designer must continually think about the plan while the idea of the setting is being developed. The plan grows with the design, pushed one way for aesthetic reasons, altered another way for practical ones, modified for staging purposes, and finally solidified into the key working drawing and information center—the ground plan.

All phases of production seek information from the ground plan. To explain the design of the set adequately, the designer refers often to the plan. The carpenter consults it to lay out the set pieces properly. The director and stage manager cannot map out the staging without understanding and studying it. The setup, rigging, and lighting depend on information in the ground plan to complete the final assembly of the set on the stage.

Analagous to the top view in an orthographic projection, the ground plan is a horizontal section (with the upper portion of the set removed). As we mentioned in Chapter 4, the cutting plane is at a level that shows the most characteristic view of the shape of the set, the standard being 3 feet above the stage floor. Because a stage set is made up of many small units of scenery, the ground plan is also an assembled view. It reveals the horizontal shape of the set, locates it on the stage with all the pieces assembled, and labels the units and pieces that make up the complete setting. This will include any walls of the set, furniture, and **masking.** Masking is any piece of scenery—walls, black drapes, and so forth—that is used both to complete the stage picture beyond openings such as doors or windows and to hide the workings of the backstage area.

masking Any piece of scenery that is used to complete the stage picture and prevent the audience from seeing the backstage area.

The ground plan also includes the position of any furniture, although some designers draft a separate plan to include that. In addition, any piece of scenery that will be used in more than one position should be shown in both. The position where the scenic unit is most often used is drafted in solid line. The other position, called **alternate position,** is shown in dotted line.

alternate position Any secondary position of a piece of scenery, drafted in dotted line.

The sightline points from the extreme house right and house left seats in the front row and is marked on the ground plan as a cross overlapping a circle. This enables the designer to place some kind of masking beyond an open door, a window, or any other opening in order to control what any audience member can and cannot see.

hanging chart A chart included on the ground plan and section that indicates the placement of each piece of scenery that hangs or flies from a batten, including line set number, distance from the plaster line, and trim.

trim Height of something above the stage floor.

On one side of the drafted ground plan, the designer will usually include a **hanging chart.** This provides information about any piece of scenery that flies or hangs from a batten: line set number, the scenic unit, its distance from the plaster line, and its **trim** or height above the stage floor. A set that has no hanging scenery does not need to include the chart on the ground plan.

All walls should be labeled. A simple number or letter system is best. It is also not a bad idea to label any drops, scrims, and even sometimes the masking on the ground plan. Anything out of the ordinary requires a label for easy understanding of the drawing.

Symbols

The ground plan is usually drawn at the scale of ½" = 1'-0". (Preliminary plans are often drafted at ¼" = 1'-0"). In any scale, designers must use symbols and conventions to help explain the set with a limited amount of detailed drafting. Most of the symbols shown in Figure 5-7 are standard; their

5-7

Drafting Symbols

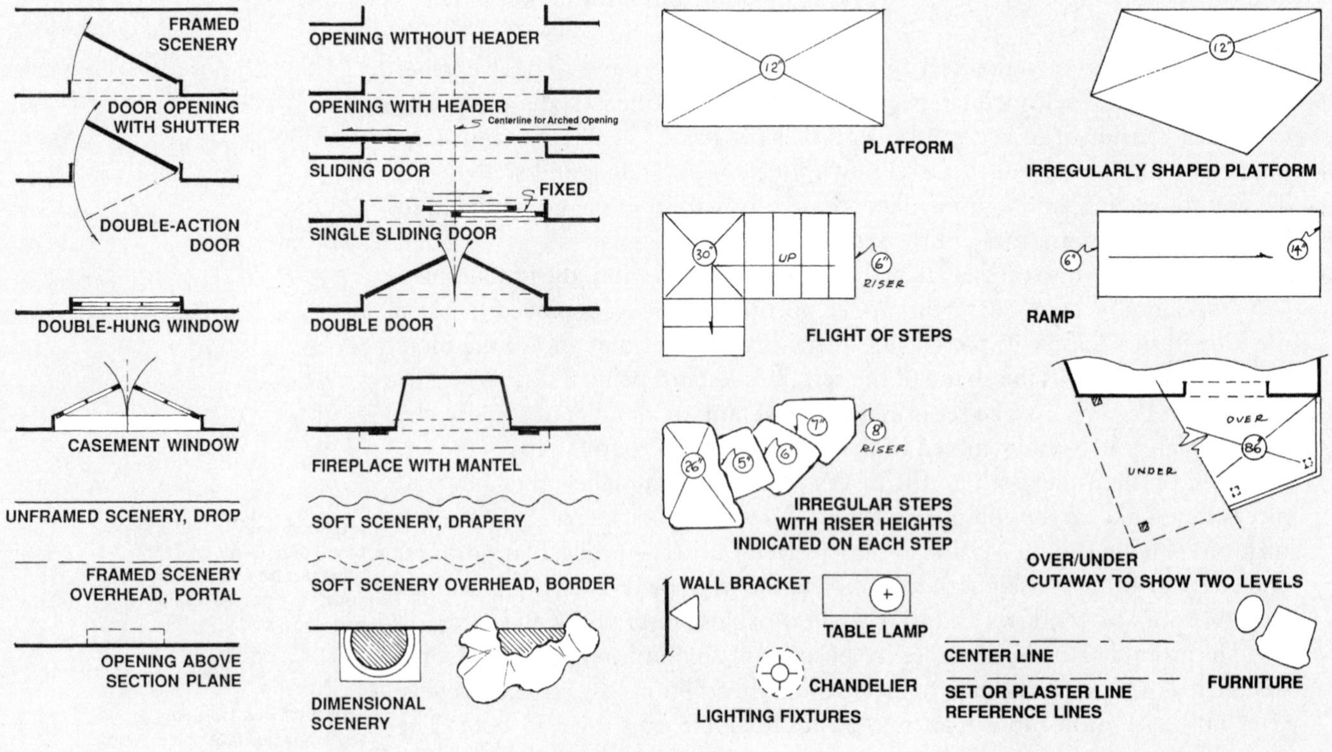

use and meanings are logical enough if one keeps in mind that a plan is a horizontal section view.

Labeling

Part of the function of an assembled view is to identify and label the parts that make up the whole. The ground plan gives this information in varying degrees of completeness, depending on the working conditions and the nature of the production. The amount and manner of labeling may depend not just on individual designers' preferences but also on the given situation. Summer stock or university and community theatres, where the bulk of the structural planning falls on the designer's shoulders, would likely require a more specific labeling of each piece of scenery than other productions would. The label becomes an easy, accurate means of identification for a single piece of scenery or assembled units of a setting.

Dimensions

A drawing needs to indicate size before the carpenter can begin building. The designer places dimensions opposite a surface in such a way as to show its exact limit and measure. Placing dimensions on a scaled drawing saves time in the shop. A properly given dimension includes the dimension line, measurement, and extension lines. There is no set rule for the amount of dimensioning on a drawing. As with labeling, every designer does it a little differently. Some designers provide only the outside dimensions of a piece of scenery; others provide the dimensions of almost every detail.

Dimensioning the Ground Plan

Any point on the stage is located by its distance right or left of the center line and its distance upstage or downstage from the plaster line. If a production will tour, the designer might substitute the **set line**, a dotted line or lightweight solid line indicating the edge of the set farthest downstage. Only major turning points or corners of a set are dimensioned. With few exceptions, no other dimensions should appear in the ground plan.

set line The edge of the set farthest downstage, usually parallel to the plaster line.

The technical director will use the dimensions to place the scenic pieces on the stage properly; the stage manager will use them to tape the set on the floor of the rehearsal space. It is not necessary to dimension the plan in great detail, because all the scenery will appear in separate elevations with complete dimensions. Figures 5-8 and 5-9 show two designers' ground plans.

Remember that the ground plan is also an assembled view; it will help to determine which dimensions the stage carpenter or the stage manager needs to know to locate and assemble the set on the stage and in the rehearsal room. After all important corners and backings are located, a few additional dimensions may be needed, such as radius dimensions of circles or arcs that may be in the ground plan. However, sometimes certain circumstances such as a more complex, multilevel set or an unusual type of unit require additional information if the plan is to be useful.

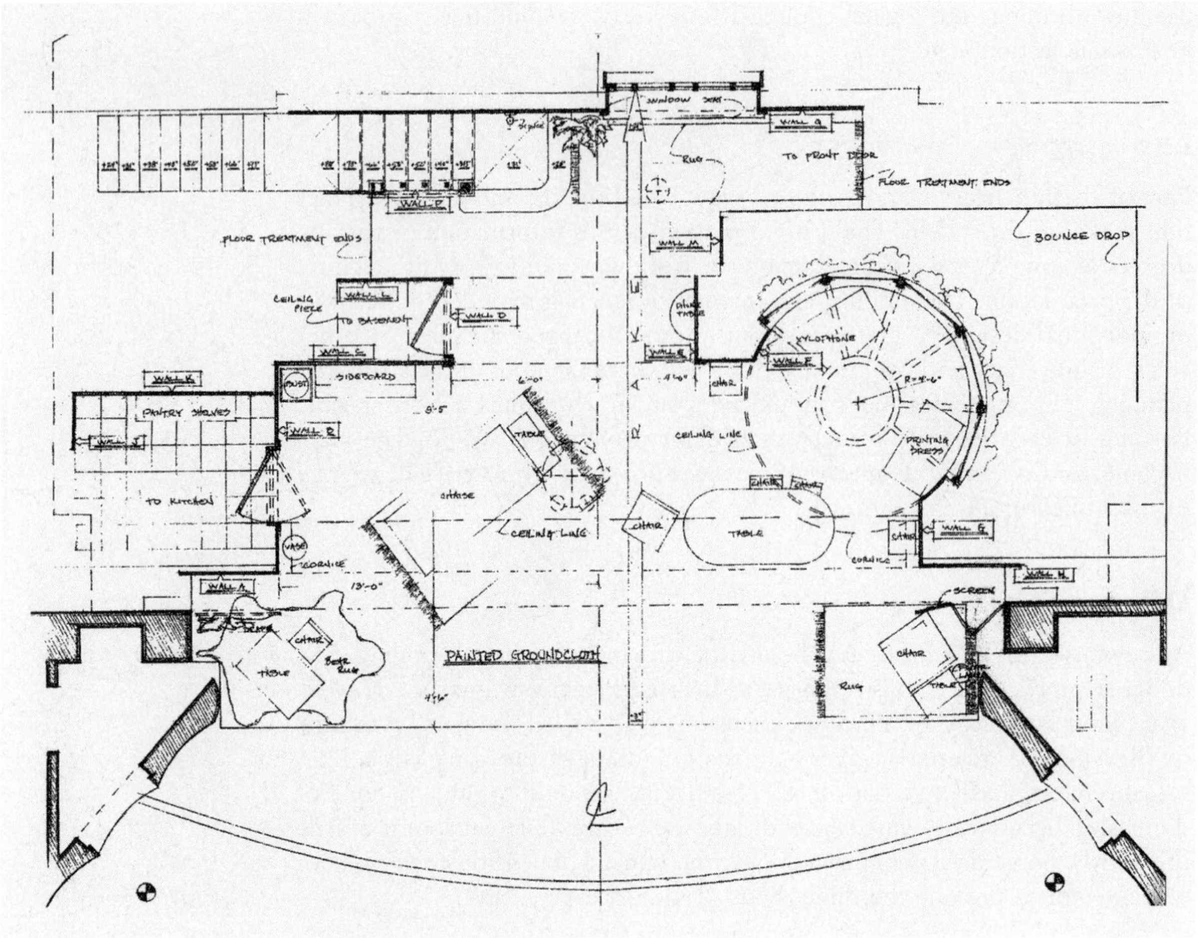

5-8

The Ground Plan

The ground plan is a horizontal section with a cutting plane usually at three feet above the stage floor. This height most often will provide the most information, although can be adjusted higher or lower if necessary. (Use the symbols from Figure 5-7 to understand the plan.) The darkest lines represent places where the walls of the set intersect the cutting plane. Medium-weight lines outline steps and platforms as seen from above. The dotted lines indicate openings (and anything else that exists above the cutting plane). Lightweight dimensions locate the set on the stage as it relates to two reference lines—the plaster line and the center line. Ground plan for *You Can't Take It with You,* designed by Dick Block.

SECTIONS

section A view of a set from one side, as if cut across vertically at the center line.

The **section,** sometimes referred to as a *hanging section,* is a view of the set looking either stage right or stage left with a cutting plane at the center line. To envision this, we can imagine that a large knife has sliced the set in half vertically at the center line and we are standing on one side looking toward the cut surface (see Figure 5-10). As the ground plan provides information about the amount of stage space taken up by the set, the section offers information about the vertical space and the heights of the set. This view, which in orthographic terms takes the place of the side view, is crucial. Without a section drawing of a set, no one can determine the necessary heights

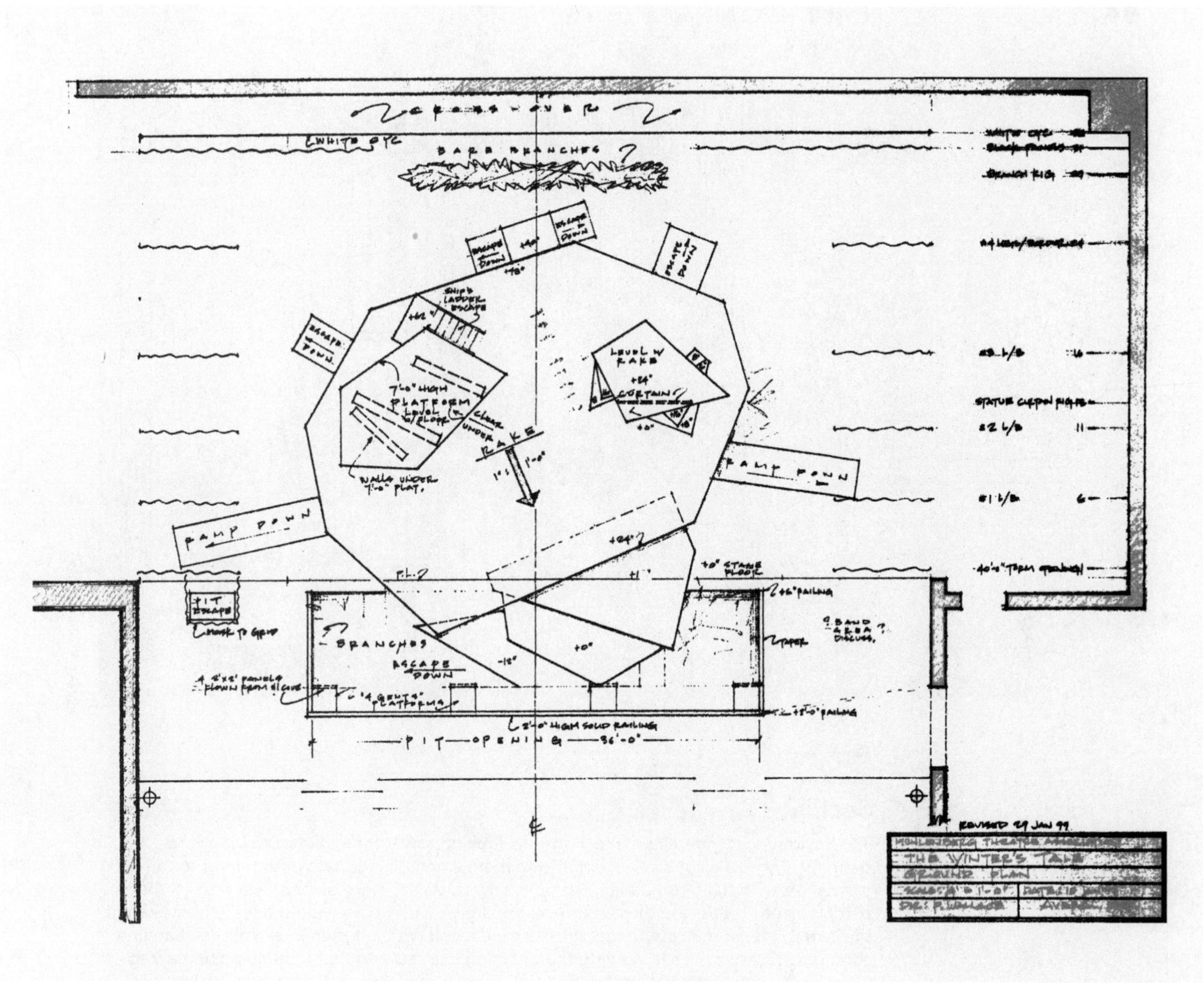

COURTESY TIMOTHY AVERILL

5-9

Ground Plan with Levels

This ground plan for *The Winter's Tale* is less about walls and opening than about platforms and ramps. Designer, Timothy Averill.

of masking walls or the placement and size of borders. In addition, the section is the most important piece of drafting for the lighting designer because it enables him or her to figure out possible lighting positions and angles.

Given the rules about line weight and orthographic projections, any place at which the walls intersect the cutting plane (almost always the center line) will be in heavy-weight line. The remaining parts of the set will be in medium-weight solid line, assuming that they are seen from the center line. If they are hidden outline, they will be in medium-weight dotted line. Any scenic pieces behind the cutting plane (for example, a stage-right window if we are looking toward the left side of the stage) will also be in dotted medium-weight line. Or, if this is too confusing, two sections can be drawn.

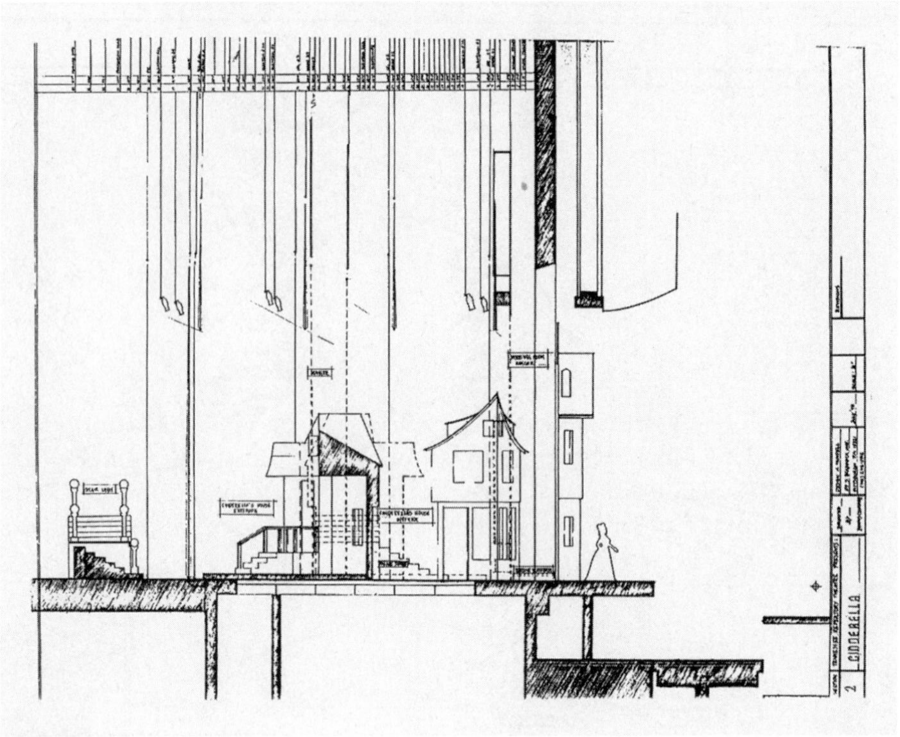

COURTESY ANNE MUNDELL

5-10

Section

The drawing for *Cinderella* is a section view looking toward stage left. Drawn by the designer, it shows all of the scenery information, emphasizing that which relates to the vertical. As with the ground plan, the points at which any piece of scenery intersects the cutting plane, in this case the center line, are drawn with heavy-weight lines. Objects behind the center line (in this case, stage right) are indicated with a dotted line. Note the hanging chart drawn above the set showing the use of all line sets and the sightline point marked with a cross. Lighting positions are also suggested in the section. Designer, Anne Mundell.

The only dimensions needed on the section are the vertical openings of any portals, including the false proscenium if there is one, and the trim height of any borders. In addition, there should be a hanging chart aligned to the set above the section drawing including the batten line set number (indicating which pipe the scenic piece uses), and the unit of scenery that is hanging on the line set and its distance from the plaster line and trim height, if any (the same information that appears in the hanging chart on the ground plan). Any piece of scenery that flies should be shown in its "in" position and its "out" position. The predominant position should be in solid medium-weight line; the alternate position should be in dotted line as in the ground plan.

The designer needs to decide whether the stage-right or the stage-left section will be more informative. This is often obvious. The lighting designer in particular will want to be able to see any openings in the set that will allow for light. If one view shows clearer information about windows, arches, and doors, then that is the view that should be drawn.

As in the ground plan, sightlines figure strongly in the section. In this view, the designer can check the verticals, again making sure that the audience can see all that is necessary and nothing that they should not see. The sightline point allows the designer to make sure that any flying scenery is completely out of sight when in the "out" position. If the theatre has a balcony, those sightlines need to be checked as well.

The designer soon discovers that flying space is quickly filled with lighting equipment, traveler tracks, masking curtains, and the like. A certain amount of juggling may be necessary in order to get all of the pieces to fit and work easily. Once the lighting designer has had a chance to look at the section, there may be some negotiation about the best use of the fly space to allow for needed lighting positions.

DESIGNER'S ELEVATIONS

Almost equally as important as sections are the designer's elevations (Figure 5-11). Compared with the ground plan, which is an assembled view showing the relationship of many parts, the elevations are, in a sense, a disassembled or dismantled view of the individual parts. Because the elevation of an assembled set as it would appear in a normal front view offers little as a working drawing, the scene designer uses another technique. The set is "taken apart and flattened out," and each piece of scenery is shown in orthographic projection at the scale ½" = 1'-0". The setting is drafted to show

5-11

Designer's Elevations

The front of every element of scenery is shown in a flattened-out view. The basic outside dimensions and interior openings are indicated. Side notes give specific directions to the scene shop. Design for *A Streetcar Named Desire,* with design and drafting by Tim Saternow.

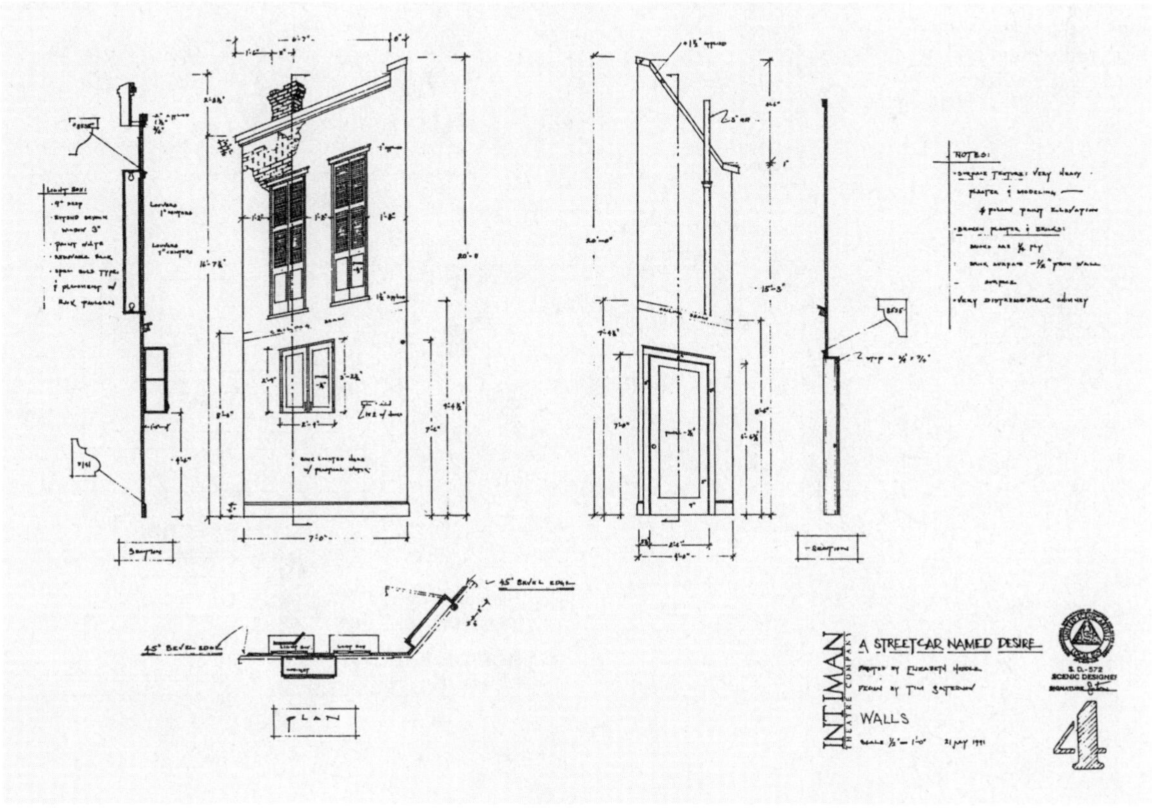

COURTESY TIM SATERNOW

all pieces of scenery laid out in order, piece by piece, most often from stage right to stage left.

Each piece of scenery—be it a flat, a platform, or a three-dimensional piece—is drafted with as many views as needed to explain its size, shape, and function. The front view is the most important, but most scenic pieces will need to have a plan view as well. This may sometimes seem excessive, but even a simple wall will be better understood when drawn from more than one view. Depending on the individual piece, a side or section view may be needed (Figure 5-12). Any wall that has an arch, a door, or a window should have a section view that intersects the opening. This will allow the designer to explain the relationship of the wall, reveals, attendant molding, and any other added elements.

5-12

Section Views

a Revolved section, drawn directly on the elevation to indicate contour.

b Removed section, a revolved section that has been removed and set to one side of the elevation. Each section is labeled, A–F.

c Section B-B is a vertical section, and A-A is a horizontal section (often called a *plan*).

d Half section, used on a symmetrical object combining the section and front elevation views.

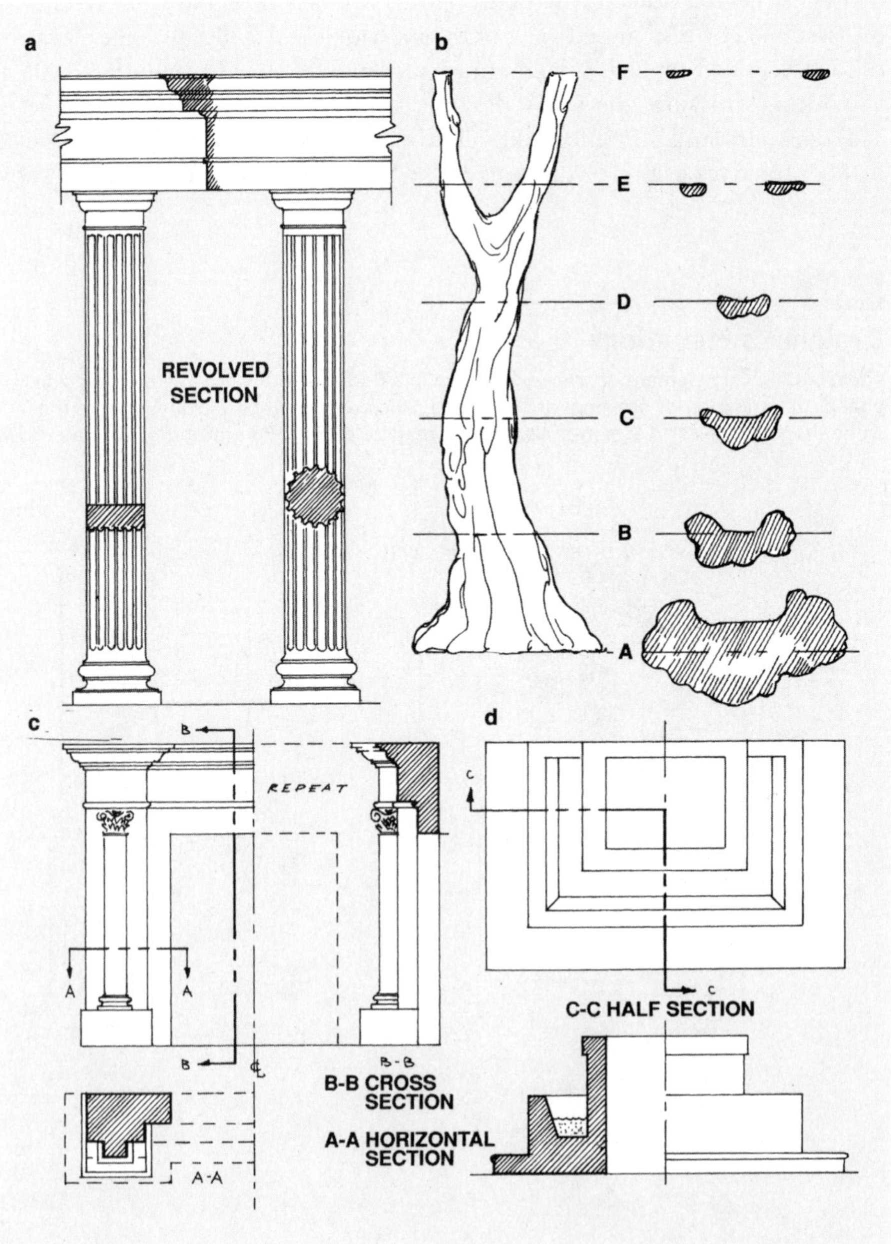

The main purpose of the design elevations is to explain each piece of scenery in order for the shop to determine the best method of construction. Clarity in the drawing is of great importance. The designer should remember that the people reading the drawings know only the information that is provided (Figure 5-13).

5-13

Dimensioning the Elevation

a A portion of a design elevation showing different forms of dimensioning.

b The irregular outline of a set piece presents different problems in dimensioning. In this case, only outside dimensions are needed. A grid can be laid over an elevation for ease in replicating difficult shapes. If the scene shop does not have a carpenter who is skilled at layout work, a scenic artist will be called in to draw out the piece.

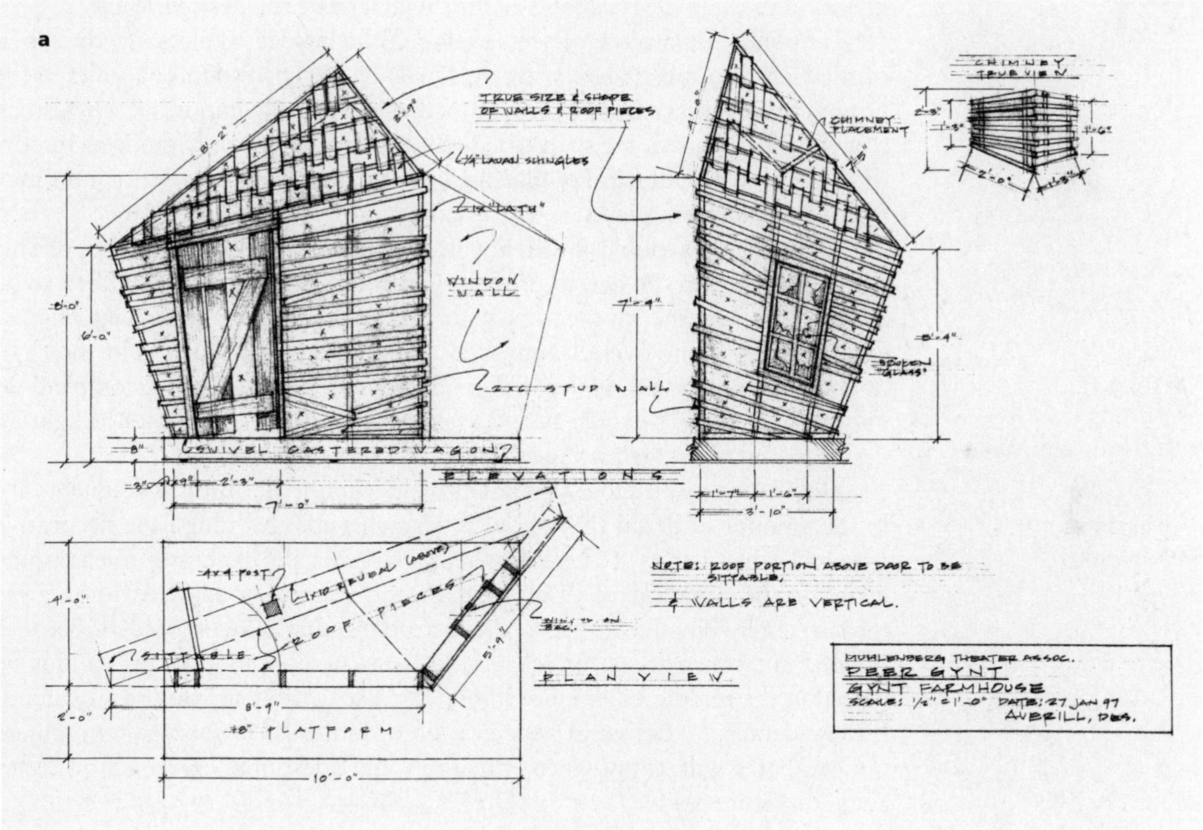

a COURTESY TIMOTHY AVERILL

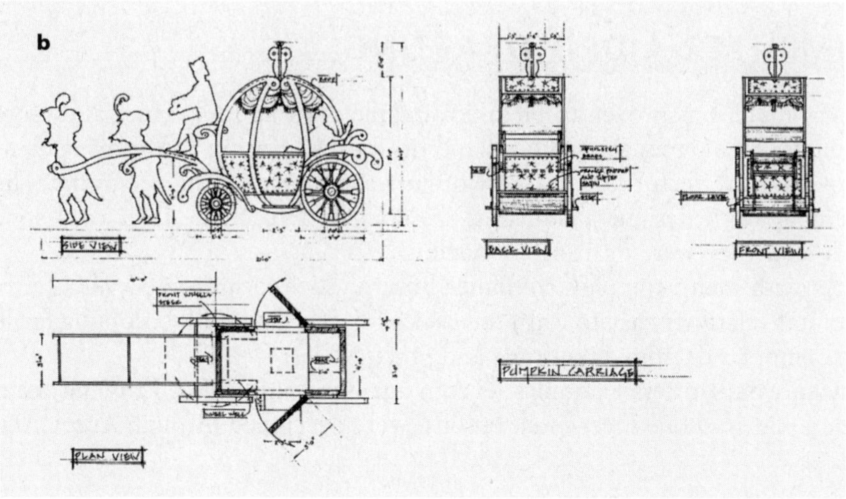

b COURTESY ANNE MUNDELL

On the design elevation, the designer should include information about materials that should be used and any information that might affect the construction. For example, if an actor will get thrown against the wall, it needs extra bracing. The same is true if a door will get slammed or someone will crawl through a window. An indication of how the walls or other pieces of scenery are to be treated by the scenic artist will inform the shop how to "finish" the piece. If a wall is to be painted, the hard-covered flat should be covered with canvas; if it is to be wallpapered or textured, there is no reason to cover the lauan surface. The more thorough the information provided in the drawings, the better the technicians can plan for the final result.

Most shops have a standard method of building flats and platforms, but some indication of how the scenery should be built can be useful. On more unusual pieces, the shop will often make suggestions for a better method of construction or have ideas about cheaper materials. A wise designer will pay attention to these ideas as long as they will achieve the desired result.

Each individual piece of scenery should be labeled. Obviously, the labels of the elevation must agree with the labels of the corresponding units in the ground plan. The accuracy of cross-labeling is especially important when stock scenery is being used, for such labeling is the carpenter's only guide as to how the pieces are assembled. For clarification, the plan view of a scenic unit may include the adjacent pieces.

The designer should thoroughly discuss final draftings with the shop. This is a critical step in the design process. Questions always arise and need to be addressed before the shop can provide estimates of time and money. Further explanations of the overall approach to the design may also help the shop understand what the designer is trying to achieve with the set. A complete set of draftings should be made available to the shop, the scenic artist, the lighting designer, and the stage manager.

How much detail should designers include in the elevation? Designers vary in the amount of detail they show at ½-inch scale. Although the decorative trim and other details are best shown at a larger scale, including at least some detail on the elevations is wise. Any trim shown in the design elevation gives the carpenter some idea of special construction that may be needed. Because of the light construction of scenery, pictures or lighting fixtures cannot be placed in the middle of a wall without extra structural support from behind. If these details are drawn in the elevation or indicated in some other manner, the carpenter will know where to supply the additional construction (refer again to Figure 5-11).

COMPUTER-AIDED DRAFTING

The computer has proven to be an invaluable drafting tool. More and more designers are moving away from hand drafting and using programs such as AutoCAD and VectorWorks, the two most common drafting programs. The programs allow designers skilled at the computer to create their own style much as if they were drafting by hand.

URL http://www.nemetschek.net

As with many complex computer programs, the learning curve is fairly steep. It is relatively easy to learn the basics but, like any skill, becoming facile with computer drafting takes time and practice.

Figure 5-14 offers examples of computer drafting. These drawings of a ground plan and one sheet of elevations, were developed through AutoCAD.

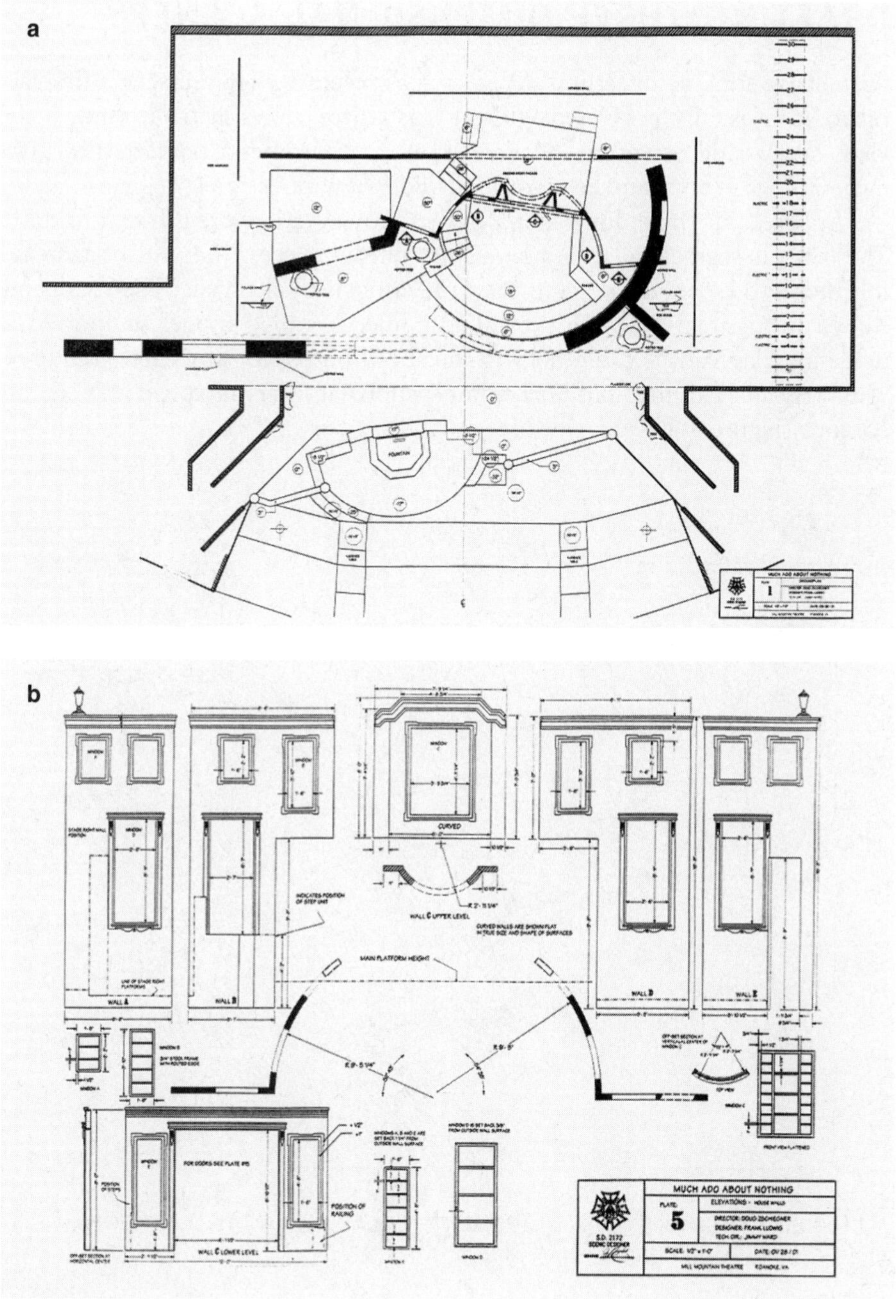

a & b COURTESY FRANK LUDWIG

5-14

Computer-Aided Drafting

a CAD ground plan for *Much Ado About Nothing,* designed and drafted by Frank Ludwig. Only the speed—not the conventions—of drafting changes when the work is done on a computer.

b CAD design elevations for *Much Ado About Nothing.*

Although many theatre groups find drafting programs too expensive, such programs are becoming more and more common.

The use of a computer does not replace the need for knowledge and skill in drafting. Designers still need to study drafting techniques, symbols, and conventions as they apply to the theatre.

DRAFTING THREE-DIMENSIONAL SCENERY

As we have seen, architectural forms such as columns, step units, or a fireplace mantel are usually presented with at least three views: a front view, a top view, and a side or vertical section. Most of the time, a section view gives more information than the traditional side view does.

An irregular three-dimensional object, however, is more difficult to draft. The form is segmented into a series of contour pieces that will be fastened together and covered to create the three-dimensional object. The tree trunk shown in Figure 5-12b is a typical example. A scaled model sculptured in modeling clay can be a big help to the shop, but is not absolutely required. The carpenter can then cut horizontal sections at intervals to get an accurate contour (Figure 5-15).

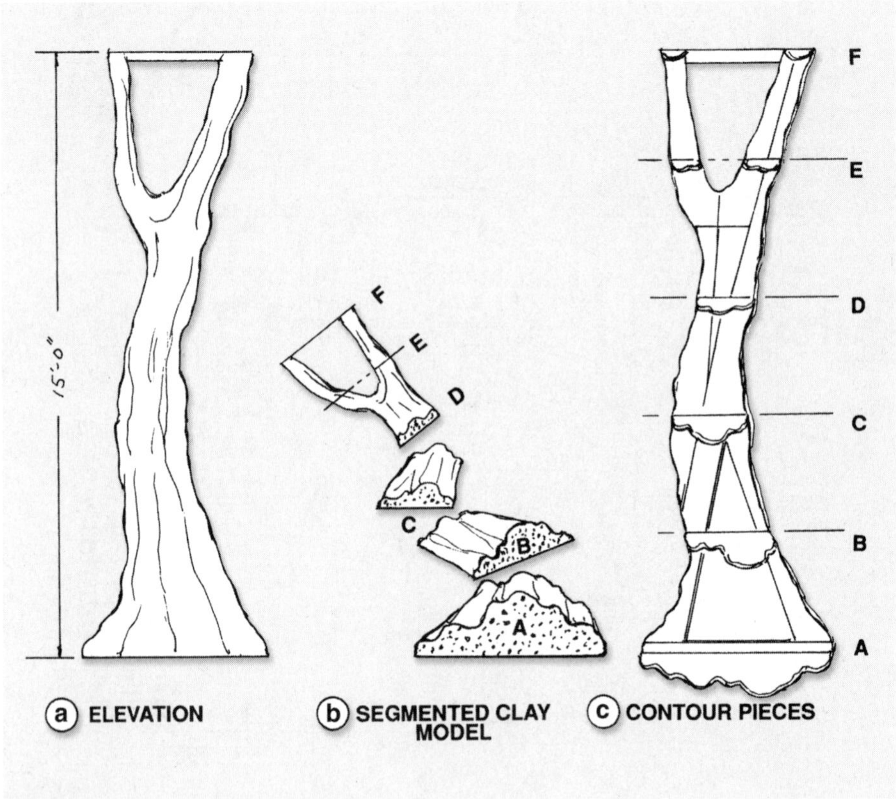

5-15

Drafting an Irregular Three-Dimensional Form

This three-dimensional form represents a tree trunk. The designer's elevation provides an accurate outline of the trunk and, in this case, a clay scale model shows the contours of the trunk. A clay model can be immensely helpful to the designer. The series of sections through the trunk are critical for the artisans building the tree.

a The outline of the tree trunk is framed.

b The clay model is segmented at intervals that reflect the dimensions of the surface material. Each cut is a scale section at that interval.

c The contour pieces are constructed and placed at measured intervals on the tree trunk's frame. The scene shop will then proceed with a screen or similar covering to achieve the shape, contour, and texture of the tree trunk.

PLANNING PROPERTIES

The designer is responsible for the selection of properties, for the design of specially built pieces of furniture, and for the general arrangement of properties in the setting.

In planning the properties, the designer's chief concern is to coordinate design needs with those of the director. A meeting of minds can be achieved easily if the designer shows—through sketches, clippings, or photographs—what is planned and provides a plan to indicate the size and position of set properties as they appear in the setting.

The construction of a special prop, like any three-dimensional piece of scenery, requires a working drawing. The usual plan showing front and side views will suffice; or, if the piece is not too complicated, a dimensioned pictorial drawing will serve (Figure 5-16). Again, the designer will find it wise to study all the important details at full scale.

5-16

Freehand Pictorial Drawings

For a relatively simple object, usually furniture, a freehand drawing will suffice in lieu of a formal drafting. There is enough information on a drawing such as this for the carpenters to begin building. Throne/catafalque for *Dido and Aeneas,* designed and drawn by Timothy Averill.

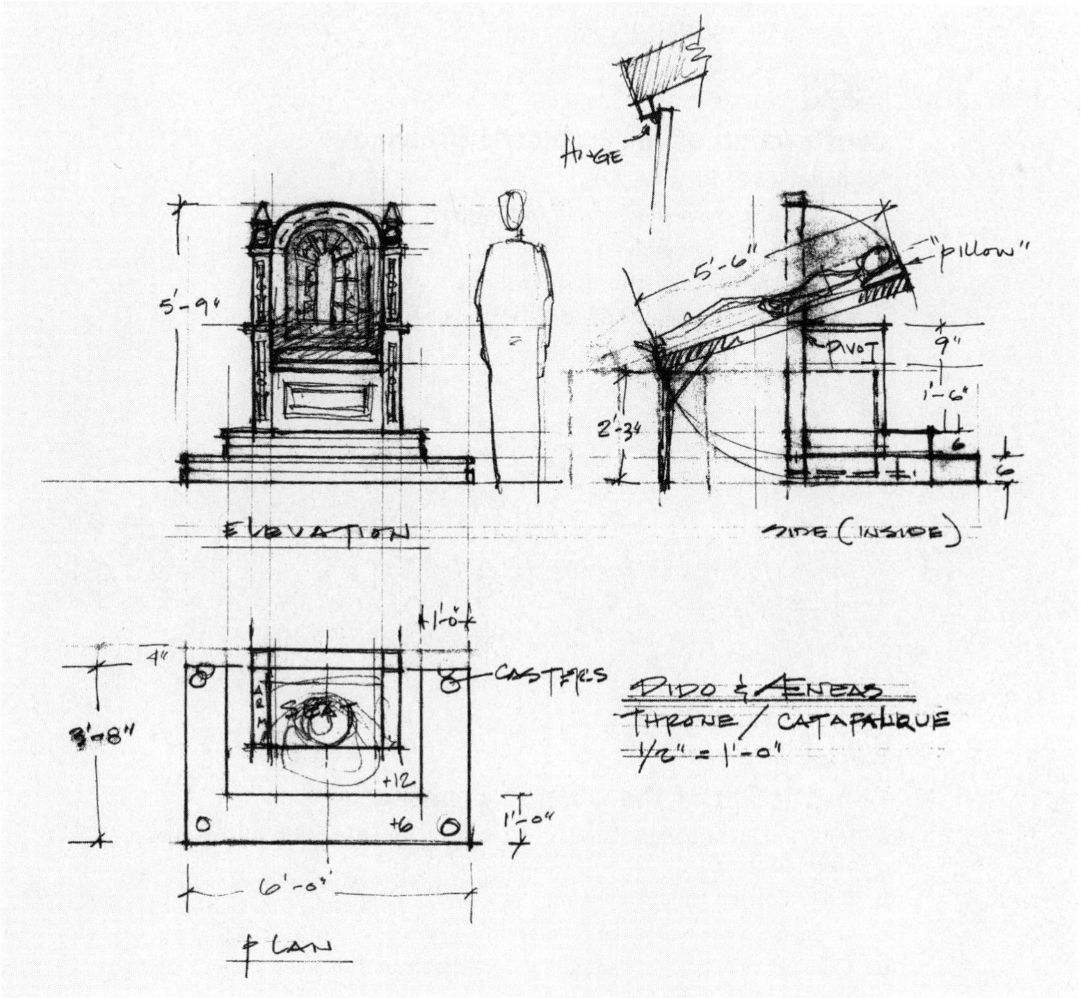

COURTESY TIMOTHY AVERILL

PICTORIAL DRAWINGS

The designer's sketch is a type of pictorial drawing, but because it is in perspective it cannot be used as a working drawing. But imagine a pictorial drawing with the edges of the receding surfaces not converging and the sides not foreshortened. Such a drawing can be done to scale and used as a supplementary view to the working drawings. The lack of perspective makes it possible to draw to scale, although the object may look distorted.

The two basic kinds of pictorials are the isometric and the oblique drawings. Their difference stems from the angle of the view. An *isometric drawing* represents an object as seen from one corner and slightly above (Figure 5-17). An *oblique drawing* shows the object as seen opposite one face with the side angled off to the right or left (Figure 5-18).

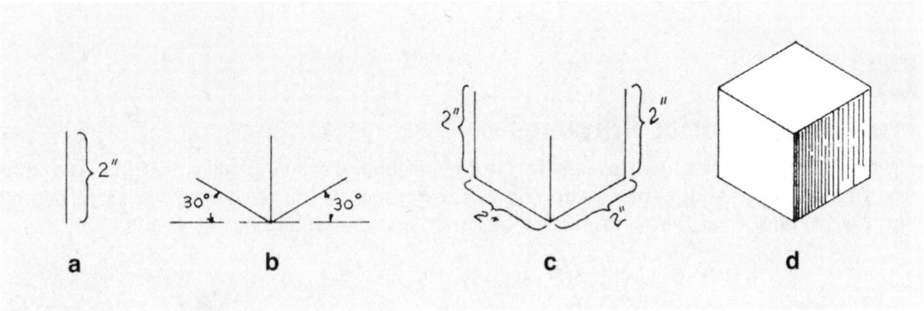

5-17

Construction of the Isometric Drawing

The object is a 2-inch cube.

a Vertical axis, the nearest corner of the cube.

b Slanted axes, right and left.

c Slanted lines and uprights drawn to scale.

d The completed isometric drawing of the cube.

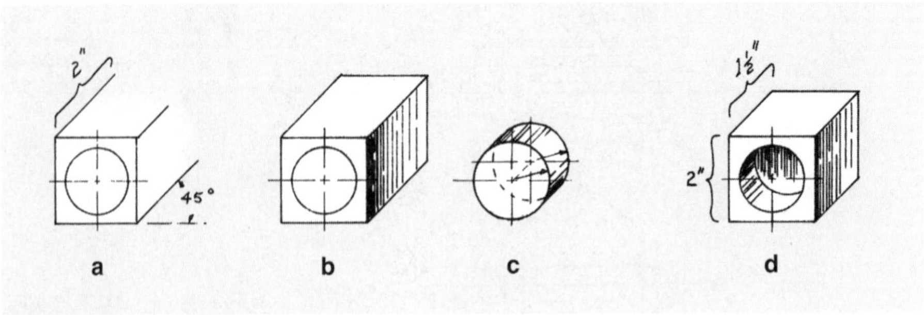

5-18

Construction of the Oblique Drawing

a The principal face with slant line drawn to the right or left. All the lines are drawn to scale.

b The completed oblique drawing.

c An oblique drawing of the circular disk.

d A cabinet drawing. All slanted lines are drawn at a reduced scale to minimize the distorted look of an oblique drawing.

Isometric means "equal measure" (as opposed to the foreshortened distances or unequal measure of perspective). An isometric drawing has three axes to represent the principal planes of the object. The first is a vertical line to indicate all the upright edges; the second, a slanted line to the right, 30 degrees to the horizontal, to represent the horizontal edges of the right plane; and the third, a 30-degree line slanted to the left to represent the horizontal edges of the planes to the left. These lines, and all lines parallel to them, are known as *isometric lines.* Conversely, lines that are not parallel to any of the three axes are *non-isometric lines.* Heights and distances can be measured on isometric lines, but a non-isometric line cannot be drawn to scale (Figure 5-17).

Because irregular edges, curves, and angles are distorted in an isometric view, a designer may want to change the direction of the view to show them at a better vantage. By moving the object around until the complicated surface is parallel to the plane of the paper, or frontal position, the designer can draw the irregular edge or curve without distortion. A view from this direction is an *oblique* drawing.

The same general pictorial characteristics are present in the oblique drawing as in the isometric, with the exception of a more pronounced distortion in appearance. Because of the frontal position of one of the principal planes, two of the oblique axes are at right angles to each other. The angle of the third axis, representing the plane of the sides, may vary from 30 to 45 degrees to the horizontal. It can be drawn either to the right or left and slanted either up or down (Figure 5-18). By placing the side that contains the irregular outlines, angles, or curves in the frontal position, drafting time can be saved and the appearance of the view made more attractive.

To reduce the distortion and improve the looks of the oblique drawing, the draftsperson sometimes uses a *cabinet drawing* (Figure 5-19). It is constructed with the complicated face parallel to the picture plane—like the obliques—but lines parallel to the angled axis are reduced in scale. A ratio of 2:3 or 3:4 between the frontal planes and the angled axis produces a pleasing

5-19

Cabinet Drawing

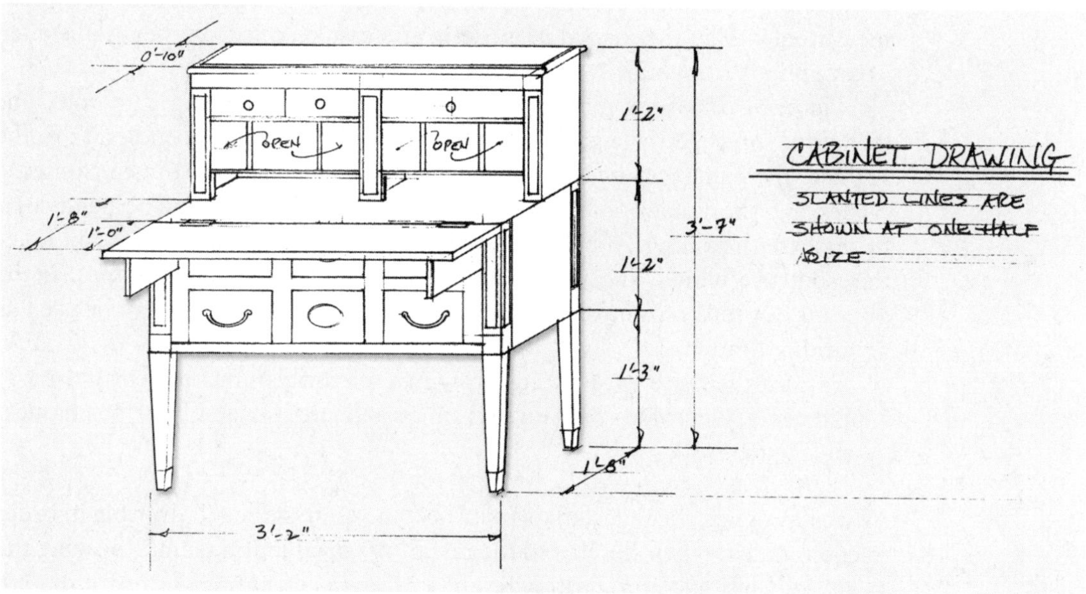

5-20

Pictorial Drawings

a An exploded isometric drawing to show how certain pieces of scenery fit together.

b Isometric drawing used to explain a complicated pivoting movement.

c An oblique drawing of a decorative bracket.

d An isometric drawing using a horizontal axis instead of the usual vertical axis.

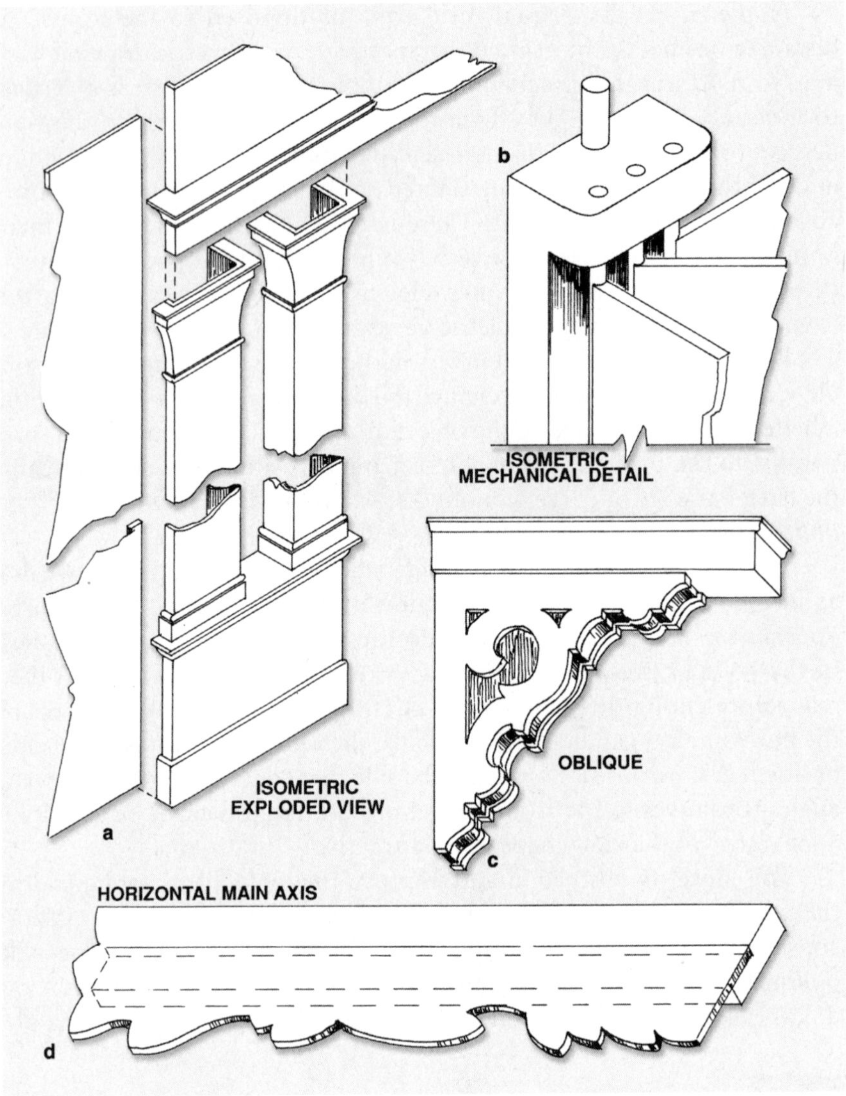

proportion. By always labeling the cabinet drawing and giving the ratio of the measurements on the angled axis, designers can keep it from being mistaken as an oblique drawing.

Pictorial drawings may be dimensioned like a working drawing. The technique, however, is slightly different. Instead of being perpendicular to the surface, the extension lines are drawn as extensions of one of the isometric planes, and the dimension line is parallel to the object rather than perpendicular to the extension line. To help give the feeling that the dimension is in one of the isometric planes, the figures are slanted with the extension lines. If the object is not too complicated, a dimensioned pictorial drawing can be used as a working drawing.

Besides their use as working drawings, pictorials are frequently used as supplementary views to explain bits of complicated assembly or mechanical detail (Figure 5-20).

As we have seen, then, designers must become quite skilled at drafting in order to communicate their designs to the rest of the production team. Knowing the tools, conventions, and approaches of drafting is essential to theatre design.

PART II

Realizing the Design

"Between the initial idea and the finished piece lies a gulf we can see across, but never fully chart. The truly special moments in art-making lie in those moments when concept is converted to reality—those moments when the gulf is being crossed. Precise descriptions fail, but it connects to that wonderful condition in which the work seems to make itself and the artist serves only as guide or mediator, allowing all things to be possible."

DAVID BAYLES AND TED ORLAND
ART AND FEAR

6

The Scene Shop, Tools, and Equipment

Before the ideas of the designer can reach the stage, the designs, in the form of working drawings, have to go through a preparation or construction period. The scaled model is transformed into full-scale elements of scenery, the graded wash in the sketch becomes a carefully painted backdrop, and what appears to be an insignificant spot on the elevation is fashioned into a particular bit of detail. Step by step, all the scenery is fitted together on the stage, under lights, and in final form.

Although the study of technical production is placed here in the logical order of the development of a stage setting, it presents knowledge a scene designer should possess *before* beginning a design. For this reason a study of technical production is a necessary part of a scene designer's training and background. As the architect understands building techniques and materials, so should the scene designer know about methods of constructing and handling scenery as well as the uses of theatrical materials and techniques. A logical place to begin is with a survey of the tools and materials that are used to make scenery and an examination of the working procedures of a scenery shop.

THE SCENERY SHOP

Often, scenery is built and painted under the adverse conditions of an inadequate shop. Designers soon learn that an ill-equipped shop with sparse working space limits the types and amount of scenery that can be built and painted. Occasionally they find themselves in the enviable position of being able to plan their own shop or at least asked to specify the space requirements of the ideal scenery shop. In preparation for such an occasion, the designer should have some knowledge of the space requirements and layout of a good scenery shop.

Space Requirements

The overall area of a scenery shop depends on four things: the size of the stage the shop is to serve; the location of the shop in relation to the stage and storage areas; the number and kinds of productions to be produced in an average season; and the nature of the shop's working procedure and personnel.

The size of the stage, or in some cases several stages, that the shop will serve determines the size of the shop itself. Because a large stage requires large elements of scenery, its shop would need an expansive space in which to make them. Similarly, if a shop will serve more than one stage, it will need to have enough space to accommodate large quantities of scenery.

The location of the scenery shop may also affect its size. For example, a shop near the stage can sometimes use stage space to construct scenery; the shop therefore could be relatively small. This assumes, of course, that the stage is not occupied by a production during the building period. On the other hand, a shop in a remote location might need additional space to store scenery and properties as well as supply construction and painting areas. Although a distant shop requires the handling of scenery from the shop to the stage and back again, it does allow workers to operate free of preperformance uses of the stage. A shop adjacent to the stage will need to consider factors such as soundproofing and careful scheduling to avoid problems. Further, traffic in and out of the shop from users of adjacent spaces may present difficulties, depending on the building layout. Some conflict with rehearsals and performances may be unavoidable, which will render the shop inoperative much of the time.

The specific uses intended for a shop also determine its size. Does this organization produce strictly dramas on a small scale? Will the space be rented to outside users or other departments? Will it be used as a roadhouse for big touring productions? Does it function as the maintenance shop for a larger facility? The answers to these and similar questions help determine the space requirements of a scenery shop. A repertory company, for example, would require enormous storage space to preserve the scenery of numerous productions, even though it creates only one or two new productions a year. A group producing opera or musical-comedy would have a greater demand for scenery than would a company that mounts intimately scaled productions.

The final factors influencing the overall size of the shop are the shop procedures and personnel. The nature of the shop's personnel and working hours may vary from a staff of full-time professionals to scattered groups of part-time student apprentices or volunteers. A small, highly skilled staff working steadily can use building space more efficiently than can large sporadic groups requiring sufficient space to do many separate jobs at once. A further evaluation of the space requirements resulting from shop procedure includes an analysis of the areas of work, tools and equipment, and materials of the average scenery shop.

Work Areas

The shop is divided into areas related to the various steps in the process of building and painting. These areas correspond to the following functions: (1) receiving materials, (2) storing materials and tools, (3) layout, (4) cutting and working lumber, (5) framing and covering basic units of scenery, (6) the

6-1

Scenery Shop

Here is a plan of a scenery shop for a modest theatre. Notice that the layout is based on the various functions of the shop.

1 The shop needs areas for cutting and framing scenic units as well as tool and lumber storage. The major power tools normally include a radial arm saw, table saw, band saw, drill press, sander, mitre saw, and panel saw. Two work tables are essential, as well as a dust-collection system. There must also be storage space for short and long pieces of lumber (and metal) and an office for the technical director or project manager.

2 The prop construction and maintenance area contains a spray-painting booth, wood lathe, work bench, and furniture work table. Note that this area should have forced ventilation.

3 The metalworking shop also has forced ventilation. In the room are a welding table and electric welder, a work bench with vise and bench grinder, an anvil, gas welding tanks, and various cutting tools.

4 The paint and trial assembly area must have enough space and height for a trial assembly of all or a portion of a set (ideally the same size as the full stage). There is enough floor space to stretch the largest drop used onstage, and enough height to accommodate a vertical paint frame. Paint storage is adjacent.

5 A sewing room for draperies and drops has a storage room as well.

6 The area for working plastic is well ventilated. Vacuum forming, printing, and an area for constructing small properties are located here.

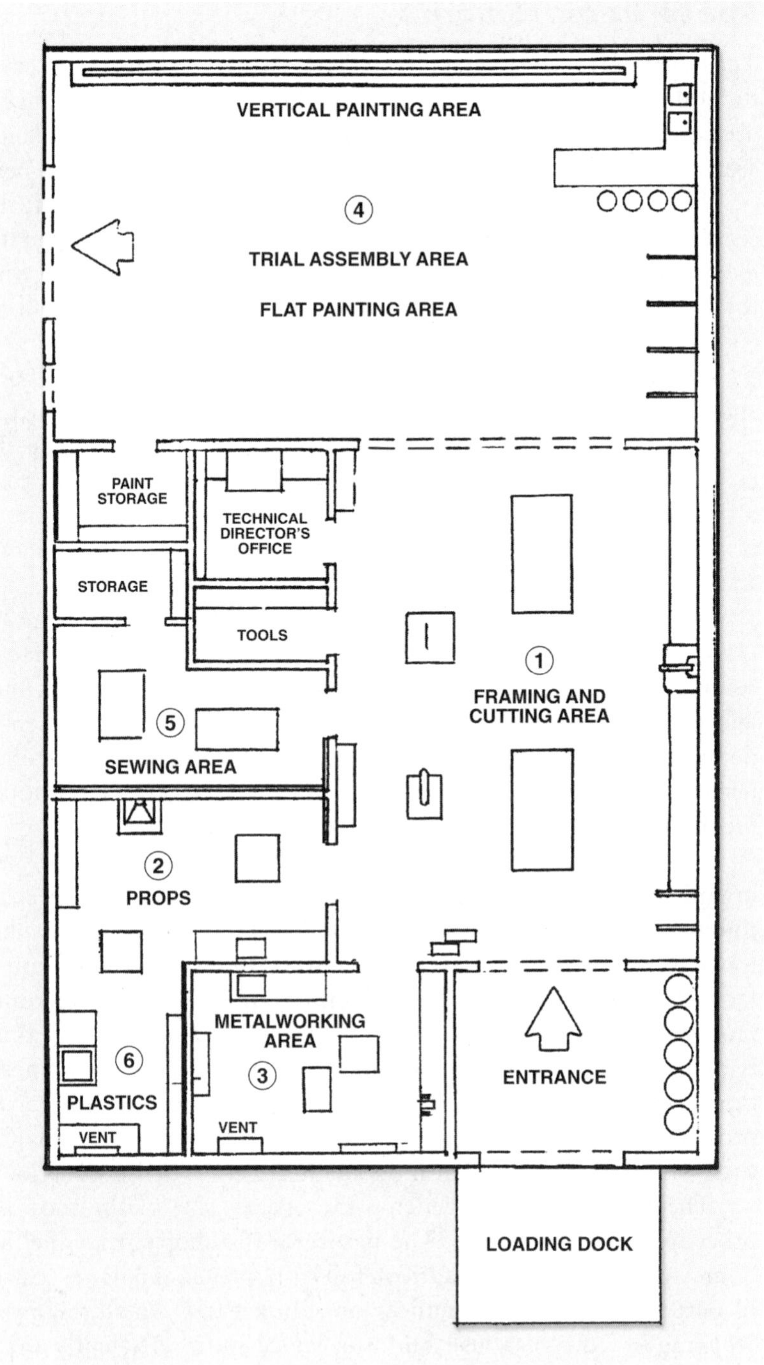

trial assembly of basic units into portions or all of the complete setting, (7) metalworking, (8) plastic working, (9) property preparation, and (10) scenery painting. (See Figure 6-1 for a sample shop plan.)

1. *Receiving.* The first area to be used in the shop is the receiving area, into which all major materials will arrive from a loading dock. Receiving should be large enough to hold a palette, enabling easy movement into the shop.

2. *Storage.* All shops need space for storing materials and small tools. This means that the space must accommodate lumber racks, pipe and structural

steel racks, paint bins, and hardware cabinets. Provisions should also be made for the storage of brushes near the painting area and of small tools near the woodworking area.

3. *Layout.* In planning how all of the pieces of scenery will work together, it is often necessary to draw out the larger pieces. This part of the building process can save immense amounts of time later.

4. *The woodworking area.* In this area the lumber is worked (bored, planed, cut, and so on). There should be space for the large power tools such as a table saw, band saw, drill press, and panel saw, as well as workbenches. A large shop would include an air compressor and storage tank for pneumatic tools. A heavy-duty compressor can also serve the painting area and property shop.

Careful consideration should be given to the lighting of the woodworking area as well as the other work areas. The location of power outlets convenient to the working positions of power tools in all areas is essential. Also, each power tool should ideally have its own dust collection system to contain waste as the work is being done.

5. *The framing area.* The framing and covering of scenery can take place in the center of the shop, often on template benches, but the joining or hinging of units of scenery together must take place in a larger area. Template benches are waist-high work tables on casters so they can be moved easily out of the way. A base size of 5 feet by 10 feet allows for the easy construction of a 4 by 8 platform. Add-on tables of 5 feet by 5 feet and 2½ feet by 10 feet are ideal.

6. *The assembly area.* This space ideally should be as large as the stage area and high enough to stand the scenery upright. Besides being a trial assembly area, it can offer enough floor space to paint flats and to lay out full-scale patterns of irregularly shaped scenery.

7. *The metalworking area.* This area should be near the assembly area, because some metalwork is used to brace scenery or to support weight-bearing forms. This is where metal will be cut, bent, and joined (bolted or welded). The welding area should be well ventilated, have a concrete floor, and be separate from the other areas, if only by a welding screen.

8. *The plastic-working area.* The working of plastic in all forms (foam casting thermoplastic and the sculpturing of foam) needs a separate space. Because of the fumes and dust, ventilation is critical. Occasionally, plastic working can be done in part of the property area.

9. *The property preparations area.* The most frequently neglected area in shop planning is the space to build properties. The altering, repairing, upholstering, and finishing of furniture is a specialized operation that requires different tools, materials, and paints from those found in the scenery shop. It should be in an area protected from the dust, spattering paint, and general confusion of the scenery shop.

10. *The painting area.* This area should be near a sink, gas or electric burners, and the paint bins. Vertical painting, which occupies the least amount of floor space, requires enough overhead clearance to stand the scenery upright. The

simplest vertical painting method is to mount the scenery on a fixed frame against a wall and paint from a rolling platform (see Chapter 9).

Certain painting techniques require horizontal painting and, in fact, many scenic artists prefer this method. It requires a large floor on which to lay the scenic pieces. A wooden paint deck allows for easy attachment of drops to the floor.

The lighting in this area must be bright and, if fluorescent, color corrected.

Scenery Materials and Tools

An ideal scenery shop is well stocked with appropriate materials and tools. Here we consider briefly most of the materials that are used for making scenery. To compile a comprehensive list is, of course, next to impossible, because designers and technicians are constantly bringing new materials into the theatre every day as well as discovering new uses for old materials.

Materials can be divided and classified as follows:

1. Structural (lumber and metal)
2. Cover stock (fabrics and sheet goods)
3. Hardware (joining and stage hardware)
4. Rigging (rope, cable, wire, and chain)
5. Paints and related supplies (to be discussed in Chapter 9)

Please note that the number of kinds of tools and materials used in the theatre are truly limitless. Because of the special needs of theatre scenery, designers and technicians can "borrow" from any other industry. Often, the scene shop includes inexpensive tools and materials developed for reasons completely unrelated to theatre construction but nonetheless have proven to be quite helpful in the scene shop.

BUILDING SCENERY WITH WOOD

Types of Wood

Lumber is one of two principal structural materials used in the theatre (the other is metal, to be discussed in the next section). Because the availability and cost of lumber varies from region to region, we cannot specify which specific type of lumber should be used. Shops use the kind of lumber that is most convenient and affordable at the time. Some have even turned to lightweight structural steel in addition to or instead of wood for framing.

Recycled wood is more readily available than ever, although it can be more expensive than regular wood or require a shop equipped to resize salvaged lumber. Some shops use *synthetic wood* products (such as Trex, by Mobil Oil Corporation), which are made of recycled plastic grocery bags and salvaged wood chips. Manufactured wood products available today include I-beams, Microlam, and Perra-lam. The latter two are wood fibers shredded and manufactured to form a board the same length and width as a 2 by 4. These are useful as structural framing members.

URL http://www.trex.com

To fill the general needs of scenic construction, lumber must be lightweight, strong, straight, and inexpensive. White pine offers the best combination of weight and strength, but it is not readily available in all areas. Although woods such as spruce are lighter, they do not have the strength, and they tend to splinter and split. The hardwoods are stronger, of course, but weigh and cost too much and are more difficult to work.

Although lumber selection and construction techniques vary from region to region, many types of lumber are widely found in scene shops. The use of plywood as a cover stock for framed scenery construction is one example. Other common types of lumber include Duron, lauan, Masonite, MDF (medium density fiberboard), and OSB (commonly called chipboard).

URL http://www.masonite.com

The type of materials and construction used need to fit the specific needs of the production. The approach to a one-night-only production and the materials used are likely to be quite different than that of a tour or a show that is expected to have a long run.

Grades and Sizes of Lumber

At the lumberyard, wood is classified by quality, determined by the straightness of the grain and freedom from knots. Hence, clear white pine is the highest quality of pine. Wood is further classified according to its expected use. A board that is to become trim or a finished surface is of a higher quality than one to be used as a structural member hidden from view. Prices vary regionally.

The *select grades* of lumber are designated by A, B, C, and D. Hence B-select or better is a high-grade pine. C-select is used in the construction of paneled doors, window sashes, turned work, and architectural moldings.

The *common grades* are numbered 1 to 5. They are not intended for a finished surface, although many times 1- and 2-common are used as knotty pine paneling. In general, 2-common is the usual framing material for scenery unless better grades of pine are available at reasonable prices. Assuming a long run, a higher quality might be used, but at considerable expense. Construction grade and pressure-treated lumber (for outdoor use) are also available but very expensive.

The *stock sizes* of lumber refer to its rough-cut size—not to the finished dimension after the wood has been dressed (planed or smooth on all sides). Thus 1 by 3 is really ¾ inch by 2½ inches. Stock lengths vary but the most common are 8, 10, 12, 14, and 16 feet (the longest stocked length). Longer lengths can be obtained on special order.

Because 2 by 4's are so commonly used in home building, a "pre-cut stud" used in housing construction will often be 93 inches (as opposed to the 96 inches in 8 feet). This is because the common height for a room in a modern home is 8 feet. In framing a home, there is a top and a bottom 2 by 4 plate, each at a thickness of 1½ inches. Subtracting this 3 inches from a total height of 8 feet leaves us with 93 inches. When ordering 8-foot lengths of 2 by 4, it is wise to be quite specific. The loss of those 3 inches could be critical.

Most often, lumber is sold by the linear foot as just described. The common unit of measurement for lumber used to be the **board-foot,** and occasionally it is still used, particularly for finer types of wood such as cherry, walnut, and maple. A board foot is the equivalent of a 1-inch-thick board that is 1 foot square. A 16-foot length of 1 by 3, for example, contains 4 board-feet. A piece of lumber of any size can be reduced from its linear dimensions into board-feet.

board-foot A measurement of lumber equivalent to a board 1-inch thick and 1-foot square.

Special shapes such as "rounds" are stocked in diameters from ¾ inches to 1½ inches and sometimes as large as 3 inches in diameter. Dowel is available in ⅛- to 1-inch diameters and 3-foot lengths made of maple and birch.

URL http://www.cyberyard.com/termsglossary

Other special shapes are stock moldings, which are made in a great variety of sizes and contours. Before specifying moldings, the designer should check local suppliers, because names and shapes vary throughout the country. See Figure 6-2 for examples of stock lumber and molding shapes.

6-2

Stock Lumber and Molding Shapes

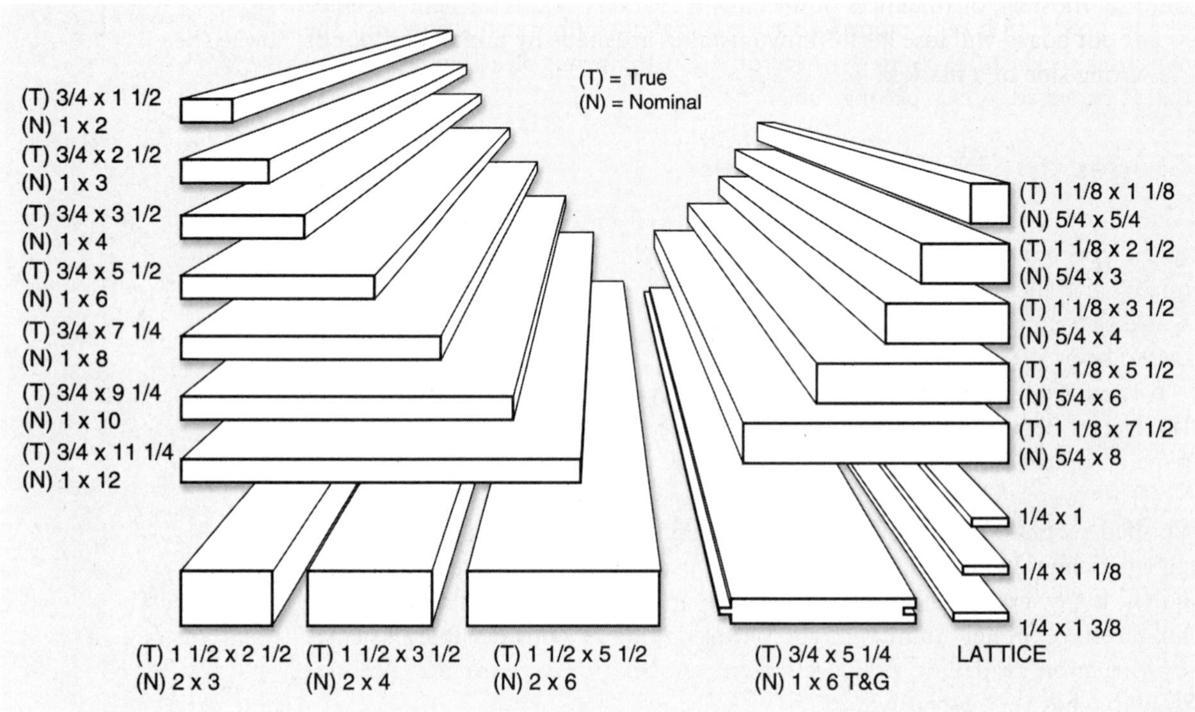

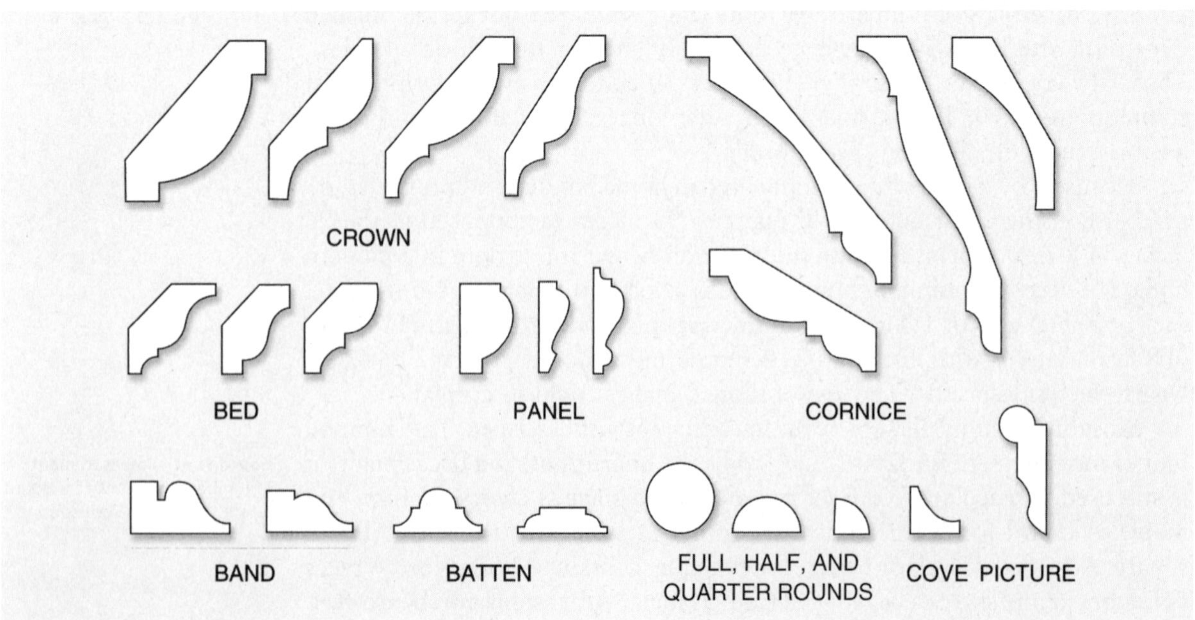

Measuring and Marking Tools

To build scenery it is necessary to cut, pare or shape, bore, and join the wood. The tools to work the wood are either hand tools for limited and special work or power tools for mass production and precision work. The working and joining of wood, however, is always preceded by careful measuring and marking.

Tools for measuring and marking are used not only with each technique of working wood but also in every step in the construction and assembly of the completed setting (see Figure 6-3). Almost all mistakes in building are directly traceable to incorrect measurements or a misinterpreted mark. The importance of accurate measurements cannot be overstressed.

Mistakes are often made, particularly by inexperienced carpenters, from ignoring the **kerf,** or thickness of the cutting blade. Wood is cut, not sheered, so any cut board will lose kerf. Many mistakes are made by taking kerf out of the wrong side of a marked line.

kerf Thickness of a saw's cutting blade.

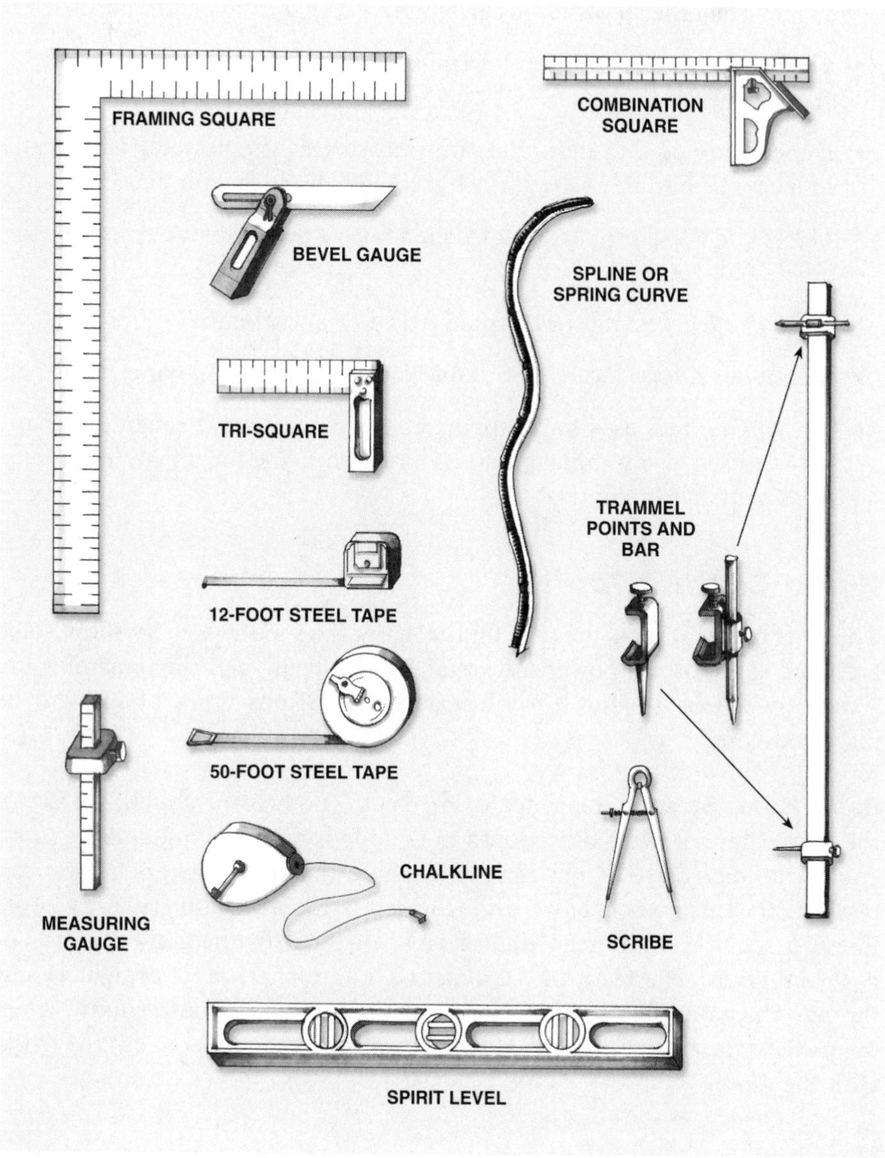

6-3
Woodworking Measuring Tools

Some tools are obviously for measuring only (6-foot rule and 50-foot tape); others are specifically for marking (tri-square, bevel gauge, scribe, spirit level, spline, and center square). A few tools, however, are designed for both measuring and marking:

- The *combination squarer,* with its adjustable sliding bar, is calibrated for measuring as well as establishing a marking guide for 90-degree and 45-degree angles.
- The *framing square,* with calibrated edges, is a useful tool for establishing a right angle for framing and in marking the angle cut of a stair carriage.
- The *marking gauge* is calibrated to mark for a rip cut, an operation that can be duplicated by the combination square.
- Within the group of marking tools, the *tri-square* is calibrated for limited measuring, although its chief function is as a marking guide for a 90-degree angle cut. The bar or beam holding the *trammel points* is sometimes calibrated to measure the radius of the circle or arc it is to swing. The other tools in this group serve as marking guides only.
- The *bevel gauge* is designed for transferring or saving a predetermined angle or bevel.
- *Dividers* are used to mark the same measurement repeatedly and scratch or mark the outline of the surface at a fixed distance with the other point.
- The *spline* is used to mark an irregular curve or to plot a curved edge in full-scale layout.
- The *spirit level* establishes a true vertical or horizontal.
- The *center square* locates the unmarked center of a circle or round stock.
- The *chalk line* is used for snapping an extremely long, straight line that may be used as a framing guide, as a reference line for full-scale layout, or as a guide for painting.

Wood-Cutting Tools

The chief cutting tool is the saw. Of the many saws in the scenery shop, some are hand saws, others power saws that are handheld, and the remaining are fixed power saws. Figure 6-4 illustrates the various types of saws to be discussed here.

Basic Hand Saws The shape of the tooth (pointed or chisel), the set of the tooth (flare of every other tooth in the opposite direction), and the tooth count (number of teeth per inch) determine the specific work a saw can perform. Because wood has a grain, which is the alternating density of its fibers, it requires a different kind of saw to cut *across* the grain than to cut *with* the grain. The teeth of a *crosscut saw* are sharp and straight to cut through the wood fibers (across the grain, so the largest tooth count), while the teeth of the *ripsaw* are angled and flat-edged like a chisel to cut the wood with the grain.

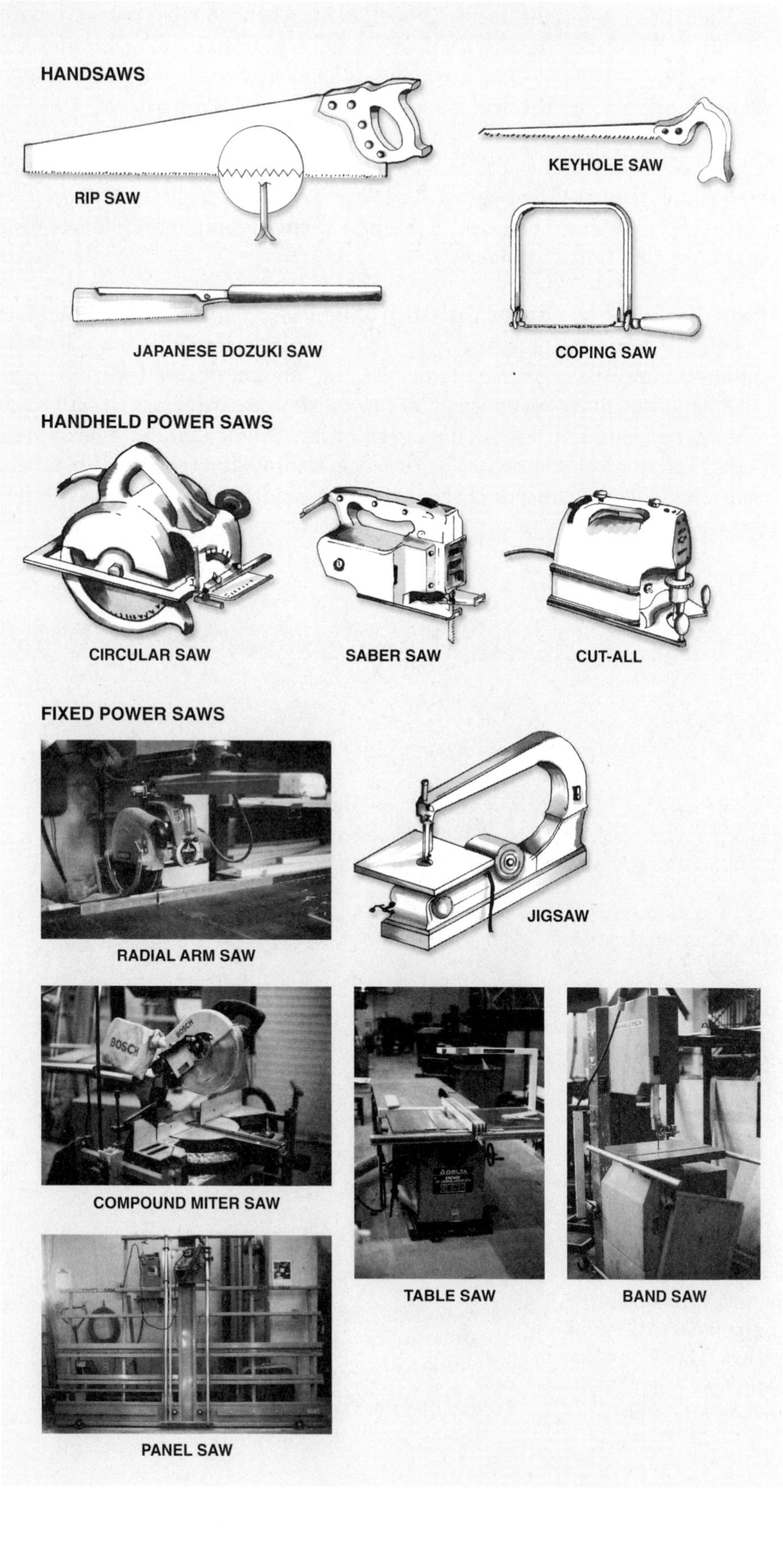

6-4

Wood-Cutting Tools

DRAWINGS BY STEPHEN FOUND, FOUND MARKETING AND DESIGN

The *set* of a saw is the degree of bend every other tooth has away from the saw blade. The set of the saw teeth keeps the saw from binding, because the width of the cut is wider than the blade. When a saw has lost its set, it begins to bind in the cut (see the accompanying box on woodshop safety).

An angled cut or miter can be cut freehand with a crosscut saw, or it can be more easily and accurately cut in a miter box with a backsaw. With a high tooth count, the *backsaw* is a stiff-bladed saw with a straight back that serves as a guide in the miter box. It is extremely useful in mitering moldings for a cornice, picture frame, or panel.

Hand Tools for Irregular Cutting Making scenery demands more than straight-line cutting. A high percentage of the cutting is irregular or scroll work. Cutouts and profile edges require the greatest amount of scroll work.

A hand saw to cut on an irregular line must necessarily have a small blade to be able to turn and follow the irregular line. The *coping saw* has a high tooth count to produce a smoothly cut edge. It also has a removable blade for inside cuts. The deep throat of the frame that holds the blade allows the saw to reach well into the work.

Safety Practice

Woodshop Safety

When working with power tools such as table saws, radial arm saws, drill presses, and handheld power tools, follow these guidelines:

1. Dress appropriately. Avoid loose clothing; net long hair. Wear goggles. For protection from high-level noise, wear earplugs.
2. Keep all blades and drills sharp to prevent chances of the wood kicking back. A dull blade can bind or skip and cause an accident. If the blade binds in the middle of a cut, do not force the cut. Shut off power while holding the wood or the tool firmly until the blade stops completely, then back the work out.
3. When using the sander, be aware of the dust hazard, especially as sawdust fumes of certain woods may be toxic. The sawdust should be gathered or handled with caution. Wear a dust mask and avoid inhaling fumes. Especially when sanding rigid foam, use a respirator, keeping in mind the importance of using the appropriate filter for the material being worked. Follow manufacturer's instructions for proper use as well.
4. Make sure the space under work is clear. Do not cut the sawhorse.
5. If you use an unusual setting on the saw or drill press, return it to a standard setting after work is finished.
6. Ask for help to crosscut or rip a long board.
7. When using a power tool, concentrate on what you are doing and pay attention to where your hands are.
8. After the work is finished, clean up and return tools.
9. Above all, listen to and follow the work procedures of the shop in which you are working.
10. Use the right tool for each job.

The *keyhole saw,* with a high tooth count, is made for heavy, coarse, and fast work. The small blade, although not as small as the coping saw, allows irregular cutting beyond the limits a coping saw can reach.

Handheld Power Saws With a *portable circular saw,* a carpenter can bring the saw to the work rather than having to bring the work to the saw. It can be used as a ripsaw or crosscut saw; because of its light weight and small blade, its depth of cut and accuracy are limited.

For irregular cutting, the *saber saw,* which is a portable jigsaw, does not limit the size of the work. It is a versatile tool for scroll cutting at any stage of assembly.

The *cut-awl* is designed for light, detailed cutting. It requires a padded bench or table for satisfactory results.

Fixed Power Saws Power tools made for straight-line cutting are the table saw and radial arm saw, as well as the portable circular saw. Each may be fitted with a rip, crosscut, or combination blade for specific work.

A 10-inch, tilting-arbor *table saw* with miter gauge and rip fence is a basic piece of equipment. It is heavy enough to do precision work in quantity. It miters and rips with ease and accuracy.

A 10- to 12-inch *radial arm saw* provides the necessary power for cutting heavy lumber. Its pullover action above the wood and long table make it an accurate crosscut and limited mitering tool. It is not an accurate ripping tool.

For both of these saws, the work of the scene shop suggests a powerful 5-horsepower saw although a 3-horsepower one is adequate. A 1-horsepower saw is fine for light use.

The Power Compound Miter Saw A **miter** cut is any cut across the grain of the wood (as opposed to a **bevel** cut, which is in the same direction as the grain) and can be done on the radial arm saw, table saw, or miter box. A simple miter is used for turning a corner with two bands of wood or molding. Each piece of wood is cut at an angle that bisects that of the corner. In a typical right-angle corner for example, each piece of molding is cut at an angle of 45 degrees.

miter Any cut across the grain of the wood.

bevel Any cut in the same direction as the grain of the wood.

When a molding changes planes as well as turning a corner (such as the molding following an angled roof line turning a corner of a house), it requires a *compound miter.* To cut a compound miter, the saw blade has to be tilted as well as angled. A compound miter saw has these features.

The *power compound miter saw* is a very specialized power tool, and some models can be quite expensive. It does, however, take the guesswork out of cutting a miter. A *sliding compound miter saw* allows for a larger capacity and cutting longer boards.

Power Tools for Irregular Cutting Power tools that speed up the production of **scroll work** are the band saw and jigsaw. With its continuous blade, the *band saw* is limited to outside cutting and to work no larger than the depth of its throat. A band saw with a 20-inch throat will serve the average need of a scenery shop if it is supplemented with other equipment to do inside cutting. The *jigsaw,* with its removable straight blade and deep throat, is made for both inside and outside scroll cutting.

scroll work Curved, detailed design resembling a rolled piece of paper.

Wood-Shaping Tools

Hand Tools The simplest tool for shaping wood freehand is the chisel. Although the hand chisel cannot compare in speed and accuracy to a power tool, it is an excellent tool for cleaning up a power-cut **dado, rabbet,** or routed area. A set of chisels in a theatre shop should include a variety of widths, from 4 to 14 inches.

dado Notch cut into a board, allowing a second piece to fit into it.

rabbet Wide groove cut into the face of a board, allowing another board to fit into it.

The paring edge of the chisel is shown in the inset of Figure 6-5. The top bevel is forged, but the lower bevel is sharpened into a cutting edge. Note that the angle is about 45 degrees. When the edge becomes dull or nicked, one can resharpen it by first reshaping the edge on the coarse emery wheel and then grinding a new cutting surface at 45 degrees. The sharpening is finished on an oil stone.

The *smoothing plane* can pare a surface to an accurate dimension. It smooths with the grain of the wood, in contrast to the small *block plane,* which works across the grain. The block plane can smooth or shape the end of a board and can be used to correct a bad saw cut or shorten a member to improve a delicate fit.

The *rasp* and *Surform,* a replaceable rasp blade in a holder, are also designed to work across the grain. They can do the same shaping faster than the block plane can, but they leave a rougher finish.

Power Tools Probably the most useful and versatile small power tool for shaping is the *router.* Depending on the particular bit being used, it can perform a wide variety of jobs. With straight bits it can cut **tenons**, dados, rabbets, flush cuts, and, with an extension guide, large circles. A wide range of molding bits are available.

tenon A projecting member in a piece of wood or other material for insertion into a mortise to make a joint.

Portable sanders are handy tools at the bench or when brought to the work area. The *disk sander* is best to use when smoothing an end cut. With coarse sandpaper it can reshape or round a cut. It is less effective sanding a flat surface because it tends to leave sanding marks.

With its continuous loop of sandpaper, a handheld belt sander can remove a great amount of wood quickly. Because this sander creates a relatively rough surface, it is often the first tool used in the sanding process.

Lightweight and economical, the *orbital sander* and the *random orbital sander* are excellent tools for smoothing a flat surface. An orbital sander uses a half sheet of regular 9-inch by 11-inch sandpaper. The random orbital sander has a round base. The entire plate orbits as the disk spins, providing the advantage of faster sanding and reducing swirl marks. This is important when the surface is to be finished and seen, as in a stained table top. There is also a small, quarter-sheet palm grip orbital sander for finish sanding.

The *power plane* does the same job as a handheld smoothing plane, but faster and more efficiently. Its rotating drum has two or three knives that do the smoothing. It deals with the end grain of a board (such as the corner top of a door) better than does a plane with nonrotating blades. The *jointer* is a type of power plane. Its rotating blades can smooth the edge or surface of a board. By setting the fence at an angle, the edge of the board can be planed with an angle.

Power tools designed to do various shaping and smoothing operations are limited mostly to special cuts. With a *rotary planer* or *joiner,* for example, a woodworker can smooth a board, size a board by changing the depth of cut,

6-5

Wood-Shaping Tools

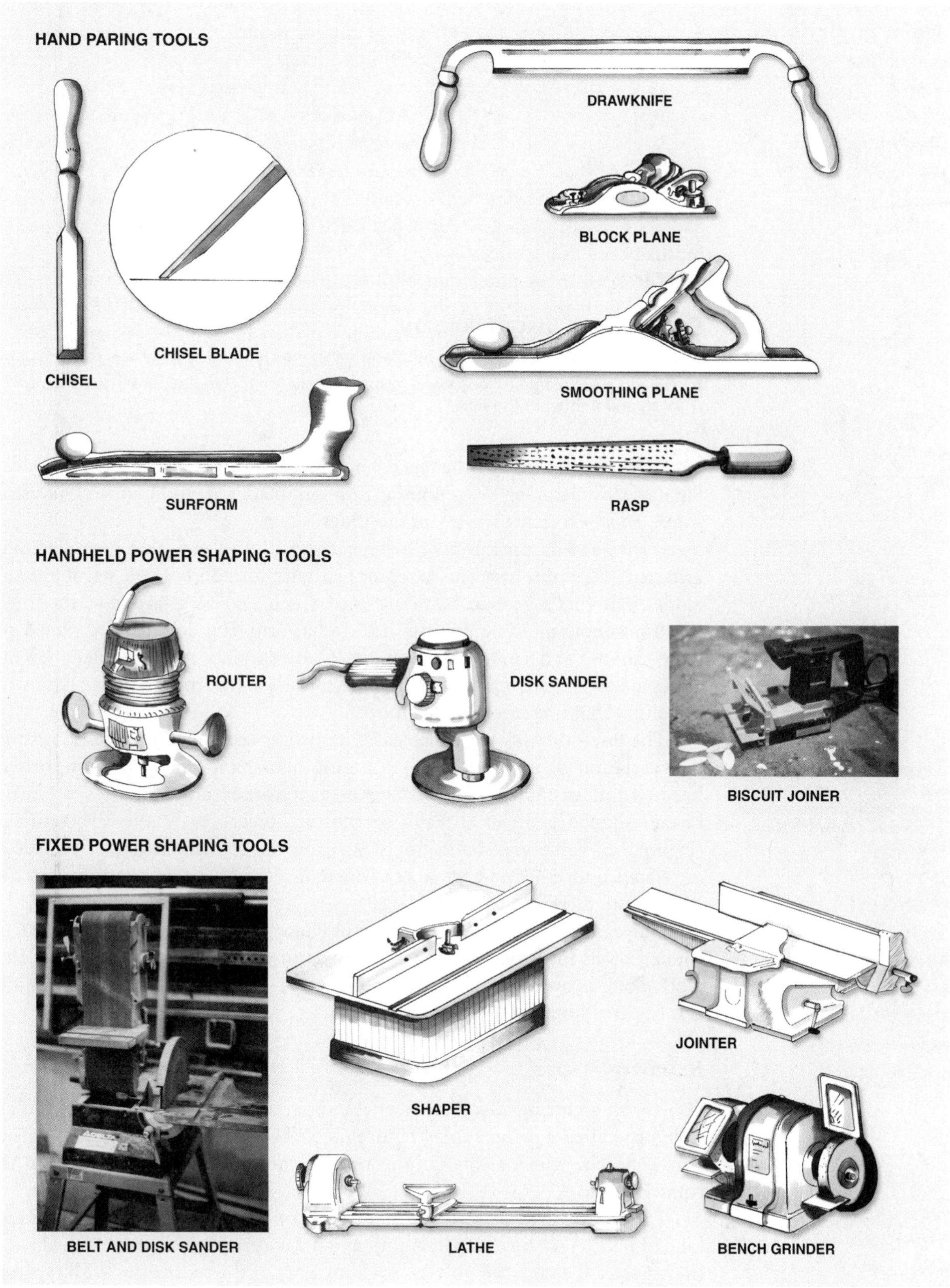

DRAWINGS BY STEPHEN FOUND, FOUND MARKETING AND DESIGN

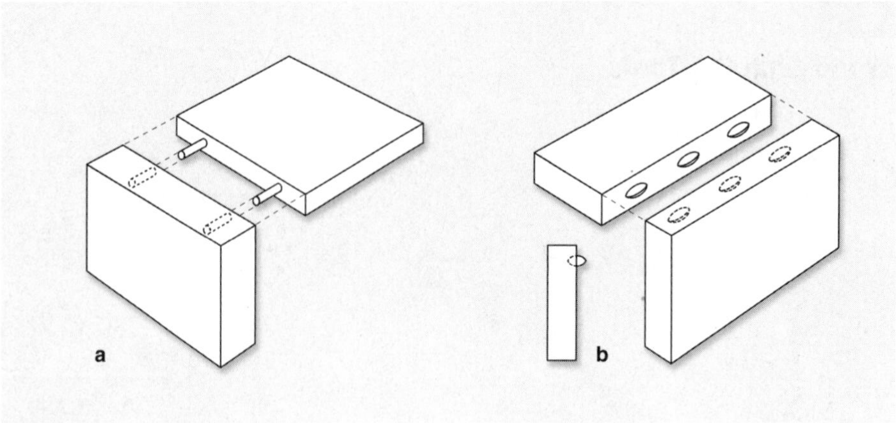

6-6

Pegging and Biscuit Joinery

a Here is a simple pegged joint, with two dowels inserted into appropriately sized holes.

b The more common method now is to use a biscuit joint. The glue causes the biscuit to swell and tighten in the hole.

bevel the edge by angling the fence, and cut a rabbet on one side of the board. Similarly, by changing or combining different blades, a woodworker can use a *rotary shaper* to cut a variety of moldings.

Some shaping operations can be performed on the table saw and radial arm saw. The table saw can be equipped with a dado head, a set of special blades that cuts a groove. Molding cutters can also be attached to the table saw for simple molding cutting. The radial arm saw can also be rigged to dado, shape, and rout. However, these adjustments must be made by an experienced carpenter as they can be extremely dangerous. It is far better to use a tool that is created for the job.

pegging Method of attaching two pieces of wood by inserting a small wooden dowel (peg) into a hole drilled into both pieces.

The *biscuit joiner* is used to ease the process of attaching two boards. It is a variation of **pegging** but uses an almond-shaped piece of compressed beechwood called a *biscuit*. The biscuit joiner cuts a series of half-biscuit-shaped grooves in each of the two pieces of wood to be joined (Figure 6-6). Glue is added to the wood and the biscuit, then the two pieces are clamped together and left to dry. The moisture in the glue causes the biscuit to swell, tightening the joint.

One can use a *wood lathe* to *turn* or shape cylinders. A block of wood is rotated on its long axis and shaped with a chisel that can be moved with the work along an adjustable rest. A baluster or spindle for furniture or stair railing can be turned on this tool.

Boring Tools

Tools with a cutting edge that revolves about a central axis to cut a circular hole are called boring tools (Figure 6-7). The tool consists of two basic parts: the bit, which is the cutting part of the tool, and the mechanism to rotate the bit.

The types of bits vary greatly, depending on the size and depth of the hole, kind of hole (clean bore, taper, ream), and the nature of the material (hardness, thickness). Likewise, the power-providing part of the tool varies with type of bit used and the speed of rotation necessary to do the work.

6-7

Wood-Boring Tools

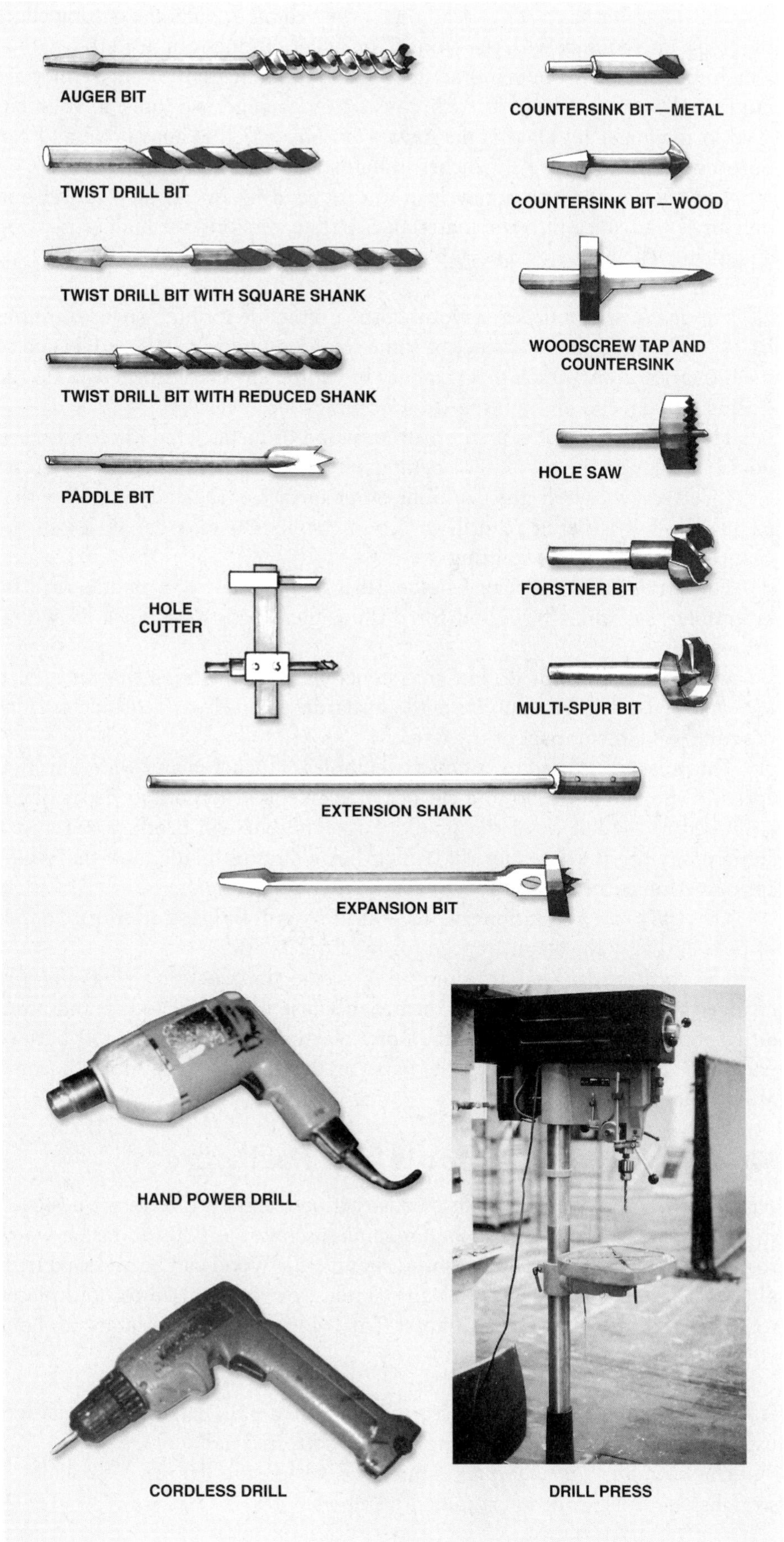
AUGER BIT
COUNTERSINK BIT—METAL
TWIST DRILL BIT
COUNTERSINK BIT—WOOD
TWIST DRILL BIT WITH SQUARE SHANK
WOODSCREW TAP AND COUNTERSINK
TWIST DRILL BIT WITH REDUCED SHANK
HOLE SAW
PADDLE BIT
FORSTNER BIT
HOLE CUTTER
MULTI-SPUR BIT
EXTENSION SHANK
EXPANSION BIT
HAND POWER DRILL
CORDLESS DRILL
DRILL PRESS

The *auger bit* has a screw lead that, when rotated, pulls the cutting edges of the bit into contact with the wood. The auger bit does not need to rotate at a high speed. Augers are manufactured in size differences of 1⁄16 inch. They are numbered by sixteenths of an inch; thus a ½-inch auger would be a No. 8 bit. Also in the auger bit class is the *expansion bit,* which is adjustable and can bore a hole 1¼ inches to 2½ inches in diameter.

Twist drills have no screw lead and depend on speed of rotation and pressure to advance into the material. Separate versions are made for wood and metal. The high-speed portable *power hand drill* is excellent for this type of work.

The *spade* or *paddle bit,* a wood-cutting bit made for high-speed rotation, has a small round shank (¼ inch) for the small power drill. The paddle end of the bit varies from ⅜ inch to 1¼ inches in width. The chisel-like edges do the cutting and depend on high speed for accuracy.

The *countersink bit* is used on either wood or metal after a hole has been bored. It enlarges the top of the opening with a beveled cut deep enough to set a flathead screw or bolt flush with the outer surface of the material. Note that in plexiglass it is better to drill the countersink first in order to lessen the chance of the plexiglass splitting.

The *extension shank* can lengthen the depth of cut of a paddle drill by extending its shank. It is good for drilling the length of a block of wood, for example.

Special bits used for drilling into concrete are called *masonry bits.* They look like twist drill bits but are made of hardened steel with carbide set into the tip to take the impact of the work.

The *hole-saw* is used to cut oversized holes (1½ inches and wider) at high speed. Although it is faster and cleaner than an expansion bit, its depth of cut is limited to the length of the shank. Two bits that will produce holes in a similar way are the *Forstner bit,* which has a smooth blade, and the *multi-spur bit.* Unlike the hole-saw, they can be used at an angle.

The *drill press* is a stationary power drill. Woodworkers can control depth of bore and vary the shank's speed for precision work.

The *cordless drill* has revolutionized scenic construction. It has literally changed the way that people do theatre, because it is easier to use and more efficient than standard drills. With improvements in the strength of its battery pack and the speed with which the batteries can be recharged, it has become an invaluable tool.

URL http://www.dewalt.com/

URL http://www.deltawoodworking.com/

URL http://www.makita.com/

Wood-Construction Tools and Hardware

Fastening wood to wood is a basic construction technique. Tools are designed to drive or set hardware such as *nails, staples, screws,* or *bolts,* to fasten wood together in a variety of combinations (Figure 6-8). Wood can be attached with glue as a primary fastener, with nails, staples, or screws used to hold pieces together until the glue dries. Chapter 7 provides specific information about construction techniques.

Hammers The *claw hammer* is used to drive a nail. The rounded claw is used to correct mistakes by pulling out a misdirected nail.

The *straight claw hammer,* sometimes called the "ripper," provides a straight claw for prying apart joined members.

6-8

Wood-Construction Tools

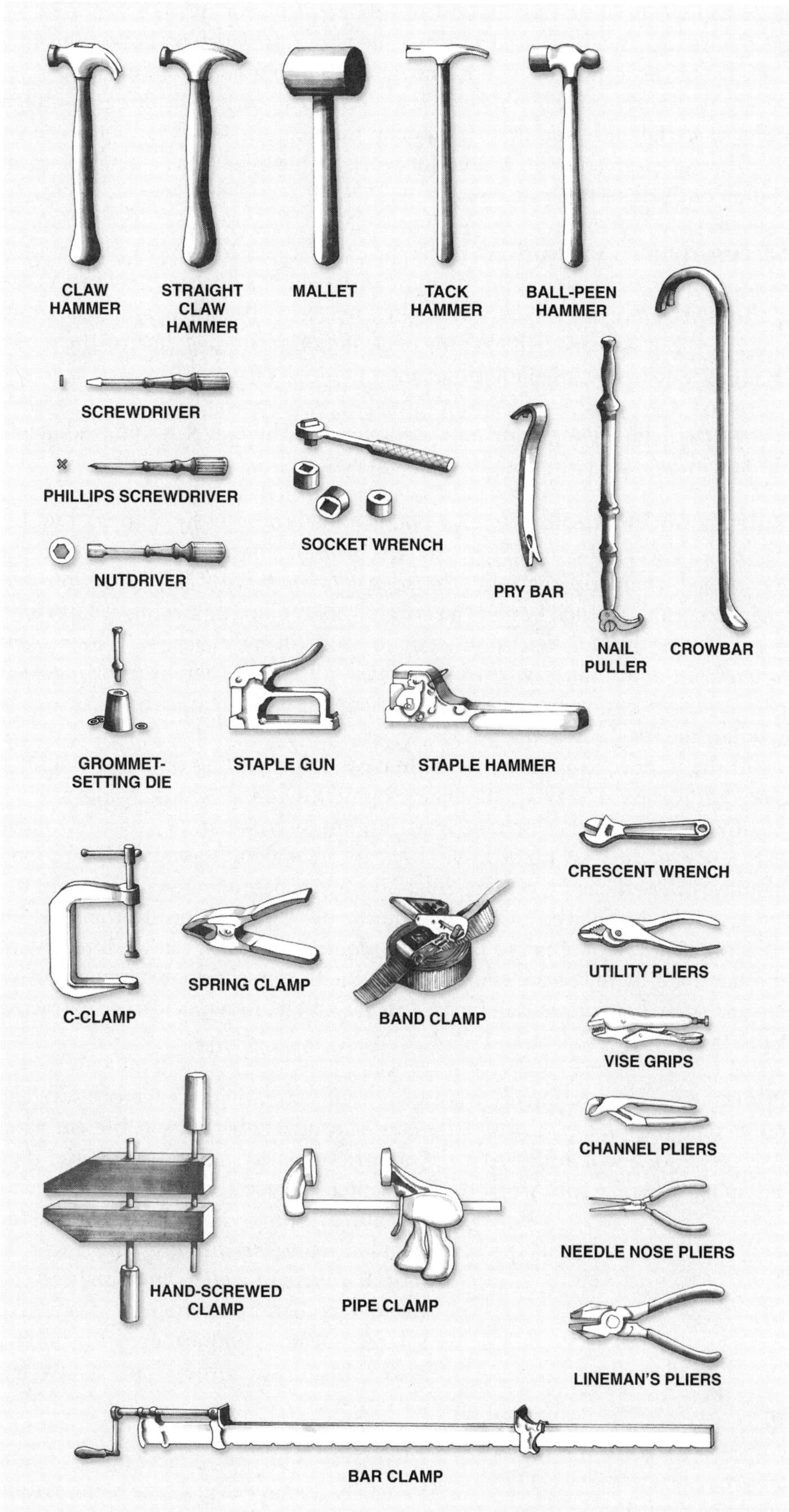
CLAW HAMMER
STRAIGHT CLAW HAMMER
MALLET
TACK HAMMER
BALL-PEEN HAMMER
SCREWDRIVER
PHILLIPS SCREWDRIVER
NUTDRIVER
SOCKET WRENCH
PRY BAR
NAIL PULLER
CROWBAR
GROMMET-SETTING DIE
STAPLE GUN
STAPLE HAMMER
CRESCENT WRENCH
C-CLAMP
SPRING CLAMP
BAND CLAMP
UTILITY PLIERS
VISE GRIPS
CHANNEL PLIERS
NEEDLE NOSE PLIERS
HAND-SCREWED CLAMP
PIPE CLAMP
LINEMAN'S PLIERS
BAR CLAMP

The *mallet,* which has a wooden, rubber, or plastic head, is not used for heavy driving. It can be used to tap a member into place without damaging the edge or surface of the wood. The mallet is also used with the chisel.

The *magnetic tack hammer* is used primarily in upholstering to attach heavy material and padding to a wooden frame.

The *ball-peen hammer* is used for working metal and has a hemispherical end on one side of the head.

Screwdrivers Screwdrivers come in several types for screws with *slotted head, Phillips head, hex head,* or *nut driver.* There are also screwdrivers for *Robertson* or recessed squarehead screws, which are becoming more and more popular. Their advantage is that the drive does not slip and destroy the screw head, as it does with the Phillips head.

Staplers The *staple gun* drives the staple when the trigger is squeezed, while the *staple hammer* requires a hammering action.

Bolt-Fastening Tools When wood is joined together by bolting, a tool is needed to tighten the nut. There are several tools, besides the nut driver just mentioned, that grip the nut. The *socket wrench* with ratchet action and interchangeable wrench heads is a very efficient tool for tightening or loosening a nut. It also has an extension shaft to work in tight places. The *crescent wrench* has adjustable jaws to fit the sides of the nut, thereby applying even pressure. As a last resort, pliers can be used, but with great care, because they can damage the sides of the nut.

If the joint is temporary, to facilitate the dismantling of a scenic unit, a *wing nut* is used. The wing nut can be tightened and loosened by hand.

To correct mistakes or take apart a joint, a *crowbar, pry bar* ("Wonder bar"), or *nail puller* is needed. All three are strong and, because of their long handles, offer efficient leverage. Their leverage is based on the principle of the *lever.* A long bar placed over a fulcrum or pivot point close to the work (a rock to be moved or a nail to be pulled) requires less energy at the long end of the bar than at the short end (Figure 6-9). If conventional methods prove unsuccessful, *bolt cutters* can be used to cut a bolt, allowing it to be extracted from the scenery.

Pliers Pliers are essentially a gripping tool with a wide range of uses. The most common—*utility* or *slip-joint pliers*—are adjustable to two different sizes. A *channel lock* will adjust to a larger variety of sizes. With *vise grips,* after clamping down on the work, the carpenter can let go while the vise grips remain gripping. For more delicate or detailed work, *needle nose pliers* will be useful. *Lineman's pliers* are used less by carpenters than by electricians. They have a large, fat nose and are used for pulling wires. In addition they have a jaw for cutting wire.

6-9

The Lever

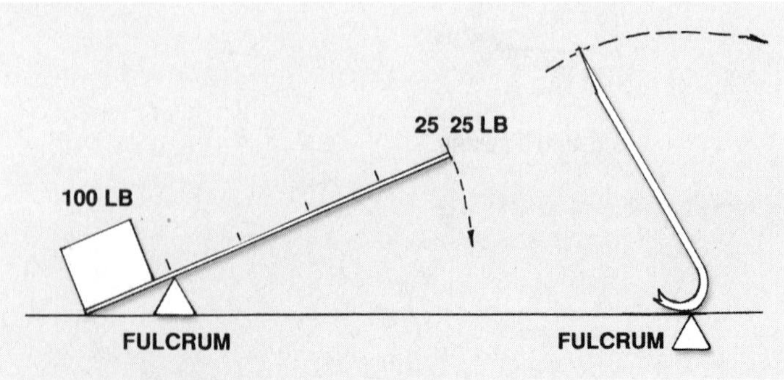

Clamps The final method of wood joining is gluing. Because glue requires time to set, one needs clamps to hold the members firmly in place while the glue dries. The *C-clamp* holds boards face-to-face, as does the *wood clamp* (also called *hand-screwed clamp or Jorgensen clamp*); however, because the latter is made of wood, it damages the surfaces less. The *bar clamp* is designed to hold the boards edge-to-edge.

There are several variations on the bar clamp. One is the *pipe clamp,* which uses a manufactured set of jaws that can be attached to any length of standard pipe. This provides an almost unlimited clamping range and a bit more flexibility than the standard bar clamp.

Besides being an easy-on/easy-off clamp for holding a joint, the heavy-duty *spring clamp* can serve the carpenter as an extra hand. This type of clamp works best on face-to-face joints. While the extra-strong spring holds the joint firmly together, the polyvinyl sleeve protects the wood. A spring clamp with a 4-inch reach is best for all purposes. A *quick grip clamp* allows for quick one-handed clamping.

A *band clamp* uses a woven strap with a ratcheting apparatus to tighten a band around an irregular or curved shape. For example, when adding a facing to a round surface, one would use a band clamp.

URL http://www.mcmaster.com

Pneumatic Tools

Tools driven by air pressure save time and energy. No well-equipped scenery shop should lack a pneumatic nailer and staple gun, which offer great speed and efficiency (Figure 6-10). With the slightest pressure of the finger, a nail or staple is set in one stroke.

6-10

Pneumatic Tools

a Cross section of a pneumatic nailer designed to set finish nails from 1-inch brads to 8d finish nails. See the text for a description of its functions.

b Pneumatic nailer for structural nails 6d to 10d common.

c Stapler for ⅜-inch to 2-inch staples. A 1-inch staple is suitable for attaching corner blocks (used in connecting the parts of soft-covered framed scenery; see Chapter 7).

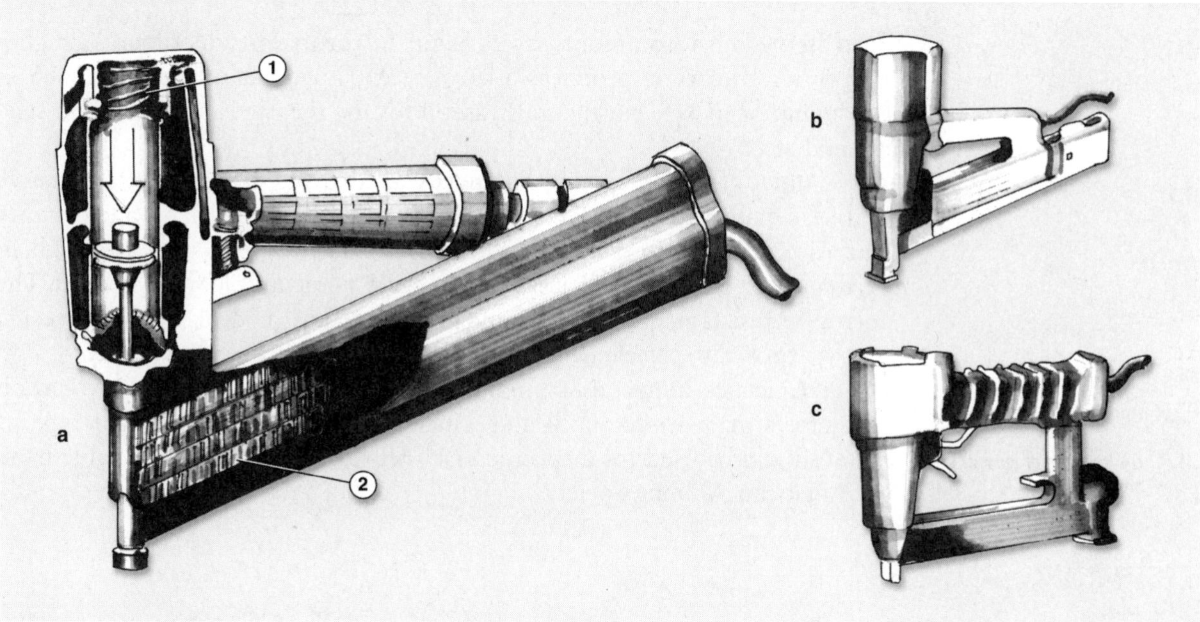

Figure 6-10a shows how a nailer works. The cross section presents the cylinder and piston to which the driver blade is attached. The piston is held to the top of the cylinder against the head bumper (1) by air from the last shot. When the trigger is released, air drives the piston, which in turn pushes the nail or staple out of the gun. The nails are stored in the nail magazine (2) and are spring-loaded to push each nail into position to be set. The nailer shown here is for brads and finish nails and can set a variety of nail sizes. All of the component parts of the pneumatic gun are proportional to the fastener being used.

Frequently the position of the nail magazine is different for the nailer than for the stapler. The nailer magazine is angled, allowing greater flexibility in choosing the placement of the nail.

The pneumatic staple gun can drive, and clinch if needed, staples from ⅝ inch to 2 inches long. The 1-inch staple is used to fasten corner and keystone blocks in the construction of flat scenery (see Chapter 7). Staples vary in (crown) width and wire gauge as well as length.

Because pneumatic tools require about 90 pounds per square inch of pressure to operate, the shop must have either a portable heavy-duty compressor or a built-in compressed-air service with connection positioned conveniently throughout the shop. The same system with a pressure regulator can provide compressed air to the painting and property construction areas to operate paint spray guns. A large shop with an air pressure system might also use a pneumatic reversible drill with socket wrench and screwdriver attachments.

BUILDING SCENERY WITH METAL

Metal has been used in the theatre as a structural material for some time. Metal is also being increasingly used as a design feature. For these reasons, the designer and technician need to understand the many forms and techniques of using metal.

Types of Metal

Steel is the most commonly used metal in theatre productions. A higher proportion of carbon produces a harder steel. Steel has other alloys such as chromium or nickel, but the most useful for the theatre is a low-carbon steel or mild steel.

Aluminum is also gaining popularity as a strong, lightweight alternative to steel in many situations. It comes in many variations of hardness and ductility (the ease with which something bends). Stainless steel, which is high in chromium or nickel, is used less often but fills a crucial role when needed. The corrosion-resistant quality of stainless steel makes it ideal when the scenic unit is exposed to the elements or is used underwater for a long time.

URL http://www.AWS.org

URL http://www.metalworkingdigest.com

Like plastics, all metals are manufactured and treated according to certain parameters in order to fulfill a specified range of needs. The right type of metal should be used for a specific task. More information is available from the American Welding Society.

Forming and Fabricating Metal

In the factory, when metal is still molten, it can be *formed* in many ways: *rolling* to produce *plate* and **sheet metal; extruding** by squeezing the molten metal through a shaped aperture to form rod, tubes, and so on; *casting* liquid metal into block forms; *drawing* the softened metal through a small aperture to make *wire;* and **forging** or stamping the metal into a prescribed shape.

sheet metal Piece of metal that has been rolled into a flat sheet, thinner than plate.

extruding Squeezing molten metal through a shaped aperture to form a shape such as a rod or tube.

forging Stamping metal into a shape.

Forming generally produces the following shapes: *plate*—rolled steel no thinner than 1/8 inch; *sheet*—rolled steel no thicker than 1/8 inch; *strip*—rolled steel narrower than plate; *strap*—narrow strip; *rod*—solid round and square; *structural* shapes such as channel and angle; *tube*—extruded round, square, and rectangular; *pipe*—round malleable iron; and *wire*—drawn carbon steel.

The *fabricating* of metal involves special techniques and tools, many of which are common in other trades as well. The table saw, for example, can be used on wood and plastic as well as on metal. The following terms are often used in the fabrication of metal: *brake forming*—the bending of plate or sheet metal; *shear*—to cut sheet metal in a scissorslike tool; *spinning*—placing sheet metal into a lathelike machine and spinning it while a blunt tool shapes the metal into bowl or bell shapes; *rolling*—cold-rolling sheet metal between large hardened steel cylinders into curved or cylindrical shapes; *twisting*—twisting a square bar into a decorative shape or a wire into cable; *blanking*—punching holes or a pattern through plate or sheet metal; *mechanical fastening*—bolting or riveting together structural steel or sheet metal; *welding*—joining metal to metal by fusing them together at a high temperature; *brazing* and *braze welding*—joining metals at a lower temperature where only the filler metal (usually a brass alloy) is made molten; and *soldering*—joining sheet metal, tubing, or electrical parts with solder (usually a tin or lead alloy).

Structural Steel Shapes Here we discuss the typical shapes of structural metal used in the theatre; cross sections of these shapes are shown in Figure 6-11. All shapes come in a variety of thickness and length; choosing the right combination of size and thickness depends on the work the structural member must do. In the beginning, the designer and technician are wise to understand all the size and weight variations of any one shape.

- *Strap.* Very thin strap is commonly used as a *sill-iron,* a horizontal strip holding the bottom of a door frame in position.
- *Strip.* This is a wide strap. Thick strip is sometimes cut and drilled for mending plates.
- *Angle.* A good reinforcing shape for stiffening or bracing scenery, this useful cross section comes in many sizes. It is often used in stage machinery construction.
- *Channel.* Its U-shaped cross section makes it stronger though not as adaptable as an angle.
- *Tee.* The tee is useful for stiffening. When it is used horizontally in a framework, it is stronger than angle. The tee also serves as a guide for the arbor in a counterweight system.

6-11

Structural Steel Shapes

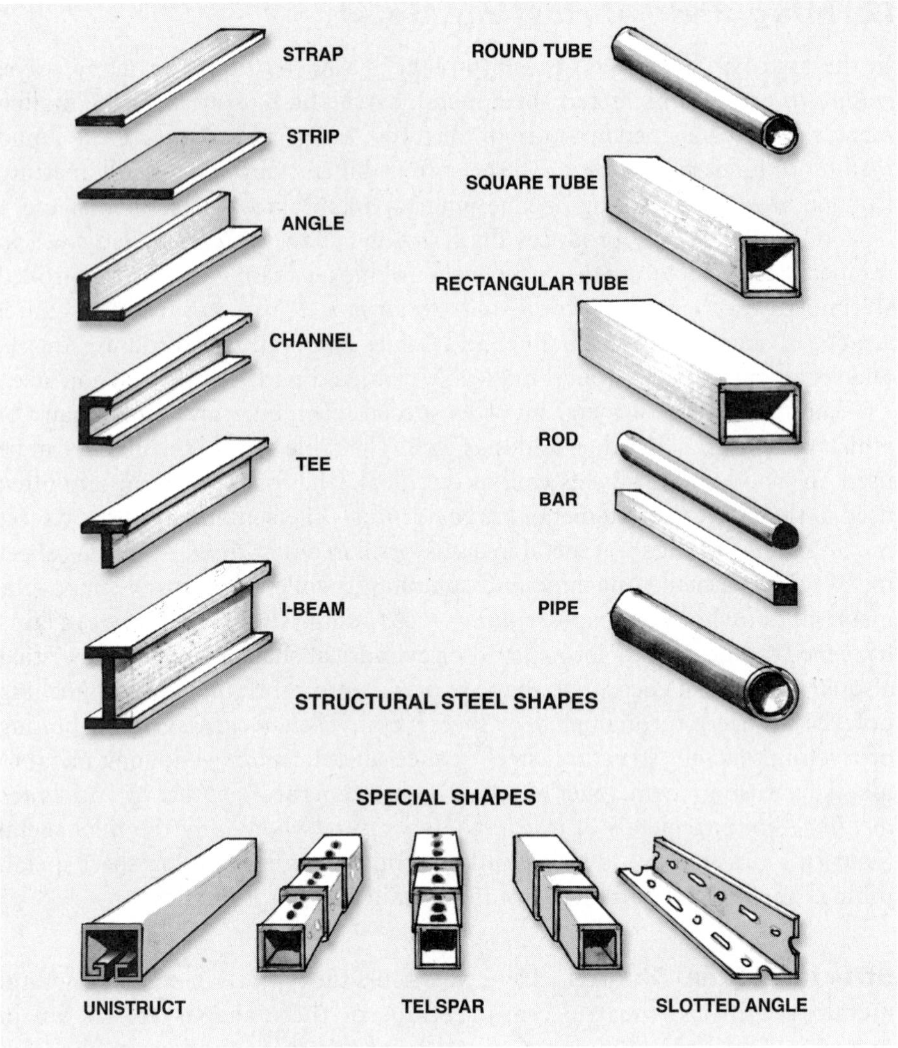

- *I beam.* As the name suggests, the I beam is best used as a beam where the top of the "I" carries the main thrust or weight.
- *Rod.* A round solid, the rod is sometimes used as the internal member of a steel truss or is easily bent into decorative shapes for scenery or props.
- *Bar.* A square solid, sometimes used as a spindle in a metal railing, bars can be bent and twisted into ornamental shapes found in wrought iron work.

  Although the terms *tube* and *pipe* are occasionally used interchangeably, this is a mistake. Tube is usually extruded and is much more precisely made than pipe. It is manufactured in a variety of shapes, listed here. Pipe is either rolled and welded or cast.

- *Rectangular tube.* This offers a good clean shape for design or structural uses.
- *Round tube.* This is one of the many extruded forms of steel. The larger tubes can become vertical support members, while smaller diameter tubes can be bent into decorative shapes (see the discussion of EMT in the subsection that follows).

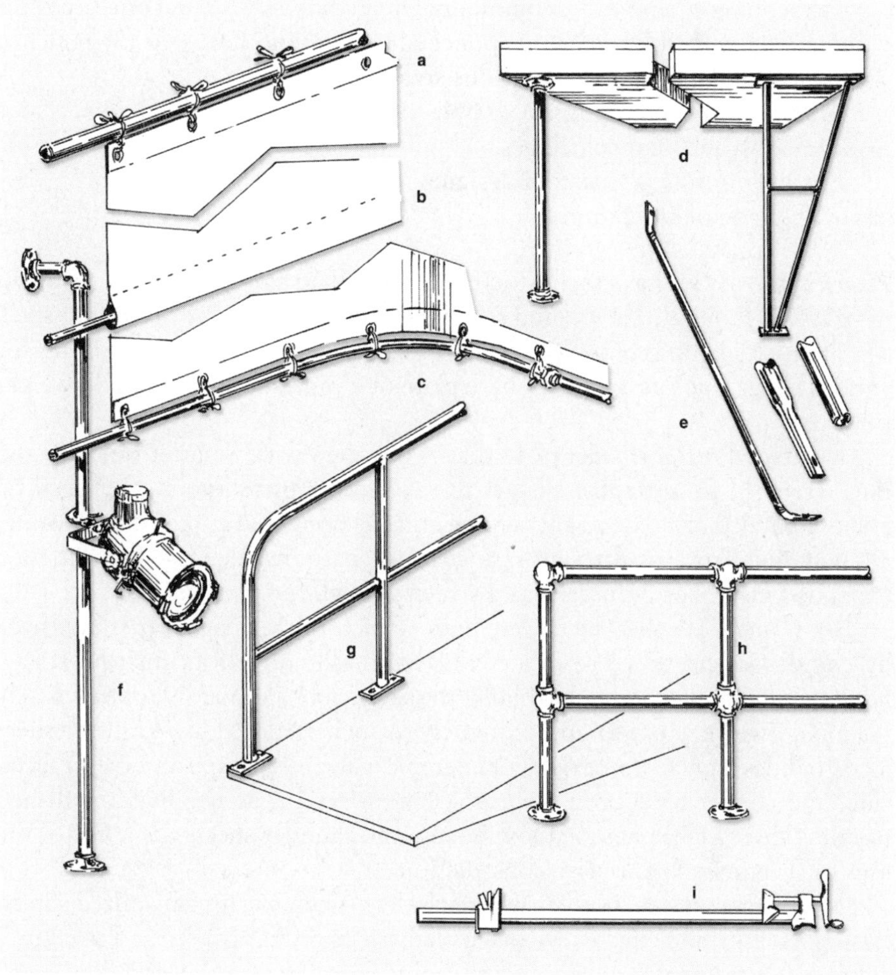

6-12

Various Uses of Pipe

- **a** Top batten for drop, cyclorama, or stage drapery.
- **b** Bottom batten for a drop pipe sleeve.
- **c** Curved bottom batten using tie lines.
- **d** Freestanding platform legs.
- **e** Special bracing.
- **f** Lighting booms and battens.
- **g** Bent pipe and welded railing.
- **h** Cut pipe and fitted railing.
- **i** Bar clamp.

- *Square tube.* This popular shape can be cut and welded into structural or decorative forms. It is the most commonly used shape overall.
- *Pipe.* With heavier side walls than tube, malleable iron pipe can be threaded and joined with fittings (Figure 6-12). Although the outside dimension (OD) remains the same, pipe is available in a variety of side-wall thicknesses.

Special Shapes Frequently, a manufacturer's name will be used so often to refer to a specific type of material or tool that it becomes the "generic" reference to the material or tool. Some of these special shapes are shown in Figure 6-11 and described here.

Unistrut, a specially formed channel-shaped steel, is used to create knock-down framing that is adaptable to platforming and trussing in the theatre. It reduces the necessity of welding and cutting and is available in different forms.

Thin-wall conduit (EMT), a type of galvanized-steel pipe, has become a very popular structural and decorative material in the theatre. With walls too thin to thread but quite easy to bend, it has many uses in scenery construction. It comes in many diameters (½-inch, ¾-inch, and 1¼-inch), in 10-foot lengths. Extra caution should be used when welding or brazing EMT because of zinc fumes.

Telescoping square tube, commonly referred to as *Telspar,* comes in three varieties: (1) with solid sides, (2) punched with round holes, or (3) punched with square holes. It comes in various styles as well.

Slotted angle iron, designed to bolt together in a variety of ways, is also made in strap and channel shapes.

Extruded forms are custom designed to suit specialty applications. They are often made of aluminum.

Flat Steel As we have seen, stock flat metal plate and sheet metal are forms of flat steel. Expanded metal and screening are other useful forms of flat steel.

Plate is rigid and comes as thin as ⅛ inch. It can be cut to order in sizes for various needs, such as a motor's base plate or a pipe-stand base to add weight to the bottom.

Expanded metal is steel plate that is punched with a pattern of slits and then stretched from opposite edges to expand the plate into a grille surface. Some expanded metal is weight bearing and has been used as platform flooring, allowing light to pass through in interesting patterns. Lightweight flattened expanded metal has been used as a screen for light projections.

Sheet metal is rolled metal less than ⅛ inch thick. Thickness is indicated by *gauge.* Gauges decrease in steps of 1.5 hundredth of an inch (0.015)—hence, the larger the gauge, the thinner the sheet. Sixteen gauge is approximately 1⁄16 inch. Twelve gauge is approximately ⅛ inch thick. Many forms of sheet metal besides regular steel exist. For example, galvanized steel, aluminum sheet, zinc, and copper have been used as scenic materials, as has highly polished stainless steel. Light pans, shadow boxes, and thunder sheets are a few of the uses of sheet metal in scenery construction.

Metal screening such as hardware cloth (¼-inch mesh), galvanized screen (1⁄16-inch mesh), and chicken wire (1-inch mesh) is primarily used as a structural material. Occasionally, galvanized screening is used to simulate window glass.

Metalworking Tools and Equipment

The use of metal in the theatre requires special tools to cut, shape, and join many forms of metal. It also requires equipment that supports various methods of fabrication. Although some woodworking tools can be used on metal, most metalworking tools have special functions. Here we discuss in turn the tools used for measuring, marking, shaping, and cutting metal (see Figure 6-13).

Measuring and Marking Tools

A measuring tape is usable for measuring long dimensions; however, a *flat steel rule* not only gives measurements, but also serves as a straightedge for marking. The large *framing square* is also useful for layouts.

Most marking on metal is done with a *scriber.* Its sharp point scratches a line on the surface of the metal. Thin permanent or wet-erase markers are also useful for less critical work. Both the *china marker,* often called a grease pencil, and *soapstone* are used for marking on metal or any other object with a hard, highly polished surface but are highly inaccurate.

The *compass scriber* will mark a circle or arc as well as scribe an irregular shape or pattern. The *center punch,* as its name implies, marks the center of a circle or provides a start hole for drilling in metal.

6-13

Metalworking Tools

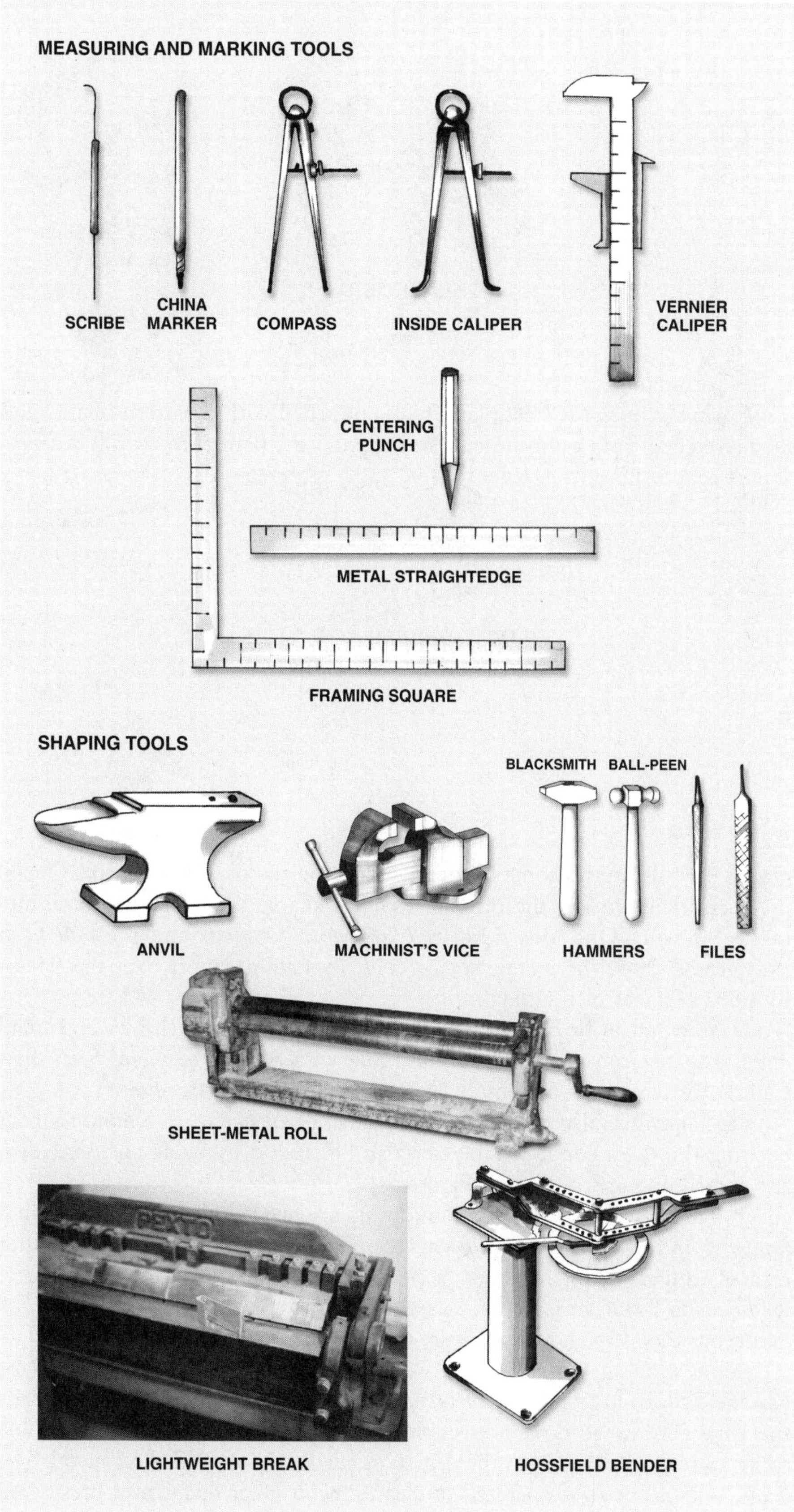

DRAWINGS BY STEPHEN FOUND, FOUND MARKETING AND DESIGN

6-14

Decorative and Structural Uses of Rod and Strap

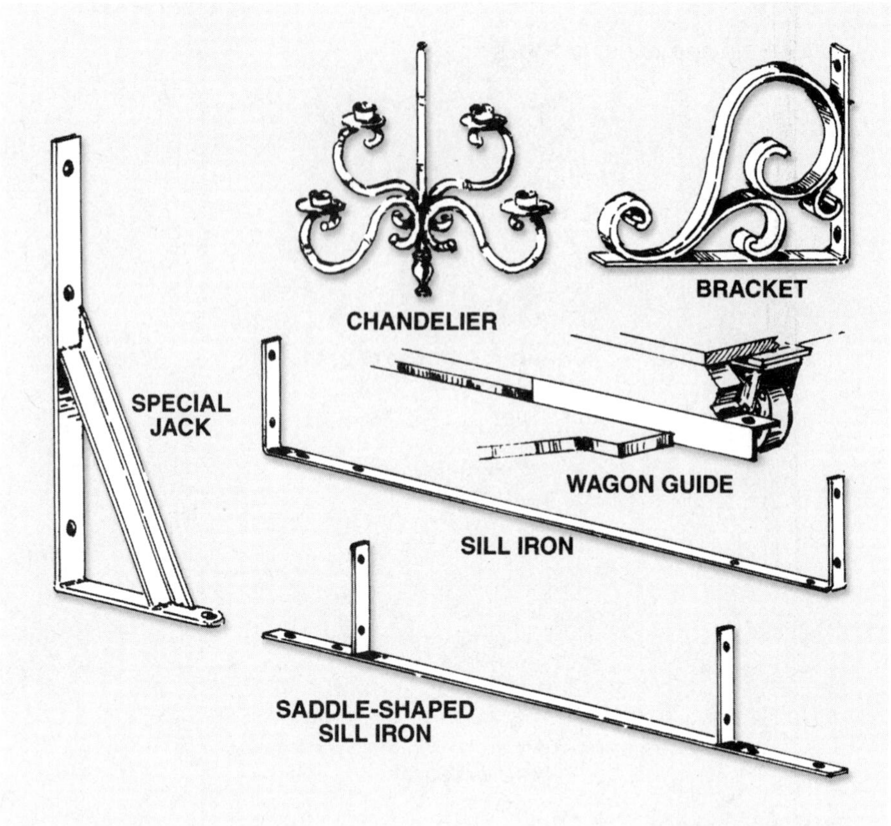

Shaping Tools

Figure 6-14 illustrates some of the many uses in the theatre for shaped metal products. The *anvil* is the original tool for shaping and bending steel and malleable iron. One uses a heavy *blacksmith hammer* and the *ball peen* hammer to shape the metal, hot or cold, by hammering it over the flat or rounded surfaces of the anvil.

Strap iron can be bent in a *machinist's vise* with its steel jaws and small anvil. The vise can hold metal for shaping with a file. The *metal files*—flat, round, or triangular—can smooth a rough cut or round an edge.

Pipe and tube also can be shaped. The *conduit bender* is a hand tool for bending thin-wall conduit. Pipe can also be shaped by being cut, threaded, and joined in numerous ways (Figure 6-12).

To cut and fit pipe, several hand tools are needed. The pipe is held in a *pipe vise* and cut with a *pipe cutter.* Technically a cutting tool, the pipe cutter rotates around the pipe to make a clean cut. The *pipe threader,* with several *die heads* to fit the various pipe sizes, cuts threads on the end of the pipe. The numerous tools are shown in Figure 6-15.

Some shaping tools, although operated by hand, are too large to be handheld tools. In using a *sheet-metal roll,* for example, a metalworker feeds sheet metal between three adjustable rollers. The position of the adjustable roller increases or decreases the degree of curl in the shaped sheet metal. The *brake* is hand or foot operated to cleanly bend sheet metal to a prescribed angle. The *Hossfeld bender* is a tool used to bend many shapes of metal—pipe, tube, rod, bar, and angle. All of these tools can be powered.

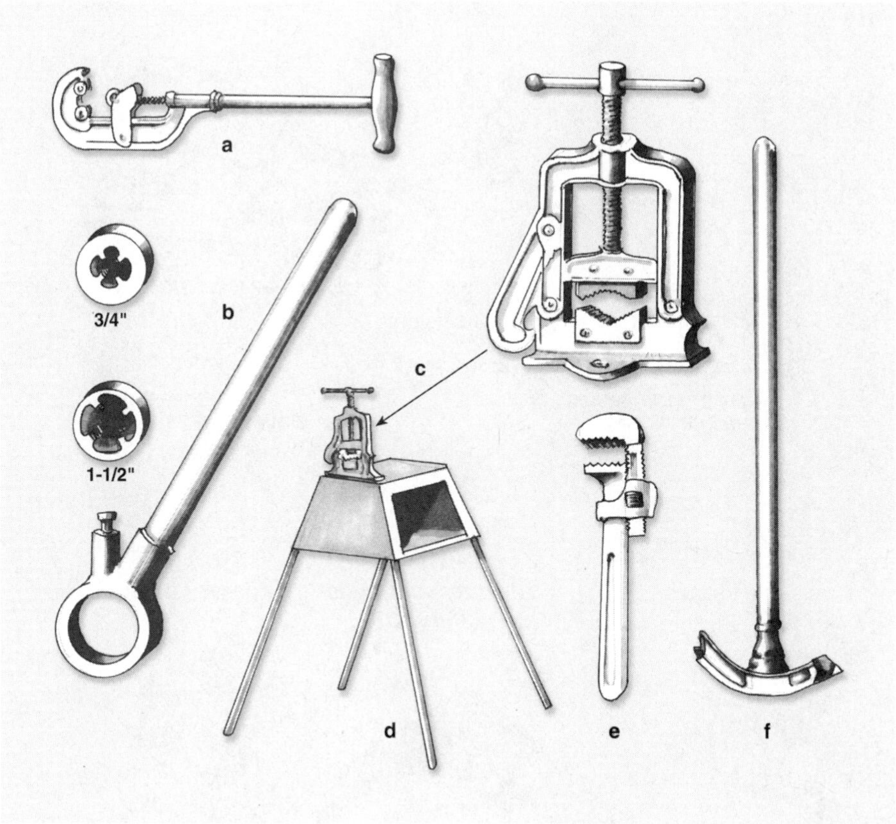

6-15

Pipe-Cutting, Threading, and Bending Tools

Hand tools used for cutting, threading, and bending pipe include the following:

a Pipe cutter.

b Pipe threader with ¾-inch and 1½-inch die heads.

c Pipe vise.

d Portable vise stand.

e Stillson wrench.

f Pipe bender.

Cutting Tools

Hand Tools A *hacksaw* fitted with a fine-toothed blade is normally used to cut metal bars or bolts (see Figure 6-16). *Bolt cutters* can be used to rough cut rod of strip stock to length.

As we have seen, a *pipe cutter* is necessary for cutting and threading pipe.

The hand tools used to cut sheet metal are the *tin shears,* for cutting a straight line; *nippers,* for end cutting; and side-cutting pliers. There is also a large stationary sheet metal shear that "chops" full sheets of metal in one cut.

A *cold chisel* can be used for breaking welds or for trimming operations.

Power Tools Figure 6-16 shows many of the standard powered metal-cutting tools. To cut sheet metal or aluminum, which come in thicker minimum gauges than steel does, a *saber saw* with a metal cutting blade is noisy but effective. Two tools designed to cut sheet metal are the *power shear,* a handheld tool that cuts a straight or curved line, and the *power nibbler,* for inside cutting. A *grinder* fitted with an abrasive cutoff wheel is also very effective.

The major tools for crosscutting pipe, tube, or any structural steel forms are the *horizontal band saw* and the *abrasive wheel cutoff saw.*

The *power hand drill* with ½-inch chuck capacity is a heavier tool than is the wood drill. The *drill press* is a fixed tool for precision work. A *drill press vise* is used to hold the work in position. Another fixed power tool is the *bench grinder.* With one coarse and one fine wheel, the bench grinder can sharpen tools or grind down a metal edge.

6-16
Metal-Cutting Tools

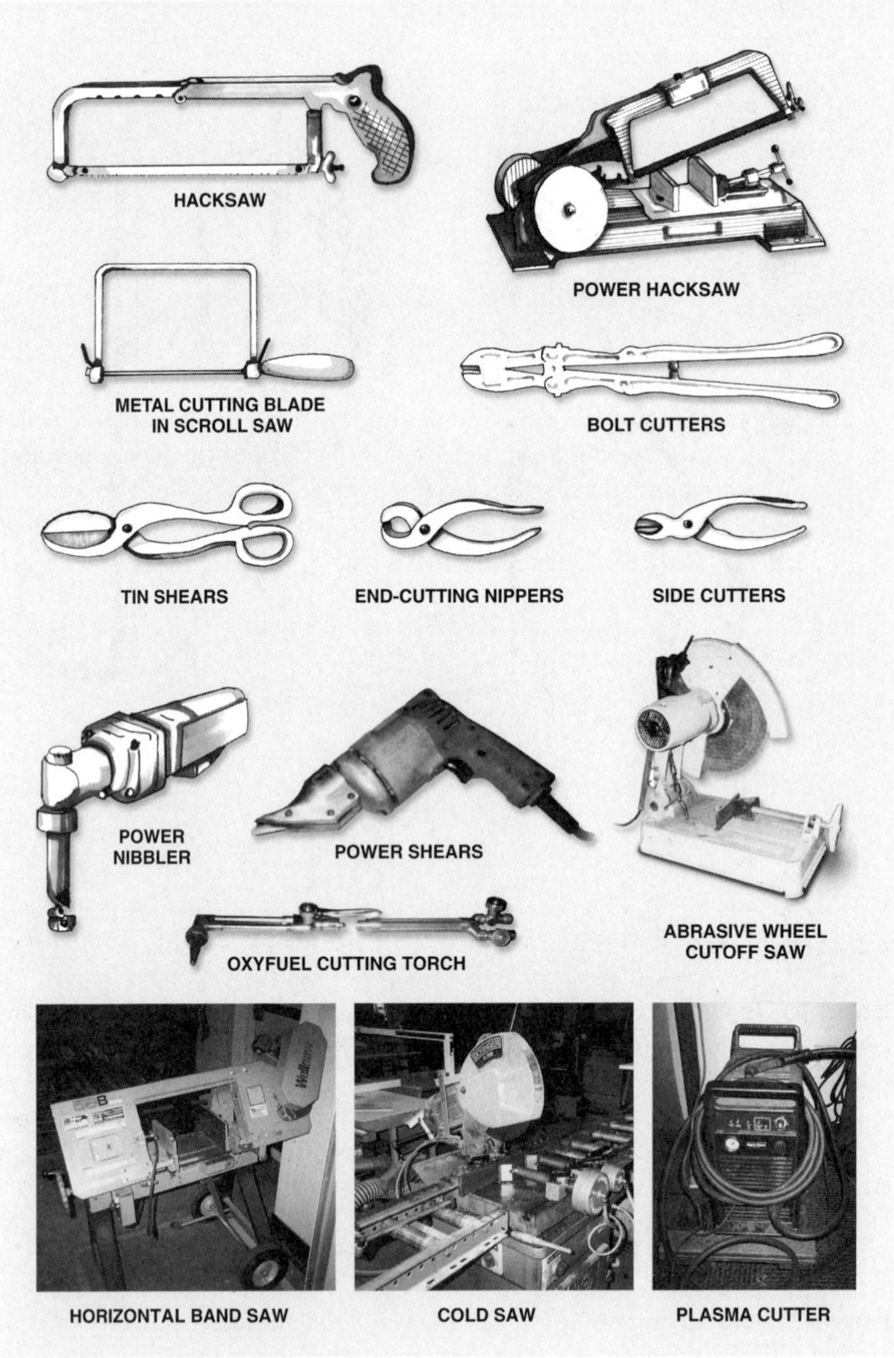

DRAWINGS BY STEPHEN FOUND, FOUND MARKETING AND DESIGN

The *cold saw* is a stationary saw that uses an extremely hard blade, low rotational speed, and a fluid coolant/lubricant. It is designed to make extremely accurate miter cuts (including 90-degree cuts).

Plasma cutters and *oxyfuel torches* can also be used to cut all sizes of metal. The plasma cutter is similar to an arc welder. With a jet of air, it melts the metal and blows the resulting puddle through the work. When one cannot bring the work to the tool, one can use the oxyfuel torch. Although this tool does not require an electrical outlet, the resulting cut is much rougher and the setup is rather bulky.

Three common types of band saws are used for cutting metal. The semiautomatic *horizontal band saw* is used for all sizes including larger stock; the *vertical band saw* often has a variable speed and is used mostly for curves in sheet material; and the *portable band saw*, a handheld unit, can be used in many situations where other tools cannot (often for lack of space).

The *reciprocating saw*, often referred to by its brand name, Sawzall, is a handheld saw that makes rough cuts. It is not good for accurate work.

Basic Metal-Joining Tools and Materials

The various forms of metal can be joined with bolts, screws, rivets, or solder or by fusing the metals together with heat. Threading on the inside or the outside of pipes allows for many configurations as well (Figure 6-17). For example, the *saddle tee* can be strapped on the surface of the pipe, providing a right-angle coupling. The *rotalock* clamps the adjoining pipe, also at a 90-degree angle (Figure 6-17). The *Stillson wrench* (Figure 6-15), which has jaws

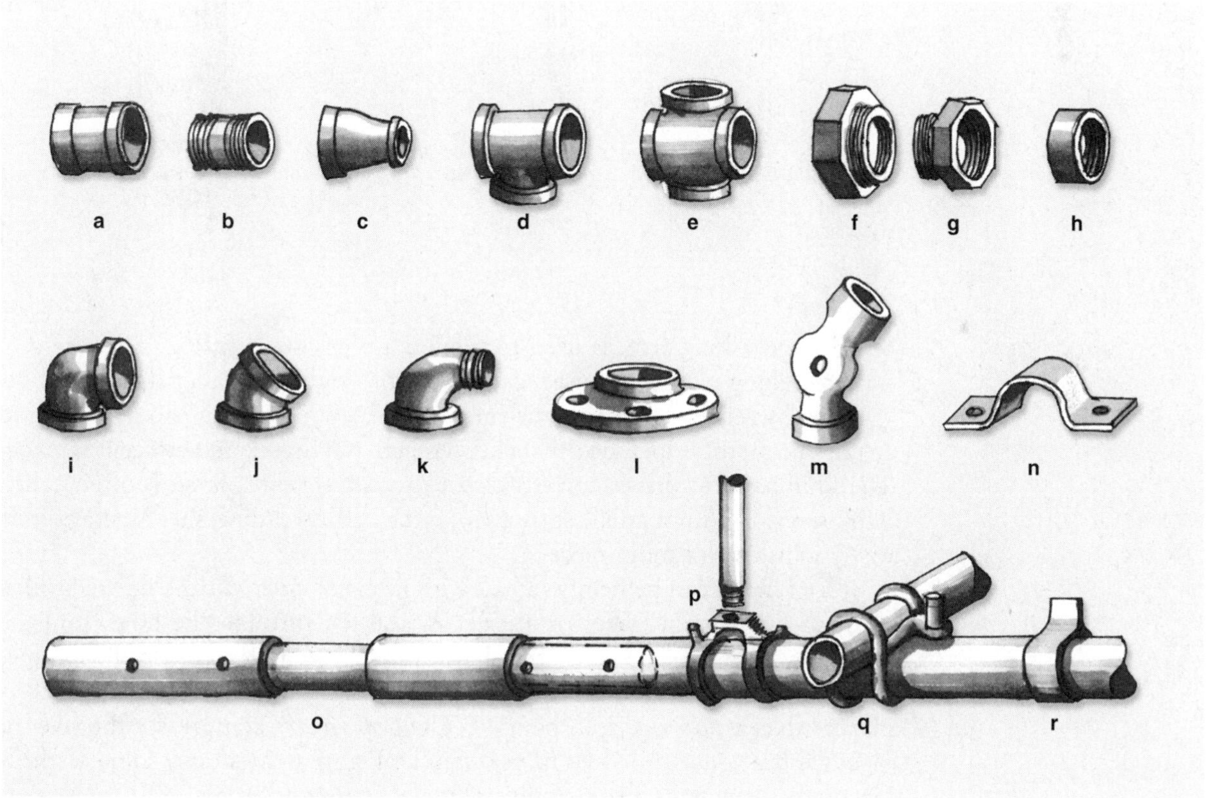

6-17

Threaded Iron Pipe System

Here are some of the screw fittings used to join sections of pipe:

a Coupling.
b Nipple.
c Reducing coupling.
d Tee.
e Cross.
f Union, ring end.
g Union, screw end.
h Cap.
i 90-degree elbow.
j 45-degree elbow.
k Street elbow.
l Floor flange.
m Adjustable elbow (railing fitting).
n Pipe trap.
o Batten inside sleeve splice.
p Saddle tee, double strap.
q Rotalock.
r Pipe hanger.

6-18

Metal-Joining Tools

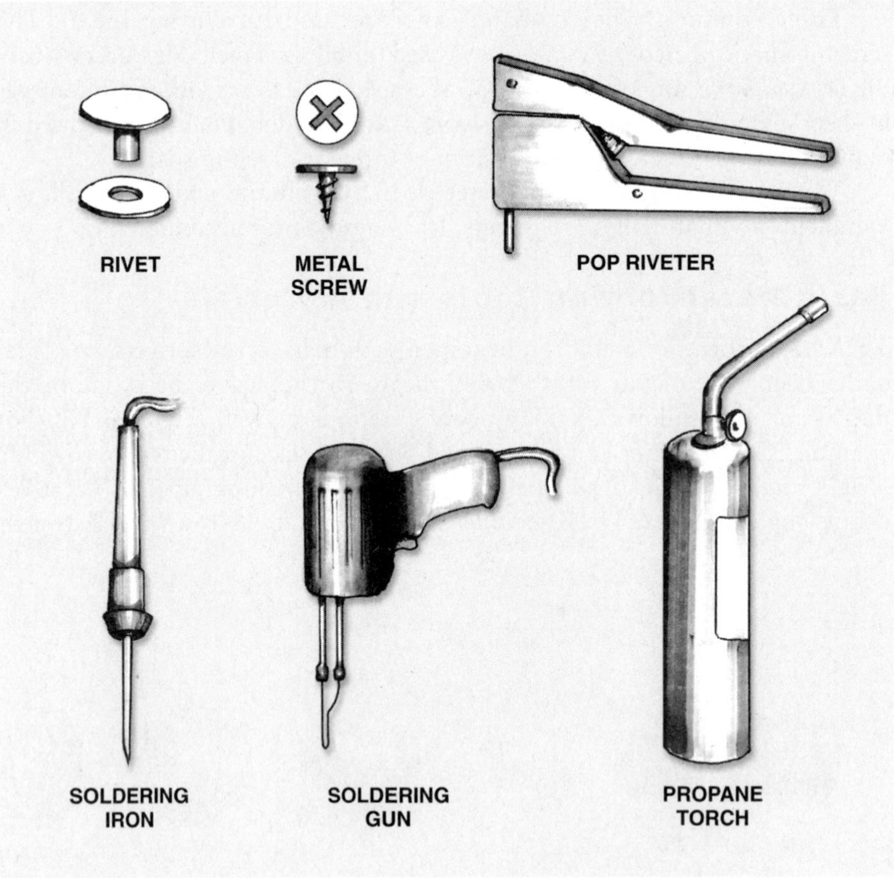

to grip and a long arm, is used to tighten a pipe into a fitting. The *vise-grip wrench,* along with other uses, can be used to tighten smaller diameter pipe.

Some wrenches and screwdrivers used in woodworking can also be used to join metal; these include the socket wrench, nut driver, and crescent wrench. The Phillips screwdriver can be used to set *sheet-metal screws,* often called *TEK screws.* With a small starter hole, the self-threading sheet-metal screw easily joins two or more pieces.

Sheet metal can be firmly joined with *rivets* or *rivet nuts.* A hole is drilled through overlapping sheets; the rivet is inserted through the hole from the back; a washer is placed over the shaft of the rivet; and, to finish the joining, the shaft is *peened* or flattened with a ball-peen hammer. When the back is inaccessible, a *pop rivet* can be used. The *pop riveter* compresses the rivet in place with a squeeze or two of the handle. Figure 6-18 shows some of these fasteners, along with views of several metal-joining tools.

Soldering

As a method of joining metal, solder functions as a *bond.* The strength of the bond depends on the preparation of the surfaces to be joined and an even application of solder. The surfaces should be free of oil, paint, and oxidation (rust). A flux, borax, or rosin is applied to further clean the metal and prevent oxidation.

Figure 6-18 shows some of the tools used for soldering. An electric *soldering iron* or *soldering gun* supplies sufficient heat at the tip to melt the solder along the joint. The soldering of pipe to a fitting requires a torch. The *propane torch* supplies heat to a large area of the fitting so that when the solder is applied it is sucked into the joint. The joint surfaces are cleaned and polished with emery cloth and coated with flux before applying the heat and solder. For the soldering of electrical connections, a rosin flux is used to prevent corrosion.

URL http://www.epemag.wimborne.co.uk/solderfaq.htm

URL http://www.jwharris.com/home

Welding

Welding is the joining of metal, often by using extreme heat, in which one piece coalesces with another. It provides a more permanent joint than soldering does; it is also faster but requires specialized equipment. The two most useful welding processes adaptable to the construction and designing of scenery are *GMAW* (gas metal arc welding) also called *MIG* (Metal Inert Gas) welding and *GTAW* (gas tungsten arc welding) also called *TIG* (Tungsten Inert Gas) welding.

Metalworking in general and welding in particular is dangerous. Proper training and extreme caution are essential. In fact, on structural elements such as platforms or on large scenic units like stairways, welding should be done by a certified welder. Certification, standards, and services are provided by the AWS (American Welding Society) and the ASME (American Society of Mechanical Engineers).

Gas-Welding Equipment Oxyfuel welding uses oxygen as a catalyst to burn a fuel gas. *Oxyacetylene welding* (OAW), the only kind of *oxyfuel welding* that is used in the theatre, ignites an oxygen and acetylene mixture to produce one of the hottest flames known. Welding is possible with or without a filler metal. Gas-welding equipment can perform a wide range of work in addition to fusing metal. It can (1) braze, or join metals with a rod that melts at a lower temperature than the two metals; (2) join metals with solder, a tin and lead alloy that melts at a much lower temperature than the two metals; (3) cut metal with a cutting attachment that concentrates the oxygen flow; and (4) preheat metal with the torch, for reshaping.

The chief disadvantage of gas-welding is heat warpage. Because heat expands metal, gas-welding can cause warping of the metal near the welded point. The choice of a welding rod that will melt at the same temperature as (or slightly lower than) the melting point of the steel will minimize the distortion.

The most cumbersome parts of a gas-welding outfit are the heavy tanks containing the two welding gases, oxygen and acetylene. A tank truck is essential to make their movement easier and keep the tanks from tipping over. The methods of acquiring oxygen and acetylene vary with the suppliers. Some gas suppliers charge a fixed deposit on the tank, which is refunded when the empty tank is returned, while others rent the container on a per diem basis. If a supplier insists on the tank-rental arrangement, it pays in the long run to purchase a set of empty tanks to exchange for each tank of gas and thereby eliminate the per diem rental charge which, though small, can mount up during idle times between productions.

A listing of the parts and attachments of a gas-welding outfit, including the gas tanks, is found in Figure 6-19.

Arc-Welding Equipment The heat of arc welding comes, as the name implies, from the arc of a high-amperage short circuit between the metal and

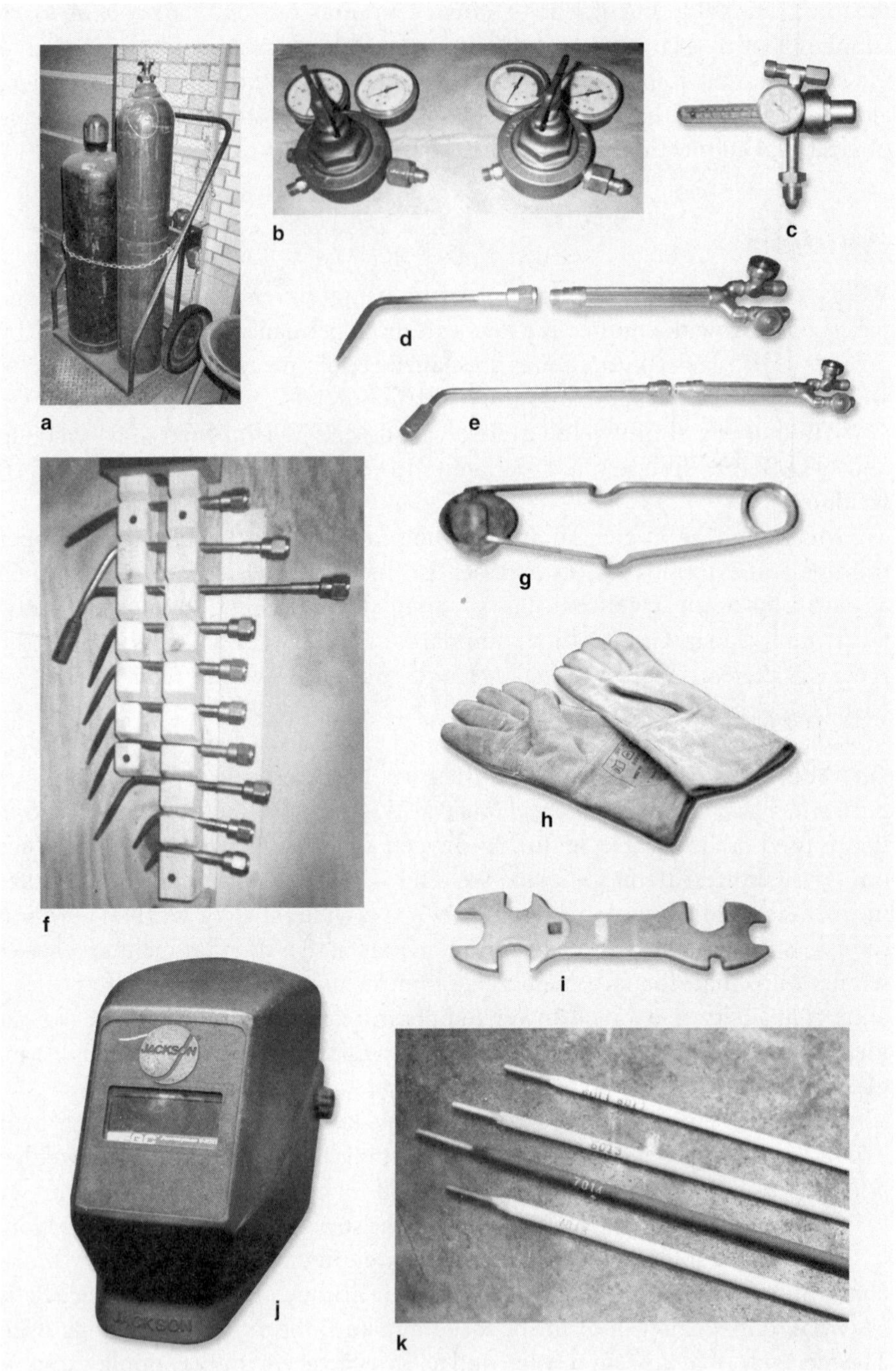

6-19

Gas-Welding Equipment

- **a** Oxygen tank with cap removed to show regulator (right) and acetylene tank (left) on tank truck.
- **b** Oxygen regulator (left) and acetylene regulator (right).
- **c** Flow meter.
- **d** Welding/brazing torch.
- **e** Rosebud tip—heating and bending.
- **f** Welding tips.
- **g** Flint striker.
- **h** Welding gloves.
- **i** Tank wrench.
- **j** Welding helmet.
- **k** Welding rods (electrodes); numbers of rods refer to material of electrode and tensile strength.

the rod or electrode. The work has to be grounded to complete the circuit from the rod to the holder, through the electrode cable and to the power source. *Shielded metal arc-welding* (SMAW), often referred to as *stick welding,* used to be the standard but has been replaced by MIG welding.

In stick welding, a rod serves as both the filler metal and as the vehicle that allows electricity to go from the source to the work. The weld is continuous through the length of the rod, which is consumed during the process. The metal rod has a shield, referred to as *flux coating,* which melts as the welding is being done. This leaves a residue, called *slag,* which as the metalwork cools becomes solid and must be chipped off.

Stick welding's chief advantage is its speed. Because a welding temperature is reached almost instantaneously and in such a small area, the amount of heat warpage is negligible. This is important in the welding of a preassembled part when its fit is critical to the final shape of the completed structure.

Gas-Metal Arc Welding A third welding process, which has become adaptable to theatre shop use, is the gas-metal arc-welding method commonly referred to as *metal inert gas* or MIG. The components of MIG equipment are found in Figure 6-20, and Figure 6-21 shows a MIG welder in action.

MIG uses a wire electrode fed through a gas hose and through the center of a gun nozzle. The arc is surrounded with an inert gas shield. The trigger of the gun nozzle simultaneously turns on the shielding gas flow, starts the power to melt the wire, and starts the pinch roller that feeds the wire. When the

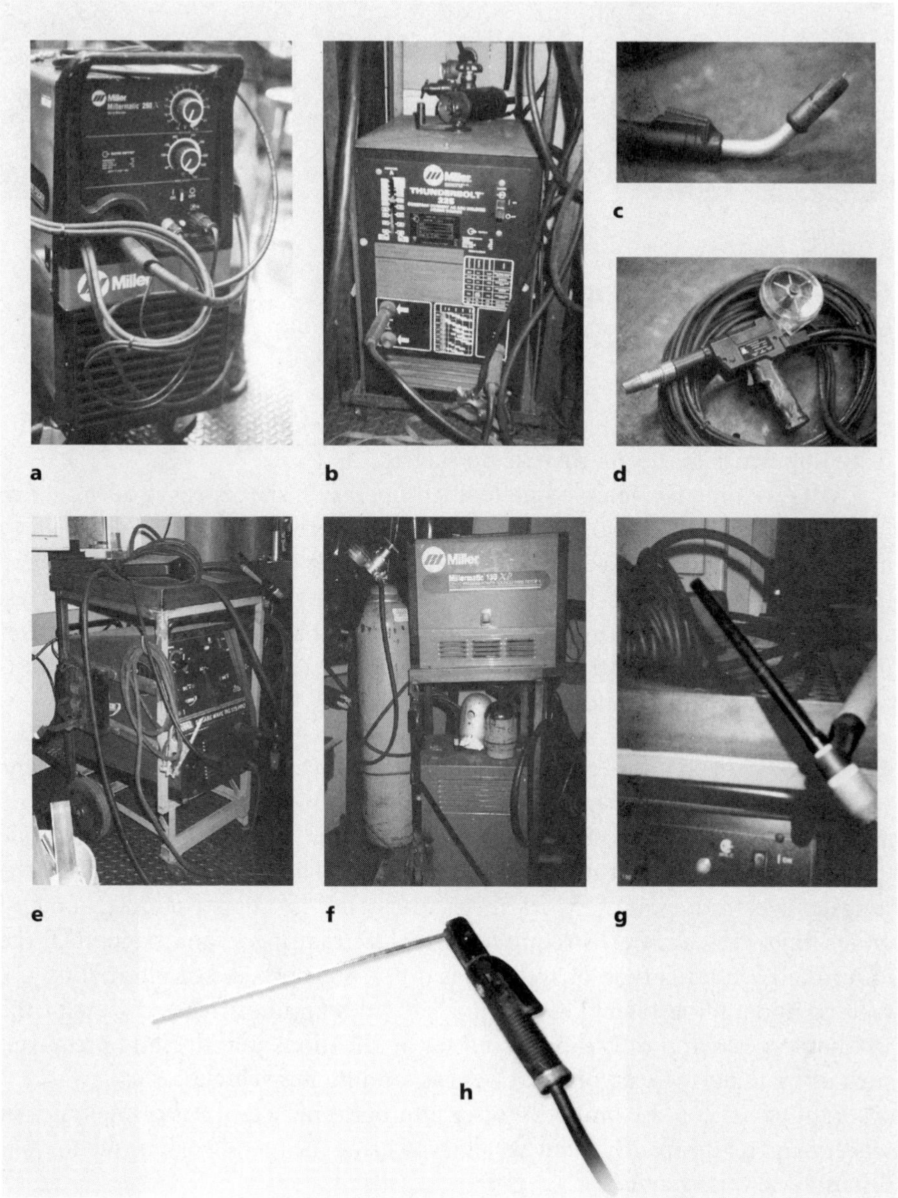

6-20

Gas-Metal Arc-Welding Equipment

a 250-amp MIG.

b Lincoln stick welder.

c Large MIG torch.

d Spool gun.

e TIG/stick welder.

f 130-amp MIG and stick combo.

g TIG torch.

h SMAW holder and electrode.

6-21

Gas-Metal Arc Welding

Note the expanded-metal welding table top.

trigger is released, all three stop. Because the shielding gas protects the wire from impurities in the air, there is no slag.

MIG welding is a simple one-handed operation that is easy to learn. The heat of the arc and gauge of the wire can be altered to weld various metals, including aluminum. A special spot-welding fitting can be attached to the end of the nozzle for temporarily tacking or permanently joining adjacent surfaces. In addition, a special form of MIG wire is available with a core that negates the need for gas. Called Flux Core Arc Welding (FLAW), using this wire is considered a separate welding process.

Gas-Tungsten Arc Welding Essentially an electric version of oxyacetylene welding, *gas-tungsten arc welding* (GTAW), or TIG welding, uses an electric arc instead of a flame. This type of welding uses a nonconsumable electrode (tungsten), meaning that it does not burn away. The arc created between the tungsten electrode and the work melts the metal, forming a puddle, some of which vaporizes. A filler is required to replace that metal and strengthen the joint; therefore, this type of welding is a two-step process of alternating the melting and adding filler. TIG welding provides an unobstructed view of the welding process and thus is preferred for applications that demand precision, such as building rockets, pressure vessels, and racing vehicles.

Figures 6-22, 6-23, and 6-24 offer photographic examples of the types of scenery and set designs that can be achieved using the metalworking techniques discussed in this chapter.

Safety Practice

Welding Safety

Gas-welding operators should wear goggles, ear protection, protective clothing, and gloves, more for protection from flying sparks than from the intensity of the flame itself. Because there are no ultraviolet rays generated in the flame by gas welding, it does not have to be isolated or shielded from other shop activity. Precautions should be taken, however, to guard flammable materials from the sparks by using sheetrock pads under and around the work. A respiratory mask should also be worn. Long sleeves are also recommended.

Arc-welding operators require the same protection, plus shielding from the ultraviolet rays of the arc. A welder's helmet with a ray-absorbing window should be worn to protect the eyes. If other workers are nearby, a portable shield can be used to protect their eyes as well.

Prolonged welding in a closed room requires forced ventilation.

6-22

Metal Scenery

Metal railings, showing details of the welded joints.

6-23

Steel Staircase

Various views (including details) of a spiral and a straight staircase for a production of Sondheim's *Company,* framed with 1-inch-square steel tube. Designer, Zach Bunker.

6-24

Use of Scaffold in Design

Design for *Viet Rock* by Dan Gray.

PHOTO COURTESY DAN GRAY

COVER STOCK

The material used to cover the structural frame of scenery, thereby providing a surface for painting, is known as *cover stock*. The frame can be covered with a fabric or a hard surface, depending on the use and handling of the particular piece of scenery. A translucent backing, for example, is framed and covered in a way different from a section of wall that must support the weight of an actor.

Covering Fabrics

The most common covering fabric for framed scenery is unbleached muslin. Muslin is also frequently used as a drop (an unframed piece of painted fabric used as a background; see Chapter 7). As with other scenic materials, the use of muslin depends on location, price, and availability. There are areas where canvas is cheaper. Almost any fabric can become a covering material to serve as a special effect or as an unusual painting surface. Burlap, velour, scrim, terry cloth, and even string rugs have been used as covering fabrics.

URL http://www.rosebrand.com

URL http://www.ushwy1.com/gerriets

Hard Surfaces

Soft-covered flats are largely the domain of schools, and even there they are becoming rare. Because audiences have become more sophisticated and the number of intimate theatres such as the thrust has increased, hard-covered flats have become much more common. They are more efficient and only slightly more expensive than soft coverings. The most frequently used hard-surface material is ⅛-inch or ¼-inch lauan. It is lightweight but still strong enough to supply a hard surface with a minimum of framing.

URL http://www.cyberyard.com/woodlibrary/woodpage.php3?selectName=17

Other hard-surface materials include ⅛-inch and 3⁄16-inch Upson board, an inexpensive board made of laminated paper; ¼-inch A-C plywood, a very sturdy but heavy board (also used for keystones and corner blocks); ½-inch Homesote, a paper-pulp board with little strength but thick enough to be carved or textured (as for stone); and Masonite, a very heavy hard surface of compressed wood pulp. Tempered Masonite is an extremely hard surface that is often used as a floor covering. Typically, shops also include ¾-inch plywood for platform tops. Most of these materials are available at the local lumber yard in stock 4-by-8-foot sheets. Occasionally, oversized sheets—such as 5 feet by 9 feet, 4 feet by 10 feet, and 4 feet by 12 feet—are stocked.

URL http://www.masonite.co.za

Plastic offers another type of hard-surface cover stock. Because the use of modern plastic as a scenery surface is usually related to a textured or relief-sculptured surface, it is reserved for discussion in Chapter 7, where the techniques of working plastics such as Styrofoam, urethane foam, and thermoplastics are discussed.

It is best to remember that every project has unique requirements. Other perhaps less usual materials might be used for various purposes. If the designer and the technicians are open to what is available, they will find a great variety of materials to use.

SCENERY HARDWARE

In the scenery shop, hardware is divided into two categories: fastening hardware and stage hardware. The first is hardware used in the construction and basic assembly of scenery; the second is for the bracing, stiffening, rigging, and onstage assembly of scenery.

Fastening Hardware

Fastening hardware is an important part of normal scenery construction. It includes all the necessary nails, screws, and bolts to fasten wood to wood or metal to wood.

Nails Driven with a hammer or pneumatic nailer, a nail is used for a relatively permanent fastening of wood to wood, such as framed scenery units or platform construction. The various types of nails serve specific purposes.

All nails are stamped out of steel wire. Each nail has a particular thickness, length, and shape of head. The weight is known as *penny* and is represented by the letter *d*—a 10d nail is longer and thicker than an 8d nail.

A *common nail* has a flat head for easy driving and extracting. The wide flat head also adds strength to the joint. Useful common nails for theatre might include 8d (2½ inches), 10d (3 inches), and 16d (3½ inches). *A box nail* is a lightweight (smaller wire) common nail, 4d (1½ inches) or 6d (2 inches). *A finish nail* is a small-wire, small-headed nail for finish work such as attaching molding or trim. A finish nail's head is set below the surface of the wood so it can be covered with wood putty or paste, thereby concealing the nail. Finish nails in stock would begin with 1-inch wire brads (very fine wire) and would include 4d (1½ inches), 6d (2 inches), and 8d (2½ inches). The double-headed *duplex nail* is used for temporary assembly and comes in sizes 6d, 8d, and 10d.

6-25

Hardware: Screws, Nuts, Bolts

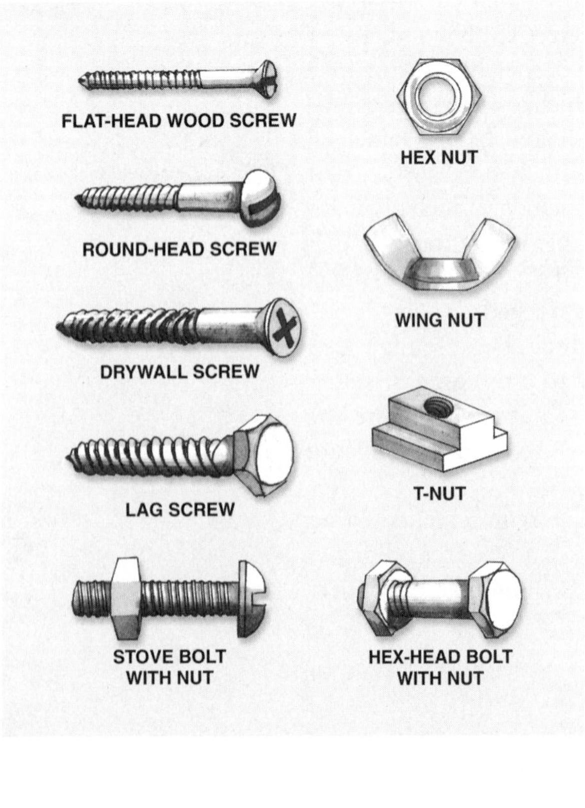

Screws The screw acts as an internal clamp in that it pulls the material into itself as it tightens. The tapered advancing threads of the screw are drawn into the wood as the screwdriver turns, providing a very firm fastening of wood to wood. The diameter of a screw is indicated by number; the length is indicated in inches. The types of heads are numerous—the *flat head* with tapered sides to countersink into the wood; the *round head* to set on the wood surface; the *bugle head,* a flat head with the silhouette of a bugle horn; the *pan head,* a flattened round; and the *hex head* of the *lag screw.* The types of recesses in the screw head for the driving tool include the *slot, Phillips,* and *Robertson* square. (See Figure 6-25 and refer again to Figure 6-8 and the subsection on screwdrivers.) The most common sizes to stock might be No. 8 screws: ¾, 1, 1¼, 1½, 2, 2½, and 3 inch.

With its deeper and steeper threads, a *wood screw* not only can hold better but can be driven faster. The industrial-quality wood screw is made of tempered high-grade carbon steel and is lubricated for easy installation. It has extruded threads, which means the threads extend beyond the diameter of the shank (most screws are turned from shank stock). The extruded threads give the screw greater holding power. Most often, screws are now being made with Phillips heads rather than slotted heads to help ease installation.

The *drywall screw* is of similar quality to and can be used in place of a wood screw. Good sizes to stock include No. 8 screws sizes ¾, 1, 1¼, 1½, 1⅝, 2, 2½, and 3 inch. Their flat heads have Phillips slots or square recesses.

A *lag screw* has wood screw threads. It is used in heavy assembly where a bolt is not feasible, and it is driven with a socket wrench. Sizes 5/16 to ½ inch in diameter and 1½ to 4 inches long are suitable for most needs.

Tacks and Staples A No. 6 or No. 10 *carpet tack* will secure a carpet, padding, or ground cloth. *Upholstering tacks* in various colors and patterns aid in the construction or remodeling of furniture for properties; usual size will be ½ inch or ⅝ inch.

The size and shape of a *staple* will vary with the type and make of the stapler as well as with the nature of the work. There are, for example, hand-powered staplers, hammer staplers, electric staplers, and pneumatic staplers—each requiring a slightly different type of staple. Staples for hand or electric staplers (for attaching fabric or metal screening to wood) are usually ¼, ⅜, 5/16, or ½ inch in size. Staples for pneumatic staplers (for fastening wood to wood) are most commonly ¾ or 1 inch, or 1¼, 1½, or 2 inches in size.

Bolts, Nuts, and Washers As fastening hardware, the bolt plus nut is stronger than the nail or screw. The nut and bolt are also easy to disassemble, allowing scenery knockdown. Bolts commonly used in theatre are the stove bolt, the machine screw, the carriage bolt, and the machine bolt.

Both the *stove bolt* and the *machine screw* have a flat head and a slotted recess and are threaded their full length. They are among the most commonly used pieces of hardware in the theatre. In short lengths and small diameters (3/16 inch), they are used to reinforce the screws in a backflap hinge or hanger iron. The flat head of the machine screw fits into a countersink, whereas the slotted round head of the stove bolt sets on the face rather than being countersunk. Both bolts are tightened using a socket wrench on the nut and a screwdriver in the slotted head. Suggested sizes are 1/36-inch diameter—1, 2, or 3 inches in length; and ⅜-inch diameter—2, 4, or 6 inches in length.

The *carriage bolt* is engineered specifically for fastening wood. The rounded head with the square shank is expected to be drawn into the wood surface and thereby resist turning as the nut is tightened. Because the bolt is not threaded its full length, care needs to be taken to select the right length bolt for each joint. Normal sizes to stock are ⅜-inch diameter—3, 3½, 4, and 6 inches in length.

The *machine bolt,* also commonly used in the theatre, has a finer thread than the other bolts discussed. It also has a square or hex head. Although it can be used for wood, it is manufactured for metal assembly such as slotted-angle and structural steel framing. The size of bolt depends on the forms of the steel and the nature of the structure. Frequently used sizes are ⅜-inch

6-26

Bolt Length

Bolt length is determined by the portion of the bolt that is recessed into the work.

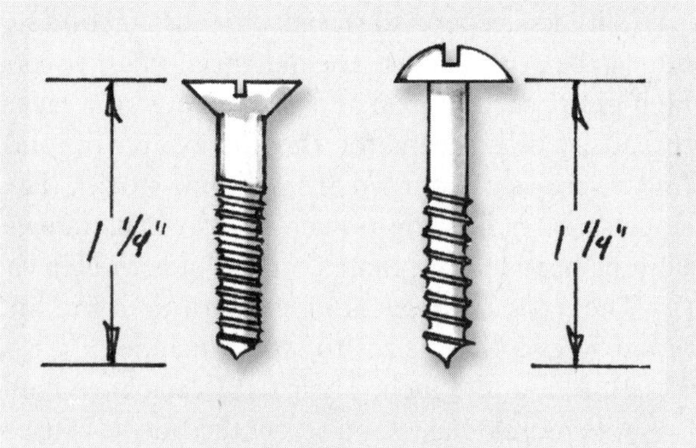

diameter—1, 1½, 2, 2½, 3, 3½, and 4 inches in length; and 2-inch diameter—6 and 8 inches in length.

Bolt length is determined by the amount of bolt that will be recessed into the work, not by the total length of the bolt.

Nuts are usually hexagonal, with inside threading that matches the bolt. Their function is to tighten the bolt in place. Although the *hex nut* has to be tightened with a wrench, the *wing nut* is designed to be tightened by hand for easy and quick assembly. A *T-nut* has sharp prongs to anchor the nut in the wood surface around a predrilled hole, thus permitting rapid fastening.

The *washer* is a flat disk of steel with a center hole slightly larger than the diameter of the bolt (Figure 6-27). It spreads the pressure of the tightened nut for a stronger fastening. The *lock washer* is a cut disk with offset ends that provide enough pressure to keep the nut locked in place. Lock washers also come in other shapes, including "star" and "wave." Washers are used under the nut—never under the head of the bolt.

6-27

Types of Washers

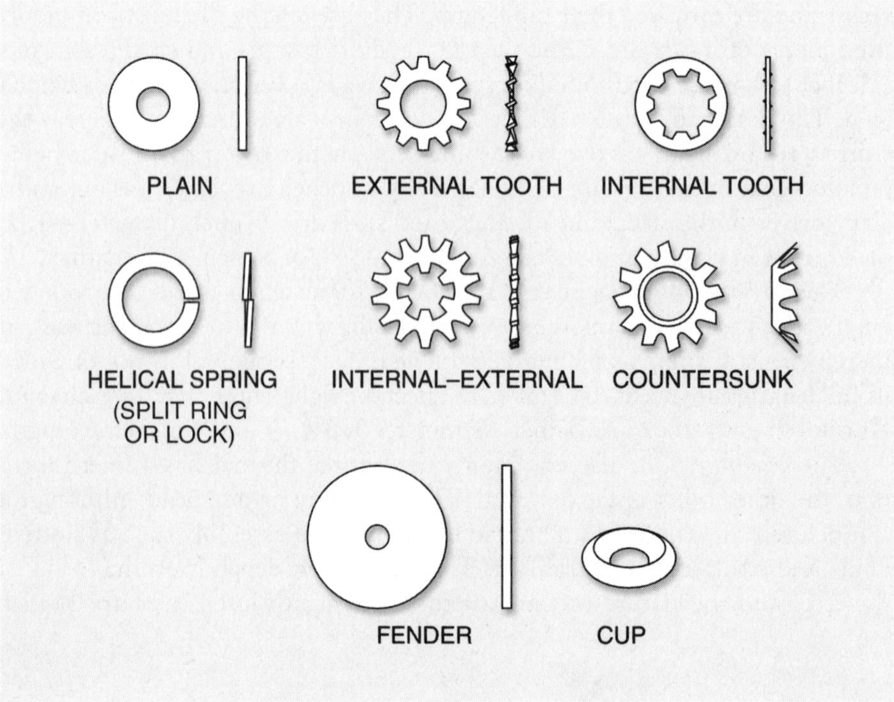

Stage Hardware

Because scenery must be portable, many pieces of hardware have been developed especially for the stage. Most of them are designed to brace, stiffen, and temporarily join units of scenery as well as to work with rigging for the flying of scenery (Figure 6-28).

6-28

Stage Hardware

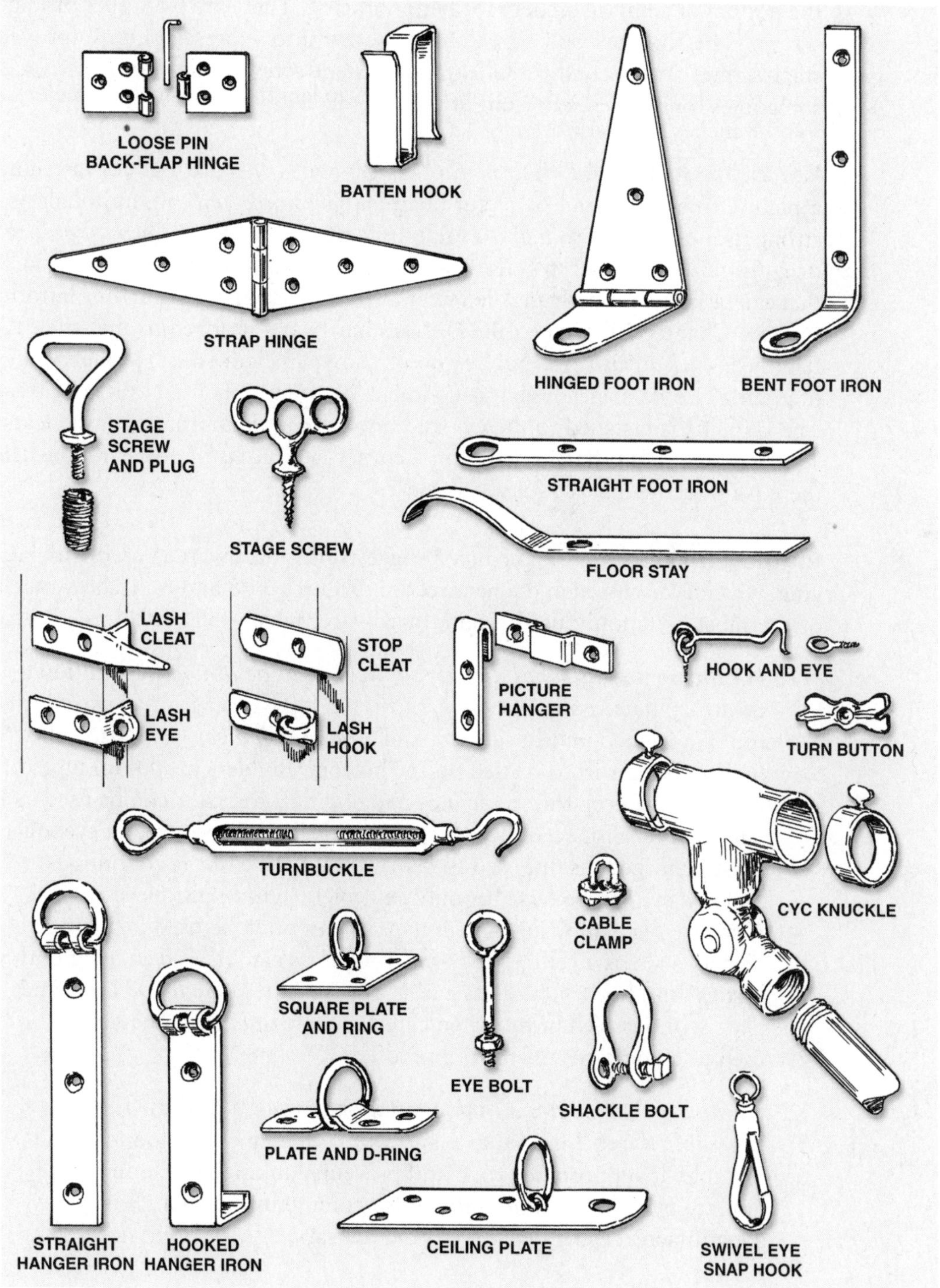

Stage hardware has been broken down into categories that relate to their function:

Stiffening Hardware The loose-pin back-flap hinge is used to attach a horizontal stiffening member to the back of two or more units of scenery. A *keeper hook* over the toggle rails of two or more units can receive a horizontal stiffener.

Bracing Hardware A *strap hinge* is used to brace and hold a door frame in position. A *hinged foot iron* and a *bent foot iron* with a *stage screw* secure the bottom of a unit of scenery for better bracing. There are two types of stage screws. The first has bolt threading to screw into a preset plug (improved stage screw). The second is the traditional stage screw. A *straight foot iron* is sometimes found on the bottom of a jack brace.

Hardware Assembly The *picture hanger* and *socket* are used for fastening a picture to a toggle rail or picture batten. The *hook and eye,* although not strong, is a quick way to make a joint, as is the *turn button.* The *casket lock,* or *coffin lock,* recessed into the edge of a wagon platform, is a hidden lock that can be unlocked with an Allen wrench through a small hole in the platform top (see Chapter 10, Figure 10-14). Lash hardware attached to the stile of a flat (the *lash cleat, lash eye,* and *lash hook*, shown in Figure 6-28) is one method of joining two flats, although it is no longer as commonly used as it once was. The lash line is fastened to the eye and hooks around alternating lash cleats. The *stop cleat* holds flats together in a corner lash. A *lash hook* is used when there is not enough space for a lash cleat.

Rigging Hardware As the name suggests, this hardware is used with rigging, which is discussed in the next section. Figures 6-28 and 6-29 show much of the most commonly used rigging hardware, which falls into three types:

URL http://www.versales.com

1. *Hardware that attaches directly to the unit to be flown.* In traditional theatrical flats, a *straight hanger iron* (or top hanger iron) is used at the top of a framed unit of scenery, and a *hooked hanger iron* (also called bottom hanger iron) is used on the bottom. Builders need both types of hardware to keep the scenic unit hanging flat. *Eyebolts* can be used as a lifting point for scenery or to guide a lift line. To be safe, an eyebolt must be forged (as opposed to bent) so that the circle is continuous. A *screw eye* can be used for only extremely lightweight pieces. A square *plate and ring* or *ceiling plate* can often be used for flying scenery such as a ceiling. A *D-ring and plate* can be used to hang both vertical and horizontal units and is also used to guide lines. The same plate without the D-ring, often called a *keeper plate,* is frequently used to guide cable off the top of a flat.

2. *Hardware that creates a usable termination in the cable or rope.* The *cable thimble* is used as a part of making an eye or loop in rope or cable. It supports the rope and prevents kinking. The loop is held in place by either a *cable clamp* (also commonly called a *Crosby,* a manufacturer's name), which is temporary, or a *swaging sleeve*

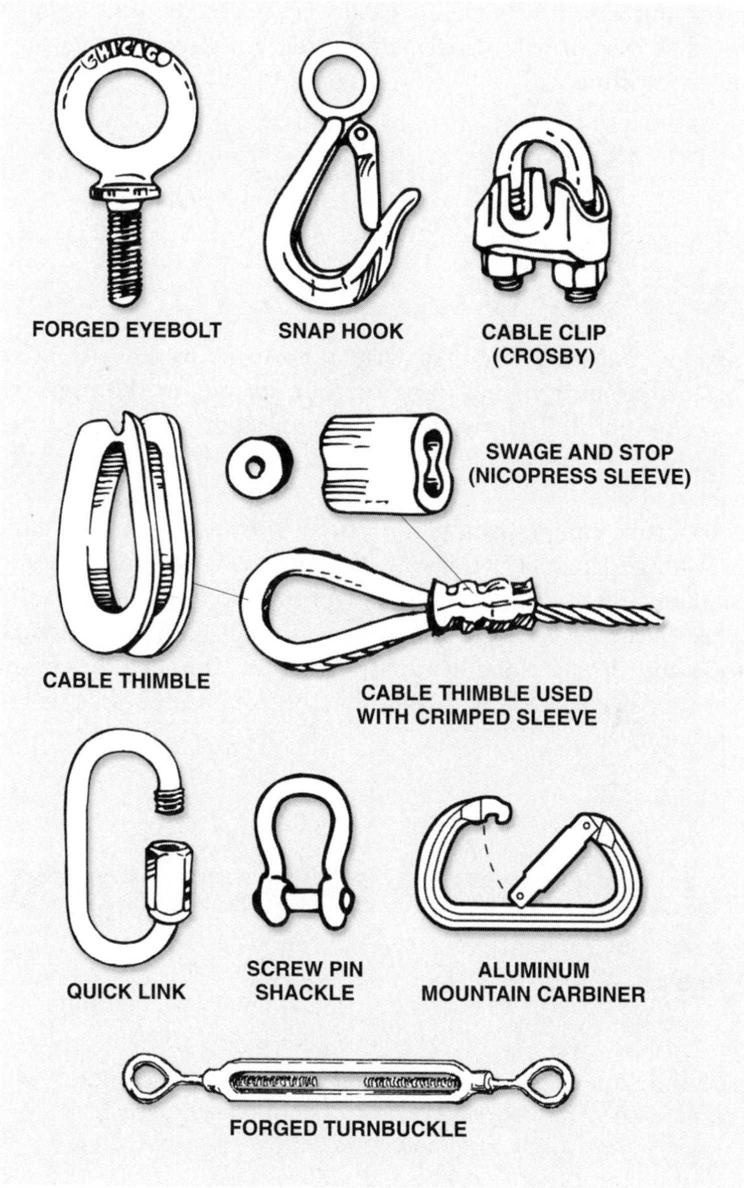

6-29

Rigging Hardware

(also called a *Nicopress* sleeve, again a manufacturer's name), which is permanent. The permanent sleeve is stronger and requires a special tool called a *swaging tool* or *Nicopress tool.*

3. *Hardware that connects the two types just discussed, allowing for adjustment and removability.* The *screw-pin shackle* is a two-part fastener consisting of an inverted U that slips through the loop of the thimble and a removable pin that passes through the ring of the attachment hardware. A *quick link* resembles a single link of chain, one side of which can open or close with a threaded fitting. The *snap hook* is a forged hook with a spring-loaded latch. Because of its open shape, it is used only for attaching sandbags. The *caribiner* is a piece of rock-climbing hardware with a spring-loaded latch that is often lockable. A *forged turnbuckle* is used to make adjustments in the level

of the scenic unit after it is in the air. Lightweight latch hooks, or *dog clips,* should be used only for extremely lightweight pieces, as they are not intended for lifting.

RIGGING

Rope

URL http://www.phoenixrope.com

Constructed of spun *fibers* that are first twisted (normally to the left) into a *strand, rope* is formed by twisting three or four strands in the opposite direction (i.e., to the right). This twisting is known as the *lay* of the rope. The opposing tensions of the lay of the rope and the lay of the strand hold the rope together.

The fibers of a rope can be from *natural* or *synthetic* sources. The most common natural fiber is manila. Relatively inexpensive, it has many uses in the theatre. Synthetic fibers such as nylon, polypropylene, polyethylene, and polyester have been incorporated into rope construction. The continuous length of synthetic fibers adds strength and flexibility to a rope. Although the cost of a synthetic fiber rope is considerably higher than one of natural fiber, its life span can be much longer.

Safety Practice

Rope Safety and Care

Those who work in the theatre should observe the following guidelines for safe use and maintenance of rope:

1. Do not overload. The rope manufacturer's listed BP (breaking point) is for new rope and under a fixed load. Rope in the theatre is run over sheaves and pulleys, tied and untied, and subjected to variable loads—all of which eventually weaken it. To avoid overloading, it is a good practice to use a safety factor of 10, or one-tenth of BP. A normal hoist line of manila rope, for example, is ¾-inch three-strand with a BP of 5,400 pounds. With a safety factor of 10, 540 pounds would be a safe load.
2. Keep a file of the installation date of all hoist and purchase lines.
3. Establish a schedule of inspection, rotation, and replacement of hoist lines, especially those of natural fiber.
4. In each inspection, check for fraying or chaffing where a rope runs over the gridiron or through a sheave. Look for damage from clewing several lines together and other stress points of stage rigging.
5. Store natural fiber rope in a clean, dry area, away from excessive heat.
6. Protect ends of rope from fraying or unwinding by binding or whipping the strands together.
7. When rope has reached the end of its useful life, cut it up into small lengths of 3 to 4 feet before throwing it away. This will prevent scavengers from using an unsafe piece of rope.

Sizes of rope most frequently used in the theatre include the following (see Chapter 10 for more):

- ⅝-, ¾-, ⅞-inch three-strand—used for purchase lines of a counterweight flying system and the lift or hoist line or a pin-and-rail system
- ¼-, ⅜-, ⅝-inch three-strand—a lightweight rigging good for breasting and bridling

Another kind of rope is *braided rope,* which is quite flexible. Cotton is the most common natural fiber used in braided rope. However, the same synthetic fibers found in stranded rope are used in braided rope. When strands of synthetic fiber are braided around a central braided core, the resulting rope carries amazing strength. It is not, however, recommended for use as hoisting rope, because it tends to stretch and lose trim. It is also very expensive. An excellent combination of fibers for theatre use is made of cotton strands braided around a central core or strand of polyester or polyethylene. Many other combinations are available.

Sizes and uses of braided rope include these:

- ½ inch (No. 10)—drawline for heavy traveler curtain
- 5⁄16 inch (No. 8)—lash line and lightweight rigging
- ⅛-inch awning cord—lightweight window-curtain rigging, trick line, and tie-lines

Cable

Sometimes referred to as *wire rope, cable* is made of flexible, high-grade steel wire twisted into strands like fiber rope. Six or more strands are twisted into one cable. A cable is identified by its diameter, plus two numbers such as 6 × 7, 6 × 16, or 6 × 19. The first number indicates the number of strands, the second the number of wires in a strand. A ½-inch 6 × 7, for example, would be a cable ½ inch in diameter, made up of 6 strands with 7 wires per strand. The same factor of 10 also applies as a safe load guide for cable rigging.

Aircraft cable is made of flexible, high tensile strength steel. Its flexibility and strength allow it to pass through small pulleys and make it useful for special rigging and winch work.

Sizes and uses of cable are as follows:

- ¼-, ⅜-inch 6 × 19—hoist line in counterweight system
- ¼-inch 7 × 19 aircraft cable—winch, turntable, and wagon drives
- 1⁄16-, 3⁄16-, ⅛-inch 7 × 19 aircraft cable—most flown scenery, some winch drives, and actor-flying rigging

Considerably more information can be found in the *Wire Rope User's Manual* published by the Wire Rope Technical Board, which is a certifying agency for the manufacture of wire rope. They can be contacted at:

Wire Rope Technical Board
P. O. Box 849
Stevensville, MD 21666
(410) 461-7030

Wire

Single wire in various sizes is used to reinforce, or guy, properties or units of scenery. Here are some special uses for two kinds of wire used in the theatre:

- *Pin wire* (No. 13 gauge)—used in short lengths as a temporary pin of a loose-pin hinge, to facilitate its easy removal during a quick change
- *Stove wire* (No. 16 gauge)—soft, flexible wire; invisible at a short distance because of its dark color; can be used to stabilize decorative properties that tend to vibrate or fall during the movement of a wagon or turntable

Chain

Chain is used to attach and trim hanging scenery by connecting the pipe on which the scenery hangs to the cable that allows the pipe to fly (see Chapter 10) and to weight stage draperies. It also serves as special rigging or for a chain drive. A chain drive, like a belt drive, transfers motion from the shaft of a motor to another shaft that directly moves a scenic unit. The advantage of a chain over a belt drive is that it cannot slip. Sizes and uses are as follows:

- ½- and ¾-inch jack chain (single or double)—curtain weight
- ¾- and ⅞-inch jack chain (24- to 36-inch lengths)—trim chain on pipe batten of the counterweight system

Although designers do not usually work directly with the rigging as well as the other materials described in this chapter, a thorough knowledge of stage materials and tools can help them envision creative possibilities and avoid problems in actualizing their designs.

7

Building the Scenery

Scene designers and technicians are interested in the construction of scenery, not only to become familiar with building techniques but also to become aware of the uses and limitations of various materials. The more they know about present-day theatrical materials and techniques, the better they can introduce new materials and original methods into designs, as well as develop a knowledgeable use of contemporary types of scenery.

The building of scenery is under the charge of the *technical director* or shop head, the person who is responsible for translating the designer's idea into reality. The better an understanding he or she has of the designer's ideas and interpretation of the production, the more profound an effect the technical director can have on the design.

Compared with standard building construction, scenery construction may seem at first glance to be unduly flimsy and unnecessarily complicated. These characteristics are due chiefly to the unique demands the theatre places on scenery. First, it must be portable and lightweight so as to move easily from the shops, on the stage, and sometimes from theatre to theatre. Second, because theatre is larger than life, scenery has to be able to assume large-scale proportions for conceptual, decorative, or masking purposes. Therefore, large expanses of scenery must be furnished with the minimum of structure and the maximum of portability. And finally, because scenery exists for only a short time—the run of the production—its construction must be economical. This does not necessarily mean made from the cheapest materials. Rather, it means balancing costs against the weight and structural demands of a material. It also implies the economical use of scenery. Higher material costs can be made affordable if a scenic element has more than one use or can be reused at a later date.

For the purpose of discussion, we have divided the various types of scenery into groups; each is similar in method of construction, function, and handling requirements. First, we broadly divide scenery into two general classifications: two-dimensional and three-dimensional.

Two-dimensional scenery includes all flat scenery, categorized by its basic shape rather than by the way it is used on the stage. Although units of flat scenery, for example, may be assembled to make a three-dimensional form on the stage, the individual pieces are still classified as two-dimensional scenery.

Two-dimensional scenery is further subdivided into two groups: framed scenery and unframed, or soft, scenery. Within these two groupings falls the bulk of the scenery that is used on the stage.

Three-dimensional scenery refers to the pieces that are built in three dimensions to be handled and used as solid forms. Three-dimensional scenery is separated into two basic groups: weight-bearing, meaning the weight of the actor and other scenic units, and non-weight-bearing.

SOFT SCENERY

Large unframed pieces such as stage draperies, drops, and the cyclorama, or "cyc," are counted as soft scenery. They all serve the same function—providing a large area of scenery with a minimum of construction and a maximum of portability. Being soft, they must hang from a batten or pipe for support and can be easily folded or rolled for transportation or storage.

Stage Draperies

Construction The large panels of stage draperies are made by sewing widths of materials together with vertical seams. There are three sound reasons for using vertical seams. First, because the direction of the weave or decoration is with the length of the fabric, it hangs and looks better in a vertical position. Second, a vertical seam is less conspicuous because it is lost in the folds of the drapery. Third, there is less strain on a vertical than on a horizontal seam, which carries the cumulative weight of each width of material from the bottom seam to the top.

The seams are sewn face-to-face to present a smooth front surface. The top is reinforced with a 3- to 4-inch jute webbing through which grommet rings are set at 1-foot intervals for the tie-lines. The bottom has a generous hem containing a chain that functions as a weight for the curtain. Occasionally, the chain is encased in a separate sound-deadening pocket, called a pipe pocket, that is sewn on the back side of the drapery.

Drapery fabrics may be sewn flat to the top webbing or gathered or pleated onto the webbing to give a fixed **fullness** to the curtain. For a front curtain or traveler curtain, fixed fullness is an advantage as it has a softer look. If used as masking, it absorbs more light than does a flat curtain panel. However, it is not as flexible, because the latter can be hung either flat or with varying degrees of fullness for a greater variety of uses (Figure 7-1).

fullness The effect achieved by gathering or pleating a given width of fabric into a narrower width.

Materials Many fabrics can serve as stage draperies. Which kind will work best depends on the budget and how the drapes will be used. Are the draperies to be opaque, translucent, or transparent? Are they to be pictorial, decorative, or simple masking? Are they to be stock draperies or used as a one-time special effect? Answering such questions helps decide the kind of material to choose and its relationship to cost and use.

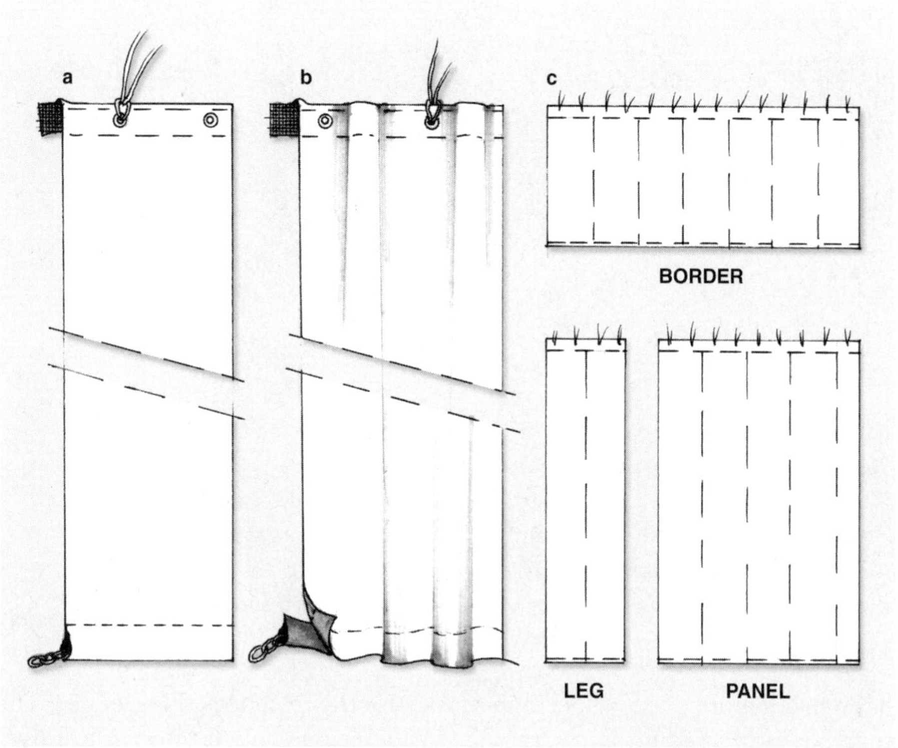

7-1

Stage Draperies

a Flat drapery construction. Webbing with grommets and tie-lines at top; hem enclosing chain weight at bottom.

b Gathered drapery. Fullness gathered on top webbing; chain pocket attached above hem at bottom.

c Types of stage draperies: border, leg, panel.

Velour, although expensive, is the favored drapery material. Its pile weave has a rich texture under the stage lights that cannot be duplicated with cheaper substitutes. It hangs and drapes beautifully, is opaque, and is easy to maintain, handle, and store.

Among the more economical fabric choices are duvetyn, commando cloth, and flannel. Commando cloth and duvetyn are almost as opaque as velour but drape poorly and lack as rich a surface quality. Flannel drapes a little better than duvetyn, and it has almost the same opacity. Its woolly nap surface has a fair texture under stage lights.

Stage draperies are made of other materials as well—not with the intention of imitating velour, but to create their own effect. Monk's cloth and many cottons have enough texture to make an interesting inexpensive curtain when hung in fullness. Corduroy is another drapery texture, which although semiopaque, drapes and hangs well.

Sometimes draperies are expected to be translucent or even transparent. Dyed muslin is the least expensive translucent fabric. It has a further advantage of coming in wider widths than many other translucent materials, such as satin or nylon crepe.

Gauze, the general term applied to all transparent materials, is available in a variety of fabrics such as cotton or nylon net, chiffon, and organdy. Although these fabrics are available at the local fabric store, their chief disadvantage is their narrow width, which increases the number of seams in a curtain. The seams become visible when the transparent curtain is back-lighted. Some gauzes, as well as muslins, are woven on wide looms especially for theatre use. Shark's-tooth scrim is a transparent material that has a rectangular or ladder pattern and is made in 30-foot widths. Bobbinet is a hexagonal net that

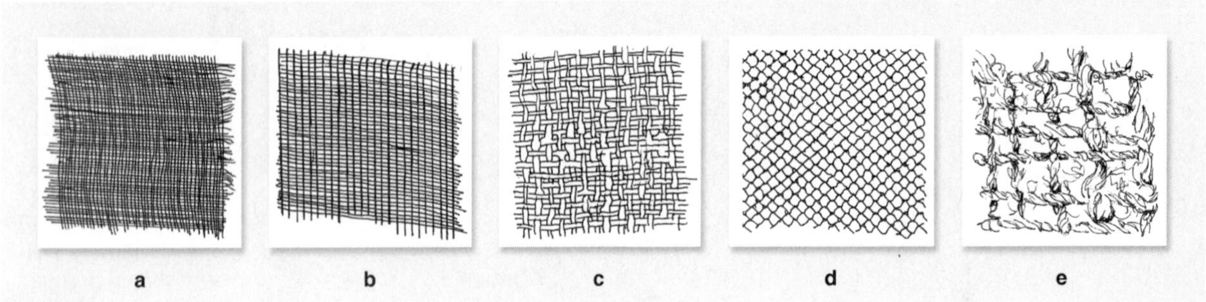

7-2

Gauzes

A variety of gauzes are illustrated to show their different weaves.

a Theatrical gauze: This fabric, which looks like surgical gauze, has very little strength.

b Shark's-tooth scrim: horizontal, ladder-weave. Strong, not as sheer as bobbinet, best for dye painting.

c Burlap: One of many weaves, this one is more open than some and is very flexible. Easily stretches out of shape.

d Bobbinet: hexagonal weave. Very transparent and strong but stretches out of shape easily.

e Erosion cloth: Designed for landscapers, this gauze has a very open weave. Can be painted and drapes easily.

URL http://www.showbiz.com

has a much more open weave than shark's-tooth scrim does (Figure 7-2). The shark's-tooth, in addition to draping well, is dense enough to provide a dye-painting surface but still become transparent when light is removed from its face. Filled scrim or leno scrim can be used as a cyc, or painted drop, for a softer look.

Drops

Another large-area piece of scenery is the *drop,* taking its name from the fact that it hangs on a batten and is dropped in. The drop is made with horizontal face-to-face seams to create a smooth surface (Figure 7-3). The horizontal seams, when the drop is hanging, are under enough tension from the weight of the material and bottom pipe to stretch into a smooth surface.

A translucent drop is painted with dye or transparent paint and is equipped with tie-lines at the top and a pipe pocket or occasionally tie-lines at the bottom (Figure 7-3). Ideally, a translucent drop is made by using 30-foot-wide muslin, although this may not be affordable. If seams in a translucent drop are necessary, their position matters. If not carefully hidden in the design, they produce a distracting shadow line. For this reason, translucent drops are sometimes made with vertical or irregularly placed seams.

For transportation, drops are made to fold. Acrylic and latex paints are flexible enough to withstand folding *only* if the paint application is thin and kept to one layer. Even then, with age and use, the paint will eventually crack.

Drops are commonly made of muslin because it is available in wide widths and is an excellent, inexpensive translucent material. Drops are sometimes made of other materials, such as burlap, often to achieve a specific desired textural quality. And, of course, drops can be made of the gauze materials. Shark's-tooth and other theatrical gauzes are used more often than other sheer fabrics because they come in wider widths.

A cut drop such as in Figure 7-3b is often backed with bobbinet, opera net, or scenery net. The cut edges of a drop can be supported with a lighter material, often with a 1-inch square mesh. When the net is dyed to match the

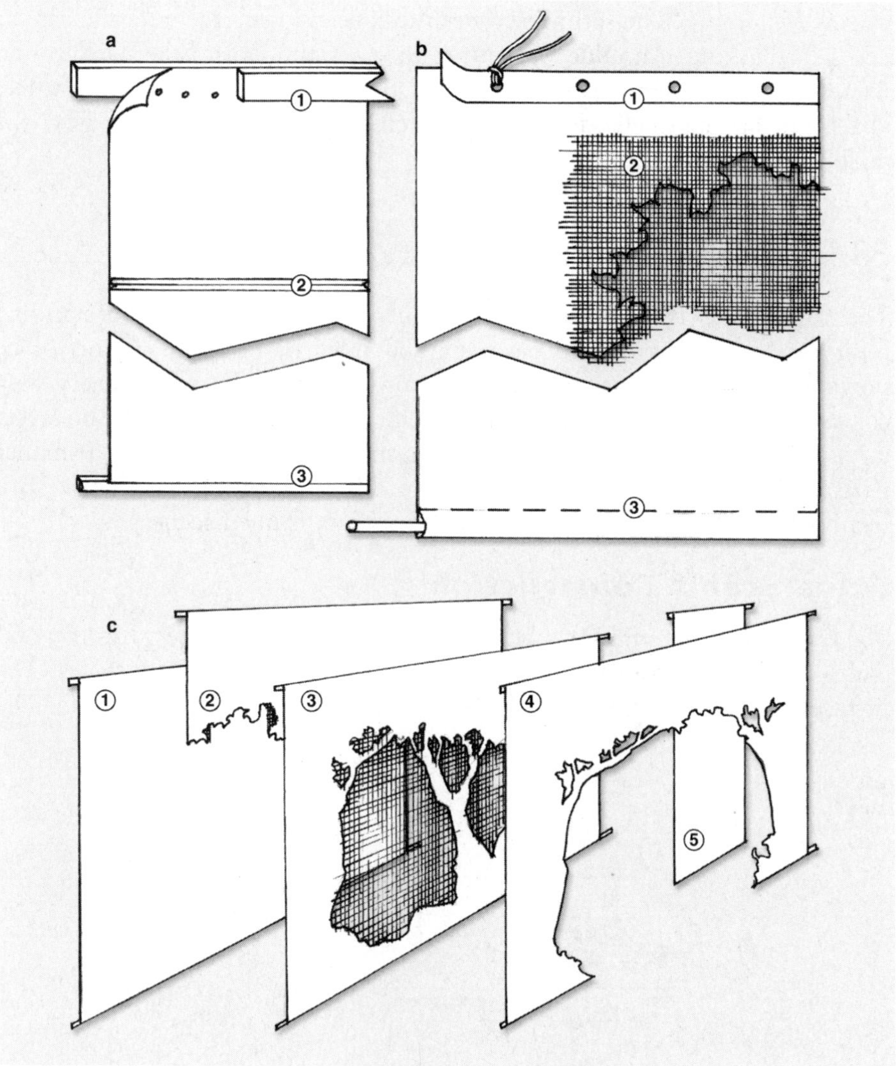

7-3

Drop Construction

a Rear view of a roll drop:
- **1** Top batten, double 1×4.
- **2** Face-to-face horizontal seam.
- **3** Bottom batten, double 2-inch half round.

b Rear view of a cut drop:
- **1** Top webbing with grommets and tie-lines.
- **2** Netting glued over openings or cut edges to support loose ends.
- **3** Drop bottom with pipe sleeve for the removal of bottom batten.

c Types of drops:
- **1** Plain backdrop.
- **2** Cut border.
- **3** Cut drop, netted.
- **4** Leg drop or portal.
- **5** Leg.

background, it becomes nearly invisible. A plastic netting of 4-inch mesh, originally manufactured to protect farm crops, is another option that works well.

The Cyclorama

The largest single piece of scenery in the theatre is the cyclorama, or "cyc." The cyclorama's most familiar use is as a sky or void, backing a setting or elements of scenery placed in the foreground. Most commonly, the cyc is hung flat across the back of the setting, although it can also extend downstage in a gentle arc on either one or both sides of the set.

The challenge in making a cyclorama is to create a large, uninterrupted, smooth surface. A seamless cyc, although ideal, can be prohibitively expensive. With a seamed cyc, the direction of the sewn seams becomes important. Because the cyc material is hung flat, the tension from horizontal seams will help pull the surface smooth.

Vertical seams round the corners better than do horizontal seams, but the former do not present as smooth a finished surface. In both cases the seams are sure to show under a high level of illumination. This can be corrected by hanging a large flat panel of shark's-tooth scrim directly in front of the canvas cyclorama. The scrim becomes the reflecting surface, and the canvas acts as a backing. An added benefit is that a scrim causes the background to appear more distant. If the scrim and the cyc can be moved several feet apart and lit separately, designers can achieve great flexibility in how the audience sees the cyc.

FRAMED SCENERY

The structure of framed scenery is planned to support itself in a standing position. Although a framed piece may be aided by hanging support or be flown altogether, the basic principle remains the same. Framed scenery, as a construction technique, does not lend itself easily to a large area. If too large, it has to be hinged to fold into a smaller size or be dismantled into smaller parts to move in and out of the theatre. Most framing, then, deals with relatively small modules when compared with unframed scenery.

Wood Scenic Construction

The traditional material for scenic construction is wood. The various wood joints are derived from the many ways of combining lumber surfaces. The surfaces of lumber are described as its *face* (flat surface), *edge*, and *end*. The

7-4

Typical Wood Joints Used in Scenery Construction

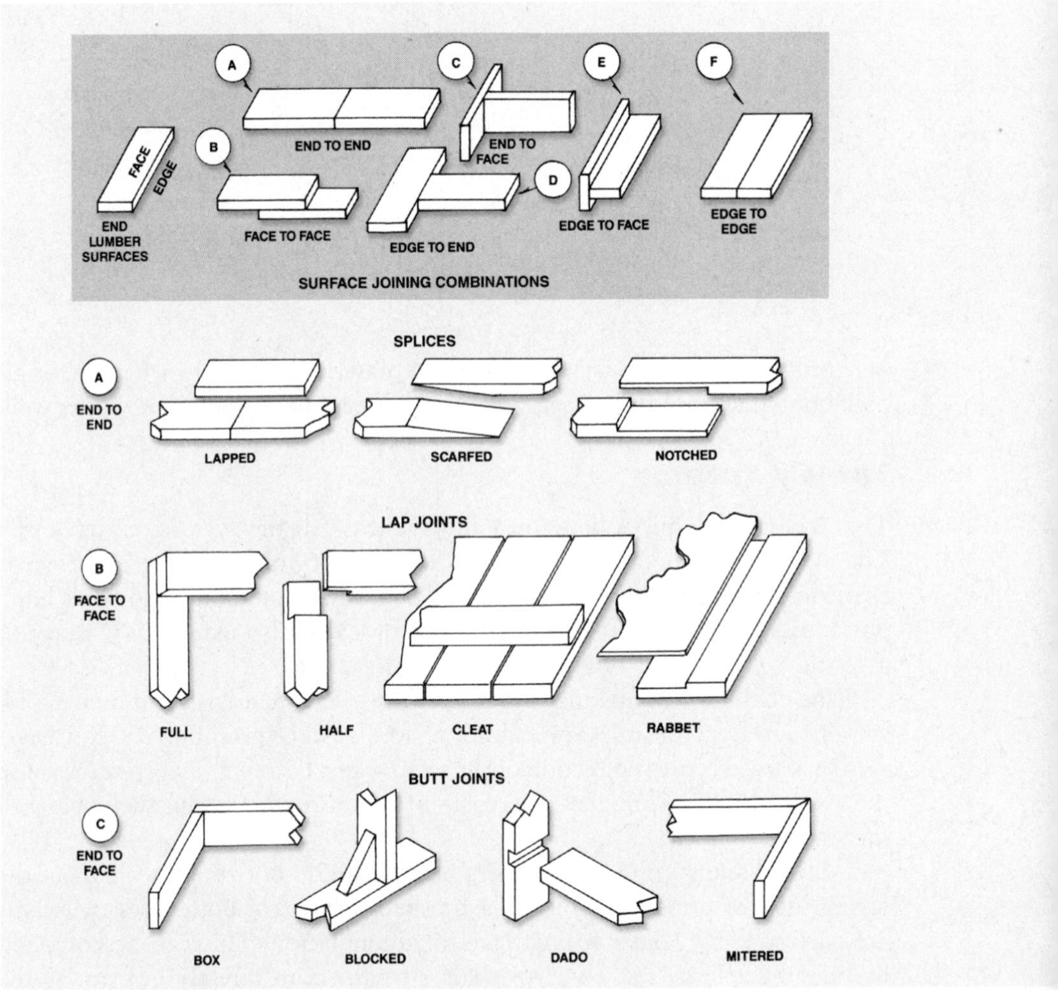

surface-joining combinations are classified as *end to end, face to face, end to face, edge to end, edge to face,* and *edge to edge,* as illustrated in Figure 7-4.

Joining lumber has two steps: first, the cutting and fitting of the joint; second, the securing of the joint with hardware or glue. Wood joints, whether permanent or temporary, are used in constructing individual units of scenery.

In Figure 7-4, the numerous joints used in scenery construction are classified into groups that combine the same surfaces. Fixed joints are secured with glue and nails, staples, or screws. Knockdown or temporary joints are held with bolts, loose-pin hinges, keeper hooks, and turn buttons.

The framing of a traditional theatrical flat, such as the one shown in Figure 7-5, illustrates the two basic techniques that are applied to any size or shape. The soft-covered flat uses an end-to-edge joint, which is strengthened most commonly with a ¼-inch-thick plywood plate called a *corner block* or *keystone.* The plywood is attached with its grain running across the joint.

The top and bottom horizontal framing members are called **rails,** while the vertical framing members are **stiles.** Internal horizontals or verticals are referred to as **toggles** and are generally spaced at 4- to 5-foot intervals.

The diagonal braces strengthen and hold square the rectangular shape. A rectangle is basically a weak structure easily racked out of shape. The triangle, on the other hand, resists a change of shape. Hence, two diagonal braces off one side of the rectangle, as shown in Figure 7-5, will resist a change of shape.

rails Top and bottom horizontal framing members of a flat.

stiles Vertical framing members of a flat.

toggles Internal framing members of a flat, usually horizontal but sometimes vertical.

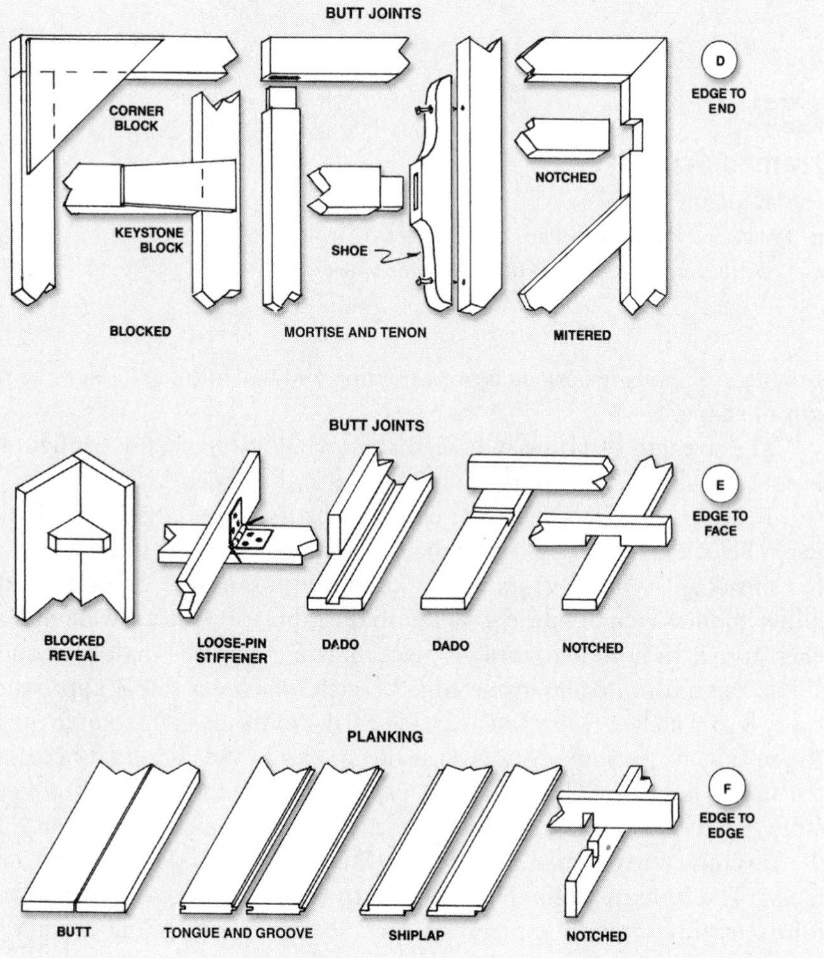

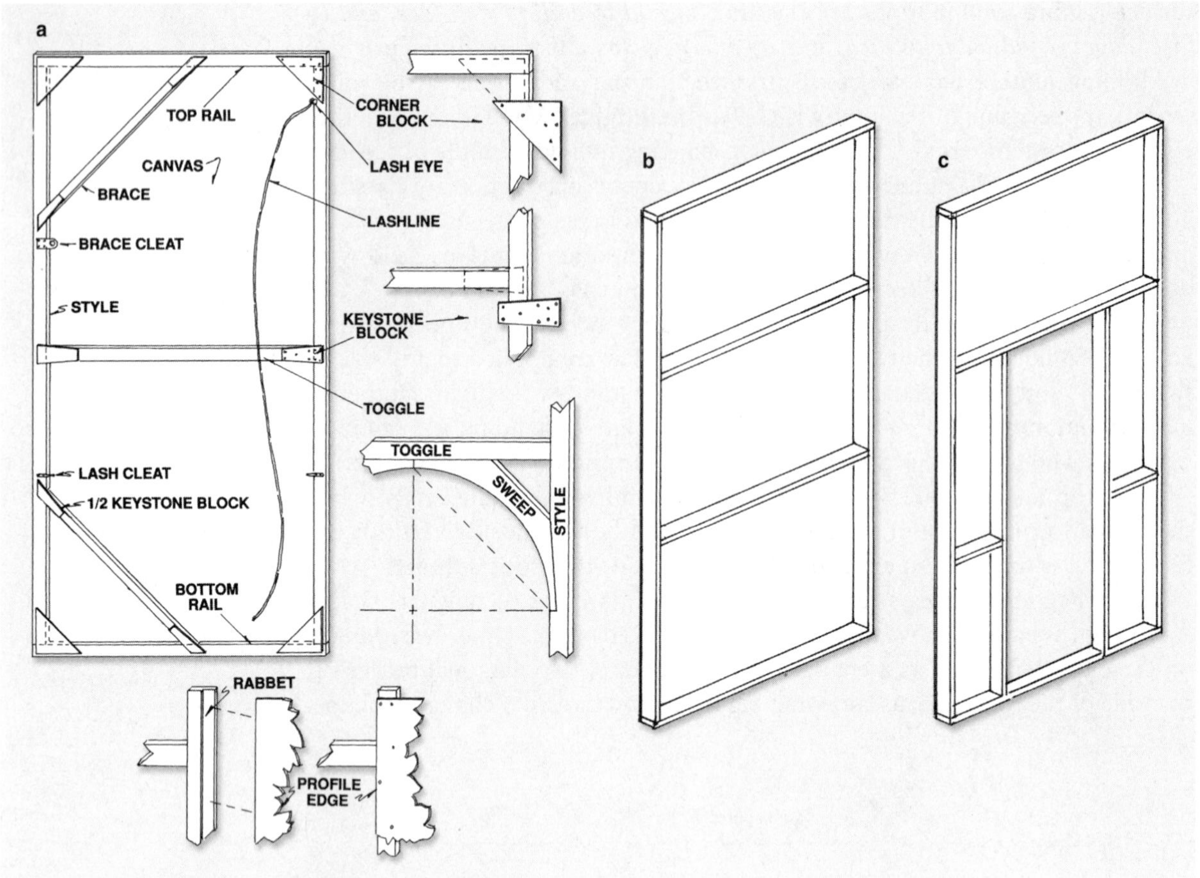

7-5

Framed Scenery

a Flat construction.

b Hollywood flat construction.

c Construction of Hollywood flat with door opening.

Bracing on opposite corners is not as strong and will allow the flat to be racked out of shape.

The strength of properly braced scenery allows for many configurations. Figure 7-6 shows some of the many uses of framed scenery.

To cover a flat with muslin, choose fabric slightly larger than the frame itself. Place the muslin on top of the frame without pulling it tight; this allows for shrinkage, which occurs when the muslin is painted. The standard is to allow about 1 inch of fabric to fall onto the table for a 3-foot-wide flat. Staple each corner to hold the fabric in place. Starting with the middle of one stile, staple the muslin to the inside edge of each, placing a staple approximately every 8 to 9 inches. Work toward each corner in this fashion. Staple the fabric to the rails in the same way. Adjust the staples in the corners if necessary so the fabric lays flat. Then glue the loose edges of fabric to the frame on all sides. After this has dried, carefully trim the excess fabric with a matte knife.

It is now fairly common for flats to be covered with sheet material such as lauan. The framing technique is similar to that of a soft-covered flat, but the joints in this method are end to face so that the framing members are

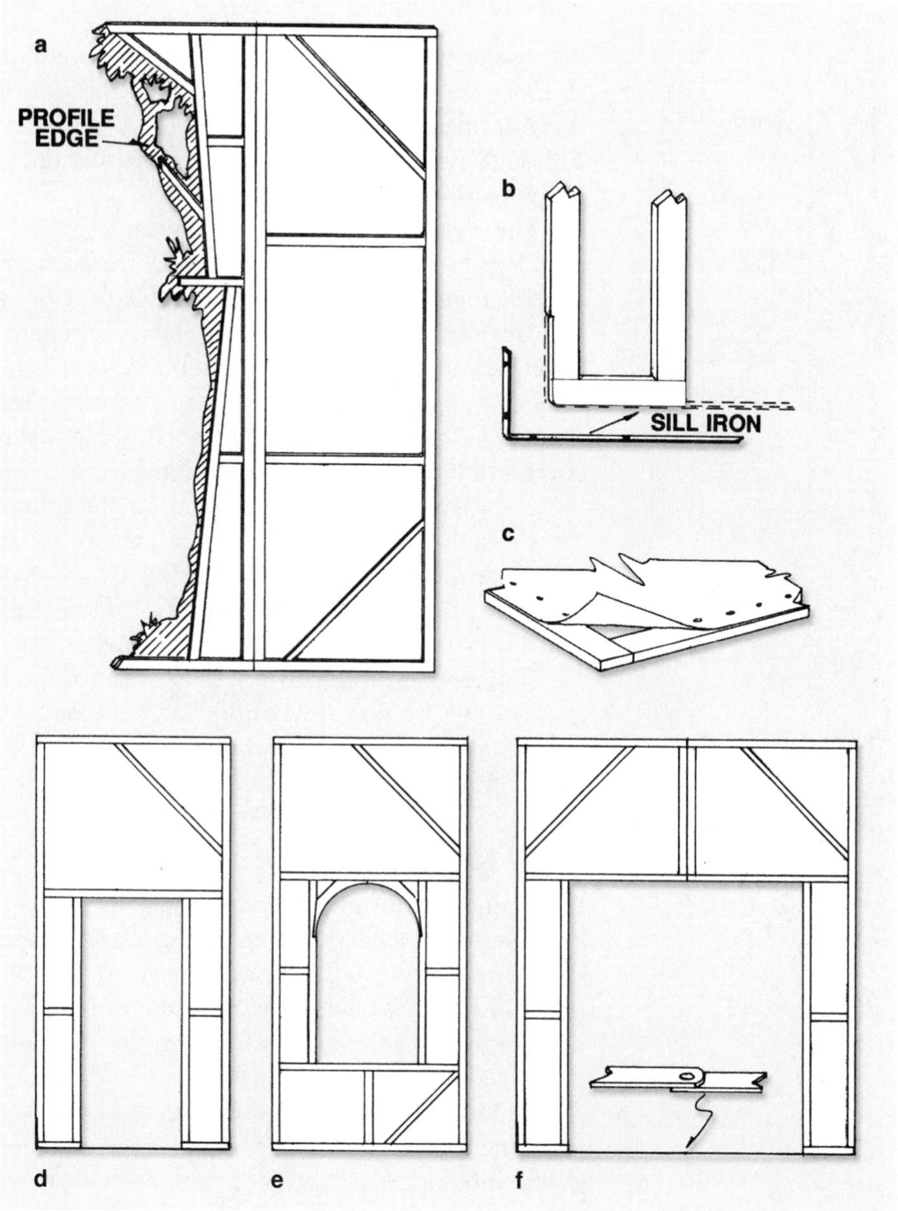

7-6

Uses of Framed Scenery

- **a** The framing of a profile flat, or a flat with profile edges of ¼-inch plywood.
- **b** Detail of sill-iron used across the bottom of a door opening in a flat.
- **c** Detail of canvas covering technique. Staples are set on the inside edge of the external framework.
- **d** Door flat.
- **e** Window flat.
- **f** Two-fold flat with double-door opening. Note hinged sill-iron.

perpendicular to the face of the flat. This is called a **Hollywood flat.** The hard cover negates the need for diagonals, corner blocks, and keystones. The advantages of hard-covered flats are greater structural integrity and the ability to accept a wide range of textural surfaces. It is preferable for the hard-covered flats to be covered with muslin to provide a good paint surface.

Hollywood flat A flat in which the framing members are on edge; the corners of the flat are end to face (as opposed to end to edge).

Framing Curved Scenery

The framing of a curved surface requires a technique similar to the one used for a Hollywood flat. All framing members are on edge rather than on the face. The toggles are sweeps, most often of plywood, cut to the desired curve of the surface. Because the covering must be firm yet able to bend, lauan or ⅛-inch ply are commonly used. Canvas or muslin is glued to the finished form to provide a surface matching the rest of the scenery (Figure 7-7).

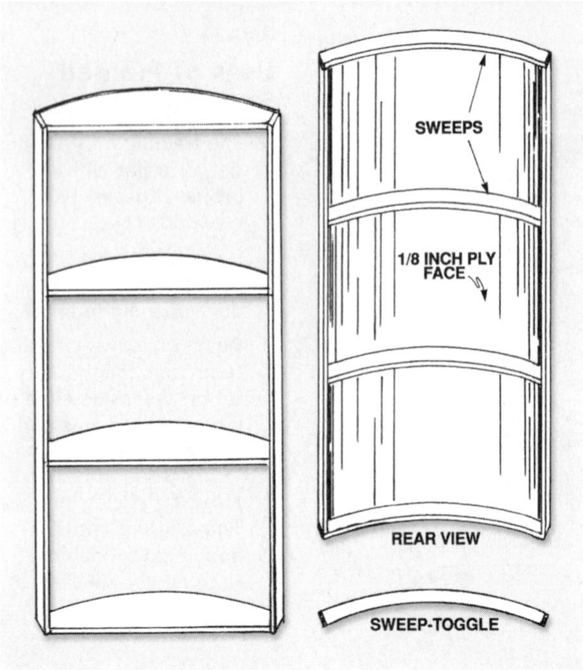

7-7

Curved Scenery

Stiles and toggles are framed on edge to stiffen a ⅛-inch lauan cover, which is most often used with curved surfaces.

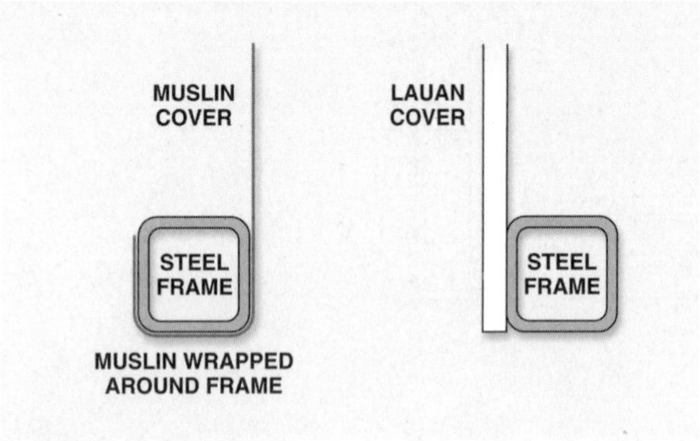

7-8

Covering Metal-Framed Flats

For soft-covered metal-framed flats, the muslin cover is wrapped around the metal frame and glued in back. Hard-covered metal-framed flats have the lauan cover attached to the face of the metal frame.

shutter The part of a door that opens and closes.

reveal The jamb (header and sides), or the edge of an opening, such as a door or an arch, indicating thickness.

Metal-Framed Scenery

Because of the recent accessibility of MIG welding to more scene shops (see Chapter 6), the use of metal-framed scenery is becoming more common. Although not cheaper than wood construction, it is comparable in cost.

The structure is essentially the same as with wood-framed flattage—an outside frame with interior toggles—but in this case welded together. The advantage of metal-framed flats is strength, stability, and durability. They can be hard- or soft-covered (Figure 7-8). Because metal frames need fewer interior supports, designers can use a scrim cover and have it lit to be transparent.

Light-gauge steel tubing is used for the frame. This can be rectangular, but square is more common, the most widely used being 1-by-1-inch (outside dimension of the tubing) 18 gauge (thickness of the tube wall) square tubing.

Unlike wood-framed flats, metal-framed units can be hung from the top of the flat, because they cannot come apart (see Chapter 10, Figure 10-5). If done this way, the flat will hang flat like a curtain.

Doors

Doors and windows are important details that can be neglected in the haste of preparing a set. A door, in a sense, is a moving piece of scenery used by the actor. In a split second, its malfunction can destroy not only the scenic illusion but also the carefully developed mood of a scene.

Building and hanging a door requires both skill and time. For these reasons, the average amateur group should make or commission a set of good stock door casings that can be used in a variety of ways.

A door unit is made up of three basic parts (1) the actual door, called a **shutter;** (2) the frame, comprising the jambs (vertical members), header or top (that together make up the **reveal**), and sill (bottom); and (3) the trim, which forms the decorative frame around the door opening. The door is always hinged to the reveal. Most often the reveal is built as part of the flat structure, as this is the easiest method of construction. The shutter is built separately and hung in the opening. The trim around the door is attached to the flat itself. One can also build the shutter, reveal, and trim as a complete but separate unit from the flat; this unit

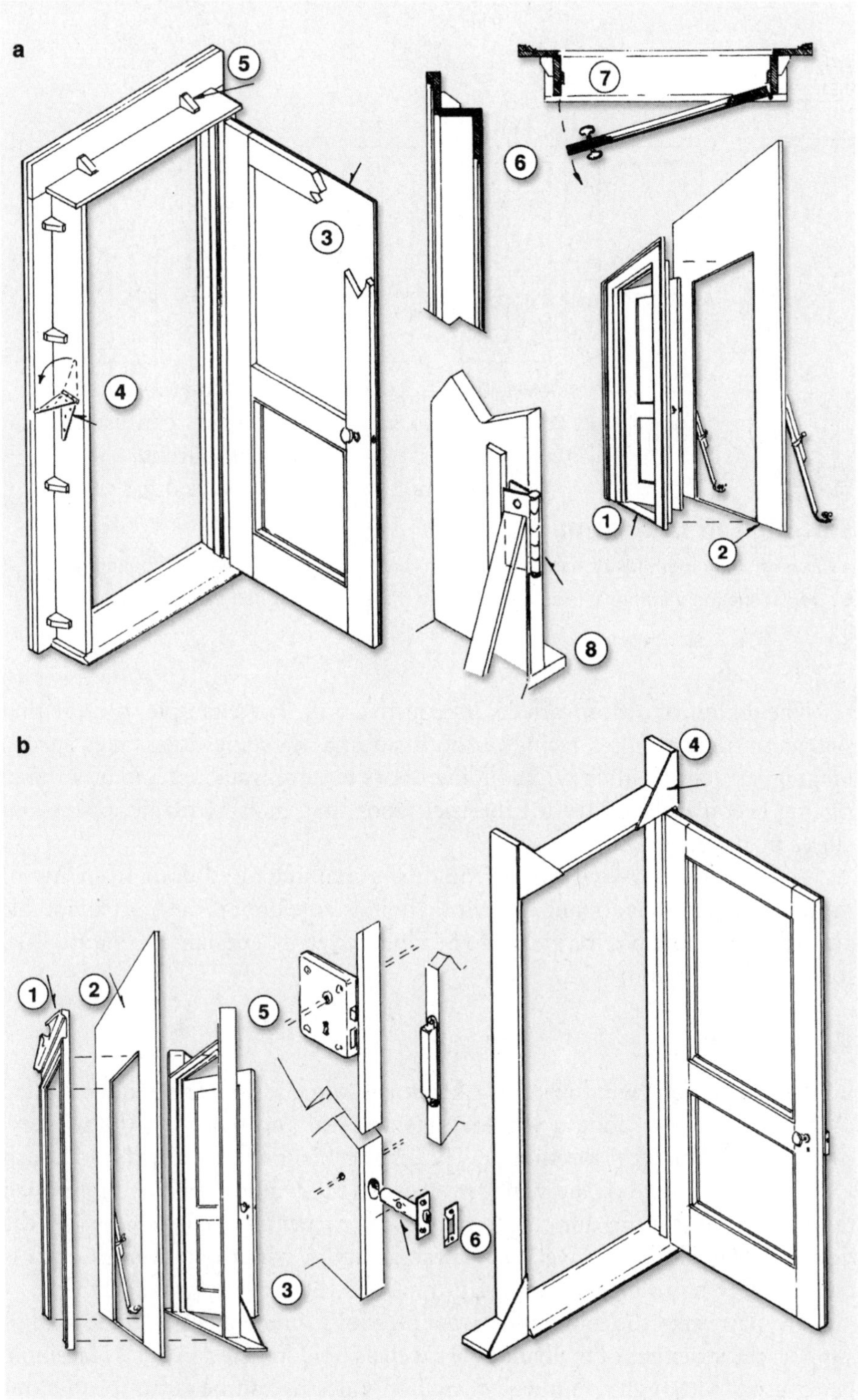

7-9

Door Construction

a Independent door:
- **1** Door reveal and trim built as one unit.
- **2** Flat with standard door opening.
- **3** Detail of door construction.
- **4** Angled strap hinge on jamb to hold door unit in the opening.
- **5** Blocks to hold trim in place.
- **6** Cross section of door unit through header.
- **7** Plan of the independent unit showing the hinging.
- **8** Butt hinge on door.

b Dependent door:
- **1** Separate trim.
- **2** Flat with a standard door opening.
- **3** Door and reveal.
- **4** Corner blocks to hold reveal square.
- **5** Rim lock. Attached on back side of door.
- **6** Tubular latch. Sets into edge of door.

is referred to as an **independent door** (Figure 7-9a). The third method is to build a **dependent door** in which the reveal structure, containing the shutter, butts up against the back side of the flat (Figure 7-9b). The trim can be completely painted or attached and set away from the opening to increase the apparent size of the doorway.

independent door A door that is a completely separate unit from the flat or wall into which it will be fit.

dependent door A door in which the reveal structure is a part of the flat or wall that frames it.

7-10

Variation in Door Trim

a Two of many methods of handling the trim around the same-size door opening.

b Door paneling variations. Doors 1, 2, 3, and 4 are standard paneled door shutters.

The action of a door affects its construction. For example, a door that swings onstage requires facing on both sides; a swinging door takes special hinging, as does a Dutch door; sliding doors involve tracking; and additional rigging becomes necessary for the trick door that, as if by magic, opens and closes by itself.

URL http://www.simpsondoor.com

URL http://www.sidl.com

A contemporary-styled door could be a manufactured door from any of the home centers that abound. The flush, hollow core door is the most adaptable and affordable and has the ability to be modified to fit a design. See Figure 7-10 for variations in door trim.

Windows

window sash Frame that contains the panes of a window.

Functional realistic windows are called for in some scripts and require skilled carpentry. Like the door, a window has a reveal and trim, but the **window sash** takes the place of the shutter. The arrangement of panes within the sash varies with the style of the window. Because the window sash is more open than a door, it is more difficult to build. The carpenter needs to consider the design of the window as well as its practicality. A window that must open is considerably more difficult to build than one that is simply decorative.

mullions Interior window-framing pieces.

The pattern of the thin **mullions,** or interior framing pieces, can be used to support the structure of the window as well as hold in place any glass facsimile being used. Although complicated mullion patterns can be cut in profile out of ¾ plywood, this works well only if the windows are far enough upstage that the audience cannot see much detail. Delicate tracery is frequently reinforced by one of several materials that can pass for glass and strengthen the mullions at the same time.

Real glass is too fragile and dangerous to use on the stage. Plexiglas, the most obvious substitute, has certain drawbacks. When the window background is darker than the onstage lights, the window reflects the lights like a mirror. Also, to avoid a Plexiglas "shimmy," it has to be at least ¼ inch thick and

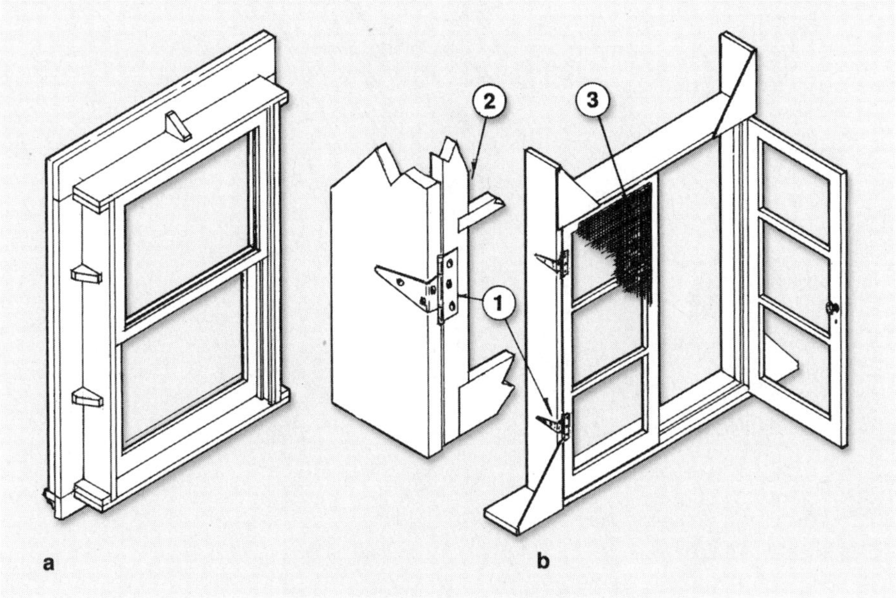

7-11

Window Construction

a Double-hung window. Trim is attached to reveal in the same manner as the independent door's trim.

b Casement window. The reveal is constructed in the same way as the dependent door with hinged sashes.

1 A bent T-strap hinge in place of the butt hinge.

2 Notched mullions.

3 Galvanized screening to strengthen the sash and simulate glass.

therefore expensive. (The use of Plexiglas windows in TV and film, on the other hand, is common practice. Reflection problems are minimal because there is only the one eye of the camera and not the 500 or more pairs of eyes of a theatre audience.)

Windows are sometimes left clear or backed with netting or screening. The net, although nearly invisible, has enough density to give the feeling of glass and will catch light coming through the window. The effect increases by contrast if the window is opened during the action of the play.

Like that of the door, window action involves sliding or swinging on hinges. A window may have the vertical sliding action of a double-hung window, or it may slide horizontally. It may have the vertical hinging of a casement window or the horizontal hinging of the awning-type window (Figure 7-11).

Because of the great variation in sash styles, it is a little more difficult to plan a set of stock windows than doors. Often-used, conventional windows can be standardized and put into stock. Also the casing (reveal and trim) may be kept in stock to be used with different sashes for each show. As with doors, manufactured windows can be used where practicable.

Trim

Decorative trim appears on a set in places other than around doors, windows, and other openings. Baseboards, chair rails, wainscoting, cornices, over-the-mantel decoration, and other kinds of trim may all contribute to scenic illusion. Such trim might need to be removable for handling or changing from one set to another, although this can severely slow down the shifting process.

The attached trim may require additional framing within the flat for support. Chair rails and baseboards are easy to attach, but the construction and hanging of a cornice is more complicated. The average cornice and other trim pieces can be made of stock moldings, even when the trim is oversized for theatrical purposes. To keep the framing lightweight, the molding is nailed to sweeps set at about 2-foot intervals and backed with 3 ply or longitudinal

7-12

Cornice Construction

A cornice is a lightly framed three-dimensional element of trim that usually runs along the top edge of a wall. The perspective view shows the block-framing technique and a method of attaching the cornice to the scenery.

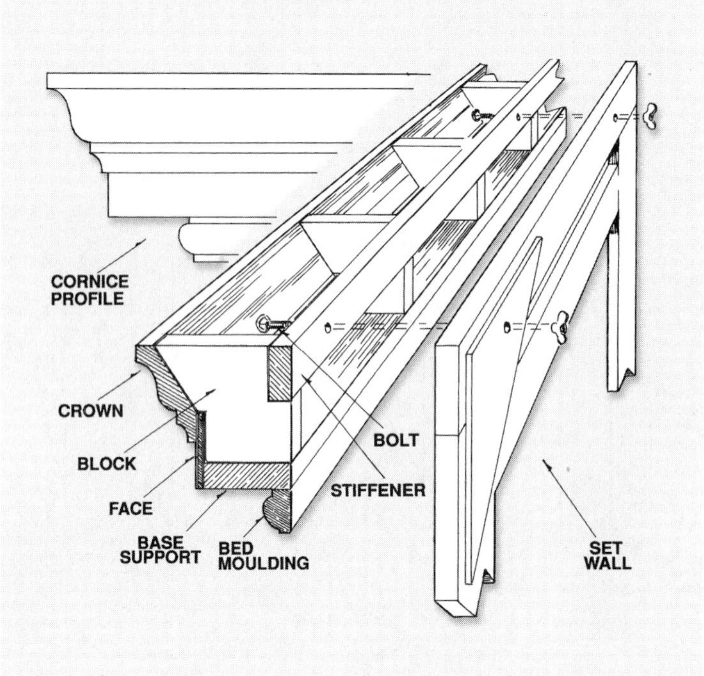

framing strips. The whole assembly is attached to the wall flats with bolts or turnbuttons (Figure 7-12).

URL http://www.flexibletrim.com

Architectural and decorative trim, of course, can be duplicated in lightweight materials such as carved Styrofoam or vacuum-formed shapes (discussed later in this chapter). Flexible plastic molding, although expensive, is also available and is useful when molding must follow a curved surface.

WEIGHT-BEARING STRUCTURES

Certain elements of scenery cannot be reduced to flat planes. Others, because they are so small, are more practically built as three-dimensional forms. This is especially important if the form is to bear the weight of a sitting or standing actor or other pieces of scenery. Weight-bearing structures take many forms: architectural shapes such as steps, ramps, and raised platforms; the irregular forms of rocks; and the free form of abstract designs. Raising a large portion of the stage floor and the use of steps and ramps brings excitement to a design composition, variation to the staging, and potential headaches to the stage technician. In the absence of mechanical means to raise sections of the stage floor, the technician must create a second floor at a specific height above the stage floor. The level must be structurally sound enough to support actors and furniture with a minimum of deflection and, at the same time, be portable and economical. A large expanse of platforming is subdivided into smaller units for ease of handling. A single unit is made to knock down into even smaller parts.

Platforms

Construction Any surface platforming technique can be broken down into the three structural members that are always present in some form or other: the top, rail, and post. In the simplest terms the perimeter shape of the platform is framed and then supported up to the desired height.

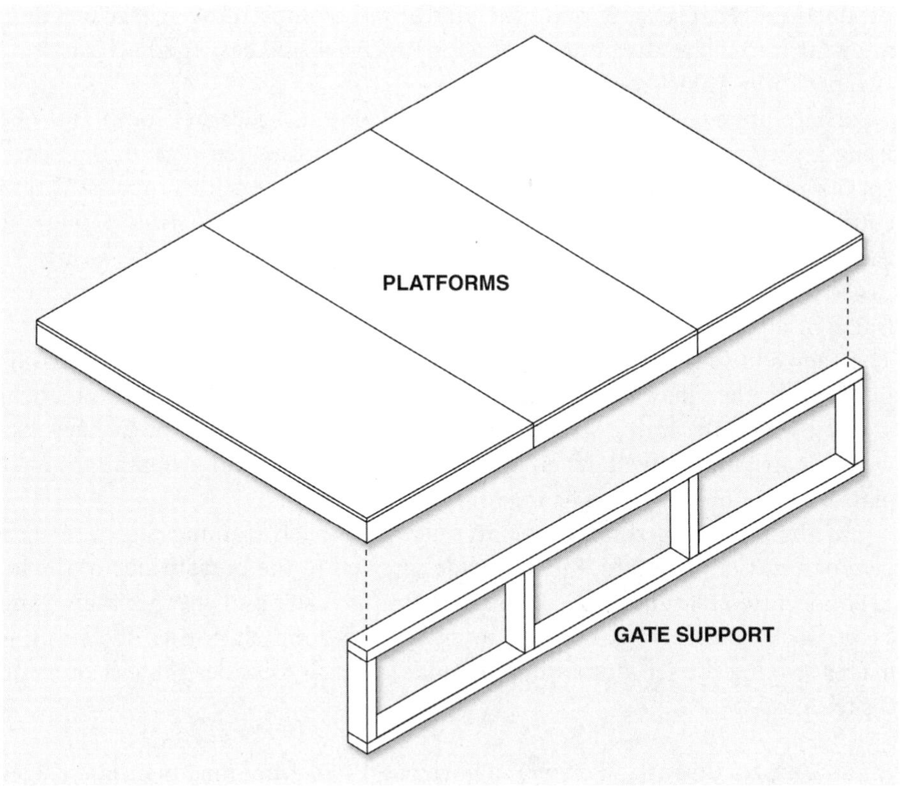

7-13

Gated Platform Support

Three 4 by 8 platforms with gate support.

Most frequently, the lid and frame structure of a platform are permanently attached to one another, sometimes referred to as a "rigid platform" and built in stock lid modular sizes (4 × 8, 2 × 8, 4 × 4, 3 × 3, 3 × 6). This typically consists of a lumber frame of 2 by 4's or 1 by 6's or a tubular steel frame. This frame is then covered with a ¾-inch plywood lid. The platform is elevated to any variety of heights using simple lumber legs, typically 2 by 4's bolted to the frame. Each leg is independent of all others. This style of construction is applicable to platforms of any shape.

A more efficient type of platform support is stud wall construction, referred to as *gating*. Similar to house construction, this is an all 2 by 4 frame consisting of two horizontal members joined by a series of vertical members. The advantages of this method are quick installation, very rigid support, and the ability to create raked or angled decks easily. In this method, support members are often shared by a series or group of platforms. The framed platform is attached to the gated support (Figure 7-13). Because they are separate, each component can be made of different materials. For example, one could use a steel tubular-framed platform with a wood-framed gate (and vise versa).

The frequency of the leg support depends on the size and material of the frame. For 2 by 4's, the standard interval for legs is 24–30 inches. Obviously the thicker and wider the lumber, the fewer supports are needed.

Joining Platforms Joining two or more stock platforms together is standard practice. The cheapest and fastest way to do this is to use large C-clamps to pull together the frames of two separate platforms. The C-clamps must be thoroughly tightened and checked periodically during the run of the production, because activity on the platforms can loosen the grip of a clamp, allowing it to fall to the floor. Another inexpensive and easy method is bolting two platform frames together.

casket lock A two-piece locking device incorporating a rotating wedge that pulls both pieces together and locks them with one turn of an Allen T-wrench. Also called *coffin lock.*

There are two more desirable methods, one using **casket locks** and one using a plywood gusset plate. Casket locks are most often placed in a notch cut out of the frame of the platform. The disadvantage of this method is that cutting a notch in the frame weakens the structure. All casket locks must be the same size and placed exactly the same way in relation to the platforms. An easier method is to employ what is called *hold-back framing,* in which the frame of a platform lid is inset 1½ to 2 inches from the edge of the platform. This then allows space for the casket lock to be bolted directly to the underside of the lid rather than to the support. This method, standard in commercial scenery, leaves the frame structure completely intact. The use of casket locks works particularly well when frequent installation and deinstallation of platforms are needed, such as for touring productions.

In the second method, carpenters use hold-back framing and a ¾-inch plywood gusset plate 3 to 4 inches wide screwed to the bottom side of the lid to connect two platforms (see Figure 7-14). It is easier and cheaper than using casket locks and there is no need to crawl under the platforms. However, it makes striking the set more difficult and is generally less desirable than using casket locks.

truss A framework of wood or metal that uses triangles and is therefore considerably stronger than a simple beam.

Truss Versus Beam A *beam* is a horizontal structural member that bridges a long span between vertical supports. In the theatre, beams and cross-beams support the stage floor to provide a pattern of trap openings. Because of its necessarily heavy weight, a beam is not suitable for scenery construction. By framing a beamlike structure with a network of cross-bracing, the resulting lightweight structure, called a **truss,** can function as a beam.

7-14

Connecting Two Platforms

a The simplest way to connect two platforms is to use a plywood gusset underneath two platform lids that overhang the support.

b A better method is to use casket locks, which work most effectively with an overhanging platform lid.

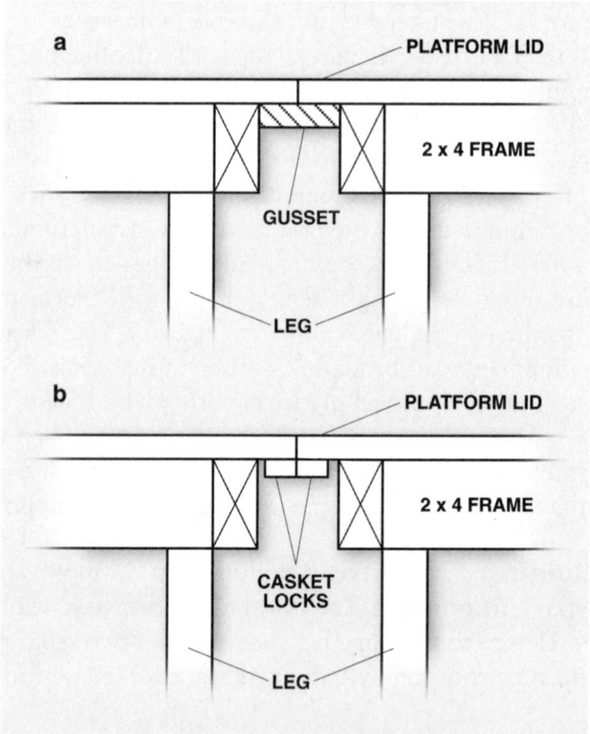

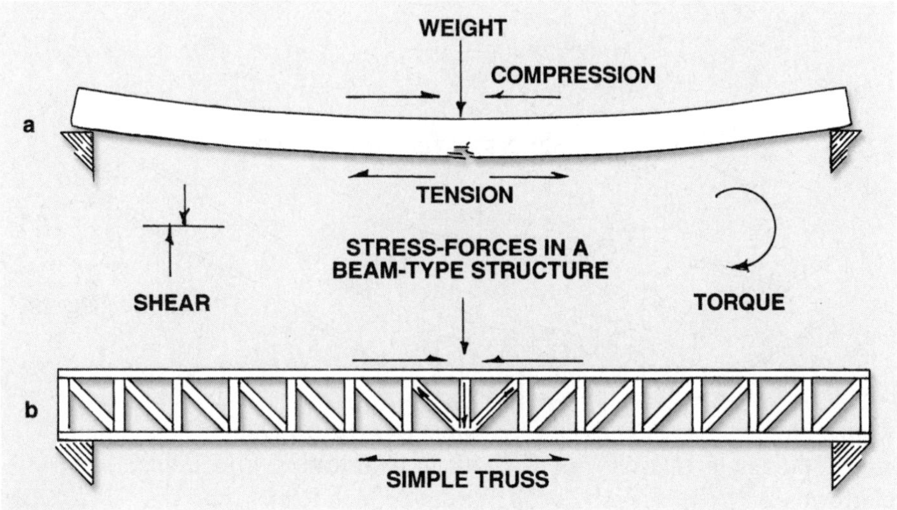

7-15

Truss

a Various types of trusses. A beam in an unstable condition illustrates the direction of stress forces.

b Simple truss showing the direction of each stress force.

Truss framing involves two long horizontal members—one on top and one on the bottom—and a series of vertical posts spotted at intervals to hold the members apart. Carpenters complete the framing by inserting a diagonal at each interval. Just as the diagonal brace strengthens the frame of a flat, so the diagonals greatly strengthen a truss. A simple truss is considerably stronger and will safely support much more weight than a beam of the same size and length.

The stress forces on a beam or beam-type structure can be illustrated by placing the beam in an unstable condition (Figure 7-15). As the beam sags, the top face is under compression while the bottom face is in tension. The stress forces within a truss are similar. When the top member is compressed in a horizontal direction, the bottom member is in tension. The vertical members are compressed and the diagonals are also in tension.

A long single truss has a tendency to torque or twist. As a result, a long span has to be stiffened with a second truss, forming a *box truss*. Repeated trusses, when used as a joist, are bridged or cross-braced.

URL http://www.howstuffworks.com/bridge.htm

Stress Skin Panels The stress skin construction technique produces a panel of great rigidity and structural strength. Typical stress skin construction consists of two plywood sheets that sandwich an internal structure, often a wood or honeycomb core (Figure 7-16). In essence, the "skins" resist the forces of compression and tension in the same manner the top and bottom of a truss do. The extra rigidity of a stress skin panel generally reduces the amount of substructural support required.

Ramps Note that ramps can be constructed in the same manner as any of the platforms just discussed.

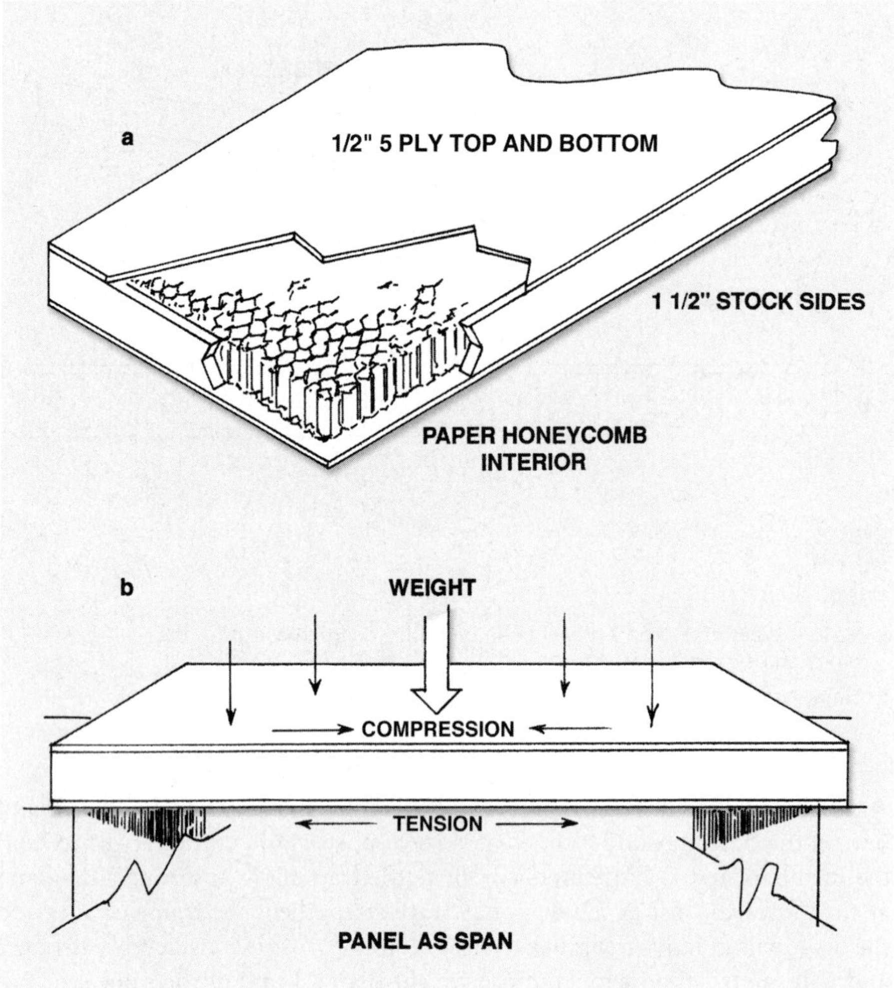

7-16

Stress Skin Panel

a Construction of panel.

b Stress skin panel as a bridge. The honeycomb interior spreads the load to support a relatively heavy weight over a limited span.

Free Forms

Irregular surfaces that cannot be reduced to a series of flat planes must be constructed as a three-dimensional unit. Examples include rocks and abstract forms that may have to bear weight.

Framing an irregular surface is, of course, more or less extemporaneous (at least within the parameters of the design) and depends on some final sculptural touches by the designer or scenic artist to complete the form. For this reason the design drawings of a free form should be accompanied by a scaled model. The form usually suggests the manner of construction; nevertheless there is a basic method that can be adapted to most irregular shapes.

One method of construction of a rock piece, demonstrated in Figure 7-17, involves the following steps. (1) The exact shape of the base of the rock is framed as a piece of flat scenery. (2) Across the shortest dimension of the base is set a series of shaped pieces that follow the contour of a section taken at that point (see Chapter 5). (3) The contour pieces are stiffened with cross-bracing, and all weight-bearing surfaces are reinforced. (4) Over the contour pieces is placed chicken wire or 2-inch screen wire, which is pinched or stretched

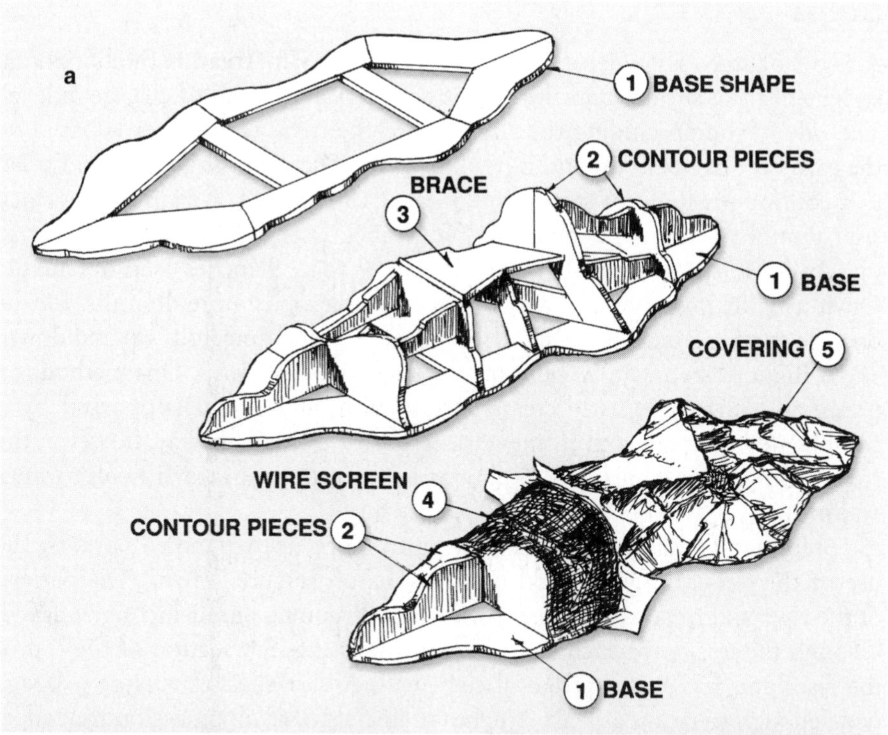

b

c

7-17

Construction of Rock Forms

a Steps in construction:
- **1** Shape of form on floor. Conventional framing.
- **2** Contour pieces.
- **3** Cross bracing.
- **4** Wire screening.
- **5** Burlap.

b Three-dimensional shape before covering with burlap.

c Same shape covered.

into the desired shape. (5) The final surface is applied to the screen wire. The kind of covering material depends on the desired texture. The best results are usually obtained with fabric. It is applied by first dipping it into a mixture of strong white glue and base color. The fabric is then draped over and tacked to the framework and allowed to harden. A form made in this manner is lightweight, inexpensive, and surprisingly sturdy. (We discuss textured and sculptured surfaces later in this chapter.)

Steps

tread Horizontal surface of a step.

riser Vertical surface of a step, often referred to as *facing*.

A flight of steps is made up of risers and treads. The **tread** is the horizontal weight-bearing surface and the **riser** is the vertical interval of change in level. The rule of thumb guiding the size ratio of the tread to the riser is based on the ease of movement up and down the steps. The sum of the riser and tread in a continuous flight of steps should equal 18 inches. For example, a 6-inch riser would require a 12-inch tread, an 8-inch riser a 10-inch tread, and so on. Any rise lower than 4 inches or higher than 9 inches is problematic. Obviously the low-riser and wide-tread combination is more desirable for the onstage steps, permitting an actor to move easily and gracefully up and down.

A flight of steps can be built for the stage in many ways. One method is a modified platform trestle construction with each tread supported by a complicated post-and-rail framework (Figure 7-18a). This way, however, the steps are a part of a bulky three-dimensional platform that is difficult to store and move.

nosing The projecting edge of a stair tread and top of stair riser; often refers to a simple molding hiding the intersection of tread and riser, particularly if the tread itself does not project.

carriage The supporting structure of a staircase tread.

Steps can be made to knock down into more easily handled parts by the use of the cut-carriage method of construction (Figure 7-18b). The pattern of the riser and tread is cut from a wide board running parallel to a line drawn through the nosing of each step. The **nosing** is the intersection of the top of the riser and the outside edge of the tread. A **carriage** is cut from a board wide enough to retain at least 3 inches of uncut board along the bottom edge. The thickness of a carriage depends somewhat on its unsupported length. Often 1-inch pine stock is used for lightweight construction, while 2-inch stock is required for a heavier structure. The use of a *metal carriage* can be seen in Figure 6-23.

The choice of carriage stock is also affected by the nature of the riser material. Is the riser made of 1-inch pine or ¾-inch 3 ply—or is it left open? As the riser material becomes lighter, the carriage stock should increase in thickness.

A flight of steps would have, typically, two carriages. Additional carriages would depend on the thickness of the tread and the width of the steps. For example, a ¾-inch-thick tread would need a carriage at least every 30 inches along its width. The lower step of the carriage sits on the floor and the top is either attached to the front of a platform or is supported by legs.

facing The edge of a platform or stair tread, used to hide the structure decoratively.

The understructure of a stair unit (or platform) is often hidden by a **facing.** One method of doing this is seen in Figure 7-18e. In this method, the stair railing, balcony, stringer, and newel post are incorporated into the facing. The carriage supports the bottom ends of the balusters. It can be an "open carriage," revealing the profile of the tread and risers, or it may be a "closed carriage," masking the ends of the steps.

NON-WEIGHT-BEARING STRUCTURES

Columns, tree trunks, and any other objects that have dimension but do not bear weight are the last type of scenery we consider in this chapter. Because these kinds of structures need only be strong enough to hold their shape, framing is lightweight in comparison to weight-bearing structures.

An irregular shape may be built in three dimensions by the use of two structural elements: the basic silhouette of the object and numerous contour pieces. In a tree trunk, for example, the basic silhouette is the vertical outline

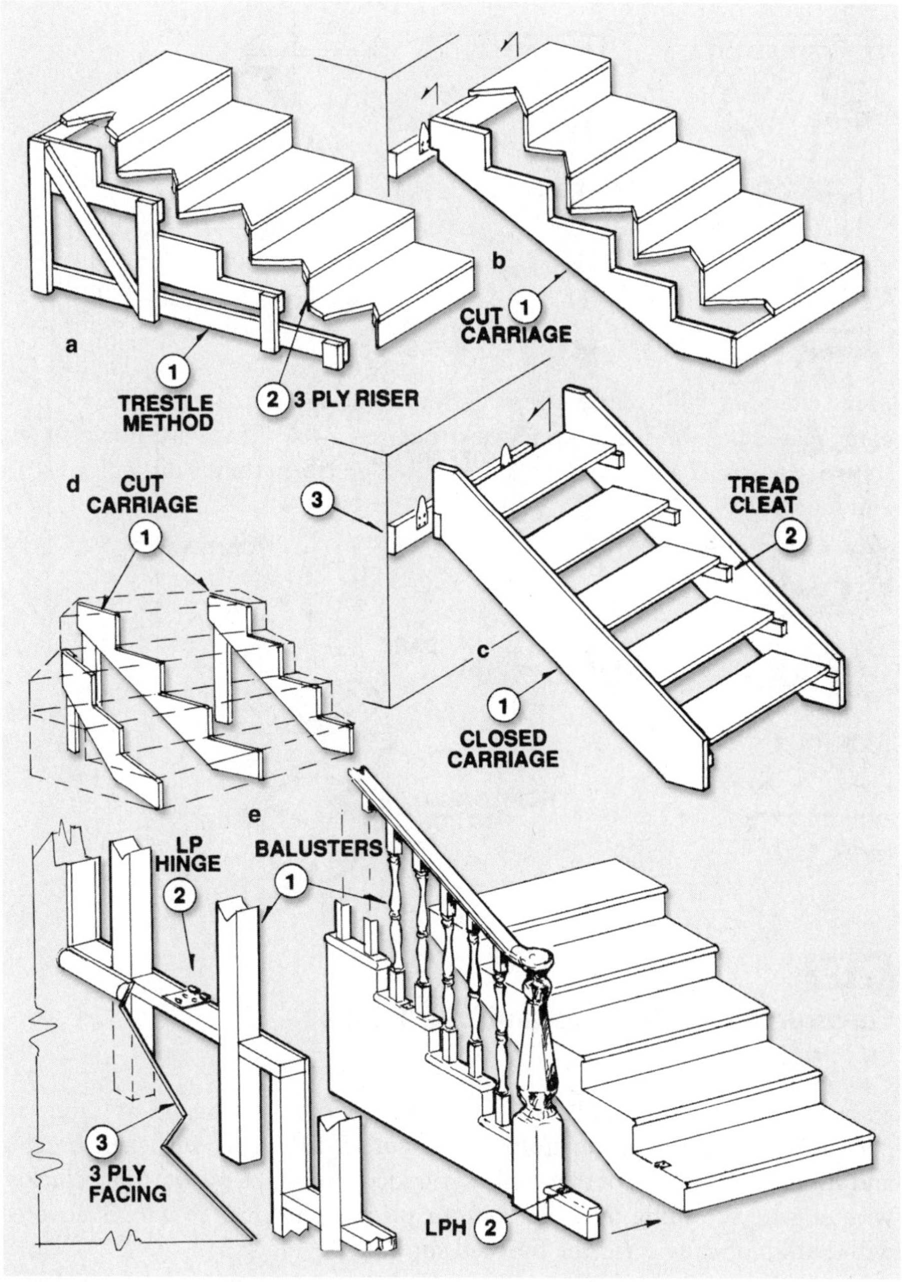

7-18

Stair Construction Techniques

a Trestle method, similar to gate:
- **1** Trestle with the top edge framed to riser-tread pattern.
- **2** For riser stock, 3 ply is used.

b Cut-carriage method:
- **1** Carriage is cut to riser tread pattern. Step unit leans on platform for support.

c Closed-carriage method:
- **1** Because the closed carriage can be used only on the outside of the stair unit, this type of construction limits the width of the stairs.
- **2** Cleat to hold tread. Note that no riser is used.

d Cut-carriage method used on an irregular-shaped flight of steps:
- **1** Carriages with same riser height but varying tread dimensions.

e Stair facing:
- **1** Framed out of 1⅛-inch baluster stock.
- **2** Facing pin-hinged to steps.
- **3** If both faces are covered with 3 ply, the facing unit becomes reversible with minimum alterations.

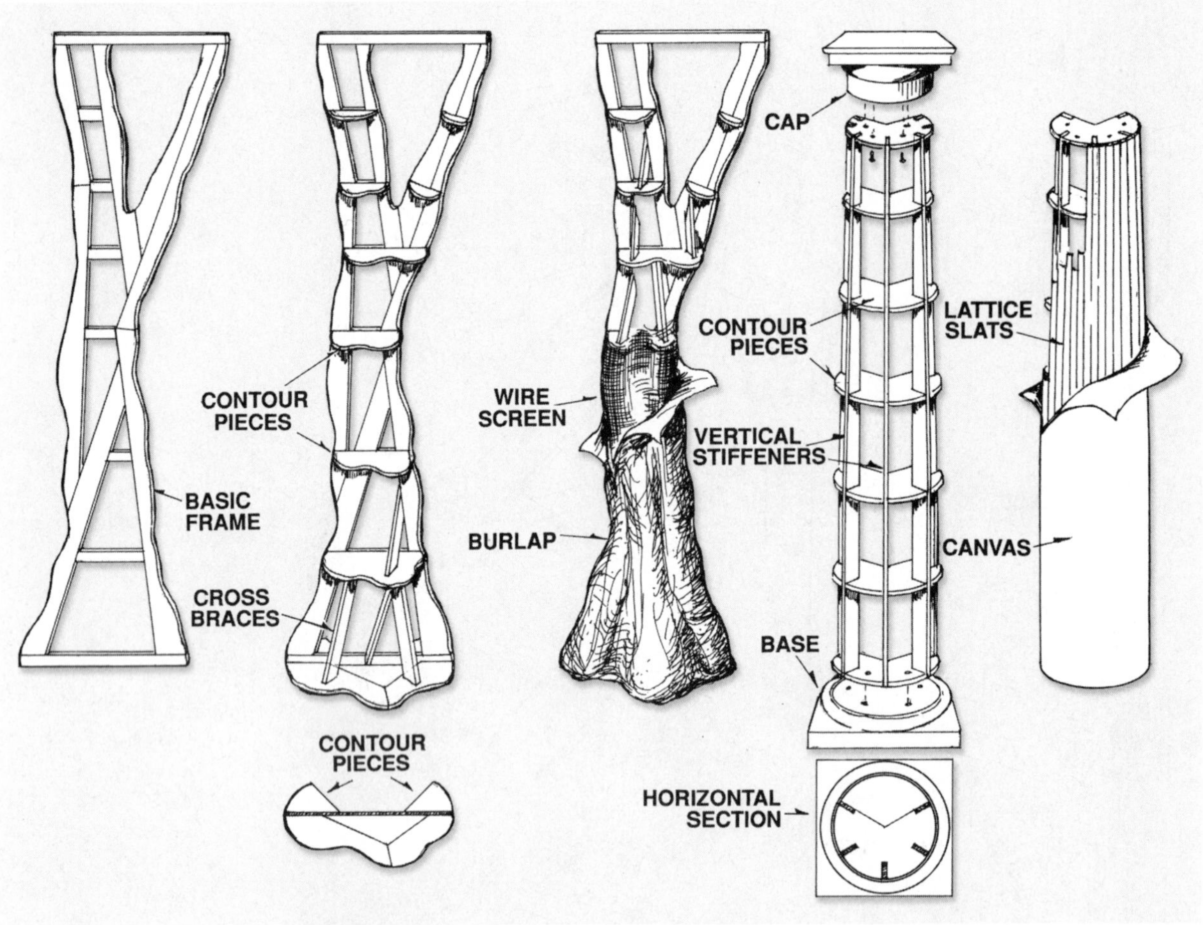

7-19

Construction of Columns and Tree Trunks

of the trunk and branches. The contour pieces are spaced at intervals perpendicular to the silhouette frame (Figure 7-19). After sufficient bracing and stiffening, the form of the trunk is rounded into shape by attaching chicken wire or wire screening over the contour pieces. The chicken wire is covered with burlap or canvas for the finished surface.

Columns have regular shapes and lend themselves to a slightly different construction method. It is not necessary to use a silhouette piece. The circular or semicircular contour pieces can be attached to a central core or be held at intervals by slats on the outer surface (Figure 7-19). The exterior surface of the column can be handled in two different ways: (1) The surface can be made up of thin vertical slats (best for a column with a taper) that are covered with canvas after all of the slats have been rounded with a plane or rasp. (2) The column can be covered with flexible ⅛-inch lauan or other thin sheeting material. Columns can also be made of Sonotube or shaped as a box column with square sides.

Textured and Sculptured Surfaces

Designers are always fascinated by a deeply textured surface. It reacts well under stage lights and gives the scenery a feeling of authenticity and stability.

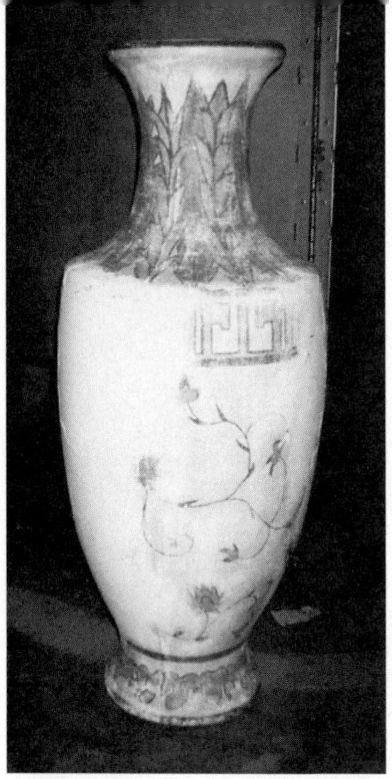

a

b

c

7-20

Carved and Turned Rigid Foam

- **a** Urn made from large block of foam turned. A makeshift lathe was needed to turn this large piece.
- **b** Relief carving of styrofoam sealed with thin layer of glue and joint compound. Carving by Jeff Hinchee.
- **c** Styrofoam relief carving of architectural detail after being sealed with joint compound and sanded. It is now ready to be painted. Carving by Delia Hauser.

A deeply textured surface like that of a stone wall can be accomplished by using the laborious technique of applied papier-mâché. New plastic foams and forming techniques have made it easier to texture a surface or to create sculptural relief, architectural details, and many three-dimensional forms. Figure 7-20 provides some examples.

Premanufactured Foams The need for greater perfection in the design and construction of decorative details on both properties and small elements of scenery has led to easier methods of simulating a sculptural form. Closeness to the audience, increased amount of handling, and change of design focus from scenic background to set properties are the basic influences on new theatre forms.

Styrofoam, the trade name of Dow Chemical's low-density, rigid polystyrene foam (RPF), has been used successfully as a lightweight material that is easy to carve into three-dimensional details or textured surfaces. Blocks of Styrofoam can be glued together or to a scenery surface for convenient carving. Styrofoam

URL http://www.polystyrene.org

Safety Practice

Foam Safety

- Because the chemical action in all foam systems is highly toxic, precaution should be taken to ensure proper ventilation and protection of the hands. Any method of shaping foams—whether hot-wire cutting, sawing, or sanding—can release toxic gases. A respirator and a well-ventilated space are a must. The use of disposable surgical gloves is strongly recommended and often necessary.
- Any area of contact of the foam chemicals with skin should be washed with soap and water immediately.
- The use of a respirator is effective *only* if it creates a tight seal (a custom fit is ideal) and the cartridge used is manufactured specifically for the type of fumes being released.
- There is no way to make some two-part foams completely safe. A self-contained breathing apparatus, such as a respirator, can be expensive and provide no more than a false sense of security.

can also be turned on a lathe, as for a balustrade. As with any foam product, any form of heat applied to it results in a chemical release of toxic gas fumes. (See the box on safety practices.)

Regular Styrofoam is low density and therefore very porous. This limits detailed carving and reduces its strength. *Urethane* is a high-density, rigid foam (RUF) that is easier to carve in detail or turn on a lathe. It also has greater strength than a low-density foam does.

Sections of rigid or flexible foams can be glued to reinforcing wood or an adjacent surface with a variety of adhesives. The manufacturer's recommendations for the use of adhesives must be followed carefully; doing otherwise could bring disastrous results.

Sculpted foam surfaces need to be sealed or primed to provide a surface that will accept paint. There are several possible methods for sealing the surface. A flexible glue alone will work if it is not touched by actors. Likewise, if there is little contact with actors, a layer of cheesecloth adhered with the glue will seal as well as strengthen the foam, but at the price of losing detail. If the foam surface will get abuse (for example, must bear the weight of actors) the best method for sealing it is to use Jaxsan, a latex roofing product. Paint can be mixed in with this product.

Foams, of course, are quite lightweight and many times have to be counterweighted or attached to heavier units of scenery to maintain stability and the illusion of reality. Nothing is more disconcerting than a supposedly quarter-ton Greek statue bouncing like a Ping-Pong ball if knocked over.

Ethafoam Rod Ethafoam rod is a commercial insulation material. It is a flexible, closed-cell foam extruded in various diameters of ½ inch to 2 inches. It can be easily cut with a band saw or knife into half-rounds or quarter-rounds and glued to a surface as a decorative relief or curved molding. Similar forms in sheets and other shapes are available. It does not, however, accept paint very well as the paint cracks as soon as it is touched.

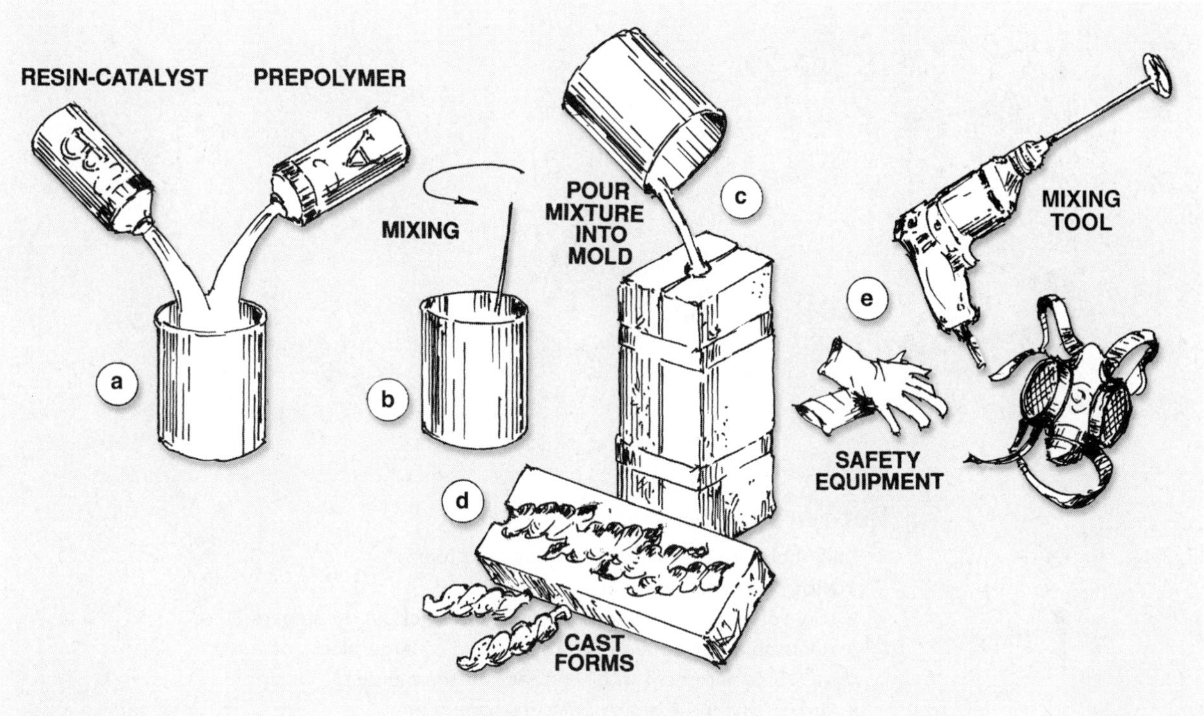

7-21

Foam Casting

Demonstrating one of the many forms plastic foam casting can take, these drawings show the steps in duplicating various forms of bakery goods.

a Mix IASCO's Prepolyer "A" with a Resin-Catalyst "B" in equal parts.

b Stir mixture vigorously for about 30 seconds.

c Pour mixture into a hollow mold prepared with parting agent.

d After liquid foam expands into the mold (about 20 minutes) remove the casting from the mold. With the excess foam cut away, the foam is ready for painting.

e Take great care in mixing by following all instructions and using the proper equipment, such as a mixing tool, disposable surgical gloves, and a respirator.

Two-Part Foams and Latex Some foams are manufactured and sold as a two-part kit. Proper mixing of the two components yields either a rigid or a flexible foam, depending on the particular ingredients. This is useful, for instance, in cases where a mold can be prepared for a sculptural element or decorative detail that recurs several times on a set. The choice of a rigid or a flexible foam is determined by its use onstage. For example, the application of relief detail on a curved or flexible surface requires a flexible foam. Figure 7-21 illustrates foam casting.

There are innumerable types of two-part foams, each one manufactured for a specific purpose. The stage technician should choose a particular type of foam according to both the specific properties of the final product and the expense.

It is critical to follow the manufacturer's instructions and recommendations when working with foams, both for ease of use and for safety. As mentioned before, all foams give off fumes, and many of them behave differently if impurities are introduced. Ammonia, for example, will make some foams collapse. Those who are especially sensitive need to take extreme care.

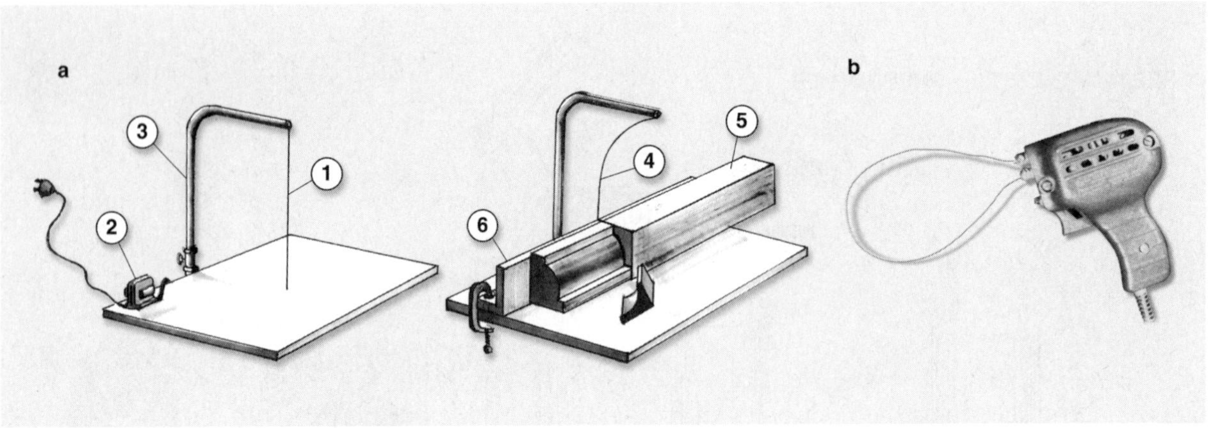

7-22

Hot-Wire Cutters

a Table hot-wire cutters for sculpting rigid foams:
- **1** Nichrome resistance wire.
- **2** Low-voltage, high amperage transformer (about 16 amperes).
- **3** Adjustable arm to facilitate the cutting of large blocks of foam.
- **4** Nichrome wire bent into the shape of the molding.
- **5** Strip of styrene foam or rigid urethane foam.
- **6** Fence guide clamped to table top.

b Handheld hot-wire cutter.

Hot-Wire Cutter The hot-wire cutter is a handy tool for cutting and shaping rigid foam. Both the table hot-wire cutter and the hand cutter using the flexible wire loop are useful to cut large blocks and to carve small forms (Figure 7-22). The wire loop is made of a high-resistance wire conductor (Chromel or Nichrome resistor wire). The wire's resistance generates enough heat to melt the rigid foam, thus enabling it to cut the block cleanly and quickly.

Thermoplastics

Another method for shaping three-dimensional details such as arabesques, props, masks, and armorplate or for duplicating real objects is the vacuum forming of sheet plastic. Formerly a manufacturing technique that was out of reach of the average scenery shop, it is now a viable construction method for hard-to-execute details.

When a thermoplastic is heated, it loses its rigid state and becomes ductile. While heated and pliant, it can be reshaped or stretched over a mold, then allowed to cool and return to a hardened state. A true thermoplastic can be reheated and reshaped without a discernible change in its physical properties, making it economically feasible for theatre use.

Of the many thermoplastics available, there are three that seem best suited for use in the theatre: high-impact polystyrene, low-density polyethylene, and cellulose acetate. They can be opaque, translucent, or transparent; come in a selection of colors or take paint and dyes; be noncombustible; and be strong enough to withstand normal handling onstage and the mechanics of fastening (nailing, stapling, and so on). The working thickness need not be greater than .004 inch (4 thousandths of an inch); it depends on how rigid or flexible the final form must be.

- *High-impact polystyrene,* as the name implies, resists high-impact damage. It also has great flexibility for intricate forming, comes in a wide range of colors, and is obtainable in opaque or translucent sheets.
- *Low-density polyethylene* is also tough and flexible. It is normally milky white (no colors) and opaque, but it turns translucent when heated and formed.
- *Cellulose acetate* is a well-known plastic with excellent forming characteristics. It is also quite sturdy and completely transparent.

Vacuum Forming To take an accurate impression of the mold, the heated thermoplastic sheet must be tightly drawn by a vacuum around or into the form, a process called *vacuum forming.* The basic steps of vacuum forming are as follows: (1) Heat the plastic sheet uniformly to the temperature that renders it flexible (750–1,000°F). (2) Transfer it quickly to a forming table, then stretch it over the mold and clamp its edges to the table to form an airtight seal. (3) Remove the air through the forming table by turning on the vacuum tank and pump, thereby sucking the heated plastic sheet over or into the mold. (4) Allow the plastic to cool and harden into its new shape. (5) Break the seal and remove the plastic form for trimming, painting, and attaching to scenery, costume, or any other formed unit.

The best material for constructing the mold is wood because it can withstand the heat needed. Most other materials will deform under the process.

The reservoir tank permits the rapid vacuuming necessary to finish the molding before the plastic cools and returns to a rigid state. The pump recovers the vacuum in the tank while the next sheet of plastic is being heated. Figure 7-23 illustrates the various components that make up a vacuum-forming machine.

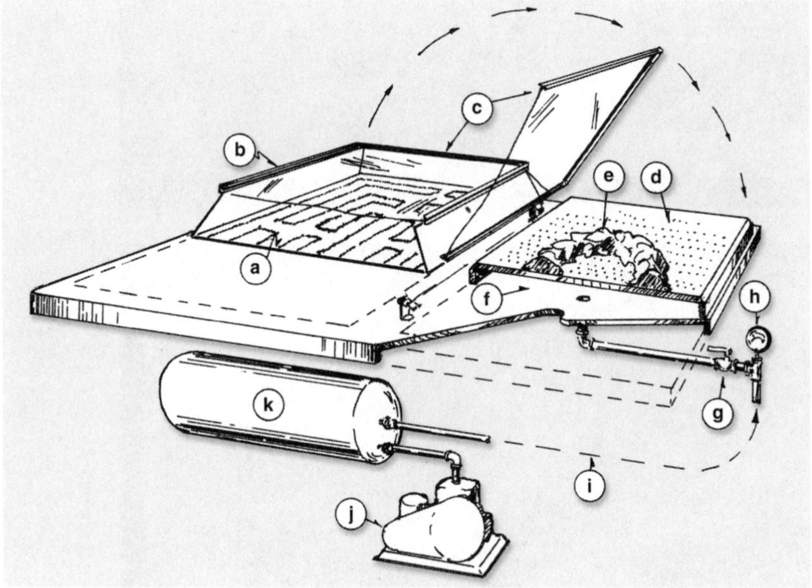

7-23

Vacuum Forming

Here is a cutaway drawing of a vacuum-forming machine suitable for a scene shop.

a The oven has slanted metal sides with sheetrock lining. The floor of the oven is covered with a pattern of coiled resistor wire forming a heating element.

b Plastic sheet in angle-iron frame.

c Frame is hinged to swing off the oven and onto the mold and forming table when the plastic sheet is ductile.

d Forming table. Floor is pierced with ⅛-inch holes spaced at one-inch intervals to vent the vacuum chamber underneath.

e Mold.

f Vacuum chamber.

g Bleed valve; can be rigged for pedal action.

h Gauge reading inches of mercury.

i Air hose or pipe to reservoir tank.

j Vacuum pump.

k Reservoir tank.

Heat Gun Useful accessories to the thermoplastic-forming process include the heat gun, which can deliver a blast of hot air (750–1000°F) from an enclosed heating element and turbo fan. This tool is used at close range to soften portions of the plastic sheet that may not have taken to the mold accurately.

Welding Gun Similar to the heat gun, the hot-air welding gun produces a fine jet of hot air (400–700°F) that, when directed at a seam or thermoplastic welding rod, can weld plastic sheets or plastic forms together. Because the welding gun needs a jet flow of air, it has to operate from an air compressor.

Other three-dimensional forming techniques such as fiberglass and the like are discussed in Chapter 11, because they relate to properties, furniture, and costume accessories. Figures 7-24, 7-25, and 7-26 show some of the pieces that can be made using the techniques discussed here. Figure 7-27 illustrates a sophisticated vacuum-forming process for theatre usage.

7-24

Thermoplastic Forms

Here are a few of the many architectural and decorative details that can be vacuum formed for stage use.

a Original pieces mounted on board and ready to be copied.

b Vacuum-formed pieces before being trimmed to shape.

a

b

a & b PHOTOS COURTESY DAN GRAY

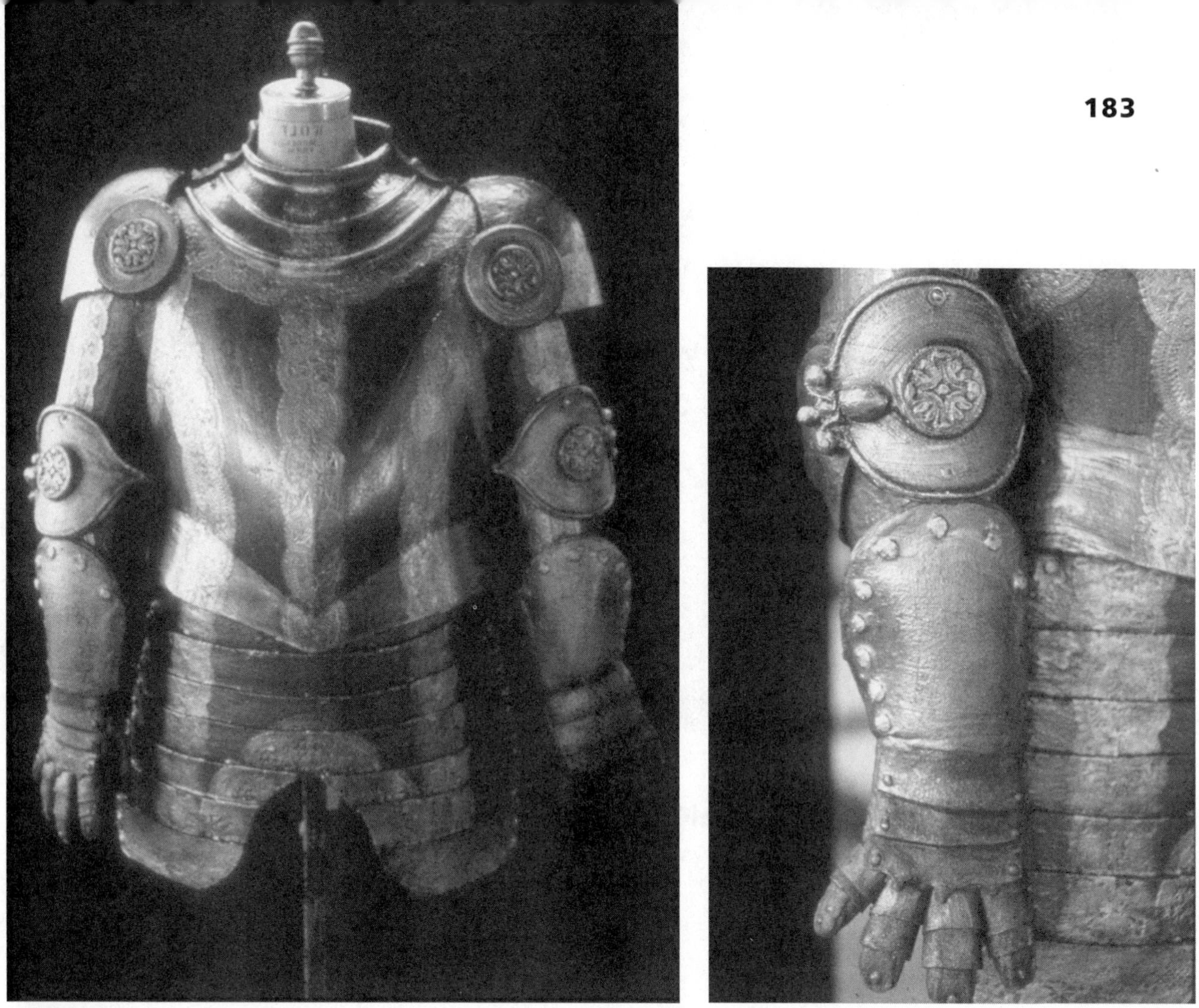

PHOTOS COURTESY BAKKOM

7-25

Fabrication of Rigid Foam

This armor is made of formed fiberglass. A one-to-one mix of 16-pound density IASCO rigid foam was used to build pea-pod form, caskets, gauntlets, and details. A latex and graphite surface with paper-doily appliqué was used as decorative detail.

PHOTO COURTESY BAKKOM

7-26

Cast Plastics

This altar for *Oedipus the King* was designed to look like an oversized, polished half of a geode. The top surface is made of layers of tinted Clear-cast, a clear polyester available at local craft shops, supported on a hollow frame of wooden ribs with a Celastic coating. The crusty edge is modeled fiberglass resin and Cab-o-sil (formed silica), an inert powder that gives the mixture body for modeling. Designed by Desmond Heeley.

PHOTO COURTESY FOX STUDIOS

7-27

Commercial Vacuum Forming of Stage Products

A newly cooled sheet of vacuum-formed brick, referred to as a "skin" in the industry, is added to the pile. The computerized machine is shown behind the craftsperson.

Mirrors

Mylar Highly reflective surfaces and optical mirror surfaces have always fascinated the scene designer as a theatrical effect. Until Mylar became commonly used in the theatre, large mirrors were heavy and awkward to handle. A Mylar mirror surface, when rigidly mounted or tightly stretched, provides the reflection of a real mirror, yet is lightweight and easy to handle.

Silver Shrink Mirror This kind of mirror begins with a vinyl-backed reflective surface designed to be tacked to a frame and then shrunk with heat to a smooth mirrorlike surface. The heat source can be a portable electric heater or a heat gun. The 54-inch width of the material, however, limits the size of the individual frame. A full stage mirror, for example, would have to be made of several frames. However, if the planes of the frames are parallel, the divisions are not noticeable.

Scrim-Backed Mirror This form of stage mirror is backed with a scrim instead of vinyl, giving it the advantage of being transparent when lighted from behind. When stretched and heat-shrunk, it serves as a mirror surface, transparent scrim, or a rear projection screen.

Mirrored Plexiglas Although expensive and difficult to handle in large sizes, mirrored Plexiglas has been successfully adapted for a large surface through the use of small mirrored squares. The joints are not visible at a distance.

SHOP-BUILT JIGS

Even the best-equipped shop will find that some often-performed tasks have special or unique needs for which no tools are manufactured. Although these tasks can be accomplished with the tools on hand, every shop, in an effort to be more efficient, will create a series of *jigs*. A jig can be as simple as a template to place bolt holes in a platform frame and leg, assuring that all legs and platforms conform and that all legs are interchangeable, which can be a helpful timesaver when building stock scenery. Some jigs are built when it is difficult to perform the job in any other way, such as splitting an ethafoam rod. The decision to build a jig hinges on cost-effectiveness. Is the job faster or more efficient with a jig? Will this job need to be repeated many times? Will the time saved be worth the time and money it will take to build the jig? If it will take longer to build a jig than to build the scenic unit, then it is a waste of time.

Certain jigs are found in almost every theatre shop. The following jigs are typical (see Figure 7-28):

- *Stop block for radial arm saw.* This jig is used to cut pieces of wood the same length. Perhaps the easiest jig to set up, almost all that is required is to clamp a piece of wood to the fence of the radial arm saw. The wood should be held off the table about ¼ inch to prevent dust

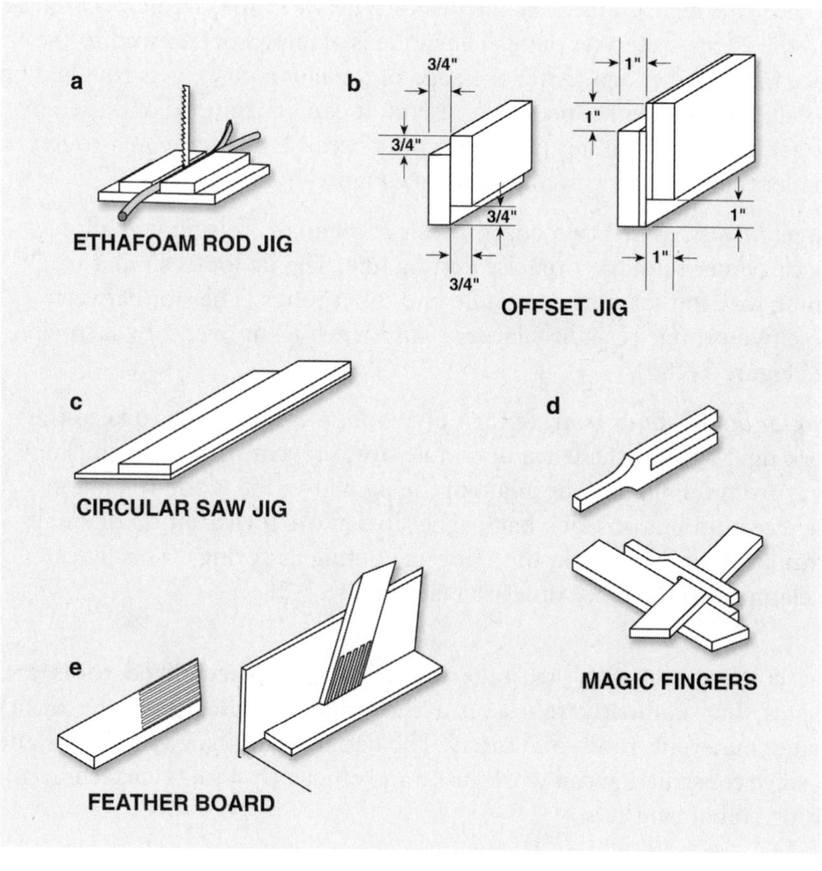

7-28

Shop-Built Jigs

a Ethafoam rod jig.
b Offset jig.
c Circular saw jig.
d Magic fingers.
e Feather board.

collecting at the point where the work touches the jig. Dust buildup will eventually affect the length of the boards being cut.

- *Ethafoam rod jig.* The use of three pieces of ¾-inch plywood can make splitting ethafoam rod easy. A bottom plate has a center line cut halfway through the piece so that it can fit around the band-saw blade. On top are attached two more pieces of ¾-inch plywood, leaving a gap in the center the width of the ethafoam rod. The entire structure is clamped to the table of the band saw. This can be used to create half-round or quarter-round shapes. Each size of ethafoam rod requires a separate jig (see Figure 7-28a).
- *Offset jig.* This jig is used with flattage when the joints are end to edge, not end to face. This is particularly useful when building soft-covered flats in order to inset corners, blocks, and keystones the right distance from the edge of the flat. The jig itself is simply two pieces of 1 by 3 stock offset ¾ inch or the thickness of a similar flat. If the flats are to be hard covered, a piece of ¼-inch lauan is added to make the distance 1 inch. If the inset is the same in both directions, it is impossible to place the jig incorrectly (see Figure 7-28b).
- *Circular saw jig.* This jig allows technicians to saw a precise, straight line with a circular saw. A length of ¼-inch lauan is attached to an equal length of ½-inch plywood. The lauan must be wider than the plywood by the same measurement as the distance between the circular saw blade and the edge of the saw plate. The guide is clamped or screwed to the piece that will be kept. After the edge of the lauan guide gets roughed up to the point where it is no longer useful, it can be trimmed and used in the same way as a router jig. This works because the plate on a router is smaller than that of a circular saw (see Figure 7-28c).
- *Magic fingers.* When two boards meet at an angle, this jig will allow the carpenter to mark a precise cutting line. The jig looks similar to a tuning fork in that it has a handle and two prongs. The slot between these two prongs is slightly larger than ¾ inch to fit over 1 by 3 stock (see Figure 7-28d).
- *Feather board.* Built from ¾-inch plywood, this jig is used to keep the work tight against the fence of a table saw, preventing it from shifting away from the blade. The angle of the jig allows the wood to pass in one direction but not kick back. The slots allow for variation or small irregularities in the work, the "fingers" acting as springs. This jig can be clamped to the fence if desired (see Figure 7-28e).

URL http://www.woodzone.com/tips.htm

Clearly, constructing for the stage involves many specialized tools and techniques, but it mostly relies on a thorough knowledge of the basics concerning materials, tools, and safety. The designer familiar with the ins and outs of stage construction can work easily and efficiently with stage technicians in creating convincing sets.

8

Color in the Design

Any discussion of color must begin with defining the word color. *This is not as easy a task as it might seem. To a physicist, color is* light, *referring to the small visible portion of the electromagnetic spectrum. An artist will refer to* paint, *while a psychologist will suggest that color is individual perception, because no two people see color in exactly the same way. Any experience of color involves all of these attributes. The theatre artist must consider all of them when using color as part of the critical analysis of and emotional response to a play.*

Although scenery, costume, and lighting designers learn about all the properties of color, they apply this knowledge in different ways. Lighting designers are more involved with the physics of color, while scene and costume designers are interested in the painting and dyeing of color as well as the manipulation of colored materials. Whatever the specific use of color may be, all areas of design eventually must come together onstage to form a cohesive visual statement. The beginning designer in the theatre must be aware of the separate uses of color and be able to explain the effects of color both as light and as paint. As such, any explanation of color in the theatre must involve not only the separate study of color in light and color in pigment, but also the integration of the two.

Clearly, then, any theatre artist, designer, director, or actor should understand at least the basic "language" of color in order to communicate clearly. It is good to be aware that not only do no two people "see" color in exactly the same way, but no two *respond* to color the same way. Color inevitably elicits an emotional response. It is certainly one of the strongest elements of design and the most difficult (if not the most important) element to understand.

THE LANGUAGE OF COLOR

The three most basic terms used when discussing color are *hue, value,* and *chroma* (see Chapter 3). One can describe a color by hue identification (red, yellow, and so on); value level, or the amount of black or white present in a color; and the degree of chroma or freedom from neutralization by mixture with another hue. Any color can adequately be described in simple semiscientific terms by referring to its hue, degree of chroma, and value level. In normal communication their use brings to mind a more consistent image of a specific color than would the use of such emotionally charged labels as "blushing pink" or "passionate purple." Because descriptive labels are so firmly a part of the advertising and merchandising of color in fabric, paint, and the light-color medium, a designer soon learns to translate them into more communicative terms. A "chocolate" shade, for example, might be described more precisely as a spectrum orange neutralized to one-half chroma but retaining its normal low-light value position. (We discuss and illustrate these concepts in more detail later in this chapter.)

Because there is no color without the presence of light, this discussion will begin with light and the physical properties of color. Only a small portion of the electromagnetic waves that are called light are visible to the human eye. When these visible wavelengths are mixed together, we see white light. Conversely (and probably more useful to us), if we break white light into its component parts, as through a prism (a process called *refraction*), we see a separation of colors into the visible spectrum. A physicist can precisely produce an accurate spectrum with wavelength values for each hue and can explain the existence of these hues, from infrared to ultraviolet. This is the beginning of understanding hue (Color Plate 8-1).

Hue

The position of a color in the spectrum determines its hue. The number of hues that can be separated or identified as principal hues in the spectrum is arbitrary. Six easily identified hues are *red, orange, yellow, green, blue,* and *violet* (Figure 8-1). Different color theories distinguish more or fewer discernible hues, depending on the intended application. For example, the mixing of paint as a color medium is not as accurate as the mixing of colors in light. Hence, the painter requires a finer separation of spectrum hues to creatively mix and use color (see "Color in Paint" later in the chapter).

primary hue One of three hues that are used to mix all other hues; in pigment the primary hues are red, yellow, and blue; in light they are red, green, and blue.

secondary hue One of three hues produced by mixing any two primaries; in pigment they are violet, orange, and green; in lighting they are yellow, violet, and cyan.

Primary hues fall within the six basic hues of the spectrum and form the basis for the mixing of color in both light and pigment. In other words, all other hues can be mixed using the primaries. In pigment, the primaries are red, yellow, and blue (see "Subtractive Mixing" later in this chapter). Red, green, and blue are the light primaries (see "Additive Mixing" later in this chapter). By mixing any two of the primaries, a series of three **secondary hues** are produced.

The Color Wheel To show the physical relationship of spectrum hues, most color notation systems use a color wheel (Color Plates 8-2 and 8-3). The circular arrangement of colors brings into view the diametric and adjacent correlation of the twelve spectral hues and thus provides designers a schematic view of primary and secondary hue relationships. For example, both the primary and secondary hues form triangles. Using the color wheel, it is easy to see how, by mixing two primaries together, we produce a secondary hue.

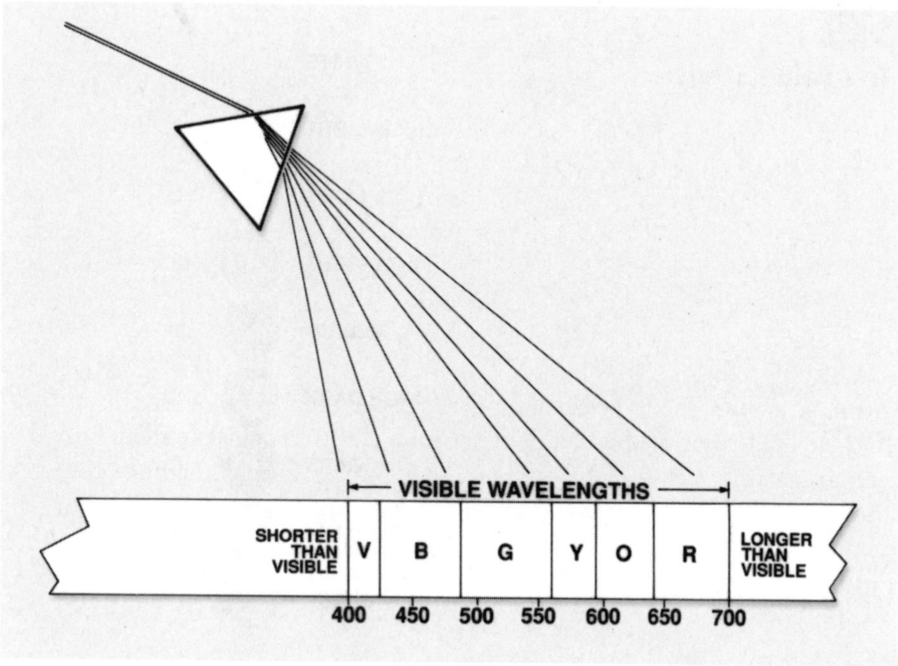

8-1

Spectrum and Six Basic Hues

Within the visible spectrum, the hues are determined by wavelength, as measured in nanometers.

Complementary Hues Hues that appear directly opposite each other on the color wheel are **complements** of each other. When any two complementary hues are placed side by side, the color contrast is so high that it produces an apparent vibration. This phenomenon involves both the physics and optics of color and will be discussed later, after all the aspects of color have been examined.

complementary hue One of two hues directly opposite each other on the color triangle.

A knowledge of complementary hues is not only necessary for mixing both light and pigment but is also important in composition. This is apparent in the choice of tints and shades in a production color scheme for both costumes and scenery. Because color in light and pigment are constantly brought together in the theatre, they must be compatible or have the same complementary colors.

Value

The light-to-dark relationship of a hue or mixed color is its *value.* The lighter values, nearer white, are known as **tints;** the darker values, approaching black, are referred to as **shades.** Both represent a variation of the true hue (Color Plate 8-4).

tint Lighter value of a hue.

shade Darker value of a hue.

The use of value as a color variant or control is more obviously the tool of the painter than of the lighting designer because of the necessarily greater range in pigment mixing. Subtle value differences are easier to accomplish in paint, particularly in the darker ranges, because in the use of colored light there is no black.

Although the number of steps in a value scale is arbitrary, the standard is seven (Figure 8-2). This is due to the eye's limited ability to distinguish smaller differences.

The value in the center of the scale is referred to as *medium (M)*. The steps above M toward white are *low light (LL), light (L),* and *high light (HL)*. Below M toward black are *high dark (HD), dark (D),* and *low dark (LD)*. Within this range the artist can create form without the use of color.

8-2
The Value Steps

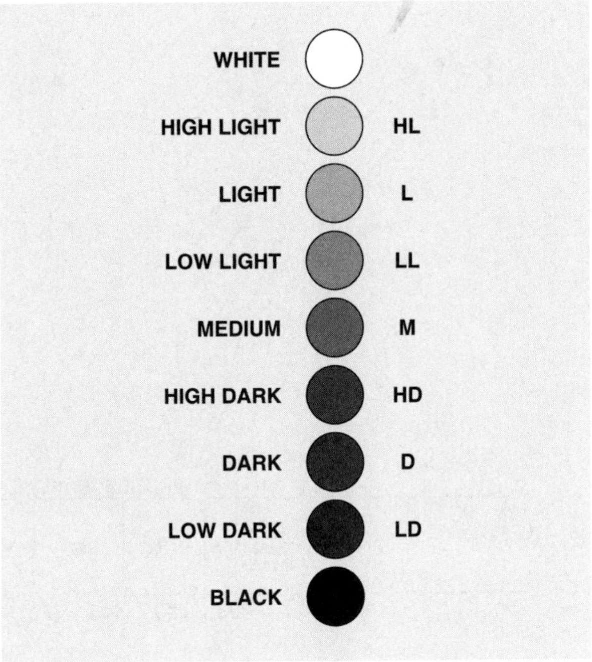

The Value Sketch The worth of the value sketch cannot be overemphasized. Using black and white tones to simulate light, an artist can model the forms in a design. This expressive method allows the designer to suggest the tone of the piece without worrying about the specifics of color. Many old masters applied monochromatic underpainting, using the values of a single hue to express form and light before overprinting in full color. Value sketches can be expressed in any medium, although marker, pencil, and pen and ink are the most common (Figure 8-3).

Value and Hue Some hues come from the spectrum with a natural value difference. A black-and-white photograph of the primary and secondary hues would place each of them at a given point in the value scale (Figure 8-4). The light-to-dark difference between yellow and violet is the most extreme example. Other hues have less value difference and some, of course, are about equal (Color Plate 8-5).

Chroma

The instant the purity of a principal hue is modified, the change is referred to as a change of its *chroma* (*saturation* and *intensity* are also common terms for this). Like value, chroma has a scale in which the degree of pureness, or freedom from neutrality, is measured in steps. Although there are an infinite number of steps from a pure hue to neutral gray, most color theories use only a few, for practical reasons. It is commonly accepted to work in quarter portions, moving from a fully saturated hue to three-quarter saturation, through one-half, then one-quarter to full neutrality. These steps are particularly useful in describing a color. Intermediate steps can be as subtle as can be perceived.

Mixing complementary hues in equal parts tends to neutralize or "gray down" each hue, placing it on the value scale at medium gray. A mixture, for

8-3

Value Sketch

Two black-and-white sketches showing light and dark.

a *Buried Child,* designed by Tim Saternow.

b *Romancin' the One I Love,* designed by Dex Edwards.

a COURTESY TIM SATERNOW

a

b COURTESY DEX EDWARDS

b

8-4

Hue and Value

Each hue has a value that corresponds to one step on the gray scale, as shown here.

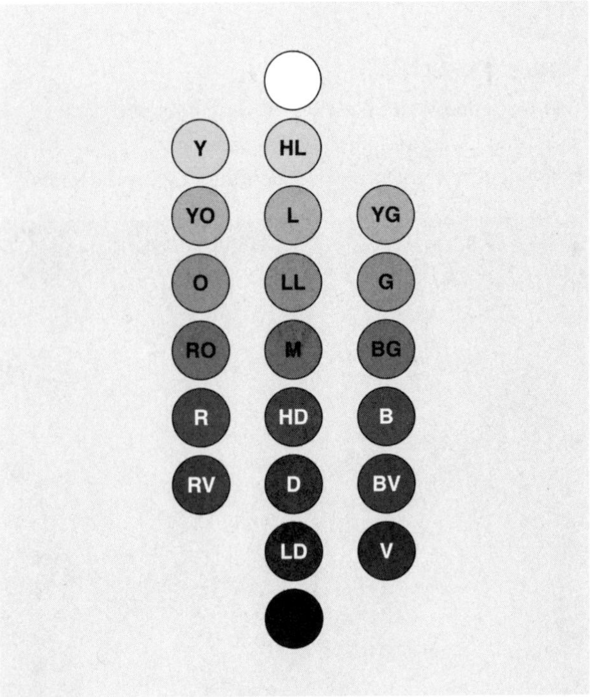

example, of red (high dark) and green (low light) results in medium gray. Complementary hues in light produce white when mixed, while their mixture in paint results in neutral tones.

Using the complement is the easiest and usually best way to control chroma through pigment, even though neutralization can be accomplished by the use of black or white paint. As a tint or shade moves a hue toward black, it is moving as well toward the gray (or value) scale. However, the use of a complementary color to neutralize a hue gives the painter a chromatic neutral that has more life under the stage lights. Black especially tends to "deaden" a color.

Color Plate 8-6 shows the value and chroma changes produced by mixing orange and blue hues. When the value of either orange or blue is raised or lowered, its chroma is also changed as the tint or shade becomes more neutral. On the other hand, the quarter steps on the direct horizontal line to the value scale represent a chroma change without a value drop. This is accomplished on the orange side by the proportional mixing of blue (the hue complement of orange) after it has been raised to the matching value of orange. In other words, it is possible to change the chroma of a hue without affecting its value, but it is impossible to change the value of a hue without modifying its chroma.

URL http://www.abelard.org/colour/col-hi.htm

COLOR MIXING

Although hue, value, and chroma are theoretical variables of color, a designer must understand them also as a way to describe a color and use them to create new shades and match old ones. Color is varied by *additive mixing* and *subtractive mixing*. Although both methods effect hue changes, additive mixing also noticeably alters value, while subtractive mixing modifies chroma.

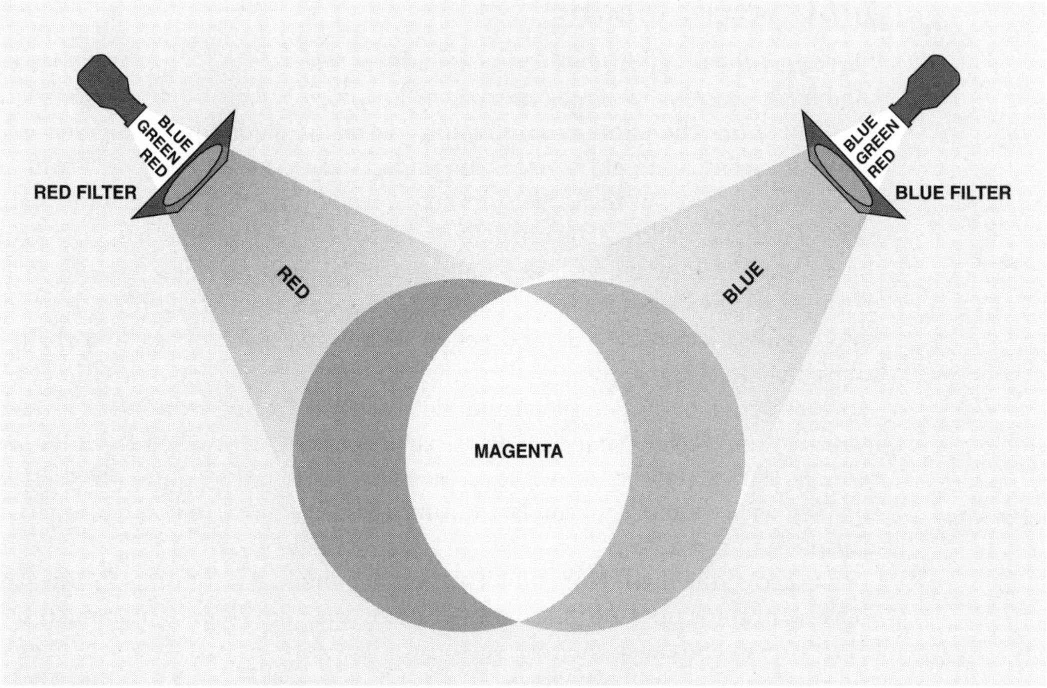

8-5

Additive Mixing

Light (represented in its primaries—red, green, and blue) is passed through a blue filter. Red and green are filtered out, resulting in a blue-colored light. A red filter absorbs green and blue, passing the red light. The fields of red and blue light overlap to create a third, magenta. Magenta is a red-violet raised in value because additive mixing raises the value of the mixed color.

Additive Mixing

The blending of colored light from two or more sources is called *additive mixing*. It is best demonstrated by the three overlapping fields of the light primary hues in Color Plate 8-7. The additive mixing of the light primaries red, green, and blue produces, first, the secondaries. Green and blue cross to make a cyan (BG); red and blue produce the light secondary violet (RV); and red and green make yellow (YO). The white in the center results from the additive mixing of all three primaries. Note that the additive mixing of two hues raises the value of the mixed color.

Figure 8-5 diagrams the physics of the additive mixing of red (R) and blue (B). A single red color filter, for example, absorbs all other hues from the spectrum and transmits only red. When red rays overlap with light from a blue filter, the colors are "added," resulting in a red-violet or magenta hue. In other words, more total light rays are transmitted—an increase in light or additive process. The additive mixing of all three primary hues in light results in a white. Remember that all colors resolve into white before being refracted into the color spectrum. (The mixing of the three primaries in pigment results in black.)

One method of applying additive mixing in pigment is to paint two translucent layers of different colors, resulting in a mixing of the two to create a third hue. Using a sponge to apply two different colors works in the same way.

Subtractive Mixing

The opposite of additive mixing is subtractive mixing—the crossing or combining of color mediums in front of a single source of light. Color Plate 8-8a illustrates the effect of combining two color mediums, blue-green and yellow, in front of a light source containing all the spectral hues. It is not as visually apparent, but the same subtractive results are present when the artist mixes blue and yellow in paint (Color Plate 8-8b). The blue paint absorbs the red and yellow, the yellow paint absorbs the red and blue—it *subtracts* the light waves of those absorbed colors. Likewise, white light on a green object will reflect only blue and yellow light waves; the object absorbs (or subtracts) all others.

Subtractive mixing in paint and light is characterized by a move toward neutrality and darker shades. This is particularly evident when the hues are complementary colors, as we have seen. The closer the colors are to true complements, the less light can be transmitted until a block or point of negative transmission is reached.

In theory, the mixing of complementary colors in paint results in a nearly black neutral for the same reason. In practice, the impurities of manufactured color in pigment cause the mixing to produce gray instead of black. Scenic artists often refer to this as "graying down" or "neutralizing" a color.

Because most pigment mixing is subtractive, the gray tone in the center of the color wheel indicates the neutralizing effect of any pair of complementary colors. Recall that the many tints and shades resulting from mixing orange and blue is shown in Color Plate 8-6, which demonstrates the flexible relationship between chroma and value. The subtlety of neutral shades and almost unlimited combinations of hues is the main advantage of subtractive mixing in pigments.

COLOR IN PIGMENT

Color in paint, of course, depends on light to realize its physical properties. The color of a surface reaches the eye by the reflection of the light that is illuminating it. Just as a lighting gel transmits a color by absorbing some hues and letting others through, so a colored surface reflects only the colors of the paint (see Chapter 16, Figure 16-4). These are the physical properties of a paint surface that begins with its coloring agent, pigment.

Pigment refers to the coloring agents in paints, dyes, and nature. It can be best explained as the chemical properties of color that create hue. At first, pigments came from natural sources; the indigo and madder plants are familiar examples. Minerals and semiprecious stones were also pulverized and made into pigments. The practices of the past established many of the names of colors still used today, such as madder lake and indigo blue.

In the mid-nineteenth century, chemical breakthroughs produced colors that had never been seen before. These dyes were made from natural materials, mostly minerals and their compounds. Although present-day pigments are often created from compounds not found in nature, many still bear the name of their earlier source, such as chrome green, alizarin crimson, and calcium red.

Theoretically, one could make any hue by using only the three primaries in pigment. However, attempting to create even the secondary hues from mixing pigment primaries is impractical because of the color impurities of manufactured paint. Hence, the painter prefers to begin with a larger palette that might include all the principal hues of the spectrum. This palette includes the primaries and secondaries as well as intermediate hues in the color wheel, often referred to as *tertiary hues* (see Color Plate 8-2). Mixing blue and green—a primary and a secondary—will result in blue-green.

URL http://www.geocities.com/~jlhagan/lessons/mainmenu.htm

URL http://www.worldwidelearn.com/art-courses.htm

URL http://www.colorcube.com

COLOR AND LIGHT

Chapter 16 provides a detailed discussion of the use of color in light. Here we look at the more general aspects of color in light, especially as it relates to pigment. For example, the arrangement of the twelve principal colors on the light color wheel (Color Plate 8-3) is the same as with pigment. The primary, secondary, and intermediate colors are developed from the additive mixing of the light primaries. Because the additive mixing of colored light tends to move toward white, the secondary and intermediate colors are lighter in value than their companion colors in the pigment wheel.

By understanding how white light can be broken up into a series of colors, the stage designer can have complete control of how objects are perceived. Colored light can modify surface color. The common use of colored light on a colored surface is unique to the theatre (although this is more frequently being used in architecture as well). Designers in the theatre have to consider not only the colors of a painted background, costumes, and other materials of a set but also the colors of the lights that will reveal them. This is especially true if the lighting for the scene is unusual, such as romantic "moonlight" or red or green hues flooding the stage to provide an unnatural effect.

A white surface lit with white light reflects rather than absorbs all of the wavelengths, allowing us to see the object as white. Likewise, unfiltered light on a black surface will be mostly absorbed, revealing the object as black, or without color. Under white light, a colored surface such as green will reflect only green wavelengths and absorb all others. Adding a colored filter to the white light will change our perception of the colored surface. A red filter will allow only red light to transmit. This mixed with a green surface will appear black. The laws of subtractive mixing dictate that the red wavelengths will be absorbed, and nothing will be reflected.

Understanding this is critical to set, costume, and lighting designers for obvious reasons. Once again, clear communication throughout the production process is essential. Without it, a grayed-out production may result. If from the start everyone is aware of how color is to be used in production, great success can result and each designer can use the others to enhance the statement he or she is trying to make.

COLOR VISION

The source of color can be scientifically explained, the mixture of color can be diagrammed, and all the variants of color can be arranged in a system of notation. However, what the eye sees and the brain interprets is an individual color experience. Although the eye functions much like a camera, it is not a scientific instrument. It receives light through its lens, which focuses the image or impression onto the layers of the retina in the inner eye. The innumerable nerve endings (*rods* and *cones*) of the retina culminate in the optic nerve, which carries the impression signal to the brain for interpretation. The eye sees value differences (intensity) through the rods and hue variations through the cones (see Chapter 16).

Intensity and Color Overload

The retina of the eye assimilates light energy. Hence, after any sudden change of intensity or color, the retina has to regenerate itself. This process takes place over a noticeable period. It takes the eye about one to one and a half minutes to adjust in a blackout, for example (rod regeneration); a color change (cone regeneration) may take as long as five minutes.

The time lag the eye experiences after a sudden change of color explains *afterimage,* a phenomenon of color vision. Until the eye has recovered, it retains an image of the object and a color impression long after the object has been removed or changed. The afterimage, however, is in the complementary hue of the original image color.

The phenomenon of afterimage, or the color-balancing tendency of the eye, also affects how a color appears in the context of another color. In 1886 M. E. Chevreul, an early color theorist, first referred to this effect as the *simultaneous contrast of color.* In 1960, Joseph Albers called the same effect *interaction of color.*

Some effects of color juxtaposition are painfully obvious, while others are extremely subtle. The degree of color interplay is a critical element in the use of color by stage designers. Aside from the mixing and creating of colors, the designer's arrangement of colors plays a vital role in stimulating an emotional or intellectual response from the audience.

The interaction of colors affects all variants of color. The value of a color can seem to change by juxtaposition, a neutral can be influenced by a surrounding color and appear to take on a *hue,* and the chroma of a color can be sharpened or deadened by its background. Color Plates 8-9 through 8-14 show a few classic examples of obvious color interactions that influence the designer's use of color.

Color Sensation and Subjective Response

The experience of color includes elements of sensation or emotion as well. Designers in the theatre must be aware of the scope of the audience's emotional response, often subconscious, when they choose colors, in both pigment and light, to establish a mood or specific atmosphere on the stage. The psychological effect of color on an audience, however, is difficult to measure. To some extent the designer must depend on a measurable individual response and hope it will multiply.

Most emotional response to color is conditioned by a lifetime of reaction to colors in nature and under natural light. We are repulsed, for example, by strong colors in light that produce unnatural flesh tones or discolor our food. We are also influenced by centuries of social and religious conventions buried deeply in the subconscious. Finally, we react to symbolism in color, some primal and others more contemporary (such as traffic lights and color-coded road signs).

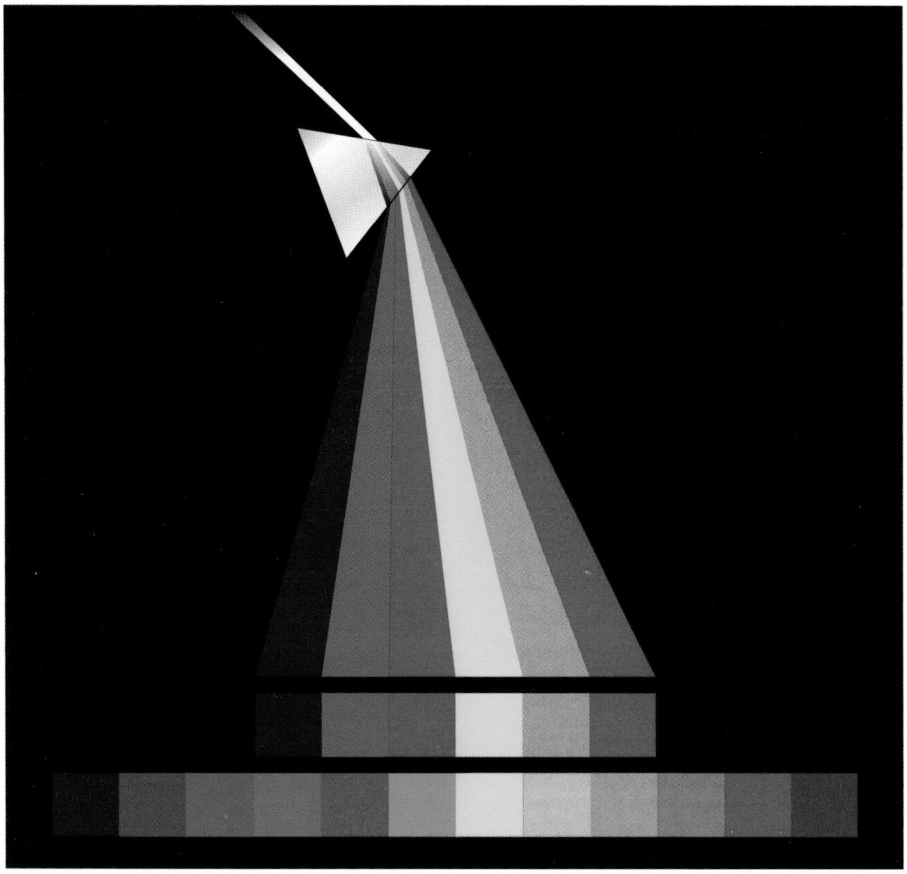

CP8-1

Spectrum Hues

The breakdown of sunlight through a prism refracts light into first six, then twelve spectrum hues.

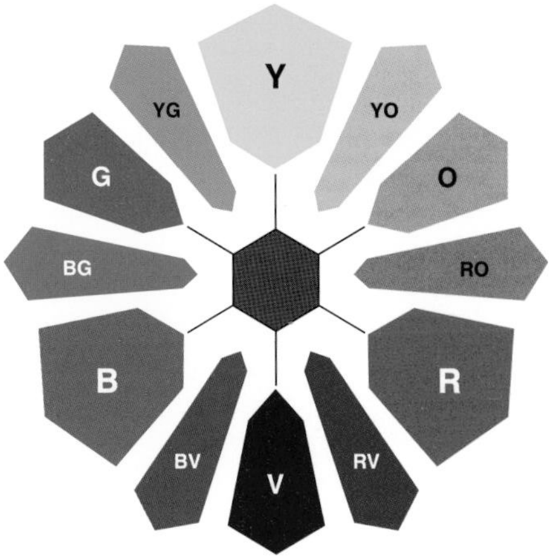

CP8-2

Pigment Color Wheel

Twelve principal hues of the spectrum arranged in a circle. Diagonals are color opposites; their subtractive mixing would produce a neutral shade similar to the gray in the center.

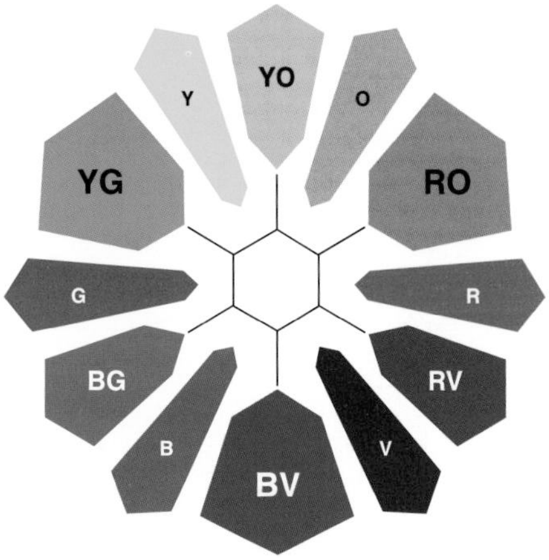

CP8-3

Light Color Wheel

The light color wheel is centered on the light primaries. The large lozenges are the light primaries YG, BV, and RO. Two adjacent primaries mix to form intermediate or secondaries that become complementary hues. The secondaries are lighter in value because of the additive mixing of the primaries. The additive mixing of all primaries is shown by the white in the center.

CP8-4

Tints and Shades

a The range of tints from primary blue to white.

b The range of shades from primary blue to black.

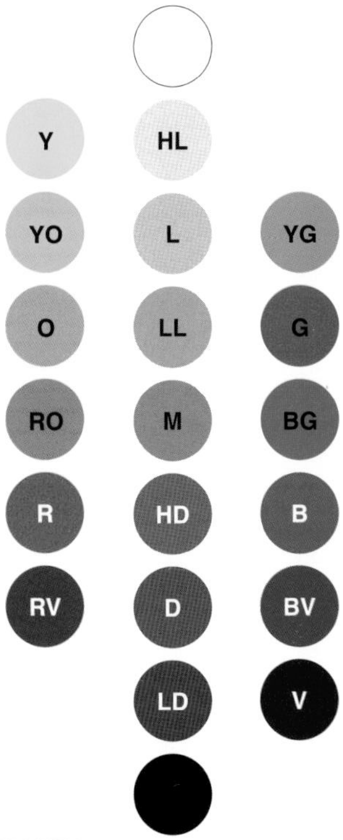

CP8-5

Hue–Value Relationship

The twelve principal spectrum hues are arranged next to the value scale in their natural light-to-dark relationship. The middle value of the seven steps between black and white is referred to as medium in value while the three steps above are known as low light, light, and high light. The lower value steps are high dark, dark, and low dark.

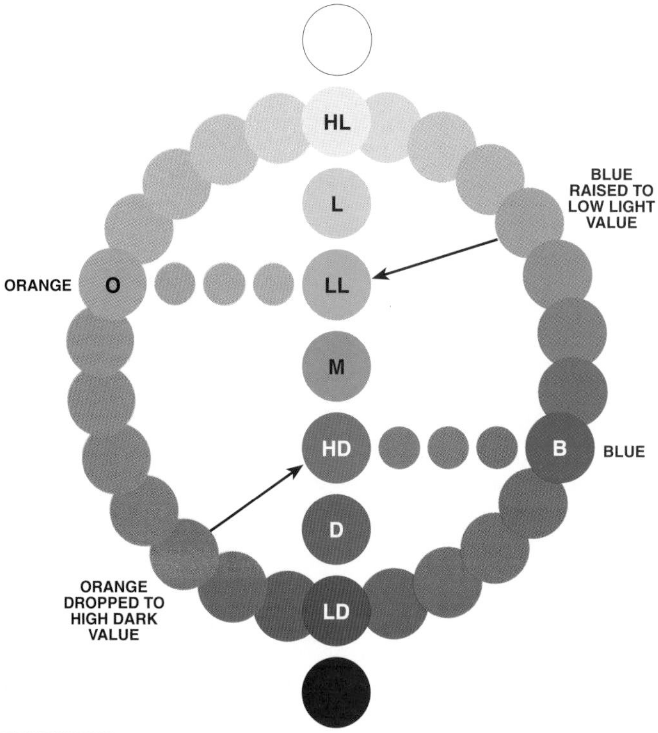

CP8-6

Value and Chroma

The complementary hues blue and orange are subjected to value and chroma changes first by alternately mixing each color with white and black in the outside ring to effect a value change. Chroma changes at fixed value are accomplished horizontally by mixing a color with its complementary hue after it has been raised or lowered to the same value (arrows). Note that to change the value of a hue automatically alters its chroma.

It is possible to alter chroma at each value step and completely fill the circle with a variety of tints and shades. This mixing procedure (although impossible to reproduce accurately), applied to any set of complementaries, serves the stage designer as a method of creating new and unusual colors as well as matching existing shades.

CP8-7

Additive Mixing

The additive mixing of light primaries by the crossing of three spotlight rays. Note that the secondary hues formed by the mixing of two adjacent primaries are lighter in value and that the mixing of three primaries results in white light.

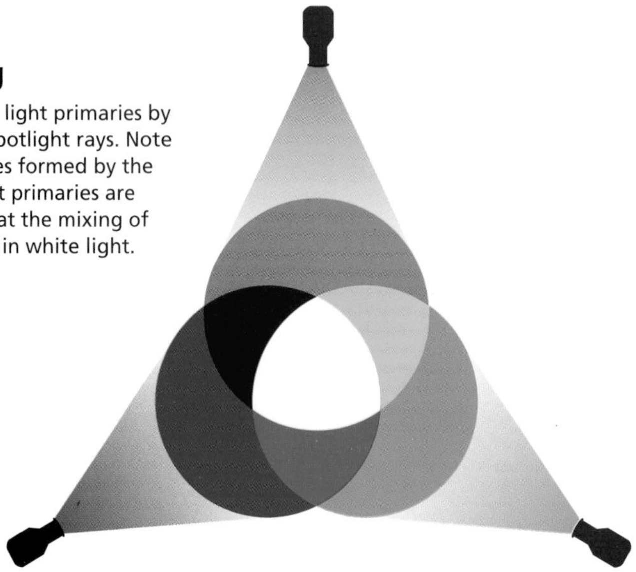

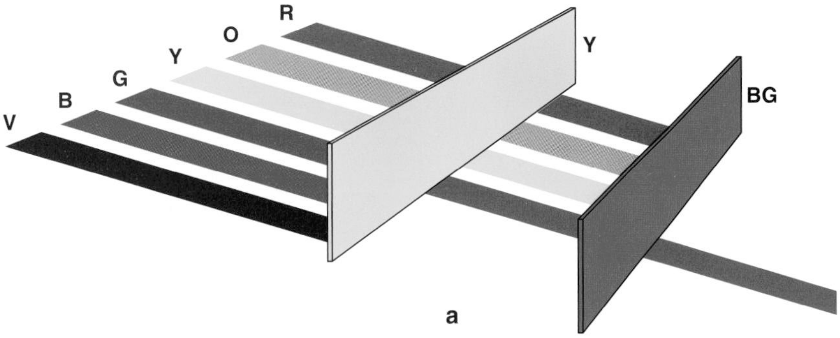

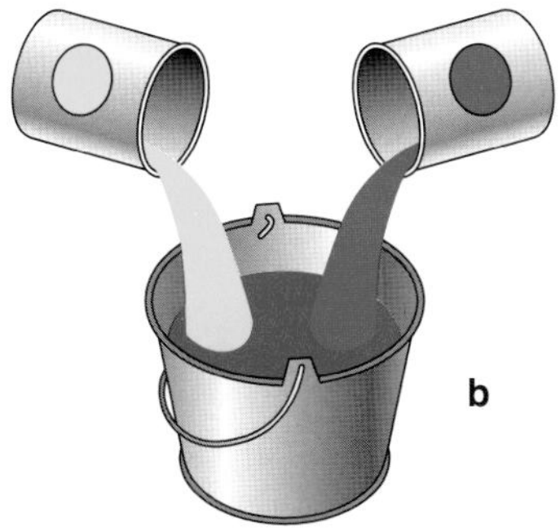

CP8-8

Subtractive Mixing

a Six basic hues of the spectrum are shown passing through two color mediums, first yellow and then blue-green. All hues except green are absorbed or subtracted by the two filters.

b Subtractive mixing in paint. The result is the same when blue-green and yellow paint are mixed.

CP8-9

Hue and Value Relationship

Color is seen in relationship to its surroundings. Proximity can greatly affect our perception of color. In this example, the center strip of violet does not change. As our eye moves from the lighter value of the orange to the darker value of the blue, the violet stripe appears to change also—darker in relationship to the orange, lighter in relationship to the blue.

CP8-10

Warm and Cool Relationship

In this example of color relationships, our perception of the light violet stripe in the center is once again affected by its surroundings. The closer to the cool blue hue, the warmer the violet appears; the closer to the warm red hue, the cooler the violet stripe appears.

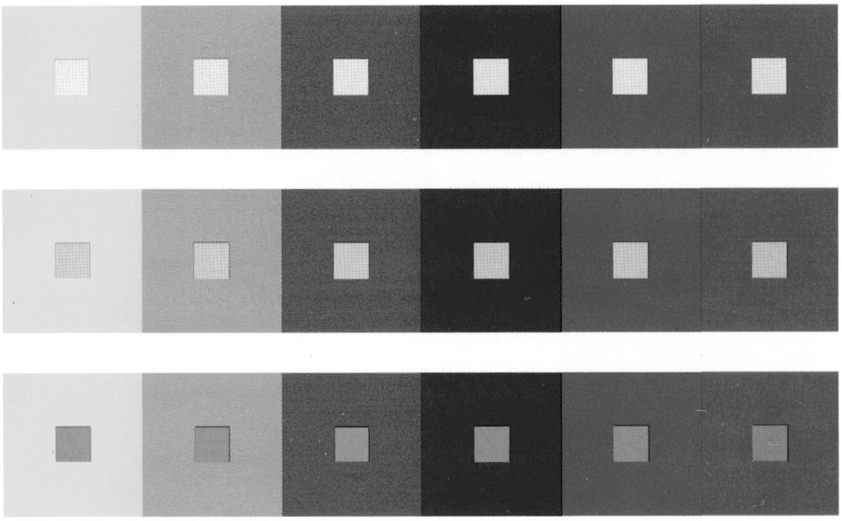

CP8-11

Hues and Neutrals

A small neutral surface is influenced by the color of the ground that surrounds it. The neutral in each of the six appears to vary slightly, depending on the background color.

CP8-12

Hue to Complement

The range of the hue red to its complement of green. Note the grayish tones in the middle of this bar.

CP8-13

Complementary Colors

Note how the blue hue appears to change when placed next to variations of the complement orange. Top to bottom: blue with orange, a tint, a shade, a lower chroma.

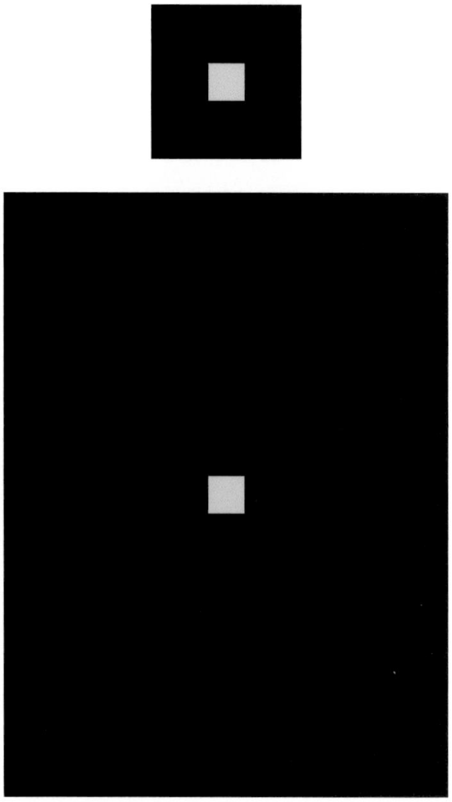

CP8-14

Hue and Field

The larger field of black makes the small amount of yellow appear brighter than it does in the smaller field of black.

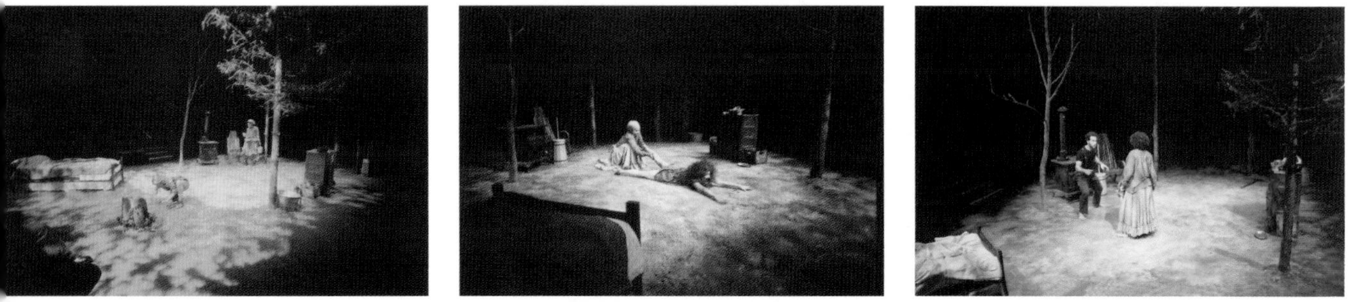

PHOTOS COURTESY CHRIS KENNEDY

CP8-15

Color Modifications

A set designer can easily use color to help the lighting designer control the overall tone of the set. In this set for *Love Talker,* designed by Chris Kennedy, the variety of color used in painting the set has allowed the lighting designer to create a wide variety of looks, from the very warm (on the left) to the very cool (on the right).

COURTESY TIM SATERNOW

CP8-16

The Artificial Jungle

Sketch designed by Tim Saternow.

COURTESY FRANK LUDWIG

CP8-17

Ain't Life Grand

Sketch designed by Frank Ludwig.

CP8-18

All My Sons

Designed by Kathleen Widomski.

PHOTO COURTESY KATHLEEN WIDOMSKI

CP8-19

Alabama Rain

Designed by Frank Ludwig.

PHOTO COURTESY FRANK LUDWIG

CP8-20

Fences

Designed by Daniel Guyette.

PHOTOS COURTESY DANIEL GUYETTE

COURTESY DUNSI DAI

CP8-21

Mame

Sketch designed by Dunsi Dai.

PHOTO COURTESY DANIEL GUYETTE

CP8-22

Othello

Model designed by Daniel Guyette.

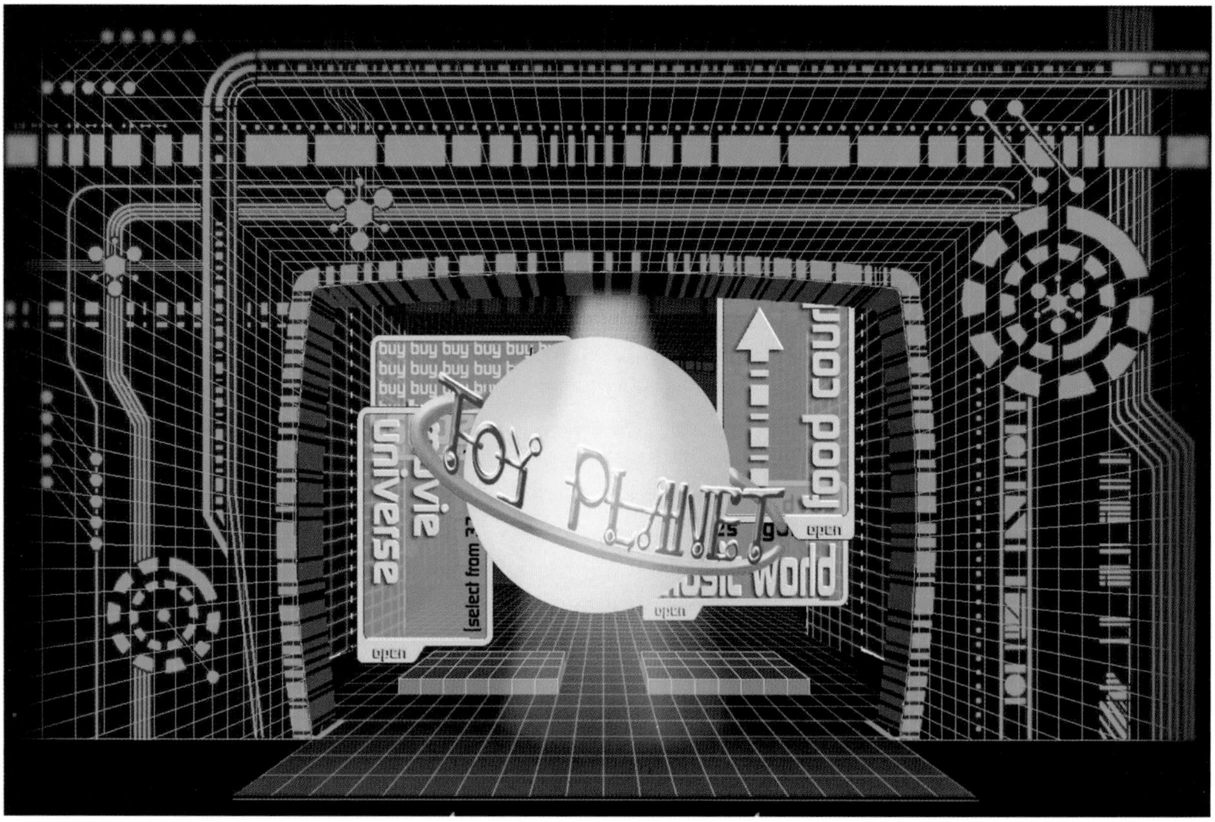

COURTESY KEVIN L. RAPER

CP8-23

Pinocchio 3.5

Sketch designed by Kevin L. Raper.

COURTESY STEVEN L. GILLIAM

CP8-24

Present Laughter

Sketch designed by Steven L. Gilliam.

The psychological description of a hue is, at best, general. As we have seen, adjacent colors can counter or modify an emotional response to a particular hue. The intercolor experience, which involves both the psychological response and the physiological limitation of the eye, can also be tricked by an optical illusion. This phenomenon of fooling both the eye and the mind is dependable enough to be considered an important part of the impact of color on a theatre audience. Color Plates 8-15 through 8-24 offer many examples—from sketches to photographs—of how designers use color onstage.

COLOR MANIPULATION

Some designers have an intuitive sense of color. The colors they put together seem right for the specific dramatic moment or atmospheric scene. A designer in the theatre, however, frequently has to suppress personal preferences in order to maintain color control (harmony or contrast) within the production. To ensure the chances of a unified color solution, all designers—scenery, costume, and lighting—rely on advance color schemes to coordinate the final color impression.

The Color Scheme

The development of a production color scheme may be as simple as deciding on the overall tonality of a single hue, or it may involve selecting several related or contrasting colors. The *harmony* or *contrast* of hues becomes the basic control of a production color scheme. The mood of the production is often expressed in the interrelationship of the colors in the scheme. All the variants of color (hue, value, and chroma) may be called on to provide interest and flexibility to the final colors in the composition.

One way to develop a color scheme is to examine the relationships of the hues on the color wheel. The closer the hues are on the color wheel, the more harmonious they will appear together. Increasing the distance of two hues on the color wheel increases the contrast, the limit being complementary colors.

Typical color schemes include the following:

- *Monochromatic.* A **monochromatic** scheme uses one hue and its variations in value (addition of black or white) and chroma. The complement to the hue is used only to neutralize or gray down the color.
- *Analogous.* An **analogous** color scheme has little contrast because it uses three hues that are adjacent on the color wheel (yellow, yellow orange, and orange, for example). This is one way to maintain a very tight palette.
- *Complementary.* The perception of vibration when placing complementary colors next to one another has already been discussed. Increasing the contrast of one complement in either value or chroma can often alleviate this problem. It is easier on the eyes if the chroma of one complementary hue is reduced.

monochromatic Using only one hue, black and white, and the complement to reduce the chroma.

analogous Using any three adjacent hues of the color wheel.

- *Black and white.* Although this color scheme can be severely limiting, it can also be extremely elegant. This obviously suggests high contrast, but it could just as easily mean the use of many grays. The use of warm and cool grays can enable the designer to create interest and contrast quite subtly. One variation is to use one hue sparingly in addition to black and white. The Edward Gorey design for *Dracula* is a good example. The set was entirely black and white—no grays—with a single element of red in each set (such as a rose in a bud vase or a glass of red wine).

The color scheme serves as a guide to color composition within a design or throughout a production. Besides providing a means of color communication among collaborating designers, the color scheme is also a device for explaining color relationships and analyzing the dramatic use of color. There are, of course, innumerable color schemes; every production calls for a unique way of looking at color and every designer has a unique way of exploring it.

The Color Plot

The control of color within a composition is only a portion of the color planning that occurs in designing for the theatre. The color scheme for each setting of a multiscene play must also be considered in the context of the entire production.

Some scene designers and many costume designers use a *color plot* to make preliminary studies of the entire production. Although it is a view of the show the audience will never see, it does serve as a color guide for the lighting and costume designers. Through the color plot, the overall development of color can be studied. The functional relationship of colors is clearly visible. The progressive unfolding of color change within a scene or throughout a production, as well as moments of high contrast or subdued uniformity, can be demonstrated in the color plot. The color plot also establishes the progression of colors from scene to scene and act to act.

Because it shows the overall relationship of all costumes in the production, the color plot is very important to the costume designer. It enables him or her to plot small scenes and families of color that may help to visually define sympathetic characters and rival groups or individuals. The focus or center of attention in a large group scene can be planned, as well as the control of the overall emotional impact or mood within the scene.

Color Modification

We have seen how color can be changed by mixing, can be influenced by interaction with other colors, can be created by optical illusion, and can be modified by colored light. Fortunately, color modification is not quite as complicated as it seems. The effect of colored light on a colored surface is a result of subtractive mixing. In other words, if a red light is thrown on a yellow surface, the yellow is modified into orange.

The modification of a color in a costume or on scenery by colored light is a theatrical example of the joining of two color mediums, pigment and light. Designers in the theatre are constantly aware of how colored light and pigment influence each other. They are always prepared to compensate in either medium to create a natural effect or to deliberately cause dramatic reversals of color.

9

Painting Scenery

Scenery painting is a highly skilled and specialized portion of creating a setting. It is also a critical and fascinating part of the scene design process. After deciding on the look of the scenery, a designer communicates with the scenic artist, who then uses the designer's ideas to create painted scenery. Many of the methods and techniques of handling scene paint are familiar to anyone with training in the visual arts. The main difference between scenery painting and easel painting is one of scale and distance of the work from the spectator. Instead of painting at a small drawing board, the scenic artist paints on a life-size or larger canvas for an audience that will often view it from afar.

Because the scale of scene painting is so large, the scenic artist uses a broad technique, sometimes so broad that clear forms appear only when viewed from a distance. Learning to paint this way may be an adjustment for the visual artist. A basic understanding of scenic design is certainly helpful, as are painting skills of any kind. Sketching and painting from still life or landscape not only improve the student designer's drawing and painting ability but also increase his or her perception of texture, light, and color in nature. Color especially comes into play in theatre painting; a thorough grounding and understanding of how to use it is essential.

PAINT AND COLOR

The design of a setting can succeed or fail on the strength of the scenic art or painting. Hence, the designer in collaboration with the scenic artist should carefully plan how the scenery will be painted. A good scenic artist can greatly enhance a design if allowed to work with the designer in determining painting procedures. Perhaps the most important and certainly the most difficult consideration is the use of color. A scene designer must be familiar not only with the mixing and use of pigments but also with the effects of colored lights (see Chapters 3 and 8).

Components of Paint

URL http://www.rosebrand.com/A_Com/Category.cfm?&DID=6&CATID=7

URL http://www.ppgaf.com/school.htm

Scene paint is composed of three basic components: *pigment* (color), *binder,* and *vehicle.* The pigment and binder are suspended in a liquid (the vehicle) that allows the paint to be brushed or sprayed onto a surface. As the vehicle evaporates, the binder holds the pigment to the surface. Most of the paint that is used for scenery is ready-mixed, meaning that the pigment, binder, and vehicle have been premixed, although unmixed dry pigment is still on the market.

Scenic Paint

The scenic artist's first act is to create a working palette of scene paint that will relate to the twelve principal hues of the spectrum. The size of the palette will vary, depending on the individual artist's tastes and working methods, on the requirements of the design, on the pureness of hue and mixing behavior of the available pigments, and finally on the relative cost of individual colors.

Designers need to know the wide range of types of paint available. In choosing the type of paint to use, they must determine the types of surfaces to be painted as well as the type of work to be done. Some paints are general purpose while others are designed to be used in specific situations. The most commonly used paints for scenery are the water-based *latex* and *acrylic. Casein,* or milk-based paints, are less common in the paint shop than they used to be. Whenever possible, it is wisest to use a water-based paint such as those previously mentioned, because they are generally the safest and easiest to use. There are so many new products on the market that there is a water-based paint made for almost any given circumstance, even painting Plexiglas. When using one of the many paints that are not water soluble, such as enamel, lacquer-based, or acetone-based paints, it is important to note the solvent required and to carefully follow safety precautions. These may, at the very least, require the use of gloves, a respirator, and a well-ventilated area in which to paint.

Color Matching The designer must also judge how the color of a commercial paint matches the corresponding color in the design. Because designers use an infinite variety of colors rather than only those from the color wheel, it is often necessary to compensate by stocking two pigments instead of one. For example, because a true spectrum yellow is not obtainable, two yellows are usually stocked—one that will mix easily with blue or green, and one that will mix with orange.

In preparing a list of stock scenic colors, artists compare the quality of the pigments' hues with the twelve principal colors of the color wheel. A good scene-painting palette includes them as well as some special colors and the earth colors.

Color matching is one of the scenic artist's most important skills. Practice allows the artist to become familiar with the available manufactured pigments as well as to develop a better eye for color. Each pigment has its own idiosyncrasies, but with practice, choosing the best combinations for matching a designer's color choices will get easier.

Dry Pigment Dry pigments are ground specifically for theatrical use and therefore are available only at supply houses specializing in scenic paints and supplies. Formerly the industry standard, dry pigment is used only occasionally today. Many shops will use what remains from years past, but few shops stock these pigments on an ongoing basis.

When dry pigments are used as scene paint, the pigments are suspended in water (the vehicle) with a water-soluble glue as the binder. A filler such as whiting (an inexpensive chalk, sold in powdered form) is frequently added to the mixture to give the paint body and opacity. Some care should be used, however, because whiting affects the value of the color.

The binder used for dry pigment is called *size*. Traditionally, the size was made from a casein, gelatin, or animal glue that was manufactured in granular form and required soaking then boiling in water before use. It is common practice now to use other glues such as a flexible glue as a binder for dry pigment. Once prepared, the size can be mixed directly with the dry pigment. However, certain colors, such as Prussian blue and Van Dyke brown, will not suspend if mixed directly with the size. They must first be soaked in denatured alcohol. Once the pigment has been mixed into a paste form, the size can be added slowly.

To match a specific shade of color with dry pigment, the scenic artist can mix colors dry before adding the size. Although this may achieve an accurate match, it is a hazardous process. The fine powder of dry pigment can easily become airborne and then inhaled. It is vital that the user wear a dust mask while mixing dry pigment or any other powder.

Although large-scale painting with dry pigment has fallen into disuse, generally because of its time-consuming preparation, it is sometimes a convenient medium to have in the shop. Dry pigment can be mixed in small quantities with other binders such as shellac, flat varnish, or clear acrylic for a semigloss effect or for wood graining.

Ready-Mixed Paints With ready-mixed paints, the pigment, color, binder, and vehicle are premixed in proper proportions into a creamy paste. Caseins often have too little binder, and under a series of washes (painting with little pigment and much water) casein undercoat tends to come off. Adding a binder such as a clear acrylic or a polyvinyl acrylic (PVA) to the paint is sometimes best. The many commercial scenic paints vary in quality and potential use, particularly in terms of color richness. The price varies as well. Another vinyl scenic paint, "supersaturated," has recently become more popular. It is the most expensive paint but has excellent color richness. It can also be diluted yet retain its depth of color.

Latex and acrylic paints can be used almost interchangeably. Although caseins offer a wide range of color, they tend to be chalkier and stickier than other paints. They also can take longer to mix during color matching. Latex paints are often used as a cheap substitute for caseins but in general they are less intense in color. The latex paints high in chroma tend to be as expensive as caseins.

Aniline Dyes

Aniline dyes are available in almost all the standard colors. They are used for thin wash glazes, translucencies, and dip-dyed fabrics that do not come in contact with skin. Because aniline dyes are toxic, gloves and a respirator must be worn during the mixing process.

Dyeing or painting with dyes is a different process than painting with scene paints. Scene paint changes the color of a surface by covering it with a pigment that is held in place by a binder. Dyeing, on the other hand, is a chemical process. The dye color becomes a part of the material to which it is applied. If the dye and material do not have an affinity for each other, a complete chemical action will not take place.

To dye cotton duck or muslin, adding a small amount of acetic acid or vinegar to the dye solution is sometimes needed. The acid increases the affinity of the cotton for the dye, causing the fabric to absorb more color. The addition of a small quantity of salt also helps to increase the amount of absorption. Salt counteracts the tendency of dyestuffs to go into solution, making it easier for the dye color to be absorbed by the material. However, too much salt in the mixture, possibly from salted dyes or flameproofing compounds frequently mixed with the dye bath, can keep the dye from going into solution. Because dye comes in powder form (hence the need for a respirator), it is important to make sure all crystals dissolve, or streaks of concentrated color will appear on the surface of the canvas. If the dye has a tendency to separate, the addition of some alcohol will ensure a complete solution. Normally, the crystals go into solution in hot water without any trouble.

For extensive *dye painting*—when painting a translucent drop, for example—the muslin is prepared with a starch size (discussed later in this chapter). If the painting is being done on a fabric that cannot be sized with starch, such as velour or silk, a small amount of starch can be added to the dye mixture to keep it from spreading ("bleeding") on the fabric. To prevent this on detail painting, the dye can be mixed with *methocel,* which thickens the dye.

Because aniline dyes are so strong in color and relatively inexpensive, dip-dyeing can be used for large gauze pieces with excellent results. The preparation of the dye for dip-dyeing is the same as for dye painting except, of course, for the increase in quantity. Artists must be sure to mix enough dye, for to run out of dye mix in the middle of a dipping is disastrous. The color of the mix should be checked by dipping a sample of the fabric before preparing it for dipping.

Before dipping the fabric into the dye, the fabric is first soaked in water. If it is new material, it should be washed first to remove any sizing. After excess water has been wrung out, the still-damp fabric is dipped into the dye mix and stirred carefully to ensure the dye penetrates the fabric evenly. After squeezing or wringing out the excess dye, the artist should stretch it out to dry or hang it in place and stretch it back into shape as it dries.

URL http://www.woodfinishsupply.com/tecAniline.html

Dip-dyeing will take out any flameproofing that might have been in the material. It has to be reflameproofed later, or better still, flameproofed directly by a mixture added to the dye. As always, testing this procedure on a sample piece before proceeding is best.

Toxicity of Paint and Dye

The daily contact of paints, dyes, and their solvents—all of which often contain toxic chemicals—can become a health hazard unless they are handled carefully. Toxic chemicals can enter the bloodstream in many ways: absorbed through the skin, ingested, or inhaled.

Although the paints and dyes discussed in this text are relatively safe, basic precautions are critical, especially because individual tolerances can vary. For example, some people have a multiple chemical sensitivity (MCS), while others are allergic to the touch and smell of paints. Every product has an MSDS (Materials Safety Data Sheet), which can be easily obtained from the manufacturer by request; these sheets should be posted in the shop and read by all personnel. A stock of latex gloves and respirators with the appropriate types of cartridges for the product being used should be kept available, and any painting with toxic materials should be done *only* in a well-ventilated area.

Solvents Used as a vehicle to put pigment into a solution, a solvent is basically a paint thinner. Water is the principal solvent for most paints used for scenery, although an occasional chemical solvent is used on a stubborn mixer, in the manufacturing of ready-mixed paints, or for a particular project.

Some familiar solvents used in the theatre are *alcohol* (methanol or wood alcohol), *turpentine, mineral spirits* (a substitute for turpentine), *ammonia,* and *formaldehyde* (in ready-mixed acrylic paints). If any of these toxic solvents enter the respiratory tract or bloodstream, it can cause damage to the central nervous system, kidneys, or bladder. Any contact with the eyes should also be avoided.

Most solvents are volatile and will therefore evaporate quickly in a well-ventilated shop. Even under the best painting conditions, the eyes should be protected with goggles, the hands with gloves, and the lungs with an air-purifying respirator. This is especially important when mixing with solvents.

URL http://www.clean.rti.org/altern.cfm

Pigments As we have seen, the color or hue of a paint is its pigment. The source of a pigment helps to establish its degree of toxicity. Most pigments used in theatre are either inorganic or synthetic organic in origin.

Inorganic pigments come from the earth or minerals. Earth colors—such as ochre, burnt and raw sienna, ivory black, Prussian blue, and titanium white—are considered nontoxic. Pigments from mineral sources—such as cadmium yellow, raw and burnt umber, and cobalt blue—may have some lead content and should be treated as toxic.

Synthetic organic pigments are human-made colors created in part from organic materials. Although the organic source may not itself be toxic, toxic chemicals are often used in the pigments' manufacture. Such pigments as chrome yellow, chrome green, and molybdate (moly) orange should be used with extreme caution.

Dyes Aniline dyes in their original organic state are quite toxic. Present-day aniline dyes, however, are synthetic and are prepared especially for cotton (duck and muslin). Although considered nontoxic, they are hazardous in powder or crystalline state. As with any powder, extreme care should be taken to avoid inhalation when handling dye crystals before they are put into a liquid state. As with dry pigment, when mixing dyes it is wise to wear a respirator. To avoid potentially dangerous mixing during the pressures of a heavy work schedule, some shops prepare dyes ahead of time, storing them as a concentrated liquid. When painting with dyes, avoid skin and eye contact. Protect an open cut with rubber gloves.

URL http://www.straw.com/sig/dyehist.html

Frequently materials other than cotton—such as rayon, wool, or silk—have to be dyed. Commercial dyes are available in small quantities and for all kinds of fabrics. Packaged or household dyes may be potentially hazardous. Read the directions and handle these dyes with extreme caution.

URL http://www.prochemical.com

URL http://www.dharmatrading.com

For additional and more detailed information about solvents, pigments, and dyes, write to the center of Occupational Hazards, 5 Beekman Street,

URL http://www.epa.gov/ttn/atw/hlthef/aniline.html

New York, New York 10038. Literature on most aspects of painting can be obtained. Enclose a stamped, self-addressed envelope. As well, the books *Artist Beware* by Michael McCann and *Stage Fright* by Monona Rossol deal with artists' materials and are filled with invaluable information.

PAINTER'S ELEVATIONS

Designers must thoroughly prepare for scene painting even if they plan to do it themselves. Painting ideas are expressed in painter's elevations, which, unlike sketches, remove all the atmosphere of stage lighting to show true colors and exact form. This is the point in the process when the designer must think through the appropriate painting technique and procedure for a design. The painter's elevation is a scaled drawing showing in detail the line work and the actual color of each piece of scenery, as well as a clear indication of the technique to be used for each. The scale of the elevation varies with the designer. The larger the scale, however, the more accurately it can be interpreted. The painter's elevations for most settings can be done at ½-inch scale.

To provide the most complete information for the scenic artist, designers should include a black-and-white line drawing of the scenic piece, especially a drop. Any portions of the work that have been obscured through the painting of the paint elevation may be clarified in the line drawing.

Painter's elevations can also provide clear information to the costume designer and especially the lighting designer, so that they have a full picture of what the set will be. The color information that these provide can be vital.

PAINTING PROCEDURE

It would seem likely that enlarging the drawing from the paint elevation would be the first task in creating a drop. But this cannot happen until the fabric has been prepared. There are three steps in preparing a surface for decorative painting: applying the size, prime, and base coats. Their individual use or omission varies in accordance with the complexity of the design, the nature of the surface, and the painting technique. Figure 9-1 illustrates the overall painting procedure, from the painter's elevation to the finished piece.

Size Coat

When working with soft-covered flats and muslin drops (or any piece of scenery that is covered with canvas or muslin), the first step in the painting process is preparing the surface. This is done with a *size coat,* which shrinks the fabric and glazes the surface without filling it. Starch is most often used. The starch size prepares a canvas or muslin for dye-painting on translucent work or for very thin opaque paints. It can also serve as a surface for opaque paints, especially if the opaque coat will not completely cover the surface but will be applied to leave areas of unpainted background. Starch size can be made by adding a cup of cooked Argo starch (the "blue box") to a 16-quart bucket of hot water at about a 20-to-1 proportion. The temperature of the water and the amount of humidity in the air will affect the strength of the

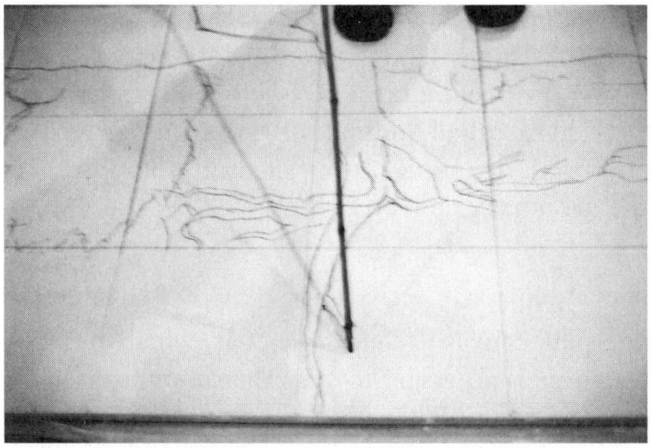
a

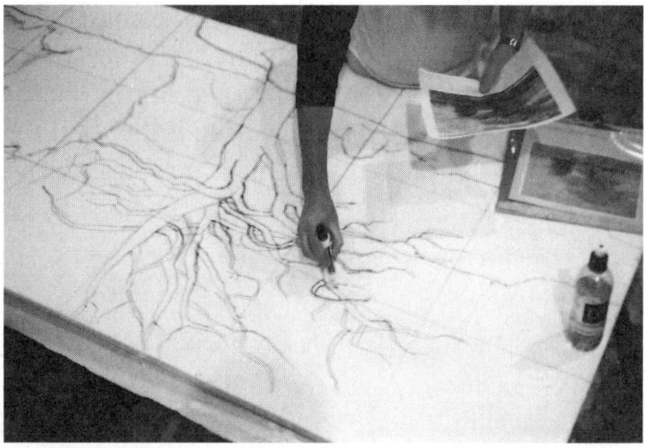
b

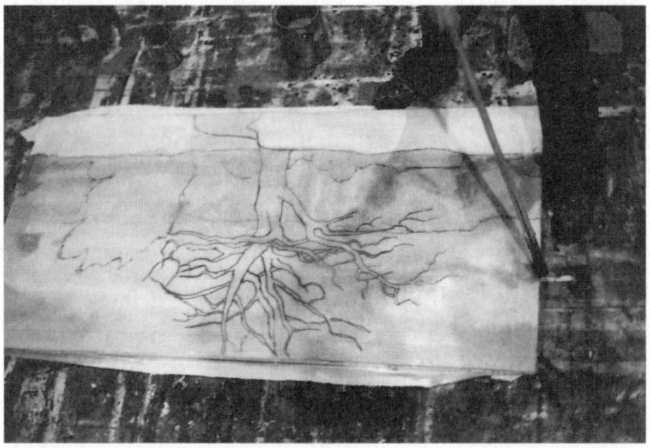
c

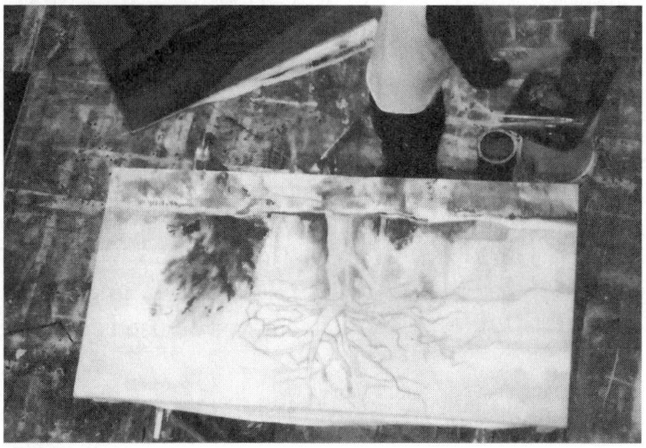
d

e

9-1

Scenery Painting Procedure

- **a** Painter's elevation of a flat prepared by the designer. This scale drawing has been gridded with 2-foot squares in preparation for the full-scale drawing on the drop.
- **b** Proportional enlarging on the sized muslin drop. It has been gridded with charcoal and a snap line to full scale, matching the grid on the elevation. The design is cartooned, or sketched out, with charcoal so that mistakes in construction lines can easily be "flogged" or dusted off.
- **c** Inking the drawing. The charcoal drawing of the design is fixed to the muslin with a thin marker.
- **d** Painting the flat: wash backgrounds and laying in basic shapes and colors.
- **e** Detail painting can proceed without fear of losing the drawing, because the marker lines will bleed through the paint and remain visible.

starch size. Also, every scenic artist has his or her own preferences as to how thin or thick to mix the starch size. (This comes with experience.) A touch of dye can be added to make the size coat more visible for brushing onto the fabric. The resulting coat is a taut, slightly glazed surface that is excellent for dye as well as paint.

floating Lifting a wet drop off the floor by blowing air underneath while the paint is wet.

When sizing a drop, the artist must allow air underneath during the painting and drying process; otherwise, the drop will adhere to the floor below. With a *bridge* to lift up one corner of a drop and a box fan to blow air underneath, the drop is lifted off the floor. This is called **floating** the drop. Unless the drop is extremely large or is a soft portal, one bridge is sufficient. It is important to keep the air flowing until the drop has dried.

Prime Coat

The second step in preparing new canvas is the prime coat, which serves to fill the canvas. Filling a new canvas is necessary to keep the colors from losing brilliance. This phenomenon is quite noticeable when old canvas is used beside new canvas on a flat. The prime coat serves to guarantee that both paint surfaces will be the same.

The type of prime coat used depends on the kind of painting that will be done and how the piece of scenery will be used onstage. A translucent drop will most often be prepared with a thin layer of starch. White latex is often used for flats because it is inexpensive. There are primer coats manufactured specifically for metal (well cleaned) and for plastics. If dry pigment will be used, a prime coat is made of working size and whiting with a touch of color to facilitate the application. Whatever is used as a prime is kept thin to keep from overloading the muslin. Most prime coats tend to be opaque and therefore cannot be used over areas that are to be translucent or dye painted.

Cartooning

cartooning The drawing, usually in charcoal, of a paint elevation on a drop or flat.

Working from the painter's elevations, the scene painter can proportionally enlarge the drawing to full scale (see Figure 9-2a, b). The drawing out of the paint elevation is called **cartooning.** A grid of horizontal and vertical lines is placed over the drawing; this grid is scaled to match the grid that will be drawn on the canvas. A 2-foot full-size grid is common, but every situation is different and the decision of grid size should be determined by the complexity of the painting. Sometimes a 4-foot grid is enough, but a 6-inch grid might be needed for minute details. It is often tempting for the inexperienced scenic artist to draw a very small grid. A too-small grid will perhaps allow the scenic artist to more easily draw a detail but will hinder the connectivity of all the parts of the drawing. Whatever the size, a grid that replicates the one on the painter's elevation at full scale is drawn on the priming coat of the surface to be painted.

Ways of numbering or lettering the grid vary and have to do with the personal taste of the artist. Some artists prefer to number the spaces, while others favor numbering the lines. Proceeding square by square, the painter transposes the small-scale elevation into a full-scale layout of the design.

All cartooning or layout drawing is done in charcoal on the prime coat. If the line drawing is Xeroxed, several artists can cartoon the piece for more efficiency. It is not unusual with a complicated drawing to use an overhead or opaque projector to speed up the process. After the drawing is completed, key points or portions of the cartoons are "inked" in, using an industrial marker supplied with replaceable felt tips. Excess charcoal is "flogged" or dusted off the surface in preparation for the base coat. The inked-in portions of the design will bleed through the base coat and serve as a guide for detailed painting.

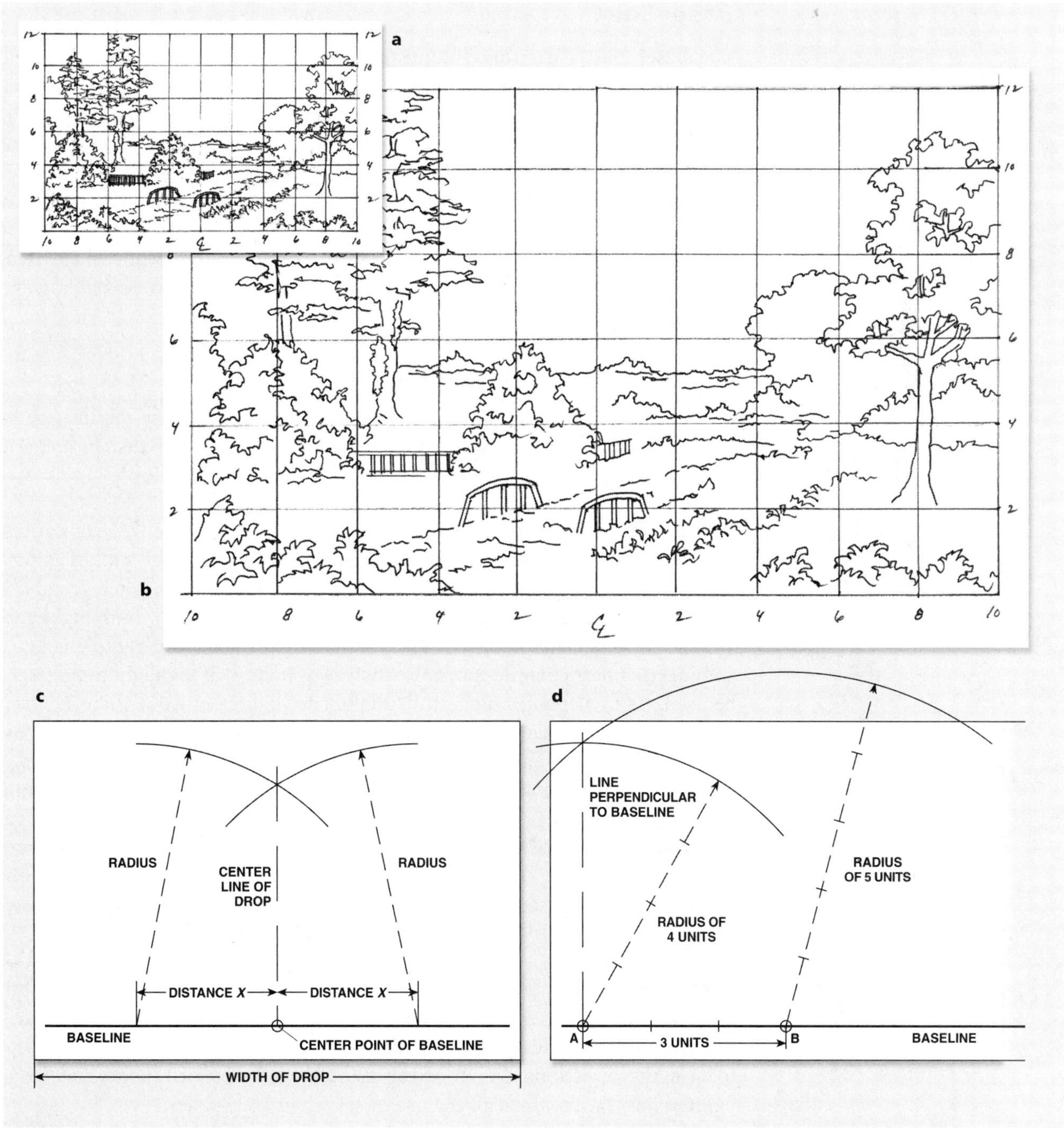

9-2

Methods of Enlarging

a The designer's elevation with a grid of 2-to-4-foot squares. Lines are numbered from the center line out to the left and right as well as from bottom to top.

b Full-scale layout of the drawing with the same labeling method.

c **Finding the center line of the drop:** Establish a baseline for the drop, then find the center point of the baseline. Swing two arcs from a point equidistant from the center of the baseline. Connecting the intersection of these two arcs with the center point of the baseline will establish the center line of the drop.

d **Squaring the drop:** Again, establish a baseline for the drop. Using a convenient unit of length, measure 3 units along the baseline from one corner (point A). Swing an arc 4 units long from the same corner (A). From the other end of the 3-unit length along the base (point B), swing an arc of 5 units long toward the edge of the drop. Drawing a line between the intersection of the two arcs and point A will establish a perpendicular.

Base Coat

The base coat is the underpainting for the final decorative painting and texturing. As a mixture, the base coat is kept thin in order not to overload the canvas. The application and color of the base coat is determined by the finished surface of the scenery. For example, a base coat may be one tone as a basis for a slick, modern paneled wall; it may be a **scumbling** of two or three tones in preparation for an antiqued, weather-beaten surface; or it may be a graded wash to go under a stenciled wallpaper design. In this way, the scenic artist can use the base coat to start to suggest the final surface. This technique is especially helpful in creating texture or when a particular light source is integral to the painting.

scumbling Intermixing of two or more colors on the scenery in a random pattern, allowing some areas to blend.

Detail and Decorative Painting

The final step in scene painting is the definition of form, or the illusion of form, through the various painting techniques of lining, texturing, creating foliage, stenciling, and pouncing.

Lining The technique of **lining,** freehand or with a straightedge, helps artists represent in two dimensions the complicated surfaces of the moldings in a cornice, chair rail, panel, or door trim (Figure 9-3). Careful lining helps establish highlight, shade, and shadow. The specific choices of color for both highlights and shadows depend on the design as well as the principles of complementary colors. For a particular design, more than two shadow or highlight tones might be used. As their names suggest, highlights are lighter in value than the local color, and shadows darker. Because they tend to recede, cooler colors are most frequently used for shadows, but warm tones can also create them successfully.

lining Using a small brush to paint lines, most often used in painting highlight and shadow in painted molding.

The order of lining for a panel or cornice is determined after first studying a cross section of the molding and the direction of the light that would reveal the molding if it were real. The positions of windows or artificial light sources offer clues for fixing the general direction of light for each wall in the set, but it is critical for the set designer and scenic artist to consult with the lighting designer to coordinate light direction for painted scenery.

Texturing To avoid the starkness of a single tone and to bring more depth to a flat surface, the painter uses various texturing techniques. Many natural shadows and reflected-light tonalities are eliminated because the stage is lit from many directions. Much of this natural variation of tonality has to be painted into the set through the use of texturing techniques.

One of the simplest texturing techniques is to **wet-blend** two or more tones of a color on a surface. Using a separate brush for each color, the two or more artists use both at the same time to blend the different tones together on the canvas. The result is a gradation of one color to another. This technique is handled on a broad scale with either subtlety or obviousness depending on the contrast or harmony of the tones.

wet-blend To blend two or more colors on the scenery while they are wet.

The artist can also use wet-blending to begin the suggestion of light. If, for example, a wall has a well-lit portion and a shadowed area, a wet-blend in the base coat will greatly help to indicate this and will save time in the more detailed painting to follow.

A blending technique can also be done over a dry surface by blending the tones together with **dry-brushing** or **feathering.** Dry-brushing, as the name implies, is done with the tip of a relatively dry brush in order to cover the

dry-brushing Pulling the brush across wet paint in such a way that the bristles of the brush leave a streaky brush stroke.

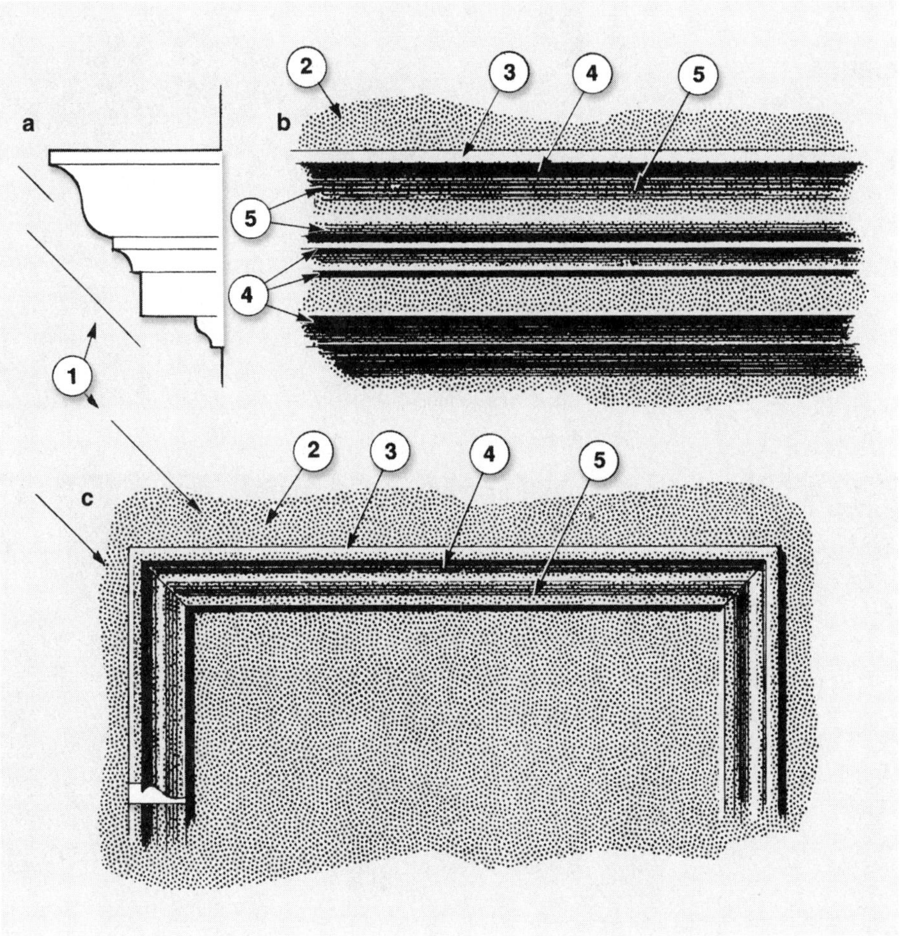

9-3

Lining Techniques

a Profile of cornice to be painted.

b Lining of cornice.

c Lining of raised panel molding.

1 Assumed direction of light.

2 Local or base color.

3 Highlight.

4 Shadow, darkest tone.

5 Shade.

undersurface only partially, letting the dry surface show through. *Feathering* refers to the direction of the brush stroke. The brush is drawn from the wet surface toward the dry so that the stroke ends in a featherlike pattern.

Other texturing techniques on a smaller scale include **sponging, stippling, spattering,** stamping, combing, rolling, and spraying. Each technique creates an appearance of texture by applying tones to form a vibrant surface (Figure 9-4). Many of these scenic art techniques have become extremely popular in interior decorating. Many widely available books provide step-by-step instructions for these techniques, and many paint companies provide brochures with similar information at most paint retailers.

Although these are fairly standard methods of painting textures, every project presents a unique set of problems and solutions. Using the basic techniques that have been mentioned, the scenic artist should find a specific method that will satisfy the needs of the project at hand.

All the techniques just discussed can be used to simulate the textural qualities of a specific material such as stone, plaster, or wallpaper. Some materials, however, require texturing techniques that border on decorative painting; wood and wood graining are prime examples (Figure 9-5).

The painting of wood graining employs the same use of color found in the other techniques. The grain pattern, of course, varies with the type of wood and its use in the design. Is it to be matched-grain walnut veneer on a late Empire breakfront secretary, or knotty pine vertical paneling? Any attempt at

feathering Pulling the brush from a wet painted surface to a dry one so that the stroke ends in a featherlike pattern.

sponging Using a sponge to apply paint.

stippling Using the tips of the brush to apply paint in an up-and-down motion.

spattering Method of applying painted texture by sharply tapping a loaded brush against the heel of the hand, leaving droplets of pigment on the work.

9-4

Texture-Painting Techniques

a Wet blending.
b Combing or dry brushing.
c Scumbling.
d Stippling.
e Spraying.
f Spattering.
g Rag rolling.
h Feather duster.
i Paint roller.

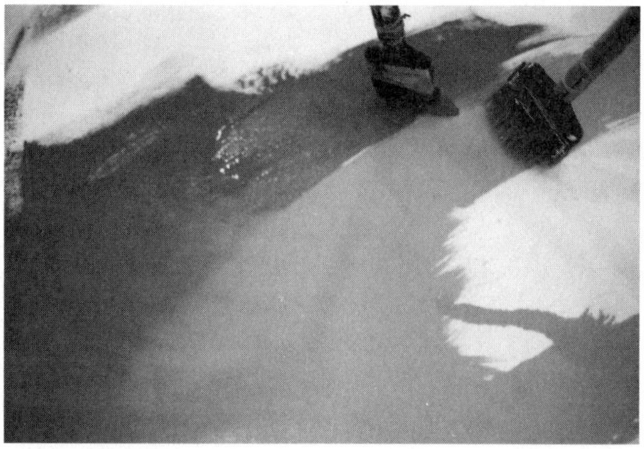

a

b

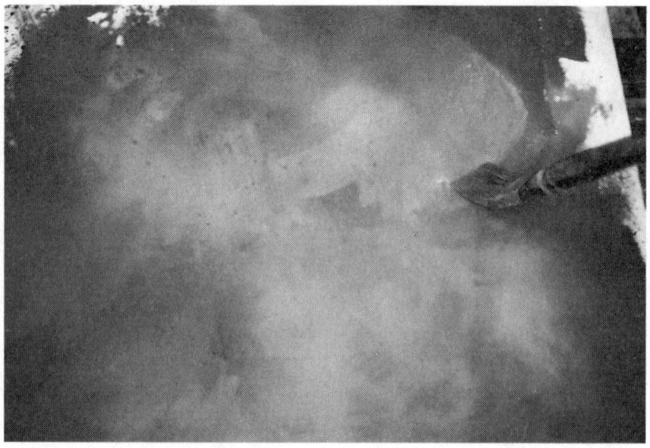

c

d

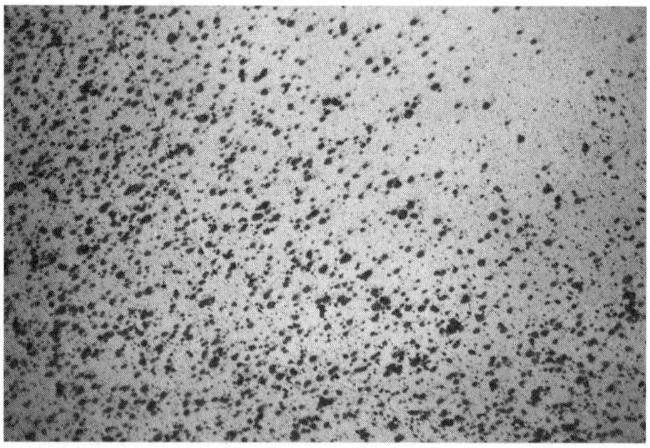

e

realistic representation of wood graining on the stage should be preceded by a careful study of the real wood's color and grain characteristics.

glazing Painting a transparent or semitransparent layer on top that subtly tones a surface or provides a finish (such as gloss, semigloss, or matte).

If the painted "wood" needs a varnished finish, **glazing** might work. Glazing, however, not only reduces the contrast between colors but also lowers their value. This must be taken into consideration in the preparation of the grain colors.

The glazing of grain can be accomplished in several ways. One method is to grain the surface first, then apply a shellac, clear acrylic, or flat-varnish glaze. Glazing can also be effective in subtly toning scenery, by adding a thin layer of yellow to warm up a wall, for example.

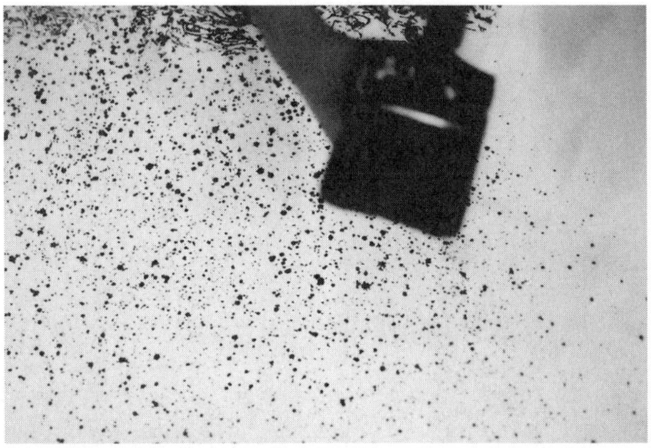

f

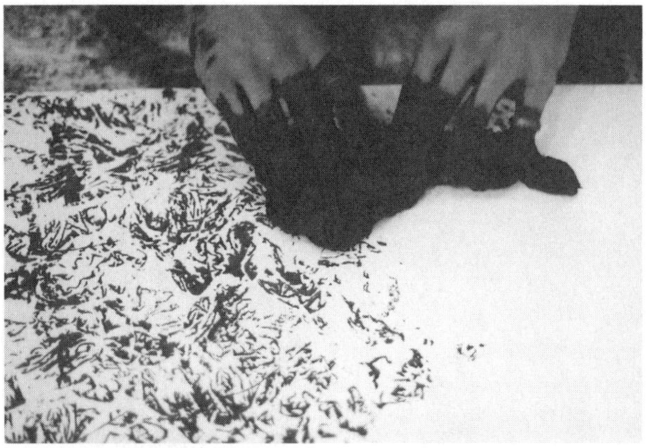

g

h

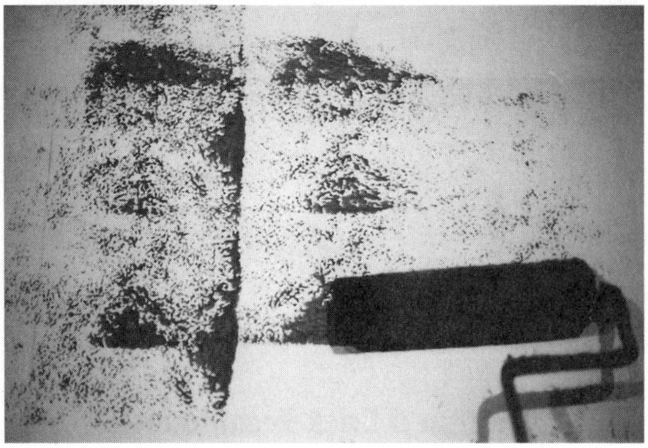

i

In many cases, it is possible to mix a clear gloss or clear flat acrylic with the paint. This eliminates the step of painting a surface finish. Dry pigment can be mixed with shellac or varnish, which serves as binder as well as providing a sheen. Glazed surfaces created in this way must be handled with caution as they are harder to control and there is the danger of creating a surface that is too reflective.

Creating Foliage The designing and painting of trees and foliage requires practice and a study of natural forms. So much of what the designer and the scenic artist must do is *observe* what is around them. The designer should first study trees in their natural state, perhaps painting them in watercolors. A designer will soon learn to see the overall mass of foliage, then the subdivisions of smaller units relating to the branches of the tree's structure, and finally the detail of a single leaf. Careful observation will allow the artist to see how light reveals the forms, passing through translucent areas. Some branches catch light, while others are silhouetted.

The conceptual treatment of a tree onstage can assume many forms. Stage foliage can be translucent, opaque, or textured. The tree style may be real or stylized, or it may even be suggested with light patterns. Foliage can be carefully painted leaf by leaf or boldly painted in block areas loosely suggesting the organic form.

A landscape artist often starts with the darkest tones. Leaf masses in the shadow or silhouette are blocked in first. The lighter shades and highlights are

a

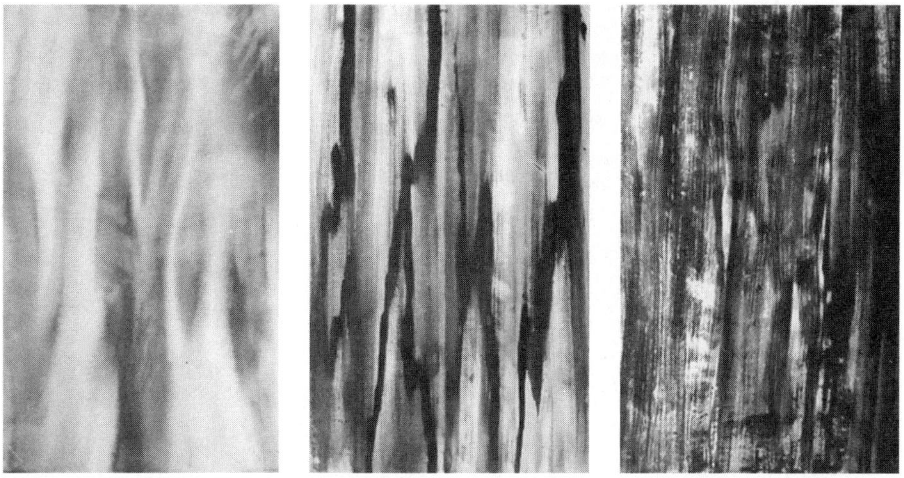

b

9-5

Wood-Grain and Brick Techniques

a Wood technique: A standard wood-grain technique is shown here in three steps. The beginning is a two- or three-color base coat establishing the direction, scale, and general color of the grain. Larger graining lines are painted in, following the movement in the base coat. More texture in the form of spatter and drag (pulling a dry brush over a wet spatter coat), smaller graining, and toning finish the wood grain.

b Brick technique: The size and shape of the bricks is drawn out carefully. An uneven spatter coat is done to establish some background texture for both the brick and the mortar. Individual bricks are painted in using a variety of colors, the number and range depending on the nature of the design. The brick is finished by adding highlights and shadows and more texture as necessary.

These descriptions are somewhat simplified; it takes time to perfect the skills required to paint these standard textures. Even more importantly, there are an infinite number of ways to approach any of these standard textures. What appears here is simply one method.

painted last in opaque paint. If the foliage of the tree is to be translucent and painted with dyes, the technique is reversed. The lighter tones are painted first and the darker shades last. There are, of course, an infinite number of ways to paint foliage. The particular method will, as always, depend on the needs and style of the design (see Figure 9-6).

Stenciling The chief use of stenciling is for a painted wallpaper (or something similar) in which a design motif is repeated in an interlocking overall pattern. The cutting and printing of a stenciled design is the fastest and most effective method of repeating a small motif. After the means of interlocking the motif have been carefully figured out in relation to the size of the wall area, the motif is traced onto a sheet of paper strong enough to withstand the abuse of repeated brushing and layers of paint.

Stencil paper is a tough, oil-impregnated paper made especially for the task. It is readily available in art shops or paint and wallpaper stores, or it can be made by applying a half-and-half mixture of linseed oil and turpentine to heavy kraft paper. Oak tag is a cheaper and thinner substitute for stencil paper but it must be treated the same way. Both are good only for light usage, as they wear out quickly. Thin Plexiglas can be used, although it is harder to cut. More common now are thin plastic and Upson board.

A well-planned stencil has at least one full motif with portions of adjacent motifs to key the stencil into an interlocking scheme. The size of the motif and the amount needed for interlocking the design more or less determine the size of the stencil sheet. Care should be taken not to create too large a stencil that might become awkward to handle. The motif is cut out of the paper with a sharp knife, razor blade, or X-acto knife. Be sure to leave some tabs within the open parts to support the loose ends and strengthen the stencil as a whole. Two or more stencils can be cut at one time, for it is wise to have more than one stencil, especially if there is a large area to cover. They can be alternated in use so as to minimize the tendency of a stencil to become damp and misshapen from hard use. The stencil is coated on both sides with clear shellac or any water-repellent plastic spray as an additional protection from the water-soaking effect of scene paint.

COURTESY KARL BRAKE

9-6

Foliage

A portion of a painter's elevation of foliage, designed and painted by Karl Brake.

After the stencil is cut, it is framed at the outside edges with 1 by 2 on edge. This strengthens it and also provides a shield if the paint is being applied with a spray gun.

Artists can make a stencil print by spray gun, brush, or sponge. The spray gun is fast but sometimes messy and hard to control. Stenciling with a brush is slower. The brush should be kept fairly dry and stroked toward the center of the openings to avoid dribbles. The use of a sponge or soft cloth to apply the paint works best on an open stencil (Figure 9-7).

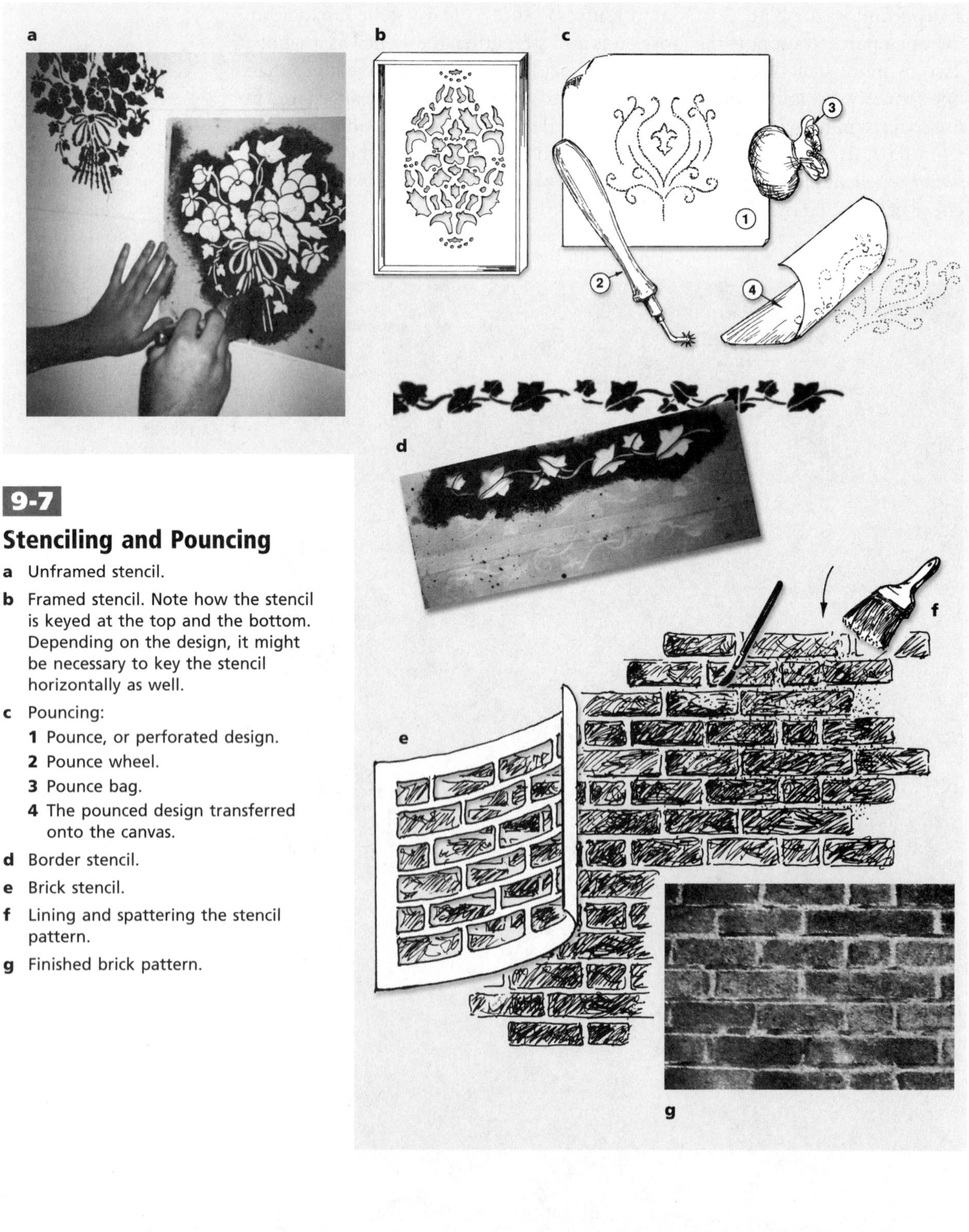

9-7

Stenciling and Pouncing

- **a** Unframed stencil.
- **b** Framed stencil. Note how the stencil is keyed at the top and the bottom. Depending on the design, it might be necessary to key the stencil horizontally as well.
- **c** Pouncing:
  - **1** Pounce, or perforated design.
  - **2** Pounce wheel.
  - **3** Pounce bag.
  - **4** The pounced design transferred onto the canvas.
- **d** Border stencil.
- **e** Brick stencil.
- **f** Lining and spattering the stencil pattern.
- **g** Finished brick pattern.

Pouncing Another method of transferring a repeating design motif is the use of a **pounce.** It is generally used when the motif is too large for a stencil, does not repeat enough times for one to bother cutting a stencil, or is repeated in reverse. Pouncing differs from stenciling in that only the outline or drawing of the motif, rather than the painted print, is transferred (Figure 9-7c).

pounce A drawing, done on kraft paper, that has been perforated in order to transfer it to the scenery to be painted.

The pounce pattern is made by first drawing the design on a piece of brown kraft paper and then perforating the outline with a pounce wheel. The best type of pounce wheel has a small swivel-mounted perforating wheel. It works better on a padded surface, such as a blanket or fold of canvas or velour, than on a hard tabletop or floor.

After the design is perforated and the rough edges of the back side are lightly sanded, the paper is laid on the canvas in the desired position. The pattern is rubbed with a pounce bag made of a thin material such as cheesecloth filled with charcoal dust. After the pouncing, the outline is strengthened with marker, as in a cartooned drop, and the excess charcoal dust is flogged off.

In the commercial theatre, an entire drop will often be drawn as a pounce and transferred to fabric. If a second production such as a tour is produced, this method saves the company a great deal of time and money.

Textured Surfaces

We have discussed the illusion of texture created by paint in the theatre, but surfaces that have a truly textured surface are sometimes desirable as well. Important points to consider before texturing a surface include these: (1) A textured surface cannot be reclaimed for a different use without re-covering the piece of scenery. (2) Deeply textured surfaces may not stand up to excessive handling or wear. (3) If any texturing is done, the lighting designer must know all the details in order to light it properly. As well, the costume designer needs to know the type of texture in order to prevent fabric snags or other problems with costumes.

Scenic artists are always looking for new, inexpensive, and fast methods of creating a texture. Some of the most commonly used materials to do this follow (see also Figures 9-8 and 9-9).

9-8

Textured Surfaces

a Preparation for textured surface: Random shapes of Upson board are glued to the surface of scenery units.

b The appliquéd surface is covered with a mixture of joint compound and glue. It is helpful to add some of the base color into the texture mix. If some of the texture subsequently breaks off, what remains will be similar in color to the rest of the design instead of white. This can save much time in touching up the painting. When dry, the surface is painted in dark tones, and then higher surfaces are dry-brushed with lighter tones.

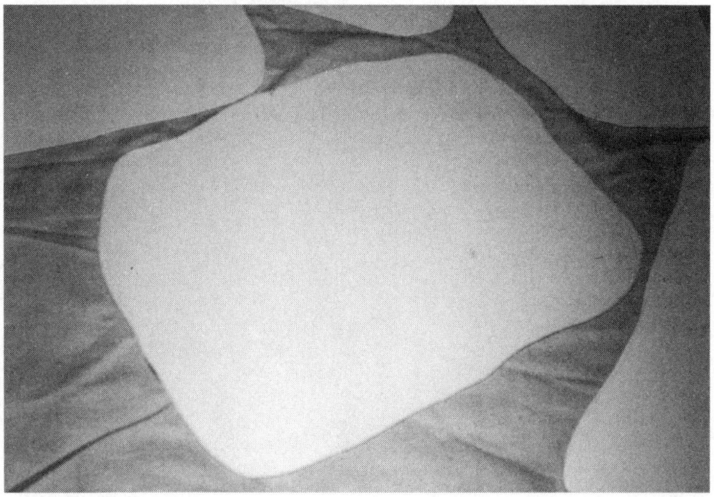

a

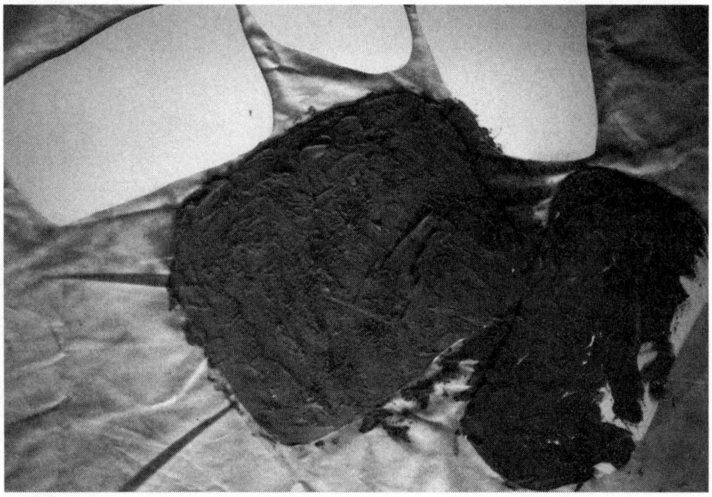

b

9-9

Textured Details

Any number of inexpensive and easy-to-use materials can be used to create texture. Some samples:

a Cheesecloth dipped in a mixture of glue and pigment after being ripped into random shapes can be glued onto a surface and shaped according to need.

b Muslin can be treated the same way. It is less pliable and more difficult to shape but can provide an excellent texture.

c A mixture of joint compound, flex glue, and sawdust gives a much rougher texture. With careful application, and perhaps a bit of sanding afterward, a wide variety of textures can be created.

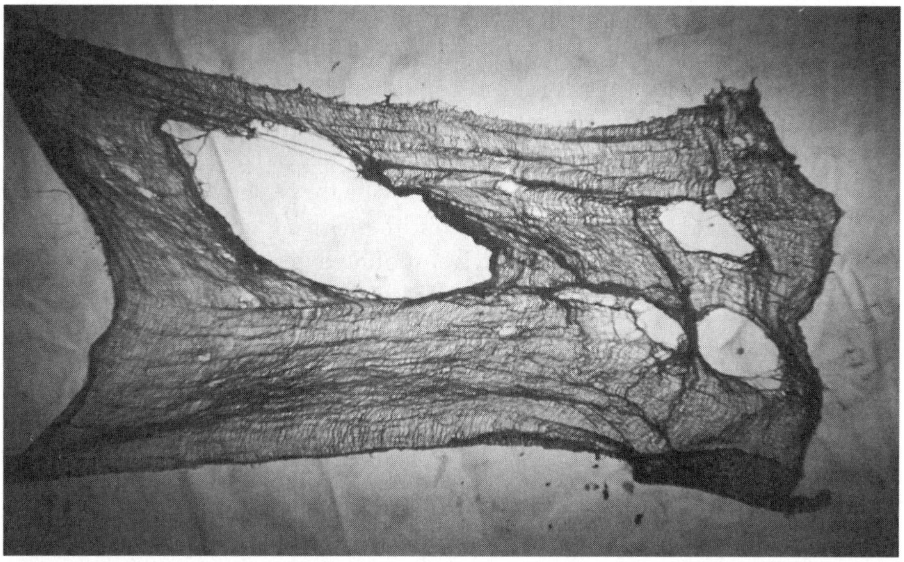

a

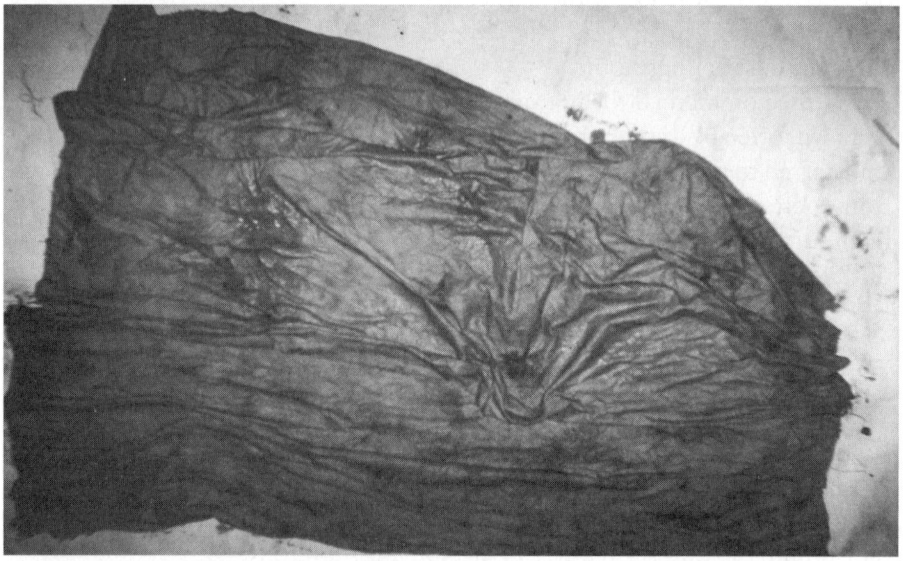

b

c

Joint Compound A compound developed commercially to cement tape over drywall joints in house construction, joint compound will hold a deep texture if a little white glue is added to it before application. It is inexpensive, applies with little trouble, and dries hard. If pigment from the final color of the set is added to the mixture before application, any of the texture that chips off will match the set and not be the white of the raw material. This can save touch-up time.

Sawdust Coat Sawdust or wood chips can be mixed directly with scenic paint and applied as a texture coat. The binder should be stiffened a little to adhere the sawdust firmly. A sawdust coat requires less preparation and dries more quickly than does joint compound, but it does not provide a deep texture.

Water Putty Durham's Water Putty, a commercial surface repair mixture in powder form, can also be used as a texture coat. It works best on a hard surface such as wood and can be combed or stippled into a deep texture. Although it dries off-white, it can be colored either with dye during the mixing or with paint after it has dried. When hardened it is tough but subject to chipping. It can also be used to coat fabric on a curvilinear piece. Best used for smaller projects, this medium is handy in the prop shop.

Surface Materials

Any surface treatment is usually the responsibility of the scenic artist. Surface materials used mainly for textural purposes take a variety of forms. Each has its special handling and individual effect.

Irish Linen Irish linen has, of course, long since disappeared from the U.S. theatre as the standard covering for framed scenery. Its durability and excellent texture, however, have not quite been matched by the scene canvas in common use.

Canvas Canvas, usually 8-ounce cotton duck, has been discussed as a painting surface. Along with muslin, canvas is the professional standard and most frequently used painting surface for all framed scenery. All other surfaces are limited in use to a special effect.

Muslin Unbleached muslin is the next most frequently used covering material. Although it lacks the texture and durability of canvas, its lightweight weave is useful for other purposes. As was mentioned, muslin is an excellent dye-painting surface for translucencies.

Scrim In addition to its general use as a dye-painted transparency, scrim can be used as a painting surface. Unbacked scrim can also be painted with thin scenic colors. They are not as good as dyes, for they tend to stiffen the scrim, which is a disadvantage if it has to fold or roll. If large areas of scrim must be painted, it is best to use a spray to avoid stretching the scrim out of shape.

The open mesh of a scrim can be filled to create opaque areas. One means of doing so is to squeeze pure undiluted clear latex, mixed with a casein color to a paste consistency, onto the scrim to fill the mesh. A mustard squeeze bottle serves as a good applicator. If the scrim is to be filled while it is in a horizontal position, steps should be taken to prevent the latex from sticking to the floor. Polyethelene, a clear transparent plastic, is a good separator. More expensive, premixed fillers are also available (for example, Roscofiller).

Burlap Burlap is frequently used as a covering material chiefly for its texture. Burlap should be backed or fastened to a firm surface, for it is made of jute and may stretch or sag under a heavy coat of paint. Sometimes it helps to paint and dry burlap horizontally. Burlap needs to be heavily sized to keep the color from "striking in." However, this may be a desirable effect in approximating an old tapestry or wall hanging.

Wallpaper Occasionally the scenic artist will be expected to hang wallpaper. Figure 9-10 illustrates the proper technique.

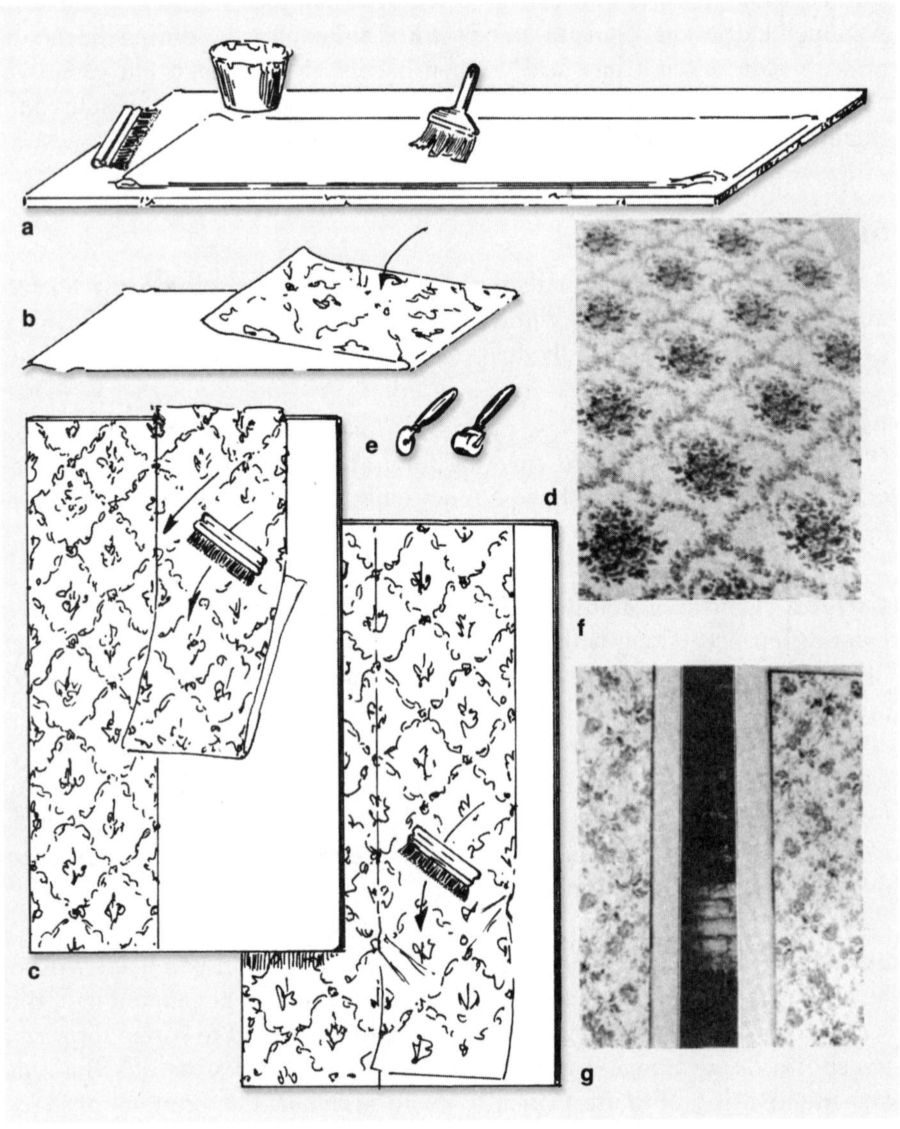

9-10

Wallpapering

Occasionally the scenic artist will have to hang wallpaper. This should be done on a hard surface, not a canvas-covered flat.

a Wallpaper strips long enough to cover the vertical length of the surface are laid face down on pasting board. Store-bought wallpaper paste is used. Adhesive that is already on the back of some wallpaper will not hold well enough.

b Paste-covered strip is folded by one-third, as shown. This is for easier handling of a long strip.

c Exposed portion of pasted strip is smoothed onto wall. Care must be taken to match the pattern. Bubbles are smoothed out with a wallpaper brush.

d Strip is unfolded and brushed flat.

e Cutting wheel and roller. Top edges are trimmed and vertical seams rolled.

f Wallpapered unit of scenery.

g Wallpapered panels.

METHODS OF PAINTING

As we have seen, scenery is painted in two different positions, horizontally and vertically. The various methods of painting are devised to facilitate either way of painting. A good scenic artist trains in both methods.

URL http://www.fcc.net/cobaltstudios/

Horizontal Painting

Painting on the floor is the oldest and simplest method and requires the least mechanical assistance. Long handles on the brushes, charcoal holders, and straightedges help to take the backache out of horizontal painting. The most essential requirement is lots of smooth floor space (preferably wood) and good overhead illumination (Figure 9-11).

Although some painting techniques are best employed horizontally, others are accomplished more easily in a vertical position.

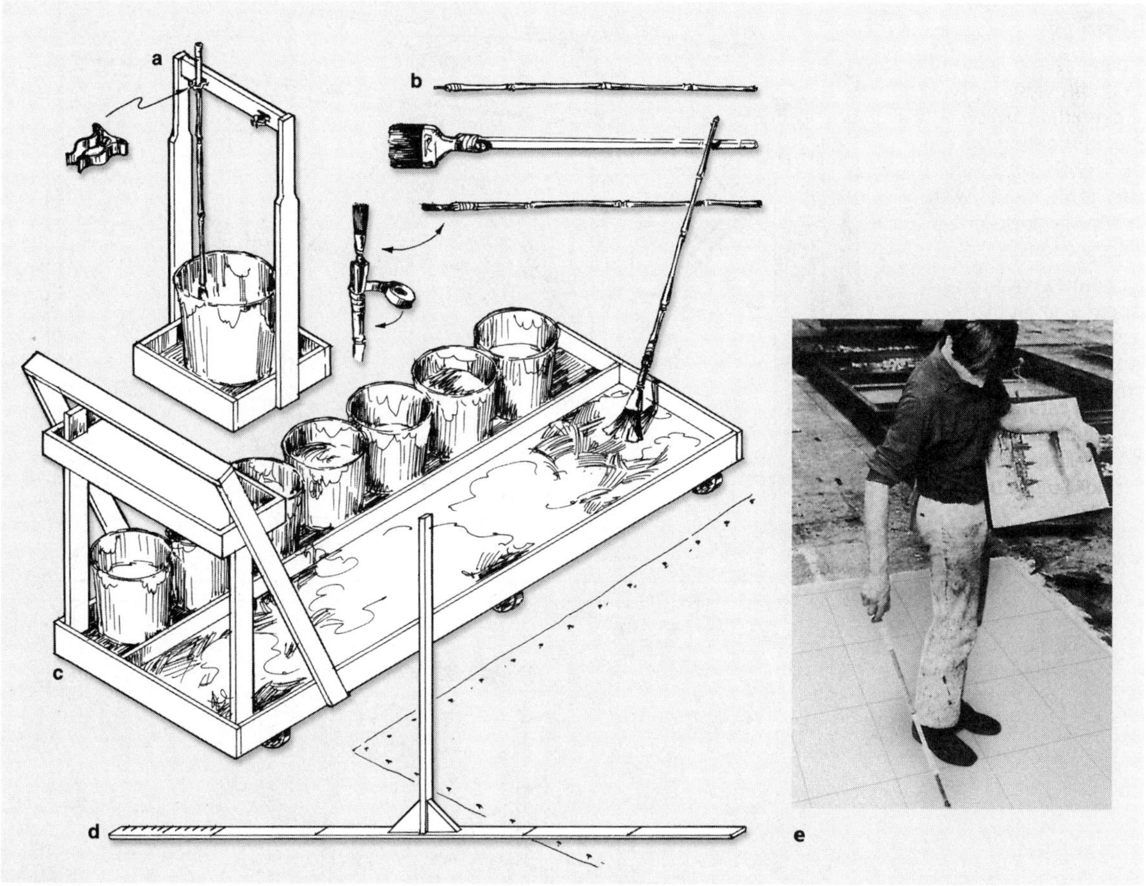

9-11

Painting on the Floor

Extensive floor painting is made easier with the use of proper tools and the right types of brushes.

- **a** Individual paint-bucket carrier.
- **b** Long handles for brushes.
- **c** Paint cart with palette area for mixing paint. (Fewer and fewer painters use a palette area like this.)
- **d** Straightedge with handle.
- **e** Painter using a piece of bamboo to hold the brush, allowing the artist to stand and get some distance from the work while painting.

Vertical Painting

Moving Frame The moving paint frame that can be raised or lowered past the working level brings the greatest flexibility to vertical painting (Figure 9-12a). The frame lowers into a well or to a second painting level. Some unusually high frames often have two or three decks so that the painters can work at different levels at the same time.

boomerang A rolling platform, usually with several levels, that allows scenic artists to work on several areas of a drop simultaneously when painting vertically.

Stationary Frame and Boomerang It is easy to fasten scenery against a wall or on a stationary frame along a wall, but it is not so easy to paint all areas without using a ladder. A rolling platform, or **boomerang,** provides the painter with two or three painting levels (Figure 9-12b).

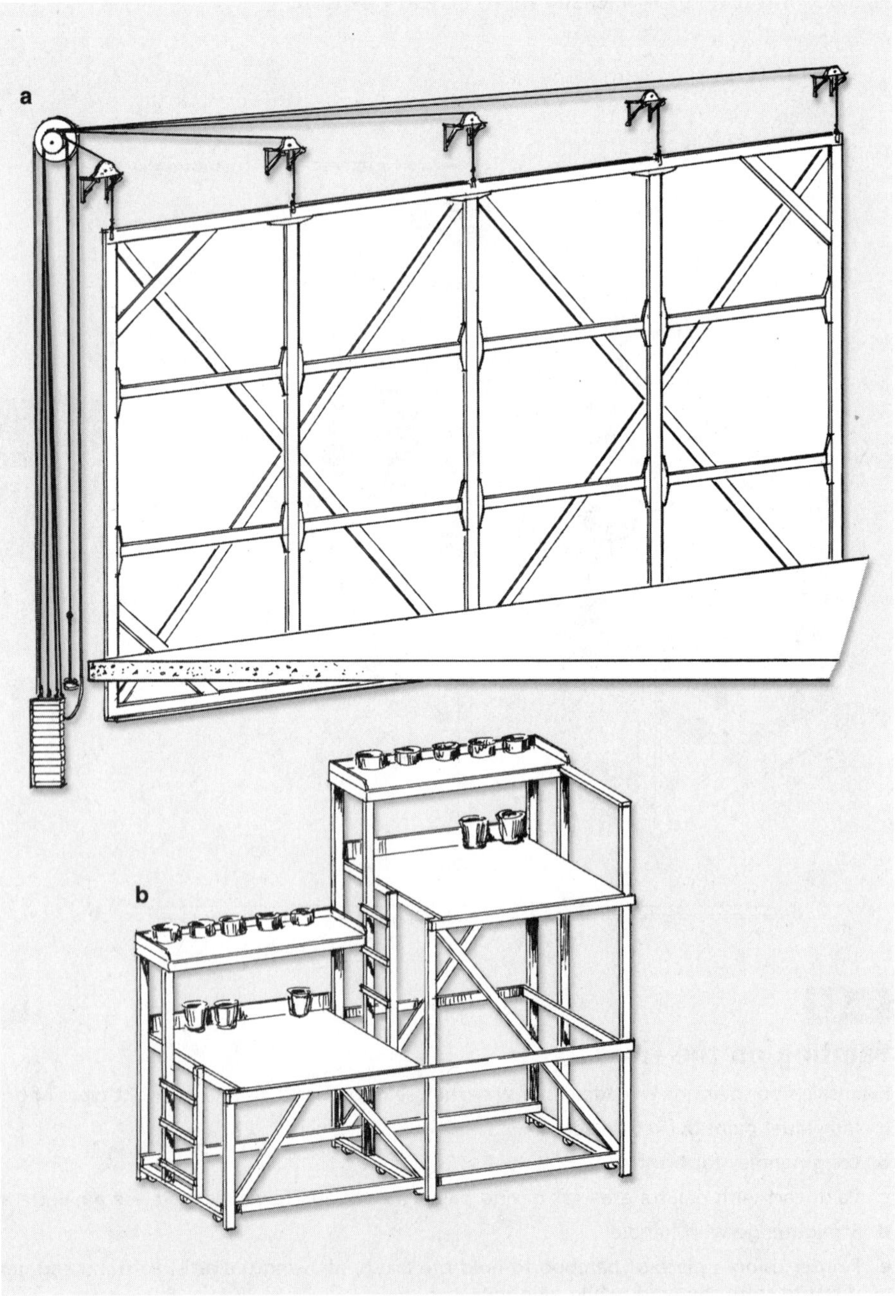

9-12

Vertical Painting Methods

a The paint frame is raised from and lowered into a well extending below the main working-deck level. Scenery attached to the frame moves with it to allow painting of various sections.

b The boomerang, a stepped-level platform on casters, provides a variety of working levels for the painter.

BRUSHES AND OTHER EQUIPMENT

The painter's most important tool is, of course, the *brush*. A good brush should have long bristles and a full shape. (Avoid hollow centers.) Pure bristles are so expensive, especially in the larger sizes, that many painters have turned to nylon brushes. A nylon brush with sandblasted tips is about half the price of the pure-bristle brush of the same size. The difference in price is offset by the slight disadvantage of nylon, for watercolor tends to run off nylon, causing it to hold less paint than a pure-bristle brush does.

Because scene-painting brushes are used predominately with watercolors, the bristles should be rubber set. Some brushes set in glue are suitable for oil paint but will break down with continued use in watercolor.

Types of Brushes

The types of brushes for scene painting are classified by the work they do, such as priming, base-coating or *lay-in*, decorating, and lining (Figure 9-13).

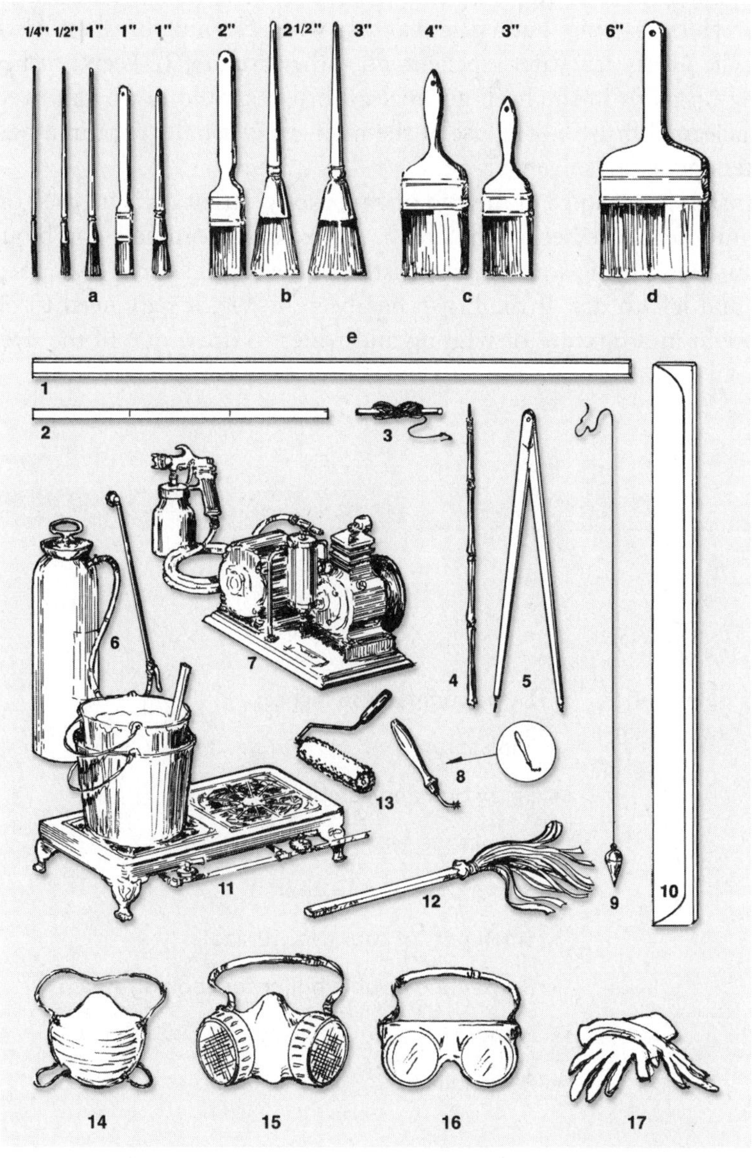

9-13

Brushes, Tools, and Safety Equipment

Scene-painting brushes:

a Lining brushes—flat and oval.
b Decorating brushes.
c Lay-in brushes.
d Priming brush.
e Painting tools and accessories:
1 Beveled straightedge.
2 Yardstick.
3 Snap line.
4 Charcoal and holder.
5 Large compass.
6 Tank spray.
7 Spray gun and compressor.
8 Pounce wheel.
9 Plumb bob.
10 Bow snap line.
11 Burner and double boiler for starch size.
12 Flogger.
13 Paint roller.
14 Dust mask.
15 Air-purifying respirator mask.
16 Goggles.
17 Rubber gloves.

priming brush Wide brush (6 inches is common) used for covering very large areas.

lay-in brush Brush, usually 3 to 4 inches wide, used for painting large areas; often used for base coating, spattering, and other techniques.

fitch Flat brush with a long handle; varies in size from ½ inch to 3 inches.

liner Narrow, long-handled brush (often ¼ inch) used for details, most often in painting molding.

The **priming brush** is the widest brush (6 to 8 inches). It holds a large quantity of paint, which makes it good for spreading size and prime coats quickly and efficiently.

The **lay-in brush,** about 4 inches wide, is used for the more careful painting of a base coat, blending, spattering, and similar techniques.

The **fitch** is a flat brush with a long handle, varying in width from ½ inch to 3 inches. It is used for decorative painting such as architectural details or the foliage of a tree. A pure-bristle brush made especially for scenic painting, the fitch can be quite expensive. A *sash tool,* which is a flat, long-handled brush for painting window sashes, can be used as an inexpensive decorative painting brush. The sash brush, however, is not made any wider than 2 inches.

Liners, or lining brushes, are also long-handled brushes varying in width from ¼ to 1 inch. Liners should have long, pure bristles to perform well. A 1-inch sash tool can do limited lining, but there is no substitute for the smaller brushes.

How to Clean Brushes

Water-based paints "set up" more quickly than most oil-based paints. This is an advantage while painting, but a disadvantage when cleaning brushes. Also, latex and acrylic paints are water-repellent when they are dry. To keep brushes from building up paint in the heel, an unclean brush should not be allowed to dry. An uncleaned brush not in use at the moment is usually kept in a pail of clean water (or other solvent).

When brushes are cleaned at the end of a workday, attention is focused on getting all paint out of the heel of the brush. A wire brush can help comb out stubborn paint. After being washed, the bristles of the brush should be shaped while damp and left to dry. If the brush has been in dye, it may need to be soaked overnight in a mixture of whiting and water to draw out all the dye.

Tools of the Trade

Painting Tools

In addition to brushes and paints, the painter uses other necessary painting tools, including these:

- Beveled straightedge (6 feet)
- Rule or steel tape
- Snap line (50 feet)
- Bow snap line (6 to 8 feet)
- Plumb bob
- Charcoal stick and holder
- Large compass (36 inches)
- Tank sprays
- Spray gun and compressor
- Pounce wheel
- Buckets (14 and 16 quarts)
- Small pots or cans (No. 10 size)
- Burner and double boiler for cooking starch
- Flogger
- Paint roller

Tools of the Trade

Additional Painting Supplies

- White shellac: For glazes, water-repellent finishes, binder, and hardener
- Alcohol solvent: For shellac; speeds the dissolving of colors that are poor mixers
- Flat varnish: Glaze finish and paint binder
- Turpentine solvent: For varnish and oil paints
- Liquid wax: Glaze finish and paint binder
- Metallic paints: Powder mixed with strong size or clear acrylic for metallic surfaces; all right for scenery, but not for props; spray cans (Krylon) have harder finish, good for props, more expensive
- Glycerin: Added to paints for slow drying
- Lysol: Preservative
- Alum: For alum-size preparation
- Flame-proofing chemicals: Formula—1 pound borax, 1 pound sal ammoniac, 3 quarts water

Other Painting Tools and Supplies

In addition to brushes and paints, the painter uses other implements for preparation, layout, and safety in creating scenery. These tools include measuring devices, buckets, rollers, and so forth. Many of them are pictured in Figure 9-13e and listed in the box on painting supplies.

FLAMEPROOFING

Every city has very specific laws dealing with fire regulations and safety. Canvas, wood, and muslin can be purchased already treated with a flame-retardant, but they tend to be quite expensive. A mixture of 1 pound of sal ammoniac, 1 pound of borax, and 3 quarts of water is an inexpensive flameproofing formula. For the best results, it is brushed or sprayed onto previously dampened material. Sheer materials, such as scrim or bobbinet, should be dipped to ensure successful flameproofing. There are, of course, many commercial flame-retardants available on the market.

Because the flameproofing mixture is highly corrosive to metals, brushes and spray cans should, after use, be washed thoroughly in cold water. A small amount of acetic acid in the water helps to counteract the corrosive action. A separate sprayer should be designated to be used exclusively for flameproofing. Also be aware that the fumes of the flameproofing mix can be toxic to some individuals; therefore, any prolonged exposure during the flameproofing procedure requires good ventilation and the use of an air-purifying mask.

The term *flameproofing* does not mean that a treated fabric will stop a flame; it means that it will *not support* a flame. Hence when an obscure section of a drop or flat is *tested*—by bringing a lighted match to the surface—the flame will burn a hole, but the fabric will stop burning when the flame is removed, if the fabric is flameproof.

URL http://www.l-weiss.com/products/stage/fabric/

Testing and other fire regulations vary across the country. It is the responsibility of the designer and the shops to become familiar with local regulations before beginning production and adhere to them strictly.

The scene painter clearly has many responsibilities, from aesthetic choices to safety procedures. The designer who keeps these considerations in mind will create set designs that are more likely to be fully realized, compared with the designer who has little knowledge of the possibilities and limitations of paint as well as the paint shop.

Safety Practice

Scene-Painting Safety

Scene-painting safety considerations include the following:

Goggles: These protect the eyes from dust and splashing paint during spray-painting.

Gloves: The EPT Neoprene type are best for all purposes.

Dust mask: These cover the nose and mouth to prevent the inhaling of dust from dry pigment or dye crystals during mixing.

Air-purifying mask: Wear a mask with twin air filters to protect against toxic fumes during prolonged spray-painting. Filters must be checked repeatedly.

Clothing: Avoid bare arms. High-top shoes not only support the feet better through long hours of standing but also provide protection against paint spray or splashing solvent.

Respirators: Various filters and cartridges are made for various chemicals. Be sure that the correct one is being used. Proper fit and training are a must.

OSHA regulations: OSHA establishes safety rules in the workplace for a reason. It is good to be familiar with them. They should be posted in the paint shop.

Fire hazard precautions: Oil-based paints, Krylon spray cans, and solvents such as alcohol and turpentine should be stored in a separate fireproof chamber. Care should be taken to ensure proper ventilation when using them. There should be no smoking, no open flame, and no sparks in the area.

10

Handling Scenery

Confronted with a multiscene play, a designer has to consider, early in the planning, a method of handling the settings. A production scheme is developed from the numerous ways of moving scenery, and this scheme frequently influences the design approach. Consequently, the more designers know of the mechanics of the modern stage and of theatrical techniques for moving scenery, the closer they can come to realizing their design fully. This is especially true when a designer has to be clever enough to overcome limited funds and a poorly equipped stage. Thus, technical knowledge can help a designer solve scenery-shifting problems with an ingenuity that often becomes inventively original.

FACTORS INFLUENCING THE HANDLING OF SCENERY

The basic methods of handling scenery, in the order of increasing complexity and amount of construction needed, are: (1) the manual running of scenery on the floor; (2) the flying of scenery; (3) the moving of scenery on casters, including such large units as wagons and revolving stages; and (4) the handling of scenery through the stage floor by elevators or lifts.

Before we discuss these particulars, we need to look at the four main factors that influence which handling methods will be employed in a given production: (1) the *play;* (2) the *theatre,* including its stage and available personnel and resources; (3) the *design* of the production, both conceptual and visual; and (4) the *budget.*

The Play

The primary factors affecting the handling of scenery are the form of the play and its plot structure. For instance, a play may have many unrelated episodic scenes, flashbacks, several simultaneous scenes with continuous action, or a conventional three-act form. The structure of the play (and in some cases the particulars of the production) determines the number of scenes or locale changes and their order of appearance or reappearance; it also establishes the *kind* of changes that take place.

The interval for a change of scene most often occurs between acts. The act change, which can be quite short (less than one minute) or as long as fifteen minutes or more, presents no great problem under optimum conditions, assuming the stage has adequate flying and offstage space. Even under limited stage conditions, an act change usually allows enough time to maneuver the scenery, although some changes require more ingenuity and hard work than do others.

A change within the act, or a scene change, can be almost instantaneous or considerably longer than one minute. This inherently fast change can be handled in several different ways. It may be a *hidden* change, taking place behind a curtain or under cover of a blackout. It may be a *visible* change (**a vista**) made in full view of the audience with a display of theatrical magic or by actor-stagehands openly moving elements of scenery as a part of the action. In contrast to the other kinds of changes, the *a vista* change becomes a part of the play by calling attention to the movement of the scenery. As a theatrical technique, it obviously fits only certain types of plays and production schemes.

a vista In view of the audience.

The Theatre

The shape of the theatre and the size of the stage greatly influence the movement of scenery. The amount of flying space and equipment; the placement, number, and size of any existing traps; the extent of offstage and wing space; the size of the proscenium arch and sightline conditions—all obviously help determine the way scenery can be handled.

Some stages have more elaborate mechanical aids or stage machinery for shifting scenery, such as a built-in revolving stage, tracking and offstage space for full stage wagons, or elevator stages. Having one or more of these mechanical aids often influences scenery-handling techniques.

Touring productions must deal with other scenery-shifting considerations as well. Instead of one theatre and stage, the designer has to consider the size and sightline conditions of many stages and auditoriums as well as the physical limitations and extreme portability expected of scenery for a road show. Elaborate scenery-moving devices such as turntables and treadmills are sometimes duplicated in order to reduce the setup time in each theatre. Sometimes referred to as a "jump set," this allows a crew to set up the scenery in one city while the production is playing in another. This means less down time for the production, which equals fewer days without a paying audience and less money lost in setup time.

The Design

The scene designer reconciles the needs of the play and the physical stage and adds a third factor—the design of the production. Recall that the designer's production scheme stems from the kind of scene or locale change inherent in the play, the physical limitations of the stage, and the specifics of the production (see Chapter 4). Like every other element of the production, the movement of the scenery needs to fit into the conceptual parameters that have been determined by the artistic team. A designer cannot design a large production, however, without thinking through a basic scheme for handling the changes.

The Budget

By determining the overall scale of the production, and specifically the set, the budget directly influences the handling of scenery. Although the operational budget has little direct effect on the form of the physical stage, it does influence its operation through the provision of funds for an adequate production staff. A large stage with a small production run staff, for example, would limit the amount of scenery that could be efficiently handled manually.

Several factors affect the operational budget. A Broadway show with a prolonged run, for example, can reduce its operational costs by investing in costly mechanical aids to shift the scenery, thereby cutting down the number of stagehands on the weekly payroll. In venues such as universities or community theatre, labor can be paid or volunteer. People-intensive solutions are often used when labor is free (although this should not give designers free reign for abuse). Material costs, labor costs, and reusability all must be balanced against each other.

BACKSTAGE ORGANIZATION

Anyone who has seen a fast change from a backstage vantage point has been amazed by the teamwork and precision with which the large pieces of scenery, properties, and actors move. Due in part to careful rehearsing, this efficiency is largely the result of the normal division of responsibility in backstage organization. Under the coordinating management of the stage manager, a production has two major divisions: acting and technical. The technical responsibilities are divided among the scenery, electrical, property, sound, and costume departments.

Stage Manager

The stage manager is the conduit through which information flows among the entire company, although he has more everyday contact with the director and the actor than with other members. The stage manager officiates at the first technical rehearsal, sometimes without actors, to allow all hands to become familiar with the timing of shifts, light and sound cues, and the placement of properties.

Once the production is onstage, the stage manager becomes fully responsible for running a smooth operation. He or she starts each performance, gives all cues, calls the actors, and posts all daily calls. The stage manager is charged with maintaining both onstage company discipline and the production standards set by the director and designers.

Stage Carpenter

Although taking cues from the stage manager, the stage carpenter is in charge of the shifts, the rigging, and the general condition of the scenery. The crew, made up of deckhands (stagehands) and flymen, report to the stage carpenter.

Master Electrician

The responsibilities of the master electrician include hanging and focusing lighting instruments, maintaining all electrical equipment, and sometimes operating the control console for the lighting cues.

Property Master

The property master's duties include the care and maintenance of the set and hand props. They also include supervising the handling of props during a shift, helped by crew assigned to the property department.

Sound Technician

A typical production usually involves one or more of the three types of sound support: (1) the reinforcement of live voice, (2) recorded music or sound as background or accompaniment, and (3) recorded or live sound effects. The sound technician is responsible for placing microphones and speakers as well as operating the sound mixer during the performance and according to the specifications of the sound designer. The sound technician is often responsible for rigging the audio communication system, providing instant communication among all department heads.

Wardrobe Supervisor

The care and maintenance of all costumes is the responsibility of the wardrobe supervisor (and, during a fast costume change, of the actors as well). The backstage organization of community and university theatre often places the supervision of makeup in the costume department as well.

MANUAL RUNNING OF SCENERY ON THE FLOOR

As mentioned at the beginning of this chapter, the manual running of scenery is the simplest handling method and requires the least construction. If the units are strong enough to be self-supportive, little additional bracing may be needed. Because the needs of every production differ, determining the type of needed support always presents a new challenge. Required support might include horizontal stiffening, vertical bracing of a piece in an upright position, or a quick and easy method of joining together the various parts of the set. Occasionally the extreme height of scenery combined with its traditional thinness makes moving it difficult for anyone not experienced in handling scenery.

Handling

Some of the many ways of handling single flats, two-folds, and partially assembled units of scenery on the floor are illustrated in Figure 10-1.

footing Using a foot to prevent a flat from sliding in the process of walking it up.

Figure 10-1a illustrates how a large unit of scenery is raised. The stagehands on the backside are **footing**, or holding, the bottom edge with their feet while the other two stagehands "walk-up" the piece by pushing on solid surfaces, such as the stiles.

To "edge-up" a single flat is a similar maneuver (Figure 10-1b). With the flat on edge, one stagehand holds the corner of the flat down and pulls while the second walks-up the unit by pushing along the edge.

To "run" a single flat (Figure 10-1c), the stagehand has one hand low and the other high for balance. By lifting the lead corner slightly off the floor and keeping the trailing corner on the floor, the stagehand handles the flat in perfect balance.

10-1

Manually Handling Scenery

The running or "gripping" of scenery is the simplest handling method although, occasionally, the awkward shape or extreme size of a piece may require experienced stagehands to handle it successfully.

a "Walking-up" a stiffened two-fold.

b "Edging-up" a single flat.

c Running or "gripping" a single flat.

d Making a lash.

e Running a two-fold.

f Three stagehands running a top-heavy piece.

g "Floating" down a single flat.

Lashing is a method of joining two flats in their playing position with lightweight rope (Figure 10-1d).

Running a two-fold (Figure 10-1e) requires two stagehands, while running top-heavy and other special pieces requires three or more (Figure 10-1f). On the other hand, "floating" (Figure 10-1g) requires only one person to move a large piece from a vertical to a horizontal position.

Stiffening, Bracing, and Joining

Because scenery has to travel in small and lightweight units in order to get in and out of theatres, the joining or unfolding of these smaller units into larger shapes is necessary. The new larger shape requires stiffening to be safely handled in a shift.

stiffener Usually a 1 by 3 or 1 by 4 used horizontally on edge to keep several flats in place, most often on the same plane.

jack brace A triangular structure used to support or brace a vertical flat.

A **stiffener** is usually a horizontal member (a 1 by 3 or a 1 by 4 on edge) that is loose-pin hinged into place as the set is assembled. A **jack brace** (often shortened to *jack*) is a triangular form with a small base providing maximum bracing. A jack can be loose- or tight-pin hinged to the scenery it is bracing.

Bracing and stiffening can take a variety of forms, depending on the shape and size of the scenery being reinforced (Figure 10-2). The three categories of joining are related to the portable nature of scenery and the degree of

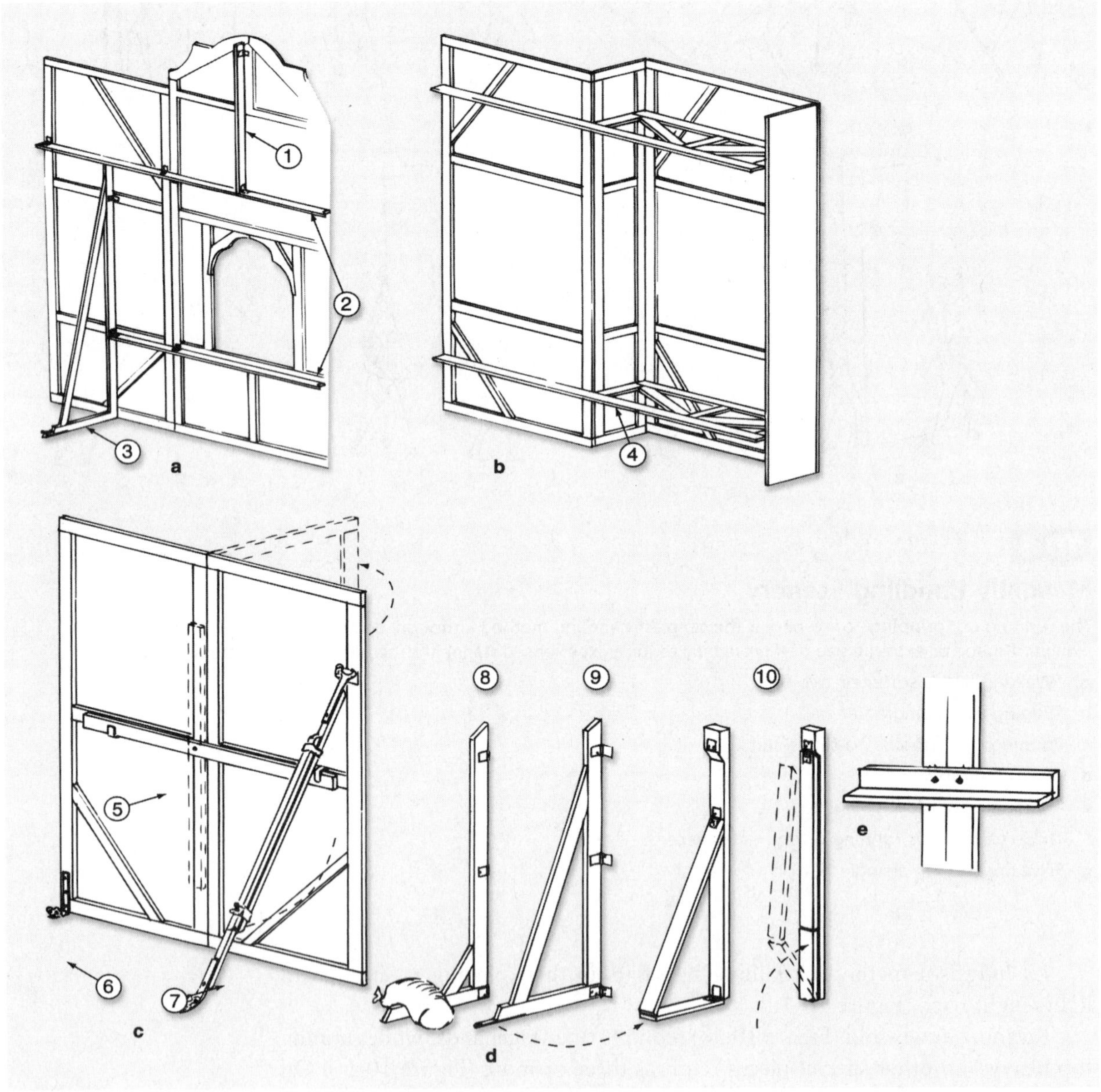

10-2

Bracing and Stiffening

a Stiffening a flat wall:
- **1** Vertical stiffener.
- **2** Horizontal stiffener.
- **3** Jack brace.

b Stiffening a jogged wall:
- **4** A framed stiffener that conforms to the shape of the wall.

c Other bracing and stiffening techniques:
- **5** A swivel keeper bar and keeper hooks.
- **6** Bent footiron and stage screw (rarely used).
- **7** Adjustable stage brace (rarely used).

d Jacks:
- **8** L-jack and sandbag.
- **9** Hinged jack
- **10** Folding jack.

e A stock stiffener referred to as the "hog trough"; fastened across the stiles with screws.

permanence of the joint. Elements of scenery may be joined together by (1) fixed or permanent joining or (2) temporary joining. The kind of joint and its location often affect the design, for the designer and technical director will seek ways to avoid a crack or open joint in a conspicuous area of the setting.

Fixed joining occurs as the scenery is being built (with use of nails, screws, staples, and so on). A fixed hinged joint is made with **tight-pin hinges** so that units composed of several small pieces may unfold into larger sizes. A **dutchman** is a thin strip of fabric (same material as that covering the flat) glued to the face of a flat in order to cover the tight-pin hinges installed on the face. The smaller pieces remain fixed together and travel or move folded from shop to stage, to be unfolded and stiffened into their final shape in the theatre (Figure 10-3a–d). The typical joining of Hollywood flats uses either bolts or screws through the stiles.

tight-pin hinge A hinge in which the center pin cannot be removed.

dutchman A thin strip of fabric used to hide the joint on the face of two adjacent flats.

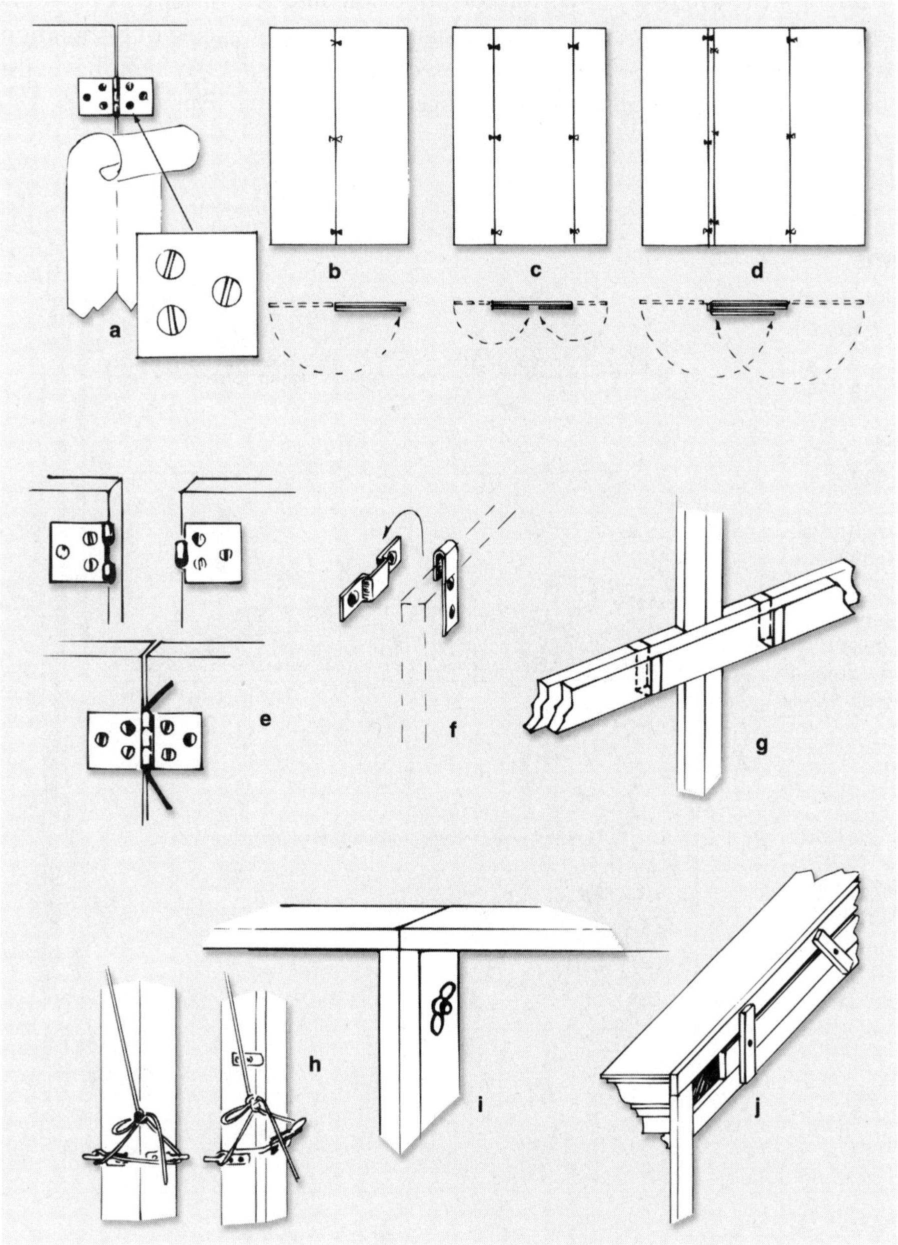

10-3

Scenery Joints

A few methods of fastening scenic elements together for either easy handling or for a quick scene shift.

Fixed joining:

- **a** Tight-pin hinge and dutchman.
- **b** Two-fold: two flats hinged together.
- **c** Three-fold: two jogs and a flat hinged together.
- **d** Three-fold with "tumbler" to hinge three full-width flats together.

Temporary joining:

- **e** Loose-pin hinge.
- **f** Picture hanger.
- **g** S-batten hook.
- **h** Lashing, flush, and around corner (rarely used).
- **i** Bolting Hollywood flats with bolt and wing nut.
- **j** Turnbuttons.

loose-pin hinge A two-piece hinge in which the pin can be removed.

On the other hand, large areas of scenery may be made in separate small pieces to be assembled in the theatre. **Loose-pin hinges,** screws, bolts, wing nuts, and turn buttons are also frequently used. Larger units are stiffened and braced. The joining of scenery during an act change commonly uses loose-pin hinges, coffin or casket locks, lashing, and stage screws (Figure 10-3e–j).

FLYING SCENERY

line-set A group of three or more lines using the same counterweight to lift a batten or unit of scenery.

batten Pipe batten; horizontal pipe hung from a line-set of a fly system.

The designer is always interested in the size of the stage house and type of flying system, if any, over the stage. A stage house designed to handle scenery in the air will have an adequate flying system and a generous amount of hanging space, which means a high and wide loft. The two most common methods of flying scenery are the *hemp* and the *counterweight systems,* shown in Figure 10-4. Both start with an iron grid placed over the stage to support a pulley structure that allows for control of the **line-sets** or **battens** from one side of the stage. They differ in complexity of the rigging, cost of installation, and flexibility of use. Other systems, such as the dead lift system, have also been developed to meet ongoing changes in the theatre over the years.

10-4

Flying Systems

a Counterweight system:
1. Pipe batten, a fixed line-set.
2. Cable for lifting lines.
3. Head block, multigrooved.
4. Trim chains on top of arbor.
5. T-track attached to an arbor for weights.
6. Purchase line.
7. Lock and safety line on lock rail (may be located on the stage deck or a fly floor).
8. Pulley.

b Hemp system:
1. Short line.
2. Center line.
3. Long line.
4. Tandem head block.
5. Pinrail on fly floor.
6. Trim clamp on a line-set.
7. Sandbag counterweight.

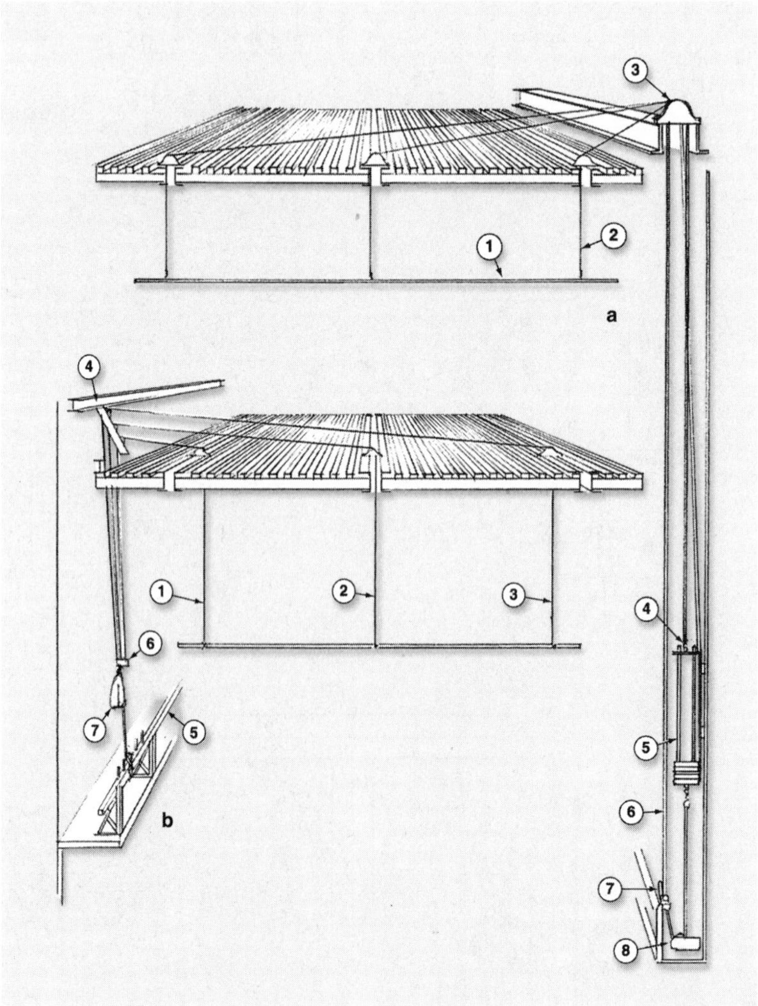

Grid

As the name implies, the *grid* is an open floor of iron high over the stage. The average grid has three to seven openings, or *wells,* that run up- and downstage. Across each opening, usually 6 to 8 inches wide, are the loft blocks through which each **liftline** runs toward the stage floor.

The space between the wells is typically floored with strips of 3-inch channel iron running parallel to the wells. The channel iron strips are set far enough apart to allow the placement of additional sheaves for special **spotlines** (Figure 10-4).

Recent gridiron designs employ the use of **loft blocks,** or pulleys, suspended above the gridiron floor from beams over each well. This keeps the grid floor walkable and clear for the placement of additional spotlines.

liftline The line running from the batten through the loft blocks and the head block on top of the arbor in a fly system.

spotline (1) Line rigged specially for one production; not part of the standard rig of the theatre. (2) A single rope and pulley used in remote position on the grid, often used to fly scenic pieces that are not parallel to the plaster line.

loft block Any block, or pulley, placed in the grid.

Line-Sets

A *line-set* is a grouping of three or more lines to be handled as a single unit. The **sheaves** of a line-set are usually placed over each well and are all the same distance from the proscenium, thus forming a line parallel to the plaster line.

The number of lines in a line-set depends on the number of wells in the individual grid. A stage with a wide proscenium opening might have as many as five lines in a set, while a smaller stage usually has only three lines to a set.

The lines are named by their length and position on the stage. The line nearest the control side of the stage is called the *short line* and the line to the far side of the stage is the *long line.* The line in between is the *center line.* A four-line set would have two center lines (a long center and a short center), and so on.

sheave Pulley; the part of a block that rotates.

The Hemp System

The hemp system is the older and more flexible of the two flying systems. It is less costly to install but does require more skill and more people to operate. The hemp system typically uses 4-inch manila rope for liftlines. As illustrated in Figure 10-4b, the individual line in a line-set (1, 2, and 3 in the figure) comes up from the stage, passes through the loft block, and travels horizontally to one pulley in the **head block** (4) located on the left or right stage wall. From the head block, in which the pulleys are mounted in tandem, the lines are brought together as a set and tied off at the **pinrail** (5). The lower rail of the pinrail is usually the **trim** tie for the scenery in its "in" or working position (**in-trim**), and the top rail receives the tie for the "out" or stored position (**out-trim**). A line-set can be bound together by a **trim clamp** (6) and sandbagged (7) to counterweight a heavy piece for easy handling. The trim clamp is also used to adjust the length of each individual rope in a line-set to keep the batten level.

As can be seen, the hemp system has great flexibility in its ability to use only part of a line-set, add a spotline to a line-set, or in some instances cross line-sets. Adding a spotline involves using a single rope and placing a loft block in a remote position on the grid; this allows stagehands to fly a piece of scenery at an angle to the plaster line. Because the cables from the lighting instruments can get in the way of moving battens, a spotline is often used to pull them up after the show is hung and cabled.

head block A grouping of pulleys that carry the lines from individual blocks to the arbor in a counterweight system and to the pinrail in a hemp system.

pinrail The rail where lines are secured in a hemp system, often by the use of belaying pins.

trim Height of something above the stage floor.

in-trim Position of scenery as it should be when in use, the "in" position.

out-trim Position of scenery when it is not in use, the "out" position.

trim clamp A two-piece metal clamp that is used to bind together the lines in a hemp system, for ease of operation. Also referred to as a *Sunday.*

The chief disadvantage of a hemp house is in the number of hands required to run a show, as well as the professional skill necessary to rig and safely counterweight heavy pieces of scenery.

The Counterweight System

Unlike the hemp system, which can separate lines or add a single line to the line-sets, the counterweight system uses fixed line-sets. Although the counterweight system was born in an era of box sets and raked scenery, it is rigidly based on wing-and-drop staging. It keeps the lines in sets fixed to a pipe batten parallel to the plaster line.

The system, as illustrated in Figure 10-4a begins at the pipe batten (1) and the permanently attached wire-rope liftlines (2). Lifting the batten, the lines pass through the individual loft blocks at each well, then over a multigrooved, single-pulley head block (3). They attach to the top of the counterweight arbor (4). The arbor is guided by a T-track (5), or guy wire, and controlled by a separate purchase line (6). Typically made of manila or synthetic rope, the purchase line is also attached to the top of the counterweight arbor and passes through the large groove in the head block. It then turns toward the floor and, after going through the lock (7) on the **fly rail** and around the idler pulley (8), fastens to the bottom of the arbor.

fly rail Any part of a fly system where the lines are moved in and out and locked into place. Also referred to as *locking rail.*

Pulling down on the outside purchase line lifts the arbor and lowers the scenery hanging on the batten. A corresponding amount of weight placed on the arbor balances the weight of the scenery—the arbor should weigh the same as the scenery hanging on the batten (in contrast to the hemp system, which must be slightly batten-heavy for the system to work).

This kind of system is designed for scenery that hangs parallel to the plaster line. The fixed line-sets make this system somewhat inflexible. Most of the rigging time used to hang an angled or raked piece is spent in overcoming rather than using the system. As in the hemp system, spotlines are used, the difference being that in the counterweight system, they are placed individually rather than as part of the entire system.

URL http://www.feeneywire.com

Typically the counterweight system includes a mechanism for adjusting the level or trim of the batten relative to the stage floor. These mechanisms generally consist of either turnbuckles or trim chains that connect the liftlines to the batten or the arbor.

The Dead Lift System

URL http://www.PRG.com

Both the hemp and the counterweight systems use weights in some fashion to keep the system in balance. This is what allows for ease in movement of the scenic pieces in both the "in" and "out" directions. A third way to fly units of scenery is the *dead lift system.* The name implies the lack of counterweights. Instead, the work is accomplished through the use of electrical **winches** that have been designed for this purpose. It is most often used for a specific effect such as the falling chandelier in *Phantom of the Opera.* A cable is wrapped around the large grooved drum of the winch. The grooves allow for the ability to control the path of the cable as the drum rotates.

winch A hand-cranked or motor-driven drum rigged with a cable that is used to move scenery.

Rigging

In either a hemp or counterweight system, stage rigging begins with the relatively simple process of hanging scenery and includes the more complicated maneuvers of breasting and tripping scenery elements. The handling of stage curtains (such as traveler, tableau, and contour curtains) and the unframed drop is also a part of stage rigging.

Hanging Scenery An early and critical step in rigging is the preparation of scenery to hang. To do this, carpenters use hardware or other means to attach the scenery to liftlines. For example, hanger irons or D-rings are used on framed scenery. These should be bolted to a vertical member of the framing for greater strength. Except on extremely lightweight pieces, two rings are used, the one at the top serving as a guide for the liftline that is attached to the bottom. Lifting the load from the bottom not only is safer than lifting from the top but also provides a convenient position from which to trim each line (Figure 10-5).

Cable Clamps Often, framed scenery is hung a distance below the batten with wire rope that is attached to the scenery with special hardware. Although the cable may be flexible, it is important not to allow a kink to form, or the cable will lose its strength.

Figure 10-5 illustrates various methods of termination used to secure the cable to the batten and the scenery. Cable clamps are used on cable as small as ⅛ inch. Alternatively, the *Nicopress* clamp is a very secure, though permanent, fastener. These soft-metal tubes are designed to slide over the cables and are crimped into place with a Nicopress tool (Figure 10-5d).

Unframed pieces of scenery, such as drops and borders, are hung from their tops and can be fastened to a pipe or picked up by a set of lines in many ways, the most common being the use of lines tied directly to the batten (Figure 10-5c). If a wooden batten at the top of a drop is used, numerous pickup points about every 6 feet are needed to keep it from sagging and thereby spoiling the trim of the drop. *Bridling* can help in this task, as will be discussed shortly.

Knots Safe stage rigging requires the use of a modest number of knots, and the technical director and anyone who supervises rigging should be skilled in the use of at least a few of the knots and hitches that appear in stage rigging. Some of the most frequently used knots are illustrated in Figure 10-6. A more detailed and comprehensive manual of knots and splices can be found in the catalogs of cordage companies (see Additional Reading, at the back of this book).

However familiar we are with square knots, they are to be avoided in stage rigging because they can undo themselves quite easily. As there is some level of danger anytime a piece of scenery involves rigging, a great amount of care and caution should prevail.

Breasting Scenery Regardless of which flying system is being used, two pieces of scenery cannot occupy the same space at the same time, although the

10-5

The Hanging of Scenery

a Hanging hardware:
- **1** Top hanger iron, straight.
- **2** Ceiling plate and ring.
- **3** Bottom hanger iron, hooked.

b Trim adjustments:
- **1** Trimming hitch (or trucker's hitch) using hemp rope or sash cord.
- **2** A snatch line and hook. The snap hook on the end of the liftline makes it possible to unhook a flown piece of scenery.
- **3** Turnbuckle on wire cable—another way to adjust the trim of a flown piece of scenery.

c Various methods of hanging a drop:
- **1** Tie around batten.
- **2** Tie through batten.
- **3** Drop holder.
- **4** Tie lines to batten.
- **5**, **6** Floor stays.

d Cable clamps and Nicopress.

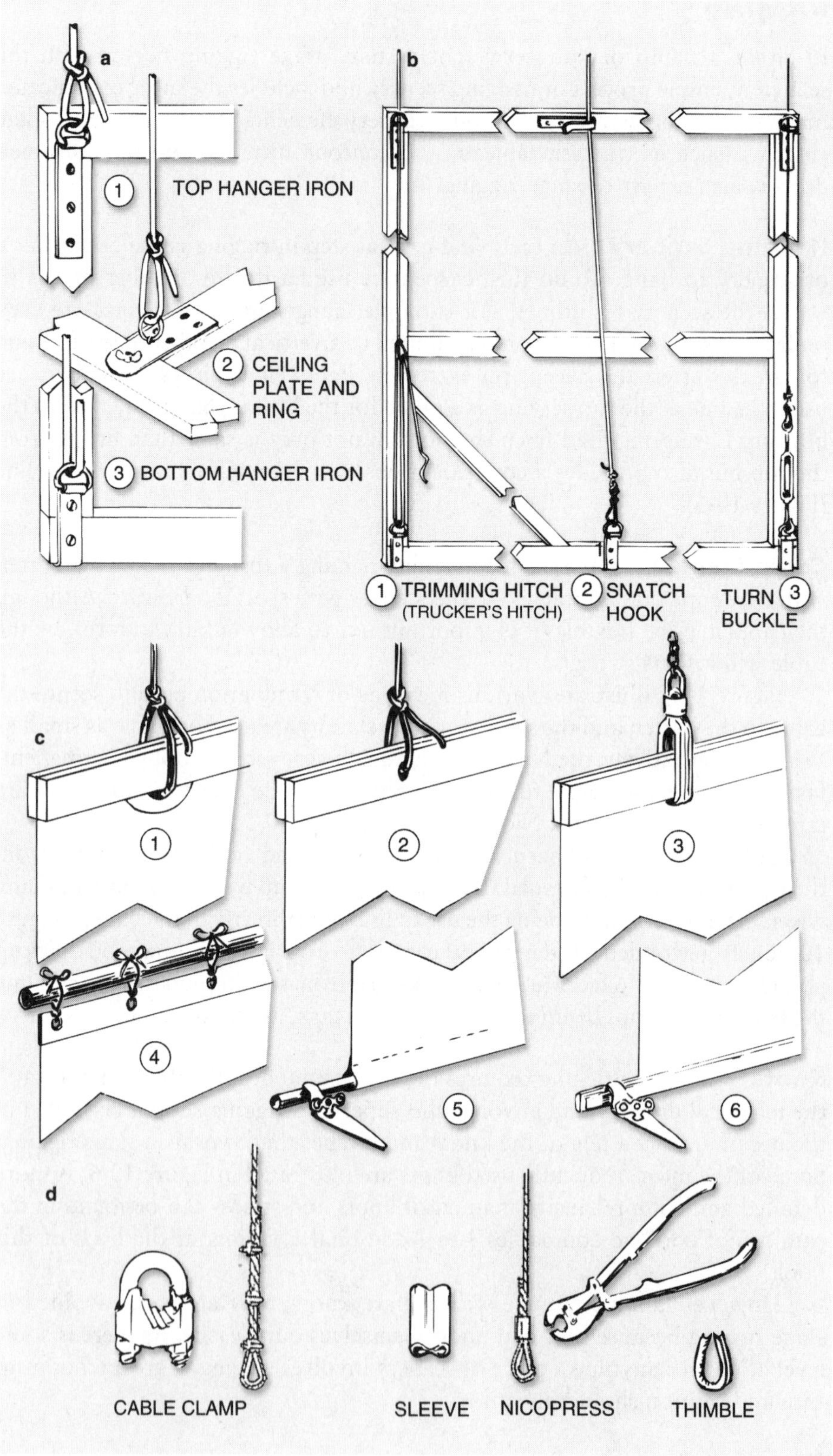

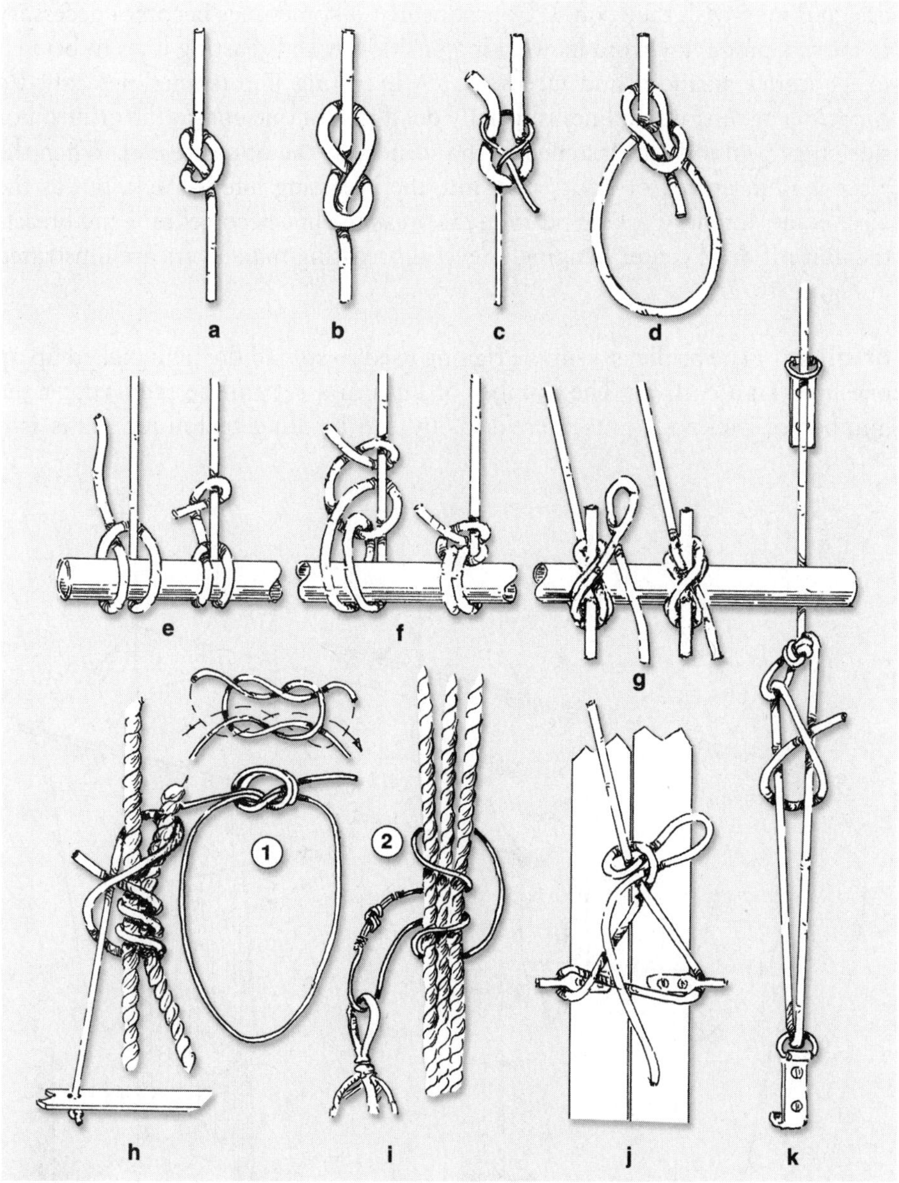

10-6

Knots Used in Stage Rigging

a Half hitch or overhand knot.

b Figure eight. Used to put a knot in the end of a line to keep it from running through a pulley or eye.

c Sheetbend. Knot of choice for joining two ropes of equal or different size.

d Bowline. A fixed loop used on end of liftline through ring.

e Clove hitch on a batten, finished with a half hitch. It grips firmly under tension, but it is easy to adjust or untie.

f Fisherman's bend. Excellent for a tie onto a batten. Not as easy to adjust as the clove hitch.

g Half hitch over a belaying pin. Used as a tie-off on a pinrail.

h Stopper hitch, made with a smaller line in the middle of a larger rope. The safety line on the counterweight lock rail uses a stopper hitch on the purchase lines.

i Sunday:

1 A method of joining the ends of a small loop of wire cable without putting a sharp kink in the cable.

2 The loop is then used to clew a set of rope lines together so as to counterweight them with a sandbag.

j Lashline tie-off.

k Trimming hitch, to adjust the trim of a hanging piece of scenery.

breasting Moving a hanging unit of scenery away from its working position in order to make room for (usually) another piece of scenery or an electric.

designer may wish they could. Consequently, it sometimes becomes necessary to move a unit away from its working position with breasting lines to bring it to its stored position, and vice versa. A **breasting** line (sometimes called a *checkline* or restraining line) is usually dead-tied at one end to the gridiron or side-stage position and fastened to the scenery at the opposite end. When the piece is in its stored or "out" position, the breasting line is slack, but as the piece comes into its working position the breasting line becomes taut and breasts the unit off dead-center hanging. (Several breasting maneuvers are illustrated in Figure 10-7.)

bridling Extending the line-set by adding a length of pipe and tying it diagonally to the liftlines.

Bridling The **bridle** is a simple rigging used to spread the load picked up on one line (Figure 10-7). The number of lines in a set can be reduced, or the number of pickup points increased, by the bridling technique. This is a

10-7

Bridling and Breasting Techniques

- **a** A simple bridle.
- **b** A bridle of a set of lines to support the overhang of an extra-long batten.
- **c** Breasting a drop up- and downstage:
  - **1** Stored position.
  - **2** Working position.
- **d** Breasting across stage.
- **e** Twisting a batten into an angled position.
- **f** Breast lines on the side-tab arms of a drape cyc:
  - **1** Stored position, arms hanging down.
  - **2** Working position, arms pulled by breast lines into spread position.

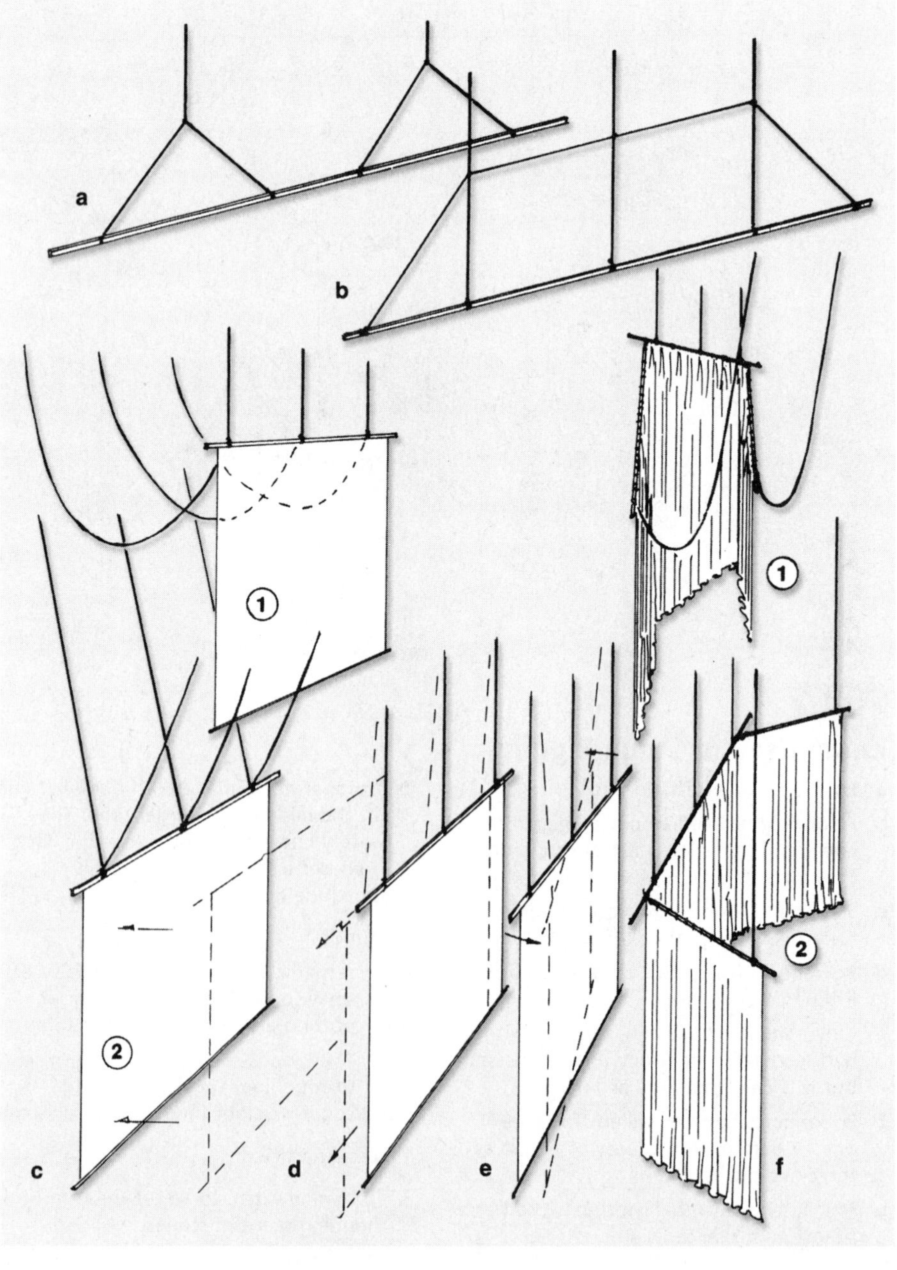

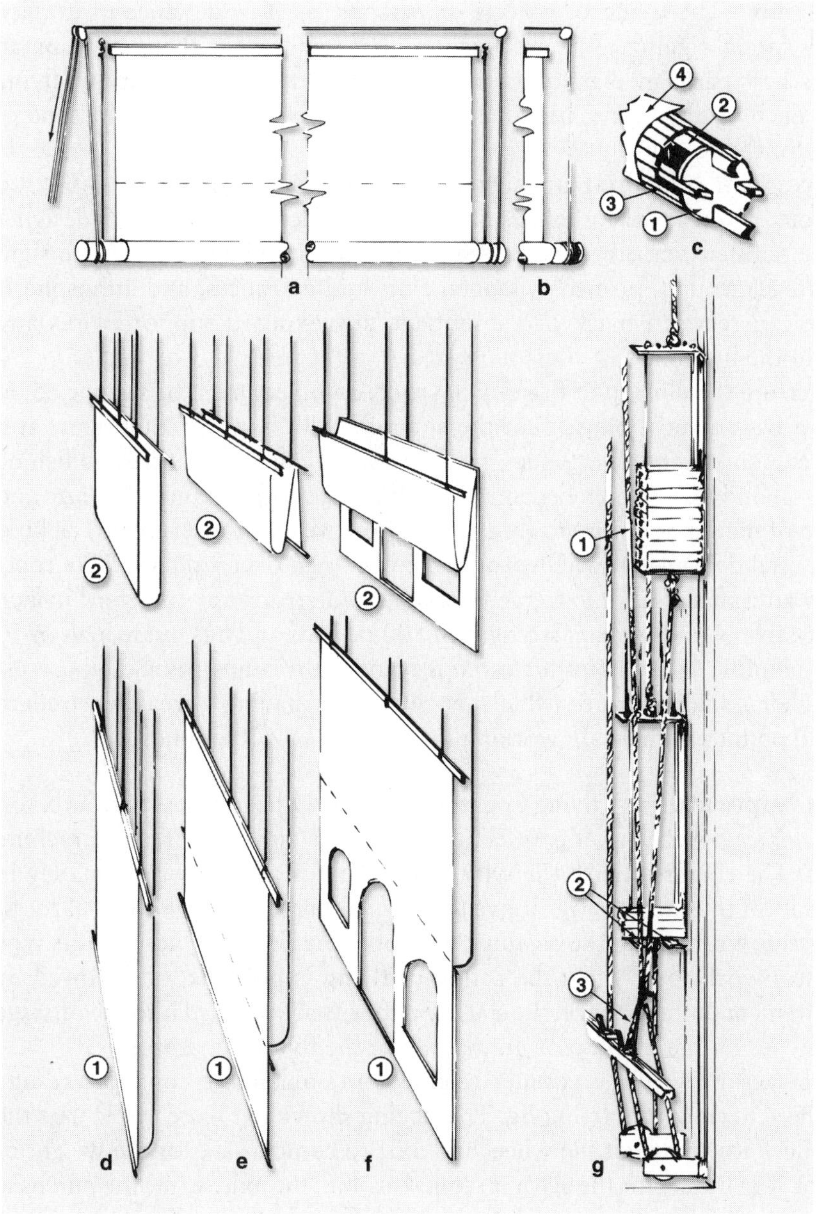

10-8

Tripping Techniques

a The roll (oleo) drop, which rolls on the bottom batten or drum. *Note:* The rigging of the rope gives the operator a mechanical advantage or two. The drop is made with horizontal seams to make it roll flat.

b An alternate rigging. The liftline has equal turns on the end of the drum, in reverse direction of the drop. When the liftline is pulled, it unwinds as the drop winds onto the drum and thus rises.

c Detail of drum construction:
1 Contour pieces.
2 Linear stiffeners.
3 Lattice slats.
4 Padding and final cover.

d Tripping a drop. Back set of lines is attached to bottom batten:
1 Working position.
2 Stored or *tripped* position.

e Tripping in thirds. Upstage batten is attached at one-third height of the drop off the floor.
1 Working position.
2 Tripped position.

f Tripping a drop that has the lower portion framed:
1 Working position.
2 Tripped position.

g Carpet hoist, handling a variable load:
1 Free arbor (no batten attached) carrying counterweights.
2 Working arbor with batten that handles the variable load.
3 Free arbor locked off at top position, allowing working arbor to run free of counterweight after load has been removed from batten (rigging is usable only on light loads of 100–150 pounds).

particularly useful technique when it is necessary to extend a batten farther offstage than other techniques would allow.

Tripping Scenery Many rigging problems result from too low a grid or the complete absence of one. **Tripping,** which can be used only on soft or semisoft scenery, is one way of flying scenery in a limited space (Figure 10-8d–f). By picking up the bottom of a drop as well as the top, it can be flown in at half the height necessary to clear a full drop. The height can be further reduced by picking up the drop a third of the height off the floor and thereby tripping it in thirds.

A **roll drop** or *oleo drop* is an extreme variation of tripping. In this method, the drop is wrapped around a drum attached to the bottom edge (Figure 10-8a–c). Many old opera house and vaudeville drops were rigged in this manner, and it still is a good way of flying a drop on a stage with reduced flying space.

tripping Picking up the bottom of a drop as well as the top when there is not enough room to fly it completely out.

roll drop A drop wrapped around a long horizontal roller (usually like a big blind). Also called an *oleo drop.*

URL http://www.flybyfoy.com

URL http://www.zfxflying.com

Levitation The flying of objects or persons, as if in defiance of gravity, requires special rigging. Any circumstance that requires the flying of a human being is best performed by a company that has made a specialty of flying actors. Each of these companies has developed it own proprietary method of rigging for flying.

This is *not* something an untrained person should try as it is far too dangerous. To create a workable setting for flying actors or objects, a designer must be familiar with the spatial requirements for a flying effect. The right kind of background, properly planned exits and entrances, and atmospheric lighting can serve to mask or camouflage any exposed support wires and highlight the illusion.

To create the illusion of floating in space, an object must be supported on as fine a wire as possible so that the support will disappear from view at a distance. Lightweight objects such as a bat or bird can be supported on fishing line (20-pound test), which becomes invisible at a short distance. The size and strength of the support wire to fly an actor, however, is more critical. The kind of wire used depends on whether or not it has to go over a pulley. Wire rope, such as aircraft cable, is extremely flexible and strong for its size: 1⁄16-inch aircraft cable has a breaking strength of 500 pounds and has a safe load of 50 to 100 pounds; 1⁄8-inch aircraft cable is standard for most flying apparatus. Although it is slightly more visible, it is much safer, having a breaking strength of 2,000 pounds with a safe working load of 200 to 400 pounds.

Flying Apparatus A flying apparatus begins with a harness for the actor. Made of strong webbing, it is fitted about the legs and chest like a parachute harness. The ring, to which the wire is attached, is placed approximately in the middle of the back, a little above the actor's center of gravity. The harness, of course, is worn under the costume with only the ring protruding. This type of harness works best when the action of flying is preceded or followed by free movement of the actor on the stage. Brief exits are planned into the offstage wings to permit the hookup or unhooking of the flying apparatus.

If the actor's weight is counterweighted, an unbalanced condition results when the actor is off the flying rig. The rigging shown in Figure 10-9d uses the mechanical advantage of the wheel and axle to compensate for the weight of the actor. The liftline for the actor is wound around the axle, while the purchase line for the operator encircles the wheel. This method sacrifices distance or length of rope, however.

For lateral movement, the rig employs a pendulum technique, which means that if the actor is airborne a certain distance from the center he or she will swing, on a diagonal, to an equal distance opposite of center. With rehearsal, this technique can be used to fly from one part of the stage to another. Similarly, the actor can fly in large circles by running circles on the stage before being airborne. For diagonal or transverse movement, the pulley of the center drop line can be rigged to move on a track.

If the flying actor stays in the air and the direction is fixed, the rigging is different. Because the actor is in the air longer, the harness should provide more support, such as a lightweight framing and a higher center of gravity for the point of suspension (Figure 10-9e).

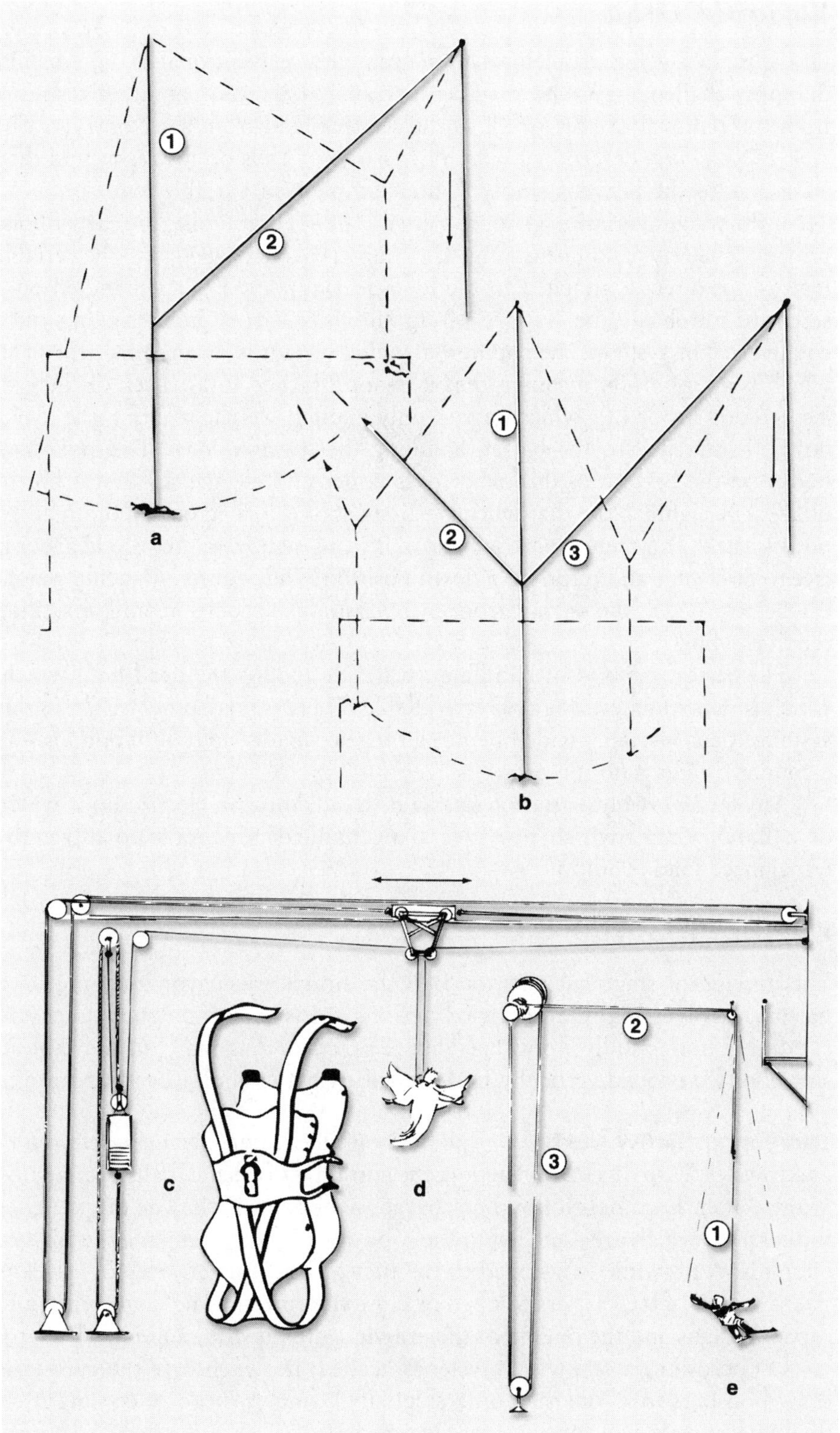

10-9

Levitation

Types of rigging for flying objects or persons:

a Pendulum and breast line:

- **1** Pendulum line, placed off center, has long arc when swinging free of breast line.
- **2** Breast line shortens arc and lifts object up and out of sight.

b Pendulum and double breast line:

- **1** Pendulum line.
- **2** First breast line.
- **3** Second breast line.

c Harness for actor.

d Flying rig for limited pattern. The actor can fly a lateral pattern across the stage.

e Schematic diagram of a flying rig using the wheel and axle for lift control:

- **1** ⅛-inch aircraft cable lead to the actor.
- **2** Rope or larger cable feeds through swivel sheave at grid to axle.
- **3** Operating line around the wheel. The ratio of the axle's smaller radius to the larger radius of the wheel provides a mechanical advantage for the operator. Because a counterweight is not involved, the actor is free to detach the rig when on the floor.

Variable Load

Of the many rigging problems experienced with conventional flying systems, the most challenging is the variable load or unbalanced condition resulting from the removal of part or all of the scenery load from a set of lines. The *deus ex machina,* descending with a live cargo of gods or goddesses and then ascending to the heavens empty, is an example of a variable load.

If the weight variation is not too great (100–150 pounds), the carpet hoist provides one way of compensating. The counterbalancing weight to the variable load is not directly attached to the load-bearing batten but is handled on a separate purchase line. Figure 10-8g shows a carpet hoist rigging on a counterweight system. The counterbalancing weight is on the first arbor (1), which is a *free arbor,* meaning that it is not attached to a batten or line-set. The second arbor (2), which carries only enough weight to bring the arbor down, is attached to the batten handling the variable load. The extending hooks on the bottom of this arbor pass under and engage the first arbor to utilize its weights. Note that when the first arbor is locked or tied off in an up position at the moment the variable load is being removed, the second arbor is free to disengage and return to a down position. The counterbalancing weight can be returned to the second arbor by reversing the procedure and unlocking the first arbor.

dead haul winch A winch that lifts a load that has not been counterweighted.

The easiest method of handling a variable load is the **dead haul winch,** which is unfortunately not always available. There is no counterweight in this system. It has instead a wide operating range of load—up to 400 pounds—so a counterweight is not necessary.

Any larger weight variation has to be handled by an electric floor winch or a hand winch, which provides a mechanical advantage to offset the unbalanced load condition.

Curtain Rigging

The moving of stage curtains, beyond the simple raising or lowering on a batten, involves many and varied actions. Most commonly, curtains are (1) drawn horizontally from the sides, (2) tripped diagonally into a tableau shape, or (3) tripped vertically into the varied patterns of a contour curtain.

traveler Any curtain that is drawn in a horizontal direction. Also called a *draw curtain.*

Traveler or Draw Curtain The horizontally drawn curtain is referred to as a **traveler.** With this kind of action, the curtain is divided in half, overlapping at the center. Each half follows a separate section of track. The track guides the carriers, which are attached to the top edge of the curtain at about 1-foot intervals. A drawline is fastened to the first or lead carrier, which pushes or pulls the rest of the carriers to open or close the curtain. The many track and carrier designs and the rigging of the drawline are illustrated in Figure 10-10.

On occasion, a one-way traveler is needed, in which case the curtain is drawn onstage from one side on a single long track instead of coming from the two opposite sides of the stage (Figure 10-10b). Also illustrated is a rear-fold device that causes all carriers to move at once rather than being pushed or pulled by the lead carrier (Figure 10-10c).

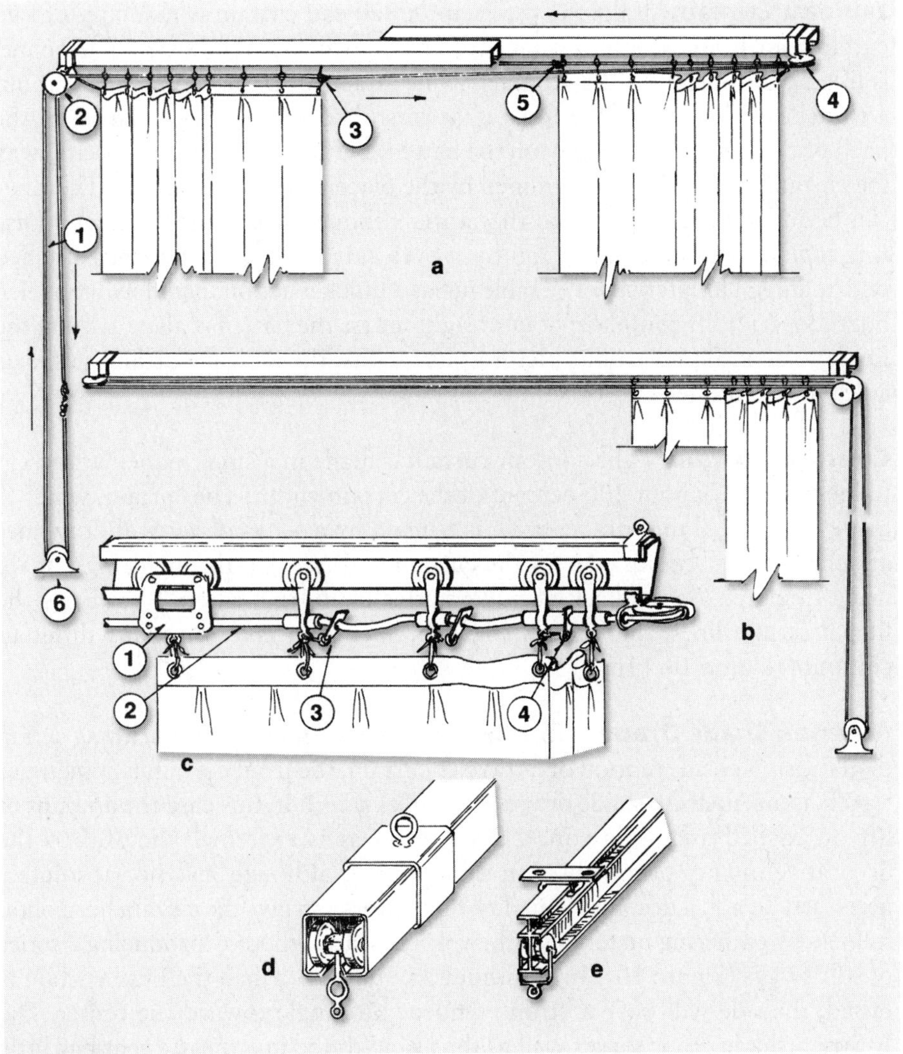

10-10

Traveler Curtains and Tracks

a Rigging of a draw curtain or two-way traveler:

- **1** Drawline.
- **2** Head block.
- **3** Lead carrier on downstage curtain, fastened to drawline.
- **4** Change-of-direction pulley.
- **5** Lead carrier on upstage curtain also fastened to drawline.
- **6** Floor block.

b One-way traveler curtain.

c Detail of rear-fold attachment. All carriers move at once with drawline and curtain folds offstage rather than bunching onstage.

- **1** Lead carrier.
- **2** Drawline.
- **3** Rear-fold attachment grips drawline until the attachment is straightened up by bumping into the next carrier.
- **4** Drawline now passes through the rear-fold attachment.

Two types of traveler tracks and carriers:

d Square steel track with double-wheel carrier.

e I-beam track (hospital curtain track for lighter-weight drapery).

tableau curtain Two overlapping panels of fabric that are rigged to pull open on a modified (curved) diagonal.

Tableau Curtain Like the traveler, the **tableau curtain** is made up of two curtain panels hung with a center overlap and from a single batten. Each panel is lifted or tripped by a diagonal drawline attached to the central edge, about a third of its height off the floor, that runs through a series of rings on the back of the curtain to a pulley on the batten (Figure 10-11a). The specific way the curtain will drape is determined by the placement of these rings. The rings can be individually sewn onto the fabric although it is more efficient to use *ring tape,* a narrow band of tightly woven fabric with plastic rings stitched onto it at regular intervals. The tableau has a quicker action than does a traveler, but it does not lift completely out of sight unless the batten is also raised at the final moment. Because of its picturesque quality, the tableau curtain is used as a decorative frame.

contour curtain A curtain that is rigged with several separately operated drawlines that can create a variety of shapes when the curtain is open.

Contour Curtain The **contour curtain** is made in a single panel with great fullness, usually about 200 percent of the curtain width. The curtain, which is made of material that drapes well, is tripped by a series of vertical drawlines attached to the bottom edge of the curtain and running through rings, again using ring tape, on the back to pulleys attached to the batten. By varying the lift on certain lines, the bottom edge of the curtain takes on many different contours (Figure 10-11b).

Austrian shade drape Sometimes referred to as a *brail curtain,* a curtain that is rigged with a series of vertical drawlines that lift at the same time and at the same speed.

Austrian Shade Drape To achieve a faster and more desirable lifting action than the slower side motion of a traveler curtain, the front curtain is sometimes rigged as an **Austrian shade drape** (or *brail curtain*). In this case the amount of lift on each drawline is equal. Some fullness is extremely helpful to the decorative quality of an Austrian shade drape, although it is not absolutely necessary. To add a decorative quality, fabricators can give the curtain horizontal fullness by gathering material on the vertical seams, thereby producing a series of soft swags (Figure 10-11c). Without any fullness, when the brail curtain is raised, the side will have a strong tendency to angle toward the center. The Austrian shade drape serves well as the grand drape in a theatre that has little or no fly space.

SCENERY ON CASTERS

Mounting a three-dimensional piece of scenery on casters makes moving it on the floor easier and faster. Such mounting can vary from a single caster on the edge of a hinged wing to the large castered platform or wagon to move an entire set.

Casters

URL http://www.bmisupply.com

The stage places special demands on casters. A good stage caster should first of all run quietly, which requires a rubber wheel or a rubber-tired wheel. The rubber-tired wheel is a better long-term investment because the tires can be replaced as they wear. One must balance the softness of the wheel against its capacity and resistance. The softer the wheel, the harder it is to move and the lower the capacity, or load, it will take.

Second, the caster wheel should have as large a diameter as possible ($3\frac{1}{2}$ to 4 inches). The larger the diameter, the smaller the resistance. A wagon on 4-inch-diameter casters rolls with little effort and is not easily stopped by small obstructions such as rugs, padding, ground cloth, or lighting cables.

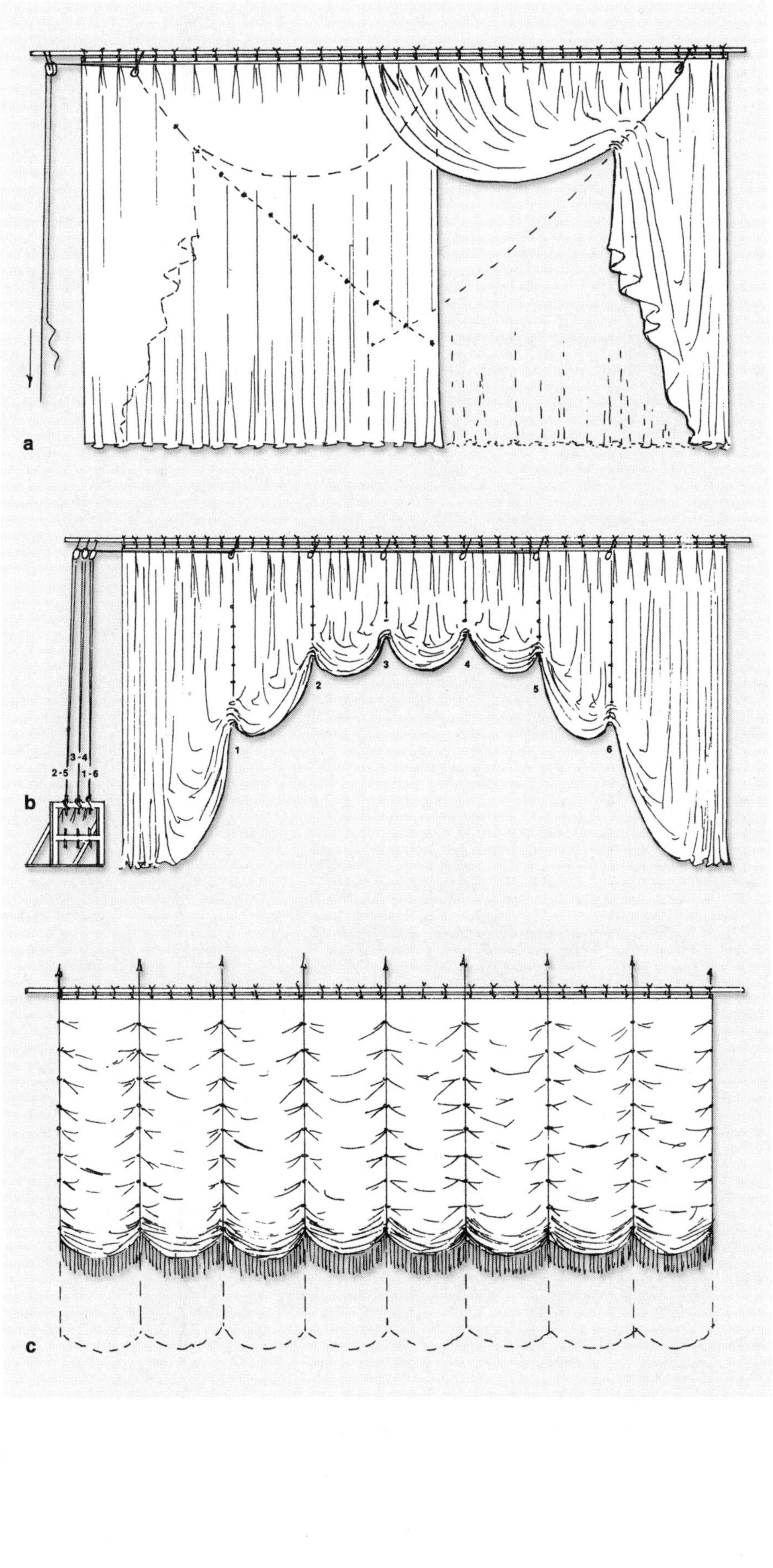

10-11

Front Curtain Riggings

a Tableau curtain.

b Contour curtain. The lift-lines are numbered 1–6. The lines are paired 1–6, 3–4, and 2–5.

c Austrian shade drape.

With the softness of rubber but less resistance and greater durability, polyurethane wheels are becoming the standard. They wear like steel, are rugged, and cost about the same as good rubber.

swivel caster A caster that allows movement in any direction.

fixed caster A caster that allows movement in only two directions.

triple swivel caster Also called a *zero-throw caster,* a caster mounted on three wheels around a central point for easy turning.

Casters are of two general types: those made to move freely in any direction and those made to move in a fixed direction. The **swivel caster** has a free action that allows it to move in any direction. Changing the direction of a swivel caster, however, requires force to alter the "throw" or direction the caster is facing. The **fixed caster** is limited to one direction. A refinement of the typical swivel caster incorporates a mechanism that locks the swivel action, thereby creating the equivalent of a fixed caster. (See Figure 10-12 for examples of casters.)

A third type of caster, the **triple swivel caster** or *zero throw caster,* is mounted on three wheels around a central point. This allows for easy turning. Changing directions requires minimal effort compared with moving the swivel caster.

10-12

Castering Techniques

- **a** Single caster mounted on rear of flat.
- **b** Single caster mounted in corner.
- **c** Outrigger wagon.
- **d** Tip jack:
  - **1** Scenery tipped back to rest on casters.
  - **2** Scenery upright; blocked-off caster in working position.
- **e** Castered jack:
  - **1** Side view showing how scenery is held clear of floor.
  - **2** Caster jack on a hinged or "wild" piece of scenery.
- **f** Flat-top swivel caster.
- **g** Flat-top fixed caster.
- **h** Stem-type swivel caster for furniture.
- **i** Small stem-type ball caster for furniture.
- **j** Large stem-type swivel caster; mounts into bottom of scaffolding pipe.
- **k** Triple-swivel caster (zero throw caster).

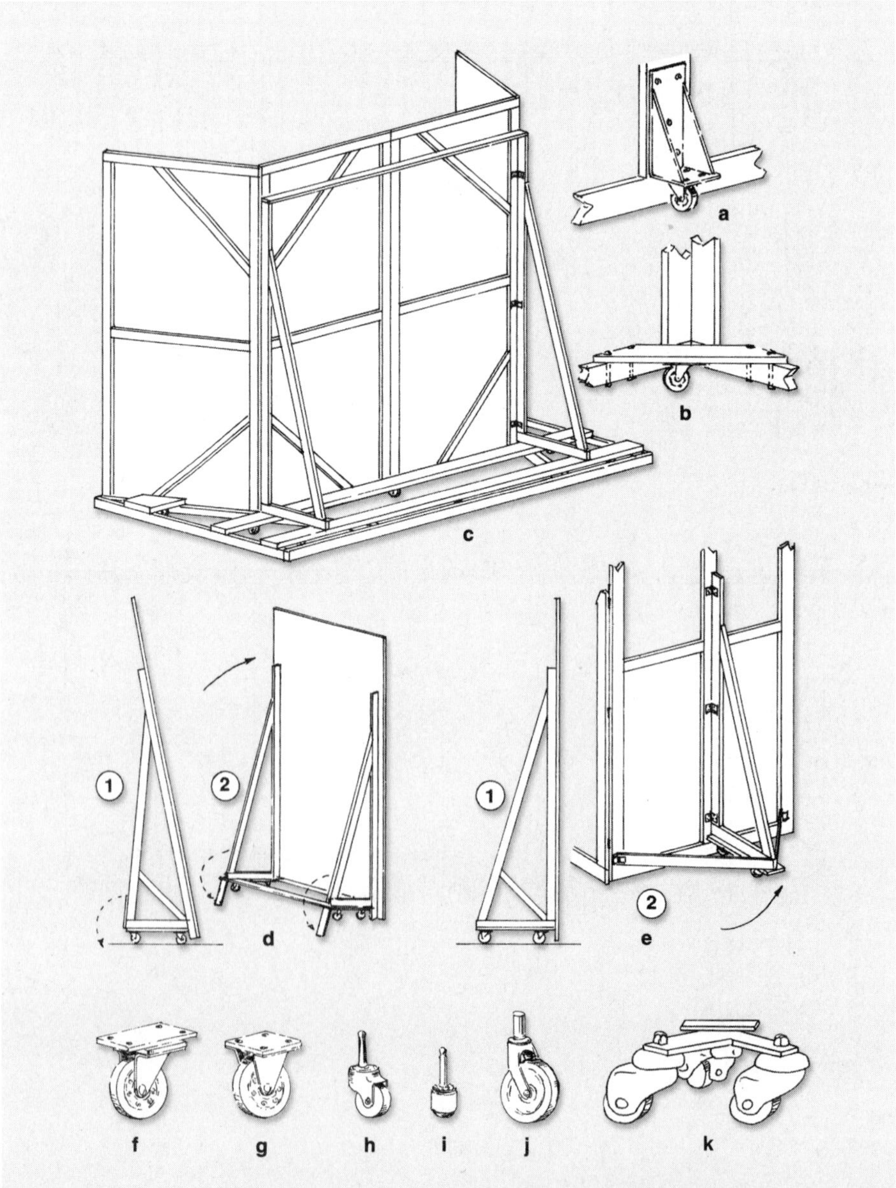

Lift and Tip Jacks

Mounting scenery on casters in order to make it move easily creates the paradoxical problem of anchoring, or preventing the unit from moving at an undesirable moment. *Lift* and *tip jacks* lift the scenery off the floor and onto the casters. With the tip jack, the scenery is literally tipped back onto the castered structure. The lift jack has a simple mechanism to force the casters to the floor. In both cases, the scenery sits firmly on the floor when it is in its working position.

Another way to anchor a castered platform or a bulky three-dimensional piece of scenery is to attach it to units that are sitting on the floor or by tipping the piece onto casters mounted on its offstage or upstage edge (Figures 10-12d and 10-13e).

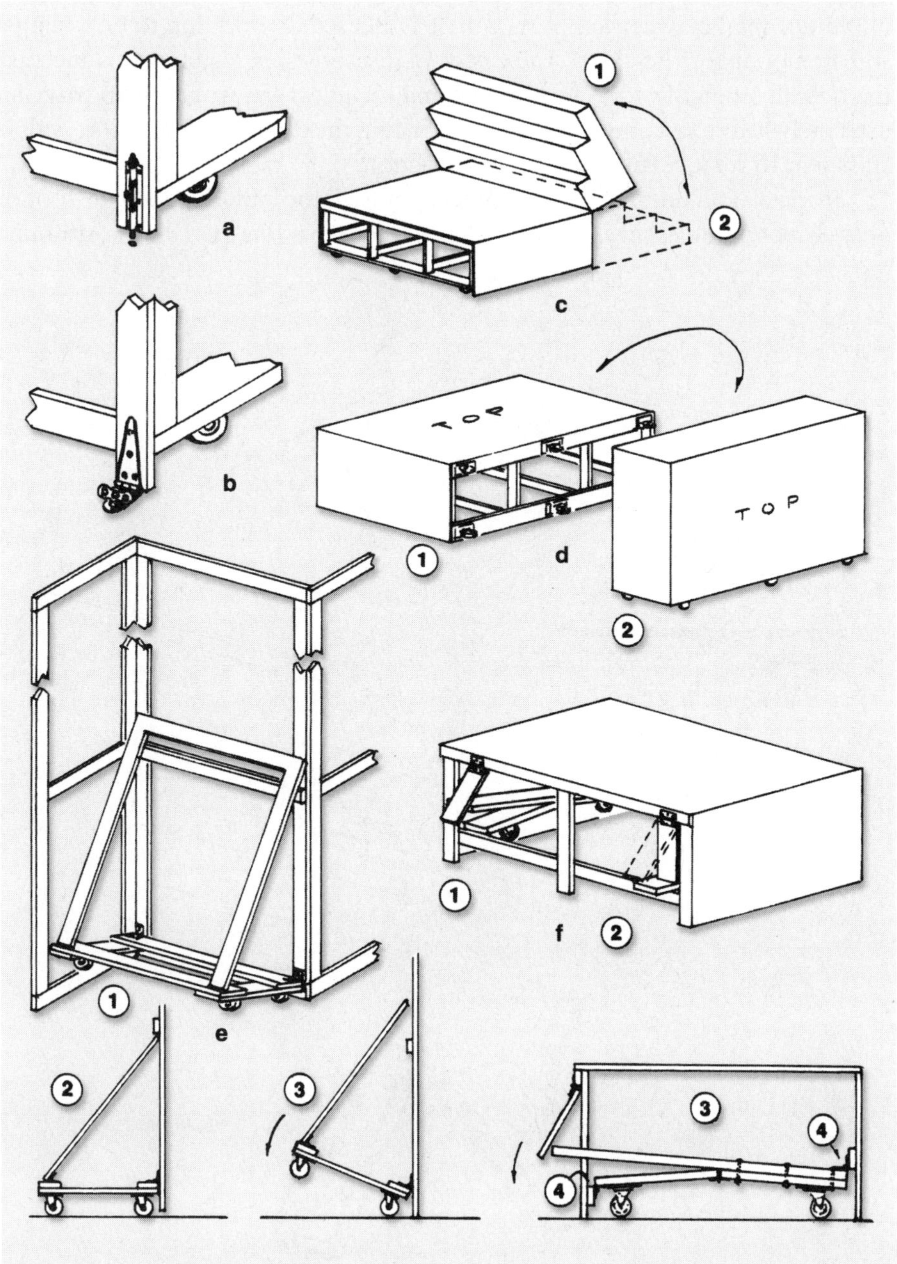

10-13

Methods of Stabilizing Castered Units

a Barrel bolt fits into hole in stage floor.

b Hinged footiron and stage screw.

c Portion of platform not on casters:
  1 Steps hinged to castered platform fold on top for easy movement.
  2 Unfolded and resting on the stage floors, the steps stabilize the platform unit.

d Casters on offstage edge of platform:
  1 Platform in working position, casters on back edge.
  2 Platform tipped onto casters for easy movement.

e Lift jack:
  1 Full view of lift jack.
  2 Side view showing jack lifting scenery.
  3 Jack released, scenery resting on floor.

f Lift jack under a platform:
  1 Jack released.
  2 Jack depressed to lift platform on casters.
  3 Sectional view.
  4 Note the eccentric hinging.

Outrigger Wagons

An *outrigger wagon* is essentially a pattern of castered jacks or braces around the outside of a set or portion of a set. The scenery remains on casters. This skeleton wagon braces and casters the scenery. The action of the scene is played not on a wagon but on the stage floor (Figure 10-12c).

Wagons

The low-level platform (6 to 8 inches) on casters, called a *wagon,* can carry a large portion of a setting including the set props. Large wagons often carry an entire setting, which can be swiftly and easily moved into place for a scene change. Although it requires ample floor space, the wagon is a flexible and efficient method of handling scenery.

Wagon construction is basically the same as platform construction, with the casters serving as "legs." If the casters are mounted on caster planks, the minimum span between supports can be increased. In addition to providing a sturdy mount for the caster, the caster plank serves as a support to increase the overall strength of the wagon. Normally, unless the wagon is to carry an extremely heavy load, such as a piano, spacing the casters at 3-foot intervals is sufficient to remove any noticeable deflection.

Stock wagon units made in a convenient size for handling (3-by-6-foot or 4-by-8-foot modules) are joined to make larger units (Figure 10-14). Although

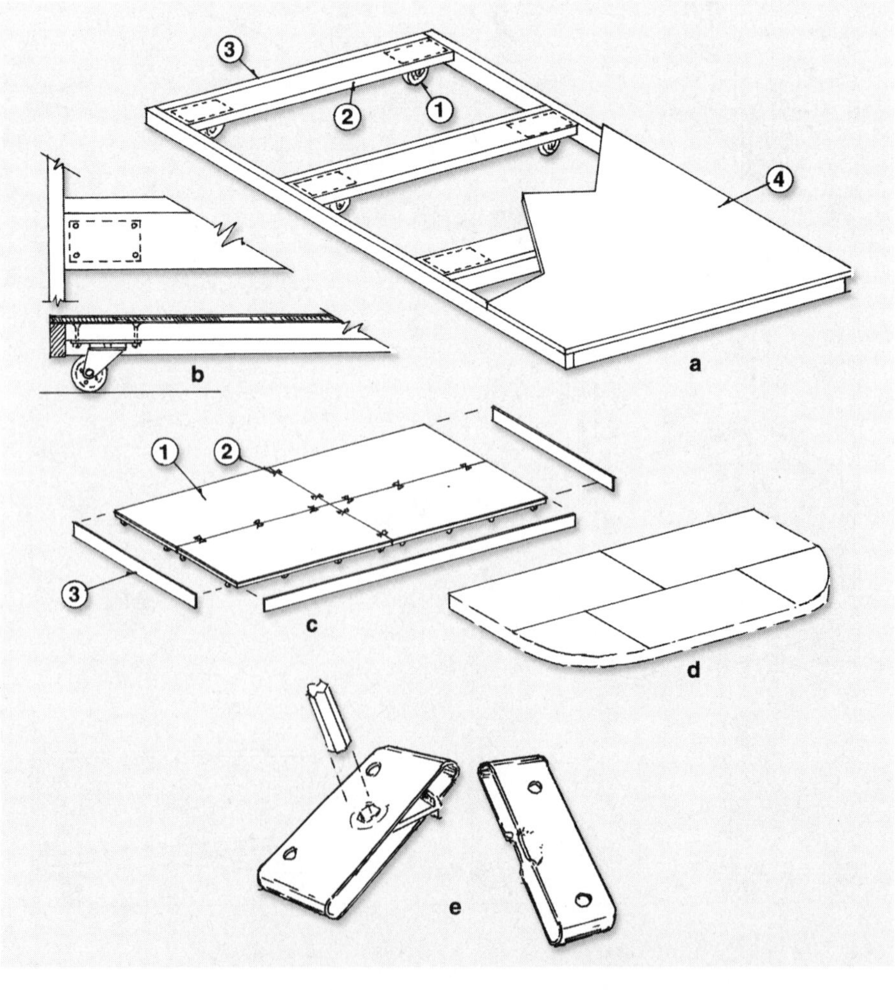

10-14

The Wagon Unit

a Construction of a stock wagon:
- **1** 4-inch swivel casters.
- **2** 2 by 6 caster planks.
- **3** 2 by 4 frame.
- **4** 4-by-8-foot, ¾-inch plywood top.

b Sectional view.

c Large wagon made up of stock units:
- **1** Stock unit.
- **2** Units pin-hinged together.
- **3** Facings.

d A different shape made of three stock wagons and two special corner pieces.

e Casket locks to lock wagons together.

stock wagons use more casters than are necessary for the total area covered, the flexibility of arrangements and handling and ease of storage justify the module system.

There are times when a wagon with a very low profile is needed; this is called a **pallet** or *skid*. These very low platforms are often used to carry furniture and actors onstage. A pallet could be a thin sheet of plastic (the problem being high resistance) or ¾-inch plywood on glides. A hard surface such as a polyurethane seal on the stage deck will facilitate a smooth operation. If possible, the pallet should be built of two layers of ¾-inch plywood skinned with Masonite or another finished surface. Small rollers are then embedded into the structure to allow for movement. The plywood can be beveled to soften its edges, making it less intrusive visually.

pallet A wagon with a very low profile. Also called a *skid*.

Wagon modules can be fastened together to make up a larger wagon unit with a hidden fastener, the casket lock. The two halves of the lock are mounted opposite each other in countersunk slots. Through an access hole in the top, the two halves of the fastener are locked together with an Allen wrench–type key (Figure 10-14e).

The Air-Bearing Caster

The air caster lifts a wagon or heavy unit of scenery on a film of air for easy movement on- or offstage. The air supply can be from one of two sources, a low-pressure air blower or a high-pressure air compressor. The low-pressure air blower delivers an even flow of air at a constant pressure and is more economical but entails a larger air caster unit. The air compressor can use a smaller lift unit, but it is more expensive and requires a storage tank to maintain an even pressure. Even so, many shops already have a fixed air compression system with hookup positions in the scenery shop for pneumatic tools, in the paint shop for spray gun painting, and on the stage for setup and touch-up. To avoid a loss of pressure during prolonged use of the air caster, an extra storage tank can be added to the system.

Preparing the Floor Having the right floor surface is crucial for air casters to work: It must be smooth and level. The average stage floor is soft wood, pierced with floor traps. Because the clearance of an air-castered unit is only ¾ inch, there cannot be dips or abrupt rises on the floor of more than ⅛ inch in 10 feet. Surfaces such as linoleum, vinyl, or smooth-sided Masonite boards are recommended. All joints and cracks should be sealed so as not to leak air.

Positioning the Air Caster The manufacturer recommends a perimeter placement of the air caster, partly for easy access to the caster for maintenance and replacement. For large units, this may complicate the construction of the wagon. The internal structure must be strong enough to bridge the width with minimum deflection. If internally placed air casters are to be used, access through the platform floor should be planned.

Figure 10-15 shows two types of air casters from different manufacturers. The round-pad unit has an air-off support built into the unit, while the square-pad unit's air-off support is built into the platform. The round pad is a more visible caster and is better adapted for moving scaffold-type structures or a pipe-sculptured scenic unit.

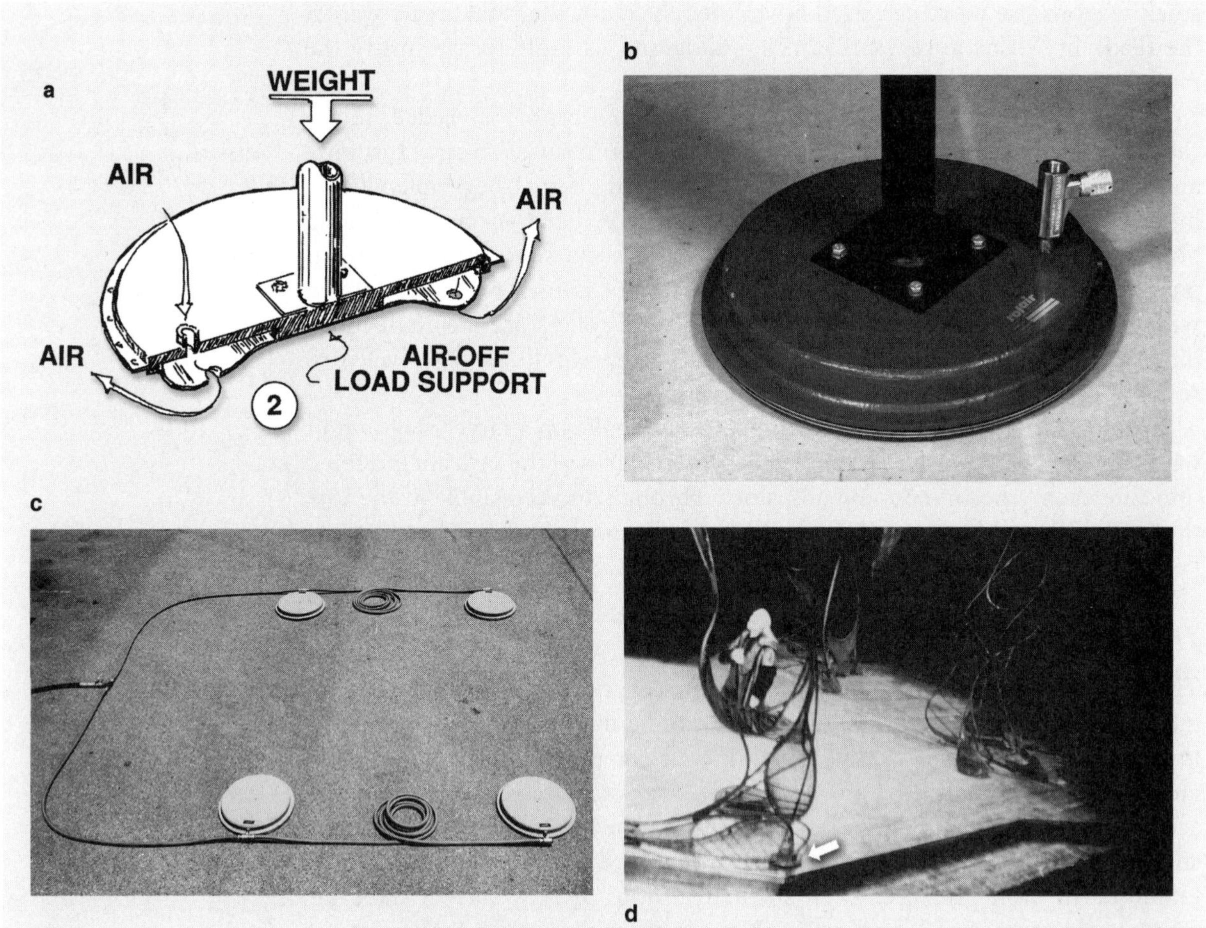

b & c PHOTOS COURTESY ROLAR SYSTEM INC., SANTA BARBARA
d PHOTO COURTESY BAKKOM

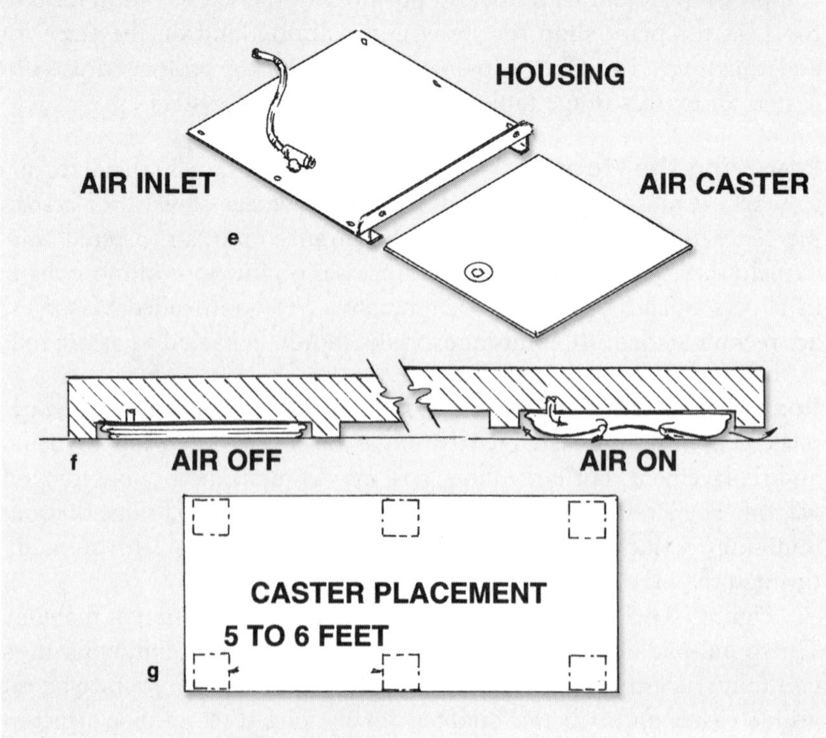

AIR CASTER CORPORATION, DECATUR, IL

10-15

Air-Bearing Casters

Round-pad air caster:

- **a** Sectional view. Note the built-in air-off support.
- **b** Single pad.
- **c** Distribution of casters.
- **d** Use of round-pad air caster in a production of *The Tempest* at the Guthrie Theatre. The arrow indicates one of several air casters placed at strategic points on a giant wire sculpture, which pivots and rotates to indicate the many locations on Prospero's magical island.

Square-pad air caster:

- **e** The air-off load support has to be built into the platform structure.
- **f** Section showing position of wagon with air on and air off.
- **g** A perimeter placement of casters is recommended for easy access.

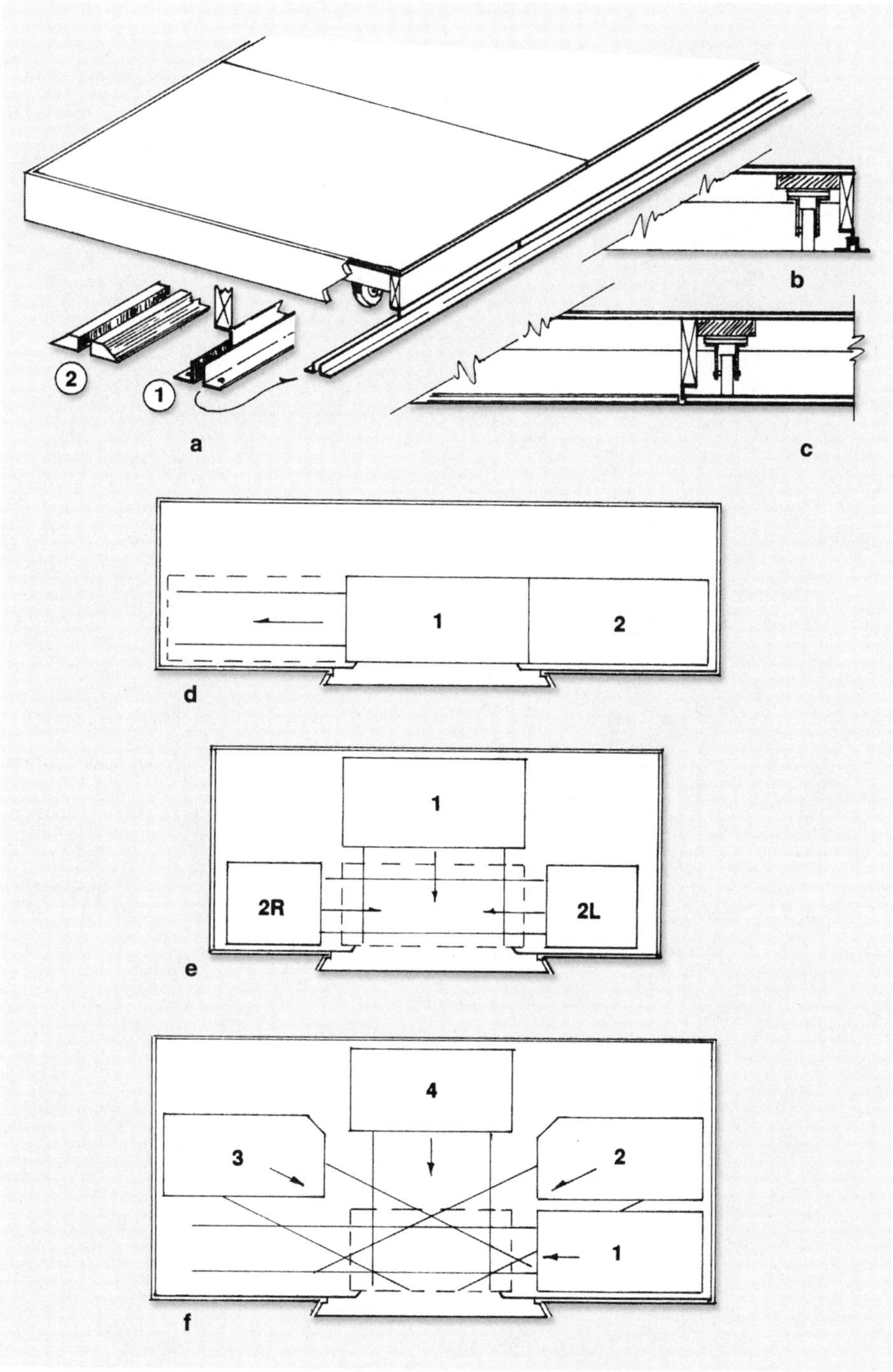

10-16

Tracked Wagon Movement

a Tracks on top of the stage floor. This technique is inherently problematic if actors need to walk in the area of the stage where there is tracking.

1 Steel angle irons.

2 Beveled wood; quieter than steel on steel, but more subject to wear.

b Sectional detail.

c Section showing track cut into the stage floor. In an elaborate tracked wagon scheme such as those diagrammed in (d), (e), and (f), a temporary stage floor is installed with space beneath the track groove for cables to drive the wagon unit by hand winch from an offstage position.

Types of tracked wagon movement:

d Transverse movement.

e Slit transverse wagons and a large single wagon moving up- and downstage.

f Multimovements: transverse, diagonal, up-, and downstage.

Wagon Movements

Aside from the free movement of a wagon carrying a full or partial set, there are several controlled movements that can become a scheme of production for handling scenery entirely on casters. These involve the construction of tracks either above the stage floor or recessed into it (Figure 10-16). The scheme is sometimes based on a pair of alternating wagons, allowing the scenery and props to be changed on the offstage wagon while the alternate wagon is in the playing position. The transverse, jackknife, and split-wagon movements operate on this principle (Figure 10-17). Cables drive the platforms

10-17

Pivoted Wagon Movement

a Pivot mounted on corner of wagon.

- **1** Pivot detail.
- **2** Socket fastened to floor at pivot point. Although the pivot and socket positions are often reversed in a turntable installation, it is best under the illustrated conditions to place the socket on the floor. Besides being an awkward mounting position, a corner pivot may also have to bear weight because the nearest caster is usually about four feet away.
- **3** Fixed caster set perpendicularly to radius.

b Jackknife wagons.

c Jackknife in combination with split wagons.

d Pivoting a half circle.

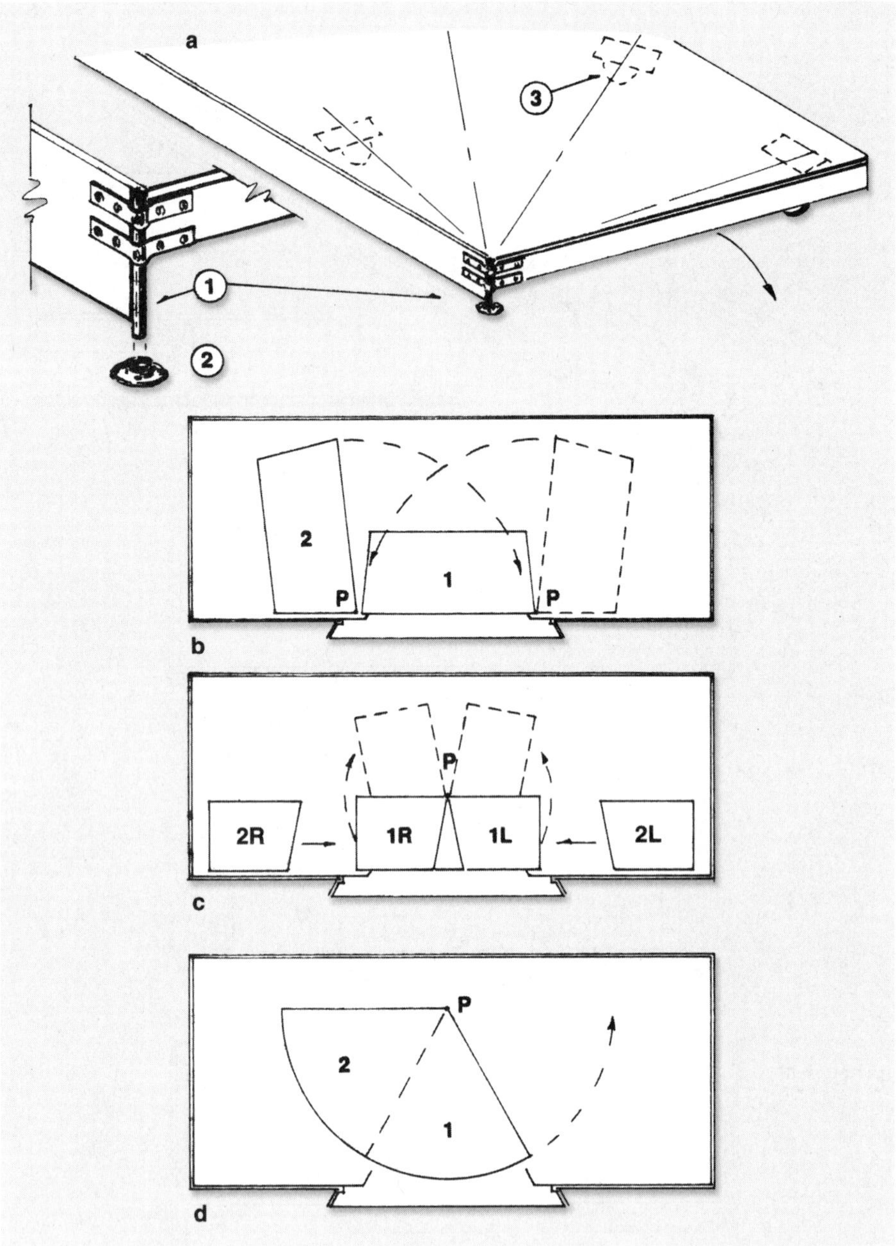

10-18

Cable Drive for Moving Wagons

The drive cable is hidden from view under a raised stage floor and attached to wagon guides, right and left. The cable turns on the drum of the winch to pull the wagon to the right or left.

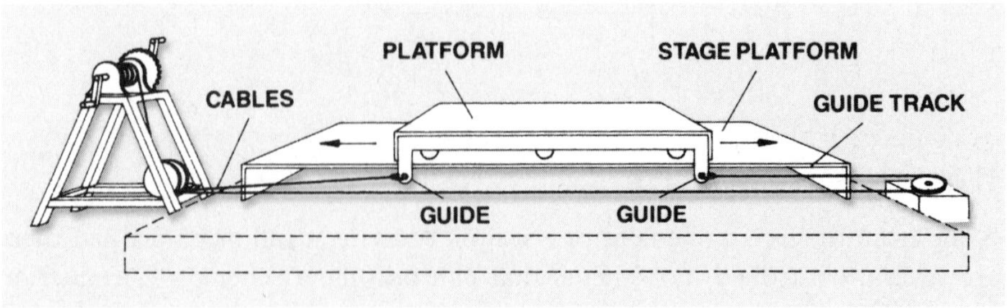

along the tracks (Figure 10-18). Although scenery rigged in this manner is most often manually operated, it is becoming more common to see the use of automation as the technology increases and the expense becomes less prohibitive.

When a production uses small sets, keeping each set intact on separate wagons works best at times. The stage then becomes packed with wagon sets and the shifting is accomplished by shuttling each wagon into position. The pattern of movement varies with the size and shape of the sets, their order of appearance in the play, and the design.

Current technology has made the electric motor winch the standard for moving scenery, the biggest hurdles being the expense and the added time needed to set up the mechanism. As well, any winch is also rather large, so the initial plan must provide a convenient space. Advances in the control of electric winches have made it easier to use off-the-shelf components to build a custom mechanism. Until relatively recently, a smooth operation required all kinds of special and complicated mechanical components. New technology allows the motor itself to do most of the work. Hydraulics are still used, particularly for high-end productions and in small spaces; they take up less space than do electromechanical parts.

The Automated Deck

Modern, large-scale productions often involve extensive use of automated movement. The standard today is for a multiple tracking system that is accomplished through the use of an *automated deck*. All of the component parts needed to move scenic units are built into this deck (as opposed to on top of it, for example). One or more tracks in the deck are controlled by using electrical winches. The movement is almost always linear.

This closed-loop system allows the scenic unit to be pulled in either direction along each *track*, or long, narrow slot built into the deck. To each piece of scenery is attached a *drop knife*, or metal plate approximately ¼ inch by 4 inches, which fits through the track. A cable following the direction of the track is wound about the winch on one side and a pulley on the opposite side, forming a long loop. Connecting the drop knife to the scenic unit is a *dog* that allows the scenic unit to follow the path of the track pulled by the cable. The previously mentioned pallets or skids are usually moved in this manner.

The drop knife can be removed in order for one winch or the same track to be used to move multiple pieces of scenery. In other words, one track can be used to move more than one wagon.

Because of the amount of scenery and the lack of wing space in many of the Broadway houses, scenic units that come offstage are often released from the dog and then lifted by chain motors into the air to keep them out of the way. It is not unusual in a big musical to see a vertical line of scenery hanging in the air backstage.

The Revolving Stage

Another controlled movement is that of a castered unit around a fixed pivot: a revolving stage. Such a stage, which is not permanently built into the stage floor, has a structure similar to that of the wagon. To remain portable, a turntable is made in smaller sections that are fastened together (Figure 10-19). The fixed casters are mounted in a pattern to support each unit properly and are fixed in a position in which the axle of the caster is on a radius line drawn from the pivot point. If the casters are carefully mounted, the turntable will revolve about its pivot point with little effort.

10-19

The Revolving Stage

A portable revolving stage or turntable can be built many ways. Shown here are two methods.

a Turntable made up of stock wagon units with special-shaped wagons to form the curve of the outside edge:

1 Stock wagon.

2 Special wagon to complete circle.

3 Casters blocked perpendicularly to radius.

4 Section.

b Turntable made of wedge-shaped units around central core; fewer casters are used, creating less noise:

1 Basic wedge-shaped unit.

2 Top removed, showing the position of casters.

3 Central core.

4 Sectional view.

c Turntable construction, reverse castering:

1 Basic wedge-shaped unit.

2 Central core; ball-bearing pivot.

3 Single unit viewed from underneath to show framing.

4 Bearing surface in path of casters; ¾-inch plywood or particle board.

5 Casters mounted on the stage floor in patterns that have the same circumference as the caster-bearing surface on the underside of the turntable.

6 Spirit level and rotating bar to check the level of each caster mount to ensure smooth rotation.

Although the reverse caster turntable takes longer to assemble, it is quieter and easier to turn than the conventional castered unit.

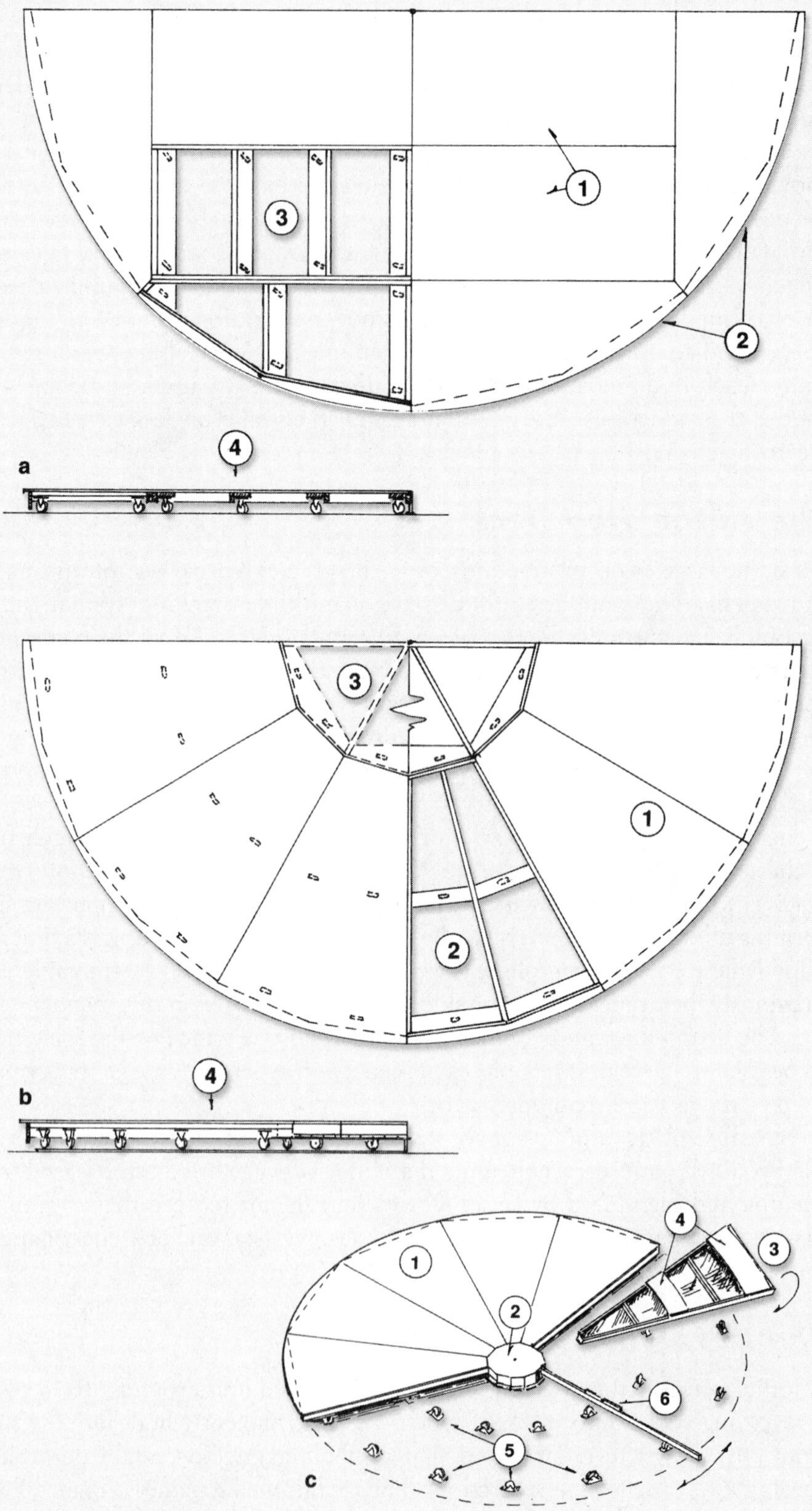

Another method of assembling a turntable is to reverse the normal position of the casters under the table and place them upside down on the stage floor (Figure 10-19c). The casters are placed in concentric circles as bearing points on a prepared rolling surface on the underside of the table. Each caster is shimmed to the same height to ensure a level turntable floor. This compensates for any irregularities in the stage floor. Although the assembly time is longer and the table is a little higher off the stage floor, the result is a smooth-running, quiet turntable. Figures 10-19 and 10-20 illustrate the assembly steps as well as the motorized cable drive for powering a revolving stage.

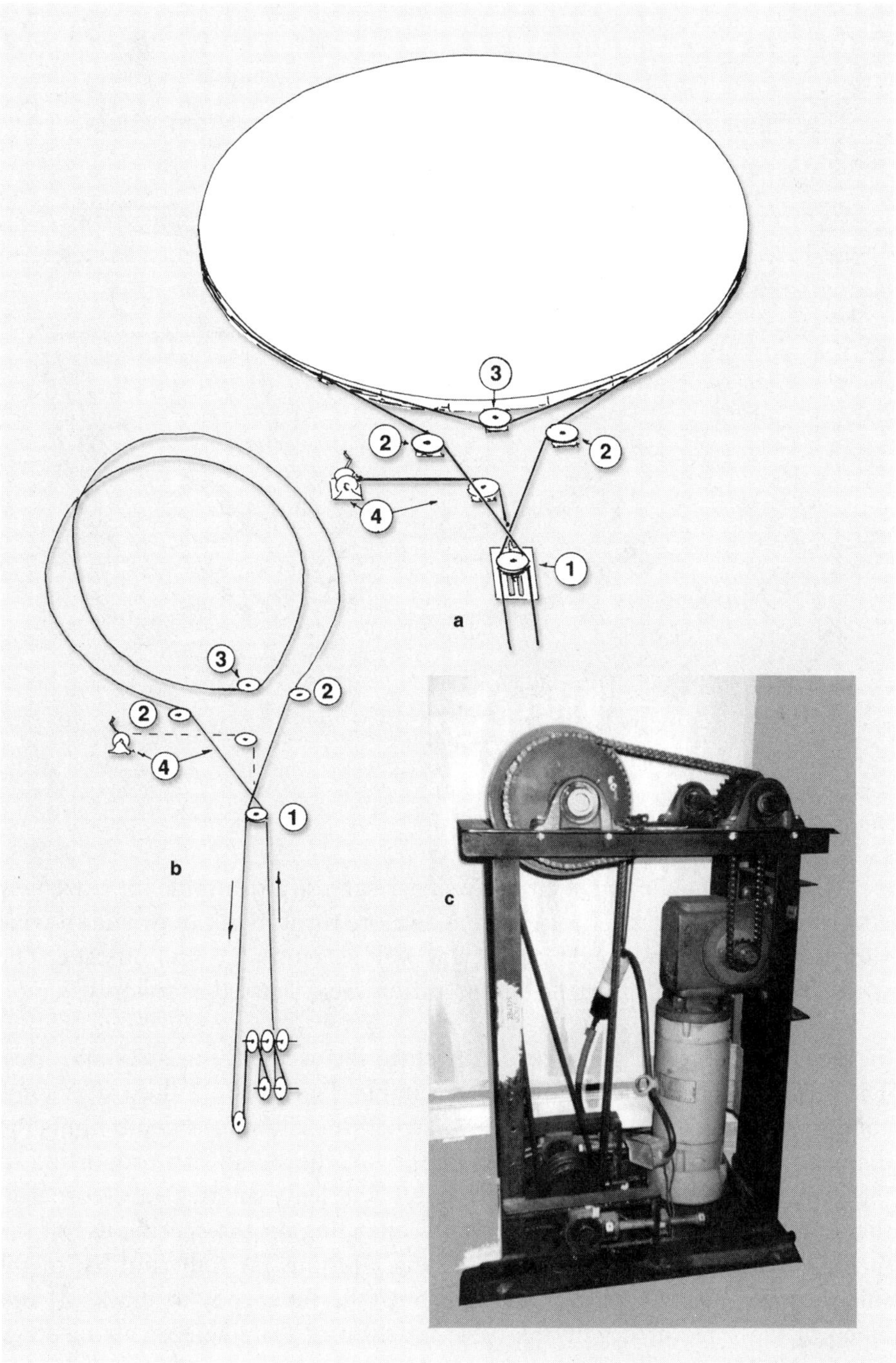

10-20

Motorized Cable Drive for a Single Turntable

a Basic turntable:

- **1** Tension idler.
- **2** Mule pulley to change direction of cable.
- **3** Centering pulley, which keeps cable from creeping and binding as it winds and unwinds on the edge of turntable.
- **4** Winch to control cable tension.

b The threading of the cable, which is ¼ inch of flexible steel long-spliced into a continuous loop (see (a) for number descriptions).

c Motorized cable drive.

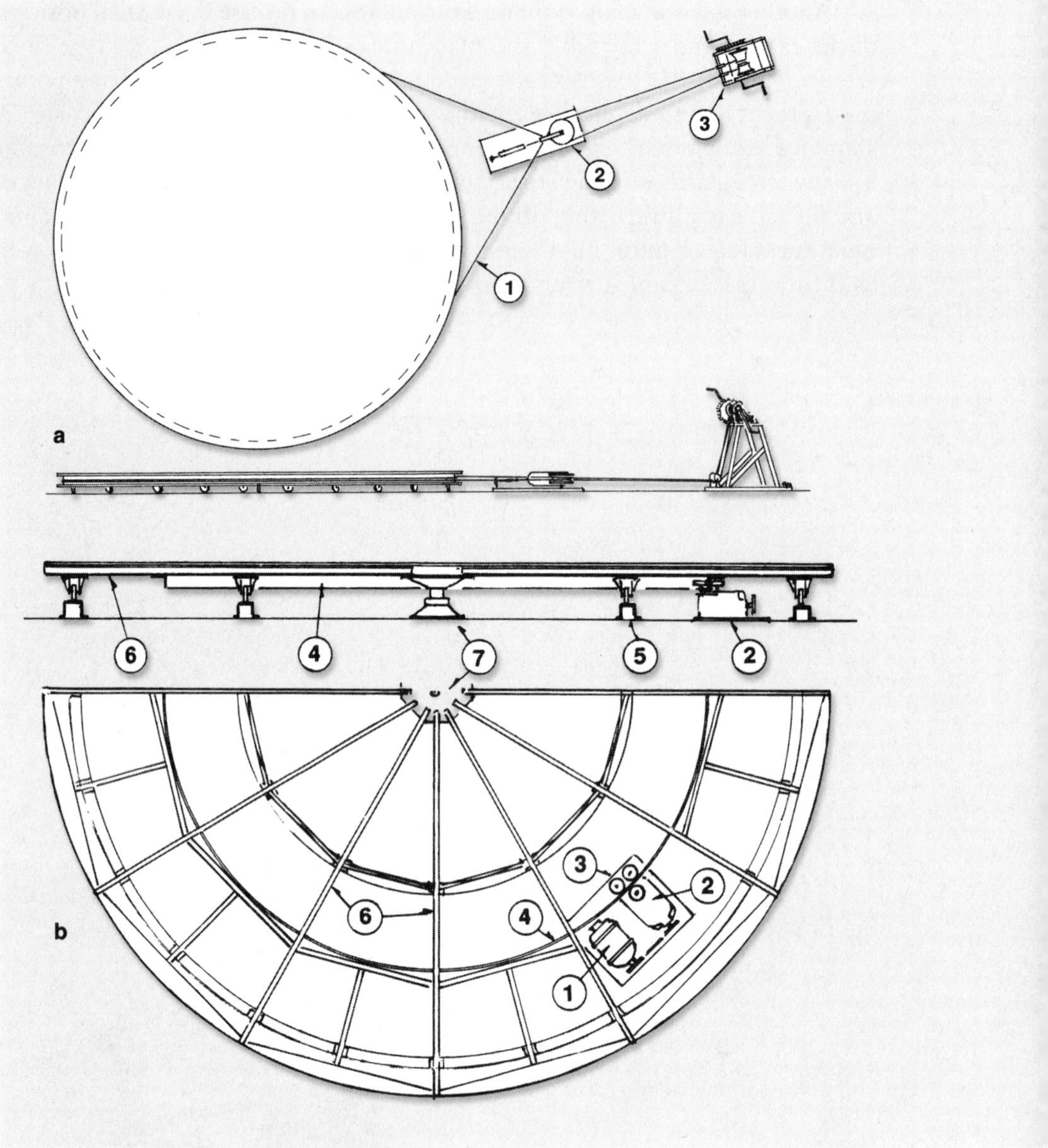

With careful planning, a clever designer can use a turntable for extremely effective scene changes. The use of one or more turntables can provide a wide variety of patterns in moving scenery as well as actors on- and offstage. The standard methods of turntable configuration are discussed as follows.

Single Turntable The revolving stage has a variety of sizes and uses. The most familiar is the large single turntable. Figure 10-21 illustrates some commonly used methods to power this structure. The stage's depth limits the diameter of a turntable. If the stage happens to be shallow in proportion to the proscenium opening, a single turntable will leave an awkward corner in the downstage right and left positions. Depending on the specific use of the turntable, a show portal masking the stage portions far right and left might solve this problem. However, caution must be taken not to mask off too much of the stage or negate the basic function of the single revolving stage (Figure 10-22a).

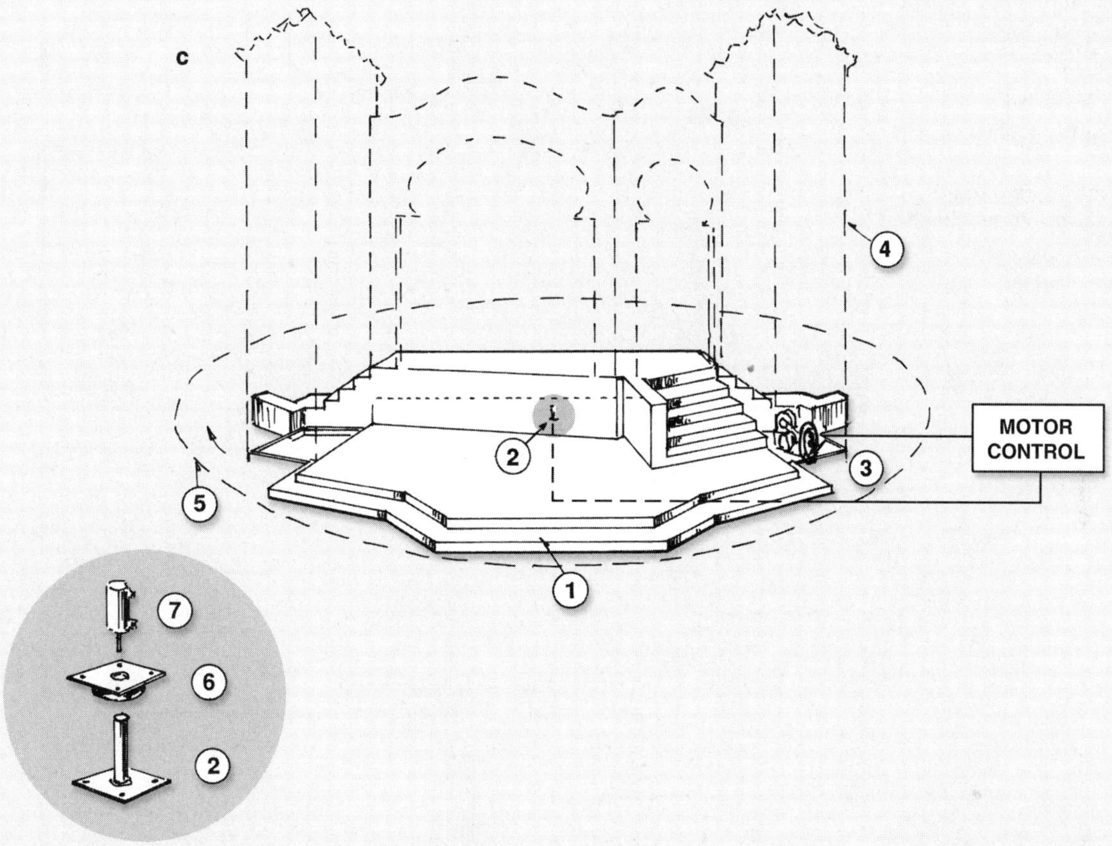

10-21

Three Methods of Powering a Single Turntable

Both (a) and (b) turntables are usually surrounded by a raised temporary stage floor flush with the top of the turntable.

a Cable and winch:
- **1** Spliced cable with one turn around the outside edge of the turntable; held taut by tension idler.
- **2** Tension idler; powered by hand winch.
- **3** Hand winch.

b Top and sectional views of a motor-driven turntable—a reversible and variable-speed electric motor underneath a highly mounted turntable:
- **1** Motor.
- **2** Reduction gear box.
- **3** Spring-loaded friction drive wheels, or bevel gears.
- **4** Drive ring for friction drive, or gear ring for bevel gear drive.
- **5** Raised, fiber-padded track for fixed caster.
- **6** Steel channel-beam framework.
- **7** Roller-bearing pivot.

c Motor-controlled turntable. There are many varieties, but they all get information about the position of the turntable from an *encoder* (a device for registering the position of the turntable) and send it to the motor control, which in turn sends power to the motor.
- **1** Basic platform structure on fixed casters perpendicular to radius.
- **2** Pivot located off the center of the platform and positioning device indicating electronically where the turntable is.
- **3** Wheel drive power unit hidden by superstructure.
- **4** Superstructure of the setting.
- **5** Path of rotation.
- **6** Ball-bearing socket fixed to the platform.
- **7** Encoder, or turn indicator device.

10-22

Turntable and Ring Combinations

a Single large turntable.
b Two small turntables.
c Large turntable with two small disks.
d Large turntable with ring.
e Two small turntables with rings.
f Semi-revolving ring segment and small turntable.
g Single turntable in a transverse wagon.
h Pair of rings.

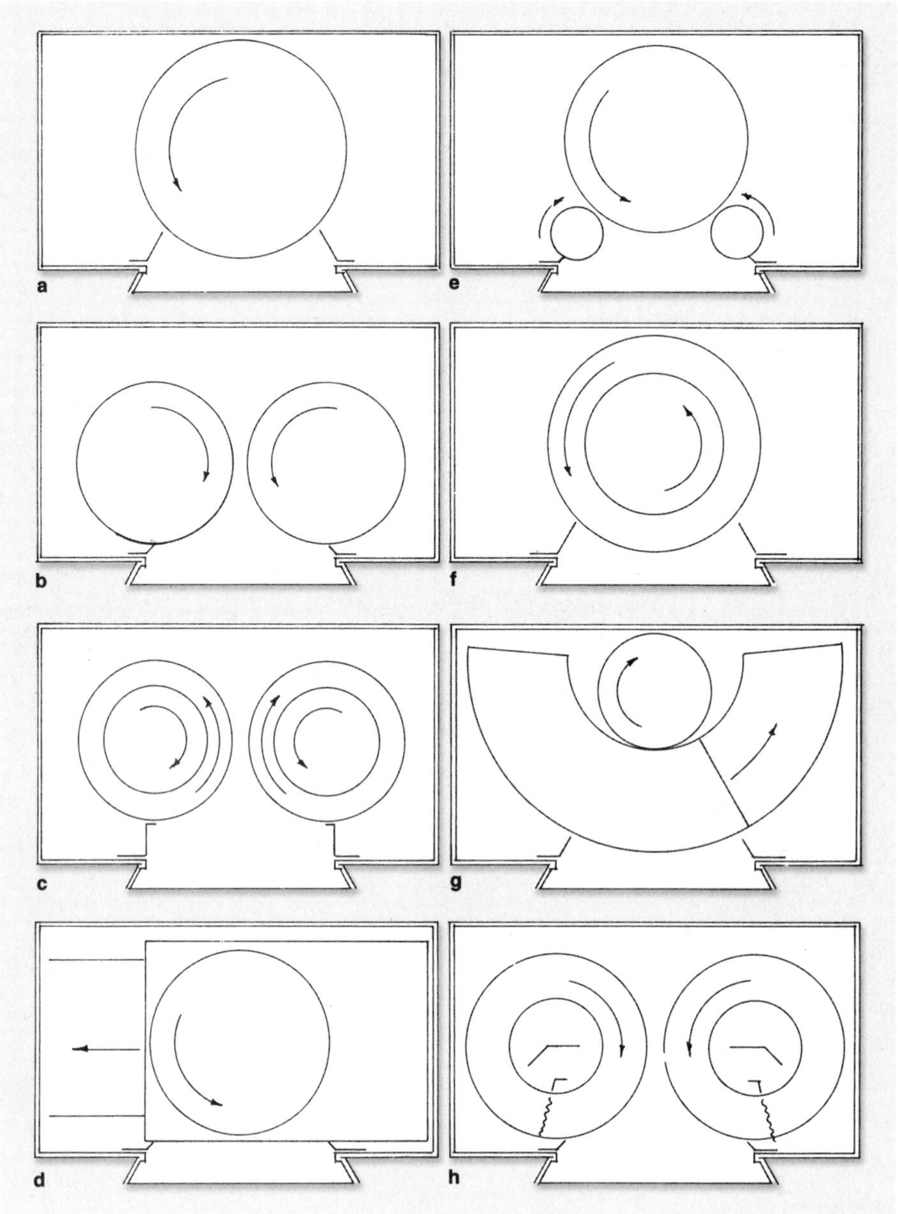

Two Turntables A shallow stage is adaptable to the use of two turntables that are slightly apart at center stage. This method removes the awkward corners of the single turntable, but it creates a design problem—that of joining all the sets in the center (Figure 10-22b).

Three Turntables Occasionally, a large turntable is combined with two small disks in the downstage right and left positions. The small disks either carry scenery related to the large set in the center or are small independent sets (Figure 10-22c).

Ring and Turntable A great deal more variety of movement is achieved by using a ring and turntable combination (Figure 10-22d). The ring and turntable are individually powered so that they can turn in the same direction at identical or different speeds, or they can revolve in opposite directions. The possible combinations of fixed units on the ring and turntable are almost endless. If the changes are made a vista, this configuration becomes a delightful scheme of production.

Two Rings and Two Turntables Although less adaptable to revolving fixed units than the single ring and turntable, two rings around two turntables provide a flexible method of changing elements of scenery and properties (Figure 10-22e). This was demonstrated in the production of *Lady in the Dark,* designed by Harry Homer. With the help of flown pieces of scenery, the settings were able to blend from one scene to the next in full view of the audience.

Semi-Revolves and Combinations There are even more variations of the revolving technique using the semi-revolving stage and a combination of a turntable and a wagon.

The semi-revolving stage is a portion of a ring or turntable tracked to swing in an arc (Figure 10-22f). The semi-revolving stage may be large or small, used singly or in pairs, or combined with a turntable.

A combination of revolving and lateral movements can be accomplished by building a turntable into a full-stage transverse wagon (Figure 10-22g). This combination works best when a portion of one set is reused many times during the show. The lobby of *Grand Hotel,* for example, was saved in this manner. Most of the lobby settings remained on the left side of the wagon while a portion moved on the turntable. The smaller rooms and other scenes in the hotel occupied the remainder of the turntable and were moved into better sightlines by sliding the wagon to the left. The scheme can be varied by setting the turntable into the center of the wagon and having elements of scenery on both sides instead of on one side.

The Air Caster for the Revolving Stage Air casters can be used on a turntable or for any pivoting motion. A semi-revolve is not a problem, but if the motion is a complete revolve the air hose may become tangled. To avoid this problem, portable air compressors and air blowers can ride on the revolve. However, although they are equipped with noise suppressors, they still need to be covered with music or some other appropriate sound. If the theatre has a trap room, the air hose can feed through an enlarged center pivot.

Conventional drive systems such as cable or rim drive can be used on the air caster. An air-castered wagon can be tracked and driven by cable, or just pushed.

LIFTS AND ELEVATOR STAGES

As a means of moving scenery, the elevator and the lift require sophisticated stage machinery. If the installation is a permanent part of the theatre architecture, it is referred to as an **elevator.** If it is built for a specific production, it is called a **lift.**

Unless the theatre will make constant use of the elevators or can use them, for example, as a scenery and property lift to and from remote storage areas, installation would be extravagant. With few exceptions (the Metropolitan Opera House, Radio City Music Hall, and similar presentation houses), the use of an elevator or lift to change scenery is not common (Figure 10-23). As for all other methods of moving scenery, the vertical motion must fit into the concept of the production.

elevator A mechanism built to move an actor or scenery vertically; an elevator is a permanent part of a theatre, as opposed to a *lift,* which is a temporary structure built for the same purpose.

lift A mechanism built for a specific production in order to move an actor or scenery vertically. Compare *elevator.*

10-23

Elevator Stage

A backstage view of the elaborate elevator installation at the Metropolitan Opera House, New York.

The financial organization and scale of production of numerous state theatres in Europe make the elaborate elevator stage a more feasible method of handling scenery than could be supported by the unsubsidized theatres of the United States.

Small Lifts and Traps

trap Any hole in the stage floor.

Although the average stage may not have an elevator system, it usually has a portion of the floor area made in sections of **traps** that may be used to raise small elements of scenery through the stage floor. The traps can be removed to give access through the stage floor into a room below the stage, referred to as the *trap room.* Entrances by stairs or ladder can be made from below through such an opening. Trap openings are made between structural beams supporting the stage floor. The designer must be aware of the specific position of the traps in a given theatre.

Figure 10-24 shows the construction of a temporary lift that can be used for scenery or actors. Lifts can vary greatly in size. The example illustrated is a small unit; a larger lift would require more guides and lifelines.

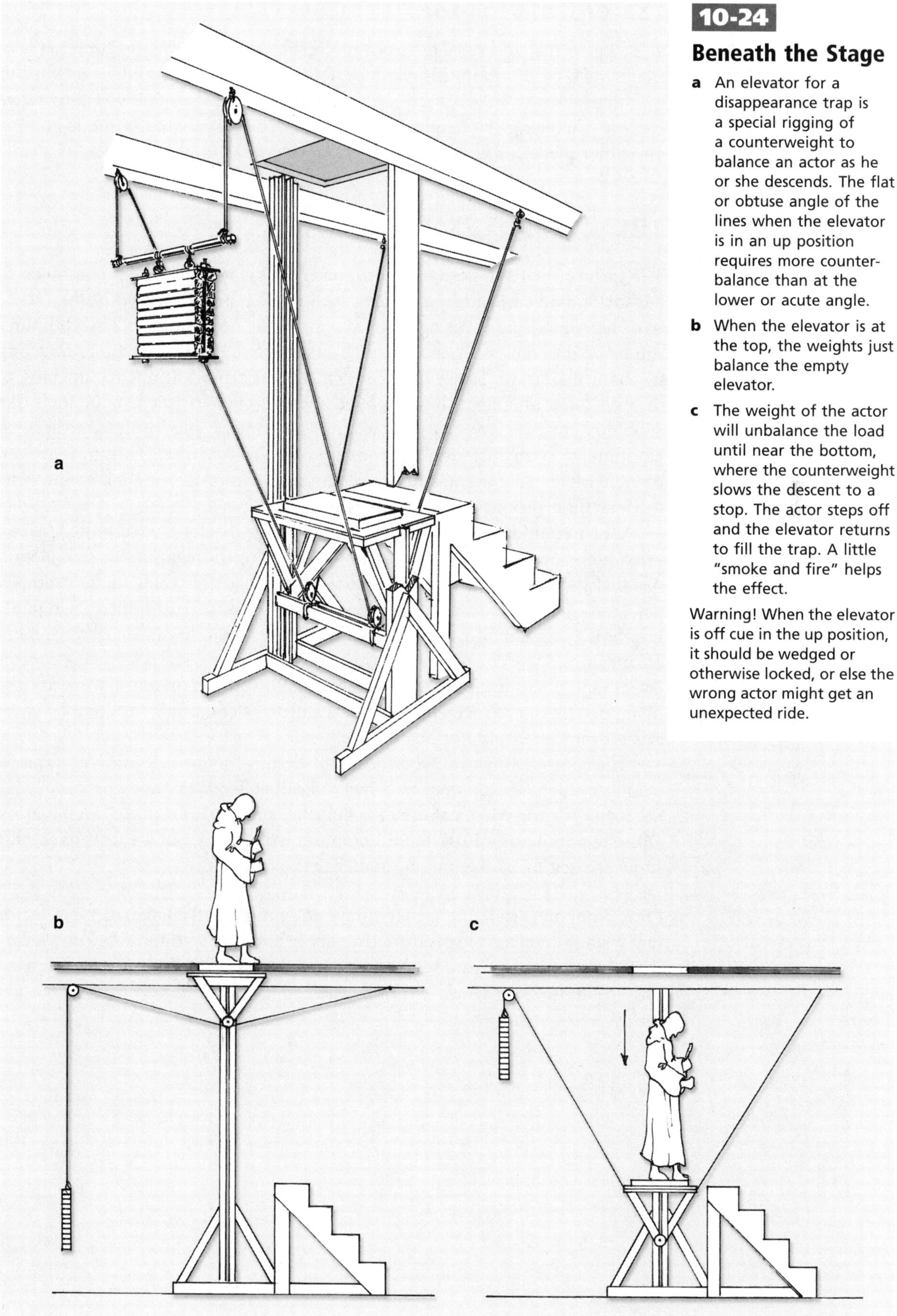

10-24

Beneath the Stage

a An elevator for a disappearance trap is a special rigging of a counterweight to balance an actor as he or she descends. The flat or obtuse angle of the lines when the elevator is in an up position requires more counter-balance than at the lower or acute angle.

b When the elevator is at the top, the weights just balance the empty elevator.

c The weight of the actor will unbalance the load until near the bottom, where the counterweight slows the descent to a stop. The actor steps off and the elevator returns to fill the trap. A little "smoke and fire" helps the effect.

Warning! When the elevator is off cue in the up position, it should be wedged or otherwise locked, or else the wrong actor might get an unexpected ride.

The Elevator Floor

Some performance spaces incorporate elevators whose primary function is to shape the stage floor. In this instance, elevators can raise or lower sections of the stage floor to make levels or pits, but this is not usually done to move scenery. Changing the height of portions of the stage floor without moving any other pieces of scenery can considerably alter the appearance of a set.

THE COMPUTER BACKSTAGE

The influence of the computer on scenery-moving technology continues to advance rapidly. Blockbuster shows such as *Cats* and *Phantom of the Opera* have been pioneers in using advanced backstage technology. The computer can be used to control hydraulic and scissors lifts, electric winches, and flying mechanisms, as well as various scenic effects. In addition, technicians in theatres large and small have applied the computer to such mundane tasks as maintaining an inventory of all units of scenery, platforms, and lighting equipment, with instructions for assembly and strike. This has proven particularly useful for tracking stock furniture and properties and scenic units for television production companies.

When computer control is reinforced with a television monitor, it can provide the operator with a situation report as to the accuracy or completion of a tricky scenery maneuver. The basic acting area for *Miss Saigon,* for example, was framed on three sides with panels of oversized rustic shutters. Each panel was flown individually, providing considerable flexibility in the arrangement of openings. In order to achieve this, the liftlines of each panel were motor-driven and computerized. A TV monitor allowed the operator to verify the final position of each screen. Without the use of a computer, the complexity of this movement would not be possible.

The computer has allowed the scenic designer great flexibility in terms of complex movement of scenery. It has radically altered the body of knowledge necessary for the technical director and the stage technician. In combination with the popularity of spectacle, computer technology can create a backstage show as exciting as the one the audience is experiencing.

From computers to flying scenery, stage equipment and its management factor into a stage designer's plans from the very beginning. Without this knowledge, the designer would create beautiful interpretations likely to remain unrealized onstage in the "real world" of the theatre.

11

Stage Properties and the Designer

In addition to being responsible for large scenic background elements, the designer designs and selects stage properties and smaller bits of scenery used by the actors. This may vary from finding a marble-topped Louis XV console table to making an exotic sofa for a Turkish cosy-corner, or from borrowing a Victorian tea set to fashioning tree leaves. Whether borrowed or constructed, each property must be carefully coordinated into the design, compositionally and conceptually, and must also be checked for size and ease of use by the actors.

Stage properties are in essence the design details of the overall visual composition. Their contribution cannot be overemphasized, even in unrealistic settings. Stage properties often provide the accent or artistic touch that makes or breaks a stage setting. The audience usually does not notice how carefully chosen props enhance the overall design and help the actors. However, they do notice sloppy prop work, which can seriously detract from a performance.

On thrust and arena stages, properties sometimes take on relatively greater responsibility for establishing the locale. Because of the physical audience-to-stage relationship in both cases, the finished detail and quality of all properties are subject to closer inspection than they are on the proscenium stage.

Because every production of a play is unique, designers must consider the suitability of each stage property to a particular interpretation. In other words, designers must ask questions that relate not just to the text but to the approach of the production as well. The initial discussions will be with the director and then with the props mistress or master.

Ultimately, the design of props entails three areas of concern: style, function, and size.

- *Style:* What is the world of the play? When and where does the play take place? Is it realistic or abstract in some way? Is the prop crude, plain, rustic, plain?
- *Function:* How will the property be used? Will it sit on a shelf never to be touched or be thrown against the wall? Will an actor stand on the table? Are the swords functional or decorative only?

- *Size:* How high can the table centerpiece be before it gets in the way of sightlines? Does the gun need to fit into a coat pocket?

Because such questions may well affect all other aspects of the production, designers must ask them at the start. The selection and designing of furniture and properties is done in close collaboration with the director in order to ensure their appropriateness for the play and to check how they fit into the staging. In addition, there must be some consideration of how props may affect the other elements of design. Is the lamp a usable light source? Will the liquid in the glasses stain fabric? Again, no design decisions are made without input from the full artistic team.

Real furniture is, of course, used in the modern theatre, although it is often altered to work well onstage. For example, scale and color are sometimes changed to improve stage composition. How the furniture will be used also matters a great deal. If, for example, a chair gets thrown on the floor, or someone will stand on it or it will in other ways be treated roughly, it may have to be reinforced. Finally, real furniture can take on a theatrical look, suggesting—sometimes faintly, sometimes openly—that it is no longer real. The term *property,* or "prop," is often synonymous with the unreal or theatrical.

Properties should be planned and built at the same time as the rest of the scenic elements, if for no other reason than to maintain unity. Their importance to the design and production scheme is sometimes overlooked in the planning period, particularly if the designer cannot evaluate each property in terms of its use, both textually and conceptually, and its decorative qualities. Fully staffed theatres retain a props master or mistress, who must see that all of the properties necessary for the production are built, bought, borrowed, or otherwise obtained. If instead the designer must do this, he or she must be careful to give it as much careful consideration as the rest of the set.

URL http://www.restorations.net/mainstyl.htm

URL http://www.time-warp.org

To make efficient use of their time, designers should know about historical furniture styles and period decorations and be thoroughly acquainted with the traditional uses of properties in the theatre. No one expects a designer to know the specifics of every period, but a general knowledge of each is important. More important is the ability to do research. Every design project, even a modern-dress play, requires some research, if only to get fresh ideas about the period.

PROPERTIES VERSUS SCENERY

What is a prop? When does a small piece of scenery become a property or a large property become scenery? The decision about whether a piece is a prop or scenery (or a costume, for that matter) often depends on the staffing of the particular theatre and who is best qualified and has enough time to create the prop. Few shops have hard-and-fast rules about this. Indeed, pieces often easily fall into several categories. The categories that follow offer no more than a guide.

Definition of Properties

Stage properties are traditionally defined as (1) all objects carried or handled by the actors; (2) separate portions of the set on which the actors may stand or sit, such as rocks, stumps, or logs; (3) decorative features not permanently built or painted on the scenery, such as pictures and draperies; (4) the ground cloth and rugs; and (5) all sound and visual effects that are not electrically powered, such as a gunshot or snow.

The average production follows these definitions when categorizing properties, but exceptions or collaborations are made all the time. Hence, a tree trunk may be scenery and foliage a property; a pair of eyeglasses discovered on the stage is a property while a pair brought onstage by the actors might be considered costumes. Heavy properties often become scenery because of their size or because they need to be fastened to the scenery for movement.

Costume design can also affect categorization. Some props such as the earlier-mentioned eyeglasses, watches, and handkerchiefs are generally the responsibility of the costume shop. There is, again, no hard-and-fast rule. If the prop is integral to the design of the clothing or is designed by the costume designer, it is usually considered a costume prop. Of course, if it could more easily be created by the prop shop, then that is where it should be built.

Classification by Size and Use

Properties may also be classified according to their size and use, although one should not be wedded to these categories. As we have seen, properties can be designated as hand, set, or dress properties or as visual- or sound-effect properties. Here we briefly discuss the first three types.

Hand Properties The small objects handled by the actor on the stage are hand props. They include such items as teacups, books, fans, and letters.

Set Properties As the name implies, set properties are the larger elements somewhat related to the scenery but still used by the actors. This group often includes furniture, stoves, sinks, rugs, ground cloths, and other large domestic objects. Exterior set props consist of small rocks, stumps, bushes, foliage, real dirt, grass mats, and so on.

Set properties are under the care of the property person, who supervises the placing of the set prop on the stage and its removal to a stored position offstage.

Dress Properties Dress properties are integral to the setting. They function chiefly to decorate the stage and to help establish the atmosphere and character of the environment through detail. Dress properties consist of all the elements not specifically used by the actors that serve to fill in and complete or dress the set. Window curtains, pictures, wall hangings, and floral arrangements are a few typical dress properties.

Dress properties can be a strong decorative feature in a setting. Because they are usually not used by the actors, they can often be "faked" in order to be created more easily than the other set props. Bookcases, for example, may have false bookbacks attached to the scenery. The shelves behind a saloon bar are often dressed with fake plastic or papier-mâché bottles to cut down the weight. A period piano or spinet, hard to find and harder to borrow, can be easily built as a dress prop. These are, of course, just a few of the many, many types of dress properties one can fake with simple construction.

GENERATING A PROP LIST

The first step in choosing the properties for a production is to generate a prop list. Either the designer or the property master will do this by first including the properties mentioned in the text. The designer will add to this list any set, dress, or hand props necessary to complete the design. Some scripts include a prop list in the back. Although at times a valid place to start, this list has been generated from a specific production quite different from the one being planned; designers need to keep this in mind.

In the planning stage, the prop list is discussed thoroughly with the director in the same way that the set, light, costume, and sound designs are discussed. As with all of the other elements of design, the props must work within the conceptual ideas of the production. Additions and cuts will be made throughout the rehearsal process, according to the needs of the director and other evolving concerns.

SELECTING PROPERTIES

The designer is responsible for the compositional unity, period continuity, and color relationships of the set and all properties. Their first notation appears in the designer's sketch, which may or may not clearly indicate the real form. Once the general idea of the design has been accepted, the designer can turn to a more careful study of the period and availability of each piece.

The designer makes the final decision on each piece of furniture, with the director's approval. To help reach this decision at an early stage in the planning, the designer uses individual sketches, research, pictures, or whatever else the designer thinks will communicate his or her ideas to the director. The selection of set properties can be further facilitated by the use of a ground plan that includes all furniture and that provides exact references to the size of an individual piece in relation to its surroundings. Well in advance of technical rehearsals, the director and designer must make decisions on the specific choices of the props. This allows the actors time to explore how best to use them in the context of the action of the play.

Polaroids of potential props are another great way to communicate with out-of-town directors. The use of e-mail and digital cameras has increased the ease and speed with which designers can work with both the props mistress and the director.

Period Style and Decorative Form

A designer needs to have a full understanding of period architecture, interior design, and furniture styles. The more familiar the designer is with the historical background of a period style, the easier it will be to design the setting (whether realistic or not), select the set and dress properties, and create the appropriate environment. (This applies to the costume designer also.) The director may ask for a specific period style, which suggests both limits and opportunities for a design. The broader the knowledge of the designer, the stronger the ability to respond to the script and the director.

A period style reflects the historical era in which it developed (Figure 11-1). It is evident in the architecture, interiors, and furniture of each period in history; indeed, furniture alone can establish the historical period of a setting. Most

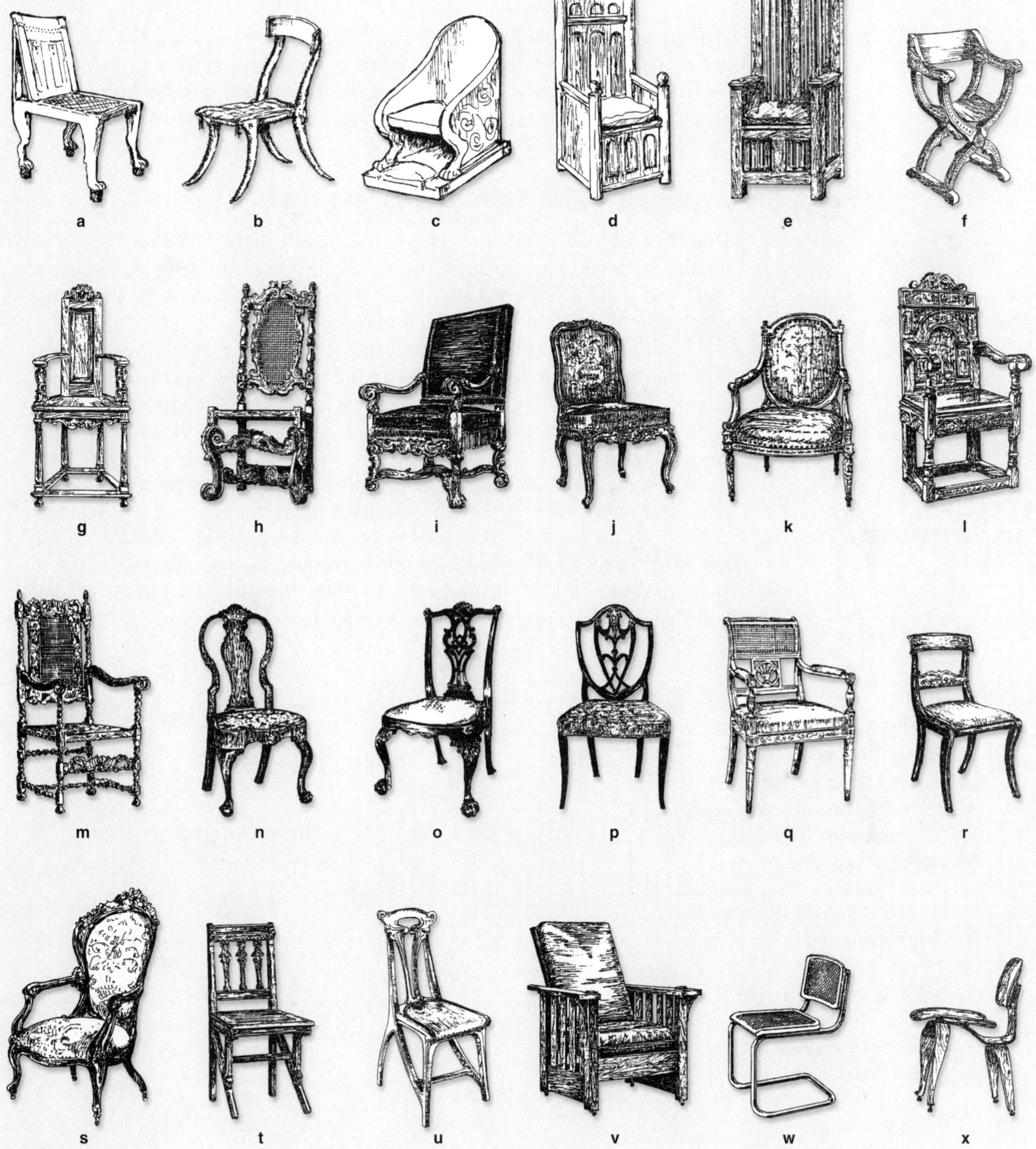

11-1

Period Chairs

- **a** Egyptian.
- **b** Greek klismos.
- **c** Roman throne.
- **d** Romanesque.
- **e** Gothic high-back.
- **f** Italian Renaissance Dante.
- **g** French Renaissance Caquetoire.
- **h** Louis XIII.
- **i** Louis XIV French Baroque.
- **j** Louis XV Rococo.
- **k** Louis XVI Neoclassic.
- **l** English Wainscot.
- **m** Restoration.
- **n** Queen Anne.
- **o** Georgian Chippendale.
- **p** Georgian Hepplewhite.
- **q** Georgian Sheraton.
- **r** Empire side chair.
- **s** Victorian.
- **t** Eastlake.
- **u** Art Nouveau.
- **v** Morris.
- **w** Bauhaus.
- **x** Eames.

changes in form, from period to period, are logical transitions, but some are reactionary. Occasionally a style is eclectic, borrowing from a period in the past. The chair provides a clear example of style trends through history. The earliest chairs are functional, then increasingly decorative, and eventually more comfortable.

Draperies and Window Dressings

URL http://www.victoriandrapes.com/index.html

URL http://www.amazondrygoods.com

Draperies are one of the main decorative details that bring character to an interior setting. Their elegance or cheapness, period, style or lack of style, and even their complete absence contribute immeasurably to the visual expression of the kind of place and people in the play.

From historical references, the designer can plan to use draperies that, depending on the period, may hang on a window, door, fireplace mantel, picture, or mirror. The designing of draperies is based on a knowledge of the look of a period, the way material drapes or hangs, and the methods of cutting and assembling material into desired shapes.

A designer needs to prepare a carefully scaled and dimensioned drawing of the assembled drapery, specifying the material and the action, if any. Window curtains, for example, may have to be opened or closed for a tableau during the action of the play. As with the rest of the set, the designer is expected to guide the execution of the draperies and therefore needs to have a general knowledge of drapery patterns and assembly techniques (Figure 11-2).

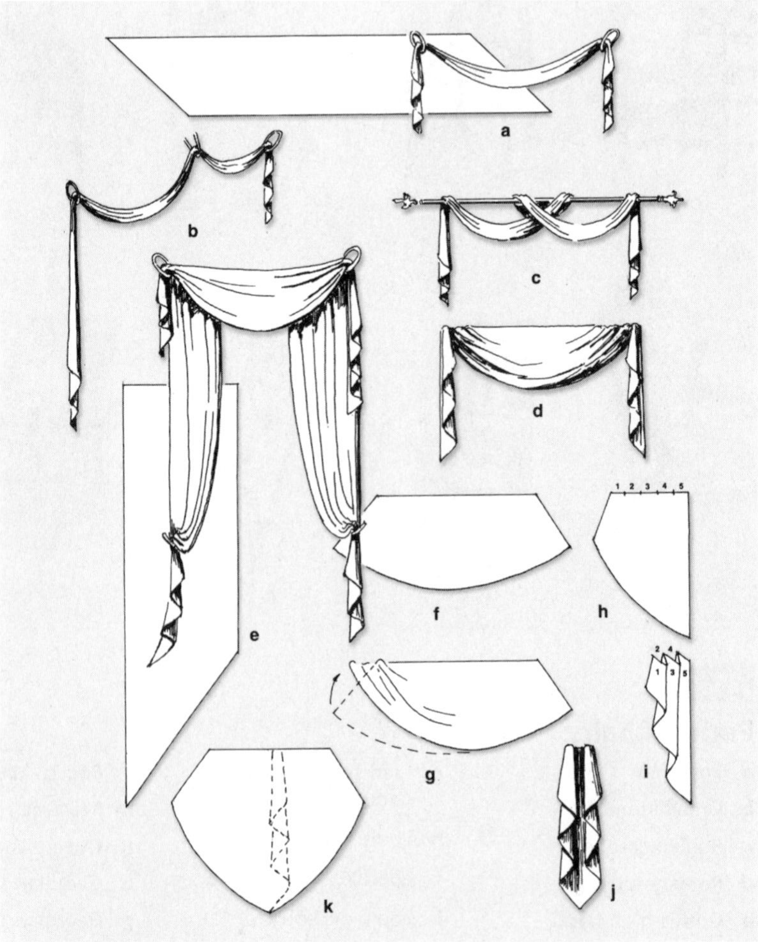

11-2

Drapery and Valance Patterns

- **a** Festoon valance and pattern.
- **b** Eccentrically draped festoon valance.
- **c** Crossed festoons as valance.
- **d** Valance of swag and tail piece.
- **e** Festoon valance and side draperies showing pattern for side drapery.
- **f** Swag pattern.
- **g** Draping swag.
- **h** Pattern of tail.
- **i** Draping or folding a tail.
- **j** Double or central tail.
- **k** Pattern for central tail.

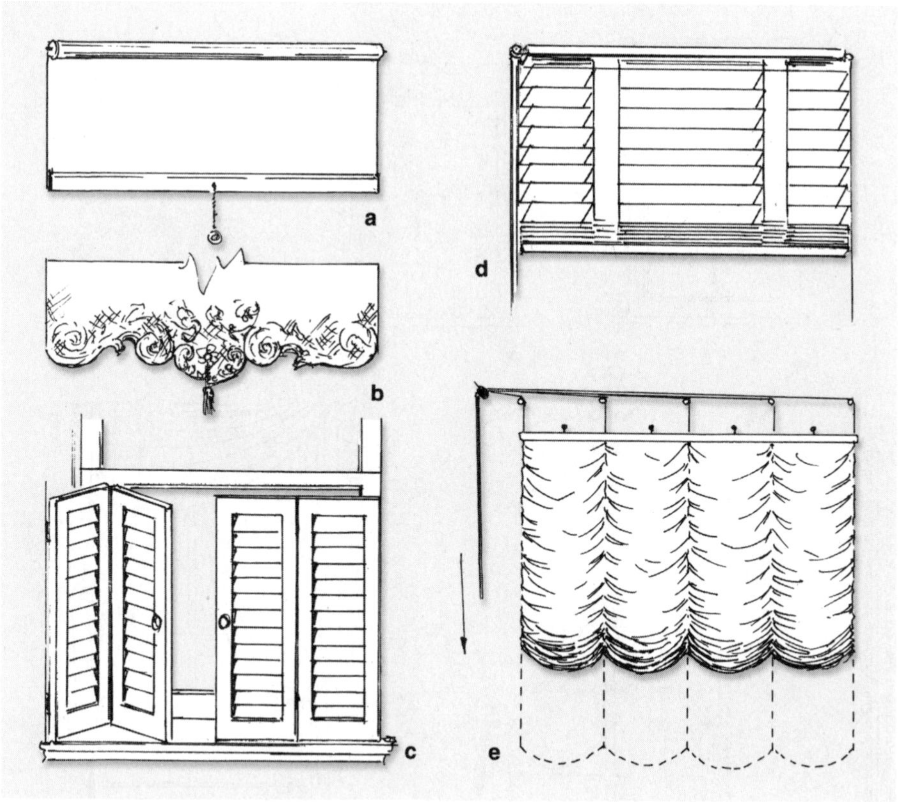

11-3

Blinds, Shades, and Shutters

a Roller blind.
b Decorative roller blind.
c Shutters.
d Venetian blinds.
e Austrian shade drape.

Although draperies may serve in many places in a setting, the fundamental parts making up the decorative portion are the same as those used to dress windows. The basic parts of a window dressing—all of which may or may not be used in the same treatment—are the **blind** or *shade,* the **glass curtain,** the **overdrapery,** and the **valance.** The overdrapery and valance are the frame, so to speak; the glass curtain diffuses the outside light; and the blind cuts off the view into the room from the outside.

The Blind or Shade Early blinds were shutters, both outside and inside the window. They offered protection from weather and break-ins. Recall from Chapter 10 the Austrian shade drape, which can be used for a grand window as well as a stage curtain. In both applications it is pulled up from the bottom by a series of vertical liftlines that have been threaded through rings on the back of the curtain. Roller blinds, both plain and decorative, as well as Venetian blinds are common (Figure 11-3).

blind A window covering used to block out light. There are various types, the most common being Venetian blinds and roller blinds. Also called a *shade.*

URL http://www.shutterblinds.com

The Glass Curtain Usually made of a translucent material or lace, the glass curtain is used to diffuse the outside light. It may be rigged to draw closed or may tie back in a soft drape. On some occasions, the curtain might be the final decorative feature, with no overdrapery. A half curtain is often used on a smaller window.

glass curtain A sheer or translucent fabric used to allow light inside a room and not allow a viewer from outside to see inside.

The Overdrapery Made of a rich and heavy material, the overdrapery serves as the vertical frame for the window. It adds a decorative and color accent to a room. An overdrapery may have the same action as the curtain, such

overdrapery Draped or gathered fabric, usually heavy and opaque, used as a decorative window treatment. Sometimes permanent, sometimes functional, it is often used in conjunction with a glass curtain.

11-4

Window Drapery Treatments

Drapery treatments vary for different window types.

as drawing from right to left, or may be draped to a hook or tieback. A fixed overdrapery can be made to a pattern that enhances its drape (Figure 11-4).

valance The uppermost decorative frame of a window drapery treatment. Sometimes a valance is draped fabric, as in a swag, or a hard surface either painted or covered with fabric.

The Valance The decorative potential of a window dressing lies mainly in the valance, which accordingly requires a great variety of draping techniques. A valance is made up of swags, plaits, tails, and wing pieces—sometimes incorporated into one drape, such as the festoon valance (Figure 11-2a). More often, though, the valance is made of separate swags and wings that are joined together to look like a single piece of fabric (Figure 11-2d, e).

A valance can be boxed and crowned with a cornice or an architectural feature, or the swags may be padded or stiffened into a fixed silhouette. Figure 11-5 illustrates a few options.

Drapery Materials The materials for window draperies are divided into three groups:

1. The transparent or sheer fabrics for glass curtains and some types of draped shades

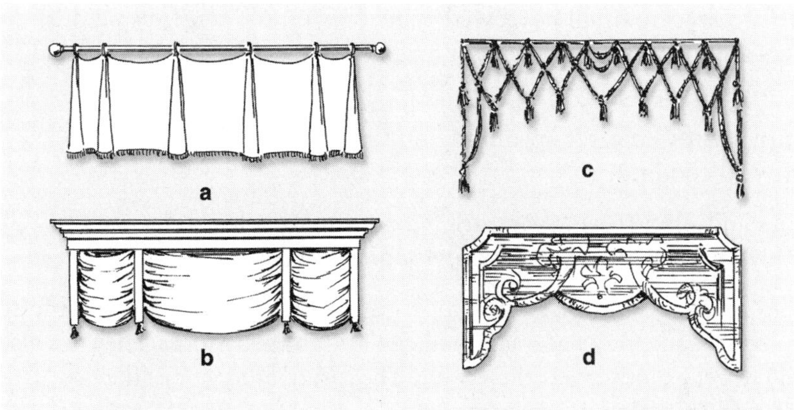

11-5

Valances

a Café curtain as valance.

b Boxed festoon.

c Draped rope or braid.

d Rigid valance covered with fabric.

2. The usually translucent but sometimes opaque materials for the shade
3. The opaque materials for the overdrapery and valance

The sheer materials include chiffon, organdy, net, or theatrical gauze, to name a few. Muslin, silk, and handkerchief linen are examples of translucent fabrics. Although the opaque materials for overdraperies are numerous, they are usually fabrics that will drape well, such as velour, velveteen, corduroy, or monk's cloth.

Borrowing or Renting Properties

Nonprofessional and professional producing groups alike must rely on renting and borrowing furniture or else maintain in storage a collection of stock period furniture for continuous use. Storing select period pieces is by far the most satisfactory method of securing properties for a repertory or stock company. Stock furniture can be varied with new upholstery and painted for reuse in future productions. However, storage is not always feasible, because of space limitations.

A producing group that depends on borrowing furniture and other articles must make an effort to maintain goodwill with the community. It pays to be businesslike and courteous when borrowing properties. Unfortunately, many a property room has been furnished with unreturned props—which is obviously not the way to build goodwill. Developing a positive relationship with local vendors and other props people in the area will always pay off in the long run. A few simple rules for borrowing will help create a friendly but professional way of handling a loan:

URL http://www.proppeople.com

1. Make a list of each borrowed article, including the name and address of the owner, date borrowed and date to be returned, estimated value, description noting condition (scratches, cracks, or parts missing), and remuneration (cash, complimentary tickets, or program credit). Request a signed receipt from the owner upon return of the article. Most lenders will insist on this for their own records.
2. Have just one person, rather than different people, do the borrowing for each production. It is easier to develop a relationship with a lender if the same person always does the borrowing.
3. Never borrow priceless heirlooms or irreplaceable antiques.

4. Take special care of all borrowed properties on the stage, using dust covers and padding to prevent damage during use in production and in storage.
5. Return borrowed pieces promptly on the date promised and in the borrowed condition.
6. Secure and file a receipt. Records become an excellent resource for quickly locating and reborrowing for another production.

Purchasing properties instead of borrowing them allows a company to alter the pieces in any way necessary and can add to their stock. They are also more likely to get exactly what they want. The disadvantages are the probable higher cost and increased need for storage.

Borrowing or renting often means less time building props and less money used on unique pieces that are not likely to be used again. Renting is usually cheaper than buying. The downside of borrowing or renting includes the inability to alter the piece in any way. As well, extreme care must be used with these props onstage. Of course, using the same props in future productions means paying to rent them again.

MAKING AND REMAKING FURNITURE

Prop shops are often called on to build pieces of furniture, a difficult and time-consuming task. Further, not all shops have a props artisan who can make complicated pieces. There are, however, several styles of furniture that may more easily be made than found or borrowed. The pieces shown in Figure 11-6 can be made without extremely fine furniture-building skills. If the furniture is to be painted rather than stained, cheaper and varied materials can be used and screw heads can be hidden with spackle; this is faster and easier than worrying about fine detail. The newly constructed pieces in Figure 11-7 require somewhat more expertise.

11-6

Easy-to-Make Furniture

These pieces require minimal time and skill, especially if they are to be painted rather than stained.

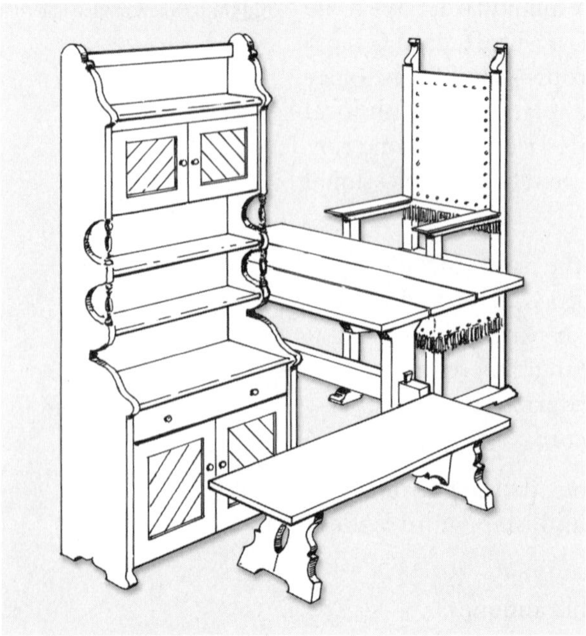

Furniture can sometimes be altered, especially if the alteration involves a reduction in size rather than an increase. Of course, it all depends on the piece at hand and what the designer wants. The practiced eye of the designer or props person will be able to see in an otherwise hideous late Victorian "masterpiece"—after a little painting, reupholstering, and trimming away excess parts—a Louis XIV side chair that would fool Molière. Given enough time, patience, and skill, a props artisan can turn a secondhand furniture store into a treasure house of "antiques" (Figure 11-8).

When sundry set properties are brought together on the stage for the first time, some or all of the furniture may have to be upholstered for either color or compositional reasons. Extensive reupholstering on borrowed pieces can be done only with the express permission of the lender, although

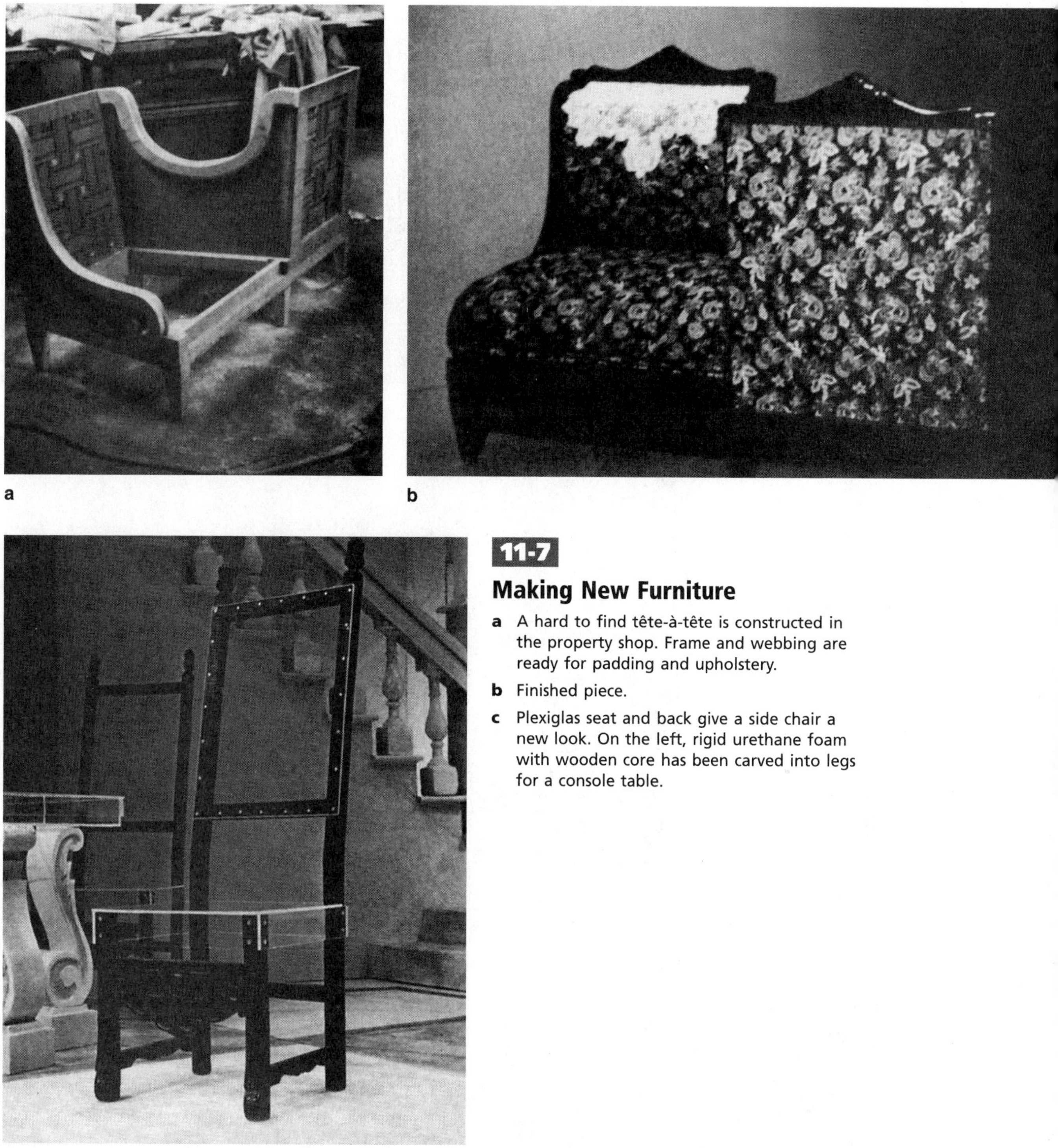

a b c

11-7

Making New Furniture

a A hard to find tête-à-tête is constructed in the property shop. Frame and webbing are ready for padding and upholstery.

b Finished piece.

c Plexiglas seat and back give a side chair a new look. On the left, rigid urethane foam with wooden core has been carved into legs for a console table.

it is sometimes possible to cover the existing surface with a new material by catching it lightly with a needle and thread. (There are those situations in which the piece is lent only on condition that it be reupholstered, repaired, or strengthened, but one cannot count on this.) Real antiques of course require greater care. Any treatment of furniture pieces must also take into account its use onstage. If the furniture is borrowed, the props department must obtain permission for any surface treatment or structural change.

11-8

Remaking Furniture

Remodeling a sofa:

a Before alterations.

b Back removed, reupholstered, and freshly painted.

Tufting:

c Tufted sofa.

d Rear view of ties used to form tufts.

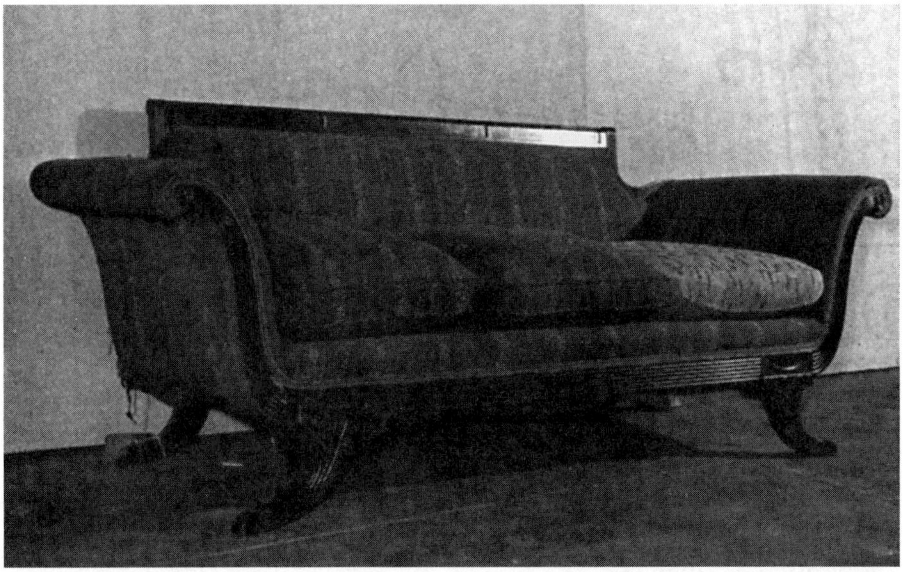

a

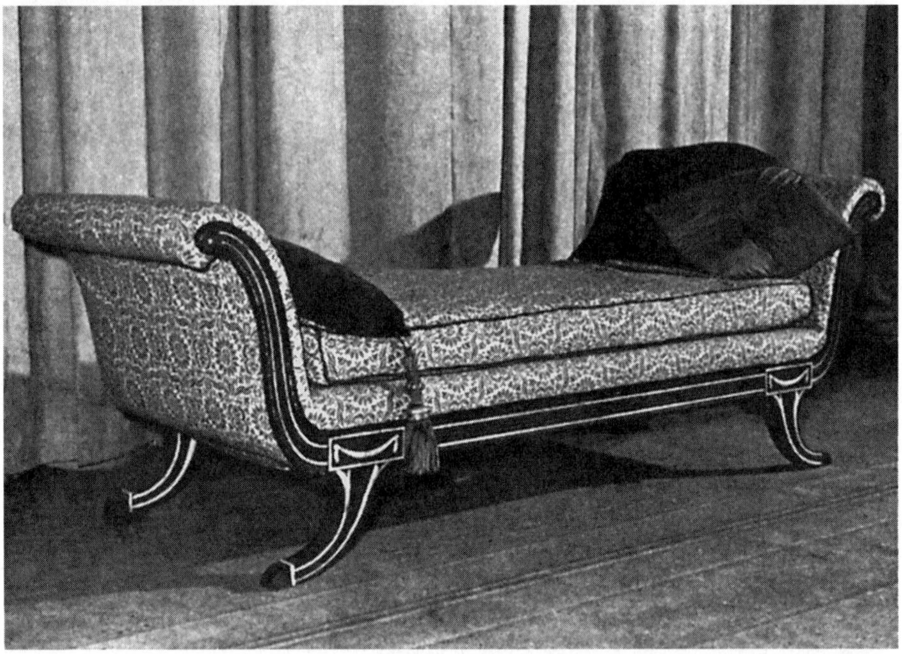

b

c

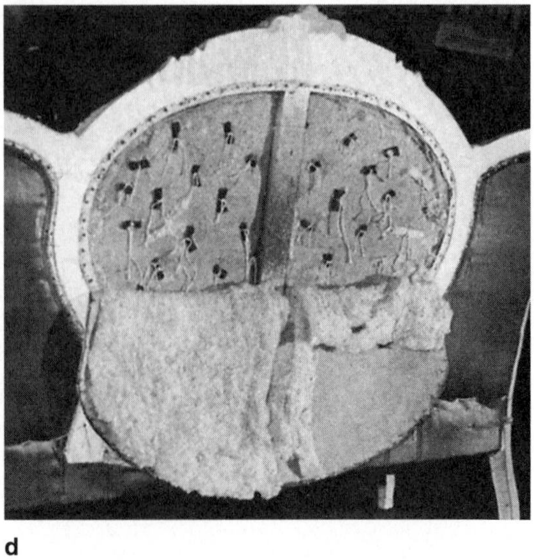

d

a–d PHOTOS COURTESY GENE DISKEY

To reupholster furniture that belongs to the theatre, it is best to follow the same method of covering used originally. If the old covering is removed carefully, the pieces can serve as a pattern for cutting the new material. This can save hours of time. While the upholstering is off, repairs can be made to the springs, webbing, and padding, and the piece can be painted. If the furniture is going to be kept in stock, the padding should be covered first with muslin, which serves as a base for any future changes in upholstering.

Expert upholstering will hide or cover any tacks or staples used. This may be accomplished in many ways. The material can be tacked on a hidden edge in back or underneath, or tacked to a surface that is later hidden by a covered panel. Exposed tacks can be covered with a decorative gimp braid or fringe. Studded tacks can be left exposed as a decorative feature in themselves. Pleating that is done to shape fabric around a curve can also be used as a form of decoration (Figure 11-9).

URL http://www.upholster.com

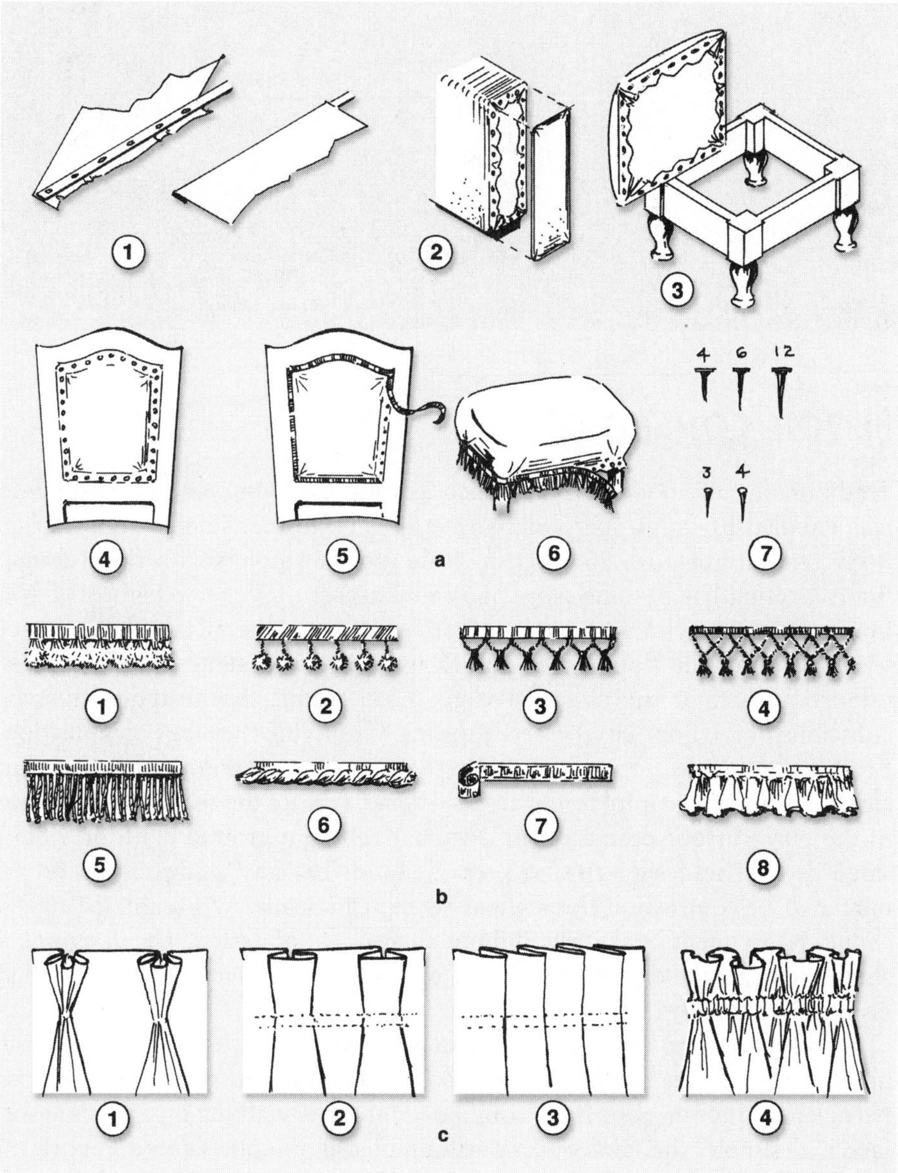

11-9

Upholstering Techniques

a Tacking:
- **1** Hidden tacking.
- **2** Tacking covered by panel.
- **3** Tacking kept on an unexposed surface.
- **4** Decorative tacking.
- **5** Tacking covered with gimp braid.
- **6** Tacking covered with fringe.
- **7** Upholstering tacks (4, 6, 12) and gimp tacks (3, 4).

b Fringes, braids, and ruffle:
- **1** Fringe.
- **2** Ball fringe.
- **3** Tassel fringe.
- **4** Tassel fringe.
- **5** Bullion fringe.
- **6** Braid.
- **7** Gimp braid.
- **8** Ruffle.

c Pleats:
- **1** Pinch pleat.
- **2** Box pleat.
- **3** Accordion pleat.
- **4** Gathering.

PHOTO COURTESY ALBERT FILONI

11-10

Floor Covering

Ramped floor for a production of *Macbeth*. The wood frame and cover are textured with fiberglass. Designer, Albert Filoni.

FLOOR COVERING

Traditionally, any floor covering (such as rugs, carpeting, and ground cloth) was handled by the property department, as it was considered set dressing. In present-day theatre, however, with its greater emphasis on floor design, floor covering has become more and more a part of scenery (Figure 11-10). In a proscenium with an increased seating gradient that allows the audience to see more of the floor, or on the thrust and arena stage, the floor is an important part of the overall design. As a result, the designer must be conscious of the floor covering as a means of unifying the stage composition. Even if the floor is not overly visible to the audience, the proper treatment can be immensely helpful to the actors trying to create the reality of the world of the play. A floor design might involve painting a ground cloth or a built stage deck. The designer must keep in mind that any stage setting on an unrelated or contrasting floor seems to float in space. When this occurs, it should be an intentional effect and not an accident of design. The design plan should indicate the texture, materials, or patterns that will anchor the design visually to the floor.

If affordable, an applied material might be used. An example of this is the use of lauan pieces for a parquet floor or painted tempered Masonite or particleboard for marble. If the sound of characters walking on a specific surface is desirable, the choice of flooring materials becomes more important. As always, this choice depends on cost and on the needs of the production. An arena or thrust stage increases the need for the use of real materials.

Latex and acrylic-based paints are durable enough to use on rigid surfaces, especially when they are later glazed with clear latex or acrylic. Such a surface can be damp-mopped and polished to perfection for each performance.

There are many examples of unusual floor coverings that go beyond conventional ground cloth or painted floor: real dirt in *Tobacco Road,* for example, or artificial snow in *Ethan Frome.* There have been productions in which the entire stage floor and scenery were covered with free-form overstuffed canvas, which obviously encouraged very unconventional movement. The designer must be open to any and all kinds of materials.

A stage floor may have to be covered for purely technical rather than artistic reasons. An entire stage, for example, may have to be built up to surround a turntable or to provide slots to guide wagon movements. Stage floors are also notorious for their poor condition, a situation that bothers dancers the most. To correct this, most ballet companies and dance groups cover an imperfect floor with one of several available vinyl coverings. Some dance companies even carry their own portable floor. For example, D'Anser, the trademark name of a portable modular floor, was designed by Ronald Bates and Perry Silvey of the New York City Ballet. Transported in 4-by-8-foot units, this floor is 3 inches thick, with offset wooden supports that allow for the "bounce" dancers want. The units connect with interlocking hardware and can cover an entire stage area.

URL http://www.stagestep.com

FABRICATING AND CASTING TECHNIQUES

Properties often require decorative details or bold relief at an exaggerated scale, beyond that of conventional furniture. These and other forms (such as architectural details, costume armor plate, small properties, and various free forms) are often made in the shop to obtain the exact shape and dimension the designer seeks. The forms may be fabricated or cast from a real object or from the prepared mold of a three-dimensional shape. These same techniques can be used to adapt a "found" object.

URL http://www.wizardsden spfx.com

Papier-Mâché

The term *mâché work* has grown to include all techniques and materials used to mold or fake carved relief detail on furniture or scenery. The original papier-mâché technique used paper or paper pulp, which was either modeled directly on the surface or, in order to duplicate a pattern repeatedly, was fashioned from a plaster mold.

When modeling directly with papier-mâché, the props person uses a porous paper, such as tissue, paper toweling, or newsprint. After being torn into convenient strips and dampened in water, the paper is dipped into a binder consisting of wheat paste and strong glue size. Any excess binder is lightly squeezed out of the now near-pulp mass, which is then applied to the furniture surface and modeled into the desired shape. If the relief is high, some preliminary modeling can be done with wire screening, to which the mâché is applied as the final surface. The technique is similar to that described in Chapter 7 for the construction of large irregular shapes.

To duplicate identical forms, the same process can be applied to a greased positive or negative mold. As mâché dries, it shrinks noticeably; when molding, the props person needs to consider what the final size will be.

URL http://www.paperclay.co.uk/papierm.htm

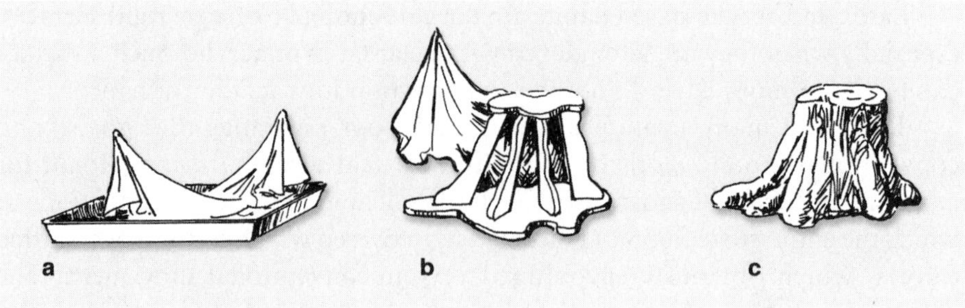

11-11

Fabric and Glue

- **a** Fabric soaked in glue and water.
- **b** Glue-soaked fabric draped over prepared understructure.
- **c** Final form after fabric and glue have dried.

Alternatives to Papier-Mâché

Because papier-mâché is fragile, a sturdier substance is often needed. The easiest and cheapest method is the use of muslin and glue (Figure 11-11). The muslin (or any other fabric) is soaked in glue and shaped or molded in a negative or positive mold. As the glue dries, the fabric hardens in the desired shape.

The industry standard for this kind of work used to be Celastic, a cheesecloth material impregnated with cellulose nitrate and a fire retardant. However, because working with it requires the use of acetone, Celastic should *never* be used. The fumes from acetone can be deadly, getting into the bloodstream and eventually causing brain damage, after much exposure. At the very least, acetone can cause a serious rash if left on the skin.

URL http://amaco.co.uk/friendly.htm

Several products on the market today serve just as well and are much safer. "Friendly Plastic" and Wonderflex are two examples. These products are thermoplastics that become soft enough, after immersion in hot water, to form over positive molds. Available in a variety of thicknesses, they yield various degrees of strength and capacity for detail.

URL http://www.sculpturalarts.com

Sometimes stronger products are required. Sculpt-or-Coat can be used to create irregular forms or used with felt or towels to build up forms in a mold. It is available in 1- or 5-gallon buckets.

URL http://www.Koolseal.com

Another alternative is an elastomeric (polymer with similar qualities to rubber) roofing compound such as Kool Seal and Jaxan. Both are readily available at home-improvement centers. Paper towels dipped in Kool Seal are first pulled through the fingers to remove the excess, just as with papier mâché, and then draped over a form to create a tough, flexible, and waterproof coat that will not chip or crack.

Styrofoam

URL http://www.rosco-ca.com/products/scenic/foamcoat.html

URL http://www.barbizon.com/reference/paint.html

Architectural detail, sculptural pieces, and out-of-the-way dress props may often be fashioned out of Styrofoam. The big advantage of Styrofoam is that it is easy to carve and quite lightweight (Figure 11-12). However, Styrofoam is fragile, and its surface needs to be protected or hardened. Either a seal of flexible glue alone or cheesecloth adhered with glue or Foamcoat (a water-based, nontoxic coating manufactured especially for coating Styrofoam) will work, but one must still be careful.

URL http://www.dow.com/craft/index.htm

URL http://www.aeromfg.com.au/styrofoam.html

More importantly, the user also needs to be aware of the dangers inherent in using Styrofoam. It has high flammability (as do all other foams), and it releases toxic gas when heated. This means that cutting it with any kind of power tool, including a hotwire, will produce toxic fumes. Care should also be taken when gluing Styrofoam pieces. Most adhesives contain solvents that

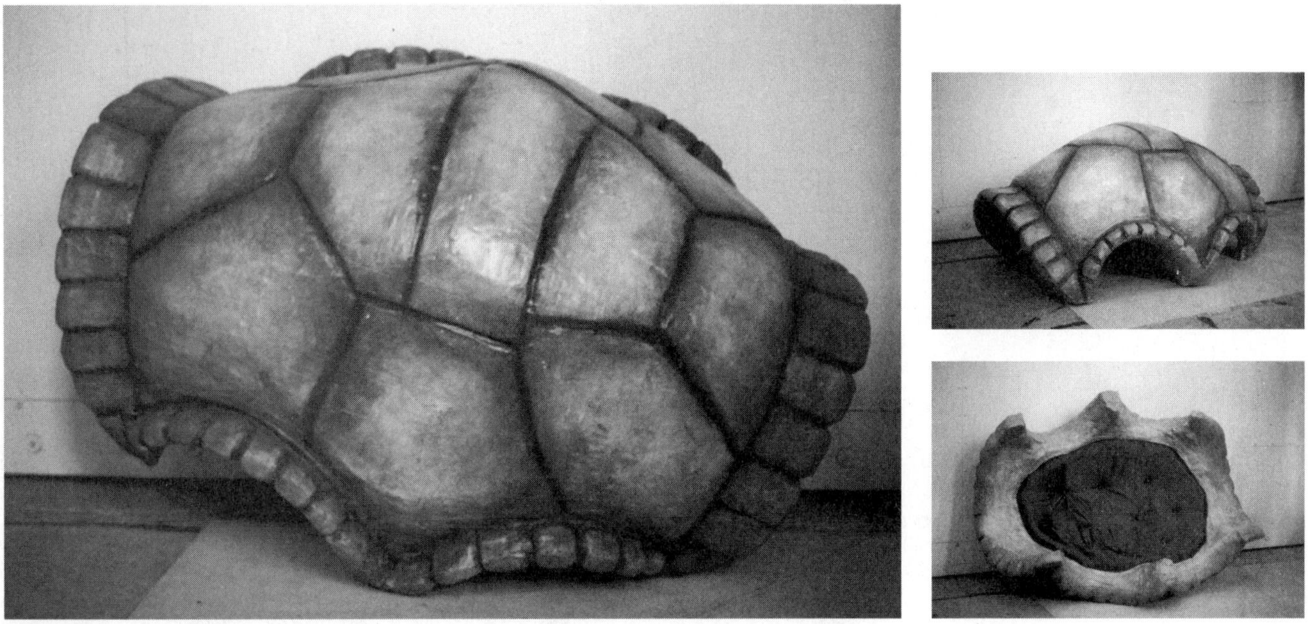

11-12

Styrofoam Turtle Shell

This turtle shell needed to support weight and was seen on all sides. Carved out of wood and Styrofoam for a production of *the Tempest.*

will dissolve Styrofoam. A panel adhesive or mastic should be used, but they are generally not heavy duty. Liquid Nails is one adhesive made specifically for foams.

URL http://www.liquidnails.com

Fiberglass

Fiberglass is another medium for creating three-dimensional details on scenery or properties. The technique is similar to working with papier-mâché. The artist shapes a fiberglass cloth over a positive form or into a negative mold after first coating the mold with a releasing agent. However, fiberglass is used only rarely in the theatre because of its expense, toxicity, and inherent danger (working with tiny pieces of glass fiber). The only reason to use fiberglass is if the scenery is to be used outdoors and must be waterproof. Even then, extreme precautions must be taken. It should be used when absolutely no other product will work.

A safer alternative to fiberglass is a product called Aqua-Resin. This is used and worked exactly like fiberglass but is completely nontoxic.

URL http://aquaresin.com/

Mask Making and Body Armor

Some of the mâché techniques can be applied to the making of full or partial masks, or, in some cases, to appear as decorative details on scenery. Figure 11-13 illustrates the designing and making of masks. Many forming techniques can be used, such as papier-mâché, Sculpt-or-Coat, rubber latex, Wonderflex, and Aqua-Flex. As with any prop, the type of mold used and the qualities and use of the finished piece determine the choice of materials. One must also consider the build time available as well as the skills of the prop shop.

a

b

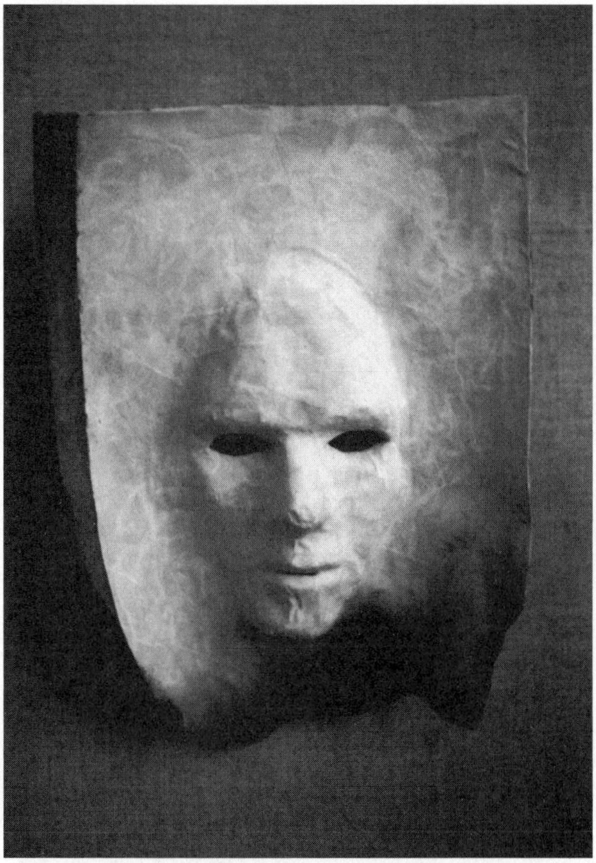

c

d

c PHOTO COURTESY LINDSAY LEADER
d PHOTO COURTESY JESSICA NOBLE

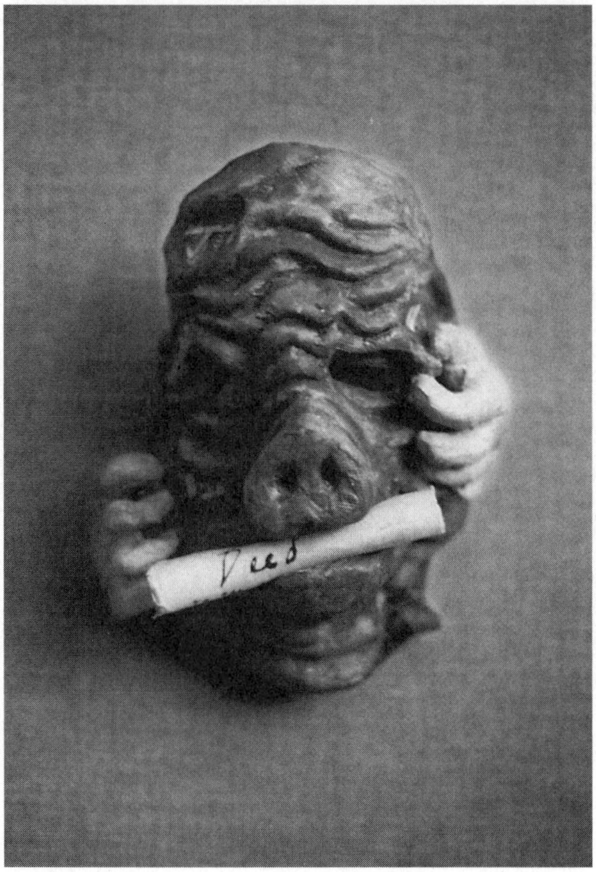

e

e PHOTO COURTESY MARIE WAGNER

11-13

Mask-Making Techniques

a Mask variations based on single mold (viewed bottom center).

b Full and half masks using a variety of materials.

c Project for *Hedda Gabler* done as a movement piece. This mask, for the character of Eilert Lovborg, uses a store-bought neutral mask as the base. Designer, Lindsay Leader.

d Another mask for *Hedda Gabler* for the character of George Tesman. Rather than create a new "face" for the character, this mask frames the actor's face, essentially using negative space. Designer, Jessica Noble.

e A heavily textured and dimensional abstract mask for Big Daddy in *Cat on a Hot Tin Roof.* Designer, Marie Wagner.

11-14

Vacuum-Formed Properties

A few of the innumerable vacuum-formed articles.

a Prop telephone, architectural details, armor breastplate, and other articles in various stages of assembly and surface finish from Tobins Lake Studios.

b Full armor and shields, vacuum-formed from vinyl plastic sheets. The swords are made of tempered steel.

a

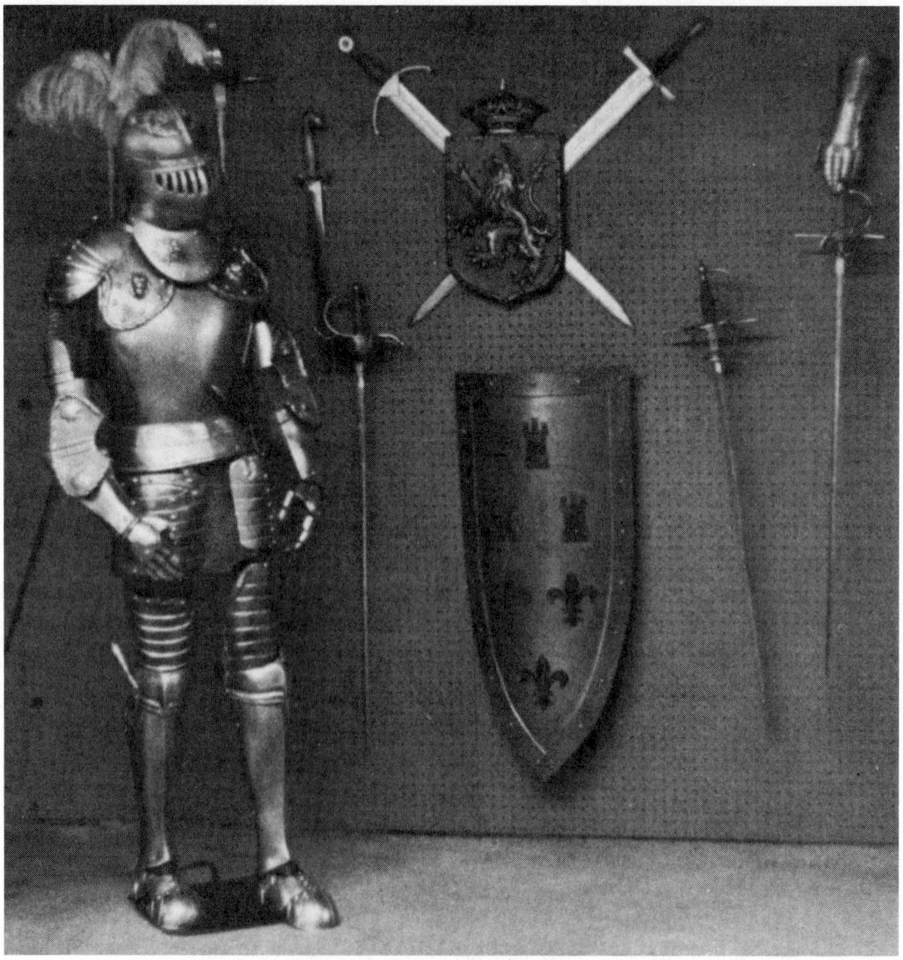

b

Leather is also a good option for making masks. It requires some time to learn the best techniques for working and shaping it but can result in extremely intricate shapes that will last a long time if cared for.

Body armor can be made from vacuum-formed vinyl. Figure 11-14 shows such armor and other props, as well as some of the molds used to create them.

VISUAL EFFECTS

Visual effects can either be simple to produce or require special skills and knowledge. Although many are electrified, most are still produced mechanically. Smoke, fire, and flash explosions are usually electrically controlled; however, smoke also can be made without electricity by combining solid carbon dioxide (dry ice) and water.

Some familiar visual effects created mechanically are the snow cradle and rain pipes. These and other special effects call on the ingenuity of the stage technician and property person to rig and trigger on cue (Figure 11-15).

URL http://www.technicreations.com

Breakaways

Many times pieces of furniture, dishes, or other objects have to break onstage. A chair that collapses, a flagpole that falls down, or a railing that breaks during a fight scene are a few examples of properties or scenery breaking on cue and in a predetermined manner.

In Figure 11-16, a railing breakaway is prebroken and lightly glued together. Thin strips of wood are tacked to the back of the repair to give a convincing splintering sound as the railing breaks again. Balsa wood should be used because it is the least likely to be dangerous. The pattern of the break

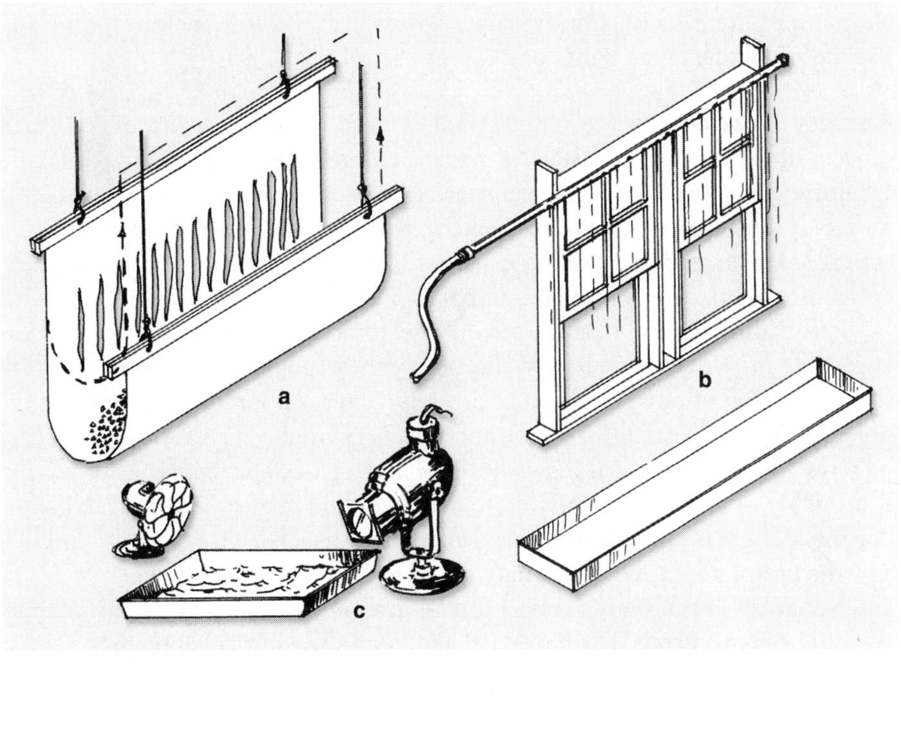

11-15

Tools for Visual Effects

a Snow cradle.

b Rain pipe.

c Water reflection trough.

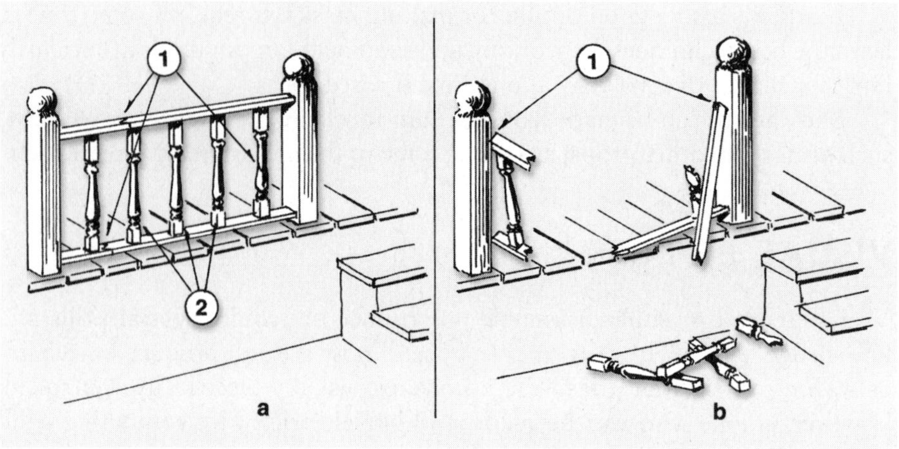

11-16

Breakaway Railing

a Railing prepared for breaking:
- **1** Prebroken spots, lightly glued.
- **2** Loose spindles, lightly glued.

b Railing after breaking:
- **1** Prepared hinge points.

is carefully planned in order to control the fall of the pieces in the same manner for each performance.

Breakaway Windowpanes and Mirrors Breaking real glass onstage is dangerous and must be avoided at all costs! There is no easy way to simulate this onstage, but there safe substitutes exist.

Although it can be cost-prohibitive, commercially manufactured breakaway glass is readily available. "Poured glass," which is really plastic, can also be used. Making poured glass is time-consuming, and getting the "recipe" exactly right can be difficult.

URL http://www.thegizmoshop.com/breakaway.html

One familiar substitute is candy glass, or hardened sugar and water. Candy glass is prepared like old-fashioned rock candy. After a supersaturated solution of sugar and water is brought to about 260 degrees Fahrenheit, it is poured onto a smooth surface, where it forms a thin sheet. The sheet hardens into a clear, transparent solid. Candy glass, however, has a low melting point and may soften under stage lights or excessive handling.

Pottery Breakaways Opaque shapes such as teacups, dishes, or small objects of art are much easier to make into breakaways than are glass and furniture. Because they are not transparent, inexpensive pottery or china pieces may be prebroken and lightly glued together again to ensure their breaking onstage. As the second breaking usually shatters the piece beyond reclaiming, a separate breakaway should be prepared for each performance.

If the authenticity, both in sound and look, of the breakaway object is extremely important to the play, a replica can be made by slipcasting. A clay slip or solution of powdered water clay and water is poured into a mold of the object and, after setting for a few minutes, is poured out. A thin shell of clay adheres to the mold, making a hollow casting of the object. After drying thoroughly (48 hours), the raw-clay casting is fired in a ceramic kiln to bisque hardness. A great number of props can be prepared this way. The time needed and the use of a kiln, however, may make this method unsuitable.

Neoprene (a synthetic rubber) can be used in the same fashion as the clay slip but needs no firing. The hardened neoprene shell shrinks enough to release it from an unsealed plaster mold. Commercially made breakaway pottery is also available.

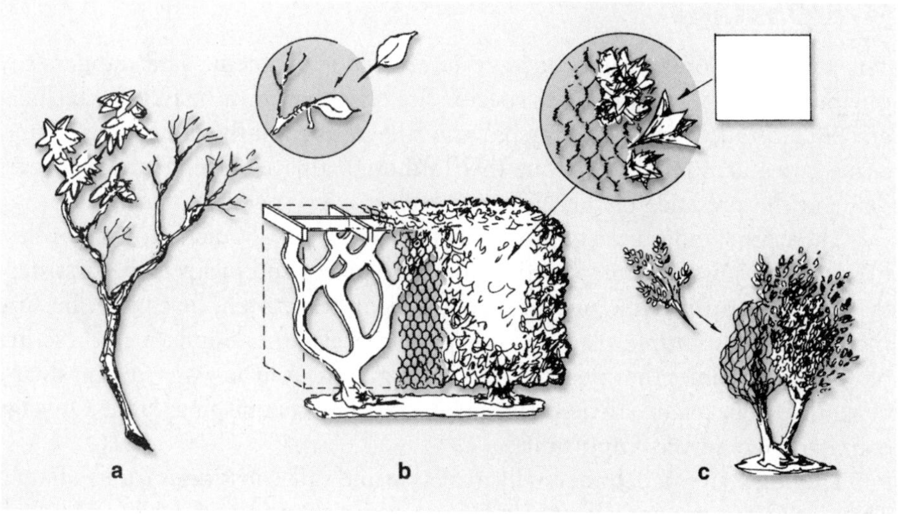

11-17

Foliage

a Artificial leaves wired or taped to real tree branches.

b Trimmed boxwood hedge made of frame covered with 1-inch-mesh chicken wire. Fabric squares or artificial leaves are pushed into openings (two or three shades of green used for a more convincing color).

c Chicken wire shaped over basic frame and filled with sprays of artificial boxwood.

Foliage

Artificial flowers and the foliage of hedges, bush pieces, and small trees are considered properties, as are live flowers, potted plants, and sprays of real leaves used to dress the setting. The expression *prop bush* means that the bush is not real but also implies that it is shaped in three dimensions, as opposed to a flat, painted set piece.

Lifelike artificial flowers can be obtained easily from display houses, local variety stores, or the home-decoration section of a department store. Numerous companies specialize in the manufacture and sale of artificial foliage. Although artificial flowers are more expensive than real ones, with proper care they can be used over again.

Stylized or caricatured blossoms have to be specially made. Their scale and design determine the material used. Exotic tropical flowers in a musical comedy, for example, have been made of velveteen or satin, with leaves made of wire loops covered with sheer chiffon. This is really a lost art, and for good reason—the process is extremely time-consuming and expensive.

A fairly realistic box hedge can be made of chicken wire holding sprays of artificial boxwood or flex leaves. Large-mesh chicken wire can support clumps of leaves on a tree branch or compose a hanging border related to a tree trunk. The leaf material, which can be either paper or fabric, should have sufficient stiffness to hold a leaflike shape, or else it will have to be stiffened with wire (Figure 11-17). Window-shade stock, which comes in several shades of green, makes a good leaf fabric to staple onto a branch or chicken-wire frame. Any of these methods requires fireproofing of the materials.

Fire Onstage

The use of an open flame onstage is always a problem. The dangers are obvious. As such, every city has specific fire laws that must be followed. Under any circumstances, the Fire Marshall must be notified of the use of open flame. Some cities are quite lax about this (although this is getting rarer); others demand the presence of the Fire Marshall at every performance.

There are standard safety procedures that everyone should follow regardless of what is required. Flameproofing all scenic pieces and props is the first step. If there is an open flame onstage, be it a cigarette, match, or candle, be sure that there are multiple places to extinguish the flame. Sometimes these are obvious, sometimes they need to be well disguised. A little water in an ashtray or sand in a bucket are efficient and cheap ways of extinguishing flame. Offstage containers are just as important.

There are several commercially available and safe substitutes for live flame. They are pricey, but not necessarily less expensive than paying the Fire Marshall every night. Candle substitutes are probably the easiest to find and use. Battery-operated candles can be built fairly easily or bought relatively cheaply. Flickering bulbs meant to look like live flame are now very convincing. They are safe and can be controlled by the actors.

SOUND EFFECTS

There was a time in theatre history when visual and sound effects were the main concern of the property department. Before the advent of high-tech recording, many sound effects were created mechanically by the property person. Most of these old machines are now gathering dust in the property room.

An adequate sound system and a good sound designer can bring any effect to the audience with a truer quality and more sensitive control than any mechanical sound effect could. There is one possible exception: the effect of offstage gunfire. The recordings of distant battle scenes are fairly convincing, but close rifle or revolver shots are better when a starter's gun with blank cartridges is fired backstage. Due to the inherent danger of firearms, it is getting more difficult to find ones that can be used onstage. Every state, and some cities, have very strict laws requiring permits for even a starter pistol or a gun that shoots only blanks. Although generally harmless when used properly, they can pose a real danger. It is *vital* to check with the local police to determine the local laws and how a prop gun can be legally obtained.

Figure 11-18 shows some of the mechanical sound effects that have traditionally been a part of the property department. Directors, on occasion, have requested old mechanical sound effects for their conceptual reasons rather than having the realism of electronic sound. However, most of these machines are not used anymore.

ADHESIVES

Most of the prop-building techniques that have been discussed required some kind of adhesive, and there are numerous types readily available. It is important that the right kind of adhesive be used for the specific material

11-18

Producing Sound Effects

a Wind machine.
b Rain (shot in rotating drum).
c Rain (shot in tray with wire-screen bottom).
d Thunder sheet.
e Rumble cart.
f Falling rubble after an explosion.
g Wood crash.
h Gun shots.
i Slap stick.
j Horses' hoofs.

being used. There should also be some consideration for the function of the prop. One that gets extremely hard use might need a strong adhesive in order to last through the production.

URL http://www.adhesivesmart.com

URL http://www.mmm.com

The most useful adhesives for porous materials such as paper and wood are white glue and hot-melt glue. White glue is the universal glue, useful for most jobs. Inexpensive and easy to use, it dries overnight. Hot-melt glue is more expensive but still cheap. It dries very quickly but can be dangerous—it is easy to burn one's fingers because the glue gets extremely hot.

For nonporous materials, epoxies work best. Industrial-strength epoxies are readily available, usually in two parts that must be mixed together to work.

There are many adhesives designed for specific materials. Mastics for foam have already been mentioned. Contact cement or rubber cement are both excellent for laminating porous materials. A variety of spray glues are available for gluing porous to nonporous materials.

Whatever adhesive is used, caution must be taken. Many adhesives must be used in well-ventilated areas, some with respirators and gloves and some used only if nothing else will work.

THE COMPUTER AND PROPS

As with every other aspect of theatre, the computer has proven to be of invaluable use in the prop shop. The most obvious use of the computer is for research. A large number of Web sites, some mentioned in this chapter, deal with prop-related issues. The Web offers chat rooms devoted to prop problems, directories of props artisans, and the sites of companies that cater to the theatre world.

URL http://www.cclabels.com/label-galleria.html

In addition, AutoCAD and similar software provide an excellent method for developing patterns to be cut out of plywood or other materials. Profile pieces or even three-dimensional objects such as a cabriole leg can be patterned in the computer and then printed in full scale to be traced onto the material. A light layer of spray adhesive will adhere the pattern to the work and can be easily removed if applied while still wet (not tacky).

The plotter and color printer can also be used with software such as Photoshop and any of the varied drawing and painting programs to create full-size or even oversized posters, menus, and any other printed materials.

Clearly, the stage designer needs to know a great deal about stage properties and how they are created. In the next section, we turn to another important aspect of theatre design—sound.

PART III

CHAPTER 12
Sound and Music in the Theatre

CHAPTER 13
Sound Systems and Equipment

Sound for the Theatre

"Music expresses, at different moments, serenity or exuberance, regret or triumph, fury or delight. It expresses each of these moods, and many others, in a numberless variety of subtle shadings and differences. It may even express a state of meaning for which there exists no adequate word in any language."

AARON COPLAND
WHAT TO LISTEN FOR IN MUSIC

12

Sound and Music in the Theatre

The use of sound and music in theatre is not new; its origins go back to primitive rituals that combined dramatic action with music and dance. However, sound as a separate theatrical design element on a par with scenery, costume, and lighting is a fairly recent development. Not so many years ago, theatre sound comprised primarily mechanical effects supervised by the properties department, while sounds requiring electricity, such as bells and buzzers, were relegated to the lighting and electrics department.

With the advent of high-fidelity recording and playback equipment in the 1960s, sound reproduction became a practical tool for the theatre. The next decade brought about more-sophisticated equipment for recording and playback. The synthesizer, a revolutionary electronic keyboard developed by Robert Moog, could reproduce a multitude of musical sounds. Digital technology followed, introducing compact discs, DAT (digital audio tape) recorders, sampling, hard disk recording, and advanced sound processing by means of digital audio workstations.

In a very short time, then, technology and a seemingly insatiable desire for more design freedom on the part of sound designers and technicians has revolutionized the art of sound design in the theatre. The venerable audio tape is now a thing of the past, having been replaced with recordable CDs and MiniDiscs. Today the sound designer/technician works his or her magic on a computer equipped with digital sound editing software. As a new permanent member of the design team, the sound designer offers exciting potential for enhancing today's theatrical production.

FUNDAMENTALS OF SOUND

Whether it be a favorite tune playing on a Discman, the environmental sounds of an afternoon spent in the park, or background chatter from an unwatched television, we are constantly surrounded by sound. The brain controls what we hear, through its remarkable ability to focus on a particular sound or reject it in order to concentrate on something else. As the composer Aaron Copland indicates, music affects us emotionally. It can heighten or relieve tension. In the theatre it can alter our perception of dramatic action. And, because of its temporal nature, music can alter our perception of time. The responsibility of the theatrical sound designer is to manipulate music and sound to enhance the effect of dramatic action.

The Phenomenon of Sound

We are most familiar with sound as air waves or vibrations within a certain range on the electromagnetic spectrum (Figure 12-1). However, nearly all of us have experienced hearing under water, which illustrates that sound moves more or less easily through nearly all materials. In fact, sound moves slowly through air, compared with most other mediums—only about 1,130 feet per second (approximately 1 foot per millisecond). It follows that sound cannot travel through a vacuum, because nothing exists from which waves can be created.

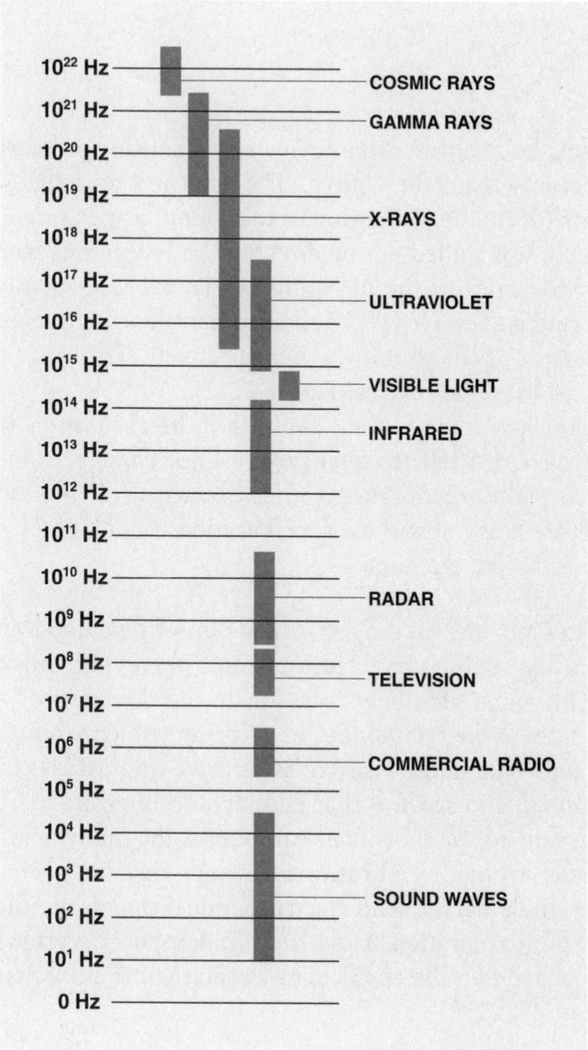

12-1

The Electromagnetic Spectrum

The normal range of human hearing is generally 20 to 20,000 hertz (cycles per second).

12-2

Sound Wave

A single cycle waveform.

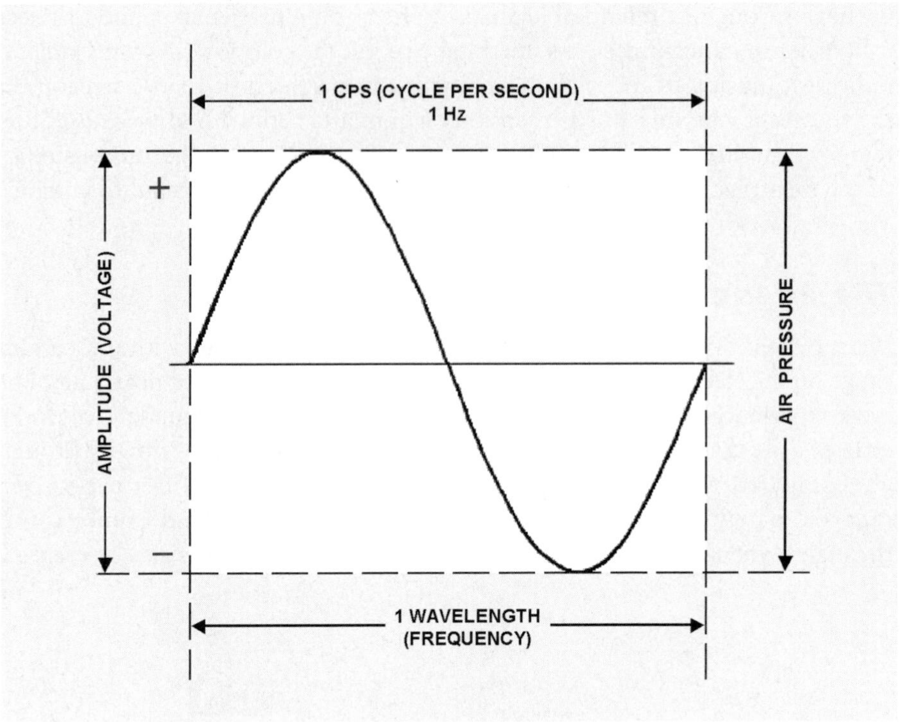

Sound is produced when a body at rest is made to vibrate, causing pressure waves to move in all directions from the source. The rate and amount of vibration play an important role in our perception of the sound. For example, when a harp string is plucked, it is pulled in one direction and rebounds past its original resting place. Molecules in the air mimic the movement of the string and thereby create sound waves. How far and how fast the string moves determine the height and length of the sound wave, respectively. This can be illustrated in graphic form as a series of cycles (Figure 12-2).

As sound waves move through the air, they diminish in height (loudness or **amplitude**), but the wavelength itself (**frequency**) does not change. Some surfaces absorb sound waves, while others cause them to bounce off. If a sound is reflected several times before being absorbed, **reverberation** occurs. Finally, the sound may reach a receptor, like our ears.

amplitude Measured in decibels (dB), amplitude is synonymous with volume or intensity. Amplitude is determined by the height of a sound wave.

frequency The rate at which a sound vibrates, measured in cycles per second or hertz (Hz). The length of a sound wave determines frequency. A sound's frequency determines its pitch.

reverberation The combination of multiple, blended sound images caused by reflections from walls and other surfaces. If reverberation time is long enough to discern individual sound, then it is referred to as an *echo*.

The Ear As can be seen in Figure 12-3, the ear is made up of several parts. The *pinna,* or outer ear, acts like an antenna to collect sound waves and direct them into the *ear canal.* The pinna also helps one locate the direction of a sound. The ear canal terminates at the *tympanum,* or eardrum, which vibrates in reaction to the sound waves. The middle ear contains three tiny *ossicles* or bones (called the *hammer, anvil,* and *stirrup*) that take up and intensify these vibrations. The fluid-containing *cochlea,* or inner ear, houses the many nerve endings that receive pressure from the vibrations through tiny hair cells. Responding to the pressure, these nerves send electrochemical signals via the auditory nerve to the brain for interpretation. Much important input concerning loudness and frequency is gathered in the cochlea; however, the brain is what selects and analyzes sounds.

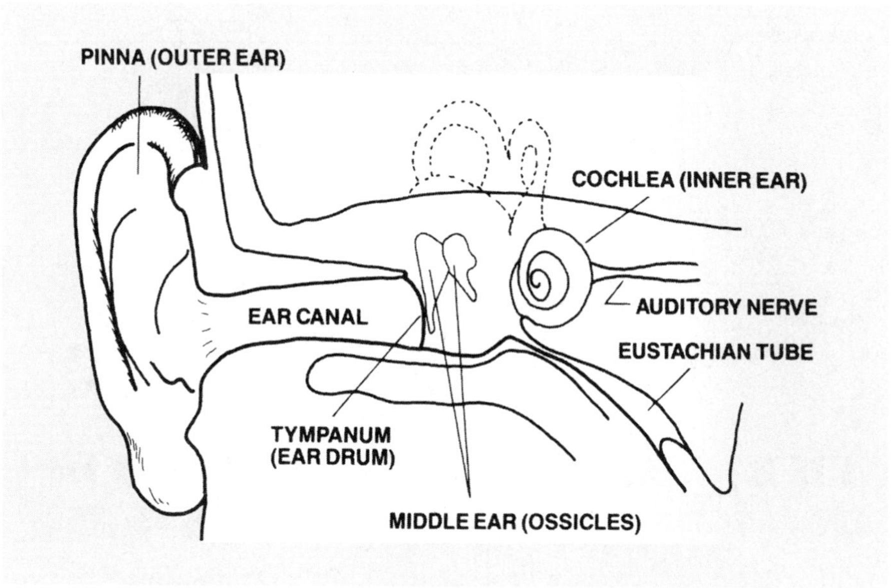

12-3
The Human Ear

Digital Audio

As we have seen, sound waves flowing through the air create a pattern analogous to the vibration of their source (as in the harp string). If received by a microphone, a copy or *analog* of these waves can be reproduced electronically and sent through a wire to a recording device such as a CD. However, in a *digital reproduction,* the direct action of a sound wave is not recorded; instead, a sound wave is measured, and the measurement (a numerical representation of the wave) is recorded. In essence, a "snapshot" of the sound wave is taken and recorded as a binary number on a CD or other recording device. To record all audible sound waves accurately, one must take a minimum of 44,100 measurements or "snapshots" of a wave *per second.* Known as the **sampling rate,** 44,100 samples per second is the rate used to produce a commercial CD. The digital recording of sound has allowed huge advances in the manipulation and playback of sound and music in the theatre.

sampling rate The number of times per second that an analog to digital converter (ADC) freezes and assigns a numerical value to the analog signal (voltage). A sampling rate of 44.1 thousand times per second is referred to as *CD quality.*

Measuring Sound

To describe a given sound, one needs a technical vocabulary that defines the components specifically enough to be meaningful. Although very few sounds are made up of a single frequency, all sounds can be broken down into their various component frequencies and amplitudes.

Frequency The length of a sound wave is defined according to its *frequency* in time and is measured in cycles per second or **hertz** (Hz). There is a direct relationship between *pitch* and frequency: the high-pitched sounds from a flute have high frequencies (shorter waves); the low-pitched sounds from a cello exhibit low frequencies. Frequency is the main characteristic that allows us to discern one sound from another. The normal human ear can hear frequencies from 20 Hz to 20,000 Hz (representing wavelengths from approximately

hertz A unit of measurement used to identify the frequency of a sound. Hertz (Hz) are equal to cycles per second or CPS.

12-4

Frequency Ranges

A comparison of musical sounds and their frequency ranges.

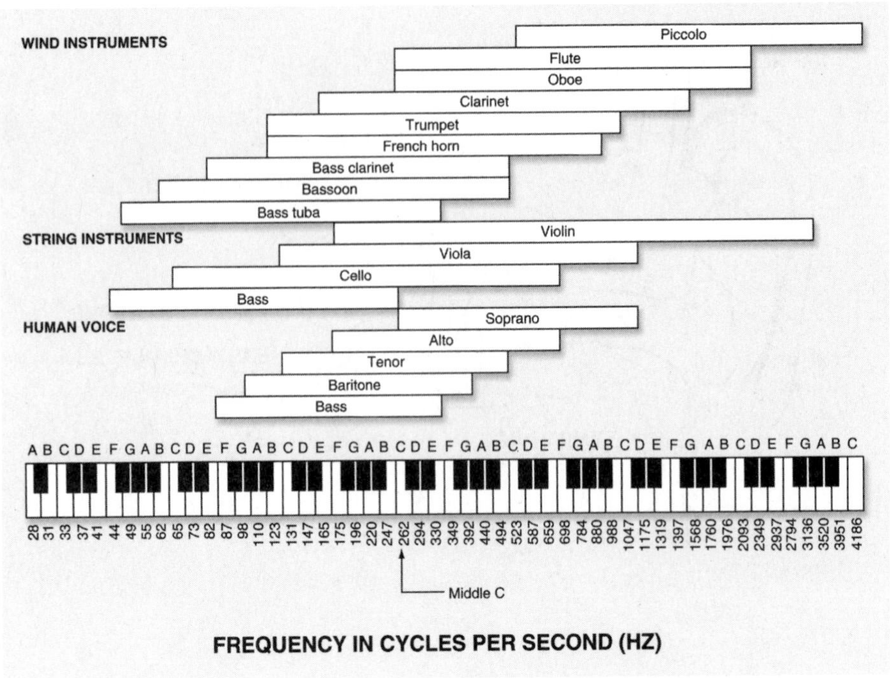

fifty-six feet to ⅔ inch long). Figure 12-4 shows some common frequency ranges for musical instruments and the human voice.

Amplitude The height of a sound wave is called its *amplitude,* which is synonymous with the volume or intensity of sound. The most common measure of amplitude is the **decibel** (dB), with 1 dB being the smallest difference that can be distinguished by the normal human ear. The decibel measurement is not on a linear scale, however; it is instead a ratio of two intensities. The next chapter provides more on decibel levels.

Here are some important terms and concepts concerning the volume of sound. **Sound pressure level (SPL)** is a standard measurement of loudness that uses decibel values (Figure 12-5). **Threshold of hearing** refers to the quietest sound human beings can hear, or 0 dB SPL. The **dynamic range** of a sound is the difference between its smallest and greatest amplitudes. In live situations, dynamic range is the difference between the ambient sound of a theatre auditorium (referred to as the "noise floor") and the loudest sound level. Finally, it is important to remember that sound intensity drops off by the square of the distance from the source *(inverse square law).*

decibel A measurement of sound intensity, the decibel (dB) describes a ratio of two quantities. One decibel is a measurement of electrical or acoustic power equal to ⅒ of a Bel (a unit named after Alexander Graham Bell).

sound pressure level (SPL) The measurement of acoustic pressure level in decibels.

threshold of hearing Normally defined as 0 dB SPL, this equates to the quietist sound that the ear can discern.

dynamic range The difference, measured in decibels, between the quietest and the loudest portion of a segment of sound. In a live situation, this usually is the difference between the loudest portion and the noise floor of the theatre.

Timbre and Harmonics As stated earlier, very few sounds are pure (containing a single frequency and amplitude). Most sound is made up of a combination of frequencies and amplitudes, which are perceived as a single sound. The relationship between the various frequencies and amplitudes determines the quality, or **timbre,** of the sound. Timbre is the distinction in sound between two different musical instruments playing an identical note at the same volume.

timbre The tonal quality of a note, sung or played on a musical instrument, that includes the fundamental frequency of the note combined with all of the harmonics (overtones) created. Timbre is what distinguishes the sound of two different musical instruments playing an identical note at the same volume.

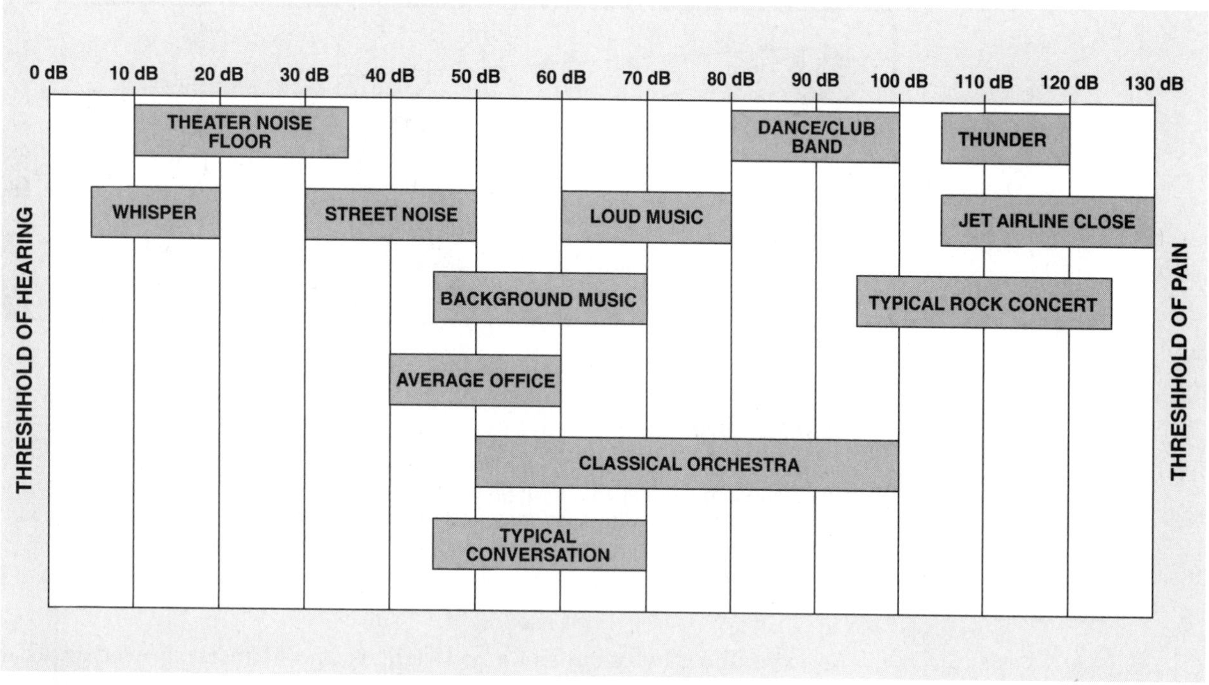

12-5

Sound Pressure Levels (Loudness)

A range of various sound pressure levels between 0 dB, the threshold of hearing, and 130 dB, the threshold of pain.

A determining factor in timbre is **harmonics**, a musical term for frequencies that are multiples of a primary or fundamental frequency. Harmonics are present in all complex sounds and contribute greatly to the uniqueness of a sound. Timbre is also affected by the sound instrument's *resonator.* Normally the body or case of the instrument, the resonator helps to create a sound unique to that instrument.

harmonics The overtones that are created when a note is played on a musical instrument. Normally these are multiples of the root frequency.

Perception

Sound and vision are the tools we use to recognize our surroundings. Vision is unidirectional, while sound perception is omnidirectional. The two work together to determine our environmental sensitivity. By a process of *triangulation,* our two ears give us the ability to locate generally the sound of, say, a chirping bird. We then look in the direction of the sound to discover more information (Figure 12-6). Because of the placement of our ears, locating a sound on the horizontal axis is easier than doing so vertically.

To learn how to manipulate sound effectively, the theatrical sound designer must be acquainted with additional principles of sound perception concerning distance and loudness, masking, recognition, and reverberation.

Distance and Loudness The inverse square law tells us that the loudness of a sound decreases significantly over distance. In addition, air absorbs sound energy. The higher the frequency, the greater the absorption. As a result, distant sound is not only perceived as softer than close sound, it also lacks higher frequencies.

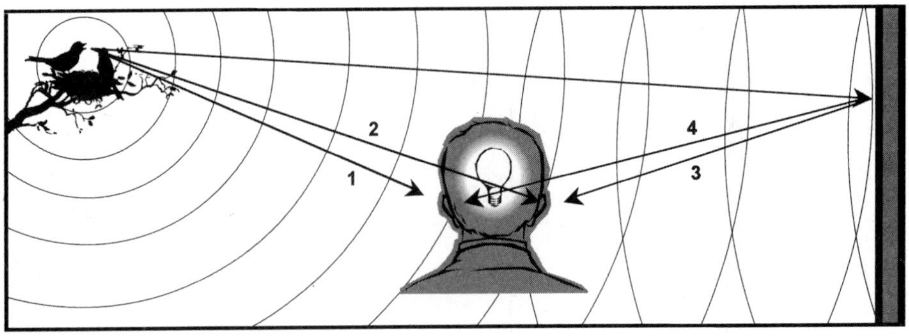

12-6

Locating a Sound

Compared with the speed of light, sound travels relatively slowly. Our brain can discern which ear hears a sound first and, through triangulation, knows the direction the sound comes from. In addition to direct sound, reflected sound offers other information about our surroundings: size and placement and texture of walls, height and surface treatment of ceilings, and so forth.

An experiment by two men named Fletcher and Munsen showed another important feature of loudness perception over distance. They discovered that the frequencies we hear best are between 2,000 and 4,000 Hz and that this apparent midrange acuity becomes more pronounced as loudness decreases. In other words, distant and quiet sounds are perceived as having limited dynamic range—their lower and higher frequencies are not heard as well. It follows that our brain's most accurate indication of the distance of a sound is through frequency identification. The sound designer needs to capitalize on these factors when preparing distant sounds for theatrical playback.

masking When one sound or event demands our attention to such a degree as to negate other sounds or events.

Masking The phenomenon of **masking** occurs when one sound or event demands our attention to such a degree that it negates other sounds or events. Sound masking is most often the result of a louder sound taking over quieter sounds, but masking may also occur if a sound is unusual or out of place. A sound is too obvious the moment it unintentionally takes dramatic focus.

At equal volumes, a lower frequency will mask the frequency just above it. This is significant, especially when a designer makes selections for *underscoring* (playing music under dialogue). Masking may occur if underscoring frequencies are lower than those of the dramatic dialogue.

Recognition As we have seen, decreasing the amplitude of a sound does not by itself give the sound a sense of distance. Likewise, merely increasing the amplitude will not necessarily allow people to hear a sound better. Recognition of a sound depends on the interaction of its *duration, familiarity,* and *volume.* A sound must last long enough to be understood. Familiar sounds are the most easily recognized. And, to a point, a louder sound is more readily perceived than a softer one. When making sound effect choices, the designer must take all three of these factors into account.

Reverberation Our ears receive sound waves directly from a source as reflected off various surfaces. As we have seen, these multiple reflections are known as *reverberation.* One of the primary means we have of identifying our immediate surroundings is an analysis of the relationship between direct and reflected sound. Remember that our ears receive a reflected sound moments after the original. The brain then compares the reflected waves with the original in terms of timing and quality and forms a "picture" of our environment for us. For instance, if the delay between direct sound and reflected sound is long and the sound has not been greatly muted, our environment is felt to be cavernous. A sound is perceived as "rich" if it contains a certain degree of reverberation; it is flat or "dry" if it does not. The sound designer can manipulate the mood of a sound or a piece of music through frequency as well as reverberation control.

Acoustics

Acoustical measurements of a room or a theatre refer to how that specific space responds to sound. The study of **acoustics** is a subject of its own; here we discuss the basic factors that are most significant to the sound technician and designer.

acoustics The scientific study of the total effect of sound, especially as produced in an enclosed space. In the theatre this may relate to reflection, absorption, and creation of harmonics that characterize a theatre's reverberant field.

Acoustical Reverberation A major element in acoustical study, *reverberation* must be controlled in order for sound to be heard well. As noted earlier, too little reverberation makes a room sound "dead," lacking in richness and fullness; too much causes complete lack of intelligibility. In a performance space, the key to good sound is directly related to the reflective qualities of the room; however, the matter is complicated by the fact that the ideal reverberation time for speech is not the same as the one for music. Between .8 and 1.4 seconds of reverberation time is preferable for the speaking voice. Musical instruments require more time for their sounds to blend well—from 4 to 5 seconds.

Reflective Surfaces Because sound emanates in all directions from a source, it is reflected by many different surfaces in a typical theatre. Scenery onstage, as well as the walls, floor, and ceiling of the auditorium, all reflect sound. If the side walls of an auditorium are parallel to each other, sound is bounced back and forth between them, creating reverberation that may destroy intelligibility. A hard, flat ceiling can act as a valuable sound reflector, but a convex ceiling serves better because it disperses the sound more evenly (Figure 12-7).

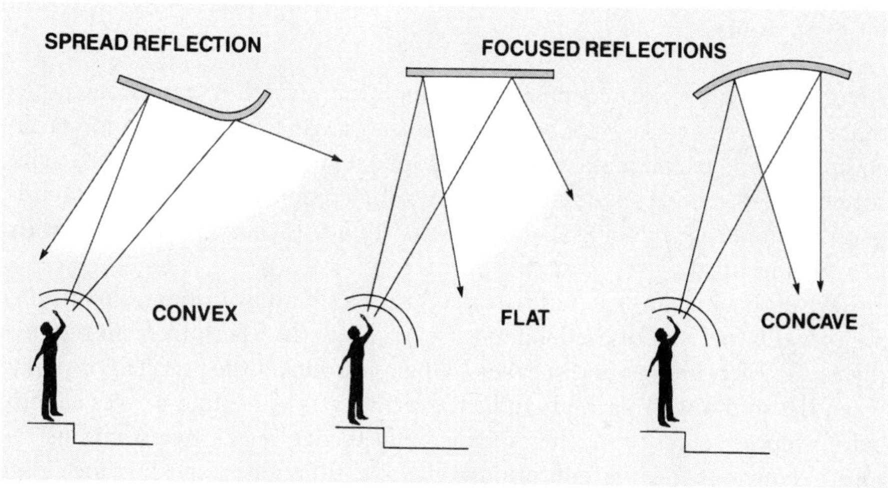

12-7

Sound Distribution

The shape of a ceiling, as well as the walls and floor, affects the distribution of sound in a room. As indicated, concave reflectors focus the sound and can cause echo.

To control reverberation, acousticians treat walls and ceilings with absorptive materials. They carefully design the shape and interrelationship of the walls and ceiling and pay close attention to the *rake* (slope) of audience seating, the seats themselves, and floor treatment. Still, there remain several uncontrollable variables, such as number of people in the seats (people absorb sound), scenery on the stage, and quality of sound reinforcement. Large multipurpose auditoriums are built with adjustable ceilings and side walls that either increase or decrease reverberation time in order to accommodate both speech and musical instruments.

URL http://www.siasoft.com

Recent developments in acoustical analysis software have made a big difference in how much influence a sound designer can exert over a space. Software such as SIA SmaartLive and SIA Smaart Acoustic Tools can perform acoustical analyses previously possible only with highly sophisticated measuring devices.

SOUND IN THE THEATRE

In addition to the performer's natural voice, sound in the theatre can be divided into four functional categories:

- Reinforcement
- Live music
- Audio communications
- Production design/playback

Reinforcement

reinforcement The electronic amplification of actors or musical instruments onstage. Typically used to do the following: (1) Help the audience hear the actors or hear an offstage actor in larger theatres. (2) Blend and balance the vocals and musical instruments in a musical theatre production. (3) Add an effect or change the quality of a voice on- or offstage.

Perhaps the most difficult of sound tasks, **reinforcement** is the amplification (and sometimes processing) of a live sound. In the theatre such sounds are most often, but not restricted to, performers' voices or musical instruments. What makes this endeavor difficult is the usual desire to maintain as natural a sound quality as possible. Reinforcement is typically necessitated by either poor acoustics or the desire to balance two or more sounds. Musical theatre is an obvious example, in that balancing an orchestra and a singing voice is a common necessity. However, over the years, theatre audiences have become so used to amplification that they have come to expect it in all but the most intimate venues.

Amplification Greater emphasis on amplification in the theatre has required that sound designers become proficient in using a wide variety of reinforcement equipment and techniques. Wireless microphones amplify a single actor's voice, sophisticated mixing equipment provides for complex balancing of sounds, and digital delay units make sure that the sound reaches the audience at the proper time.

We determine the exact source direction of a sound by distinguishing either *the sound heard first* or the loudest of several sounds. Reinforcement requires the use of microphones and speakers, which introduces the problem of timing when the sound will reach an audience member. If live sound arrives slightly before reproduced sound, the audience will recognize the live sound as the source. However, in large auditoriums or in situations where speakers are closer

PHOTO COURTESY SOUNDCRAFT, HARMAN INTERNATIONAL INDUSTRIES LTD.

12-8

A Mixing Console

Soundcraft Series FIVE mixing console positioned in the back of a theatre.

to the audience than performers are, the sense of source direction is distorted by the audience hearing the sound from the speakers first. Because sound sent electronically to a speaker moves significantly faster than live sound travels through the air, the former must be delayed. Digital delay equipment allows reinforcement systems to do this, so that the apparent source remains onstage.

Requirements for a musical theatre reinforcement system will most likely change for each and every production. The design of such systems involves speaker selection and placement, microphone selection and placement, and a sophisticated mixing control console that must be located in the auditorium. The mixing console operator must hear what the audience hears (Figure 12-8).

A final reinforcement concern is amplification done for the *performer.* Such an arrangement is called a **foldback system.** It consists of speakers that allow performers to better hear recorded or live music as well as themselves. Individually controlled speakers, called either foldback or monitor speakers, are placed so as to direct their sound to the performers. Foldback systems may also be necessary for certain pieces of the orchestra to hear themselves as well as for the conductor to hear the singers and/or musicians. Obviously, each foldback system needs to be controlled and mixed separately from the others and from the main sound system.

foldback system Typically a separate set of amplifiers and speakers placed to direct their sound to the actors/singers so they can hear the orchestra and themselves. Also placed in the orchestra for musicians to hear themselves and the actors/singers.

Sound Processing The act of treating sound with electronic equipment in order to change its quality is called **processing.** Extremely valuable in both production design and reinforcement, processing used to involve routing the sound through numerous pieces of equipment such as various effects processors or delay units or equalizers. Today we can employ specialized computer software and hardware such as the Sabine Graphi-Q or BSS OMNIDRIVE to do the job (Figure 12-9).

An **equalizer** is a particularly useful processing tool. Depending on the circumstance, both the female and male voice, as well as most musical instruments, can benefit from proper and judicial *equalization*—a process of

processing Altering the audio signal in a nonlinear fashion. Equalizers, effects units, and compressors are examples of signal processors.

URL http://www.sabine.com

URL http://www.bss.co.uk

equalizer An electronic device that alters a specific frequency or frequency range. The two most common types are graphic and parametric.

12-9

Sound Processing

This is a screenshot of the Sabine Graphi-Q, which combines graphic EQ, feedback eliminator, compressor/limiter, delay, and parametric EQ in one software-controlled unit.

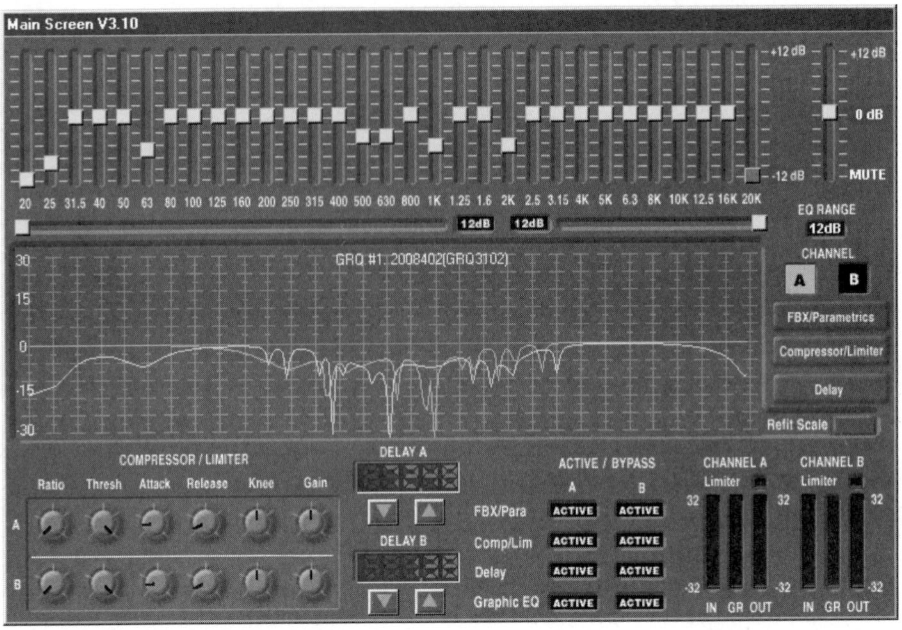

COURTESY SABINE INC.

electronically boosting or cutting selected frequencies. Because of their particular acoustics, many auditoriums require equalization in order to control undesirable resonant frequencies. An equalizer will often be found as an integral part of the reinforcement system. (This tool will be discussed in greater detail in the next chapter.)

Live Music

Although live music in the theatre is certainly not limited to the musical theatre orchestra, a full orchestra tends to demand the most elaborate electronic sound requirements. The live orchestra is an important part of the magic and attraction of musical theatre, an art form having its roots in the theatre of the United States. There are occasions when the live musical requires no electronic treatment of sound at all, but these tend to be the exception rather than the rule.

The Orchestra Traditionally found in a pit located at the front of the stage, the musical theatre orchestra of today may just as likely be found backstage behind a scrim, or on a side stage, or on the stage itself. Such changes have been brought about by the healthy desire to break with the traditional structure of the American musical, as well as by an increased interest in stages other than the proscenium. However, moving the orchestra is often fraught with numerous problems, including sound. Individual musical instruments, instrumental sections, or even the entire orchestra may need to be miked in order to provide sound that is properly balanced with that of the performers. Even a small orchestra requires a great deal of physical space that must include room for music stands and lights, details that might fall under the auspices of the sound department. As mentioned earlier, *foldback speakers* may also be necessary for certain parts of the orchestra to hear themselves or the singers.

The Conductor An orchestra's conductor often has no special sound requirements, with the possible exception of foldback speakers as well as necessary communications (discussed later). It may seem obvious, but the conductor must be able to see the stage, and the actors and musicians must be able to see the conductor. These seemingly minor details can require extensive treatment, often demanding closed-circuit television. A single camera set up to cover the stage can suffice for the conductor equipped with a small video monitor. A second camera focused on the conductor, along with several large monitors situated about the stage or on a balcony rail, may be necessary to enable the performers to see the baton. If this is the case, sufficient light must be provided on the conductor to accommodate a television signal.

Audio Communications

Production Headsets Many people scattered all over the theatre need to be in constant touch with the stage manager and each other during a performance. A flexible and reliable system of audio communication is therefore crucial. Usually such a system is built into the theatre. If not, a portable system is necessary, and the sound technician may have to attend to it. Headsets are the most common and useful system, and several companies manufacture a sturdy and reliable product (Figure 12-10).

URL http://www.clear-com.com

URL http://www.telex.com

Certain locations in the theatre are best served by speaker stations as well as headsets. These include the fly rail and loading dock, where stagehands cannot wear headsets, and perhaps soundproof booths such as the lighting control booth. Wireless headsets are available and much more reliable than in the past. Obviously, not being attached to a wire is a big plus for users such as backstage personnel, but this system's cost and susceptibility to interference remain an obstacle for performances.

Assistive-Listening Devices Many larger theatres have a built-in audio system designed to assist audience members who have special hearing needs. This system is normally completely separate from the other stage audio systems, having its own input microphones, amplifiers, and transmitters. An audio signal from the stage is sent to an infrared or radio frequency (RF) transmitter that, in turn, sends a signal to special headsets being worn by the hearing impaired.

URL http://www.sennheiser.com

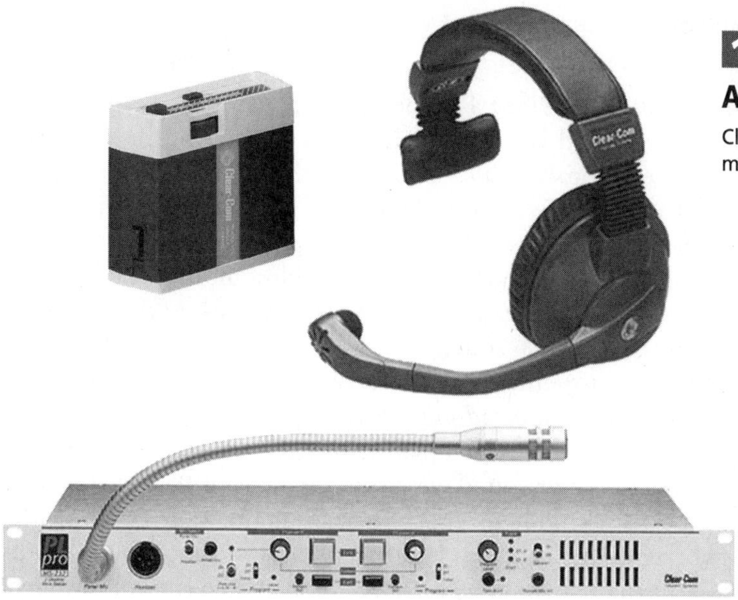

PHOTO COURTESY CLEAR-COM INTERCOM SYSTEMS

12-10

Audio Communications

Clear-com belt pack, headset, and multichannel main station.

Sound Advice

Headset Suggestions

- A system with more than one channel is often very useful, sometimes imperative.
- Use headsets with one earphone rather than two, so that live sound can be heard also (an exception might be in high-volume situations such as rock concerts).
- Always have working spare headsets and the belt packs that power them available and readily accessible.
- Treat headsets with the care and respect they deserve—they are fragile instruments.
- Know what to do if headsets fail—have a backup system.

Functions of Sound Design

The design of musical and audio effects for theatrical production is certainly the most creative and perhaps the most important function of sound in the theatre. Such design requires that a person have a strong background in general theatrical production, a good knowledge of sound equipment, and an interest in and familiarity with music and sound. In addition, music composition skills are a big plus. Fortunately, recent developments in compositional software have made this area of sound design much more accessible than before. The ways sound design can contribute to theatrical production fall into three categories:

- Evoking atmosphere or mood
- Reinforcing the action
- Commenting on the action

Evoking Atmosphere or Mood One familiar way sound can evoke a specific atmosphere or mood is by using environmental sounds in a realistic manner. Such use can establish *locale, environmental conditions, period,* and *time of day,* as well as mood. Examples abound: bright chirping of birds for a cheerful morning scene, ominous rolls of thunder preceding a storm, or sad notes of a lone violin. Although it must be handled with some degree of caution, realistically motivated sound is one of the easiest to use because of the audience's inclination to readily accept such sound.

The designer can also use either nonrealistic or unmotivated sound to evoke an atmosphere or mood. *Unmotivated* sound has no apparent source; *motivated* sound does, as in music coming from a piano onstage. **Musical underscoring,** the process of playing music or sound effects under a performer's dialogue, is often unmotivated. This technique is most appropriate for less-realistic styles of production, where it is easier for an audience to accept. However, it can be extremely effective in any style of production. A subtle touch is recommended.

musical underscoring Playing music or sound effects underneath the dialogue of a scene.

A designer must never forget the power of silence. The artful device of establishing an atmospheric sound, such as crickets chirping, then suddenly cutting off the sound, can be more dynamic and effective than any other device.

Further examples of the use of atmospheric sound are pre- and post-show music and incidental or **change music.** The selection of such music depends completely on the style of production as determined by the director and artistic team during their early collaborative meetings. In some stylized productions, *punctuation effects* may be appropriate. These are sounds used, often at the entrance or exit of actors, to comment on their characters or on a particular situation.

change music Music used to cover the time and possibly the noise of a scene change.

Reinforcing the Action Using sound in a realistic manner to reinforce the action of a play helps to keep the audience informed of current or upcoming events. Sound coming from a television just switched on is an example, as is the ringing of a telephone or the sound of an approaching delivery truck. Such sounds are not chosen arbitrarily, for the designer must remain faithful to the period and style of the production. And, even though the sound is primarily reinforcing the action of the play, there is often room for comment. The sound from the television may have a sharp and nagging tone, the telephone ring may be insistent, or the delivery truck may screech to a halt to express urgency. These sounds usually fall into the category of effects. In addition, offstage voices or "voice-over" effects might be used to reinforce a central action.

Commenting on the Action The designer can comment on an action by using sound in a symbolic manner. Such usage may or may not be motivated, and a wide variety of approaches might be taken. For example, a tympani roll on the entrance of a character might be either comic or sinister depending on its treatment, and comic music playing under a serious scene will certainly affect the audience's reaction to the scene. Underscoring serves as a powerful technique for commenting on the action. In every case, however, the designer must be extremely sensitive to the stylistic approach of the production and be sure that the sound is in every way appropriate.

ELEMENTS OF SOUND DESIGN

The building blocks of any sound design are the tools with which the designer works. The script and the approach to the production, as arrived at by the design team, determine the choice of these tools, including the following:

- Music (live or recorded)
- Sound effects (live or recorded)
- Synthetic and processed sound
- Speaker placement

Music

Most of today's productions use either live or recorded music to enhance the performance. This music may be either found or composed by the sound designer.

incidental music Music that occurs other than during the actual play, such as before and after the show or at intermission.

Incidental Music Preshow music is played as an audience enters the theatre. Selection of this **incidental music** is never left to chance, for the designer would be wasting a great opportunity to put audience members in the proper frame of mind for the upcoming performance. Preshow music can establish the period of the ensuing production, comment on the action that is about to take place, or hint at the style of the production. In addition, a particular type of sound (electronic music, for instance) to be used elsewhere in the production can be introduced at this time in order to acclimate the audience to the sound.

In making selections from existing music, the designer must proceed with great caution. Music carries with it associative memories that stick with people for a long time—sometimes all their lives. *Also Sprach Zarathustra* (used in the film *2001*), the much-played *1812 Overture,* and almost any Beatles tune are just a few examples of music that would have to be used with great care. Most designers like to work with original music in order to avoid audience associations. Teaming up with a composer or using composition software such as Sonic Foundry's ACID PRO or Cakewalk's SONAR is highly recommended in situations where music will play a major emotive role in the production.

URL http://www.sonicfoundry.com

URL http://www.cakewalk.com

Change Music Music accompanying a well-choreographed scene change can make a potentially painful experience pleasurable. Yet, music used solely for covering changes (and nowhere else in the production) may appear obvious and out of place. Of course, this *change music* must be as carefully selected as any other. The designer may select the music to reflect on the scene just past or set the tone for the one to come. He or she must always remember to allow for greatly varying scene change lengths from performance to performance.

Underscoring As mentioned earlier, the powerful technique of underscoring involves playing music or other sounds during character dialogue. It is perhaps the trickiest way to use music in a production. The danger lies in competing with the spoken word to the extent of distraction or masking. In addition, the technique itself, which is used commonly in television and film production, can become obvious and ridiculous. The camera focuses an audience's attention to a much greater degree than theatre does, where the normal field of focus is considerably broader. Therefore, the designer must approach underscoring in the theater with particular care and consideration. Many stage directors may at first find underscoring distracting to the point of being unacceptable as a technique. However, it can be used effectively if the sound designer introduces the music at low levels using limited dynamic range and remembers the principles of masking.

effects Music or sounds that are prerecorded and played back during a scene, such as that from an onstage phonograph or radio.

Effect Music When music is used as an **effect** (motivated by a phonograph playing, a radio, a piano in the sitting room, an orchestra, or a jazz combo across the street), selections require careful attention as to their appropriateness. Being true to the *source* of the music, as well as the style and period of the play, is critical. For example, a jazz combo playing onstage will exhibit a great deal of dynamic range and sound quite different from that same combo heard on the radio or even across the street.

Sound Effects

Although one could argue that *any* use of sound in a stage production is an effect, it is helpful to consider most music and processed sound to be separate from effects. Sound effects can be found prerecorded, be self-recorded, or be created. Sources of sound effects are only as limited as the designer's imagination.

Prerecorded Sound Prerecorded sound effects can be downloaded from the Internet or found as libraries on compact discs. Several of the better sound effect libraries that sell prerecorded effects include the following:

- *Gefen, Inc.*: Sells numerous SFX Libraries; http://www.gefen.com
- *The Hollywood Edge:* SFX Library; http://www.hollywoodedge.com
- *Network Music:* SFX Library; http://www.networkmusic.com
- *Sound Ideas:* SFX Library; http://www.sound-ideas.com
- *Valentino:* SFX Library; http://www.tvmusic.com

Here are several other Web sites of interest to the theatrical sound designer:

- *The Theatre Sound Design Directory:* http://www.theatre-sound.com
- *A library of sound effects, production effects, and musical recordings:* http://www.networkmusic.com
- *Commercial online sound effects library:* http://www.sounddogs.com
- *Music and sound effects libraries to order off the Web:* http://www.killersound.com

Music stores carry various small collections, which are the least expensive, although their quality varies. The purchase of an effects library represents a significant investment, but the ready availability of effects is an absolute necessity for even the modest production studio. Although the Internet and a computer with composition software along with synthesizers and samplers have elevated sound production to new heights, they have not negated the value of an effects library.

Other sources of prerecorded effects might be local radio stations or professional recording studios, where both the quality and cost will be high. Become familiar with the studio nearest you; its personnel are usually audio experts and can offer great assistance.

Self-Recorded Sound The sound engineer can also directly record environmental sounds, the playing of musical instruments, or the human voice. Recording on location can be fraught with problems that range from special equipment demands to the need for sound isolation. Although not to be totally avoided, this technique of sound gathering should never be left to the last moment, and a backup plan is advisable. Studio work is much safer, and a wide range of recordings can be accomplished in a well-equipped studio space.

To keep unwanted noise at a minimum, sound engineers often place a microphone close to the sound source in live recordings. In doing so, they must pay attention to the **proximity effect.** Because various frequencies can differ greatly in wavelength, a directional microphone placed less than two feet away from a source will exhibit an increase in low-frequency response. The results can be balanced by using an equalizer.

proximity effect The increase in low-frequency response when a microphone is placed very close to the sound source. This is an inherent characteristic of directional microphones and is usually associated with singers using handheld microphones.

In addition, close-up recording accentuates sounds that otherwise would be indistinguishable. A good example of this effect is the squeak of a guitar

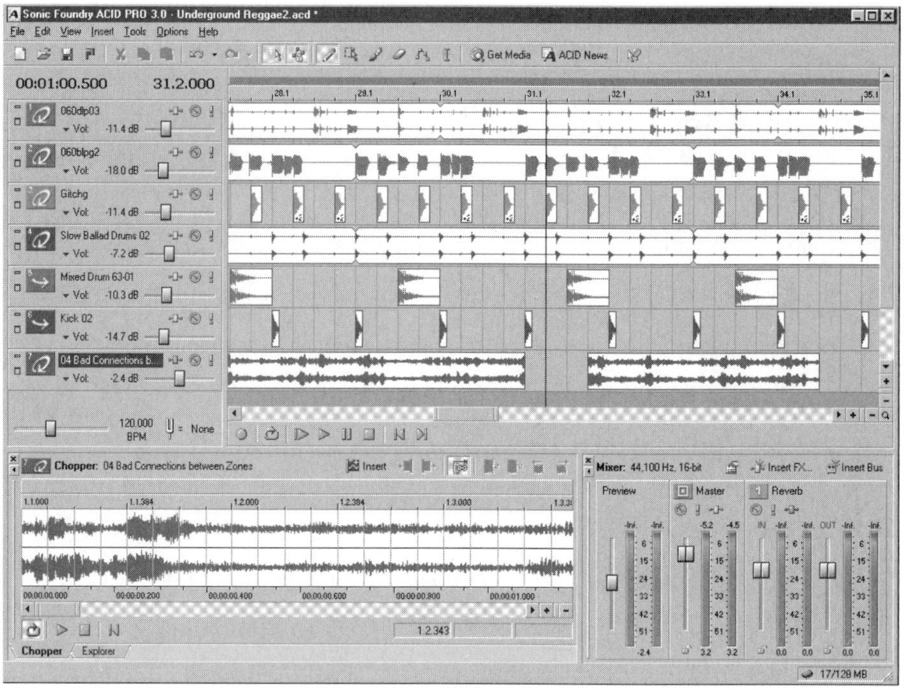

12-11

Created Sound Effects

A screenshot of Sonic Foundry's ACID PRO 3.0 loop-based music creation software showing multiple tracks of audio loops synced to a common tempo.

COURTESY SONIC FOUNDRY MEDIA SERVICES

string as the musician's finger moves. Such sounds are nearly impossible to process out of a finished recording. Recording engineers must give special consideration to this problem.

Created Effects Created effects, by far the most interesting, offer great potential for exciting design results. Found objects such as pieces of metal, noise-making machines, and everyday things such as squeaky screen door hinges all have possibilities for interesting effects. Sound designers investigate objects made up of as many different materials as possible (tin interacting with fiberglass, metal tubes striking glass, for example) and imagine how each sound might be used—they also keep a written record of their findings. Finally, the possibilities for creating sound by using a computer with software such as the earlier mentioned ACID PRO or SONAR are endless (Figure 12-11).

Synthetic and Processed Sound

Some of the greatest potential for creating exciting music and effects falls under the categories of synthetic and processed sound. The production and manipulation of sound as a design tool has been made possible by technological advances beginning with the *synthesizer,* followed by *samplers* and *digital effects processors* and, most recently, *digital audio workstations.*

Synthesizers and Samplers The most common type of synthesizer is either an electronic keyboard or computer software that can simulate an array of sounds, including those of various musical instruments. Synthesizers come in a variety of types and price ranges, one type being primarily intended for performance and another for production. *Digital synthesizers,* currently the most sophisticated and versatile type available, can sample sound. *Sampling*

COURTESY SYNTRILLIUM SOFTWARE CORPORATION

12-12

Digital Audio Workstation

A screenshot of Cool Edit Pro digital-audio editing software showing a stereo waveform and the various editing controls.

keyboards closely resemble synthesizers and have many of the same functions. Additionally, they receive and store audio data in digital form. After the sound is converted to digital data, it can be manipulated, combined with other sound or sounds, and played back with no loss in quality. *Samplers* can record, store, and manipulate sound without the addition of a keyboard. The possibilities are almost endless as the sound designer learns to use this equipment to produce and/or alter sound to fit the mood or style of a production.

Digital Audio Workstations For most applications, the *digital audio workstation* (often a computer with various software) has replaced the need for vast amounts of hardware, including dedicated synthesizers and samplers (Figure 12-12). Available software enables the sound designer to import sound and alter it with the stroke of a mouse. Wave forms can be viewed, processing performed, and effects created in an astonishingly short time. Learning curves vary, but most elementary programs are extremely simple to learn. In fact, most of today's new computers come equipped with a sound card that contains some kind of sound editing program. This hardware and software has indeed revolutionized the way theatre sound designers think and work.

MIDI A further advantage of digital technology is the ability to interface between different pieces of equipment. For this to happen, various manufacturers had to agree on a common digital "language." *Musical Instrument Digital Interface,* or **MIDI,** was born out of this need. MIDI is the standard protocol for digital communication between one component and another. As the name implies, MIDI was originally developed for musical instruments, but today people use it in much broader ways. For example, *MIDI Show Control* enables computers with MIDI ports to "speak" to lighting control consoles, sound systems, and automation devices.

MIDI Musical Instrument Digital Interface is a standard for representing musical information in digital format. Through MIDI Show Control, its use has been expanded to include communication and the control of all types of theatrical equipment.

Processed Sound Samplers, digital effects processors, and digital audio workstations offer ways to alter sound in order to create a particular effect. One of the most popular is *speed distortion:* the process of speeding up or slowing down a recorded sound in order to change its quality. As a sound is slowed, its pitch is lowered, resulting in a "bigger" sound; for instance, a small engine can be made to sound like a huge turbine by slowing the playback speed. This was the primary reason for having a variable-speed tape machine in the sound studio of the past.

Other valuable techniques are mixing *sound on sound,* playing back in the *reverse direction, filtering* using an equalizer or equalization software, adding *echo* or *reverberation,* and *pitch shifting* (altering frequency). Sound-on-sound mixing through the use of multitrack waveform editing software can be quite subtle, adding a "richness" to the sound; alternatively, its effect can be quite abstract and bold. Using equalization to filter sound can reduce or eliminate low frequencies, conditioning a piece of music to serve as underscoring. It can add as well as subtract hiss and noise in a recording, and it can subtly adjust the quality of a music selection or sound by attenuating (turning down) or boosting certain frequencies. All of these techniques can be achieved by using the proper editing software, including the following:

- *Digidesign:* Pro Tools (complete music production system/DAW); http://www.digidesign.com
- *Sonic Foundry:* Sound Forge, Vegas Audio (digital audio recording, editing, and mixing software); http://www.sonicfoundry.com
- *Syntrillium:* Cool Edit Pro (digital audio recording, editing, and mixing software); http://www.syntrillium.com

Speaker Placement

The final tool available to the sound designer is control over how the sound will reach the audience. Although the selection of speaker type (discussed in the next chapter) significantly affects a sound's quality, the placement of speakers matters even more than the type. Recall that the location of our ears gives us greater horizontal than vertical sensitivity to the direction of a sound source. Therefore, principles of sound reinforcement state that speakers should be located above the stage in order to maintain a proper directional sense of the performer. This is a good rule to remember but may not always apply to performance music and sound effects.

For effects that have a distinct source (for example, a gutted radio prop located onstage), the speaker should be located inside or as close as possible to the object. Speakers come in a variety of sizes, and good sound is being reproduced from some very small speakers these days—so locating the speaker right onstage is usually achievable. Distant effects can often be helped by speakers aimed in some direction other than at the audience. The theatre's grid and auditorium ceiling are also valuable speaker positions.

Many sound designers like to hang their speakers above the stage. This is desirable for a variety of reasons: clearing valuable deck (stage floor) space, keeping sound cable in the air (off the floor), and providing source direction. If plans include hanging speakers, the scenic and lighting departments must be advised well in advance; they also need that air space and, if consulted, will less likely place a black border immediately downstage of the speaker position.

A valuable rule of thumb is that a speaker must be able to "see" the audience in order to deliver good sound.

Finally, flexibility of speaker placement is absolutely necessary for good production sound. Although not true for reinforcement, playback requires that the designer have the ability to place speakers in any position.

THE PROCESS OF DESIGNING SOUND FOR THE THEATRE

The best design in the theatre is a result of good collaboration. The production sound designer must be involved in the collaborative process from the start. This is when the style of production is determined, a factor that will heavily influence sound decisions; this is when the scene designer can be made aware of special sound needs such as speaker placement; and this is when creative ideas can be shared with the director and other designers. Like the lighting designer, the sound designer normally has a bit more time to develop his or her ideas than do the scenic or costume designers. This means that the sound designer may have the luxury of attending rehearsals before final design decisions must be made.

The Sound Designer and the Design Team

Several references have been made to qualities that a designer of sound for the theatre should possess: a working knowledge of theatre production in general and sound production specifically; a passion for music, with interest in all types and periods; a technical knowledge that provides understanding of the equipment involved in sound production; and a keen environmental awareness that will facilitate design creativity. In addition, every designer in the theatre must have the ability and desire to share in the design process—to be a member of a design team. Of all the arts, theatrical design is unique in its collaboration. Relating to other designers and their ideas in a positive manner not only is exciting but also forms the very basis of collaboration.

The sound designer is involved with the production and the production team from their inception. An approach to a production is the result of script analysis and design meetings with all the designers, the director, and perhaps the playwright. This approach is the product of much thinking and input; it will guide the manner in which the story will be told—including, but not necessarily limited to, which period, thematic elements, and production style will predominate. From this information will grow design ideas that will be unified by the fact that each stemmed from a common approach. Only then will the sound designer be ready to begin the exciting process of making specific choices.

The process of sound design can be broken down into four stages: design, preproduction, a sound plot, and production. Each will be discussed in turn.

Design

Design for the theatre always begins with the script, for it embodies the playwright's ideas, on which all production choices are based. The first time the designer reads a script, it should be read as if it were a novel. Subsequent

12-13

Sound Score

Sample from a sound score. The score helps the designer formulate and present early sound ideas to the director and other designers.

SOUND SCORE
12TH NIGHT

SOUND DESIGNER: JEFF LADMAN

NO.	PAGE	DESCRIPTION
1	1	Extension of boat entrance as Viola leaves the boat and steps foot onto the Illyrian sands
2	1	Viola moves farther onto Illyrian soil
3	2	Strain of music from Orsino's group in the distance. It is coming from the portable gramophone, but will open out more generally as they come onto the stage. Will need to be timed to end. Something excruciatingly romantic
4	3	Orsino's "love" music; repeat of section of previous
5	3	Exit of Orsino as group moves away and exits. In the same vein as preceding. Might be the beginning of the piece to which we only heard the later part.
6	4	Pull down on Viola/Orsino motif that runs through the show.
7	15	Toby entrance music with cart, et. al. ("Arise, Arise"?) Music is coming from the jukebox on the cart, then opens up to a more general sound.
8	15	Olivia mourning music (interrupts or overlaps the preceding). A kind of dirge which needs to cover a cross-over by Olivia and her entourage. Will be interrupted by a large belch from Sir Toby in the middle of it. So, may need to be constructed in two parts.
9	21	Live dance cues

SCORE COURTESY JEFF LADMAN

readings will allow the designer to begin formulating a sense of the sound for the production. After meeting with the collaborative team, the designer will develop a **sound score.**

sound score A preliminary, written description of all possible ideas for sound cues that the designer might have. The sound score facilitates discussions with the director and other designers and acts as a springboard for developing the final cues for a production.

The Sound Score The early sound score (Figure 12-13) is a visual representation of what the sound eventually might be like. It embodies a preliminary presentation of mood, style, and period, which may or may not include specific cues. This valuable paperwork helps the designer present his or her ideas to the rest of the production team and acts as an initial outline of the final sound design. Although there are no set rules concerning what information the score should contain, here are some things that should be included:

- The *name* of the sound cue or idea
- Script *location*
- *A description* of the cue in terms of its content, mood, style, and other information, including special treatment
- The *purpose* of the cue (could be as simple as the telephone ringing or as complex as underscoring intended to affect the audience psychologically)

A great deal of thought goes into the creation of a sound score, with all decisions being based on the script and production approach.

Research The period in which the production is set will undoubtedly affect the ultimate style and quality of the sound. Period research, an essential step toward any good sound design, must take place as soon as possible, for a sound score cannot be developed without proper research. Of course, films

Sound Advice

Design Steps

1. Script reading and collaborative meetings with director and design team to determine production style, period, and mood
2. Research and study resulting in sound score
3. Collection and storage of music and sounds
4. Creation of a director's CD and attending rehearsals
5. Creation of a rehearsal CD, if necessary
6. Development of the sound plot
7. Creation of the final show sound

and actual period music are good research sources—but the designer should also consider reading about the period, reading books from the period, and looking at art and photographs from the period. Photographic records of architecture, clothing, and interiors will be a tremendous aid in discovering the feel of the times.

Preproduction

Once the sound score is complete, the designer may start to collect the required music and effects as well as begin the recording process. The time required for this work varies greatly, depending on the complexity of the design. The designer must allow at least three weeks before technical rehearsals begin; however, complex production designs may take several months to complete.

Master Computer Files As sounds are found, they should be stored in a *Master Folder* and carefully labeled for content. This folder will store all sound and music being considered for the production. Further "generations" of a sound can be stored in other folders as the designer works toward the final product.

The Director's CD As soon as a significant amount of sound has been collected, the designer must produce a special CD for the director containing representative selections of music and sound effects. The purpose of this **director's CD** is to gain imperative feedback concerning the style and mood of the selections as well as their appropriateness to the production. This is also a good time to attend rehearsals in order to get a better feeling for the atmosphere created by the actors, the pace of the production, and overall directorial intent. Keeping in close contact with the director and stage manager of a production in rehearsal just makes good sense.

director's CD Selections of possible sound cues for the director to evaluate.

rehearsal CD Sound effects or music given to the director or stage manager for use in rehearsal; useful for timing or giving the actor a chance to work with underscoring, songs, or sound effects before technical rehearsals.

The Rehearsal CD A director may need a **rehearsal** CD well in advance of the actual show sound in order to coordinate actor timing or familiarize the actors with particular sounds. Necessary sound and music should be recorded onto a CD for ease of playback and should contain sound that is as close to the final product as possible. Preparing a rehearsal CD can prove to be of great advantage to the sound designer, often cutting hours off a technical rehearsal.

Sound processing such as equalization or digital reverberation treatment should happen next, followed by the construction of the show CD, MiniDisc, or computer files. However, before the final show sound can be created, the designer must produce a sound plot.

Sound Plot

sound plot The actual working list of the cues for a production; normally includes cue numbers, speaker assignments, fade times, and so forth.

Another planning tool for the designer, the **sound plot** is similar to the sound score—but much more detailed and technical (Figure 12-14). Components and format can vary, and some playback software will generate sound plots. However, every sound plot must include the following information:

- Sound cue number
- Script page number
- Cue description and length
- Playback device information
- Speakers in use

12-14

Sound Plot

A screenshot of the cue list from SFX theatrical playback and show-control software.

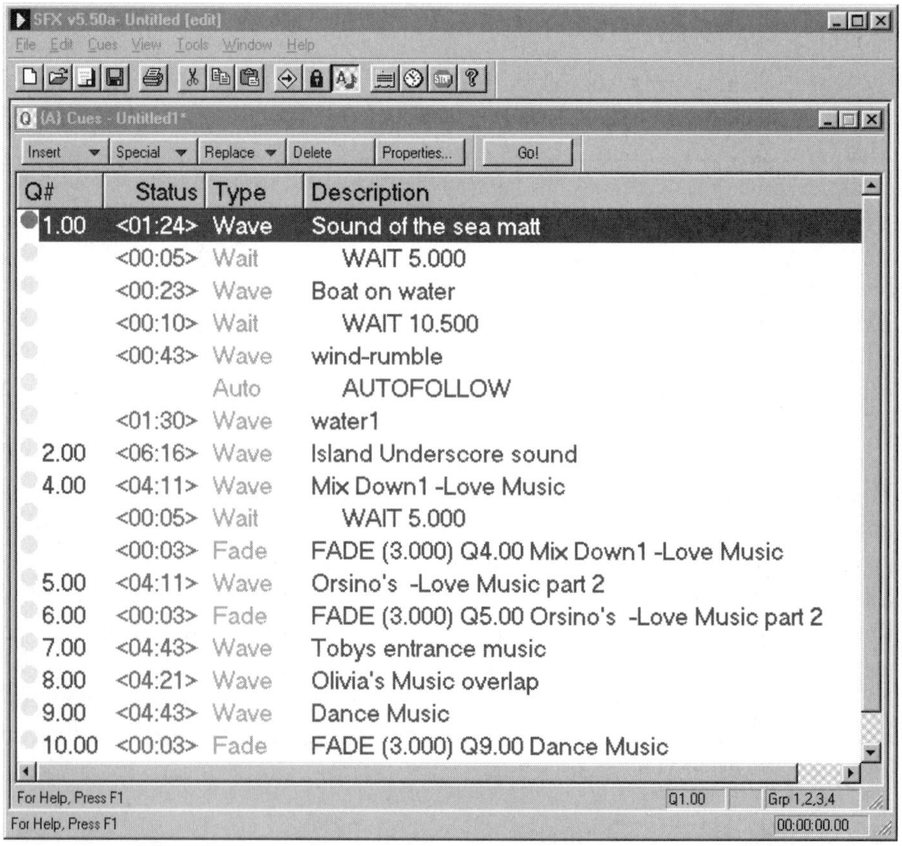

COURTESY STAGE RESEARCH, INC.

This is the design step where the designer plans exactly how the production sound will be run—how many playback devices are necessary, exact speaker requirements and control, how many cues there will be, and how long each one should last. Often the stage manager can help and should at least be consulted for last-minute changes. Formulating the sound plot will give the designer enough information to proceed intelligently with the creation of the final show sound, but the final sound must never be attempted without finishing this paperwork. Here are two popular suppliers of playback software:

- *Richmond Sound Design Ltd.:* AudioBox, ShowMan, E-Show (Audio and show control hardware and software); http://www.richmondsounddesign.com
- *Stage Research:* SFX (Theatrical playback and show control software); http://www.stageresearch.com

In addition, if sound requirements are complex, with many overlapping cues, it is advisable to do additional charts (sometimes referred to as *work sheets*) detailing in a time line each cue playing.

Production

Whether the production period begins with a sound rehearsal or technical rehearsals, the sound designer needs to have several details taken care of prior to this time. Cues should be written into the stage manager's script several days before the technical or sound rehearsal. Because the director may wish to be present at this session, it should be scheduled well in advance. Each of the stage manager's cues should have a specific call placement so that changes made later can be done in an exact manner.

Pre-Tech System Check It is wise for the sound designer to take a quiet moment in the theatre before the first sound or technical rehearsal and set preliminary sound levels for each cue, checking speaker functions at the same time. This is also a good time to brief and check out the operator on the equipment, allowing plenty of time for problem solving. If the headset communication system is the responsibility of the sound department, the sound designer should find out the number and location of headsets from the stage manager and prepare and check out the equipment. Leaving these details for the day of the technical rehearsal is a serious mistake and will waste much time. Good preparation and planning is never more evident than at the technical rehearsal; every effort should be taken to make this experience a painless one.

Sound Rehearsal The sound designer should arrive a bit early for the sound or technical rehearsal and be sure that the sound operator and the equipment are ready to begin on time. Every sound cue should be run under performance conditions so that its length and level can be properly judged. (An audience will absorb roughly 3 dB of sound, a factor that the designer must allow for.) The designer sits at the "tech" table and makes sure that both the stage manager calling the cues and the operator take careful notes of all changes. Nothing is more frustrating than mistakes being repeated because changes were not properly noted. The entire crew (including the designer) needs proper breaks to do their job well.

Dress Rehearsals Often the designer will need to make adjustments after the technical rehearsal and before the dress rehearsals begin. These changes will usually be minor if everything has gone well, but they may require a great deal of studio time if there are problems. The corrected sound must be ready for first dress, so planning ahead is important. Once the dress process has begun, sound problems must be dealt with while the run goes on. The sound designer may not stop a dress rehearsal for a problem unless it is an emergency. He or she must make sure to touch base with the director, stage manager, and operator after every rehearsal. A backup of the final show sound must also be readily available in case of emergency.

The Run Before each performance, the sound operator needs to check the entire system to ascertain that everything is in proper working order. It is good practice to record a series of sounds that can be used as preshow tests; this recording can be done at the beginning of the *show sound,* or the sound to be used in the show (often recorded on a CD). Each speaker should be tested individually and a show cue should be run to check volume levels.

As this chapter has shown, designing sound for the theatre involves many specialized areas of knowledge as well as an ordered collaboration with other designers. The next chapter discusses in detail the equipment used for sound design in the theatre.

13

Sound Systems and Equipment

Mastering the art of theatrical sound, like other aspects of design, involves not only artistry but also technology. The functions of various pieces of equipment and how they interrelate matter a great deal to the sound designer/technician. Technology has driven the evolution of theatrical sound design—what follows is a closer look at that technology.

THE SOUND SYSTEMS

Music and sound play several different roles in the theatre, and the requirements of a sound system vary with each. Here we discuss the three theatrical systems:

- Recording system
- Playback system
- Reinforcement system

Each of these systems requires an **input source.** Anything that sends a sound signal to the system is considered an input source. Two commonly used methods of transmitting and storing a source's signal are *analog* and *digital.* Although the two cannot be used interchangeably, an analog signal can be converted to digital and vice versa by means of an analog/digital (a/d) or a digital/analog (d/a) converter.

input source Any device that sends an audio signal to the sound system.

Analog signals have been with us for a long time. As noted in Chapter 12, they are electrical waveforms carried through wires that duplicate sound waveforms. Because of their relatively low voltage and current, analog waveforms are quite susceptible to induced noise and interference. More recent digital technology has provided a solution to some of the problems inherent in analog signals. In the digital process, an analog signal is converted to a rapid series of on-or-off (binary) pulses. These pulses can be read, recorded, and

analog signal Audio information represented by a continuous variable measurement of physical quantities, such as length, width, voltage, or pressure. An analog audio recording is a continuous curve, as opposed to a digital recording, which is based on discrete samples.

manipulated with great precision, resulting in more flexible and accurate storage and reproduction.

The Recording System

digital audio workstation (DAW) Typically, a personal computer with software and hardware configured for audio work. In a large studio this is most likely a dedicated computer system.

A theatrical recording system is used to record and process voice, music, and sound effects intended for use in a production. Modern recording systems comprise numerous input sources and a **digital audio workstation (DAW).** Input sources vary by application, while the DAW is typically a computer with software that enables the designer to record, edit, mix, and process sound in the creation of production cues. The recording system is best located in its own studio, one that has been adequately soundproofed for live recording.

Input Sources for Recording Input sources for the recording system can be categorized as follows:

- Microphones
- Tape media
- Optical media
- Records
- Keyboards or other electronic instruments
- Computers

transducer A device, such as a microphone or speaker, that converts input energy of one form into output energy of another. In the case of a microphone, it transduces acoustical energy in the form of sound pressure waves in the air into electrical energy.

Specialized *microphones* used for recording come in various types, depending on the specific application. A microphone is a **transducer** in that it receives acoustic sound waves and converts them to an analog electrical signal. As noted earlier, the electrical signal produced by a microphone is not powerful; it has quite a low voltage. Therefore, the wires carrying this signal must be adequately shielded from other electrical interference, and the signal must be either converted to digital or electronically boosted to a higher level (called *line level*) before being processed.

Tape media provide a common input source because of their ability to store sound and play it back. The tape's film is coated with ferrous oxide particles, which can be magnetized, allowing the storage of either analog or digital signals. When recording, a tape player receives an electrical signal and transfers it to the tape by means of a small electromagnetic head. A second head can read the signal stored on the tape so it can be transmitted to other pieces of audio equipment, such as the DAW. The most universal type of tape media used for analog recording is the familiar *cassette.* Currently two tape formats are common for digital recording: DAT (digital audio tape), a two-track tape that comes in small cassettes, and MDM (modular digital multitrack), a larger multitrack version. MDM machines record multiple tracks onto tapes such as those commonly used for 8mm or VHS-C video recording. Tape quality varies. Poor recording tape can stretch in playback and/or "print through" when stored, rendering the tape useless. Being magnetic, recording tape is sensitive to all magnetic fields. An entire cassette of tape may be erased by using an electromagnet called a bulk eraser.

The most recent input sources, *optical media,* represent a significant advance in sound recording. Optical media store sound waves in digital form on a disk such as a CD or a MiniDisc. Tiny divots representing a binary code are etched in the surface of the disc; they can then be read by a laser for playback. Optical media can store much more information than recording tape can and are not as susceptible to damage. Current optical media used for theatrical sound recording include these:

- CD (compact disc)
- CD-R (recordable compact disc)
- CD-RW (recordable and rewritable compact disc)
- DVD (digital video disc)
- DVD-R (recordable digital video disc)
- MiniDisc (compressed format digital disc)

Of this group, the CD-R is the most common of the recordable media because its playback device, the CD player, is almost universally available. DVDs can store more information than CDs can, because DVDs allow storage of information in numerous layers rather than on the surface only. Although smaller, a MiniDisc stores about as much as a CD because the digital information is *compressed* before it is stored.

Compression of sound in order to allow for greater storage capacity is not a new idea; a standard for compressed audio was adopted in 1991 by the Moving Picture Expert Group (MPEG) and has been evolving ever since. Two of the more popular formats are MP3 (short for MPEG-1 Layer 3), used to compress audio files found on the Internet, and ATRAC (adaptive transform acoustic coding), used by Sony for MiniDisc compression. Both types of compression remove sounds that theoretically would be masked and, therefore, not perceived by the human ear. MiniDisc compression ratio is 5:1; MP3 is higher, usually around 10:1. With greater compression comes the danger of removing sound that could be heard.

There remains some music that can be found only on vinyl discs or *phonograph records*. Therefore, a good recording studio will still have a turntable available for the rare occasion when only a phonograph record will do the job. Sometimes audio designers want to record the unique sound of a phonograph record. Phonograph records are recorded with special equalization. As a result, a turntable preamplifier that corrects for the equalization must be used in order to achieve proper sound. That is, the turntable cannot be plugged directly into a mixer without its specialized preamplifier.

Keyboards such as *synthesizers* and *samplers* can generate a vast array of sounds. Sampling keyboards record or "sample" a sound into RAM (random access memory), allowing instant access to the sound for editing and processing. The length of the sample is limited by the amount of memory. Digital samplers can record and store these sounds for subsequent playback and therefore function as an input source. A synthesizer can also act as an input source.

The final input source is the *computer.* A computer equipped with the proper software can function as a synthesizer or sampler. It can store *loop libraries* as well as other computer-stored libraries. It can also access the Internet, a vast source of sound and music. Today's computer is the most versatile of input sources.

PHOTO COURTESY DIGIDESIGN, INC.

13-1

An Early Digital Audio Workstation

This digital audio production system manufactured by Digidesign is a Macintosh-based system for recording directly to a hard disk. It allows visual editing of wave forms and playback of multiple tracks.

Digital Audio Workstation (DAW) Early digital audio workstations (Figure 13-1) were dedicated computer systems with built-in software enabling them to edit music and sound and record it onto some sort of storage media (often a hard disk). Today, the sound designer is most likely to use a nondedicated computer along with a personal selection from the various available software. The modern DAW allows the designer to edit a piece of sound by displaying its specific audio waveform on a monitor; the visual waveform can then be cut and pasted in any manner. In addition, complex processing can be performed on this waveform, including adding such effects as equalization, reverb, pitch shifting, noise reduction, and compression. After processing, the DAW provides the potential for a multitrack "mix down" of multiple wave forms to prepare the sound for playback. Finally, the system archives the finished sound onto a storage device such as a hard drive, recordable CD or DVD, or MiniDisc.

The Playback System

The *playback system* takes the sound prepared by the recording system and puts it in a format suitable for production playback. It must be able to store a great deal of music and sound, providing instant access to each cue for production playback. For many years, this task was accomplished by bulky reel-to-reel tape decks or even less-desirable cassette players, which fed their sound to a *mixer,* which subsequently sent it to amplifiers and speakers.

Two types of playback systems are in common use today:

- Input sources connected to a playback mixer
- Computer playback system

PHOTO COURTESY SOUNDCRAFT, HARMAN INTERNATIONAL INDUSTRIES LTD.

13-2

Playback Mixer

The Soundcraft Spirit FX16: A compact 16-channel playback mixing console.

Input Sources Connected to a Playback Mixer Modern playback input sources include digital audio tape, recordable CDs, MiniDiscs, recordable DVDs, and computer hard drives. These storage devices take sound created by the digital audio workstation and store it in a form that is easily retrieved for production playback. The sound is then routed through a **mixing board** located in the sound booth and run by the sound operator.

mixing board A device used to preamplify, combine, and adjust sounds from a variety of sources and assign them to various outputs. A mixing board usually includes some provision for limited equalization along with supplying phantom power to devices that require it. Also known as a *mixer.*

The mixer in a playback system serves mainly to combine or "mix down" several input signals and route them into one or more output channels. In addition, a mixing console provides volume control as well as some equalization for each of the input signals (Figure 13-2).

Computer Playback System The future of production sound playback almost certainly lies with the computer. Equipped with software programs such as SFX from Stage Research or ShowMan from Richmond Sound Design, the computer provides the same functions that the input sources just discussed do when connected to a mixer—and more. The computer's hard disk stores the production sound as well as all necessary cue information. The system acts much like a lighting control board, with the sound cue sheet displayed on the monitor and the operator pushing "go" for a cue to begin. Fade rates, volume levels, and speaker assignments are recorded and automatically played back with each cue (Figure 13-3).

13-3

Playback Monitor Screen

A screenshot of the playback screen from SFX theatrical playback and show control software showing the cue and note list, track status, and GO button.

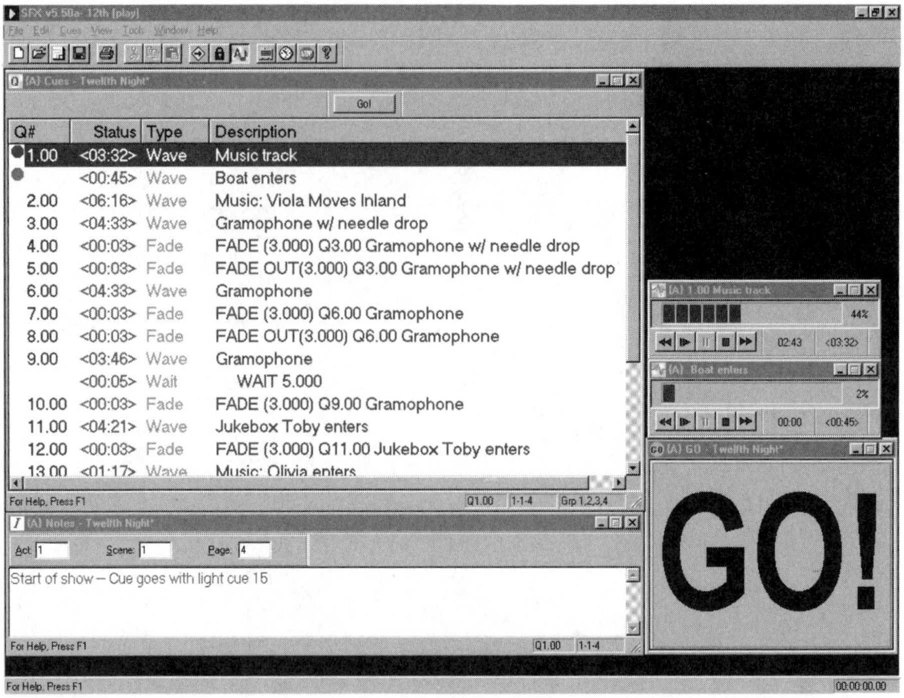

COURTESY STAGE RESEARCH, INC.

Speakers in the Playback System As discussed in Chapter 12, a theatrical playback system requires great flexibility in terms of speaker selection and location. Because a theatre audience expects sound effects and music to come from their apparent source, speaker placement is critical to good sound design. Specific selection criteria will be covered later in this chapter, but concern for placement should be utmost in the designer's mind from the beginning of the process.

The Reinforcement System

A theatrical *reinforcement system* is used to amplify, process, and mix live music and sound—principally actor's voices and orchestral music. This system is made up of various input sources connected to a *reinforcement mixer* that, in turn, is connected to amplifiers and speakers. Theatrical reinforcement can be fairly simple or extremely complex; a trade magazine article reporting on the reinforcement system for a recent Broadway musical stated that nearly 100 input sources were used. This is a huge number of audio signals to access, control, and mix down to output channels.

Reinforcement Input Sources The vast majority of input sources in a reinforcement system are *microphones*. Some signals will likely come from traditional wired microphones placed onstage, backstage, or in the orchestra. These mikes may take the form of *floor microphones* used onstage for general vocal reinforcement; *stand mikes* used backstage or in the orchestra for vocal or musical instrument pickup; or specialized musical instrument microphones used to amplify the orchestra. In musical productions, the performers will likely wear *wireless microphones*, with their audio signal sent by a transmitter to a receiver and then through wires to the mixer. In addition to microphones, input sources may include **direct boxes** or other line-level inputs from the orchestra (more on line levels later). Playback system inputs such as a CD, MiniDisc, or a computer can also be routed through the reinforcement mixer.

direct box Also referred to as a *DI box* or *direct injection box,* this device takes an unbalanced line-level sound signal from an electronic musical instrument such as an electric guitar or synthesizer and provides an isolated low-impedance microphone-level signal to a mixing board.

The Reinforcement Mixer The primary difference between a playback mixer and a reinforcement mixer is that the latter normally has a greater number of input channels and more sophisticated control. Their functions are similar in that they both do the following:

- Mix down (combine) several input signals
- Adjust volume levels
- Provide some tone control
- Route the signal through various processing equipment (equalizers, compressor/limiters, effects processors, feedback eliminators, and so forth)
- Send the final signal to selected amplifiers and speakers

The reinforcement mixer (Figure 13-4) is located in the auditorium, usually toward the rear of the main floor, so that its operator can hear exactly what the audience is hearing. The operator "rides" the sound levels—bringing up a mike when needed, taking it out when not required, and balancing the sounds from more than one microphone or other input source. Some of the more sophisticated playback mixers have MIDI-Mute groups, which provide computerized control over many input channels, allowing "presets" and cues to be written, stored, and played back in a way similar to how a lighting control console functions.

13-4

Reinforcement Mixer

Soundcraft Series FIVE mixing console: Provides for multiple inputs controlled through MIDI-Mute groups and extensive output metering and routing.

PHOTO COURTESY SOUNDCRAFT, HARMAN INTERNATIONAL INDUSTRIES LTD.

The reinforcement mixer contains several output channels so that specialized sound mixes can be sent to different locations. The *main house speaker system* is the primary location, but others may include a variety of *foldback* locations, including the stage itself, the orchestra, and the conductor; the *stage monitor* system with speakers located in the dressing rooms, green room, and elsewhere; and perhaps the *assistive-listening* system.

Combination Systems

patch panel A matrix of plug points used to interconnect various pieces of audio equipment. Usually divided into rows of inputs and outputs, the patch panel provides an organized central location for their routing.

To save money and space, a smaller theatre company may combine equipment used for recording, playback, and reinforcement. Examples include using a sound computer as both a digital audio workstation and a playback device, using a single multipurpose mixer for both playback and reinforcement, and using processing equipment such as an equalizer for recording as well as playback. Such systems may benefit from an electronic patch system or a **patch panel,** both of which provide flexibility in connecting one piece of equipment to another.

The traditional patch panel provides convenient routing of sound signals from one component in the system to another. It comprises a confusing-looking collection of jacks that allow an operator to connect any input source into any signal-processing unit. Depending on the needs of the job at hand, a CD's output could be patched into the equalizer or into the mixer or into another recording device. The patch bay is made up of single ⅛- or ¼-inch diameter jacks that are labeled by function. For instance, "MIX 3 IN" translates to "mixer channel number 3 input." Once the purpose of a patch panel is understood and the various pieces of equipment in the system are known, using it becomes a fairly easy task.

URL http://www.richmondsounddesign.com

Compared with the patch panel, an electronic patching system, such as the AudioBox from Richmond Sound Design (Figure 13-5), saves time and space. Besides patching, such a system provides volume control, equalization, and delay for each of the input and output signals along with the option of having eight tracks of hard disk audio playback. There is no doubt that the traditional hard patch panel will soon go the way of lighting autotransformer dimmers (see Chapter 17).

THE EQUIPMENT

The sound designer or technician must have enough knowledge of how and why a piece of equipment works to make intelligent choices about using or specifying equipment. The following section describes in detail the functional aspects of input, processing, and output equipment.

Microphones

mike level Signal voltage levels from a microphone to a mixing board, normally in the millivolt (thousandth of a volt, or mV) range.

As stated earlier, microphones convert sound waves into electrical energy for transmission to another location. By their nature, microphones are analog devices. If their low, **mike level** signals are not converted into digital, they

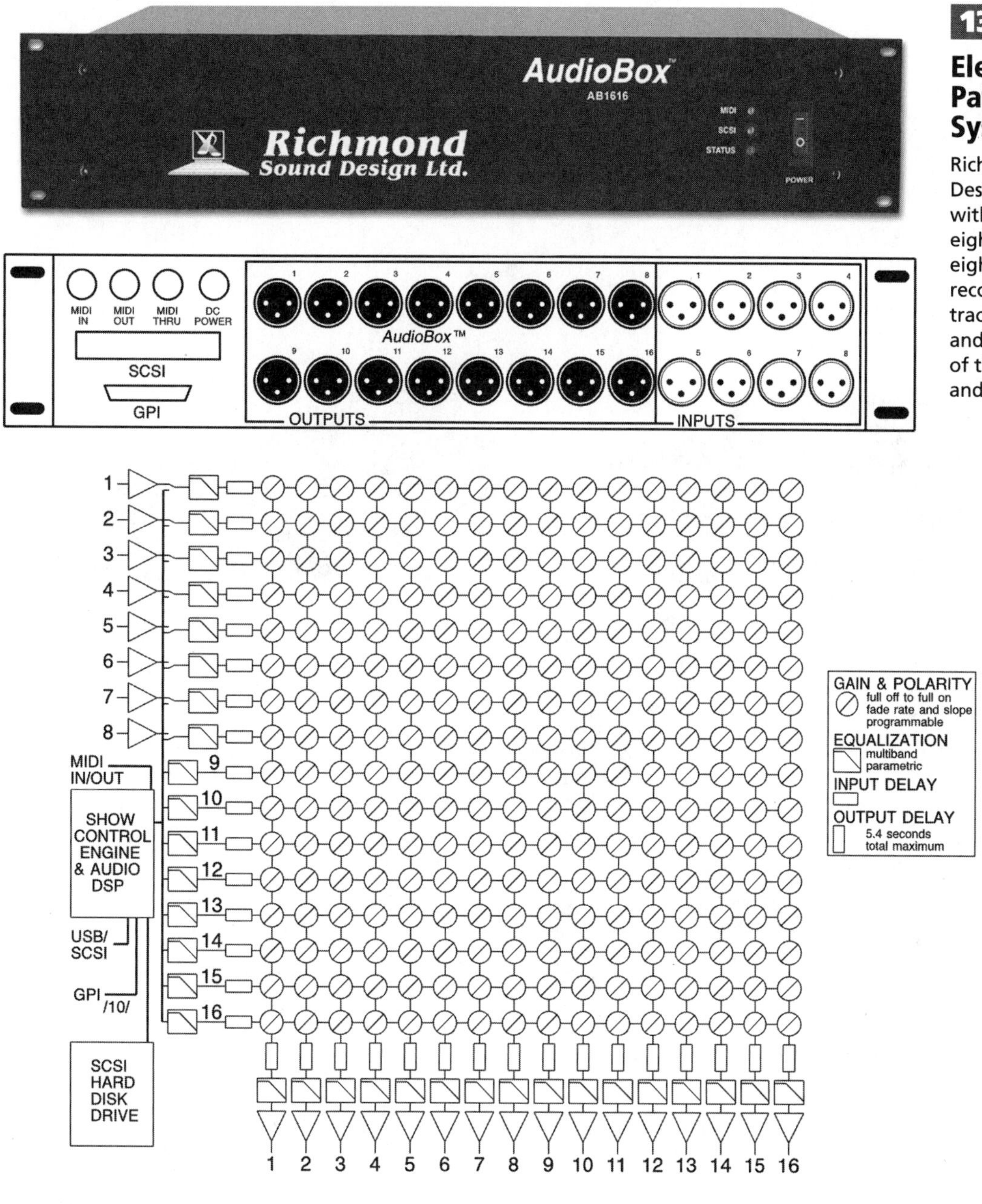

13-5

Electronic Patching System

Richmond Sound Design AudioBox with provisions for eight input channels, eight hard-disk-recorded sound tracks, equalization, and delay on all of the inputs and outputs.

PHOTO COURTESY RICHMOND SOUND DESIGN LTD.

need to be boosted to a higher power level called **line level** before they can be processed. This is normally accomplished by the **preamplifier** or "preamp," located in the mixer. If the mixer is digital, the mike-level signal will be converted to digital rather than boosted by a preamp.

line level Signal voltage levels from various pieces of audio equipment to speaker amplifiers; ranging from 77.5 millivolts to 24.5 volts, with 4.5 volts across 600 ohms equal to 1 watt.

As Figure 13-6 shows, microphones come in a variety of sizes and shapes. The handheld *vocal microphone* (Figure 13-6a) is a good choice for multipurpose use, although most tasks are performed best with specialized mikes. As one might expect, a vocal microphone is particularly sensitive to frequencies in the vocal range. The sound produced by a large, handheld vocal microphone is unique because it has a specialized frequency response and boosts low frequencies (the proximity effect).

preamplifier The first circuit encountered by the sound signal from a microphone into the mixing board, it amplifies the microphone level signal to line level.

a & b PHOTOS COURTESY SHURE, INC.

c & d PHOTOS CROWN AUDIO, INC.

e PHOTO COURTESY SENNHEISER ELECTRONIC GMBH & CO. KG

13-6

Microphones

- **a** Shure Beta 58a handheld dynamic vocal microphone.
- **b** Shure Beta 57a dynamic vocal/instrument microphone.
- **c** Crown PZM (pressure zone microphone). A condenser microphone with a typical hemispherical pickup pattern (depending on boundary shape).
- **d** Crown PCC (phase coherent cardioid) condenser boundary microphone with a half-cardioid pickup pattern.
- **e** Sennheiser MKE2 miniature electret condenser microphone—the microphone type most commonly used in wireless microphone systems.

The *instrument microphone* (Figure 13-6b) is engineered to have a "flat" frequency response, meaning that it responds fairly equally to all frequencies.

General area reinforcement uses surface-mounted or **boundary microphones** placed along the front of the stage. Two types of boundary microphones manufactured by Crown International are the pressure zone microphone or PZM (Figure 13-6c) and the phase coherent cardioid or PCC (Figure 13-6d). The primary difference between these two microphones is that the PZM accepts sound from all directions while the PCC rejects sound from all directions but one (the *cardioid pickup pattern,* to be discussed shortly).

boundary microphone A microphone placed extremely close to and facing a flat (boundary) plate. Rather than responding directly to pressure in the air, this microphone picks up pressure variations from the air gap between the element and the plate.

URL http://www.crownaudio.com

Specific reinforcement of selected performers is accomplished by using *personal microphones,* either handheld or miniature (Figure 13-6e). The popularity of wireless miniature microphones has grown as they have become more dependable and cost-effective. If used properly, modern wireless microphones work well for most stage reinforcement applications.

Microphone Types Most microphones are categorized in two ways:

1. By how they perform the task of changing sound into electrical energy

2. By their pickup patterns

Although there are many types of microphones, in the theatre we are primarily concerned with only two: the *dynamic* microphone and the *condenser* microphone.

dynamic microphone A microphone housing an element that consists of a diaphragm directly coupled to a coil of wire that moves back and forth in a magnetic field. As the air pressure moves the diaphragm, the coil's movement in the magnetic field induces a flow of alternating electricity in the microphone cable that is analogous to the alternating waves in the air.

The **dynamic microphone**, short for "dynamic moving coil," uses a diaphragm, similar to the eardrum, to receive sound waves. This vibrating diaphragm causes movement of a metal coil inside a magnetic field which, in turn, generates an electrical signal—an *analog* of the sound waves. Probably the most common microphone, the dynamic can be designed with any sound pickup pattern. It is the least fragile of types and can be of excellent quality.

condenser microphone A microphone housing an element consisting of two metallic-coated plates separated by a small volume of air. The top plate, which is charged with an electrical voltage, acts as a diaphragm. Its movement back and forth (changing the distance of the air gap between the two plates) alters the electrical charge induced in the back plate. Because of the very low voltage generated, all condenser microphones require an internal amplifier as well as a source of power—either a small battery or phantom power from the mixing board.

The **condenser microphone** receives sound waves on electronic plates that generate a signal. However, so little initial power is created that a small amplifier must be located nearby. The amplifier, housed in the microphone, may be powered by a DC (direct current) power supply in the form of a small battery, or more likely by an electrical supply from the mixing board referred to as **phantom power** (Figure 13-7).

phantom power Power for condenser microphones, which is supplied through the microphone cable from the mixing board.

While being the highest quality available, the condenser microphone is also more delicate and expensive than the dynamic. Because of its added sensitivity, the condenser microphone is normally chosen for more demanding or critical sound tasks.

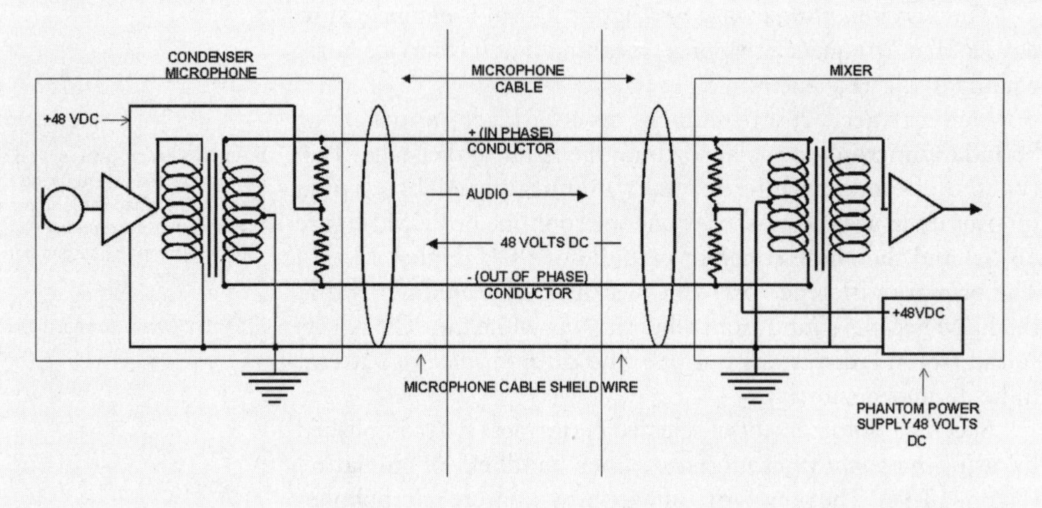

13-7

Phantom Power

Phantom power wiring showing the 48 volts DC applied to both conductors of a balanced microphone line. Because the DC voltage is applied to both lines in a balanced system, the signal is invisible (phantom) to the audio circuit, which looks only at the difference in voltage between the two conductors carrying the audio signal.

Microphone Pickup Patterns A microphone without a restricted pickup pattern receives sound equally from all directions. For instance, such a microphone located on the floor at stage front would receive direct sound from a performer's voice, bounced sound from the floor, and sound from the orchestra and audience. Restricted pickup patterns help a microphone be more selective. Figure 13-8 illustrates four common pickup patterns: omnidirectional, bidirectional, cardioid, and supercardioid.

As the name implies, an *omnidirectional* pattern microphone receives sound from all directions. This pattern is used for body mikes, monitor mikes, and pressure zone microphones (PZMs), as well as in situations where all sound is

13-8

Microphone Pickup Patterns

The choice of pickup pattern is determined by the specific task.

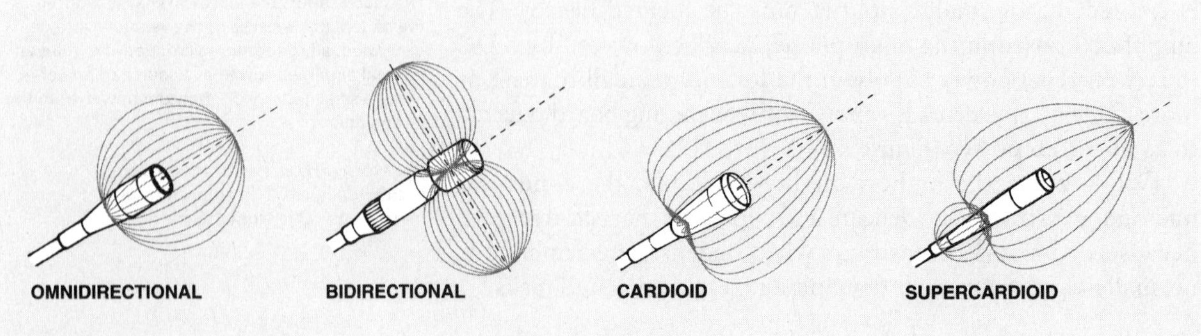

required, such as group recording. **Feedback,** in which sound from a speaker is picked up by a microphone and continuously reamplified, can be a particular problem with this pattern (see "How to Control Feedback" near the end of this chapter).

feedback An audio loop created between a microphone and its speaker. As a speaker's volume is increased, a point is reached where sound from the speaker entering the microphone is greater than the original sound from the actor. This "loop" then becomes self-feeding (hence, *feedback*), locking onto in-phase frequencies and amplifying them uncontrollably.

A bidirectional pattern looks like the figure eight. It works well in recording two-person interviews or in any other situation where the desired sound comes primarily from two opposite directions.

A cardioid pattern is the most useful for general theatrical applications. Rejection of sound increases as one moves around the microphone and is most effective at the rear, lessening the possibility of feedback.

For long-range directional pickup, the supercardioid pattern is desirable. This pattern is used by the phase coherent cardioid (PCC) microphone, which is commonly placed along the downstage edge of the apron and used for general vocal pickup.

Wireless Microphones A microphone without the nuisance of a cable is very desirable, particularly for vocal reinforcement. The wireless microphones shown in Figure 13-9 are actually miniature FM radio stations. The tiny body mike is wired to a low-power transmitter worn by the performer. This transmitter sends a radio signal of specific frequency to a receiver located offstage. The receiver picks up only that frequency and sends the analog-converted signal through a wire to the sound system for amplification. The transmitter and receivers can be made to operate on a variety of matched frequencies in order to isolate one microphone from another when several are in use.

This type of system is fairly delicate, and the better ones are expensive. However, the negatives are outweighed by the convenience of the system and the quality of its sound reproduction. Performers often wear the tiny omnidirectional microphone over the ear or on the forehead at the hairline, with the wire running through the hair and down the back. This technique, as

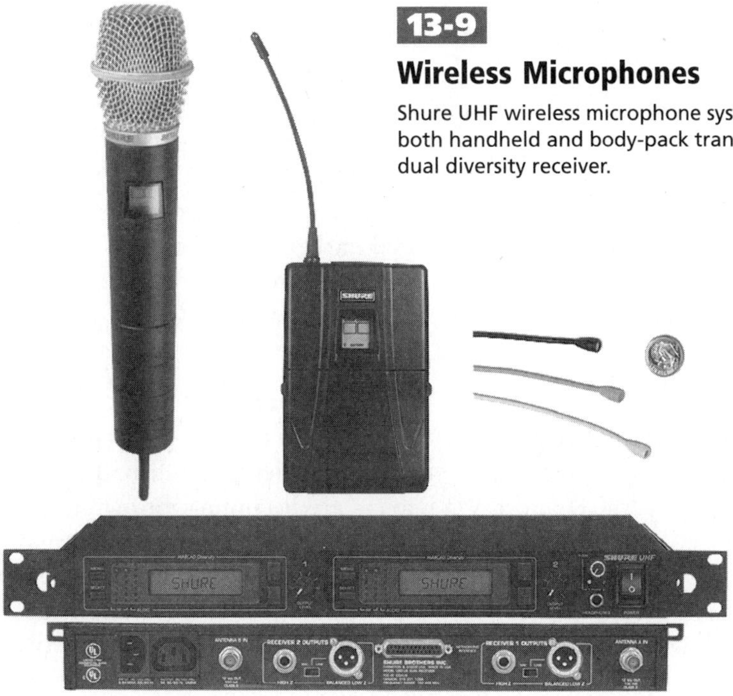

13-9

Wireless Microphones

Shure UHF wireless microphone system showing both handheld and body-pack transmitters and a dual diversity receiver.

PHOTO COURTESY SHURE, INC.

Sound Advice

Microphone Care

To perform well over their life span, microphones need to be properly cared for:

- Never blow into a microphone to test it.
- Store microphones in a cool, dry cabinet on a padded shelf or in their cases.
- Do not thump or bang microphones on a hard surface.

opposed to the familiar clipping onto a piece of clothing, avoids noise created by the clothing and prevents variation in sound level as the head turns from side to side. Another option is for the performer to wear a headset-type miniature microphone. The armature allows the microphone capsule to be placed close to the performer's mouth, providing the sound of a large vocal microphone while minimizing feedback.

In this case, a directional pickup pattern such as cardoid is used to reject sounds other than the performer's voice. The sound designer must work closely with the costume department when using wireless body mikes; the placement of relatively bulky transmitters can be tricky, and the costume department can offer invaluable assistance. For further information on the use and care of wireless equipment, see the "How to Work with Wireless Microphones" section at the end of this chapter.

Tape Playback Equipment

DAT (digital audio tape) and MDM (modular digital multitrack) machines record a digital signal on magnetic tape for storage and playback. Advantages over analog recording are ease of editing, greater dynamic range, and improved sound quality that is due to significant reduction in tape noise. Compared with other storage and playback systems such as CDs or DVDs, digital tape systems have some disadvantages, including slow random access when editing and, until recently, start-up delay. As stated earlier, tapes come in cassettes and can be multitrack, although two-track is most common for theatrical use. Even digital storage on magnetic tape is inferior to that on optical media.

Optical Playback

MiniDisc players like the one shown in Figure 13-10 became popular optical playback devices because they were relatively inexpensive and had a quick start-up time. However, CD and DVD players are becoming more and more popular as their cost comes down and the general public learns how easy it is to record on a CD. The audio world received the compact disc with open arms for a variety of reasons. Disc players are simple to use, may be controlled remotely, and allow quick and easy access to tracks. Recordable compact discs

PHOTO COURTESY TASCAM/TEAC AMERICA, INC.TASCAM/T

13-10

MiniDisc Player

TASCAM MD-801R MKII MiniDisc recorder/player.

have made it possible to use this superior storage medium for theatrical playback. Recordable DVDs, which have a greater storage capacity than CDs, will likely be the optical playback source in the future.

Digital Audio Workstations

The computer has replaced numerous pieces of audio equipment once found in the theatrical sound studio. Computers have not only lowered the cost of sound processing but also greatly reduced the editing time involved in creating sound effects and music for a theatre production.

As we have seen, *digital audio workstations* are computer-based systems that allow visual editing and processing of sound waveforms. With appropriate software, the same computer may be used as a playback device for theatrical production. For processing, the DAW will have sampling software, synthesizer software, loop-based software, and editing software. For playback, it acts as a control system for the sound operator.

Mixers

Both digital and analog mixers are available in a wide variety of styles depending on function. As mentioned earlier, theatrical mixers may need to serve several purposes—in-house reinforcement mixing, studio recording, and show playback. Mixer capacity is specified in terms of input and output channels; eight to twelve channels in and two channels out is a minimum requirement; sixteen to thirty-two or even forty inputs, with six to eight output channels, is more normal.

The mixer is a complex piece of equipment. It must control a large number of inputs and direct them to various output channels. In an analog mixer, each input channel has a line-level as well as a low- or mike-level input. Because the power of a microphone's signal is relatively slight, an analog mixer contains preamplifiers that take these low-level signals and increase them to the higher line level.

trim pot Also referred to as *input level, input gain,* or *pad,* it is a sound mixer's volume control over the input signal.

pan pot The potentiometer that controls the left/right assignment to a sound mixer's output bus.

The low-level microphone input is wired directly to a preamplifier located within the mixer. The sound signal then travels to an input attenuator or **trim pot** used to adjust the volume level, and on to equalizer controls. Next is another fader called a **pan pot** that determines how much volume will be routed, by switches, to the selected output channels. Yet another fader masters the level of the selected output channel. Finally, the VU meter registers the resulting sound. An operator can monitor the sound either completely mixed just before the VU meter or unadulterated just before the input fader (called PFL or pre fade listen).

The digital mixer receives an analog signal and immediately converts it to digital, thereby eliminating the need for signal amplification. Being digital, the signal processing and routing is more sophisticated.

Auxiliary feeds for processing equipment are standard on many mixers. A mixer can be custom designed for a particular use.

Signal Processors

Signal processors alter sound in a specific way. They include multi-effects processors, compressor/limiters, and delay units as well as equalizers.

Equalizers An equalizer serves three basic functions for theatrical sound in doing the following:

1. Adjusting selected frequencies of an output source in accordance with room acoustics or for the control of feedback
2. In a playback system, altering voice, music, or sound frequencies to improve tone quality
3. In the recording system, processing sound to make its effect more appropriate to the action

Although a mixer provides some degree of equalization through its tone controls, an equalizer allows for much more precise adjustment of specific frequencies.

Two main types of equalizers exist: *graphic* and *parametric.* The graphic type has sliding faders permanently assigned to frequency bands that are typically between one-third and one octave in width. The parametric type allows the operator to select specific frequencies for control and to adjust the band width individually. Each type serves well in particular applications. If an equalizer is used only to adjust room acoustics, for example, it should be of the parametric type and left alone to do its job. However, equalizers used to control tone quality will need to be adjusted according to each task. In this case, an easily accessible graphic equalizer is preferable.

URL http://www.sabine.com

Modern pieces of equipment such as the Sabine Graphi-Q (Figure 13-11) combine graphic and parametric equalization into a single unit. In addition, the Graphi-Q offers compression and delay features. Equalization is a very important technique for reinforcement, recording, and playback.

Other Processing Equipment *Multi-effects processors* are particularly valuable because they can perform a wide variety of processing tasks (Figure 13-12). They can alter sound in varying degrees—from making it richer by adding a slight amount of reverberation to giving it an echo (repetition of a whole sound). In addition, they can provide pitch shifting, flanging, auto-pan,

PHOTO COURTESY SABINE, INC.

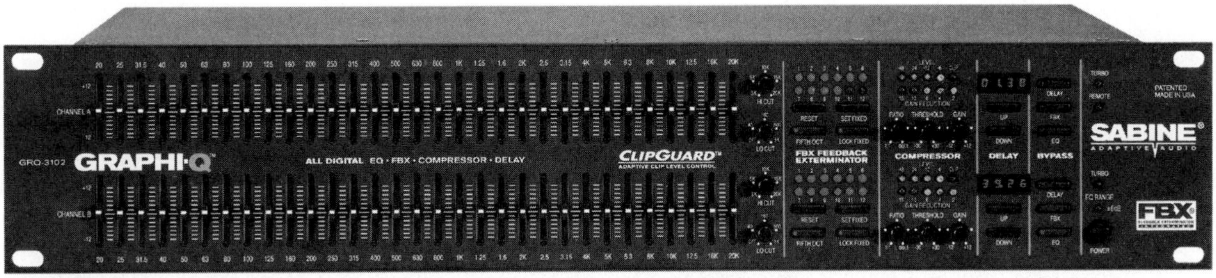

13-11

The Equalizer

The Sabine GRAPHI-Q GRQ-3102, dual channel with front panel controls for feedback eliminator, compressor/limiter, delay, and parametric EQ.

PHOTO COURTESY LEXICON, INC.

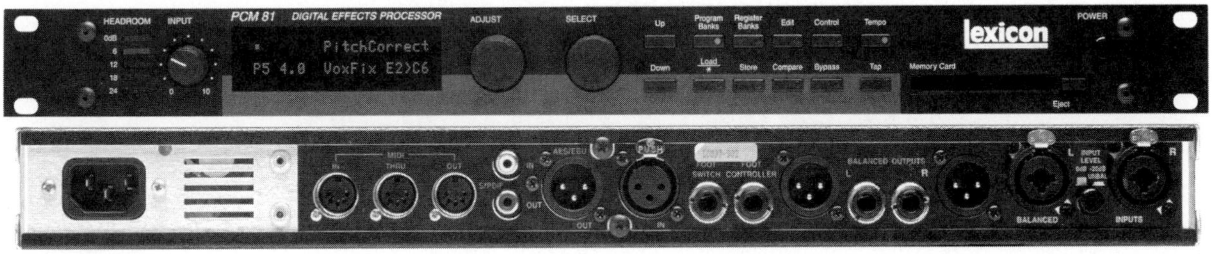

13-12

Multi-Effects Processor

The Lexicon PCM 81 Digital Effects Processor.

and so on. *Compressor/limiters* are used to ensure that a sound signal does not "over drive" an amplifier and speaker. They either compress or limit the dynamic range of an audio signal as needed. *Delay units* were mentioned previously in conjunction with the need to delay sound from speakers to the audience. They are important in maintaining the actor as the source of the sound in the theatre.

Amplifiers

Line-level voltage is not enough power to make a loudspeaker work (in technical jargon, to "drive" the speaker). Therefore, an amplifier matched to the loudspeaker's power rating is assigned to each speaker in the system. Rack-mounted amplifiers are commonly placed in the ceiling of an auditorium between the sound control booth and the majority of the speakers. The amplifier receives a line-level signal from the control booth, amplifies it to **speaker level,** and sends it on to its assigned speaker.

Power amplifiers such as the one shown in Figure 13-13 have come a long way since the days of metal boxes filled with glowing tubes. However, one thing has not changed: amplifiers and speakers must be compatible. Proper matching involves a speaker's **impedance** (similar to resistance in a DC circuit, measured in ohms) as well as its RMS power rating. **RMS** (root mean square) is a way of describing the power or wattage capacities of amplifiers and speakers. Under normal conditions, an amplifier's RMS power rating (measured

speaker level Signal voltage level from an amplifier to its speaker. 24.5 volts and up is enough to drive a speaker.

impedance The measurement of resistance in alternating current circuits, including audio signals. It is used in speaker specifications (typically 4 to 16 ohms) and in sound equipment input and output specifications.

RMS Root mean square is used to give an average power value to an alternating current or audio circuit as it would compare with that of a direct-current circuit. RMS can be used to describe both peak (instantaneous) values as well as the more useful continuous power output.

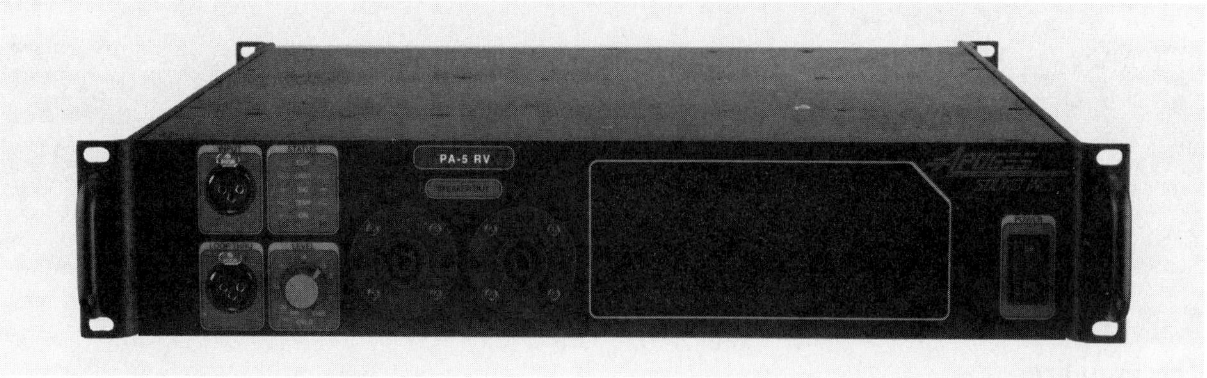

PHOTO COURTESY APOGEE SOUND, INC.

13-13

Amplifier

Shown is an Apogee PA-5 RV 400-watt processor-amplifier that incorporates both specialized signal processing and power amplification into one unit.

in watts) must never exceed that of the speaker. Although loudspeakers can have impedances varying from 2 to 30 ohms (most common are 8 and 16 ohms) and amplifiers usually are designed for loads of 4, 8, or 16 ohms, they must be matched for proper sound reproduction. It is highly recommended that a theatrical sound system have compatible amplifiers permanently assigned to each speaker.

Loudspeakers

Like microphones, loudspeakers are specialized and come in a wide range of sizes, types, and prices. They receive the sound signal from the amplifier and transduce it back into pressure waves that we can hear. The more accurately a speaker performs this task, the better it is for theatrical use; quality varies greatly.

Speaker Types Two general speaker types exist:

- The *cone speaker* (Figure 13-14a)
- The compression driver speaker (Figure 13-14b)

In both cases, a moving diaphragm generates pressure waves. The larger cone speakers have a plastic or paper diaphragm, while compression drivers have a diaphragm made of a stiff material such as aluminum or titanium. A metal diaphragm is more capable of producing sounds in the higher frequencies, while a cone speaker is better for lower frequencies. A horn such as that shown in Figure 13-15 is usually coupled with a compression driver to control the sound dispersion. The extent of directionality depends on the shape and size of the horn, which can be designed for specific tasks.

crossover network An important speaker element, this electronic device is used to divide and route frequency bands to the appropriate speaker component—either as a passive set of electronic components located inside the speaker cabinet or as an active electronic device that divides a line-level signal into frequency bands and sends them to separate power amplifiers.

Most speakers will be enclosed in a cabinet, which plays a significant acoustic role in the sound production (Figure 13-16a). Sometimes housed in or attached to the cabinet is a **crossover network.** This electronic device receives the sound signal from the amplifier and separates the frequencies into ranges acceptable to the individual speakers. Low frequencies are handled by the *woofer,* a large cone whose size is determined by the sound volume it is required to generate—the more volume, the larger the cone diameter.

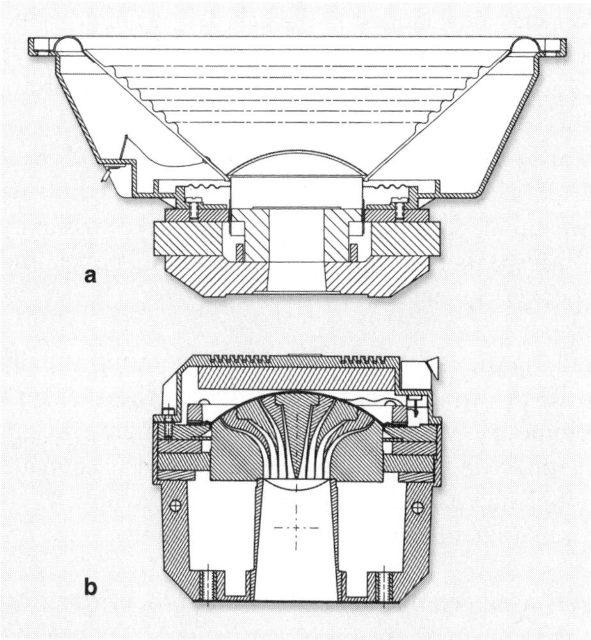

a & b DRAWINGS COURTESY JBL, INC.

13-14

Sectional Drawings of Two Speaker Types

a A cone-type driver.

b A compression driver without its horn.

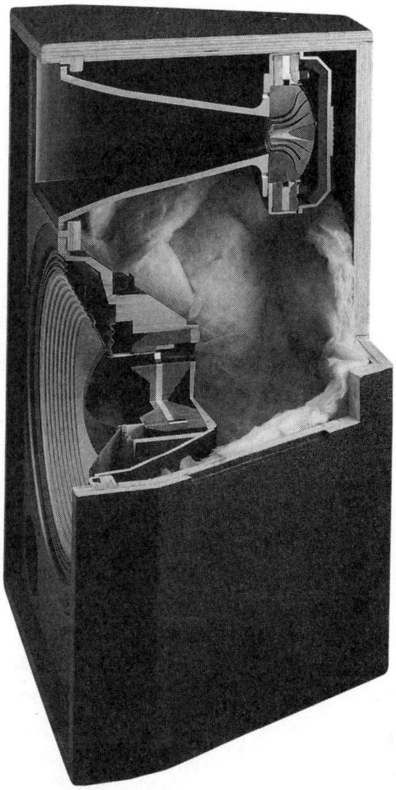

PHOTO COURTESY JBL PROFESSIONAL

13-15

Compression Driver with Horn

Cutaway of a JBL Array Series loudspeaker with a biradial horn and a 14-inch low-frequency woofer.

13-16

Speaker Systems

a An Apogee two-way cabinet speaker with an outboard processor/amplifier.

b An EAW EP3, three-way self-powered, full-range speaker system.

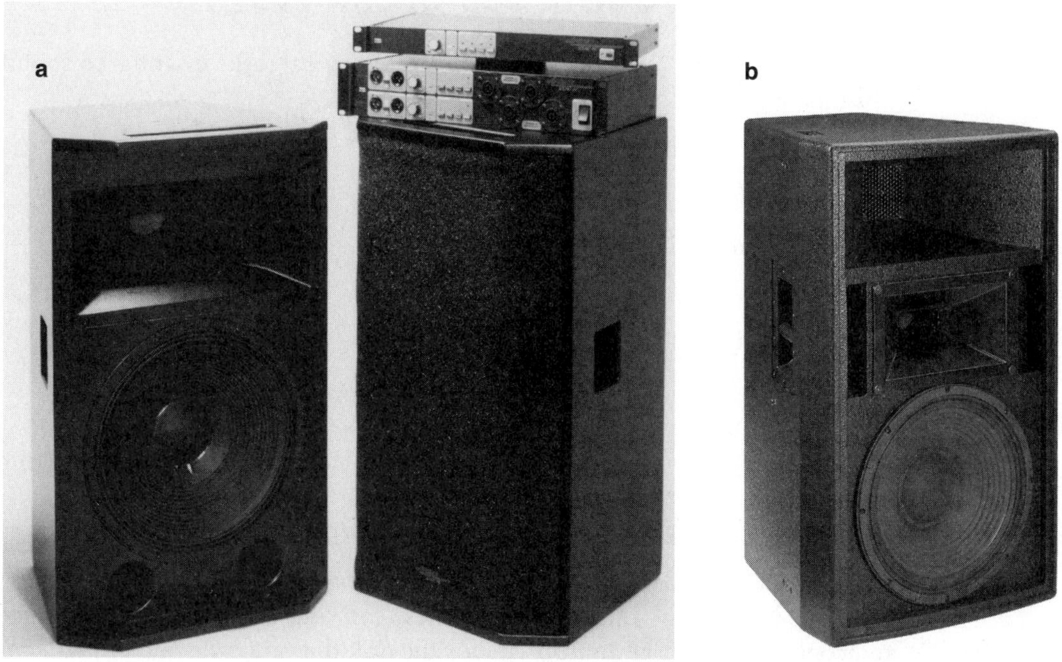

a PHOTO COURTESY APOGEE SOUND, INC..
b PHOTO COURTESY EAW, INC.

Although a midrange speaker may be included in the cabinet, the middle and high frequencies are normally handled by a single compression driver. These horn-type speakers are occasionally attached to the top of a cabinet but are more often contained within.

The current trend is toward *self-powered speakers* (Figure 13-16b). These speakers contain an amplifier, a crossover network, and signal-processing equipment within each of their cabinets. Such a system eliminates the possibility of mismatching amplifiers with speakers—one need only plug AC power and a line-level signal into the speaker cabinet.

Power Ratings As noted, speakers have an RMS power rating usually measured at 8 ohms. The RMS rating serves as a guide to the speaker's performance in terms of volume. However, some speakers are more efficient than others. Rather than rely on RMS figures alone, sound engineers compare them with the speaker's efficiency as indicated by sound pressure levels published by the manufacturers (SPL at 1 meter with 1-watt input).

Phasing When hooking up speakers, one needs to ensure proper electrical phasing. This simply means that one must always pay attention to the positive and negative connections from amplifier to speaker, never crossing them. Doing so will cause the diaphragm of one speaker to move in, while that of another moves out, potentially canceling sound.

Selection Speaker selection is determined by application. Theatre speakers should be able to produce 115 dB of sound pressure level without distortion, they should have as wide and flat a frequency response as possible, and they should be kept to a minimum physical size. All this translates into money. Theatre companies pay top dollar for their speakers. Because speakers are the weakest link in the audio system, they must be of the highest quality to make up for this fact.

ESSENTIAL SOUND DESIGN SKILLS

This section covers "how to" instructions for several tasks essential to sound design:

- How to do wiring and use connectors
- How to work with digital audio
- How to make live recordings
- How to work with wireless microphones
- How to control feedback
- How to select and place performance microphones
- How to place speakers

How to Do Wiring and Use Connectors

The power of sound signals varies in voltage from low-level mike signals (less than 1 volt) to high-voltage speaker lines (carrying up to 70 volts). Wiring and connectors must be appropriate for the task they are called on to perform.

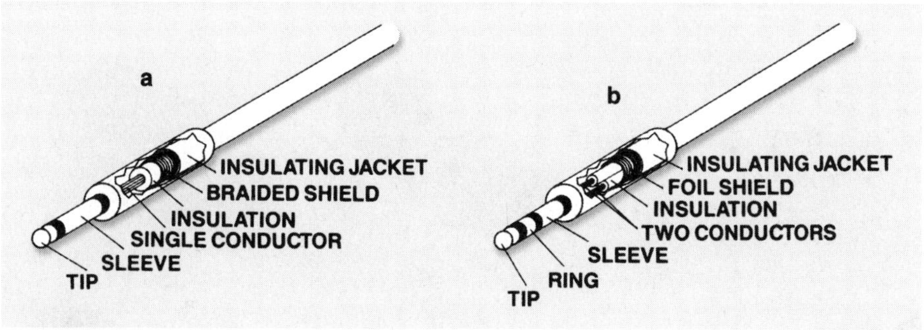

13-17

Balanced and Unbalanced Lines

a An unbalanced line with a matching jack plug.

b A balanced line with matching jack plug.

Balanced and Unbalanced Lines Two types of wiring are used to connect one piece of audio equipment to another: balanced and unbalanced lines. An **unbalanced line** is a cable made up of a single conductor with a metallic shield wrapped around it (Figure 13-17a). The single conductor is the positive wire, while the shield acts as both the negative and ground. A **balanced line** has two conductors with a shield (Figure 13-17b). These negative and positive conductors carry the signal, while the shield acts simply as a ground.

Unbalanced lines are less expensive but are subject to electrical interference. They are typically used in consumer equipment to carry a signal from one piece of equipment to another. Balanced lines are used for microphone lines and other long runs of cable. It is most desirable to have the entire system balanced, as is the case in professional systems. Even with a completely balanced system, however, it is best to keep audio cable away from higher-voltage electrical lines (such as lighting cables), which produce a significant magnetic field able to interfere with the sound signal.

unbalanced line A method in which the audio signal is carried on a single center-conductor in a shielded cable. This method is used primarily for consumer electronics and is very susceptible to noise and interference.

balanced line A method in which the audio signal is carried on two wires in a shielded cable, with one signal being 180 degrees out-of-phase from the other. Sometimes called *differential input,* this input signal is only read in terms of the difference between the two wires; therefore, any noise induced on both of them will be ignored. Balanced lines are standard in professional equipment and can be used for very long cable runs.

Speaker Lines Connections from amplifiers to speakers deserve special attention because of the relatively high voltage requirements. If the distance from amplifier to speaker is short, one need only be sure that the wire is large enough (14 gauge is fine). However, if the run is long or several speakers are being driven, wire gauge may need to be increased to ensure that the speaker or speakers receive adequate power.

Connectors Figure 13-18 shows some common connectors associated with professional audio equipment. The RCA phono connector is used only for unbalanced signals and is often found on consumer equipment. The ¼-inch phone connector can be either balanced or unbalanced and is typically used for line-level devices. It is less desirable than the XLR connector because it does not lock in place and does not at first make a complete connection when being plugged in. An XLR connector is a much better choice. It locks, has good strain relief, and makes a clean connection. However, XLR connectors cannot handle the higher voltages of speaker lines.

Because of their higher voltage and current, professional speakers should have specially designed connectors used with them. Two common connectors

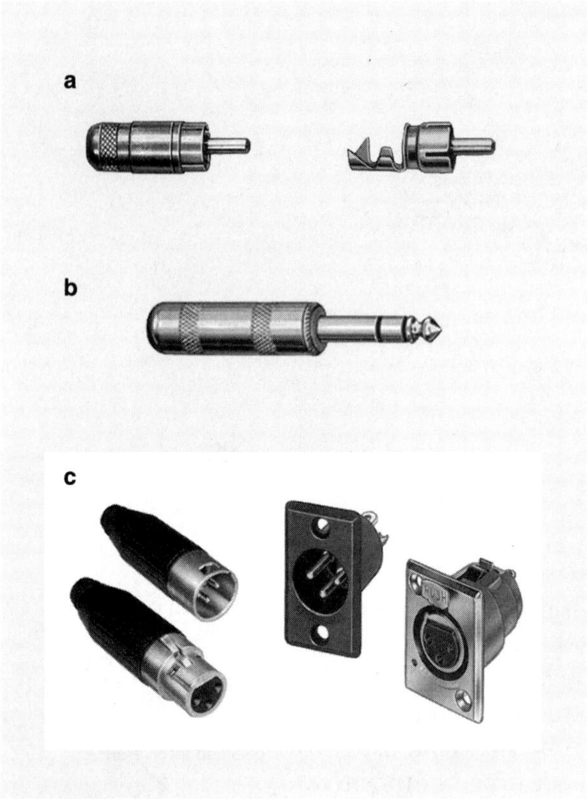

13-18

Audio Connectors

a An unbalanced RCA phono connector.

b A balanced ¼-inch phone connector.

c A pair of balanced XLR connectors with wall mounts.

PHOTO COURTESY NEUTRIK USA, INC. SPEAKON IS A REGISTERED TRADEMARK OF NEUTRIK.

13-19

Speaker Connectors

Neutrik Speakon high current, locking speaker cable connectors.

URL http://www.neutrik.com

URL http://www.switchcraft.com

are the Neutrik Speakon connector (Figure 13-19) and the comparable Switchcraft HPC-Series connector. Developed by Neutrik specifically for speakers, these connectors lock in place, allow for quick disconnect, handle high current, and are available in 2-, 4-, or 8-contact versions for multiple speaker connections. Some speakers still come equipped with ¼-inch phone jacks—they are to be avoided.

Sound Advice

Line-Level Voltages

Be aware that line-level voltages are not the same in consumer and professional equipment:

- Consumer equipment line level = –10 dBm or 245 mV (.245 volts)
- Professional equipment line level = +4 dBm or 1.23 volts

How to Work with Digital Audio

Digital audio is a numeric (binary) representation of sound. When an analog signal is changed into digital by an analog to digital (a/d) converter, the device is measuring how strong the signal (voltage) is at a given moment. This is called *sampling* (Figure 13-20a).

Sampling To represent an analog wave form accurately in binary terms, a great number of samples must be taken: normally 44,100 per second. This number is derived from the **Nyquist Sampling Theorem,** which states that one must sample an analog signal at twice the rate of the highest frequency in order to reconstruct that signal accurately. The quality of a digital reproduction, then, depends largely on adequately high sample rates and resolution.

The accuracy of each sample is further determined by the number of values assigned to each—this is referred to as the **sampling resolution.** High-quality audio samples assign 65,536 different values (2^{16}, which is equivalent to 16 bits or 2 bytes). The value of each sample may be recorded and stored in a

Nyquist sampling theorem Theorem that states that accurately reconstructing an analog sound signal in digital form requires that it be sampled at twice the rate of the highest frequency.

sampling resolution The number of different values available to assign to a digital audio sample. Resolution directly affects the quality of sound reproduction.

13-20

Digital Sampling

a Screenshot of a section of a sampled wave form.

b Screenshot of a section of a sampled wave form with digital clipping. Notice the chopping off of the tops of the waves, causing digital distortion.

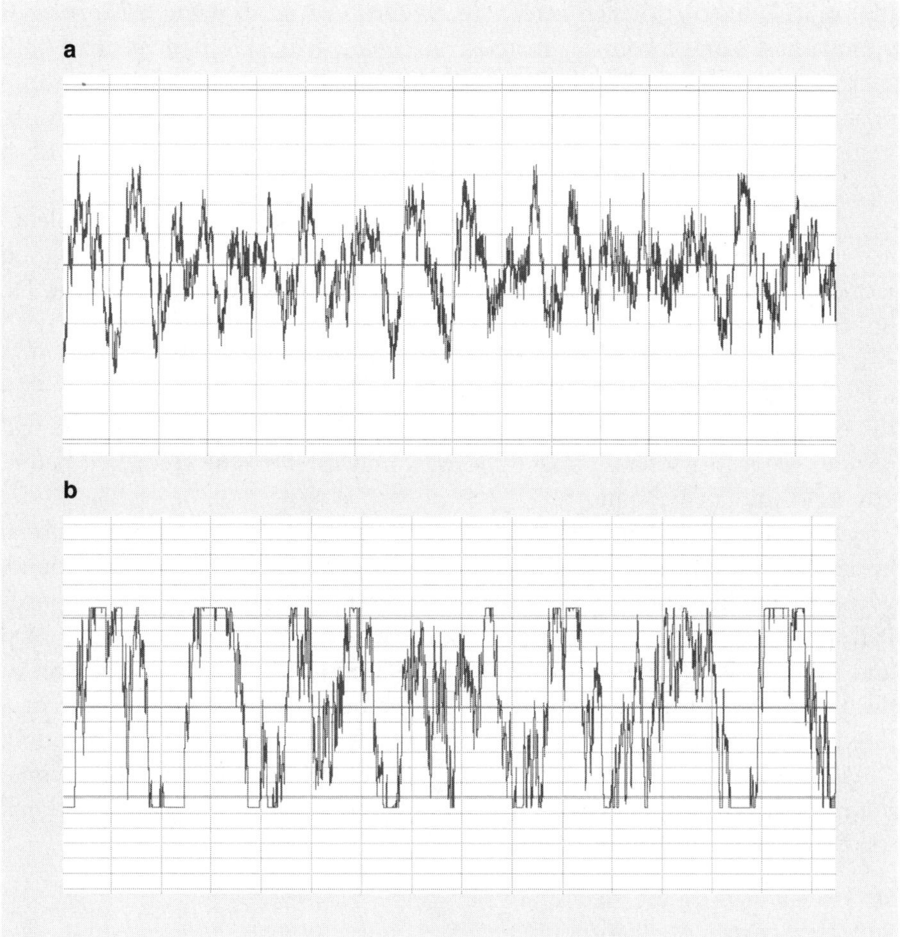

computer's hard drive, for instance. One minute of CD-quality audio contains the following:

60 seconds × 2 bytes (16 bits) × 44,100 samples per second × 2 tracks (stereo)

That is about 10 megabytes! One can certainly take fewer samples per second or assign fewer values to each sample, but some quality or resolution is lost.

digital clipping In sound recordings, a harsh distortion caused by inaccurate digital recording of frequencies beyond the sampling range.

aliasing In sound recordings, a distortion caused by a sampling rate below the Nyquist frequency.

Digital Clipping and Aliasing When converting an audio signal from analog to digital, one must consider the problem of **digital clipping.** It is a harsh distortion caused by inaccurate digital recording of frequencies beyond the sampling range (Figure 13-20b). Recording at the highest possible volume (voltage) produces the best resolution. However, a ceiling exists that reflects the highest sampling number available. Above this ceiling, clipping occurs (Figure 13-20b).

Aliasing is another severe form of distortion. It is the result of a sampling rate below the Nyquist frequency. Analog to digital converters should use low-pass filtering to remove all signals above the sampling rate.

How to Make Live Recordings

Live recording of a synthesizer or other electronic equipment is simply a matter of patching its output into the recording device, but recording sounds with a microphone is another matter entirely. The microphone input should be routed through a mixer and then into a recording device, allowing the operator volume and mixing control. In most instances, it is safest to record "flat" (without equalization) and make adjustments later. The recording studio normally should be quite "dead," with walls and floors covered with absorbent material (carpeting works well). In addition, any ambient sound must be eliminated.

Ample time must be allowed for any recording session. Before the "talent" arrives, all equipment should be checked out to be sure that it is in good working order. Make a recording only of the room to see what you hear. Do not be afraid to experiment; mistakes often reveal valuable techniques. Try a variety of different microphones as well as placements. Remember that microphones (especially omnidirectional ones) pick up *everything,* including the sound of the equipment and computer and ventilation fans. At the end of your recording session, take a moment and listen to the recording before you send the talent home.

When recording the speaking voice, a directional or an omnidirectional microphone may be used. The directional mike eliminates more ambient sound, while the omnidirectional provides more "presence" and is less likely to "pop." Place the microphone six to twelve inches away from the person being recorded and run a series of tests with the talent talking into the mike. The effect of distant sound is best achieved with the person off-axis or to one side of a directional mike; it can also be added later with equalization and reverberation.

Recording a group of voices can be done with a single omnidirectional mike. If stereo recording is necessary, try a stereo microphone or two directional mikes crossed as in Figure 13-21.

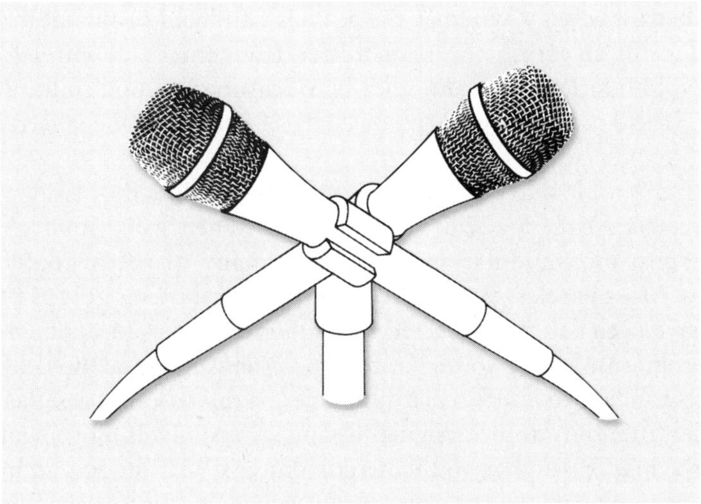

13-21

Stereo Microphone Arrangement

Microphones crossed to achieve stereo pickup.

How to Work with Wireless Microphones

Available either as handheld or as miniature body mikes, wireless microphones are a major element of any reinforcement system. In addition to understanding wireless technology, the sound designer must take care to observe several practices that improve wireless use.

Sound Quality Miniature body wireless microphones are available in two types: omnidirectional and cardioid. Selection depends on where the performer wears the microphone. In most cases, the omnidirectional type is chosen for theatre use because the mike is placed on the performer's head. Unfortunately, problems with sound quality, feedback, and interference are more common with omnidirectional pickup patterns. Sound quality lacks proximity effect and selected frequency response exhibited by larger mikes. Some degree of equalization should be used to offset this effect.

Attaching the Body Mike The body mike is attached either at the hairline or over the ear. When attaching the mike over the ear, a metal support must be used to hold the mike cable and capsule in place. Any malleable metal with a rubberized coating will do, such as solid-core copper electrical wire with rubber coating. With tape, attach the mike cable to a three- or four-inch length of the wire, allowing the mike capsule to extend beyond the end of the support wire by an inch or so. Then bend the wire over the performer's ear and tape it to the skin behind the ear using clear medical adhesive tape. Additional tape may be necessary, but attempt to keep the mike capsule slightly off the surface of the performer's skin to avoid excess moisture. Use bobby pins to attach the mike at the hairline. If this proves too unstable, try attaching a more substantial clip to the mike cable and then to the hairline.

In either case, the mike cable can be run down the back of the performer to the bodypack transmitter. The costume shop can help to provide a fabric pouch to hold the transmitter. The pouch may be attached to the costume itself or to the body of the performer.

Transmitting Frequencies Whether the mike is handheld or miniature, care must be taken in selecting the transmitter frequencies of wireless microphones to avoid interference from other broadcasting. A good solution is to use vacant VHF (30 to 300 megahertz) or UHF (300 to 3,000 megahertz) television channel frequencies.

intermodulation Additions to a processor's original audio signal produced within the components themselves.

Another potential problem to be aware of is **intermodulation,** the complex relationship between a frequency and its harmonics. When using multiple wireless microphones, intermodulation will render many of the available frequencies useless. Most wireless systems come with several preset groups of frequencies that have been carefully selected by manufacturers using sophisticated computer programs. Trying to integrate two systems manufactured by different companies can lead to interference difficulties; in this case, the designer must pay particular attention to the assigned frequency groups. If a problem still exists, he or she may have to go to the manufacturer's Web site to obtain compatible frequency numbers. Before every performance, it is wise to change the batteries that power the bodypack transmitters.

Receiver Placement Proper placement of the wireless receiver is essential for good sound quality.

- Place the receiver as close to the transmitter as possible. Many designers choose the orchestra pit or just offstage for receiver placement.
- Try to assure that the transmitter can always "see" the receiver.
- Do not place the receiver close to metal or other dense material.
- Avoid placing the receiver near computers or other RF-generating equipment.

Maintenance Try to keep the miniature microphone capsule dry—sweat from the performers can significantly reduce the life of the capsule. Keep the beltpack transmitters dry. Inspect microphones after every performance and do a thorough test before each performance.

How to Control Feedback

As we have seen, *feedback* is the annoying sound produced by a reinforcement system amplifying a certain frequency or frequencies over and over again. Usually this condition occurs when a microphone is placed too close to a speaker. Sound from the microphone is sent to an amplifier and then on to the speaker. When the sound from the speaker is as loud as that from the performer using the mike, it may be picked up by the microphone and reamplified. In this event, a sound loop occurs, resulting in feedback. There are several ways to stop feedback, listed here from most obvious to least:

1. Turn down the gain on the microphone.
2. Move the microphone away from the speaker and/or place the performer's mouth closer to the microphone.

3. Use a more directional microphone and/or speaker.

4. Use an equalizer to attenuate those frequencies that are feeding back. Under normal conditions, one or several frequencies will be causing the sound to feed back. If these frequencies can be identified, an equalizer can be employed to eliminate the problem.

How to Select and Place Performance Microphones

Vocal Other than body mikes, the best solution for vocal microphone selection and placement in the reinforcement system is floor mikes placed downstage in the footlight position. The best microphone for this task is the supercardiod PCC-type with rear sound rejection. Position the mikes about ten feet apart, keeping in mind that an odd number of mikes is best so as to provide a center position. They will be effective approximately fifteen to twenty feet upstage.

Difficult-to-reach positions often require some theatrical ingenuity. Mounting a PCC- or PZM-type microphone on the scenery can effectively solve a tough reinforcement problem. Suspending a small condenser mike above the playing area is another possible solution.

Keeping the number of microphones in use to an absolute minimum is an important rule to follow. As the number of live microphones increases, the possible volume before feedback decreases significantly. A good operator will never have a microphone turned on if it is not needed.

Musical The sound from any electronic musical instrument should be fed into the mixer by means of a direct box (see earlier discussion). Sometimes referred to as a DI box (direct injection box), this small electronic circuit makes it possible for the signal from the instrument to go directly into the microphone input of the mixer.

Most other instruments can best be miked by placing a directional microphone as close to the sound source as possible. In addition, special microphones are manufactured specifically for musical instrument pickup. Some are standard microphones and others, called *contact microphones,* react to sound vibrations. A PZM mounted inside a partially closed piano lid produces good sound. Manufacturers' catalogs provide additional information on the various microphones made for musical pickup.

How to Place Speakers

As we have seen, it is best to place reinforcement loudspeakers above and just in front of the performer. However, other locations may be necessary if the designer wishes to approximate the direction of a sound source. Physical limitations of the performance space may also compromise speaker placement.

If stereo sound is required, two speakers separated by some distance will be necessary. This can be achieved by placing speakers above and to each side of the performer, perhaps with a fill-in center speaker. Be aware that this arrangement may be fine for sound effects and music but will cause the spoken word to be less intelligible.

Speakers for the arena stage should be located as close as possible to center, above the performance space, pointing out toward the audience. The dispersion pattern of the high-frequency horns should be narrow enough to direct the sound to the audience and not to the acting area. If such an arrangement causes feedback, the speakers will have to move toward the audience until the problem is alleviated. Cabinet-type speakers may work well for the small arena.

Clearly, sound designers need to know the complexities of using sound in the theatre—from effects to equipment. The next aspect of design, stage lighting, is quite complex as well and will be discussed in the next several chapters.

PART

IV

Stage Lighting

"The basic concern in theatre lighting is with the dramatic intention of a particular moment. The visibility, or the kind of light, in which you see the actors and the scenery, the place, must have a logic. The logic is based on tying all of these in with the idea of being there, in the scene, in the first place."

JEAN ROSENTHAL

THE MAGIC OF LIGHT

14

Introduction to Stage-Lighting Design

Although each one of us reacts uniquely to our environment, it is generally true that we take light and lighting for granted. Like the veterinarian who is aware of things in an animal that even its owner does not notice, the lighting designer must be acutely aware of the presence of light: its quality, color, shadow and direction, warmth or coolness, texture, and movement. The first thing a student of lighting seeks to develop is such an awareness—not for theatrical lighting, for that will come later, but for the light that surrounds us each and every day.

The design of lighting begins with an *idea*. In the theatre, this idea results from interpretation of the script by the director and the production design team (lighting, scenic, costume, and sound designers). In dance, the idea comes from the choreographer and the movement and the music. In opera and concert lighting, it begins with the music. In advertising, it is inspired by the product. It does not matter if the lighting designer works in a theatre or a theme park or a film studio or an exhibition hall—the design will be based on a collection of impressions, an idea.

The theatre has historically been the source of lighting design and continues to be a prime training ground for today's lighting designers, no matter what the field. As such, this chapter will focus primarily on stage lighting.

STAGE LIGHTING

What is the magic of stage lighting? The demands on it are many. The costume designer, while considering period, silhouette, color, and character in choosing the fabric for a costume, also wonders how it will look *under the lights*. The scene designer, in selecting the colors of draperies and upholstery or deciding the scale of detail on the scenery, hopes they will show well *under the lights*. The actor in the dressing room ponders if the makeup will look right *under the lights*.

The primary concern of stage lighting is, and will always remain, *visibility* (a rule that the designer must never forget). Yet, visibility is much more than simple intensity or brightness of light. *Contrast* has a great influence on visibility: intensity contrast, color contrast, and contrast in direction. Good lighting ties together the visual aspects of the stage and supports the dramatic intent of the production. The lighting designer is also concerned with the revelation of form, the mood of the scene, and the composition of the stage picture.

Scripts may call for special effects such as a hearth fire, a bolt of lightning, or projected images—all of which fall under the auspices of the lighting designer. Most often, however, the concern is with lighting the actor: a moving target that can be illuminated in an endless variety of moods and degrees of visibility. Herein lies the real challenge and excitement of stage-lighting design.

The Scene Designer

Unlike the other visual arts, scene design depends enormously on the use of light as a part of the final composition—the dramatic picture. Stage lighting contributes so much to the total visual effect that every designer should be familiar with its potential.

The design of lighting may begin with the scene designer's sketch, which presents a suggestion of the light that will illuminate the scene. It may appear to be coming from natural sources, such as the sun, the moon, or a fire, or from artificial sources, such as table lamps or ceiling fixtures. Alternatively, the light may appear to have no particular source and serve solely to support the desired mood or composition of the scene. The sketch or rendering, as opposed to the model, is the scene designer's best means of conveying a sense of mood (Figure 14-1).

Such sketches, however, are only the beginning. A sketch represents an artistic vision that must be technically sound to be properly realized. The ground plan and section that accompany the sketch give the first clues as to the credibility of the designer's lighting ideas. Many a beautiful sketch has been based on a floor plan that revealed, on closer study, impossible lighting angles and insufficient space for the lighting instruments.

Today's production design team is normally made up of four designers and the director. A unified approach or concept for a production is imperative for a successful design. Diverse ideas and views must be brought together into a single outlook by active and open communication among the members of this collaborative team as well as strong leadership from the director.

The Lighting Designer

The history of modern stage lighting is relatively brief, beginning not much more than a century ago with the advent of electricity and the invention of the incandescent lamp. Except for a few scene designers who enjoyed lighting their own scenery, the lighting of most Broadway productions up until the middle of the twentieth century was neglected and became, by default, one of the innumerable duties of the stage manager or house electrician. It was inevitable that lighting specialists would eventually move into this neglected field and demonstrate with startling results what could be done if one person devoted sole attention to the planning of lighting. This trend continued as lighting designers developed their art and craft, inspired by the work of people such as Stanley McCandless, Jean Rosenthal, and Abe Feder.

14-1

Scene Designer's Sketches

The planning of stage lighting may begin with the scene designer's sketches, which indicate the kind of illumination and its distribution, color, and general atmosphere. These sketches were done by the designer Beeb Salzer for *La Giaconda* by Gabriele D'Annunzio.

- **a** Act I: The Sculptor's living room.
- **b** Act II: Outside the sculptor's studio.
- **c** Act III: The sanatorium.

a

b

c

a–c COURTESY BEEB SALZER

Today the potential of light as a design element is recognized well beyond the theatre. The value of light as a merchandising tool in sales and retail stores has finally been realized; the significance of light to the appreciation of a meal in a fine restaurant is no longer a secret; and light as a means of establishing mood and atmosphere in the entertainment industry has never been more recognized. As a result, people trained in lighting design are in demand by many diverse industries as well as the theatre.

As a collaborative artist, the theatre-lighting designer must understand and appreciate the total design effort, particularly because he or she is the only member of the visual design team who does not submit, in advance, a complete statement of what is intended. Costume and scene designers present a multitude of sketches, material samples, and models as visual examples of their intent. Lighting designers, on the other hand, may submit **lighting storyboards** or computer-generated light renderings (Figure 14-2), but they most often rely on verbal exchanges until the time comes to draft the light plot (discussed later). Of course, this mode of operation points to the need for a strong collaborative process. Fortunately, the lighting designer commonly has the advantage of attending rehearsals before the final plot is completed.

lighting storyboard A series of value sketches or color renderings depicting the quality of light for the various "looks" of a production.

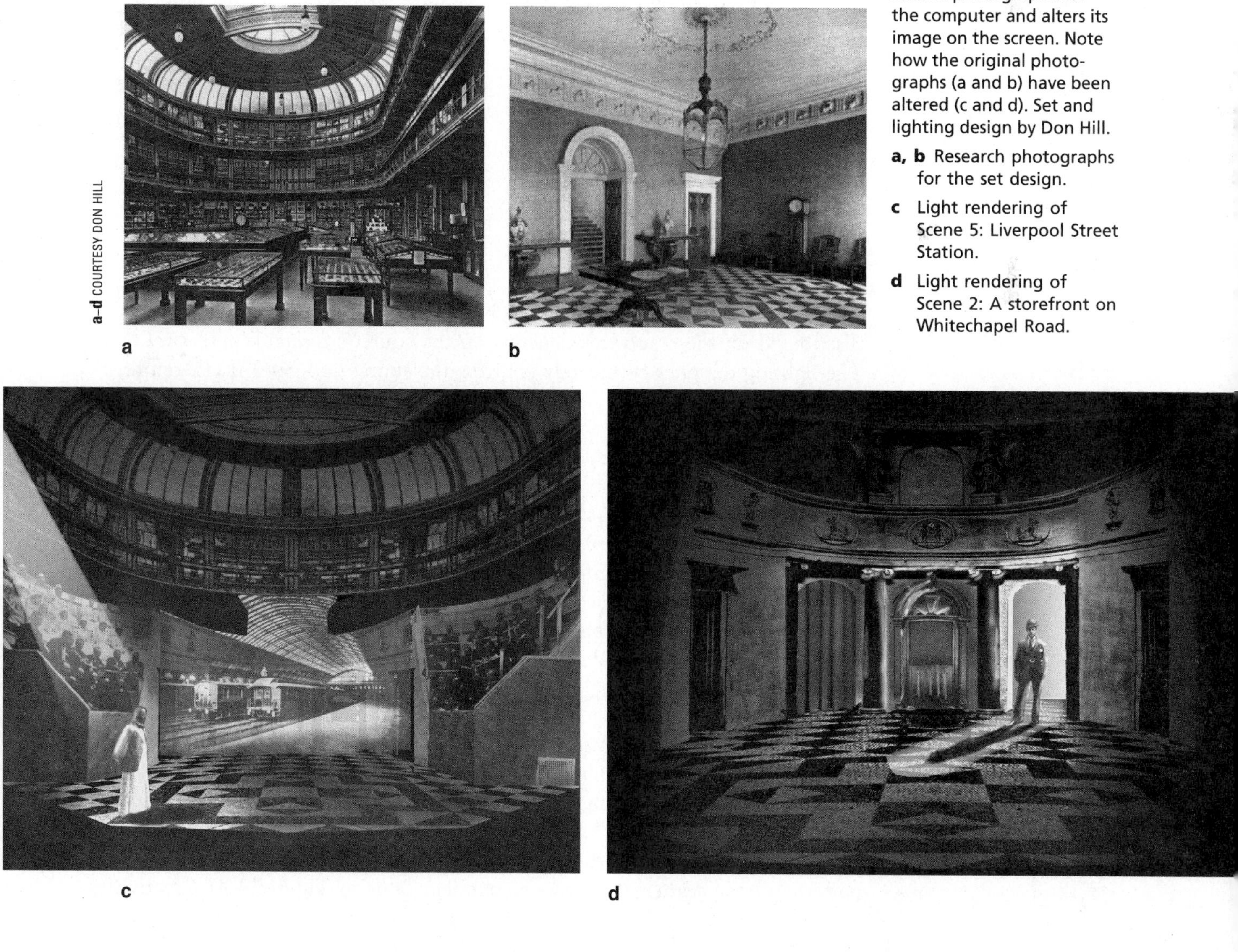

a–d COURTESY DON HILL

a b c d

14-2

Computer-Generated Light Renderings

Computer-generated rendering for a production of *Elephant Man* using Adobe Photoshop software. In this technique, the designer scans a photograph into the computer and alters its image on the screen. Note how the original photographs (a and b) have been altered (c and d). Set and lighting design by Don Hill.

a, b Research photographs for the set design.

c Light rendering of Scene 5: Liverpool Street Station.

d Light rendering of Scene 2: A storefront on Whitechapel Road.

Setting aside the technical aspects of electricity, instrument and control design, and details of plotting, the lighting designer is concerned first with the aesthetics of light. To develop a sense of composition, movement, and taste in color, a lighting designer must start with qualities and limitations of the medium itself.

QUALITIES OF LIGHT

Just as paint has traits particular to its medium, so light conforms to its own set of attributes. The physical characteristics of light in relationship to scenery are discussed in Chapter 3. The study of light as applied to stage lighting involves these same qualities: intensity, distribution, color, and movement.

Intensity

The first and most obvious quality of light is its *intensity* or brightness, which may be actual or comparative brightness. The actual brightness of the sun, for example, can be compared with the relative brightness of automobile headlights at night. Lighting instruments in a darkened theatre offer the designer the same comparative brightness under more-controlled conditions. To some degree, apparent intensity is also influenced by the color and distribution of light.

The entire composition of a stage picture depends on varying intensities of light. In addition, intensity greatly affects a scene's mood and atmosphere.

foot-candle A measurement of intensity of light reflected off a surface. Average stage brightness is approximately 70 foot-candles.

Varying the intensity of a light source is most often achieved by means of a *dimmer.* Groups of dimmers working together can direct audience focus as well as alter stage composition. Intensity is commonly measured in **foot-candles.**

Distribution

Most often we see light as it is reflected off various surfaces. How it is distributed on these surfaces depends on the source's *direction* and *quality.* The lighting designer completely controls the source of light and, therefore, its direction and quality.

Direction The visibility of an object greatly depends on the direction of the light striking it. Light can strike an object from above or below, from the rear or the front, or from the side at a high or low angle. A change in lighting direction can radically alter the perception of the size and/or shape of any form (Figure 14-3). Highlight and especially shadow are the best indicators of direction. A theatre audience feels most at ease with light coming from the natural direction of above and in front of the performer. Like intensity, direction has a strong effect on mood and atmosphere.

Quality The concept of quality is closely related to texture and depends on a source's intensity and diffusion. A highly diffuse light tends to have divergent rays, while a less-diffuse light has coherent and parallel rays. Diffuse light is perceived as soft and lacking in intensity. More-coherent light is harsher and more intense and creates harder edges. Quality can be altered by adding diffusion filters to a light beam. Blatant texture can be created by introducing pattern into the beam in the form of a template or **gobo** (Figure 14-4). Creative

gobo A pattern, normally cut into a thin stainless steel plate, which is placed at the aperture of an ERS to project an image.

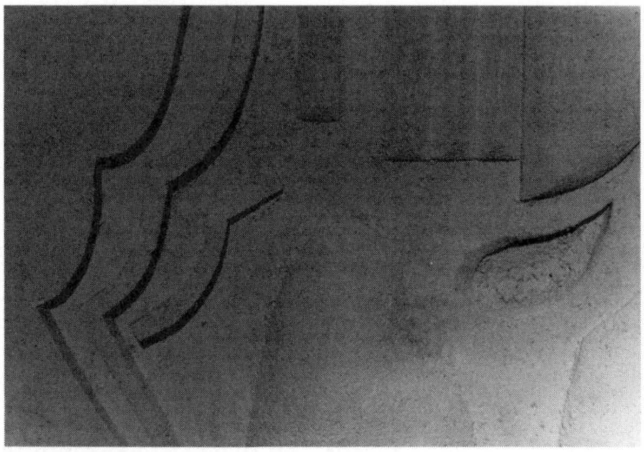

a

b

14-3

Distribution

Changing the distribution of light on a highly textured surface can produce amazingly varied effects.

a A low-relief sculptural form lit with a single source from the front.

b The same form lit with two side-angle sources of different intensities or colors.

14-4

Gobo Texture

Patterns created by gobos can enhance both mood and locale, as in this scene from *A Christmas Carol* by the San Diego Repertory Theatre. Lighting design, Peter Maradudin; scenery, Kent Dorsey; costumes, Nancy Jo Smith.

use of the direction and texture of light introduces highlight, shade, and shadow into the stage composition.

Color

The third property of light is its ability to transmit and reveal color. A forceful element in all areas of theatre design, color is often considered the most effective and dramatic quality of light. The use of colored light to enhance the mood of a scene is a common theatrical technique. The lighting designer may use color in a theatrically realistic way to convey time of day or atmospheric conditions. On the other hand, color choices may be heightened or exaggerated in order to stylize the look of a production.

Colored light is created through the use of filters. However, the beginning lighting designer needs to recognize that light sources have an intrinsic color that can vary greatly from one type of source to another. This difference in the **color temperature** of various light sources can be a useful design element.

color temperature A measurement in degrees Kelvin (°K) of the color of light emitted from a source. Stage-lighting instruments with incandescent lamps have a color temperature of about 3,200°K. Candlelight is a warm-colored 1,800°K and arc light is a cool-colored 6,000°K.

The ability of colored light to alter the color of a surface it strikes also makes it a powerful design tool. Modification of the natural color of a scenic form or costume by colored light is a design technique unique to the theatre. Color modification and the additive mixing of colored light are two rather basic concepts of color as a quality of light that all designers in the theatre must understand.

Movement

Although it is not an intrinsic quality of light, movement is an extremely important characteristic of stage lighting. Besides the physical movement of a light beam, movement includes a change in intensity, distribution, or color that might be as subtle as a slow progression from predawn to daybreak or as blatant as a blackout. Although most light movement is controlled by means of dimmers, physical movement from today's automated fixtures can have a powerful effect. Theatre audiences have long been accustomed to moving light in the form of follow-spotting, but recent use of automated fixtures has added a significant new tool to the designer's palette. A lighting **cue** in the form of a shift from one "look" to another involves movement. Movement can take and control focus. Movement alters composition.

cue The movement of light from one stage "look" to another. A cue is usually assigned a specific number.

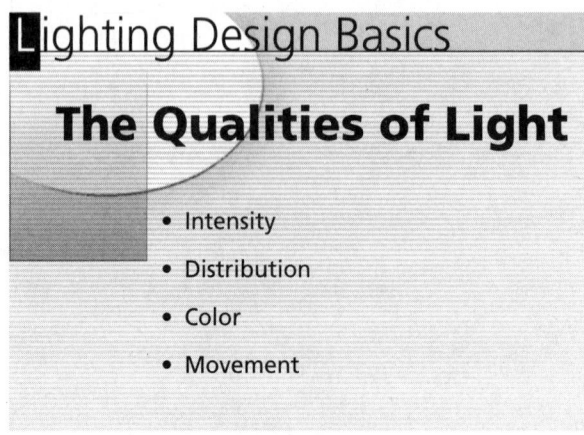

Lighting Design Basics

The Qualities of Light

- Intensity
- Distribution
- Color
- Movement

STAGE LIGHTING AND THE ELEMENTS OF DESIGN

The principles of composition are the same for the lighting designer as they are for the scene designer or any graphic or visual artist. Recall that **composition** is the organization of the visual elements of design into a unified form or arrangement of forms. Lighting reveals composition; in addition, it is the unifying and fluid force of the stage composition.

composition The organization of design elements into a unified form. Light reveals composition.

The role of the lighting designer as a member of the design team demands acute awareness of the elements of design that the scenery and costume designers work with in developing their ideas. The elemental factors that make up any visual form or arrangement of forms, as discussed in Chapter 3, can be listed in the order of their importance to the creative process:

- Line
- Movement
- Color
- Scale
- Light
- Texture

Line

As an element of design, line defines form. Its force is present in a composition in many ways. Line can enclose spaces as an outline creating shape (two-dimensional form) or as a contour line suggesting three-dimensional form. Strong back-lighting, for example, emphasizes the silhouette or outline of a form, while directional side-lighting reveals its contour. Light has the power to deny, alter, or accentuate line (Figure 14-3).

Line can appear in a composition as a *real line* in many different modes (straight, curved, spiral, and so on) or as a *suggested line* that is simulated by the eye as it follows a sequence of related shapes (as in optical motion, discussed shortly).

When line creates a path of action, it also tends to assume a direction. A strong beam of light revealed by haze in the air cannot help but establish direction. The *linear shape* of the beam coupled with a concentration of brightness creates a strong focus in the composition (Figure 14-5).

14-5

Line Created by Light

Directional light can create line and focus, as in this production of Brecht's *Edward II.* Lighting design, R. Craig Wolf; scenery, Robert Darling; costumes, Zelma Weisfeld.

Scale

As we have seen, scale is concerned not only with the size of an individual shape or mass but also with the contrasting relationship of the size of one shape to another—large to small, large to large, and so on. Accordingly, the size of the space between two objects has a definite effect on their apparent mass. Control of light on either the object or the space also influences the dimension of one or the other.

By accentuating vertical surfaces, light can make an object look taller. Lighting from directly above, or *top-lighting*, can cause an object to appear squat. Light can make a two-dimensional shape look three-dimensional and vice versa.

Movement

optical motion The movement of the eye through a composition. In the theatre, such eye movement may be dictated by light focus.

The action of form, and the kinetic energy of composition, is movement. Motion within a stage composition can be either real or optical.

Optical motion is the movement of the eye through a composition. When a form or group of forms is static, optical motion depends on the sequential arrangement of those forms. Because a form is seen only as well as it is lit, lighting plays an important role in optical motion. Note the movement of your eye through the painting by Rembrandt in Figure 14-6.

Movement of the eye can easily be altered by selectively shifting the light intensity on one or more forms, thereby also changing the composition. Strong directional light rays or the sequential arrangement of light sources are examples of the use of light as optical motion.

14-6

Optical Motion

Artists use light to cause eye movement through a painting, thereby increasing visual interest.

Light

Without light, form cannot be revealed. Given its basic role in all areas of stage design, light must be discussed from the very start of the creative process. Awareness of the significance of light as a design element is as important to the scenery and costume designers as the appreciation of all the elements of design is to the lighting expert.

Color

As an element of design, color serves as a powerful stimulus within a composition. Color can also alter form in many ways. It can change the dimension of form, reverse the direction of line, alter the interval between forms, and generate optical motion. As we have seen, color in the theatre comes from two basic sources: pigment or dye, present on the surface of the form, or colored light that affects the color of the form.

Texture

The tactile aspect of form is referred to as *texture*. Textural treatment of surfaces is of great interest to the lighting designer. Surfaces that are highly polished, rough-hewn, or rusticated will each reflect light differently, casting interesting shadows. Three-dimensional texture is best revealed by directional side-lighting, while painted or simulated texture appears more real under a wash of light that has no strong sense of direction.

In its simplest form, texture in light is the product of a specific type of lighting instrument. One of the considerations in selecting an instrument involves the textural quality of its light. In addition, the designer can create texture in light by adjusting focus, using diffusion media, or breaking up the light with gobo patterns (Figure 14-7).

PHOTO COURTESY RALPH FUNICELLO

14-7

Texture in Light

A soft texture can be created by the use of frost or diffusion media. Note the soft quality of light in the air and on the floor in this production of *King Lear* directed by Jack O'Brien for the Old Globe Theatre, San Diego. Scenery design, Ralph Funicello; lighting, David Segal; costumes, Robert Morgan.

STAGE LIGHTING AND THEATRICAL FORM

Several factors greatly influence the development of a lighting idea and the subsequent light plot. The production approach and resulting scenery and costume designs influence color palette as well as style. The scenery may affect the specific placement of lighting instruments. The style of the production as well as the script guides the lighting designer toward an approach. Finally, budget and the physical form of the theatre will impact the lighting design.

Production and Lighting Style

As we have seen, the term *style* is subject to overuse and misunderstanding (see Chapter 4); nevertheless, we use it here in its broadest sense. In a recent conversation with a gathering of students, scene designer Ming Cho Lee commented, "I don't know what style is. I think Howard Bay referred to it as a peculiar way of drawing." An individual artist's work possesses a unique look—a particular flair or technical approach referred to as a *signature.* If Monet and van Gogh had painted the same landscape, their works would appear quite different—the difference being a collection of techniques composing the artist's style. In the professional theatre, like the art world, designers are known and often hired for their particular style.

To complicate matters, a theatrical production also has a style of its own. A production's style (defined earlier as "degree of reality") is related to and often a result of the production team's approach. After analysis of the play, the director and designers agree on an approach that includes a style for the production. The designers then contribute their own techniques to this style, resulting in a unique interpretation of the dramatic work.

Two basic techniques that contribute to style are motivational and non-motivational lighting. Strict **motivational lighting** is based on the desire to duplicate a specific source of light such as the sun, a candle, or a streetlight. Environmental conditions such as time of day, weather, time of year, and locale are all taken into consideration (Figure 14-8). In providing **nonmotivational lighting**, the lighting designer ignores concerns about realistic light. Instead, he or she chooses lighting colors, instruments, and angles in response to a desired mood, a compositional requirement, or simply a "feeling" about the scene. Of course, strict motivational and nonmotivational styles stand at either end of a spectrum that includes endless variations and combinations of the two.

motivational lighting The theatrical use of light based on an actual source or sources.

nonmotivational lighting Light used as a pure element of design, without reference to any actual sources. Often such use is based on the designer's emotional reaction to the script.

The beginning lighting designer should start by concentrating on motivational lighting while realizing that a nonmotivational approach can be quite as valid and sometimes more expressive and exciting. The production style helps the designer select an approach that will employ one or perhaps a combination of these basic lighting techniques (Figure 14-9).

Physical Plant

The physical theatre itself has great influence over lighting potential in terms of distribution. Where lighting instruments may be placed and, therefore, how their light strikes the actors and scenery are chiefly determined by the space's architecture. Beginning with the *proscenium theatre* and its traditional audience and stage arrangement, lighting is essentially shadow-box illumination that caters to theatrical realism or illusory theatre. Although it is common today to see a proscenium theatre with lighting totally exposed,

PHOTO COURTESY RALPH FUNICELLO

14-8

Motivational Lighting

Motivational lighting is often required to support realism, as in this production of *Tartuffe* directed by Dan Sullivan for Seattle Repertory Theatre. Scenery design, Ralph Funicello; lighting, James F. Ingalls; costumes, Ann Hould-Ward.

a

b

a PHOTO COURTESY MOUNTAIN MIST
b PHOTO: T. CHARLES ERICKSON. COPYRIGHT © THE HARTFORD STAGE COMPANY.

14-9

Lighting Styles

a Highly stylized motivational lighting in *You Can't Take It with You.* Scenery design, Doug Grekin; lighting, R. Craig Wolf.

b Abstract nonmotivational lighting in *A Midsummer Night's Dream.* Scenery design, Michael Yeargan; lighting, Pat Collins.

traditional proscenium lighting called for its instruments to be concealed behind masking legs and borders onstage and in ceiling "ports" or "beams" or "coves" front-of-house. In older theatres, front-of-house positions were limited, sometimes to only a balcony rail. Scenery permitting, the proscenium stage is the most versatile form for side-lighting possibilities.

The *thrust stage,* with its audience on three sides, minimizes the use of scenery and gives the lighting designer greater responsibility for creating illusion. This new–old form of theatricality (popular in the sixteenth century) relies chiefly on lighting, costumes, and properties for its visual composition. Additionally, in most thrust houses the audience's viewing angle makes the stage floor quite prominent. In some cases the floor is more of a background to the actor than are any upstage scenery or properties. The lighting designer must keep this in mind when choosing color and texture in the light. Thrust staging requires full-coverage lighting (360 degrees). An exciting and challenging theatre form, modern thrust theatres provide flexibility in lighting positions both front-of-house as well as over stage.

Arena staging increases the demands on stage lighting and virtually eliminates scenery, because the audience surrounds the stage area. Like thrust, the arena requires 360-degree coverage but is often a bit more restrictive in terms of lighting possibilities. The floor of most arenas is also quite prominent, requiring special attention from the lighting designer. A good arena theatre will be equipped with a lighting grid that covers the entire space and allows total flexibility in hanging position.

Flexible or *black box staging* should not be neglected, for it can provide, on a small scale, any of the aforementioned audience–stage arrangements and more. By its sheer flexibility, it supports a frankly impromptu form; its exposed lighting instruments and temporary seating arrangement allow great latitude. Like the arena, the ideal black box offers unrestricted lighting positions by virtue of a grid covering the entire space.

FUNCTIONS OF STAGE LIGHTING

The basic obligation of stage design is to give performers *meaning* in their surroundings, providing an atmosphere in which the role may be logically interpreted. Through the manipulation of light in all its aspects—intensity, color, distribution, and movement—the lighting designer assists in creating an environment for the play by achieving *selective visibility,* by providing appropriate *composition* and *revelation of form,* and by *establishing mood* and *reinforcing the theme.*

Selective Visibility

The actor must be seen in order to be heard. *Visibility* cannot be defined as a fixed degree of brightness or an established angle of distribution; rather, it is the amount of light needed for a moment of recognition deemed appropriate for that point in the action of the play. "To see what should be seen" may mean revealing the mere silhouette of a three-dimensional form, the solidity of its mass, or the full decorative and textural detail of all surfaces. Although visibility certainly relies on intensity, contrast also plays a significant role in achieving good stage visibility.

14-10
Composition
This work of Giorgio de Chirico emphasizes the significance of light and shadow as an element of composition.

Composition

Stage composition begins with the scenic design and floor plan, is further defined by the placement and movement of actors, and is completed when lit by the lighting designer. More than any other design element, light directs the audience's eye and controls what is and is not seen. Points of visual focus are determined by the blocking and the action. Because light possesses the additional quality of incredible fluidity, stage composition can be altered with relative ease.

The study of art can reveal much about composition. For instance, cast shadows and highlights significantly influence the composition of *The Philosopher's Conquest* by Giorgio de Chirico (Figure 14-10).

Although light can have composition of its own (projected patterns, for example), its chief function is to selectively reveal actors and stage forms in the proper relationship to other forms and to the background. Here the complexity of compositional lighting begins. Compositional lighting means

a

b

b PHOTO COURTESY CHRIS PARRY

14-11

Composition

Supporting the stage composition is one of the lighting designer's most important tasks.

a Focus is clearly created by costume and light in this production of *Richard II,* while the dramatic stage composition is accentuated by the lighting. Lighting design, R. Craig Wolf.

b Composition is created by strong use of light and shadow in this production of *Midsummer Night's Dream* by the Royal Shakespeare Company. Lighting design, Chris Parry.

lighting one form and not another; controlling shadows, keeping them off the background; lighting three-dimensional forms to make them look three-dimensional (not as easy as it seems); and other similar problems, including the most significant—lighting the actor (Figure 14-11).

Revelation of Form

Figure 14-12 illustrates that a form can be revealed in a variety of ways. The appearance of scenic forms as revealed by light can be varied greatly by the simple movement of several dimmers. On the other hand, the three-dimensional form of the actor must be shown in a consistent and predictable manner while moving through space—something best not left to chance. Even in the proscenium theatre with the audience viewing principally from the front, light is focused on the sides and backs of actors in order to enhance their dimensionality. However, form is often best revealed if the various sources of light playing on it have some degree of contrast—either in intensity or color. Altering form is one of light's greatest powers.

Establishing the Mood

After researching, reading the script, and talking with the collaborative team, the lighting designer begins to get a feeling for the overall mood of the play. A color impression comes from the mood, as does a suggestion of the intensity and distribution of light. The word *mood* tends to suggest dark and gloomy surroundings, but bright comedy or nonsensical farce also indicate a type of mood.

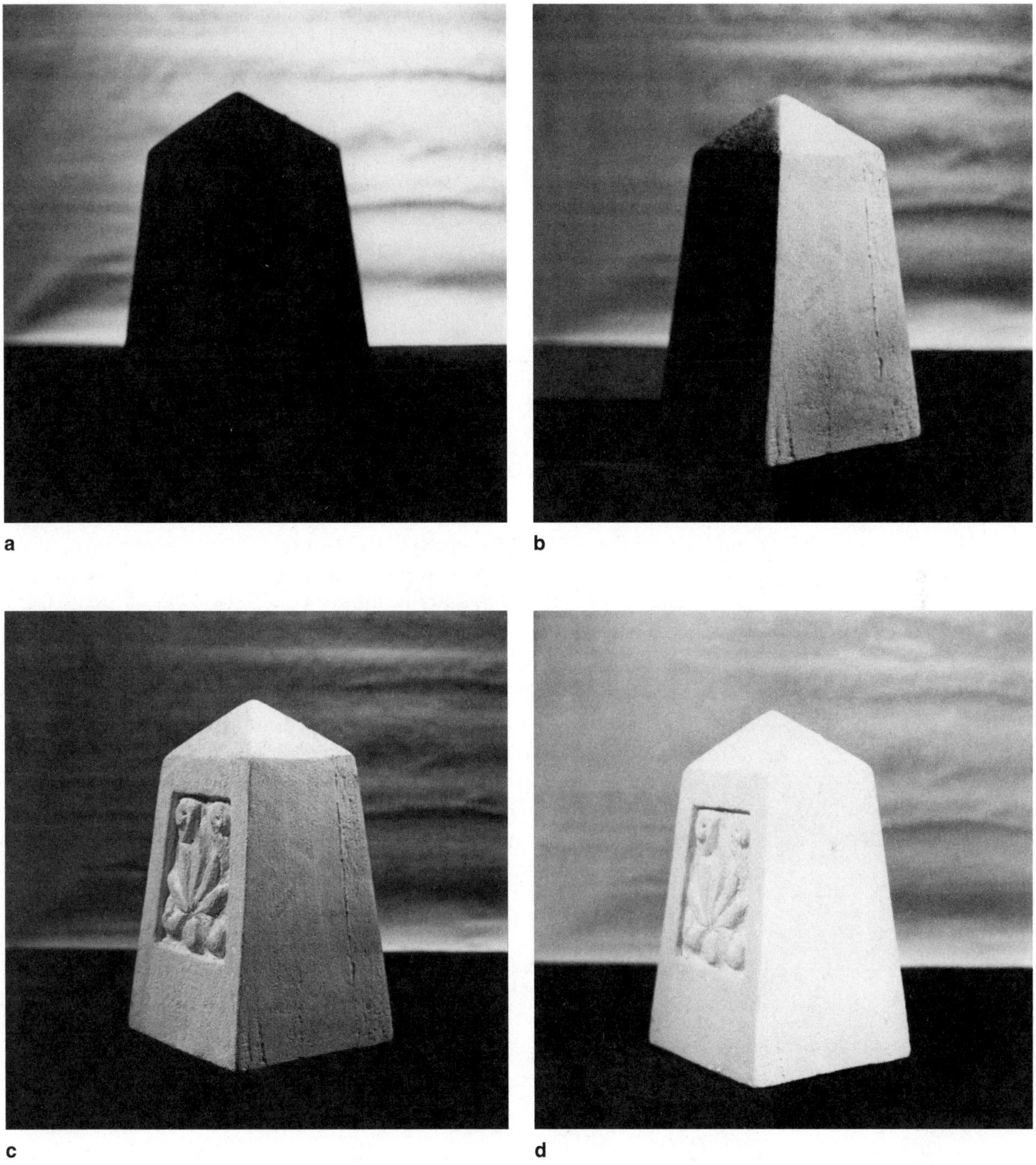

14-12

Selective Visibility

Here lighting provides stunning effect through four different kinds of visibility.

a An object lit from behind is visible in silhouette only.

b With front light added, the object is visible as a three-dimensional form.

c With the addition of another direction of light, the object's detail becomes visible.

d Detail and form can become less visible with too much light.

Occasionally a lighting designer will allow concern for mood or atmosphere to override all else, sacrificing other functions, including visibility. Unfortunately, this has happened frequently enough for directors to have become wary of "mood lighting" and shy away from any such discussion. Two things must be understood:

1. Mood and atmosphere are unavoidable features of light; to ignore this is as dangerous as overstating the mood.
2. Mood is only one of five equally important light functions; to slight any one for another must be a conscious decision made by the entire design team and director.

Although an abstract or dramatic mood is more impressive and eye-catching than the realistic visibility of a conventional interior setting, it is also far easier to accomplish with light.

Reinforcing the Theme

The lighting of a scene must reinforce, or support, the action. The visual expression of theme depends on the collaborative team's interpretation of the script. To tell the story most effectively, the lighting designer must always keep the playwright's message foremost in mind. As always, lighting the actor is key, but thematic lighting requires a concern with compositional revelation of the thematic forms of the setting as well. The theme-dominated play by Tennessee Williams, *A Streetcar Named Desire,* offers a good example of how various light qualities can support thematic action (Figure 14-13).

In the more extreme theme-oriented or documentary plays of Bertolt Brecht, the theme is often stressed by showing the play under a clear, uncolored wash of light, thereby eliminating the theatricality of stage lighting. Lighting reinforces the theme visually through the use of projections that take the form of propaganda pictures or subtitles.

Lighting Design Basics

Light Functions

- Selective visibility
- Composition
- Revelation of form
- Establishing mood
- Reinforcement

PHOTOS COURTESY RALPH FUNICELLO

14-13

Reinforcing the Theme

Tennessee Williams's *A Streetcar Named Desire* is an example of a theme-dominated play. The lighting designer supports the theme of the play through the use of various qualities of light. This production was directed by John Hirsch in the Avon Theatre for the Stratford Festival, Ontario. Scenery design, Ralph Funicello; lighting, Michael J. Whitfield; costumes, Debra Hanson.

THE ROLE OF THE LIGHTING DESIGNER

Each designer in the production team functions differently according to the demands of his or her specialty. The scenic and costume designers must begin their work well in advance of the production in order to allow sufficient time to purchase materials and build the show. The lighting and sound designers have the advantage of more time to assimilate and observe the production process as it unfolds, but they also have the added responsibilities implicit in that knowledge.

It has been made clear that *all* designers are involved in the creative development of an approach to the production. This collaborative process is the only time when the production team shares ideas. It is the time when the lighting and scenic designers work closely together in order to anticipate any lighting requirements that may affect scenery (attempting to add an onstage follow spot position after the scenery drawings have gone into the shops is terribly expensive if not impossible). It is the time when the style of the production is determined and critical design choices are made. It is the time when all of the designers can discuss color palette and the desired "look" of the show.

Preparation

Designers must first and foremost know the script. The number of readings depends on the individual designer as well as the script; however, at least three readings are necessary. In the first, designers simply enjoy the play as a piece of literature, reading it like a novel; in the second, they identify technical concerns, such as time of day, effects, and specific lighting action; and in the third they read for characterization and thematic elements.

Solid research is as important to the lighting designer as it is to the rest of the production team. He or she should study the various works of the playwright, as well as critical reviews, in order to discover more about point of view and style of working. The play's time period and locale must be carefully researched—primarily for atmosphere, but also for technical details. Any music involved in the production should be investigated for style and mood qualities. A knowledge and appreciation of music as well as art of the period will greatly enhance the lighting designer's creative work. Simply put, good research results in a superior creative product—every time.

Finally, lighting designers must study set and costume designs. In particular, they must carefully analyze scenic masking in terms of over-stage lighting positions, examine the scenery itself for potential lighting positions, and consider costume and scenery color.

Rehearsals

Attending rehearsals is richly rewarding for the lighting designer and must be taken advantage of if at all possible, for here the true depth and dimensions of a production are discovered through the interaction of the director and actors. To witness the development of characters, designers should attend rehearsals early on as well as later to study timing and movement patterns. Designers should speak with the director beforehand about attending rehearsals, if for no other reason than as a courtesy.

The various reasons for attending rehearsals may seem obvious, but many directors believe that blocking is the lighting designer's only concern. Although blocking and space usage are important, other benefits include increased awareness of the director's intent, deeper understanding of how the director works, and a feeling for both mood and pace. Planning for compositional lighting is extremely difficult without prior knowledge of blocking; however, every rehearsal need not be a run-through to satisfy other equally important lighting needs.

Preproduction

The light plot, which has been developing in the designer's head from the start, is usually drafted one or two weeks before the lighting move-in day (assuming that a large rental is not required). Although every designer has individual ways of working, most create to some degree while they are drafting. If a drawing of the theatre does not already exist (hopefully as a CAD file), it must be copied from some other source. After necessary scenic elements are drawn in, lighting areas can be determined. Next, specific instrumentation and distribution methods are chosen. Finally, color is solidified and control choices are made.

Good and thorough preplanning is of the utmost importance. Lighting cues are written and conveyed to the stage manager, who will call them during performances. The designer or an assistant is present to answer questions during the hanging of equipment (the "hang"), but crews are supervised by a master electrician who is well acquainted with the theatre facilities and equipment. A focus session follows the load-in and if lucky the designer and crew will have the theatre to themselves for the several hours required to aim and adjust the beams of light from the various instruments.

Production

Before technical rehearsals begin, the designer should write dimmer readings for each lighting cue. This can be done on paper or, if the control system allows, remotely recorded on disc. In this way, cues can be entered into the light board well in advance. It is wise to adjust these levels visually during the acting rehearsal previous to technical rehearsals. This procedure allows the technical rehearsal to be just that—a *technical* rehearsal rather than a *lighting* rehearsal. If the designer prefers to build the show visually or if the production is complex enough to require a separate lighting rehearsal, it should be scheduled to take place before the technical. During subsequent dress rehearsals, the lighting designer watches from the auditorium and makes level and timing changes, a procedure that may continue through previews.

THE ASSISTANT LIGHTING DESIGNER

As the art of lighting has become more complex, many designers have turned to young people interested in the craft to act as their assistants. In this way both parties have benefited, as novice lighting designers learn by observing the work of those more experienced and established than they.

Although the assistant's duties vary by designer and situation, paperwork is nearly always the responsibility of the assistant. Some designers hire an assistant to draft the light plot, in which case a solid working knowledge of CAD is imperative; some place their assistants in charge of paperwork such as shop orders, instrument schedules, focus charts, hookups, and the like, requiring familiarity with a good software program; and some designers expect an assistant to call channels during the focus and take notes during technical rehearsals. Be aware that designers today use several computer drafting programs; prospective assistants need to make sure they know which program is preferred. No matter what their duties, assistants can closely observe the designer's work as well as that of the entire production machine.

Every beginning designer should seek work as an assistant. It is advisable to assist several different designers, in a variety of theatres, in order to meet different people and learn various ways of working. A good assistant is a silent observer who is not afraid to ask questions when necessary. In this way, the assistant learns what to expect and how to be flexible. As an assistant, you should not be intimidated by the designer—he or she will enjoy and appreciate your contribution. The proper way to obtain an assistant position is to submit a résumé to the designer, along with a cover letter indicating your availability.

THE LIGHTING LABORATORY

More and more institutions that are genuinely committed to training lighting designers are seeking and finding the space and equipment for lighting labs. The light lab comes in many sizes and forms; most exist in found spaces that have been equipped by students and faculty with a limited budget. The available equipment is often ancient and may be less than useful in an actual production. However, the lab is also the place for experimentation with state-of-the-art instrumentation; many facilities select for purchase one or two new pieces of equipment each year to be used in the lab.

Ideally the light lab will be on a human scale, with a grid somewhere between 12 and 15 feet high. It should have its own control system and circuitry, although neither need be elaborate. If space is an issue, an intelligent arrangement is to combine the lighting lab with a makeup classroom, for makeup instruction often requires stage lighting. Lab exercises vary from reproduction of light in a painting to demonstrations of color, angle, and quality of light. A variety of laboratory exercises are available in a publication by the United States Institute for Theatre Technology (USITT) titled *Practical Projects for Teaching Lighting Design, A Compendium* (2nd ed.).

URL http://www.usitt.org

It is an observable fact that today's student learns better in a lighting laboratory than in any other environment. The student is less intimidated by scale and equipment when working in the lab as opposed to the theatre. The hands-on experience of laboratory work accelerates learning and solidifies conceptual material received in the classroom. Further, if students have free access to the lab, they can learn at their own pace.

Figure 14-14 offers an excellent example of the use of a large-scale model for demonstration in the lighting lab. Note the various uses of light angle for texture and composition.

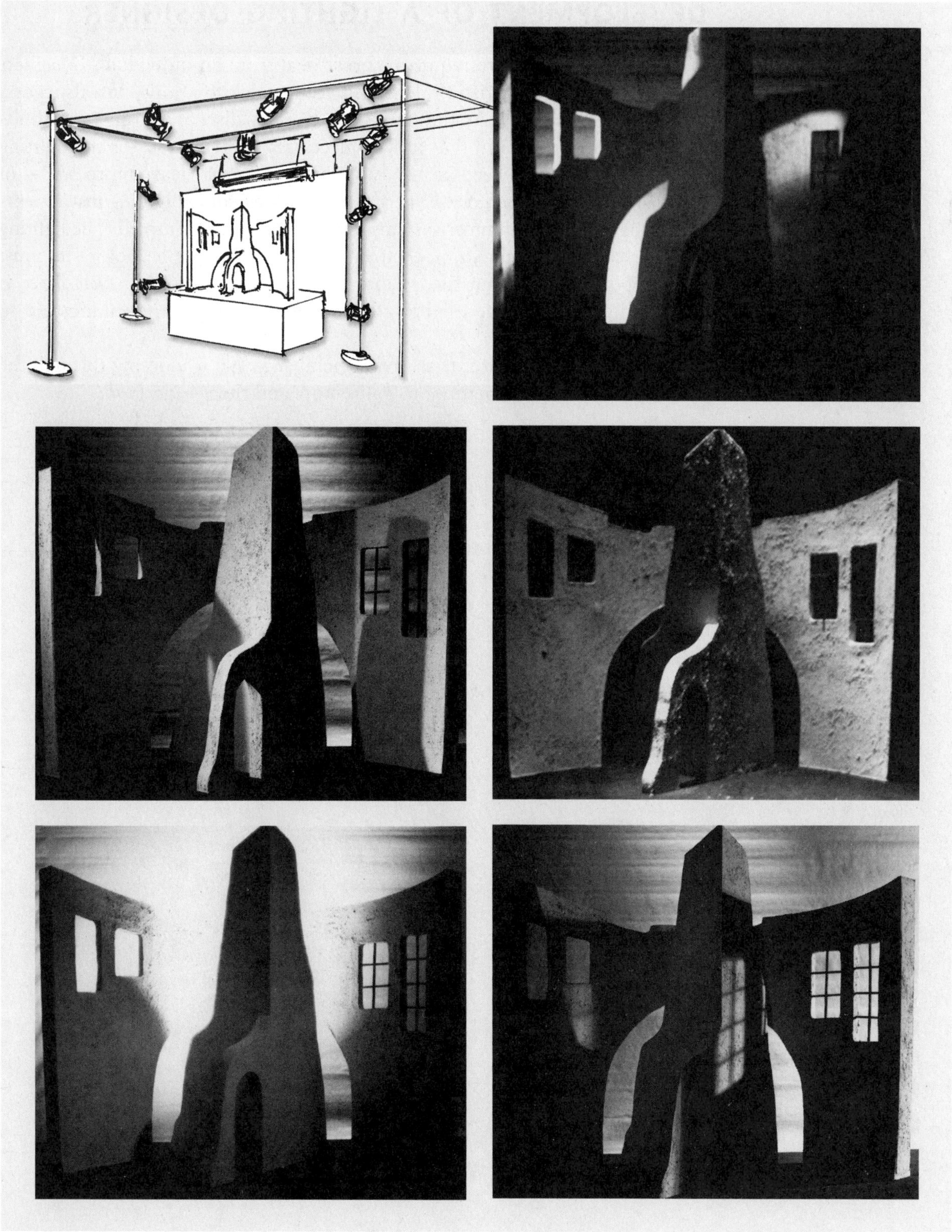

14-14

Compositional Lighting in the Lighting Lab

With a large-scale model in the lighting lab, the student lighting designer can reconstruct lighting angles and direction for any stage form—proscenium, arena, or thrust—and experiment with compositional properties of light. In this example the scenic form purposely contains a variety of surfaces. Sweeping curves, sharp corners, openings, and texture lend interest. The photographs show some of the effects.

DEVELOPMENT OF A LIGHTING DESIGNER

Designing for the theatre requires a great deal from an individual. Designers must have not only artistic talent and technical know-how but also good communications skills. As the next few chapters discuss the nuts and bolts of lighting, keep in mind that it is all necessary information for the lighting designer. And always keep in mind the importance of "learning to see"—of establishing a visual memory. Experimentation is essential: lighting instruments should be examined, dimmer systems operated, and colors mixed. The lighting designer can learn only so much from theory and example; he or she must have opportunities to put theory into practice. Because production space is always in great demand, a lighting laboratory becomes a tremendous aid to practical training.

Perhaps most important, always remember, while wandering through the maze of technical information, to pause now and then—and *look*.

15

Stage-Lighting Practice: Distribution

The four qualities of light, as mentioned earlier in this book, are color, distribution, intensity, and movement. ***Distribution*** *refers to where a lighting instrument is placed, what type of instrument it is, and how it is focused. It is one of the most critical and complex choices the lighting designer makes. Distribution determines how the actor will be seen and the scenery will be revealed. It involves choices of direction, angle, and quality of light.* Direction *refers to whether the light is coming from the front, the side, or the back.* Angle *relates to the height of the light source (for example, is the light coming from low on the horizon, or is it high like noonday sun?).* Quality *centers on the diffusion and texture of the light (for example, is it harsh or soft, broken up or smooth?).*

Advances in technology have gone hand in hand with increased demands on lighting in the theatre. Designers have responded in a variety of ways, but by far the most significant has been in the area of distribution. More and more equipment is being used to provide greater flexibility regarding angle and direction of light. At one time it was common for designers to have two or three **lighting systems** at their disposal in a given production. Today, a moderately complex show may call for a dozen systems, resulting in greatly improved distribution.

In the study of distribution, it is best to begin with motivational lighting. Accordingly, the early part of this chapter includes a discussion of types of light from familiar sources such as daylight, night light, and artificial light.

distribution The specific manner in which light falls on a surface—influenced by the direction, quality, and texture of the light itself.

lighting system An arrangement of lighting instruments of similar type, color, and/or direction that produces a specific lighting "look." A system may be used alone or in combination with other systems.

LIGHTING THE ACTOR

The primary concern of a stage-lighting designer is lighting the actor. The actor must have good visibility, be lit in a manner appropriate to the play, and be seen in proper relationship to the background. Distribution is of primary importance because it involves the angle, direction, and quality of light that reveals the actors, especially their faces, in natural form.

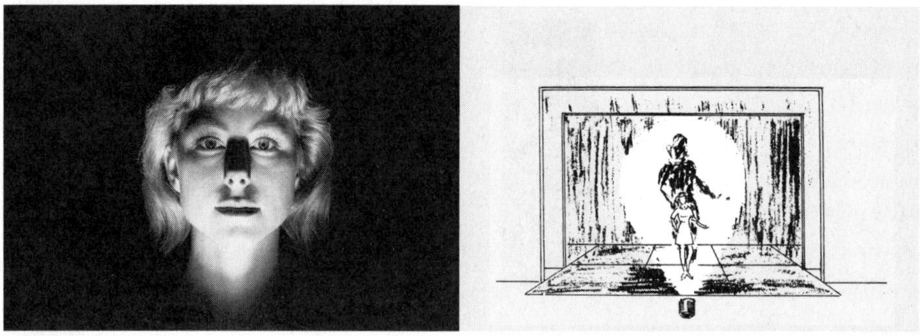

15-1

Lighting the Actor: Light from Below

Upward angle from the footlight position or apron. An unnatural, though dramatic, angle.

Natural Lighting

The expression "in natural form" is the designer's clue to appropriate lighting. It means that the actor's face should usually be seen as it appears under natural lighting. In imitating nature, theatre uses reality as a basis from which to deviate. Accordingly, the lighting designer must be keenly aware of the various attributes of natural light.

Our eyes have been schooled by a lifetime of seeing people under sunlight or interior light coming from above. We are so accustomed to seeing the features of a face disclosed by light from an overhead direction that to light it from below, for example, produces an unnatural look (Figure 15-1).

Artists and architects have long rendered their drawings as though light were falling on the subject from over the artist's shoulder at an angle of roughly 45 degrees. Following the lead of Stanley McCandless, a man who more than any other might be considered the founder of lighting design in the United States, theatre-lighting designers have adopted this same practice. Light at a 45-degree angle enhances visibility and appears natural. At the same time, this angle of light creates interesting highlights and shadows on the actor's face. Intentional deviation from this angle in order to heighten an effect or create a particular mood is also common design practice in today's theatre.

Highlight and Shadow

The primary way to determine the angle and direction of a light source is to observe the *highlight* and *shadow* created. Time of day is determined by the position of the sun, and, subsequently, the length of shadows cast by objects such as trees and buildings. The shadow of an object lit at an angle of 45 degrees is the same length as the height of the object.

The shadows in Figure 15-1 are what make the subject look unnatural. Highlight and shadow, which give dimension to a form, are controlled by the angle and direction of the light source. Figure 15-2 further illustrates the relationship of highlight and shadow to perception. We are so accustomed to seeing light from above that changing this angle has the power to alter appearances.

Highlight and shadow offer interest to scenic objects as well as to an actor's face. In addition, they often become important aspects of the stage composition. Shadowless illumination is uninteresting and actually reduces visibility.

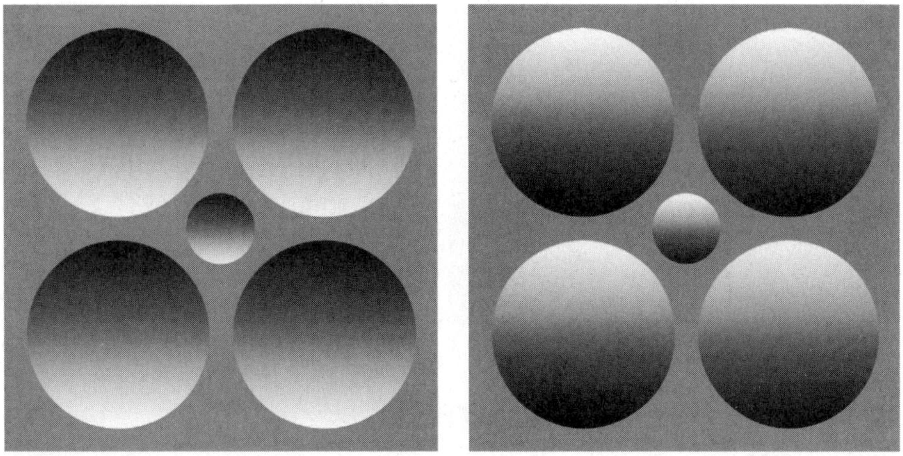

15-2

Perception as Influenced by Lighting Angle

An illustration of how we assume the direction of light to be from above. Figures (a) and (b) are identical rectangles, each containing five convex domes.

a Lighting from below—the domes appear to be concave.

b Lighting from above—the domes appear convex.

ANGLES AND DIRECTION OF LIGHT

Angle of light is commonly measured in degrees. The horizon (normally at the height of an actor's head—5 to 6 feet) is considered to be at 0 degrees, and light from directly above is at 90 degrees. *Direction* of light can also be measured in degrees but is most often referred to as front-, side-, or back-lighting. Each direction of light possesses its own attributes, with visibility being the most important attribute of front-light.

Front-Light

Theatrical front-lighting is seldom directly front-on to the performer. Such light, especially if it is low angled, flattens facial features and lacks interest (Figure 15-3). Moving the light to one side of the performer creates a much

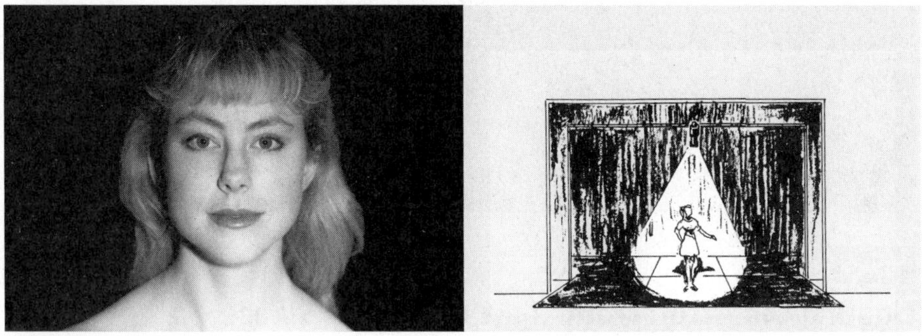

15-3

Lighting the Actor: Low-Angle Front

Low-angle, straight-front light. Note the lack of definition.

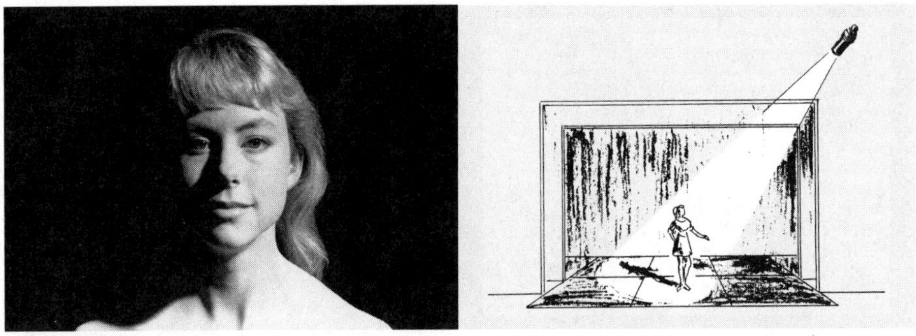

15-4

Lighting the Actor: Stage-Left Front

Front-light from stage left only at a 45-degree angle. Note the lack of visibility on the dark side of the face.

more interesting sense of directionality. Shadows are produced, and the actor's face suddenly has dimension. However, although highly theatrical, a deep shadow on the opposite side of the face reduces visibility (Figure 15-4). A second light is often necessary to fill in this shadow.

45-Degree/45-Degree System Stanley McCandless, mentioned earlier, claimed that two front-lights were desirable, one with its beam shining from 45 degrees above and to the right of the actor, and the second instrument shining from 45 degrees above and to the left of the actor (a total of 90 degrees horizontal between lights). In addition, placing a warm tint in one spotlight and a cool tint in the other creates contrast and has a pleasing, natural effect. Further varying the color or intensity of these lights increases the sense of directionality. The primary source or **key-light** comes from the warmer or more intense light, and the shadow or **fill-light** comes from the cool or dimmer light (Figure 15-5). In the 1930s, McCandless felt that this was the most natural way to light an actor with good visibility—and it was.

key-light The primary source of light in a composition—normally the brightest. Key-light may imitate a motivational source.

fill-light The secondary source of light in a composition. An important factor in visibility, fill-light is often thought of as bounce light or shadow.

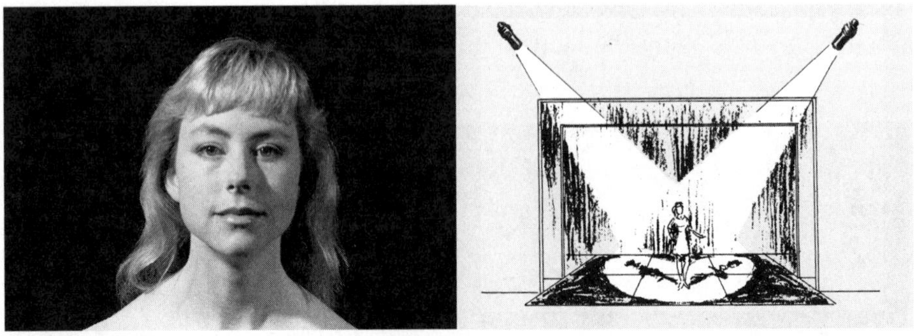

15-5

Lighting the Actor: Front-Light from Both Sides

Front-light from the left and right at a 45-degree angle. The stage-right side of the face has a higher intensity light, suggesting the direction of the motivating or "key" source.

Jewel Lighting In the early days of Broadway, New York theatres were not equipped to place lighting instruments at an angle of 45 degrees to the performer. Lights could be hung off a pipe running along the front of the balcony (balcony rail), but the angle was terribly low. Lights could be hung on pipes over-stage, but that angle was too steep. So Broadway designers convinced their producers to let them use the closest audience box on either side of the auditorium as a lighting position, and the **box boom** was born. While these seats offered poor visibility for patrons, the lighting angle to the stage was fairly good. However, the direction was much more side than front.

The performers acting downstage were lit with three lights: one from each box boom, creating good highlight and shadow, and one from the balcony rail, filling shadows and making eyes sparkle (hence, the term **jewel lighting**). Although lighting positions have improved, one can still see the roots of this system in the work of today's Broadway designers.

box boom A vertical hanging position for lighting equipment, located in the side walls of the auditorium close to the stage. Named after the placement of light booms in audience side boxes, these positions create a low to medium side angle a bit to the front of the performer.

jewel lighting An early Broadway technique of lighting involving the use of a low-angled source from the balcony rail in combination with lights from each box boom.

Front-Lighting from Below In nineteenth-century theatres, lighting positions located along the edge of the stage's apron were permanent installations. These **footlights** consisted of a row of lights used to wash the scenery with light and color, as well as fill in shadows on the actor's faces created by harsh, high-angle front light. When lighting became more sophisticated, footlighting went out of vogue, considered to be old-fashioned and capable of producing nothing but unsightly shadows. Ironically, today's designers are again using lighting from the apron position—for many of the same reasons that it was originally developed. It can color-tone actors and scenery, it can fill shadows on actors' faces, and, at a higher intensity, it can be used to create unusual effects. If a source from the footlight position is strong enough, it can create wonderful special effects—much like a spotlight from below. Small MR16 instruments are often placed in this position for just such an effect.

footlight Low-angled light sources often placed at the front edge of the stage apron—at the "feet" of the actors.

Altering Angle and Direction The most interesting kind of stage lighting employs many angles and directions of light. Over the years designers have demanded an ever greater number of lighting instruments for their productions. The total number of units in a light plot has doubled and tripled. The principal motive behind this increase has been the desire for a greater variety of angles and directions of light. The use of automated fixtures in the theatre has further increased the possibilities of variable lighting angles and direction. With moving lights (or moving mirrors), one light serves the purpose of many. It changes color, beam quality, and texture—most importantly, it changes angle and direction.

The only rule of visibility lighting is that there be at least one source somewhere from the front. It can be filled by a source from the side or by a second front-light. A creative lighting designer determines angle and direction by considering the desired effect. If a natural effect is desired, a 45-degree angle with a direction somewhat to the side of the performer might be chosen for the key-light. If a harsher effect seems appropriate, the angle might be increased to 60 degrees or the direction moved more to the side. If a softer, less angular feeling is the goal, the angle might be lowered to 30 degrees or the direction changed more to the front.

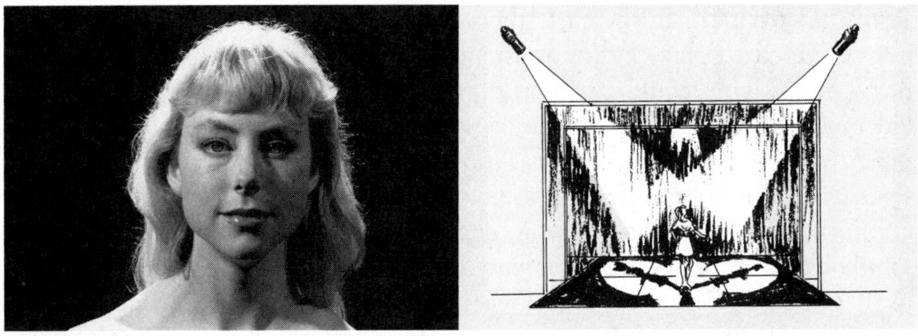

15-6

Lighting the Actor: Front- with Back-Light

Three directions of light: right and left front-light, each at 45 degrees, and back-light. Note the superior revelation of form.

Altering the look of a scene through lighting was once primarily done by changing color. Today, new looks are achieved just as often through changes in angle and direction. Designers should be aware that in order for a change to be noticeably different, the new lighting angle or direction needs to be roughly 30 degrees from that of the old.

Back-Light

Light coming from behind an actor creates dimensionality. It also separates performer from background. It can color-tone the stage floor and add contrast to the scene. Compare Figures 15-5 and 15-6; the difference results from back-light.

The use of back-light adds three-dimensionality to scenery and especially actors. In separating actors from their background, it allows the lighting designer to put a brighter light on the background than would otherwise be possible. It permits scenic and costume designers to use colors without fear of the actor blending into the background. Because the color of back-light does not affect an actor's skin tone or costume, stronger colors than those used in front-lighting may be considered. Creative use of back-light color can help to establish an overhead motivational source or simply color and texture the stage floor for a specific effect.

Angle and Direction Just as with front-light, back-light need not be directly behind the performer. Light from a back-side direction strikes more visible surface area and becomes more apparent. Two back-lights, one from each side, offer a greater degree of visible light and more intensity than does a single light shining directly behind an actor.

The ideal angle for back-light is between 45 and 60 degrees (Figure 15-7). An angle steeper than 60 degrees appears more like top-light (Figure 15-8). In many situations, care must be taken to prevent back-light from shining into the audience. The temptation is to increase the back angle, creating more of a top- or down-light. But the designer must remember that top-light is not at all the same as back-light, for it tends to "squash" rather than "edge" an actor.

Intensity Because back-light strikes so little visible surface, its intensity normally needs to be roughly one and a half times that of front-light. If it is

15-7

Lighting the Actor: Back-Light Only

Back-light providing a halo or "rim" effect.

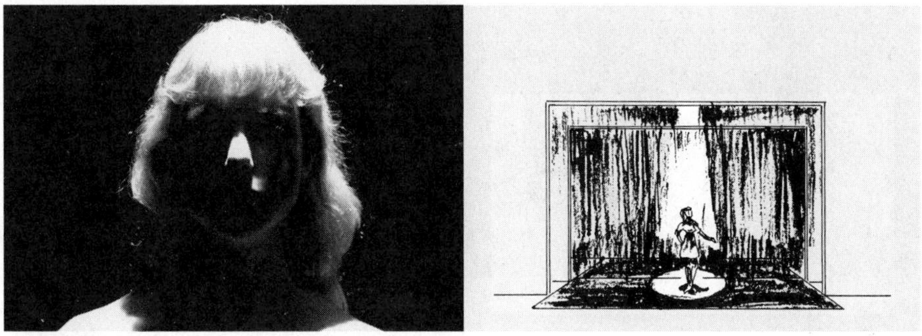

15-8

Lighting the Actor: Top-Light Only

Down-light or top-light at a 90-degree angle (straight-top). Normally not a complementary angle.

too bright, however, a halo effect will be created on the head and shoulders of the performer. When back-lighting is kept in proper balance with front-lighting, the actor is etched clearly against the background.

Side-Light

The most important attribute of side-light is revelation of form. Side-lighting gives the designer additional flexibility in defining form. Both color and angle add variety as side-lighting is used in combination with front-lighting. Using side-light as a key source is a highly dramatic and effective technique. Like back-light, side-light can be used to establish a motivational source through color, angle, and intensity. The amount of visible surface lit by side-lighting is considerably greater than that lit by back-lighting.

Low Side Dance lighting designers like to use side-light coming from a low angle to sculpt the figures of the dancers. Such light is hung on floor stands called **booms** located in the **wings.** Low side is angled from 0 degrees (the horizon) to about 30 degrees (Figure 15-9). The best direction for dance side-light is straight to the side, neither in front of nor behind the performer.

booms Vertical hanging positions for lighting instruments. Portable types often consist of 1½-inch black pipe screwed into a heavy base. Also called *lighting trees.*

wings Vertical masking pieces on the sides of a proscenium stage. The name is derived from "wing and border" scenery. Wings also refer to the offstage right and left spaces in the proscenium theatre.

15-9

Lighting the Actor: 30-Degree Side-Light

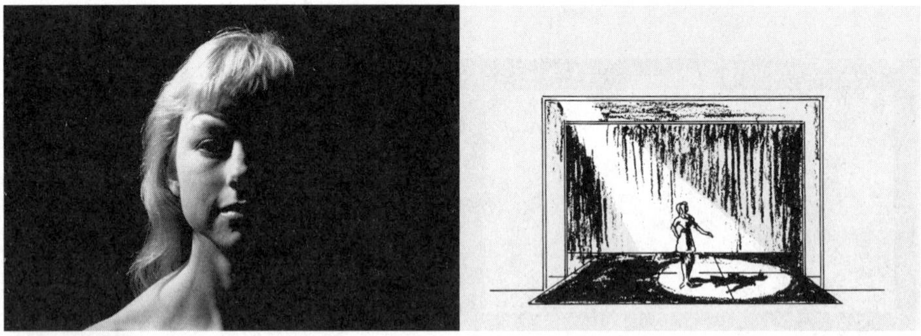

15-10

Lighting the Actor: 45-Degree Side-Light

Although low side used in a stage play can create dramatic effects, it is often fraught with problems. Assuming that an adequate hanging position is available, the designer must be concerned with the light striking scenery in an undesirable manner.

High Side A more practical angle for dramatic productions, high side is usually angled between 45 and 60 degrees (Figure 15-10). As with back-light, an angle higher than 60 degrees begins to act like top-light, beating down on the performers. High side is as common as front-light in today's theatre. Its effect is *sculptural,* revealing the actors and scenic elements in a sharp, dramatic angle of light. When used with no color or a cool tint, high side is at its harshest; when used with color, it creates a strong and directional quality without tampering too much with costume color. It can be hung from the top of booms, from lighting **ladders** located in the wings, or from the ends of over-stage pipes. It can face any direction, from front-side to straight-side to back-side, depending on the desired effect.

ladders Hanging positions for lighting instruments that derive their name from the fact that, with vertical uprights and horizontal "rungs," they look like a ladder. They may be permanently fixed or, more likely, able to be hung in a variety of positions.

Lighting Positions

The proscenium theatre offers numerous possibilities for varying the angle and direction of a light source. Figure 15-11 shows various standard positions available in a simplified proscenium house. Those positions on the audience side of the proscenium arch—referred to as "front-of-house" (FOH)—present

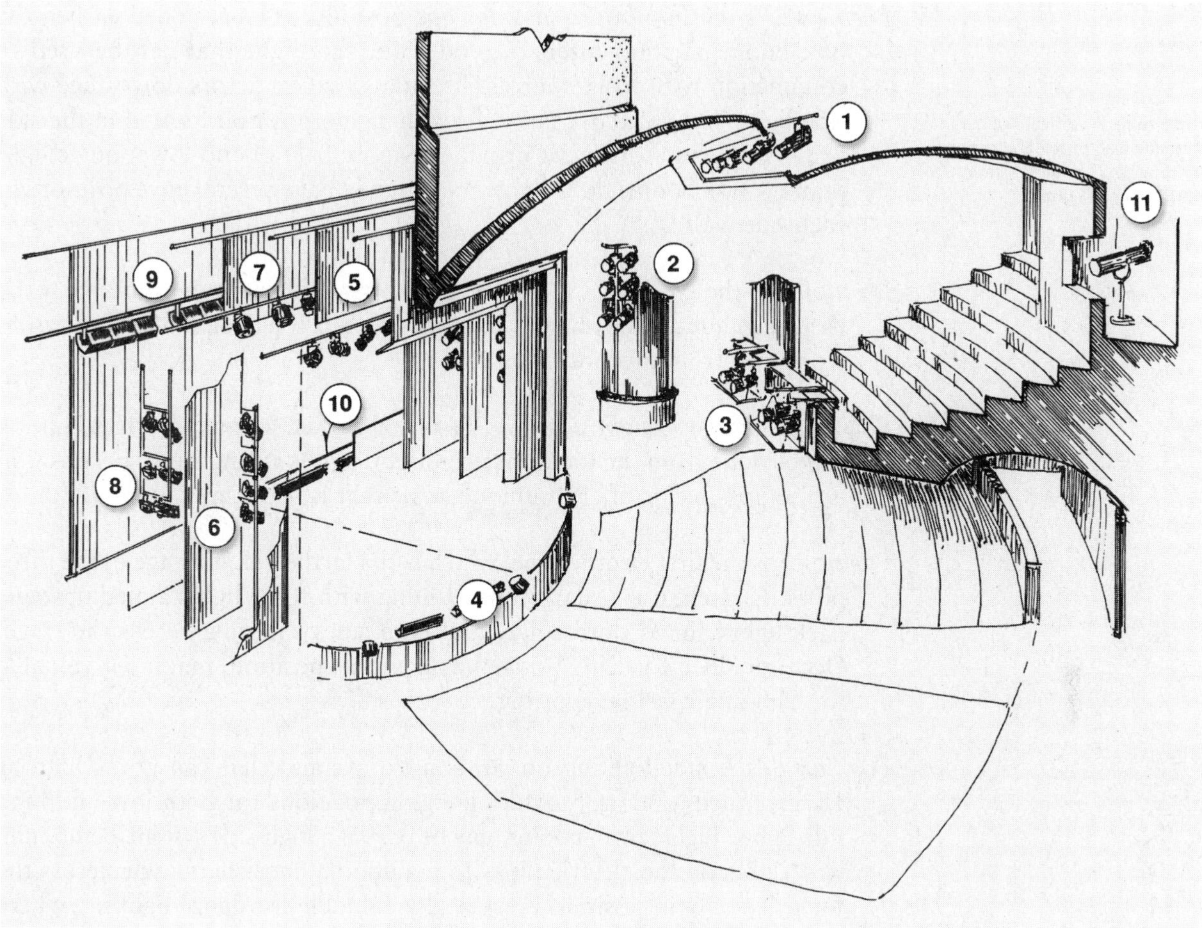

15-11

Lighting Positions in the Proscenium Theatre

1 Ceiling beams or ports.
2 Box booms or side coves.
3 Balcony front or balcony rail.
4 Apron or footlights.
5 First electric pipe or bridge (upstage front light position).
6 Floor stand or boom.
7 Second electric pipe (midstage back light position).
8 Ladder.
9 Third electric (back-light, backdrop, or cyclorama lighting).
10 Ground row (backdrop or cyclorama lighting).
11 Follow spot.

the designer with a good variety of angles from the front. The over-stage positions offer even greater variety, including lights from side, top, and back as well as front. Most of these hanging positions are equipped with electrical circuits for conveniently plugging in equipment.

Position 1 in Figure 15-11 is the **ceiling beam or port.** This is a primary position for front-light visibility. Well-equipped theatres have multiple ceiling positions to allow for a variety of lighting angles. A close position such as the one illustrated might be used to light midstage at about a 45-degree angle. A position farther back in the auditorium would light downstage areas at roughly a 45-degree angle, and a position even farther back would provide low-angle front-light. The first electric (position 5) could light an actor upstage at a 45-degree angle. High-angle follow spots can be used with good results from most ceiling positions.

ceiling beam or port A slot cut in the auditorium ceiling, providing a position for hanging and focusing front lights.

Position 2 is the *box boom* or *side cove* position. As mentioned earlier, the box boom position offers a good front side-light that can be used in conjunction with front sources. It can also sculpt actors downstage with side-light. The **side cove** is a vertical hanging position located in the side walls of the auditorium. It provides a more frontal and lower angle light than the box booms do. A large theatre may have several cove positions in each side wall.

side cove A vertical slot cut in the side wall of the auditorium to provide a hanging location for side-front light.

Position 3 is the *balcony rail.* Although a low angle, it can be valuable when used in conjunction with more extreme angles. Projections and color washes work well from this position.

Position 4 is the *footlight* position. As noted earlier, low-angle effect lighting can be done from the footlight position. Color washing from this position is also possible. It offers a unique angle that is sometimes quite useful.

Position 5 is the first electric pipe, which is the farthest downstage of the three pipes. As such, it is usually heavily hung with front-lights aimed upstage, back-lights aimed downstage, and high sides shooting across the stage. Occasionally a focusing bridge hangs in this position, making it valuable for high-angle follow-spotting.

Position 6, the side-lighting boom, is a floor stand that can go as high as 16 feet. Such a boom provides hanging positions for both low and high side-lights. Lights from booms may be part of a high-side system, combining with lights on the electric pipes to maintain a consistent angle across the stage. The boom position is especially valuable for dance lighting, where low side-lighting booms may be located in each of the side wings.

Position 7 is the second electric pipe. It provides a good back-light angle to downstage areas as well as a location for midstage high-side lights. Top-light may also be hung in this position.

Position 8 is a ladder located in the wing. This is usually hung from the end of an over-stage pipe, but it may also be suspended from the grid. Ladders are used for high side-light and have an advantage over booms in that they do not take up valuable floor space. A ladder can also **trim** higher than a boom can.

trim To hang pipes or scenery above the stage floor.

Position 9 is the third electric pipe, located the farthest upstage of the three. One pipe in this position is used for upstage back-lighting and a second to light the cyclorama or backdrop. Three electric pipes are a minimum, with larger theatres having as many as seven or eight.

Position 10 is called the **ground row.** It is used to light the cyclorama or backdrop from the bottom. Sunsets and special sky effects are created from this position.

ground row A row of strip lights located upstage and used to illuminate the background from the bottom. A *scenery ground row* is a horizontal masking device used to hide the lighting ground row.

Position 11 returns front-of-house to the traditional follow-spot position. This position provides the low-angle light that is the trademark of traditional musical theatre. If subtlety is desired, a higher angle should be chosen.

LIGHTING THE ACTING AREA

Lighting someone from various positions and angles is relatively simple if the subject remains in a fixed position. An actor, however, usually moves. In order to produce consistency in lighting a moving person, the lighting designer must constantly duplicate the focus of lighting instruments on many similar areas over the entire playing space. This is the basis of the **area-lighting method,** which aims at lighting the stage evenly and in a consistent manner. The principles of area lighting should be understood completely before the young designer considers other methods.

area-lighting method An organizational method of lighting in which lighting areas are assigned throughout the acting area and instruments are focused on those areas in the same ways, thus providing consistency in lighting the actors as they move about the stage. Also called *area method* and *area system.*

The Area-Lighting Method

Dividing the acting space into convenient areas and then lighting each area with the same number of lighting instruments provides a balanced illumination. This technique, first developed by Stanley McCandless in the 1930s, has proven to be quite efficient and systematic. Used for setting focus points for automated fixtures as well as fixed lighting instruments, it allows the designer to view the stage as a grid of overlapping lighting focus areas.

As scenery styles have changed and lighting instrument design has improved, the area method has been modified and expanded. Today, numerous instruments are assigned to each area, providing great flexibility in terms of color and distribution. The number of lighting instruments used in some shows is staggering. Although the area method was first developed for the proscenium theatre, it has been readily adapted to other theatre forms such as thrust and arena (see Chapter 23).

Area Alignment In using the area system, one of the things a designer learns is that areas must overlap considerably. If not, the actor will pass through dark spots ("dips") in lighting when moving from one area to another. A properly adjusted stage-lighting instrument shines a light that has maximum intensity along the center line of its beam and falls off in brightness toward the edge. If light beams are overlapped so that the fall-off of one beam is compensated for by that of an adjacent light, a smooth and even coverage is achieved (Figure 15-12).

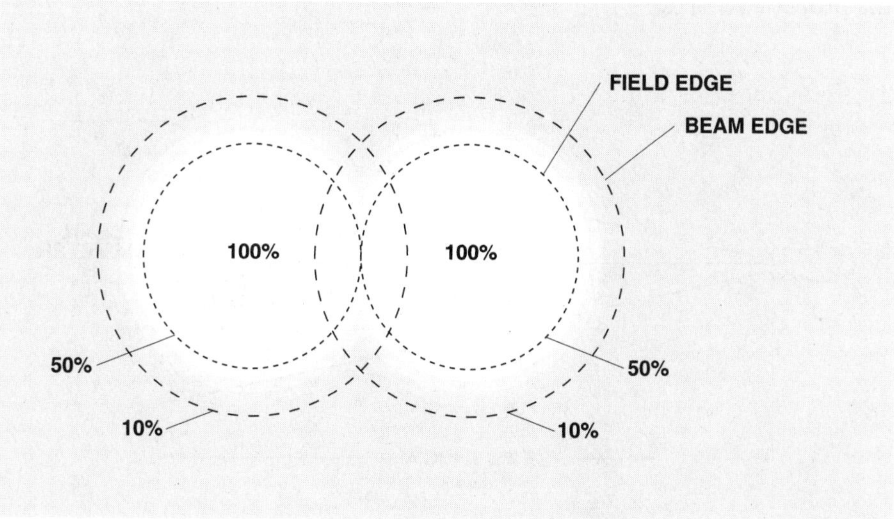

15-12

Beam Alignment

For smooth and even coverage of the acting area, light beams must be overlapped as shown. The numbers represent the percentage of light intensity.

focusing The process of aiming and adjusting lighting instruments to suit the needs of an individual production. Focusing is normally done by the lighting designer and a crew of electricians.

Focusing The process of focusing a show takes time to learn. **Focusing** involves (1) aiming a lighting instrument so that its beam falls exactly in the desired location, (2) adjusting the quality of light and/or size of the beam, and (3) shaping the beam. It is at once a technical and creative endeavor as the designer begins to discover how the light that has been planned so carefully is actually going to take form. The focus session is really the first time that the light comes to life.

When they focus, television and film designers often check for intensity variation by using a light-sensitive meter. Readings are taken at head height throughout the playing space. If meter readings indicate that intensity levels are uneven, the designer adjusts the focus or adds instruments to fill in the gap. The acceptable degree of variation is determined by camera sensitivity or film stock.

On the other hand, live-audience designers (for theatre, concerts, industrials, and the like) visually check instrument focus for even coverage, relying on experience and their personal perception of design requirements. Although less precise than studio focus, this method promotes a higher level of intuitive design during the focus process.

In either case, focus techniques and procedures are passed along from designer to designer; apprenticing is very much alive and well in the relatively small world of lighting design. A beginning designer is wise to observe the focus sessions of as many experienced designers as possible, for each will exhibit individual methods and techniques.

Area Size Lighting instruments are manufactured so that their intensity is appropriate for stage lighting when their beams of light are approximately 10 feet in diameter. Normal lighting areas vary from 8 to 12 feet in diameter, with 10 feet being a good average.

Most lighting instruments give off a beam of light that has a predetermined size or spread. Being cone-shaped, this beam may be measured either in degrees or by the diameter of its circle of light at a given distance from the source. As Figure 15-13 shows, the diameter of a light beam when it strikes a surface is determined by the distance from the source, or *throw* distance, as well as the beam angle or spread.

Normally using front-light as a basis, the designer first determines optimum lighting-area size. Then he or she chooses specific instruments that will provide the proper coverage.

15-13

Light Beam

As the light beam spreads, its diameter increases and its intensity decreases.

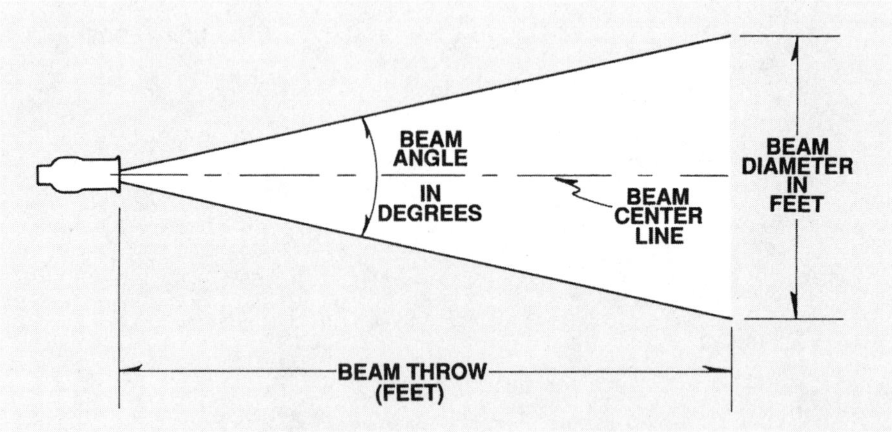

Area Placement The placement and choice of the number of areas is the lighting designer's decision. It is based on the size and shape of the playing area, as determined by the scenic ground plan, as well as the amount of control desired. Here the term **control** refers to the ability to alter light on each portion of the stage independently. The more lighting areas, the greater the control possibilities. Figure 15-14 shows some examples of lighting-area placement.

control The degree to which a designer can isolate a specific section of the acting area. Control depends on dimmers and lighting-area size.

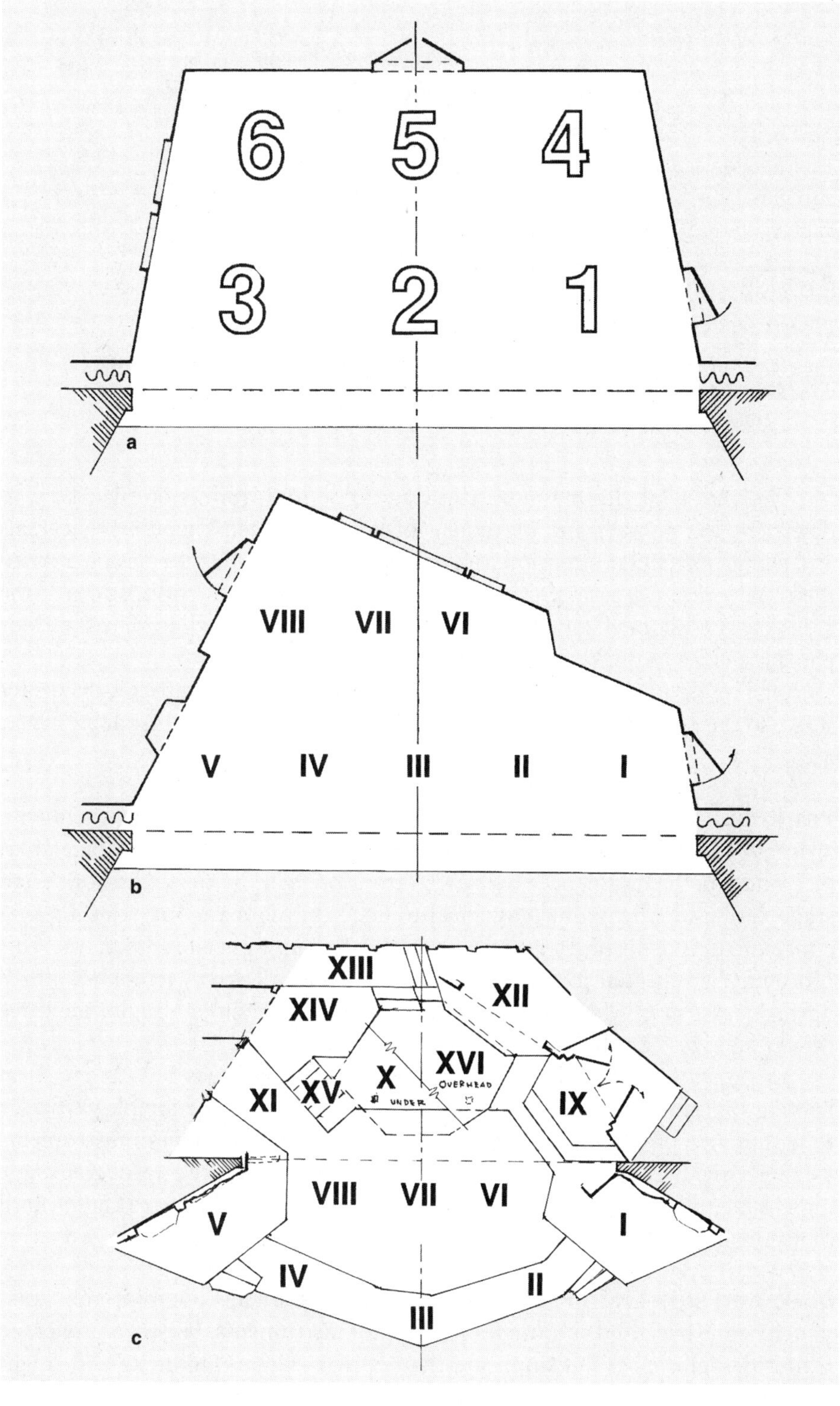

15-14

Lighting Areas

a A conventional box setting. Note the numbering of the areas from downstage left to upstage right. The total number of areas varies with the size of the acting area, the shape and number of settings in the production, and the desired degree of control.

b An irregularly shaped interior setting with the larger number of lighting areas providing greater control. Some designers prefer to designate the areas with Roman numerals to avoid confusion with other numbers on the plot.

c A complicated set. Using many levels often requires the definition of more lighting areas.

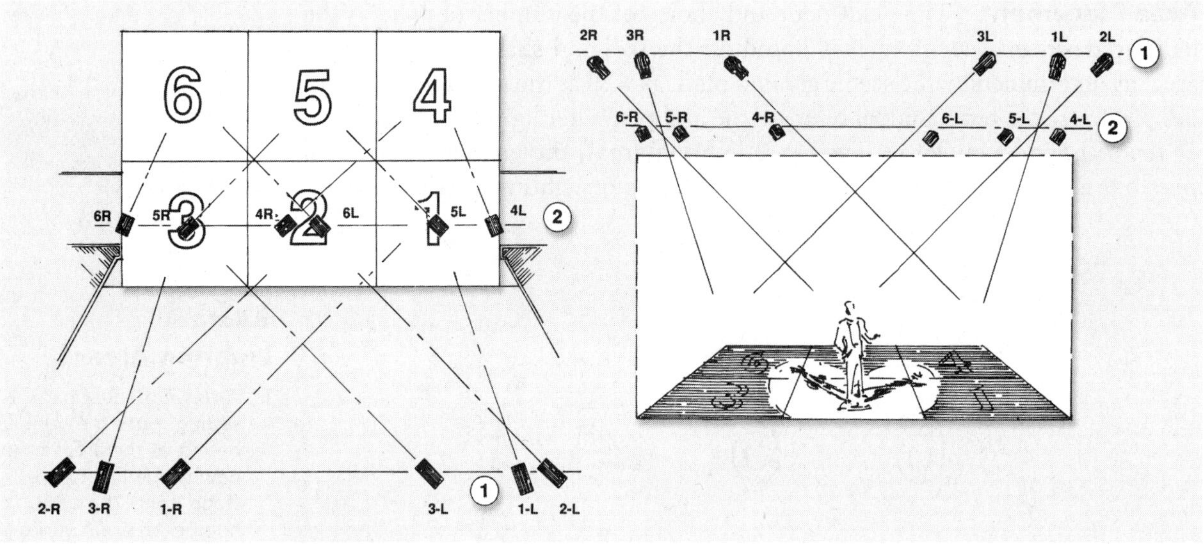

15-15

Lighting the Acting Areas: Front-Light

The area system with a minimum of front-lighting. A ceiling position (1) covers the downstage areas, while the first electric position (2) lights the upstage areas.

The action of the play and the staging of the production also help to determine the number and placement of lighting areas. Attending rehearsals and paying particular attention to blocking will greatly help the designer when the time comes for assigning areas. In a multiscene production, some of the areas can be planned for use in more than one set, providing that the floor plans are close to the same configuration.

One bit of advice: Most actors have a tendency to gravitate toward center stage, so the prudent lighting designer will be sure to have a controllable center area.

Front-Light Placement Figure 15-15 illustrates front-light placement with a simple 45-degree two-front-light area system. Looking at the upstage areas 4, 5, and 6 in the figure, note that each area is being lit by two lights: one from stage left and one from stage right. Each light beam hits the area at approximately a 45-degree vertical angle and from opposite directions. This procedure is repeated for each lighting area until all are covered. The three upstage areas are lit from the first electric. To keep a similar angle, the three downstage areas are lit from the ceiling position.

Next, examine the instruments lighting downstage areas 1, 2, and 3. Ideal lighting angles and direction often must be compromised. An example particular to lighting the proscenium stage is illustrated by the placement of instruments 1-L and 3-R. Because the proscenium arch makes the desired 45-degree angle impossible to maintain, these instruments must be shifted toward center until they adequately cover the area.

Back- and Side-Light Placement Designers normally use front-light areas to determine back and side angles and to plot instruments. However, coverage from side-lights does not duplicate that of front-lights (Figure 15-16). Light

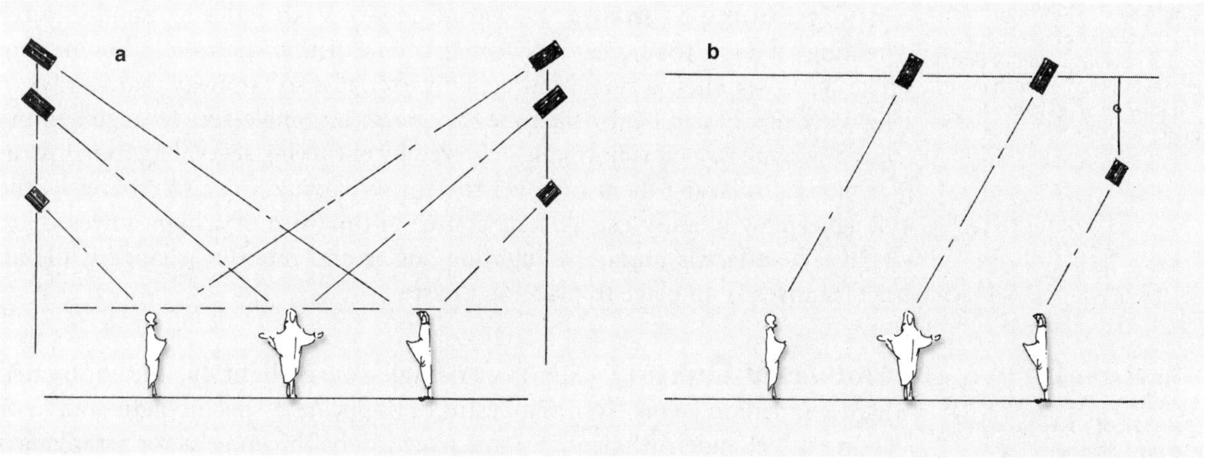

15-16

Lighting the Acting Areas: Side-Light

Side-light areas do not have the same shape as front-light areas, because the beams are oval.

a Three side-lights on booms from right and left light across the stage in a "zone." They are at a 35- to 40-degree angle.

b High side-light from an over-stage position and a drop-pipe or ladder lights the actor at a 60-degree angle.

projected at an angle to a surface produces an oval-shaped beam. Front- and back-light ovals run upstage and downstage, while sidelight ovals run across the stage. Normally this presents little problem unless the side-light is being used as a key source. In this case, it is advisable to develop a second area layout exclusively for side-lighting angles.

Figure 15-16a illustrates a side-light angle of approximately 45 degrees. For these and lower angles, a boom is the appropriate hanging position. However, for higher angles, a boom or a ladder in conjunction with an over-stage pipe must be used (Figure 15-16b).

Other Methods

Area lighting is an important, but not exclusive, method of lighting the stage. There are a variety of other techniques as well, which may or may not be used in combination with area lighting.

Variable Areas A deviation from standard area lighting, **variable area lighting** can provide a dramatic key-light with excellent control. Two sets of areas, one smaller than the other, are plotted over the stage. The smaller area is lit with narrow-beamed instruments from a fairly steep angle (60-degrees). This light provides good isolation and a strong, bright key source. The larger areas are lit in a more traditional manner, acting to fill the steep key-light.

variable area lighting Large as well as small lighting areas are arranged throughout the acting area. The small areas offer greater control and are used in conjunction with the larger areas.

Wash Lighting The term **wash lighting** refers to the use of general illumination to cover the entire playing space. Normally coming from a single direction, wash light is excellent for color-toning the stage and actors. Various angles, directions, and colors of wash light are used in conjunction with higher intensity *accent* lights to achieve variety, interest, and good visibility.

wash lighting Use of general illumination to cover the entire acting area; this technique offers little, if any, control.

single-source lighting Creating the quality of one distinct source of illumination by clustering several lighting instruments together or by using one large, bright source.

Single-Source Lighting A variation on wash lighting, **single-source lighting** attempts to re-create the feeling of one distinct source of illumination. The sun, after all, is a single source. However, it is so far away that its rays of light are nearly parallel by the time they reach us. Single-source stage lighting has diverging rays. It is normally achieved by clustering several lighting instruments and focusing them to cover the entire playing area. Alternatively, the designer may literally use a single source in the form of a high-powered arc light. The effect is unique, as lighting angles and intensity change while an actor moves from place to place on the set.

motivated lighting Lighting sources arranged to duplicate the effect of a specific source such as a chandelier.

Motivated Lighting Similar to single-source lighting, the **motivated lighting** method stems from the desire to duplicate a specific light source or sources. A chandelier hanging center-stage can be the impetus for arranging a series of lighting instruments in a circle above, cross-shooting to light actors in the manner of the chandelier. Such a source is normally the key-light, being filled by other instruments that are positioned relative to the direction of their particular key source.

Lighting Flexibility

As the demands on stage lighting increase, so do the demands of designers for greater flexibility. The ability to change angle, direction, and color depends solely on equipment. Designers in the past have answered this need by specifying ever greater numbers of instruments. Rather than depending on quantity, however, today's designer may specify more technologically advanced equipment.

Double and Triple Hanging Designers often want to improve on the limited flexibility that using one instrument from each direction into an area provides. To do this, they may double- or even triple-hang instruments. Two instruments hung side by side with different color filters allow for variable color. By duplicating the area coverage on each side, as illustrated in Figure 15-17, designers can create several possibilities for color control, including the following:

- Change the warm–cool direction from one side of the stage to the other
- Change the area color by independently mixing the colors from either side
- Flood the stage with only one of the two area colors

Hanging a third instrument offers even greater flexibility. The third instrument added to area 2 in Figure 15-17 can adjust focus and intensity in this center area. It can also be designed to alter the quality of light into the area through the use of a diffusion filter or perhaps a gobo.

color changer A DMX remotely controlled device placed at the front of a lighting instrument in order to change color filters. Often called *scrollers*.

Color Changers Double- and triple-hanging allows for greater color flexibility and can provide some degree of focus control; however, a better solution might be remotely controlled **color changers** (Figure 15-18). Called *scrollers* or *faders,* this auxiliary equipment offers the designer a wide range of color. They are quiet, dependable, and easily controlled.

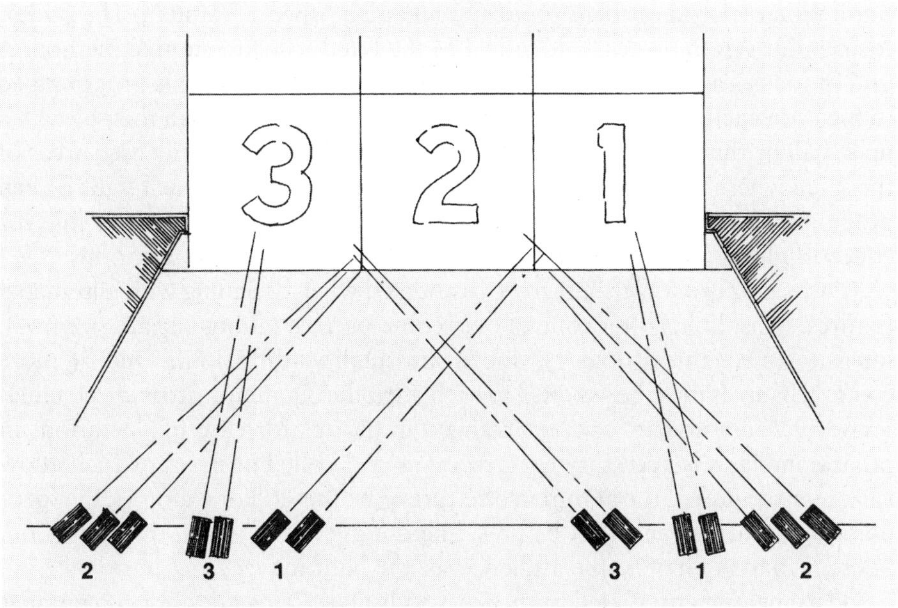

15-17

Double and Triple Hanging

Triple hanging on area 2, with double hanging for areas 1 and 3. The center area has both a tight and a more open focus while all areas provide variable color and direction of key and fill sources.

15-18

Color Changers and Automated Fixtures

Side-lighting towers used for a Kenny Loggins concert. Shown are remotely controlled color changers and an Intellabeam automated fixture.

Automated Fixtures Now common in stage use, **automated fixtures** provide a new flexibility for the designer (Figure 15-18). Designing with them, though, requires a slightly different approach from that of nonautomated fixed instruments.

automated fixtures DMX remotely controlled lighting instruments that, at a minimum, can change focus and color. Often called *moving lights*.

Like any other instrument, automated fixtures must be focused on a particular area. The coordinates of that focus are then stored in computer memory for recall when needed. There are currently two systems of automated fixture focus: a grid or *focus point* system and a "special" system. The grid or focus point system is nearly identical to the fixed-instrument area method. A grid of focus areas is determined, and each automated fixture is programmed to focus on each one of the grid points or areas. That focus can then be called up at will by the designer. The "special" system identifies heavily used areas of the stage where automated fixtures are likely to be needed. Each light is then programmed to those selected areas. While the "special" system is fine for concert lighting, the grid system is best for most theatrical applications.

Focus is only one attribute to be considered when designing with automated fixtures. Most lights offer control over color, pattern (gobos), beam size (iris), intensity (mechanical douser), and beam quality (diffusion). One or more control channels must be assigned to each attribute. Common attribute channels for several instruments can be arranged in groups for ease of operation. In programming, it is necessary to write extra cues called **dark sets,** which allow various attributes of the automated fixture to be preset. For example, the focus point of an instrument must be preset before the cue in which the light is on, in order to avoid having the audience see the light move.

dark set Special lighting cue written and inserted into the cue list to cause color changers or automated fixtures to change their color or focus without being seen.

Placement of automated fixtures depends on the effect desired and number of instruments available. They may work alongside fixed instruments as specials or perhaps as key-lights. Because of their intensity and high color temperature, automated fixtures are quite effective as specials. Otherwise, high-angle front- and side-lighting are the most popular applications.

Specials and Follow Spots

Lighting instruments that are additions to the standard production lighting add interest and focus. However, designers must carefully consider whether the use of specials will be appropriate to the style of the production.

specials Lighting instruments used in addition to the regular production lighting.

Specials Instruments that are used in addition to the regular production lighting are called **specials.** Their normal function is to emphasize a part of the setting or an actor in a specific location. Examples include a *door special* (a light carefully framed to brighten an actor standing in a doorway), a *couch special* (extra illumination where an important scene takes place), or a *pin spot* (a narrow beam of light that is held a moment longer on an actor's face during a final fade-out). Specials influence composition by attracting the eye to a desired center of attention.

Enhanced visibility may involve specials that follow the moving actor. This can be achieved in one of two ways: (1) the actor may be lit by a series of instruments focused along the path of movement, with each light dimming up or down at the proper moment; or, (2) the actor may be lit with a follow spot.

follow spot A specially equipped light operated by a stage electrician to follow an actor or actors about the stage.

Follow Spots Actor movement is followed by a single, freely mounted spotlight. The **follow spot** has long been used for musicals, revues, and other presentational productions where realism is of minor importance. It usually appears as a sharply defined, hard-edged circle of light that is brighter than all the other stage lights. Its use in this manner is frankly presentational.

A subtler method of follow-spotting is high-angle follow-spotting (sometimes called European follow-spotting, referring to the practice of placing lights and operators on the first light bridge). A soft-edged incandescent follow spot is used to highlight the action unobtrusively. To keep the light off the scenery and minimize shadows around the actor, the follow spot should be hung at an angle close to 60 degrees. Even if the moving light is noticed, audience members soon become accustomed to it and accept it as a stylized element of the production.

LIGHTING THE BACKGROUND

Even though the lighting designer deals chiefly with lighting the actor, lighting the scenery and backgrounds also require a great deal of consideration. For example, light on a background or sky cyc contributes significantly to mood and atmosphere.

Walls

In the case of a conventional interior or box setting, normal actor illumination usually lights the walls sufficiently. However, several precautions are necessary. Too often a box set's stage-right walls seem to be a totally different color from its stage-left walls. This mistake is a result of poor color mixing from the front-lights. It is corrected by making sure that all frontal colors hit the walls with relatively equal intensity. Instruments lighting the walls of a box set should be softly focused in order to blend well and reduce shadows.

Shadows on the walls from actors or furniture can be a difficult problem. The best solution is to change the angle of light causing the shadow, but at times this is impossible. A wall wash comprising lights specifically hung, focused, and colored for this purpose may help. Fresnel-type instruments are a good choice (see Chapter 18).

Backings

Lighting backings offers its own set of challenges. For example, the backing behind a doorway is rarely seen for more than a moment, and then not directly by most of the audience, but it must be lit. Designers do not need elaborate equipment to give these backings adequate illumination. The objective is to provide enough light so that an actor, when leaving the stage, does not seem to be retiring into a dark closet. Such attention to detail can make the difference between an adequate and a good design.

Of course, backings can assume greater proportions than a doorway. A painted exterior seen through a large window offers one example. Rooftops or the exterior walls of an adjoining building may be visible in a more detailed backing. Such scenic elements demand greater attention to distribution and color control than does the simple doorway backing.

Backdrops and Sky Cycs

It is not unusual to have vast areas of sky behind the performers. These backdrops or cycloramas require lighting instruments specially designed to provide the proper amount of light as well as even distribution and blending of color over the entire surface. Such instruments are hung above the drop and sometimes placed on the stage floor as well (Figure 15-19). The designer may have to mix several colors if he or she wants to change the atmosphere created by the background during a performance.

15-19

Lighting the Background

a A painted backdrop, sky drop, or cyclorama lit from above with cyc lights and from below with strip lights. When lighting from below, a *scenery ground row* is necessary for masking.

b The backing lit only from above with strip lights. This technique often requires two sets of lights, one aiming high and the other low.

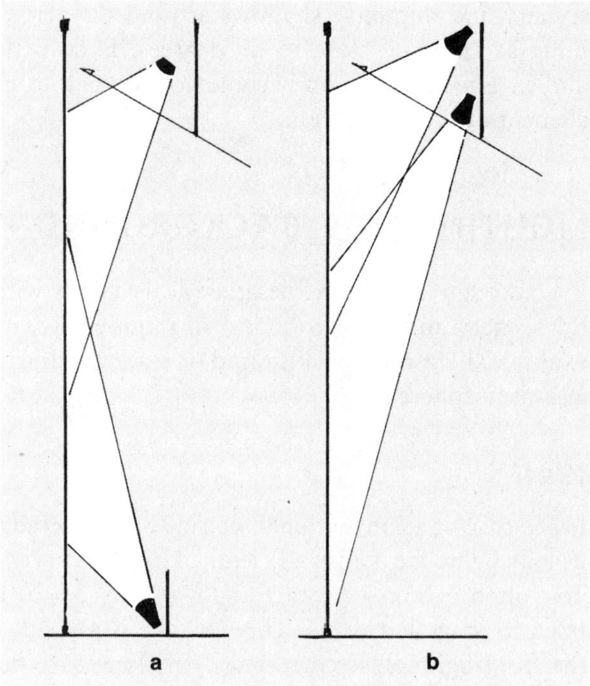

scrim An open-weave fabric used in the theatre for its transparent properties.

Scrims Open-weave material called **scrim** is particularly useful in the theatre because of its capability to appear either opaque or transparent. A scrim hung in front of a backdrop or cyclorama adds a hazy quality to the backing that adds a sense of distance. The scrim itself can be lit, or, better yet, the drop behind the scrim can be illuminated, as shown in Figure 15-20.

15-20

Lighting the Background: Scrims

A scrim (1) is placed in front of the backing (2). The scrim is lit from the front and the backdrop is separately lit from both above and below.

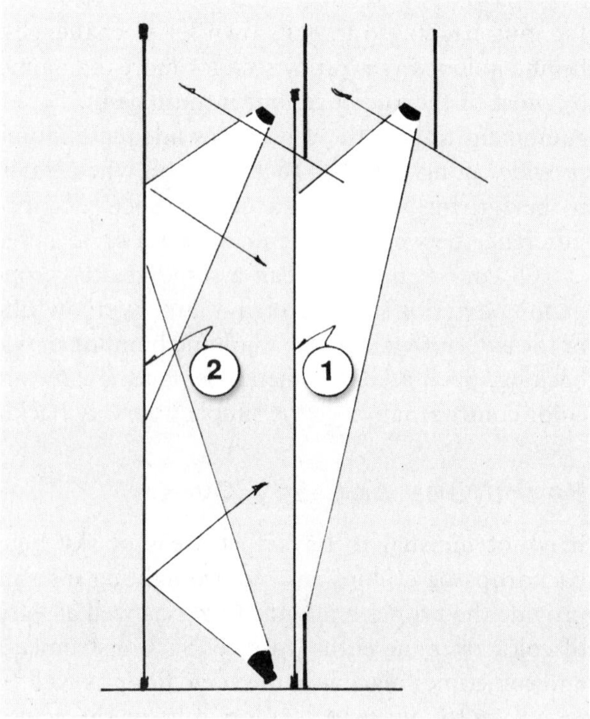

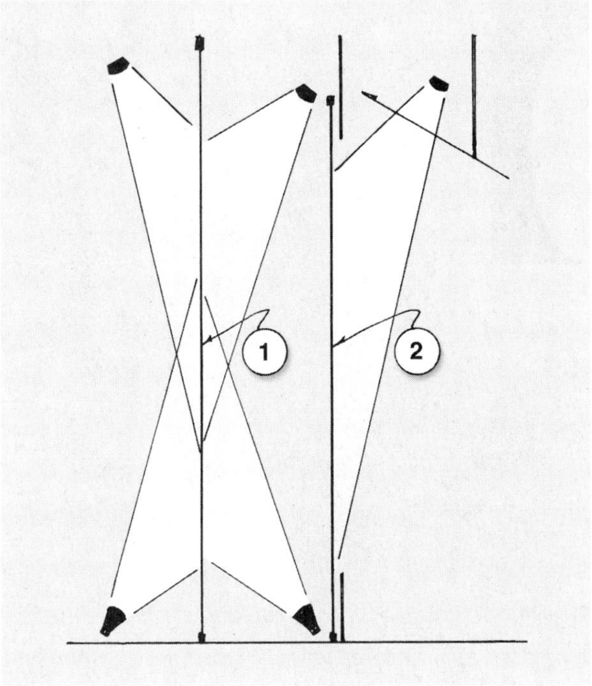

15-21

Lighting the Background: Translucencies

A translucent drop (1) is positioned upstage of a scrim (2). The drop has both front- and back-lighting to change effect, and the scrim is lit from the front to add depth and atmosphere.

Scrim may also be used by itself as a drop. In this case the designer must pay close attention to the light that falls directly on the scrim as well as behind it. Using high-angle top-light is the best way to opaque a scrim. To make a scrim transparent, the designer keeps as much light as possible off the material itself while illuminating objects behind it.

Translucent Backings A **translucency** allows for the possibility of dramatic changes in the look of a backdrop through lighting. A backdrop may be partially or completely translucent, with the translucent areas often painted with dyes rather than regular pigment. If lit from the front, the drop will appear one way; if lit from behind, it can have a completely different look (Figure 15-21).

translucency A fabric that can be either opaque or translucent depending on how it is lit.

Hanging Space Successful background lighting depends on the close cooperation of the lighting and scene designers. For instance, all too often the scene designer does not leave enough space between ground rows and the backdrop or between borders and the cyclorama for proper lighting. No matter how good the equipment, a certain distance is required for colors to mix and blend well on a backdrop. Or sometimes backgrounds representing distant fields are so close to a window or door that it is impossible to avoid shadows from area lighting. Any illusion created by good painting is then destroyed. Most of these and other potential problems can be avoided by consultation and careful study of the scene designer's floor plan.

In any case, the lighting designer must know the properties and tools of distribution in order to ensure a quality product. The next chapter explores the specific qualities of color in light.

16

Color and Light

Color, one of the four primary tools of theatre lighting, is a powerful force in stage composition. It can be subtle or dramatic, decorative or atmospheric, symbolic or realistic. Color in light animates the scene. The energy of light reveals, brightens, and adds color to actors and scenery, thereby increasing their vitality.

The history of the use of color in the theatre goes back well before electric light and plastic color filters. Designers have always known that colored light conveys a sense of mood or atmosphere in a way unlike that of any other medium. The use of colored light in the modern theatre has gone through many variations, including a recent trend toward designing with no color at all.

Of the design elements, color often seems to be the most complex. It is for this reason that it was first discussed at length in Chapter 8 and again here. As discussed, designers must pay attention to color in dye and pigment as well as in light because they always interact. Fully learning the subject of color usage, of course, takes time and experience. The beginning lighting designer can, however, learn the basic principles of color physics, psychology, and physiology, such as the following:

- An object has a particular color of its own—its surface color.
- Light is always colored—even if its color is white.
- The color of light affects the color of objects.
- Certain perceptual factors influence how we see color.

COLOR IS LIGHT

Color would not exist without light. As anyone who has used a prism knows, white light is actually made up of a variety of colors or hues. If we perceive a light as white, the receptors in our eyes are actually receiving a mixture of colors that our brain interprets as white. The color receptors in our eyes are

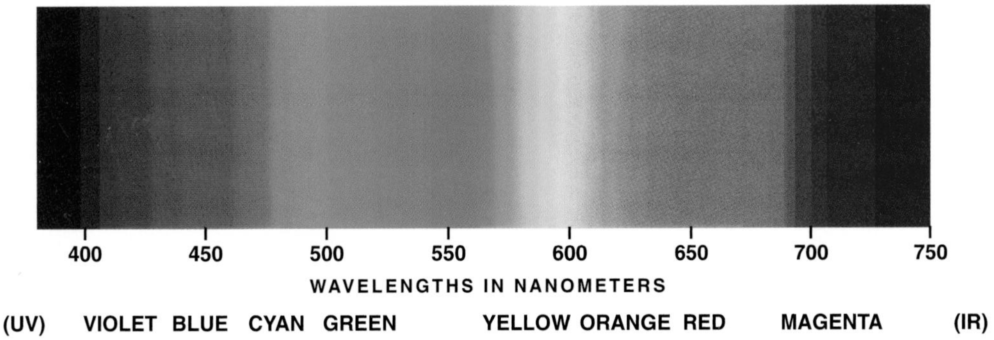

CP16-1

The Color Spectrum

The spectral hues and their respective wavelengths measured in nanometers.

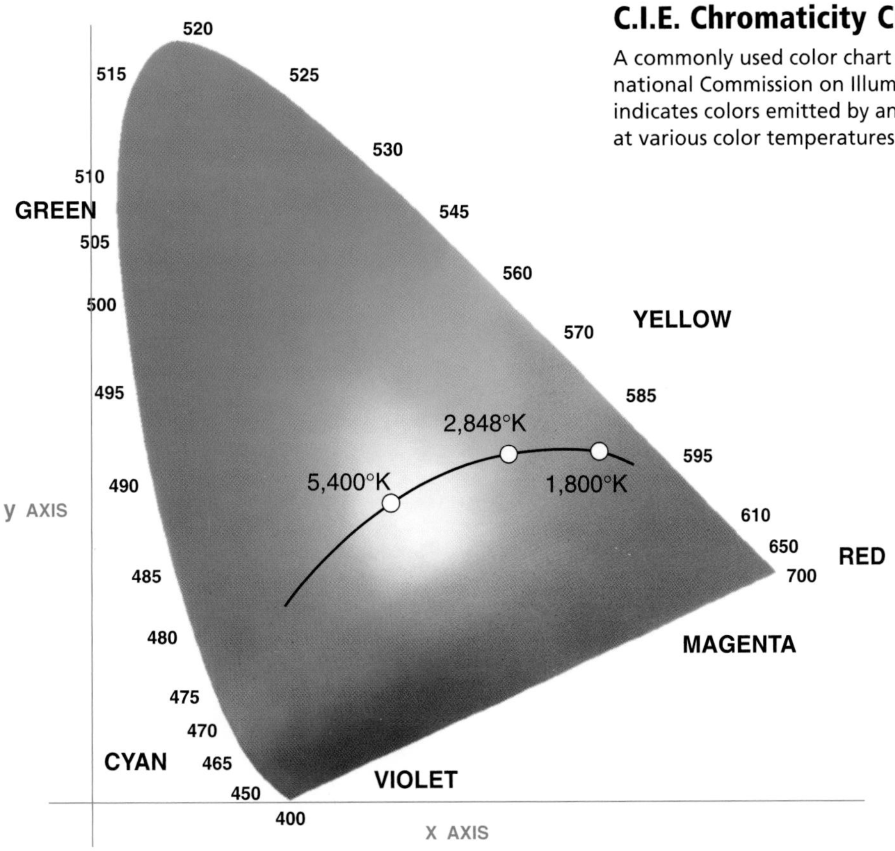

CP16-2

C.I.E. Chromaticity Chart

A commonly used color chart developed by the International Commission on Illumination. The black line indicates colors emitted by an incandescent light source at various color temperatures (degrees Kelvin).

CP16-3

Kelvin Temperature

These three light boxes illustrate the visual difference (recorded on tungsten film from left to right) among a source at 1,800 degrees Kelvin, such as candlelight; a source at 3,200 degrees Kelvin, such as stage lighting; and a source at 5,700 degrees Kelvin, such as daylight.

CP16-4

Color Mixing

When the three primary colors of light are mixed, white light is the result. Any two primaries mix to form secondary colors.

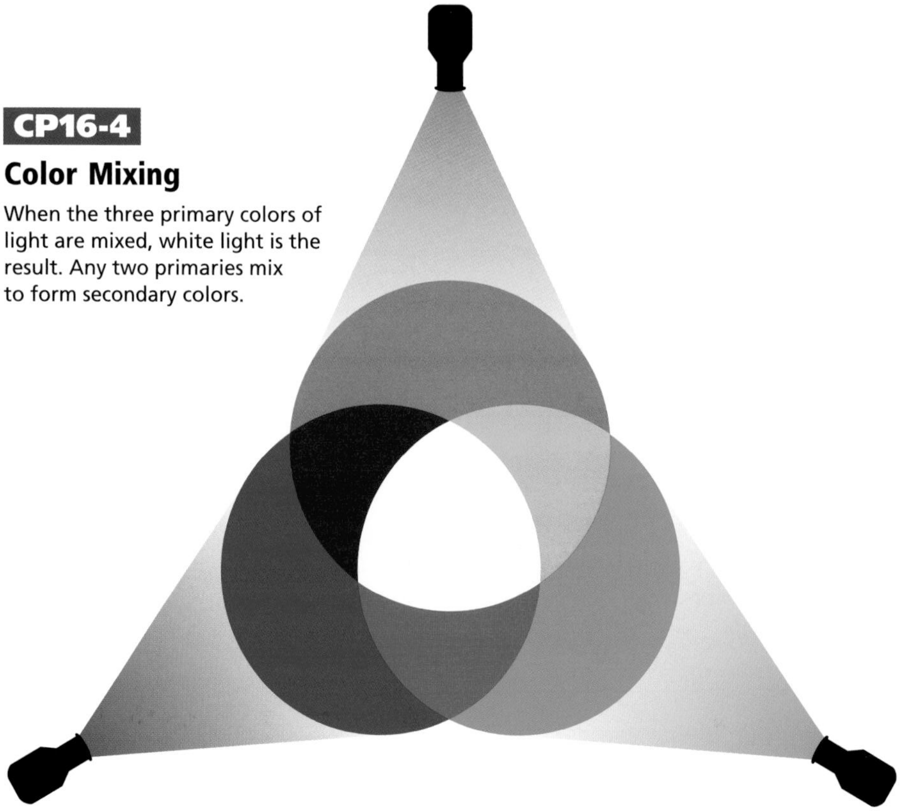

PHOTO BY MARCUS BRYAN-BROWN

CP16-5

Complex Scenic Projections

Use of large-scale projections in the Broadway production of *The Who's Tommy.* The light plot for the Broadway tour of *Tommy* can be found in Chapter 24, Figure 24-2. Director, Des McAnuff; scenery design, John Arnone; costume design, David C. Woolard; lighting design, Chris Parry; projections, Wendall Harrington.

CP16-6

Color on a Scene

These examples from *As You Like It* illustrate the strong effect of color on a scene.

PHOTO BY BRIAN RINK

CP16-7

Ultraviolet Effects

In the Tacoma Actor's Guild production of Shakespeare's *The Tempest,* the galaxy design on the scrim was visible only under ultraviolet light. Director, Pat Patton; scenery design, Jeffrey T. Cook; costume design, Susan Edie; lighting design, Scott O'Donnell.

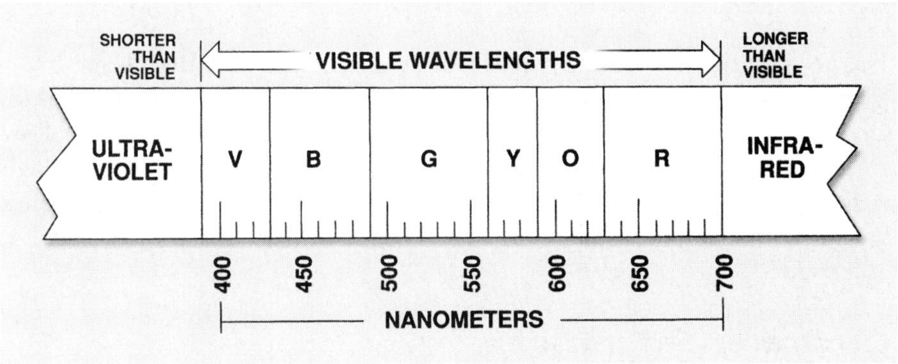

16-1

The Electromagnetic Spectrum

The six principal colors are violet, blue, green, yellow, orange, and red. Their wavelengths are measured in nanometers, equal to one-billionth of a meter (see also Color Plate 16-1).

most sensitive to three color wavelengths: red, green, and blue. The combination of these **primary hues** creates white light. Note that the primaries of light (red, green, and blue) are different from those of pigment (red, blue, and yellow).

primary hue One of three hues that are used to mix all other hues; in pigment the primary hues are red, yellow, and blue; in light they are red, green, and blue.

The Visible Spectrum

The visible wavelengths of the electromagnetic spectrum provide color and light (Color Plate 16-1). Every color has a different spectral wavelength. These wavelengths are measured in **nanometers,** with one nanometer being equal to one-billionth of a meter. The visible portion of the spectrum is a minute section with wavelengths of anywhere from 400 to 700 nanometers (Figure 16-1). The shortest wavelengths in the visible spectrum, 390 to 430 nanometers, produce what we call violet light. The next length is blue, followed by green, yellow, orange, and finally red light (at 630 to 700 nanometers). The wavelengths shorter than 390 nanometers are called **ultraviolet** (beyond violet), and those longer than 700 nanometers are **infrared** (below red).

nanometer A measurement in billionths of a meter used to define certain wavelengths (colors) of light.

ultraviolet Light energy with wavelengths just shorter than the shortest visible wavelengths (violet)—literally "beyond violet."

infrared Light energy with wavelengths just longer than the longest visible wavelengths (red)—literally "below red."

C.I.E. Chromaticity Chart

The color chart shown in Color Plate 16-2 was developed by The International Commission on Illumination (CIE) to indicate visually the relationship of any hue with another. It shows color mixing quite clearly—specifically, how various hues are derived from the mixing of the three primaries. Saturated hues are located at the perimeter of the chart and become less saturated as they mix, moving toward the white center. The curved black line (called the black body locus) indicates the exact color emitted by a light source at any given color temperature.

THE LANGUAGE OF COLOR

In describing a color, lighting designers need to use a common language that will be understood by other designers and coworkers. The three variants of color in pigments and dyes are hue, chroma, and value (discussed in Chapter 8). The lighting designer begins with these variants as a basis of color terminology. In light, color can be described in simple terms by referring to its hue (blue, yellow, and so on) and its chroma or saturation (purity).

Hue

The position of a color in the spectrum determines its hue. Recall that hue is what allows us to differentiate one color from another or from a gray of the same value (brightness). Six easily identified hues are red, orange, yellow, green, blue, and violet. As mentioned earlier, our eyes respond most strongly to the three primary hues: red, green, and blue. The lighting designer often finds it useful to think of any hue as a mixture of these three primary colors in light.

Chroma or Saturation

tint Lighter value of a hue.

In the context of lighting, the term *saturation* is preferred to that of *chroma.* Saturation refers to the amount of pure spectral hue present in a color. Primary blue, for example, is a highly saturated color. Lee Filters No. 075, evening blue, is more saturated than Lee No. 063, pale blue. The instant the purity of a spectral hue is modified by mixing, the result is a difference in saturation. Colors low in saturation, referred to as **tints,** represent a large admixture of white to the spectral hue.

Color Temperature

The lighting designer has yet another concern: the color of the source of light itself. We tend to think of light emitted from the sun and almost any incandescent lamp as being white. In reality, the actual color of light from one source can be quite different from that of another. One method of identifying the exact color makeup of any light source is called *color temperature,* measured in degrees Kelvin (after the British physicist, William Lord Kelvin).

Unlike literal temperature, a higher Kelvin temperature indicates a cooler-colored source—that is, one that has more blue in it. A source with low Kelvin temperature is rich in warmer colors such as red and amber. Candlelight, which tends to be a warm, yellow-red, is rated at 1,800 degrees Kelvin (°K); light from a standard incandescent household lamp is close to 3,200°K; and daylight is surprisingly blue at a cool 5,700°K. Color Plate 16-3 illustrates the approximate color of each of these sources. (Detailed information about Kelvin temperature will be covered in Chapter 22.)

COLOR FILTERING

Most stage-lighting instruments produce a light that people consider "white," rated at approximately 3,200°K. Currently, the only practical means of significantly altering this color is by interrupting the beam of light with a filter. Placed in front of candles, clear glass vessels containing red wine and other colored liquids were once employed as filters. Modern stage lighting uses the same technique with filters of colored plastic or dichroic glass.

As the name implies, a filter placed in front of a light source causes selected colors to be filtered or blocked from passing through. This is an important concept to understand. When white light is shone through a blue filter, the red and green wavelengths are blocked; only the blue wavelengths are allowed to pass. In theory, if a pure blue light is shone through a pure red filter, no light at all will pass through (Figure 16-2).

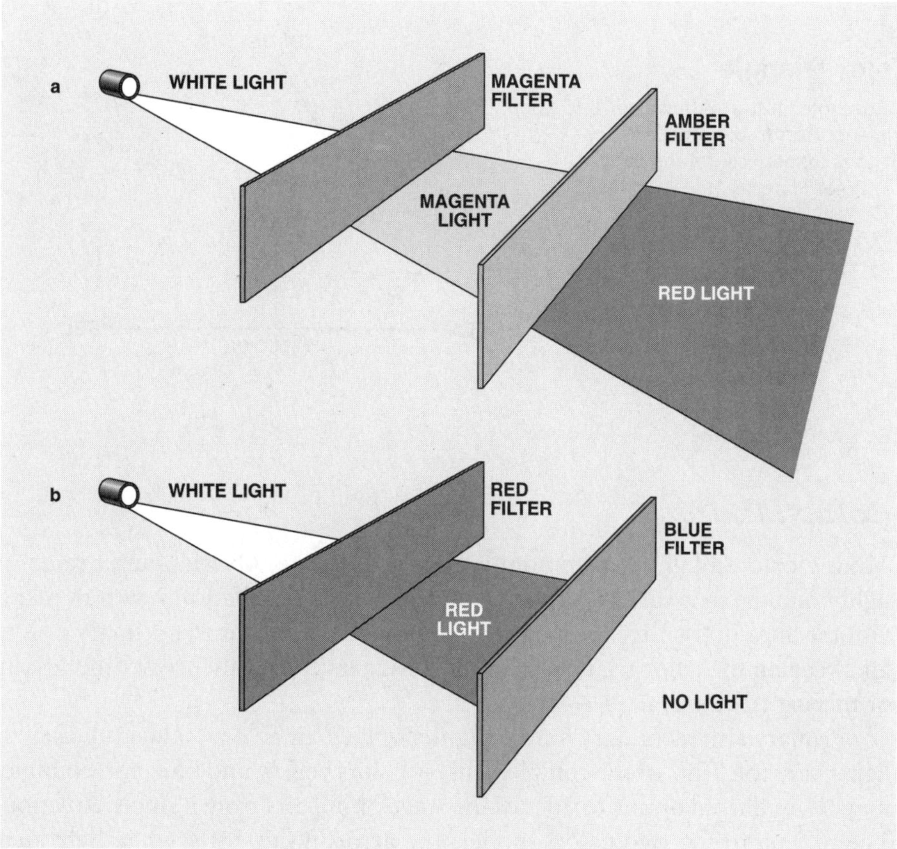

16-2

Color Filtering

- **a** White light, when filtered through two secondaries such as magenta (made up of blue and red) and amber (made up of red and green) results in red, the secondaries' common primary.
- **b** White light, when filtered by two primaries, is completely absorbed so that no light emerges.

COLOR INTERACTION

Color in light and pigment can be varied by mixing. When two lights of different colors strike a white surface, the result is a mixture of those colors. If the surface itself is colored, mixing still takes place, but the surface color interacts with the light to produce a particular reflected color. This is called color modification.

The Color Triangle

A good way to illustrate color mixing is by using a color triangle such as Figure 16-3. Each of the three primary colors is located at one of the points of the triangle. The center of the triangle represents the mixture of all three primaries to create white light.

Secondary Hues If any two of the primary colors are mixed along the edge of the triangle, a **secondary hue** is the result. Mixing primary red and primary blue results in violet. Mixing primary green and primary blue results in cyan. Mixing primary red and primary green results in yellow. Like the primaries, these three secondary hues, if mixed together, create white light.

secondary hue One of three hues produced by mixing any two primaries; in pigment they are violet, orange, and green; in lighting they are yellow, violet, and cyan.

Complementary Hues Directly across the triangle from any color is that color's **complement.** Violet is the complement of green, cyan is the complement of red, and yellow is the complement of blue. As the triangle indicates, mixing a color with its complement results in white light.

complementary hue One of two hues directly opposite each other on the color triangle.

16-3

The Color Triangle

The color triangle illustrates how the three primary colors (red, green, and blue) mix to secondary colors and to white (see Color Plate 16-2).

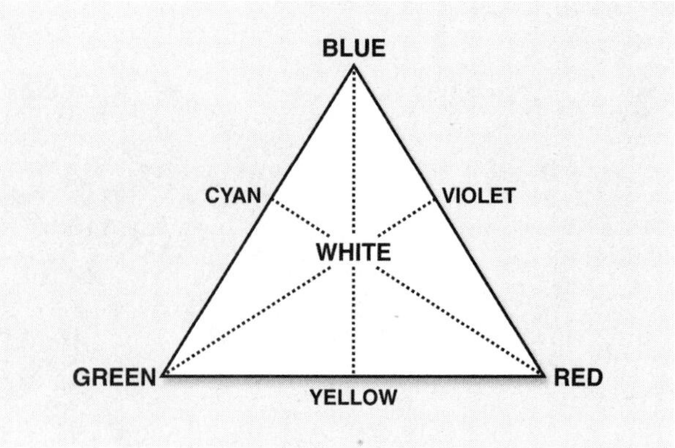

Color Mixing

Mixing colored light is commonplace in the theatre. Overlapping beams of light combine in a variety of ways, filling each other's shadows with rich and vibrant hues that enliven a scene. By thinking in terms of the primary colors and keeping the color triangle in mind, designers can easily predict the results of mixing (Color Plate 16-4).

Primary and secondary hues in lighter values (tints) are frequently used to light the actor. Tints of the complementary colors yellow and blue, for example, may be used from opposite sides of the stage or in pairs from a single direction. The mixing of the two colors models the actor in flattering white light that can be warmed or cooled by changing the intensity of the spotlights.

Color Reflection

Just as light allows us to see an object, it also reveals the object's color. The eye sees the color of a surface by means of *reflection.* Specifically, a colored surface lit by white light reflects its own color while absorbing all others (Figure 16-4). So a colored surface acts somewhat like a color filter except that it selectively reflects color rather than allowing it to pass through. For example, if an actor wearing a blue costume is lit by unfiltered white light, the costume absorbs most of the red and green wavelengths while reflecting primarily the blue. This is why it is cooler to wear white clothing than black; black absorbs all color, turning the light energy into heat.

color modification The alteration of a surface's color by colored light.

When colored light strikes a differently colored surface, **color modification** takes place. This means that the surface color of the object being lit is altered to some degree. Ideally, lighting designers use color modification to their advantage. For instance, it is common practice to use certain warm tints that are complimentary to skin tones to make an actor's face appear pink and healthy.

Using the example of a blue costume again, picture what happens when it is lit with yellow or amber light. If the fabric is any hue other than primary blue, it will contain some amount of red or green or both. Let us assume that the blue is actually a cool blue, containing more green than red. Yellow light is made up of red and green. Therefore, under yellow light, the cool blue costume will appear greener than it would under white light (Figure 16-5).

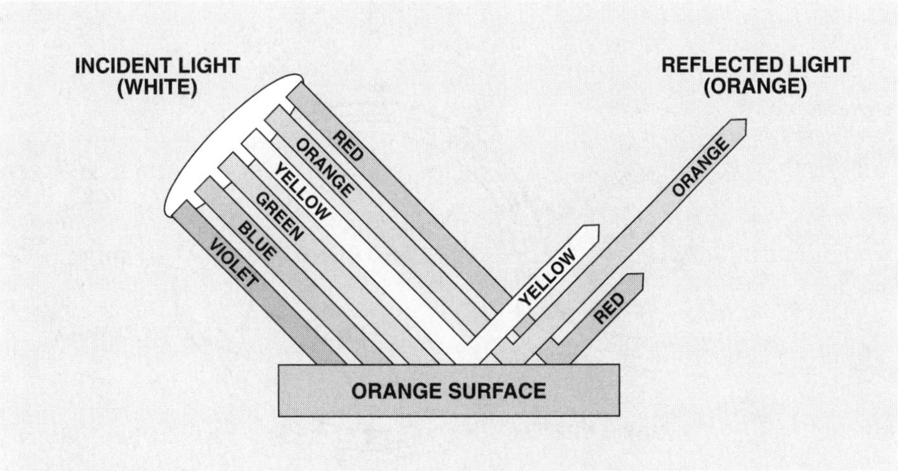

16-4

Selective Color Reflection

The horizontal orange strip represents an orange-colored surface (a costume, for instance). It appears orange under white light because only the red, yellow, and orange hues of the spectrum are reflected. The other hues are absorbed by the surface.

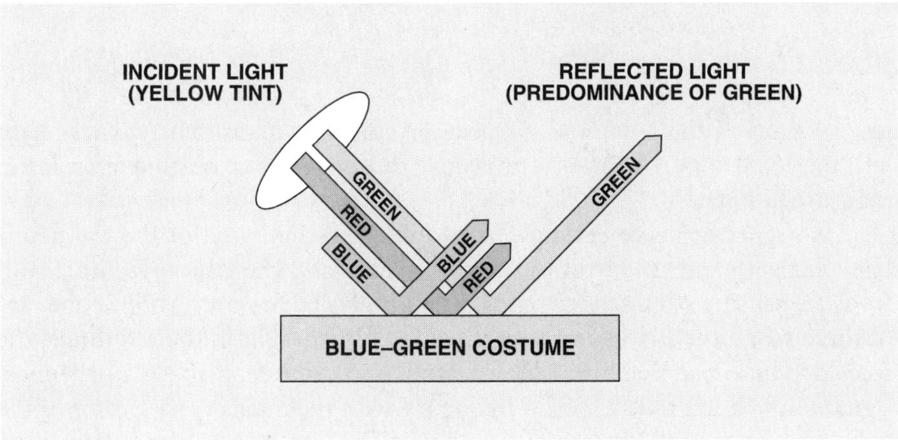

16-5

Color Modification

The horizontal strip represents a blue-green costume. Yellow light (made up of red and green) shining on the costume makes it appear more green than it would under white light.

Color modification of scenery or costumes can present a problem, or it can be used to the designer's benefit. It is simply a matter of knowing how colored light will react on a colored surface. Once again, thinking in terms of the primaries is beneficial.

COLOR PERCEPTION

Knowledge of *how* we see color is perhaps of greatest interest to the lighting designer than to other designers in the theatre. Understanding the physiology of the eye as it relates to color vision gives the designer some indication of how an audience may react to both intensity and color.

Color Physiology

The lens of the eye is capable of focusing on objects between distances of approximately 8 inches and infinity by changing the curvature of its surface—in effect, changing its own focal length. The iris contains the pupil, located

16-6

The Eye

The rods located in the retina are sensitive to brightness. The cones are most sensitive to the primary colors in light (red, green, and blue).

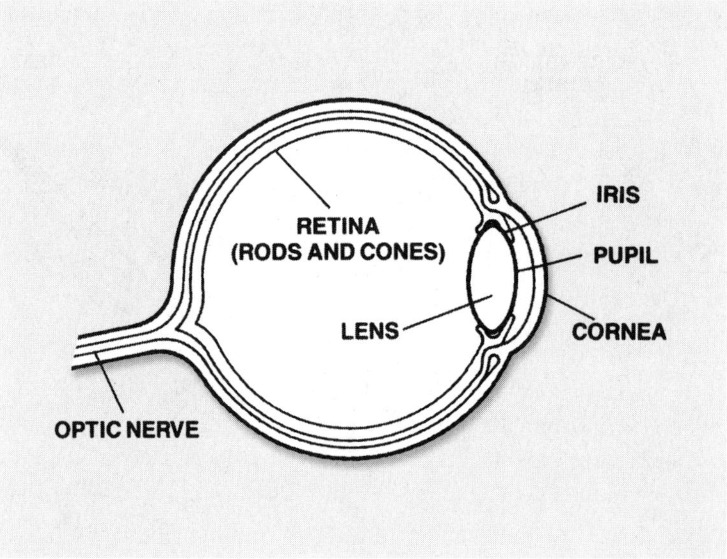

just in front of the lens, which opens or closes to allow more or less light into the eye (Figure 16-6). As a protective device, it can close quite a bit faster than it can open.

Two types of nerve endings located in the retinal area of the eye detect light intensity and color, respectively: the rods and the cones (Figure 16-6). **Rods** are sensitive to intensity or brightness only. The color-sensitive **cones** are of three types: the first is most sensitive to colored light in the red range, the second to blue, and the third to green. Rods and cones send an electrochemical signal to the brain that varies in frequency with the intensity and color of the light. The brain then *interprets* the signal. This interpretation is affected by many factors, including viewer expectation and need.

rods Light receptors located in the retina that are sensitive to intensity.

cones Light receptors located in the retina that are sensitive to color.

Intensity and Color

The eye's sensitivity to high or low levels of illumination affects the color we see. The rods of the retina, which produce most low-intensity or night vision, are most sensitive to wavelengths in the green-blue range. This sensitivity adds a greenish-blue cast to all hues seen under low levels of illumination. Moonlight appears to have a blue tint, even though it is the reflection of the sun, greatly reduced in intensity. For this reason, theatrical tradition calls for indicating nighttime with a blue tint of light.

Color-receptive cones function best under moderate to high levels of illumination. This accounts for our reduced color vision at night. At high levels of illumination, the cones are more sensitive to red and green wavelengths of light. The sun at noon, although a brilliant white, appears to have a yellowish tint (combination of red and green). The stage convention that sunlight is yellow is based on this audience expectation.

Retinal Fatigue

The retina of the eye receives and assimilates light energy. Like a microphone, it is a transducer in that it changes energy from one form to another. When it becomes saturated, the effect is twofold: (1) color impressions become weaker (less saturated), and (2) intensity appears to be lower. Regeneration takes place over a noticeable period. Intensity-sensitive rods take roughly one and a half minutes to return to normal. The color-sensitive cones may take as long as five minutes to regenerate.

Intensity Fatigue Visual fatigue becomes a factor when stage pictures remain static for long stretches of time. For example, if a scene offers little visual contrast for ten minutes, fatigue may cause viewer discomfort. Seeing well becomes difficult. Light levels appear to be low. The lighting designer may be required to slowly boost intensity levels in order to achieve visual parity with the earlier scene.

Color Fatigue The classic example of color fatigue as it occurs in the theatre is the annoying predominance of yellow light in a day scene that has immediately followed a night scene. The night scene, lit with an abundance of blue light, causes the retina's blue receptors to fatigue. The "white" day scene then appears too yellow because the red and green cones are much more responsive than the blue. Color contrast in the blue scene can help to reduce the effects of retinal fatigue. Likewise, shifting the color of the daylight toward blue can cause that scene to look more natural.

Interaction of Colors

How we perceive a color in relationship to an adjacent hue or to its background is known as **color interaction.** A working knowledge of color interaction is a basic element of color selection. Knowing how to use contrasting colors in particular is a valuable tool for the lighting designer. For example, hue opposites such as blue-green and red-orange seem to vibrate when right next to each other, creating a sense of tension. Such colors might be considered when a strong separation between actor and background is desired.

color interaction How the perception of a color is influenced by the presence of another color.

Because of differences in wavelength, certain colors appear to recede while others come forward. When viewed next to each other, cool colors such as blue and green seem to be more distant than warmer colors such as red and yellow. A designer may choose to create an artificial sense of depth by subtly layering colors from warm to cool.

DESIGNING WITH COLOR

In everyday life, we make many subconscious color choices. The interior designer, fashion designer, and theatre designer, however, must force such choices to the conscious level, analyzing how and why specific color determinations are made.

Before we examine color usage in greater detail, several points should be made. First of all, the term *white light* is most often used to describe the color of unfiltered light. In fact, the color makeup of this light can be highly variable. Our eye accepts an astonishing range of colored light as "white," depending on circumstances. For this reason, the term *no color* (abbreviated N/C) is preferable to "white" in discussions of color and filtering (the British use the term *open white* or OW). Understanding how color temperature works (see earlier section) is also key in discussing color.

Color Correction

Developed primarily for the film industry, color-correction filters adjust the color temperature of a light source. Anyone who takes photographs is aware that correct film type (either indoor or daylight) must be used in order to achieve proper color rendition. This is due to the large color disparity between indoor (incandescent) and daylight sources. If a cinematographer needs an incandescent source to be the color of sunlight, a color-correction filter such as Lee No. 201 may be used to correct the color temperature from 3,200°K to 5,700°K. With the popularity of designing with "white" light, theatre designers have found these filters to be quite useful.

Amber Drift

The lighting designer must always keep in mind the effect of dimming on the color of a light source. In most cases the intensity of a theatrical lighting instrument is controlled by means of a dimmer. Dimming lowers or alters the electrical flow sent to the instrument's lamp. As a result, the lamp's filament burns less brightly.

amber drift The color shift of an incandescent lamp as it is dimmed.

As a lamp is dimmed, it radiates a warmer color of light, a phenomenon known as **amber drift.** The more a lamp is dimmed, the greater the shift in color. By the time a dimmer reaches 50 or 60 percent of original intensity, the color of light has changed significantly. This effect is particularly harmful to colors in the blue range. A blue filter in front of an instrument shining at 100-percent intensity emits a very different color from that of the same filter in front of an instrument at 70-percent intensity. Like many other lighting phenomena, this quality can either represent a problem for a designer or be used to advantage.

Mixing on a Surface

Mixing occurs any time two differently colored lights are used on the same area. The resultant color depends on several variables:

- The colors of the light sources
- The direction of the light sources
- The contour of the surface being lit
- The natural color of the surface being lit

If two light sources strike a surface from different angles, and if the surface is three-dimensional and sculpted (an actor's face, for example), many interesting things happen. First of all, one source will cast shadows that are filled or partially filled by the other source's light and color. Second, an overall even color mix will not be achieved, because the sources are coming from different directions. What will be seen instead is a heavy coloration from one source that merges gradually to an even mix with the second color and finally moves into the color of the second source. Such coloration adds three-dimensionality to a figure onstage and can help establish a direction of light (Figure 16-7).

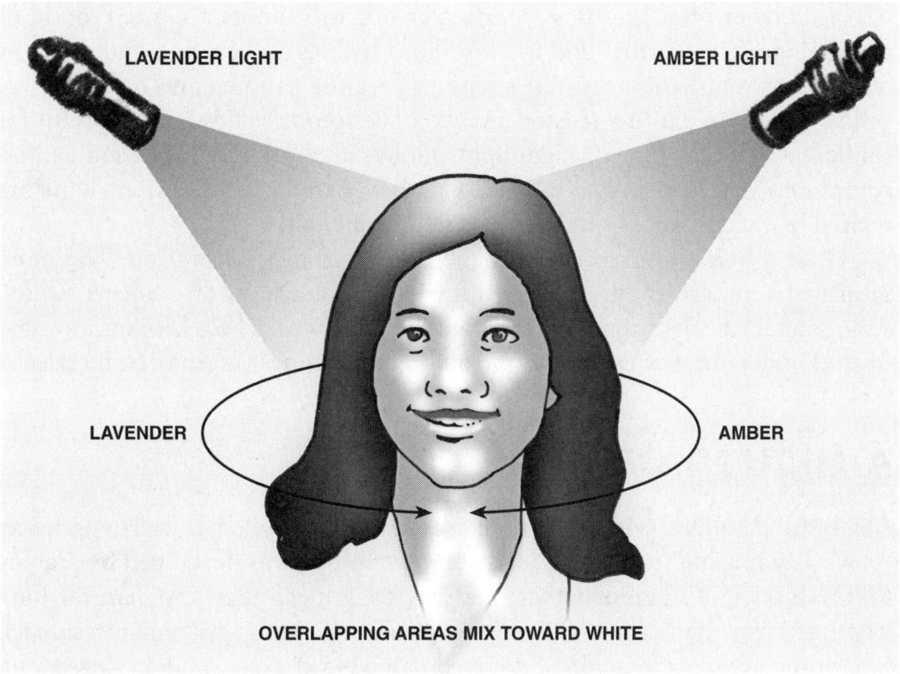

16-7

Color Mixing

Two complementary colors striking a three-dimensional object (such as an actor's face) from different directions will gradually mix toward white.

Mixing in the Air

Another form of color mixing involves placing two or more light sources very close to one another, effectively acting as a single source. The most common example of such mixing in the theatre is the use of striplights or cyc lights on a cyclorama or backdrop. Designers can also employ this technique for area lighting by using spotlights placed very close to one another (double- or triple-hanging). This allows the designer a large range of color options through mixing, while using only two or three lighting instruments. Of course, this type of mixing depends on dimming, and therefore each instrument must be under separate control.

Choosing Color

Most often the lighting designer's challenge centers not on whether to use color, but on which color to choose. The designer's job in this respect is made easier by the fact that most design teams determine a production's color scheme early in the design process. The scenic and costume designers will have made their color choices based on these earlier discussions; the lighting designer should follow suit.

The designer chooses colored light for one of four reasons:

1. The light is motivated by a specific source (the sun, a lamp, the fireplace), and colored light helps convey the motivation.
2. The mood of a scene is reinforced by the light; color heightens the effect.
3. A visual contrast between light sources is desirable; color enhances that contrast.
4. Change or dramatic effect for its own sake is desired.

A designer often chooses a particular hue to support a desired mood or atmosphere. The warmer and brighter hues such as ambers and pinks convey high energy and happiness. Blues tend to be more calming and restful, while yellow and cyan express tension. As we have seen, a yellow tint is useful for sunlight and a blue tint for night light. Violets and lavenders are good neutral colors and can also indicate dusk. Candlelight and incandescent light are relatively warm sources often represented by an amber tint.

Once a hue is chosen, the designer must consider saturation. The more saturated a color is, the greater effect it will have on any surface color it strikes. As a general rule, lighting an actor from the front works best with unsaturated tints. As the light moves around the actor, color saturation may be increased.

A METHOD OF USING COLOR

Successful designing with color depends on taste, knowledge, and experience. As we saw in Chapter 15, one important technique was developed by Stanley McCandless. He suggested that one way to achieve the most natural look when lighting the actor onstage is to position lighting instruments to each side of the actor at an angle of approximately 45 degrees, and 45 degrees up from the horizontal (Figure 16-8). Two complementary colors are then placed in the instruments—such as a light blue in one and a warm amber in the other. The amber acts as a *key* or primary source light, while the blue reads as *fill* or reflected light. The colors mix with each other on the actor's face and body front to a shade of white. This technique has formed a basis for color use in modern lighting design.

Note in this example that two complementary colors are used to mix toward white light. An audience views the warmer of two equally intense light sources as primary (the "key"); the cooler source serves as shadow (the "fill").

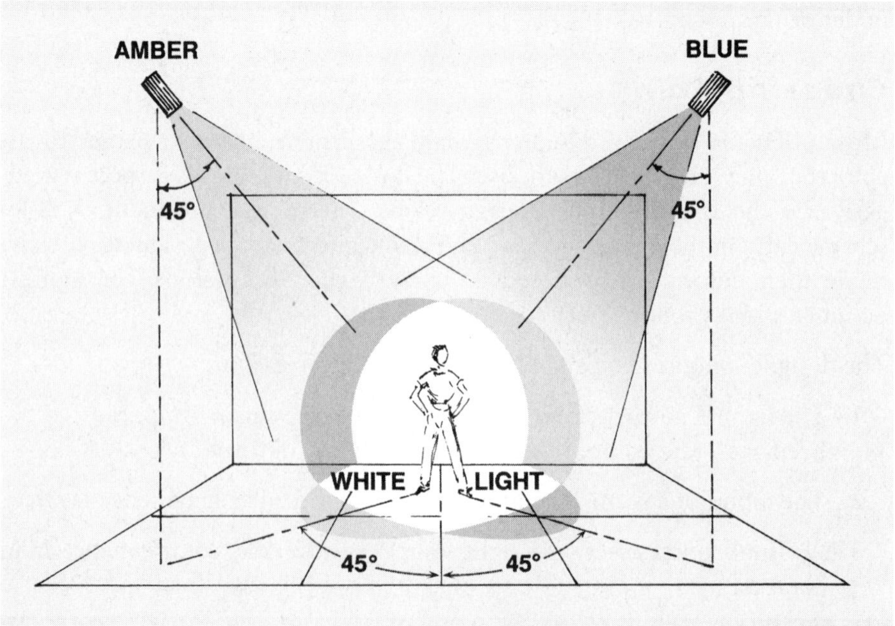

16-8

45-Degree–45-Degree Mixing

A stage-left blue fill source and a stage-right amber key source mix toward white light at the center of the actor's body.

Warm and Cool Colors

Typical Associations Most people consider the color red as bloodlike, typifying violence, anger, and perhaps war. Amber is likely to be perceived as sunlight, warm and comfortable. Blue typifies restraint and coolness, while green may be seen as restful. When selecting stage colors, designers take these and similar audience associations into consideration. However, placing too much emphasis on the psychological effects of color is a mistake. Cultural differences as well as the personal nature of color perception cause color symbolism to be fraught with conflicting theories.

There is one psychological effect, however, that should not be ignored: the relative warmth and coolness of colors. Few people would deny that bright red-orange suggests warmth; most would agree that brittle blue-white gives an impression of coolness. Color Plate 16-6 is a good example of the warmth and coolness of colors being used in a literal manner to convey temperature. Color warmth and coolness used in a more abstract manner can also have a strong effect on the mood of a scene.

Given samples of twenty different tints and shades, rarely will two people list them in exactly the same order from warm to cool. But in general the reds, oranges, and ambers are considered in the warm group, while the cool group consists of blues, violets, and greens. Some mixtures of hues from the opposing groups seem to be on the borderline. The particular effect they give at any moment depends on which color is viewed in relationship to them (color interaction and contrast).

Color Contrast Without contrast, a stage picture appears dull and lifeless. In lighting, contrast is first achieved by varying distribution—the angle and direction of the sources. Contrast is further achieved through differences in intensity and/or color.

The precise feeling conveyed by most tints depends purely on comparison. A pale blue that seems positively icy next to a bastard amber appears quite warm when placed adjacent to a stronger shade of blue-green. Unsaturated pinks and lavenders are frequently used on the stage as neutral tints whose effect can be reversed merely by changing the hues used in association with them.

Unfiltered light may also appear to be warm in one situation and cool in another. Opposite a cool color, such as the palest of blues or greens, uncolored light appears quite warm. In comparison to a pink or pale amber, white light will definitely be on the cool side.

When using pale tints or white light, the effect of dimming on the color of the light becomes particularly significant. A clear light source at full intensity is not only brighter than one reading at lower dimmer levels but also cooler and harsher in color. Intensity as well as color contrast is achieved—without the use of filters.

Using Color Modification

All designers in the theatre have to consider not only the colors of a painted background, costumes, and other materials of a set, but also the colors of the lights that will reveal them.

Fortunately, color modification is not quite as complicated as it may seem. The effect of colored light on a colored surface is the result of mixing. If a red light is thrown on a yellow surface, the yellow is modified into orange tones.

The modification of a color in a costume or on scenery by colored light is a theatrical example of the joining of two color media—pigment and light. Designers in the theatre are constantly aware of how colored light and pigment influence each other. The lighting designer may enhance the mood of a scene by washing the stage with pale blue light. Perhaps this effect alters the brown walls or floor of the set, resulting in a cooler, gray feeling. The reverse could be achieved by using a pale pink tint on the scene.

Colored Light and the Actor

The designer must always consider the general or large-scale effects of lighting the actor or scenery (see Chapter 23). In acting-area front-lighting, for example, it is best to avoid saturated and unnatural shades that will adversely affect the faces and costumes of the actors. Tints of either blue or yellow that contain green can be detrimental to skin tones, while warmer tints are often complimentary.

Preserving the color integrity of costumes can be a difficult task. Often the acting areas are illuminated with tints of pinks and ambers, flattering enough to the human face but deadly to green costume materials. Because the scene may definitely call for such colors in the light, the lighting designer must at all times keep abreast of the costume designer's color palette.

Breaking down the colors into primaries simplifies the task of determining what will happen to a given costume under colored light. For example, assume a yellow dress is lit by a cool blue light from one angle and a straw or cool amber from another. The cool blue light contains a mix of green and blue. The cool amber is made up of red and green. The yellow dress reflects red and green. The conclusion, reached by simply noting the preponderance of green, is that we are probably going to be in trouble. A warmer blue or lavender and a warmer amber light would be a better choice.

If a scene calls for strong color, using it in back-light should be considered. Colored back-light does not affect the costumes or faces of the actors and can tone the floor in an effective manner. A strongly contrasting back-light color acts to separate performers from their background.

Colored Light and the Scenery

In choosing lighting colors, designers need to consider two main types of scenery: three-dimensional scenic forms, which are sculpted and colored by the light, and two-dimensional, flat scenery, which is most often painted.

Three-Dimensional Scenery Sculptural three-dimensional scenery provides the lighting designer great opportunities to create and alter composition. Direction of light is most important, but color plays a significant role. Color creates life, especially in the shadows cast by three-dimensional forms. Color can make forms appear to come forward or recede and can alter the apparent space between objects. Of course, it can also change the surface color of the object.

Two-Dimensional Painted Scenery Unless otherwise informed, designers always assume that the scene designer has painted the settings the way they should appear. Thus, for a lighting designer to attempt to improve on the scene designer's artistry would be impertinent. Enhancing it is fine, but only in strict accordance with the scene designer's wishes. Close collaboration between scene and lighting designers is crucial. The result will usually be that nearby scenery, such as the walls of an interior setting, will receive acting-area tints of light only.

Here is a good rule of thumb: If you are debating whether or not to light two-dimensional scenery—don't. Generally, light on scenery such as flats and drops will cast unwanted shadows and possibly create a situation where the walls and the actors are competing for focus.

On the other hand, color washing the scenery (including the floor) can help to create some harmonious and useful effects. Nearly any scenic or costume color can be made to appear warmer or cooler—more or less inviting— through the use of colored light. A scene designer may, in addition, actually paint the set in several different colors that can be selectively accentuated or deemphasized by colored light.

Color on the Sky

Lighting designers are frequently called upon to use color on a backdrop or cyclorama. A **sky-drop** is a large expanse of cloth that may be lightly colored but is not painted with any kind of sky or landscape. A **cyclorama** ("cyc") is a curved sky-drop.

sky-drop A backdrop that is not painted with anything representational.

cyclorama A curved sky-drop. Generally called a *cyc*.

Careful consideration and experimentation must go into choosing cyc colors. If at all possible, colors under consideration should be examined by projecting them onto the actual background. The color of the drop itself will affect the lighting choice, for sky-drops can vary from numerous shades of white to blue. If the drop is unavailable, experimentation on a similar surface in the lighting lab is recommended.

Is it better to select a single color medium that gives the exact hue desired, or is a blending of several colors preferable? Of course, if there is to be a color change during the scene, then more than one color must be provided. More delicate and precise shadings can also be achieved if several different colors are blended into one. However, mixing the three primaries is a traditional, but often wasteful, method of achieving variable cyc color. Designers rarely use primary red or green by itself.

Tints are seldom useful as sky color. They are too pale and tend to do nothing but muddy the drop. Unlike acting areas, cycs require more saturated lighting colors. Unfortunately, light transmission from primary colors, particularly blue, is extremely low. This presents a problem because near-primary blue is an important sky color. A possible solution is to double the output by using two circuits of blue and mixing it with other secondary hues.

Selecting Color

As we have seen, color choice is a complex issue. Many factors might enter into the equation: mood, time of day, motivational source, dramatic effect, color contrast, scenery, costumes, or actor skin tone. One thing is certain—experimentation is key to good color selection.

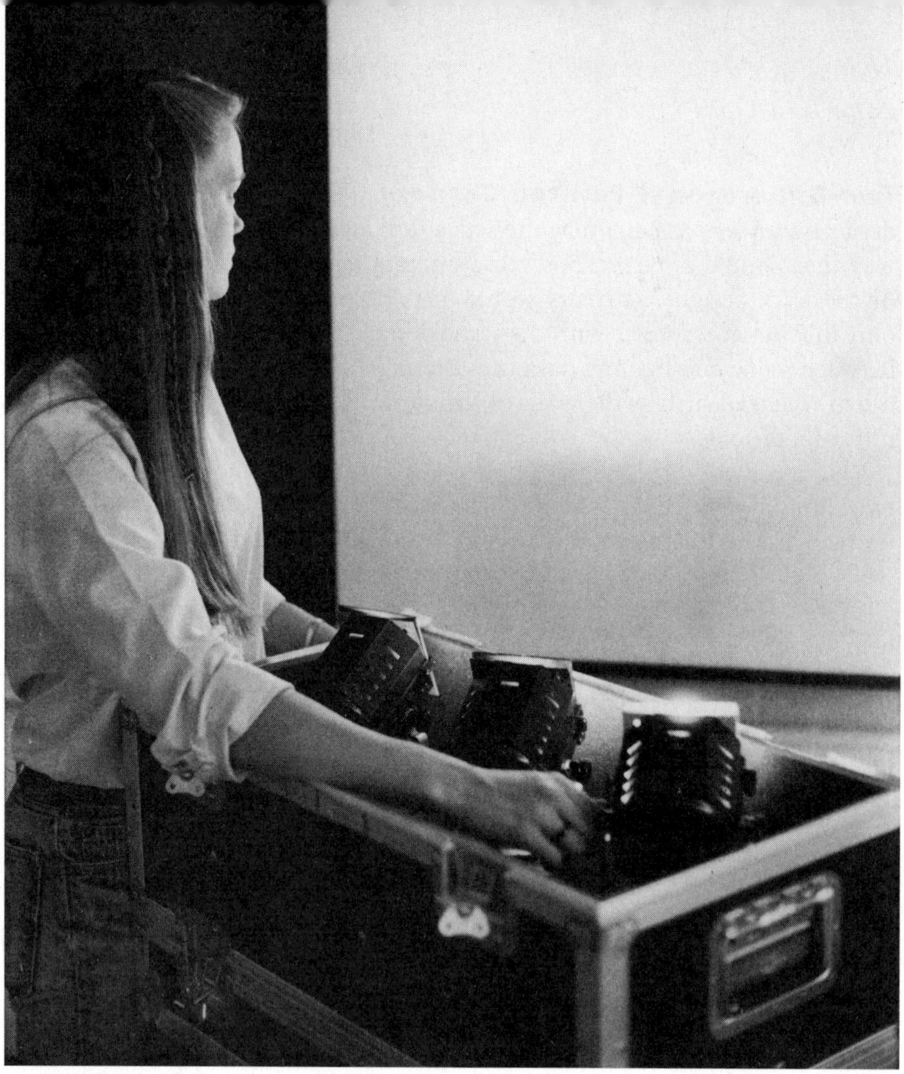

16-9

The Color Mix-Box

Three Fresnels on dimmers allow the designer freedom to mix colors in a space other than the theatre.

Experimenting with color mixing is especially important for the beginning lighting designer. Colors projected by stage-lighting instruments can be examined in the theatre or in a lighting laboratory—in fact, any place that has dimmers.

A particularly useful tool for color experimentation outside the theatre is the *mix-box* (Figure 16-9). Three-inch Fresnels and three common household dimmers are used in the mix-box shown. The box is portable and can be plugged into any household circuit. To use a mix-box, a lighting designer must have available a file box of color media that contains a frame-size cut of every color the designer may need.

COLOR MEDIA

gels A short name for color filters; derived from the word *gelatin.*

It is common in the theatre to refer to color filters as **gels,** being short for *gelatin,* the first material to be manufactured as a color medium. However, except for very special applications, gelatin is no longer used. Today designers can choose from three main types of color media: plastic, colored glass, and dichroic glass.

Plastic Media

Plastic filters made of polyester or polycarbonate were developed for use with the hotter, quartz stage-lighting instruments. These filters are available

PHOTOS COURTESY ROSCO LABORATORIES, INC., GAMPRODUCTS, INC., AND LEE FILTERS

16-10

Color Swatch Books

Color sample books, called swatch books, are available from the three major manufacturers.

by the roll or in 20-by-24-inch sheets. Frame-size cuts can be catalogued and stored for future use. Three companies supply stage filters in the United States: Great American Market (GamColor), Lee (Lee Filters), and Rosco (Roscolux). A huge range of colors is available, as indicated by the "swatch" or sample books shown in Figure 16-10.

Swatch Books GamColor is conveniently arranged in color-order, using numbers in the 100s through 900s. Lee Filters numbering begins with 002 and goes into the 700s. Roscolux is arranged in color-order and begins its numbering at 001 and goes into the 100s. In adding new colors, Roscolux found it best to insert a color number between two others. The inserted colors are numbered in the 300s. For example, Rosco added a new color, pale violet, between existing colors No. 55, lilac, and No. 56, gypsy lavender. The new color's number is 355.

To avoid confusion caused by different manufacturers using the same numbers, the following practices can help designers designate a color clearly:

- Use an "R" or "X" prefix before Roscolux numbers
- Use an "L" prefix before Lee Filter numbers
- Use a "G" prefix before GamColor numbers

It is good practice to replace swatch books every two or three years, keeping abreast of newly added colors. Never trust the names that the various manufacturers assign to their colors. Names are given to individualize the color, making it easier to remember. However, their descriptive accuracy is suspect. One need only compare Gam's "light steel blue" (G720) with Roscolux's color of the same name (R64) to fully understand why such labels are meaningless.

Handling Plastic Media It is easy to cut sheets of color media down to size by using a large paper cutter. The color-frame size of the new enhanced ellipsoidal reflector spotlights is 6¼ by 6¼ inches. The color-frame size for most 6-inch lighting instruments is 7½ by 7½ inches and for an 8-inch instrument it is 10 by 10 inches. Electricians should always check the frame size before cutting.

Colored Glass

Colored glass filters are expensive and break when dropped. Although plastic may be cut to any size or shape desired, glass must be ordered for exactly the purpose required. It comes in few colors, is heavy, and is bulky to store. Glass does offer three advantages, however: It never fades, it resists heat, and it can be molded like a lens in order to spread light.

roundel Round glass color filters made to fit into strip lights.

Roundels Colored glass **roundels** can be obtained with the following features:

- *Plain:* For color filtering only
- *Stippled:* For color and also to diffuse the beam
- *Spread:* For color and also to spread the beam laterally, so that the various colors will blend more readily
- *Stripped:* Very thin glass in narrow strips to color the light from instruments with extremely hot beams

Variegated Glass Filters Rosco has introduced a new line of glass filters that fit into the gobo slot of an Ellipsoidal Reflector Spotlight. There are three types: Colorizers, Prismatics, and ColorWaves. The Colorizers offer rather subtle variegated multicolor effects (Figure 16-11). The Prismatics are made up of broken chips of dichroic glass and produce a stronger texture and shape than the Colorizers do. The ColorWaves produce a more distinctive multicolored pattern than either of the other two. Any one of the three types can be used in conjunction with a gobo pattern. Although they cost about $50 each, they produce a unique and interesting effect.

Dichroic Glass

dichroics Glass color filters that reflect rather than absorb unwanted wavelengths.

Thin pieces of glass treated with a dichroic coating can act as superb color filters. Whereas plastic filters absorb the unwanted color wavelengths, turning their energy into heat, **dichroics** reflect the unwanted color back toward the source. The dichroic reflection process provides colors that exhibit a greater purity, richness, and saturation than do the colors produced by plastic. Currently being used in automated fixtures, several dichroic filters in combination can produce a wide range of colors (Figure 16-12).

Remarkable for its purity, the color from dichroics is unobtainable with standard colored glass or plastic. The major drawback of dichroic filters is their expense. The cost of a 6-inch filter is prohibitive except for theme parks and architectural applications where alternatives are equally expensive.

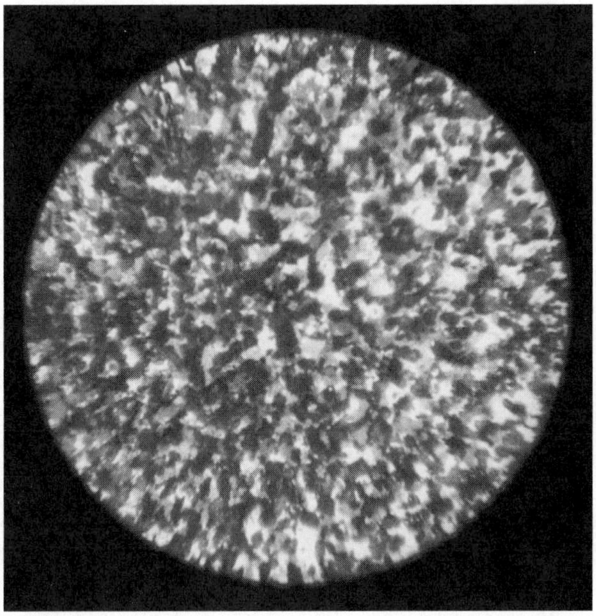
a

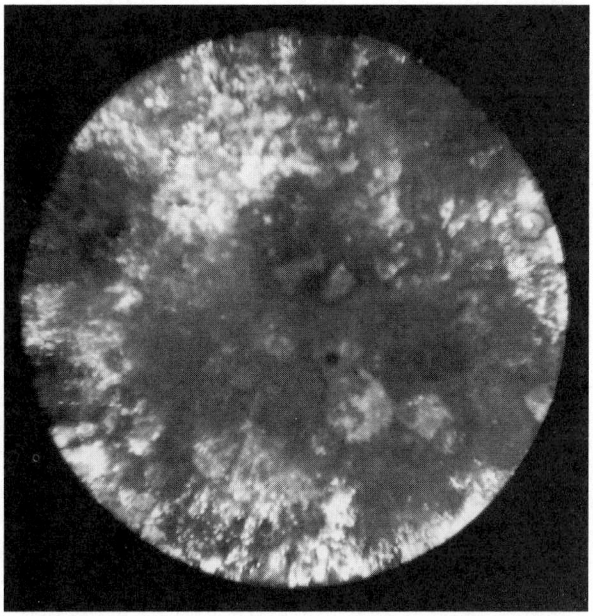
b

a & b PHOTOS COURTESY ROSCO LABORATORIES, INC.

16-11

Rosco Colorizers

Colorizers are glass filters placed in the gobo slot of ellipsoidal reflector spotlights to create multicolored effects. They require a glass gobo holder and may be used in conjunction with metal gobo patterns.

a Stippled series.

b Free Flow series.

PHOTO COURTESY MARTIN PROFESSIONAL

16-12

Dichroic Color Wheel

The color wheel from a Martin automated fixture containing dichroic color filters.

Automated Color Changers

URL http://www.wybron.com

URL http://www.morpheuslights.com

URL http://www.aclighting.com

gelstring A series of plastic color filters taped together and rolled to form the scroll of a color changer.

Remote control of the color projected by a stage-lighting instrument is a valuable design tool. The theatrical use of automated color changers has become widespread because one lighting instrument can serve as several.

Figure 16-13 shows several of the changers in use today. Some systems, such as Wybron's CXI or Morpheus Lights's S Fader, achieve their color by mixing. Others like AC Lighting's Chroma-Q or Wybron's Coloram use a **gelstring:** a series of plastic colors taped together and rolled to form a scroll.

A metal box containing the color, two rollers, and a motor slides into the lighting instrument's color holder. A DMX signal is sent from the lighting control console to the changer, instructing the motor what to do. Some scrolling changers can hold up to thirty-two different colors.

In using color changers, designers must alter the way light cues are normally written. Up to three control channels are necessary to operate each changer independently. Color changes are written into the memory of the lighting control board just like light cues. However, in order to imperceptibly change from one color to another, the instrument must dim out, change color, and dim up again. Dimming out in order to change color is referred to as a dark set (see Chapter 15).

16-13

Remotely Controlled Color Changers

a Wybron Coloram II.
b Wybron Forerunner.
c Morpheus S Fader.
d AC Lighting Chroma-Q.

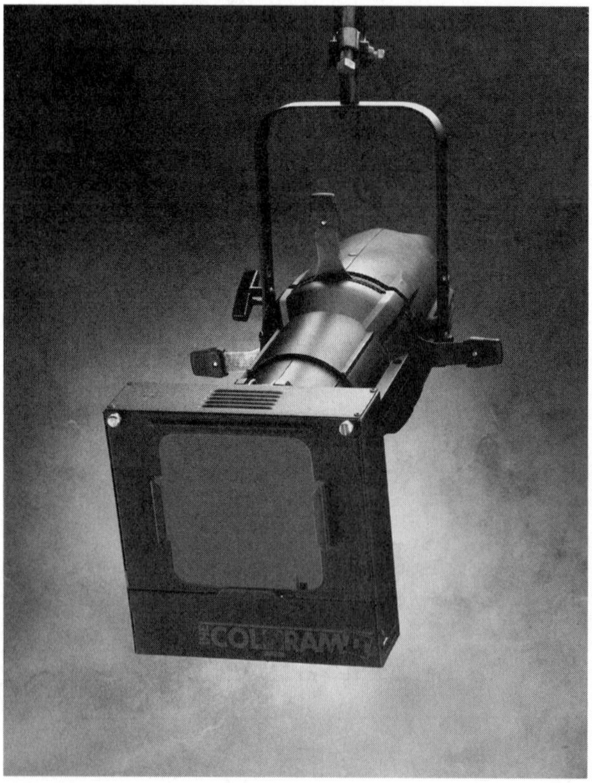

a

b

a & b PHOTOS COURTESY WYBRON, INC.

c

d

c PHOTO COURTESY MORPHEUS LIGHTS

d PHOTO COURTESY AC LIGHTING, INC.

Diffusion Material

Diffusion material, often called **frost**, diffuses light from an instrument and softens or even eliminates a shutter cut or beam edge. Although not a color medium, it is manufactured by the same companies that produce color media. Frosts are listed in the color swatch books and are commercially supplied in sheets.

frost A plastic light-diffusion medium.

A wide range of diffusers are available—from a very light frost, which barely takes the edge off a sharply focused instrument, to a heavy frost, which makes a beam edge all but disappear. In addition, several densities of "silk" are available, which cause the beam of light to spread in two directions only (Figure 16-14).

Most diffusion material has limited application in front-of-house positions, because of the amount of unwanted spill light that is produced. Although any use of frost reduces light intensity to some degree, some heavy frosts cause nearly as much light to come out of the side of the filter as the front. The variety of frost media available provides a lighting designer with many options and is an important tool of the trade.

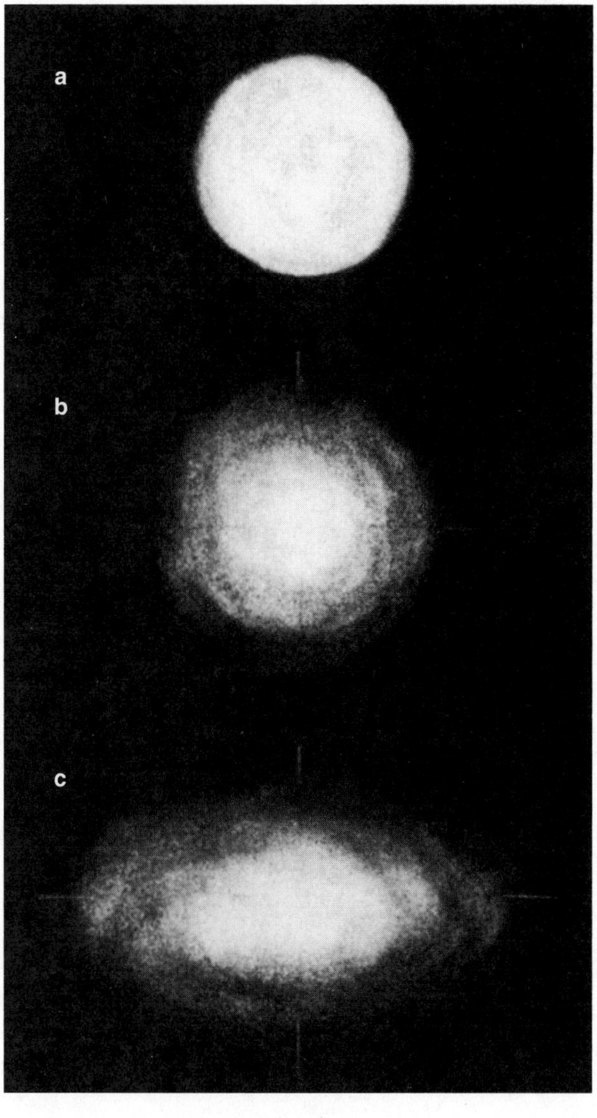

16-14

Diffusion Material

The effects of three different diffusion materials.

a A light frost such as Rosco's "Hamburg Frost"—R114.

b A heavy frost that keeps a hot center similar to Rosco's "Tough Frost"—R103.

c A spread frost such as Rosco's "Tough Silk"—R104.

Tools of the Trade

Obtaining Color Samples

To obtain color swatch books, go to your local theatrical supply house or contact the following manufacturers:

GamColor
The Great American Market
826 North Cole Avenue
Hollywood, CA 90038
http://www.gamonline.com

Rosco
Rosco Laboratories, Inc.
52 Harbor View Avenue
Stamford, CT 06902
http://www.rosco.com

Lee
Lee Filters
2237 North Hollywood Way
Burbank, CA 91505
http://www.LeeFilters.com

With a basic understanding of color, and the media that produce it, the beginning lighting designer can start to learn through experience the more subtle aspects of stage lighting. The next chapter presents yet another important aspect of lighting—intensity control.

17

Intensity Control

Intensity, the third property of light to be explored in this book, refers to the brightness of a light source. In the theatre, subtle fading of light is often more aesthetically appropriate than abrupt switching on or off. To achieve this, designers use dimmers. An audience's attention can be gently shifted by fading the light down on one scene and up on another. Time change can be indicated with the help of dimming. The mood of a scene can be altered by a cross fade from one color to another. Depending on the desired effect, dimming speed can be fast or slow.

A dimmer is the lighting designer's paintbrush. Broad strokes are accomplished by controlling several lighting instruments with one dimmer or by grouping dimmers together. Detail work requires individual control over lighting instruments. Well before installing the equipment, the designer must determine exactly how each instrument will be controlled.

Dimming a lighting instrument is normally achieved by reducing the electrical current sent to the lamp. This causes the lamp's filament to glow less brightly and give off a warmer light. The process of bringing up one group of lights while dimming out another group is called a **cross fade.**

cross fade The process of bringing up one group of lights while dimming out another.

Throughout theatre history, lighting designers have wanted more dimmers than were available. Many felt that lack of control was the most limiting factor in a production's design. Difficult and time-consuming choices had to be made as to which instruments would be controlled independently and which would be ganged together. A mistake in dimmer assignments was always costly.

Finally, in the 1970s, a revolution in lighting control took place. The electronic dimmer was developed and became affordable and practical for use in the theatre. Soon after, computerized control consoles became a reality. The lighting designer was free to create as never before.

THE HISTORY OF DIMMING

The history of dimming offers much perspective on lighting design today. The demand for dimming in the theatre began as soon as productions moved indoors. On seventeenth-century stages, cans suspended by cords were lowered over candles to vary the light. In the eighteenth century, candles in the wings were mounted on vertical boards that could be revolved to turn the light away from the stage or back toward it.

Light fueled by natural gas was introduced in the nineteenth century. *Gas tables* were the first vestiges of modern lighting-control systems. A series of valves located backstage controlled the flow of gas to various jets arranged about the playing space. Rubber tubes connecting gas jets to control valves made the location of the jets flexible. Theatre fires were commonplace.

With the incandescent lamp came crude forms of electrical dimming. All utilized the principle of dimming by means of variable electrical resistance: the dimmer created resistance to the flow of electricity, and the amount of resistance could be varied. The carbonpile and saltwater dimmers were among these early forms, but the most popular and long lasting was the resistance dimmer.

Resistance Dimmers

Most commonly found in the form of a large disk, the resistance plate consisted of lengths of wire used to create electrical resistance. When properly loaded, these dimmers could fade a light source or sources evenly and smoothly. A "road board," such as that shown in Figure 17-1, consisted of several plates mounted next to each other. Typically, several were arranged backstage, close to the power supply. A jungle of stage cable ran from the

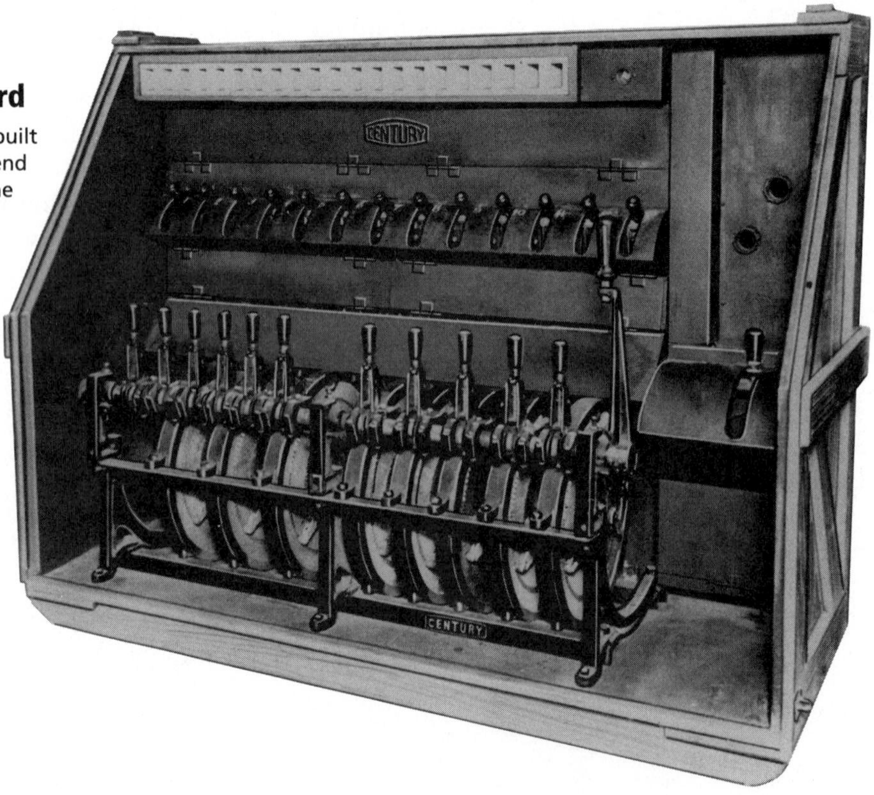

17-1

Resistance Dimmer Board

Example of an early switchboard, built into a box for travel. At the right end of the row of dimmer handles is the long interlock handle, and beyond it is the master switch.

PHOTO COURTESY STRAND LIGHTING

dimmers to lighting instruments located over stage and front-of-house. As many as six or eight electricians operated the switches and dimmer handles on cue from the stage manager. Road boards remained a part of rental house stocks well into the 1970s, when they were replaced by the electronic dimmer.

Resistance dimmers had many disadvantages. In reducing electrical current flow to the lamp, a resistance dimmer converts electrical energy into heat. Not only did this process waste electricity, but it also generated overwhelming amounts of heat. In addition, resistance plates were heavy and bulky. However, the greatest disadvantage from an artistic point of view was their fixed capacity. That is, the plate's electrical capacity was dictated by the length of wire it contained. Accordingly, a lamp or lamps plugged into a resistance dimmer had to total the same wattage as the dimmer; otherwise, the dimmer could not dim the light(s) completely out. To load a dimmer to its capacity, extra lights were plugged in. Often placed out in the alley behind the theatre, these "ghost loads" faded up and down in unison with the lights onstage.

Autotransformer Dimmers

Many of the problems with resistance dimming were solved by the autotransformer dimmer, put into use in the 1940s. This device consisted of copper wire wound around a large doughnut-like core made of iron. The autotransformer was wound in such a way that the magnetic fields created when electricity flowed through the wiring worked against each other, restricting the flow of current. This phenomenon is called back-electromotive force (back-EMF) or back-voltage. When the wire is arranged properly, a variable current is created along the coil. A sliding contact called the brush makes an electrical connection with the bare wires of the coil. As the brush moves along the coil, it conducts a variable flow of electricity to the lamp.

The autotransformer is not load sensitive. Any wattage lamp within the capacity of the dimmer can be dimmed smoothly and effectively between full out and full up. Little heat is created, and autotransformers are not quite as bulky as resistance plates.

The most common housing configuration for the autotransformer was the *package board* (Figure 17-2). The "package" usually consisted of six dimmers, circuit breakers, and a plugging panel. The board shown in Figure 17-2a includes a large-capacity dimmer that can be used to "master" the others. The model shown in Figure 17-2b had dimmer handles that could interlock with each other, allowing one person to run all six dimmers. Although heavy,

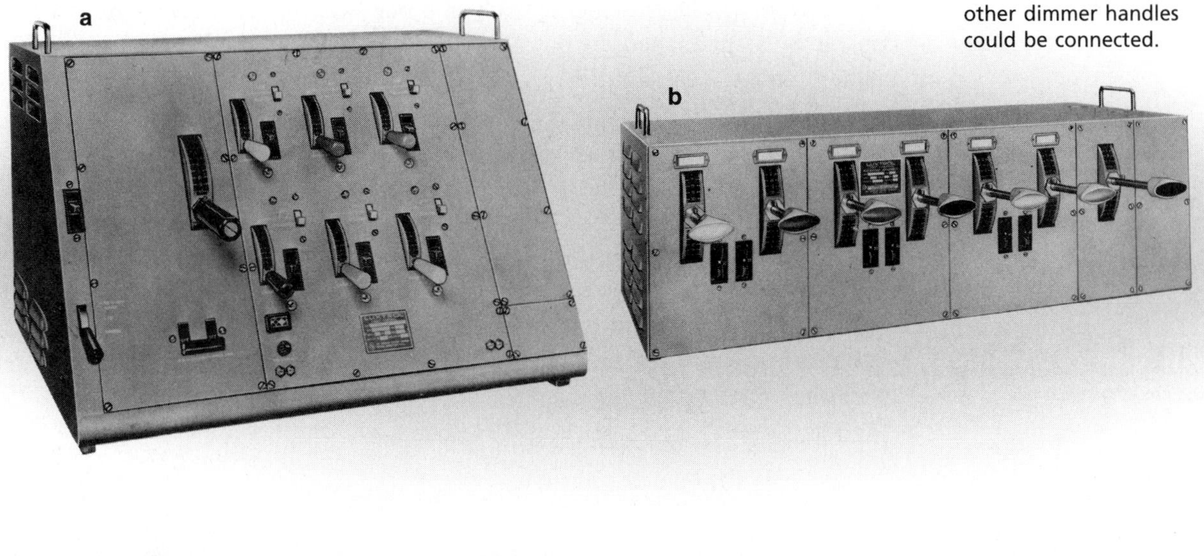

a & b PHOTOS COURTESY SUPERIOR ELECTRIC

17-2

Autotransformer Package Boards

a A package containing six 1,300-watt autotransformer dimmers and a master of 6,000-watt capacity. By means of the white switches, one or more of the small dimmers could be put under control of the large one, thus providing proportional dimming of up to 6,000 watts.

b A package with six 2,500-watt dimmers and an interlock handle to which several or all of the other dimmer handles could be connected.

17-3

An Early Two-Scene Preset Console

The transparent disks with the white handles are the controllers for thirty dimmers, one apiece for each preset. Below them is a row of on/off switches for each circuit. At the right end of the white plate is the crossfade handle.

PHOTO COURTESY GEORGE IZENOUR

these boards were transportable and were a popular means of control for many years. In the early 1980s, the final package board rolled (or lumbered) its way off Superior Electric's assembly line—the electronic dimmer had finally and rightfully taken over the entire market of intensity control.

Preset Systems

preset console A control system with at least two rheostats or controllers per dimmer located on the control console. One set of controllers can be preset for the next lighting look, while the other set represents what is "live" onstage.

The first truly electronic dimming system was put into operation by George Izenour in 1947 at Yale University. The two-scene **preset console** shown in Figure 17-3 was built by Izenour in 1955. It served as a model for preset systems throughout the next two decades.

Remote Control With the electronic dimmer came the possibility of remote control. Control consoles were developed that could be located front-of-house, away from the dimmers. This represented a huge breakthrough for lighting designers; finally the operator could see the action onstage. Low-voltage cables sending an analog signal connected the control console to dimmers located backstage or in the basement. Each dimmer was represented at the control console by a small rheostat or controller. When the controller was set at 50-percent intensity, the dimmer responded in kind.

Preset Consoles In addition to control of each dimmer from the console, preset systems provided one or more additional sets of controllers. The Izenour console shown in Figure 17-3 controlled thirty dimmers. As a two-scene preset board, it has two rows of thirty controllers each. While the controllers in the active row are communicating with the dimmers, the operator can preset the inactive controllers for the next lighting look. The looks are numbered, and each one is called a **preset.** A single lever, the cross-fader, is then used to fade from one preset to the next.

preset The name given to a lighting look—especially when the preset system is being used.

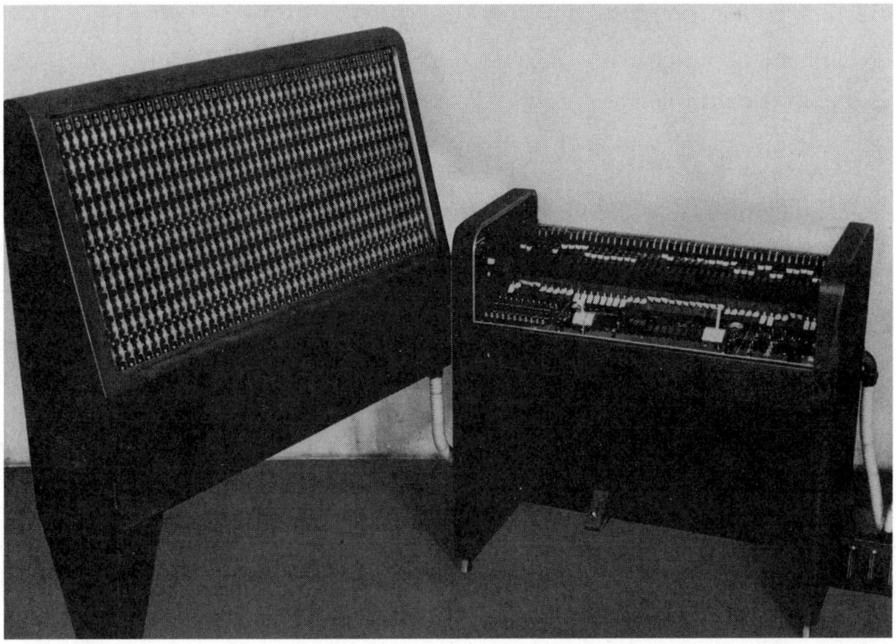

PHOTO COURTESY GEORGE IZENOUR

17-4

An Early Ten-Scene Preset Console

To the left is the preset panel with ten rows of forty-five controllers, one for each dimmer. The operator's console at the right contains another forty-five controllers across the top with preset selector buttons and a cross-fader on the lower tier.

A limitation of the two-scene preset was the time it took an operator to arrange the controllers for the next preset. To overcome this difficulty, manufacturers developed multiple-scene preset systems. Figure 17-4 shows a ten-scene preset system capable of controlling forty-five dimmers. Such a system often required several operators and took up a good deal of space. Today, these larger multiple-scene preset systems are things of the past, having been replaced by computerized control.

ELEMENTS OF ELECTRONIC CONTROL

With older methods of control, a simple shift of emphasis in stage lighting required the designer to direct several operators who likely could not see the results of their actions. If the desired effect was achieved once in five times, the designer was considered fortunate.

Electronic control changed all that. The principal advantages of today's electronic control are these:

1. More sophisticated lighting control, due to computerization
    a. Only one operator, located front-of-house
    b. Ease of control over large numbers of channels
    c. Instantaneous access to a large number of presets
    d. Multiple lighting functions, due to computer software
    e. Related automated functions such as color changers and automated fixtures
2. Dimmer-per-circuit

Electronic Dimming

An electronic dimmer comprises several components, but the basic element is a silicon controlled rectifier.

SCR dimmer A modern electronic dimmer. The silicon controlled rectifier (SCR) is the electronic component that controls the current.

Silicon Controlled Rectifiers Usually referred to as the **SCR dimmer,** its name should be interpreted to mean "a silicon rectifier under control." A silicon controlled rectifier is the electronic component that actually does the dimming in the vast majority of theatrical dimmers. The SCR controls the flow of electricity to the lamp in a unique manner: it quickly switches on and off—120 times per second! The electrical current actually reaches the filament of the lamp in bursts, occurring so rapidly that they cause no adverse visible reaction. The longer the SCR remains on before switching off, the greater the electrical flow to the lamp and the brighter it burns. Because this switching action does not result in reduced voltage to the lamp, SCR dimmers, unlike autotransformers, cannot be set to drive low-voltage devices.

Two SCRs are required for each dimmer, but the actual SCR is only the diameter of a nickel and ½-inch thick. These little "buttons" are mounted back-to-back in the middle of a doughnut-shaped coil called the *choke.* The choke functions to reduce dimmer noise as well as smooth out the "spike" of electricity generated by the SCRs. Early SCR dimmers were the size of a shoe box but are now less than half that size (Figure 17-5). The other major

17-5

SCR Dimmer Modules

a Strand SLD dimmer modules. **b** ETC Sensor dimmer module.

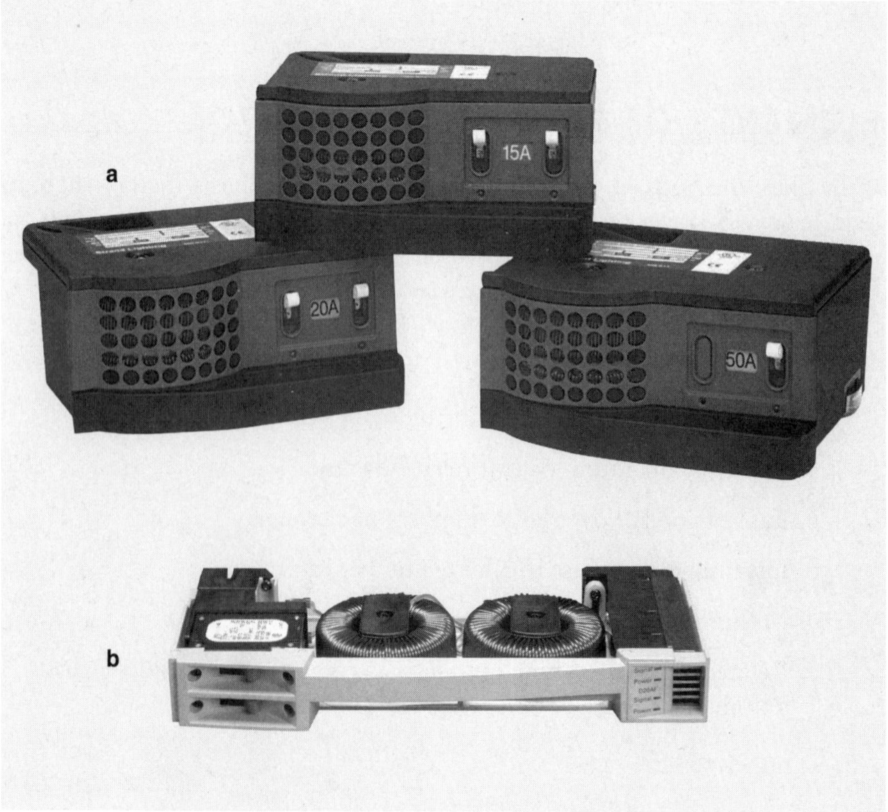

a PHOTO COURTESY STRAND LIGHTING

b PHOTO COURTESY ELECTRONIC THEATRE CONTROLS

components are a magnetic circuit breaker provided to protect the SCR electrically, a finlike "heat sink" that dissipates the heat generated by the rapid switching of the SCR, and a solid-state relay.

Normally, two dimmers are enclosed in modules that fit into racks of various sizes. The twelve-dimmer rack shown in Figure 17-6 is a standard portable size. The dimmer module can be slid out of its rack for servicing; electrical connection is made by virtue of plugs located at the rear. One must always remember to turn off the circuit breaker(s) in the front panel of the module before removing or replacing the dimmer. Miniaturization of components has allowed for the creation of high-density dimmer racks; a full-size rack contains ninety-six dimmers in a relatively small space (Figure 17-7).

PHOTO COURTESY ELECTRONIC THEATRE CONTROLS

17-6

Twelve-Dimmer Rack

The ETC Sensor portable dimmer rack.

a

17-7

High-Density Touring Dimmer Racks

a ETC SP 36 Sensor touring rack.

b Avolites ART 2000 touring rack.

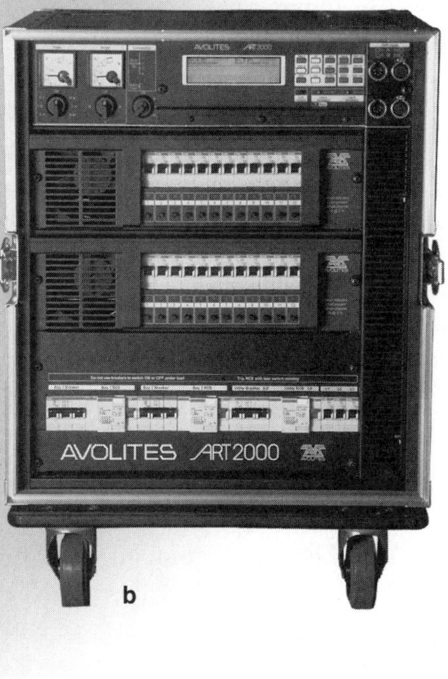

b

a PHOTO COURTESY ELECTRONIC THEATRE CONTROLS
b PHOTO COURTESY AVOLITES

a

b

17-8

Distributed Dimming

a Rosco/Entertainment Technology IPS dimmer strip (six 1,200-watt dimmers).

b Rosco/Entertainment Technology IPS dimmer box (six 1,200-watt dimmers).

a & b PHOTOS COURTESY ROSCO LABORATORIES, INC.

distributed dimming Placing groupings of dimmers directly on electric pipes near the instruments rather than in a remote location.

URL http://www.rosco.com

Distributed Dimming A new type of electronic dimmer called the IPS dimmer has recently been introduced to the theatrical market. IPS (intelligent power system) dimming is an improved form of **distributed dimming.** The concept of distributed dimming is not a new one to the theatre. It involves placing dimmers near the lighting equipment, thereby avoiding long cable and high amperage wire runs. Problems with earlier attempts at such a dimming system included large and bulky equipment, dimmer noise, and unreliability. The IPS dimming system, developed by Rosco/Entertainment Technology, uses a microprocessor and two insulated gate bipolar transistors (IGBT) per dimmer to control the current flow to the lamp. The dimmers are available in strips that resemble electrical wire-ways or in drop-down boxes (Figure 17-8). This new distributed dimming system is quiet, efficient, and reliable.

The Interconnect System

patch panel A flexible system allowing the connection of any stage circuit to any dimmer; used in non-dimmer-per-circuit systems.

In the days when SCR dimmers were large and expensive, a flexible system was necessary to allow the connection of any stage circuit to any dimmer. The major component of this system is called the **patch panel.**

Figure 17-9 illustrates the flow of power through a patch panel interconnect system, from the service entrance of a theatre to a lighting instrument. In all

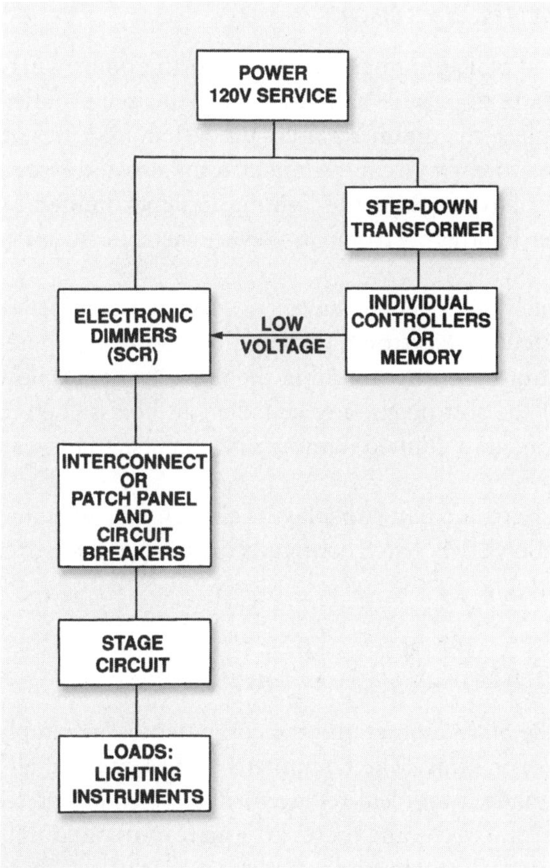

17-9

Typical Theatrical Power Flow

Power flows from service entrance through control and to a lighting instrument. A dimmer-per-circuit system would eliminate the interconnect or patch panel.

17-10

Telephone-Type Interconnect or Patch Panel

Single plugs representing each circuit in the theatre are plugged into one of several receptacles assigned to each dimmer. Circuit breakers for each individual circuit are located on the face of the panel. Repatching during a show is often accomplished by throwing the appropriate circuit breakers.

but the smallest theatres, having many more stage circuits than dimmers was normal. The advantage of the patch panel was that it allowed the connection of any lighting instrument to any dimmer. In addition, it provided for plugging multiple instruments into a single dimmer. This flexibility was important to the lighting designer.

Patch panels are still in use today in smaller and older theatres that have not yet converted to dimmer-per-circuit (see next section). Several types of patch panels exist, but the simplest and most common is the plug-patch. All of the stage circuits terminate in numbered plugs at the end of retractable cables, much like an old-fashioned telephone switchboard (Figure 17-10). The dimmer connections, also numbered, end in jacks mounted in the panel. Any plug can be inserted into any jack. Accordingly, any instrument can be controlled by any dimmer. Several jacks are assigned to each dimmer, providing a simple way to gang more than one instrument onto a single dimmer. The only precaution is to make sure that the total instrument wattage does not exceed that of the dimmer.

The Dimmer-per-Circuit System

dimmer-per-circuit A dimming system that permanently assigns an individual dimmer to each lighting circuit in the house.

By the early 1980s, the cost of SCR dimmers had fallen to the point where it became reasonable for a theatre to provide a dimmer for each circuit (outlet) in the house. As its name implies, the **dimmer-per-circuit** system allocates an individual 2,400-watt dimmer to each circuit. Dimmer numbers and circuit numbers are one in the same. No longer is the lighting designer limited by lack of individual control over lighting instruments—every instrument in use can have its own dimmer.

soft patch An electronic patching system present in most lighting consoles that allows the connection of any control channel to any dimmer/circuit.

channel The dimmer controller in a memory system.

With dimmers permanently assigned to circuits, control flexibility is achieved by means of **soft patch,** an electronic patching feature of computer control. The familiar rheostat or controller found in the preset system is now called a **channel.** By virtue of the soft patch, any channel can be assigned to any dimmer/circuit. In addition, an unlimited number of dimmers/circuits can be assigned to a single channel.

Figure 17-11 shows the electronic patch display of an ETC Expression 3 lighting control console. Selecting a new patch configuration is simply a matter of several keystrokes.

Early Computerized Memory Systems

Concurrent development of the SCR dimmer and the computer led inevitably to the computerized control of lighting. The computer's ability to store and rapidly retrieve information made it an ideal replacement for manual preset systems. With computerized memory, cue and preset information are randomly recalled with push-button speed. These systems made it easy to keep track

17-11

Electronic Patch Screen

The channel-to-dimmer arrangement of the ETC Expression 3 electronic patch display, called "soft patching."

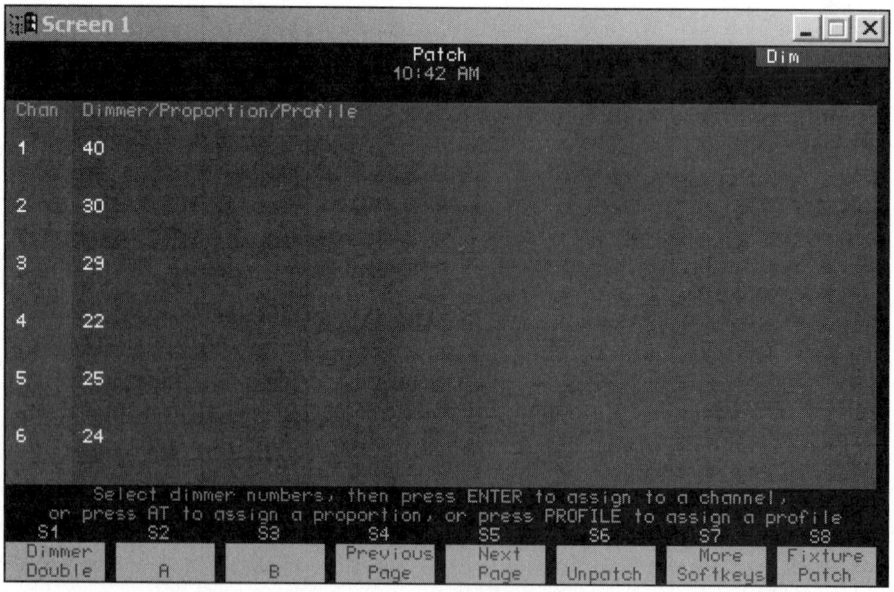

COURTESY ELECTRONIC THEATRE CONTROLS

of the numerous control channels in a dimmer-per-circuit system. Current-day control of automated fixtures would be impossible without computer assistance.

Compared with those being manufactured today, early memory systems were large and bulky. They often had a single set of manual controllers as well as a keyboard; operators could enter preset information into memory by setting levels on the controllers or by typing levels in by means of the keyboard. A split fader, a timed fader, and group and/or submasters were often standard equipment. The primary memory storage was either disc or core—only later was disc or magnetic tape **library storage** added as a standard feature. The control signal was a low-voltage analog signal sent from the console to the dimmers. The dimmers were designed to respond to varying electrical voltages. However, voltage ranges were not standard from manufacturer to manufacturer, so one manufacturer's control console could not run another manufacturer's dimmers.

library storage A permanent means of recording lighting control information (dimmer channels and levels), usually on disc.

Q-File, developed jointly by Thorn Electrical Industries of Great Britain and Kliegl Brothers in the United States, was one of the first systems to eliminate a full set of controllers and add library storage (Figure 17-12). Autocue, manufactured by Skirpan Lighting Control Corporation, introduced the video monitor to the world of control systems. More complex than necessary, Autocue was the forerunner of modern state-of-the-art equipment.

Kliegl took Q-File off the market and replaced it with its popular Performance system. Colortran introduced Channel Track, a bulky system that was soon replaced by the Prestige series of consoles. Strand Lighting developed Multi-Q and Micro-Q, predecessors of their popular Light Palette. Finally, a new company, Electronic Theatre Controls (ETC), introduced a line of user-friendly control systems that would soon become industry favorites.

URL http://www.colortran.com

URL http://www.strandlighting.com

URL http://www.etcconnect.com

17-12

An Early Memory Control Console

The Q-File console, shown here, was the first successful preset memory system. Originally developed for television, it was designed and manufactured by Thorn Electrical Industries, Ltd.

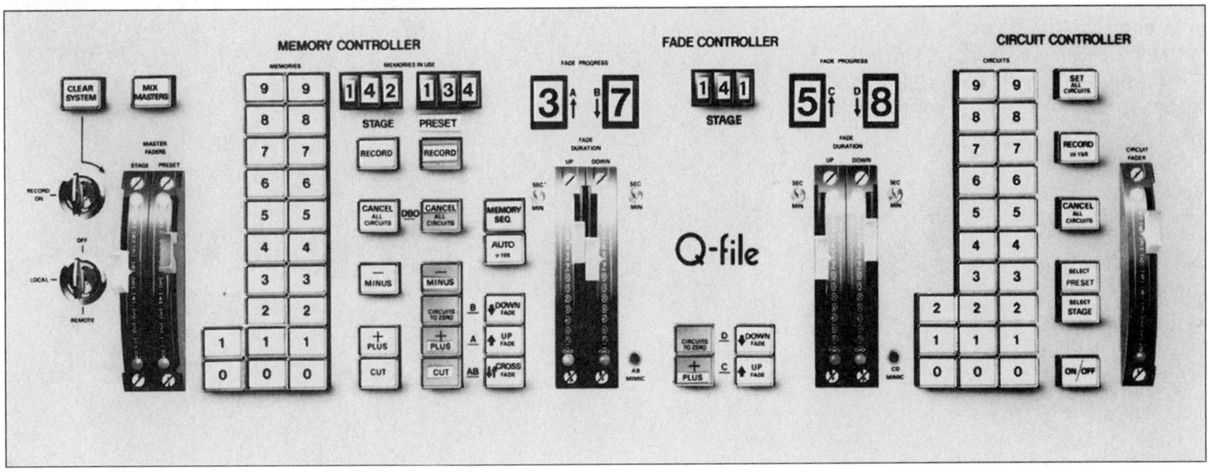

PHOTO COURTESY KLIEGL BROTHERS

TYPES OF ELECTRONIC CONTROL

For all practical purposes, only two types of electronic control exist: the manual system and the memory system. Memory systems are computer based; manual systems are not. Manual systems always consist of at least one controller per dimmer as well as a master controller. They may be quite sophisticated and flexible, offering several presets, masters, submasters, and group masters.

Manual Systems

The simplest and least expensive of the manual electronic control systems provides one controller per dimmer and might very well be contained in a single housing (Figure 17-13). Although these systems are inexpensive and portable, they are also inflexible and can be poorly built. When purchasing such a control system, one should ask the following questions:

- Are the dimmers themselves easily accessible for repair?
- Have the dimmers been properly protected from power surges?
- Is proper dimmer ventilation provided?
- Are chokes installed to prevent excessive lamp filament vibration?
- Is a master controller provided?
- Do the controllers work smoothly and seem sturdy?
- Can the system be expanded?

The only advantage these systems provide over the older autotransformer package boards are compactness, lightness of weight, and electronic mastering.

17-13

Portable Control

In this six-dimmer controller with master and circuit breakers, each dimmer has a capacity of 2,400 watts. Circuit plug-ins are located on the rear panel. In front is a remote-control unit.

PHOTO COURTESY ELECTRONICS DIVERSIFIED, INC.

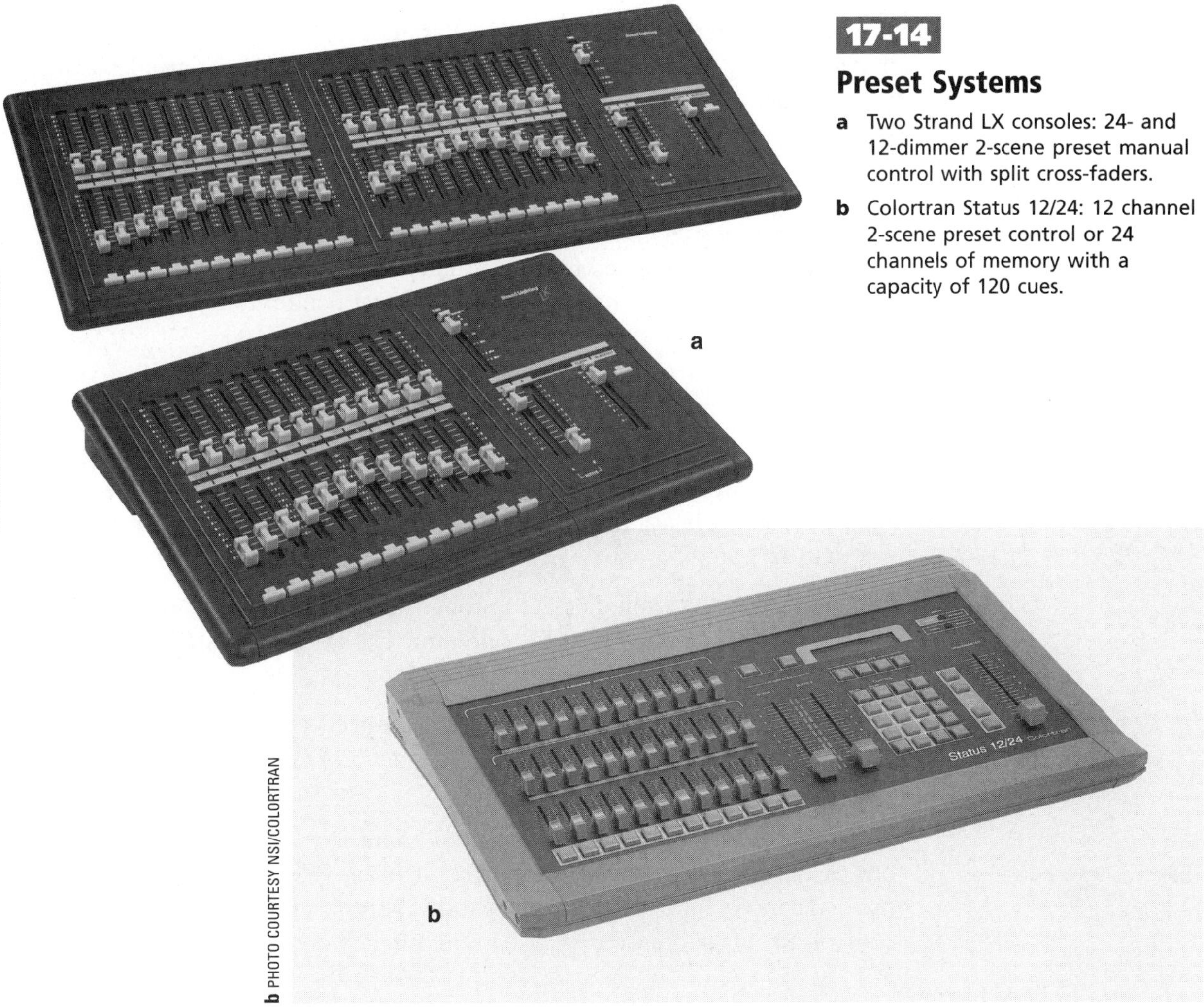

a PHOTO COURTESY STRAND LIGHTING

b PHOTO COURTESY NSI/COLORTRAN

17-14

Preset Systems

a Two Strand LX consoles: 24- and 12-dimmer 2-scene preset manual control with split cross-faders.

b Colortran Status 12/24: 12 channel 2-scene preset control or 24 channels of memory with a capacity of 120 cues.

Preset Systems As mention earlier, preset systems allow an operator to cross-fade between sets of controllers. Such systems are inexpensive and may be perfectly adequate in certain applications. Figure 17-14 shows two of the systems currently on the market. They control between 500 and 1,000 dimmers and are equipped with timed, split cross-faders; a grand master; and bump buttons.

The very small facility would benefit from a system such as the Scenemaster Six from Dove Systems (Figure 17-15). The model shown provides six dimming channels at 1,000 watts each, a two-scene preset, a timed cross-fader, and a grand master control. What makes it unique is that it plugs into two ordinary household electrical outlets. Care must be taken to plug into two different circuits and not to exceed the capacity of those circuits.

URL http://www.dovesystems.com

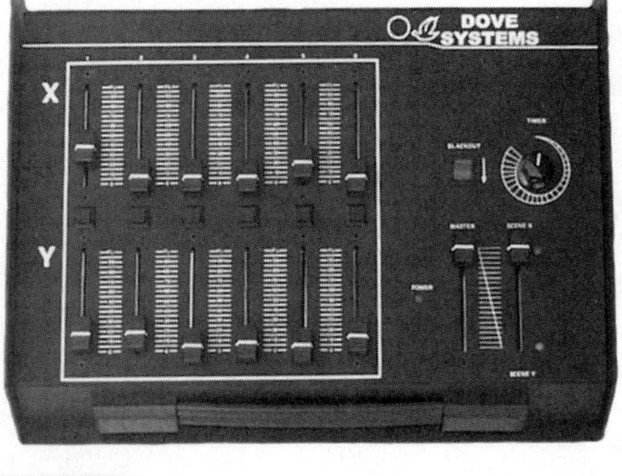

PHOTO COURTESY DOVE SYSTEMS

17-15

Small-Capacity Dimming

This portable 2-scene, 6-channel control system is unique in its ability to be powered by two normal household circuits.

Control Features Manual control systems can offer numerous features that add flexibility and increase the potential for complex lighting effects. Most common are the following:

- *Electronic mastering.* A single controller acts as a proportional master over all active controllers. This is useful for fading all dimmers to black.
- *Submastering.* A single controller acts as a proportional master over all controllers assigned to it. Any number of controllers can be assigned to a **submaster.** Submasters offer additional flexibility to a standard preset system.
- *Split cross-fading.* In a preset system, the cross-fader is a single controller that lets the operator fade from one preset to another. A **split cross-fader** consists of two faders, one for each preset, allowing the fade time of one preset to be different from that of the other. The most common application is to fade up an incoming preset more quickly than an outgoing one.
- *Timed fades.* A timing device automatically executes a cross fade at a predetermined rate set by the operator. The fade is initiated by the press of a "go" button.
- *Effects.* A limited number of prewritten effects (such as a channel chase) are available.

submaster The name given to a single lighting master controller to which any number of individual control channels has been assigned.

split cross-fader Two faders: one assigned to those lights going down in intensity and the other assigned to those lights going up in intensity. This tool allows for variation in up and down fading times.

Group Mastering The group master board is a control console that grew out of the specialized needs of concert lighting (Figure 17-16). It divides a manual console into various groups and subgroups, each with its own master control. As in a submastering system, lighting channels are assigned to group

URL http://www.avolites.com

17-16

Group Mastering Consoles

a The ETC Insight 3 has a preset-style operation of 512 channels. There are 10 pages of 108 submasters, 6 pages of 5 moving light attribute encoders, and up to 500 groups.

b The Avolites Diamond 4 is a control board designed for rapid access to a large number of channels. It offers 200 pages of 128 direct-access programming palettes with 28 cue playback masters.

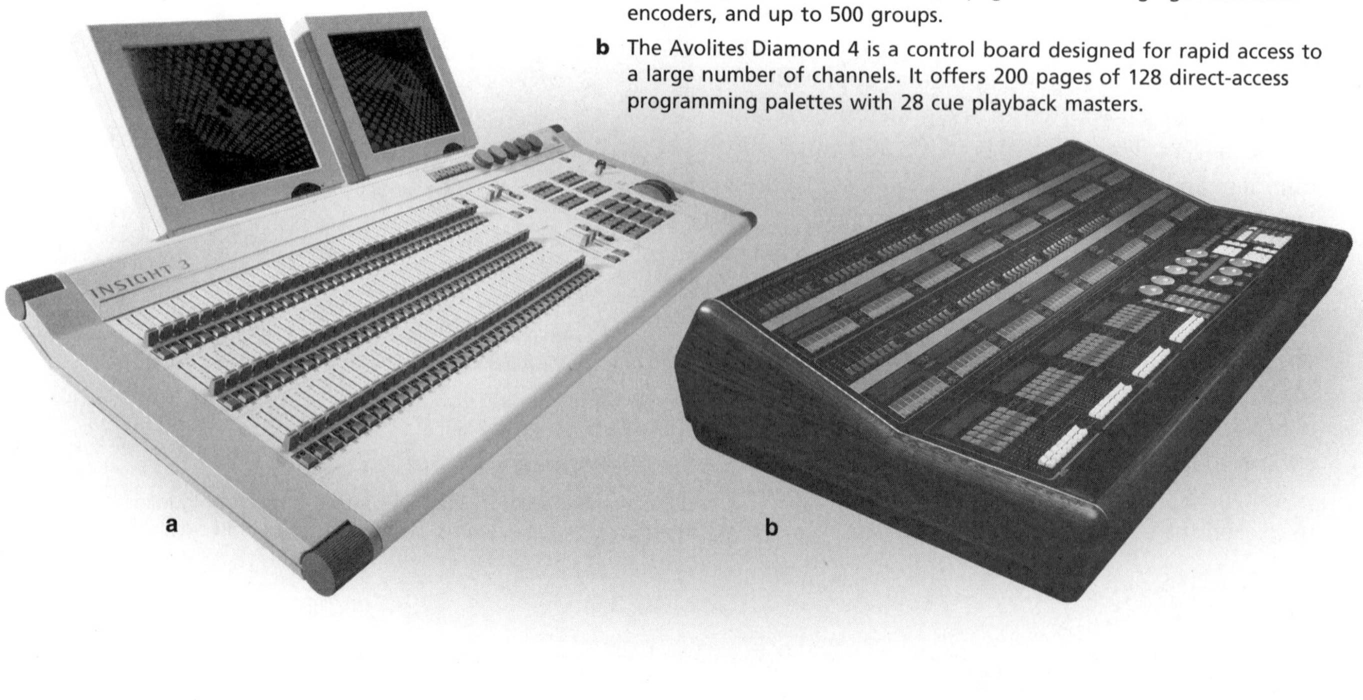

a PHOTO COURTESY ELECTRONIC THEATRE CONTROLS
b PHOTO COURTESY AVOLITES

masters. The **groups** may be used independently of each other like presets, or they may be combined to create a multitude of effects. In addition, most of these systems provide memory storage of presets.

groups Similar to lighting submasters in that any number of individual channels can be assigned to one group master. Submasters can also be assigned to groups.

This system is a favorite of concert designers, who often act as their own operators. It offers the flexibility required in many concert situations, as when the lead performer decides to add a new number or change an existing one. It also lends itself to creativity; each performance can be lit a bit differently. However, such systems are too complex to operate if many changes are needed in rapid succession. It is not ideal for theatre, because there are too many things for an operator to keep track of during a swiftly moving play.

Combination Systems The most desirable manual system combines the virtues of presetting with those of group mastering and submastering. A large variety of such control systems exists today, each with its own idiosyncrasies. Having evolved from earlier preset systems, most combination systems offer presetting with many extra features. The systems shown in Figure 17-17 offer submasters and electronic patching along with the normal features of a preset system. In addition, the ETC Expression 3 can control 500 groups and has six pages of five moving-light attribute encoders. Combination systems are economical and portable, and they offer a good alternative to small, computer memory control.

17-17

Combination Systems

a The Strand Mantrix MX is a 2-scene preset manual console with memory. The MX is available in 12 or 24 channels, has 4 pages of submasters/cues, and offers 24 programmable effects.

b The ETC Expression 3 has a preset-style operation that can control up to 1,200 channels. It has 10 pages of 24 submasters, 6 pages of 5 moving light attribute encoders, and up to 500 groups.

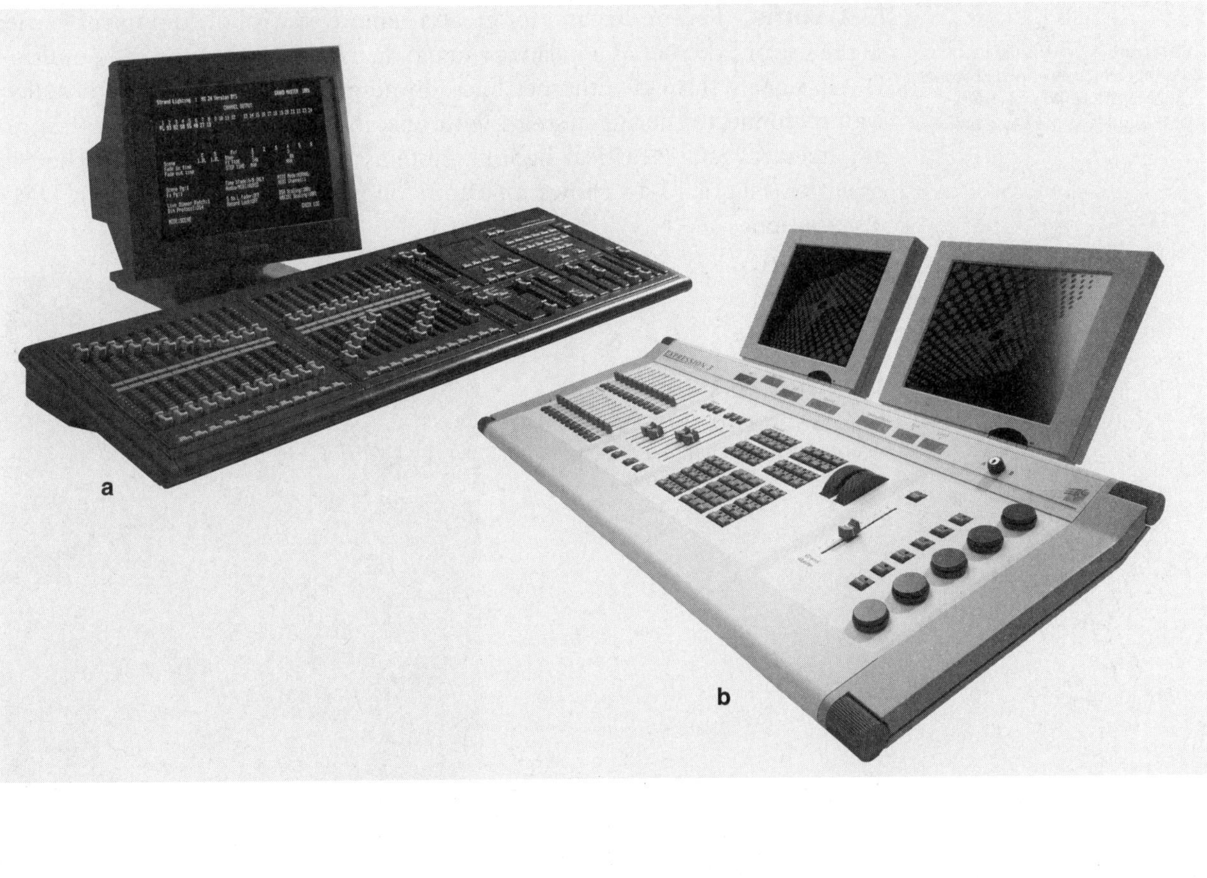

a PHOTO COURTESY STRAND LIGHTING
b PHOTO COURTESY ELECTRONIC THEATRE CONTROLS

State-of-the-art Memory Systems

Although the design of early memory systems varied a great deal from manufacturer to manufacturer, current consoles tend to be similar to one another. Trial and error has determined which features and functions designers and operators prefer in a control system. Modern systems are less complex to operate and take less time to learn. Designer interface with the system is easier and continues to improve. Size and cost have generally been reduced. However, the most significant advantage of modern control systems is their reliability. In the not-so-distant past, system failure was commonplace. The computer would "go down," often losing all of its memory. Countless hours were spent reprogramming shows. Those designers who failed to keep an accurate "hard copy" were never seen again. Thankfully, today's computers are more robust.

Interfacing from Controller to Dimmer

As mentioned earlier, the first control signals from remotely located control consoles to their dimmers were analog electrical signals. Their voltages varied roughly from 15 volts to 0, depending on the system, and no two systems were compatible. This irritated users until, finally, manufacturers developed systems based on a new digital protocol called DMX.

URL http://www.usitt.org

DMX Thankfully, members of USITT (the United States Institute for Theatre Technology) were concerned enough to develop a standard digital language for communication between control consoles and dimmers. It was called DMX-512 (the "512" referring to the amount of information transmitted). This standard digital signal allows almost any manufacturer's equipment to "speak" to that of any other manufacturer.

DMX-512 A standard communication protocol for lighting-control systems.

Networks Recent demand for greater remote control of equipment has led to the use of **Ethernet** as a means of signal distribution. One can send multiple DMX signals through Ethernet lines. In addition, Ethernet is a convenient way to connect differing systems with one another. For instance, a theatre's architectural and theatrical lighting systems can be connected together via Ethernet. Figure 17-18 shows a Strand "Shownet" network node for DMX distribution.

Ethernet A universally used digital communications protocol capable of carrying numerous DMX signals at the same time.

17-18

Ethernet Networks

Strand's SN103 network node provides remote DMX and handheld remote control using Ethernet lines.

PHOTO COURTESY STRAND LIGHTING

Types of Systems

Four categories of theatrical memory control systems currently exist:

1. Nondedicated control systems
2. Small-capacity dedicated systems
3. Large-capacity dedicated systems
4. Automated-fixture control systems

Nondedicated Control Systems The term *nondedicated* refers to a control system that uses specialized software with a standard computer to perform the tasks required of a lighting-control system. Perhaps the most popular nondedicated system on today's market is Rosco's Horizon/IPS Lighting Control Network. Horizon 2000 Basic software runs with Windows on any Pentium PC. Figure 17-19a shows the control portion of the Horizon system. The operator can select on-screen displays of soft patches (or channel levels or

a

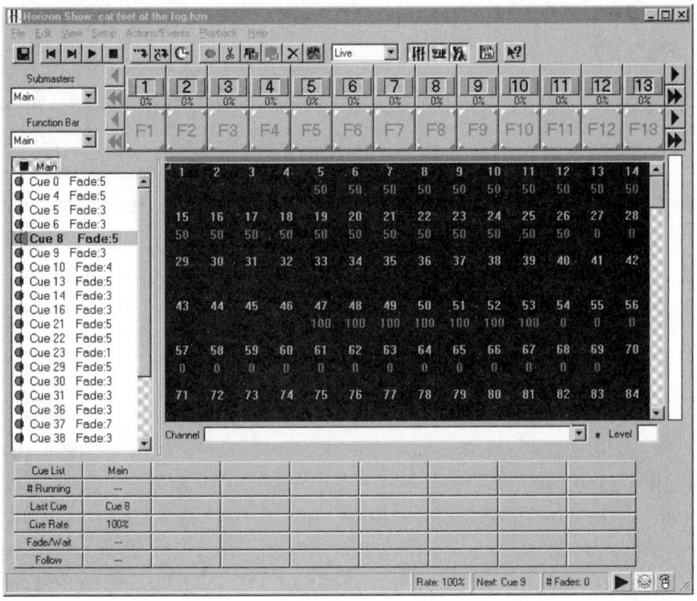

b

a & b PHOTOS COURTESY ROSCO LABORATORIES, INC.

17-19

Nondedicated Memory Control

The Horizon control system from Rosco/Entertainment Technology.

a The system, showing monitor, keyboard, submaster wing panel, and 512 channel DMX interface. The Horizon system uses any Pentium-class PC to create a command-line, tracking-style console.

b A monitor screen showing the cue list, function buttons, and an active cue.

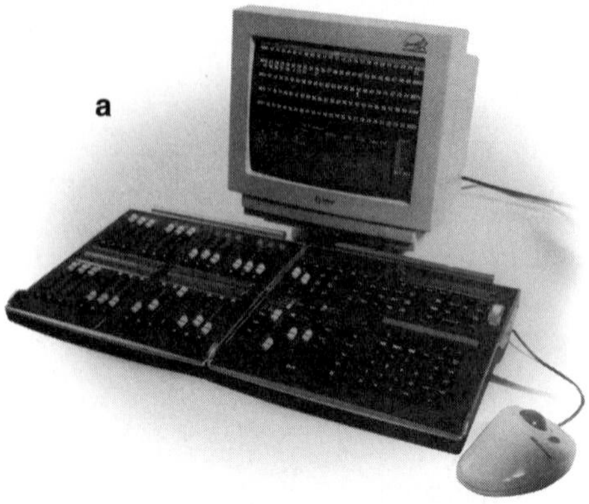

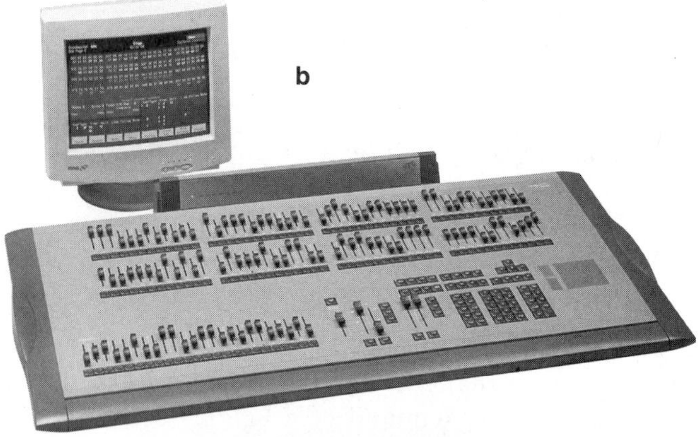

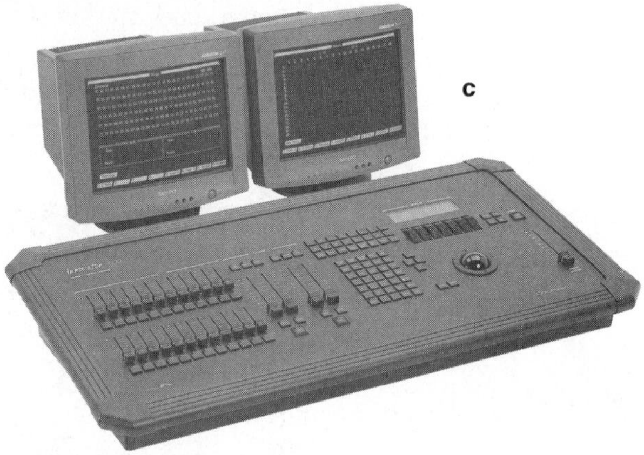

a PHOTO COURTESY STRAND LIGHTING
b PHOTO COURTESY ELECTRONIC THEATRE CONTROLS
c PHOTO COURTESY NSI/COLORTRAN

17-20

Small-Capacity Memory Control Systems

a The Strand 300 Series console is available in seven formats with capacities from 125 to 600 channels. All consoles have a minimum of 24 submasters.

b The ETC Express series of five consoles offers from 24 to 250 channels. Features include preset-style operation with 10 pages of 24 submasters, 600 cues, and 500 groups. The model shown here is the Express 48/96.

c The Colortran Innovator 600 console has 600 channels and 24 submasters with 8 pages each.

cue sheets) used during playback. Figure 17-19b is a close-up of the system's cue sheet. The main body of the screen is dedicated to a sequential list of cues, fade times, and channel levels for the active cue. Above and below are listed operational functions from which the operator can choose.

The advantages of the nondedicated system are its low cost and the fact that the computer can be put to uses other than stage lighting. Bookkeeping, box office, and a host of other software programs can all be run on this single computer. The disadvantages of the system include lack of functions and relatively difficult operation.

Small-Capacity Dedicated Systems Figure 17-20 shows three typical small-capacity dedicated systems. Such systems offer all the standard operational features as well as some specialized ones depending on the manufacturer. They are categorized as small systems because of their low cost and limited number of channels, dimmers, and cues. A good example is Express, the fine yet inexpensive system from ETC. Express consoles operate a maximum of 96, 192, or 250 channels depending on the specific console; they control 1,024 dimmers and can have 600 cues.

Small systems normally have one video monitor that displays various information according to operational needs. A quality system includes a reliable battery backup, an easy-to-use entry keyboard, a video monitor for the operator, and an optional remote monitor for the designer. Important functions include the ability to insert additional cues into an existing cue list, soft patching, the ability to link one cue to the next, split time fades, and a help display for the operator.

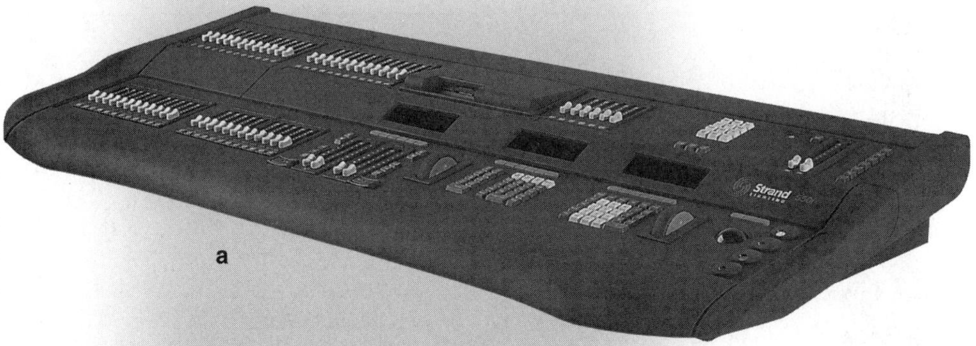

a

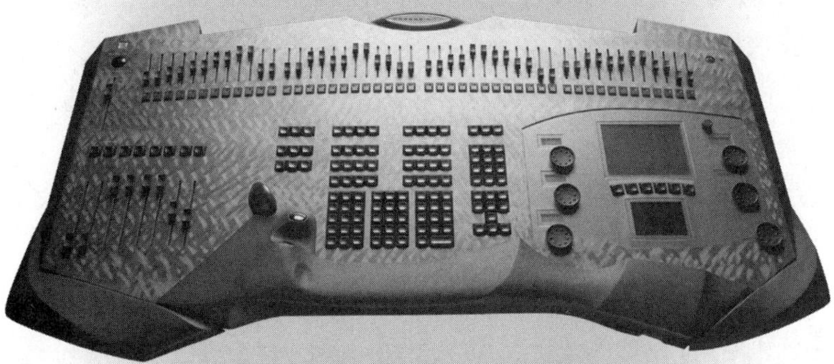

b

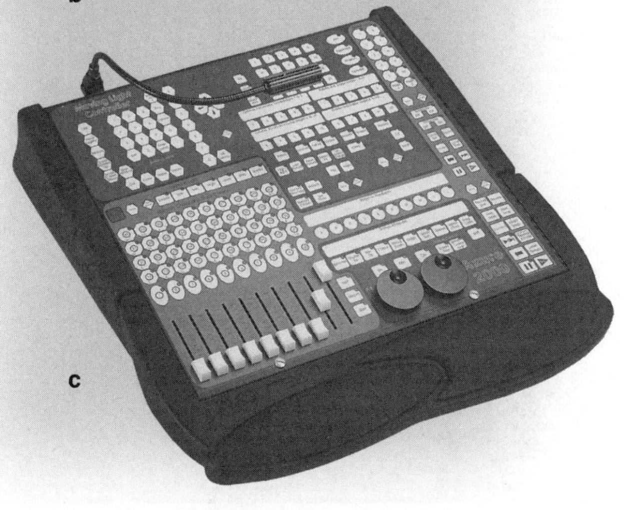

c

a PHOTO COURTESY STRAND LIGHTING

b PHOTO COURTESY ELECTRONIC THEATRE CONTROLS

c PHOTO COURTESY AVOLITES

17-21

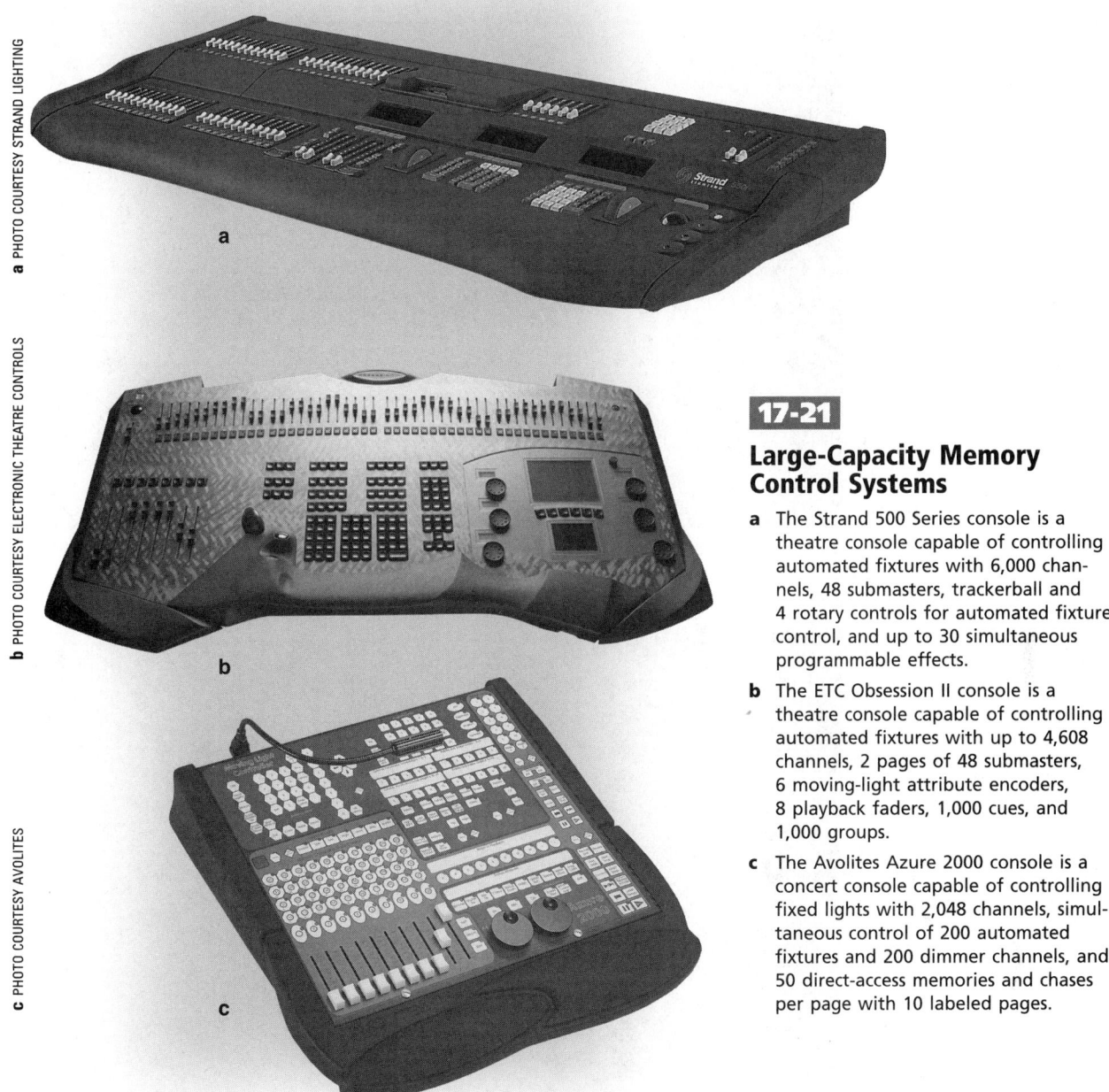

Large-Capacity Memory Control Systems

a The Strand 500 Series console is a theatre console capable of controlling automated fixtures with 6,000 channels, 48 submasters, trackerball and 4 rotary controls for automated fixture control, and up to 30 simultaneous programmable effects.

b The ETC Obsession II console is a theatre console capable of controlling automated fixtures with up to 4,608 channels, 2 pages of 48 submasters, 6 moving-light attribute encoders, 8 playback faders, 1,000 cues, and 1,000 groups.

c The Avolites Azure 2000 console is a concert console capable of controlling fixed lights with 2,048 channels, simultaneous control of 200 automated fixtures and 200 dimmer channels, and 50 direct-access memories and chases per page with 10 labeled pages.

Large-Capacity Dedicated Systems As lighting control has been called on to perform more and more functions, demand for larger-capacity systems has increased. In the 1980s the need to control more than 100 channels was unusual. Today, with the control demands of color scrollers and automated fixtures, more than 1,000 channels may be necessary. Several large-capacity systems are shown in Figure 17-21, including ETC's Obsession II console (b). Depending on the model, this system has a capacity of 750 to 4,608 control channels and 1,536 to 8,192 dimmers with 1,000 cues and 1,000 groups. Compare this with its smaller cousin, the ETC Express, discussed previously and shown in Figure 17-20b.

Nearly all of the larger systems have two monitors with selectable on-screen displays. During normal operation, the cue sheet is displayed on the primary screen, with channel levels or other information as needed on the second screen.

17-22

Monitor Screen Displays

Screen displays from an ETC Expression 3 console.

a Cue sheet display.

b Channel display.

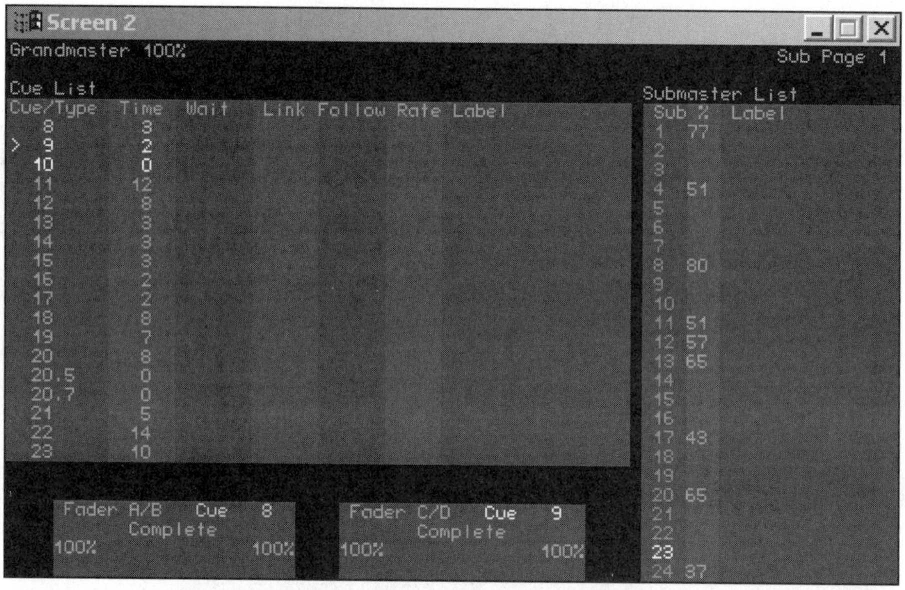

a

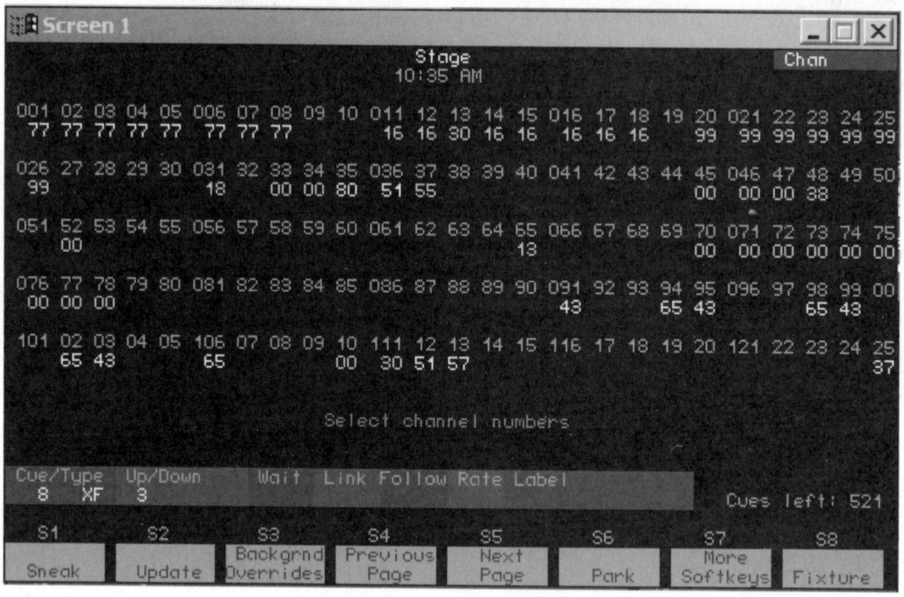

b

a & b COURTESY ELECTRONIC THEATRE CONTROLS

The displays shown in Figure 17-22 are from an ETC Expression 3 control system. The cue sheet display includes cue number, time, and other playback information such as cue parts, delays, and effects. The channel display lists each control channel along with its assigned level in the designated cue (in this case, the live cue onstage).

One of the major functional advantages of the larger and more sophisticated control systems is programmable effects. Several systems offer "effect packages" that allow a limited number of effects such as a forward chase or a random flicker (useful for fire effects), but only a few allow for operator-designed effects. To be most useful, such a program must be easy to both write and operate and be flexible enough to accommodate any kind of effect desired.

Automated-Fixture Control Systems Automated fixtures, sometimes erroneously referred to as moving lights, come in a wide range of types and sizes (as did early computerized control systems). Each manufacturer has created its own version, with nearly all of them offering unique and valuable features. Until recently, control over any of these fixtures was the exclusive domain of its manufacturer. For instance, when a Vari*Lite system was rented for a concert tour, both the control console and the operator were part of the package. When Intellabeams were rented, a control unit designed and manufactured by High End Systems had to be included. It soon became clear that such proprietary activity was not acceptable to users; manufacturers responded with compatible and user-friendly systems.

Automated fixtures have several remotely controlled features called parameters or attributes, such as a color wheel that provides variable color selection. Each of a light's attributes requires one or more channels of control. The Cyberlight, High End Systems's powerful moving mirror fixture, needs twenty control channels to operate all attributes. A bit of simple math tells us that a great number of channels are necessary to control modern automated fixtures. Although a control system's capacity is an important factor, ease of operation is equally significant. Early control systems were extremely complex and cumbersome to operate, in some cases requiring manufacturer-trained operators.

URL http://www.highend.com

A new generation of computerized control systems has finally arrived (Figure 17-23). Vari*Lite has developed the new Virtuoso DX console, which can control 2,000 multiple parameter luminaries with between 2,000 and 10,000 cues per fixture. Flying Pig Systems, manufacturers of the impressive

URL http://www.vari-lite.com

17-23

Automated Fixture Control

a The High End Whole Hog II console has 2,048 channels expandable to 3,584 with unlimited multipart cues and 8 playback masters.

b The Vari*Lite Virtuoso console has 2,000 multiple parameter channels, 30 submasters, and 3 encoders dedicated to intensity, pan, and tilt with 6 soft encoders for other functions.

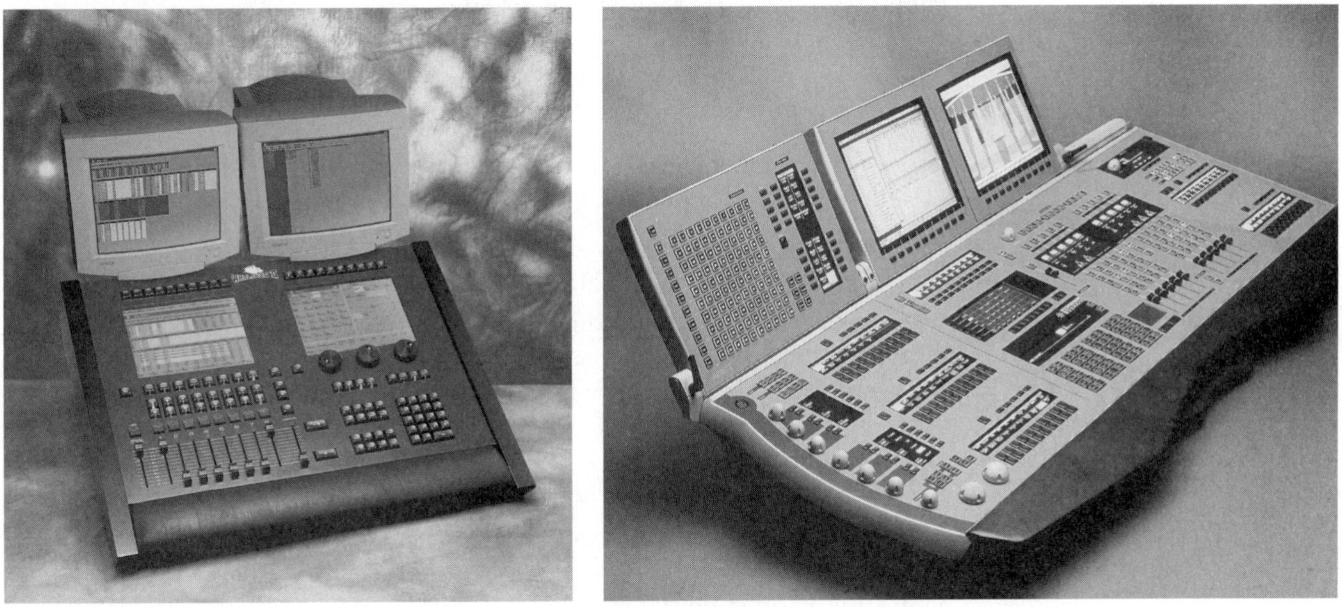

a **b**

a PHOTO COURTESY HIGH END SYSTEMS
b PHOTO COURTESY VARI*LITE

Whole Hog control system, recently merged with High End Systems and introduced the Whole Hog II. This ideal system controls everything: moving lights, color scrollers, and conventional fixed lighting instruments. Features of the Whole Hog II may include 6,000 control channels, twenty master controllers, two built-in touch screens, and easy access to all attributes.

DESIGNING WITH ELECTRONIC CONTROL

In 1975, when the designer Tharon Musser insisted on a Light Palette control system for her Broadway production of *A Chorus Line,* it became obvious that even New York was going to accept memory lighting control. There is no doubt that lighting designers have achieved a higher level of artistry as a result of computerized control. Cue writing is simplified, the potential for complex and sophisticated cues is greatly increased, and changes are made quickly and accurately—every time.

Limited Dimmer Control

Well before a production goes into the theatre, a designer must consider *control.* If not working in a dimmer-per-circuit situation, the designer faces the task of assigning instruments to dimmers. Color control is normally a high priority. Seldom is it desirable to have two instruments of differing colors on the same dimmer. Area control is the next priority: which stage areas should be controlled individually and which should be "ganged" or grouped together? The latter is a critical decision, for the designer must work with the chosen control flexibility throughout the production. Before a choice is made, the designer should view rehearsals and discuss control-related questions with the director.

In a situation where dimmers are limited, there are no absolute rules concerning control priorities. However, the following priorities, from most important to least, are suggested as a beginning:

1. Control of front-of-house "visibility" area lighting
2. Area control of side-light
3. Area control of back- or top-light (least important *unless* the stage floor and its composition are visible to the majority of the audience)

Most specials require their own control channel. Designers also need to assign control for practicals, house lights if necessary, and curtain warmers or stage toners. Reserving two or three dimmers as spares is good practice, though difficult. These dimmers will save the day in case of a dimmer failure or discovery that additional control is required.

Control and Patching

Before the days of electronic control, dimmer board layout was a critical operational concern for the designer. He or she had to anticipate the best way to aid the various operators in performing their sometimes octopus-like maneuvers. Although today these concerns are less critical, channel layout is still important to the designer for the following two reasons:

1. Channels that are frequently controlled together should be grouped together. Operationally it is much faster and easier to keystroke, say, channels 23 through 31 than a random series of nine channel numbers.
2. Channel numbers should be assigned with some sort of logic to help the designer remember them. If, for instance, front-of-house lights are always assigned lower channel numbers, the designer can identify them more easily than if they are randomly assigned.

Soft Patch Capability The computer's electronic patch system makes logical dimmer/circuit-to-channel assignments an easy task if the designer follows basic guidelines. If using an area-lighting method, designers should assign all the instruments lighting a given area to a logical sequence of channels. For example, all instruments lighting area 1 should be assigned to channels 1, 11, 21, 31, 41, and so on. The front-light for area 2 is assigned to channel 2, the side-light for area 2 is assigned to channel 12, the back-light for area 2 is assigned to channel 22, with other assignments following in the same manner.

Some soft patch systems include a feature called *proportional patching*. This simply means that if two dimmers (or circuits or instruments) are ganged on a single control channel, one of them can be assigned a proportional intensity level. For instance, if lighting instrument A is assigned a proportional level of 90 percent while instrument B is assigned nothing (the default being a level of 100 percent), the intensity readings of A will always be 90 percent of those of B.

Part of the setup procedure before beginning to write a show is the creation of patch assignments. If the system's patch is left unassigned, dimmer-to-channel will default to a one-to-one relationship. Patch assignments never need to be touched during playback—a good reason for using the "record lock" key switch found on many control consoles.

Features of Electronic Systems

As noted earlier, available functions vary from one system to another. However, the designer can normally depend on several fairly common operational features, including submasters, split time fades, cue copying, and the ability to insert and/or link cues. Other features, which may or may not exist on a given system but deserve comment, are tracking and cue-only functions, groups, tracking of channels, follow cues, a level/rate wheel, simultaneous cue playback, channel or dimmer parking, and direct dimmer access.

Common Features As discussed earlier, *submasters* allow the control of several channels with one fader. When writing cues, the designer can save time by using a submaster to access channels commonly used together, such as same-colored cyc lights. In addition, submasters can be extremely helpful in programming moving lights.

Movement of light is greatly enhanced by the previously discussed split time fade. Rather than be restricted to a simple linear cross-fade, the designer can customize a fade to perfectly coincide with action onstage.

One of the most time-saving features in writing cues live is the ability to copy them. It is often desirable to alter an existing cue rather than begin from scratch. Normally this is performed by assigning a new cue number to an existing cue after adjustments are made.

cue insertion The ability to insert a new lighting cue between two existing cues in the cue list.

point cue An additional lighting cue that is assigned a decimal point number placing it between two whole-numbered cues.

cue linking A feature that allows the linking of one lighting cue to another out of normal cue-list order.

tracking An operational mode in which a channel or dimmer level remains the same in all lighting cues until told otherwise.

For making corrections and additions, **cue insertion** is a must. Most control systems allow **point cues** to be inserted between whole-number cues. An example would the insertion of cue 3.5 between cues 3 and 4. Many designers like to assign point cues to specialized functions such as scrollers or dark sets. **Cue linking** is also handy and can be used in some cases to form effect "loops" (link cue 6 to cue 10, then cue 10 back to cue 6).

Specialized Features The operational concept of **tracking** is a holdover from the days of resistance dimmers. When a dimmer level was set at a certain reading, it remained there until the operator was instructed to change it. In tracking-only systems, such as early Light Palettes, a channel assigned to a level in a cue retains that level in all subsequent cues until told otherwise. Although this makes perfect sense, tracking can sometimes be confusing, with channels apparently popping up out of nowhere. Many newer systems provide the designer with the option of working in either a tracking or a *cue only* mode. As its name implies, cue only means that a channel's level is set for the active cue only and will not track into subsequent cues.

The concept of *groups* originated with the preset type of control and, as noted earlier, is popular for concert lighting-control systems. Any number of selected channels can be labeled a group and accessed as such with a single command. This tactic is valuable for the rapid building of various stage looks. For instance, all the blue side-light channels could be grouped together for easy access.

Tracking of channels is a useful feature offered by some systems. It allows the operator to view the levels of a single channel throughout all the cues in the show. Figure 17-24 shows the channel track screen from an ETC Expression 3 control console.

follow cues An important lighting control function that allows one cue to follow another automatically with a single press of the "go" button.

The action of one cue automatically following another is normally not desirable for live performance. If the timing onstage changes, the timing of the light cues must follow suit. However, **follow cues** can be valuable for a sequence effect or for timing to something other than live action. Follow cues are quite useful in programming automated fixtures.

The operational term *delay* has different meanings depending on each system's manufacturer. In general, the *delay function* usually provides a preset time delay between the execution of one cue and the execution of a second, following cue.

level/rate wheel A wheel or touch pad that can control individual lighting channels, groups of channels, or an entire cross fade.

With proper use, the **level/rate wheel** greatly facilitates both writing cues and playback. Anything from a single channel to an entire preset can be assigned to this wheel. If a group of dimmers is "put on the wheel" and the wheel is rolled down, the intensity levels of all channels in the group are lowered. If an active fade is suddenly assigned to the wheel ("captured"), the speed of the fade in progress can be altered. In other words, the operator can seize control of any fade speed by using the rate wheel. An experienced console operator performs a great number of operations with the aid of this wheel.

Simultaneous playback of several cues is a valuable feature that most control systems provide. The slow sunset can now continue undisturbed while other lighting movements take place.

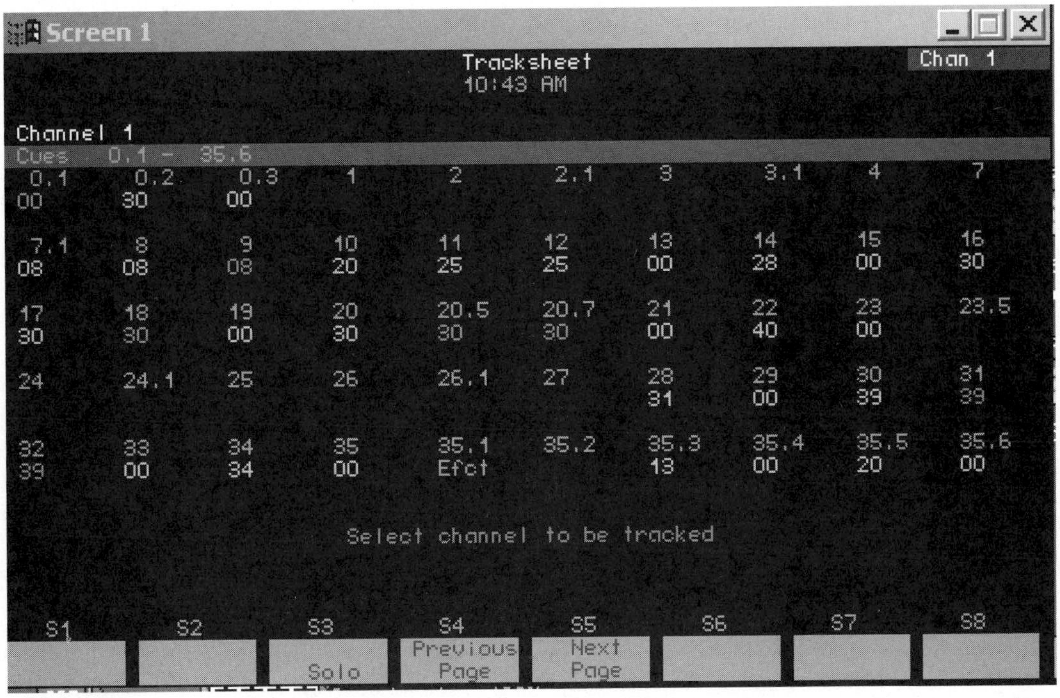

COURTESY ELECTRONIC THEATRE CONTROLS

17-24

Tracking of Channels Screen Display

The Expression 3 channel track sheet shows readings of a selected channel (channel No. 1 in this case) in all programmed cues.

A useful feature when visually writing levels into the control board is **channel or dimmer parking.** When a designer records a lighting look into memory, the value of a "parked" channel or dimmer will be ignored and not recorded. This means, for example, that he or she could write cues but still leave the house lights up by parking them. Finally, although *direct dimmer access* is not used very often, it is extremely helpful when needed. When several dimmers have been soft patched onto a single control channel, this option allows the operator to access any of the individual dimmers.

channel or dimmer parking A lighting control-board feature in which the intensity level of a channel or dimmer will not be recorded in a cue.

Every control system comes with an operation manual that, despite the fact that some are poorly written, should be read by both the designer and operator. Systems vary enough that the designer will discover new and exciting possibilities by reviewing the manuals of unfamiliar boards.

THE OPERATOR AND REMOTE CONTROL

As we have pointed out, the low amperage and low voltage used by modern control systems permit the operator to be placed at any distance from the stage and in any location that seems appropriate. The rear of the main floor of the auditorium is unquestionably the most practical place, because the view of the stage is good and because it is away from backstage activities. During rehearsals, moving the control console into the house, near the lighting designer, allows the operator and lighting designer to easily and directly communicate with each other, the director, stage manager, and other designers.

The operation of a memory control system is quite a different task from that presented to an electrician standing backstage manipulating several large and heavy handles. Often the control apparatus is delicate and complex, not at all like a bank of simple and rugged resistance or autotransformer dimmers. An error could very well result in every light on the stage assuming the wrong reading. Although a good memory control system will lessen the chances of operational error, a highly competent operator is still essential.

All computer memory control systems provide a backup disc for library storage. It is extremely important for the operator to keep this copy of a production's cues and dimmer levels up-to-date. As changes are made, periodic copying to disc is good practice, but something the designer may forget.

A good operator will have confidence, a cool head, and enough understanding of the control system to rectify an error before it gets out of hand. The operator must know the show and fully understand the lighting designer's intentions. He or she *must watch the stage.* Cues may be taken from the stage manager, but if the show is being called from backstage, the operator should take sight and sound cues from the stage action itself.

Perhaps most of all, the operator requires a sensitivity and sense of timing akin to an actor's. An operator does not merely snap lights on—he or she dims in gently, with feeling, perhaps at a varying pace to best suit the action on the stage. If the actors are fast in their pace one night, an adjustment must be made to the new tempo. A large part of the success of a production depends on the operational skills of the stage manager and light board operator.

This dependency on good operation continues with the next task of lighting designers—controlling distribution. The following chapter shows the specifics of this task and explores the optical components that determine distribution.

18

Distribution Control: Lighting Instruments

Recall that the term distribution *refers to quality of light as well as angle and direction. Is the desired light soft or harsh? Is it textured and broken up or coherent and smooth? Does it have sharp, linear edges or a soft, rounded shape? A lighting designer matches an instrument's properties and capabilities with the specific design requirements of a production. To do this effectively, the designer must be familiar with the sometimes subtle differences among stage-lighting instruments.*

CHOOSING THE RIGHT INSTRUMENT

When the designer has a visual image of what is desired, the next step is to determine which type of lighting instrument is most capable of producing that specific quality of light. Several factors affect this determination:

1. Instrument inventory and budget
2. Physical restrictions
3. Quality of light
4. Intensity and color temperature of the source
5. Beam shaping and control

Instrument Inventory and Budget

If a production's lighting equipment is rented, the designer has free choice of instrumentation. However, rental expenses must remain within an allocated budget, possibly limiting instrument choice (see Chapter 24 for more on renting equipment).

Many designers work with a fixed instrument inventory. Such inventories can vary from all new equipment to a variety of types and styles purchased over the years when funds were available. Because a theatre's instrument inventory seldom provides everything a designer requires for a production, compromises must often be made. The success of mixing and matching various pieces of equipment depends on familiarity with the instruments and begins with a basic knowledge of the types of instruments. Particularly when working with older inventories, designers are wise to confirm the accuracy of an equipment list.

Physical Restrictions

The physical features of a theatre invariably affect lighting possibilities. Throw distances (distance from lighting instrument to target) vary greatly from theatre to theatre. The type and amount of offstage space for side-lighting positions may influence design decisions. Space limitations in front-of-house ceiling and side-cove positions dictate maximum instrument size as well as number. The number of hanging positions front-of-house and over stage matters significantly as well. Finally, control and circuit limitations may be a factor in instrument usage and selection.

Quality of Light

Because quality of light greatly determines mood, a designer always considers the quality of light provided by a specific type of instrument. Ellipsoidal reflector spotlights and some automated fixtures offer variable light qualities. On the other hand, the quality of light from Fresnels and PAR instruments cannot be altered.

A Fresnel delivers a soft beam of light with fuzzy edges and an even field. The beam from a PAR has fuzzy edges, but the light itself is harsh and the field is uneven. The beam from an ellipsoidal reflector spotlight has hard edges that can be softened by various means. It is harsher than a Fresnel but less harsh than a PAR. Automated fixtures and ellipsoidals are the only instruments that can take gobos or patterns which alter the texture of the light.

Intensity and Color Temperature of the Source

A question the designer constantly considers is whether a chosen instrument can deliver the appropriate amount of brightness for the task involved. Many lighting instruments can take lamps of varying intensities, but facilities with fixed inventories normally have chosen a specific lamp to be used in each instrument. Designers need to know not only what instrument is in an inventory but also what lamp it has. Besides the lamp, the beam spread of an instrument also greatly affects how bright the light will be. A wide-angle 50-degree ellipsoidal spreads the light over a much greater area than does a narrower 20-degree one.

The color temperature of a source has become an important design tool in the theatre. Theatrical light sources vary in color temperature from a warm 2,800°K to a harsh and crisp 5,600°K. The visual difference is huge. Using differences in color temperature in a design can be very effective; ignoring variations in color temperature can be equally detrimental. Recall that higher color temperature sources are perceived as being brighter, harsher, and cooler than are lower ones.

Beam Shaping and Control

The ability to alter the shape and size of a light beam is an important design tool. Each type of stage-lighting instrument is very different in this respect.

Ellipsoidal reflector spotlights are the most versatile in terms of beam shaping and control. To a lesser extent, the beams from a Fresnel and from an automated fixture can be altered as well. The beam of a PAR is oval and nearly impossible to alter.

THE PHYSICS OF REFLECTION AND REFRACTION

The quality of light from an instrument is determined by two things: (1) the light source itself and (2) how the light is manipulated after it leaves the source. The latter factor is controlled by the **optics** of the lighting instrument. Understanding the laws of reflection and refraction is an important step in learning how to use light.

optics Reference to the optical features of a stage lighting instrument—most significantly the reflector and lens or lenses.

All stage-lighting instruments use reflectors to increase the efficiency of their light sources. Most use lenses to gather and redirect the light, focusing it into a usable beam.

Specular Reflection

The law of **specular reflection** explains what happens to a light beam when it strikes a smooth, shiny surface such as a mirror: the angle of incidence is equal to the angle of reflection. This means that light is reflected at an angle equal to the angle at which it struck, but in the opposite direction. If the beam strikes a specular surface head-on, it will be reflected directly back over the same path (Figure 18-1). Variations of specular reflection are spread reflection, diffuse reflection, and mixed reflection. Figure 18-2 illustrates these three phenomena.

specular reflection Light reflection off a shiny surface. The angle of incidence is equal to the angle of reflection.

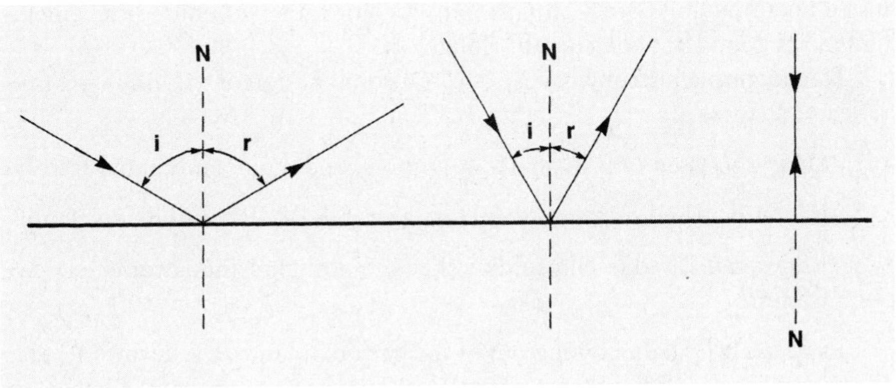

18-1

Specular Reflection

The angle of incidence is equal to the angle of reflection.

i = incident light

r = reflected light

N = the normal (a perpendicular drawn to the surface)

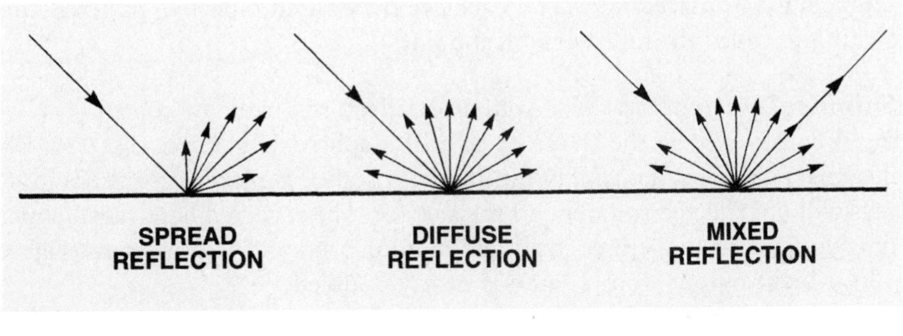

18-2

Types of Specular Reflection

Spread Reflection If a beam of light strikes a surface with slight irregularities (such as textured paint or metallic fabric), the law of specular reflection applies. However, because the light encounters various small surfaces set at different angles, the reflected rays are somewhat scattered. While maintaining the basic reflected direction, the rays diverge. This phenomenon is known as *spread reflection.*

Diffuse Reflection Highly textured surfaces or soft cotton fabrics cause *diffuse reflection* of light. Such surfaces have many small reflectors that lie at varied angles, resulting in reflected light that exhibits no single direction. The entire surface appears much the same regardless of the angle from which it is viewed.

Mixed Reflection A combination of specular and diffuse reflection is known as *mixed reflection.* A piece of pottery with a high glaze produces this type of reflection. The rough ceramic surface creates diffusion, while the shiny glaze acts like a mirror.

Types of Reflectors

Early stage-lighting reflectors were molded-glass mirrors, some of which may still be found in carbon arc follow spots. In the 1950s, reflectors began to be constructed of a lightweight spun metal. The metal shell was given a highly reflective and durable surface treatment referred to as *Alzak processing*. The Alzak reflector became an industry standard.

dichroic reflector In a theatrical spotlight, a glass reflector with a dichroic coating, which allows some wavelengths of light to pass through while reflecting others.

Recently, a new dichroic-coated glass reflector has been put to use in many lighting instruments (Figure 18-3). The advantage of a **dichroic reflector** is that it can be designed to allow ultraviolet and infrared light rays to pass through the back, so that only visible light is reflected. This produces a light beam of significantly cooler temperature. As a result, the internal parts of the instrument function better and last longer, color filters do not fade as quickly, and metal gobos last considerably longer.

Stage-lighting instruments use one or a combination of the following three reflector shapes:

1. *Spherical:* Used in Fresnels, follow spots, and many automated fixtures
2. *Parabolic:* Used in beam projectors and PAR-, MR-, and R-type lamps
3. *Ellipsoidal:* Used in ellipsoidal reflector spotlights and automated fixtures

focal point of reflectors The specific point at which a light source must be placed in relationship to the reflector in order to achieve the desired reflective pattern.

By redirecting light coming out of the back of a lamp, a reflector increases the amount of usable light from any source. The shape of a reflector determines how the light is redirected. Every reflector has a specific point where a light source must be placed in order to achieve the desired reflective pattern. This location is called the reflector's **focal point.**

spherical reflector A reflector cast in the shape of part of a sphere, which returns light back to its focal point. Found in Fresnel spotlights.

Spherical Reflectors The **spherical reflector** is made of coated glass or metal constructed in the shape of part of a sphere. The exact center of the imaginary sphere is its focal point. If a light source is placed at this point, its rays will be reflected squarely off the surface. The reflected light rays bounce directly back to the source itself and continue to spread from there (Figure 18-4). Light output from a lamp is nearly doubled.

18-3

Dichroic Reflector

Glass dichroic-coated reflector of an ETC Source Four ellipsoidal reflector spotlight.

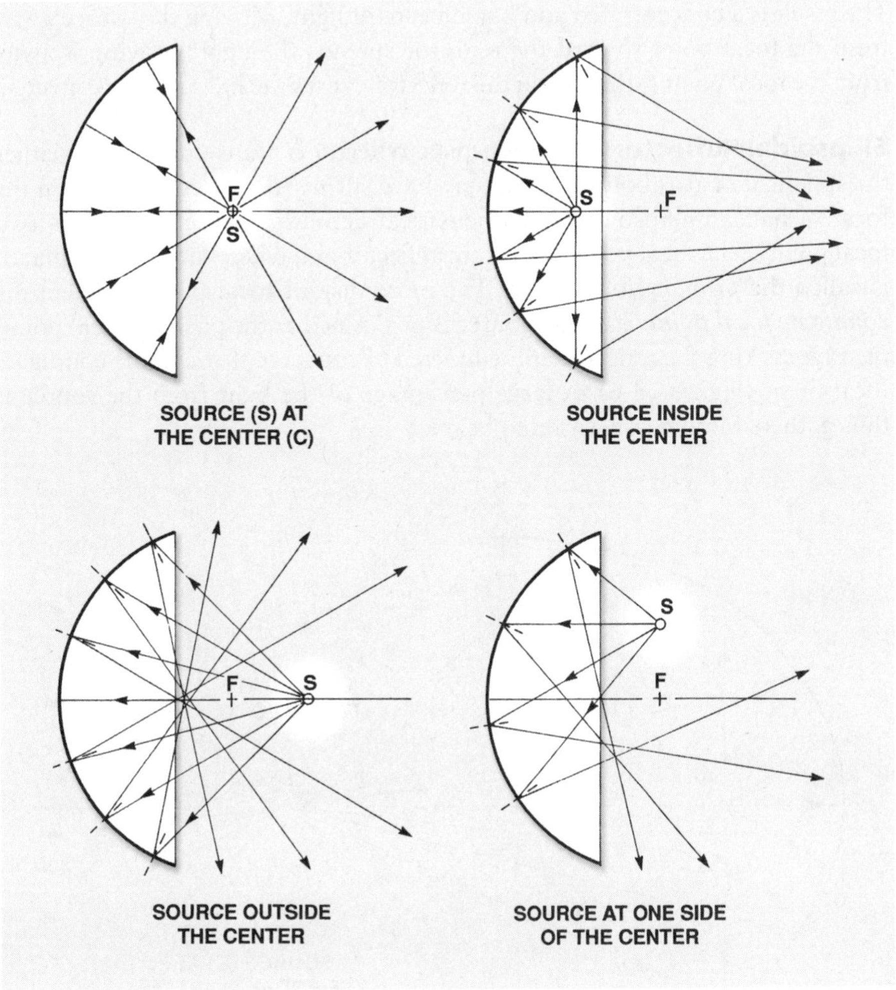

18-4

The Spherical Reflector

If a light source (S) is placed at the focal point (F) of a spherical reflector, the reflected rays are returned directly to that focal point. Illustrations show the result of the source being placed in other locations.

18-5

The Parabolic Reflector

If a light source (S) is placed at the focal point (F) of a parabolic reflector, the reflected rays are parallel. Note that nonreflected rays from the front of the source will not be parallel—they will diverge.

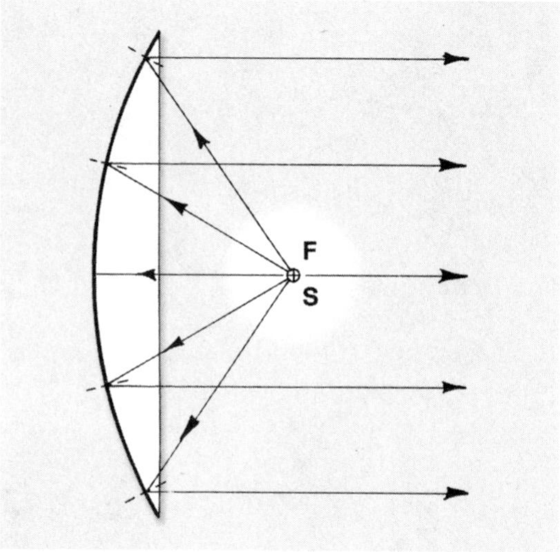

parabolic reflector A reflector cast in the shape of part of a parabola, which reflects light in parallel rays. Found in PAR fixtures.

Parabolic Reflectors A **parabolic reflector** is unique in that it produces parallel rays of light. The parabolic reflector is constructed in the shape of part of a parabola. If the light source is placed at the parabola's focal point, rays striking the reflector bounce off parallel to one another (Figure 18-5). The result is a concentrated and harsh beam of light. Moving the source away from the focal point toward the reflector spreads the light. Moving it away from the focal point farther from the reflector causes the light rays to converge.

ellipsoidal reflector A reflector cast in the shape of part of an ellipsoid, which reflects light back to its secondary focal point. Found in ellipsoidal reflector spotlights.

Ellipsoidal Reflectors An **ellipsoidal reflector** is more efficient than either the spherical or parabolic. As you may have surmised, it is constructed in the form of half an ellipsoid. By mathematical definition, an ellipsoid has two focal points. The focal point nearest the reflector and where the source is placed is called the *primary focal point.* The more distant focal point is called the *conjugate focal point.* If a light source is positioned at the primary focal point, the rays striking the reflector are redirected to converge through the conjugate focal point (Figure 18-6). A large percentage of the light from the source is thus gathered into a concentrated beam.

18-6

The Ellipsoidal Reflector

If a light source (S) is placed at the primary focal point (F') of an ellipsoidal reflector, the rays converge at the conjugate or secondary focal point (F2).

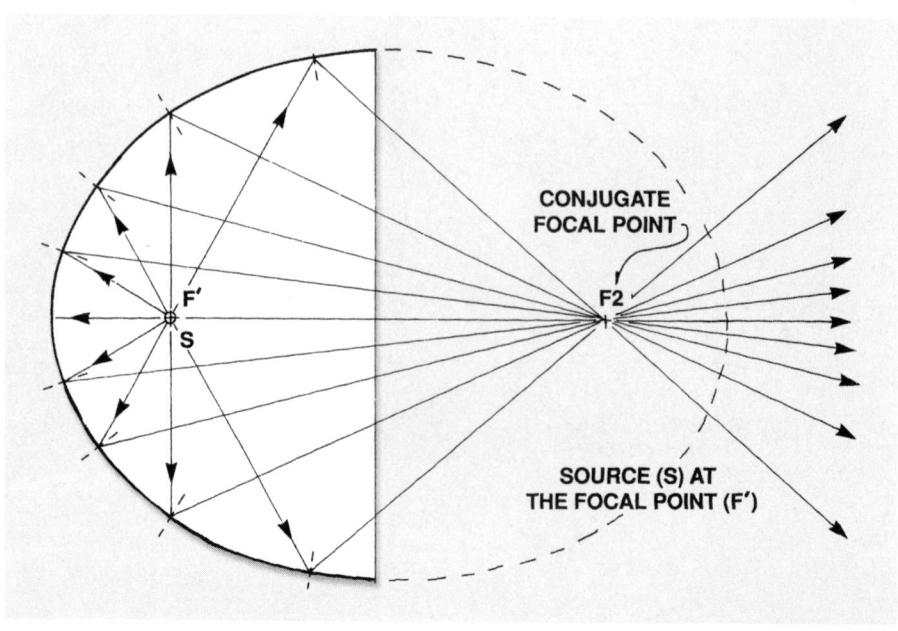

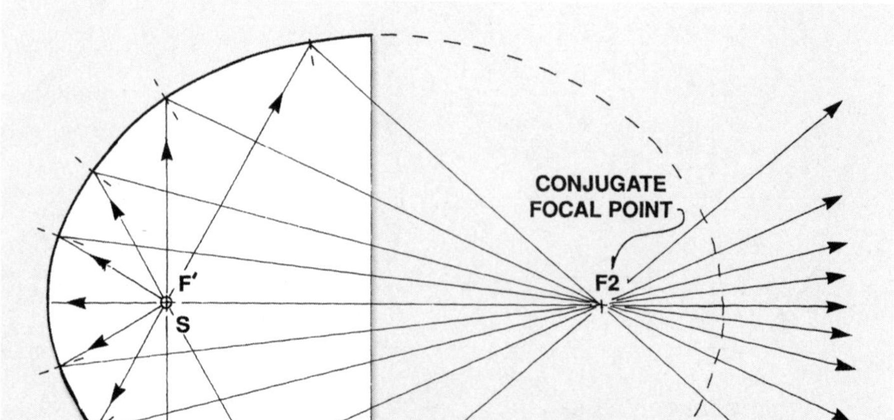

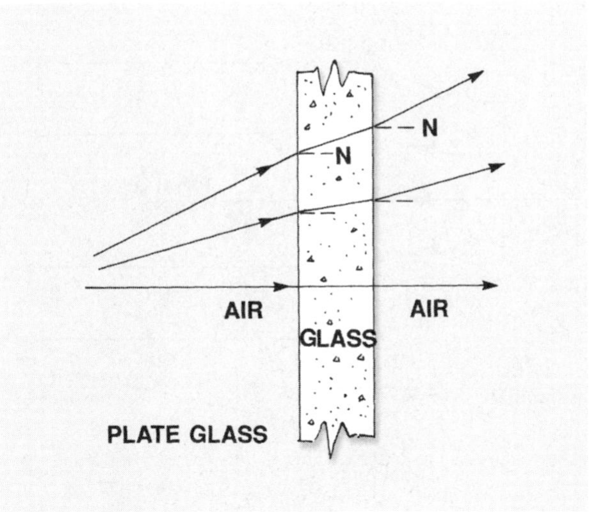

18-7

Refraction of Light

This drawing illustrates the refraction (bending) of rays of light passing through a medium denser than air, in this case a sheet of glass.

N = the normal (a perpendicular drawn to the surface)

Refraction of Light

Refraction refers to the bending of light. The law of refraction states that when a ray of light passes into a denser medium (for example, from air into glass) it is bent toward a perpendicular drawn to the surface at the point of entry. When it reemerges into the less dense medium, it is bent away from a perpendicular drawn at that point (Figure 18-7).

refraction The bending of light rays as they pass through mediums with different densities, as in a light beam traveling through air bending from its original track when it goes through glass.

The two surfaces of the piece of glass illustrated in Figure 18-7 are parallel. In such an instance, the emerging ray of light is slightly offset but continues parallel to its original course. Lenses have nonparallel surfaces, causing light to bend in a different, though equally predictable, manner.

The Plano-Convex Lens Light from a stage-lighting instrument must be intensely concentrated in the shape of a cone. A lens is used to redirect the spreading rays of light coming from the source and the reflector. The principal lens used in stage-lighting instruments is **plano-convex.** It has a flat (plano) surface on one side and an outwardly curved (convex) surface on the other. It is the simplest and least expensive lens for concentrating spreading rays into a compact and bright beam of light (Figure 18-8).

plano-convex lens A lens with one flat (plano) side and one outwardly curved (convex) side. Found in ellipsoidal reflector spotlights.

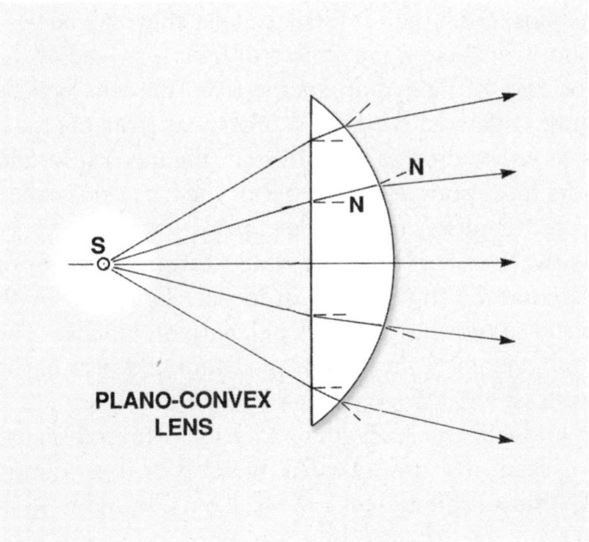

18-8

The Plano-Convex Lens

Shown is the refraction of diverging light rays as they pass through a plano-convex lens, the type used in ellipsoidal reflector spotlights.

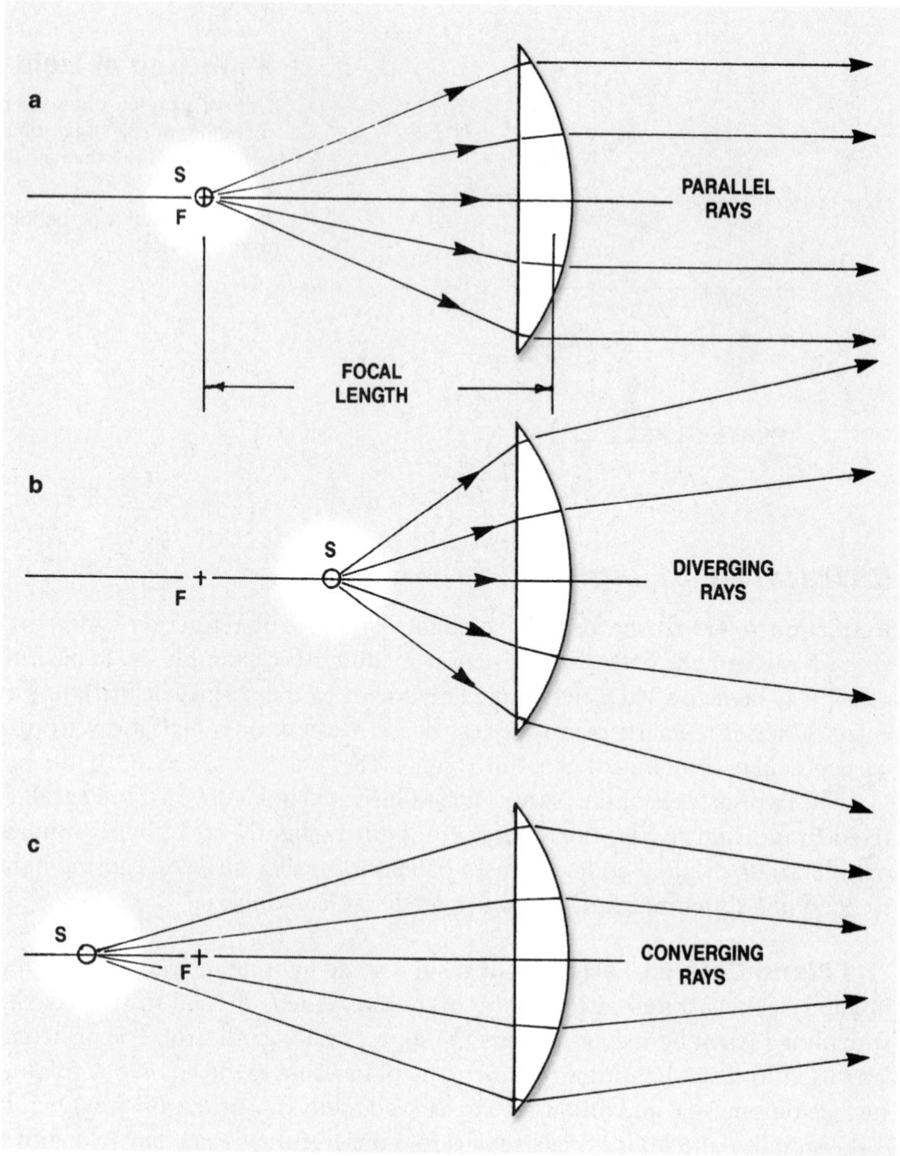

18-9

Plano-Convex Refractions

The location of a light source affects the pattern of refraction caused by a plano-convex lens.

a Source (S) at the focal point (F) of the lens. Note the focal length of the lens.

b Source inside the focal point of the lens.

c Source behind the focal point of the lens.

Focal Point and Focal Length Like reflectors, lenses have a **focal point.** If parallel light rays (such as those from the sun) strike a lens, they will be bent to converge at the focal point. Conversely, if a source of light is placed at the focal point of a lens, all the rays of light that emerge from the lens will be parallel to one another (Figure 18-9a). Moving the source away from the focal point causes the light rays to either diverge or converge (Figures 18-9b and 18-9c). The distance from the focal point to the center of the lens(es) is called its **focal length** and is measured in inches or millimeters.

focal point of lenses The point at which parallel rays of light converge after passing through a lens.

focal length The distance between the center of a lens and its focal point.

Lenses are identified by two numbers. The first indicates the diameter of the lens in inches and the second the focal length in inches. Thus, a 6-by-9-inch lens (6 × 9) has a diameter of 6 inches and a focal length of 9 inches. The greater the curvature of the convex face, the greater the bending power of the lens. Therefore, a thick lens has a shorter focal length than a thin one.

It is usually desirable to know the focal length of a lens. However, because this information is rarely marked on lenses, a quick method of determining focal length is valuable. If the sun is shining, take the lens outside and hold it,

PHOTO COURTESY STRAND LIGHTING

18-10

Modern P-C Spotlight

Strand's Alto PC 2,000-watt plano-convex spotlight provides beam spreads from a narrow 4 degrees to a wide 57 degrees.

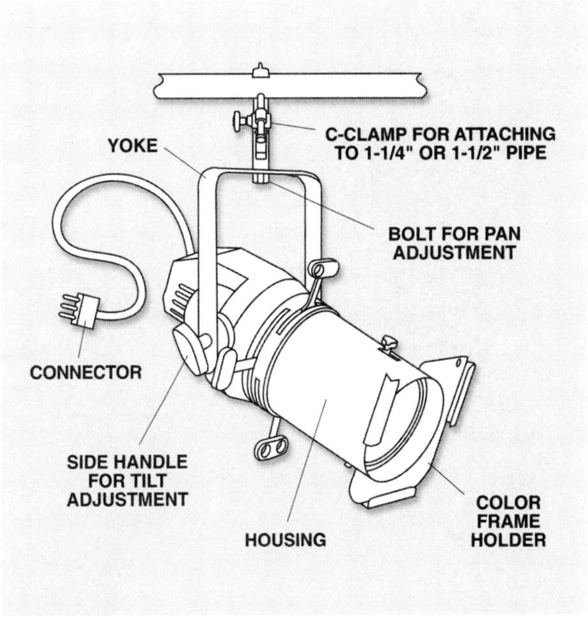

18-11

Instrument Parts

Parts common to all types of lighting instruments.

plano side down, so that the sun's rays are concentrated on the ground. Using a ruler, measure the distance from the ground to the lens. Focal lengths of lenses used in stage-lighting instruments are measured in even inches.

THE PLANO-CONVEX SPOTLIGHT

The first theatrical spotlight, and for many years the only kind, was named after its plano-convex lens. It consisted of a simple metal housing containing a spherical reflector, a lamp, and a lens. The lamp and reflector could be moved forward or back in order to increase or decrease the diameter of the beam of light.

In the United States, the plano-convex spotlight ("P-C") has been replaced by the ellipsoidal reflector spotlight. However, in many European countries it remains the standard stage-lighting instrument. Built and operated much like a Fresnel spotlight, the modern P-C gives off a high-quality, sharp beam of light that is adjustable in size (Figure 18-10).

THE ELLIPSOIDAL REFLECTOR SPOTLIGHT

The **ellipsoidal reflector spotlight** (ERS) is by far the most important lighting instrument on the modern stage. Throughout the years it has been known as a "Kleiglight" or a "Leko" or a "Cannon" or, most recently, a "Source Four."

Figure 18-11 illustrates several features of the ERS that are common to all stage-lighting instruments. The instrument is attached to a lighting batten by means of a **C-clamp.** The C-clamp is bolted to the instrument's **yolk.** Loosening

ellipsoidal reflector spotlight (ERS) Stage-lighting instrument that uses an ellipsoidal reflector. The ERS is the most efficient and versatile instrument in use today. It creates a concentrated, sharp light and has a built-in beam-shaping capability.

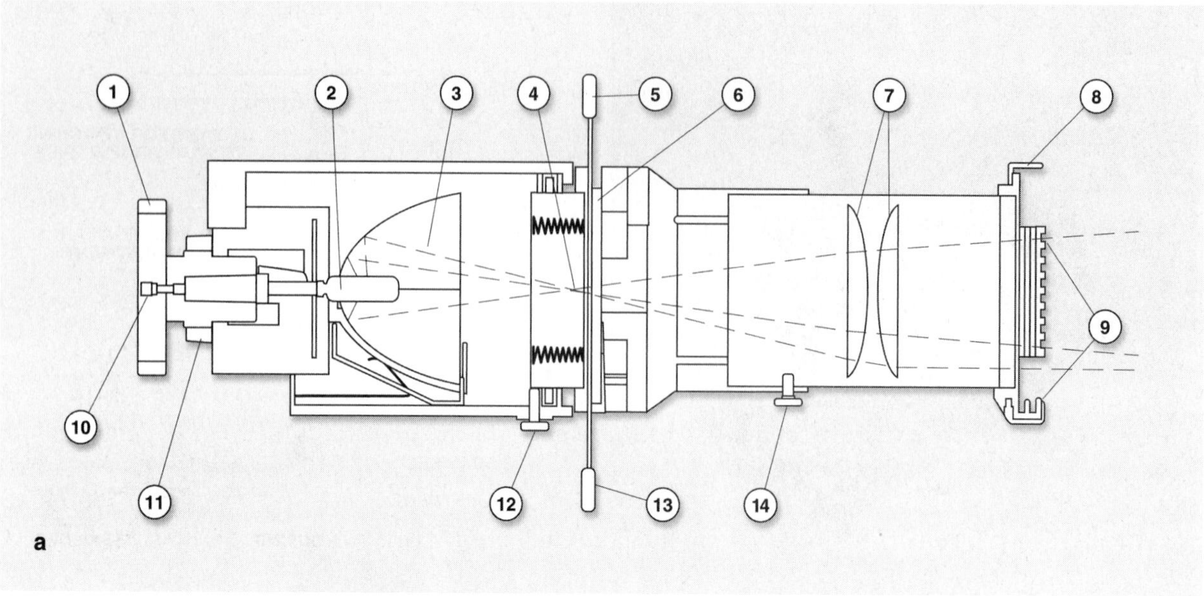

18-12

Ellipsoidal Reflector Spotlight

a The parts of an ERS:

- **1** Protective rear ring handle.
- **2** High-performance lamp.
- **3** Dichroic glass or metal-coated ellipsoidal reflector.
- **4** Aperature, or gate, with reflected rays crossing at the conjugal focal point.
- **5** Top shutter, which shapes the bottom of the beam.
- **6** Gobo/iris plate slot.
- **7** Dual plano-convex lenses.
- **8** Gel frame retainer.
- **9** Two-slot gel frame holder.
- **10** Lamp focus control.
- **11** Centering lock knob.
- **12** Rotation knob.
- **13** Bottom shutter.
- **14** Retaining screw for barrel focus.

b ETC Source Four ellipsoidal reflector spotlight.

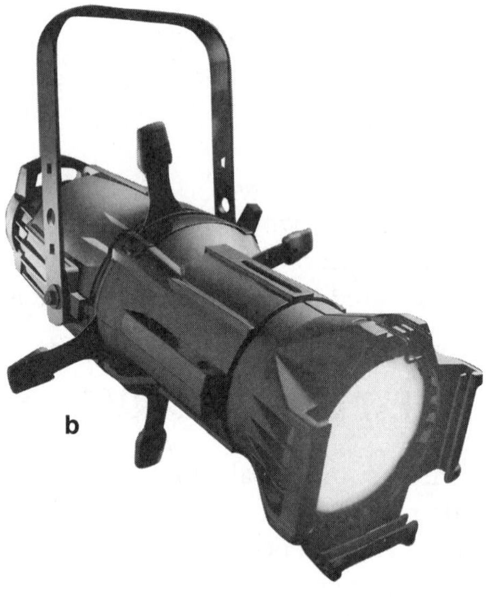

PHOTO COURTESY ELECTRONIC THEATRE CONTROLS

C-clamp A clamp, shaped like a C, that is used to attach a lighting instrument to a pipe batten.

yolk On a lighting instrument, the U-shaped part that holds the C-clamp and allows the instrument to tilt.

the C-clamp's bolt allows the instrument to be turned from side to side (to *pan*). The yolk is attached to the instrument's *housing* by means of one or two handles that can be loosened to allow for tilt adjustment. At the front of the instrument, holders can accommodate a color frame.

A cutaway view of an ERS, Figure 18-12 shows how the ellipsoidal reflector receives light from the lamp and redirects it to the conjugate focal point. At this point sits a metal baffle that has a circular opening called the *aperture* or **gate.** This baffle cuts off stray rays, allowing only the useful light to continue on to the lenses. The sharp, round beam typical of an ERS is actually an image of the gate. Four beam-shaping **shutters** are positioned immediately adjacent to the gate. An **iris** or a gobo is also located right next to the gate and can also be used to shape the beam. The lenses illustrated are examples of a fixed-lens system, meaning that the diameter of the beam of light cannot be significantly changed. The barrel can move back and forth only enough to soften or sharpen the beam edge. A **zoom ellipsoidal** reflector spotlight offers variable focus lenses that allow for a range of beam sizes.

gate In an ellipsoidal reflector spotlight, the position at which shutters, iris, and gobos are located. The gate is also close to the reflector's secondary focal point, where the light rays cross.

shutters Moveable metal plates, inserted at the gate of an ellipsoidal reflector spotlight, that allow the beam to be shaped in a linear manner from any of four directions.

iris A device, located at the gate of an ellipsoidal reflector spotlight, that makes the beam's circumference larger or smaller.

zoom ellipsoidal An ellipsoidal reflector spotlight with moveable lenses that provide an adjustable beam diameter.

ERS Beam Shaping

One of the features that makes an ERS a unique and valuable stage-lighting instrument is its built-in beam-shaping capability. As we have seen, the beam of light from an ERS is naturally round, but its shape and size can be altered by means of shutters, an iris, or a gobo.

Shutters The ellipsoidal's four shutters are standard equipment. These metal plates have heat-insulated tabs or rings attached to the part extending out of the housing. One or more shutters can be pushed into the aperture, cutting into the beam of light with a straight edge. Remember that shutter action is reversed because the light beams cross at the aperture—that is, the bottom shutter creates the top cut. Light beams crossing at the gate create high temperatures that cause even the best shutters to bend and warp, particularly in instruments without dichroic reflectors. Therefore, to avoid overheating, completely opening the shutters of an ellipsoidal as soon as the instrument is hung is good practice. Modern enhanced ellipsoidals are equipped with a rotating shutter assembly that allows virtually any angle of cut to be achieved.

Iris An iris is an optional feature of a standard ERS. Its metal leaflike fingers act to reduce the diameter of the beam in a circular manner. Like shutters, the metal iris gets extremely hot and can warp to the point of being unusable. Some brands of ellipsoidals have irises that are permanently fixed near the gate; however, most modern ones provide a drop-in slot at the top of the instrument for an iris assembly. An iris is a necessity if the ERS is being used as a follow spot.

Gobos All ellipsoidal reflector spotlights have a slot in the top of their housing that is made to receive a template commonly called a gobo. This template is a metal plate with a pattern cut in it. It fits into a holder that positions the pattern near the gate and squarely in the center of the light beam. When positioned, this simple plate turns the ERS into a shadow projector. Images of an endless variety of words or patterns can be projected onto scenery, actors, or the stage floor. By moving the lens barrel, electricians can sharply focus the pattern or turn it into soft, indistinguishable texture. Instruments equipped with a slot big enough for a drop-in iris can accommodate a gobo rotator capable of spinning a standard pattern. (The next chapter provides specific information concerning gobos.) In using gobos, electricians must remember that the pattern image is inverted because of the crossing of the light rays. Consequently, the gobo should be placed upside down in its holder.

ERS Lenses

There are currently three types of ERS lens systems:

1. *Fixed lens:* Allows an adjustment in beam edge but not in size (diameter)
2. *Interchangeable lens:* Usually provides three different beam sizes
3. *Zoom lens:* Provides a variable beam spread within a fixed range

All three of these systems use a combination of plano-convex lenses, and each has its own distinct advantages.

Fixed Lenses This system uses two plano-convex lenses mounted belly to belly in a barrel. Two lenses are used rather than one because they are lighter and less likely to crack from the heat of an instrument. A fixed-lens system is the least expensive of the three systems. It produces superior quality light with a smooth and even field.

Interchangeable Lenses An interchangeable lens system allows for movement of lenses in relationship to one another or the substitution of one lens for another. In either case, the size of the light beam is changed. An example of an ERS with this capability is the Colortran Mini-Ellipse (Figure 18-13). Electricians can remove the lens barrel from the instrument's housing and, by loosening four screws, expose the lenses. Moving the front lens to one of three different positions provides field spreads of 30 degrees, 40 degrees, or 50 degrees. The flexibility of interchangeable lenses is quite attractive. Although less convenient than zoom ellipsoidals, interchangeable lens instruments cost less.

URL http://www.colortran.com

18-13

ERS with Interchangeable Lenses

The Colortran Mini-Ellipse has interchangeable lenses that can be set for beam spreads of 30, 40, or 50 degrees. It is a compact 4-inch instrument designed for short-throw applications.

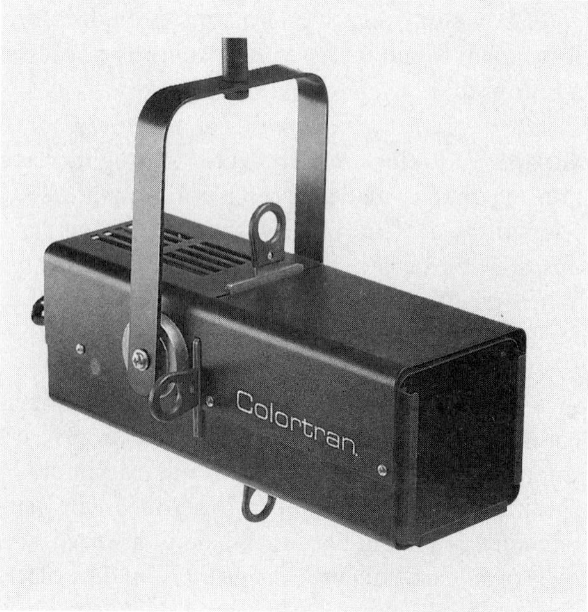

PHOTO COURTESY COLORTRAN

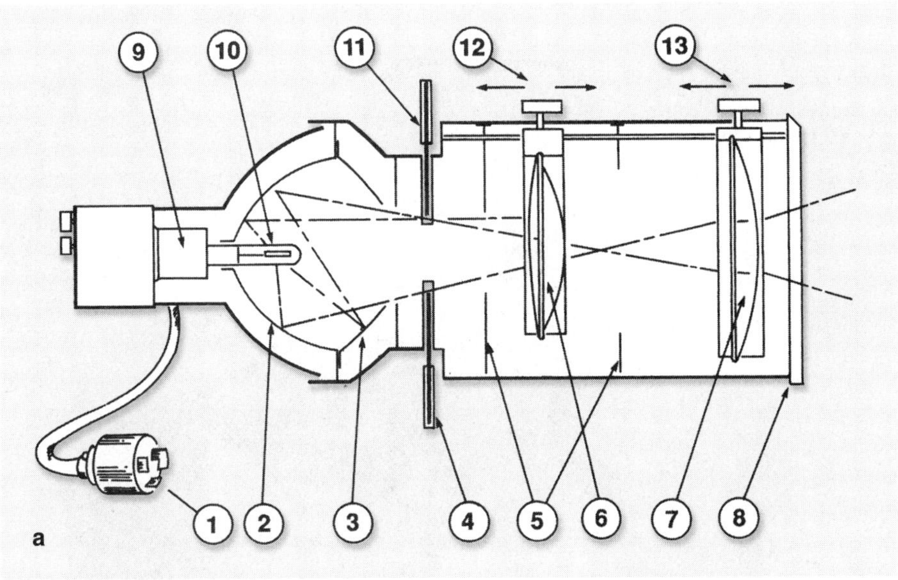

PHOTO COURTESY ELECTRO CONTROLS, INC.

18-14

The Parellipsphere

a The parts of the Parellipsphere:

1 Twist-lock connector.
2 Parellipse part of the reflector—the apex is parabolic in action.
3 Kickback reflector with slight spherical configuration.
4 Bottom shutter.
5 Baffles to trap stray unusable light.
6 Nonsymmetrical biconvex lens.
7 Plano-convex lens.
8 Color-frame holder.
9 Prefocus medium base socket.
10 Quartz lamp.
11 Top shutter.
12 Lens adjustment knob to change focal length of objective lens system.
13 Lens adjustment knob to change beam spread.

b The Parellipsphere was the forerunner of the modern zoom ellipsoidal.

Zoom Lenses One of the first practical zoom ellipsoidals was the Parellipsphere, manufactured by Electro Controls of Salt Lake City (Figure 18-14). Rather than two plano-convex lenses, this instrument used a large plano-convex lens in combination with a smaller biconvex lens. Each of the lenses moves forward and back to achieve variable beam spreads. When Electro Controls was purchased by Strand Lighting, the Parellipsphere was discontinued. However, the market for zoom ellipsoidals had been established, and several manufacturers responded with their own versions.

URL http://www.strandlighting.com

18-15

The Zoom Ellipsoidal

The ETC Source Four zoom provides adjustable beam spreads from 25 to 50 degrees.

PHOTO COURTESY ELECTRONIC THEATRE CONTROLS

The example shown in Figure 18-15 is a modern zoom ellipsoidal. Rated up to 750 watts, it has variable field spreads from 25 to 50 degrees and a single knob for moving the lenses. A zoom ellipsoidal is more expensive than comparable fixed-lens or interchangeable-lens instruments. In certain applications, however, the convenience and flexibility is well worth the extra expense.

ERS Beam and Field Angles

beam edge In a spotlight beam, the point where the light drops off to 50 percent of maximum intensity.

field edge In a spotlight beam, the point where the light drops off to 10 percent of maximum intensity.

When an ellipsoidal reflector spotlight is properly aligned, its cone-shaped beam of light is most intense along the center line of the beam. Intensity drops off evenly from the center to the edge of the beam. The point at which the light's intensity drops to 50 percent of maximum is called the **beam edge.** Farther outward, the place where light intensity drops to 10 percent is called the **field edge.**

As noted earlier, lenses are traditionally identified by two numbers: diameter in inches and focal length in inches. In the theatre it is most convenient to classify spotlights by the diameter of the light beam, measured in degrees. The figure used is technically the angle of the *field* rather than the *beam* (Figure 18-16). For example, a 6-by-12 ellipsoidal is called a "30 degree," referring to the instrument's nominal field angle of 30 degrees.

The table in the box lists typical beam and field angles as well as appropriate throw distances for 6-inch ellipsoidal reflector spotlights with various focal lengths. Note that these figures are approximate and may not correspond exactly to the performance of any specific instrument. Consult manufacturer specifications before using.

Many modern ellipsoidals allow for adjustment of the light source in respect to the focal point of the reflector. By moving the lamp either in or out, an

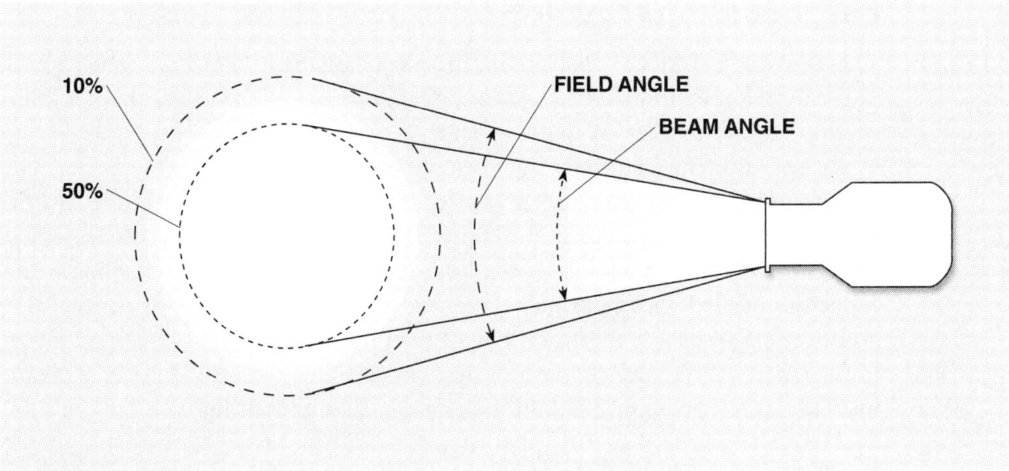

18-16

Beam and Field Angles

In a typical ellipsoidal reflector spotlight, 100-percent intensity is found at beam center. The beam and field angles are designated in degrees.

electrician can change the distribution of light from an extremely "hot center" to a "flat field." The hot center concentrates a greater amount of light into the center of the beam. The flat field evens the intensity throughout the beam. This adjustment does not alter the effective field angle but does change the beam angle considerably.

Light Reading

6-Inch ERS Beam and Field Angles

If the intensity of light from an ellipsoidal is considered in terms of percentages, and the beam's illumination along the center line is 100 percent, the beam and field angles are defined as follows:

Lens Type	Beam Angle	Field Angle	Throw
4½ × 6	33°	50°	12–20 feet
6 × 9	24°	40°	15–30 feet
6 × 12	18°	30°	25–40 feet
6 × 16	15°	20°	35–55 feet
6 × 22	8°	15°	50–75 feet

Beam angle is the point where the illumination falls off to 50 percent.

Field angle is the point where illumination falls off to 10 percent.

ERS Beam Characteristics

The ellipsoidal reflector spotlight throws a powerful beam of light capable of creating harsh and sharp shadows. Yet, this instrument offers the flexibility of altering the quality of light in nearly any manner.

Stage lighting requires tightly controlled beams of light. Stray light illuminating the architecture of the theatre or unintended scenery is both distracting and unacceptable. The ERS is by far the most successful of conventional instruments in controlling light. The precision of the ellipsoidal reflector coupled with clear plano-convex lenses accounts for this control. The addition of gobos can texture the light in endless ways. Frost diffusion placed in the color frame can achieve a variety of softening effects. There is no better instrument for providing flexibility as well as control of light.

ERS Sizes

Ellipsoidal reflector spotlights are available in several sizes for different applications. In general, the smaller instruments use lower-wattage lamps and are designed for short-throw applications. For instance, Colortran's Mini-Ellipse has 4-inch diameter lenses and takes a 500-watt lamp. However, even with lenses set at 30 degrees, it is not effective for throw distances beyond 25 feet. The Source Four Junior (Figure 18-17a) uses the popular 575-watt HPL lamp and has options for beam spreads of 26 degrees, 36 degrees, and 50 degrees.

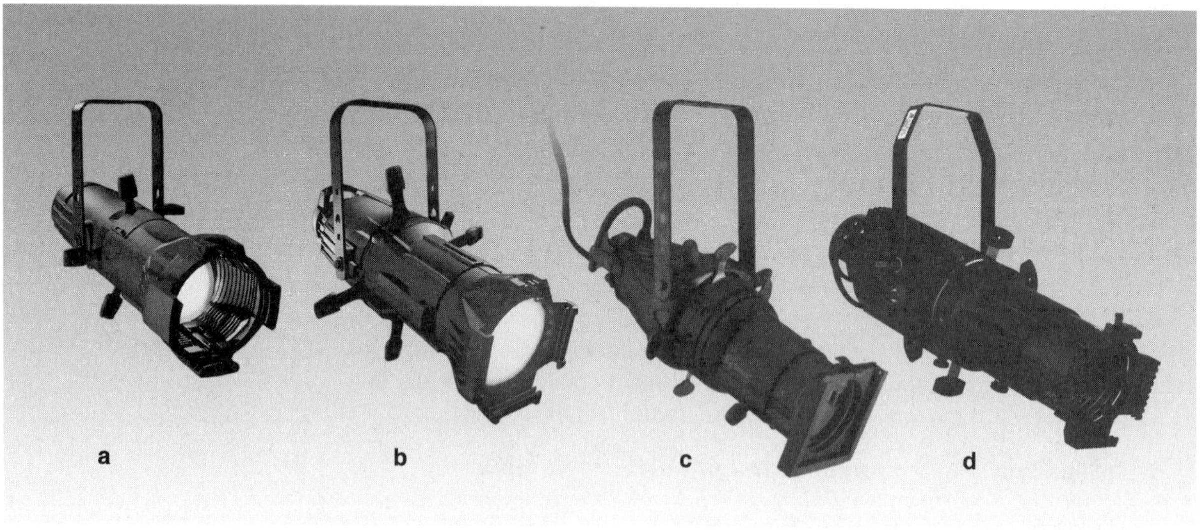

a & b PHOTOS COURTESY ELECTRONIC THEATRE CONTROLS
c PHOTO COURTESY STRAND LIGHTING
d PHOTO COURTESY ALTMAN STAGE LIGHTING CO.

18-17

Modern Ellipsoidal Reflector Spotlights

a ETC Source Four Junior. Smaller than the standard Source Four. Takes a 575-watt lamp and an "M" size gobo.

b ETC Source Four. Takes a 575- or 750-watt lamp and has a dichroic reflector and rotating shutters. Interchangeable lens tubes provide field angles of 19, 26, 36, and 50 degrees.

c Strand SL. Takes a 575-watt lamp and has a dichroic coated glass reflector. Interchangeable lens tubes provide field angles of 19, 26, 36, and 50 degrees.

d Altman Shakespeare. Takes a 600-watt lamp (FLK) and has features similar to ETC's Source Four. Lens barrels available with field angles of 20, 30, 40, and 50 degrees.

a & b PHOTOS COURTESY ELECTRONIC THEATRE CONTROLS

18-18

Narrow Beam Ellipsoidal Reflector Spotlights

a Source Four 10-degree ERS.

b Source Four 5-degree ERS. Has all the features of a standard Source Four, with a long lens providing a 5-degree field angle.

By far the most popular size is the 6-inch ellipsoidal. As seen in the box on ERS Beam and Field Angles, field spreads range from a narrow 15 degrees up to a wide 50 degrees. Standard 6-inch ellipsoidals use lamps ranging from 500 to 1,000 watts and are valuable for throws up to 70 feet (Figure 18-17). Larger 8- and 10-inch ellipsoidals have been replaced by 6-inch ellipsoidals with special lenses that can produce narrow field spreads of 5 and 10 degrees. These instruments allow throw distances up to 100 feet (Figure 18-18).

The Source Four line of enhanced ellipsoidals from Electronic Theatre Controls (ETC) made a huge impact in the theatre-lighting world. The Source Four was designed around a new high-intensity 575-watt lamp comparable in brightness to a standard 1,000-watt quartz lamp. The energy efficiency alone made the development of this instrument significant, but it also features an innovative "cool mirror" dichroic reflector and a rotating shutter assembly. A higher-intensity 750-watt lamp is now also available. Altman's Shakespeare series offers similar features and uses a compact 600-watt lamp. Strand followed suit with their SL Series of ellipsoidals, which take a 575-watt lamp.

URL http://www.etcconnect.com

THE FRESNEL SPOTLIGHT

The **Fresnel** (pronounced Fra-*nel*) gets its name from the inventor of its unique lens, Augustin-Jean Fresnel (1788–1827). The instrument is simpler than an ERS, consisting of only a spherical reflector, a lamp, and the Fresnel lens. As shown in Figure 18-19, the Fresnel's spherical reflector returns the light back to the filament of the lamp. The light then travels on to the lens, where it is redirected into the cone-shaped beam typical of spotlights.

Fresnel spotlight Named after the inventor of its lens, the Fresnel is a theatrical spotlight with a spherical reflector and the ability to change beam size. It produces a soft, even field of light.

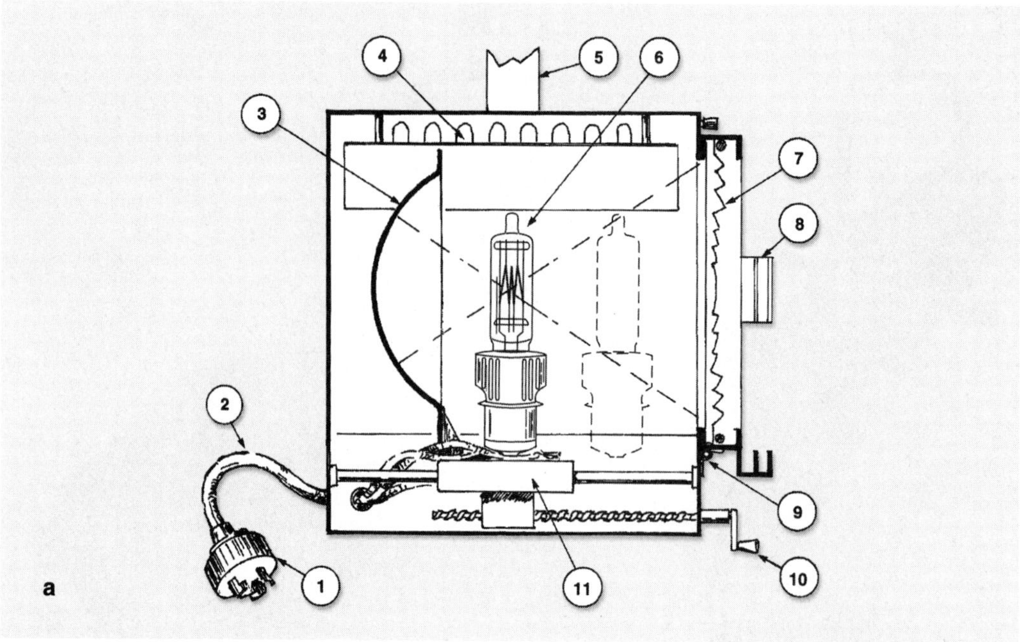

PHOTO COURTESY STRAND LIGHTING

18-19

Fresnel Spotlight

a Cutaway view of a typical Fresnel:
- **1** Twist-lock connector.
- **2** Rubber-coated lead wires.
- **3** Spherical reflector.
- **4** Ventilation holes.
- **5** Yoke.
- **6** Quartz lamp with a prefocus base.
- **7** Fresnel lens.
- **8** Color-frame holder.
- **9** Hinged lens front for interior access.
- **10** Worm-screw drive for moving the lamp and reflector carriage.
- **11** Movable carriage.

b Strand 6-inch Fresnel. Takes up to a 1,000-watt lamp and offers a wide range of field spreads.

The Fresnel Lens

The thick glass of a plano-convex lens with a short focal length has a tendency to crack because of excessive heat from the source. As we have seen, ellipsoidal reflector spotlights compensate for this deficiency by using a combination of two lenses rather than one. Another solution is to reduce the thickness of the lens by removing unnecessary glass.

The important parts of a plano-convex lens are the two surfaces, one flat and the other curved. Fresnel knew that if the curve of the convex surface was retained while "steps" were cut into the glass to reduce thickness, the lens would work like a plano-convex (Figure 18-20). In fact, such a lens (called a

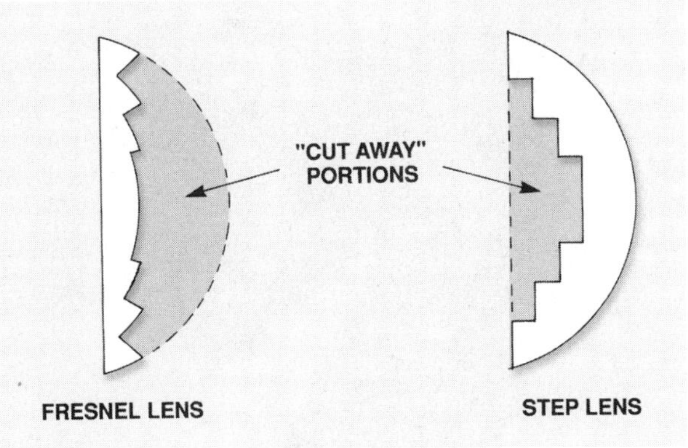

18-20

The Fresnel and Step Lenses

These simplified diagrams show how the Fresnel and step lenses are derived form the plano-convex lens.

step lens) was used in ellipsoidal reflector spotlights for a short period of time. Unfortunately, disturbing ring patterns from the step risers were apparent in the light beam. In addition, the quality of light was not as sharp and crisp as that from plano-convex lenses. Use was quickly discontinued.

In order to avoid similar difficulties, the plano surface of a theatre Fresnel lens is broken up by either a light frosting or by a series of dimples molded into the glass. This slight diffraction results in the smooth and soft illumination distinctive of the Fresnel spotlight.

Fresnel Operational Features

The Fresnel spotlight has variable beam-spread capability. As shown in Figure 18-19, the lamp and reflector are both mounted on a sliding carriage that can be moved closer to or farther from the lens.

Spot Focus and Flood Focus When the lamp is moved all the way forward, the light beam achieves its largest diameter, or **flood focus.** As the lamp is slid back away from the lens, the light beam becomes narrower. All the way back is called **spot focus.** Movement of the carriage is accomplished by means of a worm screw or a simple thumbscrew extending from the bottom of the instrument. The box lists field angles for typical 6- and 8-inch Fresnels at both spot and flood focus.

flood focus The largest of the variable beam sizes of a Fresnel spotlight.

spot focus The smallest of the variable beam sizes of a Fresnel spotlight.

Light Reading

Fresnel Field Angles

	Spot Field Angle	Flood Field Angle
6-inch Fresnel	16°	60°
8-inch Fresnel	14°	50°

PHOTO COURTESY STRAND LIGHTING

18-21

A Fresnel with Barn Doors

The four-way barn doors at the front of the instrument slide into the color-frame holder and allow for beam shaping.

barn door An accessory for the Fresnel spotlight that attaches at the color-frame holder and allows for linear beam-shaping from four sides.

top hat An accessory for the Fresnel spotlight that attaches at the color-frame holder and reduces spill and glare from the instrument's lens.

Beam Shaping Although internal beam shaping is not possible, an accessory called a **barn door** can be added. Placed in the color frame holder of the instrument, a barn door effectively shapes the beam by cutting it in a linear manner from any of four sides (Figure 18-21). Most barn doors can be rotated to allow cuts of any angle. The well-equipped theatre has barn doors for every Fresnel in its inventory.

Many newer Fresnels are provided with a top locking device as part of the color frame holder. Even so, it is wise to "safety" a barn door to the pipe or yoke of the instrument by means of a small chain or wire rope. This is particularly important for larger Fresnels, whose barn doors are heavy and easily dislodged by scenery flying on an adjacent batten.

Another accessory, useful for any instrument but particularly valuable with a Fresnel, is the **top hat** or *snoot.* A top hat is nothing more than a tin can, open on both ends and attached to a rectangular metal frame sized to fit into the color holder. Painted flat black inside and out, the top hat controls lens flare by absorbing stray light refracted by the risers of the Fresnel lens. If a lens is in audience sight, light flare from it can be quite distracting; therefore, top hats are most often used in backlight and box boom positions.

Fresnel Beam Characteristics

The beam of light from a Fresnel is soft in quality, with a smooth, even field. Its light appears to wrap around a figure; shadows are soft-edged, not harsh. The Fresnel is useful for "washing" walls and drops with smooth and even coverage. It is excellent in short-throw applications, blending one acting area with another.

The light from a Fresnel exhibits a good sense of direction. It can be used to simulate the soft quality of candlelight, an overcast sky, or any other diffuse source. In a proscenium theatre the Fresnel's usefulness is generally limited to over-stage positions, because its scattered beam characteristics cause too much illumination in the auditorium.

Fresnel Sizes

Fresnel spotlights come in several sizes, the smallest of which has a 3-inch lens and takes up to a 150-watt lamp (Figure 18-22). Fondly called an "inky,"

a

b

b PHOTO COURTESY COLORTRAN

18-22

Fresnel Sizes

a A 3-inch "inky," which takes a 150-watt lamp and can hide in a small space.

b A 10-inch, 5,000-watt studio Fresnel.

this little instrument does not possess much punch but is handy for tucking into small corners.

The most common Fresnel is the 6-inch, which uses 500- to 1,000-watt incandescent lamps. Short- to medium-throw distances of 15 to 25 feet are best suited to the 6-inch instrument. This spotlight is valuable for lighting upstage acting areas, where its soft-edged beam fades away on the scenery.

For larger stages and longer throw distances, the 8-inch Fresnel is recommended. It takes up to a 2,000-watt incandescent lamp and delivers a powerful beam with the typical smooth Fresnel pattern. The Fresnel spotlight is also available with lenses from 10 to 20 inches in diameter and lamps of 5,000 or even 10,000 watts. These instruments, primarily intended for television and film use, deliver a vast amount of soft illumination.

THE PAR FIXTURE

The heart of the **PAR fixture** is the parabolic aluminized reflector lamp, which was invented by Clarence Birdseye, the pioneer of frozen foods. The 1,000-watt PAR-64 version of this lamp soon became the mainstay of concert lighting. The PAR lamp is a self-contained instrument, lacking only a housing and conventional plug. The PAR fixture's extruded-metal housing, sometimes called a "PAR can," secures the PAR-64 lamp in place by means of a large spring ring. It also acts like a top hat, absorbing some of the abundant flare caused by the built-in lens of the lamp (Figure 18-23). The butt of the housing hinges open to allow access to the lamp and socket. Color-frame holders, including a top safety clip, are fixed to the front of the fixture.

PAR fixture A lighting instrument using the parabolic aluminized reflector lamp. It produces a strong and harsh beam of light that is oval with soft edges. Its field is rather uneven.

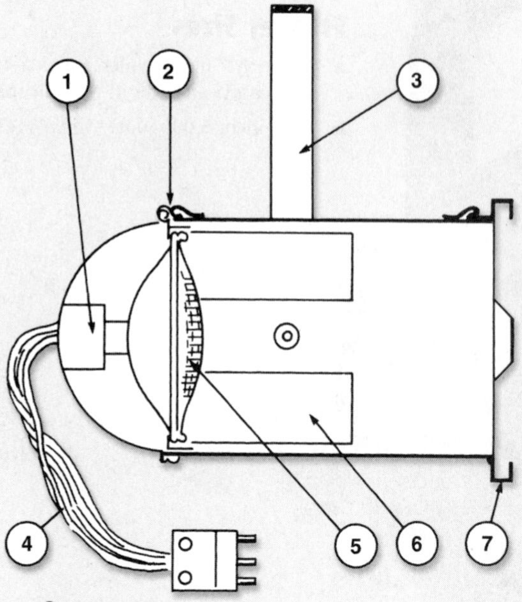

a

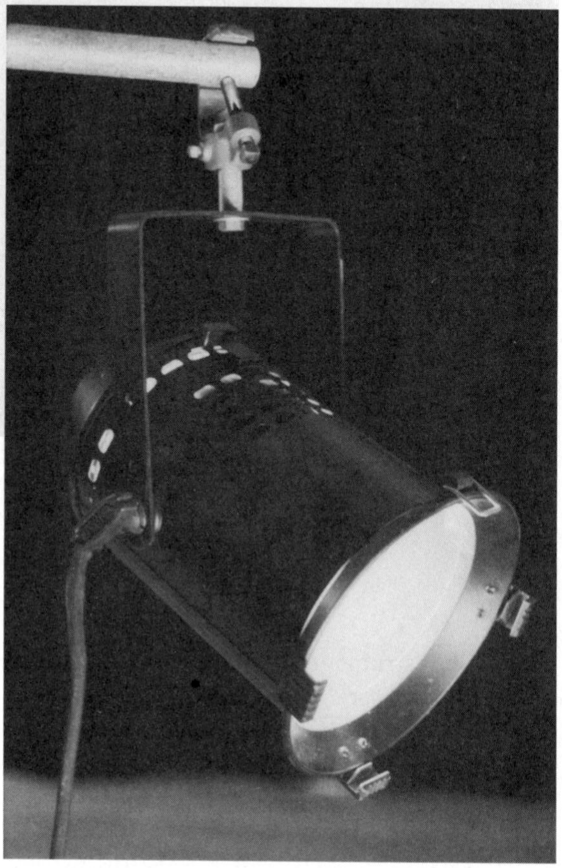

b

18-23

The PAR-64 Fixture

a Illustration of the PAR fixture:
  1 Lamp socket.
  2 Rear latch allowing access to lamp.
  3 Yoke.
  4 Three-wire cord and pin connector.
  5 1,000-watt PAR-64 lamp.
  6 Light baffle.
  7 Color-frame holder.

b An actual PAR-64 fixture. Note flare from the lamp on the inside of the housing.

The PAR-64 Lamp

Incandescent PAR-type lamps are available in many sizes, but the 8-inch PAR-64 is the theatrical standard. The lamp's parabolic reflector causes reflected light to leave the lamp in parallel rays. The lens serves only to redirect those nonparallel rays of light emanating from the front of the filament. A unique feature of the PAR-64 lamp is its oval beam, which is more than twice as tall as it is wide. PAR-64 lamps are available with four different beam sizes, as shown in the box.

The Source Four PAR

ETC developed a new PAR-type fixture based on Source Four technology. It takes the same lamp that a Source Four ellipsoidal does, it is more compact than a traditional PAR, and the 750-watt version is considerably brighter than standard PARs. The instrument comes with four interchangeable lenses that mimic the beam spreads of a PAR-64 lamp. The beam is oval, and the lenses can be rotated (Figure 18-24).

If the lens of a Source Four PAR is visible to the audience, it is best to add a top hat to the front of the fixture to cut down on the typical PAR lens flair. Standard 6-inch top hats and barn doors fit the Source Four PAR.

PAR Characteristics

The oval beam of light from a PAR fixture cannot be effectively altered or adequately controlled. The use of barn doors tends to dim rather than shape the beam of light. However, the direction of the oval can be changed by simply rotating the lamp within its housing.

Because of its parabolic reflector, the quality of light from a PAR fixture is harsh. In contrast, the beam edge remains quite diffuse because of the lens. Because PAR fixtures deliver a very bright light, they make good back-lights. However, evenly blending several PARs with one another is difficult. Like the Fresnel, the use of PAR fixtures is normally limited to over stage.

Relative to other stage instruments, the PAR-64 fixture is nearly indestructible, making it ideal for touring. Its fairly inexpensive lamp lasts a long time as well.

PHOTO COURTESY ELECTRONIC THEATRE CONTROLS

18-24

Source Four PAR

ETC Source Four PAR uses a 575- or 750-watt HPL lamp instead of the common PAR-64 lamp. Interchangeable lenses adjust the beam spread in a fashion similar to a standard PAR.

Light Reading

PAR-64 Beam Sizes and Spreads

The Incandescent PAR-64 lamp is rated at 1,000 watts and is available in the following beam spreads:

Beam Size	ANSI Code	Beam Angle	Field Angle
Very Narrow	FFN	6° × 12°	10° × 24°
Narrow	FFP	7° × 14°	14° × 26°
Medium	FFR	12° × 28°	21° × 44°
Wide	FFS	24° × 48°	45° × 71°

OTHER THEATRE INSTRUMENTS

In addition to the ERS, Fresnel, and PAR, theatre lighting employs various other instruments for more specialized needs. These include the following:

- Other parabolic reflector instruments
- Automated fixtures
- High intensity discharge (HID) fixtures
- Follow spots
- Cyclorama and backdrop lighting fixtures
- Floodlights
- Borderlights

Other Parabolic Reflector Instruments

The parallel rays of light produced by a parabolic reflector serve well as a harsh theatrical source of light. However, designers who use parabolic reflector instruments have always had to contend with the diverging light rays that come out of the front of the lamp.

URL http://www.pani.com

The Beam Projector The *beam projector* is a parabolic reflector instrument without a lens. The most recent manifestation of this instrument is Pani's P 500 Parabolic Spotlight (Figure 18-25). It uses a 24-volt lamp, which has a very small filament, allowing superior control of its light. This is a bright, harsh source that has been used successfully as a short-range follow spot.

The Source Four PARNel Another new instrument developed by ETC is the PARNel. As its name implies, this fixture combines the strong, bright light of a PAR with the even beam and adjustability of a Fresnel instrument. The

18-25

Beam Projector

Pani's P 500 parabolic spotlight uses a 500-watt, 24-volt lamp and produces a highly concentrated beam of light.

PHOTO COURTESY PANI

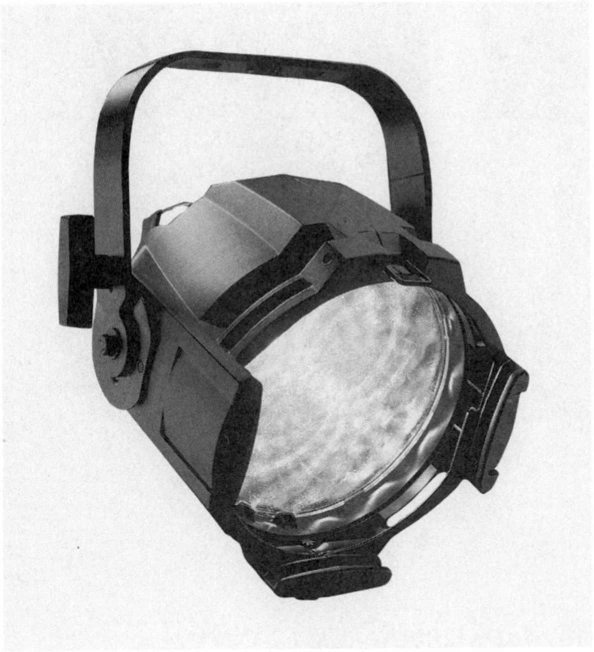
PHOTO COURTESY ELECTRONIC THEATRE CONTROLS

18-26

Source Four PARNel

ETC Source Four PARNel is a spotlight with the light characteristics of a PAR and the adjustable beam spread of a Fresnel. It uses the 575- or 750-watt HPL lamp and has field angles from 25 to 45 degrees. Beam size is changed by rotating the lenses.

PARNel can take a lamp up to 750 watts and offers an adjustable field spread of 25 to 45 degrees. A single knob makes the adjustment from spot to flood (Figure 18-26).

Automated Fixtures

In the next few decades, some theatres may very well be equipped exclusively with automated fixtures. Even today, lighting equipment for big name concert tours often comprises automated fixtures alone. Although the trendy popularity of moving light may wane, the potential offered by the technology cannot be denied.

The minimum requirement of an automated fixture is that it must accurately and repeatedly reproduce a focus assignment. To do so, remotely controlled pan and tilt motors receive a DMX signal from the control console. Normally, a single channel of control is assigned to each of the fixture's functions. Sophistication varies greatly, but the most advanced instruments change focus, intensity, color, beam size, gobo pattern, and light quality.

There are two basic types of automated fixtures: (1) a *moving fixture,* often called a **moving head,** and (2) a fixed instrument whose light moves by virtue of a *moving mirror.*

moving head The type of automated lighting fixture in which the entire body (rather than simply a mirror) moves to change focus.

Moving Fixtures There is little dispute that the leader in moving fixture design has been Vari*Lite. In the early years, its two primary lighting fixtures were the VL2 spot luminaire and the VL4 wash luminaire (Figure 18-27). Both are still available for rent. The VL2B version of the VL2 uses a 600-watt HTI arc lamp, and the VL4 uses a 400-watt arc lamp; both produce an extremely bright light with color temperatures of 5,000°K.

URL http://www.vari-lite.com

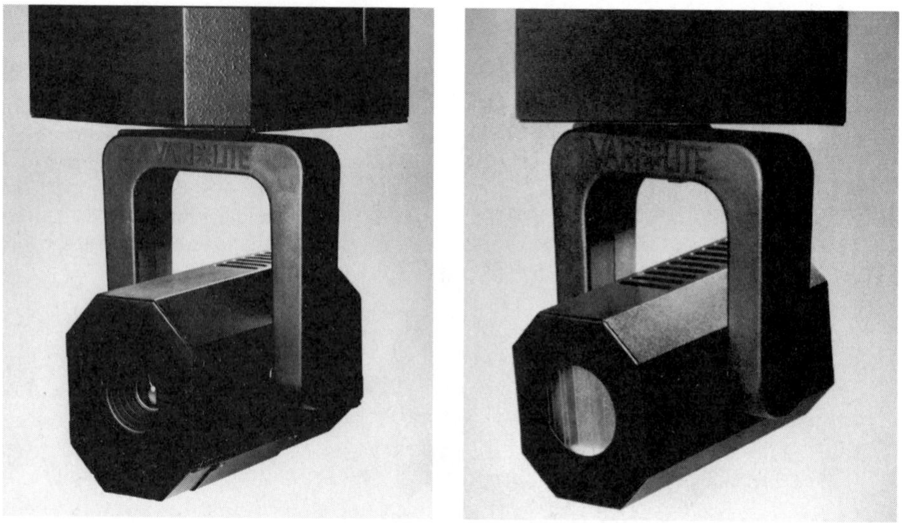

a b

a & b PHOTOS COURTESY VARI*LITE

18-27

Early Vari*Lite Spot and Wash Luminaires

These two arc lamp automated fixtures were Vari*Lite's primary concert lighting fixtures for many years.

a VL2B spot luminaire. **b** VL4 wash luminaire.

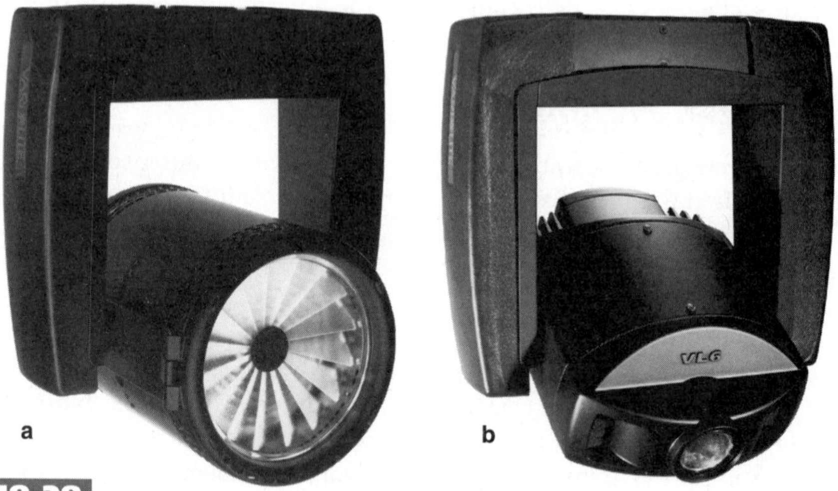

a b

a & b PHOTOS COURTESY VARI*LITE

18-28

Vari*Lite VL5 and VL6 Automated Fixtures

Vari*Lite's first instruments suitable for theatrical applications.

a VL5 wash luminaire. **b** VL6 spot luminaire.

In the early 1990s, Vari*Lite introduced what many considered to be its first theatrical fixture, the VL5 wash luminaire (Figure 18-28a). Cooled by convection and therefore quiet, it uses a dimmable 1,000-watt tungsten halogen lamp with a color temperature of 3,200°K. Internal dichroic color filters provide a wide range of colors. Interchangeable front lenses in conjunction with textured glass panels acting as beam diffusers offer a variety of beam shapes, sizes, and qualities. Soon to follow was the VL6 spot luminaire (Figure 18-28b). This fixture uses an arc lamp and provides a limited range of colors and gobos.

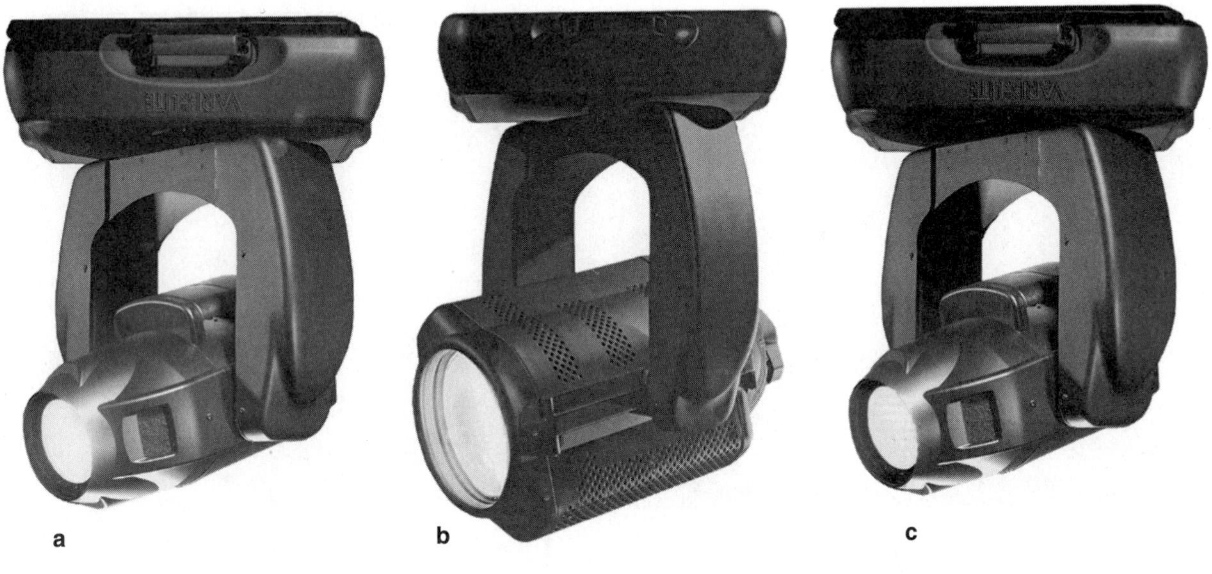

a–c PHOTOS COURTESY VARI*LITE

18-29

Modern Vari*Lite Automated Fixtures

This latest line of fixtures from Vari*Lite can be rented or purchased.

a VL2202 spot luminaire. **b** VL2416 wash luminaire. **c** VL2402 wash luminaire.

It has an iris and offers hard to soft beam-edge control. Perhaps the most important feature of the VL5 and VL6 is their capacity to be controlled by any DMX-512 control console. Both fixtures remain available for rent.

The latest line of fixtures from Vari*Lite, the VL2200 spot luminaire series and the VL2400 wash luminaire series, can be rented or purchased. (Vari*Lite's recent decision to sell equipment is a significant and welcome policy change.) In addition, the 2000 series of luminaires can be controlled by any DMX system. The VL2202 spot luminaire (Figure 18-29a) is based on the VL6B. Its features include the following:

- 400-watt metal halide arc lamp with color temperature of 5,500°K
- Variable field spread of 13 to 35 degrees plus a mechanical iris
- Full mechanical dimming and strobe effects
- User-configurable eleven-position color wheel
- User-configurable eleven-position gobo wheel
- Five rotating gobo positions
- Variable beam focus for soft or hard edges
- Requirement of seventeen DMX control channels

The VL2416 wash luminaire (Figure 18-29b) is based on the VL5. It has the following features:

- 1,200-watt short arc lamp with color temperature of 5,600°K
- Variable field spread of 5 to 55 degrees
- Internal mechanical douser for intensity control

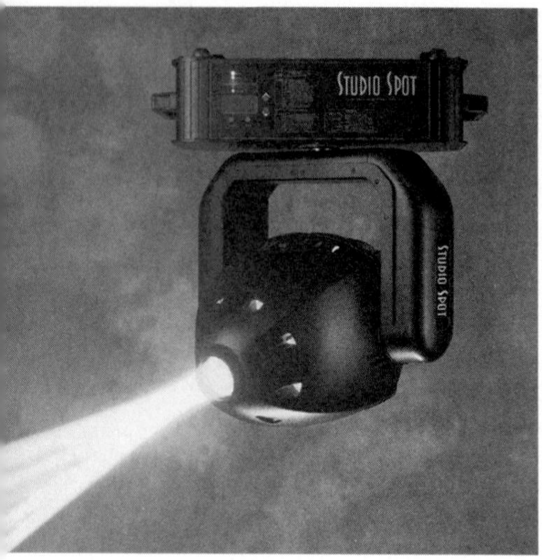

a

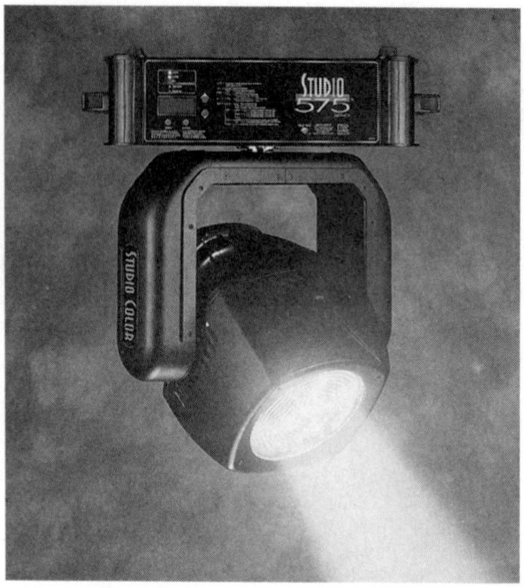

b

c

a–c PHOTOS COURTESY HIGH END SYSTE

18-30

Modern High End Automated Fixtures

a Studio Spot CMY.

b Studio Color 575.

c X.Spot, offering a zoom range of 11 to 45 degrees.

CYM color mixing A color-mixing system involving the use of the secondary colors in light: cyan, yellow, and magenta.

- Radial color changing mechanism using **CYM color mixing**
- Requirement of fifteen DMX control channels

The newest of Vari*Lite's wash luminaries is the VL2402 (Figure 18-29c). It is the same size as a spot luminaire (hang on 19-inch centers). It has the following features:

- 700-watt metal halide short arc lamp with color temperature of 5,600°K
- Variable field spread of 12 to 56 degrees
- Full mechanical dimming and strobe effects
- Cross-fading CYM color-mixing system
- Eleven-position fixed dichroic color wheel
- Requirement of fifteen DMX control channels

URL http://www.highend.com

High End Systems, known for the popular Intellabeam moving mirror instrument, entered the moving head market with their Studio Spot and Studio Color luminaries. The Studio Spot CMY shown in Figure 18-30a has CYM color mixing, ten rotating gobo patterns, a variable iris, and a mechanical strobe. Its arc lamp produces a color temperature of 6,200°K, and control requires twenty-four DMX channels. The Studio Color 575 luminaire shown in Figure 18-30b has color mixing plus five fixed dichroic colors, variable frost, beam shaping, and a mechanical strobe. Its 575-watt arc lamp produces a color temperature of 6,200°K, and control requires sixteen DMX channels. The newest addition to High End's moving head line is the X.Spot. This spot

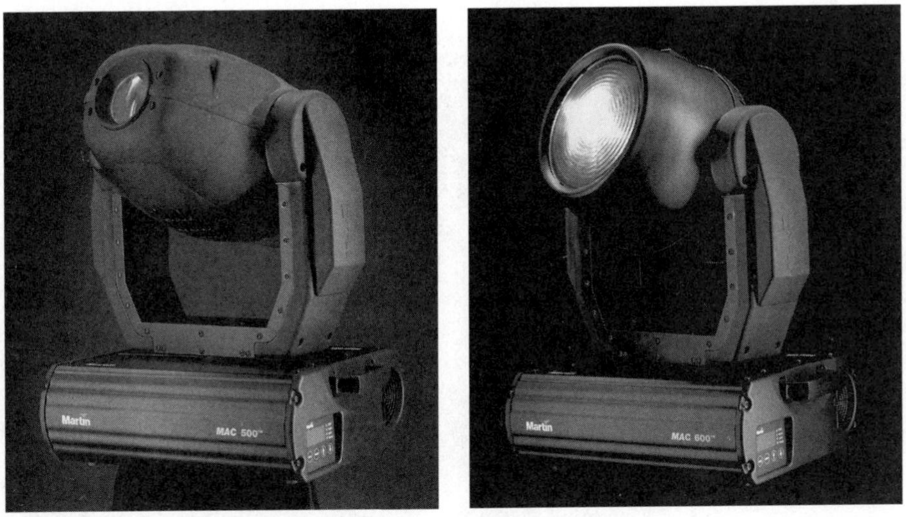

a b

a & b PHOTOS COURTESY MARTIN

18-31

Modern Martin Automated Fixtures

a MAC 500 spot luminaire.

b MAC 600 wash luminaire.

fixture has an impressive zoom lens range of 11 to 45 degrees. It is bright, offers fourteen gobo patterns and seven effects, and has internal color mixing and a variable iris (Figure 18-30c).

A third company who manufactures quality moving head fixtures is Martin. They have a large range of fixtures, from the compact MiniMAC to the impressive MAC 600. The MAC 500 (Figure 18-31a) is a spot luminaire using a 575-watt arc discharge lamp. It has two color wheels with nine replaceable dichroic color slots, a rotating prism, a motorized iris and focus, two rotating gobo wheels with five slots each, and a requirement of sixteen DMX channels. The MAC 600 (Figure 18-31b) is a wash luminaire that also uses a 575-watt arc discharge lamp. It has a CYM color-mixing system plus a four-position fixed color wheel, full-range continuous dimming, beam shaping, and diffusion.

URL http://www.martin.dk

All of these moving lights are highly sophisticated and remain fairly expensive, although prices are coming down as demand increases. The best news is that previous difficulties with control consoles have been addressed—nearly all new equipment runs off DMX. The biggest problem with moving heads is noise. When several units move at the same time, the noise is too loud for a quiet moment in the theatre.

Fixtures with Moving Mirrors Although moving heads seem to be the most popular form of automated fixtures, several manufacturers produce instruments with moving mirrors. As noted earlier, High End Systems and Lightwave Research established themselves in this market with the Intellabeam 700HX automated fixture. Soon after, the impressive Cyberlight was introduced, followed by Trackspot and Technobeam (Figure 18-32). Trackspot is a small luminaire with limited features and intensity too low for most theatre applications. Technobeam has a 6,500°K lamp, but its lumen output is only 4,000 lumens (compared with 9,000 from the Studio Spot CMY). It has twelve fixed dichroic colors, seven fixed and seven rotating gobo patterns, 11- to 17-degree beam spread, and a mechanical strobe. The variable iris is a highly recommended option. Technobeam has proven to be a good, reliable moving mirror fixture, but its low intensity cannot cut through bright stage lighting.

Martin, who manufactures MAC moving head luminaries, also produces a line of quality moving mirror fixtures. The PAL 1200 (Figure 18-33a) has a

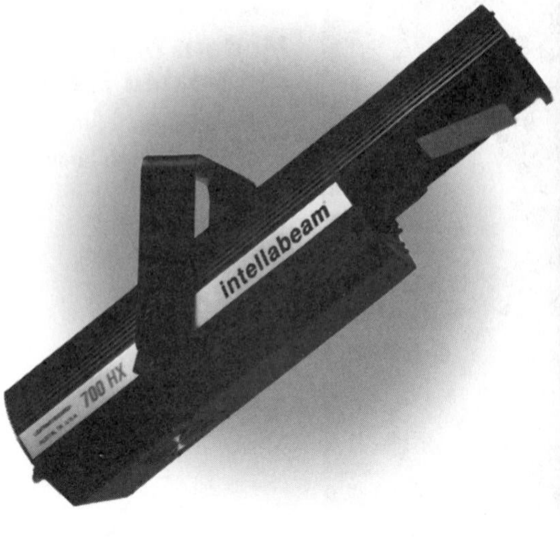

a

b

a & b PHOTOS COURTESY HIGH END SYSTEMS

18-32

High End Moving Mirror Automated Fixtures

a Intellabeam 700HX—an early industry standard in moving mirror fixtures.

b Technobeam.

1,200-watt arc discharge lamp producing a color temperature of 5,500°K. Its features include the following:

- CYM color mixing
- 16- to 26-degree zoom as well as mechanical iris
- Variable dimming
- Variable frost
- Fixed dichroic color wheel
- Gobo wheel with four rotating positions
- Effect wheel with three rotating positions
- Requirement of up to twenty DMX channels

Martin's RoboScan Pro 918 moving mirror fixture (Figure 18-33b) has a 575-watt arc lamp, which is nearly as bright as the PAL 1200. Its features include the following:

- Two color wheels: one with nine fixed and one with nine replaceable dichroic filters
- Two gobo wheels: one with nine fixed and one with five rotating replaceable gobos
- Dimmer/shutter with mechanical strobe
- Three-facet rotating prism
- Variable iris
- Requirement of up to sixteen DMX channels

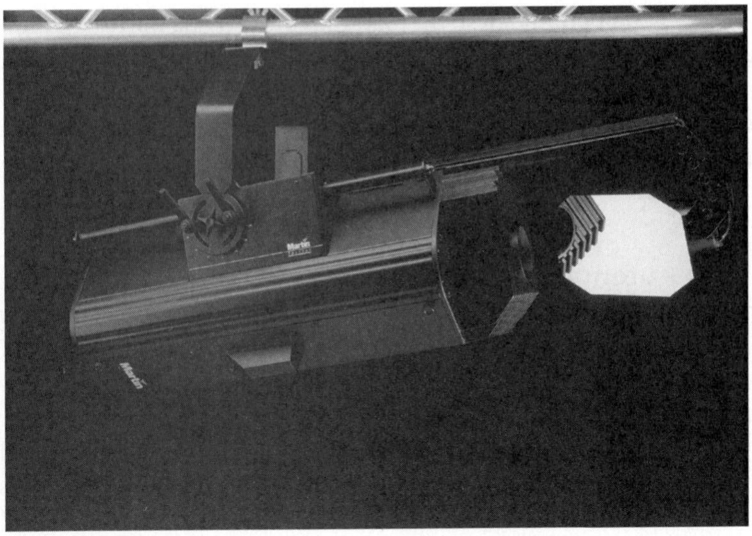

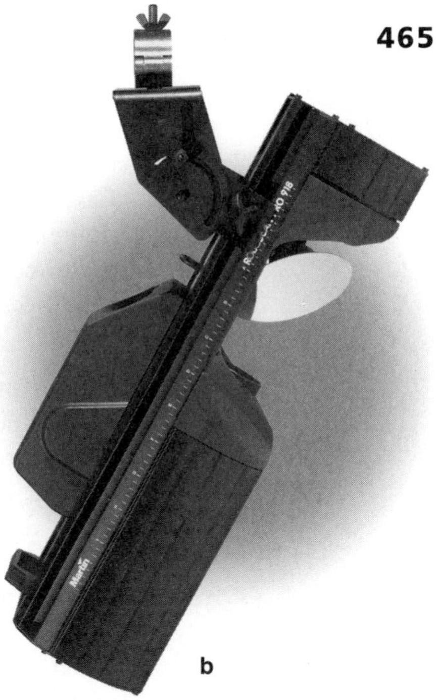

a & b PHOTOS COURTESY MARTIN

a b

18-33

Martin Moving Mirror Automated Fixtures

a PAL 1200.

b RoboScan Pro 918.

A third company manufacturing both moving head and moving mirror fixtures is Clay Paky. Known for its popular Golden Scan, Clay Paky now has a full line of moving mirror luminaries that include Golden Scan HPE and Stage Scan (Figure 18-34). Golden Scan HPE offers a bright, 1,200-watt HMI arc lamp, a large selection of color, a mechanical iris and dimming, and prism effects. The new Stage Scan also has a 1,200-watt HMI lamp with a color temperature of 5,600°K and offers the following features:

URL http://www.claypaky.it

- Interchangeable lenses for beam spreads of 13 to 25 degrees
- Two gobo wheels: one with four fixed and one with four rotating interchangeable gobos
- RGB (red, green, blue) color mixing
- Special effects, including four rotating and one static prism
- Variable iris
- Variable dimming and mechanical strobe

None of the fixtures just discussed are small. The Technobeam is almost 3 feet long and weighs 42 pounds. Martin's PAL 1200 is nearly 5 feet long and weighs in at a hefty 135 pounds!

18-34

Clay Paky Moving Mirror Automated Fixtures

a Golden Scan HPE.

b Stage Scan.

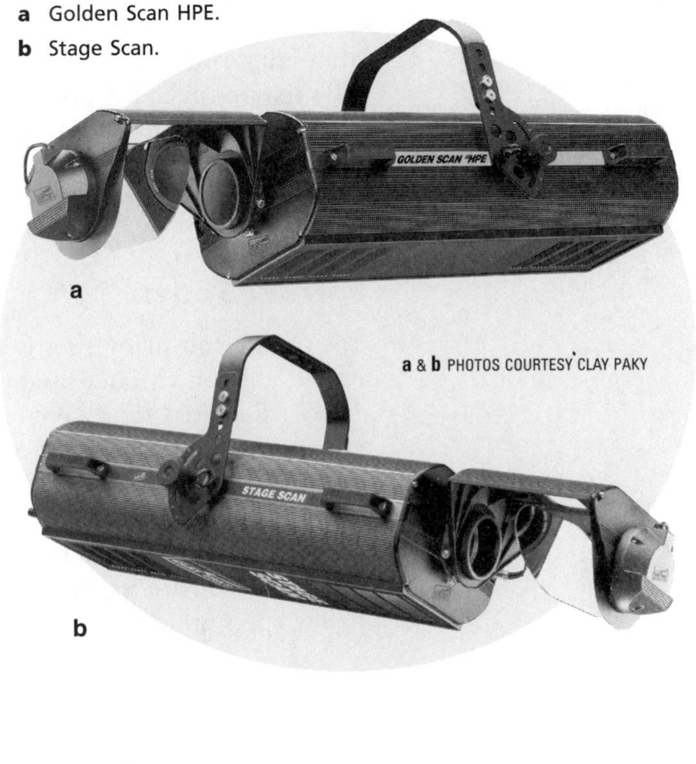

a b

a & b PHOTOS COURTESY CLAY PAKY

Both Clay Paky and High End Systems manufacture moving mirror fixtures that are even more powerful and sophisticated: the Super Scan Zoom and the Cyberlight Turbo. This generation of automated fixtures offers remarkable options. They are actually effects projectors that, incidentally, can light a performer. As such, they will be discussed in the following chapter on projection and effects.

Designing with Automated Fixtures Improvements in control systems have made theatrical design with moving lights considerably simpler. It is now possible to control a limited number of automated fixtures with any DMX console. However, such control is painstakingly slow unless a console specifically designed for moving lights is used.

Certainly, a single automated fixture can do the job of several fixed instruments. Although the automated fixture is a valuable tool, it remains to be seen how completely the theatre will embrace this technology. Successful designing with light requires as much control as possible over color, angle, distribution, and movement. In many ways automated fixtures offer much more control than standard fixtures do. However, unless used in great quantities, automated fixtures lack a certain flexibility, because the angle of light remains dependent on a fixed source. In this way, several conventional fixed instruments are more flexible than one automated fixture.

High Intensity Discharge (HID) Fixtures

HID lamps are arc sources that provide great intensity and light with a high color temperature. However, arc sources vary a great deal in terms of the color makeup of their light and therefore how they render color onstage. Some of the better arc sources are HMI (heavy metal iodine), metal halide, and xenon. Generally, xenon is too unstable for small lighting applications, but HMI and metal halide sources are common in automated fixtures and follow spots. In its quest for new and bright sources, the theatre has begun to put HID fixtures to use. They have been available for several years in the form of PAR lamps and in Fresnel fixtures (Figures 18-35 a and b). NSI Colortran makes an arc Mini-Ellipse (Figure 18-35c) and ETC manufactures a line of Source Four HID fixtures intended primarily for architectural use (Figure 18-35d).

Being arc sources, HID lamps require a heavy, bulky ballast and cannot be electronically dimmed. Use in the theatre requires the addition of a mechanical dimmer or **douser** such as the Eclipse from Wybron (Figure 18-36).

douser A mechanical device, commonly found in follow spots, used to dim the light. Sometimes spelled *dowser.*

URL http://www.wybron.com

Follow Spots

The traditional follow spot is a specialty instrument intended to produce a bright and concentrated beam of light over a long throw distance (Figure 18-37). Required for a certain style of Broadway musical, the instruments and their operators are most often situated at the very rear of the auditorium in the uppermost balcony. In concerts, multiple follow spots are used to highlight lead singers and musicians. In large venues, with some audience members several hundred feet away from the performers, extremely high levels of illumination are required for visibility. Sometimes as many as six or eight follow spots are concentrated on one performer.

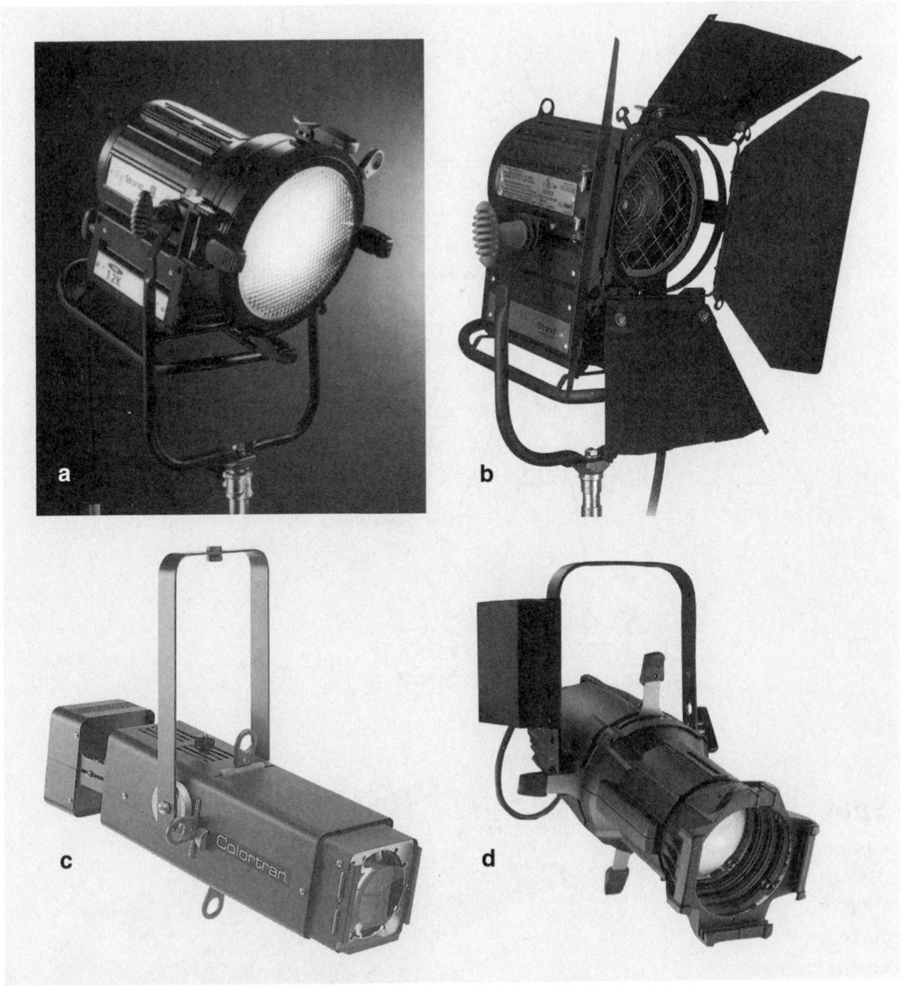

a & b PHOTOS COURTESY STRAND LIGHTING

c PHOTO COURTESY NSI/COLORTRAN

d PHOTO COURTESY ELECTRONIC THEATRE CONTROLS

18-35

High-Intensity Discharge Arc Light Fixtures

- **a** Strand's QuartzColor 1,200-watt arc light PAR fixture.
- **b** Strand's 575-watt HMI arc light Fresnel.
- **c** Colortran's 70- or 150-watt arc light Mini-Ellipse.
- **d** ETC's 150-watt HID Source Four. All the features of a Source Four ERS, with an arc light source added.

PHOTO COURTESY WYBRON, INC.

18-36

Remotely Controlled Mechanical Douser

Wybron Eclipse DMX-controlled mechanical dousers offer cross fades up to 60 seconds long and 5 "fast cuts" per second.

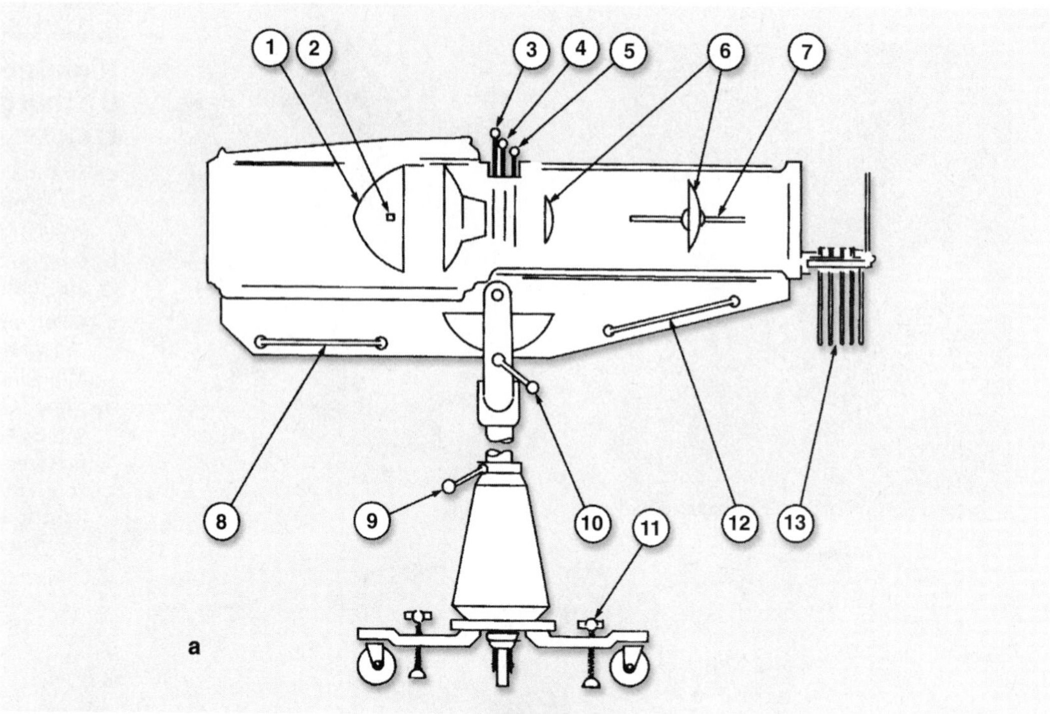

a

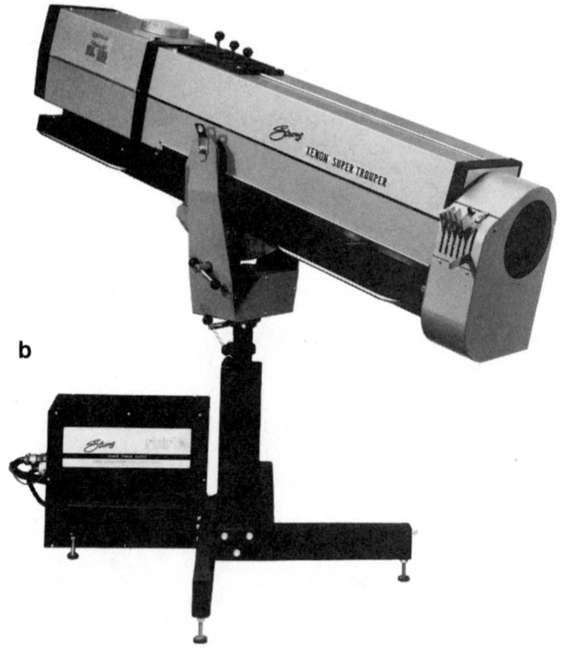

b

PHOTO COURTESY STRONG ENTERTAINMENT LIGHTING

18-37

The Follow Spot

a The major components of a long-throw follow spot:

1 Spherical reflector.
2 Arc lamp source.
3 Dimming control (douser).
4 Horizontal shutter control.
5 Iris control.
6 Lens system.
7 Zoom track.
8 Rear pan/tilt handle.
9 Pan lock.
10 Tilt lock.
11 Lock-down stabilizer.
12 Front pan/tilt handle.
13 Six-color boomerang.

b Strong Super Trouper with a xenon arc lamp.

color boomerang A device, located in the front of the barrel of a follow spot, that holds several color filters, allowing for quick color changes.

A spherical reflector is used to help direct the light to an aperture similar to that of the ERS. An iris and a douser are located near the aperture. Also in this vicinity is a mechanism variously called a "damper" or a "clipper" or "curtain shutters" that chops the beam of light in a horizontal manner. Mounted in a long barrel in front of the aperture is a lens, or lenses, that can be moved to adjust beam size and sharpness. A device called a **color boomerang,** which normally holds six color filters, allows for rapid changes.

Truss-Mount Follow Spots The design of a follow spot depends on its function and throw distance. Some follow spots such as the Strong Truss

a PHOTO COURTESY STRONG ENTERTAINMENT LIGHTING
b PHOTO COURTESY LYCIAN STAGE LIGHTING
c PHOTO COURTESY PHOEBUS MANUFACTURING

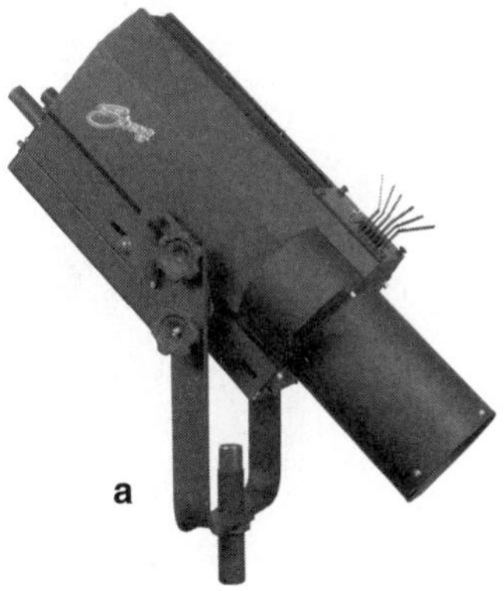
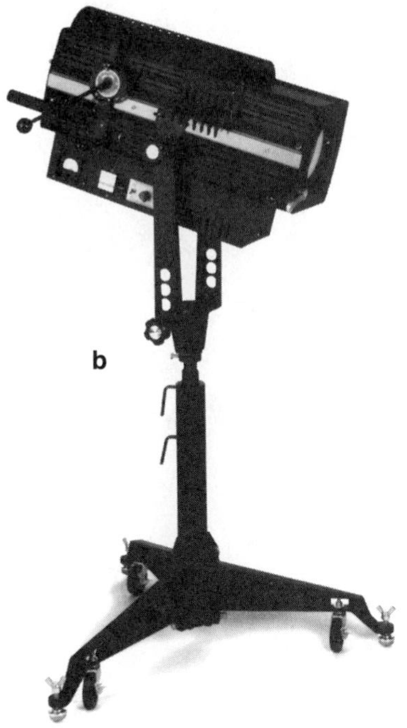
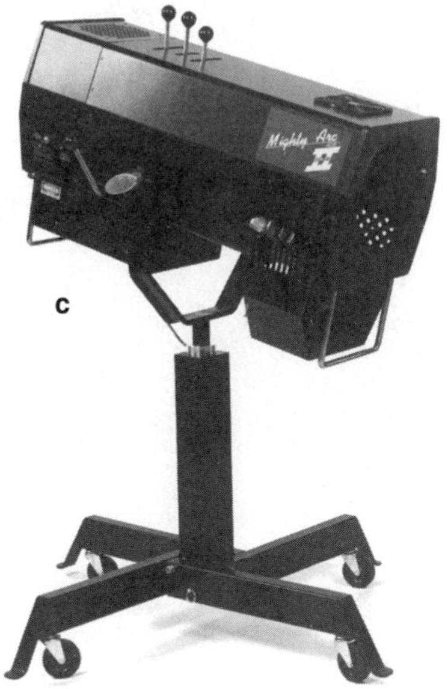

18-38

Truss-Mount Short-Throw Follow Spots

a Strong Truss Trouper.
b Lycian Super Arc 400.
c Phoebus Mighty Arc II.

Trouper, Lycian Super Arc 400, and Phoebus Mighty Arc II are designed for truss mounting (Figure 18-38). They are used primarily in concert situations where the fixture and an operator work from a **lighting truss** located above the performance space. They also serve well for high-angle theatrical follow-spotting from over-stage or ceiling positions. Strong's Truss Trouper uses a 1,200-watt HMI arc lamp and has interchangeable lens assemblies for short, medium, or long throws. The unit is only 29 inches long with the short-throw lens and weighs about 100 pounds. The Lycian Super Arc 400 uses a 400-watt HTI metal halide arc lamp with light output similar to the Truss Trouper. It is 32 inches long and weighs 93 pounds. The Mighty Arc II from Phoebus uses a 400-watt HTI metal halide arc lamp with a color temperature of 5,600°K. It is 33 inches long.

URL http://www.strongint.com

URL http://www.lycian.com

URL http://www.phoebus.com

lighting truss Metal tubing, often aluminum, welded together in a crossing pattern for strength; used to support lighting equipment.

Long-Throw Follow Spots Long-throw follow spots must deliver a high-intensity light. Carbon arc, the original source, has been replaced by metal halide or xenon arc lamps. The first Strong Trouper carbon arc follow spot was introduced in 1948. The xenon arc Super Trouper was placed on the market in 1975. Today, Strong International manufactures a line of ten follow spots recommended for throw distances from 30 to 500 feet. Figure 18-39a shows Strong's new Super Trouper II. It is smaller, lighter, and brighter than previous Super Troupers. It has a xenon lamp and features a manual dimming control. The Ultra Arc II follow spot from Phoebus (Figure 18-39b) uses a 400-watt HTI metal halide arc lamp. An optional auto zoom feature is available; it maintains a sharp focus as beam angle is changed. Clay Paky, the manufacturer of Golden Scan automated fixtures, has introduced a remotely controlled follow spot called Shadow (Figure 18-39c). Depending on the required throw distance, the Shadow uses either a 575- or 1,200-watt arc lamp. The control panel is normally rear mounted and allows the operator push-button control of intensity, color, and beam size. The Shadow uses a variable-speed dichroic filter color wheel instead of the conventional color boomerang.

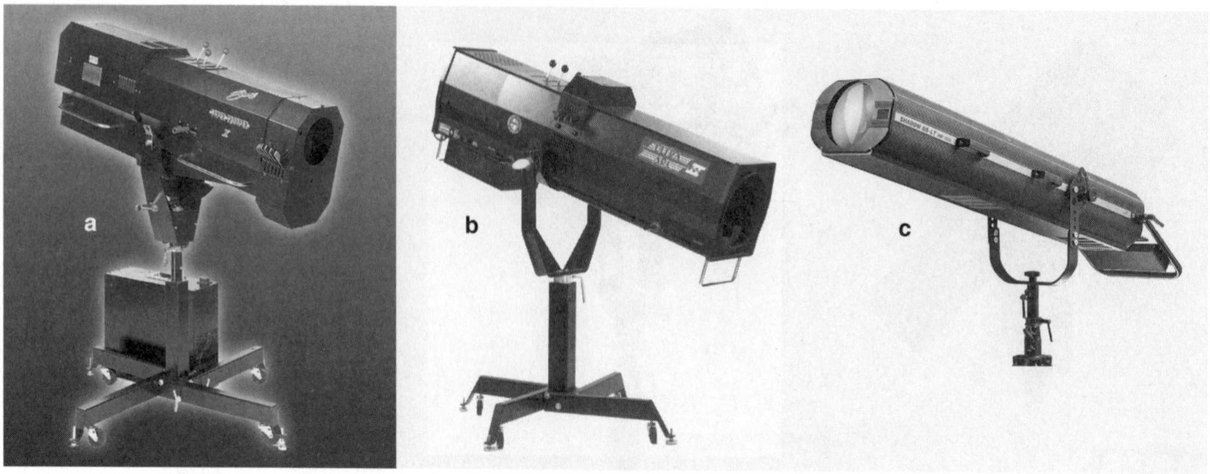

a PHOTO COURTESY STRONG ENTERTAINMENT LIGHTING
b PHOTO COURTESY PHOEBUS MANUFACTURING
c PHOTO COURTESY CLAY PAKY

18-39

Long-Throw Follow Spots

a Strong Super Trouper II.
b Phoebus Ultra Arc II.
c Clay Paky Shadow.

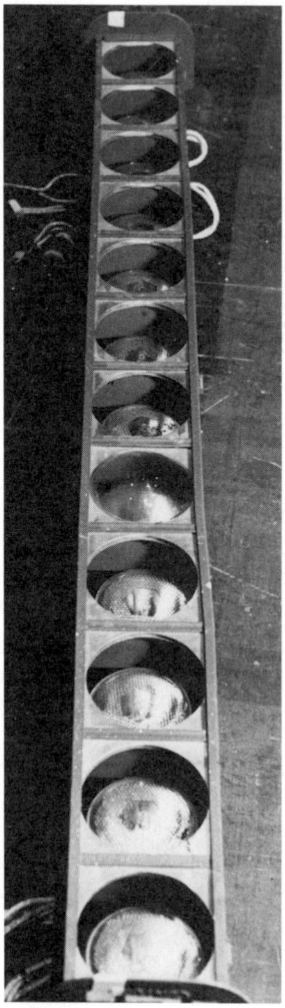

Cyclorama and Backdrop Lighting Fixtures

Lighting large surfaces such as cycloramas or scenic drops requires specialized equipment. The lighting instrument must be able to project a "wall" of light over a considerable distance while maintaining a smooth and even field. Drops are most often lit from above, although occasionally from below also.

Striplights One form of stage-lighting instrument that predates electricity is the **striplight,** which is a line of light created by multiple sources—formerly candle or gas, but now electric—placed adjacent to each other. Striplight lamps are usually wired in three or four color circuits. In a three-circuit, twelve-lamp striplight, the first, fourth, seventh, and tenth lamps operate together. A great variety of color can be attained by placing different colored filters in each circuit and mixing them by controlling their respective intensities. The lamps must be close together so that their various colored beams will blend.

For many years the basic type of striplight was the 6-foot section containing twelve PAR-36 or R-40, 150-watt lamps (Figure 18-40). With their common screw bases and built-in reflectors, these lamps produced a broad and relatively smooth sheet of light. The R-40 floodlight was used for short throws and the R-40 or PAR-36 spot provided a longer throw. Although one can still purchase striplights designed to use these or similar lamps, other light sources have proven to be more efficient.

striplight A row of lamps in a single housing used to create a wide and even wash of light; commonly used to illuminate backdrops.

18-40

Reflector-Lamp Striplight

A three-circuit striplight with PAR-36 spot lamps for a longer throw. An R-type flood lamp is normally used for short to medium throws.

a PHOTO COURTESY ALTMAN STAGE LIGHTING
b PHOTO COURTESY STRAND LIGHTING

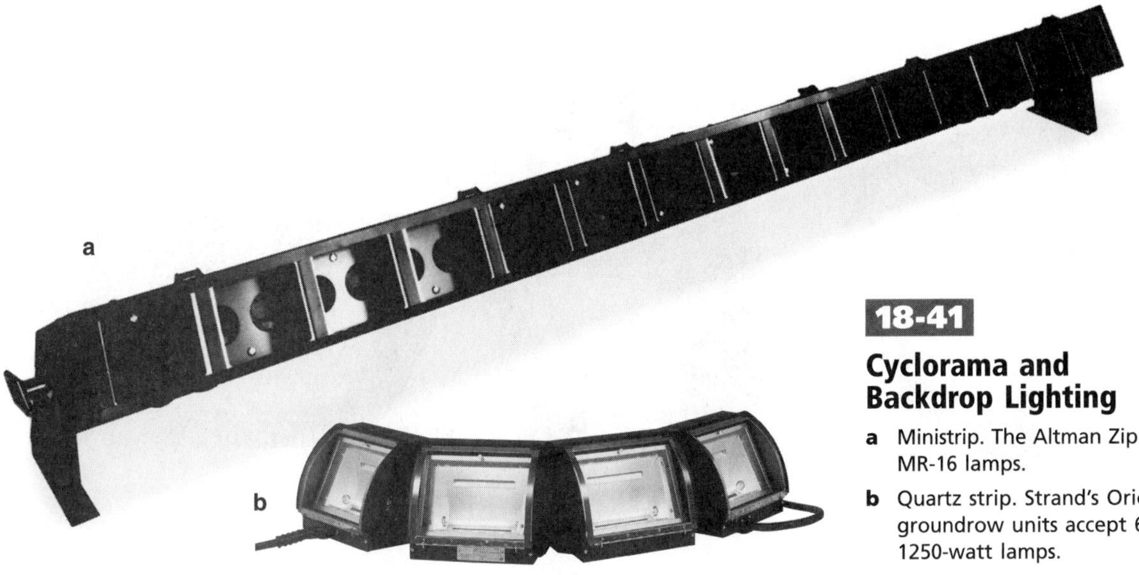

18-41

Cyclorama and Backdrop Lighting

a Ministrip. The Altman Zip Strip uses MR-16 lamps.

b Quartz strip. Strand's Orion groundrow units accept 625- and 1250-watt lamps.

Modern striplight sections use one of two light sources: **quartz strips** burn elongated 500-watt quartz lamps and throw a bright and even beam of light. **Ministrips** use concentrated-filament MR-16 lamps. Although both offer superior intensity with a smooth field, the ministrip is particularly useful because of its compactness (Figure 18-41).

quartz strips Striplights using long quartz lamps.

ministrips Striplights using MR-16 lamps.

Cyclights With the advent of the quartz lamp came a superior new design in cyclorama and drop lighting fixtures. Colortran was the first manufacturer to develop what they called the Far Cyc. Although each manufacturer uses a different trade name for its particular fixture, they all burn 1,000- to 2,000-watt quartz lamps and are available with one to four lamp compartments per section. As can be seen in Figure 18-42, the reflector is curved in an inverted J shape to project more of the light to the bottom of a backdrop or cyclorama.

PHOTO COURTESY COLORTRAN

18-42

The Far Cyc

A modern four-window cyclorama light developed by Colortran.

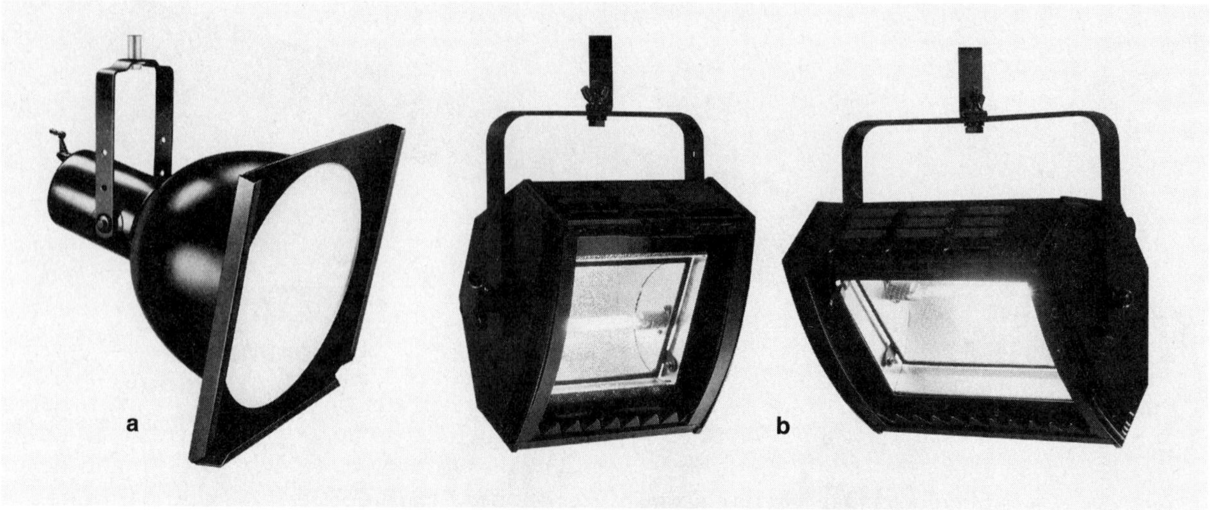

a PHOTO COURTESY ALTMAN STAGE LIGHTING
b PHOTOS COURTESY STRAND LIGHTING

18-43

Floodlights

a An ellipsoidal reflector floodlight, often called a *scoop,* can take a 1,000-watt lamp and provides a soft and even wash of light.

b Strand's Nocturne floodlight is available with 500- or 1,000-watt lamps and delivers a wide, even wash of light.

Floodlights

scoop Ellipsoidal reflector floodlight used to create a bright, even wash of light.

broad A rectangular floodlight that produces a bright and fairly even wash of light.

A floodlight, as its name suggests, is designed to throw a broad wash of light over a wide area. For many years, the **scoop,** an ellipsoidal reflector floodlight, has been the standard instrument for such a purpose (Figure 18-43a). It has a reflector with a matte finish that distributes light smoothly and without a sharp edge to the beam. Most scoops are 16 to 18 inches in diameter and take lamps up to 2,000 watts. A single instrument can light a fair-sized window backing. Banks of scoops have been used to light a drop and are especially useful for washing a curved surface.

The **broad** is a floodlight borrowed from television and film lighting. It contains a quartz lamp up to 1,500 watts and produces a wide field with even light distribution. The Nocturne, a broad-type floodlight from Strand, is shown in Figure 18-43b.

Borderlights

borderlight A striplight using PAR-type lamps, typically hung over stage and used to wash the stage with color.

The **borderlight** is a striplight lamped with 500-watt PAR-56 or 1,000-watt PAR-64 lamps. Such fixtures are frequently used over stage to produce a bright wash-illumination. They can be colored with glass filters.

CARE AND HANDLING

Although the care and handling of instruments naturally vary by situation and locality, certain good practices should be observed everywhere. By far the most important concern should be maintenance of equipment. Instrument hanging, circuiting, and focusing are made much simpler if equipment is in good condition (see the box on safety practice).

Safety Practice

Instrument Safety

The best way to prevent accidents from happening is to keep equipment in good operating order. Sticking shutters, bent bolts, and missing knobs or handles all frustrate an electrician and encourage mistreatment. At least 25 percent of all lamp "burnouts" are caused by an angered electrician attempting to free a stuck part by giving it a tap with the old wrench.

Almost all theatres require that lighting equipment mounted overhead be secured to the pipe with a safety chain or wire in addition to the C-clamp. Although the likelihood of an instrument falling during a performance is slim, nothing could be more unnerving for a theatre patron than to have an ERS fall from 30 feet and land nearby. To prevent accidents, the safety cable should ideally be attached to the instrument itself (as opposed to the yolk) and then around the pipe. A second cable clipped to the color frame will ensure that it stays with the instrument. Safety cables should be constructed of wire rope with rated hardware. Other theatres may require that a wire mesh separate all instrumentation from the auditorium.

Older instruments can be valuable if they are used properly and taken care of. Do not attempt to increase the light output of an older instrument by exceeding the recommended lamp wattage. These older instruments simply do not dissipate heat as well as newer equipment and they were made for lower wattage lamps—use them that way.

The single most important factor in instrument maintenance is keeping everything clean. Lenses can be washed in mild soap and water or with a good glass cleaner. Reflectors should be wiped with a soft cloth or washed with vinegar and water. Keep body parts as free of dust as possible. A clean spotlight dissipates heat better, thereby increasing lamp life and decreasing warpage. It also delivers more light.

Commonly needed spare parts such as shutters, knobs, and lenses should be kept on hand so that repair is not delayed by waiting for a parts order. Further, most instrument manufacturers require a fairly large minimum charge for parts orders and, adding insult to injury, take forever to fill the order.

By knowing the various kinds of lighting instruments and how they function, the designer can create plans that will actually work when electricians try to implement them. This prevents frustration and even failure. The next chapter presents further creative alternatives in discussing projections, practicals, and effects.

19

Projection, Practicals, and Effects

This chapter covers several diverse subjects, the most significant being the use of light as a scenic element. When light is used as scenery, its design requires extensive collaboration between the director, scenic designer, and lighting designer; execution is normally the responsibility of the lighting department. Whether designing something as simple as a pair of sconces on the wall of a realistic box set or as complex as multiscreen video projection, the lighting designer must be involved from the beginning. A projection specialist is often part of the staff of an extremely complex projection show such as the popular production of The Who's Tommy *(Color Plate 16-5).*

LIGHT AS SCENERY

Light begins to be a scenic element the moment a light source is visible to the audience. Motivating sources such as candles and chandeliers add a sense of mood and style to a production. Exposed light bulbs in signs or strung about the stage create a carnival-like atmosphere. Concert lighting with beams of moving light revealed by haze in the air is one of the most recent manifestations of light as scenery. When exposed, stage-lighting instruments themselves become a scenic element. All of these examples would make a strong visual contribution to the total design. However, they normally would serve as supporting elements, not the basis for a scheme of production.

The Development of Light as Scenery

Designer-directors such as Robert Edmond Jones (1887–1954), Edward Gorden Craig (1872–1966), and Adolphe Appia (1862–1928) envisioned using light as a central production scheme in their work. However, the technology of the time could not support their imagination. It took the genius of the Czech scenographer Josef Svoboda (1920–2002) to show the theatre world what could be accomplished with light. An example of his work is illustrated in Figure 19-1, scenery developed for Wagner's *Tristan und Isolde.*

19-1

Light as Scenery

A column of light created by high-intensity, low-voltage light sources. The light is reflected off a special aerosol spray of minute, electrostatically charged oil-emulsion droplets capable of staying suspended in the air for a prolonged time. This early use of "cracked oil" was developed by Josef Svoboda for Wagner's *Tristan und Isolde.*

At his theatre in Prague, Svoboda experimented extensively with low-voltage light sources. He was the first to develop, on a large scale, a way to suspend electrostatically charged particles in the air to act as reflectors of light. His use of projected images has pioneered new ways of thinking about scenic projection.

New technology in brighter light sources, color-mixing LEDs, digital imaging, and automated fixtures continues the trend toward greater use of light as scenery.

Light as a Scheme of Production

Light used as a scheme of production has been most common in the relatively abstract presentation of modern dance and performance art. As early as the late 1800s, the dancer Lois Fuller created lighting instruments and effects in order to heighten the dramatic impact of her dance performance. Light can not only be projected on actors and dancers, but it can also serve as a character in itself. For example, the modern-dance/performance-art piece *First Light* was choreographed only after a lighting "score" was developed (Figure 19-2). The

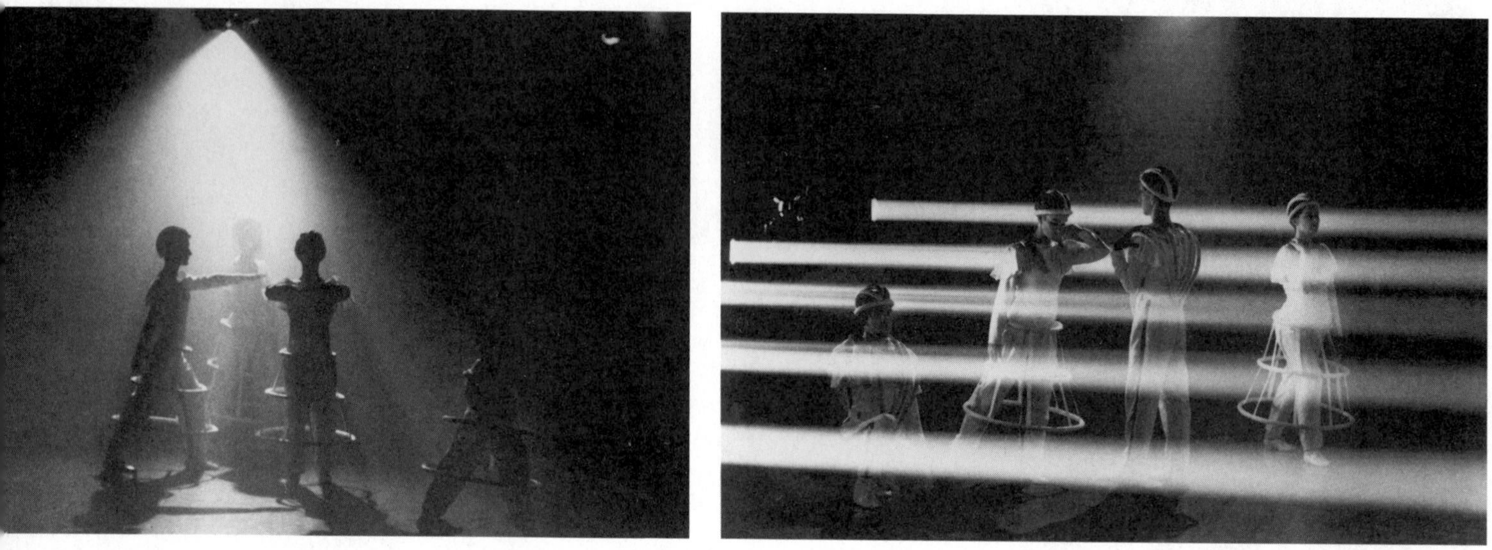

19-2

Light as a Scheme of Production

These photographs of a production of *First Light* performed by Nancy Karp + Dancers, a San Francisco–based modern dance company, illustrate the use of light as a scheme of production. Choreography, Nancy Karp; visual design, Wolfram Erber; costumes, Sandra Woodall; lighting, R. Craig Wolf.

air is filled with fog to accentuate the narrow beams of side-light. The dancers move with and react to the intense beams of light, which change the composition of the space by turning on and off throughout the dance. Costumes and support lighting were designed after the piece was conceived.

The English National Opera's production of Britten's *The Turn of the Screw* presents another quite different but equally effective use of light and projection (Figure 19-3). Expanded metal screens were reception surfaces for both front and rear projection (Figure 19-3a). Kodak Carousel projectors, Pani 5,000-watt projectors, and Strand Patt 752 projectors were used from front-of-house

19-3

Projection as a Scheme of Production

Bly, a gloomy Victorian country house, is the locale for the English National Opera's production of *The Turn of the Screw* by Benjamin Britten. Projected scenery enhances the eerie mood and facilitates the opera's rapid action through fifteen variations.

- **a** Line drawing showing the arrangement of screens that form the basic setting.
- **b** Floor plan showing the relationship of screens and location of projectors.
- **c** Two of the settings. Scene design and projections, Patrick Robertson; lighting, David Hersey.

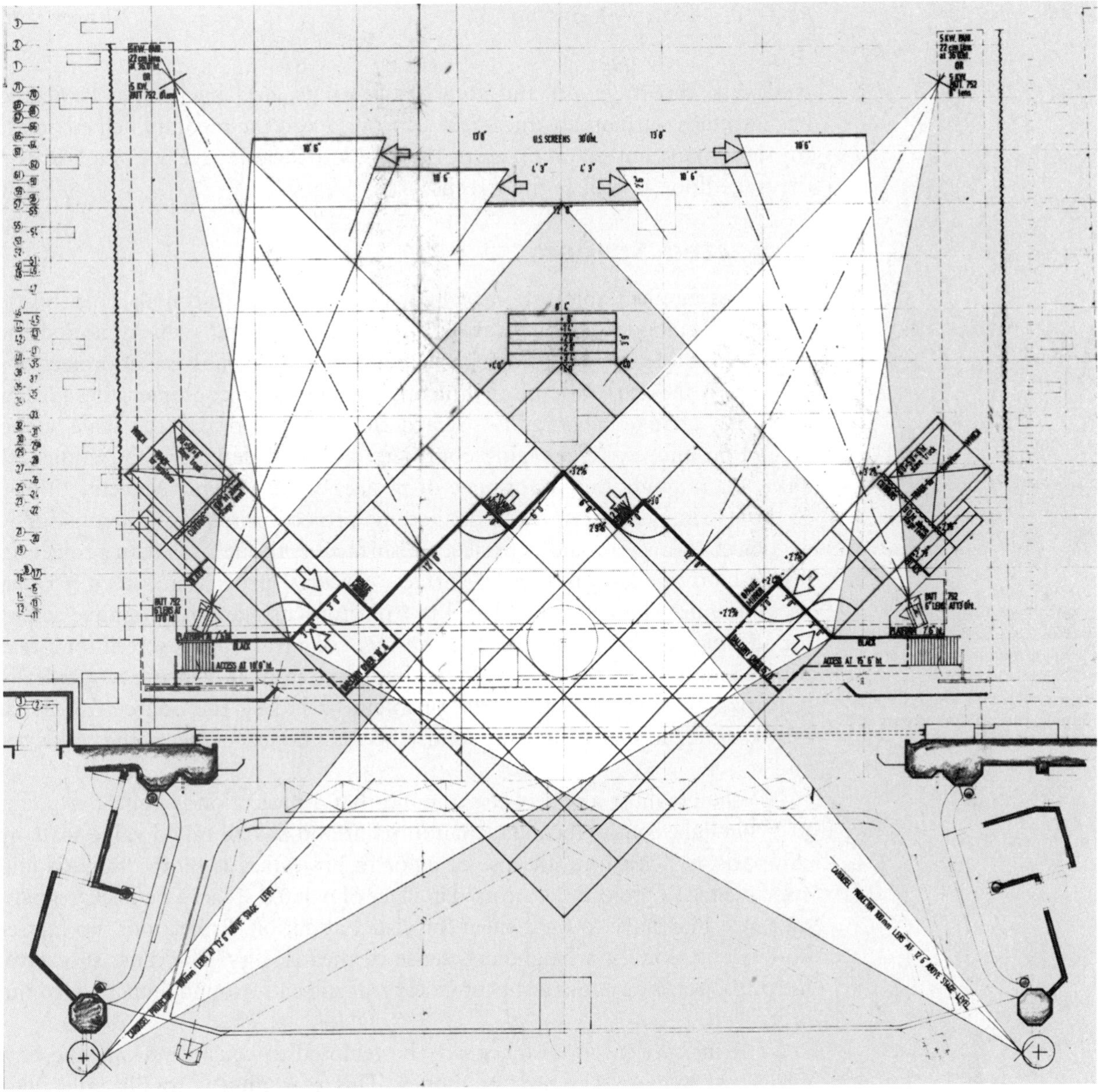

b

c

PHOTOS COURTESY NOEL STAUNTON, TECHNICAL DIRECTOR,
ENGLISH NATIONAL OPERA, LONDON COLISEUM

positions, the stage-left and stage-right wings, and backstage. Projected backgrounds with an abstract style appropriate to the medium helped create the right mood and setting (Figure 19-3c). Note the effective use of texture on the stage floor as well as the screens.

Projected Scenery

The most familiar application of light as scenery is projection. Theatre use of projections goes back as far as the "magic lantern," which entered the theatre in the 1860s, predating the incandescent lamp. The use of projections in modern theatre is the result not only of improved equipment design but also of a change in attitude toward their use. Today, large-scale video projection and digital imaging continues to excite designers and audiences alike, maintaining the importance of projection as a scenic element.

In its simplest form, traditional scenic projection requires a light source, an object or a slide, and a projection surface. Although one can project an image onto almost any type of surface, a special projection screen is often used. The projector may be placed in front (downstage) of an opaque screen for a **front projection** or at the rear (upstage) of a translucent screen for a **rear projection.** In front projection hiding the source from audience view is usually required. In rear-projection, the problem of hiding the source is solved. However, clear space backstage must be maintained between the projector and screen.

front projection The technique of projecting an image onto a screen from the front.

rear projection The technique of projecting an image onto a special translucent screen from the rear.

Designers must always keep in mind that a projection is light, not paint. Color in light is more brilliant than in paint and has a limited value scale by comparison. Therefore, the use of color in projection is more dramatic and eye-catching. If projections are used in place of painted scenery for backgrounds, the actor may have to fight them for visual attention. Projections, no matter how subtle, convey a heightened sense of theatricality. The most successful use of projection is not as a substitute for realistic background, but as a medium of its own.

The inexperienced designer may be tempted to consider projection as a means of saving either time or money. This reasoning is totally fallacious. Good projections require a great deal of effort and often more lead time than standard theatrical scenery does. Projections must never be considered a last-minute production detail. In addition, projection equipment is very expensive to buy and often difficult to rent.

The Projection Surface

The innovative use of the projection surface by designers such as Svoboda made a significant contribution to the imaginative use of light as scenery. In a very short time, projected scenery graduated from a large single-screen background to multiscreen compositions in a great variety of sizes, shapes, and three-dimensional forms. For example, Figure 19-4 illustrates an exciting scheme of multiscreen front projection for a production of *The Journey.*

As soon as the use of projections has been confirmed as the desired technique for a given production, the designers turn to consideration of surfaces. Any material capable of reflecting light can be used as a front-projection surface. Of course, some materials reflect more light than do others. Further, one surface may reflect light differently from another (see Chapter 18). Brightness and proper dispersion of the projected image are of primary concern to the designer.

PHOTOS REPRINTED FROM *THE SCENEOGRAPHY OF JOSEF SVOBODA*, WESLEYAN UNIVERSITY PRESS. COPYRIGHT 1971 BY JARKA BURIAN.

19-4

Multiscreen Technique

The use of many screens is well illustrated by the work of its originator, Josef Svoboda. This production of *The Journey* uses a rectangular screen, but the technique can involve screens of various shapes and sizes, each with its individual slide projector.

Rear Projection Single-screen rear projection has been used as background for dramatic productions for some time. The original location of the projector was behind the screen, because early projection required an operator.

A rear-projection screen must be translucent enough to diffuse the bright spot of the projector's source, yet transparent enough to transmit the image. Few materials can do so. The stage-left and stage-right shadow projections in Color Plate 16-6 are rear-projections on common plastic drop-cloth material.

The sources show through the plastic and are distracting. To solve this problem, professional rear-screen material must be used.

A professionally made rear-projection screen is constructed with the greatest density in the center to offset the hot spot of the projector's source. It is seamless and polarized to allow for equal distribution of light. Because of its high density, a rear-projection screen causes a good deal of light to be lost by absorption and reflection. Consequently, rear projection requires a brighter source than front projection does to create a similar effect. An advantage of rear projection is that the projectors can be centered behind the screen and are hidden from audience sight. As we shall see, front projection most often requires a light pitched at a high angle.

Projectors can be equipped with lenses of various focal lengths. However, even the widest of lenses can achieve only a 1:1 ratio of image size to throw distance. In other words, for a 10-foot image, a rear projector must have at least 10 feet of depth upstage of the screen. Some theatres have been designed with extra depth or a special rear-projection booth. However, many stages in the United States are simply too shallow to accommodate rear projection on any large scale.

URL http://www.rosco.com

Before making a final decision on using rear-screen projection for a production, the designers must consider the cost of purchasing or renting a screen. Projecting onto surfaces other than good rear-screen material will produce an inferior image. Rear-screen material is available in many sizes and colors from several theatrical suppliers, including Rosco.

Front Projection The greatest advantage of front projection is that the image can be projected onto a variety of surfaces. It allows for much greater creativity in the design of the screen. Front-projection surfaces can be three-dimensional or be broken up to allow for action behind or through the screens. Figure 19-5 illustrates dual-screen front projection used to comment on the action of *Oh What a Lovely War.*

19-5

Front Projection

Front-projected slides in *Oh What a Lovely War* are used to comment on the action.

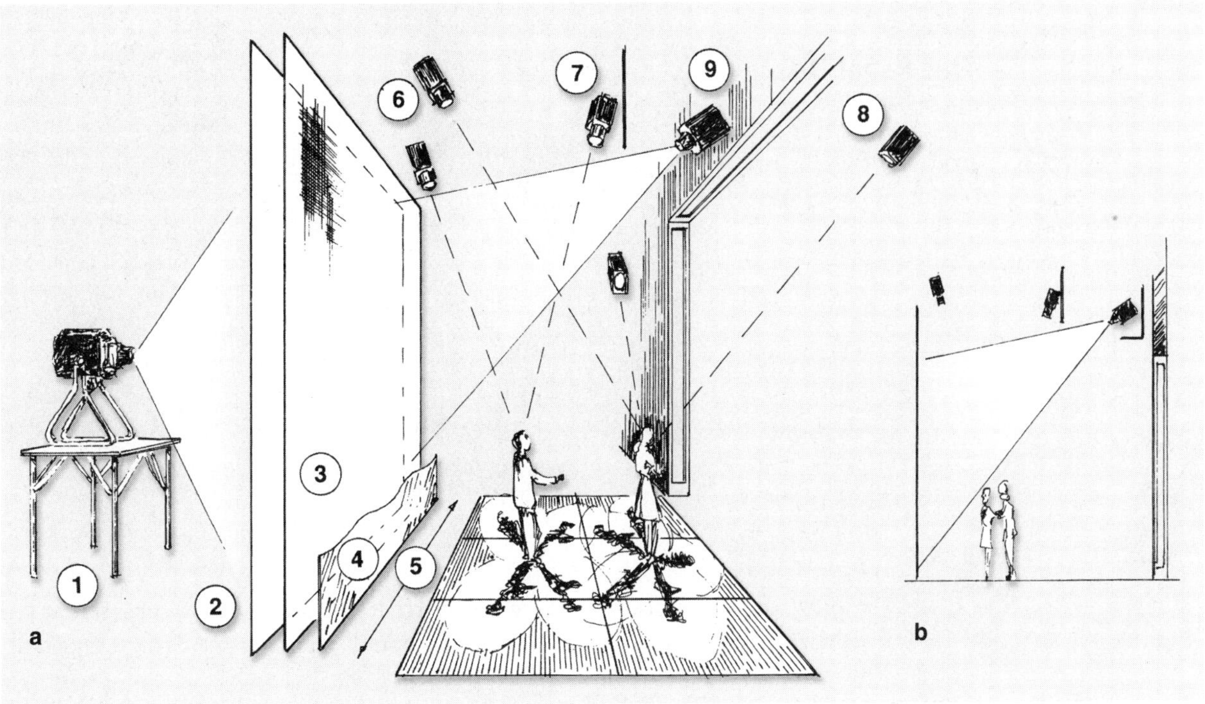

19-6

Projections and the Actor

a The effective use of large-scale projections as a background requires special lighting techniques:

1 Rear-projector.

2 Rear-projection screen.

3 Black scrim hung in front of the screen to absorb reflected light from the front.

4 Ground row.

5 "Neutral zone."

6 Back-light on actors.

7 Upstage area lights at a high angle that keeps light and shadows off the screen.

8 Downstage area lights, which do not have to be at as steep an angle.

9 Center of the first electric or bridge position for front projection.

b A front-projection arrangement. The lighting of the actor remains the same. The black scrim is removed to allow projections from the front. The angle of projection is planned to miss actors at the edge of the neutral zone.

Svoboda has developed a simple technique of slide production for screens with complex shapes. Once the screen and projector are in position, the electrician places a piece of unexposed photographic film in the projector where the slide would normally go. Shining a light on the screen exposes the film, producing an exact image of the screen shape and size for the slide.

As mentioned earlier, front projection has to throw from a more extreme angle or a greater distance than does rear projection (Figure 19-6). A high projection angle causes an image to distort, because the top of the screen is so much closer to the projector than the bottom is. Angled front projection therefore requires slides that have counterdistortion built in. With modern high-intensity lamps, light loss associated with long projection throws is less of a problem than it was in the past.

19-7

Flat Panel Display

The PlasmaSync 61MP1, a 61-inch plasma video monitor from NEC.

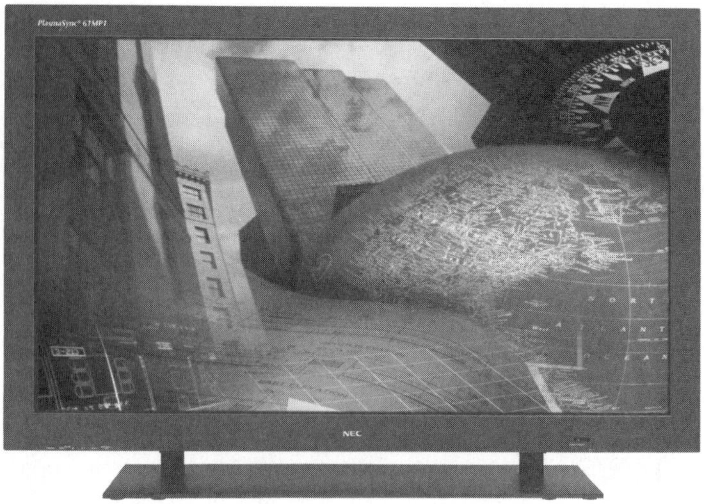

PHOTO COURTESY NEC TECHNOLOGIES

Not all distortions need to be corrected. There are times when the distortions of an angled projection are accepted as part of the design, especially if the image is abstract or nonobjective in style.

Video Projection Of course, video can be front or rear projected also. But, in addition to traditional surfaces, video can be shown on a flat panel display. Plasma monitors such as the one shown in Figure 19-7 are currently available in sizes ranging from 40 to 60 inches. Clusters of monitors can be used to project a video image of any dimension.

Lighting the Actor

Lighting actors in relation to a projected background requires special attention. Light from acting-area instruments that hits the screen causes an image to wash out. As such, designers must take care to choose lighting angles that will not hit the screen or cause light to bounce off the floor onto the screen. Side-light is particularly useful here. Additionally, back-light is important for separating the actor from the projected background. Ellipsoidal reflector spotlights are the best instrument choice because they produce the least amount of light flair. Top hats are recommended for all instruments in the vicinity of the screen. (See Figure 19-6.)

Bounce light can be minimized in ways other than control of distribution. The reflectivity of the floor can be deadened with a cover of black or gray cloth or carpeting. Even a common ground cloth can reduce floor reflection. In the case of rear projection, technicians can keep reflected light off the screen by hanging a seamless black scrim about a foot downstage of the screen. It serves to absorb the reflected light without adversely affecting the quality of the image.

The problem of reflected light can also be helped by the design and position of the screen or the image on the screen. A projected image is less likely to suffer from bounce light if it begins 3 or 4 feet above the stage floor. In addition, it is best if a so-called neutral zone of approximately 4 feet is maintained between the screen and acting areas. This practice makes it easier both to light the actor properly and to preserve the projected image.

PROJECTON TECHNIQUES AND EQUIPMENT

Projections can be achieved by a variety of methods. One can achieve large-scale shadow projection by using a simple arrangement of slide and light source. A common ellipsoidal reflector spotlight makes an excellent pattern projector. Video projection and digital imaging require specialized projectors that accept computer, DVD, or HDTV inputs. Most recently, companies such as Color Kinetics and Daktronics have been using color mixing LEDs (light emitting diodes) for large image projection. Varying the intensity of the red, green, and blue LEDs results in a huge number of possible color combinations. This technology is exciting but remains expensive. For scenic projections, a lens projector is the most commonly used device. Lens projectors for both moving and still projection come in various sizes and types. The requirements of a specific task dictate which projector is best suited for the job.

URL http://www.colorkinetics.com

URL http://www.daktronics.com

Lens Projectors

A lens projector uses two sets of lenses, each having its own separate function. As illustrated in Figure 19-8, the **condensing lens system** concentrates the light from the source onto the slide. The image of the illuminated slide is then transmitted through another lens or set of lenses called the **objective lens system.** A reflector is most often used to increase the light output of the lamp.

Normally the body of a projector includes the reflector and lamp, condensing lens, and slide holder, as well as a fan for cooling. To provide a choice of image sizes, the objective lens assembly is housed in a separate **lens tube.** Much like the lens barrel of an ellipsoidal reflector spotlight, this tube fits into the front of the projector body.

condensing lens system The first lens or set of lenses in a projector; the condensing lens(es) concentrate the light from the source onto the slide.

objective lens system The second lens or set of lenses in a projector; the objective lens system receives the image of the slide and transmits it to the screen in a size determined by the spread (focal length) of the lens.

lens tube The housing for the objective lens(es) of a projection system. The housing is normally interchangeable to provide a variety of beam spreads.

Choice of Lenses Projector lenses are available in different focal lengths, with the shortest focal lengths providing the widest spread and largest images. The size of a projected image is determined by three things: slide size, focal length of the objective lens system, and throw distance from projector to screen. A designer normally knows the desired image size first. The throw distance is found next by determining where in the theatre the projector can best be located.

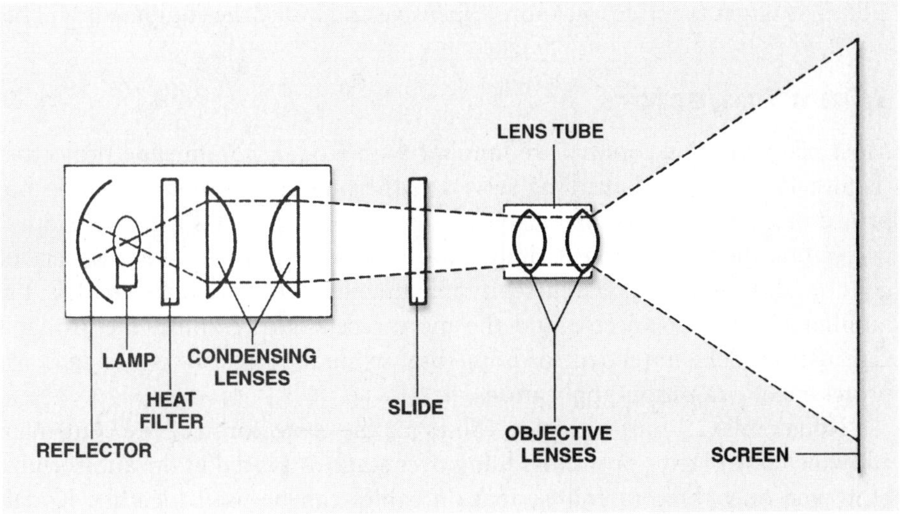

19-8

The Lens Projector

The optical train of a typical lens projector.

Choosing Your Tools

The Mathematics of Lens Projection

To eliminate trial-and-error methods of selecting lenses and placing projectors, use the following simple formulas:

$$F = \frac{D \times S}{I} \qquad D = \frac{F \times I}{S} \qquad I = \frac{D \times S}{F}$$

F = Focal length of lens

D = Projection throw distance

S = Slide size

I = Image size

Note that all these measurements must be expressed in the same units, normally inches. If the slide is not square and its horizontal dimension is used, the horizontal dimension of the image will be obtained; if the vertical measurement of the image is needed, the vertical measurement of the slide must be used.

Finally, the proper lens is selected by using the formulas presented in the box on lens projection.

The 35mm slide is by far the easiest to produce and project, but its image size and intensity have limits. If large and bright images are required, the designer must select from larger-format projectors.

Choice of Projectors The choice of scenic projectors is quite small and limited further by application. One important factor, slide size, greatly affects an image's brightness. The size of the slide a projector uses varies from the convenient 35mm (1.346 by 0.902 inches) to the large continental size of 9 by 9 inches. However, any given projector will accept only one size. Determining which projector is most appropriate involves three main considerations:

1. The longer the throw or the larger the image, the brighter the light source should be.
2. The larger the slide, the brighter and clearer the image will be.
3. The larger the slide, the more expensive and bulky the equipment will be.

35mm Projectors

URL http://www.kodak.com

Most people in this country are familiar with Kodak 35mm slide projectors (Figure 19-9a). They have long served as the best choice of standard 35mm projectors for a variety of reasons: their light output is superior to other projectors, their operation is simple and reliable, and they take a variety of good-quality lenses. Kodak currently manufactures two projector models: the familiar Carousel projector and the more recent Ektagraphic line. Today's Carousel model is intended for home use, while the Ektapro is designed for professional projection applications.

Kodak sells 25-foot extension cables for the projector's remote controller, allowing control over projectors hung over stage or placed in the auditorium. However, only three or four extension cables can be used together. Kodak projectors operate on a gravity-feed principle for changing slides. For this

a PHOTO COURTESY EASTMAN KODAK COMPANY
b & c PHOTOS COURTESY BUHL OPTICAL COMPANY

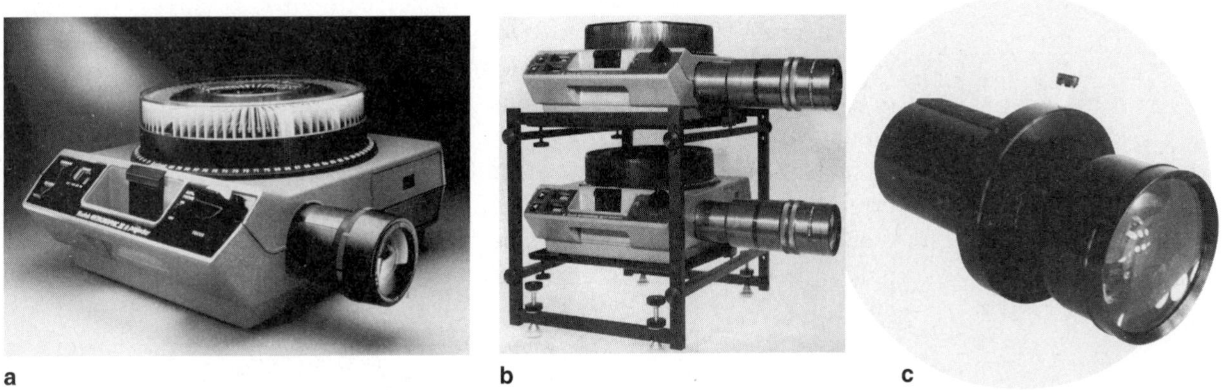

a b c

19-9

35mm Slide Projector and Lenses

a The Kodak Ektagraphic IIA 35mm slide projector.

b Two Kodak projectors with Buhl SF-7 zoom lenses mounted in a stacking dissolve rack.

c The Buhl "Keystopper" antikeystoning lens.

reason, the projectors cannot be tilted too extremely in any direction without danger of slides jamming. Attempting to use slide trays that accept more than eighty slides will cause them to jam.

Kodak sells a large range of its own lenses, but Buhl Optical Company manufactures an even larger range of superior lenses (Figures 19-9b and c). Focal lengths of Buhl lenses made to fit the Kodak projector begin at a wide-angle 1.38 inches and go to a very narrow 20 inches. These lenses are available in varying speeds, with the faster lenses being best for scenic projection. Zoom lenses are also available, but lens speed is sacrificed for the convenience of variable focus.

URL http://www.buhloptical.com

Using Your Tools

Using the Kodak Ektagraphic Projector

Keep in mind the following valuable bits of information about the Kodak Ektagraphic projector:

- The standard lamp recommended by Kodak is the FHS (300-watt, 82-volt, MR-13), with a life of 70 hours. The EXR (300-watt, 35-hour life) and the EXW (300-watt, 15-hour life) are acceptable substitutes. Although the life of the EXW is only one-half of that of the EXR, its light output is greatly increased. The EXW enables the Ektagraphic projector to be a viable scenic projection unit.

- Although Kodak manufactures a dissolve unit that will cross-fade two projectors, as wired the Ektagraphic cannot be dimmed with stage dimmers (because of its fan and slide changer motors). However, it is possible to add an external dimmer without any rewiring. A two-pin male plug fits into a pair of holes in the rear of the projector and interrupts power to the lamp. The power need only be directed through any remote dimmer of 300-watt or greater capacity. *Caution:* Power is supplied from the projector, through the dimmer, to the lamp—one may not connect the projector to a conventional stage circuit and dimmer without causing a short circuit.

Anyone with access to a 35mm camera can produce slides that project very well in a Kodak Ektagraphic projector. For copying other photographs or designs, a copy stand is a must. Plastic slide mounts are fine, but glass mounts protect the film better.

When doing slides for a complex production with a large number of projections, designers have found that it is best to shoot many more slides than necessary. When making final selections, the director and designers can pick and choose among many possibilities. This practice ultimately saves time and money.

Large-Format Projectors

Three companies manufacture large-format slide projectors commonly used in the United States: Ryodensha Company of Japan, Ludwig Pani of Austria, and E/T/C Audiovisuel of France. Some of these machines are pictured in Figure 19-10. These projectors are quite specialized, with the brightest models costing more than $50,000.

URL http://www.gamonline.com

The Ryodensha Company's machines are distributed in the United States by GamProducts. The GAM Scene Machine uses a 4-by-5-inch glass slide and is available in three models: the 1,000- or 2,000-watt Incandescent Scene Machines and the 2,500-watt HMI Scene Machine. Lenses come in a range of focal lengths between 4 inches (23 centimeters, 50-degree beam spread) and 16 inches (59 centimeters, 12-degree beam spread). A manual as well as a remote-control slide changer with a capacity of five slides can be purchased. Optional effect equipment includes a film loop machine, an effect disc machine, a prism machine, a flicker machine, and a kaleido machine. A douser is necessary for dimming the HMI model. The Scene Machine has proven to be a good, reliable projector.

URL http://www.fourthphase.com

Pani projectors are distributed in this country by Fourth Phase. Two incandescent-lamp projectors are available: the 2,000-watt BP2 (about 52,000 lumens) and the 2,500-watt BP2-2500. HMI arc lamp projectors are available in five models: the 1,200-watt BP 1.2 (about 110,000 lumens), the 2,500-watt BP 2.5 CT (Figure 19-10b), the 4,000-watt BP 4 Compact (about 410,000 lumens), the high-power 6,000-watt BP 6 GT (about 850,000 lumens; Figure 19-10c), and the super-bright 12,000-watt BP 12. All except the BP 12 take slides that are 18 by 18 centimeters (roughly 7 by 7 inches). Optional equipment includes remote-control slide changers holding fifteen slides, film loop machines, effects attachments, and a lightning generator. Lenses for all but the BP 6 and BP 12 are available with focal lengths from 60 centimeters (8-degree beam spread) to 11 centimeters (65-degree beam spread). Two zoom lenses are also available. The BP 6 and BP 12 offer eleven lenses having beam spreads from 8 to 71 degrees.

The PIGI *(Projecteur d'Images Geantes Informatise)* projection system manufactured by E/T/C Audiovisuel is also distributed in the United States by Fourth Phase. PIGI projectors can be used for slide projection but are most valuable as moving film projectors. The single and double film scrollers available can be used with either PIGI or Pani projectors. Lenses for PIGI projectors have focal lengths from a wide 11 centimeters to a very narrow 80 centimeters. They come with xenon lamps that range from 4,000 to 7,000 watts. The newest PIGI projector is the PIGI "S"—a "compact" projector weighing 132 pounds!

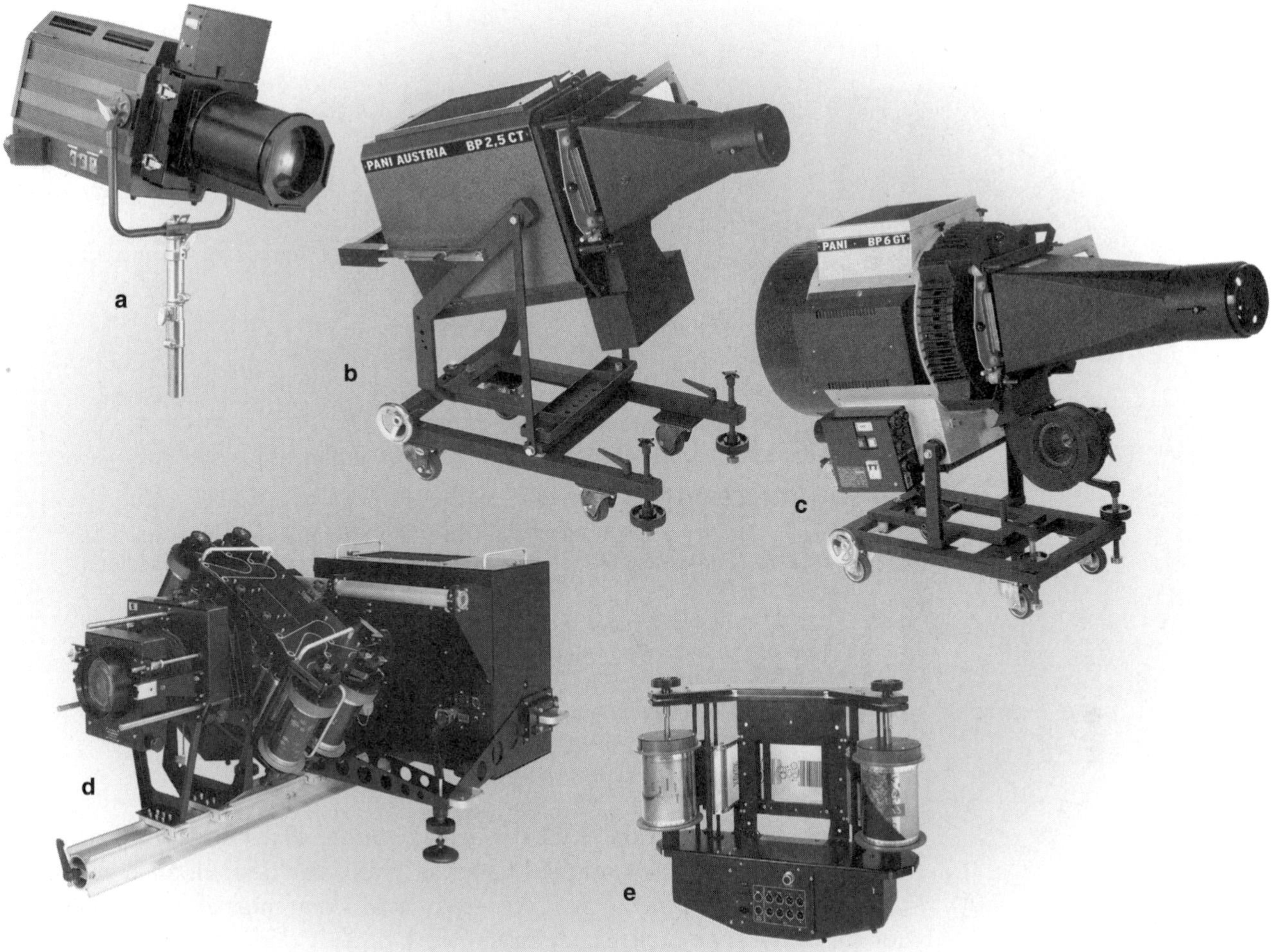

d & e PHOTOS COURTESY E/T/C AUDIOVISUEL   b & c PHOTOS COURTESY PANI   a PHOTO COURTESY GAMPRODUCTS, INC.

19-10

Large-Format Slide Projectors

a The GAM Scene Machine, a modular multipurpose projection system, is available in both incandescent and HMI versions with lenses ranging from 12 to 50 degrees.

b The Pani BP 2.5 CT projector, a 2,500-watt HMI projection system for long throws and bright images, offers lenses with 8- to 65-degree spreads.

c The Pani BP 6 GT projector is a 6,000-watt HMI projection system with high-grade optics and a cold mirror reflector, making this one of the most powerful projectors on the market.

d The PIGI "S" projector, a 2,500-watt HMI projection system, is shown here with a double film scroller. Unlike other projectors, the PIGI "S" offers dichroic color mixing and an internal dimming shutter.

e A PIGI single scroller, adaptable to the entire range of Pani projectors.

It has a 2,500-watt HMI lamp that produces more than 90,000 lumens with a 46-centimeter lens. This new projector offers dichroic color mixing and has an internal dimming shutter.

Slides for large-formal scenic projectors are expensive. The glass alone costs several times more than a complete 35mm slide does. If transparencies are used, they are normally sandwiched between two pieces of glass held together in a metal frame. Common sizes are 4 by 5, 5 by 5, and 7 by 7 inches.

a PHOTO COURTESY BOXLIGHT
b & c PHOTOS COURTESY NEC TECHNOLOGIES

19-11

Video Projection

a The Boxlight FP-97t, a bright (3,300 lumens) LCD projector with a 440-watt metal halide lamp, is suitable for short to medium throws and small to medium images in the theatre.

b The NEC XT 5000 is a compact high-output (4,500 lumens) projector with a 1,000-watt short arc Xexon lamp. Zoom lenses are available with focal lengths from 1.5 to 7 inches.

c The NEC XT 9000, a very bright (8,000 lumens) video projector, is suitable for longer throws and larger images in the theatre.

Photographic production houses can make either black-and-white or color transparencies from any original material in any size desired. Such slides are expensive and take time to produce—two factors that must always be allowed for. Of course, one can transfer design work directly onto the clear glass slides of large-format slide projectors. Rosco manufactures a transparent dye called Colorine designed to be used on glass.

Video Projectors

The television or video projector is a complex and highly specialized piece of equipment that can project a video, computer, or live televised image. Although large-scale video projection equipment has been available for several years, it remains extremely expensive. The problem is simply one of achieving enough image intensity for stage production. However, as demand for video projection becomes greater and greater, projector prices decrease and intensity increases. Figure 19-11a shows a projector from Boxlight that has a brightness of 3,300 lumens. The projectors in Figure 19-11b and c are manufactured by NEC and have brightness levels of 4,500 and 8,000 lumens, respectively.

URL http://www.boxlight.com

URL http://www.nectech.com

Other Projectors

Many theatrical effects can be created using the foregoing lens projectors and available accessories. There are also several more specialized types of projectors whose effects range from simple shadows to the extraordinary.

Effect Projection Effect projection can be achieved by using one of a variety of effects projectors or by attaching an effects module to the front of an ellipsoidal reflector spotlight. Phoebus manufactures a 575-watt HMI projector head that takes a 3-by-5-inch slide and is compatible with Scene Machine

URL http://www.phoebus.com

PHOTO COURTESY PHOEBUS MANUFACTURING

19-12

Effect Projection

The Phoebus Universal Projector, a 575-watt HMI projector head, is compatible with GAM Scene Machine effects and lenses.

accessories (Figure 19-12). Rosco and GAM manufacture variable-speed animation motor units that can be remotely controlled (Figure 19-13). Animation discs with various patterns create a good sense of movement and can be used in conjunction with gobo projection.

Automated Fixtures Highly sophisticated automated fixtures, such as Clay Paky's Super Scan Zoom and Cyberlight from High End Systems, fall under the category of effect projectors (Figure 19-14). These are moving mirror

a PHOTO COURTESY ROSCO LABORATORIES, INC.
b PHOTO COURTESY GAMPRODUCTS, INC.

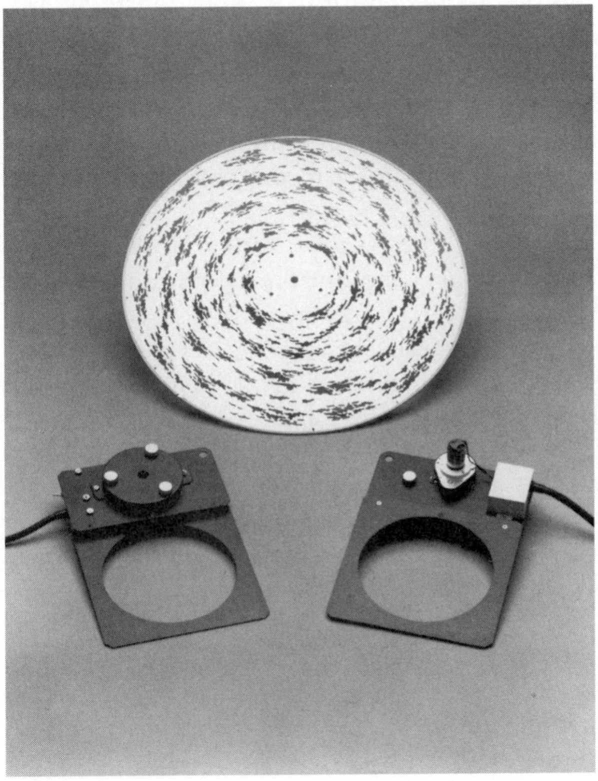

a

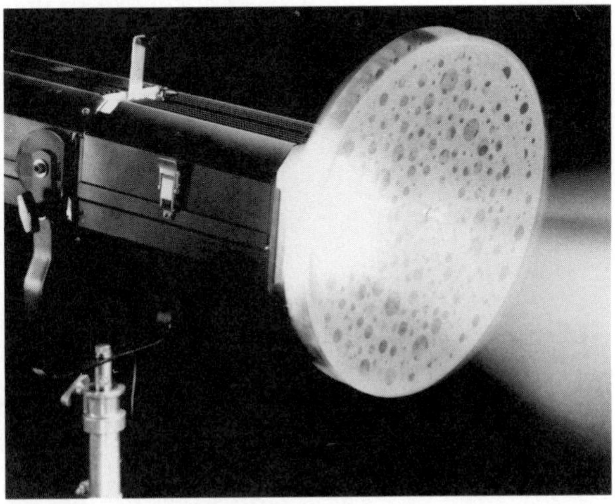

b

19-13

Effect Wheels

a Rosco's Animation Effect System offers fixed or variable-speed motor units with several animation discs to choose from. It can be mounted in the color frame of any 4- or 6-inch lighting instrument.

b The GAM Spin/FX has a variable speed double-disc drive.

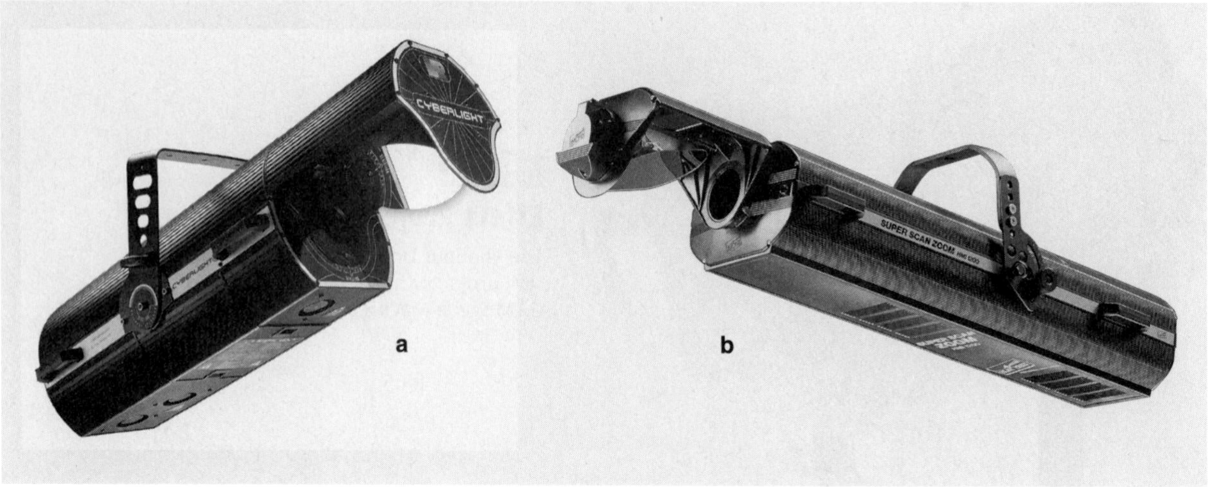

a PHOTO COURTESY HIGH END SYSTEMS
b PHOTO COURTESY CLAY PAKY

19-14

Automated Fixture Effects Projection

a The Cyberlight Turbo from High End Systems is an extremely bright automated fixture effects projector. It has a dual, rotating gobo system; a fixed dichroic color wheel as well as a color mixing system; variable frost and diffusion; and a multi-image prism. It uses a 1,200-watt MSR arc lamp with a color temperature of 5,400 degrees Kelvin and is available with two zoom lenses ranging from 13 to 26 degrees.

b The Clay Paky Super Scan Zoom offers similar features. It has two rotatable prisms and uses a 1,200-watt HMI arc lamp. Its zoom lens offers beam spreads 8 to 16 degrees.

units with remote control over an amazing variety of effects and light qualities. Both are big and heavy.

The smaller of the two, Cyberlight is 3.5 feet long and weighs 46 pounds. Twenty control channels are needed to control its various functions. It is available in four models including the Cyberlight SV, which operates more quietly than the others and is therefore more suitable for theatrical applications. The Cyberlight Turbo uses a MSR 1200 SA arc lamp, which delivers 12,500 lumens. Two zoom lenses provide variable beam spreads from 13 to 36 degrees. Both the Turbo and the SV have internal color mixing, offering an infinite variety of color.

The Clay Paky Super Scan Zoom is nearly 5 feet long and weighs in at a hefty 100 pounds. It has a 1,200-watt arc lamp, and the zoom feature provides beam spreads from 8 to 16 degrees. It can project beams of light consisting of four colors, two concentric colors, or a rainbow effect. Sixteen gobo pattern combinations and variable-speed pattern rotation are provided. It has two variable-speed rotating prisms that greatly add to its repertoire of effects.

Gobo Projection Recall that a standard gobo is a sheet of highly heat-resistant material (usually stainless steel) from which some shape, pattern, or design has been cut (Figure 19-15). When the gobo is placed at the gate of an ellipsoidal reflector spotlight, the lenses project its pattern onto any appropriate surface.

Gobo projection is an important theatrical design tool. Gobos may be projected as sharp-edged, distinct patterns or may be thrown out of focus to create texture. Many textural qualities can be achieved with the large variety

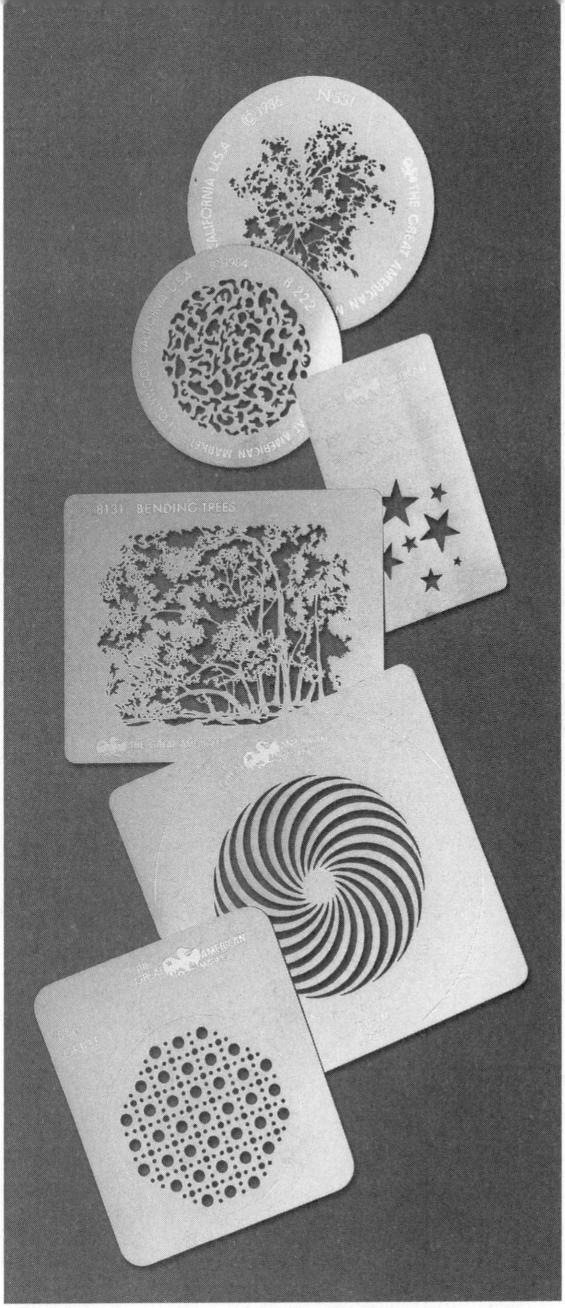

a

b

a PHOTO COURTESY GAMPRODUCTS, INC. b PHOTO COURTESY ROSCO LABORATORIES, INC.

19-15

Gobo Projection

a Several of the many gobo patterns available from GAM.

b Rosco's "Realistic Leaves" gobo and the image it projects.

of templates available. Further, gobos can be rotated at variable speeds to create moving texture. Rosco manufactures single and double gobo rotators and GAM offers the TwinSpin, which rotates two patterns in opposite directions (Figure 19-16). All these rotators fit into the drop-in iris slot of a 6-inch ellipsoidal reflector spotlight.

Custom glass gobos are becoming more and more popular for projected effects. The smash Broadway hit *The Producers* used images of actor Matthew Broderick's face projected on the walls of the set by ellipsoidal reflector spotlights equipped with glass gobos. The process of getting these gobos made has become simple and fairly quick. Cost is still a bit high but can be warranted by the quality of the effect.

Commercial equipment houses sell metal gobos in a variety of designs; some are realistic, but most are abstract patterns. Catalogs are available from Rosco, Lee, GAM, and Apollo. Custom gobos can be made from any design at a reasonable cost.

URL http://www.leefilters.com

URL http://www.internetapollo.com

a b

a PHOTO COURTESY ROSCO LABORATORIES, INC.
b PHOTO COURTESY GAMPRODUCTS, INC.

19-16

Gobo Rotators

a Rosco's single gobo rotator, available in fixed or variable speeds.

b GAM's TwinSpin II, a variable-speed, double-pattern rotator with DMX speed control from the lighting console.

Patterns can be home-designed and cut from heavy aluminum foil or the bottom of a cheap metal pie plate. An especially useful effect is clouds cut from foil, which can be wrinkled slightly to give out-of-focus soft edges. Unfortunately, gobos made from such materials do not last long under the high temperatures created at the gate of an ellipsoidal.

Linnebach projector A projector with no lens that is used in the theatre for large-scale shadow projection.

Shadow Projection A basic instrument for straight-line shadow projection, which has seen theatrical use for many years, is the **Linnebach projector** (Figure 19-17). Named after its inventor, Adolphe Linnebach, this projector is simply a large metal housing containing a lamp. Along the edge of the open side of the housing is a slot to hold the slide. The large slide size allows a Linnebach shadow projection to cover an entire backdrop. However, low intensity may be a problem.

Because the Linnebach projector is so simple, a production crew can make one themselves. The most important part of the projector is the lamp, whose socket should be mounted to allow adjustment toward and away from the slide. The lamp itself must be high intensity with as small a filament as possible. This indicates a low-voltage source such as the 150-watt, 24-volt FCS quartz lamp, which has a brightness of 6,000 lumens. The smaller the filament, the clearer the image.

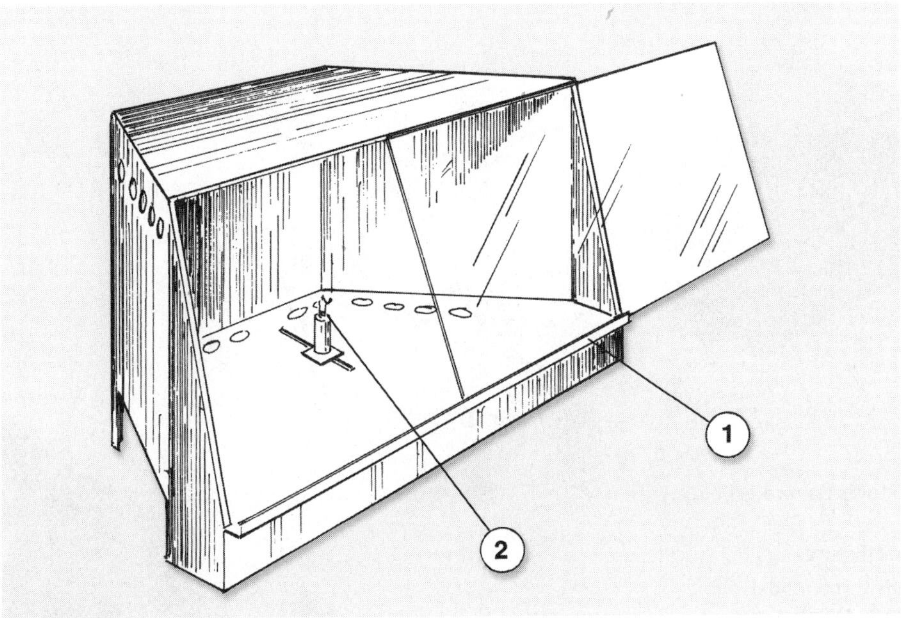

19-17

The Linnebach Projector

A low-voltage, high-intensity Linnebach—a specially built shadow projector using a small light source for sharp projection. Key components include:

1 Slide holder.
2 Concentrated-filament lamp.

Laser Projection The term *laser* is an acronym of *light amplification by stimulated emission of radiation.* Laser light is unique because it consists of a single, in-phase wavelength of light. In the relatively few years since their development, lasers have appeared in hundreds of applications, ranging from surgical tools to supermarket bar-code scanners. Lasers in the theatre have been used primarily for effects, one the most popular being Tinker Bell in *Peter Pan.* Low-power lasers are harmless, but their light output is normally insufficient for stage use. Class II lasers (power up to 1 milliwatt) are usually bright enough but can cause eye damage if improperly used. Because higher-power Class III lasers can be extremely dangerous, their use is carefully regulated. *Holograms,* three-dimensional projections in space, can be achieved by laser projection. Lasers and their related control equipment are expensive to purchase or rent.

Ultraviolet Projection Ultraviolet light is not visible to the human eye, but it causes certain materials to fluoresce, or glow brightly. Designers can create startling and exotic stage effects by using ultraviolet light and fluorescent materials (see Color Plate 16-7). For many years the best source of ultraviolet light was the carbon arc follow spot equipped with a U-V filter. Today, companies such as Wildfire and Strong Entertainment Lighting manufacture long-throw ultraviolet lighting fixtures as well as fluorescent paints and materials (Figure 19-18).

URL http://www.wildfirefx.com

URL http://www.strongint.com

a

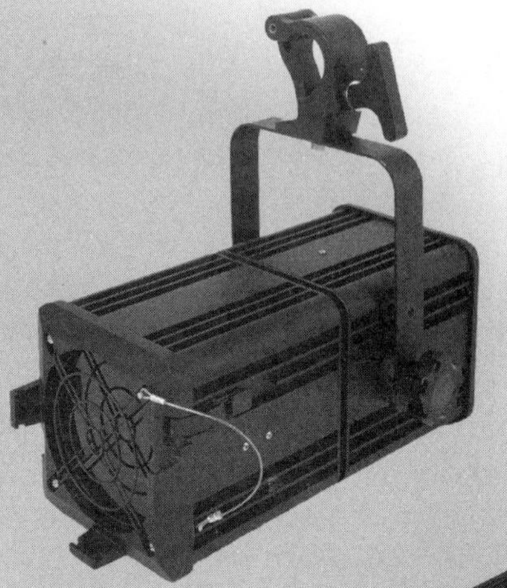

b

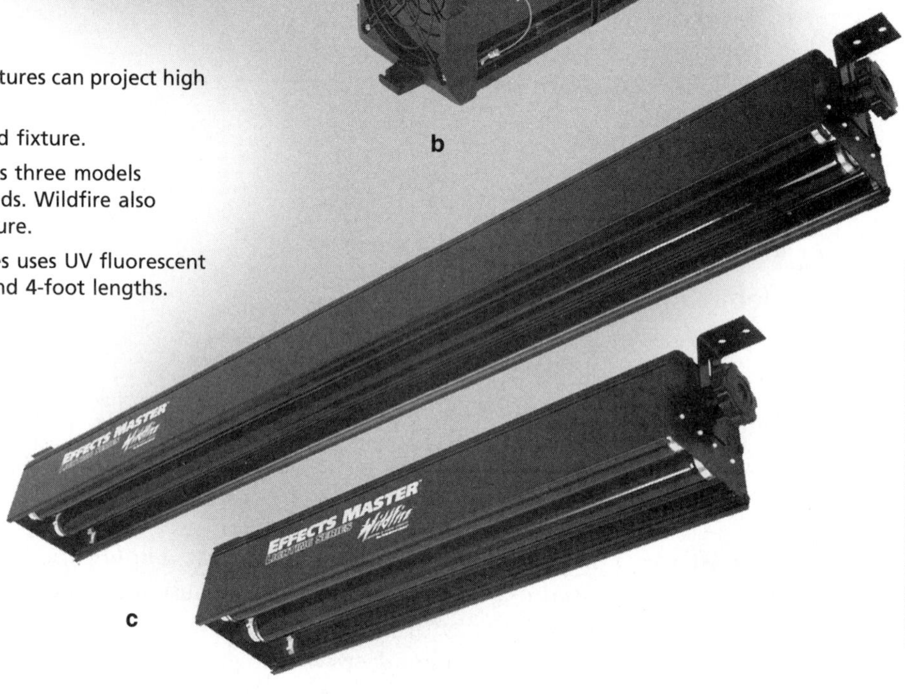

c

19-18

Ultraviolet Projection

With special filters and lamps, fixtures can project high intensities of UV light.

a Strong Nocturne 600 UV flood fixture.

b Wildfire's 250 Series comprises three models providing various beam spreads. Wildfire also manufactures a 600-watt fixture.

c Wildfire's Effects Master Series uses UV fluorescent tubes and is available in 2- and 4-foot lengths.

a & b PHOTOS COURTESY WILDFIRE, INC.

c PHOTO COURTESY STRONG ENTERTAINMENT LIGHTING

PRACTICALS

Practicals are onstage, working light sources such as lanterns, lamps, fireplaces, or candles. The design of practicals is the responsibility of the scenic designer and the property department. The wiring and maintenance of such units is the responsibility of the electrics department. Their use is sure to be a concern of the lighting designer. Playwrights or scene designers specify the use of practicals for any of several reasons, including these:

- Enhancing the desired mood of a scene
- Indicating time of day, season, or other time period
- Reinforcing the reality of a scene or location

Fire Effects

Often prohibited by fire codes, open fires on the stage are rarely convincing and are difficult to control. However, all too often the demands of a script force the designer to put a fire in full view of the audience.

Hearth Fires If no flames are required from a hearth fire, a glow from lamps buried among burnt logs and scraps of color media will do nicely. If flames must be shown, several options are available. An old stage method that works well from a distance is to shine light on thin streamers of chiffon or China silk as they are blown upward by a small fan. A light smoke effect supports the illusion. A slowly rotating drum covered with crumpled foil and lit with low-wattage MR-16 or R-type lamps can provide a convincing reflection of fire. These light sources and the drum mechanism can be partially concealed by logs.

Electronic options include flicker generators or a random chase effect programmed into the control system. Flicker generators are available from several companies and can produce a fairly realistic effect.

Torches and Lanterns Torches are particularly difficult to simulate. If actual flame is allowed, a can of Sterno mounted in the top of a torch can be convincing. GAM makes a very good and safe torch that burns solid paraffin. LeMaitre has a torch that is not real flame, but looks the part (Figure 19-19a). Liquid fuel must *never* be used.

URL http://www.lemaitrefx.com

Not surprisingly, lanterns actually burning oil must never be used on the stage. To begin with, their use is strictly against all fire rules and insurance regulations. They present a potentially extreme hazard. In case of an accident,

a

b

a PHOTO COURTESY LEMAITRE SPECIAL EFFECTS, INC.
b PHOTO COURTESY ROSCO LABORATORIES, INC.

19-19

Fire Effects

a The LeMaitre Flame provides the appearance of a burning flame without the use of fire.

b Rosco's flicker candle looks realistic under most viewing conditions. It can be powered with a 9-volt battery or dimmed with the use of an AC adaptor.

the stage could become flooded with blazing oil. Fortunately, oil lanterns conventionally have glass chimneys that can be realistically smoke stained to hide a small light bulb. If the lantern needs to be carried about, a flashlight battery can be hidden in the base of the lantern.

Small lamps can be colored by using Colorine, a commercial transparent dye manufactured by Rosco. Fabricators should always test the color first. Amber works well, and good results can also be achieved by mixing various colors.

Candles Unlike oil lanterns, candles, which usually extinguish themselves when dropped, are permissible on many stages if properly handled. In some locations they must be encased in transparent mica shields. Candles that self-extinguish when tipped are available commercially. Local fire authorities should be consulted if there is any doubt concerning the legality of using candles onstage. In no case should candles be placed near draperies or other flammable materials.

Even if allowed, candles probably should be avoided. Their bright light, and particularly their flickering in any air current, can distract the audience. A small battery and lamp or pencil flashlight hidden in a white paper tube can produce an effective simulation. In addition, Rosco and others make convincing flicker candles. Complete candles are available, or just the flame module can be purchased for custom work (Figure 19-19b).

Lighting Fixtures

Chandeliers, wall sconces, table lamps, and similar household lighting fixtures generally offer no problems except for the wattage of the lamps actually used in them. This is particularly true when the fixtures have bulbs visible to the audience. If at all bright, they create a most annoying, even blinding, glare. Bare bulbs must always have extremely low wattage, and even then may have to be dimmed. Because little usable light emanates from such fixtures, supplemental stage lighting is needed to illuminate the actor properly. Designers

Safety Practice

Fire Safety

It is best not to use open flame onstage at all.
If you absolutely must do so, take these precautions:

- Have a crew member with a fire extinguisher stationed on both sides of the stage ready to react to any emergency.
- If performers make any entrances or exits with open flame, establish the policy that anytime the flame is offstage it is handled by crew only.
- Never use a filled oil lantern onstage.

should never depend on low-wattage fixtures to produce all the light that seems to emanate from them. However, if lamp bulbs are shielded by shades, the glare is hidden and extra-large wattage lamps may be used to give a more realistic effect. Such shades must be quite opaque, or they can be lined with brown paper. An additional baffle over the bulb may be necessary to prevent an undesirable hot spot on the walls and ceilings of a box set.

Practical lamps should be controlled at the dimmer board. As such, when switching on a major motivating practical, an actor must hold the moment until the stage lighting responds. The light board operator simply cannot respond instantaneously to the actor's motion.

SPECIAL EFFECTS

Uses of light that are not directly involved in lighting the actor or illuminating the scene are grouped in the category of **special effects.** Examples include explosions, fires, lightning, and strobe effects. Working out special effects is almost always enjoyable but can take a great deal of time. It should never be left to the end as an afterthought.

special effects Uses of light other than lighting the actor or illuminating the scene.

Moon and Stars

Creating a believable moon and stars is not as easy as it might seem. A gobo or effects machine can be used for either front or rear projection. A good full moon can be created by using a Fresnel to form the outer edge in conjunction with an iris ellipsoidal forming an inner disk.

Stars can be quite effective but are tricky to handle. Even tiny "twinkle" lights appear as great blobs of light against a dark sky. One can, however, tape the bulb so that only the very tip of the envelope is exposed. If a dark blue or black scrim is hung a few feet downstage of the sky-drop, it will help cut down excessive brightness and hide the wiring to the star bulbs.

Another method of creating a good star field is to punch small holes in a black drop and shine light on a white bounce drop located upstage. If a shimmer curtain is placed between the star field and the bounce drop, a wonderful twinkling effect can be achieved.

By far the best stars are created by using fiber optics. A light source located at one end of a tiny thread of glass is conveyed the length of the thread and emitted with little loss of intensity. Bundles of these threads can be sewn onto a drop with their ends arranged to create a wonderful star field. The drawback to fiber optics is their expense.

Lightning

Many scripts call for lightning, which can be produced by several methods, depending on the desired effect. A convincing display of forks of light springing from the sky is quite difficult. However, one can achieve distant effects through either gobo or slide projection. Fortunately, presenting only great bursts of high illumination will usually suffice. A Hollywood company called Lightning Strikes manufacturers an extremely bright fixture (Figure 19-20).

URL http://www.lightningstrikes.com

Intense flashes of light can also be achieved by strobe lights, flashbulbs, or photoflood lamps. Today's strobe lights can be very bright and remotely

PHOTO COURTESY LIGHTNING STRIKES!

19-20

Lightning Effects

Lightning can be produced in a variety of ways: arc-discharge units, photo flood lamps, or specialized lightning generators such as the Lightning Strikes fixture shown, which comes in two sizes: 70,000 watts and 250,000 watts. It is bright!

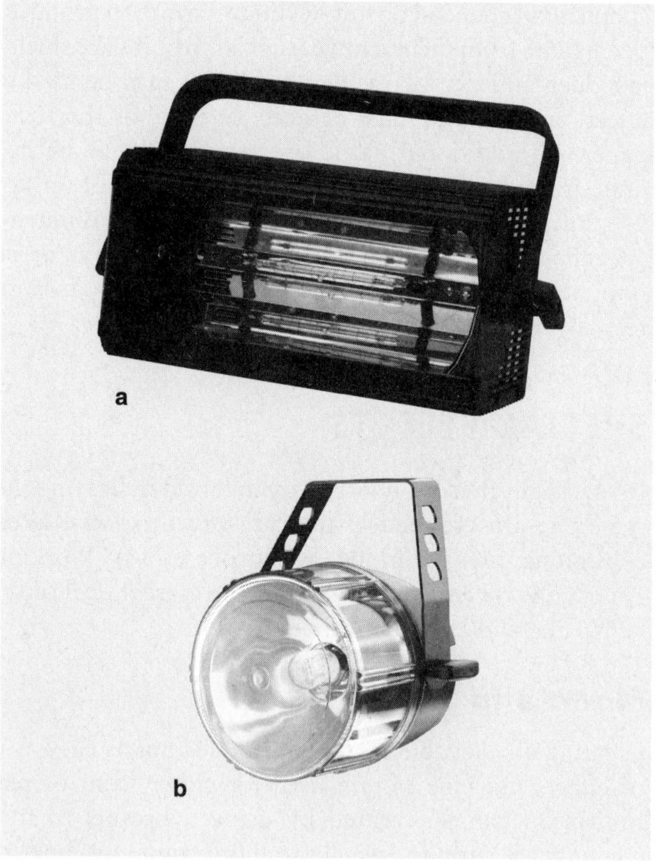

a PHOTO COURTESY DIVERSITRONICS, INC.

b PHOTO COURTESY HIGH END SYSTEMS

19-21

Strobe Fixtures

Strobe lights, available in many sizes and intensities, create special effects; many types can also be used for lightning effects.

- **a** The Diversitronics Linear Strobe Fixture can be controlled by DMX and comes with a 1,500- or 3,000-watt xenon lamp.
- **b** High End's Dataflash AF1000 offers continuous illumination or pyrotechnic simulation and is controlled by DMX.

URL http://www.diversitronics.com

controlled. Several companies—including Diversitronics and High End Systems—manufacture high-intensity strobe units, most with xenon arc sources (Figure 19-21).

Large photoflash bulbs, although fairly expensive, create a wonderfully bright burst of light. The larger lamps can be mounted in homemade housings to eliminate unwanted spill and hung over stage. Smaller lamps can easily be placed about the stage and hidden by properties or scenery.

A final method is to switch several intense sources on and off rapidly. Momentary contact switches or a control board's "bump buttons" work well for the switching. To be effective, lamps need to have small filaments that respond quickly. This indicates low-voltage sources. However, 120-volt photoflood lamps can be quite effective. Two good choices are the 500-watt, medium screw base R-40 DXB (45,000 lumens) or the 300-watt medium screw base R-30 BEP (11,000 lumens). Because the color temperature of lightning is very high, it is best to use color-correction filters or select lamps with color temperatures around 5,000 degrees Kelvin.

Explosions and Flashes

To produce explosive flashes from offstage, one can use the same general techniques for creating lightning. Sound can be added as appropriate. If the script calls for these effects to take place in view of the audience, a **flash pot** is necessary. A flash pot is a device that ignites a highly explosive powder called flash powder. Available from special effects supply houses, flash powder was once used as a light source for still photography. Figure 19-22 shows Pyropak, one of several flash-pot systems available from reputable manufacturers such as Luna Tech and LeMaitre. Use of homemade flash pots is illegal and extremely dangerous.

flash pot A device made to hold and ignite a highly explosive powder for onstage special effects.

URL http://www.pyropak.com

PHOTOS COURTESY LUNA TECH, INC.

19-22

Pyrotechnics

Flash-pot systems are dangerous and should be used with great caution. Shown are the Pyropak concussion mortar and a two-channel, six-circuit controller. Although the concussion mortar is designed for maximum report volume, Luna Tech manufactures several devises for various effects.

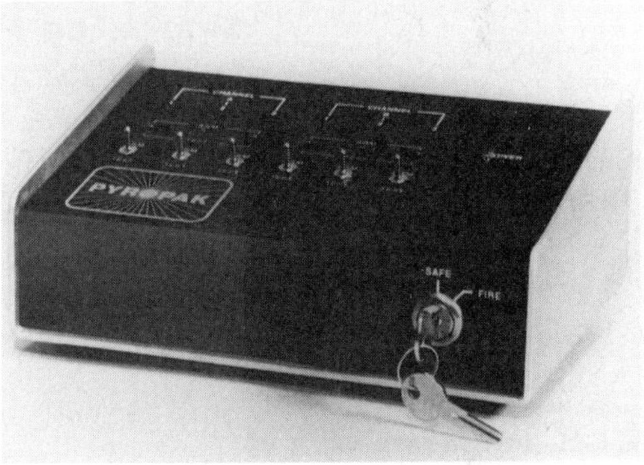

Safety Practice

Flash-Pot Safety

Flash pots are extremely dangerous. Serious injury can result if they are misused. Use only the safe, commercially available flash-pot systems—and always follow the directions carefully. Never fire a flash pot close to flammable materials or to people.

Some chemicals and materials that in the past were commonly used in the theatre have been found to be unhealthy. Asbestos is one of these, and another is ammonium chloride (sal ammoniac), used to produce smoke onstage. The use of any substance except pure ammonium chloride is harmful to the lungs and should be discontinued. In addition, even pure ammonium chloride must never be heated in contact with metal.

Smoke, Fog, and Haze

Dry ice and smoke machines have been used in the theatre for many years to create effects intended to enhance the mood of a scene. The recent popularity of using smoke and haze in the air to accentuate light beams has led to the development of newer and safer methods of production.

Dry Ice Fog As the name implies, dry ice acts more like fog than smoke; it tends to cling to the floor and creep along at low levels. Solid carbon dioxide (dry ice) changes from its solid state to a vapor without becoming a liquid. The rapidity of the change is increased if the dry ice is exposed to hot water.

Machines that produce dry ice fog are easily and cheaply built or can be purchased from various theatrical suppliers. To make such a machine, technicians need only a 55-gallon drum, an electric immersion heater like those used in home hot-water heaters, and a wire basket to suspend the dry ice. When the water is hot, dry ice is dropped in, producing a good deal of fog. This fog can be directed over a short distance by using flexible dryer hose connected to a vent in the lid of the 55-gallon drum.

Such fog gives a splendid effect, although it dissipates rather rapidly. When the dry ice is exposed to the water, it makes a loud bubbling noise. Store dry ice in an insulated cooler and avoid dry ice burns by wearing gloves when handling.

Smoke/Fog Machines Several manufacturers make excellent portable machines that produce smoke by heating up a special liquid called **fog juice.** The mist tends to rise but an attachment that cools the smoke can keep it on the ground. Hiding plastic hose about the stage is a good way to make the smoke appear wherever wanted. Smoke/fog machines are available in several models varying in the density or quantity of smoke delivered over a period of time. All have the capacity for remote control, and some are quieter than others (Figure 19-23).

fog juice The liquid used in fog and smoke machines.

19-23

Smoke/Fog Machines

Smoke rises in the air; fog hugs the ground.

a The LeMaitre G150 Fog Machine uses a water-based fluid and has an air option that expands the range of possible effects.

b The Rosco Delta 3000 Fog Machine uses Rosco's water-based fog fluid and is DMX controlled. It produces a large quantity of smoke in a short time.

c The Rosco 1600 Fog Machine is a good machine for most applications. It delivers a large quantity of smoke, is dependable, and can be DMX controlled with an interface.

a

a PHOTO COURTESY LEMAITRE SPECIAL EFFECTS, INC.

b

c

b & c PHOTOS COURTESY ROSCO LABORATORIES, INC.

Haze Machines The difference between a smoke machine and a haze machine or hazer is that the latter uses either liquid nitrogen, cracked oil, or a water-based liquid to create a long-lasting haze in the air. Extended use of cracked oil in a confined space is not recommended, for health reasons. Haze is not as dense as smoke and does not dissipate as quickly. Hazers are favored for concerts, which are often performed outside under poorly controlled conditions. Manufactured in a variety of types, hazers are more expensive than either dry ice or smoke machines (Figure 19-24).

Controlling Smoke Anyone using smoke of any nature on the stage is frequently faced with the problem of preventing it from flowing or blowing to where it is not wanted. Heavy fog that tends to hug the stage floor may easily spill over the apron into the auditorium—a touch that is seldom appreciated by the audience (not to mention an orchestra).

The lighter-than-air smoke that rises is subject to the slightest breeze or draft. A ventilator at the top of the stage house may draw it swiftly upward or a cross-draft may set up unwanted eddies and swirls. An exhaust fan that evacuates stale air from the auditorium can bring the smoke billowing into the house.

Each theatre and auditorium will affect smoke and fog in a different manner. The only way to discover how best to use these effects in a given space is to experiment in that facility under conditions that are as close to performance as possible.

a & b PHOTOS COURTESY LEMAITRE SPECIAL EFFECTS, INC.

a **b**

19-24

Haze Machines

Haze machines produce a light smoke effect that remains suspended in the air longer than standard smoke does.

a The LeMaitre G300 Fog Machine produces high quantities of smoke or haze.

b The LeMaitre LSG Low Smoke Generator couples with the G300 to create large amounts of low-lying fog.

ELECTRICALLY TRIGGERED EFFECTS

electrical solenoid An electromagnet that can be used for remote control of special effects.

Designers and technicians are constantly searching for new methods of creating stage illusions. Breakaway properties, pictures falling off the wall, or any number of magical occurrences can be achieved with the help of a device called an **electrical solenoid.**

The magnetic power of the solenoid coil can be used to withdraw the support of a picture on the wall or as a trigger for any other breakaway (Figure 19-25). When a current is passed through its coil, the solenoid becomes an electromagnet that draws the spring-loaded center pin into the coil. When the circuit is broken, the pin is released with considerable force. Either action can be used to trigger a breakaway.

Specialized lighting techniques clearly involve a wide range of instruments and effects, the most complex being the use of light as scenery. The next chapter shows how designers can create a thorough light plot, which covers all the stage-lighting plans for a production.

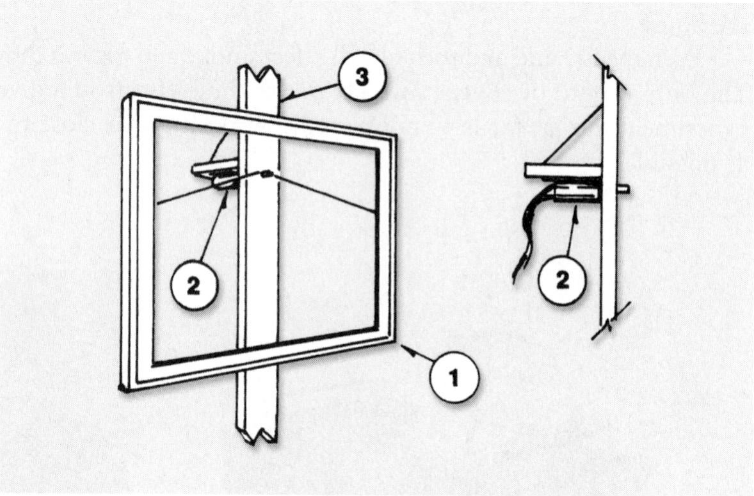

19-25

Electrically Triggered Effects

In its off position, the spring-loaded pin is extended through the batten to hold the picture frame in place. When current is sent into the coil, the pin withdraws and the picture falls.

1 Picture frame in place.
2 Solenoid coil mounted on rear of picture batten.
3 Picture batten.

20

Stage-Lighting Practice: The Light Plot and Production

We now come to a discussion of the lighting designer's basic communication tool: the light plot. The purpose of a light plot is to convey to the production electrician exactly how and where each lighting fixture is to be hung. The plot normally specifies color, circuiting, control, and related information concerning each individual instrument. A great deal of time, preparation, and thought goes into this plot, which represents the lighting designer's "working drawings." Creating a light plot is exacting work, for little time is available in the theatre to remedy any serious mistakes.

DESIGN DECISIONS

The lighting designer must make many decisions concerning the type and position of instruments, color filtering, and dimmer readings. Before we go into the specifics of plotting the lights, however, we should review the following all-important design considerations: instrumentation, angle and direction, color, and control (Figure 20-1).

Choice of Instrument

As previously noted, a designer will choose a particular stage-lighting instrument because it comes closest to satisfying the three requirements of intensity, coverage, and quality of light.

Ellipsoidal Reflector Spotlights Adjustable beam spread and shaping, high intensity, and variable quality of light make the ERS the lighting designer's most valuable instrument (Figure 20-2). In addition, it is the only conventional instrument capable of creating texture and pattern by means of a gobo. Although an ERS is the logical choice for front-of-house applications, this versatile unit also serves well backstage and should be considered along with the Fresnel and PAR fixture.

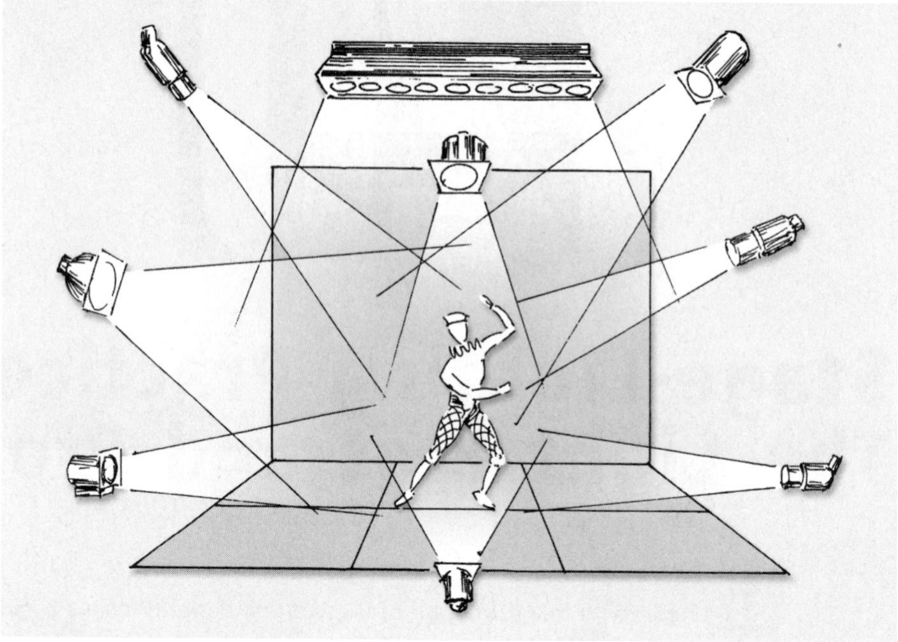

20-1

Design Decisions

Choice of Instrument. Does it provide the proper quality of light, control possibilities, and beam size/intensity?

Choice of Angle and Direction. Does it create the desired mood and visibility?

Choice of Color. Does it provide the proper mood, work with the costumes and scenery, and offer the necessary contrast?

Choice of Control. Is it used on its own or can it work with others?

Fresnels These instruments deliver a soft light whose beams blend very easily and therefore are ideal for short throws and upstage areas of a box set (Figure 20-3). Because of their variable beam spread capability, Fresnels can be used over a wide range of throw distances. The 6-inch Fresnel, lamped from 500 to 1,000 watts, has an effective throw of up to 20 feet. The 8-inch, with lamps up to 2,000 watts, can be useful up to 40 feet. Attached barn doors allow for reasonably good beam shaping. The soft light of a candle, the quality of dusk or an overcast sky, or the scattered, almost shadowless illumination from fluorescent tubes can be reproduced with a Fresnel.

PAR Fixtures and Beam Projectors The light from these instruments cannot be shaped, but their near-parallel rays come closest to resembling those of the sun (Figure 20-4). This quality can serve as a motivational source, while Fresnel and ERS light act as fill or bounce. The PAR fixture has a lens that breaks up the light, softening the edge of its oval beam. Yet it still delivers a sharp and intense light, harsh in quality. PAR fixtures make good back-lights and work well for dance.

Automated Fixtures Now available in many types, these remotely controlled instruments produce an intense light that outshines the brightest ERS and PAR fixtures. Although automated fixtures have a limited role in the theatre, compared with their use in concerts, theatre designers have embraced these technological wonders with open arms. They make superb specials

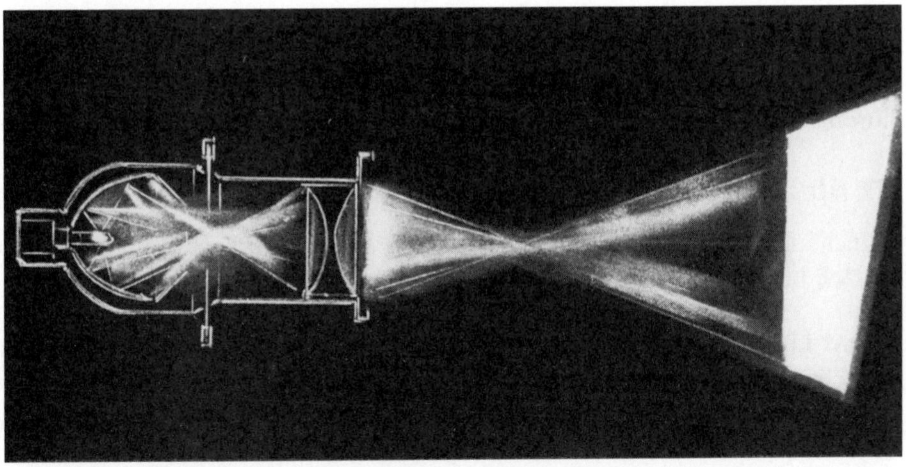

20-2

Choice of Instrument: The Ellipsoidal Reflector Spotlight

The versatile ERS has internal beam shaping, can take a gobo, and comes in a variety of beam sizes.

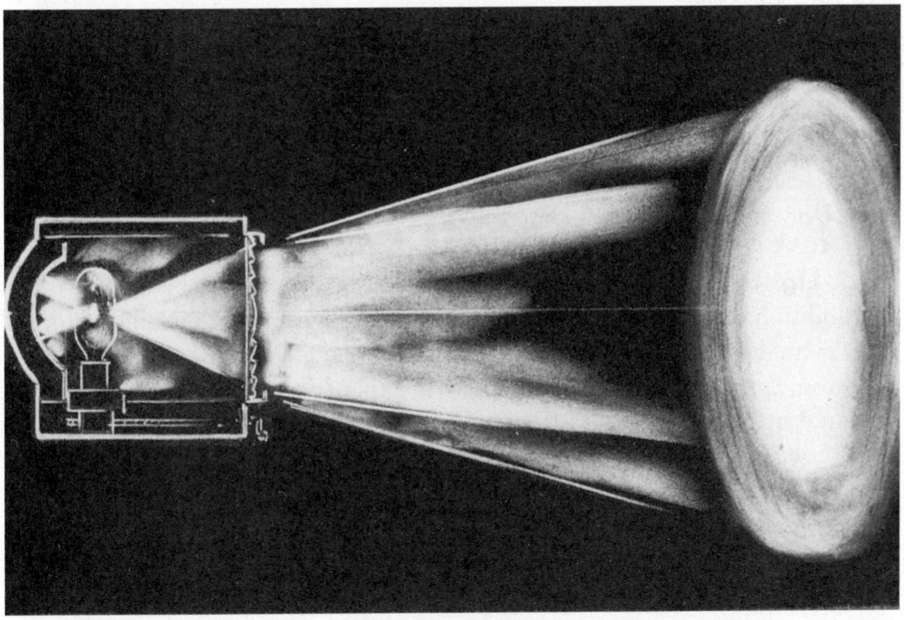

20-3

Choice of Instrument: The Fresnel

The Fresnel spotlight can take barn doors for beam shaping and allows for variable beam spreads. It delivers the softest quality of light of all types of instruments.

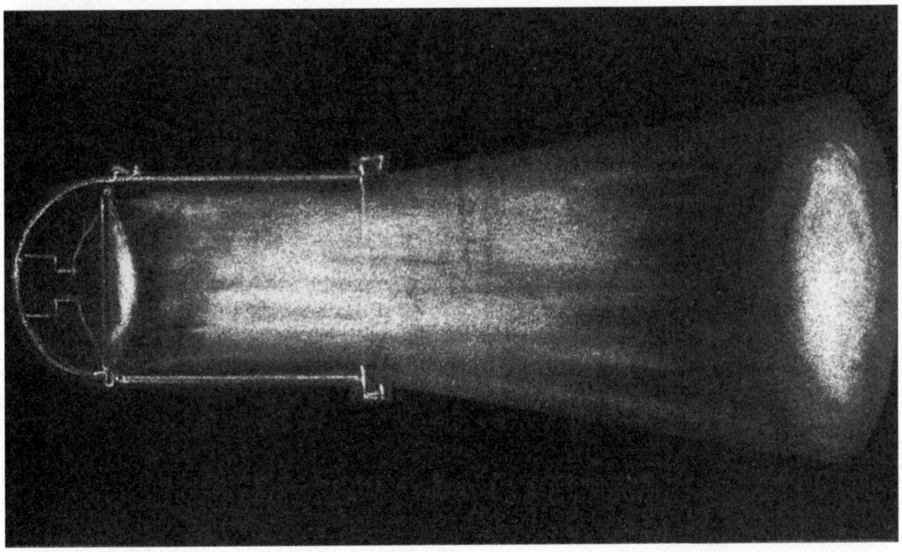

20-4

Choice of Instrument: The PAR Fixture

The PAR fixture is durable and bright, but its oval beam is impossible to shape. 1,000-watt PAR-64 lamps are available in four different beam spreads.

because of their high color temperature or can act as intense and flexible side-lighting instruments. Built-in gobo patterns and color versatility can instantaneously change the texture and mood of a scene. The flexibility alone of automated fixtures makes them a light source worth considering.

Choice of Angle and Direction

Which angle and direction of light to use is one of the most difficult choices for the beginning designer to make.

Front-Light The purpose of using two front-lights at various angles to each other, rather than a single unit straightaway, is to add dimension to the actor's body and face. As the angle of front-light is lowered, it tends to flatten features. As the angle is raised, features become sharper, with deeper shadows. Remember that front-light provides visibility more than any other direction of light does.

Side-Light Whether it is a bit frontal or straight out of the wings, side-light offers an exciting direction for both variety and revelation of form. The low-angled side-light commonly used in dance lighting evenly lights the entire height of the body. A slightly higher-angled side (from 30 to 60 degrees) is often used for theatrical productions to avoid spill on the scenery. The designer can begin to use richer and more expressive colors in side-light to establish a motivational source or simply to set the mood of a scene.

Back-Light Primarily used to create three-dimensionality, back-light offers the additional benefit of separating the actor from the background. Colored light from the back is extremely useful in toning the stage floor, and the choice of colors can be more aggressive than in other kinds of lighting. Back-light textured by gobos can be of great help in establishing mood. Compared with front gobos, rear ones are not as noticeable on the actors; yet, they texture the stage floor well, creating a broken light through which the actors move. Back-light angles should be kept between 45 and 60 degrees.

Choice of Color

Confidence in color selection requires experience—experience in traditional theatrical usage, experience in how colors mix with each other, and experience in how particular colors behave onstage. Lighting laboratories and color mix-boxes help, but a lighting designer ultimately must experiment with the real thing. A masterful use of color is the goal of every lighting designer. Achieving that goal takes time.

Careful consideration must first be given to scenic and costume colors. Unless by intention, colored light must not significantly alter the true colors of an actor's skin, clothing, or environment.

The successful use of color depends on a lighting designer's most important color resource—a strong visual memory. People associate feelings with certain colors and remember feelings or color impressions more readily than they do actual colors. In creating mood, the lighting designer uses color to tap into those feelings. As such, designers try to analyze and choose color by feeling as well as seeing. For instance, they would consider how sunlight feels and then try to translate the feeling into color. Worrying about what sunlight *should* look like can result in less effective choices.

Remember that the color temperature of a light source influences the color rendered by any filter. Another important consideration is the varying colors of an incandescent lamp under different dimmer settings. Finally, lighting colors appear less saturated or intense over longer throw distances.

Choice of Control

At the mention of "control," one normally thinks of dimmer levels; however, control also includes the way instruments and dimmers are assigned to channels. Control involves two types of decisions: the first is whether to "gang" two or more instruments onto a single dimmer/circuit, and the second is how to assign the soft patch. If made arbitrarily, such assignments can complicate the process of cue writing and level setting. Through rehearsals, discussions with the director, and review of lighting-movement requirements, the designer can begin the necessary task of anticipating control needs.

THE COLLABORATIVE PROCESS

Throughout this book, we have emphasized the great importance of collaboration. The lighting designer must be an excellent collaborator because lighting, in the end, unites all of the visual production elements. The significance of superior collaborative skills is heightened by the fact that visual and verbal presentation of lighting ideas is limited by the nature of the medium.

Production Collaboration

The first contact between a director and the designers sets the stage for the collaborative process that follows. The success or failure of this important exchange of ideas is determined first and foremost by attitude. If a production team's collaboration begins with acceptance and openness, the process has a good chance of being a positive experience. If such an environment exists and the members of the team become excited by the prospect of shared creation, the experience can be exhilarating.

Although no formula for success exists, extensive preparation in the form of research coupled with a positive attitude goes a long way. Lighting *storyboards* and *scores* are excellent teaching tools and can serve as valuable communication devices.

The Storyboard

A **lighting storyboard** consists of a series of sketches illustrating important aspects of a production's intended lighting. A complete storyboard includes a sketch for every major lighting change in the production. The drawings are often black-and-white value sketches (sometimes referred to as "thumbnail" sketches) and concentrate on the lighting mood or atmosphere of a given scene. Figure 20-5 shows a pair of storyboard sketches for a production of *Tosca*.

lighting storyboard A series of value sketches or color renderings depicting the quality of light for the various "looks" of a production.

Obviously, a lighting designer's storyboard presentation would take place well after the initial collaborative concept meetings, for a completed scenic design is necessary. On the other hand, the lighting score is a tool that can be useful in early design meetings.

20-5

Storyboard Sketches

Storyboard sketches by designer Susan Gratch for the opera *Tosca.* Often done as value sketches, storyboards show preliminary lighting ideas.

Tosca Act I S. Gratch

Tosca Act II S. Gratch

COURTESY SUSAN GRATCH

The Lighting Score

score A chart, arranged by lighting looks and various qualities of light, that helps to describe the designer's intent.

The **score** is a chart of the lighting for each scene or other unit of time (Figure 20-6). Designers can present more information in a score than in a storyboard. For those designers who do not render and draw well, the score is less intimidating as well.

In a lighting score, designers use the left column to list various concerns and factors affecting the lighting. The time line can be constructed in a variety of ways, with the play's acts or scenes making up the most convenient divisions. French scenes can be used for productions requiring a greater number of lighting

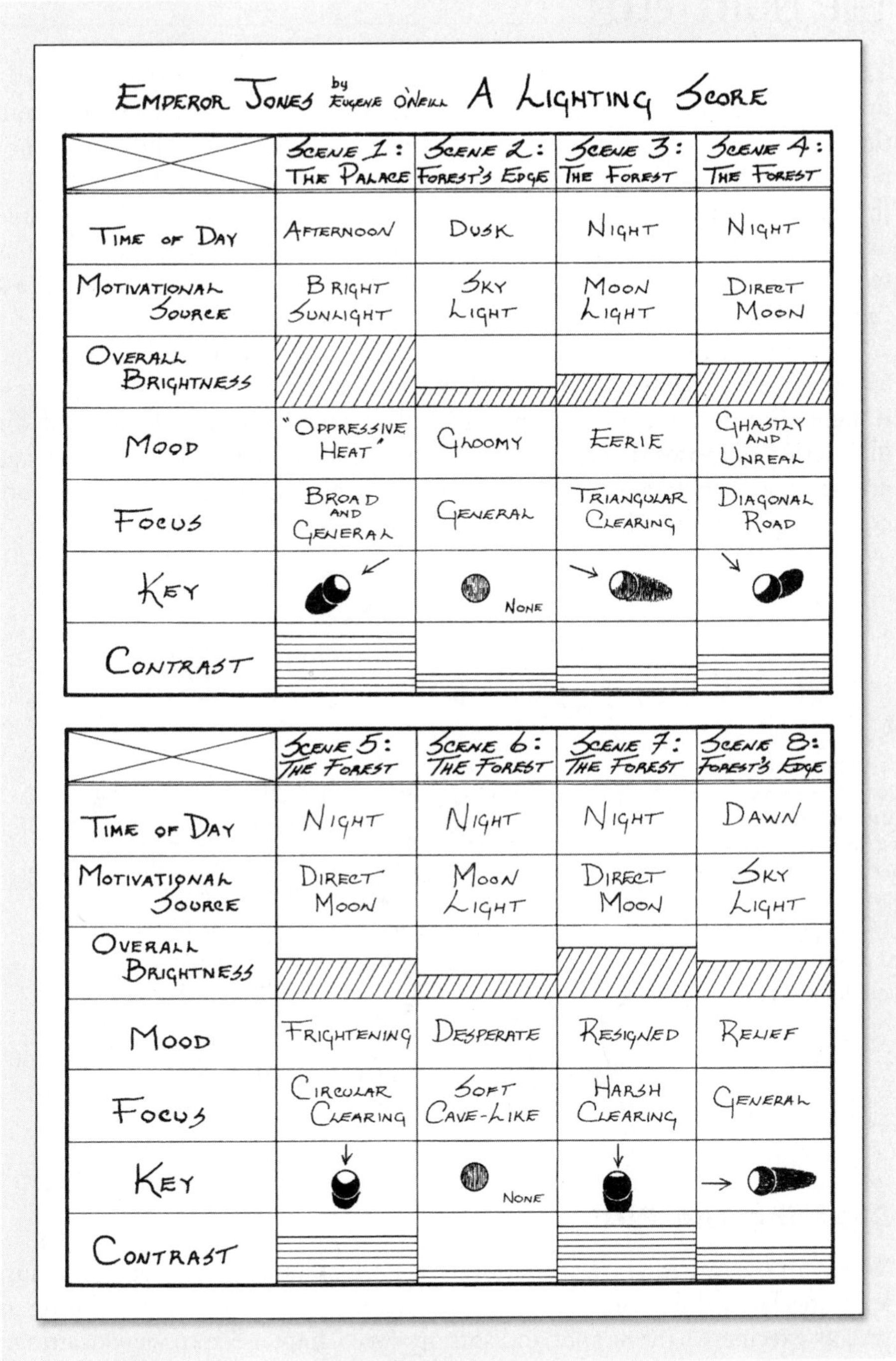
EMPEROR JONES by EUGENE O'NEILL A LIGHTING SCORE
SCENE 1: THE PALACE
SCENE 2: FOREST'S EDGE
SCENE 3: THE FOREST
SCENE 4: THE FOREST
TIME OF DAY
AFTERNOON
DUSK
NIGHT
NIGHT
MOTIVATIONAL SOURCE
BRIGHT SUNLIGHT
SKY LIGHT
MOON LIGHT
DIRECT MOON
OVERALL BRIGHTNESS
MOOD
"OPPRESSIVE HEAT"
GLOOMY
EERIE
GHASTLY AND UNREAL
FOCUS
BROAD AND GENERAL
GENERAL
TRIANGULAR CLEARING
DIAGONAL ROAD
KEY
NONE
CONTRAST
SCENE 5: THE FOREST
SCENE 6: THE FOREST
SCENE 7: THE FOREST
SCENE 8: FOREST'S EDGE
TIME OF DAY
NIGHT
NIGHT
NIGHT
DAWN
MOTIVATIONAL SOURCE
DIRECT MOON
MOON LIGHT
DIRECT MOON
SKY LIGHT
OVERALL BRIGHTNESS
MOOD
FRIGHTENING
DESPERATE
RESIGNED
RELIEF
FOCUS
CIRCULAR CLEARING
SOFT CAVE-LIKE
HARSH CLEARING
GENERAL
KEY
NONE
CONTRAST

20-6

Lighting Score

A lighting score for a production of O'Neill's *Emperor Jones.* The lighting score is a means of recording the major lighting looks of a production.

looks. The list of design considerations in the left column varies from production to production, but it almost always includes the categories of mood, focus, motivational source, and time of day. Rising and falling action, sense of conflict, brightness level, contrast, color, temperature, and atmospheric conditions are other possibilities. Lighting designers usually keep the score pictorial (as opposed to verbal), using graphs and color whenever possible and pictographs instead of words. In this way, the director, as well as the rest of the production team, can "see" the lighting images well before the actual plot is considered.

THE LIGHT PLOT

The light plot, along with its accompanying paperwork (the section and hook-up or instrument schedule), forms the link between the designer's ideas and the reality of theatrical production. The importance of the light plot cannot be overstated. It must be 100-percent accurate and complete, so that the load-in (hang, circuit, and focus) can proceed in an orderly and rapid fashion. While executing a plot, the designer discovers and remedies many artistic as well as technical problems. Careful and accurate plotting allows the designer to address these problems well before he or she sets foot in the theatre.

The rest of this chapter covers the process of developing a light plot and executing the design; Chapter 23 delves further into design considerations. A light plot and section for the musical review *Beehive* will be used for illustration purposes (Figure 20-7). The theatre is intimate, with a thrust stage and steep audience rake. Hanging positions over the thrust and audience are created by pipes on 6-foot centers.

20-7

Light Plot

The ½-inch scale light plot for a production of *Beehive*. The stage thrusts out into a steeply raked and intimate auditorium. See Figure 20-15 for the sectional.

a A portion of the plot reproduced at actual size.

b The complete light plot.

a

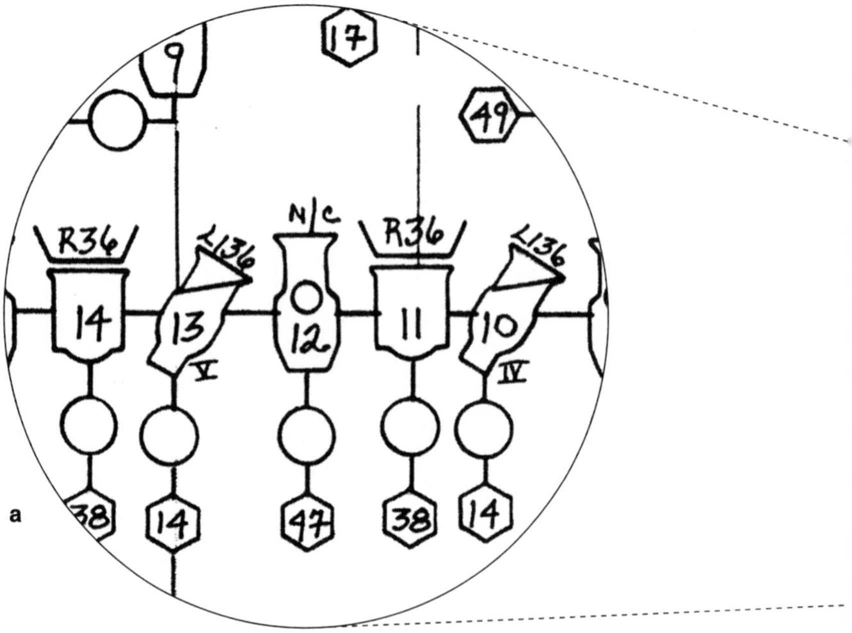

Drafting the Plot

Whether using a CAD program or drafting by hand, the lighting designer must learn mechanical drawing in order to read and understand scenic drafting as well as execute a lighting plot and section. (See Chapter 5 to review drafting.)

The light plot is drawn to ½-inch scale in a manner that allows reproduction through a process known as **blueprinting** or its variation, **blue-line printing.** The advantages of blueprinting are cost and convenience. The disadvantage is that color cannot be reproduced; it would be handy to be able to color-code rather than use some of the current drafting conventions. Black-and-white photocopying of the plot is an alternative that is becoming more cost-effective.

blueprinting A process of copying an original line drawing, which results in a blue field with white lines.

blue-line printing A type of blueprinting that produces blue lines on a white field.

The first step in drafting a light plot is to secure a copy of the plan and section of the theatre. Information from these drawings is then transferred onto the drafting plates that will soon become light plot and section. Next, details from the scenery ground plan and section are added to the two drawings. Finally, instruments are plotted, color is chosen, and control decisions are made.

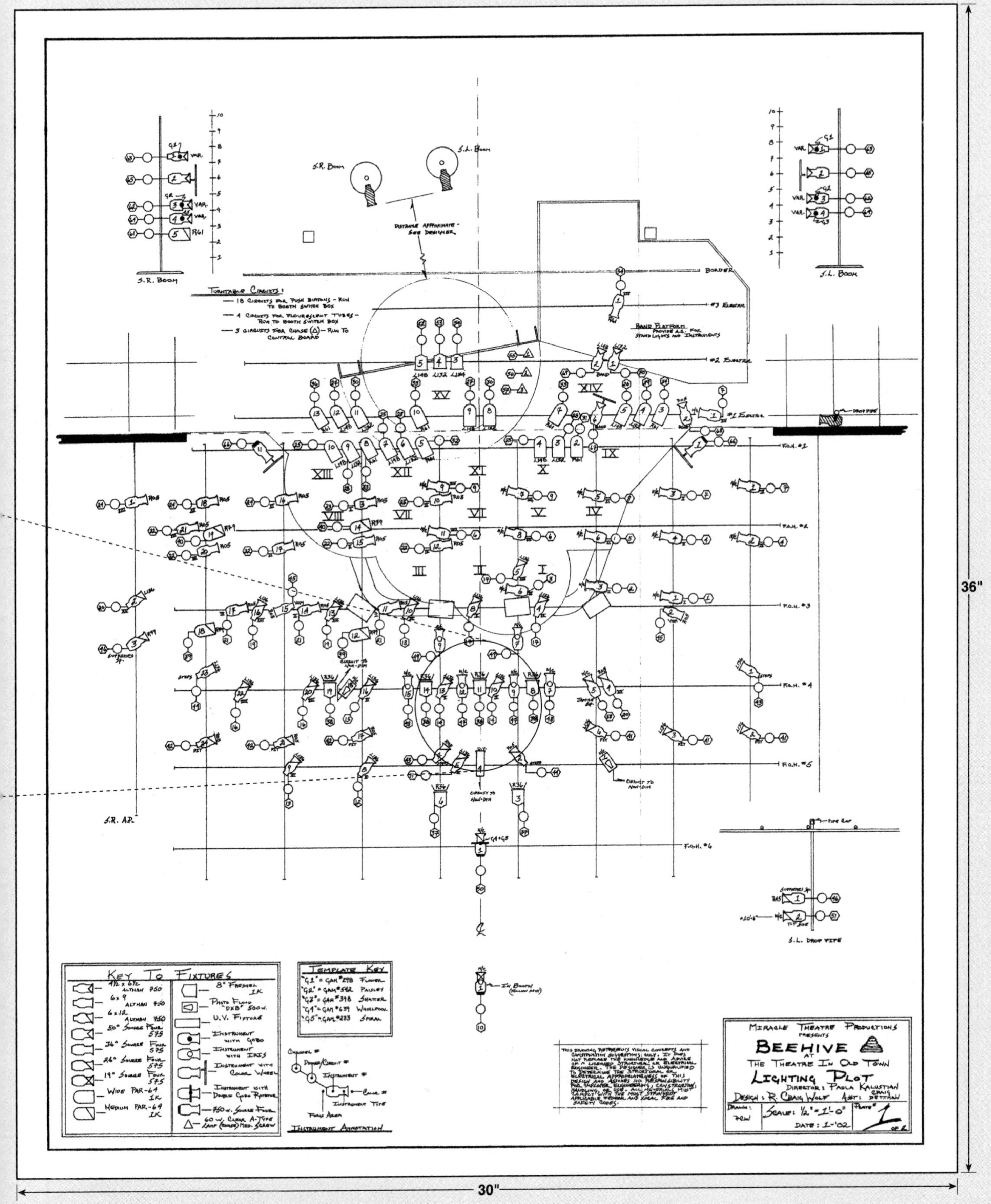

S.R. Boom
S.L. Boom
Distance Approximate - See Designer
Border
#3 Electric
#2 Electric
#1 Electric
Band Platform
F.O.H. #1
F.O.H. #2
F.O.H. #3
F.O.H. #4
F.O.H. #5
F.O.H. #6
S.R. A.P.
S.L. Drop Pipe
Key To Fixtures
Template Key
Instrument Annotation
Miracle Theatre Productions
presents
BEEHIVE
at
The Theatre In Old Town
Lighting Plot
Director: Paula Kalustian
Design: R. Craig Wolf
Scale: 1/2" = 1'-0"
Date: 1-'02
36"
30"

b

Lighting Design Basics

Light Plot Elements

Given that some standardization is desirable for any communicative tool, the light plot should include the following elements:

1. A plan of the theatre drawn to scale (preferably ½ inch—never ⅛ inch) showing and labeling all lighting positions
2. A simplified plan of the stage setting drawn to scale in lightweight lines
3. Lighting areas indicated by letters of the alphabet or Roman numerals in heavyweight lines—beginning downstage-left, working stage-right, and then upstage
4. Exact instrument placement, type and size, color, and number
5. Title block in the lower right-hand corner, instrument key, instrument annotation key, and gobo key (if needed)

Theatre Plan and Section A theatre's technical director, electrician, or production manager can provide a blue-line plan and section, hopefully in ½-inch scale. These prints should include all the information needed to draw the theatre plan onto the light plot. However, a theatre plan and section may show neither circuits nor every light-hanging position. If this is the case, designers should ask the appropriate producing agent to provide a circuit chart and/or a light-hanging plan. The house will also provide the designer with an up-to-date instrument inventory as well as control specifications. A visit to inspect the theatre is highly recommended.

The designer should transfer all rigging for the production to the light plot and section. This includes masking, flying scenery and drops, and electric pipes. Critical audience sight points, indicated by a cross, must be included on the lighting plan and section as well. If drafting by hand, designers initially indicate a lighting hanging position by a single solid line of very light weight (it will later be darkened and made bolder). Each position must be clearly labeled. To save space, a designer can show distance to front-of-house positions in a smaller scale, but this deviation should be clearly noted.

Some designers prefer to include a plaster-line scale and sometimes an upstage-to-downstage scale in order to facilitate the hanging and placement of instruments.

Designers do best to draft the basic lighting plan and section (without instruments) as early as possible in the design process—at least several weeks before the plot deadline. This allows time to digest the theatre and scenic information and saves valuable drafting time later.

Scenery Plan and Section The scenic designer should deliver to the lighting designer a copy of the scenery ground plan and section as soon as it is complete. Scenery information transferred to the light plot and section need not be as complete or detailed as it is on the scenic ground plan. It should include only elements important to the lighting, such as walls, doors, major levels, large pieces of furniture, and so forth. The scenic elements included in

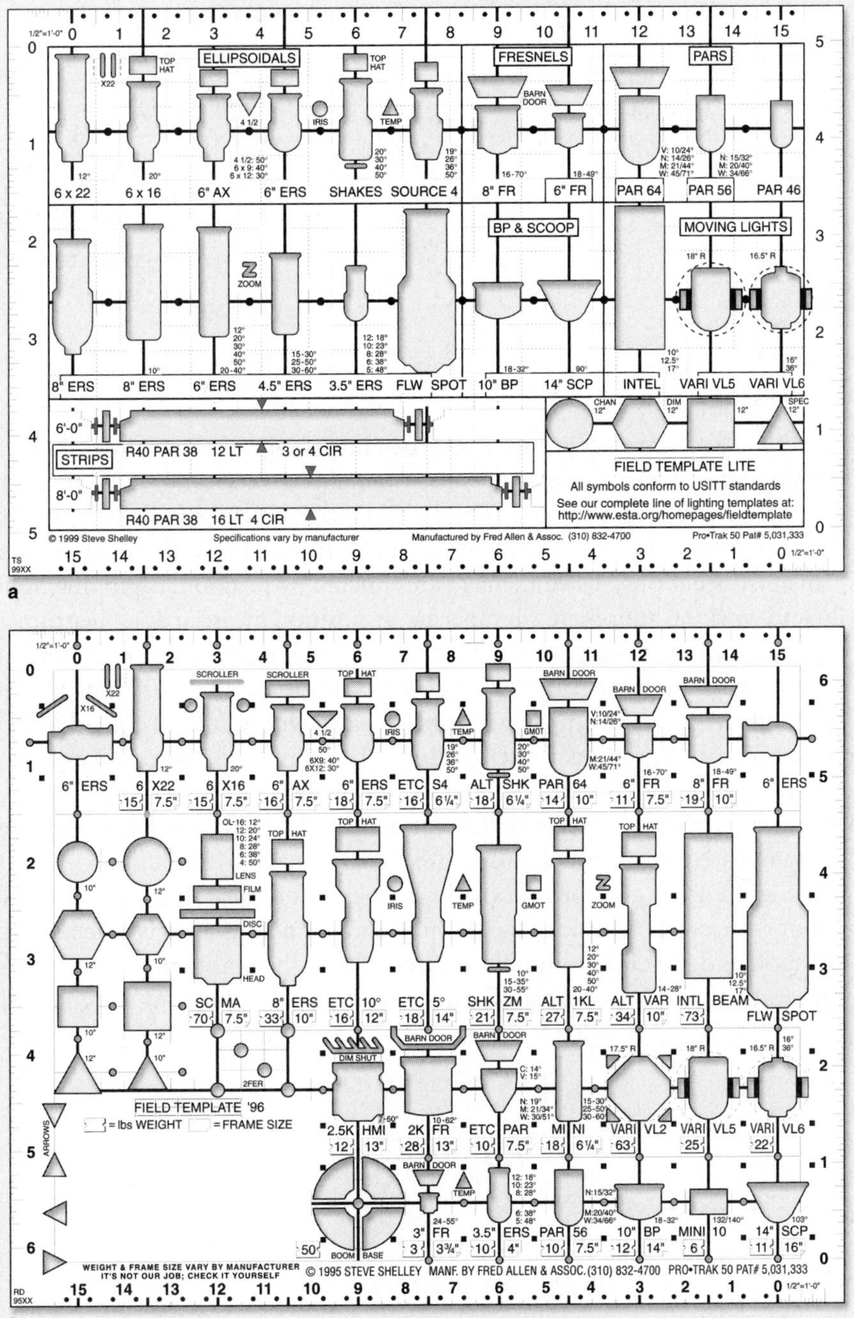

20-8

Lighting Templates

a The Field Template Lite, the educational version of the Stage Fixture Field Template.

b The Stage Plan Field Template, which includes information on beam spread, hanging weight, and cut color size.

a & b TEMPLATES COURTESY STEVE SHELLEY, FRED ALLEN & ASSOCIATES, AND FIELD TEMPLATE

the *Beehive* plot are a turntable and wall unit upstage-right, an orchestra platform upstage-left, and the thrust. All this is drafted in lightweight lines so that lighting instruments can be plotted directly over scenery lines.

Plaster line and center line should be included. If the production requires several sets, the lighting designer may use transparent overlays of each set.

Instrument Annotation One of the several available lighting instrument templates should be used to trace outlines of the various instruments (Figure 20-8). Templates can be ordered in either ¼- or ½-inch scale as well as in plan or section view. If drafting in CAD, designers may have instrument symbols as

20-9

Instrument Annotation

Some designers prefer to place the focus area in front of the instrument, along with the color number.

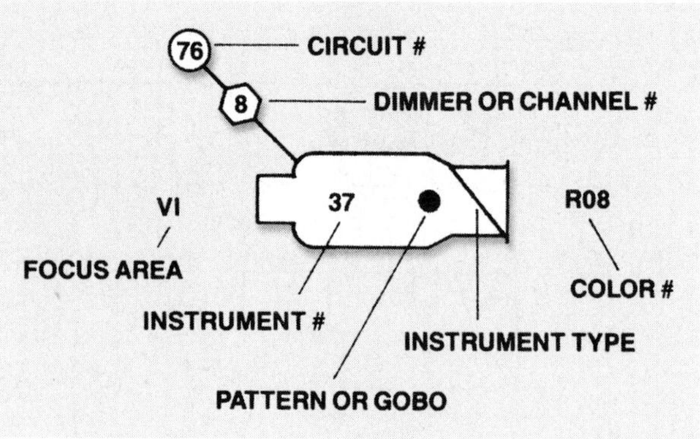

part of their software program or may be able to import them from manufacturer Web sites. These outlines must be bold enough to stand out from all the other information on the plot. The lighting instrument should intersect the lighting pipe, but the pipe itself should not be drawn through the instrument.

In most situations, instruments are numbered by position, beginning house-right and working house-left. Numbering by position means that all instruments located in each lighting position are numbered consecutively beginning with "1" (Figure 20-7). Some situations, however, may make numbering by position rather confusing (for example, a flexible theatre with a full, overhead lighting grid). In such cases, all instruments should be numbered consecutively.

The instrument annotation illustrated in Figure 20-9 is recommended. The instrument number is centered in the rear body of the instrument, the instrument type is indicated by a symbol and located at the barrel position (Figure 20-10), focus area (if used) goes behind the instrument, and the color number goes in front of the lens. In addition, the dimmer or channel number is placed within a hexagon and the circuit number is circled. Both hexagon and circle connect to the rear of the instrument as shown. If the designer does not assign circuits

20-10

Instrument Types

These symbols, used in the instrument's barrel, indicate beam spread.

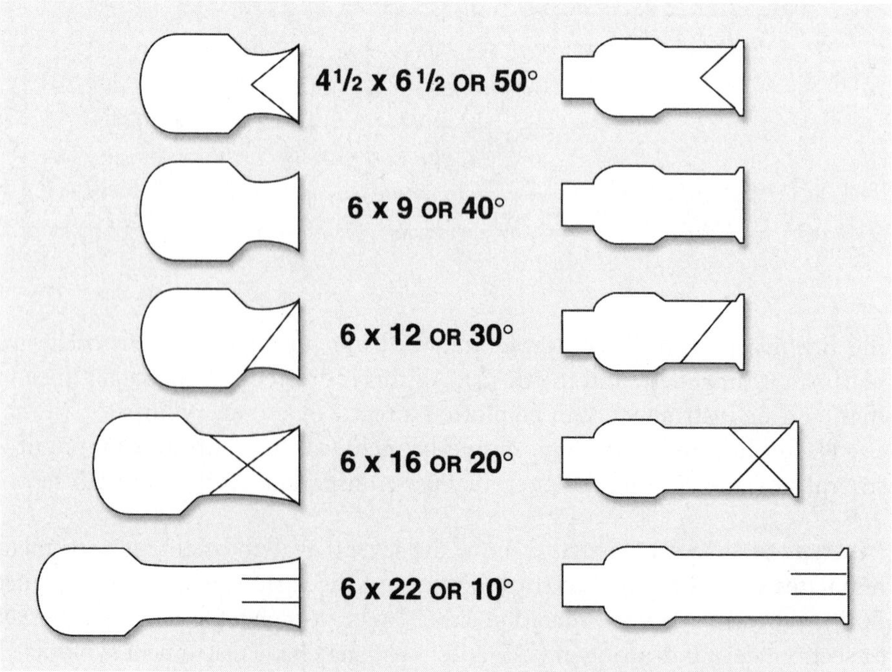

or wish to leave a place for them to be recorded, the circle may be eliminated, as in the *Beehive* plot.

Instrument, Color, and Gobo Keys The instrument key indicates exactly which symbol the designer is using for a specific instrument. This key, which should include the wattage as well as the beam spread of the instrument, is normally located in the lower-left corner of the plate.

The color key explains what numbering and lettering system the designer is using for each brand and type of color medium. For example:

"R" series = Roscolux

"L" series = Lee Filters

"G" series = GAM Color

The gobo key indicates how the designer is identifying each pattern in use:

"G1" = GAM 305: Pointed break-up

"G2" = Rosco 7795: Shattered

Booms Designers also need to represent floor stands or booms. A boom normally consists of a heavy metal base into which is screwed a length of 1¼- or 1½-inch black pipe. Any length of pipe may be used, but booms of any great height must be safely tied off from above. A lighting instrument is then hung off the boom by using a cross-pipe or **side-arm** (Figure 20-11).

side-arm An accessory valuable for hanging lights on booms or other vertical positions.

A boom can be represented on the light plot in one of two ways:

1. The boom base is drawn as a circle and located in its proper position on the plan. The pipe is drawn at scaled length and at an angle of 45 to 60 degrees directly out of its base. The various instruments are then

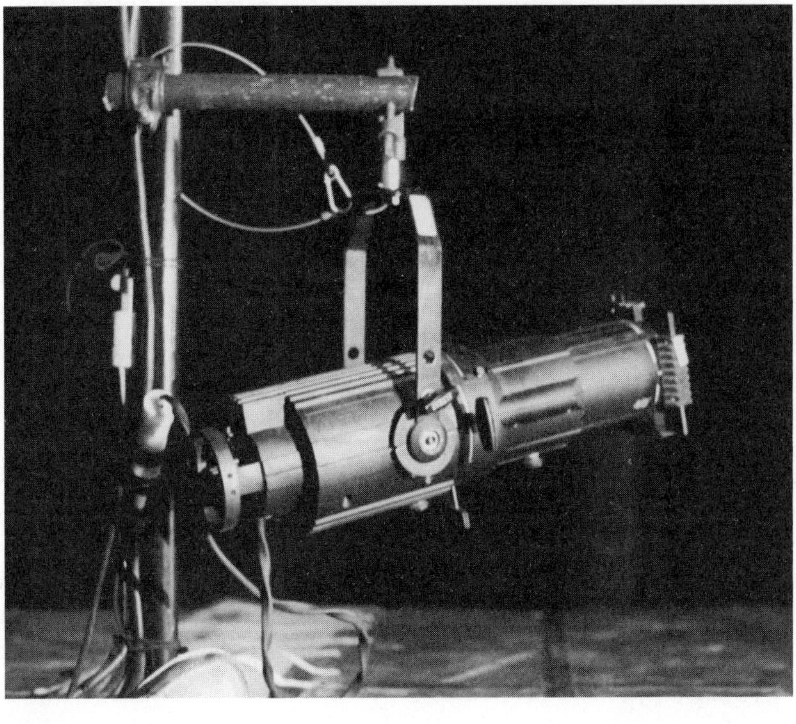

20-11

Boom with a Side-Arm

A side-arm allows one to focus an instrument more easily.

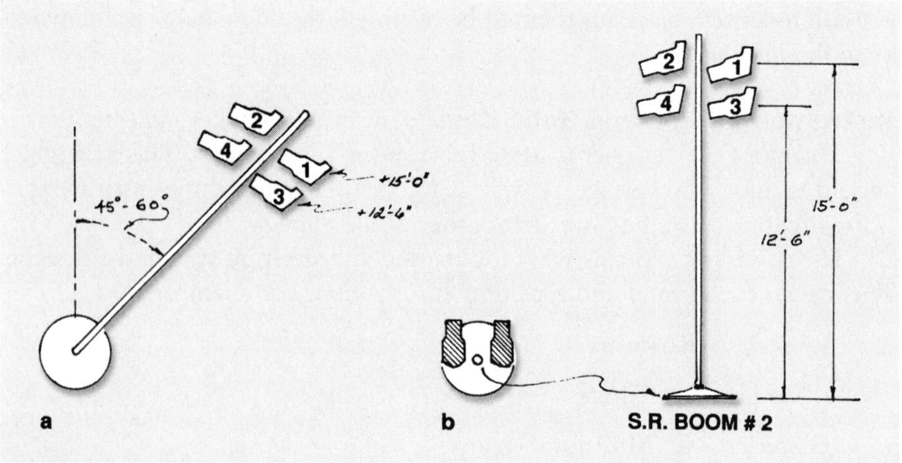

20-12

Representing a Boom on the Light Plot

a The isometric method shows the boom base in its actual position onstage.

b The plan and elevation method is often desirable when space on the plan is limited. Note the cross-hatching of the instruments in plan view.

shown in relationship to their boom pipe (Figure 20-12a). This is similar to an isometric view.

2. The boom base and pipe are drawn as circles and located in their proper position on the plan. A cross-hatched lighting instrument is drawn in proper relationship to the boom pipe, indicating that another view of the instrument appears elsewhere in the plot. An elevation of the boom is then drawn on the side or bottom of the drafting plate and labeled by position name. Instrument specifications are indicated on the elevation (Figure 20-12b; also see Figure 20-7). If a production has a large number of booms, a separate boom plate may be drawn. In both methods of plotting boom positions, instrument height must be indicated.

Similar drafting conventions should be used for ladder, box boom, and side cove positions where several instruments are stacked above each other. Note the drafting for the stage-left drop pipe in the *Beehive* plot.

Lighting Areas As discussed in Chapter 15, the lighting designer determines lighting areas by considering several factors: shape and size of the setting, degree of control desired, blocking of actors, and available equipment. The diameter of the beam of light thrown by a lighting instrument is a function of throw distance and that instrument's beam spread. The beginning designer is wise to make up beam-and-field spread templates for each of the instruments in common use. Such a template, drawn to scale on drafting or tracing paper, can be used as an overlay on a section view of the theatre and will quickly show approximate area coverage (Figure 20-13).

The heavy-weight Roman numerals or letters used as area indicators on the light plot should mark the center of the focus area (Figure 20-7). Using

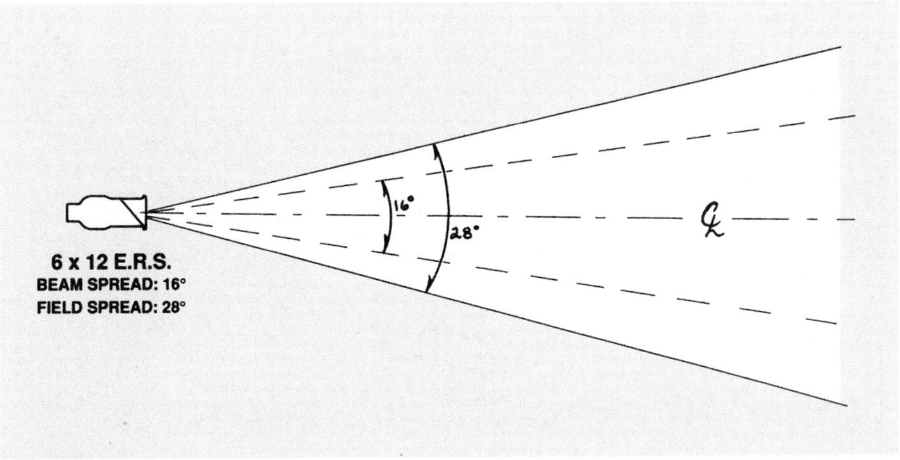

20-13

Beam Spread Template

The lighting designer can use a protractor and drafting paper to make templates such as the one shown.

Roman numerals or letters helps to keep area numbers distinct from all other numbering on the plot. Circles indicating beam or field spread should not be included.

CADD Light Plots Computer-aided design and drafting programs enable a designer to use computer graphics to create lighting plots. The new generation of lighting designers is drawing with a mouse rather than a drafting pencil. Architectural firms and much of the entertainment industry are demanding that perspective employees be CAD-literate.

The two most popular software programs are AutoCad by Autodesk and Vectorworks by Nemetschek North America. AutoCad is the industry standard in architectural, engineering, and consulting firms. Vectorworks is the preference of many theatrical lighting designers. Learning to use a CAD program takes time, and the software is expensive, but the skill is important for survival in today's highly diverse lighting design field. With access to proper software and equipment, such as a **plotter** (a drawing machine capable of drafting a light plot from computer information), the designer need only input the desired lighting instrument information and the system will generate a plot (Figure 20-14) as well as the required paperwork.

URL http://www.autodesk.com

URL http://www.nemetschek.net

plotter A mechanical drawing machine used to draft light plots and technical drawings from computer files.

The Lighting Section

A **section** is an important tool for the lighting designer. The section must be completely drafted before lighting instruments are placed on the plot. A section view helps the designer visualize the height and placement of scenery and lighting instruments, thereby improving the accuracy of the light plot. The designer consults the section for vertical sightlines, throw distances, acting levels above or below stage height, and accuracy of lighting angles. Electric trims (height of electric pipes off the stage floor) are determined by using the section (Figure 20-15).

section A view of a set from one side, as if cut across vertically at the center line.

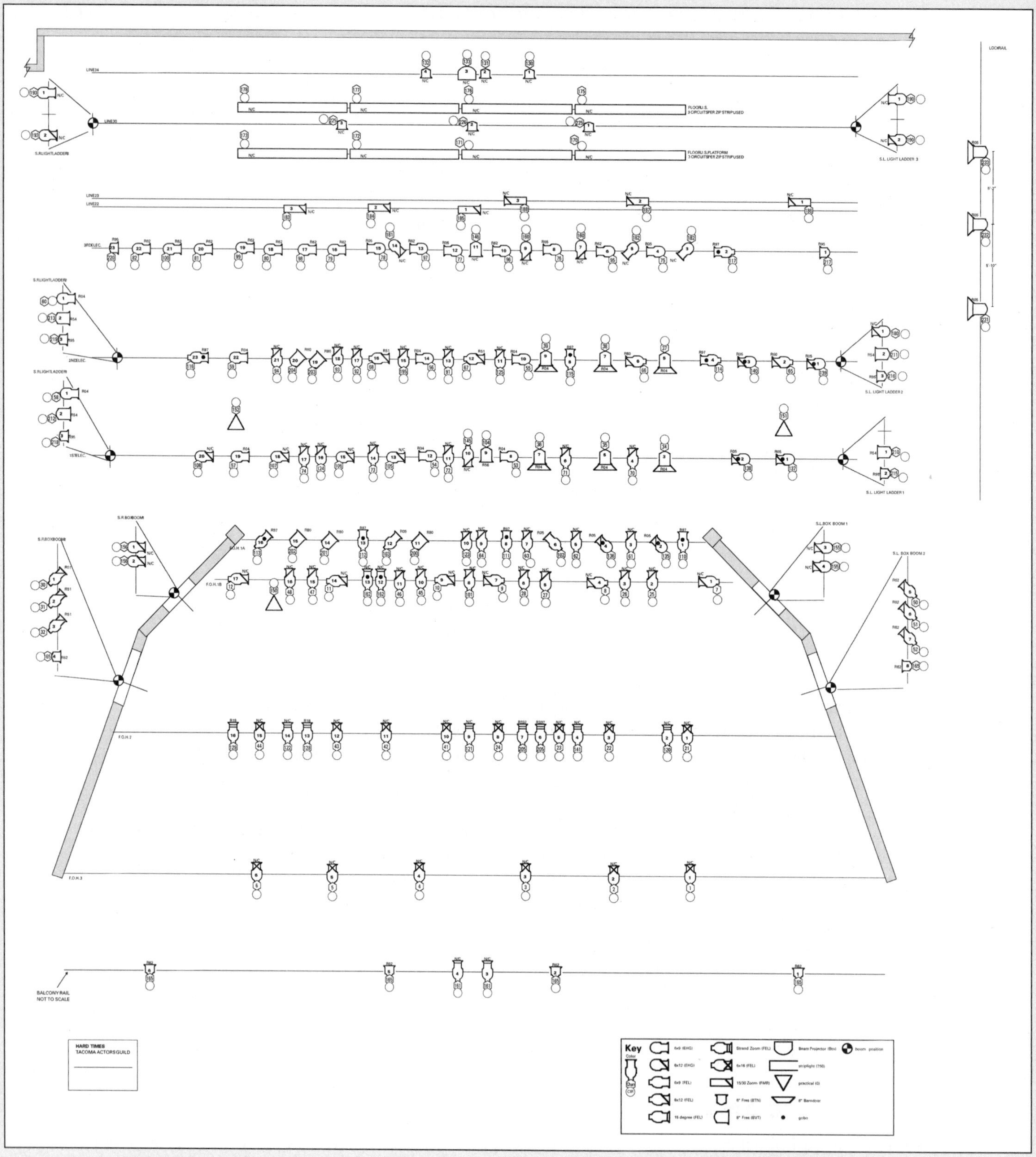

COURTESY SCOTT O'DONNELL

20-14

CADD Plot

A light plot drawn using CADD software, for a production of *Hard Times.* Design and drafting by Scott O'Donnell.

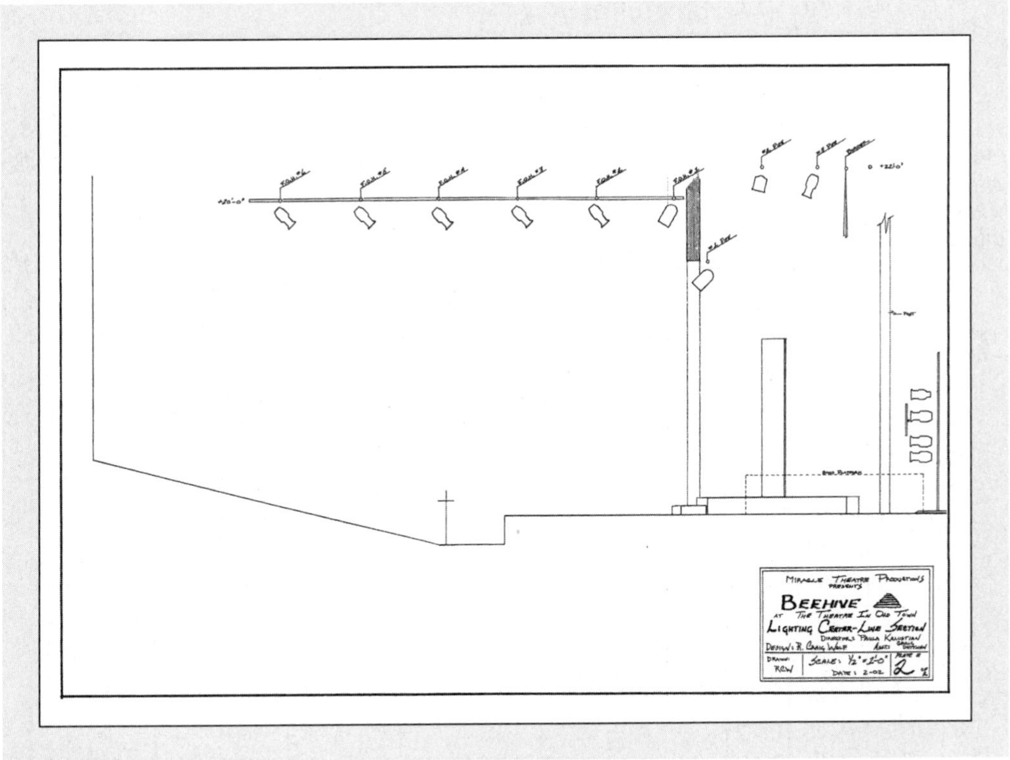

20-15

Lighting Section

The ½-inch scale center-line section of the *Beehive* light plot shown in Figure 20-7. Sections are important indicators of throw angle and distance, scenery heights, and masking.

Recall that the section view is actually a side view with the picture plane being on center line. It is as if a large cut were taken through the theatre and auditorium along the center line and we are looking into the cut surface. If the stage house is drawn on the left-hand side of the drafting plate, we are looking stage-left. If the stage house is on the right-hand side of the drafting plate, we are looking stage-right. Normally only one section view is necessary.

It should be understood that the section is primarily a lighting designer's tool. If electric trims are indicated on the plan, the production electrician need never see the section.

As noted earlier, the scene designer provides the lighting designer with a center-line section view of the stage that includes horizontal masking at trim height, critical audience sight points, and scenery placement. Occasionally various supplementary section views are necessary; the lighting designer can easily and quickly draft them.

The Hookup and Instrument Schedule

In most cases, the only paperwork item submitted with the light plot is either a hookup or an instrument schedule. Both pieces of paperwork list anything anyone would ever want to know about each instrument used in the plot. The difference between the two is the order in which they do so.

The Hookup There are two types of **hookups:** One is arranged by dimmer number and intended for installations that still use a patch panel (left column in the accompanying box); the other is arranged by channel number and used

hookup A lighting chart that is arranged by dimmer or channel number and that lists a variety of instrument information.

20-16

The Hookup

A page from the hookup for the musical *Teddy & Alice* designed by Tharon Musser.

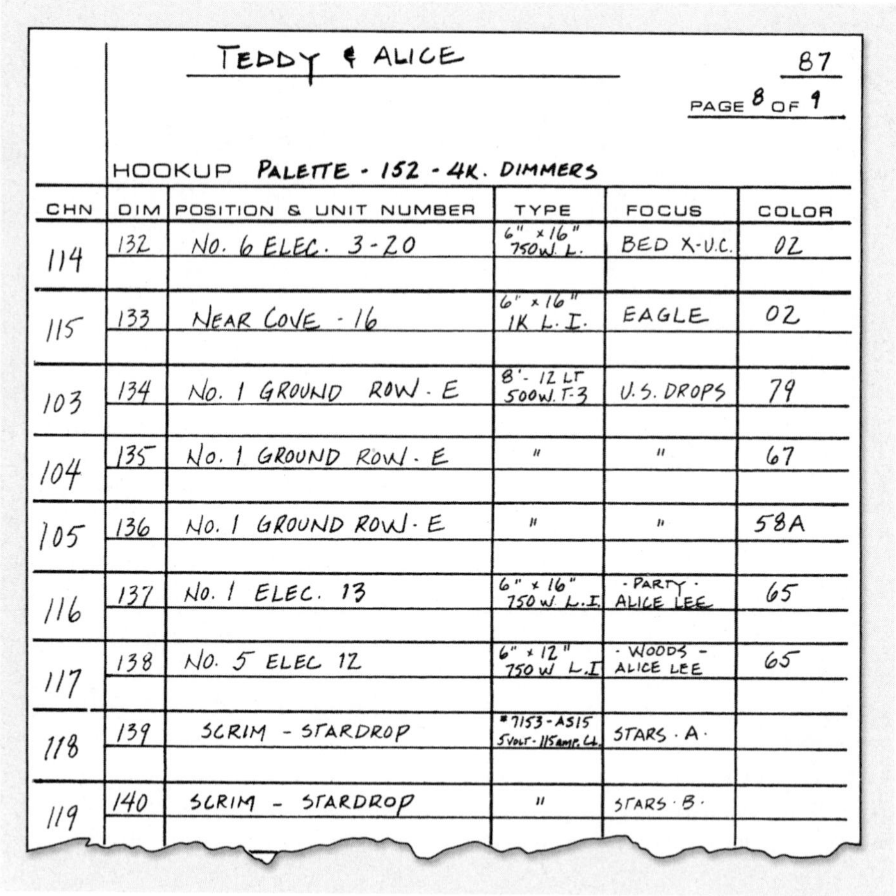

TEDDY & ALICE 87

PAGE 8 OF 9

HOOKUP PALETTE - 152 - 4K. DIMMERS

CHN	DIM	POSITION & UNIT NUMBER	TYPE	FOCUS	COLOR
114	132	NO. 6 ELEC. 3-20	6" x 16" 750W L.	BED X-U.C.	02
115	133	NEAR COVE - 16	6" x 16" 1K L.I.	EAGLE	02
103	134	No. 1 GROUND ROW - E	8'- 12 LT 500W. T-3	U.S. DROPS	79
104	135	No. 1 GROUND ROW - E	"	"	67
105	136	No. 1 GROUND ROW - E	"	"	58A
116	137	No. 1 ELEC. 13	6" x 16" 750 W L.I.	· PARTY · ALICE LEE	65
117	138	No. 5 ELEC 12	6" x 12" 750 W L.I	· WOODS - ALICE LEE	65
118	139	SCRIM - STARDROP	#7153-AS15 5volt-115amp.	STARS · A ·	
119	140	SCRIM - STARDROP	"	STARS · B ·	

with dimmer-per-circuit systems (right column). Note that items 5 through 9 in both columns contain common information.

Patch Panel Hookup	Dimmer-per-Circuit Hookup
1. Dimmer number	1. Channel number
2. Position name	2. Dimmer/circuit number
3. Instrument number	3. Position name
4. Circuit number	4. Instrument number
5. Instrument wattage	5. Instrument wattage
6. Instrument type	6. Instrument type
7. Color	7. Color
8. Purpose/focus	8. Purpose/focus
9. Remarks	9. Remarks

As is obvious from Tharon Musser's hookup for *Teddy & Alice* (Figure 20-16), not all of the information listed above is always necessary. Hookups were originally intended as a supplement to the instrument schedule. With more information included on light plots themselves, a hookup can replace an instrument schedule.

The Instrument Schedule Listing all instruments by location and instrument number, the **instrument schedule** is primarily used to provide instrument information that does not appear on the light plot. Information is listed in the following order:

instrument schedule A lighting chart that is arranged by instrument location and number and that lists a variety of instrument information.

1. Location and instrument number
2. Instrument type
3. Wattage/lamp designation
4. Color number
5. Use/focus area
6. Circuit
7. Dimmer/channel
8. Remarks

Lighting Paperwork

Proper planning and the resulting paperwork are critical to a successful design. The best lighting designers are creative as well as methodical—character traits not often found together. Designers have developed a variety of types of paperwork in order to simplify the load-in and the execution of the design. Lighting paperwork and related items include cue sheets and preset sheets, color cut lists, designer magic sheets, batten tapes, hanging cardboards, focus charts, and shop orders. Much of this paperwork can be generated by lighting software programs.

Paperwork Software Many individuals and companies have developed software programs that are intended to ease the lighting designer's paperwork load. A good example is Lightwright, developed by John McKernon and distributed by City Theatrical, Inc. Depending on the circumstances of a production, such programs can save the designer or assistant designer a great deal of time. Some initial time and effort is required to enter the lighting data into the computer. However, once the information has been entered, changes and/or additions to keep the paperwork up-to-date are extremely fast and simple. This is of particular advantage to productions that will tour or be revived. If the plot has been drafted with CAD, a supplementary software program can produce paperwork without additional data entry (Figure 20-17).

URL http://www.mckernon.com

URL http://www.citytheatrical.com

Cue Sheets and Preset Sheets Cue sheets and preset sheets are primarily used with non-computer-based control systems. However, a form of the preset sheet is valuable for writing cues "blind" for any type of control system.

Cue sheets are simply a list of a production's lighting cues in numerical order. In a preset system, information about each cue may include preset number, fade time, and description. In a computer-based system, information includes cue number, fade time, link or follow, delay, and possibly a description. A printer can produce hard copy of cue sheets from any computer-based control console.

cue sheets A list of a production's lighting cues in numerical order.

On **preset sheets**, designers record dimmer levels for each lighting cue in a production. All dimmers are listed by number, and there is space for the designer to pencil in level information. As the designer makes changes, an assistant must carefully update the preset sheets—a slow process at best.

preset sheets A means of recording dimmer levels for each lighting cue in a production.

20-17

Lightwright Hookup

Shown is the channel hookup, created by Lightwright software, from the Broadway production of *The Who's Tommy* designed by Chris Parry.

TOMMY - PINBALL "A" CHANNEL HOOKUP Page 1

Designer: Chris Parry
Associate: David Grill
PINBALL - FINAL CUT VERSION

Producer: ATP / Dodger / Pace
Head Electrician: Steve Cooksey

Note: Asterisks indicate Replug Channels

Chn	Dim	Position	Unit	Cir#	Type	Watts	Purpose	Color
(3)	84	COVE	7	6	6x16	1kw	Conductor	N/C
(6)	81	COVE	4	3	6x16	1kw	Frts CL	L203+R119
(7)	83	COVE	6	5	6x16	1kw	Frts CLC	L203+R119
(8)	85	COVE	8	7	6x16	1kw	Frts CC	L203+R119
(9)	86	COVE	9	8	6x16	1kw	Frts CRC	L203+R119
(10)	88	COVE	11	10	6x16	1kw	Frts CR	L203+R119
(17)	60	BOX BOOM L	1	1	S4-419 w/CRam w/10" TH	575w	Wash L C/C	IR H.S.+ CRam
	60	BOX BOOM L	2	1	S4-419 w/CRam w/10" TH	575w	Wash L C/C	IR H.S.+ CRam
(18)	66	BOX BOOM R	1	7	S4-419 w/CRam w/10" TH	575w	Wash R C/C	IR H.S.+ CRam
	66	BOX BOOM R	2	7	S4-419 w/CRam w/10" TH	575w	Wash R C/C	IR H.S.+ CRam
(19)	65	LO BOX L	1	6	S4-426 w/CRam w/10" TH	575w	Lo C/C L	IR H.S.+
	65	LO BOX L	2	6	S4-426 [illegible]	[illegible]	[illegible]	[illegible]

Color Cut Lists Once the plot is complete, color filters must be cut. A color cut list, organized by color manufacturer and then by color number, specifies size and quantity of each filter. This list may need to be completed quite early in order to allow time for purchasing. Paperwork software programs can generate a cut list that includes required sheet quantity. If no software is being used, electricians find it easiest to generate a color cut list from a hookup or an instrument schedule rather than the plot. If the people cutting color are inexperienced, the designer must be sure they know that a 6-inch color frame does not literally mean a 6-inch cut of color.

magic sheet Custom-designed paperwork used to assist the designer in setting and adjusting light levels. Also called a *cheat sheet.*

Magic Sheets Paperwork that aids a designer in setting and adjusting lighting levels is referred to as a **magic sheet** or "cheat" sheet. With the impressive increase in numbers of dimmers, designers needed help remembering what is assigned to each control channel or group of channels—thus, magic sheets were born.

Although each designer likes to customize his or her own sheets, and nearly as many styles exist as do designers, Figure 20-18 illustrates several of the most common types. Many magic sheets list groups of channels by either function or color. Some can be quite elaborate and pictorial. The primary objective in designing a magic sheet is to keep it clear and brief.

batten tape Strips of paper or cloth attached to a lighting batten to assist in the hanging and circuiting of instruments.

Batten Tapes To expedite hanging and circuiting the electric pipes, a designer may wish to prepare **batten tapes** for each hanging position. These consist of rolled strips of paper or cloth that have been premarked with center line and specific instrument information. The tapes are attached to the batten, and then the electricians follow the instructions on the tape. Information may include instrument number, circuit number, instrument type, color, and even focus. Tapes eliminate any measuring and chalking of the battens and, in combination with hanging cardboards, can provide so much information to electricians that they never need to consult the master light plot. Tapes are particularly valuable for touring productions or for working with inexperienced electricians.

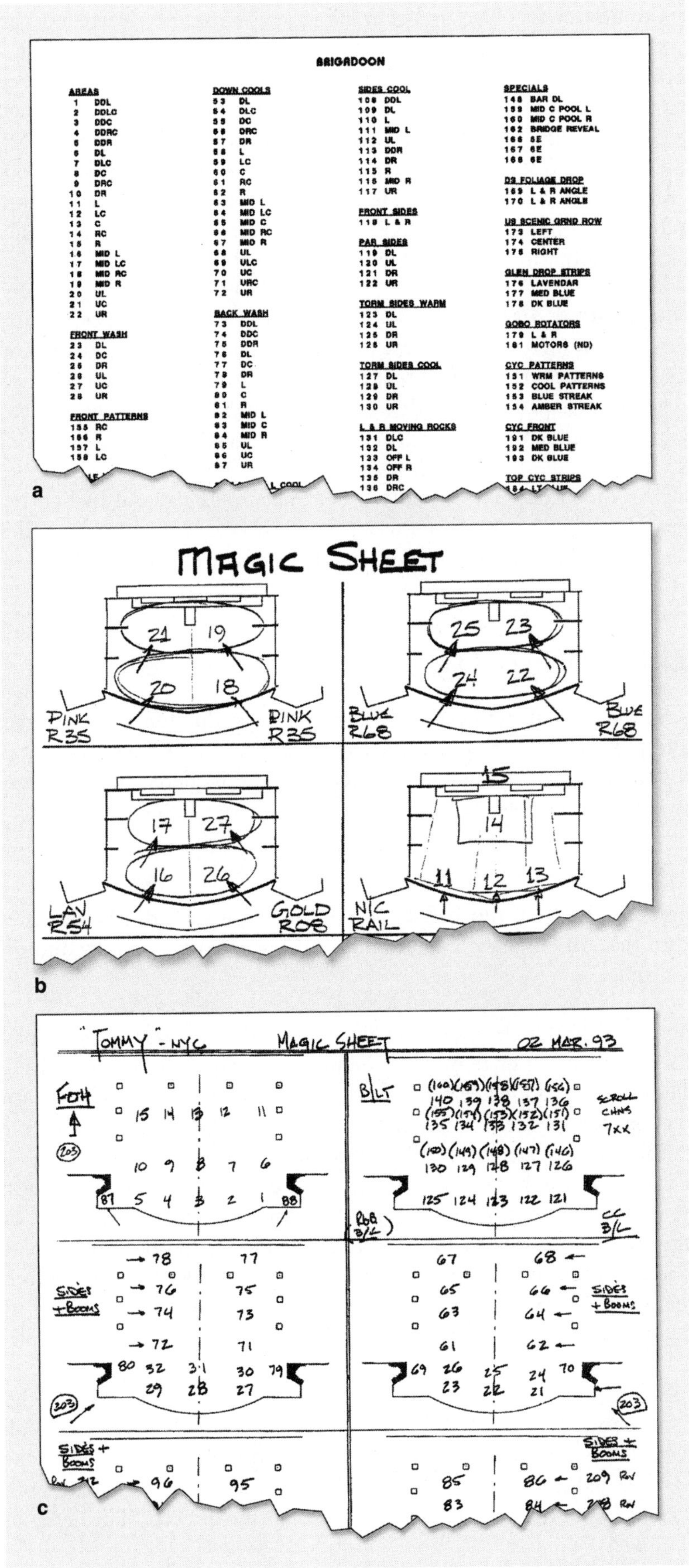

20-18

The Magic Sheet

a A magic sheet listing by function for *Brigadoon* designed by Tom Ruzika.

b A more pictorial magic sheet, used by designer Tom Schraeder.

c The magic sheet used by designer Chris Parry for his production of *The Who's Tommy.*

hanging cardboards Pieces of cardboard onto which a section of the light plot has been attached; used to assist in the hanging and circuiting of instruments.

Hanging Cardboards The assistant designer or master electrician can prepare **hanging cardboards,** pieces of stiff paper or cardboard onto which a single location and its respective instrumentation have been transferred from the master plot. Normally, a copy of the plot is cut up into positions and glued to a cardboard backing. A cardboard is given to electricians during the load-in, allowing them the freedom of hanging and circuiting the position without having to refer to the complete plot. Hanging cardboards may contain more detailed information than the plot does and, like batten tapes, are especially useful for touring situations where they can be reused many times.

focus chart Charts containing focus information for all instruments in a production; used to reproduce the focus accurately.

shop order A contract for the rental of lighting equipment and accessories that lists, in detail, all the equipment to be rented for a production; used for bidding purposes and ordering.

Focus Charts and Shop Orders Two paperwork items especially important in the commercial theatre are tour focus charts and equipment shop orders. First, a **focus chart** is a precise record of the focus information for all the instruments in a production. It allows operators to reproduce focus accurately in each venue. Like magic sheets, focus charts come in many styles and forms.

Second, a **shop order** is essentially a contract for the rental of lighting equipment and related hardware between an equipment rental house and a producer represented by the lighting designer. Both of these items are discussed further in Chapter 24.

REALIZING THE PLOT

The final and most challenging step in lighting a production is, of course, realizing the plot. This process may last only two or three days or take as long as two weeks or more. Again, any preparation completed before move-in will pay off tenfold later on.

Final Preparations

After completing the plot and before moving into the theatre, the designer must be sure that all supplies are on hand, all paperwork is ready, and all cues are written.

Cues Motivated cues such as a lamp being switched on are relatively simple, but cues to change mood or tempo can be more complicated. While lighting cues can help keep an audience's attention, the movement of light must not feel forced or inappropriate. Writing lighting cues is actually relatively simple for the lighting designer, although at first this might not seem to be the case. If a designer carefully watches several rehearsals, the *rhythm* of the production will dictate where most of the cues belong. Cues may be needed to expand or contract the space, to establish new focus, or to change mood. Noting cue placement in the script during one of the final run-throughs before move-in is a good idea. Cues can then be numbered and levels written. Cues should be numbered sequentially, with inserted cues having a decimal point (for example, Light Cue 12.1).

The cues and their placement must be given to the stage manager, who will "call" the show. This cue-writing session should take place early enough to allow time for the stage manager to properly notate each cue before the technical or first lighting rehearsal. Ideally, this session should include both the stage manager and the board operator as well as the director. The designer should set aside enough time for an uninterrupted discussion of the cues so that everyone understands why a cue happens and what the fade times are.

The stage manager must understand that some cue placements will change during the rehearsal process. Each and every cue must be assigned a precise moment when it is called, if only to facilitate changing the placement of the call. Cues should be called as follows:

"Stand-by Light Cue 12" (approximately 10 seconds before "GO")

"Light Cue 12 . . . GO"

Note that the words *Light Cue* are not prefaced by any other word on the "GO" call.

Writing Levels Setting dimmer levels for the first time is difficult and time-consuming, but it gets easier with practice. There are two ways of writing levels: "blind" and live in the theatre. Setting levels blind is a valuable skill that can mean the difference between an adequate and a good lighting design.

When writing blind, designers determine cues and dimmer levels several days before they actually see them onstage. It is important to take the time to think through each preset or stage picture: which sets of instruments should be reading highest and which control areas should take focus? Levels are recorded on a preset sheet (Figure 20-19), using one sheet for each cue. The completed sheets are then given to the board operator and entered into the memory of the control system.

Several control system manufacturers have developed software that allows a designer to use an ordinary home computer to write and edit a show. A good example is the popular WYSIWYG, developed by Cast Lighting and distributed by ETC. Most programs can be used with only that manufacturer's control system, but some software allows exchange of data between systems. Writing blind takes time to learn, but it can result in a better-looking product and can cut hours off a lighting rehearsal.

URL http://www.etcconnect.com

URL http://www.castlighting.com

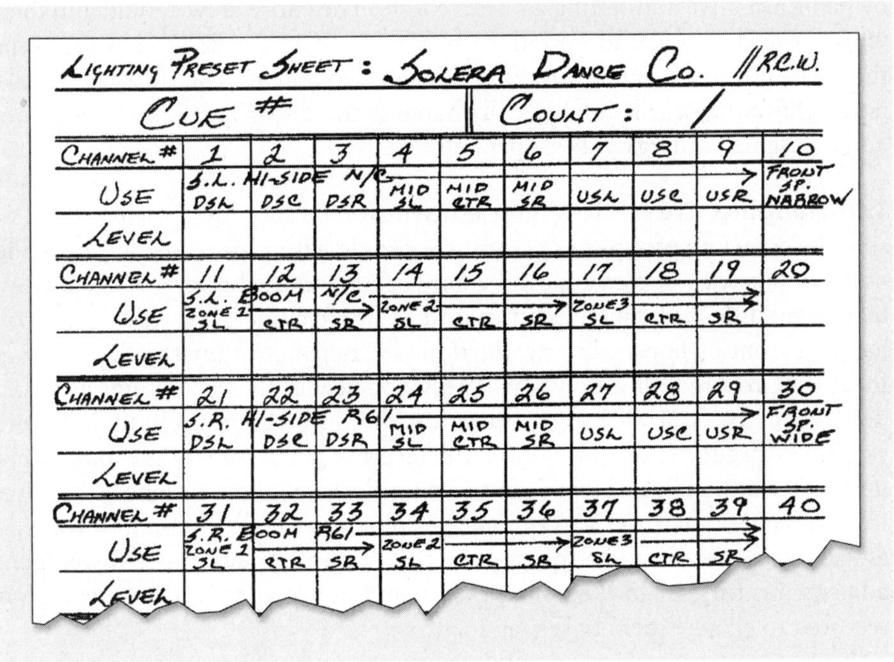

LIGHTING PRESET SHEET: SOLERA DANCE CO. //RCW.

CUE # | COUNT: /

CHANNEL #	1	2	3	4	5	6	7	8	9	10
USE	S.L. HI-SIDE N/C DSL	DSC	DSR	MID SL	MID CTR	MID SR	USL	USC	USR	FRONT SP. NARROW
LEVEL										
CHANNEL #	11	12	13	14	15	16	17	18	19	20
USE	S.L. BOOM N/C ZONE 1 SL	CTR	SR	ZONE 2 SL	CTR	SR	ZONE 3 SL	CTR	SR	
LEVEL										
CHANNEL #	21	22	23	24	25	26	27	28	29	30
USE	S.R. HI-SIDE R61 DSL	DSC	DSR	MID SL	MID CTR	MID SR	USL	USC	USR	FRONT SP. WIDE
LEVEL										
CHANNEL #	31	32	33	34	35	36	37	38	39	40
USE	S.R. BOOM R61 ZONE 1 SL	CTR	SR	ZONE 2 SL	CTR	SR	ZONE 3 SL	CTR	SR	
LEVEL										

20-19

Preset Sheet

A preset sheet used for recording dimmer levels "blind." It can also function as a designer's magic sheet.

In general, it is best to write and design for the highest dimmer levels to be between 80 and 90 percent. Then, if more light is required, the designer has room to maneuver. A rule of thumb when setting levels, is that light from two identical sources will begin to be perceived as contrasting when their intensities differ by approximately 15 percent. Depending on the curve of the dimmers, a reading of 15 to 20 percent will barely warm the filament, and a reading of 25 to 30 percent just begins to produce visible light. The saturation of color filters must be kept in mind, for the more saturated filters cut down light transmission significantly.

The Production Electrician and Crew The lighting load-in must be carefully scheduled well in advance with the technical director in order to coordinate lighting and scenery. A definite crew schedule should be published at least a week before the actual load-in of equipment. This is to ensure adequate participation by crew members and minimize any space conflicts. Equipment must be ready and waiting to be hung. Certain tasks are best accomplished by a large crew, while others are more suited to one or two people. Preparing equipment (checking lamps, lens adjustment, color, gobos, cable, and so on) is best accomplished by the production electrician and perhaps one assistant. The actual hang requires a larger group of four to eight individuals. Before the larger crew is called, the production electrician must have all necessary equipment in good working order for the hang. This simple policy allows the production electrician a fighting chance of doing a good job as crew head.

The Hang

Just as the goal of the preparation period should be to make the hang go smoothly, the goal of the hanging session should be to make the focus uneventful.

The lighting designer or assistant must be available during the load-in to answer any questions that may arise. Although the responsibility for the load-in lies with the production electrician, the designer can do a great deal of good by being attentive and setting a positive tone. The entire crew should aim their work toward a good and smooth focus session. If an electrician always keeps the focus in mind, quality of work is usually excellent. The designer should never play a major role in physically hanging the show. This is the crew's job, and a designer's energy is best spent elsewhere.

The Hanging Crew It is most efficient for the production electrician to split the crew into groups of two or three people with a group leader reporting back. In this way, one group can begin working on the booms (which always take a good deal of time), another on the first electric pipe, and a third on hanging front-of-house. The production electrician coordinates all, checking from time to time on a crew's progress and seeing that everything is being done properly. A given hanging position should be completely hung before cabling is begun. C-clamps should all face the same direction (bolts either upstage or downstage) so that the focusing electrician knows where they are. If the designer indicates focus on the light plot, instruments should be roughly aimed in that direction—this also saves valuable focus time. Instrument adjustments for pan and tilt should be snug, but not so tight that a wrench is required to change them in setting focus.

Safety Practice

Precautions During the Hang

When working overhead, remember to carry a minimum of tools and always tie off your wrench. Take special precautions to avoid falling gel frames, pens and pencils, and gobo holders.

If working with an inexperienced crew, be sure that adequate supervision is provided—even if it seems to be taking too much time.

Remember that proper crew breaks promote safety.

Circuits and Cabling Depending on the circuit layout of the house, cabling may be the most time-consuming part of the hang. The designer often leaves circuits unspecified on the light plot, thereby allowing the electricians freedom to cable to best locations. If this is the case, a single person (assistant designer) should be assigned the task of recording circuits onto the plot and subsequently doing the hookup paperwork. The only disadvantage of this system is that the patching cannot be completed until circuiting is done and recorded.

Circuiting begins as soon as each position is hung, with one or at most two electricians assigned to the task. Because of the work's complexity, cabling a hanging position is best done by a single electrician. Cable should be attached to the pipe with tie-line (cotton sash cord works well) using bow ties. Adequate slack must be left in the instrument leads to allow for free focus. If a connection is loose, it should be tied, taped, or repaired at the time rather than later during focus. A good electrician constantly anticipates the needs of the upcoming focus.

The Focus

Lighting focus takes concentration. If at all possible, electricians should have the stage to themselves during focus hours. Everyone should be prepared for the focus: be on time, be alert, and be efficient. Normally a designer focuses in order, from one instrument to the next in a position. In this case, having the assistant designer call dimmer or channel numbers to the board operator cuts down on distractions and saves a good deal of time.

The designer should never begin the focus before an accurate checkout has been completed. Interrupting focus for a lamp or a patch mistake or a bad circuit is a serious waste of time and, more importantly, concentration. Front-of-house is often focused first. Learning to focus two electricians at once and to focus with one's back to the light, looking at one's shadow, are important skills. Learning to focus fast is even more important. And giving the crew periodic breaks is essential.

A focus crew normally consists of the designer, an assistant, the production electrician, two focusing electricians, a board operator, and one or two additional electricians. The production electrician has done a full checkout and completed all necessary repairs well before the focus crew arrives. With communications in place, general focus philosophy discussed, and coffee drunk, the focus begins.

A good focus team in action is wonderful to watch. Talk is kept to a minimum as the electricians keep ahead of the designer, anticipating his or her next move. The team works like a well-oiled machine. Soon a pace is established and the job is done before the crew realizes that they are hungry or tired.

On the other hand, an unprepared and/or unskilled focus team is dreadful to observe and even more painful to be part of. Headsets do not work, lamps are burned out, one instrument is discovered without a lamp in it at all, shutters stick, cables short out, barrels refuse to budge, and three instruments are hung upside down. By lunchtime, 30 instruments have been focused with 120 left to go, and everyone is tired and feeling mean.

Lighting and Technical Rehearsals

The first time a director sees the results of the lighting designer's work is probably at the technical or lighting rehearsal. This should not, however, be the first time the lighting designer sees his or her work. The ideal situation is to look at presets during the final run-through before the technical rehearsal. The designer should explain to the cast and director that he or she will be adjusting a few lighting levels and will most probably not be in sequence with the action onstage. (He or she must simply leave them enough light for rehearsal, never blacking out the stage.) This gives the designer a good chance to see the lighting on actors without the added pressure of a technical rehearsal.

The technical and dress period is most crucial to the lighting designer, for this is when critical design decisions are made. This is also the time when the lighting designer is working the hardest and under the most pressure. Accordingly, the designer must be fresh and alert—one cannot see or think for very long with only a few hours of sleep.

lighting rehearsal A rehearsal for looking at light cues that takes place before the technical rehearsal and may take place with or without actors.

Lighting Rehearsals Some directors prefer to sit with the lighting designer and stage manager and move slowly through a production's lighting cues. This practice is usually called a **lighting rehearsal** and can take several different forms. Some directors like to take the time to build cues during these sessions. Others may want to see presets already written. The precise way of working matters little; what matters is that there be no surprises. Everyone concerned should know how the session will work and what the goals are.

Not all productions need lighting rehearsals. In fact, for many years, it was understood that technical rehearsals were the place to first see the lighting. However, with increased complexity comes a greater need for lighting rehearsals.

Technical Rehearsals Infamous for being long and laborious, technical rehearsals are disliked by technicians as well as by actors. However, with proper preparation and someone who keeps things moving, these rehearsals can be relatively painless. Good judgment must be used in determining when to stop and fix something and when to keep moving. Tactless people must be banned from technical rehearsals.

Calling this rehearsal from the house rather than an isolated booth somewhere is best, because the stage manager will be in better contact with the director, the designers, the technical staff, and the actors. Headsets must be carefully checked out well before the technical rehearsal begins. Nothing is more frustrating (and, unfortunately, more common) than communications problems during a technical rehearsal.

The purpose of a technical rehearsal is to solve technical problems—not constantly to adjust light levels, and certainly not to write lighting presets. If presets are not complete before the technical rehearsal, the rehearsal should go on without lights. This is also not the time for a director to adjust blocking, a temptation sometimes difficult to resist. If the director gives full attention to the process at hand, results will be better and the end reached sooner.

Here are a few rules of thumb: always begin a technical rehearsal on time. Pace yourself during the technical rehearsal. Never schedule an open-ended time period; always have a stopping time. Take periodic breaks, and remember that positive reinforcement works well. Remain objective, observe time deadlines, and—above all—be sure that your operators and stage manager understand and record changes as they are made.

Dress Rehearsals

A production normally has two or three dress rehearsals, with the first one devoted primarily to costumes. Lighting-level changes can be made during the dress rehearsal, but the performance must not be stopped except for an exceptionally serious problem. Second and third dresses must never be stopped. The fewer changes made during dress rehearsals, the better the stage manager and operators will learn the show.

The assistant designer should take notes so that the designer can keep his or her eyes on the stage. The designer's remote monitor enables the assistant to know what cue the designer is in. If a remote does not exist, the assistant should follow a script with the cues written in it. The director's attention is divided among a great number of equally important things during this stage of a production. The designer should never leave after a dress rehearsal without first talking to the director, the stage manager, and the operators.

Previews

Previews refer to performances with an audience that take place after the dress rehearsal process but before the official opening. The purpose is usually to expose the actors to audience reaction before the production is reviewed. The number of previews can vary from one or two to several weeks' worth; the role of the lighting designer on these occasions often depends on need. If the production's lighting is complete, the designer has no reason to attend all previews. However, if changes continue to be made during the preview process, the designer must be in attendance.

Opening

Of course, opening the show is what it is all about. By attending opening night, the designer shows support for the cast and crew. However, it is not a time to give notes. The lighting is done when the show opens. The designer should try to relax and enjoy the show as an audience member.

Clearly, much goes into realizing the light plot. This chapter has emphasized the paperwork and types of collaboration required. The lighting designer must also know how electricity works in stage lighting; the next chapter explores this topic in detail.

21

Stage Lighting and Electricity

As we have seen, lighting design requires both artistic and technical skills. A knowledge of electricity and electrical practice as it applies to stage lighting is important for the lighting designer. At the very least, designers should understand electricity and basic electronics well enough to make informed choices concerning use and safety. Unfortunately, many individuals believe that electricity is the concern of electricians only. This thinking results in a curious mystique that surrounds electrical practice and theory. Actually, electrical theory and basic electrical practice are simple and accessible.

ATOMIC THEORY

nucleus The positively charged center of an atom; composed of protons and neutrons.

electrons Negatively charged particles that orbit the nucleus of an atom.

According to presently accepted theories, all matter consists of molecules, which are made up of atoms. Each atom has a positively charged center called the **nucleus.** Around the nucleus orbit one or more negatively charged bodies called **electrons.** The nucleus of an atom consists of protons and neutrons. Neutrons have no electrical charge, but each proton has a positive charge equal to the negative charge of an electron.

Every normal atom has as many electrons surrounding the nucleus as it has protons within, thus achieving a balance of positive and negative charges. Hydrogen has one proton in its nucleus and one electron outside it. Helium has two protons and two electrons. Lithium has three of each, carbon has six, copper has twenty-nine, and so on up to uranium, which has ninety-two protons and ninety-two electrons. The electrons are in constant motion, revolving around the nucleus in much the same way that the planets orbit the sun. Figure 21-1 shows a few examples.

In the atom of lithium, the lightest of all metals, the three protons are balanced by two electrons in the inner orbit plus one in the outer orbit. Copper, the metal most commonly used in electrical wiring, requires four orbits to contain its twenty-nine electrons. The various orbits are not all in the same flat plane, but rather they are at angles to each other, somewhat like rubber bands stretched haphazardly about a baseball.

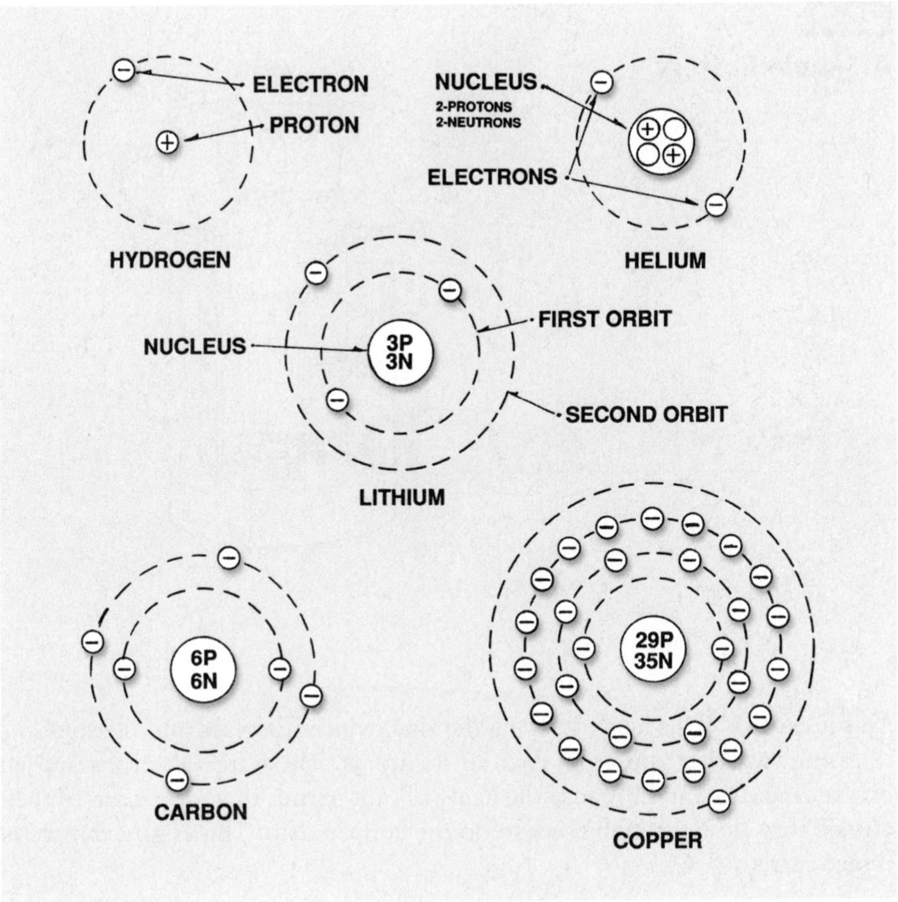

21-1

Atomic Structure of Common Elements

Note the single electron in the outer orbit of the copper atom.

The single electron in the fourth and outer orbit of copper can be easily dislodged; only a small force or voltage is necessary. An electron removed from its atom is called a **free electron** and forms the basis of the flow of electrical current. All metals are good conductors because they have electrons that are easily dislodged.

free electron An electron removed from its atom, providing the means of electrical flow.

SOURCES OF ELECTRIC CURRENT

Just as water will not flow out of one end of a pipe unless water is being poured into the other end, free electrons will not move through a conductor unless a supply of free electrons is being introduced into it. Such a supply of electrons is known as **voltage** or as an **electromotive force** (EMF). Sources of EMF include batteries; the action of friction, sunlight, heat, or compression on certain substances; and generators.

voltage or electromotive force (EMF) A difference in potential—the force that causes free electrons to move in a conductor.

Batteries

A common device for supplying EMF is a battery. Figure 21-2 illustrates how a battery works. A strip of copper and a strip of zinc are placed in a glass container filled with a dilute solution of sulfuric acid. A meter connecting the two strips shows a small electric current passing from one to the other.

21-2

A Simple Battery

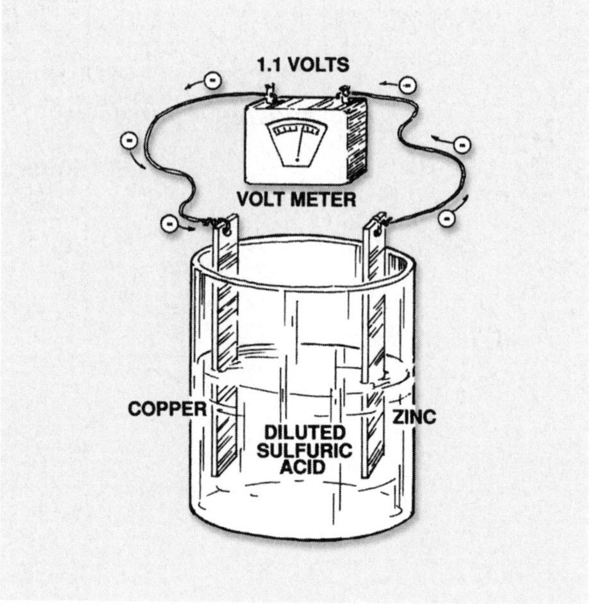

direct current (DC) An electric current flowing in one direction only.

This is caused by the acid attacking the zinc, which dissolves into the solution, releasing two electrons from each of its atoms. These free electrons are left on the zinc strip, and because the acid will not permit them to return to their atoms, they flow through the wire to the copper strip. This is an example of **direct current** (DC).

Generators

electromagnetism The creation of an electromotive force (voltage) through the use of a generator.

generator A device that creates an electromotive force (voltage) by moving a conductor within a magnetic field.

alternating current (AC) An electric current that periodically reverses direction of flow.

alternator A simple alternating current (AC) generator.

New techniques to produce electricity have been developed, but the method most important to the stage electrician is that of **electromagnetism:** the creation of an EMF by means of a **generator** powered by water, steam, or atomic reaction. A generator works by moving a conductor within a magnetic field. The conductor can be moved while the field is stationary, or the field can be moved and the conductor remain stationary. The latter is typical in large installations, but it is easier to understand the operation by considering a moving conductor within a stationary magnetic field.

The two diagrams in Figure 21-3 show a highly simplified **alternating current** (AC) generator, usually called an **alternator.** An armature in the shape of a single coil of wire is rotated through a magnetic field created between the two poles of a magnet. This action induces an EMF in the coil, causing free electrons to accumulate at slip ring 5. The electrons flow off the slip ring through the brush and the connecting wire to a voltmeter and then to slip ring 4, where they reenter the coil. In the second diagram the coil has rotated 180 degrees, reversing the position of its sides. Now the electrons accumulate at slip ring 4, pass through the connecting wire and meter, and reenter the coil at slip ring 5. Each complete revolution of the coil is called a *cycle.* For half of each cycle, the electrons move in one direction, and for the other half in the opposite direction. Thus the current is said to be alternating.

Figure 21-4 is a sine curve showing the variation of induced EMF for any portion of the complete cycle of the armature through the magnetic field.

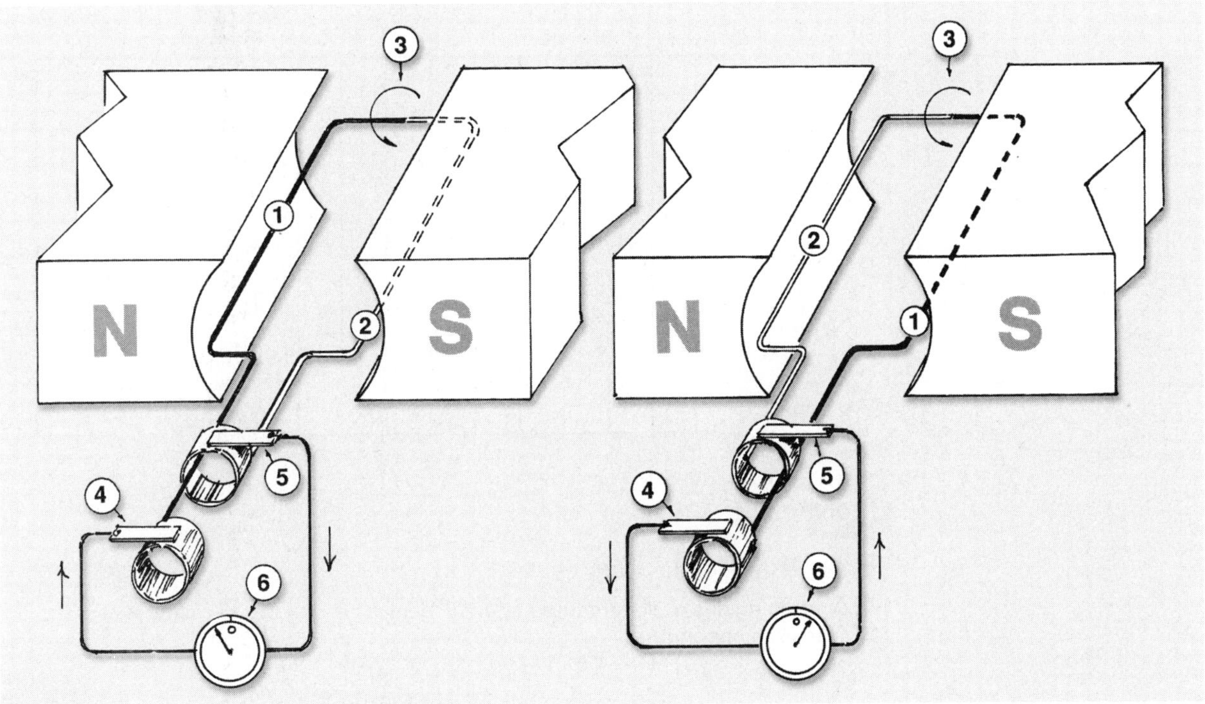

21-3

An AC Generator or Alternator

1 Side one of the coil.
2 Side two of the coil.
3 Direction of rotation of the coil.
4, 5 Slip ring and brush.
6 Voltmeter.

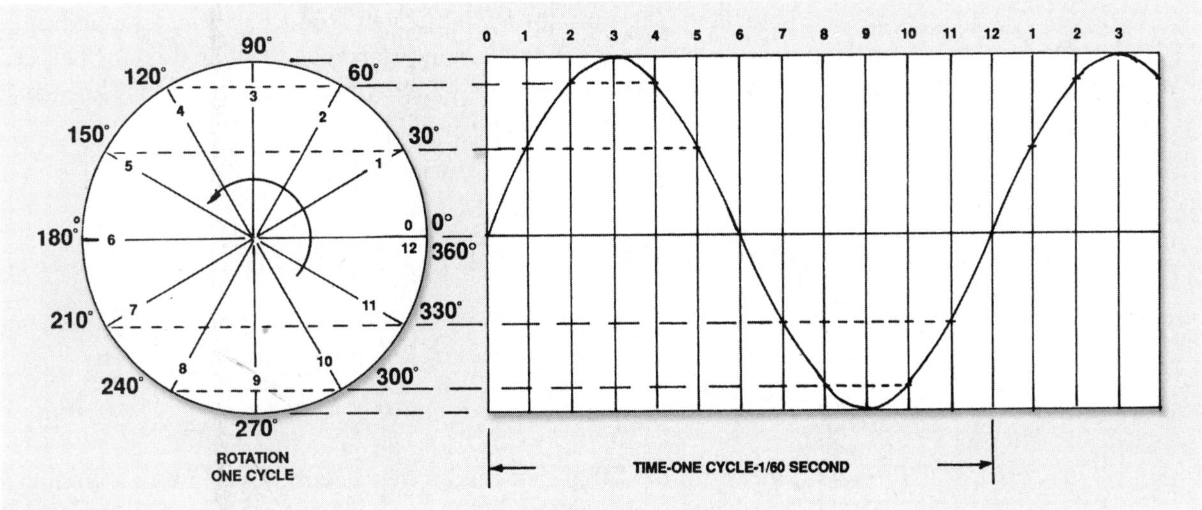

21-4

AC Sine Curve

The alternating current sine curve created by an AC generator.

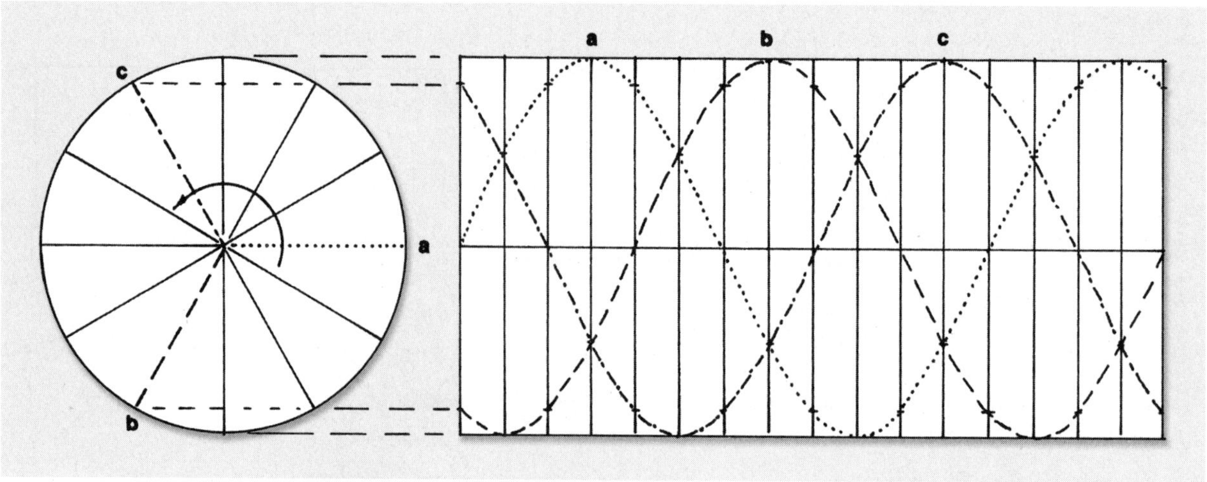

21-5

Three-Phase Sine Curves

The overlapping sine curves produced by an AC generator with three armatures at 120 degrees to one another.

At the exact instant that the armature is passing the 0-degree point in its rotation, it is moving parallel to the magnetic field, not through it, and therefore is producing no EMF at all. As it reaches the 30-degree mark, it is beginning to cut into the magnetic field and generate a small EMF. This is indicated by a line extending from the 30-degree mark to a point slightly later in time. At the 60-degree position an EMF of greater magnitude is produced, and at 90 degrees the maximum EMF is attained. After this the EMF drops back to 0, then it starts to build up in the opposite direction as depicted below the time line.

Building several armatures into a generator is economical. Because the armatures must be at angles to each other, their respective EMFs will not reach any one point at the same instant but rather will produce sine curves as indicated in Figure 21-5. Here we see the common arrangement of three armatures, each producing its own curve out of phase with the others. This is known as *three-phase current* and will be discussed later.

ELECTRIC UNITS OF MEASUREMENT

circuit An established path of electrical flow.

A **circuit** is an established path of electrical flow. Four basic measurements can be made in any electric circuit: volts, amperes, ohms, and watts.

Volts

The volt measures the *force* that causes free electrons to flow in a circuit. It is actually a measurement of the difference in electrical potential between two points in a circuit. Another way of putting it is to ask how many more free electrons there are at point A than at point B, to which they will flow if a path is opened for them. As you know, voltage is also called electromotive force (EMF); as such, its symbol is E. Standard voltage in the United States is 120 volts.

Amperes

The **ampere** is the *rate of flow* of current through a conductor. It measures how many electrons pass a given point in 1 second. The mathematical symbol for the ampere is I (for intensity of current flow). Amperage is used to describe a circuit's electrical capacity. For instance, most stage circuits carry 20 amps.

ampere The measurement of flow rate of electrons (current) through a conductor. Also used to indicate the capacity of a circuit or conductor.

Ohms

All substances offer some *resistance* to the flow of electrical current. Some, such as copper, offer very little resistance, while others, such as rubber, offer a great deal. In an electrical circuit, larger-diameter wires offer less resistance than smaller ones do. The **ohm** is the measurement of such resistance, and its symbol is R.

ohm The measurement of a conductor's resistance to the flow of electrical current.

Watts

The **watt** is the *rate of doing work,* whether it is turning an electric motor, heating an electric iron, or causing a lamp to glow. Its symbol is P for power. Wattage can be thought of as "consumption" of electricity, although flowing electrons are never actually consumed.

watt The measurement of the electric power rate, or the rate at which work is done through the use of electricity.

The Power Formula

The **power formula** expresses the relationship among wattage (P), amperage (I), and voltage (E). It states that the rate of doing work (wattage) is equal to the product of current flow (amperage) and potential (voltage):

power formula Wattage = amperage × voltage.

$P = I \times E$ (called the "pie" formula)

Or

$W = V \times A$ (using first letters of unit names—called the "West Virginia" formula)

An application of the power formula might be to determine how many 750-watt lamps *(x)* one could plug into a single 20-amp circuit, as follows:

$W = 750$ per lamp

$V = 120$ (U.S. standard)

$A = 20$ (given)

$$x \times 750 = 120 \times 20$$

$$x = \frac{2{,}400}{750}$$

$$x = 3.2$$

A 20-amp circuit will carry three 750-watt lamps.

Ohm's Law

Ohm's law presents resistance (R) in a useful formula. It states that amperage equals voltage divided by ohms:

Ohm's law A circuit's amperage is equal to its voltage divided by its resistance (measured in ohms). Used to calculate resistance.

$$I = \frac{E}{R}$$

ALTERNATING CURRENT

Direct current has never been an efficient way to transport electricity over long distances. However, it was the only way known in the early days of electricity, and for that reason it was installed in the downtown areas of many cities. Today it has been replaced by the more versatile alternating current.

Transformers

transformer A device used to increase or decrease the voltage of alternating current (AC).

Alternating current has the distinct advantage of being easily changed from low voltage to high and from high voltage to low by means of a transformer. A **transformer** consists of an iron core, frequently doughnut-shaped, around which are coiled two wires, the primary and the secondary (Figure 21-6). When an alternating current is sent through the primary coil, it sets up a magnetic flux in the iron core, and this flux in turn induces a new current in the secondary coil. There is no electrical connection whatsoever between the two coils. The voltage transformation is solely the result of fluctuating magnetic fields that surround any electrical conductor through which power is flowing.

If the primary has few turns around the core and the secondary has more, the voltage induced in the secondary will be higher than that in the primary. If the primary has more turns than the secondary, then the induced voltage will be lower. These are known as "step-up" and "step-down" transformers, respectively.

AC Service

Figure 21-6 depicts part of a typical arrangement for a modest alternating current service. At far left sits an AC generator station producing an EMF of 1,200 volts. This is fed to the substation, where a transformer boosts it to 6,000 volts. Higher voltages provide less loss in transit (some high-power lines carry up to 500,000 volts!). As the current nears the neighborhood in which it will be used, it passes through another substation, where the EMF is reduced to 600 volts. This is sent out over a local wiring system until it reaches a house, where a small transformer located on a street-side pole finally reduces it to 120 volts.

In the United States, the most common household service is 120 volts AC at 60 cycles. Other countries use quite different voltages, ranging from 105 to 240 volts, usually at 50 cycles or fewer.

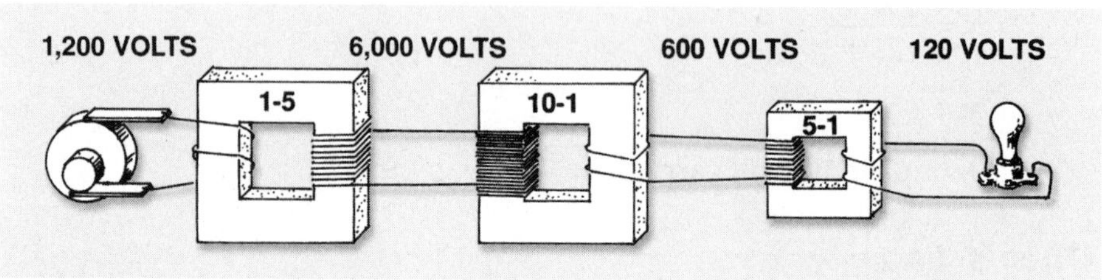

21-6

Transformers

A schematic drawing of AC transportation from generating station to a home, illustrating the function of transformers.

Two-, Three-, and Four-Wire Systems

It is essential for the stage electrician to know which of several possible wiring systems (referred to as **service power**) is carrying electricity to the theatre. This is especially true when a touring company moves into an unfamiliar building and must connect its portable control board and other equipment. Figure 21-7 illustrates the three forms of electrical distribution service.

service power Refers to the type of wiring system providing electricity to a user as well as its amperage.

two-wire system A 120-volt AC electrical wiring system consisting of two wires: one hot and one neutral.

hot wire The conductor that carries electricity to the place of work.

neutral wire The conductor that carries electricity back to the generating plant.

three-wire system A 120/240-volt AC electrical wiring system consisting of three wires: two hot and one neutral.

common neutral A neutral wire serving two or more hot wires.

Two-Wire System In a **two-wire system**, the first line is said to be **hot** and the second **neutral.** The potential between the two lines is 120 volts. Note that 120-volt service is often, in fact, closer to 115 volts and may drop to as low as 110 volts. Today's lighting equipment operates well on any of these voltages.

Three-Wire System The second form of service is the **three-wire system,** in which the two outside (hot) wires usually have a potential of 240 volts between them. However, each hot wire has a potential of only 120 volts between it and the third wire, the **common neutral.** A familiar domestic application of this service is found in many homes, where the electric lights are on two or more circuits of 120 volts each, while the electric range and clothes dryer operate on 240 volts.

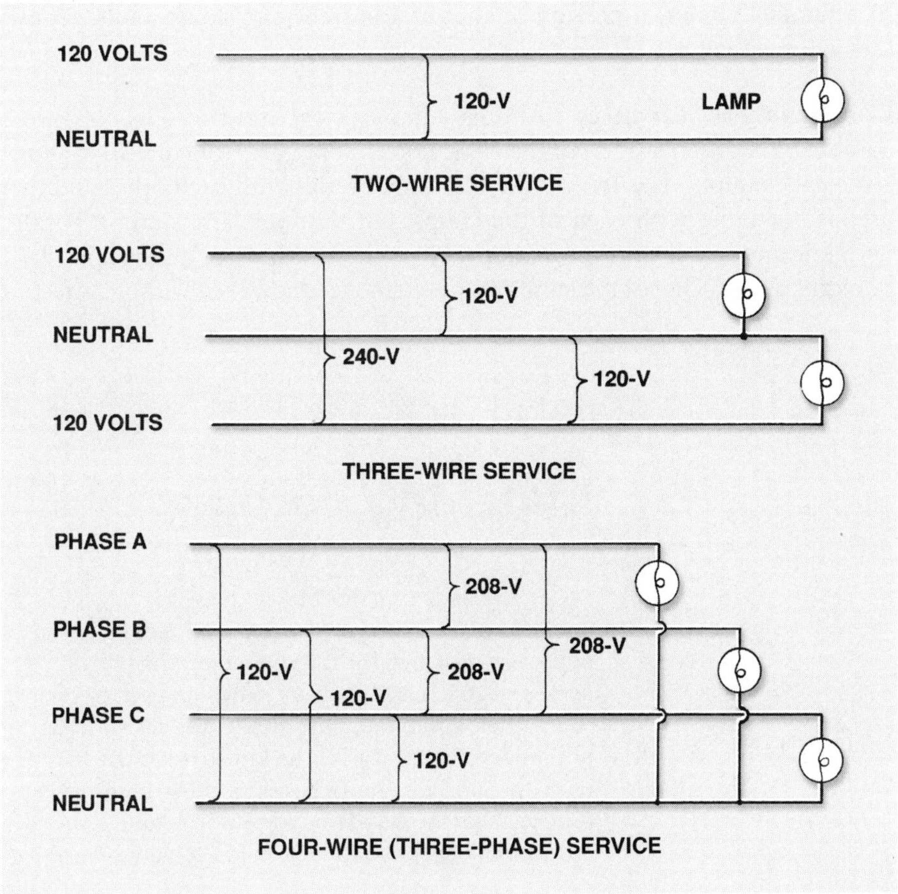

21-7

Electrical Distribution

The three kinds of electrical distribution service. Four-wire, three-phase service is found in most theatres.

Four-Wire System The third type of service is popular because of its efficiency in distribution. It is the AC 120/208-volt, four-wire system, also known as the **three-phase system.** The generation of these three phases is illustrated in Figure 21-5. The sine curve of the EMF produced by each phase is at 120 degrees to the others. If the EMF in relation to a common neutral conductor is 120 volts, then any two phases will have a potential of 208 volts (this being the product of 240 volts times the sine value of angle 120 degrees, or .8660). Many motors are built to run on 208 voltage. This type of service is quite commonly found in theatres.

three-phase system A 120/208-volt AC electrical wiring system consisting of four wires: three hot and one neutral. Also known as the *four-wire system.*

Series and Parallel Circuits

Regardless of whether the current reaches the building by two-, three-, or four-wire systems, on the inside it is distributed by two-wire systems like the one diagrammed in Figure 21-7. The various elements that work in these circuits—lamps, switches, dimmers, fuses, and the like—may be connected in either of two ways: series or parallel.

In a **series circuit,** the flow of current passes through the various elements successively. The top diagram of Figure 21-8 shows that the current must pass through each of the four lamps, one after the other, before returning by the neutral wire. If one of the lamps burns out, the circuit is broken and current cannot flow.

series circuit A type of electrical circuit in which current passes through the various elements successively. If one element fails, the current will stop.

The center diagram illustrates the same four lamps connected in parallel. In a **parallel circuit,** a portion of the total current can flow simultaneously through each lamp.

parallel circuit A type of electrical circuit in which portions of the total current flow through the various elements simultaneously.

Combination Circuits Almost all practical lighting circuits are a combination of series and parallel. The bottom diagram of Figure 21-8 shows a typical example. The switch and fuse are in series with each other and they are also in series with each of the lamps, but the four lamps are in parallel with one another. If the switch is opened or the fuse blown, all the lamps will be extinguished. One of the lamps may be removed, however, without affecting

Safety Practice

Matching Voltage

Great care must be taken with multiple-wire systems to avoid connecting any apparatus designed for 120 volts across the two hot lines. The 208 or 240 volts will blow lamps at once, ruin other equipment promptly, and provide a potential for fatal shock. The British, who use 240 volts for all their home lighting, must take precautions that would seem very irksome to us, who are used to our comparatively mild 120-volt service.

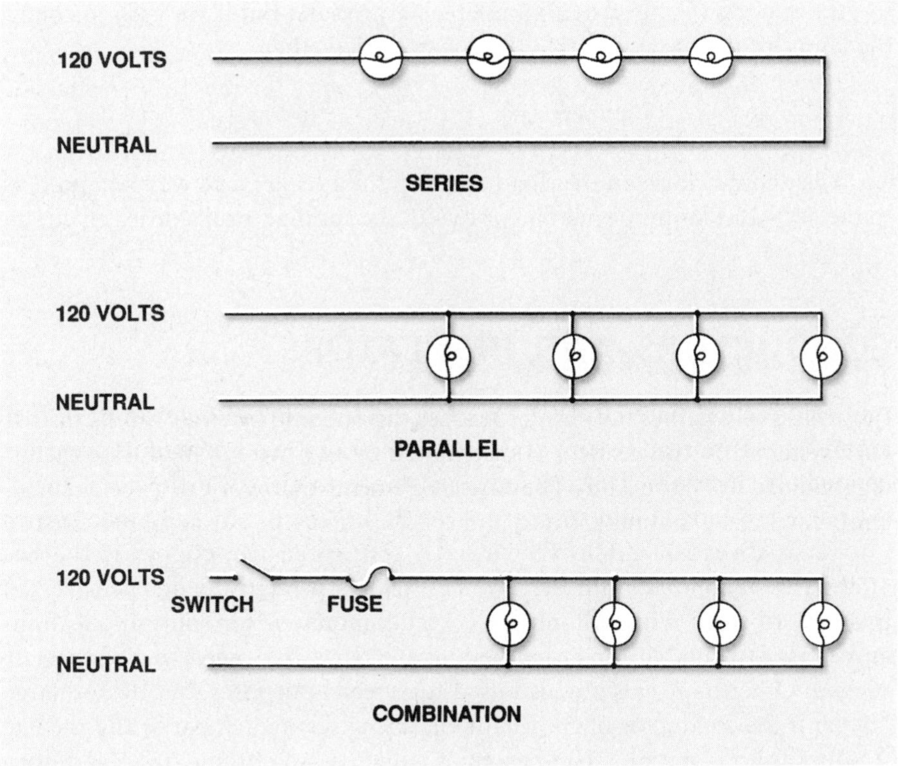

21-8

Types of Electric Circuits

The theatre uses a combination of series and parallel circuits.

the remaining three. In other words, the series portion is used to control the circuit as a whole, while the parallel portion distributes the current efficiently.

In stage lighting, switches and fuses are replaced by **circuit breakers.** These breakers and the dimmers are put in series with the stage lights for the sake of control. The circuit breaker can act as a switch, but its primary function is to protect the entire circuit against a **short circuit** or an overload that would result in a dangerously high flow of current.

circuit breaker A switch that automatically opens if the current exceeds a circuit's capacity.

short circuit An accidental path of low resistance, allowing an abnormally large flow of current; usually caused by improper wiring or broken insulation.

The stage-lighting instruments themselves are always in parallel, such as several spotlights ganged on one dimmer or the lamps in one color circuit of a striplight. In each case they are simultaneously under the control of the dimmer and the circuit breaker, but each is independent of the other. If they were connected in series, none would burn at full brightness; further, like strands of old Christmas tree lights, if one lamp were to fail, no lamps could burn (the broken filament acting like a switch).

Circuit Capacity Electricians must be able to calculate the amperage flow in a circuit quickly. This is usually necessary when several stage instruments are ganged together or several striplights are fed through each other.

Suppose we have four spotlights ganged on one circuit, each one burning a 500-watt lamp. We may invert the power formula (P = I × E) to read

$$I = \frac{P}{E} \text{ then:}$$

$$I = \frac{4 \times 500}{120} = 16.67 \text{ amperes}$$

If our circuit is fused at 20 amperes we are safe. But if we wish to change the lamps to the more powerful 750-watt variety, then:

$$I = \frac{4 \times 750}{120} = 25 \text{ amperes}$$

This would cause an overload and trip the breakers, so we must go back to the 500-watt lamps or put one or two of the spotlights on a different circuit.

CONDUCTORS AND INSULATORS

conductor Materials that allow the free motion of a large number of electrons.

insulator Materials that have few free electrons and therefore resist the flow of electricity.

As noted earlier, materials that have few electrons in the outer orbit of their atomic structure readily support flow of electricity. Such materials are called **conductors.** Everything offers some resistance to electrical flow, but metals are relatively good conductors, and silver is the best of any substance known.

Using silver for extensive wiring is too expensive; copper is the best alternative. It conducts almost as well as silver, it is relatively inexpensive, and it is easy to work with. Aluminum is seeing more use for some applications, and brass is valuable for large, permanent parts that need to be especially rugged. Other materials are also used for special purposes, but by and large, copper is the conductor of choice for electric wires, switch parts, and the like.

Just as no material is 100-percent conductive, so nothing has 100-percent insulative properties. Nonetheless, many materials serve well as **insulators.** Glass and ceramics are excellent for small permanent parts such as sockets and switches. Rubber and fiber are used for wires and cables. Many insulating plastics have been developed for assorted uses. The most useful insulator of all is dry air. If this were not so, every open socket or wall outlet would drain off current!

Safety Practice

Short Circuits

An important rule to remember is that *electricity will always follow the path of least resistance.* Some sort of insulation is necessary to prevent the electrons that are flowing in a conductor from short-circuiting—that is, escaping into other channels. This "short" may result in severe shock to anyone coming in contact with the new and unprotected channel of flow. Further, because it may offer little resistance, this new channel may allow a higher current than the legitimate circuit was designed to carry, thereby causing damage to it.

Permanent wiring such as **stage circuits,** which should be installed by a licensed electrician only, has a solid copper core through which the current flows. Temporary wiring **cable** used on the stage always has a core made up of small strands of wire. This is to provide proper flexibility in handling and laying. Standard stage cable consists of three such cores, each surrounded by strong rubber insulation. For physical strength, tough fiber cords are laid alongside the strands of wire, and everything is surrounded by a rubber and/ or fiber sheathing.

stage circuit Permanent stage wiring—normally 20-amp capacity.

cable Temporary stage wiring—normally 20-amp capacity to match stage circuits.

Grounding

National electrical codes specify that all new electrical installations be grounded. **Grounding** requires that a circuit or cable have three rather than two wires. The third, the ground wire, is designed to offer an emergency path through which the current can flow in case of a short circuit.

grounding A safety feature in modern wiring. A third wire acts as the ground wire, providing an electrical path of low resistance in case of a short circuit.

The ground wire of a stage-lighting instrument is connected to its metal housing. If a short circuit occurs and the housing becomes "hot," the current will flow through the ground wire safely to earth.

Wire Color Codes

The wires of a stage cable or circuit are always covered with rubber insulation, color-coded as follows:

black or red = "hot" line

white = "neutral" or "common" line

green = ground

Stage Cable

Electrical wire comes in different diameters, measured in **gauge.** The smaller the wire, the larger the gauge number. Each wire size is designed to carry a specific maximum current measured in amps. These limits should never be exceeded. The most useful sizes are as follows:

gauge A measurement of the diameter of a wire; directly relates to the wire's capacity.

Size (gauge number)	Capacity (amperes)
18	3
16	6
14	15
12	20
10	25
8	35
6	50

The most common (nearly standard) stage circuit has a capacity of 20 amps. Accordingly, the most common cable is No. 12, Type SO (rubber coated). Ordinary lamp cord (or zip cord), which has a 16- or 18-gauge core, may be used on occasion, but only for very small loads and very short runs.

Care and Handling When not in use, cable should be neatly coiled in large coils (diameter of 2 to 3 feet), tied with tie-line, and hung up for storage. It is a good idea to permanently attach a length of black tie-line next to the female connector on all pieces of cable. Such a line can be used to secure the cable to a batten as well as to tie the coil together when it is stored. Cable length marking codes should be maintained, and connectors should be periodically checked for proper strain relief. Cables with damaged or cracked rubber coating should be discarded.

two-fer A special cable that allows for the plugging of two lighting instruments into one circuit.

adaptor A special cable with different types of connectors on each end; allows an instrument with one type of connector to be plugged into a circuit with a different type of connector.

Cable Accessories There are two types of cable accessories. Cables that allow an electrician to plug multiple lighting instruments into a single circuit are called **"two-fers,"** "Y-connectors," "spiders," or "three-fers." They allow the electrician to plug two or three instruments into one circuit, as long as the 20-amp circuit capacity is not exceeded.

Adaptors are the other type of accessory. Simple adaptors are seldom more than 2 feet long, with a different connector on each end. They allow an electrician to plug something with one type of connector into an outlet having a different type. Applications are numerous, but an example would be plugging a backstage work light equipped with a pin connector into an "Edison" or parallel-blade socket.

STAGE CONNECTORS

connectors Electrical plugs.

Hanging placement of stage-lighting instruments must change from production to production. **Connectors** are electrical plugs that provide this flexibility. They are rated by amperage according to their electrical capacity. Ordinary household plugs with parallel blades, sometimes called "Edison" plugs, are occasionally used in small facilities because they are inexpensive and readily available. However, their use is discouraged because they are easily disconnected in error and are not designed for large amounts of current. The two connectors most commonly used in the theatre are *twist-lock* and *pin connectors.*

Twist-Lock Connectors

twist-lock connector A stage connector that provides a sure connection by means of prongs that lock within the receptacle.

Used in many educational and community theatres, the **twist-lock connector** solves the problem of two connectors pulling apart. It is designed with prongs that allow the male and female caps to be locked together easily and firmly (Figure 21-9a).

Unfortunately, manufacturers have created an amazingly large number of twist-lock blade configurations. The most common stage twist-lock has a capacity of 20 amps and comes in several styles. The most significant difference among these styles is in the grounding blade. In some models, a part of the grounding blade is bent toward the center of the plug; in others it is bent toward the outside. These two variations are commonly called "pin-in" or "pin-out," respectively, and cannot be used interchangeably.

When wiring a twist-lock, electricians must always be sure that the grounding (green) wire is connected to the grounding prong, which is marked "G" or has a green screw head. Twist-lock plugs are available in a wide variety of amperages.

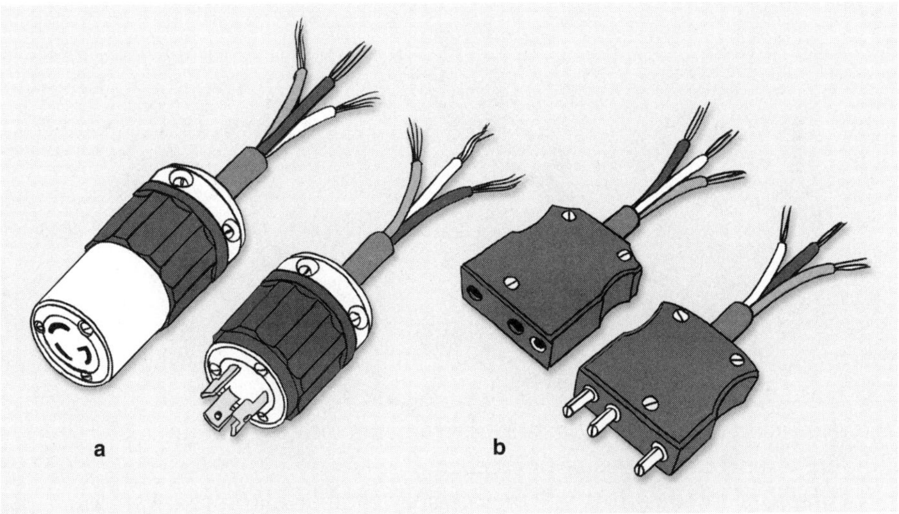

21-9

Stage Connectors

a Female and male three-wire (grounded) twist-lock connectors.

b Female and male three-wire pin connectors.

Pin Connectors

pin connector A stage connector with round brass pins that slide into holes in the receptacle.

Pin connectors had been used as stage connectors long before twist-locks were invented. The standard size has a capacity of 20 amps and consists of a heavy-duty fiber or plastic body with sturdy brass pins and sockets (Figure 21-9b). Most professional theatres use pin connectors because rental house equipment has them. They have the disadvantage of not always giving a firm electrical connection and are easily pulled apart by mistake unless the two cables or connectors are tied together.

Pin connectors have a split down the center of each brass pin (hence the name "split-pin" connector). When a pin does not make a good connection, electrical arcing occurs, causing the connector to overheat. To avoid this, the individual pins can be "split" or slightly separated with a small knife blade.

Pin connectors are available for two different types of stage cable: rubber cable (Type SO) and individual fiber-covered leads from lighting instruments. The rubber cable type has a single hole in the back of the connector, while the other type has three smaller holes. These two connector types cannot be used interchangeably.

The grounding pin is always the center pin of a pin connector. Pin connectors are available in 60- and 100-amp sizes in addition to the standard 20-amp size.

Safety Practice

Proper Grounding

In wiring plugs onto cable, electricians must take particular care to attach the ground wire to the proper pin of the connector.

Always remember: green is ground.

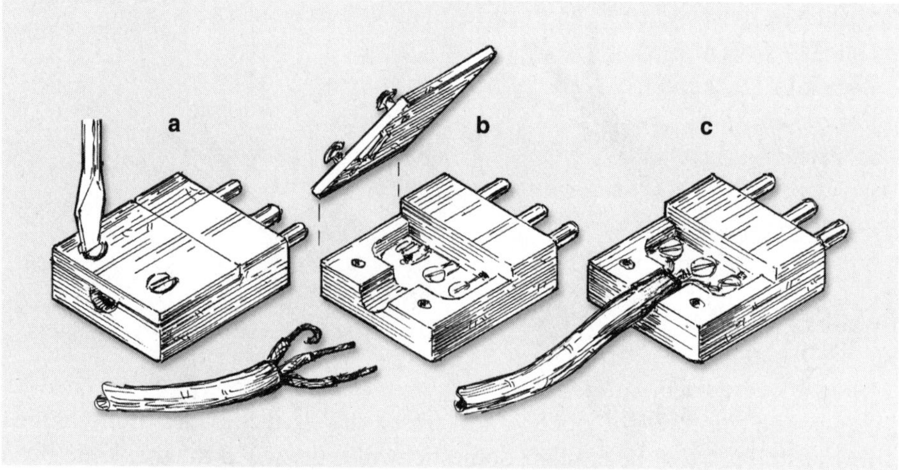

21-10

Steps in Wiring a Pin Connector

a Remove cover plate.

b Wrap wire clockwise around screw terminal, making sure the green ground wire is attached to the center screw terminal.

c Tighten screws and replace cover plate, making sure the strain relief is effective.

Wiring Connectors

Proper wiring of stage connectors ensures against short-circuiting or loose connections that can result in arcing within the plug. As pointed out earlier, stage cable consists of three groups of small strands of copper wires, each surrounded by a rubber sheathing. This rubber sheathing must be stripped away by using a cutting tool called a wire stripper.

The easiest way to wire a pin connector is to twist the small strands together in order to form a more cohesive single strand. The exposed wire is then wrapped around the connector's screw terminal (Figure 21-10). Be sure to take the following precautions:

- Expose only as much bare wire as necessary.
- Always wrap the wire in the direction the screw turns when tightened (clockwise).
- Be sure that the connector's strain relief is effective.

The strain-relief mechanism of a stage connector grips the rubber coating of a cable, ensuring that any pulling tension affects the cable rather than the connecting terminals.

A better and safer technique of wiring a connector involves "tinning" the exposed copper wire leads, that is, soldering all the small copper strands together to form one stiffer strand. This tinned lead can then be connected to the terminal in the usual way.

A third technique involves the use of a solderless terminal, a small connecting device commonly called a "Sta-kon" (Figure 21-11). The Sta-kon

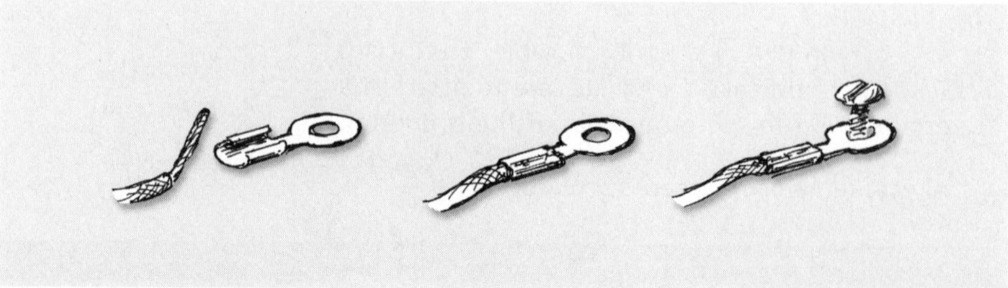

21-11

Solderless Terminals

A special crimping tool is required to secure the copper wire to the Sta-kon, which is then attached to the terminal.

is soldered (best practice) or pinched onto the exposed wire with a crimping tool. The ring is then placed around the screw terminal of the connector. A Sta-kon must be properly sized for the wire and, when in place, the three Sta-kons must not make contact with one another.

Perhaps it is obvious, but a male connector must never be "hot" or "live." For example, leads from a lighting instrument always terminate in a male connector so that it plugs into the "live," shielded female connector.

SWITCHES

A *switch* is a device that is put into a circuit to interrupt and restore the flow of current as desired (to "open" and "close" the circuit). Types of mechanical switches range from the familiar domestic wall-type switch to large knife-blade arrangements that handle hundreds of amps. Like everything else electrical, which type and size to use depends on the duty the switch is expected to perform and the load it is intended to handle.

Most theatre circuits are equipped with a circuit breaker that protects the circuit from an overload and also functions as a switch. A switch commonly found backstage in the theatre is a **disconnect box.** This heavy-duty switch is housed in a metal box that may also contain fuses (Figure 21-12). The disconnect is permanently mounted in the theatre to receive temporary lighting-control equipment, allowing quick and easy access to a power supply. A touring production might carry its own disconnect box, fused to the proper amperage for a traveling control system or other electrical apparatus. In this case, the disconnect is wired to a larger-amperage power supply in order to protect the touring equipment from a power overload.

disconnect box A switch, commonly found backstage in theatres, that supplies high amperage power for touring dimmers.

21-12

Disconnect Box

A 300-amp three-phase disconnect. Power enters at the top and goes through knife switches (shown in off position) and fuses to copper buss bars. Touring "road boards" and auxiliary equipment are connected to the buss bars by means of lugs or bolts.

contactor An electrically operated device in which a small switch controls a larger, remotely located switch.

A **contactor** is an electrically operated device in which a small switch controls a larger, remotely located switch. When operated, the conveniently located smaller switch activates a magnet that opens or closes a switch capable of handling hundreds of amps. A contactor allows high current to be kept away from the operator. Additionally, the loud noise created by large magnetic switches is kept away from the audience.

CIRCUIT PROTECTION

Fuses

If current flow increases to a dangerous level, the *fuse* gives way, breaking the circuit and preventing more serious damage. The fault is then located and corrected, and a new fuse is inserted with a minimum of trouble. Figure 21-13 shows various fuses at the voltages usually encountered in stage-lighting circuitry.

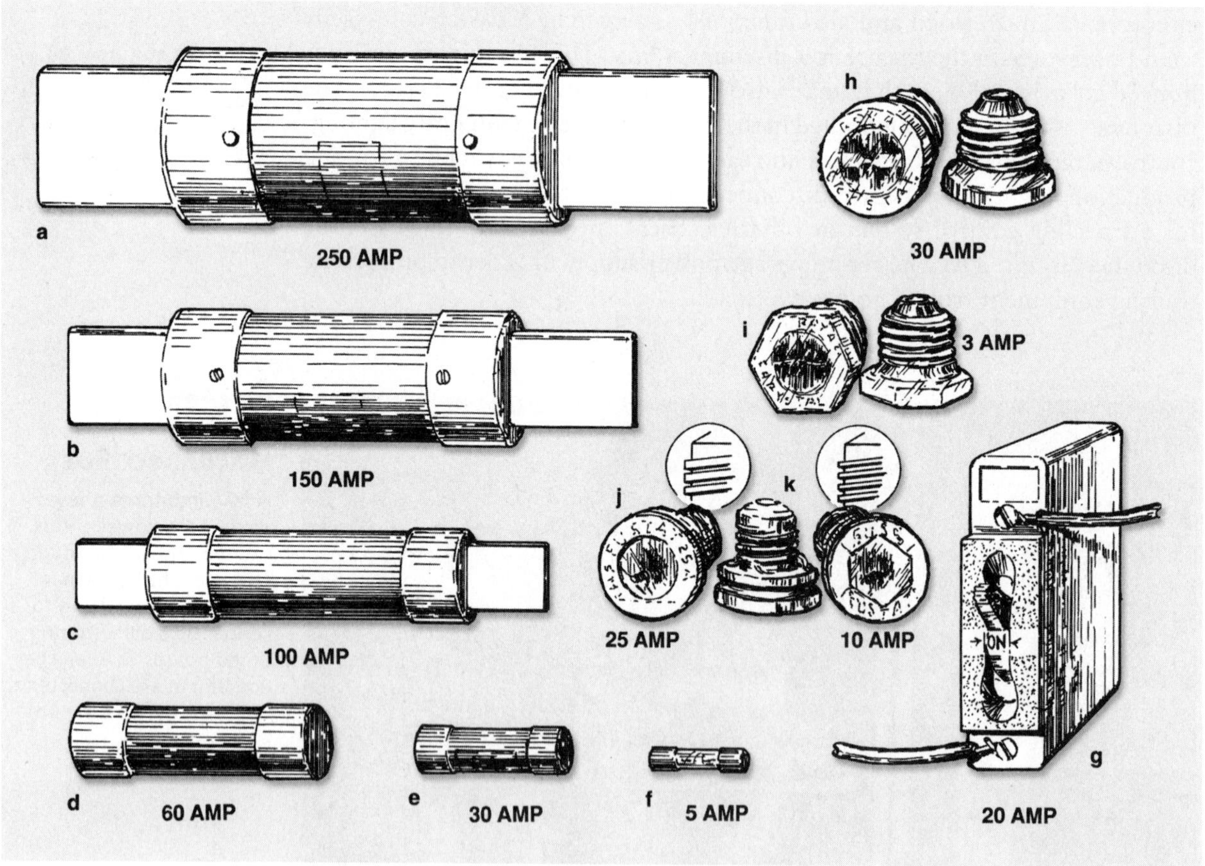

21-13

Fuses and Circuit Breakers

a, b, c Knife-blade cartridge fuses, capacities as indicated.

d, e, f Ferrule-tipped cartridge fuses.

g A typical circuit breaker.

h, i Standard plug fuses.

j, k Type-S fuses—note the difference in threads as shown in the inserts.

Tools of the Trade

Cartridge Fuses

Contact	Length	Capacity
Ferrule	2 inches	0–30 amperes
	3 inches	31–60 amperes
Knife-Blade	5⅞ inches	61–100 amperes
	7⅛ inches	101–200 amperes
	8⅝ inches	201–400 amperes
	10⅜ inches	401–600 amperes

Some older homes still use plug-type fuses that screw into a socket like a lamp. There is a special and very useful variation of this fuse known as nontamperable or Type S. It has a different screw thread for each amperage so that no one can use a fuse with a capacity that is too high. Cartridge fuses clamp rather than screw in and come in two types: ferrule and knife-blade (see the box).

If a fuse continues to blow whenever replaced, it is a sign that there is either an overload or a short circuit. Immediate steps should be taken to eliminate the hazard. Overfusing or bypassing a fuse is a dangerous and foolish practice that can cause a fire. It is good practice to keep spare fuses on hand for all equipment using them.

Circuit Breakers

Because of their convenience, circuit breakers have replaced fuses in most applications. A circuit breaker is a form of switch that automatically opens when the flow of current becomes higher than it should. A thermal circuit breaker detects excessive current flow through a buildup of heat. Magnetic breakers react to the larger magnetic field created by greater-than-normal amperage. Although more expensive, magnetic breakers are desirable because they react more quickly and can be reset immediately; thermal breakers may need a short period of time to cool before being reset.

TESTING EQUIPMENT

A stage electrician must have ready access to various testing tools in order to troubleshoot the electrical problems that invariably arise precisely when time is most critical. These tools range from the simplest test lights to sophisticated meters that combine several functions.

21-14

Neon Test Light

A handy tool for testing electrical circuits.

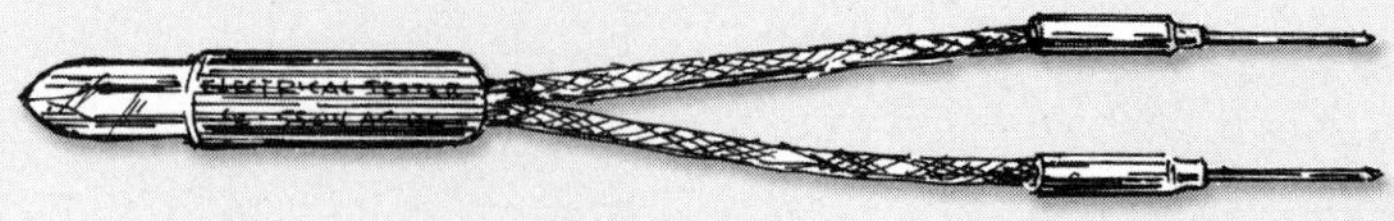

A test light such as the one shown in Figure 21-14 lights up if an electrical circuit is "live." Test lights are inexpensive, easy to carry, and hard to break.

continuity tester A piece of testing equipment that supplies a low-voltage current in order for an electrician to ascertain whether a circuit is complete or broken.

A **continuity tester** enables an electrician to test a circuit to see that it is complete (not broken). The tester's battery allows a low-voltage current to run through the circuit (or not, if the circuit has been broken).This type of tester is particularly useful for detecting burned-out lamps where the broken filament has opened the circuit. The Great American Market sells a combination circuit/continuity tester called GAM CHEK (Figure 21-15a).

Safety Practice

A Healthy Respect for Electricity

Electrical safety, like most everything else, is a matter of common sense. If you don't know what you're doing, don't do it! Attention to the following points will be helpful:

1. Always remember that electrical current will follow the path of least resistance, and your body could be that path.
2. Insulation is a good thing. Tools should be insulated with plastic or rubber handles. Soles of shoes should provide good insulation.
3. Electrical fires are most commonly caused by heat buildup resulting from arcing or a short circuit.
4. Know the locations of electrical (red) fire extinguishers.
5. Fuses and circuit breakers protect equipment and ensure circuit safety. Never attempt to bypass them.
6. Never use a metal ladder for electrical work unless it is insulated with rubber footpads on all legs. Wooden or fiber ladders are always safest.
7. Be particularly wary of damp or wet conditions. Water is a fairly good electrical conductor.
8. Strain relief in electrical connectors is important.
9. Green is ground.
10. Voltage kills.

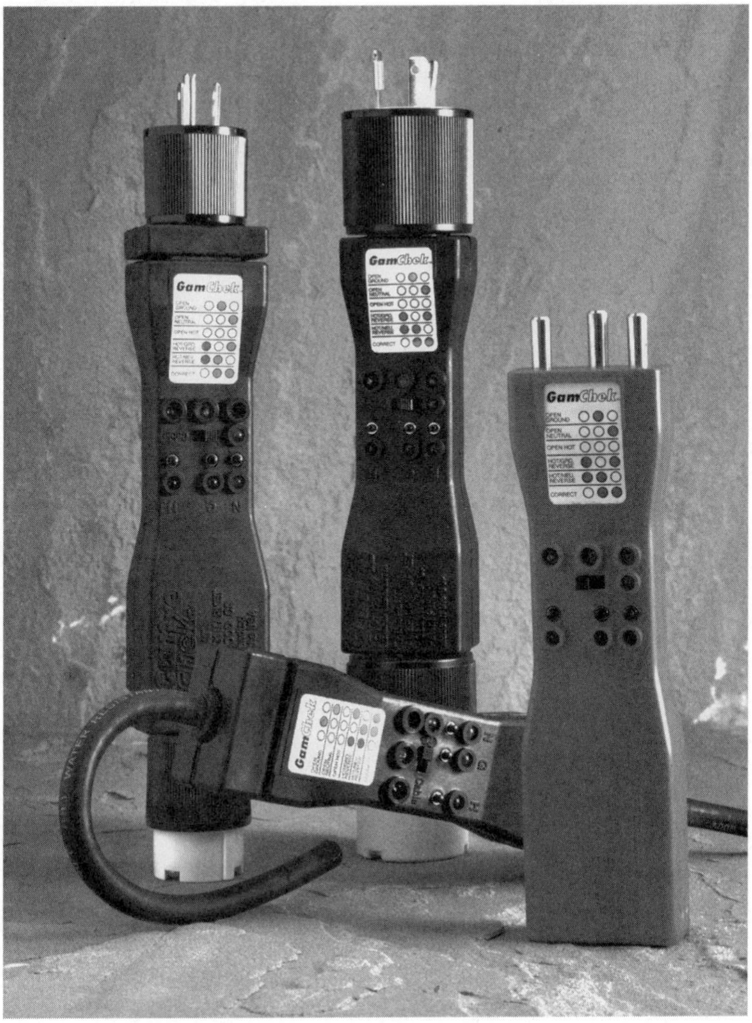

a

b

a PHOTO COURTESY GAMPRODUCTS, INC. b PHOTO COURTESY SIMPSON ELECTRIC COMPANY

21-15

Test Equipment

a GAM CHEK tools for testing Edison, twist-lock, and stage pin cables and circuits.

b A volt-ohm meter with digital readout.

More-sophisticated testing equipment in the form of meters can read voltage, amperage, and resistance in a circuit. Most meters combine several functions, such as the Simpson V.O.M. (volt-ohm meter) shown in Figure 21-15b. Amprobe manufactures a meter called an Amprobe, which measures volts, ohms, and amperage. Meters are fairly delicate and are also fairly expensive.

URL http://www.simpsonelectric.com

URL http://www.amprobe.com

An understanding of electricity lays the foundation for working with specific stage-lighting sources. The next chapter focuses on the types of sources available as well as specific properties of these sources.

22

Light Sources

Over the years there has been a steady demand for increased levels of illumination in theatrical lighting. Today's lighting designer is fortunate to have the choice of a wide variety of light sources to meet this demand. All theatrical light sources are in the form of lamps. A ***lamp*** *is composed of the* light source *(the filament in an incandescent lamp), a glass envelope or* bulb, *and a* base.

lamp A light source consisting of a filament, a bulb, and a base.

During the second half of the twentieth century great advances were made in lamp design and manufacturing. Development of the tungsten-halogen lamp in the 1950s brought about a revolution in lighting-instrument design. In 1954 the German firm Osram introduced the first practical arc lamp, which was filled with xenon gas. In 1971 a xenon arc lamp was put to use in a theatrical follow spot, the Xenon Super Trouper. This lamp is the forerunner of today's great variety of arc sources. Compact filament low-voltage lamps, combined with new reflectors, have created a source of parallel rays of light unheard of two decades ago. The HPL, a 575-watt high-performance tungsten-halogen lamp, was developed by E.T.C. for their Source Four Instruments. Because of its enhanced filament arrangement, it is brighter than standard 1,000-watt lamps. The new 750-watt version is even brighter!

More than ever before, theatrical lighting designers must be aware of the great potential provided by the various light sources at their command. The theatre uses three basic types of lamps:

1. *Incandescent.* Light is given off by a glowing metal filament.
2. *Arc.* An electrical arc gives off intense illumination.
3. *Gaseous discharge.* Light production depends on the reaction of gases to an electric arc.

INCANDESCENT LAMPS

The most common source of light used on the stage today is the **incandescent filament lamp:** a glass bulb enclosing a tungsten filament that emits light when an electrical current is passed through it. The three important parts of an incandescent lamp, to be discussed in detail later in this chapter, are these (Figure 22-1):

incandescent filament lamp A glass bulb enclosing a tungsten filament that emits light when an electrical current is passed through it.

1. The *filament,* which passes the current yet offers enough resistance to change electrical energy into light energy
2. The *bulb,* or the glass envelope that encloses the inert gas or vacuum
3. The *base* or *socket,* which holds the lamp in proper position and provides electrical contact

The glass bulb or envelope contains either an inert gas or a vacuum to prevent the metal filament from oxidizing and thus burning up. Tungsten, the same wire used in toasters and toaster ovens, is relatively resistant to electrical flow. As a result, it heats up and glows when a current is passed through it.

There are two basic categories of incandescent lamps: the *standard incandescent lamp* and the *tungsten-halogen lamp.* Thomas Edison developed the standard incandescent lamp in 1879; since then it has not changed much. The tungsten-halogen lamp is an incandescent light source with a special quartz-glass envelope containing a halogen gas. At the outset, it was a popular theatrical lamp because of its small size and increased efficiency.

Tungsten-Halogen Lamps

The development of the **tungsten-halogen lamp** (often called a *quartz lamp*) led to significant changes in the lighting industry. The most important of these was the creation of smaller and more powerful lighting instruments designed specifically to use these lamps. This new line of instruments set the lighting designer free from the restrictions of relatively archaic equipment. Not only

tungsten-halogen lamp An incandescent lamp with a halogen-family gas sealed within its quartz-glass envelope. Also called a *quartz lamp.*

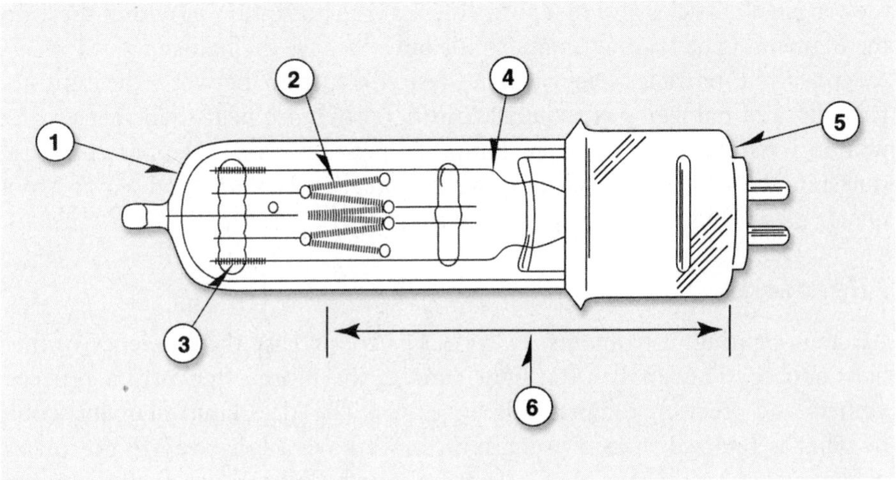

22-1

Parts of a Tungsten-Halogen Incandescent Lamp

1 Quartz-glass bulb filled with halogen gas.
2 Biplane filament.
3 Filament supports.
4 Lead-in wire.
5 Medium 2-pin base.
6 LCL (light center length).

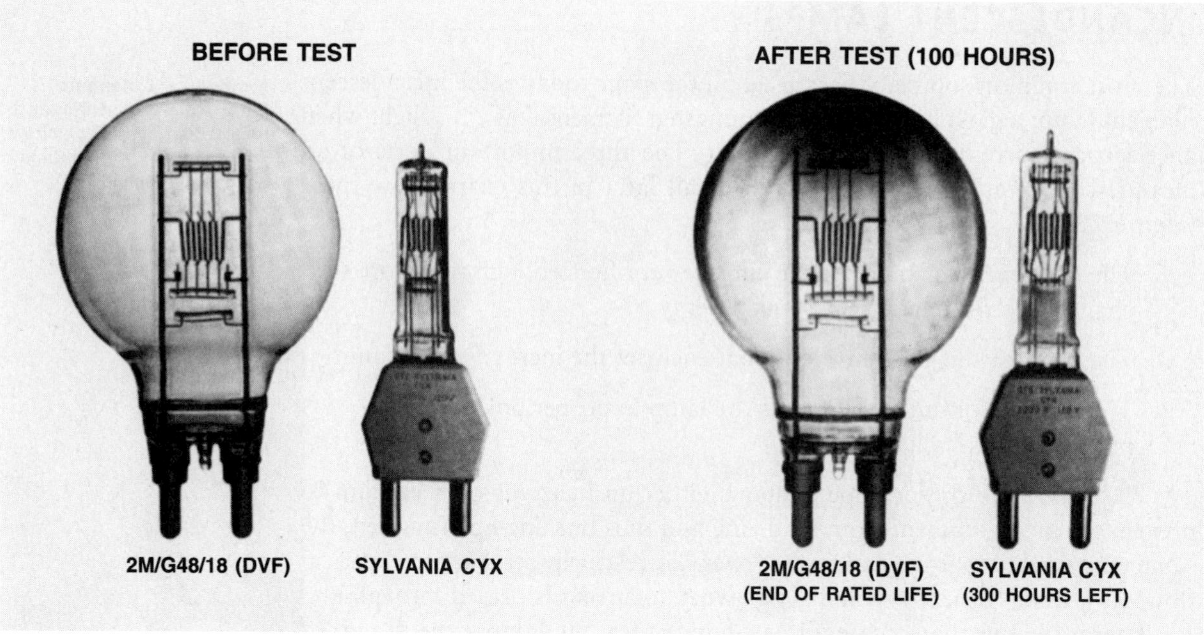

PHOTOS COURTESY OSRAM SYLVANIA, INC.

22-2

Comparison of Tungsten-Halogen and Standard Incandescent Lamps

Notice how dark the standard incandescent bulb grew after 100 hours of continuous use.

were the tungsten-halogen lamps much more compact than standard incandescent lamps, but they also maintained initial intensity throughout their life span.

The secret of this significant innovation is the halogen-family gas (usually iodine) introduced into the bulb. As a tungsten filament burns, particles evaporate from the filament and deposit themselves on the cooler glass envelope. The result of this process is a gradual darkening of the bulb and a decrease in light output (Figure 22-2). However, in quartz lamps the halogen gas collects the tungsten particles and redeposits them at the hottest point within the bulb, the filament. (The lamp ultimately fails only because the halogen gas does not redeposit the particles evenly.) The desired reaction between the tungsten particles and halogen gas requires considerably more heat than that created within a standard incandescent lamp. To provide proper temperatures, the tungsten-halogen glass envelope is made smaller and constructed out of strong quartz glass (thus the name *quartz lamp*).

Filaments

filament A thin piece of tungsten that glows and emits light from within a lamp.

All stage-lighting instruments use reflectors to increase the efficiency of their light source. The smaller the light source, the more efficiently a reflector gathers and precisely redirects the light rays. The ideal lamp **filament** would be what is referred to as a point source. We have a long way to go toward achieving such a source, but attempts have been made to make tungsten filaments as compact as possible. The tungsten wire is often coiled (designated "C") in order to maintain as small a size as possible. In the case of some tungsten-halogen lamp filaments, the wire is double-coiled (designated "CC") and called a coiled coil.

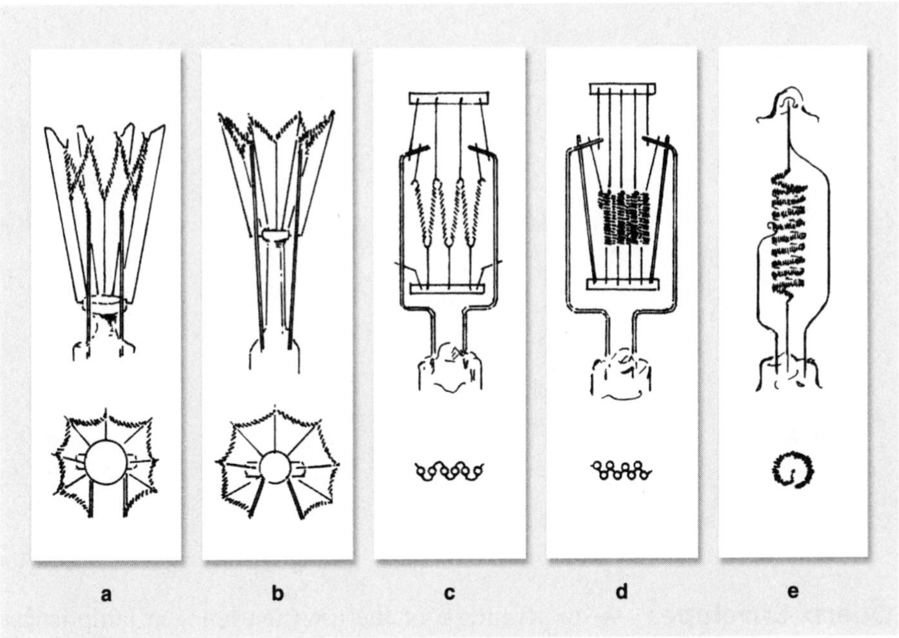

22-3

Filaments

The upper row shows a side view and the bottom row a top view of the following types of filaments:

a Barrel.

b Corona.

c Monoplane.

d Biplane.

e Coiled coil.

Filament Forms Many different filament configurations exist. The barrel and corona filaments (Figures 22-3a and 22-3b) are used for floodlights and household lamps because they distribute their light equally in all directions. The monoplane and biplane filaments (Figures 22-3c and 22-3d), used in spotlights, emit most of their light to the front and rear of the filament. This permits a larger portion of the light to be gathered and redirected by a reflector or a lens. The coiled coil, a common tungsten-halogen lamp filament, tends to be a bit longer and narrower than other filaments (Figure 22-3e).

No matter what form a filament takes, the tungsten metal becomes supple when it heats up. In this state, any excessive jarring of the filament can cause it to break. Spotlight filaments such as the biplane and the coiled coil are particularly susceptible to this sort of breakage. Lighting instruments should be handled gently when their lamps are on.

Light Center Length The LCL (**light center length**) of a lamp is the distance from the center of the filament to some predetermined place in the base. With a screw-base lamp, the measurement is to the contact button at the bottom of the base. With a prefocus base, it is to the fins; with the 2-pin, it is to the base of the pins (Figure 22-1). It is particularly important to be aware of the LCL in spotlights, where a lamp is used in conjunction with a reflector or a lens. The center of the filament must line up exactly with the focal points of such optical devices.

LCL (light center length) The distance from the center of a lamp's filament to some predetermined place in its base.

Bulbs

The **bulbs** (or *envelopes*) of standard incandescent lamps are made of ordinary glass, while the bulbs of tungsten-halogen lamps are made of the more heat- and pressure-resistant quartz glass. As a result, the normal glass envelope of the standard incandescent lamp needs to be larger than the T-H bulb in order to allow the heat given off by the filament to dissipate before it can heat up the glass too much.

bulb The sealed glass enclosure of a lamp. Also called the *envelope*.

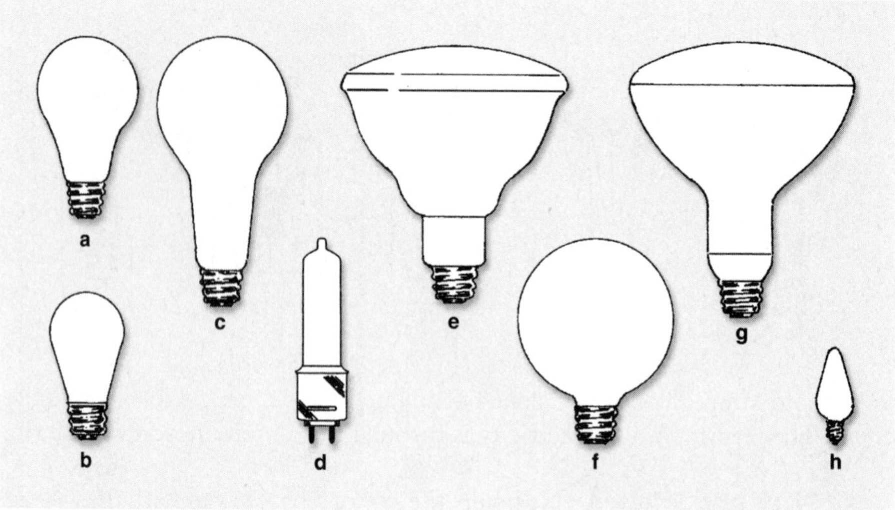

22-4

Typical Bulb Shapes

a Arbitrary (A).
b Straight-side (S).
c Pear shape (PS).
d Tubular (T).
e Parabolic aluminized reflector (PAR).
f Globe (G).
g Reflector (R).
h Cone (C).

Quartz Envelopes A disadvantage of the tungsten-halogen lamp is that the quartz glass envelope cannot be touched by fingers. No matter how clean one's hands are, oil from the skin is deposited on the glass and will react with the quartz when it is heated. The result of this reaction not only weakens the envelope (possibly causing an explosion) but also produces a frosted effect on the glass.

Shapes Bulbs come in a variety of shapes, each designated by a letter or letters (Figure 22-4). The A (arbitrary) and PS (pear shape with straight sides) are common forms of household lamps. Lamps used in stage lighting instruments were once globe shaped (G) to allow even dissipation of heat. Today's tungsten-halogen lamps are nearly all tubular (T), allowing the filament to be brought closer to a reflector. There are other shapes as well, some of which are purely decorative. The familiar R-type and PAR lamps will be discussed separately later in this chapter.

Size The size of a bulb is designated by a numbering system that may seem unnecessarily complex but is at least standardized. The diameter of the bulb at its largest point is expressed in eighths of an inch. For example, the common T-6 quartz lamp has a tubular envelope and is $\frac{6}{8}$ (or $\frac{3}{4}$) of an inch in diameter.

Finishes and Color Lamps used on the stage usually are made of clear glass, which is essential for any source used in an instrument with a reflector or lens. Common A and PS lamps are most readily available with an inner finish called *frosted.* A frosted finish diffuses the light, thereby reducing glare. These lamps can be ordered in the clear-glass style; these clear bulbs are often used in signs and for scenery effects.

There are many kinds of finishes available, some purely decorative and others for special applications. Low-wattage PAR lamps can be bought with colored lenses and small G and A lamps have colored bulbs useful for decorative purposes.

Lamp Bases and Sockets

A lamp base provides three important functions:

1. It holds the lamp precisely in a predetermined position, which is critical to the proper operation of a reflector.
2. It conducts electrical current from the socket to the filament.
3. It allows for quick and easy lamp replacement.

Similar to connectors in an electrical circuit, base and socket assemblies make changing lamps quick and easy. The electrical contact in the base is made of brass or aluminum. In the medium-sized screw base of a common household lamp, the button at the bottom conducts the electricity to the filament. The return path of electricity is through the aluminum screw-base rim.

Base Sizes and Shapes Normally the size of a base varies with the wattage of a lamp. Large bases are called *mogul,* middle-sized bases are called *medium,* and small bases are called *miniature.*

The most common theatrical bases are the screw base, the prefocus base, and the 2-pin base (Figure 22-5). Screw bases work well for low- to medium-wattage lamps whose filaments do not need to be precisely aligned. Prefocus and 2-pin bases are used on medium- to high-wattage lamps that need proper alignment. A base called the bi-post, which looks like a large 2-pin, is used for very high wattage lamps.

Most tungsten-halogen stage lamps use a prefocus, a 2-pin, or a double-ended base (Figure 22-6). The prefocus base slips into its socket and requires slight pressure downward and a turn before the lamp "clicks" into alignment. The 2-pin lamp slides straight into its socket and is held in place by a pressure plate. Excessive handling or jarring may cause this lamp to dislodge from its base, so care must be taken with instruments requiring this lamp. The double-ended lamp is held in place by two metal contacts, mounted so that they protrude through the reflector of an instrument. Depending on the design of the lighting instrument, these lamps can be difficult to get seated properly. Care must be taken not to damage either the contacts or the seal of the lamp base.

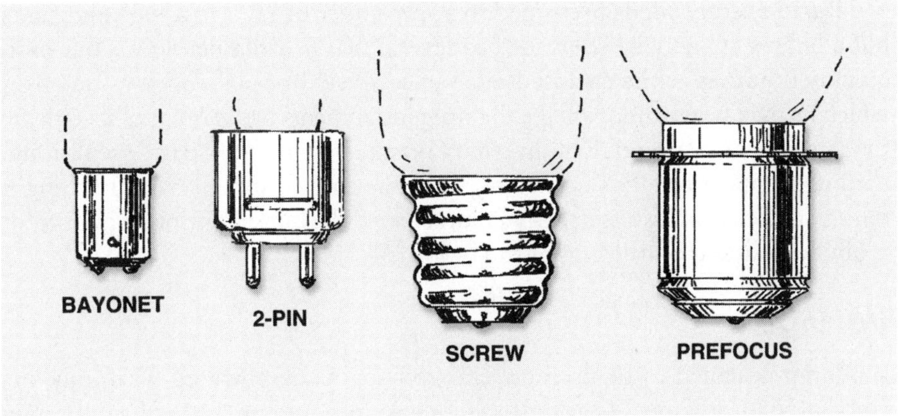

22-5
Common Base Types

22-6

Common Theatre Lamps

Four common tungsten-halogen lamp and base types.

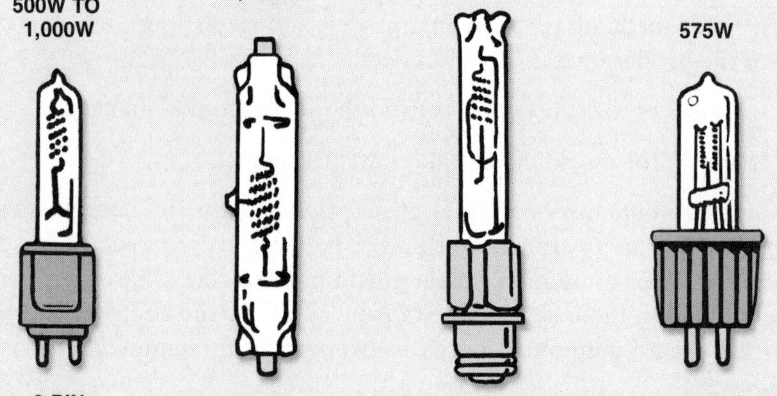

THE ANSI LAMP CODE

The American National Standards Institute (ANSI) has established a system for identifying lamps using a three-letter code called the "ANSI code." If one lamp differs in any way from another, it is assigned a separate ANSI code (Figure 22-7). Although the three-letter codes are totally nondescriptive by themselves, they have greatly simplified the process of specifying lamps. One may order a lamp simply by providing the supplier with its ANSI code.

LAMP LIFE

The rated average life for the common household lamp is at least 750 hours, but for stage lamps it can be as low as 200 hours. Rated average life is determined by the manufacturer, who burns a group of lamps under normal conditions until either (1) they burn out completely or (2) their light output drops to 80 percent of what it was originally.

Rated average life is presumed to apply under usual operating conditions, but a lamp's life may be shortened in several ways. A filament gives out more quickly if burned while enclosed in an excessively hot place such as one from which its own heat cannot escape (lighting instruments are ventilated specifically for this purpose). Rough handling may break some interior part, even though the outer appearance has not changed. In the case of some lamps, burning in the wrong position results in early failure. Proper burning position, if important, is always marked on the end of the bulb.

Voltage

If a lamp designed to be used on 120-volt service is powered with only 110 volts, it will last almost four times as long as it would on 120 volts. However, it will emit only about 74 percent as much light. On the other hand, if this same lamp is fed 130 volts, there will be 31 percent more light, but the lamp

Watts	Bulb	Description	ANSI Code	LIF Code	Product Ordering Code	Std. Pkg. Qty.	Approx. Color Temp. K	Approx. Hours Life	Approx. Initial Lumens	Filament Form	Light Center Lgth (In)	Maximum Over-all Lgth (In)	Operating Position
500	T-4	**EHD-Q500CL/TP**	EHD	—	37083	6	2950	2000	10,450	CC-8	2³/₈	4	Any
		EHC-Q500/5CL	EHC	—	37082	6	3150	300	12,700	CC-8	2³/₈	4	Any
575	T-6	**FLK-Q575T6**	FLK	—	11450	24	3200	300	16,500	CC-8	2³/₈	4	Any
		FLK/LL	—	—	39730	24	3050	1500	12,800	CC-8	2³/₈	4	Any
		GKV-Q575T6/4CL (230V)	GKV	—	35376	50	3200	250	14,000	C-13D	2³/₈	4	Any
		GLA-Q575T6/4CL (115V)	GLA	—	39145	12	3050	1500	13,000	C-13D	2³/₈	4	Any
		GLC-Q575T6/4CL (115V)	GLC	—	39146	12	3200	300	14,500	C-13D	2³/₈	4	Any
650	T-6	**FKR-Q650T6 (220V/230V)**	FKR	—	30488	24	3100	300	15,000	CC-8	2³/₈	4	Any
750	T-6	**EHG-Q750CL/TP**	EHG	—	43167	6	3000	2000	15,400	CC-8	2³/₈	4¹/₈	Any
		EHF-Q750/4CL	EHF	—	37051	6	3200	500	20,400	CC-8	2³/₈	4¹/₈	Any
		GLD-Q750T6/4CL (115V)	GLD	—	92771	12	3200	300	19,000	C13D	2³/₈	4	Any
		GLE-Q750T6/4CL (115V)	GLE	—	92773	12	3050	1500	17,400	C13D	2³/₈	4	Any
1000	T-6	**FEL-Q1000/4CL**(22)	FEL	CP77	35607	6	3200	375	27,500	CC-8	2³/₈	4¹/₈	Any
		FCV-Q1000/4(22) **(frosted)**	FCV	—	35853	6	3200	375	26,500	CC-8	2³/₈	4¹/₈	Any
		FEP-Q1MT6/4CL (230V)	FEP	CP77	31839	50	3200	300	25,000	CC-8	2³/₈	4	Any

TABLE COURTESY GENERAL ELECTRIC COMPANY

22-7

Comparison of Wattage, Color Temperature, Life, and Lumen Output

Compare in particular the 750-watt EHG and EHF lamps.

will last only a third as long. Stage lamps often last far longer than their rated life because they have been burned at low dimmer readings.

This relationship of voltage, intensity, and life must be kept in mind, especially in conjunction with "long-burning" lamps. A 75-watt "long-life" household lamp may burn twice as long as a standard one, but it burns less brightly.

Wattage and Lumen Output

Lamp manufacturers have taught the general public to equate the wattage of a lamp with its brightness. If our 75-watt reading lamp is too dim, we simply replace it with a 100-watt lamp. But, as we learned in the previous chapter, wattage is the rate of doing work—not necessarily an accurate measure of lamp intensity. Lamp manufacturers use a measure of intensity called the **lumen** to measure the light output of a lamp. Figure 22-7 shows how two lamps with identical physical specifications can be quite different in brightness (compare EHG and EHF). Note that as lumen output increases, lamp life significantly decreases.

lumen A unit of measurement of the intensity of a light source.

COLOR TEMPERATURE

As discussed in Chapter 16, most people consider the color of light emitted from an ordinary lamp to be white. However, so-called white light is relative, and the actual color of light given off by sources can vary greatly. The method we have to identify the color makeup of any light source is called *color temperature,* and it is measured in degrees Kelvin (°K).

In an effort to standardize light source color notation, a light-emitting device called a *blackbody* was developed. When heated, it emits light consisting of various color wavelengths. The blackbody responds to heat in much the same way that a tungsten filament does. It begins to glow a warm red-yellow, moves toward "white" as more heat is applied, and finally appears to approach blue when a great deal of heat is applied. The color wavelengths of light emitted by the blackbody are identified by a sophisticated meter called a spectrophotometer. Any color of light can thus be equated with the temperature of heat applied to the blackbody, resulting in a meaningful Kelvin figure (see Color Plate 16-2).

This is fairly important for a lighting designer to understand, because theatre sources vary in color—from standard incandescence, which is around 3,000°K, to much cooler arc lamps, which can be as high as 6,000°K. Obviously, the same filter placed in front of two such different sources will project very different colors. For all practical purposes, no one will notice a source color difference of less than 200°K, but any more of a difference is noticeable. The color temperature of stage lamps is often printed on their containers and is always noted in catalogs. Recall that the higher the color temperature, the cooler the light. Further, dimming a source decreases its color temperature significantly.

R-TYPE AND PAR LAMPS

The R-type (reflector-type) and PAR (parabolic aluminized reflector) lamps are discussed separately here because each is essentially a self-contained lighting instrument. Both PAR and R-type lamps have a mirrored-glass parabolic-shaped reflector that sends light to the lens in parallel rays. Low-wattage versions have standard incandescent filaments, while the brighter and larger sizes have a small quartz lamp placed at the focal point of the reflector. Both PAR and R-type lamps are extremely efficient and have found many uses in the theatre.

R-Type Lamps

All R-type lamps consist of a single-piece glass bulb that is inside-frosted to varying degrees, depending on the desired beam spread. Their field of light is generally smooth and even, with a soft beam edge. Being light and fairly fragile, they are intended for indoor use (Figure 22-8).

22-8

R-Type Lamp

The 300-watt R-40 lamp is available in flood and spot beams.

The following R-type lamps are available:

- 30-watt R-20 (20⁄8- or 2½-inch diameter); flood (40°); medium screw base
- 50-watt R-20; flood (45°); medium screw base
- 75-watt R-30; flood (60°) and spot (30°); medium screw base
- 100-watt R-40; flood (60°); medium screw base
- 120-watt R-40; flood (60°) and spot (25°); medium screw base
- 300-watt R-40; flood (120°) and spot (40°); medium screw base
- 500-watt R-40; flood (115°); mogul screw base
- 750-watt R-52; medium flood (70°); mogul screw base

The smaller R-20 variety can be tucked away in tight places for special effects or to solve a particular lighting problem. The R-40 flood and spot lamps have long been used in striplights for cyclorama and backdrop lighting. In this application, the floods are used for short throws and the spots for longer ones. The higher-wattage flood lamps are seldom used in the theatre, because PARs are brighter and have a longer throw.

PAR Lamps

The parabolic aluminized reflector lamp is made out of heavy, heat-resistant glass and can be used outdoors. It has a molded-glass lens, which determines beam spread and, to some degree, shape (Figure 22-9).

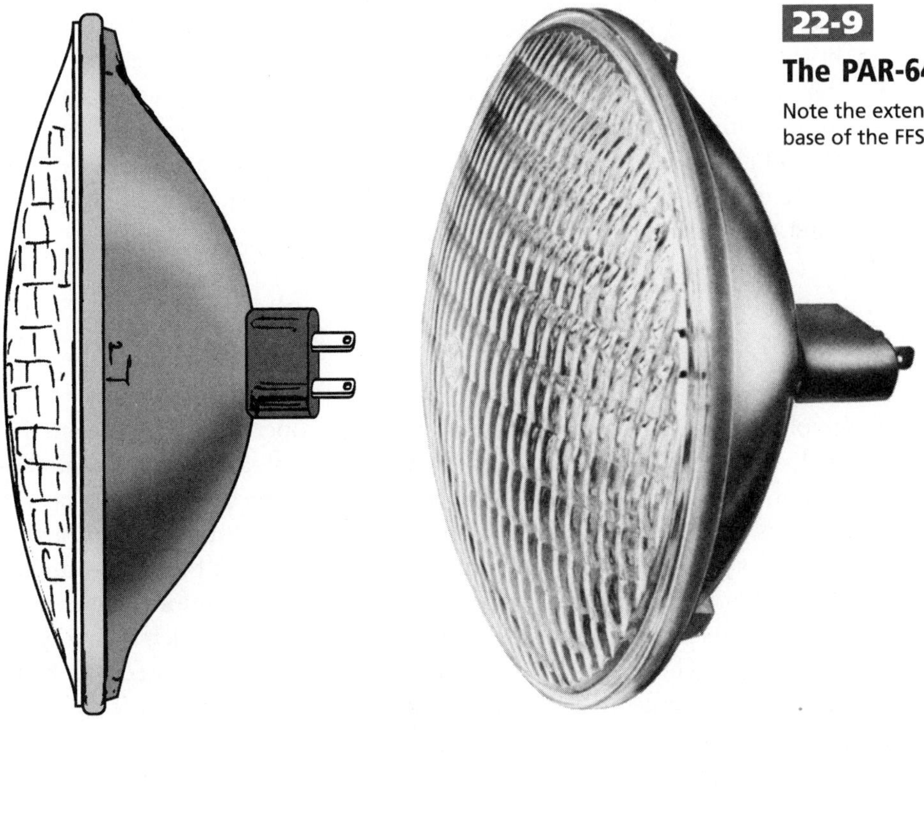

22-9

The PAR-64 Lamp

Note the extended mogul end-prong base of the FFS (wide PAR).

The range of available PAR lamps is as follows:

- 65-watt PAR-30; flood (30°) and spot (12°); medium screw base
- 75-watt PAR-30; flood (30°); medium screw base
- 150-watt PAR-38; flood (30°); medium screw base
- 200-watt PAR-46; medium flood (11° × 26°) and narrow spot (9° × 13°); medium side-prong base
- 300-watt PAR-56; wide flood (18° × 37°), medium flood (11° × 23°), and narrow spot (8° × 10°); mogul end-prong base
- 500-watt PAR-64; wide flood (20° × 42°), medium flood (11° × 23°), and narrow spot (7° × 12°); extended mogul end-prong base
- 1,000-watt PAR-64; FFS wide flood (24° × 48°), FFR medium flood (12° × 28°), FFP narrow spot (7° × 14°), and FFN very narrow spot (6° × 12°); extended mogul end-prong base
- 1,200-watt PAR-64; GFE wide flood (25° × 58°), GFA medium flood (22° × 36°), GFB narrow spot (16° × 18°), and GFC very narrow spot (14° × 16°); extended mogul end-prong base

Note that beam shape becomes oval beginning with the 200-watt PAR-46. Comparison of the beam spread of PAR lamps with that of comparable R-type lamps indicates that the PAR lamp is intended for longer throws.

Automobile headlights have used PAR lamps for years, but it took rock-concert lighting to introduce these powerful lamps to the theatre. Quartz PAR-64 lamps are mounted in a simple housing (aptly named a PAR can) and can throw a highly concentrated beam of light over a considerable distance. Because of its nearly parallel rays and its sheer intensity, the light has a distinctive quality. The color temperature is 3,200°K. The beam is oval because of the filament shape, and it has a soft and fuzzy edge, making it possible to blend one beam with another.

Par-38 and -56 lamps are used in striplights to throw an intense wash of light on a drop or act as color-toning border lights. As with R-type lamps, one can alter the beam spread of a PAR fixture by changing the lamp.

LOW-VOLTAGE LAMPS

Low-voltage light sources are lamps designed to operate with less than 120 applied volts. Sealed-beam automobile headlights operate to full potential on only 12 volts. Aircraft lamps, useful in the theatre for special purposes, operate on 24 volts. The advantage of low-voltage lamps for theatre applications lies in the intensity and quality of the light they emit. The lower the voltage applied to a lamp filament, the smaller the filament can be. Therefore, low-voltage sources have filaments that really do begin to approach the much desired point source of light. The more closely a point source is approximated, the better the light can be controlled through use of reflectors and lenses.

Power Sources

Low-voltage lamps such as aircraft landing lamps (ACLs) deliver a highly coherent light that is intense and harsh in quality. To use such lamps on the stage, however, one needs a low-voltage power supply. A variable-voltage transformer is a good equipment investment for a theatre, but it is fairly expensive. One alternative that will work in certain situations is a continuous-duty automobile battery charger. This is actually a step-down transformer from 120 to 12 volts. A second alternative is an autotransformer dimmer, which functions by reducing the voltage to a lamp (and which is not true of SCR and other electronic dimmers). By measuring the output of an autotransformer dimmer with a voltmeter, one can set it to provide any voltage up to 120.

MR-11, MR-13, and MR-16 Lamps

The MR-16 (miniature reflector, 2-inch diameter) lamp was originally developed as a light source for the Kodak Carousel slide projector (Figure 22-10). The original MR-16 was a 12-volt, T-3 (tubular, ⅜-inch diameter) tungsten-halogen lamp built into a dichroic reflector. The reflector allows nonvisible

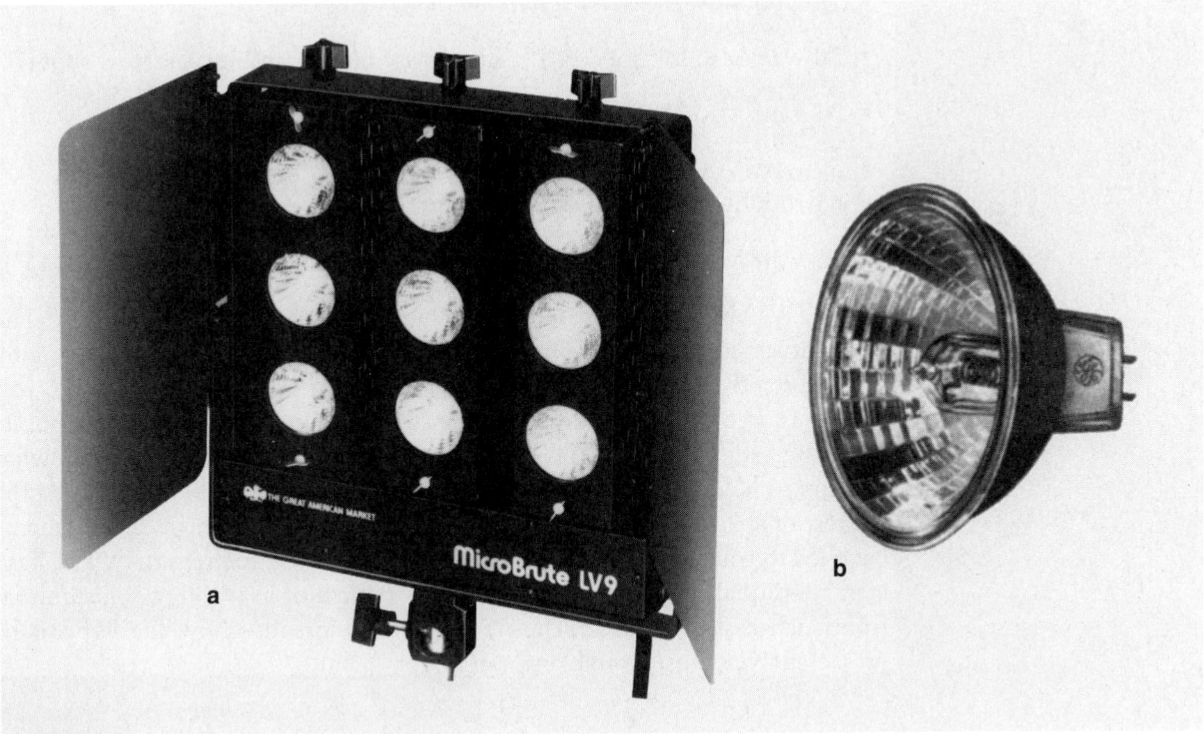

a PHOTO COURTESY GAMPRODUCTS
b PHOTO COURTESY GENERAL ELECTRIC COMPANY

22-10

The MR-16 Lamp

a Nine MR-16 lamps make up the MicroBrute LV9 fixture. Each of the three vertical rows can be aimed separately. Application is greater for television and film, but theatre can also use such a unit for special needs.

b The MR-16 lamp with its miniature 2-pin base and dichroic reflector.

Safety Practice

Calculating Amperage

When using low-voltage sources, one must take care not to overload a circuit or the transformer. Given lamps with the same wattage, the power formula (wattage = voltage × amperage) shows that as the voltage is lowered, the amperage is subsequently raised.

light (ultraviolet and infrared) to pass through, reflecting only visible rays. This results in the light beam having less heat and less harmful ultraviolet radiation. Put to wide use in display and museum lighting, these little reflector lamps are bright and extremely compact and serve as a valuable theatrical light source. Twelve-volt MR lamps are available in the following types, all with 2-pin bases:

- 20- and 35-watt MR-11; narrow flood (30°) and spot (20°)
- 20-watt MR-16; flood (40°), narrow spot (13°), and very narrow spot (7°)
- 35-watt MR-16; flood (40°) and spot (20°)
- 50-watt MR-16; wide flood (55°), flood (40°), medium flood (30°), narrow flood (30°), and narrow spot (15°)
- 75-watt MR-16; flood (40°), narrow flood (25°), and narrow spot (15°)

Today, MR-type lamps are available in a wide range of voltages. The 120-volt version is available in 150 and 250 watts with beam spreads ranging from 32 to 60 degrees. They burn very hot and require glass filters. The 12-volt MR-16 is used in a variety of lighting instruments including striplights, but its most interesting application is on its own as a tiny spotlight. Mounted in what appears to be an extremely small PAR can, this lamp can be tucked into the tightest of spaces. Although it does require low voltage, recent developments have led to transformers that can be dimmed and located remotely. The light is of good quality with a harshness that is typical of low voltage but unusual from such a small source. The narrow beam spreads allow the light to be projected over considerable distances.

ARC LIGHT

The first electric light source to be used in the theatre was an arc light form of limelight. Blocks of calcium oxide (lime) were mounted in a housing and heated until they glowed a brilliant white. Operators were required to keep the lime glowing as well as follow characters around the stage. The quality of limelight was reportedly so flattering that patrons bemoaned the installation of more modern incandescent light sources in many theatres.

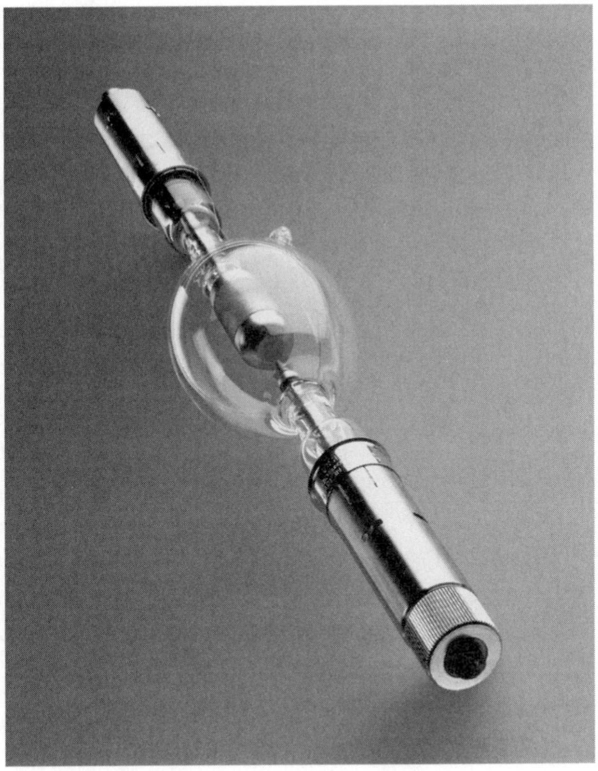

PHOTO COURTESY OSRAM SYLVANIA, INC.

22-11

Xenon Arc Lamp

An Osram XBO xenon arc lamp.

Arc light is impressive because of its brilliance. A streak of lightning during a thunderstorm is an example of arc light on a grand scale. An electric arc light source is composed of two electrodes separated from each other in order to create a gap across which the current must jump (Figure 22-11).

Carbon Arc

Carbon arc became popular as a theatrical source because of its great intensity and high color temperature. Broadway musical productions required a follow spot that could throw a high-intensity light over a long distance. The carbon arc follow spot, first marketed in 1948 by Strong International, was the solution.

Two copper-coated carbon rods, about the size of pencils, were mounted within a housing along with a reflector and lenses. Electricity was conducted to the tips of the rods via the copper coating. The rods were brought together to begin the flow of electricity and then backed off to create a gap. Air, being a good resistor, caused the arc to glow brightly. Today, a xenon arc lamp takes the place of the carbon rods in Strong's line of Trouper and Super Trouper follow spots.

Modern Arc Lamps

In today's arc lamps, two tungsten electrodes in a strong glass enclosure of gas under high pressure produce an intense light source when the current arcs between the electrodes. Because the arc is shielded from the oxygen in the air, the tungsten electrodes do not burn up as do the carbons in a carbon arc follow spot.

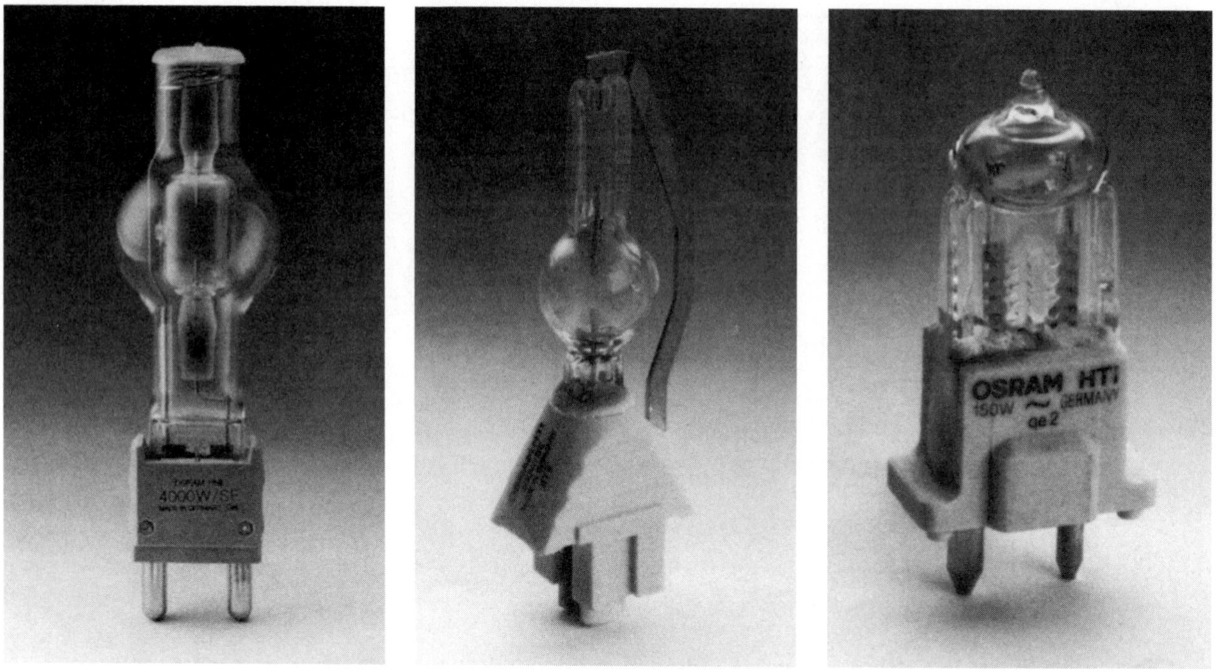

a b c

a–c PHOTOS COURTESY OSRAM SYLVANIA, INC.

22-12

Arc Sources

Three metal halide arc lamps from Osram Sylvania.

a 4,000-watt HMI.

b 600-watt HTI.

c 150-watt HTI.

xenon short-arc lamp A bright arc lamp with xenon gas sealed within its envelope; develops high pressures within the bulb.

The Xenon Lamp Developed in 1954 by Osram Corporation, the XBO **xenon short-arc lamp** was the first arc lamp light source. Filled with high-pressure xenon gas, this lamp burns with a brilliant, cool light. It maintains a color temperature of approximately 6,000°K.

A 75-watt xenon lamp is roughly as bright as a 1,000-watt tungsten-halogen lamp, and the xenon lamp's life is twice as long. Because of its efficiency and long life, it became the standard lamp for follow spots and motion picture projectors.

A drawback of xenon arc lamps is the high pressure built up within the bulb. Such sources require explosion-proof lamp housings. Like the carbon arc, the xenon arc can operate only with a DC power supply. Therefore, one needs a transformer that works with the individual lamp. Further, because few arc sources can be electrically dimmed, mechanical dimmers are provided as a part of the stage instruments that use arc sources.

HMI and HTI Two types of metal halide arc lamps commonly used in follow spots and automated fixtures.

Metal Halide Arc Lamps Several years ago GTE Sylvania and Osram Corporation joined forces to become Osram Sylvania. They have had much to do with the development of the newest arc sources: the **HMI and HTI** metal halide arc lamps (Figure 22-12). Their bulb is quartz glass filled with metal halides. Their short arc works extremely well with the optics of projectors and stage-lighting equipment. The internal pressure within the bulb is lower than in xenon lamps, eliminating the need for expensive explosion-proof housings.

Safety Practice

Proper Handling of Lamps

A good electrician follows several simple rules when working with the various light sources found in the theatre:

1. Always unplug a lighting instrument before replacing a bad lamp.
2. Lamps are expensive, so be sure to treat them with care.
3. Keep fingers off quartz bulbs.
4. The envelope of a burning lamp gets too hot to handle even with the best of gloves.

HMI lamps are available in wattages between 125 (80 volts) and 18,000 (225 volts). Their color temperatures range between 5,600 and 6,000°K. The 575-watt HMI lamp used by Clay Paky's Golden Scan automated fixture burns at 5,600°K and operates at 95 volts. Its intensity is equivalent to a 2,000-watt incandescent lamp. The 1,200-watt HMI used by Clay Paky's Superscan is as bright as a 5,000-watt incandescent lamp and has twice the life.

HMI sources are also available in the form of PAR lamps. They offer a choice of four lenses: narrow spot (7 by 8 degrees), medium flood (9 by 21 degrees), wide flood (26 by 56 degrees), and super wide flood (47 by 47 degrees). Operating on 100-volts at 1,200-watts, they are very bright and have high color temperatures and long lives.

HTI lamps are available in wattages from 150 to 4,000, with color temperatures ranging from 4,800 to 6,500°K. The 400-watt HTI lamp used by the Vari*Lite VL4 wash luminaire requires 55 volts and burns at 4,800°K. It is as bright as a 1,000-watt incandescent lamp and has a similar life expectancy. Osram Sylvania also offers a 270- and a 400-watt HTI lamp with a dichroic reflector similar to the one found in MR-type quartz lamps.

GASEOUS DISCHARGE LAMPS

The most familiar form of a gaseous discharge lamp is the fluorescent tube, which never achieved its promise of becoming a major light source in the theatre. Current passing through a pressurized mercury vapor causes a gaseous discharge, predominantly in the ultraviolet zone. This energy is absorbed by the phosphorous coating on the inside walls of the tube and is emitted as light.

Because the fluorescent tube is a line of light and not a point source, its uses in the theatre are limited to producing a wash of light on a cyclorama or backdrop. The shape of the lamp makes it difficult to achieve smooth color blending. Dimming is possible, but only with special equipment. Fluorescent hoods can be installed with black light fluorescent tubes to flood the stage with ultraviolet light for black light effects.

Tools of the Trade

Recommended Lamps

	Watts	ANSI Code	Color Temp.	Lumens	Life (hours)
E.T.C. Source Four*	575	N/A	3,265°K	16,520	300
	750 (115 V)	N/A	3,200°K	22,000	1,500
6-inch Ellipsoidals**	500	EGE	3,000°K	10,450	2,000
	750	EGG	3,000°K	15,750	2,000
	750	EHF	3,200°K	20,400	300
	1,000	EGJ	3,200°K	27,500	400
6-inch Ellipsoidals*	750	EHG	3,000°K	15,400	2,000
	1,000	FEL	3,200°K	27,500	300
6-inch Fresnels**	500	BTL	3,050°K	11,000	750
	750	BTN	3,050°K	17,000	500
	1,000	BTR	3,200°K	27,500	200

*Medium 2-pin base **Medium prefocus base

MANUFACTURER RECOMMENDATIONS

A lighting instrument is designed with a certain lamp or lamps in mind. The instrument's ventilation, base type and size, and reflector specifications may all be determined by the choice of lamp. All stage-lighting manufacturers provide specific lamp recommendations for their instruments, usually allowing a choice of several different lamps depending on the user's preference. See the box for a sampling from the catalogs of several instrument manufacturers. Note that several lamps of the same wattage are listed, but their color temperature, lamp life, and lumen output differ.

The stage electrician should be familiar with all possible variations in lamp manufacture and have access to up-to-date lamp catalog information. Not only is this information useful when ordering spare lamps, but it also offers quick access to special-application lamps such as flashbulbs, low-voltage lamps, arc lamps, and photofloods. The two major manufacturers in the United States, Osram Sylvania and General Electric, maintain online lamp catalogs.

URL http://www.sylvania.com

URL http://www.gelighting.com

Now that we have thoroughly discussed the tools of lighting design, the next chapter explores how to put those tools to good use in various types of theatres.

23

Stage-Lighting Practice: Design

This chapter presents lighting layouts for different types of productions in a variety of spaces. We examine simplified designs for a realistic interior "box set" in the proscenium theatre, an "in-the-round" production in an arena theatre, a drama designed for the thrust stage, and a modern dance piece.

The following examples have been simplified for clarity and ease of presentation. Each lighting layout is designed to show the minimum number of instruments necessary to achieve acceptable design and visibility. Additional commentary on the individual layouts offers suggestions for embellishing the basic designs with more equipment.

THE PROSCENIUM THEATRE

When a proscenium theatre is used in the traditional manner, the main action of the play takes place upstage of the proscenium line. Front-light for the downstage acting areas normally comes from a lighting position located in the ceiling of the auditorium. Front-lights for upstage areas are hung on the first electric pipe.

The theatre in our example is of medium size: it seats 600 and has a proscenium opening that is 30 feet wide and 18 feet high. Hanging positions both over stage and front-of-house are adequate. About 20 feet out from the proscenium line is a ceiling position for mounting front-lights.

A Realistic Interior

Realistic interiors often call for some variation of the conventional box setting, either with or without a ceiling piece. As one might expect, having a ceiling greatly affects lighting possibilities. The primary action takes place within the walls of this set, while the backgrounds seen through windows and doors are less important. The lighting is often motivated by apparent sources such as sunlight through the windows, light from sconces, or firelight. In practically all cases it is realistically plausible.

23-1

Realistic Interior Sketch

Figure 23-1 is a sketch of such a setting. In the upstage-left wall, a door leads into the kitchen. Upstage-center, a flight of stairs comes down into the living room, and just to the right an exterior door leads out to the porch. In the stage-right wall is a four-window alcove that looks out onto the porch.

Two lighting scenarios are involved. Act I takes place in the afternoon of a somewhat overcast day, and Act II is later that evening.

Sectional View Figure 23-2 is a center-line section of the stage and auditorium, showing lighting positions and angles. Especially useful is the elevation of the upstage landing and steps leading to it. The beam spreads shown from several of the instruments indicate the amount of coverage in a given area. The center line of the beam is used to determine vertical angle. The sight point (indicated by a cross symbol) located in the auditorium represents the eye level of the first row of the audience. Sightlines from this point past the masking borders show whether or not the borders hide the lighting instruments from the audience.

Instrument Schedule and Layout Figure 23-3a is the instrument schedule for the layout in Figure 23-3b. For ease and clarity of presentation, the instruments are numbered consecutively throughout rather than consecutively by position. The two cross symbols on the plan indicate critical sight points from the extreme seats house-left and house-right in the front row. These sight points are used to determine what the audience can see through door openings and windows and beyond side masking. (See Chapter 2 for further detail on sightlines.) Refer to the instrument schedule for details such as instrument type, focus area, color, and channel assignment. Take the time to go back and forth between the reading and the plot.

The Light Plot

The lights in this plot must accommodate both scenes of the play. The primary light source for the afternoon of Act I is daylight coming through the stage-right windows. The source of illumination in the evening of Act II is interior lighting, including the practical sconces located on the set.

The designer has chosen to use two lights from the front, colored in Roscolux R02 (bastard amber) and R60 (no-color blue). There are also two

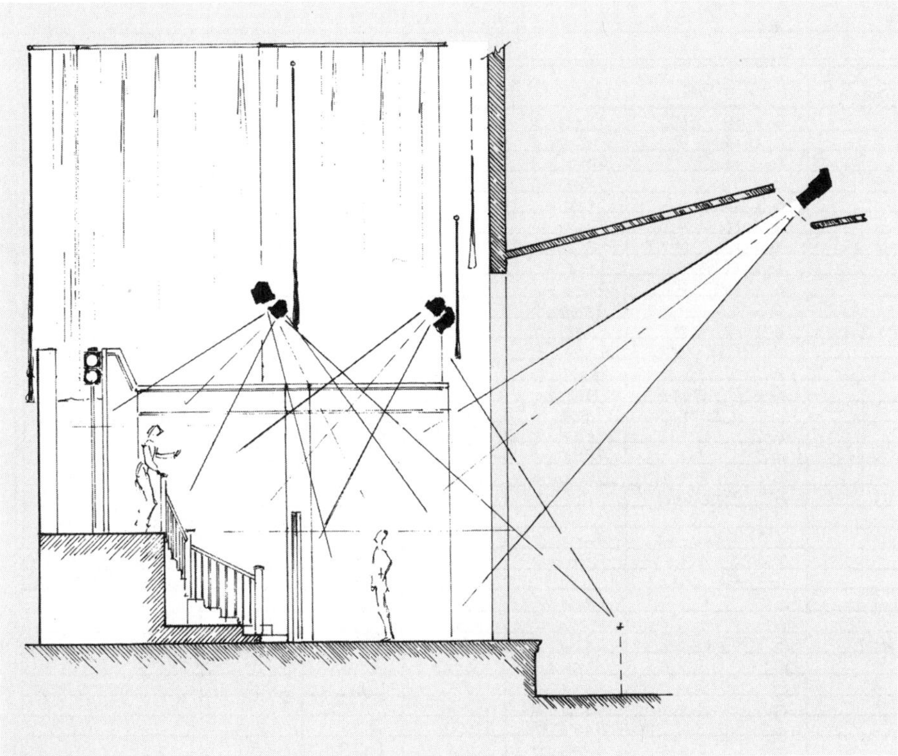

23-2

Realistic Interior: Center-Line Section

Note how the height and placement of the over-stage masking borders are determined in part by using the audience sight point and sightlines.

lights from the back in R09 (pale amber gold) and no-color. The color key in Figure 23-4 indicates position of these instruments.

Afternoon in Act I has the stage-right R60 front-light reading at 80 percent and the no-color back-light reading at 90 percent on their dimmers. The stage-left R02 front-light reads at 70 percent and the R09 back-light at 80 percent. This provides the look of natural interior day light and offers sufficient color and intensity contrast for dimensionality. Act II (evening) has the R60 front-light reading at 60 percent, and the no-color back-light is not reading at all. The R02 front-light reads at 60 percent, and the R09 back-light at 70 percent. The warmer color produced by lower dimmer readings is intended to simulate interior incandescent lighting. For color contrast, the blue front remains at a medium-high reading. Taking the no-color back-light out completely creates a sense of darkness and shadow from one direction, a good feeling for evening.

Downstage Areas In dividing the stage into lighting areas, we find that four across the front will be fine as long as a center-stage sofa special covers the overlap of areas 2 and 3. To cover these four areas, we hang 6-by-16 or 20-degree ellipsoidals in the ceiling position. The section shows that the angle from the ceiling cove to the downstage areas is roughly 45 degrees—a good angle for visibility. Because it offers good beam control, the ellipsoidal reflector spotlight is an ideal front-of-house instrument. For a shorter throw than the one in our sample theatre, or for larger lighting areas, the 30-degree 6-by-12 ERS would be a good choice.

a

INSTRUMENT NO. AND LOCATION	TYPE	USE	LAMP	COLOR	CHANNEL	REMARKS
1 - CEILING SLOT	6 x 16 ERS	AREA 2	1K	R02	2	
2 - " "	6 x 16 "	AREA 1	1K	R02	1	
3 - " "	6 x 16 "	AREA 3	1K	R02	3	
4 - " "	6 x 16 "	AREA 4	1K	R02	4	
5 - " "	6 x 16 "	SPECIAL	1K	R02	9	SOFA
6 - " "	6 x 16 "	AREA 1	1K	R60	11	
7 - " "	6 x 16 "	SPECIAL	1K	R60	19	SOFA
8 - " "	6 x 16 "	AREA 2	1K	R60	12	
9 - " "	6 x 16 "	AREA 4	1K	R60	14	
10 - " "	6 x 16 "	AREA 3	1K	R60	13	
11 - 1ST ELECTRIC	6 x 12 "	AREA 9	750	R02	27	
12 - " "	6" FRESNEL	AREA 5	750	R02	5	CIRCUIT W/ # 13
13 - " "	6" "	AREA 6	750	R02	5	CIRCUIT W/ # 12
14 - " "	6 x 9 ERS	SPECIAL	750	R02	26	STAIR + LANDING
15 - " "	6" FRESNEL	AREA 9	750	R02	8	
16 - " "	6" "	AREA 7	750	R02	6	
17 - " "	6" "	AREA 5	750	R60	15	
18 - " "	6 x 9 ERS	SPECIAL	750	R02	26	UPPER LANDING
19 - " "	6" FRESNEL	"	750	R02	28	WINDOW SEAT
20 - " "	3½" ERS	"	400	R60	37	FRAME ON TROPHY
21 - " "	6" FRESNEL	AREA 6	750	R60	15	
22 - " "	6 x 12 ERS	SPECIAL	750	R02	35	FRAME TO ARCH - AREA 9
23 - " "	6" FRESNEL	"	750	R02	28	WINDOW SEAT
24 - " "	6" "	AREA 7	750	R60	16	
25 - " "	6" "	AREA 9	750	R60	18	
26 - 2ND ELECTRIC	8" FRESNEL	AREA 1	1K	R09	21	BARNDOOR OFF SCENERY
27 - " "	6" "	STAIRS	750	R02	10	" " "
28 - " "	8" "	AREA 2	1K	R09	22	
29 - " "	8" "	AREA 1	1K	N/C	31	
30 - " "	6" "	AREA 8	750	R02	7	
31 - " "	8" "	AREA 3	1K	R09	23	
32 - " "	6" "	STAIRS	750	R60	20	
33 - " "	6" "	AREA 8	750	R60	17	
34 - " "	8" "	AREA 2	1K	N/C	32	
35 - " "	8" "	AREA 4	1K	R09	24	
36 - " "	3½" ERS	SPECIAL	400	N/C	37	FRAME ON TROPHY
37 - " "	8" FRESNEL	AREA 3	1K	N/C	33	
38 - " "	8" "	AREA 4	1K	N/C	34	
39 - BOOM # 1	6" "	KITCHEN	750	N/C	36	
40 - BOOM # 2	6" "	HALL	750	R02	25	CIRCUIT W/ # 41
41 - BOOM # 2	6" "	LANDING	750	R02	25	CIRCUIT W/ # 40
42 - SPOTLINE PIPE # 2	8" "	STREET LIGHTS	1K	R62	41	CIRCUIT W/ # 43
43 - " " # 2	8" "	" "	1K	R62	41	CIRCUIT W/ # 42
44 - " " # 2	8" "	" "	1K	R62	41	
45 - " " # 1	PORCH LIGHT	PRACTICAL	100	N/C	42	
46 - " " # 1	" "	"	100	N/C	42	FIXTURE IN VIEW
47 - " " # 1	14" ERF	WINDOW WASH	750	R02	29	
48 - HALL	9" ERF	WALL WASH	500	R02	30	
49 - "	CEILING FIXTURE	PRACTICAL	3 @ 40W	N/C	38	
50 - SR WALL	WALL SCONCE	"	2 @ 40W	N/C	39	
51 - STAIRS	" "	"	2 @ 40W	N/C	40	

23-3

Realistic Interior Schedule and Plot

a Instrument schedule.

b Lighting layout—instruments have been numbered sequentially for ease of identification.

An important skill for a lighting designer to learn is the ability to examine a light plot to determine where scenery, masking, or the architecture of the theatre might interfere with the path of light. In choosing mounting positions for the ceiling instruments, we have attempted to maintain the desired 45-degree horizontal angle. Note however that we must mount instrument 2 somewhat in from the end of the position in order to reach the extreme downstage-left corner of area 1 without being cut off by the proscenium arch. In addition, the

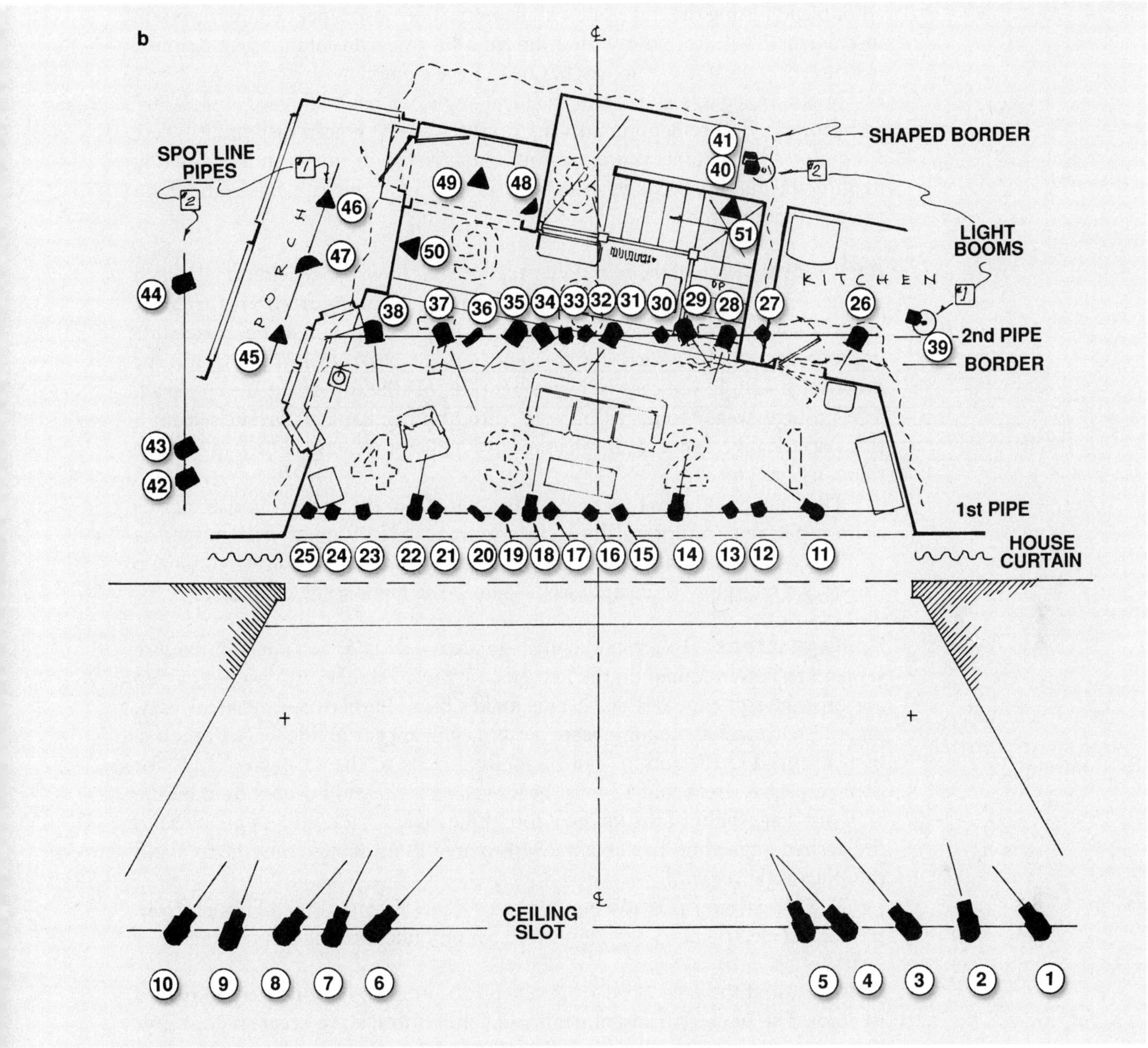

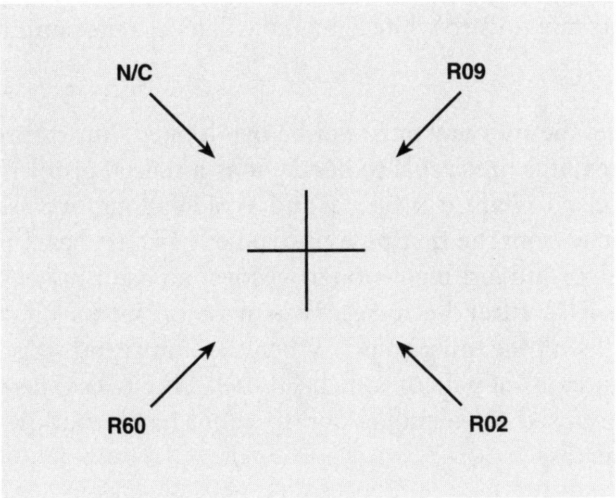

23-4

Realistic Interior Color Key

Color key for the light plot in Figure 23-3.

color blend hitting the stage-left wall from the blue instrument 6 and the warm instrument 2 will be better with 2 moved a bit toward center. In like manner, instrument 9 must move somewhat nearer the center.

In sacrificing to some extent the ideal angle, we have achieved a necessary compromise. The remaining area instruments can be placed just about where we prefer. All instruments are carefully shuttered so as not to spill distracting light on the face of the stage apron and, in the case of instruments 2 and 9, on the proscenium arch.

Back-Light Each of the four downstage areas is lit with two additional 8-inch Fresnel back-lights. A Fresnel is ideal for good blending from area to area, and the high-wattage 8-inch instrument can punch through the area lights without any trouble. Barn doors keep the light beam from spilling too far downstage and, in the case of instrument 26, off the top of the scenery wall. The upstage areas would be back-lit with another bank of Fresnels from a third electric pipe; however, for the sake of simplicity, we have chosen to exclude these instruments.

The back-light helps to separate the actors from the background and gives them a pleasing, sculptural look. In addition, its R09 color from stage-left reinforces the feeling of daylight in Act I and, when lowered on the dimmers, provides a nice glow of incandescent light in the night scene of Act II.

Upstage Areas To cover the upstage areas (areas 5, 6, 7, and 9), we use 6-inch Fresnels mounted on the first electric pipe. Fresnels are chosen for two reasons: the soft edge of their beams makes blending between the areas easy, and no sharp and distracting beam patterns will appear on the walls of the set. Instruments 13, 15, and 16 can be focused close to the 45-degree angle for their respective areas, but 12 must be moved a bit center in order not to hit the wall just stage-right of the kitchen door. Likewise, 17, 21, and 24 are close to the desired angle, but instrument 25 (into area 9) must slide onstage to avoid the stage-right set wall.

The special step area and landing (area 8) are lit with 6-inch Fresnels from the second electric pipe. See the section for an indication of vertical angle.

Color All of the area lights from one direction must be consistent in regard to color. The house-left instruments are colored in R60 to create a cool key-light in Act I and a shadowlike fill in Act II. The corresponding house-right front-lights are colored in the warmer R02. This color choice is particularly useful because the two colors mix toward white light and will look quite natural on the actors and scenery.

The Stairway Of course, the stairway must not be overlooked. But rather than consider it another area, it is preferable to handle it as a special problem because of its different levels. To light it properly and avoid spilling, we use a 40-degree ERS in soft focus from the first pipe (instrument 14). Its beam is framed to the stairs themselves and just high enough to cover an actor moving up and down. It has an R02 filter because a warm color seems most appropriate and blends well with the other colors. When the stairs bend stage-right toward the landing (area 8), a pair of 6-inch Fresnels take over. These instruments (27 and 32) are used for blending and to avoid harsh shadows on the wall behind the staircase.

Practicals There are five practicals on the set. Instrument 51 is a wall sconce at the first stair landing; 49 is a ceiling light located in the vestibule; 50 is another wall sconce on the upstage-right wall; and 45 and 46 are porch lamps. Note that the triangular "special" symbol is used for these fixtures.

All except the two porch lights should be on their own dimmers, and actual control of the fixtures should be in the hands of the light board operator and stage manager, not the actor. The actors must be instructed to mime switching the practicals on and off while the light board operator does the actual operation.

Backing and Support Lights Backing and support lights are valuable in achieving the illusion a box-set production requires. They must receive the same priority that visibility lighting does.

Beginning in the kitchen, we have hung a 6-inch Fresnel on a boom at a height of 14 feet to simulate a ceiling light (instrument 39). This light, without a color filter, illuminates an actor moving through the kitchen door and shines an interesting light into the living room when the door is open. A second boom holds two 6-inch Fresnels (40 and 41) at 16 feet off the stage floor and focused down the "hallway" at the top of the stairs. These two instruments, colored in R02, light actors coming into view from behind the wall so that they do not appear to emerge from a black hole.

The upstage-right archway is an important area lit by a special ERS (22) from the first electric. This instrument is placed in fairly soft focus and shuttered to the arch in order to light an actor entering from the porch door. In addition, the backing wall is washed with a small scoop (48) colored in the warm R02 to dissipate shadows created by the frontal ERS.

Outside the stage-right window is another larger scoop (47) that is used as a window-wash during the overcast afternoon scene. Direct sunlight would require different instrumentation in this position, perhaps PAR fixtures. In the night scene of Act II, instruments 42, 43, and 44 shine in the bay windows like streetlights, casting long and eerie shadows into the living room.

Specials These are non-area-lighting instruments used for special visibility or effect. As mentioned earlier, the center-stage sofa specials (instruments 5 and 7) from the front-of-house ceiling position are important not only because they accent action on the sofa but also because the sofa is located between two lighting areas.

Several Fresnels act as specials into the window seat area from the first electric. These instruments (19 and 23) fill in where the other lights for areas 4 and 7 do not provide adequate coverage.

Instrument 18 is a 30-degree focused onto the stair landing for special accent on an actor playing there. Instrument 20 is framed on a trophy, accentuating its symbolic significance to the play.

Control Even though we attempted to keep the number of instruments to a bare minimum, our schedule lists fifty-one units. Although several instruments (such as the exterior streetlights and the two hall-light Fresnels on boom 2) can be ganged, our layout still requires no fewer than forty-two dimmers—and this figure means that we have to gang areas together.

Two areas that might work together would be 5 and 6. If we place the two R02 Fresnels (12 and 13) into one dimmer, and the two R60 Fresnels

(17 and 21) into another dimmer, we save two dimmers. Note that like colors always are controlled together. Other ganging choices must be determined by the blocking and desired movement of light.

Possible Additions If more equipment and control were available, we might double-hang the stage-right front-lights. This would allow for more of a distinction between Act I and Act II. A better sense of night could be conveyed if the second set of instruments was colored in more saturated blue or lavender. It would also be possible to vary the angle of the two stage-right front sources, thereby accentuating the difference in time of day between the two acts.

Adding a Ceiling If the scene designer adds a ceiling, it would likely eliminate the second electric pipe. However, the first electric pipe must remain, and provisions for it must be made.

All back-light is lost with the second electric pipe. In such a case, the lighting designer must do everything possible to compensate. Extra light flowing into the room from the stage-right windows is a possibility. A set of high side instruments from the first electric pipe is another. Side cove and box boom positions could be used to provide light that wraps around the performer better than traditional front-light would. Some ceilings can have false beam structures built into them, accommodating a lighting position.

ARENA PRODUCTIONS

The term *arena* is derived from Roman amphitheaters where the audience surrounded the action on all sides and the lighting was nature's. Present-day arena theatres, such as the Arena Stage in Washington, D.C., are fine examples of modern technology working in combination with one of the oldest and most intimate of staging configurations: theatre-in-the-round (Figure 23-5).

Special Considerations

Scenery in the arena must be kept to a minimum so as not to block the audience's view. Because the audience surrounds the playing space, lighting must be from all directions. Typically, throw distances are shorter in the arena than in proscenium or thrust theatres, and the audience is closer to the actors.

Functions of Arena Lighting Visibility remains, of course, the primary function in arena production lighting. The actors should be effectively lit for all members of the surrounding audience. Lighting must focus the spectators' attention on the acting areas, providing good definition and precision of form. Tight and specific area control is often desirable in the arena, adding another requirement, this time of a compositional nature, to the designer's list. Mood can be established through intensity and color toning, but both within limited ranges. In addition, because of the audience's viewing angle, the color, texture, and compositional makeup of the stage floor takes on greater visual importance in arena than in other productions.

Accuracy of Focus With the audience arranged closely—often too closely—around the playing area, instruments that have hard-to-control beams are of little value. Ellipsoidal reflector spotlights are the best choice. Fresnels must

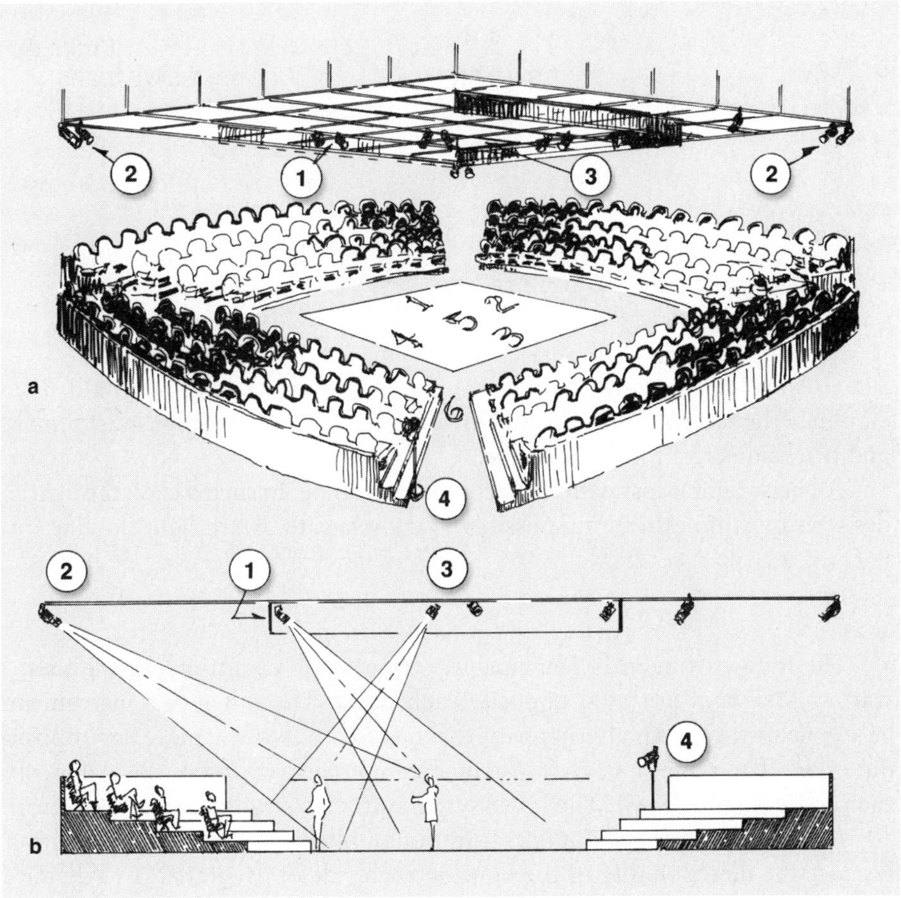

23-5

Arena Lighting Positions

a A perspective view of an arena stage showing the lighting grid.

b A sectional view of the same arena showing the various positions and angles of distribution.

1 A masking valance and the nearest frontal position behind it.

2 The extreme lighting position on the outer edge of the grid.

3 A central position over the acting area.

4 Special boom position in the aisle for a very low angle.

be focused with particular accuracy, with top hats or barn doors added to control the beam spill. Because of their extreme lens flare, PAR fixtures are seldom useful.

The smaller 3- or 4-inch ellipsoidals are quite useful in an arena space with a low grid. Because this space requires adjustable field spreads up to 50 degrees, zoom ellipsoidals are an ideal choice.

Arena Lighting Areas On the proscenium stage, each area must be covered by a minimum of two spotlights and ideally a third back-light. In an arena, however, where the actor is seen from all sides, more instruments are necessary. There are two popular area-lighting approaches in arena designs. The first uses three instruments per area, evenly distributed around the area and thus at approximately 120 degrees from one another. The second uses four lights on each area, spacing them at 90-degree intervals and shooting along the diagonals of the space.

Color in the Arena With either approach, the system of using one warm and one cool color on each area is no longer applicable. In the three-instrument plan, the third instrument is assigned a neutral color, such as light lavender. Opposite a warm filter such as light pink, the lavender appears cool. Opposite a cool filter such as a blue tint, the lavender appears warm. Light bastard amber or no-color can also be quite effective in this application.

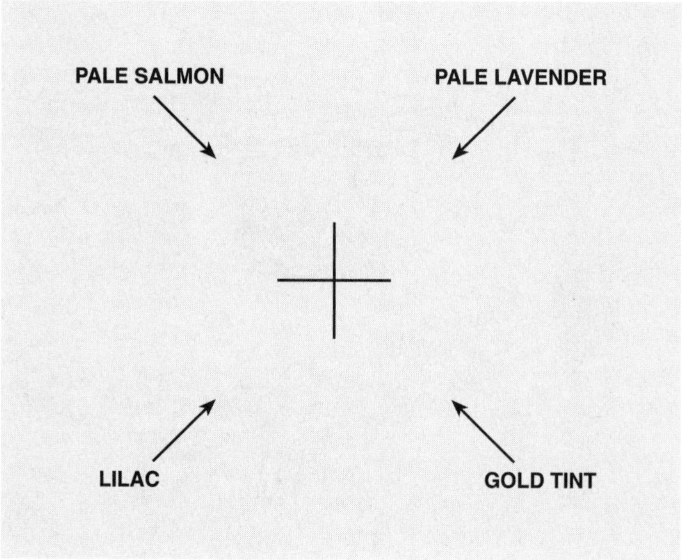

23-6

Arena Color Key

A possible color key for the arena using four lights per area and a warm/cool approach.

The four-instrument system suggests two color variations. In the first, a warm and a cool are used opposite each other. The other two instruments have a neutral tint. An alternate approach is to use two warms, each opposite the other. The remaining two instruments contain two cools, also opposite each other (Figure 23-6). The latter system often proves the most satisfactory.

A word of warning about the saturation of filters used in arena production: because the directionality of the light on each side of each area is so definite, colors appear very strong on the actors. This is more pronounced than in a proscenium production, where there is far more mixing of different beams. Or perhaps this seems true because the audience is so close to the action. In any event, use of the more saturated colors is rarely advisable.

Hanging Positions In a temporary arena setup, attempting to hide the instruments from the audience is fruitless. The lights can, of course, all have top hats and be hung and maintained in a neat manner, with wiring carefully tied off. However, if a space has been specifically designed for arena production, a false ceiling can be provided with openings through which the beams of light may be focused. Instruments can be safely hung off catwalks well above the ceiling and out of sight. Catwalks must be arranged so that an electrician can easily reach all instruments.

Another solution is the tension wire grid (look ahead to Figure 23-12). Such a grid is suspended over the entire room, allowing great flexibility of instrument placement as well as safe and simple hanging and focus. Although the initial expense of such a system is greater than that of others, safety and lower long-term labor costs more than compensate.

Lighting the Audience A difficult problem in any form of arena production is keeping beams of light out of the eyes of spectators seated close to the stage. As long as directors block their actors at the very edge of the arena stage, a compromise is necessary between a well-lighted actor and a

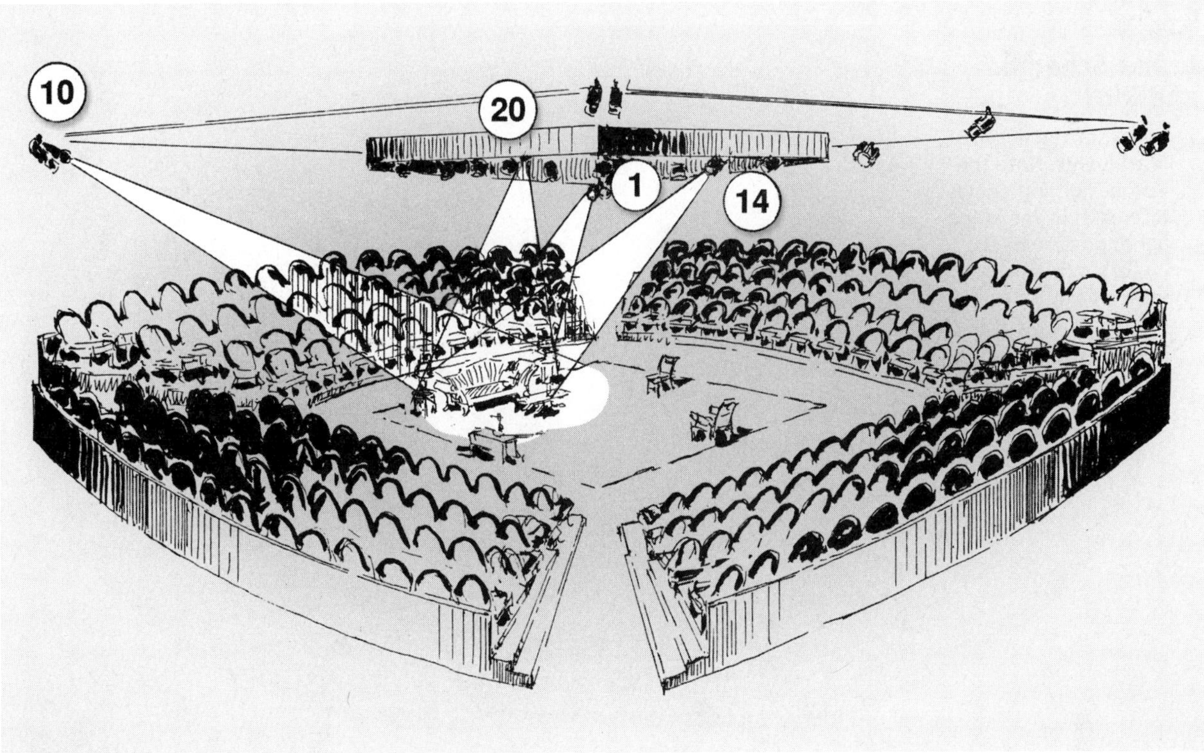

23-7

Lighting an Arena Area

Area 1 being lit from four angles. The numbers refer to instrument numbers found on the light plot in Figure 23-8.

half-blinded spectator. Further, arena audience members look across the stage at other audience members. If the people opposite are lit too brightly, they distract focus from the actors.

To solve the problem, the angle of the instruments spilling into the audience can be raised, but this compromise helps only to an extent. If the first row of the audience can be raised higher than the stage level, or be set back from it, or both, the problem can be greatly eased. In any event, this is one of the greatest challenges confronting the lighting designer in arena production.

Designing the Lighting

The lighting designer need not attempt to create the same lighting picture for everyone in the arena audience. Experience has shown that such an approach is quite restrictive and leads to fairly bland lighting. Nonetheless, the designer should always be concerned about the quality of light from all viewing angles.

Figure 23-7 illustrates a sample arena layout with properties in place on the stage floor. There are two boxes in which lighting instruments may be hung overhead. The plot and an instrument schedule for a suitable lighting design are shown in Figure 23-8. Refer to these illustrations as needed in the following discussion.

23-8

Arena Schedule and Plot

a Layout of the lighting instruments. Note the various lighting angles to area 1. In the arena, lighting instruments are often numbered sequentially.

b Instrument schedule with instruments lighting area 1 indicated.

a

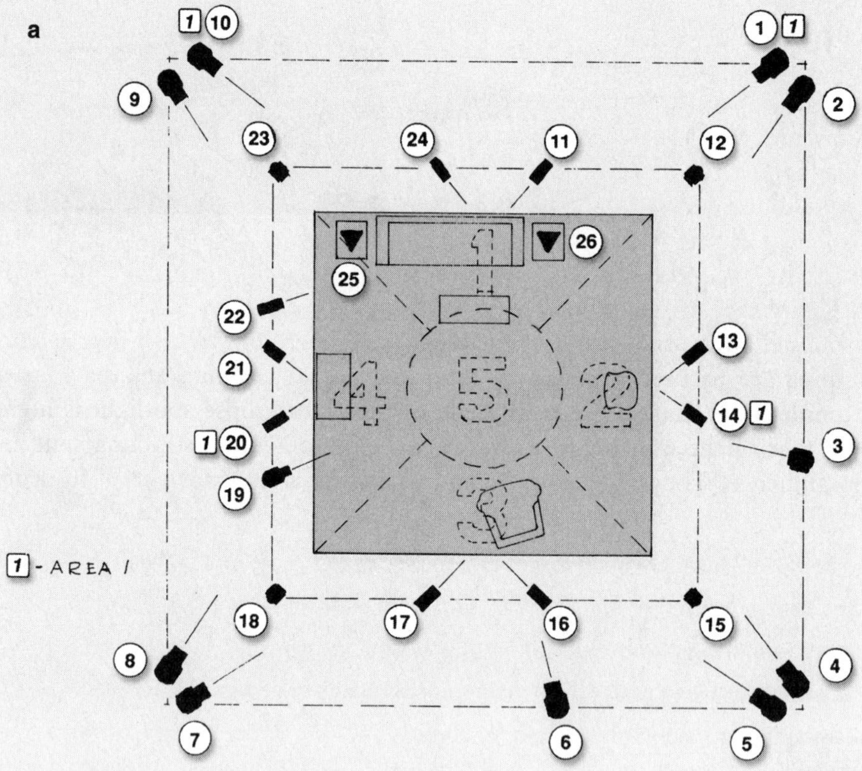

b

No.	INSTRUMENT	PURPOSE	LAMP	COLOR	REMARKS
• 1	30° 6" E.R.S.	AREA 1	750 W.	G325	
2	30° 6" E.R.S.	AREA 2	750 W.	G325	
3	8" FRESNEL	MOONLIGHT SPECIAL	1000 W.	G815	FOCUS CENTER
4	30° 6" E.R.S.	AREA 2	750 W.	G790	
5	30° 6" E.R.S.	AREA 3	750 W.	G790	
6	30° 6" E.R.S.	COUCH SPECIAL	750 W.	G105	FRAME TO COUCH
7	30° 6" E.R.S.	AREA 3	750 W.	G364	
8	30° 6" E.R.S.	AREA 4	750 W.	G364	
9	30° 6" E.R.S.	AREA 4	750 W.	G940	
• 10	30° 6" E.R.S.	AREA 1	750 W.	G940	
11	40° MINI-ELLIPSE	AREA 4	500 W.	G325	TOP SHUTTER
12	6" FRESNEL	AREA 5	500 W.	G325	TOP HAT
13	40° MINI-ELLIPSE	AREA 3	500 W.	G325	TOP SHUTTER
• 14	40° MINI-ELLIPSE	AREA 1	500 W.	G790	TOP SHUTTER
15	6" FRESNEL	AREA 5	500 W.	G790	TOP HAT
16	40° MINI-ELLIPSE	AREA 4	500 W.	G790	TOP SHUTTER
17	40° MINI-ELLIPSE	AREA 2	500 W.	G364	TOP SHUTTER
18	6" FRESNEL	AREA 5	500 W.	G364	TOP HAT
19	50° 6" E.R.S	CENTER ACCENT	750 W.	CLEAR	FOCUS CENTER
• 20	40° MINI-ELLIPSE	AREA 1	500 W.	G364	TOP SHUTTER
21	40° MINI-ELLIPSE	AREA 3	500 W.	G940	TOP SHUTTER
22	40° MINI-ELLIPSE	COUCH SPECIAL #2	500 W.	G360	SHUTTER TO COUCH
23	6" FRESNEL	AREA 5	500 W.	G940	TOP HAT
24	40° MINI-ELLIPSE	AREA 2	500 W.	G940	TOP SHUTTER
25	FIXTURE	TABLE LAMP #1	40 W.	-	GANG WITH #26
26	FIXTURE	TABLE LAMP #2	40 W.	-	GANG WITH #25

The Light Plot The designer has divided the stage into five areas numbered clockwise 1 through 4, with area 5 in the center. Dashed lines on the layout mark the approximate limits of these areas, although it is understood that they will actually overlap one another with their lights blending smoothly.

The area allocation indicated in Figure 23-8 represents an absolute minimum. If the actors play any corner of the stage, they will be poorly lit. Using nine areas, three across and three deep, would provide better coverage. It would also nearly double the number of instruments required.

The instruments have been numbered systematically, from the top, clockwise around the stage, in the outer box first and then the inner. From each corner of the outer box, a pair of 30-degree ellipsoidal reflector spotlights is focused on the two closest areas. From the inner box, two 40-degree Mini-Ellipses are focused on each of the same areas. Looking at area 1 as an example, note that the vertical angle of the Mini-Ellipse spotlight is higher than that of the 6-inch ERS. This angle helps to avoid distracting spill into the audience. The higher angle also means a shorter throw, so a 40-degree rather than a 30-degree instrument is chosen. The ERS is used here because the upper portion of its beam can be shuttered to prevent light from glaring into the eyes of the spectators.

Area 5, in the center, is lit from the four corners of the inner box by 6-inch Fresnels. Here the problem of spill light annoying the audience is less extreme than in the outer areas. Nonetheless, top hats are used on the instruments. Ellipsoidal reflector spotlights might be used, but the soft-edged Fresnel beam pattern helps to blend this center light with illumination in the adjacent areas.

Color The color system, using GAM filters, is that of opposite warms and cools. The warm light, working diagonally out of the upper-right corner of the layout, is from G325 (bastard amber). The identical color might have been employed from the lower left also, but the designer preferred to use a slightly different tint, G364 (pale honey). In like manner, the cools are not identical. From the lower right is G790 (electric blue), while opposite it is G940 (light purple). Although the light purple is not an especially cool color, the nature of the drama warrants it. For a starker and more dramatic piece, we might have selected a combination of G790 and G830 (north sky blue) for the cools. The versatile G940 might have been one of the warms, with perhaps no color at all in the opposite instruments.

Specials A few specials have been provided. On the right side of the plot is an 8-inch Fresnel with a G815 (Moody blue) filter to give the effect of moonlight for a brief scene. Instrument 6 is focused carefully on the couch and colored in a romantic G105 (antique rose) for a scene played there. Toward the upper-left corner is another couch special, colored in G360 (amber blush), for a different scene. Also on the left, a wide-beamed ellipsoidal reflector spotlight without color (instrument 19) serves as an accent on the central area for a special moment there. The two table lamps at either end of the couch are practical fixtures, meaning that they will be lit at some point in the production.

Control Twenty-four dimmers would be necessary for this simple arena layout, assuming that we can repatch one of the specials. Arena and thrust lighting almost always require tighter and more individual control than proscenium productions do.

THRUST PRODUCTIONS

Although normally larger in scale, thrust production has many of the same characteristics as the arena. Its appeal as a performance space is its intimacy, with audience members viewing the performers from three sides.

The Theatre

vomitory entrance In the thrust theatre, ramps serving as actors' entrances and exits that lead up to the front of the stage from beneath the audience.

Figure 23-9 is a perspective drawing of a thrust theatre showing lighting positions and other features of such an auditorium. Thrust theatres often have ramps that lead up to the front of the stage from beneath the audience. These are called **vomitory entrances.** Placing a lighting boom in these ramps with an instrument shooting onto the stage creates an interesting and dramatic angle of light. Lighting position 4, the tormentor boom, might very well be a permanent lighting ladder such as the one shown upstage of it. Many thrust theatres have a balcony, the front rail of which provides a useful lighting position.

23-9

Thrust Lighting Positions

A perspective view of a thrust stage showing its various lighting positions. The stage division into areas varies with each production. Note that if a balcony exists, there will also be a balcony rail position.

1 Outer valance position.
2 Second valance and over-stage grid.
3 Wing ladder for side-lighting.
4 Boom in tormentor position.
5 Vomitory rail.
6 Moat or gutter.

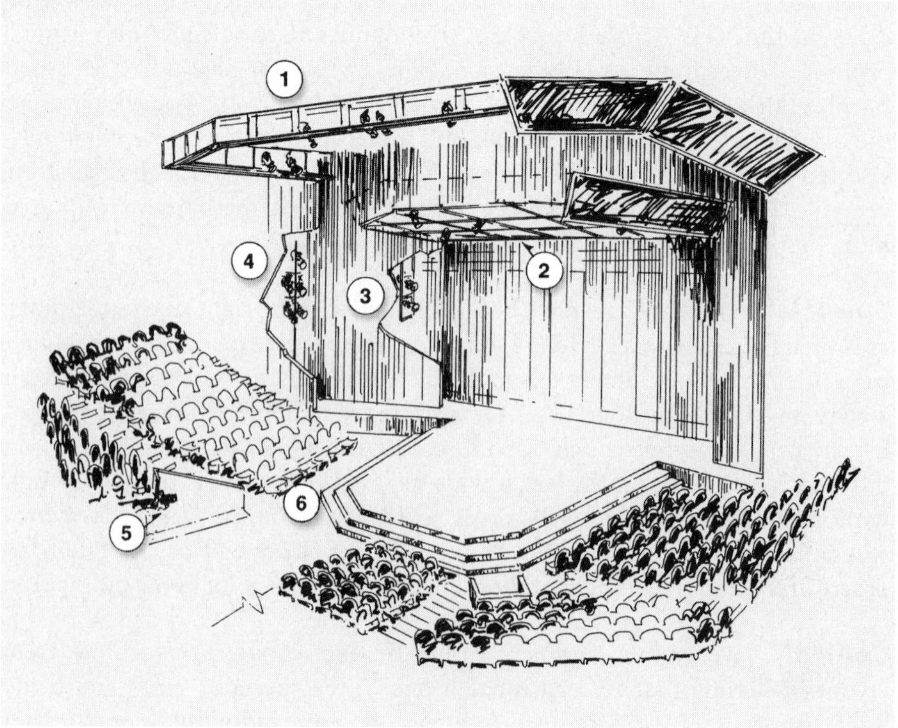

Note that an actor playing downstage is seen from all sides by the audience, which wraps well around the thrust. As in the arena, side-light for some audience members is front-light for others.

Any theatre designed with a thrust stage must provide ample mounting positions for the lighting instruments. The simplest way to do this is to hang a grid of pipes or other mounting structures over the entire stage and auditorium. It should extend in all directions at least as far from the edge of the stage as the height of the grid above the stage floor. There should be enough circuits on this grid to accommodate more than all anticipated instruments.

Boxes or valances to hide the instruments can be provided. However, these devices are not completely effective. The need to hang lights in any location on the grid makes them difficult to mask. Today's audience has come to accept exposed lighting instruments, particularly in arena and thrust theatres. Instruments neatly cabled are seldom a distraction.

The spectators in the side seats particularly will find that the lenses of instruments focused in their general direction are in full view. But as long as top hats are used, this should not be too much of an annoyance. Care must be taken to mask or frame off the upper part of the beams from such instruments to be sure they do not glare directly into the eyes of those seated facing them. Fresnels, if used, should have barn doors. Once again, a tension wire grid rather than awkward pipe grids is a good choice.

Design Considerations

The arrangement of set pieces and properties often dictates how a thrust stage is best divided into lighting areas. Each area requires several instruments focused on it from different directions. Top- or back-lighting is essential to set off the actor from the background. Care must be taken to avoid, as much as possible, light spilling into the audience. Blending and toning are best accomplished by the use of soft-beamed spotlights throwing color washes over large portions of the stage. Because of the steep audience rake, the stage floor becomes a major scenic element in most thrust houses. As in the arena, lighting color, texture, and composition are readily apparent on the floor.

Distribution The thrust theatre offers many possible variations for instrument placement. Varying the angle of instruments into an area provides good visual variety. However, because of spill into the audience, very low angles are possible only from the front. Therefore, a designer will often treat an area with a low-angle front light as well as color washes. Five to seven instruments per area is not unusual in thrust lighting. The absolute minimum is three, but this provides for little or no variety.

Color As with arena staging, strong colors are not desirable on the thrust stage—although a designer can be somewhat bolder because of the one closed side. The use of very light tints, approaching no-color, has been a popular color system for the thrust. This look is generally sharp and dramatic. Another system calls for instruments from the front to have very pale tints, with those on the side taking on stronger shades of the same basic colors. Color systems for the arena are also adaptable to the thrust. Color toning the floor is best done from back- or top-light and can add a great deal of variety to the stage picture.

Designing the Lighting

Figure 23-10 shows a sketch of a typical thrust stage with one area lit. Also shown are the plot and instrument schedule for a thrust production. Refer to these illustrations while reading the following pages.

23-10

Thrust Lighting of a Single Area

- **a** Area 4 lit from five angles and directions.
- **b** The lighting layout with area 4 instruments indicated.
- **c** The instrument schedule with area 4 instruments indicated.

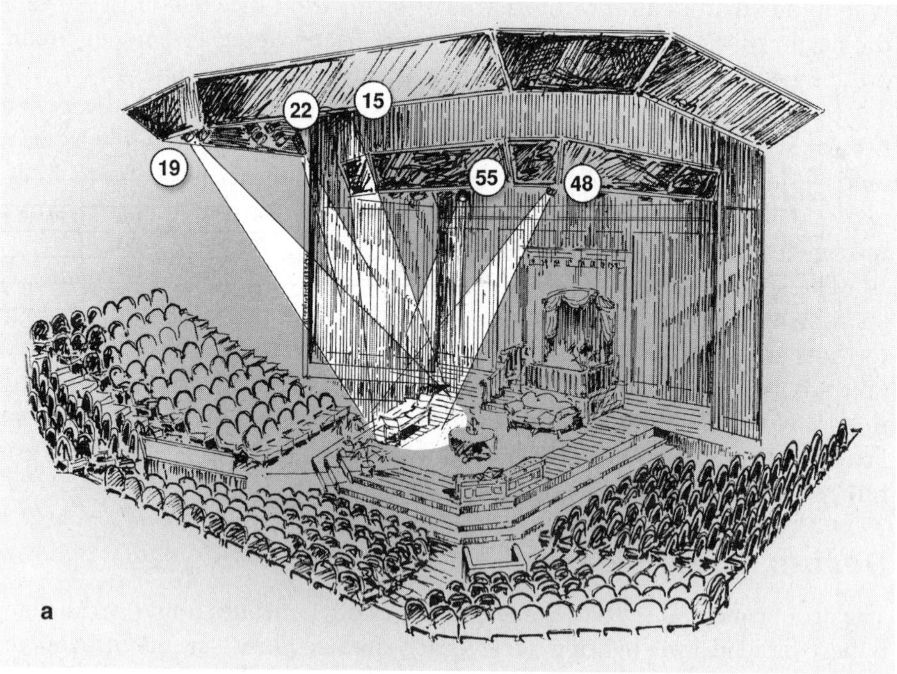

a

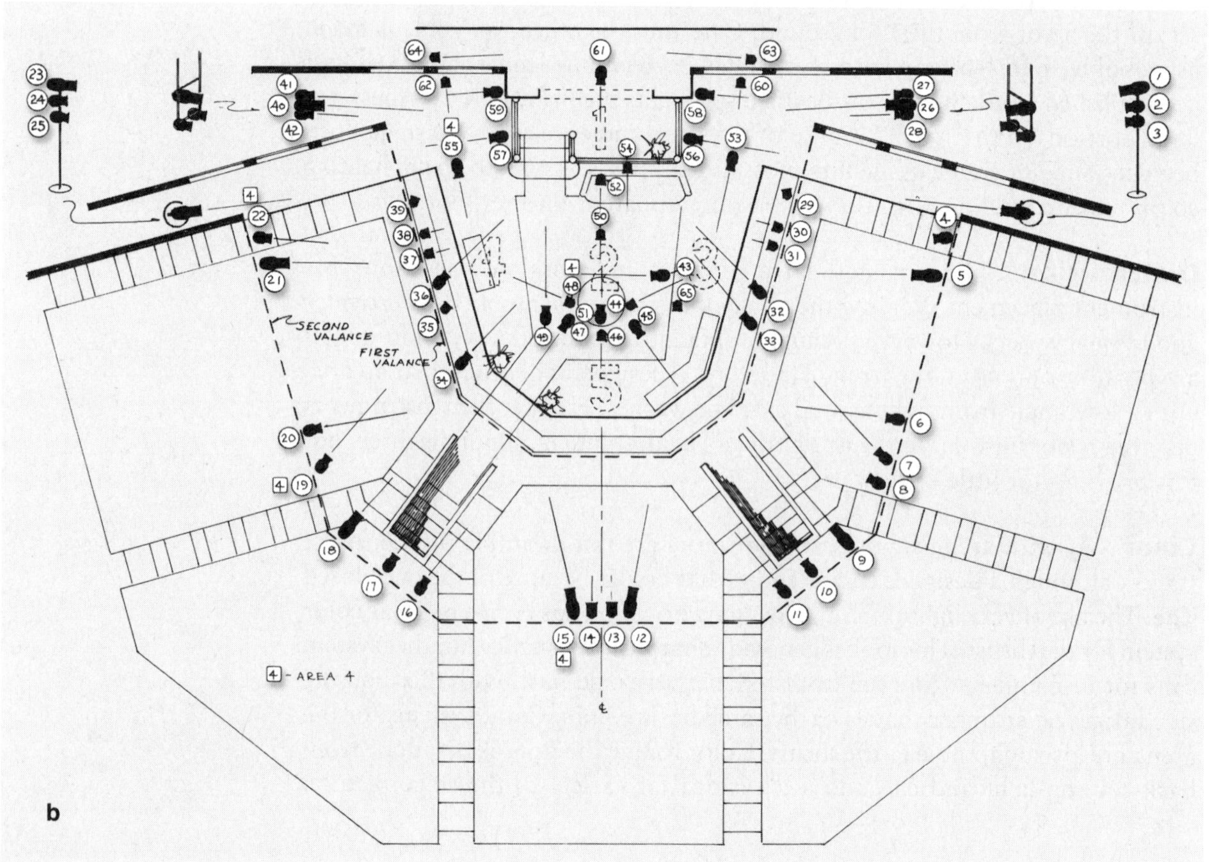

b

No.	INSTRUMENT	LOCATION	PURPOSE	LAMP	COLOR	REMARKS
1	6X16 E.R.S.	LEFT BOOM	AREA 1	1000 W.	L144	L. BOOM TOP
2	6X12 E.R.S	LEFT BOOM	WASH WARM	750 W.	L134	L. BOOM MIDDLE - SOFT EDGE
3	6X12 E.R.S	LEFT BOOM	WASH COOL	750 W.	L119	L. BOOM BOTTOM - SOFT EDGE
4	6X12 E.R.S	2ND VALANCE-L	AREA 3	1000 W.	L141	
5	6X16 E.R.S.	2ND VALANCE-L	AREA 2	1000 W.	L141	
6	6X12 E.R.S	2ND VALANCE-L	AREA 5	750 W.	L141	
7	6X12 E.R.S	2ND VALANCE-L	AREA 3	750 W.	L144	
8	6X12 E.R.S	2ND VALANCE-L	WINDOW SEAT	750 W.	L144	
9	6X16 E.R.S.	2ND VALANCE-L	AREA 2	1000 W.	L117	
10	6X12 E.R.S	2ND VALANCE-L	LEFT TUNNEL	750 W.	L142	FRAME TO TUNNEL
11	6X12 E.R.S	2ND VALANCE-L	AREA 5	750 W.	L117	
12	6X16 E.R.S.	2ND VALANCE-C	AREA 3	1000 W.	L117	FRAME OFF AUDIENCE
13	8" FRESNEL	2ND VALANCE-C	WASH COOL	1000 W.	L119	BARN DOOR-OFF AUDIENCE
14	8" FRESNEL	2ND VALANCE-C	WASH WARM	1000 W.	L134	BARN DOOR-OFF AUDIENCE
• 15	6X16 E.R.S.	2ND VALANCE-C	AREA 4	1000 W.	L152	FRAME OFF AUDIENCE
16	6X12 E.R.S	2ND VALANCE-R	AREA 5	750 W.	L152	
17	6X12 E.R.S	2ND VALANCE-R	RIGHT TUNNEL	750 W.	L142	FRAME TO TUNNEL
18	6X16 E.R.S.	2ND VALANCE-R	AREA 2	1000 W.	L152	
• 19	6X16 E.R.S.	2ND VALANCE-R	AREA 4	750 W.	L151	
20	6X16 E.R.S.	2ND VALANCE-R	AREA 5	750 W.	L153(2)	
21	6X16 E.R.S.	2ND VALANCE-R	AREA 2	1000 W.	L153(2)	
• 22	6X16 E.R.S.	2ND VALANCE-R	AREA 4	750 W.	L153(2)	
23	6X16 E.R.S.	RIGHT BOOM	AREA 1	1000 W.	L151	R. BOOM- TOP
24	6X12 E.R.S	RIGHT BOOM	WASH WARM	750 W.	L134	R. BOOM MIDDLE - SOFT EDGE
25	6X12 E.R.S	RIGHT BOOM	WASH COOL	750 W.	L119	R. BOOM BOTTOM - SOFT EDGE
26	6X16 E.R.S	LEFT LADDER	U.R. CORNER	1000 W.	L141	L. LADDER TOP - FRAME SIDES
27	6X12 E.R.S.	LEFT LADDER	AREA 1	750 W.	L141	L. LADDER BOTTOM - FRAME US
28	6X12 E.R.S.	LEFT LADDER	U.L. CORNER	750 W.	L141	L. LADDER BOTTOM - FRAME US
29	6" FRESNEL	1ST VALANCE-L	U.L. CORNER	500 W.	L117	
30	6" FRESNEL	1ST VALANCE-L	WASH COOL	500 W.	L119	BARN DOOR OFF AUDIENCE
31	6" FRESNEL	1ST VALANCE-L	WASH WARM	500 W.	L134	BARN DOOR OFF AUDIENCE
32	6X12 E.R.S	1ST VALANCE-L	AREA 1	750 W.	L117	
33	6X12 E.R.S	1ST VALANCE-L	SOFA	750 W.	L117	
34	6X12 E.R.S	1ST VALANCE-R	SOFA	750 W.	L152	
35	6" FRESNEL	1ST VALANCE-R	BENCH	500 W.	L152	
36	6X12 E.R.S	1ST VALANCE-R	AREA 1	750 W.	L152	FRAME BOTTOM
37	6" FRESNEL	1ST VALANCE-R	WASH WARM	500 W.	L134	BARN DOOR OFF AUDIENCE
38	6" FRESNEL	1ST VALANCE-R	WASH COOL	500 W.	L119	BARN DOOR OFF AUDIENCE
39	6" FRESNEL	1ST VALANCE-R	U.R. CORNER	500 W.	L152	
40	6X16 E.R.S.	RIGHT LADDER	U.L. CORNER	1000 W.	L153(2)	R. LADDER TOP - FRAME SIDE
41	6X16 E.R.S.	RIGHT LADDER	AREA 1	750 W.	L153(2)	R. LADDER BOTTOM - FRAME US
42	6X16 E.R.S.	RIGHT LADDER	U.R. CORNER	750 W.	L153(2)	R. LADDER BOTTOM - FRAME US
43	6X16 E.R.S.	GRID OVER STAGE	BENCH	750 W.	L117	SOFT EDGE FRAME OFF AUDIENCE
44	6" FRESNEL	GRID OVER STAGE	AREA 3	500 W.	CLEAR	BARN DOOR OFF AUDIENCE
45	6X12 E.R.S	GRID OVER STAGE	LEFT TUNNEL	750 W.	L103	FRAME TO TUNNEL
46	6" FRESNEL	GRID OVER STAGE	AREA 5	500 W.	CLEAR	BARN DOOR OFF AUDIENCE
47	6X12 E.R.S	GRID OVER STAGE	RIGHT TUNNEL	750 W.	L103	FRAME TO TUNNEL
• 48	6" FRESNEL	GRID OVER STAGE	AREA 4	500 W.	CLEAR	BARN DOOR OFF AUDIENCE
49	6X12 E.R.S	GRID OVER STAGE	STEPS	750 W.	L152	SOFT EDGE FRAME TO STEPS
50	6" FRESNEL	GRID OVER STAGE	AREA 2 D.S.	500 W.	CLEAR	
51	6X12 E.R.S	GRID OVER STAGE	ARCHWAY	750 W.	L103	FRAME TO ARCHWAY
52	6" FRESNEL	GRID OVER STAGE	AREA 2 U.S.	500 W.	CLEAR	
53	6X12 E.R.S	GRID OVER STAGE	AREA 3	750 W.	CLEAR	FRAME L AND TOP
54	6" FRESNEL	GRID OVER STAGE	SOFA	500 W.	CLEAR	
• 55	6X12 E.R.S	GRID OVER STAGE	AREA 4	750 W.	L117	FRAME R AND TOP
56	6X12 E.R.S	GRID OVER STAGE	LEFT RAMP	750 W.	L103	FRAME OFF R. WALL
57	6X12 E.R.S	GRID OVER STAGE	RIGHT RAMP	750 W.	L103	FRAME OFF L. WALL
58	6X12 E.R.S	GRID OVER STAGE	UL ENTRANCE	750 W.	L103	FRAME OFF R. WALL
59	6X12 E.R.S	GRID OVER STAGE	UR ENTRANCE	750 W.	L103	FRAME OFF L. WALL
60	6" FRESNEL	GRID OVER STAGE	UL CORNER	500 W.	CLEAR	
61	6X12 E.R.S	GRID OVER STAGE	AREA 1	750 W.	CLEAR	SOFT EDGE
62	6" FRESNEL	GRID OVER STAGE	UR CORNER	500 W.	CLEAR	
63	6" FRESNEL	GRID OVER STAGE	HALLWAY - L	500 W.	L104	
64	6" FRESNEL	GRID OVER STAGE	HALLWAY - R	500 W.	L104	
65	6" FRESNEL	GRID OVER STAGE	WINDOW SEAT	500 W.	CLEAR	BARN DOOR OFF AUDIENCE

Area 1 Because area 1 is so far upstage, it is lit somewhat from the front, proscenium-style, by two 30-degree ellipsoidals (32 and 36) mounted in the inner box. Two 20-degree ellipsoidals (1 and 23) strike the area from the booms placed in the ramp entrances on either side of the stage. Two more 30-degree ellipsoidals (27 and 41) are on the ladders hung in the upstage entrances. Instrument 61, a 40-degree ellipsoidal because of its short throw, acts as a back-light from above the upstage archway.

The colors, working from front to rear on the left side, are Lee filters L117 (steel blue), L114 (no-color blue), and L141 (bright blue). On the right side they are L152 (pale gold), L151 (gold tint), and double L153 (pale salmon). The back-light is clear. The other areas use these same colors for instruments working from the same angles.

Area 4 Figure 23-10a highlights the instruments being used for area 4, typical of the other three areas onstage. Instrument 15, a 20-degree ellipsoidal, strikes the area from the front with L152. Instruments 19 and 22 are 30-degree ellipsoidals colored in L151 and double L153. The double salmon (L153), which is relatively saturated, comes from the far stage-right side. Instruments 48 and 55 are both quite steep to avoid spill into the audience, and the 6-inch Fresnel has barn doors as well. The back-light ellipsoidal (55) is colored in L117 (steel blue) and the stage-left Fresnel (48) is clear.

Color Wash A pair of 8-inch Fresnels light the entire set from the front to give a tonal wash that we could vary by dimming the warm and cool instruments to different readings. Two pairs of 6-inch Fresnels located on either side of the inner box work with the 8-inch Fresnels. For the cool wash, an L119 (dark blue) is used, and for the warm wash an L134 (golden amber). The golden amber has a warming effect on the rather cool blue, resulting in lavender tones when mixed properly.

Specials A large number of specials have been hung. The extreme up-left and up-right corners, which could be considered areas in themselves, are each covered by three spots from front and sides, plus a back-light. The vomitory entrances are lit from front and back by house-right instruments 10 and 45 and house-left instruments 17 and 47. The upstage-left and upstage-right entrances are lit by instruments 56 through 59, and two 6-inch Fresnels (63 and 64) illuminate the far upstage hallway. Instrument 51, a 30-degree ellipsoidal, is framed to the upstage-center archway and colored in the versatile L103. Instrument 49 lights the steps leading to the upstage platform area. The bench, the window seat, and the sofa also have appropriate coverage.

Additional specials would be indicated by blocking and traffic patterns. Actors might, for example, be placed on the steps leading down from the platform toward the audience; this would call for suitable lighting. If the steps were used a great deal, up to five additional areas might be necessary.

We have used ellipsoidal reflector spotlights a great deal in this layout because of the good control we have over their beams. When practical, they are made soft-edged by shifting the lenses to throw the gate out of focus. If moving the lens barrel does not produce a soft enough edge, a light diffusion filter such as R119 can be added. This reduces sharp beam edges that result in abrupt changes of intensity on the stage and the actors. For the same reason, Fresnel spotlights are used when their spill light will not be critical. Barn doors or top hats are suggested for all Fresnels.

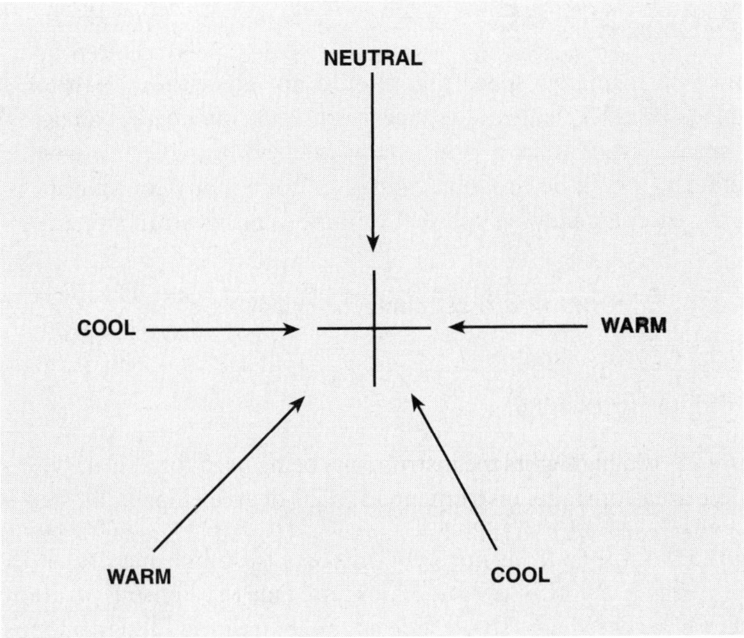

23-11

Thrust Color Key

A possible color key for lighting a thrust area from five directions.

Variations

Our sample lighting layout is designed for a comedy or a light drama with a simple interior setting. Lighting angles are standard for good visibility and the colors are chosen for their pale tints. The arrangements of color (cool on one side and warm on the other) and angles are derived from proscenium lighting and provide good coverage. However, this two-sided color approach allows for little variety or color interest and may not be desirable for a production with scenes that demand their own specific lighting.

With a minimum of five instruments on each acting area and a color arrangement as shown in Figure 23-11, the designer has several more options, as follows:

1. The two warms can act as key-light, with the cools filling.
2. The two cools can act as key-light, with the warms filling.
3. Any one instrument (except the back-light neutral) can be lowered in intensity or dropped out completely, causing a color shift as well as a compositional change.

If more than the minimum five instruments per area is possible, even greater variety of color and distribution can be achieved.

Side Angle For more dramatic productions, the vertical angle of the side-lights can be raised, with the following results:

1. Higher angle distribution causes sharper facial and body shadows.
2. Spill into side audience seating is more controllable.
3. Area control is tighter.

Texture Texture achieved by patterns or gobos can break up the sometimes flat and dull surface of the thrust stage. High side- or back-light is often a desirable angle for such treatment.

THE FLEXIBLE STAGE

Another form of performance space that should not go without mention is the popular "black box." This flexible space is primarily intended as an actor's performance space rather than a production facility, but lighting is often required nonetheless. Black box seating can be set up in many configurations, each defining a particular playing space. Common seating arrangements are as follows:

1. One-sided, or full front (a proscenium-type orientation)
2. Two-sided, or corner staging
3. Three-sided, or thrust staging
4. Four-sided, or arena staging
5. Aisle—with seats on two sides of a central aisle

Lighting the flexible space is not very different from lighting one of the several theatre forms previously examined, except that the lighting positions are generally closer to the stage. To provide adequate lighting, designers must keep hanging positions flexible. A cross-pipe grid over the entire space is a fair solution to the problem of flexibility. Such a grid allows lighting instruments to be hung in any position and focused in any direction.

A better solution, as we have seen, is the tension wire grid (Figure 23-12). One-eighth-inch wire rope is woven in all directions, forming a weight-bearing surface on which an electrician can walk. Pipes supported from the ceiling are arranged to allow complete hanging flexibility with a minimum of time and effort. The lighting instruments shoot through the thin wire mesh as shown in the photograph. This grid is ideal for the flexible space as well as extremely useful in arena or thrust situations.

LIGHTING FOR DANCE

Dance is most often performed on a proscenium stage with a formal leg-and-border arrangement. At first glance it would seem that dance requires the same sort of light that other forms of production do. There is, however, one important difference. When we attend a play we are vitally interested in the faces of the actors to convey character, thoughts, and emotion. This is not true in dance, particularly ballet, in which the position and movement of the dancer's body tell all. A knowledgeable lover of concert dance will scarcely notice a dancer's face and will surely not concentrate on it. The primary concern is movement, revealed and emphasized by light.

Design Considerations

One method of emphasizing movement is to place the principal axis of light in line with the axis of movement. Thus, a ballerina spinning in a pirouette would have the light hitting straight down on her or straight up from below. The latter, which has been used for trick effects in modern dance, would probably not be appropriate for classical ballet. Although light from directly overhead tends to make the human body appear shortened, it remains a good way to accent the rapid turning of the dance.

a

b

23-12

Tension Wire Grid

a View from the grid of the Keck Theatre at Occidental College in Los Angeles. The woven cable grid is weight bearing and offers complete access to overhead lighting positions. This full-ceiling grid was installed by Hoffend & Sons.

b View from the stage. The Keck is a unique courtyard theatre with a seating capacity of 475.

Of course it would be impractical, if not inappropriate, to attempt to cover every single movement of a dance. Fortunately, choreographers often establish several basic movement patterns and repeat them throughout the dance. These patterns echo or reinforce the theme of the dance piece, creating compositions that can be effectively reinforced by the lighting. Lighting designers can provide for some of the most significant movement and for more general lighting that will best suit the work. They must attend as many rehearsals as possible and take careful notes before developing the light plot.

dance zones Dance lighting areas that extend completely across the stage; normally determined by placement of side-lighting booms.

Dance Areas Unlike most dramatic productions, dance layouts are not organized by lighting areas but arranged in a series of **dance zones,** areas that extend completely across the stage. The number of zones is determined by the depth of the dance space and the number of side entrances. For example, if a dance concert has five side entrances, the layout will most likely consist of five lighting zones. In addition to zone lighting, a dance designer may provide diagonal lighting and numerous specials.

Side-Light When lighting a dramatic production, the designer usually begins with front visibility light and then moves on to side- and back-light angles. In lighting most dance, however, the designer begins with the side-lights. Side-lighting is the primary source of figure-modeling light (Color Plate 24-1). Although a typical theatrical light plot for the proscenium theatre has at least half of its equipment located front-of-house, dance plots often have three-quarters of their instruments backstage. Extra cabling may be required if a theatre does not have the necessary number of circuits backstage for an average dance plot.

Location of Instruments

Here are common mounting positions for dance lighting instruments (almost invariably ellipsoidal reflector spotlights):

Low Front For a low front position, lights can be mounted on a low balcony rail. Although light from this angle tends to wash out body form, a little may be desirable for the sake of visibility and/or color washing.

Medium Front Medium front-lights would be mounted on a second balcony rail or in a ceiling position. Again, this does little for the body and casts shadows of ballet costumes on dancers' legs. This angle corresponds with the 45-degree visibility light common to theatrical presentation and, if necessary, can be used as such.

High Front Roughly at a 60-degree angle, high front is much more useful for theatrical presentation than for dance. This dramatic angle casts serious costume shadows on the legs of a ballerina, but it can be used in other types of dance to emphasize mood.

Low Side For the low side position, lights are mounted very low on booms in the wings. Although an unnatural angle, it is flattering to dancers because it tends to lift the body. Low side-lighting instruments are called "shin kickers" or "shin busters" for obvious reasons. They are normally clear or colored with very light tints. Their light can be shuttered off the floor surface in order to eliminate visible scallops from the beams. Gobos placed in low side instruments enhance the sense of movement and add texture and mood to a scene. Instruments can be focused so that patterns are visible only on the dancers and not on the floor.

Medium Side For the medium side position, lights are mounted about 8 or 10 feet above the floor in the wings. This may be regarded as the basic dance lighting angle. It throws a wash across the stage with little significant shadowing. It may be desirable to mount an additional spotlight a few feet higher to carry across to the far side of the stage. A third instrument can be mounted a few feet lower to light the close side of the stage. In this case both long- and short-throw ellipsoidals are focused so that the center lines of their beams are parallel (see Figure 23-13 for details). Gobo patterns placed in medium side instruments shine on both the dancers and the floor.

High Side Light in the high side position comes from 15 to 20 feet high in the wings or from the ends of electric battens (such units are called **pipe ends**). If too high an angle is chosen, the light will tend to make the dancers appear squat. However, a 60-degree high side can be effective for a dramatic moment and is particularly useful in modern dance. Gobo patterns from high side instruments read strongly on the floor.

pipe ends Instruments clustered at the ends of light battens, providing high side-light.

Straight Back In the straight back position, light comes from above but also from behind the dancer. This is a very valuable position, for it highlights the body in space, separating it from the background. It does not cause one dancer to throw a shadow on the next one.

Diagonal Back Like the straight back position, light comes from above and behind the dancer, but from an angle to the side as well. Frequently this is more desirable than straight back because it illuminates a more visible surface area of the dancer's body.

Down-Light In the down-light position, lights are mounted directly overhead, an effect that tends to push the body down. This position is useful only for specialized moments.

Follow Spots Light from a follow spot can come from various locations in the auditorium or from some onstage position. Such use must be kept unobtrusive and should be operated by an individual capable of making it so. Of course, in musical comedy, dance, and some classical ballet, blatant use of follow spots is accepted as traditional.

Dancers' Centering Light Dancers maintain balance by finding their "center." The lighting designer can help them by placing a **dance centering light** or *spotting light* in the auditorium. This should be a small 7½- or 15-watt red lamp located at head height, dead center at the rear of the auditorium or on a balcony rail.

dance centering light A small red light placed at dancer head height at the rear of the auditorium or on a balcony rail; serves to help dancers locate front. Also called *spotting light.*

Booms

Low and medium side-lighting require floor stands or booms as hanging positions. A dance concert or ballet almost always calls for booms in each wing on both sides of the stage. This can total twelve booms for a large production. It is traditional to hang lighting instruments to the side of booms in the theatre, but for dance they should be mounted straight out from the boom pipes. In this way, the boom will take up as little wing space as possible, allowing more freedom for dancer entrances and exits (often leaps into the wings). Figure 23-13 illustrates a typical dance boom layout.

23-13

Dance Boom Layout

Instruments are hung onstage from the boom to take up as little wing space as possible. Instrument 1 lights far stage-left in the second zone, while instrument 2 lights mid-stage and 3 lights close. Instrument 4 is a low-angle "shin."

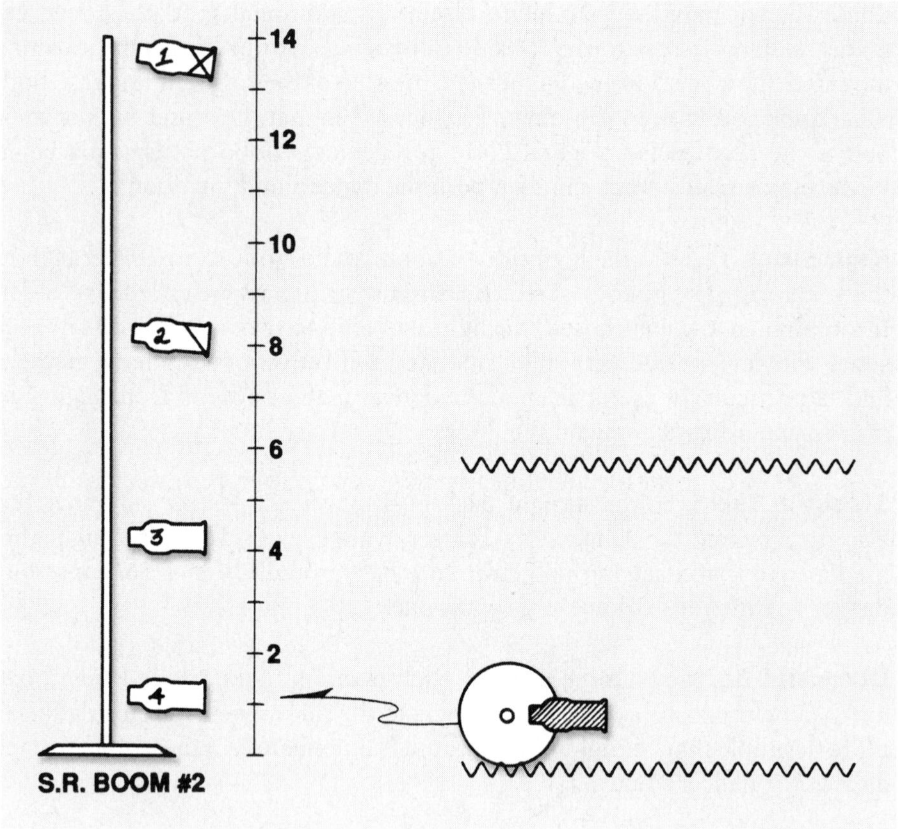

Booms must be clean and safe, each with a safety tie from the top of the pipe to the grid. Cable to booms is neatest if run up the boom and onto an electric pipe for circuiting. However, many times floor pockets must be used. If this is the case, run the cable straight offstage from the boom and then turn upstage or downstage to floor pocket locations. Cover the cable with carpeting and tape it securely to the floor.

Be aware that inexperienced dancers may try to use light booms as balance bars when warming up. Discourage this practice without being rude.

Color Considerations

For most classic ballet, strong front colors are not desirable, but a basic tint certainly is. Pale lavender is frequently used, but tradition may prescribe some other tint. Whatever color is selected becomes the neutral for the particular ballet. The other shades work in relation to it and, when blended together on the stage, approximate the neutral. Thus, if lavender is the neutral, a light rose next to it appears quite warm and light blue appears cool. The rose and blue mix together to create lavender.

Color Plate 24-2 is a photograph from the classical ballet *La Sylphide.* Principal front-light colors are lilac (R55) and pale amber gold (R09). The cool-looking back-light is no-color blue (R60).

Designers can achieve a valuable effect by using advancing and receding colors to add apparent depth to the stage. The use of slightly cooler tints on the upstage dancers makes them appear farther away than they would otherwise seem. Likewise, warmer shades on the downstage dancers bring them even farther forward. Care must be taken in using this technique, however. The tints must not be so far apart that the dancers visibly change color as they move through the zones.

As illustrated in Color Plate 24-3, modern dance requires color usage that is appropriately modern. Use of saturated colors, especially in side-light, is a common technique for expressing mood. No-color light or cool tints are often chosen to express the sometimes dramatic nature of the dance. Remote-control color changers mounted on the booms can provide needed variety for a performance comprising several dance pieces.

Cues

The rhythm of a theatrical production often dictates cue placement. This is even truer of dance. Movement nearly always corresponds to the music, and cues should do the same. The cues for a ballet should be called by the stage manager from the score. The lighting designer should become quite familiar with the music before beginning the design. Cues for modern dance or pieces without scores may need to be called from the action. This requires that the lighting designer and stage manager become quite familiar with the movement. Attending preproduction rehearsals is imperative. Using a rehearsal video tape may also help the designer review and write cues with the stage manager.

A Dance Plot

Figure 23-14 is a ½-inch over-stage light plot for a modern dance concert consisting of three separate pieces. Each of the three is quite modern, with the second piece, "Souvenir," being the most traditional (music from Tchaikovsky's *Souvenir de Florence*).

Physical Space For this performance, the Old Globe Theatre, which often plays in thrust configuration, was used in its proscenium form. Downstage and upstage edges of the dance floor are indicated on the plan. Note that the masking legs step in a bit as they go upstage. This technique accommodates the audience sightlines, which are fairly wide and typical of thrust theatres. The rake of the audience is steep, allowing a good view of the stage (and stage floor) from every seat.

Distribution This plot does not indicate front-of-house instruments. However, only twelve instruments were used from the auditorium. They included five 6-by-16 ellipsoidals colored in R54 used as a downstage visibility wash. The other seven instruments were specials for the various dances.

The over-stage hang was slightly limited by instrumentation previously hung for a dramatic production ("Blues in the Night"), which was to follow the dance concert. The lightweight instruments with no color or channel notation were hung for "Blues" and not used in the dance concert. Three sets of PAR-64 back-lights were designed, one for each dance piece. They were hung seven across the stage with their oval beams running up- and downstage. Three electrics were necessary to cover the depth of the stage. An upstage R54 front wash of 6 by 12s was located on the first electric. The various other over-stage instruments were designed as specials for each piece.

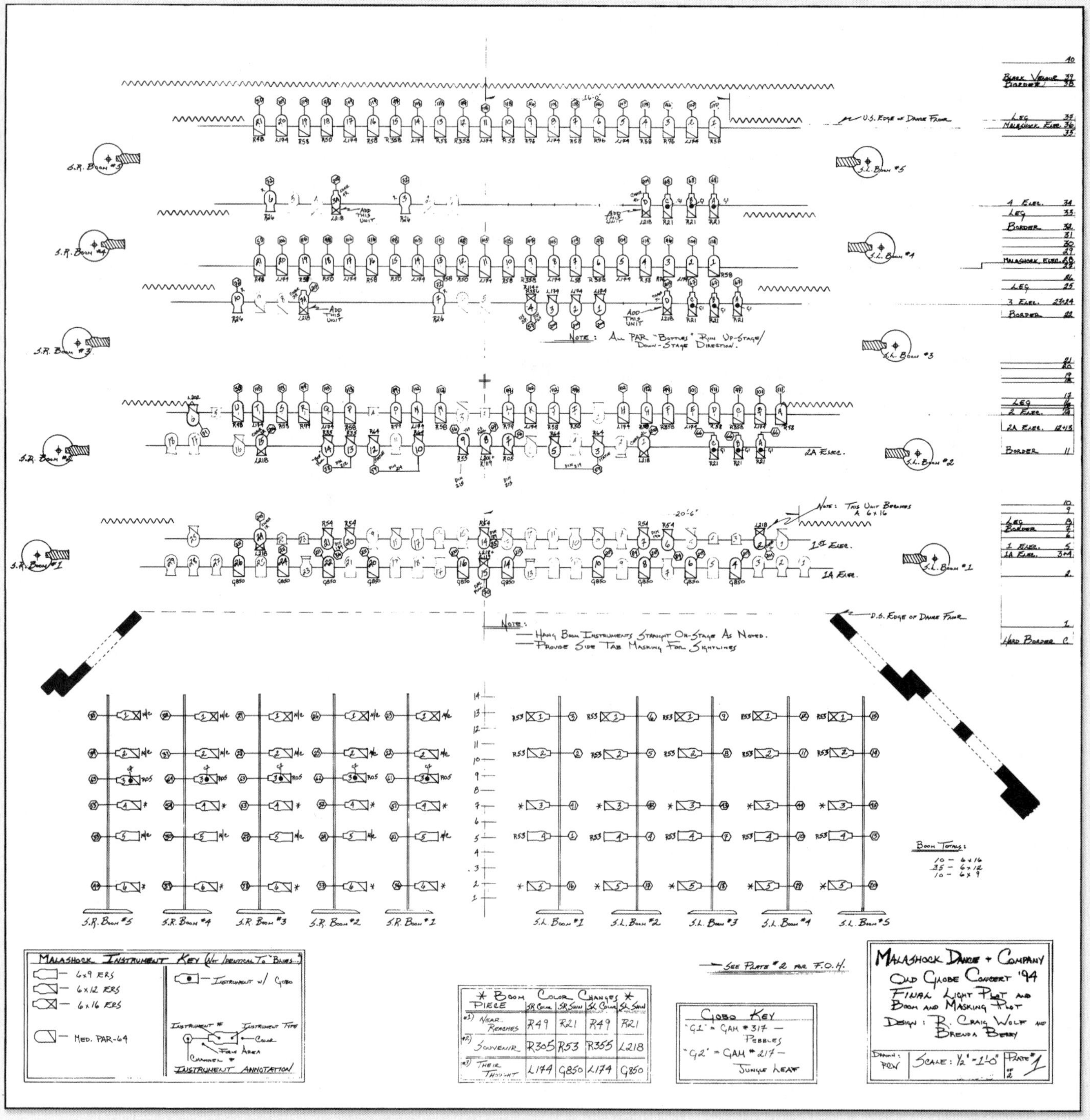

23-14

Modern Dance Plot

A ½-inch scale over-stage light plot for a modern dance concert consisting of three separate pieces. It was produced at the Old Globe Theatre and lit by Brenda Berry and R. Craig Wolf.

The booms held five instruments each on the stage-left side and six instruments stage-right. The additional stage-right instruments contained a leaf pattern, which provided a swirly breakup for "Souvenir." The top boom instrument (6 × 16) threw far across the stage and was focused a bit high to eliminate too much intensity buildup in the center of the stage. It received top and upstage shutter cuts off the black masking legs. The mid-boom instrument (6 × 12) was focused center stage with slight shutter cuts both up- and downstage. The close instrument (6 × 9) was focused to hit about 10 feet out from the wings and also received shutter cuts on up- and downstage edges. The 6-by-12 shins were tilted up just slightly and received top and side shutter cuts. Finally, the color-change instruments (6 × 12) were focused straight across the stage with minor shutter cuts.

Color One bank of back-lights was colored in L174, a medium steel blue. The second was R58, deep lavender. The third consisted of a mixture of fairly saturated colors in order to create a mottled look on the stage floor for "Souvenir."

A light tint of lavender (R53) was used in the stage-left side-light, while no-color was used stage-right. This technique offers a built-in warm and cool side, however slight. The color-change instruments generally took more saturated colors that blended with the light tints of the other side-lights. The "Boom Color Changes" key indicates the exact colors used for this performance.

An interesting color and pattern effect was created for "The Near Reaches" by the pipe-end gobo instruments on 2A, 3, and 4 electrics. Their golden amber rays were focused across the stage from a diagonal back direction. The saturated color effectively cut through the other stage lighting to create an appropriately abstract effect.

Control For this dance concert, 220 control channels were used, providing independent control over nearly all instruments. Note the channel layout for the booms, intended to make remembering individual zones and functions easier.

Dance Design

Dance, in all its forms, is an exciting design experience. The principles of theatrical lighting apply, but more freedom for creativity and innovation commonly exists. It is not unusual for a dance lighting designer to be involved in the very creation of a dance piece, an involvement rare in the theatre. Working with choreographers is a joy, for they compose visually. Dance lighting seldom pays very much money, but the experience in terms of the art of lighting is well worth it.

Clearly, different types of stages as well as productions affect in many practical ways how designers develop ideas. In the next and final chapter, we continue the discussion of designing for specific venues, starting with Broadway, and explore lighting design as a profession.

24

Lighting Design as a Profession

This chapter gives special attention to lighting for the commercial theatre as well as theatre-related professions such as themed entertainment, concerts, architecture, television and film, restaurants, museums, industrials, and displays. It also includes interviews with several of this country's finest lighting designers.

LIGHTING ON BROADWAY

New York's Broadway has always been, and still remains, the premier theatrical entertainment center of the United States. People come from all over the world to see Broadway productions. This extremely commercial theatre presents tough competition along with great rewards for achievement. Although many practices are identical to those of any commercial theatre, some are unique to the Broadway stage.

The Broadway Lighting Designer

No designers work exclusively on Broadway. Despite the potential for high pay, there is not enough work to keep more than a handful of designers busy even on a part-time basis. New York–based lighting designers spend much of their time traveling about the country, working at regional theatres and other commercial venues. Many of these individuals spent years working as assistants to more established Broadway designers before they were rewarded their first Broadway show. Some of them designed off- and off-off-Broadway for many years, learning the ropes and meeting directors and producers.

A producer hires the artistic staff for a production, but the director is normally chosen first and often consulted. It is frequently the director (or occasionally the scenic designer) who recommends an individual lighting designer for the show. Accordingly, the experience of having worked with many people on a variety of productions is essential to being hired for a Broadway show.

Designers at Work

Donald Holder

Color Plate 24-4

Donald Holder is a theatrical lighting designer with a blossoming career. He maintains a studio in New York along with several other designers and works in regional theatre, off-Broadway, and on Broadway. His wide range of credits include *The Lion King,* the Gloria Estefan Millennium 2000 Tour, *Thoroughly Modern Millie, King Hedley II and Hughie* (directed by Al Pacino) on Broadway, *The Education of Randy Newman* at South Coast Rep., the Ringling Bros. and Barnum and Bailey Circus, *Romeo and Juliet* (directed by Emily Mann at the McCarter Theatre), and Animagique, a new Disneyland attraction in Paris. He has designed at many of America's regional theatres, does architectural and residential design, and enjoys working on new scripts. He won a Tony Award for *The Lion King.*

Don grew up on Long Island, where his parents exposed him to the New York theatre as a young boy. He always had a fascination for lighting and loved the theatre. However, his more practical side determined that he would attend college at the University of Maine and major in forestry. Of his college experience, Don says, "Of course I immediately went and worked in the theatre 24 hours a day. . . . The faculty lighting/set designer there took me under his wing. . . . I learned from him that you could make a living and have a good, rich, happy life doing what you want to do—following your dream."

After graduation, Don worked several jobs while doing theatre. He eventually applied to Yale and was admitted into Jennifer Tipton's advanced lighting classes: "She gave me my first chance to light a production. Even [after] graduating, I was still worried about whether I could make a living in the profession. I remember I had the opportunity to take a job at New York City Opera or assist Jennifer off and on. It was a big decision for me. I turned down the job at the Opera and decided that I was going to be poor and assist. . . . That was a turning point for me—that I was finally willing to take the big step and go out and give it a shot. I think ultimately everybody has to make that commitment."

From then on, things began to fall into place. Don first worked with Julie Taymor on a production of *Titus Andronicus* for Theatre for a New Audience. It was a last-minute design and a difficult process, but he reports, "I really understood her style and her way of working because it was very much like mine in a way . . . and I respected her unrelenting push for perfection and her inability to accept the word 'no' . . . we became really good collaborators." About the collaboration on *Lion King,* Don says, "I got involved before they even officially hired a set designer—Julie had some basic ideas about the piece that I think informed all the other decisions. . . . When she pitched the piece (to Disney) she decided that she was going to tackle the hardest moments of the film—how to pull those moments off in the theatre—like the wildebeest stampede—and how to articulate Pride Rock. Those really informed the overall stylistic approach. . . . She had the courage and convictions to say, 'We want to keep the essence of what the story is and the characters, but we want to tell it in a completely different way and give the piece a completely new identity and a new life.'"

In terms of lighting, Don says, "She doesn't say, 'This is what I want the lighting to be here and here and here'—you have to, as the designer, figure out what the overall shape of the piece will be and then be prepared for her reaction in the theatre—you have to make choices and be prepared to shape those and change them and be flexible because she tends to respond to what she sees."

Elaborating on the issue of collaboration, Don says, "Every director is a little different. . . . It's important that you come into the process with your own point of view about the piece—I think you need to know the script well enough that you have your own ideas about what the piece should or could be—and hopefully your ideas can inform the director's vision." In collaborating with scenic designers, Don notes, "Some scenic designers seek out your input early on and others don't at all. . . . If you don't protect the interest of the lighting in the overall approach, you can run into big difficulties. I think that the earlier on you get involved, the better it is."

(continued) ▶

Don feels that he uses color in a spare, simple way: "I think as you get older, you get more comfortable with color but it's the most daunting. . . . The more I kind of absorb the way light works in the world, a lot of questions get answered for me about how to use color." In terms of how he lays out a show, Don says, "What I first do . . . is figure out how I am going to carve out the space—in other words, create the light that separates the actor from the background—that gives a three-dimensional, sculptural context—create this living light in which the actors can exist. And that, to me, typically starts with side-light of some kind." Using *Lion King* as an example, Don says, "*Lion King* is essentially a dance space—an open luminous box with luminescent cyc and legs that were intended to give the sense of an unending vista. . . . Dance is so integral to that space that it is essentially a dance light plot . . . it's so much about sunlight and about natural light. The systems of light, side-light in particular, are very much based on parallel construction—all the high side-light is very much in one angle."

In discussing light for a production style grounded in realism, Don says, "The light in nature, the rays of sunlight, are parallel. . . . To me, theatre is basically about humanity—it reflects the human condition—light is a subliminal, subconscious part of our world. . . . You need to put the play or the world in a context that (audiences) understand. . . . In order to understand how to interpret a moment through light, you have to understand how light functions in the world and you have to start with that reference."

Don offers the following wisdom to a person wanting a career in lighting: "The first thing I should say in terms of advice [is that] I think all this technology that we are being exposed to is [only] a means to an end—I think we can't forget that what's important is serving the piece, understanding the material, embracing the material, and being part of the overall vision. . . . All the technology out there is part of an ever-expanding palette, but you should not focus on that—that stuff you can always learn. My point is that, as a growing designer, you should learn about how to read a play—learn how you fit into the rest of the world—read a newspaper every day—go to museums—become a fully-rounded, fully-informed member of society—understand history, understand art, understand literature. That's infinitely more important than learning all the attributes of a moving light. [Young designers] should be getting a liberal arts education." Don believes that there is no single path to follow when breaking into the business: "The important thing is to believe in yourself, work hard, be passionate about what you do, and never settle for second best—always do your best and realize that it's a long, hard road. . . . It has to be the most important thing for you in your life—if it isn't, then maybe you should consider what else would make you happy."

United Scenic Artists Union (USA) The American union representing professional scenic artists; costume, lighting, scenic, and sound designers; art directors; and computer artists.

URL http://www.usa829.org

Before being eligible to light a show on Broadway or at many of the larger commercial theatres across the country, the designer must become a member of the **United Scenic Artists Union (USA)**, IATSE Local USA-829. This union represents professional scenic artists (painters); costume, lighting, scenic, and sound designers; computer artists; art directors; and art department coordinators. It consists of one local union (829) divided roughly into three regions: Eastern, Central, and Western.

Applicants must undergo a portfolio review (in all regions) and an interview with members of the regional examination committee in New York and Chicago. Design exams are held at least four times per year in New York, Chicago, and Los Angeles. Specific requirements vary from region to region but usually include a list of items the judges will be looking for at the portfolio review. In New York, lighting-design applicants also complete a forty-five-minute paper exercise, which replaces the former eight-hour practical exam in testing the basic skills and concepts required of a lighting designer. A nonrefundable application and examination fee of $150 must be paid in order to attempt the exam. If it is passed, the designer pays an initiation fee (currently $1,500) and becomes a USA-829 member. Dues and assessments are approximately $300 per year.

Membership in the union is often the first major hurdle faced by a young designer looking to work professionally. The interview and portfolio-review process is designed to eliminate individuals whom the committee judges to be underqualified for membership in terms of the everyday skills and techniques required of professionals working in the commercial entertainment industry.

Regional business offices are located at the following addresses:

16 West 61st Street, 11th Floor, New York, NY 10023; (212) 581-0030

203 North Wabash, Suite 1210, Chicago, IL 60601; (312) 857-0829

5225 Wilshire Blvd., Suite 506, Los Angeles, CA 90036; (323) 965-0957

Write your regional business agent for exam dates and information.

When working under a United Scenic Artists contract, a designer must receive a minimum fee. Established designers may ask for and often get a great deal more than this minimum. For example, a well-known designer may receive, in addition to a straight fee, a royalty based on a percentage of the gross receipts.

Equipment in the Broadway Theatre

Uniquely, the commercial theatres commonly referred to as "Broadway houses" have no lighting equipment of their own. There may be a dimmer for the house lights and wiring in conduit from backstage to front-of-house positions. A high-amperage company switch providing power for dimmers will be found close to the stage area. Everything else must be rented for the show: instruments and their accessories, all control equipment and cable, dimmers and plugging boxes, cable sufficient to connect all instruments to the dimmers, booms for offstage instruments, work lights, and all special rigging supplies.

Equipment Rental and Shop Orders Because all expenses related to the production must be approved by the producer or business manager, the lighting designer must work within the figures that either has in mind. The normal rental contract calls for a payment of 10 percent of the value of the equipment for the first three weeks of the rental (e.g., an ellipsoidal reflector spotlight that costs $400 rents for $40 for the first three weeks). A lower percentage is charged for the next three weeks, and rental is further reduced for the remainder of the run of the production. Most producers ask for competitive bids from the few companies that rent lighting equipment for the stage. Others have a favorite rental house and always work with this same company. A producer may depend on the lighting designer to recommend a firm. The major rental and supply houses in the New York area are Fourth Phase (Bash/Production Arts) and West Sun.

shop order A contract for the rental of lighting equipment and accessories that lists, in detail, all the equipment to be rented for a production; used for bidding purposes and ordering.

FINAL ELECTRICAL EQUIPMENT LIST
"THE WHO'S TOMMY - GOIN' MOBILE"

Manager:	George MacPherson The Pinball Touring Company ATP / Dodger 1501 Broadway Suite 2015 New York, NY 10036 (212) 391-8160 (212) 944-7616 FAX
Designer:	Chris Parry (619) 942-2697 (619) 942-2697 FAX
Associate:	David Grill (201) 825-0391 (201) 825-2643 FAX
Production Electrician:	Mark Davidson (201) 440-9224 Shop
Shop:	Steve Terry Wayne Lawrence Production Arts Lighting 35 Oxford Drive Moonachie, NJ 07074 (201) 440-9224 (201) 440-2612 FAX

GOIN' MOBILE
FINAL - Electrical Equipment List

EQUIPMENT TOTALS

15	4½x6½ 1k
6	4½x6½ Dataflash w/DMX 512 Prom
18	6x9 1k
35	6x12 1k
44	6x16 1k
17	Source 4 426 575w
45	Source 4 419 575w
1	Source 4 410 575w
2	30°-60° Baby Zoom 750w
6	PAR 16 EZK 150w
5	PAR 16 EYC 75w Short Nose
6	PAR 16 EYF 75w w/Transformer
56	PAR 46 NSP 200w
26	PAR 46 NSP 200w Custom Housing to fit into Deck
2	PAR 64 MFL 1k
38	PAR 64 NSP 1k
8	PAR 64 NSP 1k Short Nose
22	6" Fresnel 1k
26	7" Arri Fresnel 2k
12	2Lt Broad Cyc 1500w w/Hangers
10	2 Lt Ianiro Orion 1k
5	6' 9Lt PAR 56 12v 240w VNSP Motorized Lite Curtains
3	Wildfire 400w Flood UV
7	Mini 10 500w
6	Stik Up 100w
2	Pani HMV 1202 1200w Followspot
16	Vari*Lite VL-2C
5	Vari*Lite VL-4 w/Tophats
4	Vari*Lite VL-5 w/Stipple Lens
48	Data Flash w/DMX 512 Prom, Reflector, & Yoke
3	Super Nova Strobe
3	F100 Fogger w/Remote Trigger
1	Rosco Pencil Fogger
2	Fogmaster 3000
1	Theatre Magic Haze Master w/25' Output Hoses
4	Bowens Fan - Variable Speed w/Yokes
8	Color Ram w/Source 4 Plate
18	Color Ram w/PAR 64 Plate
26	Color Ram w/7" Arri Fresnel Plate
1	Wybron Scroller w/Source 4 410 Plate
12	Wybron Scroller w/PAR 64 Plate
1	Howard Eaton 4 RPM Flicker Wheels w/Diffusion Glass
2	12" Mirror Ball w/Variable Speed Motor
6	Twin Spin
2	Blue Police Beacons

Page 2

GOIN' MOBILE
FINAL - Electrical Equipment List

7	Source 4 Iris'
16	6" Tophat
22	Source 4 Tophat
10	6" Halfhat
8	10" Tophat
8	10" Barndoor
400	Safety Cables
20	Template Holders
1	Custom Addressable DMX Triggered Contact Closure w/Amiga Interface Cables and Connectors
1	Set Midi Cables (Amiga to Artisan)
4	LMI L86 96x2.4k DMX 512 Dimmer Rack
3	Opto Splitter
1	DAC
3	DMX - Data Flash Protocall Converter
8	12 Unit Color Ram Control Box
1	50 Channel Radio Control Transmitter
2	12 Channel Radio Control Receiver
6	10 amp 12v Radio Control Dimmer
6	Radio Control Battery
6	Radio Control Battery Charger
2	Obsession 600
2	Obsession LD Monitors
1	Obsession RFU
1	Obsession Printer (As fast as possible)
1	UPS
3	A-B Switch Boxes (Cue / Work Lights)
4	5' Unistrut Bar
3	7' Unistrut Bar
18	10' Unistrut Bar
6	Unistrut Cart
2	36' Genie Personal Lift
14	Custom Quick Mount VL-2C Brackets
1	Custom Quick Mount VL-4 Brackets
4	Custom Quick Mount VL-5 Brackets
3	Vari*Lite Bumpers

Page 3

GOIN' MOBILE
FINAL - Electrical Equipment List

IMPORTANT NOTES

- All units to be axial with quartz lamp, clamp, template slot and black color frame unless otherwise stated;
- All units to have clear lenses - NO green or tinted lenses accepted;
- All PAR Cans must have interior protective screening;
- Any substitutions or revisions must be fully disclosed at the time of the bid, these substitutions or revisions are not accepted without permission of the Designer;
- Bidder assumes responsibility for any additional materials that are required on site due to rental shop oversight or error;
- Allow for color scroller color and color scroller loading labor;
- Multi, cable, jumper, control cable, video cable specifics by Electrician;
- Allow for Spare Units, Lamps, Dimmer Cards, Control Cards, Fuses, Control Cables, Scrollers, etc.

24-1

***Tommy* Shop Order**

The shop order for the tour of *The Who's Tommy,* designed by Chris Parry.

COURTESY CHRIS PARRY

Even if the producer does not require competitive bids, the rental house must provide a cost estimate based on the equipment list called the shop order. This paperwork is generated by one of the various software programs as soon as the light plot is completed. It lists every piece of rental equipment in specific detail. It also specifies all necessary "perishables" (materials that will be used up and, therefore, must be purchased by the production), such as tape and tie-line.

After a bid is approved, the shop requires at least a week to gather and prepare the equipment necessary for a Broadway show. For a large show with specialized equipment such as effects projectors or unique light sources, much more lead time is needed. For this reason, the Broadway lighting designer must complete the plot several weeks earlier than a designer working primarily with in-house equipment must do.

Figure 24-1 shows part of the equipment list for the national tour of the Broadway production of *The Who's Tommy.* The production opened at the La Jolla Playhouse, and the lighting was redesigned for Broadway and again for touring. Note that the order includes everything needed, from lighting instruments to radio-control batteries.

Hiring Electricians

Even more significant than equipment rental costs are the wages paid to the electricians who set up and run the show. In New York and many commercial theatres elsewhere, these people must be members of the **International Alliance of Theatrical Stage Employees Union** (IATSE), commonly called the **IA.** Member electricians receive a substantial hourly wage, so prudent use of their time is imperative. The designer must understand and adhere to stringent regulations concerning working hours and conditions, which may vary from one local union to another.

International Alliance of Theatrical Stage Employees Union (IA) The union representing stage hands and electricians.

URL http://www.iatse.lm.com

Every large city across the country has its own IA local. The **union business agent** is the union's representative to the public. This individual negotiates labor needs with a producer and subsequently fills the crew call. Often one member of the crew is designated "union representative." This person is responsible for seeing that the rules and regulations of the union are followed and must report any violations to the business agent.

union business agent A union's representative to the public; negotiates contracts and fills labor needs.

The electrician who works most closely with the designer is the **production electrician.** Hired by the show's producer, this person, who may or may not be a union member, works with the rental house and acts as a liaison between the producers and the IA union. Obviously, the choice of who will serve as production electrician matters a great deal to the lighting designer.

production electrician The electrician in charge and who works most closely with the designer.

The Production Period

The biggest difference between designing for Broadway and elsewhere is *time.* Exciting, dramatic lighting such as that by Donald Holder for *The Green Bird* (Color Plate 24-4) requires extensive preparation and a lot of work—yet time available for the design period and production in the Broadway theatre is so compressed that only the best designers can survive. The familiar adage that "time is money" has never been more appropriate than when a designer is in the theatre with an IA crew. This is where superb preparation and an excellent production electrician really pay off.

It should be expected that focus conditions will not be ideal. At best, a sound check will be going on simultaneously. At worst, carpenters will still be rigging scenery under a blaze of work light. The job must be done quickly in order to avoid overtime wages for the electricians on the work call. It must also be done absolutely correctly. A subsequent labor call in order to adjust focus means a ladder crew of four people, each hired for the union minimum of four hours.

According to union regulations, under no circumstances whatsoever may the lighting designer or an assistant handle any lighting equipment. One of the union electricians must be requested to do so. This applies even to such innocent actions as handing a wrench to its owner or steadying a ladder on which an electrician is working.

Moving the Show

The Broadway designer, more than any other, must know how to design a production for more than one space. Perhaps, like *The Who's Tommy,* the production premieres at one of the nation's regional theatres with the intent of then going to Broadway. Nearly all successful Broadway shows tour at some point after they have opened in New York. The lighting designer thus needs to be proficient at designing for more than a single theatre.

national tour A tour that plays for a long run in a single city.

bus-and-truck tour A tour that plays short runs in numerous cities.

There are two types of Broadway tours. One is called a **national tour,** which plays for many weeks in a single large city. The second, the **bus-and-truck tour,** jumps from city to city, often playing a week but sometimes playing only one-night stands in each location.

National Tours A national tour settles into a major city. The actors get apartments, the IA crew is contracted for a long run, and the load-in period is at least several days. A light plot is usually designed for the specific theatre being used. The lighting designer normally attends technical and dress rehearsals, setting the look of the production before its run begins.

Figure 24-2 shows the light plot for the national tour of *The Who's Tommy.* It calls for seven over-stage electric pipes, extensive side-light, and very little front-of-house lighting. Trims are high, at approximately 30 feet, creating a square rather than rectangular stage

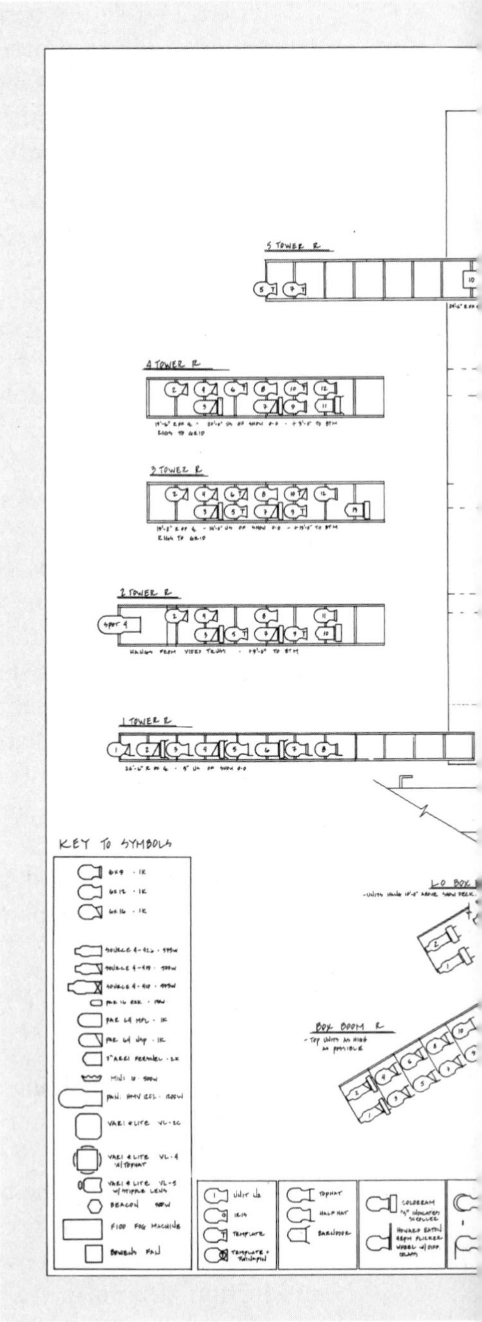

24-2

***Tommy* Light Plot**

The plot for the national tour of *The Who's Tommy,* designed by Chris Parry.

picture, as can be seen in Color Plate 24-5. Vari*Lites are used over stage, and color scrollers are used both over stage and in side-light positions.

The plot notes refer to black *Zetex*, a heat-resistant material that is hung between lighting instruments and masking borders to keep the latter from burning. In this case, the first electric pipe is close enough to the upstage masking border to require the use of Zetex.

Bus-and-Truck Tours The light plot for a bus-and-truck tour must be designed to accommodate different types and sizes of theatres. Such a production inevitably carries less equipment than the Broadway plot specified. In response to time constraints, designers have developed various techniques

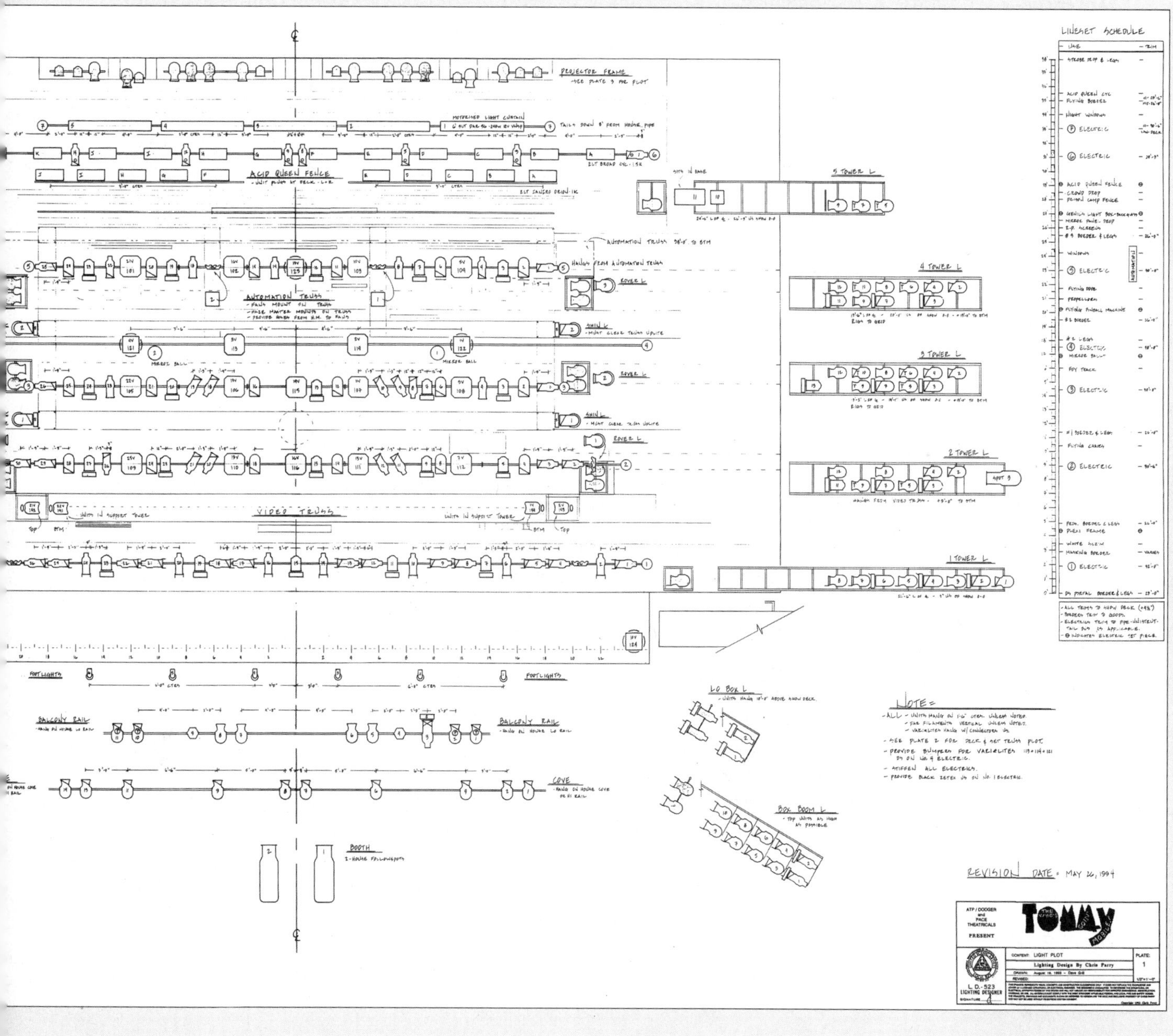

COURTESY CHRIS PARRY

to make setting up and focusing as easy as possible. The number of instruments might be reduced and their type simplified. Lengths of pipe or track with instruments already attached might be carried on the truck. Focus charts such as the one for the Broadway production of *Teddy & Alice* (Figure 24-3), as well as other time-saving devices, have been invented by designers and electricians who frequent the road.

Focus Charts A *focus chart* is a piece of lighting paperwork intended to record exact focus information for each lighting instrument in use by the touring production. It indicates exact focus location, usually using a grid method of notation. It also specifies shutter cuts and beam edge focus. Figure 24-3c is a sample page from the focus chart for the tour of *The Who's Tommy.*

road electrician An electrician for a bus-and-truck tour.

The Road Electrician If the designer is fortunate, an experienced head electrician will be assigned to the bus-and-truck production. This **road electrician** travels with the production and, along with the production stage manager, is responsible for making sure that the lighting is faithfully reproduced. Early consultation between the designer and the road electrician concerning equipment and methods of working can greatly enhance a production's success.

The designer must periodically drop in and check on a production during its run. If the lighting has slipped a bit from what was originally set, adjustments must be made.

DESIGNING FOR REGIONAL THEATRE

The middle years of the twentieth century will be remembered for the rebirth throughout the country of professional theatre, too long confined to New York and a few other large centers. Now it is a rare city that does not have at least one repertory or stock theatre, run by professional producers and directors and employing professional actors and designers.

Working in Regional Theatre

LORT houses Professional regional theatres; *LORT* stands for *League of Regional Theatres.*

Theatre Communications Group (TCG) A national service organization dedicated to assisting the not-for-profit theatre; publishers of *American Theatre* magazine and *Art*SEARCH.

URL http://www.tcg.org

Nearly all regional theatres (called **LORT houses,** after the type of union contract issued to the actors) run apprentice programs, which seldom pay much but offer exceptional experience and valuable professional contacts. **Theatre Communications Group** (**TCG**) publishes a complete list of theatres and programs; for a copy, write to TCG at 355 Lexington Avenue, New York, NY 10017-0217.

An enormous amount of exciting production is going on in regional theatre, using both national and local designers (Figure 24-4). More and more college students and graduates are working in these theatres on a full- or part-time basis. Opportunities abound for learning and making valuable contacts. The chances of assisting a designer or working on the staff are good for the talented and devoted theatre student. The first thing to do is send a résumé to either the production manager or artistic director of the theatre. Then telephone and request an interview—it is that simple. Do not be discouraged if you are turned down and seemingly ignored. These individuals are extremely busy, but you will get results if you are persistent. The following section provides an overview of lighting practices in this segment of the commercial theatre.

FOCUS CHART FOR: TEDDY AND ALICE

KEY TO ABBREVIATIONS

O.O.H. = Out of House

O.O.P. = Off of Proscenium

Off Prosc. = "

H.H. = Head High (To Fingers with Hand Held Above Head)

S.E. = Stage Edge

A.A. = As Above (Same cuts as previous lamp)

∆ = Angle Shutter

L = Stage Left

R = Stage Right

@ = At

F or FLD = Flood Focus for Fresnels

SP = Spot Focus for Fresnels

¼ SP = Lamp is ¼ way from Full Spot in a Fresnel

H = Hard Edge or Sharp in terms of focus of Lekos

S = Soft Edge or "Fuzzy" " " " " "

M = Medium Edge

℄ = Center Line

O.F = OFF FOOTS

a

FOCUS CHART FOR: TEDDY & ALICE

POSITION: UPPER BOX BOOM RIGHT.

CH / UN	PLUGGED W/	FOCUS		F	TYPE	COLOR
11 / 1	0 -2- -U.B.L. 7-8	D.L. SL OFF PORTAL SR —	• +4 @ 12L US H.H. DS O.F	S	6"x16" 1K LEKO	02
11 / 2	0 -1- U.B.L 7-8	D.L SL ∆.A. SR	• +4 @ 12L US H.H. DS O.F	S	"	35∆
12 / 3	0 -4- U.B.L. 3-4	D.L O/C SL OFF. PORTAL SR —	• +4 @ 4L US H.H. DS O.F.	S	"	02
12 / 4	0 -3- U.B.L 3-4	D.L O/C SL ∆.∆. SR	• +4 @ 4L US H.H. DS O.F.	S	"	35A
13 / 5	-6- U.B.L 5-6	D.R O/C SL OFF COLUMN. SR —	• +4 @ 4R US H.H DS O.F	S	"	02
13 / 6	0 -5- U.B.L 5-6	D.R O/C SL ∆.∆. SR —	• +4 @ 4R US H.H. DS O.F	S	"	35A
14 / 7	0 -8- U.B.L 1-2	D.R. SL — SR O.O.P.	• +4 @ 12R US H.H. DS O.F.	S	"	02
14 / 8	0 -7- U.B.L 1-2	D.R. SL — SR O.O.P.	• +4 @ 12R US H.H. DS O.F.	S	"	35A
78 / 9	10-11-12	(T) HOUSE FRONT SL O.O.P. SR —	• LEFT US OFF HEADER DS OFF FOOT	M S	" T&S	64A #210 BRANCHES
78 / 10	9-11-12	(T) HOUSE FRONT SL — SR —	• SL OF ℄ US CLIPS HEADER DS O.F.	M S	" T&S	"
7 / 11	9-10-12	(T) HOUSE FRONT SL O.O.P SR	• LEFT US OFF HEADER DS O.F	M S	" T&S	02 #294 LEAVES
79 / 12	9-10-11	(T) HOUSE FRONT SL — SR —	• SL OF ℄ US CLIPS HEADER SLIGHTLY DS O.F.	M S	" T&S	"

POSITION & NO. UPPER BOX BOOM RIGHT
PAGE NO. 1 OF 42

b

```
==================                 ============
TOMMY - PINBALL "A"                FOCUS CHARTS                        Page   1
==================                 ============
Designer: Chris Parry                                  Producer: ATP / Dodger / Pace
Associate: David Grill                            Head Electrician: Steve Cooksey
PINBALL - FINAL CUT VERSION
===============================================================================
Note:  Asterisks indicate Replug Channels
===============================================================================
====
COVE
====
Unit  Purpose                 Type              Watts   Color          Dim    Chn
===============================================================================
  1   Door Frts               6x16               1kw    L201            79   (314 )
                    @
   ----------     ----------
   US                       SR                 Sf . + . Hd
   DS                       SL                 Sp . + . Fl
   TP                       BT                 Axis:
-------------------------------------------------------------------------------
  2   Door Frts               6x16               1kw    L201            79   (314 )
                    @
   ----------     ----------
   US                       SR                 Sf . + . Hd
   DS                       SL                 Sp . + . Fl
   TP                       BT                 Axis:
-------------------------------------------------------------------------------
  4   Frts CL                 6x16               1kw    L203+R119       81   (  6 )
                    @
   ----------     ----------
   US                       SR                 Sf . + . Hd
   DS                       SL                 Sp . + . Fl
   TP                       BT                 Axis:
-------------------------------------------------------------------------------
  6   Frts CLC                6x16               1kw    L203+R119       83   (  7 )
                    @
   ----------     ----------
   US                       SR                 Sf . + . Hd
   DS                       SL                 Sp . + . Fl
   TP                       BT                 Axis:
-------------------------------------------------------------------------------
  7   Conductor               6x16               1kw    N/C             84   (  3 )
                    @
   ----------     ----------
   US                       SR                 Sf . + . Hd
   DS                       SL                 Sp . + . Fl
   TP                       BT                 Axis:
-------------------------------------------------------------------------------
(continued on next page)
```

c

24-3

Focus Charts

- **a** Key to the focus chart for *Teddy & Alice*, designed by Tharon Musser.
- **b** Focus chart for *Teddy & Alice*.
- **c** Focus chart for *Tommy*. It was generated with a Lightwright program.

PHOTO COURTESY CHRIS PARRY

24-4

Regional Theatre Production

The Gambler at the Milwaukee Repertory Theatre. Lighting, Chris Parry.

Regional Theatre Production

Many of the professional practices that apply to lighting design on Broadway are also standard for the country's regional theatres. However, accepted practice among the regional theatres also varies a great deal. Production schemes, ranging from repertory to stock, strongly influence how a lighting designer approaches his or her work. Local IA union rules and regulations differ from city to city. Each theatre has its own in-house equipment, which may be radically different from one to the next. Technical production practices and staffing are unique to each situation.

business manager Person in charge of budgeting and all other financial matters, often including fund-raising.

artistic director Person responsible for play selection, hiring of artistic staff, and sometimes fund-raising.

production manager Person in charge of the day-to-day operation of the theatre and overseeing all production matters; often hires staff and works closely with the artistic director and business manager.

electrics department head Person in charge of all electrics and sometimes sound operations of the theatre; may be an IA union position. Also called *house electrician.*

Regional Theatre Staff Most regional theatres are nonprofit organizations run by a board of directors. This is a group of community leaders who have an interest in the arts but may know little or nothing about the actual operation of a theatre. The theatre's **business manager** and **artistic director** are hired by, and directly responsible to, this board of directors. Each theatre has a permanent staff, the makeup of which depends on the unique needs of the individual theatre. There will most likely be a **production manager** and department heads, including an **electrics department head** or *house electrician.* This person's duties include maintenance of house equipment and working with each of the production's lighting designers. In addition, this individual has a strong voice in determining load-in and running crew size as well as local interpretation of union rules and regulations.

CP24-1

Dance Lighting

This scene from the Richmond Ballet Company's *Gloria* illustrates the effective use of side-light as a source. Artistic director, L. Stoner Winslett; lighting, R. Craig Wolf.

CP24-2

Classical Dance

The Richmond Ballet Company's *La Sylphide.* Staging, Frederic Franklin; lighting, R. Craig Wolf.

PHOTO BY SCOTT SUTHERLAND

CP24-3

Modern Dance

The Waters of Babylon. Choreography, Kimberly Jones; costumes, Ronald Blakely; lighting, Stephen Jones.

a

a PHOTO BY LIZ LAUREN

b

b PHOTO BY JOAN MARCUS

CP24-4

Broadway Lighting by Donald Holder

a The Chicago Shakespeare Theatre's production of *King Lear.* Director, Barbara Gaines; scenery, Scott Bradley; costumes, Miachael Krass.

b *The Green Bird* by Carlo Gozzi. Translation by Albert Bermel and Ted Emery. Produced by Ostar Enterprises, Inc. with Theatre for a New Audience at the Cort Theatre, New York City. Director, Julie Taymor; scenery, Christine Jones; costumes, Constance Hofman.

PHOTO BY MARCUS BRYAN-BROWN

CP24-5

Broadway Production

The "Acid Queen" scene from *The Who's Tommy.* Director, Des McAnuff; scenery, John Arnone; costumes, David C. Woolard; lighting, Chris Parry; projections, Wendall Harrington.

a

b

a & b PHOTOS COURTESY CHRIS PARRY

CP24-6

Regional-Theatre Lighting by Chris Parry

a *The Trojan Women* at the Oregon Shakespeare Festival. Scenic design, Richard Hoover.

b *Seagull* at the Old Globe Theatre.

a

b

a & b PHOTOS COURTESY CINDY LIMAURO

CP24-7

Opera Lighting by Cindy Limauro

Columbus Light Opera's production of *The Student Prince* by Sigmund Romberg. Director, Roger L. Stephens; scenery, Gary Eckert; costumes, John Lehmeyer.

a Exterior of the inn, evening.

b The grand ballroom, evening—opening moment behind scrim.

a

b

CP24-8

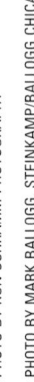

Architectural Lighting by Robert Shook

a Historic Water Tower, Chicago, Illinois.

b Alexander Calder's *Flamingo,* Federal Plaza, Chicago, Illinois.

a PHOTO BY RON SCHRAMM PHOTOGRAPHY
b PHOTO BY MARK BALLOGG, STEINKAMP/BALLOGG CHICAGO

a & b PHOTOS COURTESY DENNIS SIZE

a

b

CP24-9

Television Lighting by Dennis Size

a An MSNBC News *Special Town Meeting LIVE* from the 16th Street Baptist Church in Birmingham, Alabama.

b Diane Sawyer in the atrium windows of *Good Morning America* at Disney's Times Square Studios in New York City.

PHOTO COURTESY ANN ARCHBOLD

CP24-10

Industrial-Show Lighting by Ann Archbold

The Cadillac Exhibit at the North American International Auto Show, Cobo Hall, Detroit, Michigan.

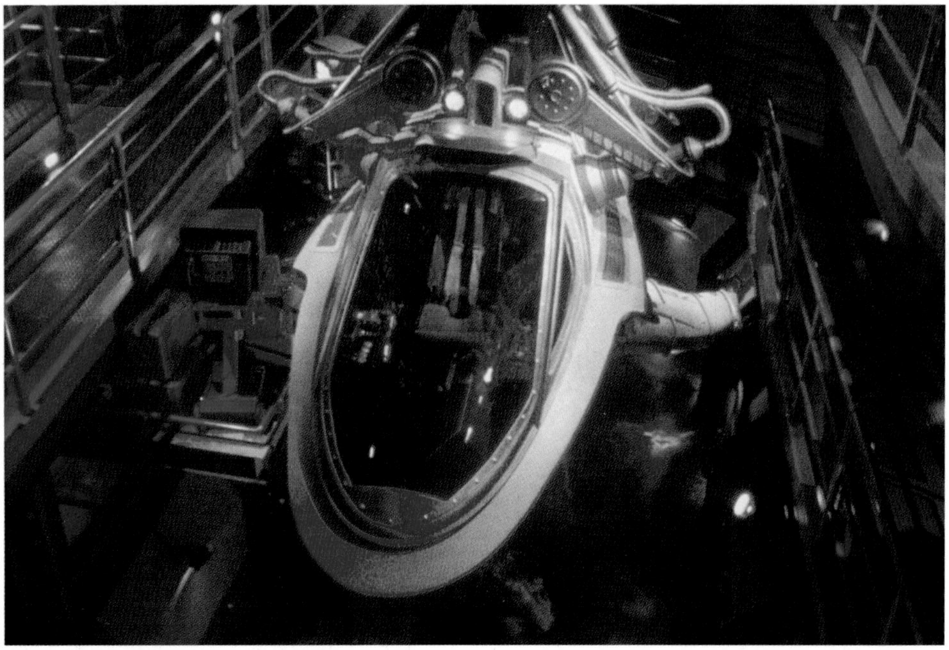

PHOTO COURTESY TOM RUZIKA

CP24-11

Themed-Entertainment Lighting by Tom Ruzika

The "Moon Pool Sub" in the SEAFARI motion-based simulator entry queue, Porto Europa Entertainment District, Wakayama Marina City, Japan.

Designers at Work

Chris Parry

Color Plate 24-6

Chris Parry is a much sought-after international lighting designer who works extensively in America's regional theatres. He grew up and was trained in England, spending thirteen years (1976–1989) in various staff capacities with the Royal Shakespeare Company. He currently heads his lighting company, Axiom Lighting, in Los Angeles (www.axiomlight.com) and teaches at the University of California, San Diego. Chris has designed for many of this country's regional theatres and has received numerous awards, including a Tony for *The Who's Tommy.*

Chris was not always interested in theatre. When he was growing up, British schools were using a system called streaming that determined at an early age whether a student showed an aptitude for science- or arts-based learning. Chris relates, "I couldn't paint or draw to save my life, so they decided that I had better be on a science track . . . so I took that. Then, about six months later, I found myself in a physics class and we were hanging the lights for the school play—lights use electricity, electricity is physics—so the whole thing kind of tied together! That was how I got hooked on theatre—in physics class—that was my introduction to [lighting] and I kept it up from there." However, as time went on, Chris continued to consider himself a technician rather than an artist/designer. He relates, "I still heard my teachers telling me that. So, when I graduated high school, I joined the phone company as a telephone engineer . . . still doing theatre in the evening . . . [then] it dawned on me one day 'you only come this way once—and you better do what you really enjoy doing.' I realized it wasn't working for the phone company, so I wrote to Richard Pilbrow . . . and said 'How do you get into this business?'" Pilbrow responded, "'Your best bet is to get a job in the regional theatre and work your way up from there as an electrician—assist people.'"

Chris continues, "I was extremely lucky; I got an interview with the Royal Shakespeare Company and was offered a job on the lighting crew at the RSC in Stratford." After putting in his time as a lighting technician at the RSC, Chris began to assist visiting lighting designers: "They didn't have a staff lighting designer in those days—they always brought in big-name designers like David Hersey—so I began to assist those people—began to watch what they were doing. Without realizing it, you just pick things up—you think 'I would never do that' or you see them do something and you think 'Wow, that's a good idea—I'll store that one away.'" Assisting led to transferring shows for the RSC—the process of re-creating the lighting for a show that was selected to tour: "That was exciting—it was scary and exciting—a big responsibility." For one such show, the director [Howard Davies] had asked the original designer to come back to re-create the design, but he failed to show up, so Chris re-created the lighting.

One year later Chris was working with Davies again: "Howard Davies directed a Christopher Hampton play called *Les Liaisons Dangereuses (Dangerous Liaisons*—it became a huge hit—it started out in a small studio theatre at Stratford called the Other Place, went to the West End, played in the West End for a year and then went to Broadway. My first show on Broadway. I was nominated for a Tony Award. Unbelievable—the first time I appeared in America I was nominated for a Tony Award!"

As can be surmised from his background, Chris feels strongly that assisting is an extremely valuable way for young lighting designers to learn: "I'm a great believer in that . . . even if you don't learn what to do, you learn what not to do . . . and you learn things without even realizing you're learning them—you learn how to talk to a director—how to keep your mouth shut in the right place; you learn the politics of designing."

In discussing regional theatre practice, Chris says, "Almost always I will not be able to see any rehearsals before the plot goes in. Often I will have a conversation or two with the director on the phone. Sometimes I'll have a meeting with the director face-to-face—it depends on the situation and logistics." In designing for regional theatre, Chris thinks that it is vital to be able to visualize how a director may use the space: "Part of what I think I'm good at for some reason is analyzing the space—you know, looking at the set—and trying to figure out how the director might use it—covering my options. . . . It means that I can go into a run-through the day before focus and there are not many surprises—I've thought about most things."

(continued) ▶

Asked if he writes cues "blind" before he goes into the theatre, Chris replies, "No, I don't. My students have a problem with that, in a way—because I teach them to write cues ahead of time and I don't do it myself, so they think I'm very hypocritical. I try to explain to them, 'Look, I've been doing this 25 years—I can work fast—you don't have that speed, that facility, so you need to have something up your sleeve.' I can create on the fly—I can write cues pretty much as fast as a tech is going—it comes with practice."

Regarding setting levels without actors, Chris says, "I really need to see the whole event unfold in front of me, in real time, rather than sit in an empty theatre with the stage manager walking the stage—there's no drive—there's no emotional connection . . . I'm not lighting the production, I'm just lighting objects out of context and it doesn't mean anything. Many regional theatres don't give you time to write cues ahead of time [in the theatre]—one day of focus, and the following day you're in tech. Regional theatre tech rehearsals normally last from two to five days, followed by one to three days of previews. That's all. It is very fast. As a result, the lighting designer relies on good crews. Unfortunately, the level of crew talent varies quite a bit from theatre to theatre."

Chris also comments on the collaborative process—in particular with scene designers: "I like to find out why the scene designer is doing what he is doing. I also like to try to find out how they think it should be lit—my thought is that if they designed the set, they must have a picture in their mind of how it's lit—and I want to know what that looks like. . . . I feel that when I finish, the set and the lighting should look like they were done by the same person. . . . I'm really affected by the set—I really want to find ways of treating the set. . . . 'How can I use it to create the atmosphere to reinforce the emotions of the play?'—I love three-dimensional scenery." Chris observes that collaboration with directors varies tremendously. He prefers directors that speak in "words that generate pictures" and says that "the more directors can be specific, the better I like it." Unfortunately, discussions with some directors prove to be totally unproductive, so the lighting designer is forced to depend solely on other things: the script, the set, and rehearsals.

When giving advice for someone entering the business of lighting design, Chris recommends good mentoring and assisting opportunities: "Mentoring is really good—learning that way. Assist as much as you can." In terms of getting into the business, Chris says, "It's getting a lucky break. It's often not what you know, it's who you know. . . . Directors will usually hire somebody that they feel comfortable with, on a one-to-one basis—it's all about personalities, it's all about who you know and making contacts and being in the right place at the right time—my lucky break was because a designer didn't show up—it just happens like that . . . you have to put yourself in the right place, too." And, sometimes: "It's almost like there's a fork in the road and you've got to make a decision. If this opportunity has presented itself to you, you had better take it, because there's a reason that it happened."

Regional Theatre Designers A few regional theatres have staff designers, but most hire designers on a show-by-show basis. The way a lighting designer is hired is similar to Broadway practice, with the theatre's artistic director acting like the New York producer. Some regional theatres hire only designers who are United Scenic Artist members, while others pay no attention to union membership. Most theatres have a list of favorite designers, although a production's director can greatly influence this decision as well.

repertory production The process of presenting a different show each night, with the number depending on the size of the repertory.

Designing for Repertory Repertory theatres have a unique scheme of production in which different shows are presented each day of the week. Traditional **repertory production** generally requires daily changeovers from show to show. It may involve as few as two or as many as eight individual productions. The lighting designer must develop a repertory plot that serves as a basis for all shows, adding special instrumentation for each individual production. Repatching and sometimes color changes may take place during changeovers, but extensive refocusing should be avoided in repertory situations. Repertory design requires much more equipment than is normal for a single production, and the demands of an individual show must often be compromised for the sake of the entire production scheme. Remotely controlled color changers are an excellent equipment investment for the repertory theatre. Equally valuable are automated fixtures, which provide the designer with tremendous flexibility in repertory production.

Summer repertory—of Shakespeare or other classics, historical reenactments, and popular fare, especially musicals—has become a tradition in the United States. Designing for repertory theatre is an extremely valuable experience for any developing lighting designer.

Designing for Stock The vast majority of regional theatres produce their shows in a **stock** arrangement, running each production continuously for two to six weeks (summer stock productions may run only one week). Such a scheme requires rapid changeovers from show to show and normally a new lighting design for each production. The stock designer must be able to work quickly and efficiently, remaining one step ahead of the production schedule at all times.

stock production The process of running a single show for several weeks.

Those theatres that run shows for more than three weeks often hire in their lighting designers for each production. Those operations with shorter runs may very well employ a resident designer. Either way, the lighting designer is always under a great deal of time pressure. Like repertory production, stock experience is invaluable for the beginning lighting designer.

What to Expect Some regional theatres have a stagehand contract with the local IA union, and just as many others have no union labor affiliation. In essence, the regional designer should expect to find a new situation and new challenges in each place he or she designs.

Most cities have their own IA local. Rules and regulations vary radically from local to local, as does the quality of work. The expertise of any local can be known only through previous experience or by word-of-mouth. Well before a production is mounted, the designer should carefully evaluate the potential workforce in addition to local rule idiosyncrasies.

As regional theatres have spread across the country, stage-lighting rental houses have grown in number as well. Some of these local businesses are surprisingly efficient and well stocked. Others are woefully ill equipped and lacking in knowledgeable personnel. The designer must anticipate the possibility of having to go to New York or some other major center for equipment needs, a situation that will surely affect budget and time considerations.

More important than commercial usage is the matter of professional standards. Designers should never consider going into any level of commercial theatre unless they plan to devote their total energy and ability to the routines and the problems that arise. Regional theatre is no place for the casual enthusiast or the dilettante, nor for the easily discouraged, the supersensitive, or the uncooperative.

LIGHTING FOR OPERA

Lighting for the opera calls for a heightened theatricality, often combining the techniques of theatre and dance. Traditional operatic scenery suggests reality, but does so on a grand scale. Modern opera design often uses exaggerated techniques that suggest reality in a distorted manner, reminiscent of expressionism. Lighting may follow suit with saturated colors to produce a heightened sense of reality. Exaggerated angles and harsh colors may be used to produce stark images. Follow spots are frequently called for in traditional opera production.

24-5

Opera Light Plot

The light plot for a production of *The Student Prince,* produced by Columbus Light Opera and directed by Roger L. Stephens. Scenery, Gary Eckert; costumes, John Lehmeyer; lighting, Cindy Limauro.

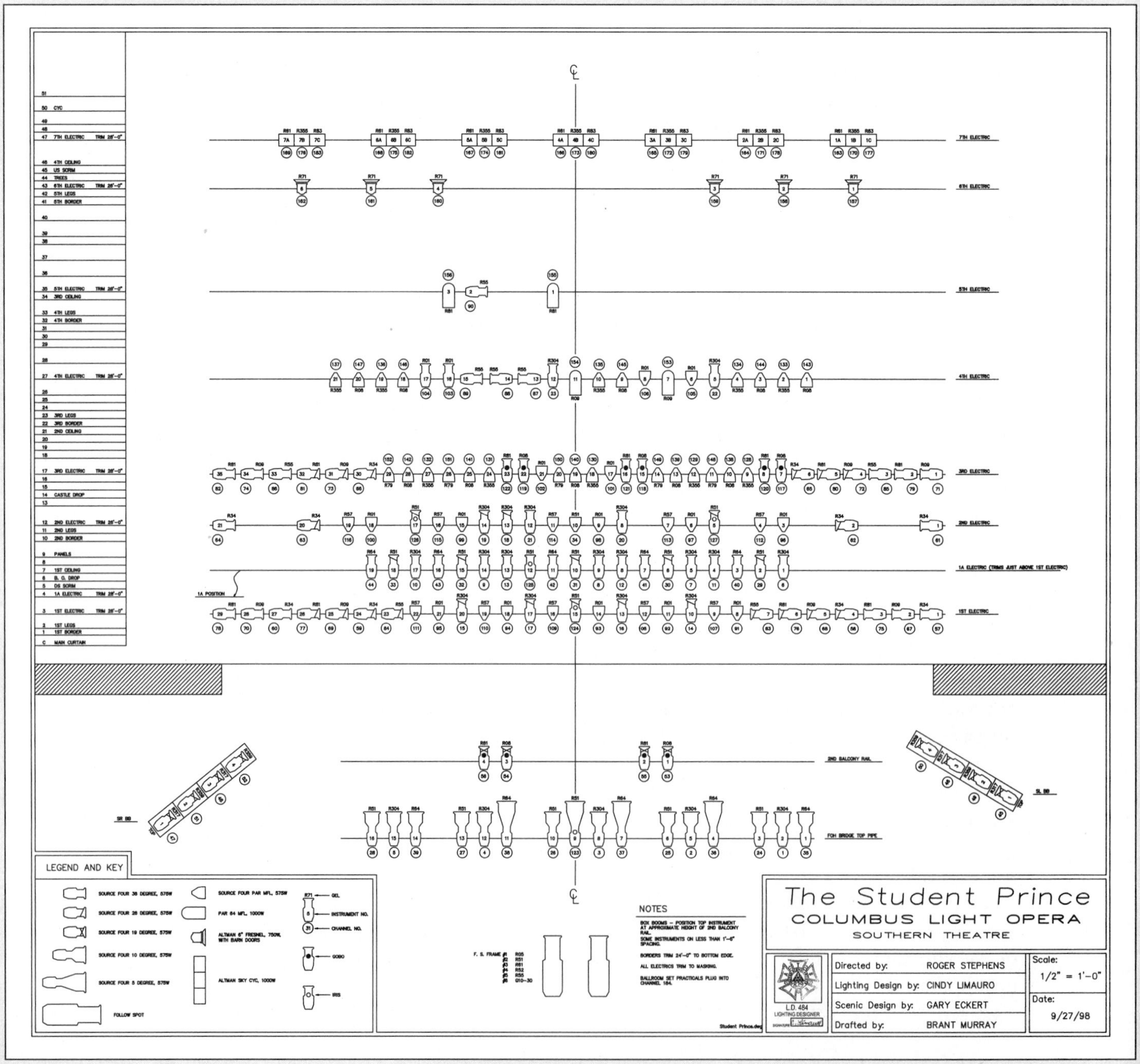

COURTESY CINDY LIMAURO

Figure 24-5 is a light plot designed by Cindy Limauro for Columbus Light Opera's production of Sigmund Romberg's *The Student Prince*. The theatre is the newly renovated Southern Theatre. It has a proscenium opening 33 feet high and 40 feet wide with two balconies, and it seats 1,700 people. Figure 24-6 is the color key for the production and Figure 24-7 is a part of the designer's hookup. Production photographs can be found in Color Plate 24-7.

Act I of this opera has four scenes and Act II has six. The primary action takes place at court in Karlsberg and at the Inn of the Three Golden Apples in Heidelberg. The opera is about Karl Franz, a young prince and heir to the throne of Karlsberg, who travels to Heidelberg for a year of study before

24-6

Student Prince Color Key

Color keys for *The Student Prince*, designed by Cindy Limauro.

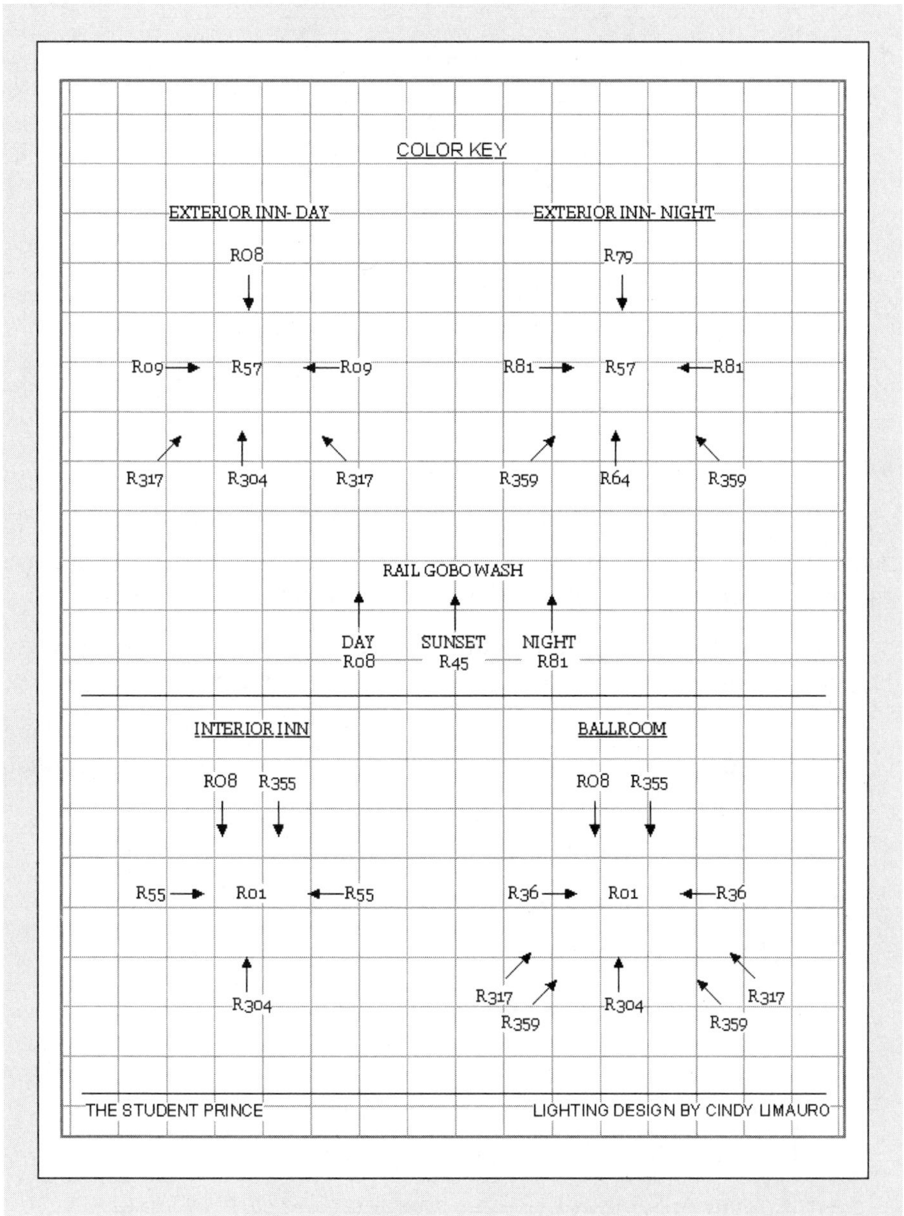

COURTESY CINDY LIMAURO

24-7

Student Prince Hookup

A page from the channel hookup for *The Student Prince,* designed by Cindy Limauro.

The Student Prince CHANNEL HOOKUP Page 1
06 Mar 2002

Channel	Dim	Position	U#	Type & Wattage	Purpose	Clr/Tmp
(1)		FOH Bridge	2	Source 410 575w	DL Front	R304
(2)		FOH Bridge	5	Source 410 575w	DCL Front	R304
(3)		FOH Bridge	8	Source 410 575w	DC Front	R304
(4)		FOH Bridge	12	Source 410 575w	DCR Front	R304
(5)		FOH Bridge	15	Source 410 575w	DR Front	R304
(6)		1A ELEC	1	Source 436 575w	ML Front	R304
(7)		1A ELEC	5	Source 436 575w	MCL Front	R304
(8)		1A ELEC	9	Source 436 575w	MC Front	R304
(9)		1A ELEC	14	Source 436 575w	MCR Front	R304
(10)		1A ELEC	17	Source 436 575w	MR Front	R304
(11)		1A ELEC	4	Source 436 575w	MCL Front INN Plat	R304
(12)		1A ELEC	8	Source 436 575w	MC Front INN Plat	R304
(13)		1A ELEC	13	Source 436 575w	MCR Front INN Plat	R304
(14)		1st ELEC	10	Source 426 575w	UL Front under plat	R304
(15)		1st ELEC	20	Source 426 575w	UC Front under plat	R304
(16)		1st ELEC	13	Source 426 575w	Bottom stairs Front	R304
(17)		1st ELEC	17	Source 426 575w	Bottom stairs Front	R304
(18)		2nd ELEC	13	Source 426 575w	Front Top of Stairs	R304
(19)		2nd ELEC	14	Source 426 575w	Front Top of Stairs	R304
(20)		2nd ELEC	8	Source 436 575w	Front Top of Plat	R304
(21)		2nd ELEC	12	Source 436 575w	Front Top of Plat	R304
(22)		4th ELEC	5	Source 436 575w	Front Top of Plat	R304
(23)		4th ELEC	12	Source 436 575w	Front Top of Plat	R304
(24)		FOH Bridge	3	Source 410 575w	DL Front	R51
(25)		FOH Bridge	6	Source 410 575w	DCL Front	R51
(26)		FOH Bridge	10	Source 410 575w	DC Front	R51
(27)		FOH Bridge	13	Source 410 575w	DCR Front	R51
(28)		FOH Bridge	16	Source 410 575w	DR Front	R51
(29)		1A ELEC	2	Source 426 575w	ML Front	R51
(30)		1A ELEC	6	Source 426 575w	MCL Front	R51

assuming his duties as king. There, at the inn, he falls in love with the barmaid, Kathie. Although their love is not destined to be, a beautiful scene between the two of them ends the opera. The scene breakdown is as follows:

Act I, Scene 1: Interior room of the palace in Karlsberg. This scene was staged to play "in one"—all the way downstage in front of a drape.

Act I, Scene 2: Interior of the Inn of the Three Golden Apples in Heidelberg. It is late afternoon. The scenery revolves to the exterior of the inn—late afternoon into sunset.

Act I, Scene 3: Same as I, 1.

Act I, Scene 4: Same as I, 2—early evening and evening.

Act II, Scene 1: Exterior of the inn—late at night.

Act II, Scene 2: Interior of the inn—the prince's suite upstairs—night.

Act II, Scene 3: Same as I, 1.

Act II, Scene 4: Grand Ballroom of the palace—evening.

Act II, Scene 5: Same as I, 1—dream sequence.

Act II, Scene 6: Same as I, 2—late afternoon and early evening.

WORKING AS A LIGHTING DESIGNER

The theatre has always been the primary training ground for lighting designers. It remains so today, despite the diverse fields in which theatre-trained lighting designers work. Not only does the theatre teach the art of designing with light, it also teaches the art of collaboration. A background in theatrical lighting can form the basis of the skills and qualities needed for work in the fields of architectural lighting, themed entertainment, film and television, concerts, and industrials.

Rarely does a graduate from a theatre training program immediately get work as a designer. The old axiom that people have to "pay their dues" is still true—experience working in the field is a significant part of becoming a designer. Whether the work is theatrical, architectural, industrial, or themed entertainment, an aspiring lighting designer probably must live in or around a fairly large city. Some cities are known for certain types of work. Obvious examples are Los Angeles for film and New York for theatre. It is simply a matter of determining what field one wishes to pursue, getting proper training, and then going where major employers in that field are located.

Architecture

Architectural lighting is done by specialists who have backgrounds in design and engineering. Some very large architectural firms have their own lighting specialists on staff, but architects usually hire a lighting firm, such as Schuler & Shook, who specialize in architectural lighting. Many architectural firms hire young people as apprentices. Individuals with theatre backgrounds are particularly welcome because they have been trained to think both creatively and practically and because they work well with other people. Chicago, Los Angeles, San Francisco, and New York are hubs of architectural activity. The ability to draft and use a CAD program is of great advantage in landing a job in the architectural world.

Designers at Work

Robert Shook

Color Plate 24-8

Robert Shook, IALD, LC, is a founding partner of the architectural lighting and theatre consulting firm, Schuler & Shook (www.schulershook.com). All the partners of this firm began their careers as theatrical-lighting designers and continue to apply this background to the practice of theatre consulting and architectural-lighting design. Bob's theatre consulting projects include the Seattle Opera, the Detroit Symphony Orchestra, and the Van Wezel Performing Arts Hall in Sarasota, Florida. His architectural-lighting projects in Chicago include the Art Institute, the Field Museum, Old St. Patrick's Church, and the Museum of Science and Industry.

Bob grew up in Louisville where, during his high school years, he was an usher at Actor's Theatre of Louisville, where he saw every show three or four times. Despite the fact that his love for theatre and architecture had been established, Bob went to Murray State University as a journalism major, but it did not last long: "By my second year of college, theatre was it. . . . From the beginning, light just fascinated me. . . . I was always interested in light

(continued) ▶

quality and light on stage." After two years, Bob transferred to the Goodman School of Drama in Chicago—"a great place to get an education and practical experience" at the same time. Bob did graduate work at Ohio University and, on receiving his M.F.A., immediately returned to Chicago: "The Chicago off-loop theatre movement was just getting started, and I was absolutely in the right place at the right time. . . . I loved working in small spaces. . . . Lighting for me was all about what light looked like on an actor's face—there's nothing more important than revealing an actor with light. . . . I loved working with actors—I would go to rehearsal all the time. I loved the rehearsal process—I loved sitting over in a corner and seeing how a scene develops—I would do all of my design work sitting in a rehearsal hall watching the director and the actors work—there is so much energy in the room and you're really sensing what's going into that scene—and I'm designing it as they're talking about it."

He also gained important foundation experience by working in the industry: "Of course, nobody could make a living just doing lighting design, so I worked for awhile at Grand Stage Lighting . . . getting a little bit of 'behind-the-scenes' in terms of the lighting-supply side of things. I worked for a couple of years at a large television studio in Chicago and learned a lot about lighting for video, and then I went to work for awhile at Art Drapery Studios, a rigging company, and learned a lot about stage rigging. I also saw, coming through that office, theatre designs that had been done by consultants—and I started learning what theatre consultants did—that's where I sort of taught myself how to read architectural drawings. I began to realize that the perfect thing for me was theatre, lighting, and architecture—[that] drove me in the direction of theatre consulting and architectural lighting." Although Bob never apprenticed or worked in an architectural firm, he says that it "would have been a good idea—I applied to a firm that I wanted to work for, but they weren't hiring. So, after awhile, I decided that I could take a stab at this myself." Bob began doing small projects as a theatre consultant and, later, as an architectural-lighting designer. In 1980, Bob met lighting designer Duane Schuler, who was lighting opera in Chicago. In 1986, Schuler & Shook was born. Today, they have a total staff of thirty-five, with offices in Chicago, Minneapolis, and Dallas/Fort Worth.

Bob explains that the firm is pretty much equally divided between theatre consultants and architectural-lighting designers and that he is "one of the few people in the firm who actually has a foot on both sides." Most architectural firms do not maintain lighting designers on their full-time staff, instead electing to hire designers on a project-by-project basis from a firm such as Schuler & Shook. Undoubtedly the founders' grounding in theatrical design influenced the firm's belief that "an open collaborative process is the key to successful design."

Regarding the process involved in a typical architectural project, Bob says, "The first thing we do is to have a sit-down meeting with the architect and, if possible, someone else [such as the owner] who may have a slant on this project. That meeting, in our view, is just to get [the architect's] take on 'What is this building about?' . . . 'What was behind your ideas to have gotten this far?' It's a process, in my view, of getting into the architect's head—understanding what he is doing with this space so that we can try to come to some idea of what the lighting should be like—what the quality of light should be in the space." Next, the firm receives a set of architectural plans, usually electronically: "Everybody in the architectural market these days is working in AutoCad—that makes it very convenient because there's one standard." They study the plans "looking for opportunities—'Where are the (lighting) opportunities in this space?'"

Bob continues, "Then, in our office, we have a studio process. . . . Everybody has an opportunity to sort of lob ideas in. . . . It's just a big brainstorming session." Then Bob and the project designer consider options for the lighting—developing them on presentation boards created from archived images or the architect's drawings. Photoshop is a useful tool at this stage. Meetings go back and forth between the project designer and the architect and, finally, fixtures are chosen and lighting plans are developed: "We produce, in our office, what we call 'lighting layouts' . . . to distinguish them from actual working drawings. . . . The architect will incorporate our drawings into the reflected ceiling plans, which show the location of the fixtures, and our information will also get passed on to the electrical engineer, who will add conduit and wiring and circuitry and that kind of information. Then, from that point on, we are sort

(continued) ▶

of reviewing what the architect and the electrical engineer are drawing."

In discussing training and breaking into the architectural lighting business, Bob says, "I have found that it's a relatively difficult transition to make from theatrical lighting to architectural lighting. The advantage of having a theatrical-lighting background and doing architectural lighting is that you're aware of the dramatic possibilities of light and you are very aware of how light behaves. . . . When you are working in a dynamic environment like the theatre, you are making those [light behavior] decisions every second; when you are working in an architectural environment, it's all about planning." He believes that there are two other areas that one must deal with in making a transition from theatre to architecture: "Actually knowing the equipment . . . learning your tools . . . it takes a long time to do that . . . [and] the third area, to me, is learning how to work with an architect." While collaborative skills learned in the theatre are extremely important, Bob feels that "if you are going to work in the architectural field, you have to like architects. You really have to understand where they're coming from, you have to sort of put yourself in their shoes, you have to understand 'Why did they design this space the way they have?' You have to figure out 'If I were the architect, how would I design the lighting for this building?'"

He goes on to say, "There are schools that are training people [specifically] to be architectural lighting designers. . . . They are almost all architectural engineering programs—and so you're really coming out of it from an engineering background—which is kind of a side-door to architectural lighting. And theatre might be another side door. And, in fact, the best of all possible worlds is if you had an office that was populated with about half theatre people and half engineering people—very interesting process." Bob explains that most offices try to "free up" those people with engineering backgrounds, while "the people that come at it from a theatre background, they need more of a technical engineering grounding: understanding how to read a photometric chart, how to run calculations, and how to draw an architectural detail."

Here is Bob's advice to theatre-trained designers who want to work in the architectural lighting field: take independent courses sponsored by local chapters of the Illuminating Engineering Society (IES) and learn to use AutoCad because "when you start you are going to be doing a lot of drafting."

The **Illuminating Engineering Society** (IES) is a national organization made up primarily of architectural lighting engineers and designers. The principal function of this organization is to provide its members an outlet for discussion and the dissemination of up-to-date information on architectural lighting. The IES is also concerned with providing better training in architectural lighting. They have an online job listing, and local chapters offer beginning and advanced classes that can greatly help one gain industry-specific information.

Illuminating Engineering Society (IES) An organization made up primarily of architectural lighting designers and engineers; publishes the IES handbook and offers courses in architectural lighting.

URL http://www.iesna.org

Television and Film

As in architecture, many lighting directors for television and film were trained in the theatre. Television and film lighting is a highly competitive field. However, one can gain entry into the industry by beginning as an apprentice or assistant. Los Angeles and New York are the major film and television centers, although most other large cities offer ample television opportunities. Some universities, such as San Diego State, offer a theatre major with a film or television minor. Most colleges and universities offer some film and television course work.

Designers at Work

Dennis Size

Color Plate 24-9

Dennis Size is Vice President of Design for The Lighting Design Group, a major broadcast-lighting design firm on the east coast (www.ldg.com). His personal television credits include designs for *Live with Regis & Kathie Lee, Nightline, 20/20, All My Children, Ryan's Hope, The Montel Williams Show, The Oprah Winfrey Show,* and *Martha Stewart Living.* He has received two Emmy awards (*Oprah Winfrey* and *All My Children*) as well as numerous Axiom awards.

Dennis studied theatrical design at the University of Scranton and in the M.F.A. program at Penn State. At that time, many of the major television networks had a "vacation relief program" in which designers would be trained to take over the lighting of an ongoing production when the staff lighting director was on vacation. Through a series of fortunate circumstances, Dennis received the opportunity to work on ABC's popular *Ryan's Hope*. After a dozen years of refining his craft, Dennis established himself among the most sought after television-lighting designers in New York. He describes his initial work in television as a "means of supporting my theatrical lighting habit" and continues to this day to design and teach design, not only for television but also for the stage.

Although Dennis believes that "the most important thing is that [he] was trained as a theatrical lighting designer," he also makes it clear that television and theatre lighting have their differences. Television lighting is so commercial. Dennis bemoans the fact that "you have to compress all of your design skills and your abilities to make it happen in an eight-hour day because God forbid you end up creating overtime." Time in the studio is so compressed that there is little margin for error and there is seldom a sense of collaboration. The television designer needs to think like a director: "I have to go into everything as though I am directing it. . . . We have to direct the attention to what the audience needs to see. If the shot is a close-up of somebody's face and it is important to see the reaction in the eyes, you want to make sure that there are not shadows on the face or wrinkles or anything that takes the attention away from the story the eyes are telling." The good television designer knows exactly what is needed for the specific program: "Nine times out of ten on talk shows or news programs [the producers] are 'content' people—they don't get involved with the visuals—that's why you're being hired—they hire the design team to come in and create something for them that makes the intended statement." The producer is concerned with content and whether the director is shooting the visuals properly.

Dennis goes on to tell about creating the lighting for an ABC late night news program. The typical news shows of the day tended to have uninteresting, flat lighting. However, the director of this particular show did not want to duplicate that look, because "it's late at night and people are working—they are prepping the news for the day—the janitors are going to be coming through—we're shooting 360 and we're going to see the whole room. So I threw all sorts of patterns around the room and I lit it very starkly—very dramatically—it made the two anchor people in the center of this cavernous space pop out—we used the qualities of white light and shadow and texture. They loved it—to me it was just another little theatrical thing." The word soon got out and Dennis moved from show to show applying his theatrical talents. His lighting "tells a story."

Dennis's use of follow spots to fill in the faces of television actors is interesting. This technique was born with his redesign of *The Oprah Winfrey Show:* "They wanted Oprah to go everywhere. We were talking about individual areas, we were talking about many lights into areas from every angle, the set was going to be on air casters, they were going to be able to lift the whole set up and move it to different parts of the studio. . . . I loved the idea of lighting the whole space—we used blues and patterns and texture—it was textural space that had a lot of color quality to it. Oprah then became an issue: 'How do you light this woman to go anywhere?'—you follow her. When I brought up the word [*follow spot*], people in television looked at me like I was nuts." The idea was to locate six very tightly irised and softly focused follow spots around the space that would fade up and down as

(continued) ▶

Oprah moved and turned from camera to camera. "The concept of the show was to really fill her face with a soft glow at all times so wherever she moves around that set there is an ethereal wash of light on her face. . . . This way you are highlighting just her face." Today, Dennis uses 5-degree Source Fours, usually running at only 30 percent.

A fundamental element of Dennis's lighting is tight control: "You want to be able to control the light—I think that's the key. . . . That's all I did at ABC when they said 'We want his style.' My style was just to put the light where it is needed, and nowhere else. You know, if you want to light the walls and make them look good, don't put that 2K Fresnel so it washes both the person and the wall." As a result, a typical Dennis Size studio hang contains a large number of Lekos (ellipsoidal reflector spotlights) used not only as set lights but also as key lights.

In reflecting on his start in television lighting, Dennis says of *Ryan's Hope:* "I was lucky enough to fall into something that fit my design aesthetic like a glove. If I had been thrown into something like the sports department . . . I would have been trained by people who only cared about getting enough lumens on somebody's face to get a picture—and that's a problem. I ended up putting in about fourteen years on soap operas doing dramatic presentations." After that, Dennis moved on to special events for ABC, where he found greater design challenges. In leaving ABC in 1997, Dennis joined forces with Steve Brill, who had designed for NBC, and they formed The Lighting Design Group: "At that time there were only about nine people on staff—now we are sixteen—between our production staff and our designers." In discussing how the firm works, Dennis explains that, even though the basic lighting for a show has been designed, "every day you're redesigning—you're setting something new—you're deciding what the look of the show that day is going to be. . . . To maintain our standards, we like one of our own lighting directors to be on a show." As part of his job as Vice President of Design, Dennis supervises the designers. He makes sure that the right designer gets placed on the right show.

In terms of breaking into the industry, Dennis says, "People coming out of school just aren't trained in television lighting—they're trained in lighting design and I think that's great because you can modify it, but . . . the company can't afford to train people. So what I usually do is have people come and observe me and our other designers, and then we'll hire them for awhile as an intern—we started an internship program about two years ago. We also created a staff Assistant Designer position . . . who also does the drafting for us." So, the necessary skills are sounding rather familiar:

- A solid basic training in theatrical lighting
- Excellent people skills
- Drafting and visualization skills such as Photoshop
- A strong desire to work in the industry

The **National Association of Broadcasters (NAB)** holds an annual convention that attracts television workers from across the country. It is a good place to meet people and learn more about the field—and perhaps find a job.

National Association of Broadcasters (NAB) An organization of individuals involved in television production.

URL http://www.nab.org

Industrials and Trade Shows

Lighting for industrials and trade shows can be a lucrative business. It is primarily done by firms that have gained reputations over the years for this type of design work. These firms are contracted by industry giants like General Motors or IBM to design and execute the lighting for their product shows. The scope of this design work varies from relatively direct and simple illumination to extremely complex and spectacular productions.

Designers at Work

Ann Archbold

Color Plate 24-10

Ann Archbold is a USA lighting designer who has worked in regional theatre, dance, opera, and, most extensively, the industrial world. Her many credits include design for the Old Globe Theatre in San Diego, the San Francisco Opera, the Pittsburgh Symphony, the Odyssey Theatre in Los Angeles, Audi and Cadillac, and Fittness Quest. She is currently the faculty lighting designer at Florida State University and has her own firm: AMA Design & Consulting. She has a B.G.S. from the University of Michigan and an M.F.A. from San Diego State University

Ann explains how she first got into the business of designing for trade shows or "industrials": "I was working in a Los Angeles area rock 'n' roll rental house in order to support my freelance theatre-lighting design habit. A job came through our rental house which involved design for a small touring exhibit featuring a new Cadillac engine. Basically it was an 8-foot tube of Plexiglas with a cutaway of this brand new engine. They wanted the display to be able to illuminate a particular feature of the engine in conjunction with a video presentation. Because of the compactness of the exhibit, we used a number of MR-16s, which lit up at the appropriate times. Cadillac liked it so much that they decided that this kind of use of light would be good for their big car shows." The rest is history. Ann became chief designer for The Secor Group, designing for Cadillac as well as other car manufacturers, and continues to this day to work in the industrial sector.

Designing for industrials often means starting with a vast empty space. Ann points out that the early industrial rigs, trussing and lights, came from concert lighting. Therefore, it is no surprise that most of the equipment in use is PAR-64s. Ann reports that at the 1986 Detroit Auto Show, "I was one of the first ones in this country to put a lighting truss over a booth—that was Cadillac. They wanted it to be a part of the overall look—they wanted to see a lot of truss and a lot of lights as part of the exhibit. Previously they were using house fixtures located far away in the ceiling—and very few of them at that. The next year at the same auto show there were dozens of rigs." One of the most interesting things that Ann emphasized was the importance of understanding the aesthetics of color temperature. She pointed out that particularly in the auto industry there exists a distinct "European aesthetic," which essentially calls for the use of light with color temperatures of 4,700–5,600°K in order to feature or highlight a product. She explained that very little color filtering is used unless it is to correct color temperature (for instance using a Lee ¾ C.T. Blue to correct a 3,000°K PAR to 4,700°K). More recently, the use of high color-temperature moving lights, low-voltage fixtures such as parabolic spots, and metal halide sources has become common practice. Clearly, a broad knowledge of fixtures and particularly sources is important in working on industrials.

Regarding the control of all these lights, Ann says, "Coming from a theatrical background, I wanted to have a lot of specific control. Cadillac had light moving with music—timed to their commercials—where I needed a lot of control. We used rock 'n' roll truss-mounted dimmers. We then hired someone to create a lighting software program that I could cue to SMPTE time code. As we got into moving lights, we hired another person to create a unit into which we could download a program off a standard light board. It was originally called 'Firefly,' which is, of course, the precursor to the Horizon System distributed today by Rosco. It was all created from within because there wasn't anything on the market that could do that. This was an innovative time because we were exploring things that nobody really knew how to do or nobody had attempted to do. Later, for big shows, we built custom lighting rigs which became more scenery than lighting. Cadillac's gear alone took up three semis between the rigging and the lighting."

Among the things unique to working trade shows, Ann lists the following:

- The large scale of a typical trade show venue (an auto display can be the size of several football fields)
- The challenge of remaining enthusiastic about lighting inanimate objects
- Working with corporate individuals whose forte is often not collaboration

(continued) ▶

- Lots of travel, interesting people, and good money
- International contacts
- Trade show union workers who are unfamiliar with the equipment

Ann says that an industrial designer must first and foremost remain flexible and patient. She points out that, more often than not, things change after lights have been hung and focused. When the Cadillac regional director does not like an arrangement of cars, there is nothing else to do but refocus. Ann also notes, "Today you must know about video—it is an important advertising tool for manufacturers. You must understand what it takes to produce video as well as how to light it. The need for this knowledge applies to still projection as well."

Finally, Ann offers advice on how to break into the field—on what kind of training is necessary and how to find work: "The eye for light and the aesthetics that one is taught in a theatre training program allow you to see light in a particular manner—a unique way that other people don't see it. The skills you develop in a design program will hold true no matter what aspect of the entertainment industry you may be in. This is the best foundation you can get." Here are her further suggestions:

- Work for equipment rental houses located in commercial centers.
- Apply to large design firms located in New York or Los Angeles.
- Work for one of the moving light companies.
- Work as an assistant for large projects designed by freelance designers.
- Try exhibit houses, which are becoming more and more interested in hiring lighting designers.

But remember: "It is necessary to keep up your theatre work. Theatre feeds that design/artist part of us that can be lost when designing a commercial product. There is more freedom of expression in the theatre."

Industrial-lighting firms are always looking for people with lighting-design talent to apprentice and learn more about the business. Such firms are generally located in larger cities and can be found in the telephone book. Prospective designers can call and ask for the name of the individual who accepts résumés.

Themed Entertainment

The rise in popularity of themed entertainment has made this another lucrative field for lighting designers. Theme parks are often owned and run by large corporations such as Disney or Universal. In this case, one should apply to the human resources department for a position. If at all possible, find out exactly who does the hiring and contact that person directly. Assuming there is work, lighting designers trained in the theatre are welcomed at these large entertainment conglomerates. At times, small firms consisting of one or two designers are contracted to do the lighting for a specific theme park or attraction. When the work comes along, these firms need help to get the job done. Sending a résumé and requesting an interview could lead to a good job and provide exceptional experience. Remember that volume of work for the smaller firms varies a great deal. Do not give up if nothing is available immediately. Be persistent without being a nuisance.

Designers at Work

Tom Ruzika

Color Plate 24-11

Tom Ruzika is the principal designer and owner of The Ruzika Company, a team of California lighting designers and theatre consultants (www.ruzika.com). The Ruzika Company specializes in architectural and residential lighting, is heavily involved in theatre consulting, and is well-known for its work in themed entertainment. Tom Ruzika began his lighting in the theatre and has a long list of theatrical credits, including South Coast Rep., the Mark Taper Forum, Berkeley Rep., and Utah Shakespeare Festival. Tom is also head of the graduate lighting program at the University of California, Irvine.

Tom is a hands-on type of person. From the very beginning of his lighting career, Tom did it all—he was the electrics person for his high school, lighting the school plays, music concerts, assemblies, and touring productions. During those years, he was able to work in an exceptionally well-equipped 1,400-seat auditorium that also served as the only road house in the area. Tom's first (and last) formal lighting course was taken at Cal Poly Pomona from friend and mentor, Aubrey Wilson. It was here that Tom learned that there was more to lighting than dimmers and Lekos—he discovered a whole new world of dramatic literature. He learned how to interpret a script, to see and talk about light, and to appreciate the power of the playwright's text. As a theatre major at Pomona, Tom was encouraged to broaden his educational horizons by taking courses in psychology, architecture, and engineering. He also took a teaching job at his former high school.

After graduation, while pursuing the thing that gave him most joy—lighting—Tom discovered that U.C. Irvine was attracting talented theatre and dance groups from across the nation to perform in their new facility. He enrolled in the M.F.A. program there and immediately began acting as lighting supervisor for visiting dance companies and teaching lighting classes, along with designing many productions. There he discovered what he describes as "the wonderful world of dance lighting—one of the most expressive ways of designing light." Tom reports, "At that time, as part of that whole dance touring project, we were getting the Paul Taylors, we were getting the Eliot Felds, we were getting Nickolais—I mean, I executed I can't tell you how many Jennifer Tipton light plots—I still have the 8½ by 11 hand-drawn Tipton light plots—and worked with their people in executing them. So I learned about Tipton's lighting and what dance lighting was by doing and watching—like when Nickolais came in with their twenty-four projectors—and what you can do with twenty-four projectors."

Tom soon became involved with The Moving Company, a regional professional dance company, and designed for them for five years. They toured up and down the west coast, playing in venues that varied from wonderfully equipped theatres to small gymnasium stages. The experience of dealing with such a huge variety of equipment and spaces was one of the most valuable to date, for it taught him to be flexible and adjust to any situation—a trait to which he attributes much of his success today. Tom's next step was to regional theatre: "Soon after that I saw my first show at South Coast Rep. and was bowled over and called them and said 'I want to work with you.'" That was in the early days of South Coast Rep. and, once again, Tom's organizational and hands-on skills proved significant: "I came into their storefront theatre—it was a total disaster—lightingwise, there was garbage everywhere. I went in there to do my first show and before I even started the show I basically cleaned up the whole place—electrically and lightingwise—and put everything in boxes—and Martin [Benson] saw that and says. 'You've got a job here forever!'" Soon after South Coast Rep. came designing at the Taper as well as the Utah Shakespeare Festival.

Tom has always had a fascination with architecture—a curiosity about how things are built—and he believes that this interest was an important force in bringing him to architectural lighting. He sees a "natural progression from theatrical lighting to discovering what light could do to buildings." After all, "it's the same light in different cans." This philosophy holds true for whatever project Tom and his firm takes on—it is all about "What can the light do?"

One day while teaching at Irvine and lighting everything he could, Tom received a call from an acquaintance who was, at the time, the entertain-

(continued) ▶

ment director at Universal Studios—they wanted him to come over and look at something they were doing. That was the beginning of design for themed entertainment—a move that prompted the creation of The Ruzika Company in the mid-1980s. The firm is made up of individuals who have expertise in a variety of design areas and who have mostly theatrical-lighting backgrounds. The senior people are project managers with whom Tom works closely; the others have supporting jobs. Estimating that "half of the work in theme parks is actually architectural lighting," Tom feels that knowledge of architectural lighting is instrumental in successful theme park design. The job begins with the proposal—normally three to five years before an expected completion date. The firm must prepare a bid package that includes design ideas and cost estimates based on client specifications. It seems that preparing the proposal is a game in itself—one that Tom does not exactly enjoy but handles well because of his organizational skills. These days more and more paperwork is involved in landing a contract; it forms a big part of the business—"The days of the handshake agreement are gone." Tom acknowledges the importance of having good people working with him in the firm—they must attend to the details that he can no longer handle, ranging from CADD work to site visits and from Photoshop presentations to travel reservations. He remains directly involved, however: "I keep my fingers on the whole business end of it and do my own negotiating of contracts. . . . If you think about it, a good lighting designer, besides being creative, is usually a good manager." Tom reports that, especially lately, clients may not even want the firm to work on a project beyond the creative stage—they simply want a schematic idea. The creators may not be involved with the evolution of the project or even see the final results. But that is the part that Tom misses and he is likely to pay a visit or two to the site whether he is contracted to do so or not.

Tom has several ideas concerning what it takes to succeed in this business. To his mind, the ability to be flexible—to think on one's feet—is of prime importance. "In getting into this business—in working in this business—that is one of the most important characteristics that an individual has to have: the ability to make it work and be flexible and be able to handle it." To succeed in the "corporate" world of lighting one must be able to exist "in the world of lighting that goes beyond what I would call a personal level. A lot of lighting—especially in the theatre—you can make very personal. You can kind of do your own thing and even though you're collaborating with the set designers, costume designers, and directors, you're in a kind of 'cocoon' world. Doing an entire theme park and working with the construction trades and people who don't really know anything about lighting or care about lighting except 'I've got to have some light there'—that's where it takes flexibility." In terms of training, Tom the educator states, "I'm a firm believer in lighting education where there are opportunities to explore the world of light." He also acknowledges the importance of learning certain skills, such as how to use AutoCad and Photoshop. But perhaps most importantly, Tom believes that the potential lighting designer must have enough interest, curiosity, and passion to have fun with light.

Lighting Dimensions International (LDI) holds a national conference each November, which many lighting designers in diverse fields attend. Such conferences offer a way to meet people and learn more about the various aspects of lighting design. Entertainment Technology Online offers job listings at the URL listed for LDI. The **Themed Entertainment Association** publishes a directory of firms working in the industry and has an online job board.

Lighting Dimensions International (LDI) Group that publishes *Lighting Dimensions* magazine and holds an annual convention for individuals working in entertainment lighting.

Themed Entertainment Association An organization made up of people working in the themed entertainment business.

URL http://www.lightingdimensions.com

URL http://www.themeit.com

Concerts

Concert lighting grew out of the need for special illumination of touring rock concerts. In the beginning, a band member was in charge of the lighting—often nothing more than a few spotlights providing a wash of color on the stage. However, things changed quickly as bands realized the dramatic effect color

24-8

Concert Design

One section of a concert truss containing both fixed and automated instruments.

and light had on their audiences. Special lighting and effects soon became a necessity. New methods of touring lights were developed, and the PAR-64 fixture became an industry standard. More recently, concert lighting provided the theatre with a whole new generation of automated fixtures (Figure 24-8).

A concert-lighting designer often tours with the band, running the lighting console for each performance. Being a part of a concert tour is an extremely valuable experience for any young lighting designer. Such tours hire electricians, and it is certainly possible to assist the designer. Jim Moody, who was trained as a theatrical designer, has written an informative book on concert lighting that anyone interested in the field should read. It is listed in the additional reading list at the back of this book.

The Theatre

Working your way up to designing in the theatre is a slow and sometimes frustrating process. Normally, producers will not hire a designer until his or her work has been seen. The paradox is this: how can someone see your work if you cannot get hired? You must be prepared to design for little or no money at first. This also means that you will need another job. In fact, most theatrical-lighting designers work in other fields. Your first choice for nondesign work should be doing something else in the theatre. Stagehands and electricians are always needed, and some get paid good wages. Assisting more experienced designers is of great advantage. Such work allows you to stay close to the theatre and meet people who may offer you work in the future. Build up a résumé and distribute it frequently.

USITT (United States Institute for Theatre Technology) is the American association of design and production professionals in the performing arts. It sponsors an annual conference usually held in March, which is invaluable for meeting other designers, keeping up with state-of-the-art techniques and equipment, and learning more about the art of design through the numerous workshops offered. USITT also provides a job placement service at its national conference. Membership is inexpensive for students and reasonable for others. For information, contact USITT at 6443 Ridings Road, Syracuse, NY, 13206-1111.

URL http://www.usitt.org

***Art*SEARCH** is a national publication listing available positions primarily in the theatre arts. You may subscribe to this TCG (Theatre Communications Group) service by writing to the following address: *Art*SEARCH, 355 Lexington Avenue, New York, NY 10017-0217.

***Art*SEARCH** A nationwide listing of available theatre jobs; published by Theatre Communications Group.

The theatre is a wonderful place to work, because theatre people enjoy what they are doing. It does not take too long to discover whether or not you are cut out for a career in the theatre. But remember—if you think you are, be persistent. It will pay off!

Glossary

acoustics The scientific study of the total effect of sound, especially as produced in an enclosed space. In the theatre this may relate to reflection, absorption, and creation of harmonics that characterize a theatre's reverberant field.

adaptor A special cable with different types of connectors on each end; allows an instrument with one type of connector to be plugged into a circuit with a different type of connector.

aliasing In sound recordings, a distortion caused by a sampling rate below the Nyquist frequency.

alternate position Any secondary position of a piece of scenery, drafted in dotted line.

alternating current (AC) An electric current that periodically reverses direction of flow.

alternator A simple alternating current (AC) generator.

amber drift The color shift of an incandescent lamp as it is dimmed.

ampere The measurement of flow rate of electrons (current) through a conductor. Also used to indicate the capacity of a circuit or conductor.

amplitude Measured in decibels (dB), amplitude is synonymous with volume or intensity. Amplitude is determined by the height of a sound wave.

analog signal Audio information represented by a continuous variable measurement of physical quantities, such as length, width, voltage, or pressure. An analog audio recording is a continuous curve, as opposed to a digital recording, which is based on discrete samples.

analogous Using any three adjacent hues of the color wheel.

apron The area of the stage just in front of the proscenium arch. Synonymous with *forestage.*

area-lighting method An organizational method of lighting in which lighting areas are assigned throughout the acting area and instruments are focused on those areas in the same ways, thus providing consistency in lighting the actors as they move about the stage. Also called *area method* and *area system.*

arena seating Also referred to as *stadium seating* in which the slope of the audience seating is quite steep. Most often found in arena and thrust theatres (as well as in sports stadiums).

arena stage Theatre in which the audience sits on all sides of the acting space. Sometimes referred to as *theatre-in-the-round.*

artistic director Person responsible for play selection, hiring of artistic staff, and sometimes fund-raising.

***Art*SEARCH** A nationwide listing of available theatre jobs; published by Theatre Communications Group.

Austrian shade drape Sometimes referred to as a *brail curtain,* a curtain that is rigged with a series of vertical drawlines that lift at the same time and at the same speed.

automated fixtures DMX remotely controlled lighting instruments that, at a minimum, can change focus and color. Often called *moving lights.*

a vista In view of the audience.

backstage All of the area upstage of the proscenium arch. Often used synonymously with *offstage.*

balance Equalization of visual weight or opposing forces within a composition.

balanced line A method in which the audio signal is carried on two wires in a shielded cable, with one signal being 180 degrees out-of-phase from the other. Sometimes called *differential input,* this input signal is only read in terms of the difference between the two wires; therefore, any noise induced on both of them will be ignored. Balanced lines are standard in professional equipment and can be used for very long cable runs.

barn door An accessory for the Fresnel spotlight that attaches at the color-frame holder and allows for linear beam-shaping from four sides.

batten Pipe batten; horizontal pipe hung from a line-set of a fly system.

batten tape Strips of paper or cloth attached to a lighting batten to assist in the hanging and circuiting of instruments.

beam edge In a spotlight beam, the point where the light drops off to 50 percent of maximum intensity.

bevel Any cut in the same direction as the grain of the wood.

black box theatre A theater that is usually small and that allows flexibility in the arrangement of audience to acting space. It is so named because the walls are usually painted black.

blind A window covering used to block out light. There are various types, the most common being Venetian blinds and roller blinds. Also called a *shade.*

blue-line printing A type of blueprinting that produces blue lines on a white field.

blueprinting A process of copying an original line drawing, which results in a blue field with white lines.

board-foot A measurement of lumber equivalent to a board 1-inch thick and 1-foot square.

boomerang A rolling platform, usually with several levels, that allows scenic artists to work on several areas of a drop simultaneously when painting vertically.

booms Vertical hanging positions for lighting instruments. Portable types often consist of 1½-inch black pipe screwed into a heavy base. Also called *lighting trees.*

border Overhead masking, usually in reference to opaque black fabric, hanging from a batten and running laterally across the stage.

borderlight A striplight using PAR-type lamps, typically hung over stage and used to wash the stage with color.

boundary microphone A microphone placed extremely close to and facing a flat (boundary) plate. Rather than responding directly to pressure in the air, this microphone picks up pressure variations from the air gap between the element and the plate.

box boom A vertical hanging position for lighting equipment, located in the side walls of the auditorium close to the stage. Named after the placement of light booms in audience side boxes, these positions create a low to medium side angle a bit to the front of the performer.

breasting Moving a hanging unit of scenery away from its working position in order to make room for (usually) another piece of scenery or an electric.

bridling Extending the line-set by adding a length of pipe and tying it diagonally to the liftlines.

broad A rectangular floodlight that produces a bright and fairly even wash of light.

bulb The sealed glass enclosure of a lamp. Also called the *envelope.*

bus-and-truck tour A tour that plays short runs in numerous cities.

business manager Person in charge of budgeting and all other financial matters, often including fund-raising.

cable Temporary stage wiring—normally 20-amp capacity to match stage circuits.

carriage The supporting structure of a staircase tread.

cartooning The drawing, usually in charcoal, of a paint elevation on a drop or flat.

casket lock A two-piece locking device incorporating a rotating wedge that pulls both pieces together and locks them with one turn of an Allen T-wrench. Also called *coffin lock.*

C-clamp A clamp, shaped like a C, that is used to attach a lighting instrument to a pipe batten.

ceiling beam or port A slot cut in the auditorium ceiling, providing a position for hanging and focusing front lights.

change music Music used to cover the time and possibly the noise of a scene change.

channel The dimmer controller in a memory system.

channel or dimmer parking A lighting control-board feature in which the intensity level of a channel or dimmer will not be recorded in a cue.

chroma The purity of a color or the amount of adulteration (neutrality); often referred to as *intensity* or *saturation.*

circuit An established path of electrical flow.

circuit breaker A switch that automatically opens if the current exceeds a circuit's capacity.

color boomerang A device, located in the front of the barrel of a follow spot, that holds several color filters, allowing for quick color changes.

color changer A DMX remotely controlled device placed at the front of a lighting instrument in order to change color filters. Often called *scrollers.*

color interaction How the perception of a color is influenced by the presence of another color.

color modification The alteration of a surface's color by colored light.

color temperature A measurement in degrees Kelvin (°K) of the color of light emitted from a source. Stage-lighting instruments with incandescent lamps have a color temperature of about 3,200°K. Candlelight is a warm-colored 1,800°K and arc light is a cool-colored 6,000°K.

common neutral A neutral wire serving two or more hot wires.

complementary hue One of two hues directly opposite each other on the color triangle.

composition The organization of design elements into a unified form. Light reveals composition.

condenser microphone A microphone housing an element consisting of two metallic-coated plates separated by a small volume of air. The top plate, which is charged with an electrical voltage, acts as a diaphragm. Its movement back and forth (changing the distance of the air gap between the two plates) alters the electrical charge induced in the back plate. Because of the very low voltage generated, all condenser microphones require an internal amplifier as well as a source of power—either a small battery or phantom power from the mixing board.

condensing lens system The first lens or set of lenses in a projector; the condensing lens(es) concentrate the light from the source onto the slide.

conductor Materials that allow the free motion of a large number of electrons.

cones Light receptors located in the retina that are sensitive to color.

connectors Electrical plugs.

contactor An electrically operated device in which a small switch controls a larger, remotely located switch.

continuity tester A piece of testing equipment that supplies a low-voltage current in order for an electrician to ascertain whether a circuit is complete or broken.

contour curtain A curtain that is rigged with several separately operated drawlines that can create a variety of shapes when the curtain is open.

contrast In scenery, dissimilarity of forms used to create interest. In lighting, a difference in color, intensity, or distribution.

control The degree to which a designer can isolate a specific section of the acting area. Control depends on dimmers and lighting-area size.

cross fade The process of bringing up one group of lights while dimming out another.

crossover network An important speaker element, this electronic device is used to divide and route frequency bands to the appropriate speaker component—either as a passive set of electronic components located inside the speaker cabinet or as an active electronic device that divides a line-level signal into frequency bands and sends them to separate power amplifiers.

cue The movement of light from one stage "look" to another. A cue is usually assigned a specific number.

cue insertion The ability to insert a new lighting cue between two existing cues in the cue list.

cue linking A feature that allows the linking of one lighting cue to another out of normal cue-list order.

cue sheets A list of a production's lighting cues in numerical order.

cyclorama A curved sky-drop. Generally called a *cyc.*

CYM color mixing A color-mixing system involving the use of the secondary colors in light: cyan, yellow, and magenta.

dado Notch cut into a board, allowing a second piece to fit into it.

dance centering light A small red light placed at dancer head height at the rear of the auditorium or on a balcony rail; serves to help dancers locate front. Also called *spotting light.*

dance zones Dance lighting areas that extend completely across the stage; normally determined by placement of side-lighting booms.

dark set Special lighting cue written and inserted into the cue list to cause color changers or automated fixtures to change their color or focus without being seen.

dead haul winch A winch that lifts a load that has not been counterweighted.

decibel A measurement of sound intensity, the decibel (dB) describes a ratio of two quantities. One decibel is a measurement of electrical or acoustic power equal to 1⁄10 of a Bel (a unit named after Alexander Graham Bell).

dependent door A door in which the reveal structure is a part of the flat or wall that frames it.

dichroic reflector In a theatrical spotlight, a glass reflector with a dichroic coating, which allows some wavelengths of light to pass through while reflecting others.

dichroics Glass color filters that reflect rather than absorb unwanted wavelengths.

digital audio workstation (DAW) Typically, a personal computer with software and hardware configured for audio work. In a large studio this is most likely a dedicated computer system.

digital clipping In sound recordings, a harsh distortion caused by inaccurate digital recording of frequencies beyond the sampling range.

dimmer-per-circuit A dimming system that permanently assigns an individual dimmer to each lighting circuit in the house.

direct box Also referred to as a *DI box* or *direct injection box,* this device takes an unbalanced line-level sound signal from an electronic musical instrument such as an electric guitar or synthesizer and provides an isolated low-impedance microphone-level signal to a mixing board.

direct current (DC) An electric current flowing in one direction only.

director's CD Selections of possible sound cues for the director to evaluate.

disconnect box A switch, commonly found backstage in theatres, that supplies high amperage power for touring dimmers.

distributed dimming Placing groupings of dimmers directly on electric pipes near the instruments rather than in a remote location.

distribution The specific manner in which light falls on a surface—influenced by the direction, quality, and texture of the light itself.

DMX-512 A standard communication protocol for lighting-control systems.

douser A mechanical device, commonly found in follow spots, used to dim the light. Sometimes spelled *dowser.*

downstage Direction toward the audience.

dry-brushing Pulling the brush across wet paint in such a way that the bristles of the brush leave a streaky brush stroke.

dutchman A thin strip of fabric used to hide the joint on the face of two adjacent flats.

dynamic microphone A microphone housing an element that consists of a diaphragm directly coupled to a coil of wire that moves back and forth in a magnetic field. As the air pressure moves the diaphragm, the coil's movement in the magnetic field induces a flow of alternating electricity in the microphone cable that is analogous to the alternating waves in the air.

dynamic range The difference, measured in decibels, between the quietest and the loudest portion of a segment of sound. In a live situation this usually is the difference between the loudest portion and the noise floor of the theatre.

effects Music or sounds that are prerecorded and played back during a scene, such as that from an onstage phonograph or radio.

electrical solenoid An electromagnet that can be used for remote control of special effects.

electrics department head Person in charge of all electrics and sometimes sound operations of the theatre; may be an IA union position. Also called *house electrician.*

electromagnetism The creation of an electromotive force (voltage) through the use of a generator.

electrons Negatively charged particles that orbit the nucleus of an atom.

elevation A view of an object in which the line of sight of the viewer is perpendicular to the object, sometimes referred to as a *projection.*

elevator A mechanism built to move an actor or scenery vertically; an elevator is a permanent part of a theatre, as opposed to a *lift,* which is a temporary structure built for the same purpose.

ellipsoidal reflector A reflector cast in the shape of part of an ellipsoid, which reflects light back to its secondary focal point. Found in ellipsoidal reflector spotlights.

ellipsoidal reflector spotlight (ERS) Stage-lighting instrument that uses an ellipsoidal reflector. The ERS is the most efficient and versatile instrument in use today. It creates a concentrated, sharp light and has a built-in beam-shaping capability.

emphasis Visual prominence using the elements and principles of design to guide the viewer to a specific area of the design.

equalizer An electronic device that alters a specific frequency or frequency range. The two most common types are graphic and parametric.

Ethernet A universally used digital communications protocol capable of carrying numerous DMX signals at the same time.

extended apron An apron that projects out into the house.

extruding Squeezing molten metal through a shaped aperture to form a shape such as a rod or tube.

facing The edge of a platform or stair tread, used to hide the structure decoratively.

false proscenium A neutral frame, most often black, that either reduces the opening of the proscenium arch or alters its shape.

feathering Pulling the brush from a wet painted surface to a dry one so that the stroke ends in a featherlike pattern.

feedback An audio loop created between a microphone and its speaker. As a speaker's volume is increased, a point is reached where sound from the speaker entering the microphone is greater than the original sound from the actor. This "loop" then becomes self-feeding (hence, *feedback*), locking onto in-phase frequencies and amplifying them uncontrollably.

field edge In a spotlight beam, the point where the light drops off to 10 percent of maximum intensity.

filament A thin piece of tungsten that glows and emits light from within a lamp.

fill-light The secondary source of light in a composition. An important factor in visibility, fill-light is often thought of as bounce light or shadow.

fitch Flat brush with a long handle; varies in size from ½ inch to 3 inches.

fixed caster A caster that allows movement in only two directions.

flash pot A device made to hold and ignite a highly explosive powder for onstage special effects.

floating Lifting a wet drop off the floor by blowing air underneath while the paint is wet.

flood focus The largest of the variable beam sizes of a Fresnel spotlight.

fly rail Any part of a fly system where the lines are moved in and out and locked into place. Also referred to as *locking rail.*

focal length The distance between the center of a lens and its focal point.

focal point Center of interest.

focal point of lenses The point at which parallel rays of light converge after passing through a lens.

focal point of reflectors The specific point at which a light source must be placed in relationship to the reflector in order to achieve the desired reflective pattern.

focus chart Charts containing focus information for all instruments in a production; used to reproduce the focus accurately.

focusing The process of aiming and adjusting lighting instruments to suit the needs of an individual production. Focusing is normally done by the lighting designer and a crew of electricians.

fog juice The liquid used in fog and smoke machines.

foldback system Typically a separate set of amplifiers and speakers placed to direct their sound to the actors/singers so they can hear the orchestra and themselves. Also placed in the orchestra for musicians to hear themselves and the actors/singers.

follow cues An important lighting control function that allows one cue to follow another automatically with a single press of the "go" button.

follow spot A specially equipped light operated by a stage electrician to follow an actor or actors about the stage.

foot-candle A measurement of intensity of light reflected off a surface. Average stage brightness is approximately 70 foot-candles.

footing Using a foot to prevent a flat from sliding in the process of walking it up.

footlight Low-angled light sources often placed at the front edge of the stage apron—at the "feet" of the actors.

forging Stamping metal into a shape.

free electron An electron removed from its atom, providing the means of electrical flow.

frequency The rate at which a sound vibrates, measured in cycles per second or Hertz (Hz). The length of a sound wave determines frequency. A sound's frequency determines its pitch.

Fresnel spotlight Named after the inventor of its lens, the Fresnel is a theatrical spotlight with a spherical reflector and the ability to change beam size. It produces a soft, even field of light.

front projection The technique of projecting an image onto a screen from the front.

frost A plastic light-diffusion medium.

fullness The effect achieved by gathering or pleating a given width of fabric into a narrower width.

gate In an ellipsoidal reflector spotlight, the position at which shutters, iris, and gobos are located. The gate is also close to the reflector's secondary focal point, where the light rays cross.

gauge A measurement of the diameter of a wire; directly relates to the wire's capacity.

gels A short name for color filters; derived from the word *gelatin.*

gelstring A series of plastic color filters taped together and rolled to form the scroll of a color changer.

generator A device that creates an electromotive force (voltage) by moving a conductor within a magnetic field.

genre A general category, such as farce, mystery, and tragedy, distinguished by form, style, content, and other characteristics.

glass curtain A sheer or translucent fabric used to allow light inside a room and not allow a viewer from outside to see inside.

glazing Painting a transparent or semitransparent layer on top that subtly tones a surface or provides a finish (such as gloss, semigloss, or matte).

gobo A pattern, normally cut into a thin stainless steel plate, which is placed at the aperture of an ERS to project an image.

gradation Transitional steps in a sequence used to create emphasis and a feeling of movement in a design.

grounding A safety feature in modern wiring. A third wire acts as the ground wire, providing an electrical path of low resistance in case of a short circuit.

ground plan A view of a set from above, as if cut across horizontally (usually at 3 feet above the stage deck).

ground row A row of strip lights located upstage and used to illuminate the background from the bottom. A *scenery ground row* is a horizontal masking device used to hide the lighting ground row.

groups Similar to lighting submasters in that any number of individual channels can be assigned to one group master. Submasters can also be assigned to groups.

hanging cardboards Pieces of cardboard onto which a section of the light plot has been attached; used to assist in the hanging and circuiting of instruments.

hanging chart A chart included on the ground plan and section that indicates the placement of each piece of scenery that hangs or flies from a batten, including line set number, distance from the plaster line, and trim.

harmonics The overtones that are created when a note is played on a musical instrument. Normally these are multiples of the root frequency.

harmony A pleasing or congruent arrangement of scenic forms, creating an aesthetic unity, often achieved through repetition.

head block A grouping of pulleys that carry the lines from individual blocks to the arbor in a counterweight system and to the pinrail in a hemp system.

hertz A unit of measurement used to identify the frequency of a sound. Hertz (Hz) are equal to cycles per second or CPS.

hidden outline The outline of an object that is hidden from view, drawn in dotted line.

HMI and HTI Two types of metal halide arc lamps commonly used in follow spots and automated fixtures.

Hollywood flat A flat in which the framing members are on edge; the corners of the flat are end to face (as opposed to end to edge).

hookup A lighting chart that is arranged by dimmer or channel number and that lists a variety of instrument information.

hot wire The conductor that carries electricity to the place of work.

hue The name of a color; the color's wavelength or position in the spectrum.

Illuminating Engineering Society (IES) An organization made up primarily of architectural lighting designers and engineers; publishes the IES handbook and offers courses in architectural lighting.

impedance The measurement of resistance in alternating current circuits, including audio signals. It is used in speaker specifications (typically 4 to 16 ohms) and in sound equipment input and output specifications.

incandescent filament lamp A glass bulb enclosing a tungsten filament that emits light when an electrical current is passed through it.

incidental music Music that occurs other than during the actual play, such as before and after the show or at intermission.

independent door A door that is a completely separate unit from the flat or wall into which it will be fit.

infrared Light energy with wavelengths just longer than the longest visible wavelengths (red)—literally "below red."

input source Any device that sends an audio signal to the sound system.

instrument schedule A lighting chart that is arranged by instrument location and number and that lists a variety of instrument information.

insulator Materials that have few free electrons and that therefore resist the flow of electricity.

intensity See chroma.

intermodulation Additions to a processor's original audio signal produced within the components themselves.

International Alliance of Theatrical Stage Employees Union (IA) The union representing stage hands and electricians.

in-trim Position of scenery as it should be when in use, the "in" position.

iris A device, located at the gate of an ellipsoidal reflector spotlight, that makes the beam's circumference larger or smaller.

jack brace A triangular structure used to support or brace a vertical flat.

jewel lighting An early Broadway technique of lighting involving the use of a low-angled source from the balcony rail in combination with lights from each box boom.

kerf Thickness of a saw's cutting blade.

key-light The primary source of light in a composition—normally the brightest. Key-light may imitate a motivational source.

ladders Hanging positions for lighting instruments that derive their name from the fact that, with vertical uprights and horizontal "rungs," they look like a ladder. They may be permanently fixed or, more likely, able to be hung in a variety of positions.

lamp A light source consisting of a filament, a bulb, and a base.

lay-in brush Brush, usually 3 to 4 inches wide, used for painting large areas; often used for base coating, spattering, and other techniques.

LCL (light center length) The distance from the center of a lamp's filament to some predetermined place in its base.

leg Side masking, usually in reference to opaque black fabric, hanging from a batten and running vertically to the floor.

lens tube The housing for the objective lens(es) of a projection system. The housing is normally interchangeable to provide a variety of beam spreads.

level/rate wheel A wheel or touch pad that can control individual lighting channels, groups of channels, or an entire cross fade.

library storage A permanent means of recording lighting control information (dimmer channels and levels), usually on disc.

libretto The text or dialogue of an opera.

lift A mechanism built for a specific production in order to move an actor or scenery vertically. Compare *elevator.*

liftline The line running from the batten through the loft blocks and the head block on top of the arbor in a fly system.

Lighting Dimensions International (LDI) Group that publishes *Lighting Dimensions* magazine and holds an annual convention for individuals working in entertainment lighting.

lighting rehearsal A rehearsal for looking at light cues that takes place before the technical rehearsal and may take place with or without actors.

lighting section A cross section of a set drawn as if cut vertically at the center line and showing the position (height) of each electric being used in a production.

lighting storyboard A series of value sketches or color renderings depicting the quality of light for the various "looks" of a production.

lighting system An arrangement of lighting instruments of similar type, color, and/or direction that produces a specific lighting "look." A system may be used alone or in combination with other systems.

lighting truss Metal tubing, often aluminum, welded together in a crossing pattern for strength; used to support lighting equipment.

light plot A plan that indicates the exact placement, type, size, color, and number of each lighting instrument being used for a production.

line (1) A form that has length and width, although the width is often so narrow it is usually not recognized. (2) In geometric terms, a series of points.

line level Signal voltage levels from various pieces of audio equipment to speaker amplifiers; ranging from 77.5 millivolts to 24.5 volts, with 4.5 volts across 600 ohms equal to 1 watt.

liner Narrow, long-handled brush (often ¼ inch) used for details, most often in painting molding.

line-set A group of three or more lines using the same counterweight to lift a batten or unit of scenery.

lining Using a small brush to paint lines, most often used in painting highlight and shadow in painted molding.

Linnebach projector A projector with no lens that is used in the theatre for large-scale shadow projection.

loft block Any block, or pulley, placed in the grid.

loose-pin hinge A two-piece hinge in which the pin can be removed.

LORT houses Professional regional theatres; *LORT* stands for *League of Regional Theatres.*

lumen A unit of measurement of the intensity of a light source.

magic sheet Custom-designed paperwork used to assist the designer in setting and adjusting light levels. Also called a *cheat sheet.*

masking (1) Any piece of scenery that is used to complete the stage picture and prevent the audience from seeing the backstage area. (2) When one sound or event demands our attention to such a degree as to negate other sounds or events.

MIDI Musical Instrument Digital Interface is a standard for representing musical information in digital format. Through MIDI Show Control, its use has been expanded to include communication and the control of all types of theatrical equipment.

mike level Signal voltage levels from a microphone to a mixing board, normally in the millivolt (thousandth of a volt, or mV) range.

ministrips Striplights using MR-16 lamps.

miter Any cut across the grain of the wood.

mixing board A device used to preamplify, combine, and adjust sounds from a variety of sources and assign them to various outputs. A mixing board usually includes some provision for limited equalization along with supplying phantom power to devices that require it. Also known as a *mixer.*

monochromatic Using only one hue, black and white, and the complement to reduce the chroma.

motivated lighting Lighting sources arranged to duplicate the effect of a specific source such as a chandelier.

motivational lighting The theatrical use of light based on an actual source or sources.

movement The action of form.

moving head The type of automated lighting fixture in which the entire body (rather than simply a mirror) moves to change focus.

mullions Interior window-framing pieces.

musical underscoring Playing music or sound effects underneath the dialogue of a scene.

nanometer A measurement in billionths of a meter used to define certain wavelengths (colors) of light.

National Association of Broadcasters (NAB) An organization of individuals involved in television production.

national tour A tour that plays for a long run in a single city.

negative space The space between two or more forms.

neutral wire The conductor that carries electricity back to the generating plant.

nonmotivational lighting Light used as a pure element of design, without reference to any actual sources. Often such use is based on the designer's emotional reaction to the script.

nonrepresentational A form of art that is abstract and ornamental, not based on real-life objects and shapes.

nosing The projecting edge of a stair tread and top of stair riser; often refers to a simple molding hiding the intersection of tread and riser, particularly if the tread itself does not project.

nucleus The positively charged center of an atom; composed of protons and neutrons.

Nyquist sampling theorem Theorem that states that accurately reconstructing an analog sound signal in digital form requires that it be sampled at twice the rate of the highest frequency.

objective lens system The second lens or set of lenses in a projector; the objective lens system receives the image of the slide and transmits it to the screen in a size determined by the spread (focal length) of the lens.

offstage (1) Direction away from the center of the stage. (2) The stage areas to the right and left of the set.

ohm The measurement of a conductor's resistance to the flow of electrical current.

Ohm's law A circuit's amperage is equal to its voltage divided by its resistance (measured in ohms). Used to calculate resistance.

optical motion The movement of the eye through a composition. In the theatre, such eye movement may be dictated by light focus.

optics Reference to the optical features of a stage lighting instrument—most significantly the reflector and lens or lenses.

orthographic projection A straight-line projection drawing of an object showing three views, typically the top, the front, and the side.

out-trim Position of scenery when it is not in use, the "out" position.

overdrapery Draped or gathered fabric, usually heavy and opaque, used as a decorative window treatment. Sometimes permanent, sometimes functional, it is often used in conjunction with a glass curtain.

pallet A wagon with a very low profile. Also called a *skid.*

pan pot The potentiometer that controls the left/right assignment to a sound mixer's output bus.

parabolic reflector A reflector cast in the shape of part of a parabola, which reflects light in parallel rays. Found in PAR fixtures.

parallel circuit A type of electrical circuit in which portions of the total current flow through the various elements simultaneously.

PAR fixture A lighting instrument using the parabolic aluminized reflector lamp. It produces a strong and harsh beam of light that is oval with soft edges. Its field is rather uneven.

patch panel (1) A matrix of plug points used to interconnect various pieces of audio equipment. Usually divided into rows of inputs and outputs, the patch panel provides an organized central location for their routing. (2) A flexible system allowing the connection of any stage circuit to any dimmer; used in non-dimmer-per-circuit systems.

pegging Method of attaching two pieces of wood by inserting a small wooden dowel (peg) into a hole drilled into both pieces.

phantom power Power for condenser microphones, which is supplied through the microphone cable from the mixing board.

pin connector A stage connector with round brass pins that slide into holes in the receptacle.

pinrail The rail where lines are secured in a hemp system, often by the use of belaying pins.

pipe ends Instruments clustered at the ends of light battens, providing high side-light.

plano-convex lens A lens with one flat (plano) side and one outwardly curved (convex) side. Found in ellipsoidal reflector spotlights.

plaster line Imaginary line on the upstage edge of the proscenium arch.

plotter A mechanical drawing machine used to draft light plots and technical drawings from computer files.

point cue An additional lighting cue that is assigned a decimal point number placing it between two whole-numbered cues.

pounce A drawing, done on kraft paper, that has been perforated in order to transfer it to the scenery to be painted.

power formula Wattage = amperage × voltage.

preamplifier The first circuit encountered by the sound signal from a microphone into the mixing board, it amplifies the microphone level signal to line level.

preset The name given to a lighting look—especially when the preset system is being used.

preset console A control system with at least two rheostats or controllers per dimmer located on the control console. One set of controllers can be preset for the next lighting look, while the other set represents what is "live" onstage.

preset sheets A means of recording dimmer levels for each lighting cue in a production.

primary hue One of three hues that are used to mix all other hues; in pigment the primary hues are red, yellow, and blue; in light they are red, green, and blue.

priming brush Wide brush (6 inches is common) used for covering very large areas.

processing Altering the audio signal in a nonlinear fashion. Equalizers, effects units, and compressors are examples of signal processors.

production electrician The electrician in charge and who works most closely with the designer.

production manager Person in charge of the day-to-day operation of the theatre and overseeing all production matters; often hires staff and works closely with the artistic director and business manager.

proportion The size of a form relative to another form.

proscenium The architectural frame that separates the audience from the performers.

proximity effect The increase in low-frequency response when a microphone is placed very close to the sound source. This is an inherent characteristic of directional microphones and is usually associated with singers using handheld microphones.

quartz strips Striplights using long quartz lamps.

rabbet Wide groove cut into the face of a board, allowing another board to fit into it.

rails Top and bottom horizontal framing members of a flat.

rear projection The technique of projecting an image onto a special translucent screen from the rear.

refraction The bending of light rays as they pass through mediums with different densities, as in a light beam traveling through air bending from its original track when it goes through glass.

rehearsal CD Sound effects or music given to the director or stage manger for use in rehearsal; useful for timing or giving the actor a chance to work with underscoring, songs, or sound effects before technical rehearsals.

reinforcement The electronic amplification of actors or musical instruments onstage. Typically used to do the following: (1) Help the audience hear the actors or hear an offstage actor in larger theatres. (2) Blend and balance the vocals and musical instruments in a musical theatre production. (3) Add an effect or change the quality off a voice on- or offstage.

repertory production The process of presenting a different show each night, with the number depending on the size of the repertory.

representational A form of art that directly relates to real or lifelike objects.

reveal The jamb (header and sides), or the edge of an opening, such as a door or an arch, indicating thickness.

reverberation The combination of multiple, blended sound images caused by reflections from walls and other surfaces. If reverberation time is long enough to discern individual sound, then it is referred to as an *echo*.

rhythm Patterns of repeated visual movement.

riser Vertical surface of a step, often referred to as *facing*.

RMS Root mean square is used to give an average power value to an alternating current or audio circuit as it would compare with that of a direct-current circuit. RMS can be used to describe both peak (instantaneous) values as well as the more useful continuous power output.

road electrician An electrician for a bus-and-truck tour.

rods Light receptors located in the retina that are sensitive to intensity.

roll drop A drop wrapped around a long horizontal roller (usually like a big blind). Also called an *oleo drop*.

roundel Round glass color filters made to fit into strip lights.

sampling rate The number of times per second that an analog to digital converter (ADC) freezes and assigns a numerical value to the analog signal (voltage). A sampling rate of 44.1 thousand times per second is referred to as *CD quality.*

sampling resolution The number of different values available to assign to a digital audio sample. Resolution directly affects the quality of sound reproduction.

saturation See **chroma.**

scale The size or mass of a form.

scoop Ellipsoidal reflector floodlight used to create a bright, even wash of light.

score A chart, arranged by lighting looks and various qualities of light, that helps to describe the designer's intent.

SCR dimmer A modern electronic dimmer. The silicon controlled rectifier (SCR) is the electronic component that controls the current.

scrim An open-weave fabric used in the theatre for its transparent properties.

scroll work Curved, detailed design resembling a rolled piece of paper.

scumbling Intermixing of two or more colors on the scenery in a random pattern, allowing some areas to blend.

secondary hue One of three hues produced by mixing any two primaries; in pigment they are violet, orange, and green; in lighting they are yellow, violet, and cyan.

section A view of a set from one side, as if cut across vertically at the center line.

series circuit A type of electrical circuit in which current passes through the various elements successively. If one element fails, the current will stop.

service power Refers to the type of wiring system providing electricity to a user as well as its amperage.

set line The edge of the set farthest downstage, usually parallel to the plaster line.

shade Darker value of a hue.

sheave Pulley; the part of a block that rotates.

sheet metal Piece of metal that has been rolled into a flat sheet, thinner than plate.

shop order A contract for the rental of lighting equipment and accessories that lists, in detail, all the equipment to be rented for a production; used for bidding purposes and ordering.

short circuit An accidental path of low resistance, allowing an abnormally large flow of current; usually caused by improper wiring or broken insulation.

show portal A decorative frame that is designed for a particular production and is used either to pull together multiple sets visually or to help establish the character of the production.

shutter The part of a door that opens and closes.

shutters Moveable metal plates, inserted at the gate of an ellipsoidal reflector spotlight, that allow the beam to be shaped in a linear manner from any of four directions.

side-arm An accessory valuable for hanging lights on booms or other vertical positions.

side cove A vertical slot cut in the side wall of the auditorium to provide a hanging location for side-front light.

side stage The area right and left and in front of the proscenium arch. Sometimes used as acting area.

sightline Line of sight from an audience seat to a point onstage.

single-source lighting Creating the quality of one distinct source of illumination by clustering several lighting instruments together or by using one large, bright source.

sky-drop A backdrop that is not painted with anything representational.

soft patch An electronic patching system present in most lighting consoles that allows the connection of any control channel to any dimmer/circuit.

sound plot The actual working list of the cues for a production; normally includes cue numbers, speaker assignments, fade times, and so forth.

sound pressure level (SPL) The measurement of acoustic pressure level in decibels.

sound score A preliminary, written description of all possible ideas for sound cues that the designer might have. The sound score facilitates discussions with the director and other designers and acts as a springboard for developing the final cues for a production.

spattering Method of applying painted texture by sharply tapping a loaded brush against the heel of the hand, leaving droplets of pigment on the work.

speaker level Signal voltage level from an amplifier to its speaker. 24.5 volts and up is enough to drive a speaker.

special effects Uses of light other than lighting the actor or illuminating the scene.

specials Lighting instruments used in addition to the regular production lighting.

specular reflection Light reflection off a shiny surface. The angle of incidence is equal to the angle of reflection.

spherical reflector A reflector cast in the shape of part of a sphere, which returns light back to its focal point. Found in Fresnel spotlights.

split cross-fader Two faders: one assigned to those lights going down in intensity and the other assigned to those lights going up in intensity. This tool allows for variation in up and down fading times.

sponging Using a sponge to apply paint.

spot focus The smallest of the variable beam sizes of a Fresnel spotlight.

spotline (1) Line rigged specially for one production; not part of the standard rig of the theatre. (2) A single rope and pulley used in remote position on the grid, often used to fly scenic pieces that are not parallel to the plaster line.

stage circuit Permanent stage wiring—normally 20-amp capacity.

staging The arrangement of actors in the environment, creating stage pictures that help to tell the story of the play.

stage left Direction to the actor's left as he or she faces the audience.

stage right Direction to the actor's right as he or she faces the audience.

stiffener Usually a 1 by 3 or 1 by 4 used horizontally on edge to keep several flats in place, most often on the same plane.

stiles Vertical framing members of a flat.

stippling Using the tips of the brush to apply paint in an up-and-down motion.

stock production The process of running a single show for several weeks.

storyboard A series of sketches that provide a moment by moment view of a scene, act, and so forth.

striplight A row of lamps in a single housing used to create a wide and even wash of light; commonly used to illuminate backdrops.

submaster The name given to a single lighting master controller to which any number of individual control channels has been assigned.

swivel caster A caster that allows movement in any direction.

tableau curtain Two overlapping panels of fabric that are rigged to pull open on a modified (curved) diagonal.

teaser A rarely used term referring to the first border upstage of the proscenium arch.

tenon A projecting member in a piece of wood or other material for insertion into a mortise to make a joint.

Theatre Communications Group (TCG) A national service organization dedicated to assisting the not-for-profit theatre; publishers of *American Theatre* magazine and *Art*SEARCH.

Themed Entertainment Association An organization made up of people working in the themed entertainment business.

three-phase system A 120/208-volt AC electrical wiring system consisting of four wires: three hot and one neutral. Also known as the *four-wire system*.

three-wire system A 120/240-volt AC electrical wiring system consisting of three wires: two hot and one neutral.

threshold of hearing Normally defined as 0 dB SPL, this equates to the quietist sound that the ear can discern.

thrust stage A stage in which the audience sits around three sides of the acting space.

tight-pin hinge A hinge in which the center pin cannot be removed.

timbre The tonal quality of a note, sung or played on a musical instrument, that includes the fundamental frequency of the note combined with all of the harmonics (overtones) created. Timbre is what distinguishes the sound of two different musical instruments playing an identical note at the same volume.

tint Lighter value of a hue.

toggles Internal framing members of a flat, usually horizontal but sometimes vertical.

top hat An accessory for the Fresnel spotlight that attaches at the color-frame holder and reduces spill and glare from the instrument's lens.

tormentor A rarely used term referring to the first leg upstage of the proscenium arch.

tracking An operational mode in which a channel or dimmer level remains the same in all lighting cues until told otherwise.

transducer A device, such as a microphone or speaker, that converts input energy of one form into output energy of another. In the case of a microphone, it transduces acoustical energy in the form of sound pressure waves in the air into electrical energy.

transformer A device used to increase or decrease the voltage of alternating current (AC).

translucency A fabric that can be either opaque or translucent depending on how it is lit.

trap Any hole in the stage floor.

traveler Any curtain that is drawn in a horizontal direction. Also called a *draw curtain*.

tread Horizontal surface of a step.

trim (1) Height of something above the stage floor. (2) To hang pipes or scenery above the stage floor.

trim clamp A two-piece metal clamp that is used to bind together the lines in a hemp system, for ease of operation. Also referred to as a *Sunday.*

trim pot Also referred to as *input level, input gain,* or *pad,* it is a sound mixer's volume control over the input signal.

triple swivel caster Also called a *zero-throw caster,* a caster mounted on three wheels around a central point for easy turning.

tripping Picking up the bottom of a drop as well as the top when there is not enough room to fly it completely out.

truss A framework of wood or metal that uses triangles and is therefore considerably stronger than a simple beam.

tungsten-halogen lamp An incandescent lamp with a halogen-family gas sealed within its quartz-glass envelope. Also called a *quartz lamp.*

twist-lock connector A stage connector that provides a sure connection by means of prongs that lock within the receptacle.

two-fer A special cable that allows for the plugging of two lighting instruments into one circuit.

two-wire system A 120-volt AC electrical wiring system consisting of two wires: one hot and one neutral.

ultraviolet Light energy with wavelengths just shorter than the shortest visible wavelengths (violet)—literally "beyond violet."

unbalanced line A method in which the audio signal is carried on a single center-conductor in a shielded cable. This method is used primarily for consumer electronics and is very susceptible to noise and interference.

union business agent A union's representative to the public; negotiates contracts and fills labor needs.

United Scenic Artists Union (USA) The American union representing professional scenic artists; costume, lighting, scenic, and sound designers; art directors; and computer artists.

unit setting A setting based on the retention or reuse of certain elements of scenery for more than one scene.

upstage Direction away from the audience.

valance The uppermost decorative frame of a window drapery treatment. Sometimes a valance is draped fabric, as in a swag, or a hard surface either painted or covered with fabric.

value The presence of white or black in a color; the lightness or darkness of a color.

value sketch A sketch that emphasizes the light and shadow of a set.

variable area lighting Large as well as small lighting areas are arranged throughout the acting area. The small areas offer greater control and are used in conjunction with the larger areas.

variation Slight or major changes in the elements or principles of a form that prevent monotony.

voltage or electromotive force (EMF) A difference in potential—the force that causes free electrons to move in a conductor.

vomitory entrance In the thrust theatre, ramps serving as actors' entrances and exits that lead up to the front of the stage from beneath the audience.

wash lighting Use of general illumination to cover the entire acting area; this technique offers little, if any, control.

watt The measurement of the electric power rate, or the rate at which work is done through the use of electricity.

wet-blend To blend two or more colors on the scenery while they are wet.

winch A hand-cranked or motor-driven drum rigged with a cable that is used to move scenery.

window sash Frame that contains the panes of a window.

wings Vertical masking pieces on the sides of a proscenium stage. The name is derived from "wing and border" scenery. Wings also refer to the offstage right and left spaces in the proscenium theatre.

xenon short-arc lamp A bright arc lamp with xenon gas sealed within its envelope; develops high pressures within the bulb.

yolk On a lighting instrument, the U-shaped part that holds the C-clamp and allows the instrument to tilt.

zoom ellipsoidal An ellipsoidal reflector spotlight with moveable lenses that provide an adjustable beam diameter.

Additional Reading

GENERAL

American Theatre Planning Board. *A Theatre Checklist.* Middletown, CT: Wesleyan University Press, 1983.

Juracek, Judy A. *Surfaces.* New York: Norton, 1996.

McCann, Michael, *Artist Beware.* Globe Pequot Press, 2001.

Rossol, Monona. *Stage Fright.* New York: Center for Occupational Hazards, 1986.

Scully, Vincent. *Architecture: The Natural and the Manmade.* New York: St. Martin's Press, 1991.

Theatre Design and Technology. The official journal of the U.S. Institute of Theatre Technology, 6443 Ridings Road, Syracuse, NY 13206-1111.

SCENE DESIGN

The Design Approach

Appia, Adolph. "Adolph Appia: A Gospel for Modern Stage." *Theatre Arts Monthly,* August 1932. Entire issue devoted to Appia's influence on present-day scene and lighting design.

Brockett, Oscar G., and Robert Ball. *The Essential Theatre.* Belmont, CA: Wadsworth, 1999.

Burian, Jarka. *Leading Creators of Twentieth-Century Czech Theatre.* New York: Routledge, 2002.

Goodwin, John, ed. *British Theatre Design, 1978–1988.* New York: Tom Doherty Associates, 1989.

Gorelik, Mordecai. *New Theatres for Old.* New York: Samuel French, 1975.

Henderson, Mary. *Mielziner.* New York: Backstage Books: Watson-Guptill, 2001.

Ingham, Rosemary. *From Page to Stage.* Portsmouth, NH: Heineman Books, 1998.

Jones, Robert E. *The Dramatic Imagination.* New York: Routledge, 1987.

Oenslager, Donald M. *The Theatre of Donald Oenslager.* Middletown, CT: Wesleyan University Press, 1978

Pendleton, Ralph. *Theatre of Robert Edmund Jones* Middletown, CT: Wesleyan University Press, 1977

Rich, Frank, and Aronson, Lisa. *The Theatre Art of Boris Aronson.* New York: Knopf, 1987.

Svoboda, Josef. *Secret of Theatrical Space: The Memoirs of Josef Svoboda.* New York: Applause Theatre Books, 1994.

Thomas, James. *Script Analysis for Actors, Directors and Designers.* Woburn, MA: Focal Press, 1999.

Design Application

Aronson, Arnold. *American Set Design.* New York: Theatre Communications, 1985.

———. *American Set Design 2.* New York: Theatre Communications, 1991.

Blumenthal, Eileen, and Taymor, Julie. *Julie Taymor: Playing with Fire.* New York: Abrams, 1995.

Dean, Alexander, and Carra, Lawrence. *Fundamentals of Directing.* 3rd ed. New York: Holt, Rinehart & Winston, 1989.

Ettedgui, Peter. *Production Design and Art Direction.* Wolburn, MA: Focal Press, 1999.

Lauer, David A., and Pentak, Stephen. *Design Basics.* Fort Worth, TX: Harcourt, Brace, 1995.

Pecktal, Lynn. *Designing and Drawing for the Theatre.* New York: McGraw-Hill, 1994.

Drawing and Painting

Albers, Josef. *The Interaction of Color.* New Haven, CT: Yale University Press, 1975.

Birren, Faber. *Principles of Color: A Review of Past Traditions and Modern Theories of Color Harmony.* Schiffer, 1997.

Chevreul, M. E. *The Principles of Harmony and Contrast of Colors and Their Applications to the Arts.* New York: Schiffer, 1987.

Color Harmony Manual, Ostwald Theory of Color. Chicago: Container Corporation of America, 1948.

Dorn, Dennis, and Shanda, Mark. *Drafting for the Theatre.* Carbondale: Southern Illinois University Press, 1992.

Dunn, Charles. *Conversations in Paint.* New York: Workman, 1995.

Edwards, Betty. *Drawing on the Right Side of the Brain.* Rev. ed. Los Angeles: Tarcher, 1989.

Itten, Johannes. *The Art of Color*. New York: Wiley, 1974.

Nicolaides, Kimon. *The Natural Way to Draw.* Boston: Houghton Mifflin, 1975.

Parker, W. Oren. *Sceno-graphic Techniques*. Carbondale, IL: Southern Illinois Press, 1987.

Woodbridge, Patricia. *Designer Drafting for the Entertainment World*. Woburn, MA: Focal Press, 2000.

Furniture and Decorations

Calloway, Stephen, ed. *The Elements of Style: A Practical Encyclopedia of Interior Architectural Details.* New York: Simon & Schuster, 1991.

Gottshall, Franklin H. *How to Make Colonial Furniture.* New York: Macmillan, 1980.

Grant, Ian, ed. *Great Interiors*. London: Hamlyn, 1971.

Lawrence, Richard Russell, and Chris, Teresa. *The Period House*. London: Phoenix Illustrated, 1996.

Meyer, Franz S. *Handbook of Ornament*. New York: Dover, 1957.

Miller, Judith. *Period-Style Curtains and Soft Furnishing.* Woodstock, NY: Overlook Press, 2000.

Molesworth, H. D., and Kenworthy-Browne, John. *Three Centuries of Furniture*. New York: Viking Press, 1972.

Payne, Christopher, ed. *Southeby's Concise Encyclopedia of Furniture*. London: Octopus, 1989.

Praz, Mario. *An Illustrated History of Interior Decoration: From Pompeii to Art Nouveau.* London: Thames & Hudson, 1984.

Strange, T. Arthur. *Historical Guide to French Interiors.* London: McCorquodale, 1903.

Thornton, Peter. *Authentic Décor: The Domestic Interior 1620–1920.* New York: Viking, 1984.

TECHNICAL PRODUCTION

Construction

Arnold, Richard L. *Scene Technology*. 3rd ed. Allyn and Bacon, 1993.

Althouse, Andrew D., Turnquist, Carl H., Bowditch, William A. and Bowditch, Kevin E. *Modern Welding*. Tinley Park, IL: Goodheart-Wilcox, 2000.

Bowditch, William A., and Bowditch, Kevin E. *Welding Fundamentals*. Tinley Park, IL: Goodheart-Wilcox, 1997.

Bramwell, Martin, ed. *The International Book of Wood.* New York: Crescent Books, 1976.

Burris-Meyer, Harold, and Cole, Edward C. *Scenery for the Theatre*. Rev. ed. Boston: Little, Brown, 1972.

Dykes Lumber Company. *Molding Catalog, No. 49*. New York: Dykes Lumber Co. (137 West 24th Street, New York, NY 10011), n.d.

Feirer, John L., and Hutchings, Gilbert R. *Carpentry and Building Construction.* 5th ed. New York: Glencoe/ McGraw-Hill, 1985.

Feirer, John L. *Cabinetmaking and Millwork.* Peoria, IL: Chas. A. Bennett, 1967.

Groneman, Chris H., and Glazener, Everett R. *Technical Woodworking.* New York: McGraw-Hill, 1966.

Krenov, James. *James Krenov, Worker in Wood.* Sterling, 1997.

O'Brien, Robert L. *Jefferson's Welding Encyclopedia.* Miami, FL: American Welding Society, 1997.

Ramsey, Charles G., and Sleeper, Harold R. *Architectural Graphic Standards*. 7th ed. New York: Wiley, 1981.

Salaman, R. A. *Dictionary of Woodworking Tools.* Mendham, NJ: Astragal Press, 1997.

The Handling of Scenery

Ashley, Clifford W. *The Ashley Book of Knots*. New York: Doubleday, 1944.

Cassidy, John. *The Klutz Book of Knots*. Palo Alto, CA: Klutz Press, 1985.

Carter, Paul. *Backstage Handbook: An Illustrated Almanac of Technical Information.* 3rd ed. New York: Broadway Press, 1994.

Glerum, Jay O. *Stage Rigging Handbook*. 2nd. ed. Carbondale: Southern Illinois University Press, 1997.

Painting and Properties

Crabtree, Susan, and Beudert, Peter. *Scenic Art of the Theatre*. Woburn, MA: Focal Press, 1998.

Gibbs, Jenny. *Curtains and Draperies*. Woodstock, NY: Overlook Press, 1994.

James, Thurston. *The What, Where, When of Theater Props.* Cincinnati, OH: Betterway Books, 1992.

Motley (Elizabeth Montgomery, Margaret Harris, and Sophia Harris). *Theatre Props*. New York: Drama Books, 1976.

Pecktal, Lynn. *Designing and Painting for the Theatre.* Harcourt Canada, 1975.

Polunin, Vladimir. *The Continental Method of Scene Painting*. Princeton, NJ: Princeton Book Company, 1980.

THEATRE SOUND

Sound Design

Bracewell, John. *Sound Design in the Theatre.* Upper Saddle River, NJ: Prentice-Hall, 1993. A very good text on sound design and technology.

Copland, Aaron. *What to Listen for in Music.* New York: Mentor Books, 1985.

Davis, Gary, and Jones, Ralph. *The Sound Reinforcement Handbook*. Milwaukee: Hal Leonard, 1990. A Yamaha publication with a great deal of valuable information covering practical material not found in other books.

Holman, Tomlinson. *Sound for Film and Television*. Burlington, MA: Focal Press, 2001.

Kaye, Deena, and Lebrecht, James. *Sound and Music for the Theatre*. 2nd ed. Burlington, MA: Focal Press, 1999.

Kenny, Tom. *Sound for Picture: The Art of Sound Design in Film and Television (Mix Pro Audio Series)*. Milwaukee, WI: Hal Leonard, 2000.

Leonard, John A. *Theatre Sound*. New York: Routledge, 2001.

Moscal, Tony. *Sound Check: The Basics of Sound and Sound Systems*. Milwaukee, WI: Hal Leonard, 1994.

Sonnenschein, David. *Sound Design: The Expressive Power of Music, Voice, and Sound Effects in Cinema*. Studio City, CA: Michael Wiese Productions, 2001.

Sound Technology

Ballou, Glen, ed. *Handbook for Sound Engineers*. 3rd ed. Burlington, MA: Butterworth-Heinemann, 2001. The most comprehensive of audio reference books.

Burris-Meyer, Harold, Mallory, Vincent, and Goodfriend, Lewis S. *Sound in the Theatre*. Rev. ed. New York: Theatre Arts Books, 1979. Outdated and out of print, but nonetheless useful for theatre acoustics.

Davis, Don, and Davis, Carolyn. *Sound System Engineering*. 2nd ed. Burlington, MA: Focal Press, 1997. Formulas needed to build a sound system.

Giddings, Philip. *Audio Systems Design and Installation*. Burlington, MA: Focal Press, 1990.

Owsinski, Bobby. *The Mixing Engineer's Handbook*. Milwaukee, WI: Hal Leonard, 1999.

Pohlmann, Ken C. *Principles of Digital Audio*. 4th ed. New York: McGraw-Hill, 2000.

Stark, Scott Hunter. *Live Sound Reinforcement: A Comprehensive Guide to P.A. and Music Reinforcement Systems and Technology*. Vallejo, CA: Mix Books, 1996.

Trubitt, David. *Concert Sound: Tours, Techniques, and Technology (Mix Pro Audio)*. Milwaukee, WI: Hal Leonard, 1993.

Periodicals

db magazine. A bimonthly publication containing articles of interest primarily to musicians and small recording studios.

Electronic Musician. Published monthly by Primedia Business Magazines and Media.

EQ. A monthly magazine aimed at project recording and sound equipment.

Journal of the Audio Engineering Society. Published ten times a year by the Audio Engineering Society (AES); often contains highly technical information and papers on new developments. The AES also publishes tapes and reprints of papers delivered at their annual conventions.

Mix. Published monthly by Primedia Business Magazines and Media, this magazine is intended primarily for audio professionals.

Prosound News. Published by United Entertainment Media, Inc.

Recording Engineer/Producer. A monthly magazine aimed at those working in the recording industry.

Schwann. A quarterly guide to all currently available CDs, LPs, and cassettes.

STAGE LIGHTING

Lighting Design

Bellman, Willard F. *Lighting the Stage: Art and Practice*. 3rd ed. New York: Broadway Press, 2001.

Burian, Jarka. *The Secrets of Theatrical Space*. New York: Applause Theatre Books, 1973.

Essig, Linda. *Lighting and the Design Idea*. New York: Harcourt Brace, 1997.

Hays, David. *Light on the Subject*. New York: Limelight Editions, 1989. A wonderful book on the basics of lighting design.

Keller, Max. *Light Fantastic*. New York: Prestel Verlag, 1999. A beautiful book by this German Lighting designer—awarded the USITT Golden Pen Award in 2000.

McCandless, Stanley. *A Method of Lighting the Stage*. 4th ed. New York: Theatre Arts Books, 1958. This little book has had more influence on lighting design in the United States than any other.

Moody, James L. *Concert Lighting: Techniques, Art, and Business*. 2nd ed. Boston: Focal Press, 1998. The first book published concerned with the field of concert lighting.

Palmer, Richard H. *The Lighting Art: The Aesthetics of Stage Lighting Design*. 2nd ed. Englewood Cliffs, NJ: Prentice-Hall, 1994. A valuable book on the aesthetics of stage-lighting design.

Pilbrow, Richard. *Stage Lighting Design*. New York: Design Press, 1997. A delightful book covering the theories and practice of this British/American designer.

Rosenthal, Jean, and Wertenbaker, Lael. *The Magic of Light*. Boston: Little, Brown, 1972 (out of print).

Shelly, Steven Louis. *A Practical Guide to Stage Lighting*. Boston: Focal Press, 1999.

Lighting Technology

Bureau of Naval Personnel. *Basic Electricity*. New York: Dover, 1962. A clear and simple presentation of the fundamentals of electricity.

Cadena, Richard. *Focus on Lighting Technology.* New York: Entertainment Technology Press, 2002.

Fitt, Brian, and Thornley, Joe. *Lighting Technology.* Boston: Focal Press, 1997.

Moody, James L. *The Business of Theatrical Design.* New York: Allworth Press, 2002.

Munn, Robert C. *Photometrics Handbook.* 2nd ed. New York: Broadway Press. The best and most complete book on the subject.

Warfel, William. *The New Handbook of Stage Lighting Graphics.* New York: Drama Book Publishers, 1990. A very helpful publication addressing lighting graphic standards and paper work. A must for the student lighting designer.

Warfel, William B., and Klappert, Walter A. *Color Science for Lighting the Stage.* New Haven, CT: Yale University Press, 1981. Color filter analysis.

Lighting History

Bowers, Brian. *Lengthening the Day: A History of Lighting Technology.* London: Oxford University Press, 1998.

Kook, Edward F. *Images in Light for the Living Theatre.* New York: Privately printed, 1963. An interesting survey on the use of projections in the theatre.

McCandless, Stanley. *A Syllabus of Stage Lighting.* 11th ed. New York: Drama Book Publishers, n.d. A historical reference book and dictionary of stage-lighting terms.

Penzel, Frederick. *Theatre Lighting Before Electricity.* Middletown, CT: Wesleyan University Press, 1978.

Supplementary Resources

Electronic Theatre Controls: Middleton, WI. Equipment catalogues.

Entertainment Design magazine published by Primedia. Covers entertainment technology and design.

General Electric Company. *Fundamentals of Light and Lighting.* Cleveland, OH: General Electric Company, 1956. Excellent material on color, sources, and behavior of light.

———. Cleveland, OH. #9200 *Lamp Catalog.*

Illuminating Engineering Society (IES). *IES Lighting Handbook.* New York: IES. Pertinent information on color, instruments, equipment, and use.

Jones, Robert Edmond. *The Dramatic Imagination.* New York: Theatre Arts Books, 1941. Just for the inspiration.

NSI/Colortran, a division of Leviton: Tualatin, OR. Equipment catalogues.

Osram Sylvania, Inc. Danvers, MA. *Osram Sylvania Product Catalog.*

PULSN: Pro Lights & Staging News magazine published by Timeless Communications. Covers the business of entertainment technology and design.

Strand Lighting, Cypress, CA. Equipment catalogues.

Theatre Design and Technology. A publication of the United States Institute of Theatre Technology.

Watson, Lee. *Handbook of Lighting Design.* New York: McGraw-Hill, 1990. Part One covers lighting design of all the specialty areas, while Part Two concerns itself with employment and working in the profession.

Index